# SCIENCE INTERACTIONS

## INVITES YOUR STUDENTS TO LOOK AT SCIENCE IN A NEW WAY

The new edition of *Science Interactions* is a three-book series designed specifically for middle school and junior high students. It combines all that is good about science curriculum reform with an approach that encourages students to think for themselves as they explore scientific concepts and processes.

Hands-on activities let your students "do" science from the first day to the last.

Real-world connections show students the links between the lessons of science and their everyday lives.

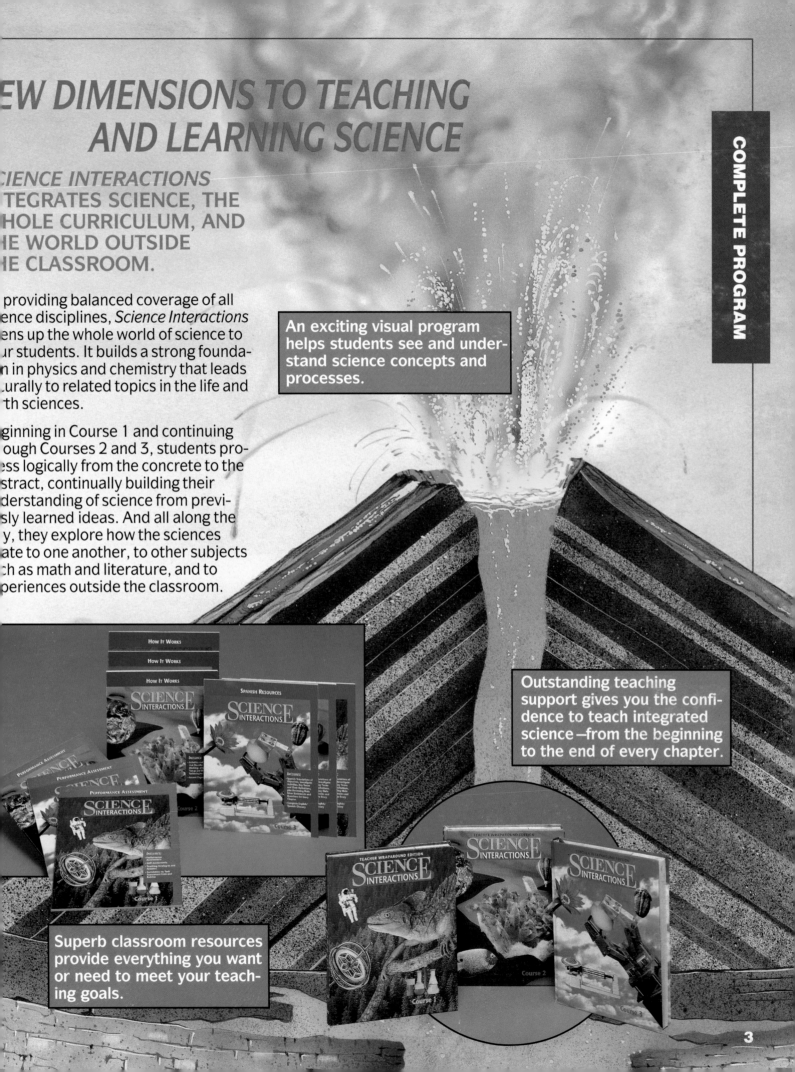

# EW DIMENSIONS TO TEACHING AND LEARNING SCIENCE

**CIENCE INTERACTIONS TEGRATES SCIENCE, THE HOLE CURRICULUM, AND HE WORLD OUTSIDE HE CLASSROOM.**

providing balanced coverage of all ence disciplines, *Science Interactions* ens up the whole world of science to ur students. It builds a strong founda- n in physics and chemistry that leads urally to related topics in the life and th sciences.

ginning in Course 1 and continuing ough Courses 2 and 3, students pro- ess logically from the concrete to the stract, continually building their derstanding of science from previ- sly learned ideas. And all along the y, they explore how the sciences ate to one another, to other subjects ch as math and literature, and to periences outside the classroom.

An exciting visual program helps students see and under- stand science concepts and processes.

Outstanding teaching support gives you the confi- dence to teach integrated science—from the beginning to the end of every chapter.

Superb classroom resources provide everything you want or need to meet your teach- ing goals.

# SCIENCE INTERACTIONS

## TO SEE IS TO COMPREHEND. VISUALS OFFER YOUR STUDENTS MORE THAN ONE PATH TO SCIENTIFIC UNDERSTANDING

No longer are science concepts locked up in page after page of text. *Science Interactions'* focus on visual learning makes concepts accessible to all students. Instead of simply reading about fundamental concepts, your students will see them illustrated in vibrant, vivid color.

Photographs and illustrations often are combined to show both the external features and inner workings of natural things and events.

### Types of Muscle

Different types of muscle in your body perform different functions. The muscles that move bones are **skeletal muscles**. At movable joints, skeletal muscles are attached to bones by tendons. **Tendons** are strong elastic bands of tissue.

You're most aware of skeletal muscles, probably because you can control the movement of these muscles. But you have two other kinds of muscles, too. The walls of your heart are made of cardiac muscle. **Cardiac muscle** pumps blood through the heart and forces blood through the rest of the body. **Smooth muscle** is found in many places inside your body, such as your stomach and intestines. Food moves through your digestive system by smooth muscle. How much control do you think you have over cardiac and smooth muscle? Compare the three kinds of muscles in **Figure 7-8**.

**Figure 7-8**

**A** *Skeletal muscle* You decide when to contract or relax skeletal muscles. All outward body movements, like doing a pull-up, are possible because of skeletal muscles.

**B** *Cardiac muscle* Months before your birth, your cardiac muscle began a pattern of contracting and relaxing that pumped blood to your body cells. Which is the only body organ made of cardiac muscle?

**C** *Smooth muscles* The movement of food through your intestines and the distribution of blood within your blood vessels are examples of the work of your smooth muscles. Do you control these actions?

Skeletal muscle

Cardiac muscle

Smooth muscle

**226** Chapter 7 Moving the Body

### Muscle Action

Body movement depends on the action of your muscles. But how do muscles work? Muscles are made up of bundles of long, stringlike structures called fiber, that can contract. When a muscle contracts, it gets shorter. In doing so, it pulls on the attached bone. The force of a muscle pulling on a bone moves a body part. Since work is done when a force moves an object a distance, the muscle works when it contracts.

Like all things that do work, your muscles need energy. Fuel of some kind is always needed to obtain the energy to do work.

Glucose is your muscles' main fuel. In your muscles, chemical energy stored in glucose changes to mechanical energy, and your muscles contract.

**Figure 7-9**

**A** Muscles are made of bundles of long stringlike cells called fibers. Muscle fibers have the unique ability to contract, or draw together. Nerves stimulate muscles to either contract or relax.

Tendon

Bundle of fibers

Membrane

Fiber

**B** When a muscle contracts, it shortens. When it relaxes, it returns to its original length. When certain muscles attached to bones at a joint contract, the bones move. Do muscles do work? Why?

7-3 Muscles **227**

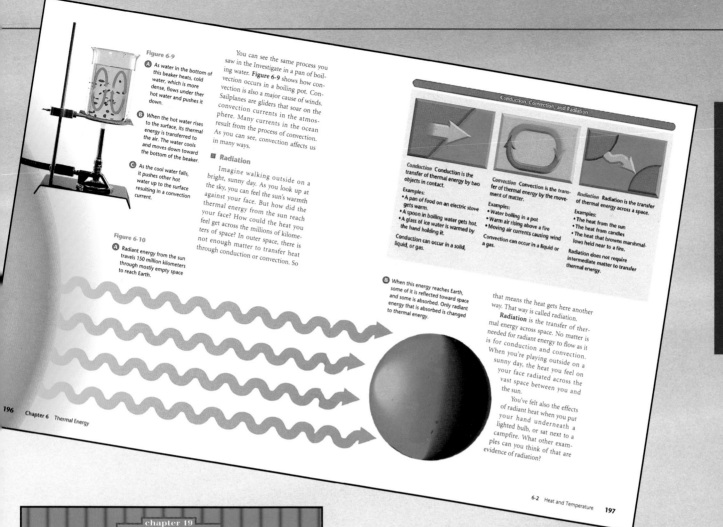

**Figure 6-9**

**A** As water in the bottom of this beaker heats, cold water, which is more dense, flows under the hot water and pushes it down.

**B** When the hot water rises to the surface, its thermal energy is transferred to the air. The water cools and moves down toward the bottom of the beaker.

**C** As the cool water falls, it pushes other hot water up to the surface resulting in a convection current.

You can see the same process you saw in the Investigate in a pan of boiling water. **Figure 6-9** shows how convection occurs in a boiling pot. Convection is also a major cause of winds. Sailplanes are gliders that soar on the convection currents in the atmosphere. Many currents in the ocean result from the process of convection. As you can see, convection affects us in many ways.

■ **Radiation**

Imagine walking outside on a bright, sunny day. As you look up at the sky, you can feel the sun's warmth against your face. But how did the thermal energy from the sun reach your face? How could the heat you feel get across the millions of kilometers of space? In outer space, there is not enough matter to transfer heat through conduction or convection. So

**Conduction, Convection, and Radiation**

**Conduction** Conduction is the transfer of thermal energy by two objects in contact.

Examples:
• A pan of food on an electric stove gets warm.
• A spoon in boiling water gets hot.
• A glass of ice water is warmed by the hand holding it.

Conduction can occur in a solid, liquid, or gas.

**Convection** Convection is the transfer of thermal energy by the movement of matter.

Examples:
• Water boiling in a pot
• Warm air rising above a fire
• Moving air currents causing wind

Convection can occur in a liquid or a gas.

**Radiation** Radiation is the transfer of thermal energy across a space.

Examples:
• The heat from the sun
• The heat from candles
• The heat that browns marshmallows held near to a fire.

Radiation does not require intermediate matter to transfer thermal energy.

**Figure 6-10**

**A** Radiant energy from the sun travels 150 million kilometers through mostly empty space to reach Earth.

**B** When this energy reaches Earth, some of it is reflected toward space and some is absorbed. Only radiant energy that is absorbed is changed to thermal energy.

that means the heat gets here another way. That way is called radiation.

**Radiation** is the transfer of thermal energy across space. No matter is needed for radiant energy to flow as it is for conduction and convection. When you're playing outside on a sunny day, the heat you feel on your face radiated across the vast space between you and the sun.

You've felt also the effects of radiant heat when you put your hand underneath a lighted bulb, or sat next to a campfire. What other examples can you think of that are evidence of radiation?

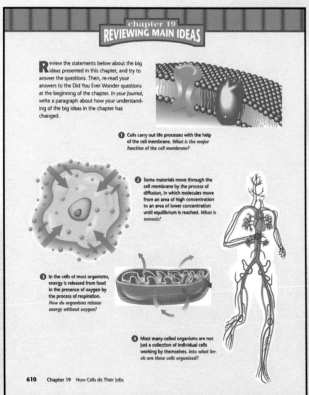

**chapter 19**
**REVIEWING MAIN IDEAS**

Review the statements below about the big ideas presented in this chapter, and try to answer the questions. Then, re-read your answers to the Did You Ever Wonder questions at the beginning of the chapter. *In your Journal,* write a paragraph about how your understanding of the big ideas in the chapter has changed.

**1** Cells carry out life processes with the help of the cell membrane. *What is the major function of the cell membrane?*

**2** Some materials move through the cell membrane by the process of diffusion, in which molecules move from an area of high concentration to an area of lower concentration until equilibrium is reached. *What is osmosis?*

**3** In the cells of most organisms, energy is released from food in the presence of oxygen by the process of respiration. *How do organisms release energy without oxygen?*

**4** Most many-celled organisms are not just a collection of individual cells working by themselves. *Into what levels are these cells organized?*

Extended captions break down complex processes into their simplest parts and focus students' attention on the main ideas.

**Reviewing Main Ideas** combines words, pictures, and probing questions to create a unique summary of chapter concepts.

NARRATIVE, VISUALS, AND CAPTIONS ARE INTEGRATED. WORKING TOGETHER, THEY BRING ALL YOUR STUDENTS THE COMPLETE STORY.

# SCIENCE INTERACTIONS

## HANDS-ON LEARNING MAKE[S] SCIENCE COME ALIVE

## SHOWS STUDENTS THAT SCIENCE IS A TOOL FOR SOLVING PROBLEMS

Hands-on activities connected by a student-friendly narrative encourage students to discover science concepts on their own and to sharpen their critical thinking and problem-solving skills.

The activities in each chapter offer a combination of open-ended and structured hands-on experiences that get students directly involved with the methods and concepts of science. The narrative guides students into and out of the activities so that students are always aware of the relationships between the activities they are doing and the science concepts they are learning.

**EXPLORE!** activities introduce students to new concepts. They are open-ended, promoting self-discovery and qualitative observations.

### Energy of Position: Potential Energy

It's fairly easy to tell that a moving object has energy. But how can you tell if an object has energy whe[n] isn't moving?

**Explore! ACTIVITY**

#### Does a softball have energy?

How can you tell if an object at rest has energy? You can explore this question in the activity.

**What To Do**

1. Hold a softball in your hand. Does it have any kinetic energy? Does it have any other kind of energy that you can tell?
2. Press a tent stake about halfway into a bucket of dirt.
3. Hold the softball about 1 m above the stake. What kind of energy will the ball have when you drop it?
4. Drop the ball onto the stake. How did the ball transfer its energy? Did the ball's energy perform work?
5. Lift the ball back up to about 1 m. Does the ball have the ability to do work, to produce change now? Does the ball have energy? If so, where did the energy come from?
6. Record your observations and answers *in your Journal.*

When you held the ball above the stake, it looked the same as it did on the ground. There was no obvious change in the ball and there was nothing to indicate that there was any energy in the ball. But as you saw, when you released the ball, it began to move toward Earth. The ball gained kinetic energy. Where did the energy come from? The only change in the ball was a change in its location. Energy was stored in the ball because of its position above the ground. Stored

**Figure 4-8**

**A** This rock has potential energy—energy stored in the rock because of the rock's position above the ground.

**B** If a strong earthquake

---

## INVESTIGATE!

### Retrieving Oil

*In this activity, you'll be an oil driller. Your objective is to find methods for pumping out the greatest amount of oil possible.*

**Problem**
What methods can be used to remove the most oil from a reservoir?

**Safety**

**Materials**
clear plastic bottle with spray pump
clear plastic tubing
100-mL graduated cylinder

1 to 2 cups of small, clean pebbles
liquid detergent
100 mL vegetable oil
100 mL hot water
50 mL cold water

Be caref[ul]
"oil well[...]
people i[...]

#### What To Do

1. Study the picture. Then, use the[...] plastic tubing, and pebbles to b[...] plastic tubing should be inserte[...] pebbles (see photo **A**).
2. Pour 100 mL of oil into your we[ll...] Seal your well.
3. Now, pump as much oil as you [...] well into a graduated cylinder. [...] and record the amount in a da[...]
4. Empty the oil out of your gradu[...] reclaiming bottle your teacher [...] your cylinder thoroughly.

## FIND OUT!

activities require students to explore certain concepts in greater depth and to collect and analyze data.

### Conservation of Energy

**Section Objectives**
■ Describe how energy changes from one form to another.
■ Understand and apply the law of conservation of energy.

**Key Terms**
law of conservation of energy

#### Energy on the Move

When you do work on an object, such as throwing, hitting, or rolling a ball, you are transferring energy from yourself to that object—the ball. You already know some ways in which energy can be transferred. Let's find out other ways in which you can transfer energy to move an object.

**Find Out! ACTIVITY**

#### How far will it go?

**W**hat's the best way to make something move? How can you give the most energy to an object? Experiment to find out!

**What To Do**
1. Obtain a set of materials, including a marble, foam cup, grooved ruler, balloon, tape, and wood splint or tongue depressor.
2. Use these objects to transfer energy in such a way that your marble travels the greatest distance when you release it. You may not throw the marble. You must simply let it go from wherever your starting point is.
3. Try to demonstrate as many different types of energy transfer as you can.

**Conclude and Apply**
1. What was the best way to make your marble move?
2. In terms of energy, why did your marble eventually stop moving?
3. Write a paragraph in your journal to describe the kinetic and potential energy present in the system you constructed. Also describe any energy changes that took place.

134   Chapter 4   Work and Energy

---

A

B

C

5. Pour 50 mL of cold water into your well (see photo **B**). Observe what happens in the bottle. Again, pump out as much oil as you can. Give the oil and water time to separate in the graduated cylinder. Then, record the amount of oil you recovered. Empty the cylinder. Do not empty this into the reclaiming bottle. Place it in a separate container that your teacher will provide. Rinse your cylinder thoroughly.

6. Using 50 mL of hot water, repeat Step 6.

7. Using 50 mL of hot water, and 8 drops of liquid detergent (see photo **C**), repeat Step 6.

This huge oil gusher on May 28, 1923, helped to bring much of the oil boom activity to West Texas. It took 21 months to drill the well, located in Reagan County, Texas, before oil flowed.

#### Analyzing

1. How many milliliters of oil did you retrieve by pumping alone?
2. What did the oil do when you added the cold water to your well? How much oil did you pump out?
3. How much oil did you pump out using hot water?
4. How much oil did you pump out using hot water and detergent?

#### Concluding and Applying

5. Tell how you would support this statement: Pumping alone is not adequate for removing all the oil from a well.
6. **Going Further** Predict the results of using detergent alone. Then, try the experiment that way.

## INVESTIGATE!

activities get students even more involved with scientific methods and processes, encouraging them to form hypotheses, manipulate variables, and collect quantitative data.

Photographs show actual students performing activities, giving your students the confidence to try them on their own.

# SCIENCE INTERACTIONS

## MAKES THE CONNECTION TO EVERY PART OF THE STUDENT'S WORLD

A key to understanding ideas is to see how they connect to other concepts. *Science Interactions* helps students see the linkages between the sciences and between science and other subject areas. Both the core text and unique feature essays help students deepen their understanding of the relevance of science in their lives.

**Technology** and **Science and Society** reveal the impact of science on today's world.

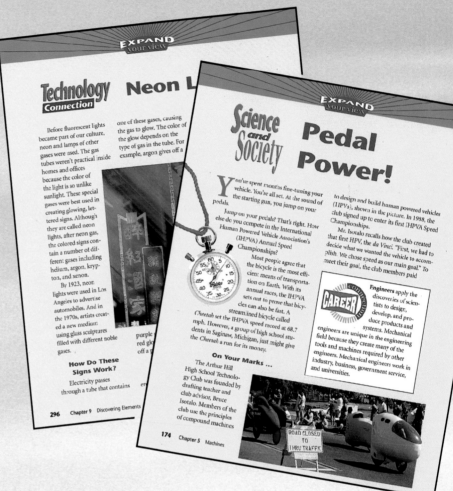

### EXPAND your view

## Technology Connection
## Neon L[...]

Before fluorescent lights became part of our culture, neon and lamps of other gases were used. The gas tubes weren't practical inside homes and offices because the color of the light is so unlike sunlight. These special gases were best used in creating glowing, lettered signs. Although they are called neon lights, the colored signs contain a number of different gases including helium, argon, krypton, and xenon.

By 1923, neon lights were used in Los Angeles to advertise automobiles. And in the 1970s, artists created a new medium using glass sculptures filled with different noble gases.

one of these gases, causing the gas to glow. The color of the glow depends on the type of gas in the tube. For example, argon gives off a [...]

purple [...]
red glo[...]
off a [...]

**How Do These Signs Work?**

Electricity passes through a tube that contains [...] er[...]

296   Chapter 9   Discovering Elements

### EXPAND your view

## Science and Society
## Pedal Power!

You've spent months fine-tuning your vehicle. You're all set. At the sound of the starting gun, you jump on your pedals.

Jump on your pedals? That's right. How else do you compete in the International Human Powered Vehicle Association's (IHPVA) Annual Speed Championships?

Most people agree that the bicycle is the most efficient means of transportation on Earth. With its annual races, the IHPVA sets out to prove that bicycles can also be fast. A streamlined bicycle called *Cheetah* set the IHPVA speed record at 68.7 mph. However, a group of high school students in Saginaw, Michigan, just might give the *Cheetah* a run for its money.

**On Your Marks ...**

The Arthur Hill High School Technology Club was founded by drafting teacher and club advisor, Bruce Isotalo. Members of the club use the principles of compound machines

to design and build human powered vehicles (HPVs), shown in the picture. In 1988, the club signed up to enter its first IHPVA Speed Championships.

Mr. Isotalo recalls how the club created that first HPV, the *da Vinci*. "First, we had to decide what we wanted the vehicle to accomplish. We chose speed as our main goal." To meet their goal, the club members paid

**CAREER** **Engineers** apply the discoveries of scientists to design, develop, and produce products and systems. Mechanical engineers are unique in the engineering field because they create many of the tools and machines required by other engineers. Mechanical engineers work in industry, business, government service, and universities.

ROAD CLOSED TO THRU TRAFFIC

174   Chapter 5   Machines

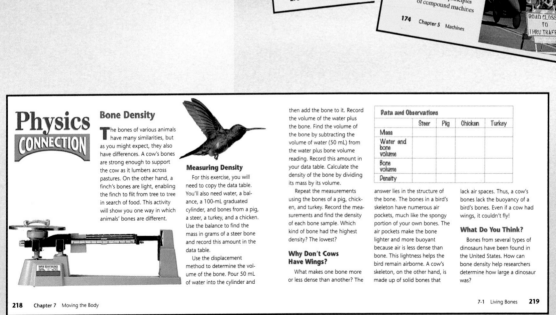

## Physics Connection
### Bone Density

The bones of various animals have many similarities, but as you might expect, they also have differences. A cow's bones are strong enough to support the cow as it lumbers across pastures. On the other hand, a finch's bones are light, enabling the finch to flit from tree to tree in search of food. This activity will show you one way in which animals' bones are different.

**Measuring Density**

For this exercise, you will need to copy the data table. You'll also need water, a balance, a 100-mL graduated cylinder, and bones from a pig, a steer, a turkey, and a chicken. Use the balance to find the mass in grams of a steer bone and record this amount in the data table.

Use the displacement method to determine the volume of the bone. Pour 50 mL of water into the cylinder and

then add the bone to it. Record the volume of the water plus the bone. Find the volume of the bone by subtracting the volume of water (50 mL) from the water plus bone volume reading. Record this amount in your data table. Calculate the density of the bone by dividing its mass by its volume.

Repeat the measurements using the bones of a pig, chicken, and turkey. Record the measurements and find the density of each bone sample. Which kind of bone had the highest density? The lowest?

**Why Don't Cows Have Wings?**

What makes one bone more or less dense than another? The

answer lies in the structure of the bone. The bones in a bird's skeleton have numerous air pockets, much like the spongy portion of your own bones. The air pockets make the bone lighter and more buoyant because air is less dense than bone. This lightness helps the bird remain airborne. A cow's skeleton, on the other hand, is made up of solid bones that

lack air spaces. Thus, a cow's bones lack the buoyancy of a bird's bones. Even if a cow had wings, it couldn't fly!

**What Do You Think?**

Bones from several types of dinosaurs have been found in the United States. How can bone density help researchers determine how large a dinosaur was?

**Data and Observations**

|  | Steer | Pig | Chicken | Turkey |
|---|---|---|---|---|
| Mass |  |  |  |  |
| Water and bone volume |  |  |  |  |
| Bone volume |  |  |  |  |
| Density |  |  |  |  |

218   Chapter 7   Moving the Body

7-1   Living Bones   **219**

The **Science Connection** feature explores in depth the relationship between two different areas of science.

**Teens in Science** shows real teenagers actively involved in various fields of science.

Teens in SCIENCE

## Flying High and Loving It

Have you ever let go of the string holding a helium-filled balloon? Did your balloon shoot straight up like a rocket, or did it seem to drift in the direction of the wind? Having trouble remembering? Just ask 18-year-old commercial hot-air balloon pilot, David Bair. He ought to know.

### Earning His Wings

David took his first ride in a hot-air balloon at the age of four. His hometown of Albuquerque, New Mexico is host to an annual festival called the International Hot-Air Balloon Fiesta. "My family met a pilot who had no crew. We volunteered to help out."

But not all the flights have been smooth. "Navigating is tricky. You don't steer a balloon as you would an airplane."

### The Science of Flight

Why is navigating a hot-air balloon so difficult? As you know, if the temperature of a gas is increased, air molecules become more active and they begin to move away from each other. When the heat source in the balloon is turned on, air in the balloon heats up. Molecular action in the balloon makes air in the balloon less dense than the surrounding air, and the balloon is pushed upward by the colder air. To go down, the heating source is simply turned off. Air in the balloon becomes more dense, and the balloon sinks. Balloon pilots can only control the up and down movements of the balloon.

"To move side to side, you have to depend on wind currents. This past summer I got caught in a severe wind. Even though I kept the balloon at a stable temperature, this wind current tossed my balloon at a speed of 400 feet a minute. Normally, ballooning is very safe, but weather is part of what makes ballooning so exciting."

478   Chapter 15   The Air Around You

---

**Connections** to art, history, literature, and other non-science subjects illustrate the relationships between science and other parts of the curriculum.

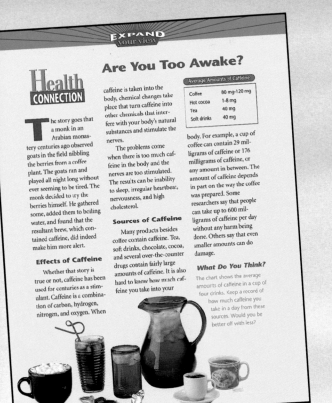

Health CONNECTION

## Are You Too Awake?

The story goes that a monk in an Arabian monastery centuries ago observed goats in the field nibbling the berries from a coffee plant. The goats ran and played all night long without ever seeming to be tired. The monk decided to try the berries himself. He gathered some, added them to boiling water, and found that the resultant brew, which contained caffeine, did indeed make him more alert.

### Effects of Caffeine

Whether that story is true or not, caffeine has been used for centuries as a stimulant. Caffeine is a combination of carbon, hydrogen, nitrogen, and oxygen. When caffeine is taken into the body, chemical changes take place that turn caffeine into other chemicals that interfere with your body's natural substances and stimulate the nerves.

The problems come when there is too much caffeine in the body and the nerves are too stimulated. The results can be inability to sleep, irregular heartbeat, nervousness, and high cholesterol.

### Sources of Caffeine

Many products besides coffee contain caffeine. Tea, soft drinks, chocolate, cocoa, and several over-the-counter drugs contain fairly large amounts of caffeine. It is also hard to know how much caffeine you take into your body. For example, a cup of coffee can contain 29 milligrams of caffeine or 176 milligrams of caffeine, or any amount in between. The amount of caffeine depends in part on the way the coffee was prepared. Some researchers say that people can take up to 600 milligrams of caffeine per day without any harm being done. Others say that even smaller amounts can do damage.

| Average Amounts of Caffeine | |
| --- | --- |
| Coffee | 80 mg-120 mg |
| Hot cocoa | 1-8 mg |
| Tea | 40 mg |
| Soft drinks | 40 mg |

### What Do You Think?

The chart shows the average amounts of caffeine in a cup of four drinks. Keep a record of how much caffeine you take in a day from these sources. Would you be better off with less?

576

---

**How It Works** applies scientific principles to the inner workings of everyday devices.

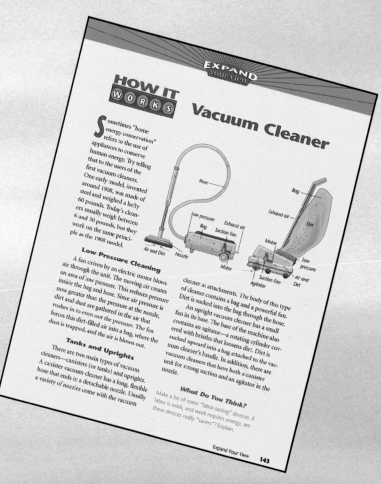

HOW IT WORKS

## Vacuum Cleaner

Sometimes "home energy conservation" refers to the use of appliances to conserve human energy. Try telling that to the users of the first vacuum cleaners. One early model, invented around 1908, was made of steel and weighed a hefty 60 pounds. Today's cleaners usually weigh between 6 and 30 pounds, but they work on the same principle as the 1908 model.

### Low Pressure Cleaning

A fan driven by an electric motor blows air through the unit. The moving air creates an area of low pressure. This reduces pressure inside the bag and hose. Since air pressure is now greater than the pressure at the nozzle, dirt and dust are gathered in the air that rushes in to even out the pressure. The fan forces this dirt-filled air into a bag, where the dust is trapped, and the air is blown out.

### Tanks and Uprights

There are two main types of vacuum cleaners—canisters (or tanks) and uprights. A canister vacuum cleaner has a long, flexible hose that ends in a detachable nozzle. Usually a variety of nozzles come with the vacuum cleaner as attachments. The body of this type of cleaner contains a bag and a powerful fan. Dirt is sucked into the bag through the hose.

An upright vacuum cleaner has a small fan in its base. The base of the machine also contains an agitator—a rotating cylinder covered with bristles that loosens dirt. Dirt is sucked upward into a bag attached to the vacuum cleaner's handle. In addition, there are vacuum cleaners that have both a canister unit for strong suction and an agitator in the nozzle.

Hose

Bag

Exhaust air

Low pressure
Bag   Suction Fan

Air and Dirt   Nozzle   Motor

Exhaust air

Dirt

Motor

low pressure

Air and Dirt

Suction Fan
Agitator

### What Do You Think?

Make a list of some "labor-saving" devices. If labor is work, and work requires energy, are these devices really "savers"? Explain.

Expand Your View   143

# SCIENCE INTERACTIONS

## OUTSTANDING TEACHER EDITIONS GIVE YOU THE TOOLS YOU NEED TO PLAN, TEACH, AND ASSESS WITH CONFIDENCE

The Teacher Wraparound Editions are comprehensive resources designed to keep you in control of the learning and teaching environment. Whether it's meeting the needs of diverse student populations, teaching science processes, or assessing student learning, the Teacher Editions give you the support to meet every challenge with confidence.

## REACHING ALL STUDENTS

**Teaching Strategies** are color-coded for individual student needs and ability levels, from those who require a little extra help to those who show exceptional aptitude.

**Multicultural Perspectives** helps you explore the contributions to science that have been made by individuals and societies from diverse cultural backgrounds.

**Meeting Individual Needs** offers teaching strategies for students who have unique challenges.

## ALTERNATE ASSESSMENT OPTIONS IN EVERY LESSON

### PREPARATION

**Concepts Developed**

In this section, students will compare open and closed circulatory systems; examine the pathway of blood through the heart, lungs, and body; and compare and contrast arteries, veins, and capillaries.

**Planning the Lesson**

Refer to the Chapter Organizer on pages 82A–B.

### 1 MOTIVATE

**Demonstration** Turn off the water supply before students arrive. Ask a student to fill a beaker with water. When no water flows, ask students why this is a problem. *You can't get what you need.* Tell students that this section will show them how the cells of an animal's body get materials that they need. L1

**Section Objectives**
In this section, you will
- Explain the role of a circulatory system in animals.
- Compare and contrast open and closed circulatory systems.
- Describe the path of blood through the heart, lungs, and body.
- Compare and contrast arteries, veins, and capillaries.

**Key Terms**
arteries
veins
capillaries

### Explore!

How can you make a model of circulation in a one-celled organism?

**Time needed** 10 minutes

**Materials** paper plate, honey, food coloring

**Thinking Processes** observing and inferring, comparing and contrasting

**Purpose** To observe food coloring diffusing through honey and compare this process to nutrient circulation in a one-celled organism.

**Teaching the Activity**

**Student Journal** Have students predict what will occur when they tilt the plate and write their predictions in their journals. L1

**Expected Outcome**

Students will observe that and flows in the direction in wh

**Answers to Questions**
**4.** The color swirls and flows in tion as the honey.
**5.** It moves as fluid in the organ
**6.** Not very efficient; seems to much the organism moves.

84    Chapter 3    Circulation

ASSESSMENT PLANNER

**PORTFOLIO**
Refer to page 81 for suggested items that students might select for their portfolios.

**PERFORMANCE ASSESSMENT**
Process, pp. 53, 54, 65, 73
Skillbuilder, pp. 56
Explore! Activities, pp. 53, 58, 60, 67
Find Out! Activities, pp. 54, 61
Investigate, pp. 64–65, 72–73

**CONTENT ASSESSMENT**
Oral, pp. 58, 67
Check Your Understanding, pp. 59, 66, 74
Reviewing Main Ideas, p. 79
Chapter Review, pp. 80–81

**GROUP ASSESSMENT**
Opportunities for group assessment occur with Cooperative Learning Strategies.

**Assessment Planner** identifies the wide range of assessment opportunities available in each chapter including performance, best-work portfolio, and group assessment.

# TEACHING SCIENCE PROCESSES

*Science Interactions* gives you all the help you want to meet your curriculum objectives for teaching science processes, problem solving, and lab skills.

To ensure the success of every hands-on activity, the Teacher Editions include practical planning and troubleshooting tips, expected outcomes, and assessment strategies.

## stems

### eed to Live

re     large organisms. However, size makes
nd     a big difference in how different
ell    organisms have their needs supplied.
e,     Those organisms that are one cell in
an     size or only a few cells thick have very
ns     different kinds of problems from larg-
ut     er organisms like yourself. Try the fol-
       lowing activity to learn about what
ut     might take place as materials circulate
nd     in a one-celled organism.

### of circulation

ne-celled organisms depend on having
ents available to all the parts of their bodies.

**To Do**

a spoonful of honey on a paper plate.

ne drop of food coloring at the edge of the
of honey.

y tilt the paper plate to make the honey flow in
ent directions. Observe what happens to the
coloring.

r *Journal*, describe what happens to the drop
d coloring as the honey flows in different
ions.

of the blob of honey as a one-celled organism.
r *Journal*, describe how materials are distributed
ghout the organism.

efficient do you think this method is for distrib-
materials in an organism's body?

### ssessment

**rmance** Have students working in
rative groups demonstrate and observe
ne membrane of a one-celled organism
Have each group stretch a piece of close-
en cloth over a basin, place small objects
of the cloth, and then pour sugar water
onto the cloth. Ask students to describe
they observe. Use the Performance Task
ment List for Group Work in **PAMSS**,
**COOP LEARN**

## Patterns of Circulation

A little one-celled organism, such as the blob of honey represented, has only a thin barrier between the inside and outside of its body. One-celled organisms are usually found completely immersed in water. Nutrients and oxygen are right there to move into the body. Once inside, these substances flow or stream through the liquid that makes up most of the organism's body. As the organism uses up these substances, wastes are produced and move out.

### ■ Open and Closed Systems

How do nutrients and oxygen reach all the body parts in larger organisms? In the chapter opening exercise, you plotted a route from the center of a city to the suburbs. You may have first moved along a four-lane highway, then onto a county road, and finally along a narrow street. Your body is similar in that it has blood vessels of various sizes going to all body parts.

The circulatory systems of complex animals are of two types, open and closed. Learn about open and closed systems in **Figure 3-1**.

**Figure 3-1**

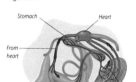

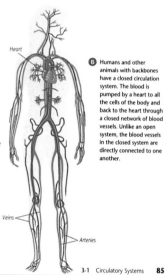

Stomach    Heart
From heart
Foot
To heart
Heart
Veins
Arteries

**A** Clams are examples of animals that have an open circulatory system. Clam hearts pump blood through blood vessels that lead to open spaces within the body. Blood washes through these spaces, and supplies body organs with a bath of nutrients and oxygen. The blood then collects in larger vessels. These vessels are squeezed by the movement of the animal, thereby moving blood back toward the heart.

**B** Humans and other animals with backbones have a closed circulation system. The blood is pumped by a heart to all the cells of the body and back to the heart through a closed network of blood vessels. Unlike an open system, the blood vessels in the closed system are directly connected to one another.

3-1 Circulatory Systems **85**

### Program Resources

**Study Guide,** p. 13
**Concept Mapping,** p. 11, The Path of Blood [L1]
**Making Connections: Across the Curriculum,** p. 9, The Red Cross [L1]
**Making Connections: Technology and Society,** p. 9, Helen B. Taussig and Heart Defects [L1]

## 2 TEACH

**Tying to Previous Knowledge**

In Chapters 1 and 2, students studied force and pressure. In this section, students learn how the action of the heart pumping produces pressure which, in turn, forces the blood through the arteries and veins.

**Theme Connection** In circulatory systems, each part interacts with the others to distribute nutrients and remove wastes throughout the body. Blood distributes the sources from which energy is released for body activities.

### Visual Learning

**Figure 3-1** To compare and contrast open and closed systems, have students use the diagrams of the clam and the human. Have students infer whether the size of an organism has any relationship to the complexity of its circulatory system.

**Inquiry Question** Have students find the root for the word *circulate*. **What do the meanings of these two words have in common?** *Something that circulates travels around in a ring or circle, returning to its starting point.* [L1]

3-1 Circulatory Systems **85**

**erformance Assessment** strategies give you ractical ways to assess tudent learning using ne activities and skill-uilder features of very lesson.

**Student Journal** activities offer diverse ways for students to record their experiences and express their thoughts.

**Portfolio** suggestions will help your students compile examples of their best work.

# SCIENCE INTERACTIONS

## UNSURPASSED TEACHER RESOURCES ARE EASY-TO-USE TOOLS THAT ENHANCE EVERY TEACHING AND LEARNING SITUATION

## HANDS-ON LEARNING

**Science Discovery Activities:** More than 50 additional hands-on, open-ended, student-directed activities give students just enough structure to enable them to select appropriate processes for making discoveries on their own.

**Activity Masters:** Copymasters of each Investigate! activity in the student text include data charts and space for student answers.

**Laboratory Manual:** One or more additional labs for each chapter, complete with set-up diagrams, data tables, and space for student responses.

**Take Home Activities:** Safe activities for students to do at home. They encourage parents to support your classroom instruction and their children's learning.

## ENRICHMENT AND APPLICATION

**Making Connections:** Three unique booklets contain activities and exercises that allow your students to explore connections to science. They are: *Integrating Sciences, Across the Curriculum,* and *Technology and Society*.

**How It Works:** Students discover the science behind how everyday things work.

**Multicultural Connections:** Biographies, readings, and activities address past and present contributions to science by individuals and societies from diverse cultural backgrounds.

## REVIEW AND REINFORCEMENT

**Study Guide:** Reinforces basic processes and content in student text. Ideal for average to below-average ability students. Also available in a consumable student edition.

**Concept Mapping Booklet:** One concept map for each chapter strengthens relationships and connections between concepts and processes. Excellent review of the chapter's big picture.

**Critical Thinking/Problem Solving:** Readings and exercises that require students to apply critical thinking and problem-solving skills. Useful with average and above-average ability students.

# SCIENCE INTERACTIONS

## INNOVATIVE RESOURCES IN THE FORMAT THAT WORKS BEST FOR YOU

## ASSESSMENT

**Performance Assessment:** A variety of skill and summative assessments help you determine your students' mastery of concepts and processes.

**Review and Assessment:** A two-page review, plus a four-page test for each chapter with a variety of question formats, to assess students' understanding of concepts, processes, and skills.

**Performance Assessment in Middle School Science:** Classroom assessment lists and scoring rubrics for more than forty different types of performance tasks.

**Alternate Assessment in the Science Classroom:** A valuable professional resource that describes a wide array of non-traditional assessment strategies.

**Computer Test Bank:** A user-friendly and flexible tool for designing and generating your own tests (IBM, Apple, and Macintosh versions).

## TEACHING AIDS

**Color Transparency Package:** Two full-color transparencies per chapter and a Transparency Masters Booklet, containing blackline masters of all color transparencies, student study sheets, and teaching strategies—all conveniently stored in a three-ring binder.

**Lab and Safety Skills in the Science Classroom** presents an overview of lab skills and safety skills related to lab activities. The booklet also contains lab and safety skills assessments for evaluating students' understanding of lab and safety skills.

# TECHNOLOGY

**Spanish Resources Booklet:** A complete Spanish-English glossary and translations of all objectives, key terms, Investigate! activities and main ideas for every chapter.

**English-Spanish Audiocassettes:** For students with reading difficulties, auditory learners, and those for whom English is a second language.

**Lesson Plan Booklet:** Complete, detailed lesson plans for every chapter help you organize your lessons more efficiently.

**Cooperative Learning in the Science Classroom:** Practical strategies for using cooperative learning techniques whenever you do activities from *Science Interactions*.

**Integrated Science Videodisc Program:** Attention-grabbing vignettes and video lessons reinforce and clarify many of the most important concepts introduced in the student edition. The interactive videodisc for each course focuses on big ideas while strengthening science thinking skills.

**Videodisc Correlation:** A user-friendly bar code directory that correlates Optical Data's Living Textbook videodiscs to every lesson in *Science Interactions*.

**Science and Technology Videodisc Series:** A seven-disc series with more than 280 full-motion video-reports on a wide spectrum of science and technology topics by Don Herbert, TV's "Mr. Wizard."

**Infinite Voyage Series** (videodiscs and video-tapes): Twenty programs from the award-winning PBS series, covering Life Science, Ecology and Environmental Education, Physical Sciences, and Archeology and Ancient History.

**Lab Partner Software** provides spreadsheet and graphing tools to record and display data from lab activities.

**MindJogger Videoquizzes:** Interactive videos that provide an entertaining way for students to review chapter concepts.

# THE SCIENCE CURRICULUM OF THE FUTURE IS AVAILABLE NOW

## A Comprehensive, Integrated Program That Engages Every Student

*Science Interactions* brings science to life and makes every student a successful learner.

## SCIENCE INTERACTIONS

| Title | Course 1 | Course 2 | Course 3 |
|---|---|---|---|
| Student Edition | 0-02-826752-4 | 0-02-826804-0 | 0-02-826856-3 |
| Teacher Wraparound Edition | 0-02-826753-2 | 0-02-826805-9 | 0-02-826857-1 |
| Teacher Classroom Resources Package | 0-02-826798-2 | 0-02-826800-8 | 0-02-826803-2 |
| *Laboratory Manual, Student Edition | 0-02-826754-0 | 0-02-826807-5 | 0-02-826858-X |
| *Laboratory Manual, Teachers' Edition | 0-02-826755-9 | 0-02-826808-3 | 0-02-826859-8 |
| Study Guide, Student Edition | 0-02-826757-5 | 0-02-826810-5 | 0-02-826861-X |
| *Study Guide, Teachers' Edition | 0-02-826756-7 | 0-02-826809-1 | 0-02-826860-1 |
| *Review and Assessment | 0-02-826758-3 | 0-02-826811-3 | 0-02-826862-8 |
| *Concept Mapping | 0-02-826759-1 | 0-02-826812-1 | 0-02-826863-6 |
| *Activity Masters | 0-02-826761-3 | 0-02-826813-X | 0-02-826864-4 |
| *Critical Thinking/Problem Solving | 0-02-826762-1 | 0-02-826814-8 | 0-02-826865-2 |
| *Multicultural Connections | 0-02-826763-X | 0-02-826815-6 | 0-02-826866-0 |
| *Lesson Plans | 0-02-826764-8 | 0-02-826816-4 | 0-02-826867-9 |
| *Take Home Activities | 0-02-826765-6 | 0-02-826817-2 | 0-02-826868-7 |
| *How It Works | 0-02-826766-4 | 0-02-826818-0 | 0-02-826869-5 |
| *Making Connections: Integrating Science | 0-02-826767-2 | 0-02-826819-9 | 0-02-826871-7 |
| *Making Connections: Across the Curriculum | 0-02-826768-0 | 0-02-826820-2 | 0-02-826872-5 |
| *Making Connections: Technology & Society | 0-02-826769-9 | 0-02-826821-0 | 0-02-826873-3 |
| *Science & Technology Videodisc Series Teachers' Guide | 0-02-826770-2 | 0-02-826822-9 | 0-02-826874-1 |
| *Videodisc Correlation (Optical Data) | 0-02-826771-0 | 0-02-826823-7 | 0-02-826875-X |
| *Transparency Package | 0-02-826772-9 | 0-02-826824-5 | 0-02-826876-8 |
| *Transparency Masters | 0-02-826773-7 | 0-02-826825-3 | 0-02-826877-6 |
| *Spanish Resources | 0-02-826774-5 | 0-02-826826-1 | 0-02-826878-4 |
| *Computer Testbank Manual | 0-02-826775-3 | 0-02-826827-X | 0-02-826879-2 |
| *Science Discovery Activities | 0-02-826776-1 | 0-02-826828-8 | 0-02-826880-6 |
| *Science Projects: Interdisciplinary Approach | 0-02-826777-X | 0-02-826829-6 | 0-02-826881-4 |
| *Science Discovery Activities Teachers' Edition | 0-02-826786-9 | 0-02-826840-7 | 0-02-826889-X |
| English Audiocassettes | 0-02-826778-8 | 0-02-826904-7 | 0-02-826882-2 |
| Spanish Audiocassettes | 0-02-826905-5 | 0-02-826831-8 | 0-02-826903-9 |
| Mind Jogger Videoquizzes Teachers' Guide | 0-02-826779-6 | 0-02-826832-6 | 0-02-826883-0 |
| Mind Jogger Videoquiz Package | 0-02-826901-2 | 0-02-826902-0 | 0-02-826900-4 |
| Performance Assessments | 0-02-826781-8 | 0-02-826833-4 | 0-02-826884-9 |
| Correlation to Science Discovery Videodiscs | 0-02-826787-7 | 0-02-826842-3 | 0-02-826891-1 |
| Testbank Package — IBM | 0-02-826788-5 | 0-02-826843-1 | 0-02-826892-X |
| Testbank Package — Macintosh | 0-02-826789-3 | 0-02-826844-X | 0-02-826893-8 |
| Testbank Package — Apple | 0-02-826790-7 | 0-02-826845-8 | 0-02-826894-6 |
| Color Transparencies | 0-02-826796-6 | 0-02-826849-0 | 0-02-826897-0 |
| Science & Technology Video Series Package | 0-02-826149-6 | 0-02-826149-6 | 0-02-826149-6 |
| Performance Assessment in Middle School Science | 0-02-827279-X | 0-02-827279-X | 0-02-827279-X |
| Lab and Safety Skills in the Science Classroom | 0-02-826853-9 | 0-02-826853-9 | 0-02-826853-9 |
| Cooperative Learning in the Science Classroom | 0-02-826430-4 | 0-02-826430-4 | 0-02-826430-4 |
| Alternate Assessment in the Science Classroom | 0-02-826429-0 | 0-02-826429-0 | 0-02-826429-0 |

*Included in Teacher Classroom Package

## AND MORE!

### Two new exciting Videodisc Series—

### Science and Technology Videodisc Series
### and The Infinite Voyage

**SCIENCE AND TECHNOLOGY VIDEODISC SERIES**
*Individual Disc Packages With Teacher Guide*
**Series Package Contains 7 Discs With Teacher Guide**

| | |
|---|---|
| Series Package | 0-02-826149-6 |

**THE INFINITE VOYAGE**

| | |
|---|---|
| Complete Video Package (20 VHS videos) | 0-02-826510-6 |
| Videodisc Series Package Dawn of Human Kind | 0-02-826517-3 |

## For more information contact your nearest regional office or call 1-800-334-7344.

**1. NORTHEAST REGION**
GLENCOE
17 Riverside Drive
Nashua, NH 03062
603-880-4701
800-424-3451
(CT, MA, ME, NH, NY, RI, VT)

**2. MID-ATLANTIC REGION**
GLENCOE
5 Terri Lane, Suite 5
Burlington, NJ 08016
609-386-7353
800-553-7515
(DC, DE, MD, NJ, PA)

**3. ATLANTIC-SOUTHEAST REGION**
GLENCOE
Brookside Park
One Harbison Way, Suite 101
Columbia, SC 29212
803-732-2365
(KY, NC, SC, VA, WV)

**4. SOUTHEAST REGION**
GLENCOE
6510 Jimmy Carter Boulevard
Norcross, GA 30071
404-446-7493
800-982-3992
(AL, FL, GA, TN)

**5. MID-AMERICA REGION**
GLENCOE
4635 Hilton Corporate Drive
Columbus, OH 43232
614-759-6600
800-848-1567
(IN, MI, OH, WI)

**6. MID-CONTINENT REGION**
GLENCOE
846 East Algonquin Road
Schaumburg, IL 60173
708-397-8448
800-762-4876
(IA, IL, KS, MN, MO, ND, NE, SD)

**7. SOUTHWEST REGION**
GLENCOE
320 Westway Place, Suite 550
Arlington, TX 76018
817-784-2100
800-828-5096
(NN, OK, AR, MS, LA)

**8. TEXAS REGION**
GLENCOE
320 Westway Place, Suite 550
Arlington, TX 76018
817-784-2100
800-828-5096

**9. WESTERN REGION**
GLENCOE
610 East 42nd Street, #102
Boise, ID 83714
208-378-4002 & 4004
800-452-6126
(AK, AZ, CO, ID, MT, NV, OR, UT, WA, WY)
Includes Alaska

**10. CALIFORNIA REGION**
GLENCOE
15319 Chatsworth Street
P.O. Box 9609
Mission Hills, CA 91346
818-898-1391
800-423-9534
Includes Hawaii

**GLENCOE CATHOLIC SCHOOL REGION**
GLENCOE
25 Crescent Street, 1st Floor
Stamford, CT 06906
203-964-9109
800-551-8766

**CANADA**
Maxwell Macmillan Canada
1200 Eglinton Avenue, East
Suite 200
Don Mills, Ontario M3C 3NI
Telephone: 416-449-6030
Telefax: 416-449-0068

**OVERSEAS**
Macmillan/McGraw-Hill
International
10 Union Square East
New York, NY 10003
Telephone: 212-353-5700
Telefax: 212-353-5894

## GLENCOE

Macmillan/McGraw-Hill
P.O. Box 508
Columbus, Ohio 43216

(SC 90907-4)
4-94

# A GLENCOE PROGRAM
# SCIENCE INTERACTIONS

Bill Aldridge                     Russell Aiuto

Jack Ballinger                    Anne Barefoot

Linda Crow                        Ralph M. Feather, Jr.

Albert Kaskel                     Craig Kramer

Edward Ortleb                     Susan Snyder

Paul W. Zitzewitz

## GLENCOE

Macmillan/McGraw-Hill

New York, New York     Columbus, Ohio     Mission Hills, California     Peoria, Illinois

# A GLENCOE PROGRAM
# SCIENCE INTERACTIONS

Student Edition
Teacher Wraparound Edition
Science Discovery Activities: SE
Science Discovery Activities: TE
Teacher Classroom Resources
Laboratory Manual: SE
Laboratory Manual: TE
Study Guide: SE
Study Guide: TE

Transparency Package
Computer Test Bank
Spanish Resources
Performance Assessment
Science and Technology
   Videodisc Series
Science and Technology
   Videodisc Teacher Guide

Send all inquiries to:

Glencoe/McGraw-Hill
936 Eastwind Drive
Westerville, OH 43081
ISBN 0-02-826857-1

Printed in the United States of America
1 2 3 4 5 6 7 8 9  VH  00 99 98 97 96 95 94

INTRODUCING THE AUTHOR TEAM

**Bill Aldridge** has been Executive Director of the National Science Teachers Association for the past 14 years. He came to NSTA after having served for 3 years in the Division of Science Education Development and Research, Science Education Directorate of the National Science Foundation. He received his B.S. degree in physics from the University of Kansas, where he also received M.S. degrees in both physics and educational evaluation. He also has an M.Ed. in science education from Harvard University. Mr. Aldridge taught high school physics and mathematics for 6 years, and physics at the college level for 17 years. He has authored numerous publications, including two textbooks, nine monographs, and articles in several journals and magazines. As Executive Director of NSTA, Mr. Aldridge has worked with the United States Congress and with government agencies in designing and producing support programs for science education. He is the recipient of awards and recognition from the National Science Foundation and the American Association of Physics Teachers.

**Russell Aiuto** is currently Senior Project Officer for the Council of Independent Colleges. Dr. Aiuto is past Director of Research and Development for the National Science Teachers Association in Washington, DC. Throughout his career, Dr. Aiuto has held several prominent positions, including Director of the Division of Teacher Preparation and Enhancement of the National Science Foundation, President of Hiram College in Hiram, Ohio, and Provost of Albion College in Albion, Michigan. He also has 30 years experience teaching biology and genetics at the high school and college levels. Dr. Aiuto received his B.A. from Eastern Michigan University and his M.A. and Ph.D. degrees from the University of North Carolina. He has received numerous awards, including the Phi Beta Kappa Faculty Scholar Award, Campus Teaching Award, and Honors Program Faculty Award from Albion College.

**Jack Ballinger** is a chemistry professor at St. Louis Community College in St. Louis, Missouri, where he has taught for 24 years. He received his B.S. degree in chemistry at Eastern Illinois University, his M.S. degree in organic chemistry at Southern Illinois University, and his Ed.D. in science education at Southern Illinois University. Dr. Ballinger has received the Manufacturing Chemists Association Award for Excellence in Chemistry Teaching.

**Anne Barefoot** is a veteran physics and chemistry teacher, with 35 years teaching experience. Her teaching career also includes biology, physical science, and working with middle school teachers in the summer at Purdue University in the APAST program. A past recipient of the Presidential Award for Outstanding Science Teaching, Ms. Barefoot holds a B.S. and an M.S. from East Carolina University, and a Specialist Certificate from the University of South Carolina. Other awards include Whiteville City Schools Teacher of the Year, Sigma Xi Award, and the North Carolina Business Award for Science Teaching. Ms. Barefoot is the former District IV Director of the National Science Teachers Association and the former president of the Association of Presidential Awardees in Science Teaching.

**Linda Crow** is an assistant professor in the Department of Community Medicine at Baylor College of Medicine. She is the project director of the Houston Scope, Sequence and Coordination (SS&C) Project. In addition to 23 years as an award-winning science teacher at college and high school levels, Dr. Crow is a recognized speaker at education workshops both in the United States and abroad. Dr. Crow received her BS, M.Ed., and Ed.D. degrees from the University of Houston. She has been named the OHAUS Winner for Innovations in College Science Teaching.

**INTRODUCING THE AUTHOR TEAM**

**Ralph M. Feather, Jr.** teaches geology, astronomy, and Earth science, and serves as Science Department Chair in the Derry Area School District in Derry, PA. Mr. Feather has 23 years of teaching experience in secondary science. He holds a B.S. in geology and an M.Ed. in geoscience from Indiana University of Pennsylvania and is currently working on his Ph.D. at the University of Pittsburgh. Mr. Feather has received the Presidential Award for Excellence in Science Teaching and the Award for Excellence in Earth Science Teaching from the Geological Society of America.

**Albert Kaskel** has 31 years experience teaching science, the last 24 at Evanston Township High School, Evanston, Illinois. His teaching experience includes biology, A. P. biology, physical science, and chemistry. He holds a B.S. in biology from Roosevelt University in Chicago and an M.Ed. degree from DePaul University. Mr. Kaskel has received the Outstanding Biology Teacher Award for the State of Illinois and the Teacher Excellence Award from Evanston Township High School.

**Craig Kramer** has been a physics teacher for 19 years. He is past chairperson for the Science Department at Bexley High School in Bexley, Ohio. Mr. Kramer received a B.A. in physics and a B.S. in science and math education, and an M.A. in outdoor and science education from The Ohio State University. He has received numerous awards, including the Award for Outstanding Teaching in Science from Sigma Xi. In 1987, the national Science Teachers Association awarded Mr. Kramer a certificate for secondary physics, making him the first nationally certified teacher in physics.

**Edward Ortleb** is the Science Supervisor for the St. Louis, Missouri Public Schools and has 37 years teaching experience. He holds an A.B. in biology education from Harris Teachers College, an M.A. in science education, and an Advanced Graduate Certificate from Washington University, St. Louis. Mr. Ortleb is a lifetime member of the National Science Teachers Association, having served as its president in 1978-79. He has also served as Regional Director for the National Science Supervisors Association. Mr. Ortleb is the recipient of several awards, including the Distinguished Service to Science Education Award (NSTA), the Outstanding Service to Science Education Award, and the Outstanding Achievement in Conservation Education.

**Susan Snyder** is a teacher in Earth science at Jones Middle School, Upper Arlington School District, Columbus, Ohio. Ms. Snyder received a B.S. in comprehensive science from Miami University, Oxford, Ohio, and an M.S. in entomology from the University of Hawaii. She has 20 years teaching experience and is author of various educational materials. Ms. Snyder has been the state recipient of the Presidential Award for Excellence in Science and Math Teaching, a finalist for National Teacher of the Year, and Ohio Teacher of the Year. She also won the Award for Excellence in Earth Science Teaching from the Geological Society of America.

**Paul W. Zitzewitz** is Professor of Physics at the University of Michigan-Dearborn. He received his B.A. from Carleton College and M.A. and Ph.D. from Harvard University, all in physics. Dr. Zitzewitz has taught physics to undergraduates for 23 years and is an active experimenter in the field of atomic physics with over 50 research papers. He has memberships in several professional organizations, including the American Physical Society, American Association of Physics Teachers, and the National Science Teachers Association. Among his awards are the University of Michigan-Dearborn Distinguished Faculty Research Award.

# Table of Contents

## TEACHER GUIDE

## STUDENT EDITION

# Responding to Changes IN SCIENCE EDUCATION

### THE NEED FOR NEW DIRECTIONS IN *SCIENCE EDUCATION*

By today's projections, seven out of every ten American jobs will be related to science, mathematics, or electronics by the year 2000. And according to the experts, if junior high and middle school students haven't grasped the fundamentals—they probably won't go further in science and may not have a future in a global job market. Studies also reveal that high school students are avoiding taking "advance" science classes.

### THE TIME FOR ACTION IS NOW!

In the past decade, educators, public policy makers, corporate America, and parents have recognized the need for reform in science education. These groups have united in a call to action to solve this national problem. As a result, three important projects have published reports to point the way for America:

- **Benchmarks for Science Literacy ...** by the American Association for the Advancement of Science.
- **Scope, Sequence, and Coordination of Secondary School Science ...** by the National Science Teachers Association (NSTA).
- **Project on National Science Standards ...** by the National Research Council.

Together, these reports spell out unified guiding principles for new directions in U.S. science education.

Glencoe's *SCIENCE INTERACTIONS* is based on these guiding principles. In fact, the leaders of

the Scope, Sequence, and Coordination project were key participants in the writing and development of *SCIENCE INTERACTIONS*.

### SCIENCE INTERACTIONS ANSWERS THE CHALLENGE!

At Glencoe Publishing, we believe that *SCIENCE INTERACTIONS* will help you bring science reform to the front lines—the classrooms of America. But more important, we believe it will help students succeed in middle school and junior high science so that they will continue learning science through high school and into adulthood.

# Science Interactions . . .

*An Innovative Series*

**Designed to Help You Prepare Your Junior High and Middle School Students *for the FUTURE!***

When you compare **SCIENCE INTERACTIONS** to a traditional science program, you'll see fewer terms. But you'll also see more questions and more activities to draw your students in. And you'll find broad themes repeated over and over, rather than hundreds of unrelated topics.

## SCIENCE INTERACTIONS FITS YOUR CLASSROOM

**SCIENCE INTERACTIONS** has the right ingredients to help you ensure your students' future. But it also has to work in today's classroom. That's why, on first glance, **SCIENCE INTERACTIONS** may look like a traditional science textbook.

Glencoe knows you have local curriculum requirements. You teach a variety of students with varying ability levels. And you have limited time, space, or support for doing hands-on activities.

No matter. Unlike a purely hands-on program, **SCIENCE INTERACTIONS** lets you offer the perfect balance of content and activities. Your students will be eager to get their hands on science. But **SCIENCE INTERACTIONS** also gives you the flexibility to use only the activities you choose ... without sacrificing anything.

## SCIENCE INTERACTIONS IS LOADED WITH ACTIVITIES

You'll choose from hundreds of activities in all three courses. These easy to set-up and manage activities will allow you to teach using a hands-on, inquiry-based approach to learning.

The **Find Out, Explore,** and **Investigate** activities are integrated with the text narrative, complete with transitions in and out of the activity. This aids comprehension for students by building continuity between text and activities.

Your teaching methods will include asking questions such as: *How do we know? Why do we believe? What does it mean?* Throughout both the narrative and activities, you'll invite your students to relate what they learn to their own everyday experiences.

### SCIENCE INTERACTIONS TEACHES CONCEPTS IN A LOGICAL SEQUENCE
### From the Concrete to the Abstract

Research shows that students learn better when they deal with descriptive matters in science for a reasonable portion of their school years before proceeding to the more quantitative, and eventually the more theoretical, parts of science. *SCIENCE INTERACTIONS* helps your students learn in this manner.

Let's look at the way you'll teach the topic of movement within and on the surface of Earth. In Course 1, students learn about the nature of Earth movements by observing that those movements bring about earthquakes and volcanoes. Learning to observe the results of Earth movement gets students to think about it in a concrete way.

In Course 2, students learn more about Earth movements by first observing how simple, everyday objects react to forces. This study of force is extended to the forces inside Earth that result in various observable phenomena—faults, seismic waves, volcanic eruptions.

In Courses 1 and 2, students have learned a lot about Earth movement by observing its results. In Course 3, they gain exposure to theoretical applications of Earth movement when they study plate tectonics.

### SCIENCE INTERACTIONS
### INTEGRATES SCIENCE AND MATH

Mathematics is a tool that all students, regardless of their career goals, will use throughout their lives. *SCIENCE INTERACTIONS* provides opportunities to hone mathematics skills while learning about the natural world. **Skill Builders**, as well as **Find Out**, **Explore**, and **Investigate** activities, offer numerous options for practicing math, including making and using tables and graphs, measuring in SI, and calculating. **Across the Curriculum** strategies in the *Teacher Wraparound Edition* provide additional connections between science and mathematics.

### SCIENCE INTERACTIONS
### INTEGRATES TOPICS FOR UNDERSTANDING

According to the experts, by using an integrated approach like *SCIENCE INTERACTIONS*, students will experience dramatic gains in comprehension and retention. For instance, the series helps you teach some of the basic concepts from physical science early on. This, in turn, makes it easier for your students to understand other concepts in life and Earth science.

But you'll be doing more than simply showing how the sciences interconnect. You'll also take numerous "side trips" with your students. Connect one area of science to another. Relate science to technology, society, issues, hobbies, and careers. Show your students again and again how history, the arts, and literature can be part of science. And help your students discover the science behind things they see every day.

### IT'S TIME FOR NEW DIRECTIONS
### IN SCIENCE EDUCATION

The need for new directions in science education has been established by the experts. America's students must prepare themselves for the high-tech jobs of the future.

We at Glencoe believe that *SCIENCE INTERACTIONS* answers the challenge of the 1990s with its new, innovative approach of "connecting" the sciences. We believe *SCIENCE INTERACTIONS* will assist you better in preparing your students for a lifetime of science learning.

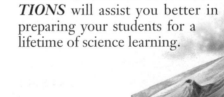

# Your Questions Answered!

### How is *SCIENCE INTERACTIONS* an integrated science program?

Although each chapter has a primary science emphasis, integration of other disciplines occurs throughout the program. Students are more likely to learn and remember a concept because they see it applied to other disciplines. This science integration is evident not only in the narrative of the core part of each chapter, but also in the **Expand Your View** features at the end of each chapter, in the *Teacher Wraparound Edition*, and in the supplements.

### How is *SCIENCE INTERACTIONS* different from general science?

There's really no comparing the *SCIENCE INTERACTIONS* program to a traditional general science text. In a general science program, the sequence of the topics and their relationship to one another is of little importance. For example, all the physics chapters in a general science text would be grouped together in a unit at the back of the book and probably have no relationship to the life, Earth, or chemistry units.

*SCIENCE INTERACTIONS* is different from general science in that chapters from different disciplines are intermixed and sequenced so that what is learned in one discipline can be applied to another.

### How is *SCIENCE INTERACTIONS* different from the "layering" or "block" approach?

In a traditional three-year course, students study life science in sixth grade, Earth science in seventh, and physical science in eighth grade. *SCIENCE INTERACTIONS* is different because it contains all of these disciplines in each course. It is true integrated science, where life, Earth, and physical science are integrated throughout the year.

### Will *SCIENCE INTERACTIONS* prepare my students for high school science?

The national reform projects agree that the best preparation is a deep understanding of important science concepts. This, rather than requiring students to memorize facts and terms, will keep your students interested in science.

Science will come alive for your students each time they pick up their textbooks. *SCIENCE INTERACTIONS'* visual format lends excitement to the study of integrated science. Students can see fundamental science concepts in living color. Learning concepts by visualizing them also increases cognitive awareness, thus giving students a more solid foundation for future science courses.

*SCIENCE INTERACTIONS* will help your students frame questions, derive concepts, and obtain evidence. When your students have mastered this language of science, they will be ready for further study.

In addition, *SCIENCE INTERACTIONS* offers your students plenty of reasons to stick with science—including unexpected career choices and examples of women and minorities achieving in science.

# Themes & Scope & Sequence

*SCIENCE INTERACTIONS*, three science textbooks for middle school, is unique in that it integrates all the natural sciences, presenting them as a single area of study. Our society is becoming more aware of the interrelationship of the disciplines of science. It is also necessary to recognize the precarious nature of the stability of some systems and the ease with which this stability can be disturbed so that the system changes. For most people, then, the ideas that unify the sciences and make connections between them are the most important.

Themes are the constructs that unify the sciences. Woven throughout *SCIENCE INTERACTIONS*, themes integrate facts and concepts. They are the "big ideas" that link the structures on which the science disciplines are built. While there are many possible themes around which to unify science, we have chosen four: Energy, Systems and Interactions, Scale and Structure, and Stability and Change.

## ENERGY

Energy is a central concept of the physical sciences that pervades the biological and geological sciences. In physical terms, energy is the ability of an object to change itself or its surroundings, the capacity to do work. In chemical terms it forms the basis of reactions between compounds. In biological terms it gives living systems the ability to maintain themselves, to grow, and to reproduce. Energy sources are crucial in the interactions among science, technology and society.

## SYSTEMS AND INTERACTIONS

A system can be incredibly tiny, such as an atom's nucleus and electrons; extremely complex, such as an ecosystem; or unbelievably large, as the stars in a galaxy. By defining the boundaries of the system, one can study the interactions among its parts. The interactions may be a force of attraction between the positively charged nucleus and negatively charged electron. In an ecosystem, however, the interactions may be between the predator and its prey, or among the plants and animals. Animals in such a system have many subsystems (circulation, respiration, digestion, etc.) with interactions among them.

## SCALE AND STRUCTURE

Used as a theme, "structure" emphasizes the relationship among different structures. "Scale" defines the focus of the relationship. As the focus is shifted from

a system to its components, the properties of the structure may remain constant. In other systems, an ecosystem for example, which includes a change in scale from interactions between prey and predator to the interactions among systems inside an animal, the structure changes drastically. In **SCIENCE INTERACTIONS**, the authors have tried to stress how we know what we know and why we believe it to be so. Thus, explanations remain on the macroscopic level until students have the background needed to understand how the microscopic structure was determined.

## STABILITY AND CHANGE

A system that is stable is constant. Often the stability is the result of a system being in equilibrium. If a system is not stable, it undergoes change. Changes in an unstable system may be characterized as trends (position of falling objects), cycles (the motion of planets around the sun), or irregular changes (radioactive decay).

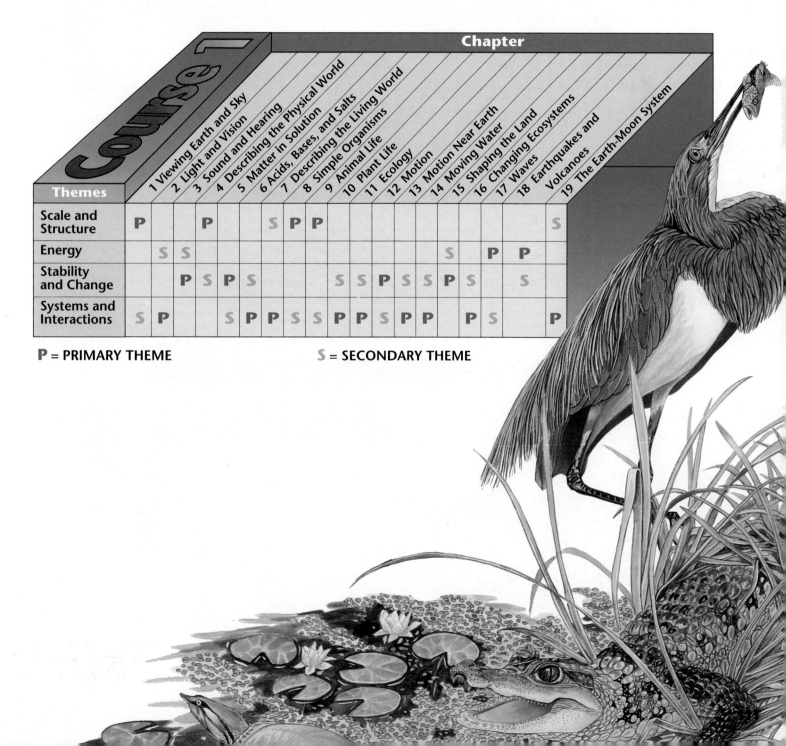

**Course 1**

**Chapter**

| Themes | 1 Viewing Earth and Sky | 2 Light and Vision | 3 Sound and Hearing | 4 Describing the Physical World | 5 Matter in Solution | 6 Acids, Bases, and Salts | 7 Describing the Living World | 8 Simple Organisms | 9 Animal Life | 10 Plant Life | 11 Ecology | 12 Motion | 13 Motion Near Earth | 14 Moving Water | 15 Shaping the Land | 16 Changing Ecosystems | 17 Waves | 18 Earthquakes and Volcanoes | 19 The Earth-Moon System |
|---|---|---|---|---|---|---|---|---|---|---|---|---|---|---|---|---|---|---|---|
| Scale and Structure | P | | | P | | S | P | P | | | | | | | | | | | S |
| Energy | | S | S | | | | | | | | | | | S | | P | P | | |
| Stability and Change | | | P | S | P | S | | | S | S | P | S | S | P | S | | S | | |
| Systems and Interactions | S | P | | | S | P | P | S | S | P | P | S | P | P | | P | S | | P |

**P** = PRIMARY THEME          **S** = SECONDARY THEME

## New Directions

### THEME DEVELOPMENT

These four major themes, as well as several others, are developed within the student material and discussed throughout the *Teacher Wraparound Edition*. Each chapter of *SCIENCE INTERACTIONS* incorporates a primary and secondary theme. These themes are interwoven throughout each level and are developed as appropriate to the topic presented.

The *Teacher Wraparound Edition* includes a **Theme Development** section for each unit opener. This section discusses the upcoming unit's key themes and explains how they are supported by the chapters in the unit. Each chapter opener includes a **Theme Development** section to explain the chapter's primary and secondary themes and to point out the major chapter concepts supporting those themes. Throughout the chapters, **Theme Connections** show specifically how a topic in the student edition relates to the themes.

### Course 2 — Chapter

| Themes | 1 Forces and Pressure | 2 Forces In Earth | 3 Circulation in Animals | 4 Work and Energy | 5 Machines | 6 Thermal Energy | 7 Moving the Body | 8 Controlling the Body Machine | 9 Discovering Elements | 10 Minerals and Their Uses | 11 The Rock Cycle | 12 The Ocean Floor and Shore Zones | 13 Energy Resources | 14 Gases, Atoms, and Molecules | 15 The Air Around You | 16 Breathing | 17 Basic Units of Life | 18 Chemical Reactions | 19 How Cells Do Their Jobs |
|---|---|---|---|---|---|---|---|---|---|---|---|---|---|---|---|---|---|---|---|
| Scale and Structure | | | | | | | | P | S | | P | | | P | | P | | | |
| Energy | | P | S | P | S | P | S | | | | | | P | | P | S | S | S | S |
| Stability and Change | S | S | | | | | S | | | P | S | | | | | | | | |
| Systems and Interactions | P | | P | S | P | S | P | P | S | P | S | | | S | S | S | P | P | P |

### Course 3 — Chapter

| Themes | 1 Electricity | 2 Magnetism | 3 Electromagnetic Waves | 4 Structure of the Atom | 5 The Periodic Table | 6 Combining Atoms | 7 Molecules in Motion | 8 Weather | 9 Ocean Water and Life | 10 Organic Chemistry | 11 Fueling the Body | 12 Blood: Transport and Protection | 13 Reproduction | 14 Heredity | 15 Moving Continents | 16 Geologic Time | 17 Evolution of Life | 18 Fission and Fusion | 19 The Solar System | 20 Stars and Galaxies |
|---|---|---|---|---|---|---|---|---|---|---|---|---|---|---|---|---|---|---|---|---|
| Scale and Structure | S | | S | S | P | | | | P | S | P | P | S | | | | | | P | P |
| Energy | P | S | P | P | | P | | P | | P | | | P | | P | | | | | |
| Stability and Change | | P | | | S | S | S | S | | S | | S | S | P | P | P | S | S | S | |
| Systems and Interactions | | | | | P | P | S | | | | | | | | S | S | S | | | |

**P = PRIMARY THEME**      **S = SECONDARY THEME**

# SCIENCE INTERACTIONS
## Contents and Primary Science Emphasis

| Course 1 | | Course 2 | | Course 3 | |
|---|---|---|---|---|---|
| Unit 1 | Observing the World Around You | Unit 1 | Forces in Action | Unit 1 | Electricity and Magnetism |
| Chapter 1 | Viewing Earth and Sky | Chapter 1 | Forces and Pressure | Chapter 1 | Electricity |
| Chapter 2 | Light and Vision | Chapter 2 | Forces In Earth | Chapter 2 | Magnetism |
| Chapter 3 | Sound and Hearing | Chapter 3 | Circulation in Animals | Chapter 3 | Electromagnetic Waves |
| Unit 2 | Interactions in the Physical World | Unit 2 | Energy at Work | Unit 2 | Atoms and Molecules |
| Chapter 4 | Describing the Physical World | Chapter 4 | Work and Energy | Chapter 4 | Structure of the Atom |
| Chapter 5 | Matter in Solution | Chapter 5 | Machines | Chapter 5 | The Periodic Table |
| Chapter 6 | Acids, Bases, and Salts | Chapter 6 | Thermal Energy | Chapter 6 | Combining Atoms |
| Unit 3 | Interactions in the Living World | Chapter 7 | Moving the Body | Chapter 7 | Molecules in Motion |
| Chapter 7 | Describing the Living World | Chapter 8 | Controlling the Body Machine | Unit 3 | Our Fluid Environment |
| Chapter 8 | Simple Organisms | Unit 3 | Earth Materials and Resources | Chapter 8 | Weather |
| Chapter 9 | Animal Life | Chapter 9 | Discovering Elements | Chapter 9 | Ocean Water and Life |
| Chapter 10 | Plant Life | Chapter 10 | Minerals and Their Uses | Chapter 10 | Organic Chemistry |
| Chapter 11 | Ecology | Chapter 11 | The Rock Cycle | Chapter 11 | Fueling the Body |
| Unit 4 | Changing Systems | Chapter 12 | The Ocean Floor and Shore Zones | Chapter 12 | Blood: Transport and Protection |
| Chapter 12 | Motion | Chapter 13 | Energy Resources | Unit 4 | Changes in Life and Earth Over Time |
| Chapter 13 | Motion Near Earth | Unit 4 | Air: Molecules in Motion | Chapter 13 | Reproduction |
| Chapter 14 | Moving Water | Chapter 14 | Gases, Atoms, and Molecules | Chapter 14 | Heredity |
| Chapter 15 | Shaping the Land | Chapter 15 | The Air Around You | Chapter 15 | Moving Continents |
| Chapter 16 | Changing Ecosystems | Chapter 16 | Breathing | Chapter 16 | Geologic Time |
| Unit 5 | Wave Motion | Unit 5 | Life at the Cellular Level | Chapter 17 | Evolution of Life |
| Chapter 17 | Waves | Chapter 17 | Basic Units of Life | Unit 5 | Planets, Stars, and Galaxies |
| Chapter 18 | Earthquakes and Volcanoes | Chapter 18 | Chemical Reactions | Chapter 18 | Fission and Fusion |
| Chapter 19 | The Earth-Moon System | Chapter 19 | How Cells Do Their Jobs | Chapter 19 | The Solar System |
| ▮ = Physics    ▮ = Life Science | | ▮ = Earth Science    ▮ = Chemistry | | Chapter 20 | Stars and Galaxies |

## Resources for Different Needs

In addition to the wide array of instructional options provided in the student and teacher editions, *SCIENCE INTERACTIONS* also offers an extensive list of support materials and program resources. Some of these materials offer alternative ways of enriching or extending your science program, others provide tools for reinforcing and evaluating student learning, while still others will help you directly in delivering instruction. You won't have time to use them all, but the ones you use will help you save the time you have.

## HANDS-ON ACTIVITIES

If you want more hands-on options, the *Laboratory Manual* offers you one or more additional labs per chapter. Each lab is complete with set-up diagrams, data tables, and space for student responses.

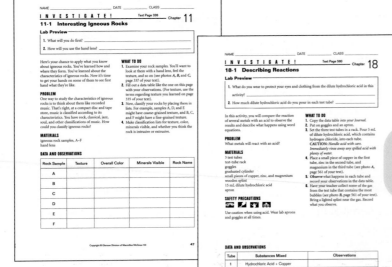

Each of the **Investigate** activities in the student text is also available in reproducible master form in the *Activity Masters* book.

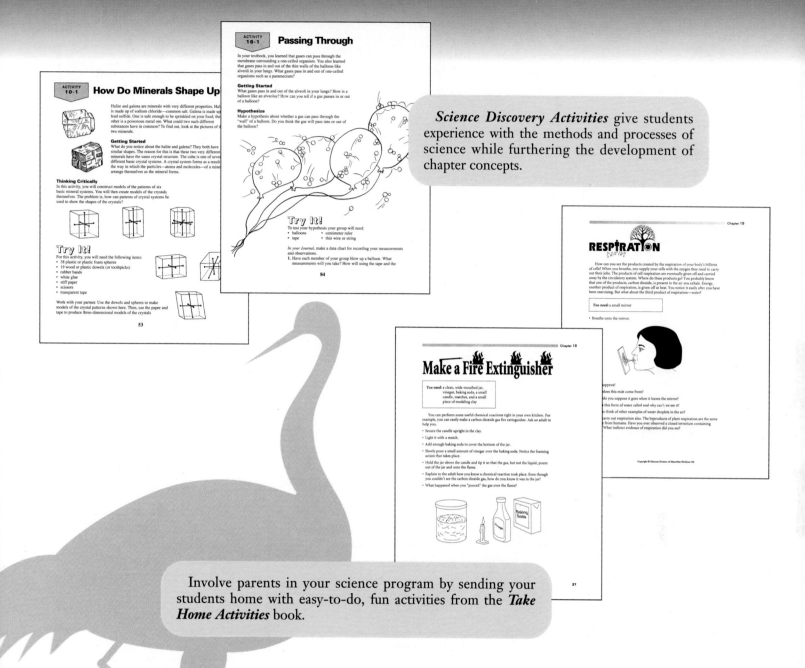

**Science Discovery Activities** give students experience with the methods and processes of science while furthering the development of chapter concepts.

Involve parents in your science program by sending your students home with easy-to-do, fun activities from the *Take Home Activities* book.

Reinforce basic lab and safety skills, including graphing and measurement, with activities from the *Lab and Safety Skills* book.

# Program Resources

## REINFORCEMENT

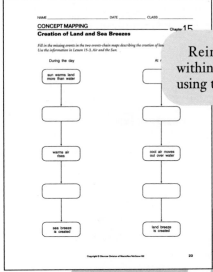

Reinforce relationships and connections within and among concepts and processes by using the *Concept Mapping* book.

Use section-by-section masters from the *Study Guide* book to reinforce the activities and content presented in the student text. Ideal for average and below-average ability students. *Consumable student edition available.*

## ASSESSMENT

*Performance Assessment in Middle School Science* provides classroom assessment lists and scoring rubrics for a variety of assessment strategies, including group assessment, oral presentations, modeling, and writing in science.

Assess student learning and performance through a variety of questioning strategies and formats in the *Review and Assessment* book. Test items cover activity procedures and analysis as well as science concepts within the four pages of reproducible masters available for each chapter.

The ***Performance Assessment*** book contains skill assessments and summative assessments that tie together major concepts of each chapter.

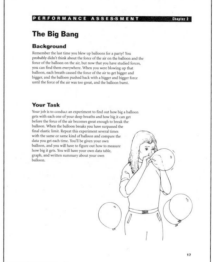

How and when to implement various assessment techniques, including performance, portfolio, observing and questioning, and student self-assessment are the focus of ***Alternate Assessment in the Science Classroom.***

***Computer Test Banks,*** available in Apple, IBM, and Macintosh versions, provide the ultimate flexibility in designing and creating your own test instruments. Select test items from two different levels of difficulty, or write and edit your own.

# Program Resources

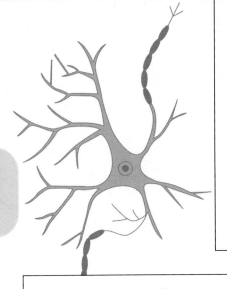

Activities and readings in the *Making Connections* series enable students to expand their understanding of the impact of science in other subjects and in different areas of their lives. The series includes: *Integrating Sciences, Technology and Society,* and *Across the Curriculum.*

---

NAME _____ DATE _____ CLASS _____

**HOW IT WORKS** ——————— Chapter 18

**How Does Photographic Film Work?**

If you've ever used a camera, you probably know that film must be kept in the dark or it will be ruined. In fact, sensitivity to light is what enables film to work.

Black and white photographic film is a thin plastic strip covered with a coating of special gelatin. The gelatin layer, called the emulsion, contains millions of silver crystals of silver-based chemicals such as silver bromide. The crystals are unusual because they have both the silver and bromine parts. But, they also contain small numbers of pure silver parts called sensitivity specks.

When light strikes film, tiny particles from the silver bromide crystals are released. The silver sensitivity specks grab and hold these particles. As more particles are trapped, the sensitivity specks begin to pull the silver away from the bromine. As they gain more silver, the specks become larger. Areas of the film that

have been exposed to more light end up with more pure silver in them. Differing amounts of silver on the emulsion form an invisible image called a latent image.

To make a latent image visible, film must be developed. Done in darkness, the developing process washes away unexposed crystals. Black-colored silver deposits remain on the emulsion. They appear as gray or black specks on the film. They are so small and close together that the image they create appears as solid color. This new image is called a negative. Clear areas on the film represent the dark parts that will be on the final picture when it is printed on paper.

Films have different types of emulsions. They vary in their sensitivity to light. Instead of having to use a flash, a photographer can often choose film made for use when little light is available.

Gelatin emulsion
Layer of silver bromide crystals
Plastic backing

**You Try It**

A photograph is made from a negative using special light-sensitive paper. Like film, this paper is also coated with a thin silver-containing emulsion. Look at a black and white photograph through a magnifying glass. Can you observe the grains that make up the shades of gray in the picture? Describe what you see.

---

With the *How It Works* book, students will see how science principles are applied in everyday devices, industry, medicine, and other technology.

---

NAME _____ DATE _____ CLASS _____

**MAKING CONNECTIONS**
**Society** ——————— Chapter 12

**The Chunnel**

In 1987, work began on tunnels beneath the seafloor under the English Channel. The tunnels cross the English Channel connecting Great Britain with France by railway. Called the "chunnel," the tunnels provide convenient and quick transportation between Great Britain and France. The chunnel enables people to travel by train under the channel in less than 30 minutes.

Two crews of diggers worked on the chunnel. One crew dug from France and the other from Great Britain. In December 1990, the two crews met for the first time in the middle of the underwater service tunnel.

The channel was completed in 1993 at a cost of over $16.7 billion. It was privately funded. With about 38.6 km of the chunnel underwater, it is the longest underwater tunnel in the world.

Huge tunnel-boring machines, or TBMs, ground the ocean floor some 30 meters beneath the English Channel. The chunnel is in a layer of Earth's crust made up almost entirely of chalk. The chalk layer is soft and does not let

water seep through. Near the French coast, however, workers had to also drill through harder materials with cracks in its surface. Water seeped through the cracks of the harder materials and caused problems for the French tunnelers. Concrete tunnel sections, which make up most of the tunnel's outer wall, were put into place by hydraulic lifters.

**What Do You Think?**

1. Would you be willing to be a passenger traveling through the chunnel? Why or why not?

2. What possible dangers could result from digging through the ocean floor?

3. Is it possible that the operation of the trains in the chunnel could have an impact on ocean life in the chunnel?

27

---

NAME _____ DATE _____ CLASS _____

**MULTICULTURAL CONNECTIONS** Use with Sections 11:1–11:3 ——— Chapter 11

**Shen Kua—Geologist in Early China**

Shen Kua (SHEN KOO uh, 1031–1095) was a Chinese writer, philosopher, ... and mathematician ... also

... *Essays* ... wrote ... erosion ... ussed ... streams ... ding earth, ... diment- ... plaining ... range is ... layered ... en Kua described how ... d once been mud and ... area. He pointed out that ... and other silt-bearing rivers ... rry sedimentary deposits to the sea year after year. He concluded that this is the way whole continents form.

The Chinese were interested in explaining the conditions of their physical environment before Shen Kua. He is one of several scholars who describe how Earth's surface was formed in terms of cycles of uplift and wearing down. The illustration is from a painting that shows sedimentary layers of exposed rock in mountains north of the Yangtze River. It was painted at about the time Shen Kua lived.

These theories were not known in Europe and other western cultures. When similar theories of Earth's geology were proposed by the European scientist James Hutton (1726–1797), they seemed strange and even revolutionary to some people.

James Hutton published his *Theory of the Earth* in 1785. It described how sedimentary rocks, deposited under ancient seas, were thrust upward and twisted into mountains by heat from Earth's interior. Molten material flowing through cracks in Earth created veins of igneous rock. Hutton completed the concept of a rock cycle by explaining how erosion wore down igneous rock, again depositing sediments into the sea, the material for new mountains.

**What Do You Think?**

Why do you think that Europeans did not learn of the Chinese theory of Earth cycles centuries earlier, when the Chinese developed the theory?

26

---

Explore past and present contributions to science of individuals and societies from various cultural backgrounds through the readings and activities in the *Multicultural Connections* book.

---

NAME _____ DATE _____ CLASS _____

**CRITICAL THINKING** ——————— Chapter 13

**Is the Oil Age Ending?**

The United States depends on oil. We use thousands of gallons every day as fuel for our cars, trucks and airplanes. We get much of our oil from Middle Eastern countries such as Kuwait and Saudi Arabia. When Iraq's military forces invaded Kuwait in August of 1990, many people were concerned that our supply of oil from that region was in danger. This caused people to wonder what it would be like if we couldn't get oil we needed. Some even think we should work toward becoming less dependent on oil for our transportation needs.

Imagine that you are developing a policy to reduce United States dependence on oil. You might consider the following items.

1. **Re-examine transportation.** Cars and trucks use as much oil each day as the nation imports each day. Three measures could reduce that demand. First, use natural gas as a fuel for cars and trucks. This would be an advantage to the environment because natural gas is a cleaner burning fuel. Second, vehicle gas mileage should be improved. A

move to smaller, more fuel-efficient cars would decrease oil demand. Third, place a tax on gasoline to encourage people to conserve.

2. **Explore for new energy sources.** Some areas are off limits for exploration in order to avoid environmental damage. Safer methods for exploration and drilling should be developed. This would allow the United States to use its own oil reserves and to protect the environment at the same time.

3. **Increase research into alternative energy sources.** Countries such as Sweden, France, Germany, and Japan make more use of nuclear power than does the United States. Nuclear power plant design has been improved. A safer way to dispose of nuclear waste or to reduce its danger should be researched. Other sources such as solar and geothermal power should be explored.

Many years ago, coal replaced wood as the primary energy source. Oil replaced coal. Now, a new energy source may be developed and bring an end to *The Age of Oil.*

**Applying Critical Thinking Skills**

1. What could result if oil companies decide to drill for more crude oil from deposits below the ocean along the shoreline at the United States?

2. You are a member of the team chosen to help develop a policy to reduce the nation's dependence on oil. What suggestions would you make?

21

---

Challenge students to apply their critical thinking and problem-solving abilities with the *Critical Thinking/Problem Solving* book. It is especially suitable for average and above-average ability students.

Chapter by chapter *Lesson Plans* will help you organize your lessons more efficiently.

**TEACHING RESOURCES**

The *Cooperative Learning Resource Guide* contains background information, strategies, and practical tips for using cooperative learning techniques whenever you do activities from *SCIENCE INTERACTIONS*.

Help your Spanish-speaking students get more out of your science lessons by reproducing pages from the *Spanish Resources* book. In addition to a complete English-Spanish glossary, the book contains translations of all objectives, key terms, Investigate activities, and main ideas for each chapter of the student text.

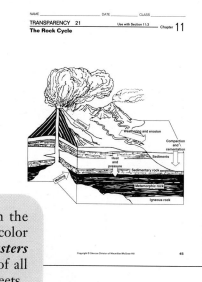

Enhance your presentation of science concepts with the *Color Transparency Package,* which includes two, full-color transparencies per chapter, and the *Transparency Masters* book. The book of masters contains blackline masters of all the color transparencies plus reproducible student worksheets.

## THE TECHNOLOGY CONNECTION

**SCIENCE INTERACTIONS** offers a wide selection of video and audio products to stimulate and challenge your students.

Attention-grabbing vignettes in the **Integrated Science Videodisc** series reinforce and enhance difficult concepts presented in the Student Edition.

Interactive videos that provide a fun way for your students to review chapter concepts make up the **MindJogger Videoquiz** series.

The **English/Spanish Audiotapes** summarize the content of the Student Edition in both English and Spanish.

## SCIENCE AND TECHNOLOGY VIDEODISC SERIES

This seven-disc series contains more than 280 full-motion video reports on a broad spectrum of topics relating to current research in various science fields, innovations in technology, and science and society issues. In addition to reinforcing science concepts, the video-reports are ideal for illustrating science methods, laboratory techniques, and careers in science.

Disc 1: PHYSICS
Disc 2: CHEMISTRY
Disc 3: EARTH AND SPACE
Disc 4: PLANTS AND SIMPLE ORGANISMS
Disc 5: ANIMALS
Disc 6: ECOLOGY
Disc 7: HUMAN BIOLOGY

### Teaching Support

The teacher guides accompanying the videodisc series show you how to use the videoreports to enrich and add excitement to your science lessons.

*Videodisc Correlation* includes a user-friendly bar code that correlates Optical Data Living Textbook videodisc programs to every lesson in *SCIENCE INTERACTIONS*.

The *Infinite Voyage Series* (videodiscs and videotapes) is twenty programs from the award-winning PBS series, covering Life Science, Ecology and Environmental Education, Physical Sciences and Archeology and Ancient History. An *Instructor's Guide* accompanies each videotape. *Lab Partner Software* provides spreadsheet and graphing tools to record and display data from lab activities.

# Thinking in Science

## CONSTRUCTIVISM IN SCIENCE

Strategies suggested in *SCIENCE INTERACTIONS* support a constructivist approach to science education. The role of the teacher is to provide an atmosphere where students design and direct activities. To develop the idea that science investigation is not made up of closed-end questions, the teacher should ask guiding questions and be prepared to help his or her students draw meaningful conclusions when their results do not match predictions. Through the numerous activities, cooperative learning opportunities, and a variety of critical thinking exercises in *SCIENCE INTERACTIONS*, you can feel comfortable taking a constructivist approach to science in your classroom.

### Activities

A constructivist approach to science is rooted in an activities-based plan. Students must be provided with sensory motor experiences as a base for developing abstract ideas. *SCIENCE INTERACTIONS* utilizes a variety of "learning by doing" opportunities. **Find Out** and **Explore** activities allow students to consider questions about the concepts to come, make observations, and share prior knowledge. **Find Out** and **Explore** activities require a minimum of equipment, and students may take responsibility for organization and execution.

**Investigates** develop and reinforce or restructure concepts as well as develop the ability to use process skills. **Investigate** formats are structured to guide students to make their own discoveries. Students collect real evidence and are encouraged through open-ended questions to reflect and reformulate their ideas based on this evidence.

### Cooperative Learning

Cooperative learning adds the element of social interaction to science learning. Group learning allows students to verbalize ideas, and encourages the reflection that leads to active construction of concepts. It allows students to recognize the inconsistencies in their own perspectives and the strengths of others. By presenting the idea that there is no one, "ready-made" answer, all students may gain the courage to try to find a viable solution. **Cooperative Learning** strategies appear in the **Teacher Wraparound Edition** margins whenever appropriate.

### And More ...

**Flex Your Brain**, a self-directed critical thinking matrix, is introduced in the introductory chapter, "Science: A Tool for Solving Problems." This activity, referenced wherever appropriate in the *Teacher Wraparound Edition* margins, assists students in identifying what they already know about a subject, then in developing independent strategies to investigate further. **Uncovering Misconceptions** in the chapter opener suggests strategies the teacher may use to evaluate students' current perspectives.

Students are encouraged to discover the pleasure of solving a problem through a variety of features. **Apply** questions that require higher-level, divergent thinking appear in **Check Your Understanding**. The **Expand Your View** features in each chapter invite students to confront real-life problems. **You Try It** and **What Do You Think?** questions encourage students to reflect on issues related to technology and society. The **Skill Handbook** gives specific examples to guide students through the steps of acquiring thinking and process skills. **Skill Builder** activities give students a chance to assess and reinforce the concepts just learned through practice. **Developing Skills**, **Critical Thinking**, and **Problem Solving** sections of the **Chapter Review** allow the teacher to assess and reward successful thinking skills.

# Developing & Applying Thinking Processes

Science is not just a collection of facts for students to memorize. Rather it is a process of applying those observations and intuitions to situations and problems, formulating hypotheses and drawing conclusions. This interaction of the thinking process with the content of science is the core of science and should be the focus of science study. Students, much like scientists, will plan and conduct research or experiments based on observations, evaluate their findings, and draw conclusions to explain their results. This process then begins again, using the new information for further investigation.

## THINKING PROCESSES

### Observing

What are the thinking processes? The most basic process is observing. Through observation—seeing, hearing, touching, smelling, tasting—the student begins to acquire information about an object or event. Observation allows a student to gather information regarding size, shape, texture, or quantity of an object or event.

### Organizing Information

Students can then begin to organize the information acquired through observation. This process of organizing information encompasses *ordering*, *organizing*, and *comparing*. How the objects or events are ordered, categorized, or compared is determined by the purpose for doing so. When ordering information, events are placed in a sequence that tells a logical story. To *classify* or *categorize* information, objects or ideas are compared in order to identify common features. By looking at similarities and differences, objects or ideas can be compared.

### Communicating

*Communicating* information is an important part of science. Once all the information is gathered, it is necessary to organize the observations so that the findings can be considered and shared by others. Information can be presented in tables, charts, a variety of graphs, or models which make it easier to consider the facts.

## Inferring

This leads to another process—*inferring*. Inferences are logical conclusions based on observations and are made after careful evaluation of all the available facts or data. Inferences are a means to explain or interpret observations. They are a prediction or hypothesis that can be tested and evaluated.

## Relating

Another process to be discussed here is *relating* cause and effect. This process focuses on how events or objects interact with one another. It also involves examining dependencies and relationships between objects and events. Since not all relationships are directly observable, the process can also be based on logical conclusions drawn from all the available data. In science, experiments involve the process of cause and relating effect. The hypothesis states an inferred relationship between objects or events. Then, as the hypothesis is tested, each variable that may interact to effect the results must be carefully controlled.

# CRITICAL THINKING SKILLS

## Making Generalizations

Identifying similarities among events or processes and then applying that knowledge to new events involves *making generalizations*.

## Evaluating Information

Developing ability in several categories of information evaluation are important to critical thinking: differentiating fact from opinion, identifying weaknesses in logic or in the interpretation of observations, differentiating between relevant and irrelevant data or ideas. Differentiating *fact from opinion* requires recognizing what can be proved objectively versus what cannot. Identifying *weaknesses in logic* requires that students be able to recognize fallacies in persuasive arguments. Differentiating *relevant vs. irrelevant* information involves recognizing details that support a central argument as well as superfluous information.

## Applying

*Applying* is a process that puts scientific information to use. Sometimes the findings can be applied in a practical sense, or they can be used to tie together complex data.

## Problem Solving

Using available information to develop an appropriate solution to a complex, integrated question is the essence of *problem solving*.

## Decision Making

*Decision making* involves choosing among alternative properties, issues, or solutions. Making informed decisions is not a random process, but requires knowledge, experience, and good judgment.

## Inquiry

The process of *inquiry* involves going beyond the present situation by asking questions or predicting outcomes of future situations. Many skills are called into play, including the ability to make generalizations, problem solve, and distinguish between relevant and irrelevant information.

## INTERACTION OF CONTENT AND PROCESS

*SCIENCE INTERACTIONS* encourages the interaction between science content and thinking processes. We've known for a long time that hands-on activities are a way of providing a bridge between science content and student comprehension. *SCIENCE INTERACTIONS* encourages the interaction between content and thinking processes by offering literally hundreds of hands-on activities that are easy to set up and do. In the student text, the **Explore** and **Find Out** activities require students to make observations, and collect and record a variety of data. **Investigates** connect the activity with the content information.

At the end of each chapter, students use the thinking processes as they complete **Developing Skills**, **Critical Thinking**, **Problem Solving**, and **Connecting Ideas** questions. **Expand Your View** connects the science content to other disciplines.

## SKILL HANDBOOK

The **Skill Builder/Skill Handbook** provides the student with another opportunity to practice the thinking processes relevant to the material they are studying. The **Skill Handbook** provides examples of the processes which students may refer to as they do the **Skill Builder** exercises.

## THINKING PROCESSES IN THE *TEACHER WRAPAROUND EDITION*

These processes are also featured throughout the *Teacher Wraparound Edition*. In the margins are suggestions for students to write in a journal. Keeping a journal encourage students to communicate their ideas, a key process in science.

In each chapter review, the *Teacher Wraparound Edition* provides **Science at Home** and **Project** ideas. Each of these indicates a thinking process skill which students will use as they complete each activity.

**Flex Your Brain** is a self-directed activity designed to assist students to develop thinking processes as they investigate content areas. Suggestions for using this decision-making matrix are in the margins of the *Teacher Wraparound Edition* whenever appropriate for the topic. Further discussion of **Flex Your Brain** can be found in the *Critical Thinking/Problem Solving* booklet of the *Teacher Classroom Resources*.

## THINKING PROCESSES MAP

On page 26T, you will find a Thinking Process Map which indicates how frequently thinking process skills are encouraged and developed in *SCIENCE INTERACTIONS*.

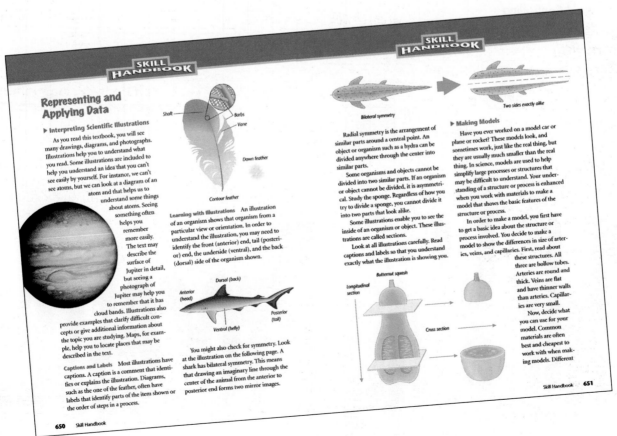

# Thinking Processes

| THINKING PROCESSES | Intro | 1 | 2 | 3 | 4 | 5 | 6 | 7 | 8 | 9 | 10 | 11 | 12 | 13 | 14 | 15 | 16 | 17 | 18 | 19 | 20 |
|---|---|---|---|---|---|---|---|---|---|---|---|---|---|---|---|---|---|---|---|---|---|
| **ORGANIZING INFORMATION** | | | | | | | | | | | | | | | | | | | | | |
| Classifying | E | I | E | FO, E | | E, SB, I | E, I | | E | | E, I | E, FO | I | FO, E | E, I, FO | | FO | E, I | | E | E |
| Sequencing | FO | FO | I | FO | | I, FO | | FO | | | | | | FO, E, I | FO, E | | E, FO, I | | FO | I | E |
| Concept Mapping | E, FO, DS | | DS | | DS | DS | I | DS | DS | DS | | DS | DS | E, DS | DS | DS | DS | DS | DS | DS | DS |
| Making and Using Tables | FO, E | I | | FO | SB, I | I, FO | SB | I | I, SB | | E, I | FO, I, E, SB | I | FO, E, I | E, SB, I | I | FO | I | I | I, E | I |
| Making and Using Graphs | | | | I | | | | I, SB | | | DS | | | | | | | I | I | E | SB |
| **THINKING CRITICALLY** | | | | | | | | | | | | | | | | | | | | | |
| Observing and Inferring | FO, E | E, FO | E, SB, FO | E, I, FO | E, FO | FO | I, E | E, FO | E, I | E, I, FO | FO, E, I | FO, I, E | E, I, FO | E, I | FO, I | E, I | E, I, FO | E, SB, FO | E, I | E, I | E, I |
| Comparing and Contrasting | FO | I, FO, E | FO, E, I | FO, E, I | E, FO, I | E, I | E, FO | E, SB, I | E, FO | E, I | E, FO | E, FO | E, I, FO | E, I | E | E, I | E | E, FO, I | I, SB | E, I | I |
| Recognizing Cause and Effect | E, I, FO, SB | E, FO, I | FO, E, I | I, E | | | E, I | E, FO | SB, E, I, FO | FO, E, SB, I, FO | E, I, FO | E, FO, I, SB | FO, I | FO | | E, FO | FO, SB | E, I | E, FO | I, SB | |
| Forming Operational Definitions | FO | E, FO | E, I, FO | I | I, E | FO | FO | FO, I | | E | | E, FO | E | E, I | FO | | I | | E, FO | E | |
| Measuring in SI | | I | | I | | | E, I | E, I | FO, I, E | FO, I | I, E | E, I | E | | | I | I | E | | I | I |
| **PRACTICING SCIENTIFIC PROCESSES** | | | | | | | | | | | | | | | | | | | | | |
| Observing | FO, I, E | I, FO, E | E, I, FO | I | | FO | | I | | | E | FO | | E | | | I | E | | | |
| Forming a Hypothesis | FO, E, I | I | FO, I, E | I, SB, E | I | | E | I, FO, E | | I | | I, E | I | I | SB | | I | | I | | |
| Designing an Experiment to Test a Hypothesis | I | FO, I | FO, I | | | | | I | E, FO, I | | I | | I | | | | I | | I | | |
| Separating and Controlling Variables | I | I | I | I | | | I | I | FO | | FO | I | I | I | | | FO, I | | I | | |
| Interpreting Data | E, I | FO, I | E | FO, I | | I, FO | FO, I | I | E, I, FO | | FO, I, E | E, I | E, I | E | FO, E, I | I | FO, I, E | E, I, FO, SB | I | I, E, SB | I |
| **REPRESENTING AND APPLYING DATA** | | | | | | | | | | | | | | | | | | | | | |
| Interpreting Scientific Illustrations | | FO, VL | FO, VL | VL | VL | VL | VL | VL | E, VL, I | VL, SB | E, VL | FO, VL | VL | I, E, SB, VL | E, VL, I | I, VL, FO | VL | VL | VL | E, VL | E, VL, I |
| Making Models | FO | FO, E | E, SB, FO, I | FO, I, E | E, I, FO | FO | I, E | I, E, FO | E, FO, I | E, I, FO | FO, E | FO | E, I, FO | E, I | FO, E | E, I | E, FO, I | FO, I, FO | | I | E |
| Predicting | I | E | E, I | I | I | | I | I, FO, FO | E, I, FO | FO | | FO | | E, I | FO, I | FO | I | I | I | | I |
| Sampling and Estimating | I | | | | | I | | I | FO | | | | E, I | | FO, I | | | E | | | I |

**Key:** I = Investigate, FO = Find Out, E = Explore, SB = Skill Builder, VL = Visual Learning, DS = Developing Skills

# Flex Your Brain

*A KEY ELEMENT* in the coverage of problem solving and critical thinking skills in *SCIENCE INTERACTIONS* is a critical thinking matrix called **Flex Your Brain**.

**Flex Your Brain** provides students with an opportunity to explore a topic in an organized, self-checking way, and then identify how they arrived at their responses during each step of their investigation. The activity incorporates many of the skills of critical thinking. It helps students to think about their own thinking and learn about thinking from their peers.

## WHERE IS FLEX YOUR BRAIN FOUND?

In the introductory chapter, "Science: A Tool for Solving Problems," is an introduction to the topics of critical thinking and problem solving. **Flex Your Brain** accompanies the text section as an activity in the introductory chapter. Brief student instructions are given, along with the matrix itself. A worksheet for **Flex Your Brain** appears in the *Critical Thinking/Problem Solving* book of the *Teacher Resources*. This version provides spaces for students to write in their responses.

In the *Teacher Wraparound Edition*, suggested topics are given in each chapter for the use of **Flex Your Brain**. You can either refer students to the introductory chapter for the procedure, or photocopy the worksheet master from the *Teacher Resources*.

**Flex Your Brain**

1. **Topic:** _____

2. **? What do I already know?**
   1. _____
   2. _____
   3. _____
   4. _____
   5. _____

3. **Q:** Ask a question

4. **A:** Guess an answer

5. **How sure am I? (circle one)**

| Not sure | | | | Very sure |
|---|---|---|---|---|
| 1 | 2 | 3 | 4 | 5 |

6. **? How can I find out?**
   1. _____
   2. _____
   3. _____
   4. _____
   5. _____

7. **EXPLORE**

8. **Do I think differently?** → yes / no

9. **? What do I know now?**
   1. _____
   2. _____
   3. _____
   4. _____
   5. _____

10. **SHARE**
    1. _____
    2. _____
    3. _____

## USING FLEX YOUR BRAIN

**Flex Your Brain** can be used as a whole-class activity or in cooperative groups, but is primarily designed to be used by individual students within the class. There are three basic steps.

1. Teachers assign a class topic to be investigated using **Flex Your Brain**.
2. Students use **Flex Your Brain** to guide them in their individual explorations of the topic.
3. After students have completed their explorations, teachers guide them in a discussion of their experiences with **Flex Your Brain**, bridging content and thinking processes.

**Flex Your Brain** can be used at many different points in the lesson plan.

**Introduction:** Ideal for introducing a topic, **Flex Your Brain** elicits students' prior knowledge and identifies misconceptions, enabling the teacher to formulate plans specific to student needs.

**Development:** Flex Your Brain leads students to find out more about a topic on their own, and develops their research skills while increasing their knowledge. Students actually pose their own questions to explore, making their investigations relevant to their personal interests and concerns.

**Review and Extension:** Flex Your Brain allows teachers to check student understanding while allowing students to explore aspects of the topic that go beyond the material presented in class.

CONCEPT MAPS

In science, concept maps make abstract information concrete and useful, improve retention of information, and show students that thought has shape.

Concept maps are visual representations or graphic organizers of relationships among particular concepts. Concept maps can be generated by individual students, small groups, or an entire class. *SCIENCE INTERACTIONS* develops and reinforces four types of concept maps—the **network tree**, **events chain**, **cycle concept map**, and **spider concept map**—that are most applicable to studying science. Examples of the four types and their applications are shown on this page.

Students can learn how to construct each of these types of concept maps by referring to the **Skill Handbook**. Throughout the course, students will have many opportunities to practice their concept mapping skills through **Skill Builder** activities, and **Developing Skills** questions in the **Chapter Review**.

## BUILDING CONCEPT MAPPING SKILLS

The **Skill Builders** in each chapter and the **Developing Skills** section of the **Chapter Review** provide opportunities for practicing concept mapping. A variety of concept mapping approaches is used. Students may be directed to make a specific type of concept map and be provided the terms to use. At other times, students may be given only general guidelines. For example, concept terms to be used may be provided and students required to select the appropriate model to apply, or vice versa. Finally, students may be asked to provide both the terms and type of concept map to explain relationships among concepts. When students are given this flexibility, it is important for you to recognize that, while sample answers are provided, student responses may vary. Look for the conceptual strength of student responses, not absolute accuracy. You'll notice that most network tree maps provide connecting words that explain the relationships between concepts. We recommend that you not require all students to supply these words, but many students may be challenged by this aspect.

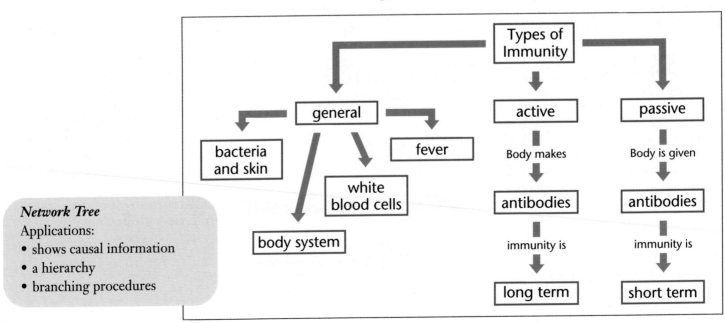

*Network Tree*
Applications:
- shows causal information
- a hierarchy
- branching procedures

## CONCEPT MAPPING BOOKLET

The ***Concept Mapping*** book of the ***Teacher Classroom Resources***, too, provides a developmental approach for students to practice concept mapping.

As a teaching strategy, generating concept maps can be used to preview a chapter's content by visually relating the concepts to be learned and allowing the students to read with purpose. Using concept maps for previewing is especially useful when there are many new key science terms for students to learn. As a review strategy, constructing concept maps reinforces main ideas and clarifies their relationships. Construction of concept maps using cooperative learning strategies as described in this Teacher Guide will allow students to practice both interpersonal and process skills.

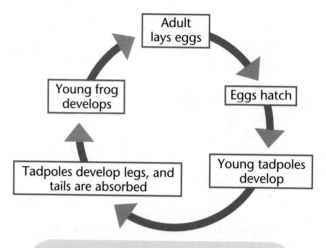

**Cycle Concept Map**
Application:
- shows how a series of events interact to produce a set of results again and again

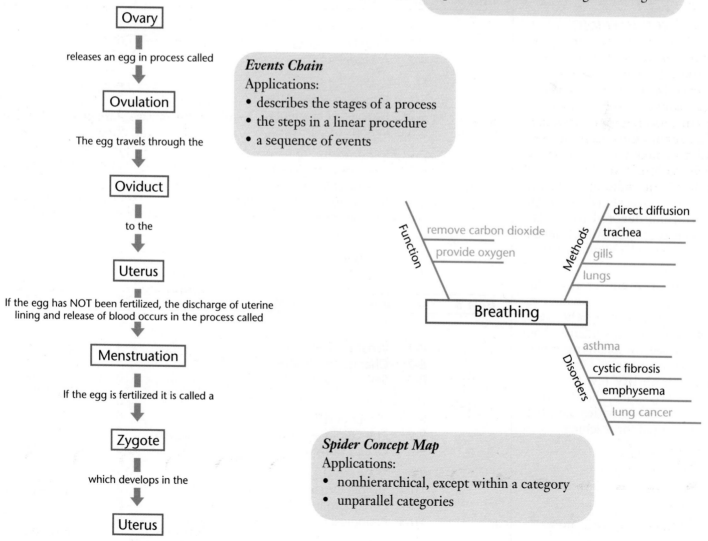

**Events Chain**
Applications:
- describes the stages of a process
- the steps in a linear procedure
- a sequence of events

**Spider Concept Map**
Applications:
- nonhierarchical, except within a category
- unparallel categories

**29T**

# Planning Your Course

SCIENCE INTERACTIONS provides flexibility in the selection of topics and content that allows teachers to adapt the text to the needs of individual students and classes. In this regard, the teacher is in the best position to decide what topics to present, the pace at which to cover the content, and what material to give the most emphasis. To assist the teacher in planning the course, a planning guide has been provided.

SCIENCE INTERACTIONS may be used in a full-year course of two semesters. It is assumed that a year-long course in integrated science will have 180 periods of approximately 45 minutes each. The sections of each chapter are classified as either core or advanced. A basic course in integrated science would include core sections, with more time devoted to fundamental concepts. An advanced course would include all sections.

Please remember that the planning guide is provided as an aid in planning the best course for your students. You should use the planning guide in relation to your curriculum and the ability levels of the classes you teach, the materials available for activities, and the time allotted for teaching.

| Unit | Chapter/Section | | Core (days) | Advanced (days) |
|---|---|---|---|---|
| Introduction | Science: A Tool for Solving Problems | | 3 | 3 |
| **Unit 1** | **Electricity and Magnetism** | | **32** | **26** |
| 1 | Electricity | | 12 | 10 |
| | 1-1 | Forces and Electrical Charges | 3 | 3 |
| | 1-2 | Electrical Charge Carriers | 3 | 2 |
| | 1-3 | Making Electricity Flow | 3 | 2 |
| | 1-4 | Resistance, Current, and Voltage | 3 | 3 |
| 2 | Magnetism | | 12 | 8 |
| | 2-1 | Forces and Fields | 4 | 2 |
| | 2-2 | Magnets | 3 | 3 |
| | 2-3 | Effects of Magnetic Fields | 3 | 2 |
| | 2-4 | Producing Electric Currents | 2 | 1 |
| 3 | Electromagnetic Waves | | 8 | 8 |
| | 3-1 | The Electromagnetic Spectrum | 3 | 3 |
| | 3-2 | The Wave Model of Light | 5 | 5 |
| **Unit 2** | **Atoms and Molecules** | | **39** | **37** |
| 4 | Structure of the Atom | | 5 | 9 |
| | 4-1 | Early Discoveries | 0 | 4 |
| | 4-2 | A Model Atom | 5 | 5 |
| 5 | The Periodic Table | | 12 | 9 |
| | 5-1 | Structure of the Atom | 5 | 4 |
| | 5-2 | Families of Elements | 3 | 2 |
| | 5-3 | Periods of Elements | 4 | 3 |
| 6 | Combining Atoms | | 13 | 11 |
| | 6-1 | Kinds of Chemical Bonds | 3 | 3 |
| | 6-2 | Chemical Shorthand | 2 | 2 |
| | 6-3 | Balancing Chemical Equations | 4 | 3 |
| | 6-4 | Chemical Reactions | 4 | 3 |
| 7 | Molecules in Motion | | 9 | 8 |
| | 7-1 | Solids and Liquids | 5 | 5 |
| | 7-2 | Kinetic Theory of Gases | 4 | 3 |
| **Unit 3** | **Our Fluid Environment** | | **37** | **43** |
| 8 | Weather | | 7 | 9 |
| | 8-1 | What Is Weather? | 4 | 4 |
| | 8-2 | Changes in Weather | 3 | 3 |
| | 8-3 | Severe Weather | 0 | 2 |
| 9 | Ocean Water and Life | | 0 | 8 |
| | 9-1 | Waves and Tides | 0 | 2 |
| | 9-2 | The Origin and Composition of Oceans | 0 | 4 |
| | 9-3 | Ocean Currents | 0 | 2 |
| 10 | Organic Chemistry | | 13 | 9 |
| | 10-1 | Simple Organic Compounds | 3 | 2 |
| | 10-2 | Other Organic Compounds | 5 | 3 |
| | 10-3 | Biological Compounds | 5 | 4 |

## Planning Guide for *SCIENCE INTERACTIONS*

# ASSESSMENT

What criteria do you use to assess your students as they progress through a course? Do you rely on formal tests and quizzes? To assess students' achievement in science, you need to measure not only their knowledge of the subject matter, but also their ability to handle apparatus, to organize, predict, record, and interpret data, to design experiments, and to communicate orally and in writing. **SCIENCE INTERACTIONS** has been designed to provide you with a variety of assessment tools, both formal and informal, to help you develop a clearer picture of your students' progress.

## PERFORMANCE ASSESSMENT

Performance assessments are becoming more common in today's schools. Science curriculums are being revised to prepare students to cope with change and with futures that will depend on their abilities to think, learn, and solve problems. Although learning fundamental concepts will always be important in the science curriculum, the concepts alone are no longer sufficient in a student's scientific education.

### Defining Performance Assessment

Performance assessment is based on judging the quality of a student's response to a performance task. A performance task is constructed to require the use of important concepts with supporting information, work habits important to science, and one or more of the elements of scientific literacy. The performance task attempts to put the student in a "real world" context so that the class learning can be put to authentic uses.

### Performance Assessment is Also a Learning Activity

Performance assessment is designed to improve the student. While a traditional test is designed to take a snapshot of what the student knows, the performance task involves the student in work that actually makes the learning more meaningful and builds on the student's knowledge and skills. As a student is engaged in a performance task with performance assessment lists and examples of excellent work, both learning and assessment are occurring.

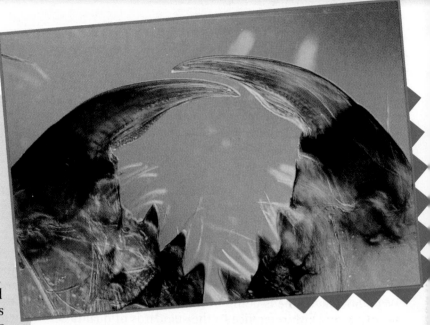

## Performance Task Assessment Lists

Performance assessment lists break the assessment criteria into several well-defined categories. Possible points for each category are assigned by the teacher. Both the teacher and the student assess the work and assign the number of points earned. The teacher is scoring not only the quality of the product, but also the quality of the student's self-assessment.

Besides using the performance task assessment list to help guide their work and then to self-assess it, the student needs to study examples of excellent work. These examples could come from published sources, or they could be students' work. These examples include the same type of product for different topics, but they would all be rated excellent using the assessment list for that product type.

## Performance Assessment in *SCIENCE INTERACTIONS*

Many performance task assessment lists can be found in Glencoe's *Performance Assessment in Middle School Science*. These lists were developed for the summative and skill performance tasks in the *Performance Assessment* book that accompanies the *SCIENCE INTERACTIONS* program. The Performance Assessment book contains a mix of skill assessments and summative assessments that tie together major concepts of each chapter. Software programs for the assessment lists are also available. The lists can be used to support **Find Out** activities; **Explore** activities; **Investigates**; and the **You Try It** and **Going Further** sections of **A Closer Look, Science Connections**, and **Expand Your View**. The assessment lists and rubrics can also be used for the **Project** ideas described in **Reviewing Main Ideas**. Glencoe's Alternate Assessment in the Science Classroom provides additional background and examples of performance assessment. Activity sheets in the Activity Masters book provide yet another vehicle for formal assessment of student products. The **MindJogger Videoquiz** series offers interactive videos that provide a fun way for your students to review chapter concepts. You can extend the use of the videoquizzes by implementing them in a testing situation. Questions are at three difficulty levels: basic, intermediate, and advanced.

## Assessment and Grading

Assessment is giving the learner feedback on the individual elements of his or her performance or product. Therefore, assessment provides specific information on strengths and weaknesses, and allows the student to set targets for improvement. Grading is an act to evaluate the overall quality of the performance or product according to some norms of quality. From the performance task assessment list, the student can see the quality of the pieces. The points on an assessment list can be summed and an overall grade awarded. The grade alone is not very helpful to the student, but it does describe overall quality of the performance or product. Both the information from the assessment list and the grade should be reported to the student, parents, and other audiences.

## ASSESSING STUDENT WORK WITH RUBRICS

A rubric is a set of descriptions of the quality of a process and/or a product. The set of descriptions includes a continuum of quality from excellent to poor. Rubrics for various types of assessment products are in *Performance Assessment in Middle School Science.*

### When to Use the Performance Task Assessment List and When to Use the Rubric

Performance task assessment lists are used for all or most performance tasks. If a grade is also necessary, it can be derived from the total points earned on the assessment list. Rubrics are used much less often. Their best use is to help students periodically assess the overall quality of their work. After making a series of products, the student is asked how he or she is doing overall on one of these types of products. With reference to the standards of quality set for that product at that grade level, the student can decide where on the continuum of quality his or her work fits. The student is asked to assign a rubric score and explain why the score was chosen. Because the student has used a performance task assessment list to examine the elements of each of the products, he or she can justify the rubric score. Experience with performance task assessment lists comes before use of a rubric.

## GROUP PERFORMANCE ASSESSMENT

Recent research has shown that cooperative learning structures produce improved student learning outcomes for students of all ability levels. *SCIENCE INTERACTIONS* provides many opportunities for cooperative learning and, as a result, many opportunities to observe group work processes and products. *SCIENCE INTER-*

*ACTIONS: Cooperative Learning Resource Guide* provides strategies and resources for implementing and evaluating group activities. In cooperative group assessment, all members of the group contribute to the work process and the products it produces. For example, if a mixed ability, four-member laboratory work group conducts an activity, you can use a rating scale or checklist to assess the quality of both group interaction and work skills. An example, along with information about evaluating cooperative work, is provided in the booklet *Alternate Assessment in the Science Classroom.*

## THE SCIENCE JOURNAL

A science journal is intended to help the student organize his or her thinking. It is not a lecture or laboratory notebook. It is a place for students to make their thinking explicit in drawings and writing. It is the place to explore what makes science fun and what makes it hard.

## PORTFOLIOS: PUTTING IT ALL TOGETHER

The portfolio should help the student see the "big picture" of how he or she is performing in gaining knowledge and skills and how effective his or her work habits are. The portfolio is a way for students to see how the individual performance tasks done during the year fit into a pattern that reveals the overall quality of their learning. The process of assembling the portfolio should be both integrative (of process and content) and reflective. The performance portfolio is not a complete collection of all worksheets and other assignments for a grading period. At its best, the portfolio should include integrated performance products that show growth in concept attainment and skill development.

## The Portfolio: Criteria for Success

To be successful, a science portfolio should:

1. Improve the student's performance in science.
2. Promote the student's skills of self-assessment and goal setting.
3. Promote a sense of ownership and pride of accomplishment in the student.
4. Be a reasonable amount of work for the teacher.
5. Be highly valued by the teacher receiving the portfolio the next year.
6. Be useful in parent conferences.

## The Portfolio: Its Contents

Evidence of the student's growth in the following five categories should be included.

1. Range of thinking and creativity
2. Use of scientific method
3. Inventions and models
4. Connections between science and other subjects
5. Readings and viewing in science

For each of the five categories, students should make indexes that describe what they have selected for their portfolios and why. From their portfolio selections, have students pick items that show the quality of their work habits. Finally, have each student write a letter to next year's science teacher introducing him- or herself to the teacher and explaining how the work in this section shows what the student can do.

## OPPORTUNITIES FOR USING SCIENCE JOURNALS AND PORTFOLIOS

*SCIENCE INTERACTIONS* presents a wealth of opportunities for performance portfolio development. Each chapter in the student text contains projects, enrichment activities, investigations, skill builders, and connections with life, society, and literature. Each of the student activities results in a product. A mixture of these products can be used to document student growth during the grading period. Descriptions, examples, and assessment criteria for portfolios are discussed in *Alternate Assessment in the Science Classroom*. Glencoe's *Performance Assessment in Middle School Science* contains even more information on using science journals and making portfolios. Performance task assessment lists and rubrics for both journals and portfolios are found there.

## CONTENT ASSESSMENT

While new and exciting performance skill assessments are emerging, paper-and-pencil tests are still a mainstay of student evaluation. Students must learn to conceptualize, process, and prepare for traditional content assessments. Presently and in the foreseeable future, students will be required to pass pencil-and-paper tests to exit high school, and to enter college, trade schools, and other training programs.

*SCIENCE INTERACTIONS* contains numerous strategies and formative checkpoints for evaluating student progress toward mastery of science concepts. Throughout the chapters in the student text, **Check Your Understanding** questions and application tasks are presented. This spaced review process helps build learning bridges that allow all students to confidently progress from one lesson to the next.

For formal review that precedes the written content assessment, *SCIENCE INTERACTIONS* presents a three-page **Chapter Review** at the end of each chapter. By evaluating the student responses to this extensive review, you can determine if any substantial reteaching is needed.

For the formal content assessment, a one-page review and a three-page **Chapter Test** are provided for each chapter. Using the review in a whole class session, you can correct any misperceptions and provide closure for the text. If your individual assessment plan requires a test that differs from the **Chapter Test** in the resource package, customized tests can be easily produced using the **Computer Test Bank**.

# Cooperative Learning

## WHAT IS COOPERATIVE LEARNING?

In cooperative learning, students work together in small groups to learn academic material and interpersonal skills. Group members learn that they are responsible for accomplishing an assigned group task as well as for each learning the material. Cooperative learning fosters academic, personal, and social success for all students.

Recent research shows that cooperative learning results in

- development of positive attitudes toward science and toward school
- lower drop-out rates for at-risk students.
- building respect for others regardless of race, ethnic origin, or sex.
- increased sensitivity to and tolerance of diverse perspectives.

## ESTABLISHING A COOPERATIVE CLASSROOM

Cooperative groups in the middle school usually contain from two to five students. Heterogeneous groups that represent a mixture of abilities, genders, and ethnicity expose students to ideas different from their own and help them to learn to work with different people.

Initially, cooperative learning groups should only work together for a day or two. After the students are more experienced, they can work with a group for longer periods of time. It is important to keep groups together long enough for each group to experience success and to change groups often enough that students have the opportunity to work with a variety of students.

Students must understand that they are responsible for group members learning the material. Before beginning, discuss the basic rules for effective cooperative learning—(1) listen while others are speaking, (2) respect other people and their ideas, (3) stay on tasks, and (4) be responsible for your own actions.

The *Teacher Wraparound Edition* uses the code **COOP LEARN** at the end of activities and teaching ideas where cooperative learning strategies are useful. For additional help refer again to these pages of background information on cooperative learning.

## USING COOPERATIVE LEARNING STRATEGIES

The *Cooperative Learning Resource Guide* of the *Teacher Classroom Resources* provides help for selecting cooperative learning strategies, as well as methods for troubleshooting and evaluation.

During cooperative learning activities, monitor the functioning of groups. Praise group cooperation and good use of interpersonal skills. When students are having trouble with the task, clarify the assignment, reteach or provide background as needed. Only answer questions when no students in the group can.

## EVALUATING COOPERATIVE LEARNING

At the close of the lesson, have groups share their products or summarize the assignment. You can evaluate group performance during a lesson by frequently asking questions to group members picked at random or having each group take a quiz together. You might have all students write papers and then choose one at random to grade. Assess individual learning by your traditional methods.

# Meeting Individual Needs

Each student brings their own unique set of abilities, perceptions, and needs into the classroom. It is important that the teacher try to make the classroom environment as receptive to these differences as possible and to ensure a good learning environment for all students.

It is important to recognize that individual learning styles are different and that learning style does not reflect a student's ability level. While some students learn primarily through visual or auditory senses, others are kinesthetic learners and do best if they have hands-on exploratory interaction with materials. Some students work best alone and others learn best in a group environment. While some students seek to understand the "big picture" in order to deal with specifics, others need to understand the details first, in order to put the whole concept together.

In an effort to provide all students with a positive science experience, this text offers a variety of ways for students to interact with materials so that they can utilize their preferred method of learning the concepts. The variety of approaches allows students to become familiar with other learning approaches as well.

## ABILITY LEVELS

The activities are broken down into three levels to accommodate all student ability levels. **SCIENCE INTERACTIONS** *Teacher Wraparound Edition* designates the activities as follows:

**L1** activities are basic activities designed to be within the ability range of all students. These activities reinforce the concepts presented.

**L2** activities are application activities designed for students who have mastered the concepts presented. These activities give students an opportunity for practical application of the concepts presented.

**L3** activities are challenging activities designed for the students who are able to go beyond the basic concepts presented. These activities allow students to expand their perspectives on the basic concepts presented.

## LIMITED ENGLISH PROFICIENCY

In providing for the student with limited English proficiency, the focus needs to be on overcoming a language barrier. Once again it is important not to confuse ability in speaking/reading English with academic ability or "intelligence." In general, the best method for dealing with LEP, variations in learning styles, and ability levels is to provide all students with a variety of ways to learn, apply, and be assessed on the concepts. Look for this symbol **LEP** in the teacher margin for specific strategies for students with limited English proficiency.

The chart on pages 38T-39T gives additional tips you may find useful in structuring the learning environment in your classroom to meet students' special needs. In the options margins of the *Teacher Wraparound Edition* there are two or more **Meeting Individual Needs** strategies for each chapter.

# Meeting
# Individual Needs

| | DESCRIPTION | SOURCES OF HELP/INFORMATION |
|---|---|---|
| **Learning Disabled** | All learning disabled students have an academic problem in one or more areas, such as academic learning, language, perception, social-emotional adjustment, memory, or attention. | *Journal of Learning Disabilities* *Learning Disability Quarterly* |
| **Behaviorally Disordered** | Children with behavior disorders deviate from standards or expectations of behavior and impair the functioning of others and themselves. These children may also be gifted or learning disabled. | *Exceptional Children* *Journal of Special Education* |
| **Physically Challenged** | Children who are physically disabled fall into two categories—those with orthopedic impairments and those with other health impairments. Orthopedically impaired children have the use of one or more limbs severely restricted, so the use of wheelchairs, crutches, or braces may be necessary. Children with other health impairments may require the use of respirators or other medical equipment. | Batshaw, M.L. and M.Y. Perset. *Children with Handicaps: A Medical Primer.* Baltimore: Paul H. Brooks, 1981. Hale, G. (Ed.). *The Source Book for the Disabled.* New York: Holt, Rinehart & Winston, 1982. *Teaching Exceptional Children* |
| **Visually Impaired** | Children who are visually disabled have partial or total loss of sight. Individuals with visual impairments are not significantly different from their sighted peers in ability range or personality. However, blindness may affect cognitive, motor, and social development, especially if early intervention is lacking. | *Journal of Visual Impairment and Blindness* *Education of Visually Handicapped* American Foundation for the Blind |
| **Hearing Impaired** | Children who are hearing impaired have partial or total loss of hearing. Individuals with hearing impairments are not significantly different from their hearing peers in ability range or personality. However, the chronic condition of deafness may affect cognitive, motor, and social development if early intervention is lacking. Speech development also is often affected. | *American Annals of the Deaf* *Journal of Speech and Hearing Research* *Sign Language Studies* |
| **Limited English Proficiency** | Multicultural and/or bilingual children often speak English as a second language or not at all. The customs and behavior of people in the majority culture may be confusing for some of these students. Cultural values may inhibit some of these students from full participation. | *Teaching English as a Second Language Reporter* R.L. Jones (Ed.). *Mainstreaming and the Minority Child.* Reston, VA: Council for Exceptional Children, 1976. |
| **Gifted** | Although no formal definition exists, these students can be described as having above-average ability, task commitment, and creativity. Gifted students rank in the top 5% of their class. They usually finish work more quickly than other students, and are capable of divergent thinking. | *Journal for the Education of the Gifted* *Gifted Child Quarterly* *Gifted Creative/Talented* |

## TIPS FOR INSTRUCTION
With careful planning, the needs of all students can be met in the science classroom.

1. Provide support and structure; clearly specify rules, assignments, and duties.
2. Establish situations that lead to success.
3. Practice skills frequently. Use games and drills to help maintain student interest.
4. Allow students to record answers on tape and allow extra time to complete tests and assignments.
5. Provide outlines or tape lecture material.
6. Pair students with peer helpers, and provide class time for pair interaction.

1. Provide a clearly structured environment with regard to scheduling, rules, room arrangement, and safety.
2. Clearly outline objectives and how you will help students obtain objectives. Seek input from them about their strengths, weaknesses, and goals.
3. Reinforce appropriate behavior and model it for students.
4. Do not expect immediate success. Instead, work for long-term improvement.
5. Balance individual needs with group requirements.

1. Openly discuss with the student any uncertainties you have about when to offer aid.
2. Ask parents or therapists and students what special devices or procedures are needed, and if any special safety precautions need to be taken.
3. Allow physically disabled students to do everything their peers do, including participating in field trips, special events, and projects.
4. Help non-disabled students and adults understand physically disabled students.

1. As with all students, help the student become independent. Some assignments may need to be modified.
2. Teach classmates how to serve as guides.
3. Limit unnecessary noise in the classroom
4. Encourage students to use their sense of touch. Provide tactile models whenever possible.
5. Describe people and events as they occur in the classroom.
6. Provide taped lectures and reading assignments.
7. Team the student with a sighted peer for laboratory work.

1. Seat students where they can see your lip movements easily, and avoid visual distractions.
2. Avoid standing with your back to the window or light source.
3. Using an overhead projector allows you to maintain eye contact while writing.
4. Seat students where they can see speakers.
5. Write all assignments on the board, or hand out written instructions.
6. If the student has a manual interpreter, allow both student and interpreter to select the most favorable seating arrangements.

1. Remember, students' ability to speak English does not reflect their academic ability.
2. Try to incorporate the student's cultural experience into your instruction. The help of a bilingual aide may be effective.
3. Include information about different cultures in your curriculum to help build students' self-image. Avoid cultural stereotypes.
4. Encourage students to share their cultures in the classroom.

1. Make arrangements for students to take selected subjects early and to work on independent projects.
2. Let students express themselves in art forms such as drawing, creative writing, or acting.
3. Make public services available through a catalog of resources, such as agencies providing free and inexpensive materials, community services and programs, and people in the community with specific expertise.
4. Ask "what if" questions to develop high-level thinking skills. Establish an environment safe for risk taking.
5. Emphasize concepts, theories, ideas, relationships, and generalizations.

# Multicultural Perspectives

American classrooms reflect the rich and diverse cultural heritages of the American people. Students come from different ethnic backgrounds and different cultural experiences into a common classroom that must assist all of them in learning. The diversity itself is an important focus of the learning experience.

Diversity can be repressed, creating a hostile environment; ignored, creating an indifferent environment; or appreciated, creating a receptive and productive environment. Responding to diversity and approaching it as a part of every curriculum is challenging to a teacher, experienced or not. The goal of science is understanding. The goal of multicultural education is to promote the understanding of how people from different cultures approach and solve the basic problems all humans have in living and learning. *SCIENCE INTERACTIONS* addresses this issue. In the **Multicultural Perspectives** sections of the *Teacher Wraparound Edition*, information is provided about people and groups who have traditionally been misrepresented or omitted. The intent is to build awareness and appreciation for the global community in which we all live.

The *SCIENCE INTERACTIONS Teacher Classroom Resources* also includes a *Multicultural Connections* booklet that offers additional opportunities to integrate multicultural materials into the curriculum. By providing these opportunities, *SCIENCE INTERACTIONS* is helping to meet the five major goals of multicultural education;

1. promoting the strength and value of cultural diversity
2. promoting human rights and respect for those who are different from oneself
3. promoting alternative life choices for people
4. promoting social justice and equal opportunity for all people
5. promoting equity in the distribution of power among groups

Two books that provide additional information on multicultural education are:

Banks, James A. (with Cherry A. McGee Banks) **Multicultural Education: Issues and Perspectives**. Boston: Allyn and Bacon, 1989.

Banks, James A (with others.) **Curriculum Guidelines for Multiethnic Education**. Washington D.C.: National Council for the Social Studies, 1977.

# Mentoring
## The role of the community in education

There are a number of ways that teachers and schools can enlist the support of their community to enhance science education.

### Parents

Continually inform parents about science classroom activities. Parents can encourage the students by asking questions about labs, following up on homework, and providing materials and support for projects.

In the *Take Home Activities* booklet of the *Teacher Classroom Resources* are simple activities for parents to do with their children. The activities require readily available materials and relate directly to the chapter contents of *SCIENCE INTERACTIONS*.

### Corporate Partnerships

A business might provide students with visits to the industry, assistance with projects, speakers for career purposes, classroom demonstrations or exhibits, or assist with curriculum development.

### Scientists in the Classroom

You may recruit a local scientist to visit the classroom about once a month to provide lessons for the students, consult with you about curriculum or lab activities, or work with students on projects. Encourage the scientist to talk about how his or her work benefits the community.

### Industrial Tutors

Encourage people with strong science backgrounds to volunteer their time to assist small groups of students who are having difficulty.

### Community Service Projects

Plan for students to study local problems such as recycling, land use, and conservation of resources. Students can then share their information with their community.

# MANAGING ACTIVITIES
## IN THE MIDDLE SCHOOL CLASSROOM

*SCIENCE INTERACTIONS* engages students in a variety of hands-on experiences to provide all students with an opportunity to learn by doing. The many hands-on activities throughout *SCIENCE INTERACTIONS* require simple, common materials, making them easy to set up and manage in the classroom.

### FIND OUT! AND EXPLORE!

**Find Out** and **Explore** activities are intended to be short and occur many times throughout the text. The integration of these activities with the core material provides for thorough development and reinforcement of concepts. Transitional statements linking the activities with core text enable students to make connections between what they read and what they do, thereby increasing cognitive awareness.

### INVESTIGATE!

What makes science exciting to students in working in the lab, observing natural phenomena, and tackling concrete problems that challenge them to find their own answers. *SCIENCE INTERACTIONS* provides more than the same "cookbook" activities you've seen hundreds of times before. Students work cooperatively to develop their own experimental designs in the **Investigates.** They discover firsthand that developing procedures for studying a problem is not as hard as they thought it might be. Watch your students grow in confidence and ability as they progress through the self-directed **Investigates.**

### Preparing Students for Open-ended Lab Experiences

To prepare students for the **Investigates**, you should follow the guidelines in the *Teacher Wraparound Edition*, especially in the sections titled Possible Procedures and Teaching Strategies. In these sections, you will be given information about what demonstrations to do and what questions to ask students so that they will be able to design their experiment. Your introduction to an **Investigate** will be very different from traditional activity introductions in that it will be designed to focus students on the problem and stimulate their thinking without giving them directions for how to set up their experiment. Different groups of students will develop alternative hypotheses and alternative procedures. Check their procedures before they begin. In contrast to some "cookbook" activities, there may not be just one right answer. Finally, students should be encouraged to use questions that come up during the **Investigate** in designing a new experiment.

### SCIENCE DISCOVERY ACTIVITIES

If you want to give your students additional opportunities to experience self-directed activities, the *Science Discovery Activities* in the *Teacher Classroom Resources* will allow you to do just that. The three activities per chapter challenge students to use their critical thinking skills in developing experimental procedures to test hypotheses. Together, all of the activities in the *SCIENCE INTERACTIONS* program form a well-rounded mix of activity types that reinforce, extend, and challenge.

# LABORATORY SAFETY

Safety is of prime importance in every classroom. However, the need for safety is even greater when science is taught. The activities in **SCIENCE INTERACTIONS** are designed to minimize dangers in the laboratory. Even so, there are no guarantees against accidents. Careful planning and preparation as well as being aware of hazards can keep accidents to a minimum. Numerous books and pamphlets are available on laboratory safety with detailed instructions on preventing accidents. In addition, the **SCIENCE INTERACTIONS** program provides safety guide-

lines in several forms. The **Lab and Safety Skills** booklet contains detailed guidelines, in addition to masters you can use to test students' lab and safety skills. The **Student Edition** and **Teacher Wraparound Edition** provide safety precautions and symbols designed to alert students to possible dangers. Know the rules of safety and what common violations occur. Know the **Safety Symbols** used in this book. Know where emergency equipment is stored and how to use it. Practice good laboratory housekeeping and management to ensure the safety of your students.

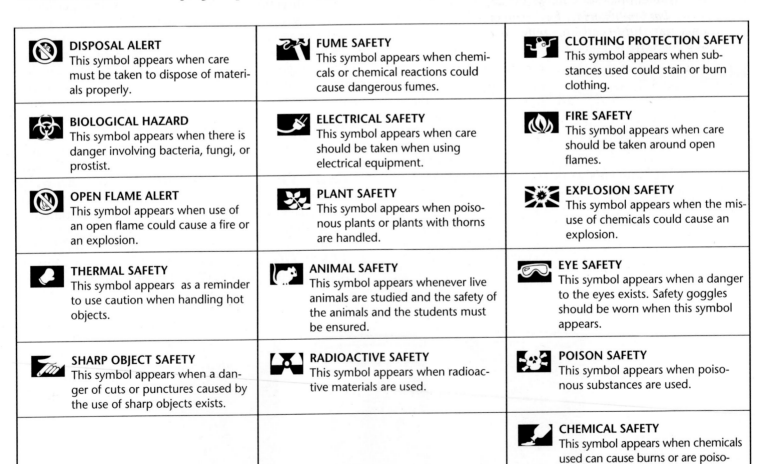

| | | |
|---|---|---|
| **DISPOSAL ALERT** This symbol appears when care must be taken to dispose of materials properly. | **FUME SAFETY** This symbol appears when chemicals or chemical reactions could cause dangerous fumes. | **CLOTHING PROTECTION SAFETY** This symbol appears when substances used could stain or burn clothing. |
| **BIOLOGICAL HAZARD** This symbol appears when there is danger involving bacteria, fungi, or prostist. | **ELECTRICAL SAFETY** This symbol appears when care should be taken when using electrical equipment. | **FIRE SAFETY** This symbol appears when care should be taken around open flames. |
| **OPEN FLAME ALERT** This symbol appears when use of an open flame could cause a fire or an explosion. | **PLANT SAFETY** This symbol appears when poisonous plants or plants with thorns are handled. | **EXPLOSION SAFETY** This symbol appears when the misuse of chemicals could cause an explosion. |
| **THERMAL SAFETY** This symbol appears as a reminder to use caution when handling hot objects. | **ANIMAL SAFETY** This symbol appears whenever live animals are studied and the safety of the animals and the students must be ensured. | **EYE SAFETY** This symbol appears when a danger to the eyes exists. Safety goggles should be worn when this symbol appears. |
| **SHARP OBJECT SAFETY** This symbol appears when a danger of cuts or punctures caused by the use of sharp objects exists. | **RADIOACTIVE SAFETY** This symbol appears when radioactive materials are used. | **POISON SAFETY** This symbol appears when poisonous substances are used. |
| | | **CHEMICAL SAFETY** This symbol appears when chemicals used can cause burns or are poisonous if absorbed through the skin. |

# Preparation of Solutions

It is most important to use safe laboratory techniques when handling all chemicals. Many substances may appear harmless but are, in fact, toxic, corrosive, or very reactive. Always check with the manufacturer or with Flinn Scientific, Inc., (312) 879-6900. Chemicals should never be ingested. Be sure to use proper techniques to smell solutions or other agents. Always wear safety goggles and an apron. The following general cautions should be used.

1. Poisonous/corrosive liquid and/or vapor. Use in the fume hood. Examples: *acetic acid, hydrochloric acid, ammonia hydroxide, nitric acid.*

2. Poisonous and corrosive to eyes, lungs, and skin. Examples: *acids, limewater, iron (III) chloride, bases, silver nitrate, iodine, potassium permanganate.*

3. Poisonous if swallowed, inhaled, or absorbed through the skin. Examples: *glacial acetic acid, copper compounds, barium chloride, lead compounds, chromium compounds, lithium compounds, cobalt (II) chloride, silver compounds.*

4. Always add acids to water, never the reverse.

5. When sulfuric acid or sodium hydroxide is added to water, a large amount of thermal energy is released. Sodium metal reacts violently with water. Use extra care if handling any of these substances.

Unless otherwise specified, solutions are prepared by adding the solid to a small amount of distilled water and then diluting with water to the volume listed. For example, to make a 0.1M solution of aluminum sulfate, dissolve 34.2 g of $Al_2(SO_4)_3$ in a small amount of distilled water and dilute to a liter with water. If you use a hydrate that is different from the one specified in a particular preparation, you will need to adjust the amount of the hydrate to obtain the required concentration.

## PREPARATION OF SOLUTIONS

**Benedict's solution** (Ch. 11): Dissolve 173 g sodium citrate and 100 g sodium carbonate in 700 mL water over a hot plate. Filter. Dissolve 17.3 g copper sulfate in 100 mL water. Slowly add to the first solution. Add water to a total volume of 1 L.

**Iodine solution** (Ch. 10, Ch. 11): Dissolve 5 g iodine crystals and 10 g potassium iodide in 500 mL water.

**Potassium permanganate solution** (Ch. 10): For a 0.01M solution, dissolve 0.16 g KMnO4 in 100 mL of distilled water.

**Sodium hydroxide solution** (Ch. 10): For a 6.0M NaOH solution, dissolve 24 g of solid NaOH in 100 mL of distilled water in a heat-resistant glass container.

# CHEMICAL Storage & DISPOSAL

## GENERAL GUIDELINES

Be sure to store all chemicals properly. The following are guidelines commonly used. Your school, city, county, or state may have additional requirements for handling chemicals. It is the responsibility of each teacher to become informed as to what rules or guidelines are in effect in his or her area.

1. Separate chemicals by reaction type. Strong acids should be stored together. Likewise, strong bases should be stored together and should be separated from acids. Oxidants should be stored away from easily oxidized materials, and so on.

2. Be sure all chemicals are stored in labeled containers indicating contents, concentration, source, date purchased (or prepared), any precautions for handling and storage, and expiration date.

3. Dispose of any outdated or waste chemicals properly according to accepted disposal procedures.

4. Do not store chemicals above eye level.

5. Wood shelving is preferable to metal. All shelving should be firmly attached to the wall and should have anti-roll edges.

6. Store only those chemicals that you plan to use.

7. Hazardous chemicals require special storage containers and conditions. Be sure to know what those chemicals are and the accepted practices for your area. Some substances must even be stored outside the building.

8. When working with chemicals or preparing solutions, observe the same general safety precautions that you would expect from students. These include wearing an apron and goggles. Wear gloves and use the fume hood when necessary. Students will want to do as you do whether they admit it or not.

9. If you are a new teacher in a particular laboratory, it is your responsibility to survey the chemicals stored there and to be sure they are stored properly or disposed of. Consult the rules and laws in your area concerning what chemicals can be kept in your classroom. For disposal, consult up-to-date disposal information from the state and federal governments.

## DISPOSAL OF CHEMICALS

Local, state, and federal laws regulate the proper disposal of chemicals. These laws should be consulted before chemical disposal is attempted. Although most substances encountered in high school biology can be flushed down the drain with plenty of water, it is not safe to assume that is always true. It is recommended that teachers who use chemicals consult the following books from the National Research Council:

*Prudent Practices for Handling Hazardous Chemicals in Laboratories.* Washington, DC: National Academy Press, 1981.

*Prudent Practices for Disposal of Chemicals from Laboratories.* Washington, DC: National Academy Press, 1983.

These books are useful and still in print, although they are several years old. Current laws in your area would, of course, supersede the information in these books.

## DISCLAIMER

Glencoe Publishing Company makes no claims to the completeness of this discussion of laboratory safety and chemical storage. The material presented is not all-inclusive, nor does it address all of the hazards associated with handling, storage, and disposal of chemicals, or with laboratory management.

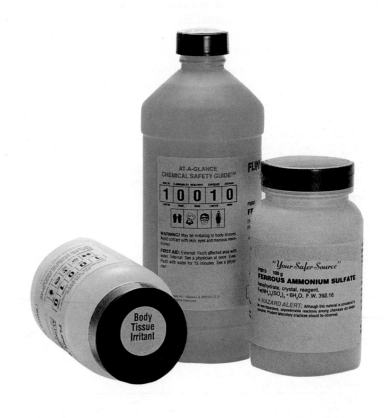

# Non-Consumables

| Item | INVESTIGATE! | Explore! | Find Out! |
|---|---|---|---|
| Apron (30) | 318, 348 | | |
| Aquarium w/glass lid (as needed) | | | 252 |
| Balance (15) | 286 | | |
| Ball, medium-sized (8) | | | 7 |
| Ball, small (8) | | | 7 |
| Ball, 12-mm steel (15) | 118 | | |
| Ball bearings (1 box) | | 129 | |
| BB pellets (150) | | 568 | |
| Beaker, 250-mL (15) | 354 | | |
| Beaker, 500-mL (30) | 38, 224, 286 | | |
| Beaker, small (45) | 198, 246 | 209 | |
| Board, 2"x4"x30 cm (15) | 68 | | |
| Bolts (1 box) | | | 122 |
| Bone (15) | | | 504 |
| Book (as needed) | 640 | | |
| Bottle, soda (15) | | 249 | |
| Bottle, 2-liter plastic (30) | | | 261 |
| Bottle, plastic (15) | | | 59 |
| Bowl (15) | 224 | 129 | |
| Box, clear plastic (15) | | | 310 |
| Box, large cardboard (2) | | | 222 |
| Brick (15) | | 111 | |
| Bulb, flashlight w/socket, (45) | | | 32, 35, 37, 40 |
| Burner (15) | | 218, 305, 322 | 59 |
| Calculator (as needed) | | | 345 |
| Camera with flashbulb (1) | | 179 | |
| Can, 1/4 pint varnish or paint w/lid (15) | | | 307 |
| Cans of equal size, metal (several each: black, white, shiny or foil-wrapped) | 88 | | |
| Chairs (long row) | | 273 | |
| Clamp, test-tube (15) | 354 | | |
| Clipboard (as needed) | 640 | | |
| Clock (1 wall) | 88 | | |
| Clock or watch (15) | 276 | | |
| Color filter (as needed) | | | 91 |
| Comb (15) | | 21 | 27 |
| Compact disc (15) | | 95 | |
| Compass, magnetic (30) | 480 | | |
| Conductivity tester (as needed) | 286 | | |
| Container, clear (15) | | 218 | |
| Container, clear plastic storage (15) | 276 | | 274 |
| Container, large, for water (10) | 12 | | |
| Container, shiny metal (15) | | | 245 |
| Container with cover (15) | 572 | | |
| Cookie sheet (15) | | 93 | |
| Cooking syringe (15) | 212 | | |
| Cork (15) | | | 274 |
| Coverslip (15) | 420 | | |

# Non-Consumables

| Item | INVESTIGATE! | Explore! | Find Out! |
|---|---|---|---|
| Crucible, open (15) | | 305 | |
| Cup, drinking (30) | 212 | | |
| Dish (30) | | 405 | 4 |
| Dish, glass baking or clear plastic storage container (15) | | | 274 |
| Dissecting pan (15) | 554 | | |
| Dropper (30) | 198, 354, 420 | 219, 322 | 4 |
| Dropper bottle (60) | 326, 348 | | |
| Earphone plug w/wires attached (15) | | | 67 |
| Electric fan (3-speed)(15) | 276 | | |
| Exercise slant board (1) | | | 356 |
| Flashlight (8 utility, 1 penlight) | | | 7, 628 |
| Flask, 500 mL (15) | | 175 | |
| Flask, 1000-mL (15) | 286 | | |
| Forceps (15) | 420, 546, 554 | | |
| Freezer (1) | | 218, 254 | |
| Funnel (15) | 38, 198 | | |
| Galvanometer (15) | | | 71 |
| Glass (45) | | 295 | 216, 356 |
| Goggles, safety (30) | 318, 348, 354 | | |
| Graduated cylinder, 10-mL (15) | 354 | | |
| Graduated cylinder, 25-mL (15) | 198 | | |
| Graduated cylinder, 100-mL (15) | 348, 354 | | |
| Hammer (as needed) | | | 307 |
| Hand lens (15) | 256, 420 | | |
| Heat lamp (as needed) | 88 | | |
| Hot plate (15) | 224, 286, 354 | | 307 |
| Ingredient lists: lawn fertilizer, dog or cat food, paint, laundry detergent or bleach (15 each) | | 185 | |
| Iron nail (60) | 60, 68 | 57 | 307 |
| Jar, large glass (15) | | 294, 295 | |
| Jar, narrow (15) | | | 284 |
| Knife, craft or razor blade (15) | | | 91 |
| Knitting needle, steel (15) | 68 | | |
| Lamp (15) | | 95 | |
| Lamp, straight filament (15) | | | 91 |
| Light (15) | 276 | | |
| Magnet, bar (30) | 68, 480 | 50, 53, 57, 65, 479 | 51, 59, 66, 67, 71 |
| Magnet, horseshoe (15) | | 129 | |
| Magnetic board (15) | 132 | | |
| Magnifying glass (15) | | 8 | 383 |
| Marbles (1 large bag) | 182 | 111 | 252 |
| Marbles, glass (60) | 118 | | |
| Marbles, steel (60) | 118 | | |
| Meterstick (15) | 38, 224, 518, 610 | | |
| Microscope slide (15) | 420 | | |
| Microscope (15) | 378, 420 | 549 | |
| Mirror (1 for class) | | 437 | |
| Model of human hand and arm bones (1 for class) | 554 | | |

# Non-Consumables

| Item | INVESTIGATE! | Explore! | Find Out! |
|---|---|---|---|
| Needle, sewing (15) | | | 59 |
| Nuts (metal)(1 box) | | | 122 |
| Object, plastic (15) | 24 | | |
| Object, glass (15) | 24 | | |
| Object, ceramic (15) | 24 | | |
| Pan (15) | 286 | 218 | 252 |
| Petri dish, w/cover (45) | 448 | | 383 |
| Pennies (up to 1500 as needed) | 572 | | |
| Pie pan or large plate (45) | | | 216 |
| Pie pan, aluminum (15) | 118 | | |
| Pliers, insulated (15) | | | 59 |
| Radio w/earphone jack, no speaker (15) | | | 67 |
| Radio, sm. battery-powered AM (1 for class) | | 81 | |
| Razor blade or craft knife (15) | | | 91 |
| Ring, ring stand (15) | 38 | | |
| Rock (15) | | 8 | |
| Rubber magnetic strips (380 pieces) | 132 | | |
| Ruler, grooved (15) | 118 | | |
| Ruler, centimeter (15) | | | 40 |
| Ruler, metric (15) | 276, 480, 600, 634 | 535 | |
| Sand, small bag of (15) | | 111 | 252 |
| Scale, bathroom (1) | | 341 | |
| Scalpel (15) | 420, 554 | | |
| Scissors (15) | 68, 96, 286, 326, 414, 448, 472, 518, 546, 610, 640 | 469, 516 | 504 |
| Shell (15) | | | 504 |
| Sink (1 for class) | | 175 | |
| Smoke detector (1 for class) | | 567 | |
| Spoon (15) | 354 | 295 | 284, 504 |
| Stirrer (15) | 198 | | |
| Stopper, one-hole w/tube assembly (15) | 286 | 175 | |
| Stopper, test-tube (45) | 198, 318 | 373 | |
| Tacks (5 boxes) | | 129 | |
| Telescope, sm. refracting (as needed) | 640 | | |
| Tennis ball (25) | | | 222 |
| Test tubes (150) | 198, 318, 348, 354 | 175, 322, 373 | |
| Test-tube holder (15) | | 322 | |
| Test-tube rack (15) | 198, 318, 348, 354 | 322, 373 | |
| Thermal mitt (15) | 212, 224 | | |
| Thermometer, Celsius (45) | 88, 224, 246 | 209 | 245 |
| Thermos bottle w/cap (15) | | 254 | |
| Timer, with second hand (15) | 38, 546 | | 537 |
| Tongs (15) | 224 | 305 | 59 |
| Towel (15) | 286 | | 388 |
| Tray or square pan (15) | | 218, 568 | |
| Tripod, small (as needed) | 640 | | |
| Tubing, plastic, polyethylene (6 meters) | 286 | | |

# Equipment List

## Non-Consumables

| Item | INVESTIGATE! | Explore! | Find Out! |
|---|---|---|---|
| Tubing, rubber, 2 sizes (15 meters each) | 38 | | |
| Washers (metal) (1 box) | 286 | | 122 |
| Wire, insulated (45 meters) | | | 32, 35, 37, 40, 67 |
| Wire, insulated 16-gauge (8 meters) | 68 | | |
| Wire, insulated 22-gauge (120 meters) | 60, 68 | | 66, 71 |
| Wire clips (45) | | | 40 |
| Wire cutter (15) | 68 | | |
| Wood block (30) | 68 | | 274 |
| Wool cloth (15) | | 21, 29 | 27 |
| World map (as needed) | 472 | | |

## Consumables

| Item | INVESTIGATE! | Explore! | Find Out! |
|---|---|---|---|
| Adding machine tape (1 roll) | 518, 610 | | |
| Aluminum foil (1 box) | | 29 | 310 |
| Apple, rotten (30) | 390 | | 310 |
| Apple, unripe (30) | | | 310 |
| Apple (95) | 390 | 305 | |
| Bacon, cooked (1 package) | 326 | | |
| Bag, paper (15) | 326 | | |
| Bag, plastic (15) | 24 | | |
| Bag, plastic, clear resealable (90) | 390 | | |
| Balloon (45) | 224 | 29 | |
| Battery, various sizes (as needed) | 60, 68 | | 32, 35, 37, 40, 66, 628 |
| Beans, dark red (375) | | | 537 |
| Beans, white (375) | | | 537 |
| Beef (2 lbs) | | | 358 |
| Bread (12 slices) | 326 | 305 | |
| Butter (1 stick) | | 324 | |
| Candy, brightly-colored, hard (45 pieces) | | 209 | |
| Candy-coated chocolates (90 red, 105 green) | 152 | 411 | |
| Candy-coated peanuts (60 red, 45 green) | 152 | | |
| Cardboard, various sizes (as needed) | 212, 246, 286, 546, 600, 640 | 111, 469, 479 | |
| Carton, milk (15) | | | 504 |
| Cellophane tape, translucent (15 rolls) | 24 | 65 | 23, 27 |
| Cheese (15 small pieces) | 326 | | |
| Chicken wing, cooked (15) | 554 | | |
| Chocolate (15 small pieces) | | 322 | |
| Clay (1 package) | | | 122 |
| Clay, green (1 package) | 586 | | |
| Clay, white (1 package) | 586 | | |
| Cotton ball (30) | 390 | | 388 |
| Cup, paper (425) | | 411, 647 | 67 |

# Consumables

| Item | INVESTIGATE! | Explore! | Find Out! |
|---|---|---|---|
| Egg (30) | | 405 | |
| Egg carton (15) | 182 | | |
| Egg white (5 egg whites) | | 322 | |
| Egg white, cooked (3 eggs) | 326 | | |
| Envelope (15) | 146 | | |
| Fabric, various (15 pieces each of different fabrics) | 24 | | |
| Filter paper (30 pieces) | 198 | | |
| Flour (1 small bag) | | | 4 |
| Gauze (15 pieces of 2-cm$^2$) | 246 | | |
| Glucose or dextrose (200 g) | 354 | | |
| Glue (15 bottles) | 414, 472 | 321, 469 | 67 |
| Gumdrops, 4 colors (10 lbs.) | | 312, 314 | 460 |
| Ice cube (30) | | 249, 294 | |
| Ice (as needed) | 224, 286 | 209 | 245 |
| Index card (1 large box) | | 192, 516 | 91, 155 |
| Label (120) | 390, 448 | | |
| Label, nutrition (10 per group) | | 343 | |
| Lacquer, clear (1 can) | | 479 | |
| Leaf, fresh (15) | | | 504 |
| Licorice rope (30 long pieces) | | | 460 |
| Magazine (variety with pictures) | | 469 | |
| Margarine (1 stick) | | 324 | |
| Marker, permanent (15) | 224 | 218 | |
| Marker (15) | 132, 480 | | |
| Marshmallow (15 small pieces) | | 305 | |
| Matches (1 box) | | | 307 |
| Meat (15 small pieces) | | 322 | |
| Meat tenderizer, commercial (1 bottle) | | | 358 |
| Milk (125 mL) | | 322 | |
| Mini marshmallow (1 bag) | | 314 | |
| Molasses (1 jar) | | | 216 |
| Newspaper (as needed) | 546 | 241, 503 | |
| Oatmeal, non-instant (1 box) | 354 | | |
| Olive oil (1 cup) | | 324 | |
| Orange juice, frozen concentrate (1 small can) | 348 | | |
| Orange juice, fresh (2 oranges, squeezed) | 348 | | |
| Orange juice, bottled (1 small bottle) | 348 | | |
| Paper, construction (30 each of black, dark red, white, and other colors) | 146, 546 | 321 | 537 |
| Paper, drawing (45 sheets) | 554, 640 | | |
| Paper, graph (45 sheets) | 88, 572 | | |
| Paper, large sheet (45) | 414, 472 | 57 | |
| Paper, plain white (250 sheets) | 132, 472, 480, 512, 600, 634 | 21, 53 | |
| Paper, shelf (30 strips, 30cm x 2m) | 96 | | |
| Paper clip (5 boxes) | 60 | 111 | 59 |
| Paper clip, colored (7 boxes) | | 321 | |
| Pencil, colored (15 sets) | 554, 572 | | |

# Consumables

| Item | INVESTIGATE! | Explore! | Find Out! |
|------|-------------|----------|-----------|
| Pencil lead (15 long pieces) | | | 40 |
| Pencil, wax (15) | | | 284 |
| Peppermint or lemon extract (1 small bottle) | | | 388 |
| pH test paper (30) | 318 | | |
| Pictures of objects made of elements (as needed) | | | 155 |
| Plaster of Paris (1 large bag) | | | 504 |
| Plastic wrap (1 roll) | 24 | | |
| Plate, small plastic (30) | | | 358 |
| Potato (2) | 326 | | |
| Potato chips (1 small bag) | 326 | | |
| Raisins (1 large box) | | 312, 314 | |
| Rubber band (15) | | | 310 |
| Saltine cracker or hard pretzel (15) | | 353 | |
| Sandpaper (30 pieces) | 68, 390 | | |
| Sawdust, white pine or oak (2 quarts) | | | 307 |
| Shortening, solid (1 cup) | | 324 | |
| Soap bubble-making equipment (15) | | 93 | |
| Soft drink and diet soft drink (10 cans each) | 12 | | |
| Soybean oil (1 cup) | | 324 | |
| Straw, drinking (75) | 60, 212 | | 356 |
| String (1 roll) | 224, 246, 600 | | 51 |
| Sugar (1 box) | | 305 | |
| Sugar, powdered (1 small box) | | | 4 |
| Syrup (1 small bottle) | | | 216 |
| Tape (15 small rolls) | 212, 246, 414, 480, 546 | | 155, 274 |
| Tape, colored (15 pieces) or paint | | | 51 |
| Tape, duct (15 small rolls) | | | 261 |
| Tape, masking (15 small rolls) | 68, 96, 348 | | |
| Thread (1 spool for class) | | 50 | |
| Thumbtack (1 box) | 600 | 50 | 51, 284 |
| Tomato, green (30) | | | 310 |
| Tomato, rotten (15) | | | 310 |
| Tomato (1) | | 305 | |
| Toothpick (6 boxes) | | 312, 314 | 122, 460 |
| Towel, paper (3 rolls) | 390, 448, 554 | | |
| Vegetable oil (1 bottle) | 326 | 373, 568 | 216 |
| Yarn (4 skeins, each a different color) | 414 | | |

# Preserved Specimens

| Item | INVESTIGATE! | Explore! | Find Out! |
|------|-------------|----------|-----------|
| Blood cells, prepared slides:<br>  human (15)<br>  fish, frog, reptile, bird (2 types, 15 each) | <br>378<br>378 | | |
| *Oscillatoria* & *Elodea*, prepared slides (15 each) | | 549 | |

# Chemical Supplies

| Item | INVESTIGATE! | Explore! | Find Out! |
|------|--------------|----------|-----------|
| Agar (15 plates) | | | 383 |
| Alcohol, rubbing (1 bottle) | 390 | 219 | |
| Baking soda (1 large box) | | 175 | 4 |
| Benedict's solution (250 mL) | 354 | | |
| Calcium sulfate solution (500 mL) | 198 | | |
| Ethanol (60 mL) | 318 | | |
| Food coloring (2 small bottles) | | 294, 295, 373 | |
| Glycerine (1 jar) | 286 | | |
| Indophenol solution (900 mL) | 348 | | |
| Iodine solution (500 mL) | 326, 354 | | |
| Iron filings (as needed) | | 53, 57, 479 | |
| Magnesium sulfate solution (500 mL) | 198 | | |
| Motor oil (1 can) | | | 216 |
| Paraffin (1 box) | | 218 | |
| Petroleum jelly (1 large jar) | | | 504 |
| Potassium nitrate (400 g) | | 322 | |
| Potassium permanganate solution (15 mL) | 318 | | |
| Salt, table (2 boxes) | 286 | 295 | 284 |
| Soap solution (500 mL) | 198 | 93 | |
| Soap (5 bars for class) | 390 | | |
| Soap, liquid (1 bottle) | | | 216, 261 |
| Sodium carbonate solution (300 mL) | 198 | | |
| Sodium hydrogen sulfate (400 g) | | 322 | |
| Sodium hydroxide solution (15 mL) | 318 | | |
| Vinegar (900 mL) | | 175 | 4 |
| Vitamin C (250 mg) | 348 | | |
| Water | 12, 88, 212, 224, 246, 276, 286, 354, 390, 420, 448 | 209, 218, 249, 294, 295, 373 | 4, 216, 245, 252, 261, 274, 284, 356, 358, 504 |
| Water, distilled (1 gallon) | 198 | | |

# Living Organisms

| Item | INVESTIGATE! | Explore! | Find Out! |
|------|--------------|----------|-----------|
| Egg, Chicken (30) | | 405 | |
| Pine Needles (300) | | 535 | |
| Tobacco Seed, green: albino (300 each) | 448 | | |
| Tulip flower (15) | 420 | | |

# References

## STUDENT BIBLIOGRAPHY

### GENERAL SCIENCE CONTENT

Barr, George. *Science Tricks and Magic for Young People.* New York: Dover Publications, Inc., 1987.

Cash, Terry. 175 *More Science Experiments To Amuse and Amaze Your Friends: Experiments! Tricks! Things to Make!* New York: Random House, 1991.

Churchill, E. Richard. *Amazing Science Experiments with Everyday Materials.* New York: Sterling Publishing Co., Inc., 1991.

Gold, Carol. *Science Express,* "50 Scientific Stunts for the Ontario Science Centre." New York: Addison-Wesley, 1991.

Herbert, Don. *Mr. Wizard's Supermarket Science.* New York: Random House, 1980.

Lewis, James. *Hocus Pocus Stir and Cook, The Kitchen Science-Magic Book.* New York: Meadowbrook Press, Division of Simon and Shuster, Inc., 1991.

Mandell, Muriel. *Simple Science Experiments with Everyday Materials.* New York: Sterling Publishing Co., Inc., 1989.

Roberts, Royston. *Serendipity Accidental Discoveries in Science.* New York: John Wiley and Sons, Inc., 1989.

Schultz, Robert F. *Selected Experiments and Projects.* Washington, D.C.: Thomas Alva Edison Foundation, 1988.

Strongin, Herb. *Science on a Shoestring.* Menlo Park, CA: Addison-Wesley Publishing Co., 1985.

Townsley, B.J. *Famous Scientists.* Los Angeles, CA: Enrich Education Division of Price Stern Sloan Inc., 1987.

### PHYSICS

Aronson, Billy. "Water Ride Designers Are Making Waves," *3-2-1 Contact.* August, 1991, pp. 14-16

Asimov, Isaac. *How Did We Find Out the Speed of Light?* New York: Walker, 1986.

Berger, Melvin. *Light, Lenses, and Lasers.* New York: Putnam, 1987.

Cash, Terry. *Sound.* New York: Warwick Press, 1989.

Catherall, Ed. *Exploring Sound.* Austin, TX: Steck-Vaughn Library, 1989.

Heiligman, Deborah. "There's a Lot More to Color Than Meets the Eye," *3-2-1 Contact.* November, 1991, pp. 16-20.

McGrath, Susan. *Fun with Physics.* Washington, D.C.: National Geographic Society, 1986.

Myles, Douglas. *The Great Waves.* New York: McGraw-Hill Book Company, 1985.

Taylor, Barbara. *Light and Color.* New York: Franklin Watts, 1990.

Taylor, Barbara. *Sound and Music.* New York: Warwick Press, 1990.

Ward, Allen. *Experimenting with Batteries, Bulbs, and Wires.* New York: Chelsea House, 1991.

Ward, Alan. *Experimenting with Sound.* New York: Chelsea Juniors, 1991.

Wood, Nicholas. *Listen ... What Do You Hear?* Mahwah, NJ: Troll Associated, 1991.

### CHEMISTRY

Barber, Jacqueline. *Of Cabbage and Chemistry.* Washington, DC.: Lawrence Hall of Science, NSTA, 1989.

Barber, Jacqueline, *Chemical Reactions.* Washington, D.C.: Lawrence Hall of Science, NSTA, 1986.

Benrey, Ronald. *Alternative Energy Sources Experiments You Can Do...from Edison.* Washington, D.C.: Thomas Alva Edison Foundation, Edison Electric Institute, 1988.

Cornell, John. *Experiments with Mixtures.* New York: Wiley, John and Sons, Inc., 1990.

Matsubara, T. *The Structure and Properties of Matter.* New York: Springer-Verlag New York Inc., 1982.

Zubrewski, Bernie. *Messing Around with Baking Chemistry: A Children's Museum Activity Book.* Boston, MA: Little Brown and Co., 1981.

### LIFE SCIENCE

Dewey, Jennifer Owings. *A Day and Night In the Desert.* Boston, MA: Little Brown, 1991.

Johnson, Cathy. *Local Wilderness.* New York: Prentice Hall, 1987.

Leslie, Clare Walker. *Nature All Year Long.* New York: Greenwillow, 1990.

McGrath, Susan. *The Amazing Things Animals Do.* Washington D.C.: National Geographic Society, 1989.

Markmann, Erika. *Grow It! An Indoor/Outdoor Gardening Guide for Kids.* New York: Random House, 1991.

Rand McNally. *Children's Atlas of the Environment.* Chicago, IL: Rand McNally, 1991.

VanCleave, Janice Pratt. *Biology for Every Kid: 101 Easy Experiments that Really Work.* New York: Wiley, 1990.

### EARTH SCIENCE

Ardley, Neil. *The Science Book of Air.* New York: Gulliver Books, Harcourt, Brace, Jovanovich, Publishers, 1991.

Ardley, Neil. *The Science Book of Water.* New York: Gulliver Books, Harcourt, Brace, Jovanovich, Publishers, 1991.

Barrow, Lloyd H. *Adventures with Rocks and Minerals: Geology Experiments for Young People.* Hillsdale, NJ: Enslow, 1991.

Booth, Basil. *Volcanoes and Earthquakes.* Englewood Cliffs, NJ: Silver Burdett Press, 1991.

Javna, John. *50 Simple Things Kid Can Do to Save the Earth.* Kansas City: The Earth Works Group, Andrews and McMeel, a Universal Press Syndicate Co., 1990.

VanCleave, Janice. *Earth Science for Every Kid.* New York: John Wiley and Sons, Inc., 1991.

Wood, Robert W. *Science for Kids: 39 East Geology Activities.* Blue Ridge Summit, PA: Tab Books, 1992.

# TEACHER BIBLIOGRAPHY

## CURRICULUM

Aldridge, William G. "Scope, Sequence, and Coordination: A New Synthesis for Improving Science Education," *Journal of Science Education and Technology*.

Banks, James A. "Multicultural Education: For Freedom's Sake," *Educational Leadership*. December, 1991/January, 1992. pp. 32-35.

Beane, James A. "Middle School, The Natural Home of the Integrated Curriculum," *Educational Leadership*. October, 1991. pp. 9-13.

*Chemistry of Life: 1988 Curriculum Module*. Princeton, NJ: Woodrow Wilson National Fellowship Foundation, 1988.

Driver, R. *The Children's Learning in Science Project, Monographs on Preconceptions in Science*. England: Center for Studies in Science and Mathematics Education, Department of Education, University of Leeds, 1984-1989.

Hazen, Robert M. and James Trefil. *Science Matter, Achieving Scientific Literacy*. New York: Doubleday, 1991.

Philips, William. "Earth Science Misconceptions," *The Science Teacher*. October, 1991. pp. 21-23.

Piaget, J., *To Understand Is to Invent: The Future of Education*. New York: Grossman Publishers, 1973.

Rutherford, E. James and Andrew Ahlgren. *Science for All Americans*. New York: Oxford University Press, 1990.

## TEACHING METHODS

Altshular, Kenneth. "The Interdisciplinary Classroom," *The Physics Teacher*. October, 1991. pp. 428-429.

Humphreys, David. *Demonstrating Chemistry*. Ontario, Canada: Chemistry Department, McMaster, University Hamilton, 1983.

Johnson, David W., Roger T. Johnson, and Edythe Johnson Holubec. *Circles of Learning*. Edina, MN: Interaction Book Company, 1990.

Johnson, David W., Roger T. Johnson, and Edythe Johnson Holubec. *Cooperation in the Classroom*. Edina, MN: Interaction Book Company, 1991.

Johnson, David W., Roger T. Johnson. *Cooperative Learning: Warm-Ups, Grouping Strategies, and Group Activities*. Edina, MN: Interaction Book Company, 1985.

Novak, Joseph. "Clarify with Concept Maps," *The Science Teacher*. October, 1991. pp. 44-49.

Penick, John. "Where's the Science?" *The Science Teacher*. May, 1991. pp. 27-29.

## CONTENT AREA BOOKS

### Physics

Arons, A. B. *A Guide to Introductory Physics Teaching*. New York: John Wiley and Sons, 1990.

Berman, Paul. *Light and Sound*. New York: Marshall Cavendish, 1988.

Gardner, Robert. *Experimenting with Light*. New York: Franklin Watts, 1991.

Urone, Paul Peter. *Physics with Health Science Applications*. New York: Harper and Row Publishers, 1986.

Walpole, Brenda. *175 Science Experiments to Amuse and Amaze Your Friends*. New York: Random House, 1988.

### Chemistry

*Element of the Week*. Batavia, IL: Flinn Scientific, Inc., 1990.

*Ground to Grits. Scientific Concepts in Nutrition/Agriculture*. Columbia, SC: South Carolina Department of Education, 1982.

Joesten, Melvin. *World of Chemistry*. Philadelphia, PA: Saunders College Publishing, 1991.

Mitchell, Sharon and Juergens, Frederick. *Laboratory Solutions for the Science Classroom*. Batavia, IL: Flinn Scientific, Inc., 1991.

Solomon, Sally. "Qualitative Analysis of Eleven Household Compounds," *Journal of Chemical Education*. April, 1991. pp. 328-329.

### Life Science

Hancock, Judith M. *Variety of Life: A Biology Teacher's Sourcebook*. Portland, OR: J. Weston Walch, 1987.

Middleton, James I. "Student-Generated Analogies in Biology," *American Biology Teacher*. January, 1991. pp. 42-46.

Vogel, Steven. *Life's Devices: The Physical World of Plants and Animals*. Princeton, NJ: Princeton University Press, 1989.

### Earth Science

Callister, Jeffrey C., Lenny Coplestone, Gerald F. Consuegra, Sharon M. Stroud, and Warren E. Yasso. *Earthquakes*. Mary Liston Liepold, ed., Washington, D.C.: NSTA/FEMA, 1988.

Lasca, Norman P. "Build Me a River," *Earth*. January, 1991. pp. 59-65.

Little, Jane Braxton. "California Town Unites to Save a Stream," *The Christian Science Monitor*. February 28, 1991.

Sae, Andy S. W. "Dynamic Demos," *The Science Teacher*. October, 1991. pp. 23-25.

# SUPPLIER ADDRESSES

## SOFTWARE DISTRIBUTORS

(AIT) Agency for Instructional
Technology
Box A
Bloomington, IN 47402-0120

Aims Media
9710 Desoto Avenue
Chatsworth, CA 91311-4409

Aquarium Instructional
P.O. Box 128
Indian Rocks Beach, FL 34635

Cambridge Development Lab (CDL)
1696 Massachusetts Avenue
Cambridge, MA 02138

(Classroom Consortia Media Inc.)
Gemstar
P.O. Box 050228
Staten Island, NY 10305

COMPress
P.O. Box 102
Wentworth, NH 03282

## COMPUTER SOFTWARE

Earthware Computer Services
P.O. Box 30039
Eugene, OR 97403

Educational Activities, Inc.
1937 Grand Avenue
Baldwin, NY 11510

Educational Materials and Equipment
Company (EME)
P.O. Box 2805
Danbury, CT 06813-2805

Focus Media, Inc.
839 Stewart Avenue
P.O. Box 865
Garden City, NY 115630

Human Relations Media (HRM)
175 Tompkins Avenue
Pleasantville, NY 10570

IBM Educational Systems
Department PC
4111 Northside Parkway
Atlanta, GA 30327

J & S Software
135 Haven Avenue
Port Washington, NY 11050

McGraw-Hill Webster Division
1221 Avenue of the Americas
New York, NY 10020

Minnesota Educational Computing
Corporation (MECC)
3490 Lexington Avenue N.
Saint Paul, MN 55126

Microphys
1737 W. Second Street
Brooklyn, NY 11223

MicroPower and Light Co.
Suite 120
12820 Hillcrest Road 219
Dallas, TX 75230

Queue, Inc.
562 Boston Avenue
Bridgeport, CT 06610

Texas Instruments, Data Systems Group
P.O. Box 1444
Houston, TX 77251

Ventura Educational System
3440 Brokenhill Street
Newbury Park, CA 91320

## AUDIOVISUAL DISTRIBUTORS

Aims Media
9710 Desoto Avenue
Chatsworth, CA 91311-4409

BFA Educational Media
468 Park Avenue S.
New York, NY 10016

Churchill Films
662 N. Robertson Blvd.
Los Angeles, CA 90069

Coronet/MTI Film and Video
Distributors of LCA
108 Wilmot Road
Deerfield, IL 60015

CRM Films
2233 Faraday Avenue
Suite F
Carlsbad, CA 92008

Diversified Education Enterprise
725 Main Street
Lafayette, IN 47901

Encyclopedia Britannica Educational
Corp. (EBEC)
310 S. Michigan Avenue
Chicago, IL 60604

Focus Media, Inc.
839 Stewart Avenue
P.O. Box 865
Garden City, NY 11530

Hawkill Associates, Inc.
125 E. Gilman Street
Madison, WI 53703

(HRM) Human Relations Media
175 Tompkins Avenue
Pleasantville, NY 10570

Indiana University
Audiovisual Center
Bloomington, IN 47405-5901

Journal Films, Inc.
930 Pitner Avenue
Evanston, IL 60202

Lumivision
1490 Lafayette
Suite 305
Denver, CO 80218

Macmillan/McGraw-Hill School Division
4635 Hilton Corporate Drive
Columbus, OH 43232

National Earth Science Teachers
c/o Art Weinle
733 Loraine
Grosse Point, MI 48230

National Geographic Society Educational
Services
17th and "M" Streets, NW
Washington, DC 20036

Science Software Systems
11890 W. Pico Blvd.
Los Angeles, CA 90064

Time-Life Videos
Time and Life Building
1271 Avenue of the Americas
New York, NY 10020

Universal Education & Visual Arts
(UEVA)
100 Universal City Plaza
Universal City, CA 91608

US Department of Energy
DOE 535

Video Discovery
1515 Dexter Avenue N.
Suite 400
Seattle, WA 98109

# SCIENCE INTERACTIONS

## Course 3

## GLENCOE

Macmillan/McGraw-Hill

New York, New York    Columbus, Ohio    Mission Hills, California    Peoria, Illinois

# Consultants

## Chemistry

**Richard J. Merrill**
Director,
Project Physical Science
Associate Director, Institute
for Chemical Education
University of California
Berkeley, California

**Robert W. Parry, Ph.D.**
Dist. Professor of Chemistry
University of Utah
Salt Lake City, Utah

## Earth Science

**Allan A. Ekdale, Ph.D.**
Professor of Geology
University of Utah
Salt Lake City, Utah

**Janifer Mayden**
Aerospace Education Specialist
NASA
Washington, DC

**James B. Phipps, Ph.D.**
Professor of Geology
and Oceanography
Gray's Harbor College
Aberdeen, Washington

## Life Science

**David M. Armstrong, Ph.D.**
Professor of Environmental,
Population and
Organismic Biology
University of
Colorado-Boulder
Boulder, Colorado

**Mary D. Coyne, Ph.D.**
Professor of Biological Sciences
Wellesley College
Wellesley, Massachusetts

**David Futch, Ph.D.**
Professor of Biology
San Diego State University
San Diego, California

**Richard D. Storey, Ph.D.**
Associate Professor of Biology
Colorado College
Colorado Springs, Colorado

## Physics

**David Haaes, Ph.D.**
Professor of Physics
North Carolina State University
North Carolina

**Patrick Hamill, Ph.D.**
Professor of Physics
San Jose State University
San Jose, California

## Middle School Science

**Garland E. Johnson**
Science and Education
Consultant
Fresno, California

## Multicultural

**Thomas Custer**
Coordinator of Science
Anne Arundel County Schools
Annapolis, Maryland

**Francisco Hernandez**
Science Department Chair
John B. Hood Middle School
Dallas, Texas

**Carol T. Mitchell**
Instructor
Elementary Science Methods
College of Teacher Education
University of Omaha at Omaha
Omaha, Nebraska

**Karen Muir, Ph.D.**
Lead Instructor
Department of Social and
Behavioral Sciences
Columbus State
Community College
Columbus, Ohio

## Reading

**Elizabeth Gray, Ph.D.**
Reading Specialist
Heath City Schools
Heath, Ohio
Adjunct Professor
Otterbein College
Westerville, Ohio

**Timothy Heron, Ph.D.**
Professor, Department
of Educational
Services & Research
The Ohio State University
Columbus, Ohio

**Barbara Pettegrew, Ph.D.**
Director of Reading
Study Center
Assistant Professor
of Education
Otterbein College
Westerville, Ohio

## LEP

**Ross M. Arnold**
Magnet School Coordinator
Van Nuys Junior High
Van Nuys, California

**Linda E. Heckenberg**
Director
Eisenhower Program
Van Nuys, California

**Harold Frederick**
Robertson, Jr.
Science Resource Teacher
LAUSD Science Materials Center
Van Nuys, California

## Safety

**Robert Tatz, Ph.D.**
Instructional Lab Supervisor
Department of Chemistry
The Ohio State University
Columbus, Ohio

# Reviewers

# SCIENCE INTERACTIONS
# CONTENTS OVERVIEW
## Course 3

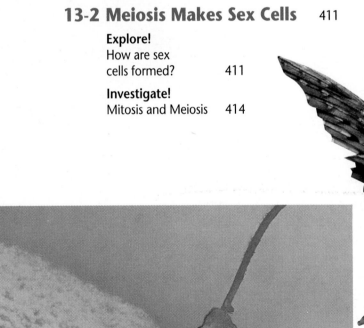

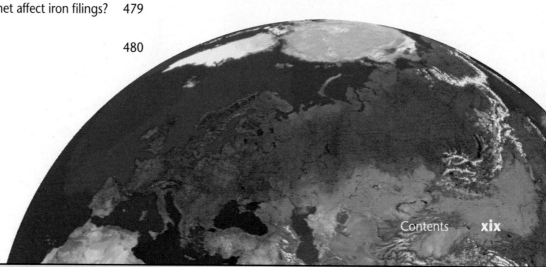

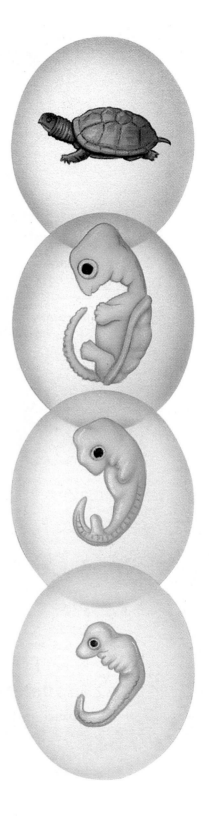

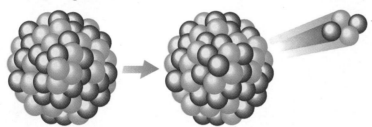

# SCIENCE CONNECTIONS

*Have you ever noticed that you really can't talk about eels without mentioning electricity? How is one science related to another? Expand your view of science through A CLOSER LOOK and Science Connections features in each chapter.*

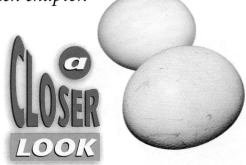

## Earth and Life Science

## Physics and Chemistry

## A CLOSER LOOK

# SCIENCE CONNECTIONS

*Science is something that refuses to stay locked away in a laboratory. In both the Science and Society and the Technology features, you'll learn how science impacts the world you live in today. You may also be asked to think about science-related questions that will affect your life fifty years from now.*

## Science and Society

## Technology Connection

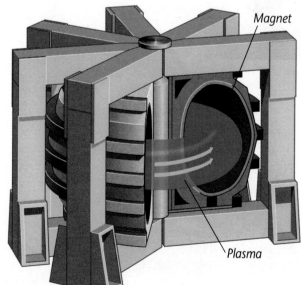

Magnet

Plasma

# CROSS-CURRICULUM CONNECTIONS

*With the EXPAND YOUR VIEW features at the end of each chapter, you'll quickly become aware that science is an important part of every subject you'll ever encounter in school. Read these features to learn how science has affected history, health, and even leisure time.*

## Health CONNECTION

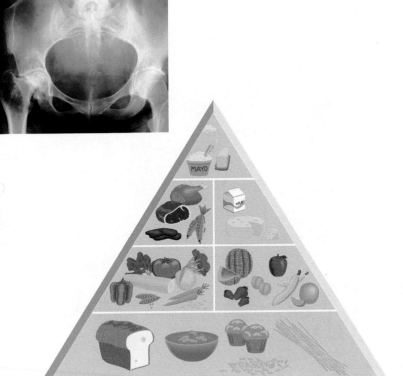

## HISTORY CONNNECTION

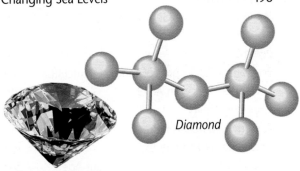

*Diamond*

## Literature Connection

## Leisure Connection

# CROSS-CURRICULUM CONNECTIONS

*What makes this thing work? What do you have to do to become a scientist? In HOW IT WORKS, learn that the workings of most ordinary everyday things are based in scientific principles. Through TEENS IN SCIENCE, you'll find out that you don't have to wear a lab coat to make science happen.*

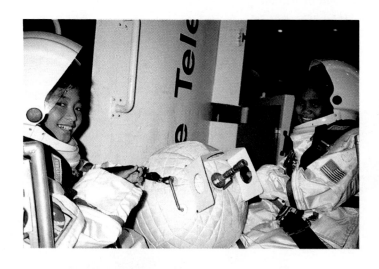

## Teens in SCIENCE

## HOW IT WORKS

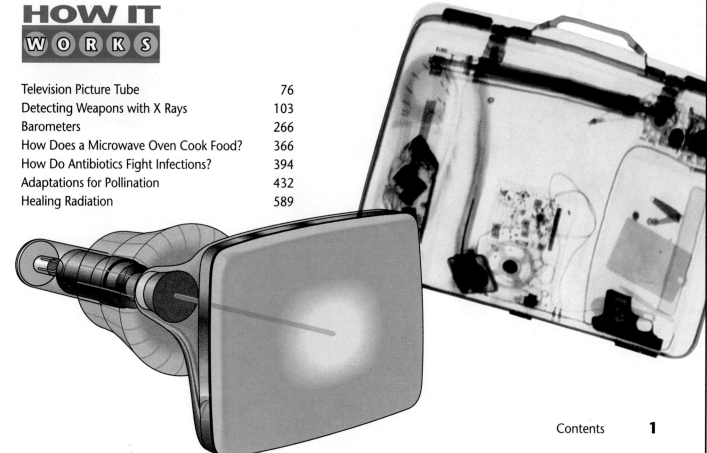

## Introducing Science: A Tool for Solving Problems

### THEME DEVELOPMENT

The primary theme of this chapter is stability and change. Scientific methods help us understand both stability and change in the natural world. After we understand a process, we are often able to improve upon it, leading to technological advances.

The chapter's secondary theme of interactions and systems is illustrated as scientific methods help us define and predict the interactions of elements within a system and of systems with other systems. Learning how systems interact enables us to modify our environment and even extend our life span.

### CHAPTER OVERVIEW

In this chapter, a class practices using scientific methods as they prepare for a science competition.

Consider challenging your class to participate in a science competition similar to the one presented in the chapter, which encourages hands-on application of scientific methods. The experience will help your students, like the class in this chapter, appreciate the practical uses of science.

#### Tying to Previous Knowledge

Divide the class into small groups and ask each group to define *scientific thinking*. Have groups share their definitions with the class, accepting all responses. Ask students to record their groups' definitions in their journals. The students' preliminary definitions may reveal preconceptions that you can address during this chapter.

# SCIENCE: A Tool for Solving Problems

**W**hat is "scientific thinking"? Does it always require beakers, magnets, or graph paper? How is scientific thinking the same as other thinking? How is it different? Do you ever use scientific thinking when you're not at school?

Follow Lee, Erin, and the rest of their science class as they prepare for a competition called Science Challenge and learn more about scientific thinking. As they prepare for the Science Challenge, the class discovers that scientific thinking can help them not only in this competition, but throughout their entire lives.

2

## Using What You Already Know

"I've been learning the periodic table for the Science Challenge," Lee told Ms. Borga and the rest of his science class. "I've memorized nearly all the elements!"

"That kind of knowledge helped this class win the school Science Challenge," Ms. Borga told him, "but you'll need more than that when we go to the regional Science Challenge in two weeks. The judges there will give you problems to solve, and you won't be able to rely on just pulling the answers out of your memory. To solve these problems, you'll need to know how to use what you've learned and how to think scientifically."

"Now we're in trouble!" Erin said. "How do you think scientifically?"

"Well, first tell me what science is," Ms. Borga asked. "Who remembers how we defined science?"

For a minute or two, everyone stared at the floor or out the window. Then Andy tentatively raised his hand. "You know, I think I remember. Science is a way of learning about things that happen in the natural world. When we understand how something works, we can use what we know to invent things or make things run more smoothly."

Ms. Borga said, "Can you think of an example?"

"Well, when you know how an engine works, you can design one that will use fuel more efficiently," Andy said.

Kisha raised her hand. "I remember an example. As scientists learn more about how our bodies work, they can make new medicines and devise new surgery techniques. They know more about what we should eat and how much exercise we should get, too."

Ms. Borga nodded. "That's basically it. Science is a way of learning about natural things and coming to appreciate them. The more we know and learn, the more we can enjoy the natural world. One way we learn is by using what we already know and applying it to new situations. Let's do an experiment to see how this works.

Science: A Tool for Solving Problems  **3**

# PREPARATION

## Concepts Developed

The goal throughout this chapter is not to help students win a science competition, but to help them understand how to use scientific methods. Getting the "right" answer to the questions in the activities is not nearly so important as learning how to use scientific methods to answer questions.

## Find Out!

### Using What You Know to Find Out What You Don't

**Time needed** 15–20 minutes

**Materials** flour, powdered sugar, baking soda, undiluted white vinegar, water, shallow dish, 2 droppers

**Thinking Processes** observing, practicing scientific methods, inferring, forming a hypothesis, making and using tables, comparing and contrasting

**Purpose** To use a scientific method to identify an unknown substance.

**Preparation** Choose one of the three powders as an "unknown." Keep track of "unknowns" used for each class or group.

### Teaching the Activity

**Safety** Remind students that no substance in a scientific investigation should ever be tasted. Students should wear goggles and avoid having substances come in contact with the skin.

**Student Journal** Have students write their hypotheses in their journals. After the experiment is completed, students should indicate whether their hypotheses were supported by observations. [L1]

### Expected Outcome

Based on previous observations of how the known solids reacted with vinegar and water, students should be able to identify the unknown.

## Find Out! ACTIVITY

### Using What You Know to Find Out What You Don't.

In this activity, you'll work with a partner to test how flour, powdered sugar, and baking soda each react with water and with vinegar. Then you'll use what you learned about these reactions to identify an unknown powder. **CAUTION:** *Never taste any powder or substance in a scientific investigation. It could be poisonous.*

### What To Do

1. *In your journal,* make a chart like the one below.
2. Pour flour into a shallow dish. Use a dropper to place a drop or two of water on the flour. Record what happens to the water when it hits the flour.
3. Use another dropper to drop vinegar on a different area of the flour. Record what happens.
4. Repeat Steps 2 and 3 using powdered sugar and then baking soda in place of the flour. Record your observations.
5. When you've completed all of your observations, ask your teacher for the final sample, the "unknown".
6. Examine the unknown sample and form a hypothesis about what it is. Record your hypothesis *in your Journal.*

Sample Data

| Data and Observations | | |
|---|---|---|
| | Reaction with Water | Reaction with Vinegar |
| Flour | water rolls off | no reaction |
| Powdered Sugar | dissolves | no reaction |
| Baking Soda | dissolves | bubbles formed |

7. Observe the reaction of the unknown with water and with vinegar. Record your observations and your conclusion about what the unknown sample is.

### Conclude and Apply

1. Compare and contrast the reactions of each solid with water and vinegar.
2. Explain how you used the "known" to find out the "unknown."

## Conclude and Apply

**1.** Water may dissolve sugar and baking soda but it will roll off flour. Vinegar will react with baking soda to release bubbles, but will not react with flour or sugar. Vinegar will dissolve sugar but not flour.

**2.** By comparing the interactions of the known substance with water and vinegar to those of the unknown substance, students can identify the "unknown."

## ✔ Assessment

**Process** Ask students to describe how they evaluated their hypotheses. *They did so by comparing observations of how the "knowns" and "unknown" reacted with water and vinegar.* Use the Performance Task Assessment List for Evaluating a Hypothesis in **PAMSS**, p. 31. [L1]

### ■ Solving a Problem—Scientifically

"Now I see what you meant." Kisha said. "After we experimented to find out how the three powders reacted, we could look at the information we had gathered and figure out what the unknown sample was."

Lee nodded. "So science is a way of using what we know to find out things we don't know. That means we can use science to add to what we already know." He looked worried. "Will the judges at

*One of Frederick McKinley Jones's refrigerated Trucks*

the Science Challenge expect us to use science to solve problems? Is that what you meant by 'thinking scientifically'?"

"Yes, but as you've already seen, it isn't that difficult," Ms. Borga reassured him. "Let's talk about different ways to solve problems scientifically. You've already done an experiment to solve a problem, using what you know to find out more."

---

### Cool Science

Thanks to a self-taught engineer who was able to apply what he knew to solve a challenging problem, we have air conditioning to cool our cars and refrigerated trucks to ship our food.

In 1937 Frederick McKinley Jones, an African American who began his career as an auto mechanic, was tired of driving around in the Minneapolis summer heat. He thought

there must be a way to put the air conditioning used to cool buildings into cars.

About the same time, Joseph Numero, the owner of a Minneapolis trucking company, had become frustrated with having truckloads of food spoil in the heat. A friend who knew both Jones and Numero got them together. Jones used his knowledge of shock-proof and vibration-proof gadgets to build a sturdy, light-weight air

conditioning unit for Numero's trucks. The two men formed a very successful refrigeration company.

---

**Discussion**

To help students recognize ways they use known information to find out the unknown, ask them how they can sometimes tell who is calling on the telephone. *They compare the unknown voice on the phone to voices they know.* L1

# 2 TEACH

**Student Journal**  Ask each student to bring in a small notebook or booklet that will serve as a journal. Students will use their journals to record their observations, charts and results of activities, and impressions. You may wish to review these journals for evaluation and assessment.

**Discussion**  Challenge students to gather examples of products or processes that have been improved or invented by applying old techniques or knowledge in new ways. Ask them to share with the class what they have learned. Encourage them to bring examples of the "old" and "improved" products to class, if possible.

### Across the Curriculum

**Language Arts**

Ask students to read a biography or an autobiography of a scientist. Have them create a poster (or make an oral presentation) sharing what they learn with the class.

Encourage students to seek out scientists who are their own gender and/or share their cultural/ethnic background.

## Content Background

American scientist Robert Goddard (1882–1945) built many models as he experimented with ways to use liquid fuel in rockets. His first successful rocket was 1.2 m (4 ft) high and 15 cm (6 in.) wide. Its fuel, a mixture of gasoline and liquid oxygen, sent the rocket 56 m (184 ft) into the air. He later built models that flew 2.4 km (1.5 miles) high. (4)

## Across the Curriculum

### History

Challenge groups of students to select an important discovery and trace the scientific methods and the people involved in making this discovery. For example, they might examine how scientists learned the organization of the solar system, the principles of electricity, blood circulation within the body, infection by contagious diseases, or another topic that had been misunderstood at some point.

Ask the groups to present what they learned to the class and create a model or other visual that illustrates the principles scientists discovered.

"Now suppose we're aeronautical engineers. We've designed a new shape for an airplane wing. Here's our question: 'Will this design increase the airflow over the wing?' We expect the answer to be 'yes.' That's our hypothesis, that the design will improve airflow. How could we test our hypothesis?"

"We could build a model of our new design," Erin suggested, "and see if it works better than the wing we're using now."

Ms. Borga nodded. "That's a scientific way to test our hypothesis:

make a model and see how it works. It's too difficult and too dangerous to put our new design on a real airplane and test it, so we make a model of the wing. Then we can test it under controlled conditions in an air tunnel."

### ■ Making a Model

"Will we need to make a model at the Science Challenge?" Andy asked. "Maybe we ought to, you know, practice."

Ms. Borga smiled. "Okay, here's a question you can answer using a model: 'What is the phase of the moon during a solar eclipse?' Remember that a solar eclipse occurs when the moon is in a position to block sunlight from reaching certain parts of Earth."

### Model Aircraft

Orville and Wilbur Wright ran a bicycle shop in Dayton, Ohio. They studied everything that was known about flight and then applied it to their airplane designs. These amateur scientists created 200 models of airplane wings, tested each one in a wind tunnel, and recorded their results on a graph. The first airplane they built, in 1903, included the wing design that had performed best in their tests up to that point.

Each new wing design they created and each flight they attempted built on what they had learned from previous trials. The brothers persevered and were able to lengthen their flights from 12 seconds to 38 minutes, after which they had to land because they had run out of fuel!

**6**

### Chinese Contributions to Science

Three Chinese contributions to science have shaped our world. They are the compass, gunpowder, and rockets, all invented centuries before they appeared in the West. In fact, the rockets that send space shuttles into orbit are based on rockets developed in China more than 5,000 years ago. Invite groups of students to research one of these contributions. Student may present their research in the form of written or oral reports, posters, or booklets. Use the appropriate Performance Task Assessment List in **PAMSS.** L1

COOP LEARN   P

# What is the phase of the moon during a solar eclipse?

You can use models to gather information when an event or a process is too big, too small, or too difficult to study directly.

## What To Do

1. Obtain a medium-sized ball (Earth), a small ball (moon), and a flashlight (sun).

2. Shine the flashlight on Earth. Then move the moon slowly around Earth to represent the moon's orbit.

3. When the sun, moon, and Earth are in a relationship that would result in a solar eclipse, observe and record the moon's phase. Record all of your observations and the answers to the questions that follow *in your Journal.*

## Conclude and Apply

1. What is the phase of the moon during a solar eclipse?

2. What are at least two other questions you could answer using this model?

3. What questions did constructing this model bring up?

4. Why is a model the best way to answer this question?

■ **Learning by Observing**

"That wasn't so hard!" Andy admitted. "The model made it easier to see what was happening."

"Right! Models can be used to help you experimental. Now here's another problem to solve scientifically," Ms. Borga said. "'Is the hole in the ozone layer getting bigger?' What could our hypothesis be in this case?"

"The hole is getting bigger," Kisha said. "That would be my hypothesis."

## Find Out!

**What is the phase of the moon during a solar eclipse?**

**Time needed** 10–15 minutes

**Materials** medium-sized ball, small ball, flashlight

**Thinking process** observing, recognizing and using spacial relationships, formulating models, formulating operational definitions, sequencing

**Purpose** To use a model to discover the phase of the moon during a solar eclipse.

### Teaching the Activity

Review the concept of an eclipse, if necessary. Divide the class into groups of four, with students taking the roles of "Earth," "sun," "moon," and observer. **COOP LEARN**

**Student Journal** Students should record their observations in their journals. **L1**

### Expected Outcomes

Students will observe that the "moon" is in its new phase, or completely dark, during a solar eclipse.

### Conclude and Apply

**1.** New phase, or completely dark.

**2.** Under what conditions does a lunar eclipse occur? How are the phases of the moon produced?

**3.** How can we make this model accurate? What can we use to make it better?

**4.** You can manipulate two elements of the model in any way you want. To study an actual eclipse, you have to wait for one to occur.

### ✔ Assessment

**Process** Have students make a model of the Earth, moon, sun system to discover the phase of the moon during a lunar eclipse. *Full.* Use the Performance Task Assessment List for Model in **PAMSS**, p. 61. **L1**

## ENRICHMENT

**Research** Another way to answer the question posed in this activity and in the Assessment activity is to search records of eclipses and correlate these dates with the phases of the moon. Have students look in recent almanacs to find dates of solar and/or lunar eclipses. The same almanacs should also list the dates of full and new moon phases. **L2**

**What's the origin of rock?**

**Time needed** 10–15 minutes

**Materials** rock, magnifying glass

**Thinking Processes** observing, forming a hypothesis, making and using tables, interpreting data, classifying

**Purpose** To apply previous knowledge in the development of a hypothesis concerning the origin of a rock.

**Preparation** Obtain samples of basalt, gabbro, rhyolite, and granite.

### Teaching the Activity

**Student Journal** Suggest that students record the characteristics of their rock, and the resulting hypothesis concerning its origin, in their journals. Students may wish to include a drawing of the rock. L1

### Expected Outcome

Students should be able to formulate reasonable hypotheses on the origin of their rocks based on data provided in the chart and observations of the rocks' characteristics.

### Answers to Questions

**4.** You could compare to rocks of various types that are in place.

### ✔ Assessment

**Process** Ask students what characteristics of their rock allowed them to formulate their hypotheses. Students should note that crystal size and rock color were the important characteristics. Use the Performance Task Assessment List for Formulating a Hypothesis in **PAMSS**, p. 21. L1

"But we can't do an experiment or make a model of the ozone layer to test that hypothesis," Lee said. "Maybe there's an instrument you could use to measure the hole in the ozone layer. If there were such an instrument, we could measure the hole again in a few months to see if it changed. Maybe we could use the space shuttle or a satellite to photograph the ozone layer."

"That's another good example of scientific thinking." Ms. Borga told the class. "Observation is a key way to gather information and test a hypothesis. We can also use observation to form a hypothesis." She held up a chunk of rock. "For example, we could use observation and previous knowledge to form a hypothesis about where this rock came from."

## Explore! ACTIVITY

### What's the origin of the rock?

**Y**ou can form a hypothesis about where a rock formed by carefully observing its physical characteristics.

#### What To Do

1. Study the chart of the characteristics that indicate an igneous rock's origin, found below. This is your "previous knowledge."

2. Use a magnifying glass to examine a chunk of rock. Record your observations.

3. Form a hypothesis about the origin of the rock.

4. Explain how you could use further observation to test your hypothesis.

#### Characteristics and Origin of Igneous Rocks

| | | Color | |
|---|---|---|---|
| | | **Dark** | **Light** |
| Mineral | **Large** | Oceanic Instrusive | Continental Intrusive |
| Size | **Small** | Oceanis Extrusive | Continental Extrusive |

---

### Meeting Individual Needs

**Learning Disabled**   Read each pair of statements below. Ask students which statement is an example of scientific thinking. Discuss why the other statement is not.

**1.** a. The dog seemed tired.

b. The dog was lying down with its head on its paws.

**2.** a. I can read that sign with my right eye, but not my left.

b. I can see better with my right eye.

**3.** a. Nine out of twelve people preferred the lemon flavor.

b. The lemon flavor tasted best.

*Students should recognize that 1a, 2b, and 3b are subjective, unmeasurable evaluations.*

## ■ Different Kinds of Observations

"So you solve problems scientifically by asking a question, thinking of the answer you expect—that's your hypothesis—and then testing your hypothesis in as many ways as possible to see if you're right. You might use an experiment or a model or observations," Erin summarized.

"That's right," Ms. Borga agreed. "In scientific problem solving, you're using the experiment, model, or observation to gather information to see whether your hypothesis is correct. Sometimes you may need to alter your hypothesis, and sometimes you discover that the initial hypothesis is wrong. That's not failure. It's progress, because now you can make a new hypothesis and test it.

"Solving problems in fields outside of science is similar, but sometimes you gather information in different ways. Let's compare solving problems in science to, say, solving problems in history. What's a good history problem?"

Andy smiled. "Here's a problem Mr. Morrow asked us to solve by next week: 'What was the real cause of the Civil War?' We sure can't do experiments or design models or make observations to find out. I'm going to

have to spend forever in the library doing research."

"You probably won't be there forever, but you'll have to read a lot of different accounts to see where they agree," Ms. Borga said. "You'll be reviewing other people's observations of what happened. However, you may

## Content Background

Rocks have three basic origins: igneous (formed by heat), sedimentary (formed by deposits of sediment), and metamorphic (one of the other two types that has been changed by heat or pressure). The four examples of rock suggested for the Explore! activity are all igneous rocks. Granite and gabbro form as magma, or melted rock, cools within Earth. Basalt and rhyolite form as lava from a volcano cools on Earth's surface.

## *Across the Curriculum*

### Daily Life

Challenge the students to ask a question about something that occurs in their daily lives, form a hypothesis (answer), and use observation to test their hypothesis.

The question could range from how many hours of television a sibling watches every evening to how quickly birds eat the seeds in a feeder. Set a time limit for the observations, such as three days or a week. Ask students to share their questions, methods, and what they learn in written or oral reports.

Galileo (1564–1642) was one of the first scientists to test hypotheses to see if they were correct. His scientific experimentation overturned beliefs people had held without questioning for centuries.

For instance, Aristotle (384–322 BC) had written that a heavier object would fall faster than a light one. He didn't test this hypothesis; it just seemed reasonable to him.

Galileo tested this theory by dropping a heavy ball and a lighter one from the top of the Leaning Tower of Pisa. (Or perhaps he rolled the balls down an inclined plane; accounts differ.) Both balls reached the bottom at the same time because gravity pulled on them equally. With this simple experiment, Galileo had disproved Aristotle's 2000-year-old theory.

Other scientists, such as the American inventor Benjamin Franklin (1706–1790) and French biologist Louis Pasteur (1822–1895), followed Galileo's example.

As late as 1752, most people believed lightning was caused by gases exploding. Franklin hypothesized that lightning was a form of electricity. Using a kite and a key, he devised an experiment that proved his hypothesis and disproved a long-held belief.

In the 1850s, many people still believed Aristotle's theory of spontaneous generation: that living things can grow from nonliving things. Pasteur decided to test this hypothesis.

In one of his experiments, Pasteur put boiled broth in glass flasks. He proved that the bacteria that spoiled the broth actually came from the air above the broth, not from the sterile broth itself.

## ■ Testing Hypotheses

Erin's group seemed to have a hundred ways to explain why one can floated and one sank. Lee thought maybe the bottling company filled one kind of can fuller than the other. Kisha thought sugar might give the regular soft drink more mass and make it heavier. Andy guessed that the diet soft drink might have more carbonation than the regular one, causing the diet can to float.

First, the group decided to see whether sugar gave the soft drink more mass. They poured exactly the same amount of each kind of soft drink into separate small cups and weighed the cups. After they compared the results to their hypothesis, they decided to test Lee's idea and determine how full each can was.

As they worked, Erin's group noticed that other groups were testing more cans of the same brand and cans of other brands to see which ones floated and which sank.

Finally, the groups were ready to share their results. They didn't all agree on the reasons the cans reacted differently, but they had used scientific methods to gather a lot of information about the physical characteristics of the cans.

## ■ Using Science Every Day

Toward the end of the discussion, Andy said, "You know, I just realized I already know how to think scientifically. When I shoot baskets, I keep experimenting with different ways to hold the ball to see which one works best."

---

## ENRICHMENT

**Activity**  This experiment will help students form and test hypotheses. Divide them into teams of eight to ten. Tell each person to make as many paper airplanes as possible in five minutes, using scrap paper. Have each team add the number of airplanes its members made.

Then ask each team to set up an assembly line in which each member performs one step in making the planes. Before they try out this approach, ask each team to predict whether it will make more or fewer airplanes this way.

This prediction is the team's hypothesis. How can they test it? After testing, discuss whether the results supported their hypotheses. What other changes might increase the number of planes a team could make? How could they test these hypotheses? L1

we'll need to know the elements before we can figure out something we don't know. The Science Challenge might be something like figuring out what that unknown sample was."

Erin nodded. "I guess that's what science is—both knowledge and a way of finding out more." Then she grinned. "But I don't know the periodic table, so I want to be on Lee's team!"

*These ways of thinking scientifically will come handy as you continue to study in the chapters ahead. You may want to look back at this chapter as you are trying to solve problems in class. But remember, scientific thinking and problem solving are not just useful in science class, they can be useful in your daily life.*

"And at this club I belong to," Kisha added, "we made different types of doormats and tried them out at home. Then we picked the best one to make and sell. That's sort of like using a model." She smiled and looked around the class. "Anyone want to buy a doormat?" Everyone laughed.

"Bird-watching is my hobby, but it's also scientific observation," Erin said. "Did I tell you I saw a great blue heron last week in the creek by the park? It was something else!"

Ms. Borga nodded. "Those are all good examples of scientific thinking and information gathering. So, do you think you're ready for the Science Challenge?"

"I think so," said Lee. "And maybe my memorizing the periodic table will come in handy. When you think scientifically, the first thing to do is review what you know, right? Maybe

**15**

**References**

**1.** Greg Pope. "Rebels with Clues." *Science World,* December 6, 1991.

**2.** Brent Filson. *Famous Experiments and How to Repeat Them.* Messner, 1986.

**3.** George Beshore. *Science in Ancient China.* Franklin Watts, 1988.

**4.** Tillie S. Pine and Joseph Levine. *Scientists and Their Discoveries.* McGraw-Hill, 1978.

# 3 ASSESS

**Check for Understanding**

Ask students whether they would use a model, experiment, or observation to answer these questions:

**1.** What is the most effective breath mint? *(experiment)*

**2.** How long does it take a product labelled *biodegradable* to break down? *(observation)*

**3.** How does increasing the size of the wheels on a toy truck affect its speed? *(model)* L1

**Reteach**

To help students understand the difference between an experiment and observation, ask why the Explore! activity on page 7 is not an experiment. *We cannot easily experiment with conditions that form rocks, but we can gather information about the origin of the rocks through observation.* Ask students for other examples of scientific observation. *These might include observing the night sky and documenting the movement of tides.* L1

**Extension**

Ask students to review the definitions of *scientific thinking* they wrote in groups at the beginning of the chapter. Ask them to work individually or in groups to revise these definitions to show what they've learned about scientific thinking. L1
**COOP LEARN**

# 4 CLOSE

**Activity**

Ask groups to demonstrate ways we can use scientific approaches in our everyday life. Each group will create a model, perform an experiment, or explain how they answered a question by using observation. Their efforts should show what they have learned about using scientific thinking to solve everyday problems. L1 **COOP LEARN**

1. You describe what has already been discovered so that you thoroughly understand the background and the question under investigation. You can also see if the question has already been addressed.

2. The subjects being studied differ, so the methods of data collection vary.

3. Sliding board—model; fertilizer—experiment; weather patterns—observation.

## REVIEWING MAIN IDEAS

Review the statements below about the big ideas presented in this chapter, and try to answer the questions. Then write *in your journal* one or two new things you learned about science as you read and thought about this chapter.

1 Science is a way of learning more about our world. *Explain why we need to study what has already been discovered.*

2 Scientific problem solving involves asking questions and gathering information to answer them. *How is this process different in history or social studies?*

3 Science includes several methods of gathering information. *Explain which method(s) you might use to determine the safest design for a sliding board, to choose the best fertilizer for a garden, and to determine any changes in the weather patterns in your area.*

# CHAPTER REVIEW

## Understanding Ideas

1. Is it possible to do an experiment with models? Explain.
2. Compare and contrast making models and observing.
3. Outline the steps you would take when designing a way to investigate a problem.

## Critical Thinking

In your journal, *answer each of the following questions.*

1. Why is someone who knows nothing about electricity unlikely to make a discovery that will add to our knowledge of electricity?
2. The people in one town cannot agree about what to build on several undeveloped acres of land. What are some questions that science could answer relating to this problem? What are some questions that depend on people's opinions?
3. What are at least two ways you do or could use scientific thinking to answer questions in your own life?

## Problem Solving

*Read the following problem and discuss your answers in a brief paragraph.*

It's winter and some young people in a Chicago neighborhood are eager to start playing ice hockey. However, no one is sure when the ice on the park pond will be frozen solid enough for a game. How could they solve this problem scientifically?

1. List at least three things the team probably already knows about this topic.
2. Write the question they need to answer. (Be specific.)
3. Form a hypothesis.
4. Think of ways they could test this hypothesis safely.
5. After the team determines whether its hypothesis was correct, what additional information will they have available next fall?

## Introduction CHAPTER REVIEW

### Understanding Ideas

1. Yes. You can use the model and simulate conditions that the real thing would be exposed to.
2. Making models and observing are two methods of testing hypotheses. To make a model, you need to observe the real thing and then build a smaller, larger, or more manageable version of it.
3. The outline should look similar to steps 1-7 of Flex Your Brain.

### Critical Thinking

1. They will not have the background to begin experimenting or to know which questions have been answered and which have not.
2. Can answer: What kind of building can the lot hold? What is drainage on the land like? Cannot answer: Is it pretty? Will it be good or bad for the community?
3. You could use scientific methods to answer questions or to help improve a way of doing something.

### Problem Solving

1. Freezing point of water, average winter temperature, depth of the water.
2. How thick must surface ice be to safely support a skater?
3-4. Hypotheses and tests will vary. Check to see that the tests actually test the hypothesis and that they are safe.
5. They will know how thick ice must be, and they may know how many days of freezing weather they have to have before the ice is safe.

# Electricity and Magnetism

## UNIT OVERVIEW

## UNIT FOCUS

In Unit 1, students will learn about electricity and magnetism. As they study this unit, they will explore the different ways they use electrical energy every day.

Ask students if they have ever used a magnet to hold a note on a refrigerator door. This unit will help students understand the special properties of a magnet that allow it to stick to certain metallic surfaces.

This unit also will explore electromagnetic waves. When students see sunlight or a rainbow, they are observing visible electromagnetic waves. If they notice that a person's skin has darkened after being exposed to the sun, they are observing the effects of invisible electromagnetic waves.

## THEME DEVELOPMENT

Energy, the ability to do work or make things move, is the primary theme of this unit. Electricity is one of the most common means by which we transfer energy, from the electromagnetic waves that transport energy from the sun to Earth to the electrical current that brings us energy from power plants. The theme of scale and structure is also important in this unit. Static cling and lightning, for example, share a common origin, although their scale and structure are very different.

### Connections to Other Units

Electrical charge is a property of matter that causes forces and interactions. Although the forces' origins are different, how they produce changes in motion and do work is the same. Electric charge interactions are one force holding atoms together. Understanding their function is one step toward understanding structures of atoms and properties of matter.

# ELECTRICITY AND MAGNETISM

**As you study this unit, you'll learn many different ways in which you use electrical energy each day. When you toast bread, pop popcorn in a microwave oven, or simply use a blender, you are using electrical energy.**

18

## VIDEODISC

Use the **Integrated Science Videodisc,** to reinforce and enhance concepts in this unit.

## Try It!

**B**ring a magnet near a refrigerator door and you experience a pulling feeling. Do you feel the same pull when you try to attach a magnet to a soft drink can? Both a refrigerator door and a soft drink can are made of metal, but why do magnets act differently with different types of metals?

### What To Do

1. Bring the magnet close to items such as paper clips, rubber bands, aluminum soft drink can tops, and paper. Based on your observations, write a general statement *in your Journal* about what a magnet does.

2. Using the materials that were attracted by the magnet, place a sheet of paper between the magnet and materials. Do you notice any difference in the way the magnet works? *In your Journal,* describe what happens.

### Try It Again

After you've learned more about magnets, try this activity again and see if your predictions change or if your original explanations were correct.

19

### GETTING STARTED

**Discussion** Some questions you may want to ask your students are:

**1. What things can you list that have to do with electricity?** Students may identify a variety of electrical appliances. They may also say *lightning, electric sockets, wires* and *transmission towers.*

**2. Which of the things you listed are similar to each other? How?** Students should find relationships among the items they listed in response to question 1.

**3. Where is the safest place to be during an electrical storm? Why?** Students may suggest a car, because the rubber tires act as insulators through which electric charge does not flow.

The way in which students answer these questions will help you to identify any misconceptions about electricity that they may have.

**Answers to Questions**
**1.** A magnet attracts certain metal objects and attracts or repels other magnets.
**2.** No. The magnet attracts the objects through the paper.
**Try It Again** Some explanations and predictions may change.

### ✔ Assessment

**Process** Have students make a data table and classify the objects according to whether or not they were attracted to the magnet. Use the Performance Task Assessment List for Data Table in **PAMSS**, p. 37. L1 LEP

## Try It!

**Purpose** To observe how a magnet affects different materials.

**Background Information** A magnet has two poles, designated *north* and *south.* Opposite poles attract each other, but like poles repel. The attractive force around a magnet, its magnetic field, is most powerful at the poles.

Electrical currents can produce magnetic fields. This phenomenon is used in some kinds of switches and in doorbells.

**Suggested Materials** Magnets, a variety of items such as soft drink can tops, paper clips, rubber bands, paper, cloth, and screws.

**Trouble Shooting** Some refrigerator magnets may not be strong enough for use in this activity. Hardware stores often sell strong rectangular magnets you may find more suitable for use than refrigerator magnets.

# Chapter Organizer

| SECTION | OBJECTIVES | ACTIVITIES |
|---|---|---|
| **Chapter Opener** | | |
| **1-1 Forces and Electrical Charges** (3 days) | 1. **Observe** the force caused by electrical charges.<br>2. **Demonstrate** the two kinds of electrical charges. | **Explore!** Can a comb pick up paper? p. 21<br>**Find Out!** Do electric charges interact? p. 23<br>**Investigate! 1-1:** Charging Up, pp. 24-25 |
| **1-2 Electrical Charge Carriers** (2 days) | 1. **Distinguish** electrical conductors from insulators.<br>2. **Describe** how a charged object attracts an uncharged one.<br>3. **Demonstrate** a variety of effects of static electricity. | **Find Out!** Do electrical charges stay put? p. 27<br>**Explore!** Do conductors hold a charge? p. 29<br>**Skillbuilder:** Determining Cause and Effect, p. 30 |
| **1-3 Making Electricity Flow** (2 days) | 1. **State** the function of a battery in a circuit.<br>2. **Light** a bulb using a battery.<br>3. **Explain** the effect of resistance on the current in a circuit. | **Find Out!** How does charge flow from a battery through a light bulb? p. 32<br>**Find Out!** How does electric current depend on the resistance in a circuit? p. 35 |
| **1-4 Resistance, Current, and Voltage** (3 days) | 1. **Control** the amount of current in a circuit.<br>2. **List** the variables that determine electrical resistance. | **Find Out!** How does increasing voltage affect current? p. 37<br>**Investigate! 1-2:** Potential Difference and Current, pp. 38-39<br>**Find Out!** How does the length of a conductor affect its resistance? p. 40 |

## EXPAND your view

**Life Science Connection** Stunning Eels, pp. 28-29
**A Closer Look** What Causes Lightning? pp. 32-33
**Science and Society** Recycling Batteries, p. 42

**Technology Connection** Latimer's Light, p. 43
**Teens in Science** Overcoming Obstacles, p. 44

## ACTIVITY MATERIALS

### EXPLORE!

**Page 21**
small plastic comb, scraps of paper; dry, wool cloth
**Page 29**
balloon, shiny balloon, piece of wool, aluminum foil

### INVESTIGATE!

**Page 24***
cellophane-tape charge detectors; objects made of plastic, glass, and ceramic; fabrics such as wool, silk, cotton, and fur; plastic bags and wrap
**Page 38***
plastic funnel, ring stand with ring, 2 1-m lengths of rubber tubing of different diameters, meterstick, 2 500-mL beakers, stopwatch or clock

### FIND OUT!

**Page 23**
removable, invisible cellophane tape
**Page 27**
plastic comb, wool, tape
**Page 32***
D-cell, flashlight bulb, wire
**Page 35**
D-cell, 3 bulbs, 3 sockets, wire
**Page 37***
D-cell, 2 bulbs rated at 3 volts, 2 sockets, connecting wires
**Page 40**
2 D-cells, lamp with socket, long thick pencil lead, ruler, 3 wires, two clips

*For adequate development of the concepts presented, we recommend that students do the activities with an asterisk.

# Chapter 1 Electricity

## TEACHER CLASSROOM RESOURCES

| Student Masters | Teaching Aids |
|---|---|
| **Study Guide,** p. 7<br>**Making Connections: Technology & Society,** p. 5<br>**Science Discovery Activities,** 1-1 | **Color Transparency and Master 1,** Like and Unlike Charges<br>**Laboratory Manual,** pp. 1–2, Electrical Charges<br>**\*STVS:** *Lightning,* Physics (Disc 1, Side 1) |
| **Study Guide,** p. 8<br>**Critical Thinking/Problem Solving,** p. 9<br>**Take Home Activities,** p. 6<br>**How It Works,** p. 5 | |
| **Study Guide,** p. 9<br>**Multicultural Connections,** pp. 5,6<br>**Making Connections: Integrating Sciences,** p. 5<br>**Flex Your Brain,** p. 5<br>**Science Discovery Activities,** p. 1-2, 1-3 | **Color Transparency and Master 2,** Series and Parallel Circuits<br>**\*STVS:** *Hydroelectric Power,* Chemistry (Disc 2, Side 2) |
| **Study Guide,** p. 10<br>**Making Connections: Across the Curriculum,** p. 5<br>**Concept Mapping,** p. 9 | **Laboratory Manual,** pp. 3–4, Wet-Cell Battery<br>**\*STVS:** *Energy Integrated Farm,* Chemistry (Disc 2, Side 2) |

| ASSESSMENT RESOURCES | |
|---|---|
| **Review and Assessment,** pp. 5–10<br>**Performance Assessment,** Ch. 1<br>**PAMSS\***<br>**MindJogger Videoquiz**<br>**Alternate Assessment in the Science Classroom**<br>**Computer Test Bank** | **Spanish Resources**<br>**Cooperative Learning Resource Guide**<br>**Lab and Safety Skills**<br>**Integrated Science Videodisc** |

## KEY TO TEACHING STRATEGIES

The following designations will help you decide which activities are appropriate for your students.

- **L1** Level 1 activities should be within the ability range of all students.
- **L2** Level 2 activities should be within the ability range of the average to above-average student.
- **L3** Level 3 activities are designed for the ability range of above-average students.
- **LEP** LEP activities should be within the ability range of Limited English Proficiency students.
- **COOP LEARN** Cooperative Learning activities are designed for small group work.
- **P** These strategies represent student products that can be placed into a best-work portfolio.

## ADDITIONAL MATERIALS

**Software**
*AC/DC Circuits,* Sunburst.
*Basic Electricity,* MicroMedia.
*Build a Circuit,* Sunburst.
*Electric Field,* EME.
*Electricity,* J&S Software.
*Superstar Science CD,* CD-ROM, Orange Cherry New Media Schoolhouse.
*Making Circuits,* Microcomputer Workshop.

**Audiovisual**
*Electricity, The Energy of Electrons,* video, SVE.
*Electrostatic Charges and Forces,* film and video, Coronet/MTI.

*Mr. Wizard's World, Electricity,* video, Mr. Wizard Institute.
*The Mystery of Electricity,* video, Hawkhill Science.

**Laserdisc**
*Understanding Earth,* Videodiscovery.
*Windows on Science, Physical Science,* Optical Data Corp.

**Readings**
Ford, R.A. *Homemade Lighting: Creative Experiments in Electricity.* TAB

\***Performance Assessment in Middle School Science**

\***Science and Technology Videodisc Series**

# Electricity

## THEME DEVELOPMENT

The themes that this chapter supports are energy, and scale and structure. This chapter describes electricity as a form of energy that can be converted to other forms, such as heat and light. Electrical charges are viewed as particles and, on a larger scale, in terms of the effects they have on matter.

## CHAPTER OVERVIEW

In this chapter, students will explore the causes and effects of static electricity and will identify the two types of charge.

Students will compare conductors and insulators. They will observe that circuits are paths for moving charges and see how the properties of resistance, current, and voltage affect circuits.

### Tying to Previous Knowledge

Arrange students in groups to brainstorm observations about electricity. Encourage students to consider experiences with devices that use electricity. Finally, have students brainstorm safety rules that relate to electricity. L1

COOP LEARN

## INTRODUCING THE CHAPTER

Have students recall memories of electrical storms. Do they know what causes an electrical storm? Tell them that in this chapter, they will find out. L1

### Uncovering Preconceptions

Students may think that friction creates charges. Be sure that students realize that charges exist in all matter, and that friction causes them to move from one object to another.

# ELECTRICITY

### Did you ever wonder...

✓ **What static cling is?**

✓ **What makes electric eels electric?**

✓ **Where is the safest place to be during an electrical storm?**

Before you begin to study about electricity, think about these questions and answer them *in your Journal*. When you finish the chapter, compare your Journal write-up with what you have learned.

A bright light and the crash of thunder awaken you one night. You watch through your window as an electrical storm moves across the sky. Bright white bolts of lightning flash and then streak outward like cracks in breaking glass. What causes this energy and draws it from the sky to Earth? Is this the same form of energy that lights lamps and heats toasters? In this chapter, you will learn about a form of energy that we take very much for granted. Without this form of energy, every aspect of our lives would be very different.

▶ **Less than a hundred years ago, this energy — electricity—was a new and mysterious novelty. In the activity on the next page, explore one of the first electrical phenomena examined.**

20

### Did you ever wonder...

• Static cling is the attraction of opposite charges on two pieces of clothes that have just been dried in a dryer. (p. 24)

• Chemical reactions, similar to those produced in a battery, make electric eels electric. (pp. 28–29)

• One safe place to be is inside a car, because the charge would flow over the outside and to the ground. (pp. 28-29, 33)

### STUDENT JOURNAL

Have students write their responses to the Did You Ever Wonder questions in their journals. After they have studied the chapter, students should read their journal entries again to see how their perceptions of electricity have changed.

## Explore! ACTIVITY

### Can a comb pick up paper?

**What To Do**

1. Take a small plastic comb and hold it over several tiny scraps of paper. What happens?

2. Now hold a piece of dry, wool cloth in one hand and brush the comb along it several times with the other hand.

3. Then hold the comb over the scraps of paper. What happens?

4. How can the comb produce a force that can overcome gravity? Why does the paper jump to the comb after brushing with wool? What did the rubbing of the wool do to the comb? *In your Journal,* explain how you think these things happen.

**21**

## ASSESSMENT PLANNER

**PORTFOLIO**
Refer to page 47 for suggested items that students might select for their portfolios.

**PERFORMANCE ASSESSMENT**
Process, pp. 21, 23, 25, 33, 37, 39 40
Skillbuilder, p. 30
Explore! Activities, pp. 21, 29
Find Out! Activities, pp. 22, 27, 32, 35, 37, 40
Investigate, pp. 24–25, 38–39

**CONTENT ASSESSMENT**
Oral, pp. 27, 29
Check Your Understanding, pp. 26, 30, 35, 41
Reviewing Main Ideas, p. 45
Chapter Review, pp. 46–47

**GROUP ASSESSMENT**
Opportunities for group assessment occur with Cooperative Learning Strategies.

### Explore!

**Can a comb pick up paper?**

**Time needed** 15 minutes

**Materials** plastic comb, scraps of paper, wool cloth

**Thinking Processes** observing and inferring, recognizing cause and effect, concept mapping

**Purpose** To observe the attraction between opposite charges.

**Teaching the Activity**

**Troubleshooting** This activity works best on days with low relative humidity. Make sure that the wool cloth is dry. Have students move the cloth vigorously along the comb.

**Student Journal** Students may relate their observations to other instances in which static electricity caused an attraction between objects. L1

**Expected Outcome**

Students will observe that when rubbed, the comb attracts scraps of paper.

**Answers to Questions**

1. Nothing happens.

3. The paper scraps are attracted to the comb.

4. Comb exerts force that attracts the paper. The paper is attracted by charges on the comb. Rubbing charged the comb.

### ✔ Assessment

**Process** Students can learn to better recognize cause and effect by thinking of other ways of producing static electricity. *By rubbing your feet on a carpet; by clothes rubbing together in a drier; by combing your hair on a very dry day, and so on.* Ask students to note if the result is an attraction between objects, repulsion, or a spark. Students could then make a concept map including this information. Use the Performance Task Assessment List for Concept Map in **PAMSS,** p. 44. L1 P

# PREPARATION

## Concepts Developed

In this section, students investigate the causes and effects of static electricity, the form of electric charge that essentially doesn't move. Students learn about the electrical nature of matter by observing the forces between charged objects. They demonstrate the induction of positive or negative charges.

## Planning the Lesson

Refer to the Chapter Organizer on pages 20A–B.

### Find Out!

**Do electric charges interact?**

**Time needed** 5–10 minutes

**Materials** cellophane tape

**Thinking Processes** observing and inferring, modeling, designing an experiment

**Purpose** To observe the interactions between charges.

**Preparation** This activity works best with 1/2-inch "invisible" tape.

### Teaching the Activity

**Discussion** Have students recall examples of charging an object. L1

**Troubleshooting** Make sure students are sticking the tape onto a perfectly smooth surface. High humidity will lessen the duration and magnitude of the effect.

**Student Journal** Students may compare the interaction between the two strips of tape before they were stuck to the desk with the interaction between the strips after they were pulled from the desk. Encourage students to form hypotheses about why the differently treated strips of tape behaved differently. L2

---

# Forces and Electrical Charges

## Section Objectives

- Observe the force caused by electrical charges.
- Demonstrate the two kinds of electrical charges.

## Key Terms

*electrical charge*
*unlike charges*
*like charges*

## Static Electricity

After you rubbed the comb on the cloth in the Explore activity, the comb attracted the tiny scraps of paper. In doing so, you repeated an experiment done by Thales about 600 B.C.E. and Gilbert in 1570. They both saw an effect of static electricity. Perhaps you've gotten a shock from touching a doorknob after walking on a carpet.

You might even have seen a spark jump. These activities result from static electricity. Lightning is a more spectacular result of static electricity.

You can explore another property of static electricity by doing the activity below.

### Figure 1-1

Ⓐ Everything contains electrical charges—people, trees, cats, and minerals. Thales, a Greek who lived around 600 B.C.E., was one of the first to describe a phenomenon related to electricity. He described what happened when amber was rubbed with a bit of wool.

*Thales*

Ⓑ This photo shows Thales's results. In 1570, English scientist William Gilbert repeated and expanded on the experiment. He named the effects *electricity* after the Greek word for amber, *elektron*.

### Find Out! ACTIVITY

**Do electric charges interact?**

Electricity is so common, we're not used to examining its properties. In this activity, you can find out one of these properties by using transparent tape.

---

## Expected Outcome

Students will observe that the two strips of tape, placed one on top of the other and quickly pulled apart, were attracted to each other. The two strips that were each stuck to the desk, then pulled off, repelled each other.

## Conclude and Apply

**1.** The strips attracted each other; they repelled each other.

**2.** Charged the strips differently

### ✔ Assessment

**Process** Strengthen students' ability to recognize cause and effect by having them design another experiment that demonstrates the interaction between opposite or like charged objects. Encourage students to be creative. Use the Performance Task Assessment List for Designing an Experiment in **PAMSS**, page 23. L1 P

## What To Do

1. Fold over about 5 mm on the end of the tape for a handle. Then tear off a strip 8 to 10 cm long. Stick the strip on a dry, smooth surface, such as your desktop. Make a second strip and put it on top of the first.

2. Quickly pull both pieces off the desk and pull them apart. Then bring the tapes close together. Observe what happens.

3. Now make two new strips of tape, but this time press each one onto the desk. Then pull them off and bring the two strips close together. What happens?

### Conclude and Apply

1. What happened when you brought the first pair of tapes close together? What happened when you brought the second pair together?

2. What did you do that might have caused the two different reactions?

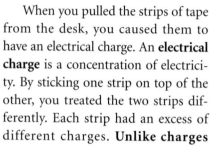

When you pulled the strips of tape from the desk, you caused them to have an electrical charge. An **electrical charge** is a concentration of electricity. By sticking one strip on top of the other, you treated the two strips differently. Each strip had an excess of different charges. **Unlike charges** attract one another. When you prepared the strips the same way, they received like charges. **Like charges** repel one another.

You can learn more about different types of charge produced by various materials in the Investigate activity on the next page.

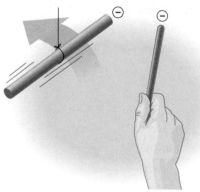

*Like charges on rods*

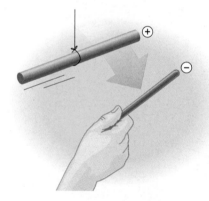

*Unlike charges on rods*

**Figure 1-2**

The two effects you saw in the Find Out activity showed you that there must be at least two different kinds of charge. Like the tape strips you prepared, the rods with like charges repel one another and those with unlike charges attract one another.

### Program Resources

**Study Guide,** p. 7
**Transparency Master,** p. 5, and **Color Transparency,** Number 1, Like and Unlike Charges L1

# 1 MOTIVATE

**Demonstrate**  Play the song "Opposites Attract" by Paula Abdul as students come into the room. Ask students to relate the main phrase of the song to the information in this section. L1

# 2 TEACH

### Tying to Previous Knowledge

Have students recall past observations by describing what can happen if you touch a doorknob after walking across a carpet. They may reply that you get a shock. Explain that friction between the carpet and shoes induces a net charge. The electric shock is a *static discharge,* or "loss" of static electricity.

**Theme   Connection**  In their study of this section, students will be exposed to the theme of scale and structure. Students will experiment with charged objects to see how charges interact. This macroscopic scale is appropriate for students who have not yet studied atomic structure. You may wish to point out, however, that it is also possible to study charge on a much smaller scale, that of individually charged particles.

### Content Background

Objects become charged through the transfer of negatively charged particles (electrons). If an object gains these particles, it becomes negatively charged. If it loses these particles, it becomes positively charged. (Because students have not yet learned about atomic structure, refer to the movement of "particles" rather than "electrons.")

## Planning the Activity

**Time needed** 20 minutes

**Purpose** To identify the two types of charges.

**Process Skills** classifying, making and using tables, comparing and contrasting, observing

**Materials** See student activity.

**Preparation** You may wish to have students work in groups of two to four. Provide one roll of tape for each group. **COOP LEARN**

## Teaching the Activity

Tell students to bring the objects and fabrics *slowly* near the tape charge detectors. Students will need to periodically refresh the tape charge detectors.

**Process Reinforcement** Ask students to compare the effect of rubbing an object with wool to the effect of rubbing the object with silk.

**Student Journal** Have students copy the data table and record their data in their journals. **L1**

## Expected Outcome

Students will classify objects according to the electric charge produced when they are rubbed together. See reduced student page for sample data.

---

# INVESTIGATE!

# Charging Up

*You're probably familiar with the static cling clothes have when they come out of the dryer. That interaction comes from fabrics rubbing together. In the following activity observe what happens when other objects are rubbed together.*

### Problem
How can charges be detected and identified?

### Materials
cellophane tape–charge detectors
objects made of plastic, glass, and ceramic
fabrics such as wool, silk, cotton, and fur
plastic bags and wrap

## What To Do

**1** *In your Journal*, make a copy of the data table. List the fabrics and objects that you plan to use.

**2** Using what you learned in the Find Out activity on page 22, make two strips of tape with unlike charges. Label the strip of tape stuck to the desk Bottom and the strip stuck to the other strip of tape Top (see photo **A**).

**3** Rub one of the objects on one of the fabrics (see photo **B**).

Sample Data

| Data and Observations | | |
|---|---|---|
| Objects/Fabrics | Wool | Silk |
| Glass test tube | Top | Bottom |
| Plastic comb | Bottom | Top |
| Plastic spoon | Bottom | Top |

---

### Program Resources

**Activity Masters,** pp. 7–8, Investigate 1-1
**Laboratory Manual,** pp. 1–2, Electrical Charges **L1**
**Making Connections: Technology & Society,** p. 5, Electrostatic Hazards **L2**
**Science Discovery Activities,** 1-1, Potato Tester

### ENRICHMENT

**Demonstration** To help students learn to interpret their observations use a Van de Graaff generator to demonstrate effects of charges. Charge up the Van de Graaff generator. Slowly approach the dome with a lighted match. The match will go out. Have students work in pairs to offer an explanation for this phenomenon. *The negative charges ionize the oxygen so it cannot be used for combustion of the match.* **L3**
**COOP LEARN**

**A**  **B**  **C**

**4** Now, bring the object near the tape charge detectors and observe what happens. If an object repels the Bottom tape and attracts the Top tape, it must be charged the same as the Bottom tape and opposite of the Top tape.

**5** Record your results. Indicate if any object attracts both tapes.

**6** Repeat Steps 3 and 4 for each object and each fabric.

**7** Identify the combination of objects and fabrics that produced the charge with the strongest force.

**8** With a plastic bag covering your hand, hold the fabric and rub the object (see photo **C**).

**9** Bring the fabric near the tapes to identify its charge. Then bring the object near the tapes to identify its charge.

## Analyzing

1. How many different kinds of charge did you produce?

2. *Compare* the charges on the object and the fabric. Are they alike or different? Explain.

3. Was there any material that did not become charged? If so, identify the material.

## Concluding and Applying

4. List two examples where rubbing the object results in a charge.

5. **Going Further** A plastic comb is rubbed with a piece of wool and is suspended from a string. What will happen if a glass object that has been rubbed with silk is brought near the comb?

---

**1.** The rubbing produces two kinds of charge.

**2.** The charges on the object and the fabric are different. When the fabric and the object are rubbed together, negatively charged particles move from one to the other. One becomes positively charged, and the other becomes negatively charged, resulting in attraction between the two.

**3.** No; all the materials became charged when rubbed.

**4.** Answers may include rubbing your shoes on the carpet or your pant legs rubbing together as you walk.

**5.** The comb will turn toward the glass.

### ✔ Assessment

**Process** Students can practice classifying additional objects by observing how these objects interact with the strips of tape. Students should expand their data tables to include these observations. Use the Performance Task Assessment List for Data Table in **PAMSS**, p. 37. L1 LEP

---

### ENRICHMENT

**Research** Have students work in groups and use reference materials to investigate Coulomb's law—the relationship among the electric force, charge, and distance between two charged objects. Coulomb's law is an inverse square law similar to Newton's law of gravitation. L3 COOP LEARN

# 3 ASSESS

## Check for Understanding

Have students answer the questions in Check Your Understanding. Pose the Apply question in terms of the movement of charges.

## Reteach

Help students recognize cause and effect by using an electroscope to detect an electric charge. Charge the electroscope with a charged balloon, then touch it with your finger. Ask students what happens and why. *The electroscope leaves fall to neutral position. Your finger and body absorb excess charges if the electroscope was negatively charged. They "donate" charges if the electroscope was positively charged.* L1

## Extension

**Discussion** Students can practice interpreting observations by explaining why the individual hairs on their arms rise when a negatively charged balloon is placed near them. *The negatively charged balloon attracted the positive charges to the ends of the hairs and pushed the negative charges down toward your arm.* L2

# 4 CLOSE

## Discussion

Ask students to explain why the electricity that causes the attraction between socks in a dryer could not be used to run a portable tape player. *The movement, or discharge, of static electricity happens rapidly and could not be used as a continuous supply of energy.* L1

**Figure 1-3**

*Photocopier*
**Copying machines use static electricity to operate in a process called electrostatic copying.**

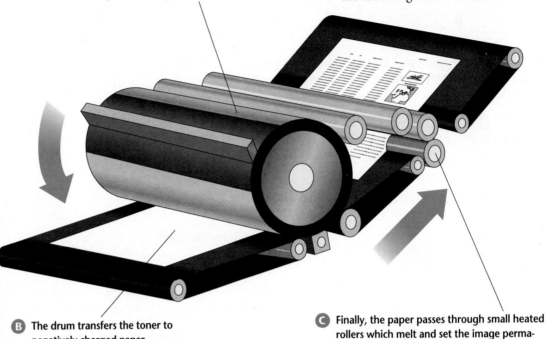

**A** Light reflected from an original image produces an invisible copy image of positive charges on the large drum. A fine black powder called toner, containing carbon particles and plastic beads, is attracted to the drum, producing a dusty, visible image there.

**B** The drum transfers the toner to negatively charged paper.

**C** Finally, the paper passes through small heated rollers which melt and set the image permanently. What properties of electricity does this process demonstrate?

In the Investigate activity you saw the interaction of charges on several materials. The two kinds of charge you observed are more commonly called positive (+) and negative (-).

As Thales and Gilbert discovered, electricity is everywhere. You often see its effects when you comb your hair, when you walk across a carpet, and in the sky during a thunderstorm. Static charges have some interesting uses as the following illustration shows.

## check your UNDERSTANDING

1. As you move two charged cellophane tapes closer together, do the forces between them become greater or smaller? Explain your answer using your observations.

2. If you rub hard rubber with a piece of wool, what charge is on the piece of rubber?

3. **Apply** Explain why your comb sometimes attracts your hair after use.

## Meeting Individual Needs

**Behaviorally Challenged** Help the easily distracted student learn to predict the effects of static electricity by experimenting at home. Have students predict what they will observe if they vigorously comb their hair in a darkened room. Tell them to record their predictions in their journal, test their predictions at home, and record the results.

## check your UNDERSTANDING

1. They become greater.
2. negative
3. The comb and hair have unlike charges after being rubbed against each other.

## Electrical Charge Carriers

### Electrical Charges

In the last section, you observed that electrical charges may be positive (+) or negative (-). What type of material moves charges from one place to another? Do all materials move charges in the same way? Do electrical charges stay put on some materials? You can answer this question by combining and expanding two activities from Section 1-1.

**Section Objectives**

■ Distinguish electrical conductors from insulators.
■ Describe how a charged object attracts an uncharged one.
■ Demonstrate a variety of effects of static electricity.

**Key Terms**

*insulator, conductor*

### Find Out! ACTIVITY

#### Do electrical charges stay put?

**A**s you've observed, electrical charges move to and from objects. What controls that movement?

#### What To Do

1. Charge a plastic comb by rubbing one end of it with a piece of wool while holding it by the other end. Bring it close to a tape charge detector.

2. Now, with your finger, touch the comb on the end you charged. Bring the comb near the charge detector again.

#### Conclude and Apply

1. *In your Journal*, describe what happened the first time you brought the comb near the charge detector.

2. What happened the second time you brought the comb to the charge detector?

3. What happened to the electrical charge?

In the Find Out activity above, you observed that the comb held a charge until you touched the charged end. Electrical charges don't move freely from one place to another through some materials such as plas-tic. If the charges had been able to move in the comb, you wouldn't have had to touch its other end to remove the charges. A material in which electrical charges do not move freely from place to place is called an **insulator**.

---

### Find Out!

#### Do electrical charges stay put?

**Time needed**   10 minutes

**Materials**   charge detector, comb, piece of wool

**Thinking Processes**   recognizing cause and effect, comparing and contrasting, modeling

**Purpose**   To infer that electric charges do not move freely through insulators.

### Teaching the Activity

**Troubleshooting**   Experiments with static electricity work best on dry, cool days.

**Student Journal**   Ask students write predictions of what will happen. L1

### Expected Outcome

Students should observe that the comb held the charge until they touched the charged end.

---

## PREPARATION

### Concepts Developed

Students observe how charges move through different materials. Students see that charges move freely through conductors, but not through insulators.

### Planning the Lesson

Refer to the Chapter Organizer on pages 20A–B.

## 1 MOTIVATE

**Discussion**   Have students sharpen their observation skills by identifying places in the classroom where electrical conductors are found. They may mention electric appliances, such as lighting fixture, classroom computer, or overhead projector. L1

**Student Text Questions**
**What types of material moves charges from one place to another?** *conductor* **Do all materials move charges in the same way?** *no* **Do electrical charges stay put on some materials?** *yes*

---

**Conclude and Apply**

1. The tape charge detector was attracted to the comb.

2. nothing

3. Somehow, touching the comb neutralized the charge.

### ✔ Assessment

**Oral**   Ask students to relate the properties of insulators to their importance to safety. *Insulators help prevent accidents by preventing the free movement of electrical charge.* Students could then write public service announcements warning of the dangers of using appliances with frayed wires. Use the Performance Task Assessment List for Oral Presentation in **PAMSS**, p. 71. L1 P

### Tying to Previous Knowledge

Ask students if they have ever shuffled across a carpet or removed a sweater and then received a shock when they touched a doorknob. Did they get a second shock if they touched the doorknob again? *no* What might have happened to the static charge? *After the first shock, the body no longer carried a charge.*

## Explore!

### Do conductors hold a charge?

**Time needed** about 15 minutes

**Materials** balloon, shiny balloon, piece of wool, small sheet of aluminum foil

**Thinking Processes** comparing and contrasting, observing, recognizing cause and effect, forming operational definitions, modeling, predicting

**Purpose** To observe how a charged object affects a nearby conductor.

### Teaching the Activity

**Discussion** Ask students if aluminum is a conductor or an insulator. *It is a conductor.* Then ask what they think would happen if a conductor were brought near an electric charge. *Accept all reasonable responses at this time.* **LEP**
**COOP LEARN**

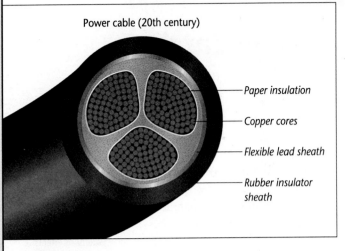

Power cable (20th century)

- Paper insulation
- Copper cores
- Flexible lead sheath
- Rubber insulator sheath

**Figure 1-4**

Insulators include paper, plastic, rubber, wood, and glass. Conductors include most metals such as copper, aluminum, gold, and silver. The copper conductor and rubber insulator of this power cable combine to safely transmit electricity.

In other materials, electrical charges can move anywhere. A material in which electrical charges can move freely from place to place is called a **conductor**. Your body is a conductor, which is why the charge left the comb after you touched it. Because your body is a conductor, electricity can be dangerous. Power cables are insulated to protect you. **Figure 1-4** shows the conductor and insulator in a power cable. The electrical cords in your home are like it—conductors wrapped in an insulating material. In the activity on the next page, you can explore an example of charges moving through a conductor.

## Stunning Eels

**M**any scientists have tried to find out why electric eels do not electrocute themselves. One hypothesis is that the brain and heart of electric eels are packed in a fatty tissue that protects and insulates these two vital organs from the strong electrical impulses. The other organs of their body apparently are able to withstand the impulses without a fatty layer.

### The Eel Circuit

The electric eel is positively charged at the head and negatively charged at the tail. The tail, which makes up four-fifths of the 6-foot-long fish, has three pairs of electric organs made of more than 5000 plates arranged like the cells in a storage battery. An eel can produce a shock of about 500 volts at a current of 2 amperes. While the electric charge can be released in a fraction of a second, an eel may need nearly an hour to recharge its batteries. By the way, an electric eel is not an eel at all. It's a fresh water fish related to carp and minnows.

### Eel Power In Use

Does it seem strange that a fish like the electric eel has electricity? All animals—even you—have electrical activity in your body. For example, your mus-

## Life Science CONNECTION

### Purpose

The Life Science Connection reinforces Sections 1-1 and 1-2 by describing the force and effects of static electricity in electric fish.

### Content Background

Explain to students that the electroplates in the electric eel, which work neurochemically, intensify what is essentially a nerve impulse. The electric field that the electroplates produce resembles the mag-

netic field of a bar magnet, which students will observe in Chapter 2.

### Teaching Strategies

Have students use the information in paragraph 2 to make a diagram of the electric eel. **L1**

### Student Writing

Have students use the information in the Life Science Connection to write a short story about the electric eel and its prey. **L2**

# Explore! ACTIVITY

## Do conductors hold a charge?

### What To Do

1. Hold a balloon that has been given a negative charge by being rubbed with wool over a few small (less than 1 cm x 1 cm) scraps of aluminum foil. Is the foil attracted to the negatively charged balloon?

2. Hold the positively charged wool over the foil. Is the result the same? Can you explain why?

3. Now, try the same experiment with a charged shiny metallic balloon like the one shown. What happens? *In your Journal, draw what you think happened and write a brief explanation.*

The Explore activity showed that conductors are attracted to both positive and negative charges. The shiny balloon didn't hold a static charge because the thin layer of aluminum on the balloon is a conductor. The charge flowed around the balloon and through you to the ground.

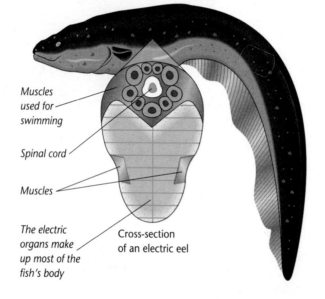

cles move because of electrical potential. Electric eels use the impulse to stun their prey. It also fends off predators, who tend to avoid the eel's electrical impulses.

The shock of an electric eel is large enough to kill an animal as large as a horse. When an animal is stunned by an electric shock, it stops breathing and drowns. Usually the electricity from electric eels stuns small prey, such as fish or frogs.

### What Do You Think?

Besides the electric eel, other animals that live in water—the electric ray, for example—use electric impulses to stun their prey and protect themselves.

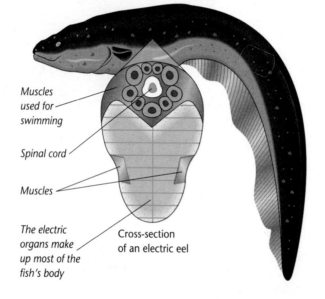

Muscles used for swimming

Spinal cord

Muscles

The electric organs make up most of the fish's body

Cross-section of an electric eel

1. Why do you think water animals use electricity in this way, while animals that live on land do not?

2. Why might it matter where the electrical impulses enter the body of an electric eel's prey?

## Answers to
### What Do You Think?

1. Answers may include the fact that impure water conducts electricity, while air does not.

2. The prey is more vulnerable in certain parts of its body. The prey might not be sufficiently stunned if the electrical impulses entered its body in a less vulnerable spot.

## Program Resources

**Study Guide,**   p. 8
**Critical Thinking/Problem Solving,** p. 9, Electrostatic Precipitator **L2**
**Take Home Activities,**   p. 6, Conducting an Experiment **L1**
**How It Works,**   p. 5, Lightning Rods **L1**

## Explore!

### Teaching the Activity

**Student Journal** Encourage students to draw diagrams showing the transfer of charge between the wool and balloon and the foil. **L1** **LEP** **P**

### Expected Outcome

Students should observe that the pieces of foil move toward the charged balloon and wool and conclude that the foil experienced a net attractive force. The metallic balloon does not attract the foil.

### Answers to Questions

1. Yes.
2. Yes. In both cases, the bits of foil are attracted to the object because the opposite charges are closer than the like charges.
3. The shiny balloon did not attract the foil because the charge flowed around the balloon, through the person, and into the ground.

### ✔ Assessment

**Oral** Ask students to propose a method for preventing the charge from flowing from the shiny balloon to the ground. *The person could wear a rubber glove on the hand holding the balloon.* Have students make a drawing showing how they think the balloon would interact with the foil. *The balloon would hold the charge and attract the foil.* Select the appropriate Performance Task Assessment List in **PAMSS.** **L1**

The positive charge on the first balloon attracts the negative charge on the tape, leaving a net positive charge on both pieces of tape. The like charges repel. A second positively charged balloon increases the effect. [L1]

---

# 3 ASSESS

## Check for Understanding

Assign questions 1–3 under Check Your Understanding. To help students answer question 4, the Apply Questions, ask whether inside a car is a safe place to be during an electrical storm. *Yes. The charge stays on the outer surface of the car.*

## Reteach

Help students learn to infer possible safety hazards from their observations of electricity. Have them discuss safety precautions for using electrical devices. They should be able to explain why you should never use electrical appliances, such as a blow dryer, while in a bathtub and why you should replace frayed electrical wiring. [L1]

## Extension

**Demonstration** Help students learn to interpret their observations by adjusting a faucet to produce a narrow stream of water. Rub a balloon to charge it. Hold the balloon to one side of the stream of water. Ask students to explain what happened. *The stream of water was deflected toward the charged balloon.* [L2]

---

# 4 CLOSE

Tell students that a continuous flow of charge can light lamps and run electrical devices. Ask students what materials would be needed to maintain this flow of charge. *conductors* [L1]

---

Like the foil, uncharged objects are attracted to charged objects. That's why you can stick a charged balloon to an uncharged wall. The charges on the balloon repel the like charges on the wall's surface. The remaining unlike charges are attracted to the charges on the balloon. The force of attraction isn't as strong as between two charged objects, but it's enough to hold up a lightweight balloon.

Lightning is a more impressive example of the spark that jumps from your finger to a doorknob after you've built up a static charge. Such small static charges can be useful as you saw on page 26. Photocopiers and electric spray painters make use of the forces between electric charges.

**Recognizing Cause and Effect**

You have two balloons, each with an equal positive charge. You bring the first one up to cellophane tape charge detectors and the pieces of tape repel. Why? You bring the second balloon near the charge detectors and the tapes repel even further. Why? If you need help, refer to the **Skill Handbook** on page 684.

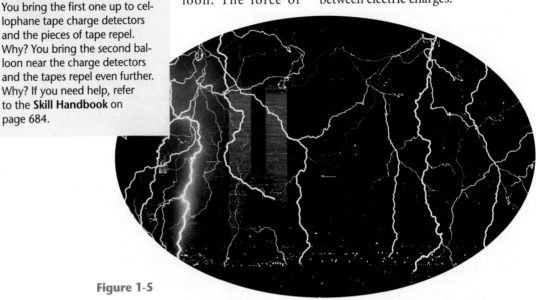

**Figure 1-5**

Lightning can travel up to 14 kilometers to reach the ground. Between clouds, it can travel up to nine times farther.

As you'll see in the next section, using conductors to control the movement of electrical charges is also enormously uselful.

## check your UNDERSTANDING

1. If a charged object touches the end of an insulator, what happens to the charge? What happens on a conductor?
2. Why does a negative charge in clouds produce a positive charge at ground level?
3. List three examples of how static charges are built up and describe the visible effects of the charges.
4. **Apply** Why is it safe to be inside a metal enclosure during an electrical storm?

---

## check your UNDERSTANDING

1. The charge on the insulator stays put. It spreads over the conductor.

2. The negative charge in the clouds attracts the positive charge on the ground and repels the negative charge at ground level. The result is a net positive charge at ground level.

3. Brushing hair—hair sticks out. Shoes on carpet—you get a shock when you touch someone. Clothes in a dryer—clothes cling together.

4. The electrical charge from a bolt of lightning would be conducted around the outside of the enclosure.

## Moving Electrical Charges

During a thunderstorm, the charge jumping from cloud to cloud or striking Earth produces a flash of light. Could you light a lamp this way? Probably not. The spark occurs for only an instant. A lamp needs energy from a continuous flow of charge to stay lit.

It takes energy to separate positive and negative charges. Till now, you've provided that energy either by rubbing or pulling tape away from a desk top. There are more convenient ways to store that energy for use later. After you study the diagrams below, try making charges flow by doing the activity on the next page.

**Section Objectives**

■ State the function of a battery in a circuit.

■ Light a bulb using a battery.

■ Explain the effect of resistance on the current in a circuit.

**Key Terms**

*potential difference*
*circuit*
*current*
*resistance*

**Figure 1-6**

*Water Wheel*

A continuous flow of electrical charge can be maintained in the same way that water in the diagram below is made to flow.

**A** The water pump works against gravity, lifting water into the reservoir. The potential energy added by the pump does work as the water escapes and turns the water wheel.

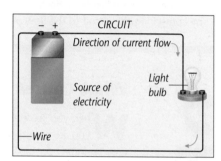

**B** Electrical charges can be made to flow and do work in much the same way as water. A chemical reaction in a battery adds potential energy as it separates charges. Charges move along a conducting wire. The potential energy does work as it lights a light bulb. What forms of energy do we use electricity to produce?

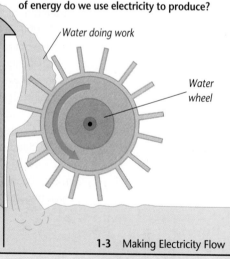

---

**Program Resources**

**Study Guide,** p. 9

**Transparency Master,** p. 7, and **Color Transparency,** Number 2, Series and Parallel Circuits **L1**

**Laboratory Manual,** pp. 3–4, Wet-Cell Battery **L2**

**Science Discovery Activities,** 1-2, Getting a Reaction

---

# PREPARATION

**Concepts Developed**

In this section, students will build on their knowledge of conductors as they learn about the conducting paths through which current electricity flows. Students will make circuits using light bulbs, wire, and a D-cell.

**Planning the Lesson**

Refer to the Chapter Organizer on pages 20A-B.

# 1 MOTIVATE

**Demonstration** Encourage the development of observation skills. Obtain a fresh lemon, a new penny, and a silver dime (one minted before 1965). Attach an alligator clip to each coin and insert the coins into the lemon about 2 cm apart. Use the leads from the coins to connect an LED to complete the circuit. Ask students what makes the LED light. (LEDs are available from scientific supply houses and electronics supply houses.) **L1**

# 2 TEACH

**Tying to Previous Knowledge**

Ask students if they have ever had a portable radio or tape player stop working due to dead batteries. Ask why the battery "dies?" *It stops producing enough voltage to operate the device.* In this section, students will learn what an electric current is and how it can be produced.

**Visual Learning**

**Figure 1-6 What forms of energy do we use electricity to produce?** *Thermal, kinetic, light, mechanical, sound.*

## Visual Learning

**Figure 1-7 How can you tell?** *The light is brighter. What does this tell you about the effect of the switch on the current?* *Each of the three "On" positions of the switch allows more current to flow through the bulb.*

## Find Out!

**How does charge flow from a battery through a light bulb?**

**Time needed** 30 minutes

**Materials** D-cell, flashlight bulb, wire

**Thinking Processes** observing, designing an experiment, interpreting scientific illustrations, sequencing

**Purpose** To observe that charge flows in a complete circuit, from the area of greatest potential to the area of least potential.

**Preparation** Have students work in groups of four. For each group, provide one battery, one bulb, and one piece of insulated wire 30 cm long from which 1 cm of insulation has been stripped off the ends.
**COOP LEARN**

### Teaching the Activity

**Safety** Direct students' attention to the CAUTION note. Have a volunteer read the note aloud. Discuss the reason for it. *Overheated wires can cause fires.*

## Find Out! ACTIVITY

### How does charge flow from a battery through a light bulb?

**E**very electrical circuit has some basic parts. Do this activity to find out some simple ways those parts go together.

#### What To Do

1. Try to connect a battery, bulb, and a wire to light the bulb.
   **CAUTION:** *If a connecting wire gets hot, immediately disconnect one end of the wire from the battery and try another connection.*

#### Conclude and Apply

1. Draw a picture of the battery, bulb, and wire. Trace the flow of charges in your drawing.
2. *In your Journal,* explain how electric current flows along this path by comparing the circuit to the flow of water.

## What Causes Lightning?

**W**hen you see city lights, you are seeing electrical energy under control. When you see lightning shatter the sky, you see electricity that is out of control. The electricity in lightning has a potential of 100 million volts, causing a temperature that ranges from 15 000 to 33 000°C—hotter than the surface of the sun!

What causes the violent discharge of electrical energy in lightning? It starts very simply with the particles in a rain cloud. Lighter particles of water in the cloud collide with heavy particles, such as hail. During the collision, the heavy particles gain negative charges from the lighter particles and become negatively charged. Since the lighter particles lose negative charges, they become positively charged. The heavier, negative particles fall to the bottom of the cloud. The lighter, positive particles drift up to the top of the cloud.

Because the bottom of the cloud is negatively charged, it repels negative charges on the ground beneath it. Because the ground is a conductor, the negative charges can flow away. This leaves a large concentration of positive charges in the ground under the clouds overhead. The number of charges makes the electrical potential energy enormous.

### Purpose

A Closer Look reinforces Section 1-2 by explaining how static charge builds up in clouds and is discharged in the form of lightning. This excursion also explains how negatively charged clouds and positively charged ground interact to produce a giant electrical spark, or lightning bolt.

### Content Background

The electric charges that move down from the clouds toward the ground just before lightning strikes, are called *stepped leaders.* Oppositely charged currents that move up from the ground toward the leaders, are called *streamers.* When a leader meets a streamer, a lightning bolt appears.

### Teaching Strategy

Have students make a class list of safety rules to observe during an electrical storm. Write the list on the chalkboard. Tell students to copy the list and encourage them to display it in their homes.

## Find Out! ACTIVITY

### How does electric current depend on the resistance in a circuit?

Examining changes in a simple working circuit will help you understand how resistance and current are related.

#### What To Do

1. Make a complete circuit containing a battery and a single bulb. Observe how brightly the bulb glows.
2. Next, add a second bulb as shown in the photograph. Note the brightness of the bulbs.
3. Finally, add another bulb to the circuit as shown. Observe the brightness of the bulbs.

#### Conclude and Apply

1. What happened when you added the second bulb to the circuit? When you added the third?
2. *In your Journal,* explain what you observed.

Each added bulb, or added resistance, decreased the brightness of all the bulbs. You could infer that less bright means less current was flowing. When the potential difference remains the same, the current decreases as the resistance increases.

Instead of static charges, you have seen dynamic charges in an electric circuit made of a complete path, a resistance, and a source of potential difference. These simple circuits are part of electric appliances and tools you use every day.

### check your UNDERSTANDING

1. Draw a circuit using a 6-V battery and a bulb that would cause the bulb to glow.
2. What happens to the potential of the charges in a 6-V battery? What happens to the potential when the charges pass through the bulb?

3. **Apply** Suppose you replaced the bulb in the circuit you drew in Question 1 with one of higher resistance. Describe the change in the current through the bulb. How would the new bulb's brightness compare with that of the bulb you replaced?

---

### Program Resources

**Critical Thinking/Problem Solving,** p. 5, Flex Your Brain

**Multicultural Connections,** p. 6, Electricity from Sunlight L1

**Making Connections: Integrating Sciences,** p. 5, Get a Charge Out of Lemons L2

**Science Discovery Activities,** 1-3, A Copper Topper

### check your UNDERSTANDING

1. Students should draw a schematic diagram to represent Figure 1-8.
2. The potential is increased by the battery. The potential decreases when it goes through the bulb.
3. The current in the bulb would decrease. The bulb would be less bright.

---

## 3 ASSESS

### Check for Understanding

Assign questions 1 and 2 under Check Your Understanding. To help students answer question 3, have a volunteer state the relationship between current and resistance. *Current and resistance are inversely related.*

### Reteach

**Discussion** To help students understand the concept of potential energy, use the analogy of an eraser on a desk. We say the eraser has potential energy because of its height. The potential energy changes when the eraser falls. The potential energy is being changed into other forms of energy such as the energy of motion as it falls and sound energy when it hits the floor.

In a battery, the potential energy at one terminal is greater than at the other. This makes it possible for electrons to move, or fall, through the circuit. L1

### Extension

**Discussion** Have students describe parts of the human circulatory system. They will probably list *heart, blood vessels,* and *blood.* Ask them what is similar about the function of the heart in the circulatory system and the function of the battery in the circuits that they made. *Each is a pump. The heart pumps blood. The battery "pumps" charge.* L2

## 4 CLOSE

### Discussion

Inform students that, in 1800, an Italian physicist named Alessandro Volta observed that two metals connected by a conducting liquid produced a continuous transfer of charges. Ask students how this phenomenon is different from static electricity. *Static electricity does not move in a continuous flow; electric current does.* L1

## Concepts Developed

Students will expand and apply their knowledge of circuits as they investigate the relationship between current, resistance, and potential difference.

## Planning the Lesson

Refer to the Chapter Organizer on pages 20A-B.

# 1 MOTIVATE

**Demonstration** Show students several batteries, each with a different voltage. Ask a volunteer to conclude which battery can light the most bulbs. *The one with the highest voltage.* [L1]

# 2 TEACH

## Tying to Previous Knowledge

Have students turn back to page 31 and review the water pump analogy. Tell students that in the upcoming Investigate activity, they will use another water model to see how changes in potential difference affect current.

---

### Visual Learning

**Figure 1-9 What does this suggest about the effect of different potential differences, or voltages, on electric current?** *It suggests that higher voltages must produce greater electric current if all other conditons are the same.*

---

### Connect to . . .

## Chemistry

Electric cells are combined in series or parallel to form batteries. A 12V car battery combines six 2.1 V electric cells in series.

---

## Resistance, Current, and Voltage

**Section Objectives**
- Control the amount of current in a circuit.
- List the variables that determine electrical resistance.

### Connect to...
## Chemistry

The reactions in most chemical electrical cells produce only slightly more than one volt. How do you think larger voltages are produced?

## Potential Difference and Current

As you saw on page 31, a battery in a circuit acts something like a pump in a water system. It increases the potential energy of electrical charges. The larger the battery's voltage, the greater the difference in potential across its terminals.

Consider a circuit containing a battery and bulb. A chemical reaction causes an increase in potential across the battery. There is an equal decrease in potential across the bulb. As **Figure 1-9** below shows, there is also a loss in potential energy of water flowing over a waterfall to a lower level. Water flowing over Niagara Falls has more potential energy than water flowing over a beaver's dam. Do the activity on the next page to see how potential difference and electrical current are related.

**Figure 1-9**

These two dams hold back water with different amounts of potential energy. As the water gates are opened, the water falls and changes potential energy to kinetic energy. The water which falls farther is flowing fastest when it reaches the bottom. What does this suggest about the effect of different potential differences, or voltages, on electric current?

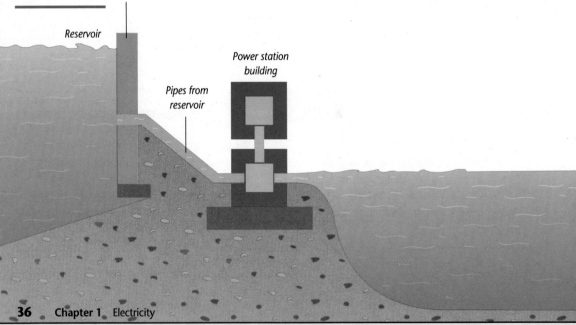

Reservoir

Dam

Pipes from reservoir

Power station building

---

### Meeting Individual Needs

**Learning Disabled** To help learning disabled students distinguish between different gauges of wire, bring in several pieces of wire in a variety of gauges. The thinner the wire, the higher the resistance and gauge number are. Have students look at and hold the wires. Ask a volunteer to put the wires in order from smallest to largest gauge (thickest to thinnest).

# Find Out! ACTIVITY

## How does increasing voltage affect current?

**W**hy do some flashlights have more D-cells than others? To find out, you'll need two D-cells, wire, and two bulbs.

### What To Do

1. Make a complete circuit with the two bulbs and one D-cell as shown. Observe the brightness of the bulbs.

2. Disconnect the circuit and add a second D-cell as shown. Be sure the D-cell connections match the photo before connecting the bulbs. Again, observe the brightness of the bulbs.

### Conclude and Apply

*In your Journal,* write to explain how the brightness in the first circuit compares with the brightness in the second circuit. Explain any differences.

If a pump lifts water to an even higher level, the water will have to fall back a larger distance. Similarly, if a battery with a higher voltage is used, the potential drop across the bulb will be greater. How will this affect the current? We can investigate this with another water model.

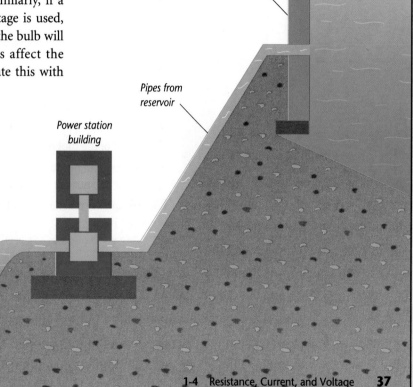

*Dam*

*Reservoir*

*Pipes from reservoir*

*Power station building*

1-4 Resistance, Current, and Voltage **37**

## Program Resources

**Study Guide,** p. 10

**Making Connections: Across the Curriculum,** p. 5, Prevent Electrical Hazards L1

**Multicultural Connections,** p. 5, The Amish and Electricity L1

## Multicultural Perspectives

### Innovations in Science

Meredith Gourdine, an African-American scientist, conducted research on producing high-voltage electricity from natural gas. His research may be applied to preserving foods, burning coal more efficiently, and desalinization. He also won a silver medal in track at the 1952 Olympic Games.

# Find Out!

### How does increasing voltage affect current?

**Time needed** one class period

**Materials** two D-cells, two bulbs rated at 3 volts, two sockets, connecting wires

**Thinking Processes** comparing and contrasting, observing, interpreting scientific illustrations, recognizing cause and effect

**Purpose** To observe that as potential difference or voltage increases, current increases.

**Preparation** Three to four students can work in one group. Assign tasks, such as disconnecting and connecting bulbs, connecting batteries, and checking the circuits against the diagrams. **COOP LEARN**

### Teaching the Activity

**Student Journal** Before beginning the activity, ask students to predict what will happen if they add another D-cell to a circuit that contains one D-cell. Ask students to write their predictions in their journals. After the activity, students can compare their predictions to their findings. L1

### Expected Outcome

Students should observe that increasing the voltage increases the current.

### Conclude and Apply

The bulbs in the second circuit shine more brightly because adding a second battery increased the potential, thereby increasing the current.

### ✔ Assessment

**Process** Ask students to draw a diagram in their journals comparing the brightness of the bulb before and after adding the second battery. Ask students to show the relationship between voltage and current. Use the Performance Task Assessment List for Scientific Drawing in **PAMSS**, p. 55. L1 **LEP** P

## Planning the Activity

**Time needed**  1 class period

**Purpose**  To design a model that provides an analogy for an electric circuit.

**Process Skills**  measuring in SI, predicting, making models, designing an experiment, forming operational definitions, comparing and contrasting, forming a hypothesis, recognizing cause and effect, observing, separating and controlling variables, interpreting data, sampling and estimating

**Materials**  plastic funnel, ring stand with ring, 2 1-m lengths of rubber tubing of different diameters, meterstick, 2 500-mL beakers, stopwatch or clock

**Preparation**  Three to four students can work in one group. Assign individual tasks, such as timer, pourer, recorder, and measurer. COOP LEARN

## Teaching the Activity

**Process Reinforcement**  Have students predict what will happen each time they lower the funnel or use tubing of a smaller diameter.

**Troubleshooting**  The water should be poured fast enough to keep the funnel full. The timer should measure the flow into the lower beaker. The tube outlet should be kept at a constant height for all trials.

The actual rate of flow depends on the diameter of the tubing and the height of the funnel.

Students may need help calculating rate of flow. The rate is determined by dividing the volume of water (100 mL) by the number of seconds needed for that volume to flow.

**Possible Hypotheses**  Students may hypothesize that an increase in potential (height) will increase flow and an increase in resistance (smaller diameter) will decrease flow.

---

**INVESTIGATE!**

# Potential Difference and Current

*Water currents aren't exactly like electric currents. However, the two are similar enough that water can be used in models of electric circuits. Investigate how a water current is affected by changes in potential and resistance.*

### Problem
How does changing the potential difference and resistance affect the current for a water system?

### Safety Precautions

### Materials
| | |
|---|---|
| plastic funnel | stopwatch or clock |
| 1-m lengths of rubber tubing of different diameters | ring stand with ring meterstick 2 500-mL beakers |

## What To Do

**1** Assemble the *model* apparatus as shown in the photo on the left.

**2** *Measure* the height from the top of the funnel to the outlet end of the rubber tubing (photo **A**). Record your data.

**3** Practice pouring water into the funnel fast enough to keep it full, but not overflowing (photo **B**).

**4** *Measure* the time for 100 mL of water to flow into the lower beaker.

---

## Program Resources

**Activity Masters,**  pp. 9–10, Investigate 1-2

**Concept Mapping,**  p. 9, Light Bulb in Circuit with Battery L1

---

**A**  **B**  **C**

**5** *Design an experiment* to explore the effect of higher and lower potential differences, and the effect of larger and smaller resistance on the flow of water. Show your design to your teacher. If you are advised to revise your design, be sure to check with your teacher again before you begin.

## Analyzing

1. The model compares water moving due to gravity with electrical charges moving due to potential difference, or voltage. Which trial corresponds to a circuit with the highest voltage?

2. If the voltage is increased while the resistance remains the same, what happens to the current?

3. What effect does the diameter of the tube have on the rate of water flow?

4. *Compare* funnel height and the rate of water flow.

## Concluding and Applying

5. What electrical property do the hose diameters represent?

6. **Going Further** If the smaller diameter hose corresponds to a greater electric resistance, what do you think will happen to the electric current if the voltage stays constant, but the resistance is increased?

**Possible Procedures** After measuring the height of the apparatus, students can measure the time needed for 100 mL of water to flow into the lower beaker. Students should complete several trials, lowering the funnel for each trial. Students can also complete several trials using tubing of a smaller diameter. Students should record their measurements in a data table and write their observations in their journals. **COOP LEARN**

**Student Journal** Ask students to write a hypothesis in their journals about the effect of potential difference and resistance on the flow of water. Students should make sure that the experiments they design test their hypotheses. **L2**

**Expected Outcome**

By observing the model, students should infer that, with a constant voltage, increasing the resistance will decrease the current.

**Answers to** Analyzing/ Concluding and Applying

1. the trial with greatest funnel height

2. It is increased.

3. As the diameter decreases the rate of water flow decreases.

4. Increasing the height increases the flow.

5. resistance

6. The current should decrease.

## ✔ Assessment

**Process** Have students imagine making a model using copper or steel wire, D-batteries, and a light bulb. Students should draw diagrams showing how current could be maximized by using these materials. *Using more batteries and copper wire will maximize current. Additional batteries increase the voltage, and copper wire is a better conductor and therefore has less resistance than steel wire.* Select the appropriate Performance Task Assessment List in **PAMSS**. **L1** **P**

**Figure 1-10 What does this demonstrate about the relationship between current and resistance?** *If the voltage remains constant, increasing resistance lowers current.*

**Figure 1-11 How would increasing the voltage affect the current in the circuit?** *Increasing voltage increased current.* **How would increasing the resistance affect the current in the circuit?** *Increasing resistance decreases current. Calculations depend on values students choose.*

## Find Out!

**How does the length of a conductor affect its resistance?**

**Time needed** 30 minutes

**Materials** two D-cell batteries, a lamp with socket, a long thick piece of pencil lead, a centimeter ruler, three wires, two wire clips

**Thinking Processes** comparing and contrasting, recognizing cause and effect, designing an experiment

**Purpose** To recognize that increasing the length of a conductor causes an increase in resistance.

**Preparation** Three to four students can work in one group. Assign individual tasks, such as connecting the elements of the circuit. **COOP LEARN**

### Teaching the Activity

**Safety** Caution students to be careful with the sharp ends of the pencil lead.

**Troubleshooting** Refer students to the figure to set up the experiment correctly.

**Student Journal** Ask students to predict what will happen as the clips get closer together and write their predictions in their journals. **L2**

The Investigate you just completed illustrates a basic principle of electricity. With a constant voltage, increasing the resistance will decrease the current. As you observed in Section 1-3, using a model is an important tool for drawing conclusions about various properties. In the activity below, you can find out another property of resistance.

## Find Out! ACTIVITY

### How does the length of a conductor affect its resistance?

It takes a special tool to measure resistance precisely, but you can see how length and resistance are related using simple equipment.

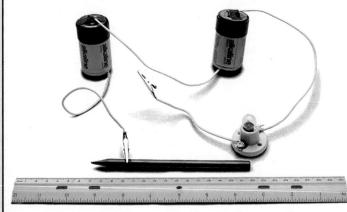

**What To Do**

1. Connect two D-cells to a light and clips as shown in the photo. Attach one clip to the end of a thick pencil lead farthest from the lamp.

2. Then, touch the second clip to the opposite end of the pencil lead. *In your Journal*, describe what happens.

3. Slowly slide the clip up the pencil lead toward the other clip. Note any changes *in your Journal.*

**Conclude and Apply**

1. What happened when you slid the clip up the pencil lead? What does that imply about the current in the circuit? How could you test your guess?

2. What conclusions can you draw about the resistance of the pencil lead?

As you've just seen, resistance of a metal wire depends on length. When you increase the length of the conductor, you increase the resistance. Thickness also affects resistance.

**Figure 1-10**

This hand-held control determines the speed of the toy electric car to which it's connected. Squeezing the triggers varies the resistance. As the resistance is lowered, the car speeds up. What does this demonstrate about the relationship between current and resistance?

### Expected Outcome

Students should observe and conclude that increasing the length of the conductor (the pencil lead between clips) increases the resistance of the circuit.

### Conclude and Apply

1. The brightness of the lamp increased. The current increased. Put an ammeter in the circuit.

2. The longer the pencil lead in the circuit, the greater the resistance.

### ✔ Assessment

**Process** Have students list other methods of increasing the resistance of their models. *By using a material that is not as good a conductor as graphite or by increasing the thickness of the graphite.* Students could then design experiments to test these methods. Use the Performance Task Assessment List for Designing an Experiment in **PAMSS**, p. 23. **L1**

## Ohm's Law

The relationship among current, resistance, and potential difference can be made quantitative by using measurements. We can say that current is equal to the potential difference divided by the resistance. The relationship can be expressed mathematically: V/R=I.

**Figure 1-12.**

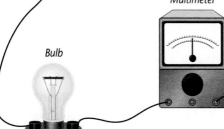

**A** These two batteries produce a potential difference of 18V. How would increasing the voltage affect the current in the circuit?

*Batteries*

*Multimeter*

**B** The fuse, resistor, and light bulb all add together to produce a resistance of 36Ω. How would increasing the resistance affect the current in the circuit?

*Bulb*

**C** Using the mathematical expression, V/R=I, the current in the circuit is 18V/36Ω, or 0.5A. Try calculating the current using two or three different values for voltage and resistance.

*Resistor*

You have discovered that there is more to electricity than simply plugging something into a wall outlet.

Batteries are a source of potential energy waiting to do work in a flashlight or tape player. Lights and appliances use the properties of resistance, voltage, and current.

### check your UNDERSTANDING

1. Two flashlight bulbs are powered by separate, identical 9-volt batteries. One bulb is dimmer. What does that imply about the resistance of the bulbs? How do the currents in the two circuits compare?

2. A piece of carbon, resistance 18Ω, is connected to a 12-V battery. Find the current in the carbon. What would be the current if a 6-V battery were used?

3. **Apply** A length of wire is cut in half, forming two shorter wires. How does the resistance of each half compare to that of the original wire? If the two short wires are placed side by side and twisted together, how does the resistance of the combination compare to the resistance of one short wire? How could you test your answers to these questions?

### Check for Understanding

Three copper wires of unequal length were connected—one at a time—to a 1.5-V dry cell and an ammeter. Copy and complete the table using $R =$ ___ L2

| Wire | Current (A) | Resistance (Ω) |
|------|-------------|----------------|
| 1 | 1.2 | *1.3* |
| 2 | 1.4 | *1.1* |
| 3 | 1.1 | *1.4* |

### Reteach

Students often have trouble rear-ranging the equation V = IR. Show them the diagram below. When the desired variable is covered, the other two variables are in appropriate mathematical order. L1

### Extension

**Demonstration** To help students relate current, potential difference, and resistance, set up a simple circuit by connecting a dry cell (or power source), a variable resistor, and a small light bulb. Have students explain what happens to the current and potential difference as you vary the resistance. L2

# 4 CLOSE

Explain that there are two main ways the parts of a circuit can be connected. Ask students to suggest different ways to arrange the elements of a circuit. L1

### ENRICHMENT

**Discussion** To help students recognize some effects of resistors, ask them why it is desirable to have resistors in some circuits, even though the circuits appear not to do any work, such as lighting a bulb or turning a motor. To help students answer this question, adjust the volume of a portable radio, or use a dimmer switch to adjust lights. *Resistors are used to regulate current in radios, televisions, and other electrical devices.* L3

### check your UNDERSTANDING

1. The resistance of the brighter bulb is higher than that of the dimmer bulb. Current is higher in the dimmer bulb.

2. Current = 0.666 A. Current = 0.333 A.

3. The resistance is less. The resistance of the two wires is less than that of one short wire. Use an ammeter.

# Science and Society

## Purpose

Science and Society extends Section 1-3, in which students observe how a battery can be used to keep charge flowing in a circuit.

## Content Background

Tell students that mercury is used not only in batteries but also in tooth fillings, fluorescent lights, fungicides for seeds, and many other products on which humans rely. In 1972, a reported 6,530 Iraqi villagers were injured and 459 villagers died after they used seed grain that had been treated with methyl mercury to feed their animals and to make bread. Fifty-two people died and 150 incurred brain and nerve damage between 1953 and 1960, when a chemical plant discharged methyl mercury into Minamata Bay, Japan. Many scientists advocate a worldwide ban both on the use of methyl mercury on seed dressings and on the discharge of mercury and mercury compounds by industry.

## Teaching Strategies

Have pairs of students read the selection together and develop a series of questions on recycling that they would like to research.
`COOP LEARN` `L2`

## Debate

Working in small groups, have students discuss the impact of batteries on the environment and debate the need for battery recycling. Some students in each group should speak from the perspective of a battery manufacturer while others speak from the perspective of a family that lives near a landfill. `COOP LEARN` `L2`

## Answers to

### What Do You Think?

Answers will vary but may include that you can recycle used

# Science and Society

# Recycling Batteries

**W**hat is as small as a button and very dangerous to the environment? The answer is the kind of battery you find in watches, hearing aids, and cameras. They make up 25 percent of the hazardous wastes from households. Tiny button batteries may have as much as 1.1 grams of mercury, a metal that can cause birth defects and brain and kidney damage. Even one battery in six tons of garbage is more mercury per ton than allowed by government standards.

### What Can Be Done?

If people used rechargeable batteries, fewer toxic metals would be discharged into the environment. Rechargeables cost three times more than ordinary batteries but last 40 times longer, so they are more economical.

Recycling is also a partial solution. Jewelry stores usually accept button batteries and turn them in at recycling centers. However, only 23 states now require stores to accept old batteries for recycling.

### What Other Countries Do

In 1983, the citizens of Tokyo discovered that one incinerator was emitting 30 times more mercury than the amount declared safe by the World Health Organization. They insisted that local facilities remove batteries from garbage before incineration.

In Austria, some recycling plants use an experimental process to remove the mercury and zinc from old batteries. These metals and the rest of the battery can be reused.

In Denmark, there is a refund surcharge on batteries. Consumers who return used batteries get the money back.

Each year in the United States, 25 million household batteries are used. In spite of the danger from toxic metals in batteries, the Environmental Protection Agency does not yet have regulations for their disposal.

### What Do You Think?

What can you and your family do to reduce the amount of lead, mercury, and cadmium in the environment? How can you make others aware of the dangers of these metals?

batteries or use rechargeable batteries. You can explain the ecological reasons for doing so to friends and relatives. You can make booklets and posters illustrating the hazards of these metals.

### Going Further ⫸

Students can work in small groups to identify whether and where in their community button batteries can be recycled. Choose one student to call the local recycling center or town hall to ask about battery recycling on behalf of the class. Then, using the Yellow Pages, assign each group

several jewelers to call. When groups have completed their research, make a class list of battery recycling stores or centers.

If students find that button batteries *cannot* be recycled in their community, you may wish to write a class letter to the mayor, city council, or newspaper, expressing the need for such facilities. Use the Performance Task Assessment List for Letter in **PAMSS**, p. 67. `L2` `COOP LEARN`

# Technology Connection

# Latimer's Light

Technology
Connection

E ver since Thomas Edison patented the light bulb, people have been trying to improve it.

One of the first to improve the light bulb was Lewis Howard Latimer. Latimer, a self-taught draftsman, worked for Alexander Graham Bell in the 1870s. Latimer's ability to draw detailed diagrams of complex electrical devices was invaluable. He drew the plans for Bell that resulted in the 1876 patent of the telephone. Latimer first became associated with Thomas Edison when Edison patented the first incandescent bulb in 1879. Latimer set about making it better. His improved method for securing the carbon filament to metal wires inside the vacuum bulb was patented in 1881. Latimer continued to work on the incandescent bulb and in 1882 received what he considered his most important patent. He improved the process for producing the carbon filaments used in light bulbs.

Latimer was the only African American invited to join the Edison Pioneers, a group of scientists and inventors who worked for Edison. He was asked to supervise the instal-lation of electrical streetlights in New York City, Philadelphia, and London.

## Making Better Light Bulbs

The part of a modern light bulb that lights up is the thin tungsten wire, the filament, in the center. When an electric current passes through it, it glows. Unfortunately, some of the tungsten molecules get so hot that they vaporize, leaving the wire and adhering to the glass bulb. When enough tungsten has left the filament, the light bulb dies.

In newer bulbs, krypton gas may be used. Krypton, is a poor conductor of heat. A light bulb full of krypton gas stays relatively cool, so less tungsten gets hot enough to leave the filament. This makes the light bulb last longer at the same brightness.

If brightness is more important than long life, the krypton-filled bulb can be operated at higher filament temperatures to give a brighter light more efficiently than non-krypton-filled bulbs. Brighter krypton bulbs are used in slide and movie projectors.

One vital use for krypton light bulbs is illuminating airport runways at night. Electric-arc lights filled with krypton pierce fog for 300 meters (1000 feet) or more.

### What Do You Think?

Think of several other places on Earth or in the solar system where krypton bulbs' greater brightness or longer life might be useful.

## Purpose

Technology Connection extends Section 1-4, in which electric current is discussed. Lewis Latimer's invention improved the way electric current was used to produce light.

## Content Background

Tell students that Lewis Latimer (1848-1928), the son of a former slave, grew up in Boston. After serving in the navy during the civil war, he began his career as a draftsman. In addition to being an inventor and patent holder, Latimer was an author. His book on the electric light bulb, *Incandescent Electric Lighting,* was published in 1890.

## Teaching Strategies

Point out that Latimer's carbon-filament light bulb was an improvement over Edison's in that it had a better connection between the filament and the wires leading in and out of the bulb. Ask students why a weak connection would be a problem. *A weak connection might melt or break when heated, and the bulb would burn out.* L2

## Answers to What Do You Think?

Answers will vary. Students may suggest such places as the ocean bottom, an underground cave, or a planet far from the sun. L1

## Going Further ⅢⅢⅢ➡

Help students learn to communicate their research by working in small groups to research and report on Thomas Edison's invention of the light bulb or on Edison's research group, The Edison Pioneers. Assign two group members the task of doing research. Assign one or two other students in each group the task of organizing the research, and one student per group the task of making an oral presentation to the class.

Students can work in small groups to make a chart that shows how light bulbs can be improved with bromine and krypton. Have students use both words and drawings in their charts. Display the finished charts on a bulletin board titled *Making a Better Bulb.* Select the appropriate Performance Task Assessment List in **PAMSS.** L2 COOP LEARN

# Teens in SCIENCE

## Purpose

Teens in Science encourages students to view themselves as potential scientists. This passage describes how, with hard work and support, young people can overcome great obstacles to achieve their dreams.

## Teaching Strategies

As students may be aware, millions of Southeast Asians immigrated to the United States during the 1970s and 1980s. Refugees of the Vietnam War accounted for many of these new Americans. Many Chinese immigrants found work assembling integrated circuits in Silicon Valley, California. Many Korean immigrants worked day and night as vegetable vendors, or greengrocers, in New York City.

Have students discuss how the hard work of these people has paid off. Suggest that students use the *Readers' Guide to Periodical Literature* to locate magazine articles on the topic. Gifted students may wish to consult a history book on immigration, such as *The Boat People and Achievement in America* (Nathan Caplan et al., 1989). L3

## Discussion

The passage emphasizes two things that enabled Sieu Ngo to succeed: his hard work and the support of his science teacher. Have students discuss how these two things worked together in Sieu Ngo's life. Ask students which, if either, they believe was more important. Ask if either hard work or adult support alone would have enabled Sieu Ngo to achieve his goal. Have students support their answers.

# Teens in SCIENCE

## Overcoming Obstacles

Nineteen-year-old Sieu Ngo was able to overcome much difficulty in his life and went on to complete an award-winning science project in electrochemistry.

Sieu Ngo is of Chinese origin. Most of his family lives in Vietnam. He immigrated to America when he was just seven years old. It was not an easy journey. Sieu was held in a refugee camp in Malaysia for more than nine months. The overcrowded camp was even more uncomfortable for Sieu because he had chicken pox!

### Sacrifices...

Finally settling in Oklahoma, Sieu began working and attending high school.

"I worked in a gas station from 11 p.m. to 7 a.m." With school beginning at 8 a.m., Sieu was exhausted most mornings. Sometimes he became discouraged.

Once Sieu even thought about giving up his science interests. "One night I was cleaning the refreshment stand. I was thinking about the kids I would be competing against. As I cleaned, I imagined them at home working on their computers or studying. What chance did I have? I almost quit."

### ...and Rewards

But Sieu Ngo's hard work and dedication had not gone unnoticed. His science teacher believed in the young man. In fact, he invited Sieu to live with his family until Sieu's project was complete.

This was just the break that Sieu needed. With more time and energy to devote, he made great strides on the project. "I spent a lot of nights in the computer lab. I was still working all night, but this time for myself, for something I believed in."

It was a race right up to the deadline. In fact, Sieu's classmates helped him finish mounting his displays on the bus ride to the competition.

Despite many obstacles, Sieu Ngo's project has earned him a good deal of respect. He also won a full scholarship to the University of Oklahoma where he studies chemical engineering. "To me, life is one big mathematical equation. The amount of hardship in a person's life is equal to the amount of personal good. I am optimistic that life is fair."

### What Do You Think?

Sieu Ngo describes life as a mathematical equation. What do you think he means?

IMPRESSED CURRENT SYSTEM
FOR CATHODIC PROTECTION IN BRIDGES

## Answers to What Do You Think?

Answers will vary but may include that the amount of hardship one has to overcome is balanced by the rewards that he or she eventually attains. L1

## Going Further ▶

Sieu Ngo describes his philosophy of life in the last paragraph. Have students compare Ngo's philosophy with their own philosophy of life in an essay or journal entry. Alternatively, have students write about a goal that they achieved by overcoming obstacles. The goal might have to do with academics, athletics, performing arts, or family life. Use the Performance Task Assessment List for Writer's Guide to Nonfiction in **PAMSS,** p. 85. L1

Review the statements below about the big ideas presented in this chapter, and try to answer the questions. Then, reread your answers to the Did You Ever Wonder questions at the beginning of the chapter. *In your Journal*, write a paragraph about how your understanding of the big ideas in the chapter has changed.

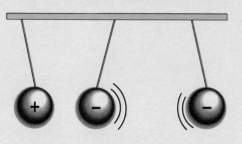

**1** There are two kinds of electrical charges, positive and negative. *How could you tell if a charge was positive or negative?*

**2** Electric charges can move easily through conductors, but not through insulators. *How could you tell if an object is an insulator or a conductor?*

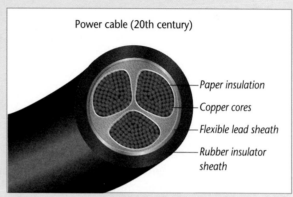

Power cable (20th century)

- Paper insulation
- Copper cores
- Flexible lead sheath
- Rubber insulator sheath

**3** Work must be done to separate positive and negative charges, producing potential, or stored energy. *What role does a battery play in an electrical circuit?*

**4** The three requirements of a circuit are a complete path, a source of potential difference, and resistance. Resistance depends on the material of the conductor as well as its length and thickness. *What does resistance describe?*

---

## Project

Have students use reference materials to research the origin and history of lightning rods. Tell them to relate their findings in a poster or written report. Display completed reports on a bulletin board titled *Safe Inside*. Select the appropriate Performance Task List in **PAMSS**. [L1]

## Science at Home

Have students demonstrate a way to produce an electrical charge. Tell them to place a piece of newspaper on a wooden board. They can rub various objects, such as plastic wrap, wool, or foil over the paper. Finally, they should lift the sheet of newspaper from the wood. If an electrical charge was produced, the paper will be attracted to the wood. Have students list the materials that produced a charge and share their lists in a class discussion. [L1]

---

Have students look at the illustrations and read the statements that go with each.

### Teaching Strategies

Have students work in groups of four to answer the question that goes with each main idea and illustration. Tell groups to explain the concept that their photograph or diagram illustrates by suggesting another way that the same concept could be illustrated.

Students can also work in pairs to select one of the images and create a poster from it. Encourage students to recreate the drawing or photograph as a picture and add a paragraph of explanation. **COOP LEARN**

### Answers to Questions

**1.** One could find out by comparing the unknown charge to a charge of known sign. How the unknown interacts with the known charge reveals what sign it is. Unlike charges attract one another and like charges repel one another.

**2.** If an object closes a gap in a circuit and current then flows through the circuit, the object is a conductor.

**3.** A battery is a source of potential energy. It separates positive and negative charges by a chemical reaction.

**4.** Resistance is measure of how much potential energy is lost as current flows through a material. Less formally, it describes how well a material conducts electricity; very low resistance means a good conductor and very high resistance means a poor conductor.

 MINDJOGGER VIDEOQUIZ

**Chapter 1** Have students work in groups as they play the videoquiz game to review key chapter concepts.

## Using Key Science Terms

**1.** A circuit is a complete path through which a charge flows. Current is the rate at which charges flow through a circuit.

**2.** A conductor is a material through which an electrical charge moves freely. An insulator is a material through which an electrical charge does not move freely.

**3.** Electrical charge is a property of matter that gives rise to a force between two charged objects. Like charges are electrical charges that repel each other, unlike charges are electrical charges that attract one another.

**4.** Potential difference is a change in total potential energy divided by total charge. Resistance is the measure of how much potential a charge loses when moving through a material.

## Understanding Ideas

**1.** positive and negative

**2.** It is high.

**3.** Thick. A thin wire has greater resistance and would get hot.

**4.** Thick. They have less resistance, so there is less drop in potential across them.

**5.** negative charge.

**6.** They have potential energy.

## Developing Skills

**1.** See reduced student page for completed concept map.

**2.** Both balloons having charges will repel each other. The charged balloon will be attracted to the cloth. The balloon having a charge and the balloon without a charge will be attracted to each other because the charged balloon (negative) induced a charge in the uncharged balloon having the positive side closest to the charged balloon.

**3.** Answers might include resistors being used in radios, computers, or television sets.

$$\frac{12V}{84\Omega} = 0.14A$$

## **U**sing Key Science Terms

circuit
conductor
current
electrical charge
insulator

like charges
potential difference
resistance
unlike charges

*Explain the differences between the terms in each of the following sets.*

1. circuit, current
2. conductor, insulator
3. electrical charge, like charges, unlike charges
4. potential difference, resistance

## **U**nderstanding Ideas

*Answer the following questions in your Journal using complete sentences.*

1. What are the names for the two types of electrical charge?
2. You observe that a very large voltage produces only a small current in a circuit. What do you conclude about the resistance in the circuit?
3. Would you connect a battery to a bulb with a thick or thin copper wire if you did not want the wire to become hot? Explain your answer.
4. Should a long extension cord needed to carry high currents be made of thick or thin copper wires? Why?
5. What type of charge would you use to attract a positive charge?
6. Why can separated positive and negative charges be used to do work?

## **D**eveloping Skills

*Use your understanding of the concepts developed in this chapter to answer each of the following questions.*

**1. Concept Mapping** Complete the concept map of electricity.

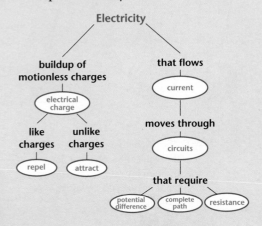

**2. Observing and Inferring** Repeat the Explore activity on page 29 using two identical balloons. Attach string to one balloon and hang it from the desk. Charge both balloons by rubbing them with the cloth. Bring the second balloon toward the hanging balloon. What happens? Bring the cloth near the hanging balloon. What happens? Remove the charge from one of the balloons and bring the other balloon toward it. Explain what happens.

**3. Interpreting Data** Review the Find Out activity on page 40 on resistance and give examples of where resistors are used. What current flows through a conductor having a resistance of 84 ohms connected across a 12-volt battery?

## Critical Thinking

**1.** The entire bird is at almost exactly the same potential as the wire. If the bird touches the second wire, there could be a difference of potential and the bird would be electrocuted.

**2.** It is the voltage, or potential difference, that is dangerous because it causes the current to flow through you.

**Program Resources**

Review and Assessment,  pp. 5–10 **L1**
Performance Assessment,  Ch. 1 **L2**
PAMSS
Alternate Assessment in the Science Classroom
Computer Test Bank

## Critical Thinking

In your Journal, *answer each of the following questions.*

1. A bird can sit on a single power line wire without harm. Why? What would happen if the bird was to touch another wire of lower potential at the same time?
2. Signs often say "Danger - High Voltage." Why don't they say "Danger - High Current"?
3. Electrical cords attached to a household appliance are constructed as shown in the diagram. Can you explain why they are made this way?

 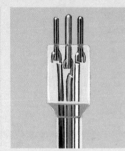

4. How does turning a dimmer light switch adjust current flow?
5. If a circuit containing 1 meter of wire and three light bulbs was changed to 0.75 meter of wire and two light bulbs, what would happen to the current if the power supply was kept the same?

## Problem Solving

*Read the following problem and discuss your answers in a brief paragraph.*

**You are playing with your friends in a field. Suddenly, there is a bright flash of light. You know that a thunderstorm is coming and you had better take shelter. Nearby there is a metal building, a car, and a tree.**

Which would be safe places to wait out the storm? Why? Which would be the most hazardous? Why?

---

## CONNECTING IDEAS

Discuss each of the following in a brief paragraph.

1. **Theme—Energy** After you receive a shock from a doorknob, touching it right away a second time probably will not produce a second shock. Why? What could you do to give yourself a shock a second time?

2. **Theme—Systems and Interactions** Many times a car will not start if one of its battery terminals is covered with corrosion. Why won't the car start? How could it be fixed? What electrical property of the corrosion causes this problem?

3. **A Closer Look** Describe the role negatively charged particles play in producing lightning.

4. **Science and Society** What are two actions that you can take to decrease the hazard caused by discarded batteries?

---

3. Wire is a conductor. Rubber is an insulator to protect whomever touches it.

4. It increases or decreases the resistance by changing the length of a resistor

5. Current would increase slightly.

### Problem Solving

Inside the car would be a safe place. The path from the lightning to the ground is not as direct in a car, due to the resistance of the rubber tires. The tree would be the most hazardous place. Because it is higher than the car or the shed, it would be struck first. Electricity would then move through the tree to Earth. The metal building would not be a safe place unless it had a metal rod to conduct lightning to the ground.

### Connecting Ideas

1. The body loses its charge in the first shock. Rub your feet again to gain another charge.

2. There is not enough contact on the battery terminal to complete the circuit because corrosion is an insulator. To correct it, clean off the corrosion.

3. Students should include the information that heavier negative particles form at the bottom of clouds. The bottom of the cloud repels negative charges from the ground beneath it, and this results in the ground becoming positively charged. The downward sweep of a lightning is a discharge in which large numbers of negative charges move toward Earth.

4. Students should mention using rechargeable batteries. Students should also recognize that they can take button batteries to a jewelry store to be recycled.

---

## ✔ Assessment

**Portfolio** Review the portfolio options that are provided throughout the chapter. Encourage students to select one product that demonstrates their best work for the chapter. Have students explain what they learned and why they chose this example for placement into their portfolios.

Additional portfolio options can be found in the following **Teacher Classroom Resources:**

**Making Connections: Integrating Sciences,** p. 5

**Multicultural Connections,** pp. 5–6

**Making Connections: Across the Curriculum,** p. 5

**Concept Mapping,** p. 9

**Critical Thinking/Problem Solving,** p. 9

**Take Home Activities,** p. 6

**Laboratory Manual,** pp. 1–2; 3–4

**Performance Assessment** P

# Chapter Organizer

| SECTION | OBJECTIVES | ACTIVITIES |
|---|---|---|
| **Chapter Opener** | | Explore! p. 49 |
| **2-1 Forces and Fields** (2 days) | 1. **Describe** the forces magnets produce.<br>2. **Identify** the north and south poles of a magnet.<br>3. **Explain** the role of magnetic fields. | Explore! p. 50<br>Find Out! p. 51<br>Explore! p. 53 |
| **2-2 Magnets** (3 days) | 1. **Explain** the effects of magnetic fields on various materials.<br>2. **Make** permanent magnets out of nonmagnetic materials.<br>3. **Make** an electromagnet and **demonstrate** its magnetic effects.<br>4. Use magnetic domain theory to **describe** how objects can be magnetized or demagnetized. | Explore! p. 57<br>Find Out! p. 59<br>Skillbuilder: p. 59<br>Investigate 2-1: pp. 60–61<br>Skillbuilder: p. 64 |
| **2-3 Effects of Magnetic Fields** (2 days) | 1. **Demonstrate** the effects of magnetic fields on wires carrying electric currents.<br>2. **Explain** how loudspeakers and electric motors work. | Explore! p. 65<br>Find Out! p. 66<br>Find Out! p. 67<br>Investigate 2-2: pp. 68–69 |
| **2-4 Producing Electric Currents** (1 day) | 1. **Demonstrate** the ability of a changing magnetic field to produce an electric current.<br>2. **Describe** the working principles behind electric generators.<br>3. **Explain** the operation of transformers. | Find Out! p. 71 |

## EXPAND your view

**Earth Science Connection** Van Allen Belts, pp. 54–55
**A Closer Look** How Can You Make a Transformer? pp. 62–63

**Science and Society** High-Tech Health Care, pp. 74–75
**History Connection** Granville T. Woods, p. 75
**How It Works** Television Picture Tube, p. 76

## ACTIVITY MATERIALS

### EXPLORE!

**Page 50**
bar magnet, thread, thumbtack
**Page 53***
bar magnet, plastic bag, sheet of paper, iron filings
**Page 57**
bar magnet, plastic bag, iron nail, iron filings, large sheets of paper
**Page 65***
transparent tape, bar magnet

### INVESTIGATE!

**Pages 60–61**
1 m of 22-gauge insulated wire, drinking straw to fit over nail, large iron nail, 3 D-cells, paper clips
**Pages 68–69**
2 m 22-gauge insulated wire, steel knitting needle, 4 nails, 2 bar magnets, 16-gauge insulated wire, masking tape, fine sandpaper, wooden board (2" × 4" × 30 cm), 2 wooden blocks, 6-V battery, scissors or wire cutters

### FIND OUT!

**Page 51***
tape, two bar magnets, string, tack
**Page 59***
bar magnet, sewing needle, paper clips, plastic bottle, Bunsen burner, tongs
**Page 66***
D-cell, 22-gauge wire, bar magnet
**Page 67**
radio with earphone jack but no speaker, earphone plug with wires attached, permanent magnet; 60 cm of insulated wire; paper drinking cup; glue
**Page 71***
22-gauge insulated wire, strong bar magnet, galvanometer

*For adequate development of the concepts presented, we recommend that students do the activities with an asterisk.

# Chapter 2 Magnetism

## TEACHER CLASSROOM RESOURCES

| Student Masters | Teaching Aids |
|---|---|
| **Study Guide,** p. 11<br>**Multicultural Connections,** p. 7<br>**Science Discovery Activities,** 2–1<br>**Flex Your Brain,** p. 5 | |
| **Study Guide,** p. 12<br>**Take Home Activities,** p. 7<br>**Concept Mapping,** p. 10<br>**Science Discovery Activities,** 2–2<br>**Critical Thinking/Problem Solving,** p. 10<br>**Making Connections: Integrating Sciences,** p. 7 | **Laboratory Manual,** pp. 5–9, Electromagnets<br>**Color Transparency and Master 3,** Domains<br>**\*STVS:** *Detecting the Body's Magnetic Field,* Human Biology (Disc 7, Side 1) |
| **Study Guide,** p. 13<br>**How It Works,** p. 6<br>**Multicultural Connections,** p. 8<br>**Science Discovery Activities,** 2–3 | **\*STVS:** *Electric Heart,* Human Biology (Disc 7, Side 1) |
| **Study Guide,** p. 14<br>**Making Connections: Across the Curriculum,** p. 7<br>**Making Connections: Technology & Society,** p. 7 | **Color Transparency and Master 4,** Electric Motor—DC Generator<br>**\*STVS:** *Wind Power,* Chemistry (Disc 2, Side 2) |

## ASSESSMENT RESOURCES

**Review and Assessment,** pp. 11–16
**Performance Assessment,** Ch. 2
**PAMSS\***
**Mindjogger Videoquiz**
**Alternate Assessment in the Science Classroom**
**Computer Test Bank**

**Spanish Resources**
**Cooperative Learning Resource Guide**
**Lab and Safety Skills**
**Integrated Science Videodisc**

## KEY TO TEACHING STRATEGIES

The following designations will help you decide which activities are appropriate for your students.

- **L1** Level 1 activities should be within the ability range of all students.
- **L2** Level 2 activities should be within the ability range of the average to above-average student.
- **L3** Level 3 activities are designed for the ability range of above-average students.
- **LEP** LEP activities should be within the ability range of Limited English Proficiency students.
- **COOP LEARN** Cooperative Learning activities are designed for small group work.
- **P** These strategies represent student products that can be placed into a best-work portfolio.

## ADDITIONAL MATERIALS

**Software**
*Electricity and Magnetism,* Educational Activities.
*Electricity and Magnetism,* CD-ROM, Videodiscovery.
*SuperStar Science CD,* CD-ROM, Orange Cherry New Media Schoolhouse.
*Fundamentals of Physical Science,* Orange Cherry New Media Schoolhouse.
*Magnets,* J&S Software.

**Audiovisual**
*Electricity and Magnetism,* video, Coronet/MTI.
*Electromagnets and Their Uses,* film/video, Coronet/MTI.

**Laserdisc**
*Physics at Work,* Videodiscovery.
*Windows on Science,* Optical Data Corp.

**Readings**
Vogt, Gregory. *Electricity and Magnetism.* Franklin Watts.
Ward, Alan. *Experimenting with Magnetism.* Chelsea House.

*Performance Assessment in Middle School Science

*Science and Technology Videodisc Series

# Magnetism

## THEME DEVELOPMENT

The themes that this chapter supports are stability and change, and energy. Students see changes as objects made of magnetic materials become magnetized in the presence of a strong magnetic field. This chapter also discusses magnetism in terms of energy. Students construct an electric motor, which changes electrical energy to mechanical energy, and learn about electric generators, which change mechanical energy to electrical energy.

## CHAPTER OVERVIEW

In this chapter, students will explore magnetism, its effects and applications, and the relationship between magnetism and electricity. They will observe and describe the behavior of like and opposite magnetic poles and the role of magnetic fields. Students will then investigate the relationships between magnetic fields and current-carrying wires.

### Tying to Previous Knowledge

Review the behavior of like and unlike electric charges, which students observed in Chapter 1. Have students work in pairs to make charge detectors out of cellophane tape and use the detectors to demonstrate how like and unlike charges behave. **COOP LEARN**

# MAGNETISM

## Did you ever wonder...

✓ How a magnet attracts or repels another magnet nearby?

✓ Why paper clips sometimes act like magnets?

✓ How a stereo loudspeaker changes electric current into sound?

Before you begin to study about magnetism, think about these questions and answer them *in your Journal.* When you finish the chapter, compare your Journal write-up with what you have learned.

**R**emember playing with toy magnets as a child? There was something magical about a piece of iron suddenly leaping off the floor and flying into the air. How did they work? And what about the mysterious behavior of a compass? A needle, jiggling on a pin to find its balance, swings back and forth a dozen times. Every time it stops moving, it's aligned north and south. Why? What causes it to turn? Why does it always point the same direction when it stops? The actions of the toys and the compass seem mysterious. They don't match our ideas of the way things work. We can't see what's happening, what's making the objects move. Since we can't see magnetism, we can figure out how it works only by observing its effects. You can observe these effects while doing the activities in this chapter. You may find that magnets play an important role in your daily life.

▶ *Do the activity on the next page and explore some everyday uses of magnets.*

48

## Did you ever wonder...

• A magnet attracts or repels another nearby magnet through the force of its magnetic field. (p. 54)

• A magnet attracts only materials whose atoms have magnetic fields. Magnetism can be induced in certain materials. (p. 57)

• A loudspeaker uses the interaction between electric current and a magnetic field to change variations in electric current into sound waves. (p. 67)

## STUDENT JOURNAL

Have students write their responses to the Did You Ever Wonder questions in their journals. After they have read the chapter, students should read their journal entries to see what they have learned about the properties and uses of magnets.

# Explore! ACTIVITY

## How are magnets used in your home and at school?

Some magnets in your home may keep doors closed. Others may keep game pieces on a board. Look for examples of magnets at home and at school. Make a list of their uses. Then, with a group of classmates brainstorm a list of ten other uses.

---

## INTRODUCING THE CHAPTER

Have students look at the photograph of an ancient compass. Ask students what they think the device is or what they think it resembles. Like the metallic ladle, early compasses were usually made of a magnetic rock called lodestone. Do they know what's special about a compass needle? Where else do we use magnets in daily life?

## Explore!

### How are magnets used in your home and at school?

**Time needed** 15 minutes

**Thinking Processes** observing and inferring

**Purpose** To find and describe uses of magnets in everyday objects.

### Teaching the Activity

**Student Journal** Have students record uses of magnets in their journals. Encourage them to also include sketches of how devices that use magnets are constructed. L1

### Expected Outcome

Students will see that magnets are used in many ways.

### Answers to Questions

Answers may include refrigerator magnets, magnetic door catches, and magnetic paperclip holders. Some students will recognize that disk drives, tape recorders, and motors also have magnets.

### ✔ Assessment

**Process** Have students design a new invention that uses a magnet. They should think of something that would be useful at home or at school. Use the Performance Task Assessment List for Invention in **PAMSS**, p. 45. L1

---

## ASSESSMENT PLANNER

### PORTFOLIO
Refer to page 79 for suggested items that students might select for their portfolios.

### PERFORMANCE ASSESSMENT
Process, pp. 49, 51, 57, 61, 65, 66, 67, 69, 71
Performance, pp. 50, 53, 59
Skillbuilders, pp. 59, 64
Explore! Activities, pp. 50, 53, 57, 65
Find Out! Activities, pp. 51, 59, 66, 67, 71
Investigate, pp. 60–61, 68–69

### CONTENT ASSESSMENT
Check Your Understanding, pp. 56, 64, 70, 73
Reviewing Main Ideas, p. 77
Chapter Review, pp. 78–79

### GROUP ASSESSMENT
Opportunities for group assessment occur with Cooperative Learning Strategies.

2-1

# Forces and Fields

## PREPARATION

### Concepts Developed

In this section, students will explore properties of magnets and discover how to map the forces in a magnetic field.

### Planning the Lesson

Refer to the Chapter Organizer on pages 48A–B.

## 1 MOTIVATE

**Demonstration** Give students the opportunity to experiment with various kinds of magnets. Provide ring magnets on a pencil, a horseshoe magnet and some paper clips and nails, and a bar magnet with coins. L1

### Explore!

**Can you make your own compass?**

**Time needed** 15–20 minutes

**Materials** bar magnet, thread, thumbtack

**Thinking Processes** observing, modeling, recognizing cause and effect, forming operational definitions

**Purpose** To observe that magnets point in a particular direction and return to that direction after being moved.

### Teaching the Activity

**Troubleshooting** If students cannot hold the thread steady, have them tie it to a meterstick supported between two desks. Be sure magnets are at least 0.5 m from any large iron or steel objects.

**Student Journal** Have students describe in their journals two or more activities in which a compass is used. For example, they might describe hiking, navigating a sailboat, or searching for buried treasure. L1

### Section Objectives

- Describe the forces magnets produce.
- Identify the north and south poles of a magnet.
- Explain the role of magnetic fields.

### Key Terms

*magnetic poles*
*magnetic field*

## Forces at Work

Besides being fun and intriguing toys, magnets play many useful roles in everyday life. Some uses are obvious. But for other uses, magnets are hidden in places you might not suspect. There are magnets as fine as powder that store images and sounds on videotape and information on computer disks. There are magnets in telephones, television sets, and radios. Some of these magnets change electric currents into sounds. Some hold doors closed or make motors turn. Magnets are all around you. You can begin to understand how magnets work by making some simple observations in the activity below.

### Explore! ACTIVITY

**Can you make your own compass?**

**What To Do**

1. Hang a bar magnet by a thread, as shown. When the magnet stops swinging, record the direction of the bar.
2. Turn the magnet slightly and then let it turn by itself. What happens?
3. Hang the magnet in another place. When it stops moving, in what direction does it point?

**Figure 2-1**

**A** More than 2000 years ago, the Greeks discovered that a certain kind of rock was attracted toward materials that contained iron. This rock was named magnetite because it was found in a region of the world that was then called Magnesia.

*Magnetite*

**B** This early compass contained lodestone, or *leading stone,* another name for magnetite. When the compass was suspended by a string, the fish's head turned to point at the lodestar. What do we call the lodestar now?

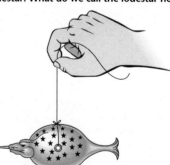

← N

### Expected Outcome

The magnet will point in a north-south direction.

### Answers to Questions

1. The bar will align in a north-south direction.
2. It returns to the previous position.
3. It always points in the same direction.

### ✔ Assessment

**Performance** Have students work in pairs to draw simple scale drawings of the classroom. Drawings should include an arrow pointing north. Students then describe in writing how to use their compasses to navigate around the room. Use the Performance Task Assessment List for Writing in Science in **PAMSS**, p. 87. L1

**COOP LEARN** P

## ■ Magnetic Poles

One end of your suspended bar magnet always pointed north while the other end always pointed south. When a magnet is allowed to turn freely, the two ends of the magnet that point north-south are called the **magnetic poles**. The end pointing north is called the north-seeking pole or just the north pole. Remember that by just looking at a magnet we might not be able to directly observe any differences between the north and south poles. Try the activity below to find out how magnetic poles interact.

### Find Out! ACTIVITY

## How do magnetic poles interact?

**W**hat happens when two magnets interact?

### What To Do

1. From your teacher obtain two magnets, tape, and string.

2. Suspend one magnet with string. After it stops moving, place a piece of tape or a dot of paint on the pole of your magnet that points north.

3. Hang a second magnet more than 50 cm away from the first magnet. Mark it as in Step 2. Then, observe what happens as you bring each possible combination of poles (N-N, N-S, S-S) together. *In your Journal,* describe

what happens as you move one magnet away from the other.

### Conclude and Apply

1. How do like poles of magnets interact?

2. How do the unlike poles of magnets interact?

3. Does distance affect the way magnets interact?

**C** These dial compasses were among the first ever developed. For what might very early dial compasses have been used?

### Program Resources

**Study Guide,** p. 11
**Multicultural Connections,** p. 7, Discovering the Compass L1
**Science Discovery Activities,** 2–1, Magnifying Magnetic Forces

### Multicultural Perspectives

More than two thousand years ago, people in China observed that a type of black rock could attract pieces of iron. Encourage students to learn more about scientific discoveries in ancient China. One good source of information is Beshore, George. *Science in Ancient China* New York: Franklin Watts, 1988.

### Visual Learning

**Figure 2-1 What do we call the lodestar now?** *North Star* **For what might very early dial compasses have been used?** *sailing, navigation*

### Find Out!

**How do magnetic poles interact?**

**Time needed** 20 minutes

**Materials** paint or masking tape, two bar magnets, string, thumbtack

**Thinking Processes** comparing and contrasting, observing and inferring, recognizing cause and effect

**Purpose** To draw inferences about how the poles of a magnet repel and attract.

**Teaching the Activity**

**Troubleshooting** It may be easier to use colored tape, rather than painted dots, to mark the north poles.

**Student Journal** Have students draw what they observe and record the answers to the questions in their journals. L2

**Expected Outcome**

Students should observe that the like poles repel and unlike poles attract each other.

**Conclude and Apply**

1. Like poles repel.

2. Unlike poles attract.

3. Yes; the greater the distance, the less the magnets interact.

### ✔ Assessment

**Process** Have students observe a round magnet used to stick notes to a refrigerator. Then have them write a paragraph explaining how they would experiment to identify the north and south poles of this type of magnet. Use the Performance Task Assessment List for Evaluating a Hypothesis in **PAMSS**, p. 31. L1 P

# 2 TEACH

## Tying to Previous Knowledge

In Chapter 1, students observed that a charged plastic comb can attract pieces of aluminum. The electric charges in the comb and aluminum interact in a certain way. Ask students to explain how magnetic forces are similar to electric charges. *A magnet attracts metal objects because clusters of atoms become magnetically aligned.*

## Across the Curriculum

### Language Arts

Have students research the origin of the word *magnet*. They should find that it comes from a Greek word meaning "the stone of magnesia." This stone was lodestone, a metallic rock that was probably the first magnet humans observed.

---

## Visual Learning

**Figure 2-2 How many smaller magnets do you suppose could be made from one large magnet?** *Answers will vary and will depend on the size of the large magnet.*

**Figure 2-3** Help students interpret this diagram by setting up a single bar magnet with four or more compasses around it. The compass needle will line up with the lines of the magnetic field. Have students compare and contrast your magnet-and-compass set up with the diagram.

---

**Discussion** Ask students to describe different kinds of attractions and repulsions. They should mention the interaction between opposite electrical charges. They may also think of gravitation. (If they need a hint about gravitation, look at the ground and jump up and down, or drop something.)

---

As you can see, the poles of a magnet act differently from each other. Two north poles repel each other. Two south poles also repel each other. But a north pole and a south pole attract each other. The distance between the magnets also affects how they react to each other. As the poles are moved closer together, the force between them becomes greater. The behavior of magnetic poles should remind you of the behavior of electric charges you studied earlier.

Can a magnet have a single pole? If you break a bar magnet in half, what happens? You get two complete magnets, each with its own north and south poles. As **Figure 2-2** shows, no matter how many times you break a magnet, you are left with more complete magnets, each with two poles.

**Figure 2-3** below shows Earth's magnetic poles and how they interact with other magnetic poles.

**Figure 2-2**

Each piece of the original magnet is a new magnet with two poles. How many smaller magnets do you suppose could be made from one large magnet?

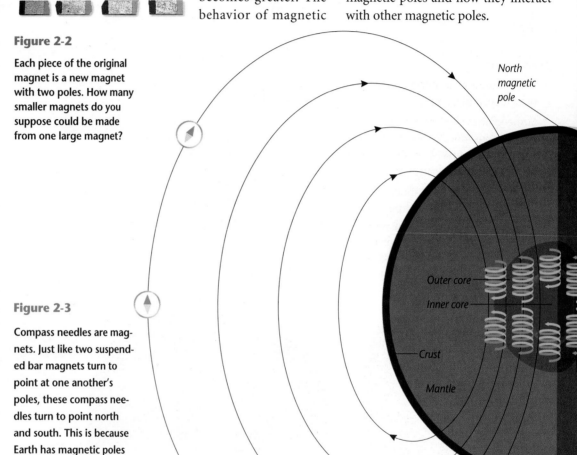

**Figure 2-3**

Compass needles are magnets. Just like two suspended bar magnets turn to point at one another's poles, these compass needles turn to point north and south. This is because Earth has magnetic poles much like a bar magnet. Scientists think Earth's magnetism is produced by materials deep in its core.

North magnetic pole

Outer core

Inner core

Crust

Mantle

South magnetic pole

---

## ENRICHMENT

**Demonstration** Anchor a tall pencil in a lump of clay. Obtain two or more ring magnets with holes in the center. Stack them with like poles facing each other; they will levitate. Ask students what causes this phenomenon. *The magnets are arranged so that like poles are facing. Like poles repel, pushing the magnets apart.*

## Program Resources

**Critical Thinking/Problem Solving,** p. 5, Flex Your Brain

---

# Revealing Magnetic Forces

You know that a force acts between magnetic poles. But you've seen only its effects on other magnets—attraction or repulsion. What is the effect of a magnet on the region around it? Do the Explore activity below and find out.

## Explore! ACTIVITY

### Can you map a magnet's force?

#### What To Do

1. Obtain two bar magnets and iron filings from your teacher.

2. Place a bar magnet on a table and cover it with a piece of white paper as shown.

3. Sprinkle iron filings onto the paper and gently tap it. Observe the pattern that results and sketch it *in your Journal*. Label the location of the magnet's poles. How far from the magnet does the pattern extend?

4. Use the paper, both magnets, and iron filings to make sketches *in your Journal* of the pattern formed by two like poles about 2 cm apart and two unlike poles about 2 cm apart. How do the patterns differ? How are they similar?

*Compass needle*

**Figure 2-4**

The iron filings around this bar magnet clump together where the force of the magnet is strongest. The compass needles also point along the lines formed by the iron filings. The force acting on the needles must also be causing the iron filings to align.

**Connect to...**
## Earth Science

Earth's magnetic and geographic poles aren't in the same place. Navigators must adjust compasses to find true north. Do you think this adjustment is the same worldwide? Why or why not?

---

**Connect to . . .**
## Earth Science

Do you think this adjustment is the same worldwide? Why or why not? *Students should be able to infer that the amount of adjustment varies depending on where you are on Earth. Point out that navigators' maps often give the number of degrees of adjustment needed for the local area.*

**Flex Your Brain** Use the Flex Your Brain activity to have students explore MAGNETIC POLES. [L1]

**Student Journal** Have students record their sketches and the answers to the questions in their journals. [L2]

### Expected Outcome

The filings around a single bar magnet should form the pattern shown in Figure 2-4. With unlike poles, the overall pattern is oval, with lines connecting the two poles.

### Answers to Questions

3. oval pattern similar to Figure 2-4; poles are at the two ends of the magnet; size of oval pattern depends on strength of magnet

4. like poles: two separate ovals with space between; unlike poles: one oval with lines connecting adjacent poles

### ✓ Assessment

**Performance** Have students predict what the magnetic field will look like when two bar magnets are positioned parallel to one another with their long sides about 4 cm apart and their north poles on the right. Have them experiment to check their predictions. Students should repeat the process with one magnet reversed so that its south pole is on the right. Use the Performance Task Assessment List for Making Observations and Inferences in **PAMSS**, p. 17. [L1]

---

## Explore!

### Can you map a magnet's force?

**Time needed** one class period

**Materials** bar magnet, plastic bag, sheet of paper, iron filings

**Thinking Processes** classifying, observing, comparing and contrasting, forming operational definitions, predicting, modeling, interpreting data

**Purpose** To model and describe the magnetic field around one or two bar magnets.

### Teaching the Activity

Ask students if they have ever used a magnet and iron filings to make a picture. *Students may mention a toy in which the magnet moves iron filings to draw hair and other features on a face.* Ask why a magnet can be used to move iron filings. *The magnet attracts the iron filings, because iron is a magnetic substance.*

**Demonstration** Allow students to observe what blocks a magnetic field.

Materials needed are a ring stand, utility clamp, needle, thread (1 m), tape, magnet, thin sheets of solids including iron and pure nickel.

Clamp the magnet to the ring stand. Thread the needle and stick the needle on the magnet. Tape the thread to the table and pull the thread until the needle is suspended just below the magnet. Slip a sheet of paper between the needle and the magnet. The needle doesn't fall; therefore, the paper doesn't block the magnetic field. Repeat the experiment with plastic, aluminum foil, coins, and other materials. Before each experiment, invite students to predict what will happen. Ask them to give logical reasons for their predictions. When a substance blocks the magnetic field, the needle will fall. L2

## DID YOU KNOW?

One ancient compass consists of a polished lodestone ladle that rests on a smooth, bronze plate. Once allowed to move, the ladle turns until its handle points south. Ancient Chinese used it in their practice of Feng Shui. In Feng Shui, the Chinese lined up buildings and cities with Earth's forces in order to harmonize with nature.

The patterns of filings form lines around the magnet. The region around a magnet where the magnetic force acts is called a **magnetic field**.

When you bring like poles together, the field lines from each of these poles bend away from the pole of the other magnet. When you bring unlike poles near each other, the filings line up to reveal that the magnetic field links the two poles.

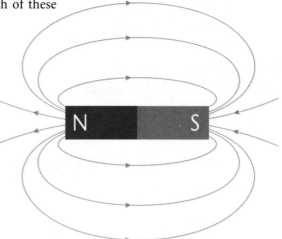

**Figure 2-5**

The magnetic lines of force in a magnetic field are not always the same distance apart. Where are magnetic lines of force most numerous and closest together? Where is a magnetic field strongest?

## Van Allen Belts

Y ou make use of Earth's magnetic field every time you find direction with a compass. You can see in the drawing how Earth's huge magnetic field extends far out in space.

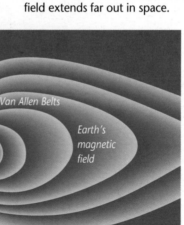

*Charged particles from sun*

*Van Allen Belts*

*Earth's magnetic field*

The field acts as an umbrella that protects us from the shower of high-energy, charged particles from space. These particles could cause cancer and genetic damage in living things.

When the first artificial satellites were launched into space, scientists discovered a previously unknown region of charged particles in space near Earth. Dr. James Van Allen of the University of Iowa suggested that the particles the satellite detected come from the solar wind, the stream of charged

*Van Allen radiation belts extend from approximately 1000 to 25 000 km above the surface of the Earth.*

**Purpose**

The Earth Science Connection reinforces Section 2-1 by describing the Van Allen Belts that exist in Earth's magnetosphere.

**Content Background**

James Van Allen discovered the two belts of charged particles with an instrument on the first U.S. space satellite, Explorer 1; it was launched in 1958.

NASA scientist Andrei Konradi hypothesizes that the number of protons in the Van Allen Belts is being reduced by space trash—broken instruments, burned-out rockets, and other debris from past space missions. The debris absorbs high-energy protons that spiral toward it in their orbit around the lines of Earth's magnetic fields. Konradi predicts that by the year 2010, space trash will be as effective as Earth's atmosphere in reducing the flow of charged particles in Van Allen Belts.

The paper and iron filings showed you only part of a bar magnet's field. The magnetic field isn't flat like paper, it's three-dimensional. The field extends around the magnet on all sides. The iron filings in this tank of mineral oil have clumped and aligned on all sides of the two cylindrical magnets inside.

particles emitted by the sun. He hypothesized that charged particles from the sun interact with Earth's magnetic field. Van Allen said that the force due to Earth's magnetic field makes the particles move in circles around the field lines. The drawing shows how the particles are trapped in regions above Earth's equator. These regions are now called Van Allen Belts in honor of the scientist who first explained them.

Occasionally, the sun emits larger than usual numbers of particles. The excess particles are pushed along Earth's magnetic field lines toward the north and south magnetic poles. There the particles interact with gases high in the atmosphere, creating spectacular displays known as the northern and southern lights, as shown in the photo to the right.

### You Try It!

Intense solar flares can disrupt the Van Allen Belts. Solar flares can lead to changes on Earth, such as interference with radio reception, surges in electric power lines, and more visible northern and southern lights. Write a newspaper story explaining such happenings as if they occurred in your area. Mention Dr. Van Allen.

*Northern and southern lights may be visible any time of the year, but they occur more frequently during periods of concentrated sunspot and other solar activity.*

---

**Teaching Strategy**

Have students do research to learn more about the mission and findings of Explorer 1. The 1958 and 1959 editions of *The Readers' Guide to Periodical Literature* might be a good place to begin. You may wish to have students increase their knowledge of social history, along with science history, by finding out what their grandparents or other adults recall thinking or feeling about the beginnings of space exploration. [L2]

**Answer to**
You Try It!

Have volunteers read their newspaper articles aloud. Post completed articles on a bulletin board titled *The Solar Storm.*

**Going Further** ⅢⅢⅢ▶

Students can work in pairs to learn more about the Van Allen Belts and other regions in Earth's magnetosphere. Suggest they research topics such as the structure of the magnetosphere, auroras, or magnetos- pheric storms. *Planet Earth,* by Jonathan Weiner (Bantam, 1986), is one source of information. Gifted students may wish to examine "Earth's Magnetic Environment," by Louis J. Lanzerotti and Chanchat Uberoi (*Sky & Telescope,* October, 1988, pp. 360–362).

After students complete their research, have them collaborate to make a drawing of the magnetosphere or write a paragraph describing something they learned about the magnetosphere. **COOP LEARN** [P]

Figure 2-7

**Visual Learning**

**Figure 2-8** **What can you observe about the magnetic poles of this stack of doughnut magnets?** *The magnets are stacked so that opposite poles are touching.*

**Ⓐ** Much geologic activity occurs under the sea near the boundaries of huge, rocky plates on Earth's crust. Liquid rock from Earth's core pushes up. This liquid rock may be magnetized by Earth's magnetic field. When the rock cools and becomes solid, the magnetic field is "frozen" in. Geologists have used these rocks to study how Earth's magnetic field has changed over time.

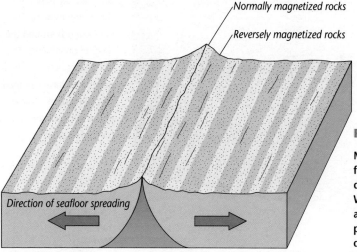

Normally magnetized rocks
Reversely magnetized rocks
Direction of seafloor spreading

# 3 ASSESS

## Check for Understanding

Have students answer questions 1–3 of Check Your Understanding. Before they answer the Apply question, encourage students to recall how poles of magnets interact. *Since the north end of a magnetic compass needle points toward Earth's North Pole, it shows that there is a force of attraction. Since opposite poles attract, this means that Earth's "north" pole is really a "south" pole.*

## Reteach

**Demonstration** Show the arrangement of the areas of intensity around the ends of bar magnets. Place a bar magnet on an overhead projector. Add a blank acetate and scatter iron filings on the acetate. L1

## Extension

**Discussion** As described in Figure 2-7, there is strong evidence that Earth's magnetic field has reversed itself many times. Ask students what would be the likely effect of this switching of Earth's magnetic poles on daily life. L3

**Figure 2-8**

Magnetic lines of force surround doughnut magnets. What can you observe about the magnetic poles of this stack of doughnut magnets?

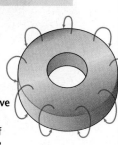

**Ⓑ** Earth's magnetic field has flip-flopped, north and south, at least 171 times. One way scientists know this is by the direction of magnetized rock on the sea floor.

Your experience with magnetic toys, refrigerator magnets, and magnetic compasses showed you that magnets acted differently from other materials. Now you've started to understand the behavior of magnets. You've seen that every magnet has two kinds of poles—north and south. Like poles repel each other and unlike poles attract each other. You've seen

that the poles are the part of the magnet where its force is strongest. You've mapped the region around the magnet, where the magnetic forces act, and identified it as the magnetic field of the magnet. The strength of the field can be found from the magnetic field lines. Earth has a magnetic field that resembles the field of a gigantic bar magnet.

## check your UNDERSTANDING

1. Figure 2-8 shows the field around a doughnut-shaped magnet. Where are this magnet's poles? How would you identify the magnet's north and south poles?
2. Figure 2-8 also shows five doughnut-shaped magnets on a pencil. Suppose the lower pole on the bottom magnet is the north

pole. Identify both poles on each of the four magnets.
3. What is the relationship between the magnetic force and the magnetic field?
4. **Apply** If a magnetic compass needle points north, what is the actual polarity of Earth's northern pole? Explain.

# 4 CLOSE

## Activity

Have students write lists of things they have learned about magnetic fields. Then work as a class to create a complete list. L1

## check your UNDERSTANDING

1. The poles are where the field is strongest, at the top and bottom surfaces. Suspend the doughnut and determine which pole faces north or experiment using a labeled bar magnet.
2. from bottom of lowest magnet to top of highest: N, S; S, N; N, S; S, N; N, S

3. The magnetic force acts within a region called the magnetic field.
4. It must be a south pole (opposite polarity) because it is attracted by the north pole of a magnet.

# Magnets

## Magnetic Attraction

In the previous section, you observed that there are magnetic fields around Earth and around bar magnets. And you know that if you break a magnet, you get two smaller magnets. But, what is a magnet? Does making a magnet require special materials? Can you make a magnet from something nonmagnetic? Do the Explore activity and find out.

### Explore! ACTIVITY

#### Can you magnetize a nail?

**What To Do**

1. Place an iron nail near one end of a bar magnet. Sprinkle some iron filings on the nail. What happens?

2. Remove the bar magnet and tap the nail. *In your Journal*, describe what happens to the iron filings.

### ■ What Makes Magnets

The iron nail you magnetized is only a temporary magnet. Its magnetism was caused by the presence of a strong magnetic field. Magnetism that occurs only in the presence of a magnetic field is called **induced magnetism**. The iron nail developed magnetic poles while it was near the magnet. When you removed the nail from the magnetic field, the nail's poles soon disappeared. Why was it possible to make a magnet? Would a piece of plastic or an aluminum nail act this way? Try it!

From the Explore activity you might hypothesize that the magnetism of materials depends on the kind of atom of which they are made. For materials attracted to the bar magnet, our hypothesis would suggest that their atoms have tiny magnetic fields. Therefore, the atoms can act like magnets.

### Section Objectives

- Explain the effects of magnetic fields on various materials.
- Make magnets out of nonmagnetic materials.
- Make an electromagnet and demonstrate its magnetic effects.
- Use magnetic domain to describe how objects can be magnetized or demagnetized.

### Key Terms

*induced magnetism*
*electromagnet*

### DID YOU KNOW?

Lightning can magnetize objects so strongly that they are capable of lifting objects as much as three times their own weight.

### Explore!

#### Can you magnetize a nail?

**Time needed**   5 minutes

**Materials**   bar magnet, plastic bag, iron nail, iron filings, large sheets of paper

**Thinking Processes**   observing and inferring, recognizing cause and effect, predicting

**Purpose**   To demonstrate how magnetism can be induced.

**Preparation**   Have students predict what happens when a magnetic material is brought near a strong magnet. Place magnets in plastic bags to keep them free of iron filings.

#### Teaching the Activity

**Troubleshooting**   To avoid scattering the iron filings, have students put the sheet of paper on the surface where they will be experimenting.  Iron filings can be saved and reused.

---

# PREPARATION

## Concepts Developed

In this section, students will explore the relationship between electricity and magnetism. Electric current is used to make electromagnets—temporary magnets that remain magnetized as long as the current flows.

## Planning the Lesson

Refer to the Chapter Organizer on pages 48A–B.

# 1 MOTIVATE

**Demonstration**   Use a "perpetual motion" toy (available in museum stores and gift shops) to show how a magnetic field and an electric coil interact. L1

**Student Text Question**
**Would a piece of plastic or an aluminum nail act this way?** *No, neither plastic nor aluminum can be magnetized.*

**Student Journal**   Have students draw the patterns made by the iron filings. L1

### Expected Outcome

Students should observe that the iron nail only attracts the iron filings when it has been magnetized. The nail quickly loses its magnetism.

### Answers to Questions

**1.** The nail attracts the filings.
**2.** The nail does not attract the filings.

### ✔ Assessment

**Process**   Have students predict what would happen in this activity using a steel needle rather than the nail. Have them test their predictions. Use the Performance Task Assessment List for Evaluating a Hypothesis in **PAMSS**, p. 31. L1

# 2 TEACH

## Tying to Previous Knowledge

Ask students why they think the topics of magnetism and electricity appear together in the textbook. Explain that motors and other devices depend on the effect that electric currents and magnetic fields have on each other. In this section, they will explore the relationship between electricity and magnetism.

---

### Visual Learning

**Figure 2-9** Ask students to think about the nail they used in the Explore activity on page 57. Which part of Figure 2-9 shows the magnetic domains in the nail? *Part A shows the domains before the nail was magnetized. Part C shows the domains after the nail was magnetized.*

---

**Theme Connection** From the Explore activity on page 57 and the Find Out activity on page 59, students should see evidence of the theme of systems and interactions. A magnet interacts with an iron object, such as the nail used in the Explore activity, or the needle used in the Find Out activity.

---

### How Do We Know?

The alignment of magnetic domains is what differentiates an iron magnet from a common iron nail. The magnetic fields of domains in a common nail are oriented randomly. If you could see their magnetic fields, they would appear to point in all directions. (See Figure 2-9A.) When you bring the nail near a strong magnet, the domains of the nail are aligned in the direction of the magnetic field of the magnet.

---

One atom produces a very weak magnetic field. Many atoms with N and S poles aligned produce a much stronger field. Groups of atoms with magnetic fields aligned are called domains. Each polygon in the figures below represents a domain containing millions of atoms. Each arrow indicates the direction of that domain's magnetic field.

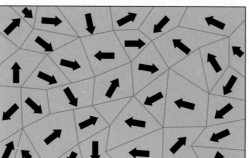
*Non-magnetic*

**B** A horseshoe magnet is one example of a magnetized substance.

**Figure 2-9**

**A** In substances that are not magnetized, all of the magnetic fields of the domains are not oriented in the same direction. If you look carefully, each arrow has an opposite arrow, which cancels its effect. Select an arrow in the diagram; can you find its opposite arrow?

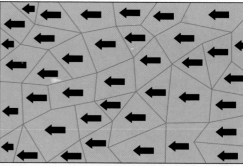
*Magnetic*

**C** In substances that are magnetized, all of the magnetic fields are oriented in the same direction.

You've already made a temporary magnet, one that works only in the presence of a magnetic field. From what you know about magnetic domains, do you think you can make a permanent magnet? Try the activity on the next page to find out.

---

### How Do We Know?

**Is there any observable evidence that magnetic atoms exist?**

Yes. A fine powder of iron oxide, also known as rust, is spread over a smooth surface of a magnetized metal. It's a little like placing iron filings around a bar magnet. The powder collects along the boundaries between neighboring clusters of magnetic atoms. These clusters are called domains. The boundaries are visible under a microscope and can be photographed. These outlines allow us to observe the way magnetic atoms interact with each other.

---

### Program Resources

**Study Guide,** p. 12

**Critical Thinking/Problem Solving,** p. 10, MAGLEV: Train of the Future [L2]

**Transparency Master,** p. 9, and **Color Transparency,** Number 3, Domains [L2]

**Making Connections: Integrating Sciences,** p. 7, Magnetic Navigation [L2]

**Take Home Activities,** p. 7, Magnetism [L1]

**Concept Mapping,** p. 10, Types of Magnetic Materials [L1]

**Laboratory Manual,** pp. 5–9, Electromagnets [L2]

## Find Out! ACTIVITY

### Can you make a permanent magnet?

**Y**ou've used magnets many times, but how are they created?

#### What To Do

1. Obtain from your teacher a sewing needle, bar magnet, paper clips, small plastic bottle, bunsen burner, and tongs or pliers.

2. Stroke the needle along the length of a bar magnet about 50 times.

3. Now, see how many paper clips the needle can pick up. *In your Journal*, use the theory of magnetic domains to explain how this magnet was created.

4. Put the needle into the plastic bottle and shake it hard for 30 seconds. Test the needle's magnetism again. Has it changed?

#### Conclude and Apply

1. Use the theory of magnetic domains to explain how the steel needle lost its magnetism.

2. Make another steel needle magnet. Then, heat it red hot using the bunsen burner and tongs. After it's cooled, test its magnetism again. Did the needle change? If so, why?

### ■ Permanent Magnets

Some materials are noticeably influenced by magnetic fields—they become magnets themselves. Materials that can be made into permanent magnets are most useful. One such material is an alloy of aluminum, nickel, and cobalt. ALNICO (ALuminum, NIckel, and CObalt) magnets retain their magnetism for a long time.

The temporary and permanent magnets you've observed have been made of magnetic materials. Can a magnetic field exist without a magnetic material? Do the Investigate activity on the next pages to find an answer.

#### SKILLBUILDER

**Observing and Inferring**

A group of students must identify the poles of three magnets. Each end of each magnet is a different color. The students suspend one magnet. It rotates until its red end points north and its silver end points south. For the second magnet, they find that the green end repels the red end, but the yellow end attracts the red. Then the students place a blue/pink magnet next to the red/silver magnet. Both the blue end and the pink end attract the red end. How should the students label the green/yellow magnet? What can they conclude about the blue/pink magnet? If you need help, refer to the **Skill Handbook** on page 683.

The green end should be labeled "north" and the yellow end "south." The blue/pink "magnet" must be only a piece of iron or steel. Its magnetism is induced by its being in the magnetic field of the other magnet. L1

---

**Student Journal** Have students record their observations in their journals. L1

**Expected Outcome**

Students should observe that stroking the bar magnet along the needle magnetizes the needle. The needle loses its magnetism when it is jolted repeatedly.

**Conclude and Apply**

**1.** The jarring destroyed the arrangement of magnetic domains.

**2.** Yes. It lost its magnetism. When the needle is heated, the atoms in domains move faster and break out of alignment.

#### ✔ Assessment

**Performance** Have students devise a way to identify the north and south poles of the steel magnet they made. *Possible answer: Suspend the needle and observe which end points north.* Then ask students to find a way to reverse the positions of the north and south poles. *Stroke the needle along the magnet in the opposite direction.* Use the Performance Task Assessment List for Designing an Experiment in **PAMSS**, p. 23. L1

## Find Out!

### Can you make a permanent magnet?

**Time needed** 20–30 minutes

**Materials** bar magnet, sewing needle, paper clips, plastic bottle, Bunsen burner, tongs or pliers

**Thinking Processes** observing, forming a hypothesis, designing an experiment, modeling

**Purpose** To explain how an object made of magnetic material can be made into a permanent magnet.

### Teaching the Activity

**Safety** Caution students to be careful when handling the sewing needle. Collect the needles immediately after students have completed the activity. Remind students to be careful around the open flame. Demonstrate how to safely use tongs to hold the needle. L1

# INVESTIGATE!

## 2-1 Making a Magnet

### Planning the Activity

**Time needed** 1 class period

**Purpose** To determine some of the factors that affect the strength of an electromagnet.

**Process Skills** observing, comparing and contrasting, formulating hypotheses, predicting, sequencing, designing an experiment, separating and controlling variables, modeling

**Materials** 1 m of 22-gauge insulated wire, drinking straw to fit over nail, large iron nail, 3 D-cells, paper clips

**Preparation** Divide the class into pairs of students or small groups. COOP LEARN

### Teaching the Activity

**Safety** Students should use the scissors carefully when stripping insulation from the wire. Make sure students avoid sharp wire ends. Magnets should only be connected briefly; wires will become hot if magnets are left on.

**Process Reinforcement** Ask students how they might measure the strength of a magnetic field. Possible answers: *The number of lines of force around the field; the weight of an object the magnet attracts.* Explain that, in this experiment, students will make a magnet and then try to find ways to increase its strength.

**Possible Hypothesis** The two variables in this experiment that have a large effect on the strength of the electromagnet are the number of coils of wire around the straw and the number of D-cells connected to the wire. Students may suggest other possibilities such as the length of the wire from the straw to the battery. Encourage them to check out their ideas.

# INVESTIGATE!

# Making a Magnet

*Can you make a magnet without using any magnetic materials? Would it be stronger or weaker than a magnet made from magnetic materials? Why might such a magnet be useful?*

## Problem
What controls the strength of a magnet made with electric current?

## Materials
1 m, 22-gauge insulated wire
drinking straw to fit over nail, cut to length of nail

large iron nail
3 D-cells
paper clips

## Safety Precautions

## What To Do

**1** Strip 1 cm of insulation from each end of the wire.

**2** Slip the straw over the nail (see Photo **A**). Leaving about 20 cm of wire free at each end, wrap the wire tightly around the straw for 30 turns. Leave about 5 mm of nail exposed at each end (see Photo **B**).

**3** Connect one bare end of the wire to a terminal of the D-cell (see Photo **C**). Hold the second to the other terminal. At the same time, touch the nail to a pile of paper clips as shown.

## Program Resources

**Activity Masters,** pp. 11–12, Investigate 2–1

**Science Discovery Activities,** 2–2, Who's Calling?

## ENRICHMENT

**Discussion** Ask students whether their family recycles aluminum and so-called "tin" cans, which are really steel cans. Have them explain why a magnet would be useful in separating these items for recycling. *The magnet would pick up only the "tin" cans because steel is a magnetic material and aluminum isn't.*

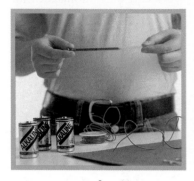

**A**       **B**       **C**

**4** Lift the nail while keeping the loose end of the wire on the D-cell terminal. Record the number of paper clips the electromagnet picked up. Then, disconnect the loose wire from the D-cell.

**5** *Design an experiment* using the materials you have to answer the question posed in the introduction. Think of things you can add or remove from the first setup. Show your plan to your teacher. If you are advised to revise your plan, be sure to check with your teacher again before you begin. Look at all the safety precautions before you begin. Carry out your plan.

## Analyzing

**1.** How does the number of batteries affect the strength of the magnet?

**2.** *Infer* how the number of turns of wire affects the strength of the magnet.

## Concluding and Applying

**3.** How does the strength of the magnetic field depend on the current?

**4.** What combination of materials produced the strongest magnetic field?

**5.** Going Further How would you use the magnet you experimented with to ring a bell?

## Multicultural Perspectives

### Aircraft Landing Systems

Lawrence Marcellus Jordan is an African-American transportation systems analyst. He develops computer programs to analyze and predict effects of electromagnetic interference on aircraft landing navigation systems. His work yields valuable information on how landing systems can be improved. Students may want to visit a library or career center to learn about transportation systems analysis and related careers.

**Possible Procedures** Encourage each pair or group of students to make at least three different hypotheses that can be tested. For example, the number of coils is directly related to the strength of the magnet. Students add coils ten at a time and test the magnet's strength.

**Troubleshooting** This is a time-consuming experiment. Monitor students' progress. If necessary, interrupt the experiment after Step 4, and have students complete it during a second class period.

**Student Journal** Have students create data tables to record the number of paper clips picked up for various numbers of D-cells and coils of wire. Have them answer the questions in their journals. **L2**

### Expected Outcome

Students should observe that the strength of the electromagnet is increased as D-cells and coils of wire are added.

**Answers to** Analyzing/ Concluding and Applying

**1.** The more D-cells there are, the stronger the electromagnet is.

**2.** The more turns there are, the stronger the electromagnet is.

**3.** The larger the current, the stronger the field.

**4.** The maximum number of D-cells and the maximum number of turns of wire.

**5.** Possible answer: Position the nail and bell so that the magnet pulls a steel clapper, which then strikes the bell.

### ✔ Assessment

**Process** Have students work in pairs to repeat the experiment using a bobby pin or steel needle instead of the iron nail. They should predict what will happen before they begin. Then they should carry out the experiment to see if changing the core metal makes a difference in the strength of the electromagnet. Use the Performance Task Assessment List for Formulating a Hypothesis in **PAMSS**, p. 21. **L1**
**COOP LEARN**

**Inquiry Question** There are situations where it is not desirable to have a magnetic field around a wire. Ask students: **How do you suppose this problem could be avoided?** *An insulated wire with current traveling in the opposite direction can be placed beside the original wire or wrapped around it. This causes the total current and the total magnetic field to be zero. Students may also suggest wrapping the wire in materials from the demonstration on TWE p. 54.*

## Visual Learning

**Figure 2-9** Have students compare all three compasses. Ask students why two compasses are different. *They're affected by the magnetic field of the wire.* Then ask why the two compasses on top of the circuits are not the same. *The polarity is reversed so that the current is flowing in the opposite direction.*

You have seen that it's possible to make a magnet out of nothing more than a current-carrying wire. Such a magnet is called an **electromagnet**. The photo below shows an example of the first evidence of electromagnetism.

**Figure 2-9**

A Danish physicist discovered what you just observed first-hand: an electrical current produces a magnetic field. He began experimenting after, by chance, he observed a compass needle move when he turned on a switch. Notice how the lone compass points north while the two compasses on top of wires point at right angles to the wires.

## How Can You Make a Transformer?

**S**imilar in appearance to an electromagnet, a transformer is made using an iron core and wire coils. The magnetic field produced in the iron core links two coils in a special way. Alternating current is transmitted to the second coil and its voltage is changed based on how many loops of wire are in each coil.

Insert a large nail in a soda straw that has been cut to the same length as the nail. Wrap 30 turns of 32-gauge wire in a tight compact coil at one end of the straw. Make a coil at the other end that has 120 turns. Use sandpaper to remove the insulating coating from the ends of the wire.

Connect the ends of the 30-turn coil to a low-voltage AC power supply. This will be the source of the voltage your transformer will change. Connect the ends of the 120-turn wire to the light bulb, the

*An electric power station*

**Purpose**

A Closer Look reinforces the ideas in this section by having students construct their own transformer. This activity also demonstrates the role of a transformer in a transmission system.

**Content Background**

By enabling power companies to transmit electric energy at high voltage and deliver it at low voltage, transformers make electricity a viable form of energy. Without transformers, power plants would have to be near power consumers.

**Teaching Strategy**

Invite a representative from the local power company to speak to the students about electric power safety. Have students prepare questions to ask the representative, such as: What safety precautions are taken when repairing a power outage? **L2**

# Electromagnets at Work

You use an electromagnet whenever you listen to a record or a tape recording, talk on a telephone, ring an electric doorbell, or dry your hair with an electric dryer. Electromagnets are useful because their magnetism

**Figure 2-10**

**Ⓐ** In a crane electromagnet, would changing the direction of the electric current change the performance of the crane?

Coil of wire

Soft iron core    Flow of electrons

**Ⓑ** How does a crane operator release an object that is held by an electromagnet?

**Inquiry Question** Ask students whether the electromagnets they have made and read about in this section are permanent or temporary magnets. *Temporary; magnet exists only when current is flowing.*

## Across the Curriculum

### Music

Have students research the function of an electromagnet in a loudspeaker. Then, have them write a clear explanation and draw a scientific diagram to illustrate how it works. If possible, have them take a real loudspeaker apart and identify its parts or have a representative from an audio equipment company come and discuss speaker construction with students. **L2**

## Visual Learning

**Figure 2–10** **How does a crane operator release an object that is held by an electromagnet?** *by turning off the current to the magnet*

user to which your transformer will transmit electricity. Observe how brightly the light bulb glows. Now reverse the position of the coils—connect the 120-turn coil to the power supply and the 30-turn coil to the light bulb. How brightly does the bulb glow in this arrangement?

Transformers are generally called step-up transformers or step-down transformers. Use your observations to determine which time your coil-wrapped straw acted like a step-up transformer. Explain your choice.

## What Do You Think?

Repeat the activity you just completed without placing the iron nail inside the straw. Record your observations. Then place several other items, such as a paper clip, a pencil lead, and a string, inside the straw. What happens? Use your knowledge of magnetism, magnetic fields, and electric fields to explain your observations.

**Answers to**

**What Do You Think?**

The transformer works poorly without the iron nail inside. Alternating current induces a current in the magnetic field surrounding the iron nail. This induces a current in the coils connected to the light bulb at the other end of the straw. A magnetic object in the turns of coil makes the transformer work much better.

**Going Further** ⫸

Have students work in small groups to make murals that show the transmission of electric energy from a power station along a power line to businesses and homes. Tell students to include both step-down and step-up transformers in their murals. Murals should also show the electric generator at the power station, transmission lines, and high towers (pylons) from which transmission lines are often suspended. (Point out to students that some transmission lines are buried.) Tell students to use labels explaining the function of each part of the transmission system shown by their murals. For example, one label might state: *Distribution transformers step down the voltage from several hundred thousand volts to several thousand volts.* One source of information is *The Way Things Work,* by David Macaulay (Houghton Mifflin, 1988), pp. 304–305. **COOP LEARN**

The magnetic field encircles the coil in the direction the fingertips point. L1

# 3 ASSESS

## Check for Understanding

Have students answer questions 1–4 in Check Your Understanding. Before they answer question 5, have students review the Investigate activity on pages 60 and 61.

## Reteach

Cut index cards into fourths. Label one end of each piece N and the other end S; scatter the pieces on the table. Tell students that these pieces represent magnetic domains. Have students label one end of an uncut card N and the other end S to represent a bar magnet. Have one student bring the south end of a "bar magnet" near the scattered "domains." Have other students arrange the domains as they would be if they were affected by the magnet. L1

## Extension

Ask students who have mastered the concepts presented in this section how they would fix a strong bar magnet that became weak. *You could try using it as a core for an electromagnet for a while, or stroking it several times along a stronger magnet.* L3

# 4 CLOSE

Show students a picture of a giant electromagnet lifting scrap metal. Ask which interaction is stronger: the magnetic attraction between the magnet and the metal, or the gravitational attraction between the metal and Earth. *The metal does not fall, so the magnetic attraction produced by the electromagnet is greater.* L1

## SKILLBUILDER

**Making Models and Observing and Inferring**

There is a rule for determining the direction of the magnetic field around a current-carrying wire when the direction of the current is shown. You think of grasping the wire in your right hand, as shown below. When your thumb extends in the direction of the current, as your fingers curl, they travel around the wire in the direction of the magnetic field. The photographs to the right show coils and iron filings. What direction is the magnetic field inside the coils? If you need help, refer to the **Skill Handbook** on pages 692 and 683.

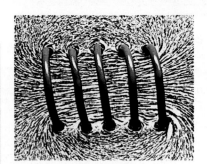

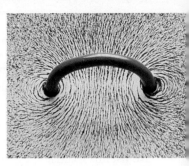

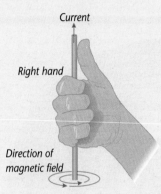

Current

Right hand

Direction of magnetic field

can be turned on and off and because they can produce magnetic fields much stronger than any permanent magnets.

When you allowed current to flow through the wire of your electromagnet the current created a magnetic field. You increased the strength of the magnet by increasing the number of batteries and by increasing the number of turns of wire. You also found that the field of the coil was stronger when an iron nail was inside the coil. The field produced by the coil realigns the magnetic domains in the iron. This adds strength to the field produced by the current in the wire coil.

In this section, you've discovered that a magnet is like a collection of tiny bar magnets, most of which are lined up in the same direction. You've made magnets that lasted for a short time and magnets that were more permanent. And, you produced a magnetic field without using magnetic materials. Next, you'll learn how magnets and electric currents interact.

### check your UNDERSTANDING

1 Why are certain materials affected by magnets while others are not?

2. Describe how you would make a permanent magnet out of a paper clip.

3. Compare and contrast an electromagnet with a permanent magnet.

4. Using magnetic domains, explain how and why a permanent magnet can lose its magnetism.

5. **Apply** You leave a box of paper clips on top of your TV. When you go to use them, you find they are stuck together. What might you infer about the TV?

**64**   **Chapter 2**   Magnetism

### check your UNDERSTANDING

1. Materials that contain magnetic domains that can be lined up are affected by magnets. Others are not.

2. Stroke it in one direction with a magnet until the domains line up.

3. Both create a magnetic field and have two poles. But an electromagnet's magnetism can be turned on and off by turning the current on and off.

4. The magnet can lose its magnetic properties by being heated or banged around. Such treatment forces the magnet's domains out of line, thus demagnetizing the magnet.

5. There is a magnetic field around the TV.

# Effects of Magnetic Fields

## Magnetism and Electric Currents

In the last chapter, you saw that an electric current can create a magnetic field. But what about the reverse situation? What effect does a magnetic field have on a static electric charge or on a current? You can combine what you learned from Chapter 1 and your new experiences with magnets to test the two parts of this question. Do the activity below to answer the first part.

### Section Objectives

■ Demonstrate the effects of magnetic fields on wires carrying electric currents.

■ Explain how loudspeakers and electric motors work.

### Key Terms

*loudspeaker*
*electric motor*

 **ACTIVITY**

### Does a magnetic field exert force on a charge?

#### What To Do

1. Obtain from your teacher transparent tape and a bar magnet.

2. Make two oppositely charged pieces of tape as in the Explore activity in Chapter 1 on page 22.

3. Bring one pole of a bar magnet near one tape, then near the other. *In your Journal*, describe what happens. (Remember that an uncharged conductor, such as your finger, will attract both tapes. So, if both tapes move, make sure you are not observing this effect.)

Now, remember what you know about circuits and currents and do the activity on the next page to answer the second part of the question.

---

**Explore!**

### Does a magnetic field exert force on a charge?

**Time needed**   15 minutes

**Materials**   transparent tape, bar magnet

**Thinking Processes**   observing and inferring, hypothesizing, modeling, comparing and contrasting

**Purpose**   To determine if a magnetic field has any effect on a static electric charge.

### Teaching the Activity

**Discussion**   Review with students how to make oppositely charged strips of transparent tape. What type of electrical charge does each strip have? *static* Have volunteers summarize how they used the charge detectors.

Before students do the activity, have them predict whether either pole of a bar magnet will attract or repel the charged strips of tape. Have them defend their predictions.

---

## PREPARATION

### Concepts Developed

In this section, students will explore the relationship between electricity and magnetism. Magnetic fields exert a force that is used in electric motors.

### Planning the Lesson

Refer to the Chapter Organizer on pages 48A–B.

# 1 MOTIVATE

**Demonstration**   Have a fan blowing in the room. Ask students what makes the blades of the fan rotate. Note that electrical energy is changed to mechanical energy (motion of the blades.) Ask students if they think electrical energy can be changed to magnetic energy. L1

**Student Journal**   Have students describe the results of the experiment in their journals. Make sure they understand observing no effect does not mean the experiment was a failure. L1

### Expected Outcome

The magnetic field produced by the bar magnet has no effect on the static charge.

### Answers to Question

**3.** Nothing happens. There is no observable change.

### ✔ Assessment

**Process**   The magnetic field around a horseshoe magnet has a different shape than the field around a bar magnet. Have students experiment to find out whether a horseshoe magnet has any effect on a static electric charge. *No type of magnet exerts force on a static electric charge.* Use the Performance Task Assessment List for Evaluating a Hypothesis in **PAMSS**, p. 31. L1

## 2 TEACH

**Theme Connection** This section supports the theme of energy. In the Find Out activity on page 66 and in the Investigate activity on pages 68 and 69, students discover that the interaction between electric current and a magnetic field can be used to convert electrical energy to mechanical or sound energy.

### Visual Learning

**Figure 2-11** Have students work in pairs to find two ways to change the figure so that the direction of the force exerted on the wire is reversed. *(1) Turn the magnet to reverse the north and south poles; (2) Reverse the wires connected to the terminals on the battery.* **L2** **COOP LEARN**

### Find Out!

**Does a magnetic field exert force on a current?**

**Time needed** 20 minutes

**Materials** D-cell; 50 cm of 22-gauge wire; bar magnet

**Thinking Processes** comparing and contrasting, recognizing cause and effect

**Purpose** To determine what effect a magnetic field has on an electric current.

**Teaching the Activity**

Before beginning the activity, have students predict whether a magnetic field exerts force on a wire in which current is flowing.

**Troubleshooting** If students have difficulty making the wire move, check to see that the magnet is positioned near the wire.

**Expected Outcome**

Students should observe that the magnet either attracted or repelled the wire.

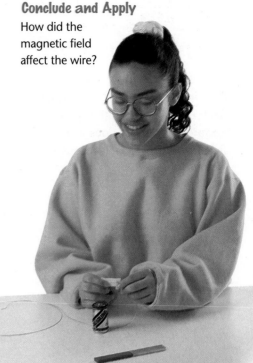

## Does a magnetic field exert force on a current?

Magnets seem to have no effect on static charges. What do they do to moving charges?

### What To Do

1. Obtain from your teacher a D-cell, 50 cm of 22-gauge wire, and a bar magnet.

2. Connect one end of the wire to the D-cell. Then, form a large, loose loop of wire and put one pole of the magnet about 2 cm away. Touch the free end of the wire to the other terminal of the D-cell. What happens?

3. Try Step 2 with as many different arrangements of magnet poles and wire connections as possible. Do the results differ? Why?

### Conclude and Apply

How did the magnetic field affect the wire?

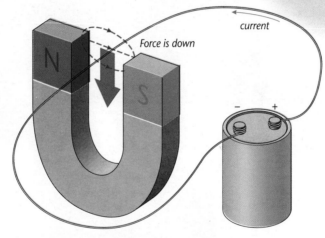

**Figure 2-11**

While current flows through the wire, the magnet exerts a force on the wire. The force is at right angles to the lines of the magnetic field and to the direction of the current. In this case, the force is down.

*current*

*Force is down*

A magnetic field has no effect on a static charge. However, you can see that a magnetic field does exert force on a wire in which current is flowing. When you placed the current-carrying wire near the magnet, the magnet pushed the wire one way or the other. The direction depended on which end of the magnet you brought near the wire. The poles of the magnetic field in the loop of wire could also be reversed—by reversing the current direction. The diagram to the left shows the direction of the current and of the force on the wire.

**Student Journal** Have students compare and contrast the effect of a magnetic field on a static electric charge and on a moving current. They should include diagrams in their written work. **L2**

**Conclude and Apply**

It repelled or attracted, depending on how the circuit was connected. Reversing the magnetic poles or reversing the direction of current in the circuit will reverse the direction of the force exerted by the magnetic field.

### ✔ Assessment

**Process** Have students predict how changing one variable in this experiment would affect the results, and design an experiment to test that variable. Students may choose to vary the strength of the magnet or the size of the dry cell. Use the Performance Task Assessment List for Designing an Experiment in **PAMSS**, p. 23. **L1**

# Changing Current Into Sound

Here's one use of magnets many people enjoy every day: radios or stereos. They run on electricity, but what comes out are voices and music, not current. The following activity will help explain how radios and speakers transform electric current into entertaining or informative sounds.

## Find Out! ACTIVITY

### How does electricity turn into sound?

**M**any appliances produce sound for your pleasure. What makes them work?

#### What To Do

1. Strip 1 cm of insulation from each end of a 2 m wire. Make a coil of 10, 1-cm in diameter turns in the middle of the wire and glue the coil securely to the bottom of a paper cup.

2. Attach one stripped end to each wire of an earphone plug from a portable radio.

3. Turn on the radio, tune in a local station, and insert the plug into the earphone jack. Then, hold the magnet very close to the coil as shown in the figure.

#### Conclude and Apply

1. What happens?

2. Why do you think this happens?

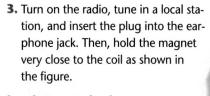

**Figure 2-12**

Your portable stereo turns electric current into sound.

The radio sends a constantly changing current through the wire. When you bring the magnet near the coil, the coil's changing magnetic field interacts with the magnet. The motion of the coil causes the cup to vibrate, creating sound waves. What you've observed is electric energy being changed into sound energy. You've built a loudspeaker. A **loudspeaker** changes variations in electric current into sound waves. Currents and magnetic fields can work in other ways. Do the Investigate activity on the next pages to see how.

---

### Meeting Individual Needs

**Visually Impaired** In each group that includes a visually impaired student, assign another student to read the instructions aloud for the Find Out activities on pages 66 and 67. For the second activity, visually impaired students could be the first to feel the effect of holding the magnet close to the wire.

### Program Resources

**Study Guide,** p. 13

**Multicultural Connections,** p. 8, Eskimos and the Aurora Borealis L1

**How It Works,** p. 6, Telephone L2

**Science Discovery Activities,** 2–3, Testing, 1-2-3

---

## Find Out!

**How does electricity turn into sound?**

**Time needed** one class period

**Materials** radio with earphone jack but no speaker; earphone plug with wires attached; small, powerful permanent magnet; 60 cm of insulated wire; paper drinking cup; glue

**Thinking Processes** observing and inferring, recognizing cause and effect, forming a hypothesis, modeling

**Purpose** To discover how electrical energy can be changed into sound energy.

**Preparation** You may wish to do this activity in two parts, over a period of two days. If so, have students set up the apparatus the first day, then let the glue dry overnight. **COOP LEARN**

### Teaching the Activity

**Student Journal** Have students diagram what is happening in this activity by using a cause-and-effect events chain. L2

### Expected Outcomes

Students should hear sound coming through the cup/loudspeaker.

### Conclude and Apply

1. You can hear the radio.

2. The coil is either attracted to or repelled by the magnetic field around the wire. The motion of the coil makes the cup bottom vibrate, producing sound waves.

### ✔ Assessment

**Process** Have students explain why the current flowing through the wire must be changing. *In order for the cup to vibrate, the coil must be moving back and forth. This will only happen if the magnetic field around the coil is changing in polarity. Thus, the current is changing in direction.* Use the Performance Task Assessment List for Analyzing Data in **PAMSS,** p. 27. L1

## 2-2 Make an Electric Motor

### Planning the Activity

**Time needed** one class period

**Purpose** To demonstrate how electric energy can be changed to mechanical energy.

**Process Skills** making models, observing and inferring, explaining cause and effect, forming hypotheses, forming operational definitions

**Materials** 2 m 22-gauge insulated wire, steel knitting needle, 4 nails, 2 bar magnets, 16-gauge insulated wire, masking tape, fine sandpaper, wooden board (2" × 4" × 30 cm), 2 wooden blocks, 6-V battery, scissors or wire cutters

**Preparation** Divide students into groups of three or four.
**COOP LEARN**

### Teaching the Activity

**Troubleshooting** It is important that none of the bare wires contact the needle. If they do so, the motor will short out and not work. Have students wrap a strip of tape around the part of the needle beneath the stripped ends of the armature wire.

**Process Reinforcement** Ask students to think about how electricity is used to power motors. Remind them that there will need to be a transformation of energy—electrical energy will need to be transformed into mechanical energy.

**Possible Hypothesis** Students should recall that holding a magnet near a moving electric current causes the wire to move. So, the combined effects of a magnetic field and a moving current can be used to create motion.

**Safety** Caution students to be careful using the scissors or wire cutters. Also caution students to avoid touching sharp wire ends.

---

# INVESTIGATE!

# Make an Electric Motor

*When you made the paper cup loudspeaker, you changed electric energy into sound. In this activity, you'll change electric energy into mechanical energy.*

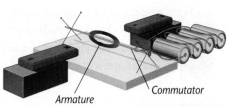
Armature          Commutator

## Problem
How can you change electric energy into motion?

## Safety Precautions

## Materials

| | |
|---|---|
| 2 m 22-gauge insulated wire | masking tape |
| | fine sandpaper |
| steel knitting needle | wooden board |
| 4 nails | (2" x 4" x 30 cm) |
| 2 bar magnets | 2 wooden blocks |
| 16-gauge insulated wire | 6-V battery |

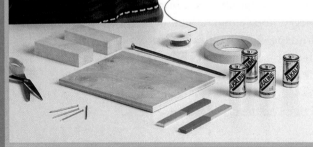

## What To Do

**1** Strip the insulation from 4 cm of each end of the 22-gauge wire.

**2** Leaving about 4 cm free at each end, form a coil of at least 30 turns by winding the 22-gauge wire around a cylinder, such as a battery. Slide the coil off the cylinder and tape the turns of wire together.

## Program Resources

**Activity Masters,** pp. 13–14, Investigate 2–2

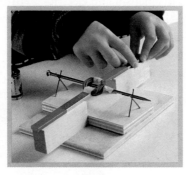
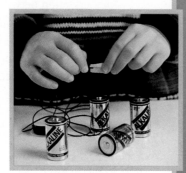

**A**                         **B**                         **C**

**3** Insert the knitting needle through the coil. Try to have an equal number of turns on each side of the needle (see Photo **A**). The coil is the armature. Tape each of the wire's bare ends to one side of the needle. This part of the motor is the commutator.

**4** Mount the needle on the crossed nails as shown in the diagram.

**5** Tape a magnet to each block and place them on each side of the coil-needle assembly as shown (see Photo **B**). Be sure the poles are placed as indicated.

**6** Take two 30 cm lengths of 16-gauge wire. Strip both ends and attach one length to each terminal of the battery (see Photo **C**). Holding only the insulated part of each wire, hold one wire gently against each bare wire of the commutator. Observe what happens to the armature.

## Analyzing

**1.** Observe that the armature is designed so that the current through it changes direction as the armature rotates. How could you test it to see if it is working?

**2.** Is there any position of the coil that makes it easier to start it spinning? Why would you hypothesize that this is true?

## Concluding and Applying

**3.** The electric motor operates on three basic principles. What are they?

**4. Going Further** Would the motor work if you replaced the armature with a permanent magnet? Explain.

**Expected Outcome**

Students have constructed a simple working motor.

**Answers to** Analyzing/ Concluding and Applying

**1.** Hold a compass nearby and see if the needle moves. A moving needle indicates a magnetic field. A magnetic field indicates current.

**2.** Yes; the coil will not start spinning easily when it is horizontal. The magnetic field of the coil isn't pointed toward the bar magnets.

**3.** Current produces a magnetic field; the direction of the current determines the location of the magnet's poles; magnetic poles attract or repel each other. As the current changes direction, the polarity changes. What had been attracted is now repelled. As this constantly changes, the armature moves.

**4.** No; if the polarity could not change, you would simply have one magnet attracting another magnet. There would be no motion.

✔ **Assessment**

**Process** Ask students to infer why most electric motors use alternating current rather than direct current. *The polarity of the electromagnet must be repeatedly reversed in order for the motor to operate. The alternating current causes this reversal.* Use the Performance Task Assessment List for Model in **PAMSS**, p. 51. L1

---

**ENRICHMENT**

**Demonstration** To help students visualize the difference between alternating current (AC) and direct current (DC), sketch a straight horizontal line on the chalkboard to represent DC. Below the DC line, sketch a transverse wave to represent AC. The crests and troughs represent changing voltage. Emphasize that in many appliances, the incoming AC is converted to DC before use. L3

# 3 ASSESS

## Check for Understanding

Have students answer questions 1 and 2 in Check Your Understanding. Encourage them to recall what they observed in the Investigate activity as they formulate an answer to question 3, the Apply question.

## Reteach

Have students list four appliances or devices in their homes that have electric motors. *Examples include hairdryers, washing machines, vacuum cleaners, electric fans.* Then, have students identify the mechanical task done by each item. *For example, a vacuum cleaner picks up dust and debris.* L1

## Extension

Ask students who have mastered the concepts presented in this section to identify one environmental advantage of an automobile whose wheels are turned by an electric-powered, instead of a gasoline-powered motor. *It would not require air-polluting gasoline to run.* Have students research the attempts of scientists and engineers to produce reliable electric automobiles. L3

# 4 CLOSE

Review the interconnection of electricity and magnetism: A current traveling through a wire produces a magnetic field. A magnetic field produces a current when a wire is moved through it. L1

---

In making the motor, you see a practical application of the interaction between magnetism and electricity. Air conditioners, vacuum cleaners, and washing machines use electric motors. An **electric motor** uses an electromagnet to change electric energy into mechanical energy, which can be used to do work. This illustration of a vacuum cleaner shows how such motors work.

**Figure 2-14**

This vacuum cleaner is driven by an electric motor which uses 120V household current. It is similar to the simpler, low voltage motors in the illustrations to the left.

**Figure 2-13**

**A** An electric motor that is powered by a battery contains a wire loop that spins on a shaft, a permanent magnet, a commutator, and brushes.

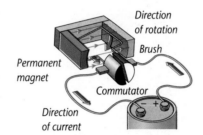

**B** As electricity is applied to the brushes that touch the commutator, a magnetic field is created that attracts one side of the wire loop.

**C** When that side of the wire loop moves past the magnet, the commutator changes the direction of the current, and the opposite side of the wire loop is attracted to the magnet.

**D** The process is then repeated many times each second, causing the motor to spin and creating the ability to perform work.

In this section, you've seen that magnetic fields can affect the direction of electric current. This interaction can be used in devices such as loudspeakers and electric motors. In the next section, you'll find out about still other useful roles that magnets play in day-to-day life.

## check your UNDERSTANDING

1. How must a loudspeaker coil and magnet be arranged to make the coil vibrate?
2. Why do most electric motors contain both a permanent magnet and an electromagnet?
3. **Apply** In what direction—with respect to a magnetic field—would you run a wire carrying a current, so that the force on it due to the field is zero?

## check your UNDERSTANDING

1. The magnetic field must be at right angles to the coil of the loudspeaker.
2. Motors work by alternately attracting and repelling poles of a magnet, causing a rotating motion. Therefore, motors use a temporary magnet, whose poles can be reversed. The permanent magnet attracts reversing poles of the temporary magnet.
3. Parallel to the magnetic field

# Producing Electric Currents

## Magnetism and Electric Current

When you made the electromagnet in the last section, you found evidence that an electric current could produce magnetism. Once again, think about the reverse situation. Can magnetism produce electricity? An American scientist and a British scientist independently discovered that it could be done. You can find out how below.

**Find Out! ACTIVITY**

### Does a moving magnet produce a current?

**E**lectric current in conductors can make magnets. What effect do magnets have on conductors?

**What To Do**

1. Leaving enough free wire to connect to the galvanometer, form a coil just large enough to accept the magnet.
2. Connect the wire ends to the galvanometer terminals.
3. Observe the galvanometer as you **a.** insert the magnet into the coil; **b.** hold the magnet inside the coil; **c.** pull the magnet out; **d.** hold the magnet just outside the coil; and **e.** move the magnet back and forth inside the coil. *In your Journal*, record your observations.

**Conclude and Apply**

1. Did the magnet produce a current? How do you know?
2. When the direction of the magnetic field changed, what happened?

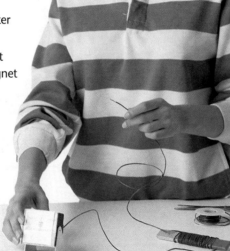

### Section Objectives

- Demonstrate the ability of a changing magnetic field to produce an electric current.
- Describe the working principles behind electric generators.
- Explain the operation of transformers.

### Key Terms

*induced current
electric generator
transformer*

## PREPARATION

### Concepts Developed

In this section, students will discover how a changing magnetic field can be used to produce electric current.

### Planning the Lesson

Refer to the Chapter Organizer on pages 48A–B.

## 1 MOTIVATE

**Demonstration** Magnetic fields around a television picture tube direct the beam of charges from the back of the tube to the screen where they produce an image. Bring a magnet near the screen of a black-and-white TV that is turned on. (A strong magnet can damage some color televisions, so be sure to use a black-and-white TV.) *The bar changes the magnetic field around the tube and the image is distorted.* **L1**

### Conclude and Apply

**1.** The magnetic field produced a current when the magnet was moving. The current registered on the galvanometer.
**2.** The pointer on the galvanometer moved the other way. This shows that the current changed direction.

### ✔ Assessment

**Process** Have students make three different sketches of the experimental set up showing the pointer on the galvanometer (1) at zero, (2) registering a positive current, and (3) registering a negative current. In each case, they should show how the magnet was moving. Use the Performance Task Assessment List for Scientific Drawing in **PAMSS**, p. 55. **L1**

**Find Out!**

### Does a moving magnet produce a current?

**Time needed**   20 minutes

**Materials**   22-gauge insulated strong bar magnet, galvanometer

**Thinking Processes**   recognizing cause and effect, forming operational definitions, interpreting scientific illustrations, modeling

**Purpose**   To analyze the relationship between a moving magnetic field and an electric current.

### Teaching the Activity

**Troubleshooting**   Refer students to the figure to ensure correct setup of the experiment.

**Student Journal**   Have students draw cause-and-effect diagrams in their journals to show how current can produce magnetism and how a moving magnet can create a current. **L1**

### Expected Outcome

The galvanometer registers a weak current when the magnet is moved inside the coil.

## Tying to Previous Knowledge

Ask students to recall from Section 2 that an electric current produces a magnetic field. Ask if they think a magnetic field might be used to produce a current. Then ask them to describe the characteristics they think the magnetic field might have to have. Why? *Students might guess that the magnetic field should be changing or moving. A static electric field won't produce a magnetic field, but a moving electric current will.*

### Visual Learning

**Figure 2-15** Have students compare this figure with the diagram of the motor in the Investigation on pages 68–69. Ask how the two devices are similar? How are they different? *Both devices contain a magnetic field and a rotating section. In the motor, the electric current causes the rotation. Here, the rotation induces the current.* L2

**Figure 2-16** **How is mechanical energy provided to the generator so it can power a light?** *By attaching the generator to the bicycle wheel so that the turns of the wheel provide the mechanical energy needed.*

**Figure 2-17** **What determines the exact voltage increase or decrease in these transformers?** *The number of primary and secondary coils*

**Theme Connection** In this section, the theme of energy is evident. Energy can be changed from one form to another. Here, the kinetic energy of rotation is changed into electric energy by a generator.

---

When you move the magnet into the coil, the galvanometer pointer moves to the left of zero, indicating a small current. When you remove the magnet, the pointer swings the opposite direction, indicating a small current in the opposite direction. If you kept moving the magnet back and forth, you would create a current that kept changing direction.

**Figure 2-15**

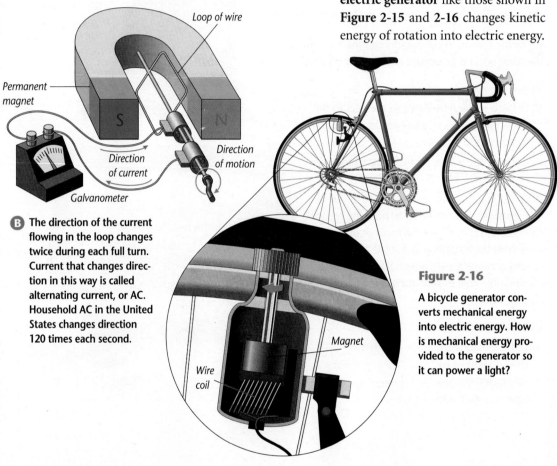

**A** One simple generator converts mechanical energy from cranking into electrical energy. It consists of a loop of wire that rotates in a horseshoe magnet. As the loop turns, it moves through stronger and weaker areas of the magnetic field. The changing magnetic field it experiences produces an induced current.

Loop of wire

Permanent magnet

S    N

Direction of current

Direction of motion

Galvanometer

**B** The direction of the current flowing in the loop changes twice during each full turn. Current that changes direction in this way is called alternating current, or AC. Household AC in the United States changes direction 120 times each second.

Wire coil

Magnet

Moving either the coil or the magnet will produce a current. It's the motion of one in relation to the other that matters. Any time a conductor, such as the coil, experiences a changing magnetic field, an electric current is induced in the conductor. An electric current produced by using a magnet is an **induced current**.

### ■ Generating Current

Induced current has made it possible for every home and business to receive electric energy from a central source. The current commonly used is produced by electric generators. An **electric generator** like those shown in **Figure 2-15** and **2-16** changes kinetic energy of rotation into electric energy.

**Figure 2-16**

A bicycle generator converts mechanical energy into electric energy. How is mechanical energy provided to the generator so it can power a light?

**72    Chapter 2** Magnetism

---

### Program Resources

**Study Guide,** p. 14
**Making Connections: Across the Curriculum,** p. 7, Audio Magnetic Tape L2
**Making Connections: Technology and Society,** p. 7, DAT Recorder L2
**Transparency Master,** p. 11, and **Color Transparency,** Number 4, Electric Motor—DC Generator L2

### Meeting Individual Needs

**Visually Impaired** During the Find Out activity, have visually impaired students move the magnet inside the coil while other students observe the galvanometer and describe what they see.

# Changing Currents

Power companies use transformers to ensure the proper voltage for the circuits of lights, home appliances, and other electric equipment in your home. Transformers also enable power companies to transmit alternating current to their users easily and efficiently. A **transformer** can raise or lower the voltage. Look at **Figure 2-17** below.

### Step-up Transformer

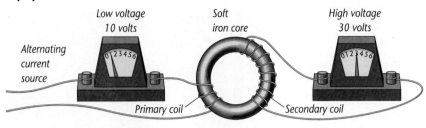

Low voltage 10 volts    Soft iron core    High voltage 30 volts

Alternating current source    Primary coil    Secondary coil

### Step-Down Transformer

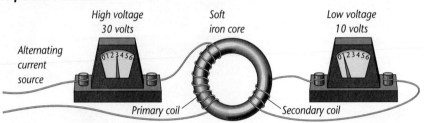

High voltage 30 volts    Soft iron core    Low voltage 10 volts

Alternating current source    Primary coil    Secondary coil

**Figure 2-17**

When an alternating current passes through the primary coil of a step-up or step-down transformer, a magnetic field is created, inducing a current to flow in the secondary coil. What determines the exact voltage increase or decrease in these transformers?

Step-up transformers raise the voltage to a level that allows the electrical energy to travel long distances with little loss. When the energy reaches the area where it will be used, step-down transformers there lower the voltage to the level needed. Like generators, transformers work by inducing currents.

In this section, you've learned that an induced current results when a magnetic field is changed in a coil. The field can be changed by moving either the magnet or the coil. Electric generators induce current by rotating a coil in a magnetic field. You're unlikely to own a generator, but you probably use electricity from one daily.

---

### check your UNDERSTANDING

1. Describe three ways in which a current can be induced in a circuit.
2. How is a generator like a motor? How is it different?

3. **Apply** Generators are used in some electric cars to transform energy from braking to electricity to recharge the car's batteries. Describe how this might work.

---

### check your UNDERSTANDING

1. Move a wire coil in a magnetic field, move a magnet through a coil, or somehow change the magnetic field around the coil.
2. Both contain coils and magnetic fields. In both cases, the coil rotates. A generator and a motor perform opposite tasks. A motor uses current to produce motion; a generator uses motion to produce current.

3. As the car brakes, the car wheel moves a magnet or a coil inside a generator. Current flows through a wire to car's batteries.

---

# Science and Society

# EXPAND
## your view

## Science and Society

**Purpose** This Science and Society reinforces Sections 2-2 and 2-3 by describing a health care application of electromagnetism. It also focuses on the theme of systems and interactions by explaining how body tissue responds in the presence of the strong magnetic field created by MRI machines.

### Content Background

MRI machines are commonly used to detect brain tumors, spinal column disorders, and multiple sclerosis. Although the usefulness of the machines is uncontested, many people say that the test is overused in the United States. A 1989 American Medical Association study found that the United States had four times as many MRI machines per capita as Germany and eight times as many as Canada.

### Teaching Strategy

Have students recall the advantages and drawbacks of MRI technology. List them on the chalkboard under the headings, "Pros and Cons." Ask students if knowing more of the facts changes the opinion they wrote about in their personal essay. **L2**

### Answers to

**You Try It!**

Sources of funds and maintenance costs will vary. An MRI machine costs $1.2 million to $2.5 million to purchase. In 1990, an estimated 5 million MRI scans were performed in the United States at prices of $600 to $1000 each.

## High-Tech Health Care

Several new technologies allow doctors to produce images of what is inside the human body without using X rays. One of the most common is called Magnetic Resonance Imaging (MRI). The machine consists of a large coil that creates a strong magnetic field. MRI works because the positively charged particles at the center of each atom making up the body act like tiny bar magnets. These bar magnets aren't usually lined up in any orderly fashion, but when put in a strong magnetic field, the magnets line up like soldiers on parade.

An electromagnetic wave is created in the region of the organ being studied. If the wave has exactly the correct frequency, it can cause the tiny magnets to flip over. The flipping requires energy—the more magnets flipped, the more energy required.

**CAREER connection**

**MRI technicians** must be able to operate imaging equipment. They also need to use probes to measure the magnetic field strength. A period of specialized training is required. MRI technicians work in hospitals and medical schools.

### Medical Uses

The frequency needed to flip the magnets depends on the tissue in which they are located. Therefore, as the frequency of the wave is varied, first one type of tissue absorbs energy, then another type. A computer creates a three-dimensional image based on energy absorption patterns.

Being able to distinguish between diseased and normal tissue while it is still inside a patient's body, without surgery, is a great breakthrough. With MRI, doctors can watch the swelling caused by arthritis shrink when medicine is applied to a swollen knee.

### Going Further ⫸

Have students reread the two questions immediately preceding You Try It. Tell students to write answers to these questions, in the form of a newspaper editorial or personal essay. Post students' writings on a bulletin board titled *What Do You Think?* **P**

Students might also debate the topic: Resolved: MRI machines should be limited to only a few hospitals. Divide students in affirmative and negative teams of four. Give each team time to prepare before debating. Remind teams to think of arguments that the opposing team may offer and possible counterarguments, or rebuttals. **COOP LEARN**

### Operating Costs

As wonderful as these advances in medical science are, they do not come cheaply. An MRI machine is very expensive and hard to maintain. The machine must be shielded from magnetic materials in the surrounding area. Even a lawn mower being run outside the hospital could affect test results. The powerful magnets could also affect other equipment in the hospital, causing it to malfunction. The cost of running MRI machinery is also high. To supply and operate a machine costs about $100,000 a year.

Some people say hospitals shouldn't purchase costly equipment because such purchases make the bill for ordinary medical care much higher than it should be. They think MRI machines should be limited to only a few hospitals. What do you think? Would your opinion change if someone in your family needed to be diagnosed with MRI?

#### *You Try It!*

Call or visit a hospital in your area that offers MRI services. Find out how much the machine cost to purchase and how much it costs to maintain. Inquire about the source of the funds for these expenses.

---

**HISTORY CONNNECTION**

# Granville T. Woods

The communications industry owes much to Granville T. Woods. In 1881, the young African-American inventor used one of the most important applications of electromagnets in recent history to design a new telephone microphone. It produced a much more distinct sound and was able to carry a voice over much greater distances than other microphones because he made use of an electromagnet. To produce the current, Woods used a thin metal disk that vibrated back and forth in response to the sound waves. When the disk moves one way, it presses against a box filled with tiny grains of carbon, a conductor. When it bends the other way, the grains no longer touch, and electrical resistance is high. This bending back and forth produces an alternating current that is sent to a telephone receiver.

As the current changes direction,  it operates a loudspeaker in the receiver. The use of the electromagnet was important because it made the metal disk in the receiver vibrate at the same frequency as the metal disk in the transmitter, thus producing amazing clarity of sound.

#### *You Try It!*

Compare and contrast Woods' telephone transmitter with a modern one. How are they similar? How are they different?

### Going Further ⫸

Arrange to have a local telephone company representative visit and explain how telephone systems work. Before the visit, have students brainstorm lists of questions they would like to have answered about telecommunications.

---

**HISTORY CONNNECTION**

### Purpose

History Connection extends Sections 2-2 and 2-3, in which students learn about electromagnets and magnetic fields.

### Content Background

Granville T. Woods had a successful career as an inventor. He held more than 150 patents dealing with communications and energy. In addition to inventions that improved the telephone, Woods also made improvements in telegraphs. One important improvement increased railroad safety because it made possible communication between stations and moving trains. Some of Woods' other inventions included a device to dim the lights in a theater, an egg incubator, and the third rail system of supplying electric power to trains. This system is still in use in many large cities, such as New York and Chicago.

### Teaching Strategy
Obtain a handset from an out-of-use telephone and take it apart so that students may see how it is constructed. L2

### Answers to
You Try It!

The principle behind the telephone receiver has not changed. Modern materials have expanded the range of sounds that can be transmitted, and have improved the clarity of sounds heard over the telephone.

# HOW IT
## WORKS

### Purpose

How It Works reinforces and extends Section 2-3 by showing an application of electromagnetic fields. This excursion also focuses on energy by explaining how the electrical energy from a stream of particles is changed to light on a television screen.

### Content Background

A rectifier in a TV set changes alternating current, which comes from the power company, to the direct current on which televisions operate. Signals transmitted from a broadcast aerial are separated in a television into picture and sound signals. The picture signal is amplified before going to the picture tube, whose operation is described in the student text. The sound signal is amplified and moved to the loudspeaker. Students can explain what happens next by recalling what they learned about loudspeakers in Section 2-3 (page 67).

### Teaching Strategies

Copy the illustration and the captions at the top of page 76 on the chalkboard. Then, go through this feature having students identify each component discussed and its function. L2

### Research

Have students use an encyclopedia to find out more about how color television reproduces a wide range of colors using images of only red, green, and blue.

### Answers to
### You Try It!

You may wish to suggest that students consult *The Encyclopedia of Science and Technology,* 6th Edition (McGraw-Hill, 1987, vol. 4) to find out how closed-circuit TV works.

# HOW IT
## WORKS
# Television Picture Tube

**S**uppose you are watching an exciting movie on TV. When you see the action, you wonder how your favorite actors appear on your television screen. Part of the answer lies in the magnetic and electric fields produced in the picture tube of your set.

Look at the illustration. At one end of the picture tube is the rectangular glass screen where you can watch the movie. Inside the television set, video or picture signals are received. These signals are sent through the air on radio waves from the broadcasting station.

A wire in the tube heats up when you turn on your TV. The heated wire sends a stream of charged particles toward the screen. The television screen is coated with a fluorescent material that absorbs electrical energy from the stream of particles. It changes the electrical energy to light. The more charged particles that hit a spot, the brighter the light. In this way, a picture of what is happening at a distance is "painted" on your screen with varying colors and intensities.

When your TV is tuned in, the signals from the TV station are processed in the TV set, and vary the stream of particles. The

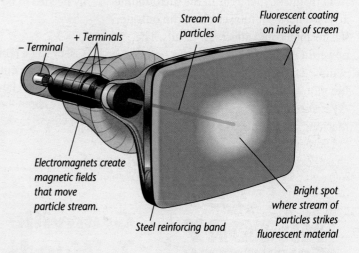

Stream of particles

Fluorescent coating on inside of screen

− Terminal

+ Terminals

Electromagnets create magnetic fields that move particle stream.

Steel reinforcing band

Bright spot where stream of particles strikes fluorescent material

number of particles then corresponds to the picture that is being broadcast.

The particles are moved across the television screen by two varying magnetic fields. One field moves the stream of particles up and down. The other field moves the stream left and right. This movement allows the stream of charged particles to sweep across the entire screen. In one-thirtieth of a second, a total of 535 lines of light resulting from the particles cover the glass tube. A full, smoothly moving picture results.

### *You Try It!*

Closed-circuit television lets you watch what is happening in another part of the building. Find out how this works. From what you have learned about television, write an article that explains how closed-circuit TV works at your school or in a building lobby.

### Going Further ⅢⅢⅢ▶

Students can work in small groups to find out how electrical equipment uses electromagnetic waves. Assign each group a device such as a radio receiver, TV camera, or video recorder. Tell groups to make a poster illustrating how their device works. Have groups present their completed posters to the class.

Students can use the drawing at the top of page 76 in the excursion as a model. To find out about the electrical device assigned to their group, students may wish to consult *The Way Things Work,* by David Macaulay (Houghton Mifflin, 1988). **COOP LEARN**

**R**eview the statements below about the big ideas presented in this chapter, and try to answer the questions. Then, reread your answers to the Did You Ever Wonder questions at the beginning of the chapter. *In your Journal*, write a paragraph about how your understanding of the big ideas in the chapter has changed.

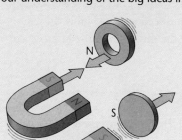

**1** Magnets have two poles, the places where the magnetic field is strongest. Like poles repel each other; unlike poles attract each other. *How could you locate the poles on an unusually shaped magnet?*

**2** Atoms themselves have tiny magnetic fields. In an unmagnetized substance, the atomic magnets point in random directions, but in a magnetized substance, they line up. *How can you make groups of atomic magnets line up?*

**3** A magnetic field is a region where magnetic forces act. *How could you identify the shape of a magnetic field around an object?*

**4** An electric current creates a magnetic field, making electromagnets and electric motors possible. *Why do electric motors turn?*

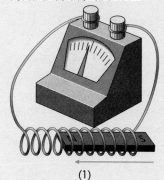 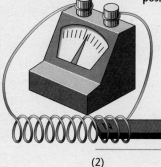

(1)                    (2)

**5** In an electric generator, a changing magnetic field induces an electric current. Transformers step up or step down a voltage. *How is the magnetic field changed in a generator?*

---

## ★ Project

Have students work in small groups to invent a device that uses an electric motor. Students can present their invention by making a poster diagram of the device. Display completed posters on a bulletin board entitled *Vroom!* Use the Performance Task Assessment List for Group Work in **PAMSS**, p. 97. **L2** **COOP LEARN** **P**

## 🏠 Science at Home

Have students make a list of where magnets are used in their homes. Tell students to add to their lists as they review this chapter and learn about magnets that are "hidden" in numerous devices and appliances. Students should add brief explanations of how each magnet is used. **L1**

---

Have students study and discuss the illustrations and text on this page.

### Teaching Strategies

Divide the class into small groups to write summaries. Have a member of each group flip a coin. Groups who get "heads" are to review those activities that helped them understand how an electric current creates a magnetic field. Groups who get "tails" are to review how a changing magnetic field induces an electric current. Reports can include summaries of activities, cause-and-effect diagrams, and events chains. **L2** **COOP LEARN** **P**

### Answers to Questions

**1.** Use a magnet with known poles and experiment to find out which parts of the unusually shaped magnet attract and repel the known magnet.

**2.** Draw the piece of non-magnetized metal through a magnetic field repeatedly, or put the non-magnetized metal in a strong magnetic field.

**3.** Observe how the field affects iron filings, or use a compass to find field lines.

**4.** The motor's coil is an electromagnet. The direction of current in the motor's coil changes direction as the motor turns. So, the coil is alternately attracted and repelled by the other magnets in the motor.

**5.** Either the coil or the magnet in a generator moves. This exposes the coil to different parts of the magnetic field. So, the wire passes through a varying magnetic field.

 **MINDJOGGER VIDEOQUIZ**

**Chapter 2** Have students work in groups as they play the videoquiz game to review key chapter concepts.

chapter 2
CHAPTER REVIEW

## Using Key Science Terms

**1.** A magnetic field is the region around a magnet where the magnetic force acts. Magnetic poles are the regions on a magnet where the magnetic field is strongest; they are also the parts of a magnet that point north and south.

**2.** A permanent magnet can retain its magnetism for a long time. An electromagnet is temporary and made with current-carrying wire.

**3.** Induced current is the current produced in a conductor by a changing magnetic field. Induced magnetism is magnetism that occurs only in the presence of an outside magnetic field.

**4.** An electric generator changes mechanical energy into electric energy. An electric motor changes electrical energy into mechanical energy.

## Understanding Ideas

**1.** Observe the patterns that iron filings form when sprinkled around the magnet, or observe how a compass or small magnet reacts to the magnet.

**2.** Electric current

**3.** Current is induced in the coil.

**4.** A transformer

**5.** It changes variations in electric current into sound.

**6.** Aluminum, nickel, and cobalt

**7.** It reverses the current to the electromagnet's coil so that the armature continues to rotate.

**8.** 1) pass the magnet through faster, 2) use a stronger magnet, 3) add loops to the coil. You could change the initial current direction by reversing the poles of the magnet.

## Developing Skills

**1.** The larger electromagnet has twice as many coils and twice as much current flowing through it. Therefore, it should pick up approximately $2 \times 2$, or four times as many paper clips.

### Using Key Science Terms

electric generator
electric motor
electromagnet
induced current
induced magnetism

loudspeaker
magnetic field
magnetic poles
transformer

*Distinguish between the terms in each of the following pairs.*

**1.** magnetic field, magnetic poles
**2.** permanent magnet, electromagnet
**3.** induced current, induced magnetism
**4.** electric generator, electric motor

### Understanding Ideas

*Answer the following questions in your Journal using complete sentences.*

**1.** What is one method of revealing a magnet's field?
**2.** What does a galvanometer detect?
**3.** What happens when a coil of wire cuts through a magnetic field?
**4.** What device is used to raise or lower voltage?
**5.** What does a loudspeaker do?
**6.** Name the three elements from which most magnets are made.

**2.** Wire with current flowing toward you produces a field counterclockwise around the wire, and wire with current flowing away from you produces a clockwise field.

**3.** The magnetic field lines form closed loops, which is characteristic of magnetic field lines.

**4.** Wind turns the windmill. The windmill turns a magnet or coil of wire in a generator. The generator produces AC power.

**7.** What is the purpose of the commutator in an electric motor?

**8.** You can induce a current in a coil by passing a magnet through the coil. What are three ways of increasing the strength of the induced current? How can you change the direction of the induced current?

### Developing Skills

*Use your understanding of the concepts developed in this chapter to answer each of the following questions.*

**1. Predicting** Refer to Investigate 2-1 on pages 60-61. Suppose you had made a magnet with 4 batteries and 60 turns of wire. Compare the number of paper clips this magnet would pick up to the number picked up by a magnet with 2 batteries and 30 turns of wire.

**2. Interpreting Scientific Illustrations** Refer to the illustration accompanying the Skillbuilder on page 64. Use this illustration to describe the magnetic field produced by 1) a wire carrying current toward you, and 2) a wire carrying current away from you.

**3. Observing and Inferring** Look at the magnetic field lines in Figure 2-8 and in the illustration accompanying the Skillbuilder on page 64. What is similar about the field lines in the two pictures?

**4. Recognizing Cause and Effect** Using the principles you've learned in this chapter, describe how a windmill-driven generator works.

### Program Resources

**Review and Assessment,** pp. 11–16 L1
**Performance Assessment,** Ch. 2 L2
**PAMSS**
**Alternate Assessment in the Science Classroom**
**Computer Test Bank**

## Critical Thinking

*Use your understanding of the concepts developed in the chapter to answer each of the following questions.*

1. If a coil of wire were placed between these magnets, and a current passed through the wire, would the coil move? Explain.

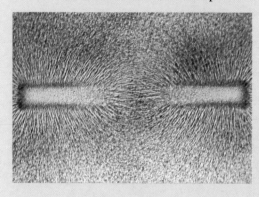

2. Is the magnetic pole in Earth's northern hemisphere like the north or south pole of a bar magnet? How do you know?

3. Explain how you could use Earth's magnetic field to help you magnetize a piece of iron.

4. Why will a magnet attract a nail to either of its poles but attract another magnet to only one of its poles?

5. What would you expect the current to be in a wire coil wrapped around a horseshoe magnet? Explain your answer.

## Problem Solving

*Read the following problem and discuss your answer in a brief paragraph.*

**Abdul has a small motor that requires 12 V of electricity. He is building a transformer to change the 120 V from the wall outlet to 12 V. If the input coil has 800 turns, how many turns will the output coil have?**

---

## CONNECTING IDEAS

Discuss each of the following in a brief paragraph.

1. **Scale and Structure** How are magnetic poles like electric charges? How are they different?

2. **Systems and Interactions** A wire carrying an electric current has a magnetic field, but a metal sphere that has a static electric charge doesn't produce a magnetic field. What do these facts suggest about the relationship between magnetism and electricity?

3. **A Closer Look** How would you build a transformer to change 12 V power to 60 V? What type of transformer is this?

4. **Earth Science Connection** How are the Van Allen radiation belts produced?

5. **Science and Society** Describe the role of the electromagnet in an MRI machine. How does this magnet allow doctors to see different body tissues?

---

## ✔ Assessment

**Portfolio** Review the portfolio options that are provided throughout the chapter. Encourage students to select one product that demonstrates their best work for the chapter. Have students explain what they learned and why they chose this example for placement into their portfolios.

Additional portfolio options can be found in the following **Teacher Classroom Resources:**

**Making Connections: Integrating Sciences,** p. 7

**Multicultural Connections,** pp. 7, 8
**Making Connections: Across the Curriculum,** p. 7
**Making Connections: Technology and Society,** p. 7
**Concept Mapping,** p. 10
**Critical Thinking/Problem Solving,** pp. 8, 10
**Take Home Activities,** p. 7
**Activity Masters,** pp. 9–10; 11–12
**Laboratory Manual,** pp. 5–9
**Performance Assessment** P

### chapter 2
## CHAPTER REVIEW

### Critical Thinking

1. The filings reveal two unlike poles facing each other. The coil would align with the magnetic field and stop.

2. It is like a south pole; it attracts the north end of a compass needle.

3. Hold the piece of iron parallel to Earth's magnetic field and strike it with a hammer. The blows disturb the iron's magnetic domains and they realign with Earth's magnetic field, producing a weak magnet.

4. The nail is made of magnetic material but is not a magnet. Domains in the nail are oriented in many directions. Therefore, it has no fixed poles. Most domains will align with a strong magnetic field. So, the nail can be attracted to either pole of the magnet. Only unlike poles attract each other.

5. Zero. The magnetic field isn't changing.

### Problem Solving
About 87 turns.

### Connecting Ideas

1. Poles are like charges in that like poles repel each other; and unlike poles attract each other. Poles differ from charges in that one pole never exists without its opposite.

2. A magnetic field is produced by moving electric charges. Static charges do not produce a magnetic field.

3. Have five times as many turns on secondary as on primary. Step-up transformer.

4. Charged particles are trapped in Earth's magnetic field.

5. A strong electromagnet causes charged particles in the body's atoms to act like bar magnets and line up. Different tissues respond differently to the electromagnetic waves generated. The signals produced are analyzed and turned into three-dimensional images.

# Chapter Organizer

| SECTION | OBJECTIVES | ACTIVITIES |
|---|---|---|
| **Chapter Opener** | | **Explore!** Do electrical appliances create disturbances? p. 81 |
| **3-1 The Electromagnetic Spectrum** (3 days) | 1. **Describe** the nature of electromagnetic waves. <br> 2. **Compare and contrast** the characteristics of waves in various parts of the electromagnetic spectrum. <br> 3. **Recognize** the uses of energy carried by electromagnetic waves. | **Find Out!** How do frequencies of electromagnetic waves compare? p. 85 <br> **Investigate 3-1:** Infrared Radiation, pp. 88–89 <br> **Skillbuilder:** Forming Hypothesis, p. 90 |
| **3-2 The Wave Model of Light** (5 days) | 1. **Explain** how diffraction through thin slits supports a wave model of light. <br> 2. **Describe** how various observations on color and light can be explained by the wave model. | **Find Out!** How is a light beam changed when it passes through a thin slit? p. 91 <br> **Skillbuilder:** Forming a Hypothesis, p. 92 <br> **Explore!** What colors are made by soap bubbles? p. 93 <br> **Explore!** Can you make rainbows in a CD? p. 95 <br> **Investigate 3-2:** Double-Slit Diffraction, pp. 96–97 <br> **Explore!** Can you see a difference in light sources? p. 99 |

## EXPAND *your view*

**Life Science Connection** Sunscreens, pp. 86–87
**A Closer Look** Long-Distance Detectives, pp. 98–99
**Science and Society** How Roomy is the Spectrum? p. 101

**Health Connection** Ultraviolet and X rays, p. 102
**How It Works** Detecting Weapons with X rays, p. 103

## ACTIVITY MATERIALS

| EXPLORE! | INVESTIGATE! | FIND OUT! |
|---|---|---|
| **Page 81** <br> small, battery-powered AM radio; several household appliances <br> **Page 93*** <br> equipment to make large soap bubbles, soap solution, cookie sheet <br> **Page 95** <br> compact disc, lamp | **Pages 88–89*** <br> 3 metal cans of equal size: one black, one white, one shiny or wrapped in aluminum foil; water, 3 thermometers, clock or stopwatch, heat lamp, graph paper <br> **Pages 96–97*** <br> 2 strips of shelf or butcher paper, each about 30 cm wide by 2 m long, scissors, masking tape | **Page 85*** <br> no special materials are required <br> **Page 91*** <br> index card, straight filament lamp, red filter, blue filter |

*For adequate development of the concepts presented, we recommend that students do the activities with an asterisk.

# Chapter 3 Electromagnetic Waves

## TEACHER CLASSROOM RESOURCES

| Student Masters | Teaching Aids |
|---|---|
| **Study Guide**, p. 15<br>**Concept Mapping**, p. 11<br>**Take Home Activities**, p. 8<br>**Making Connections: Technology & Society**, p. 9<br>**Critical Thinking/Problem Solving**, p. 11<br>**Flex Your Brain**, p. 5<br>**Multicultural Connections**, pp. 9, 10<br>**How It Works**, p. 7<br>**Science Discovery Activities**, 3-1 | **Laboratory Manual**, pp. 9–12, Investigating Invisible Waves<br>**Laboratory Manual**, pp. 13–16, Light Intensity<br>**Color Transparency and Master 5**, Electromagnetic Spectrum<br>**\*STVS:** *Images of Heat,* Physics (Disc 1, Side 1) |
| **Study Guide**, p. 16<br>**Making Connections: Integrating Sciences**, p. 9<br>**Making Connections: Across the Curriculum**, p. 9<br>**Science Discovery Activities**, 3-2, 3-3 | **Color Transparency and Master 6**, Thin Film Reflection<br>**\*STVS:** *Ultraviolet Laser,* Physics (Disc 1, Side 1) |

| ASSESSMENT RESOURCES | |
|---|---|
| **Review and Assessment**, pp. 17–22<br>**Performance Assessment**, Ch. 3<br>**PAMSS\***<br>**MindJogger Videoquiz**<br>**Alternate Assessment in the Science Classroom**<br>**Computer Test Bank** | **Spanish Resources**<br>**Cooperative Learning Resource Guide**<br>**Lab and Safety Skills**<br>**Integrated Science Videodisc** |

## KEY TO TEACHING STRATEGIES

The following designations will help you decide which activities are appropriate for your students.

**L1** Level 1 activities should be within the ability range of all students.

**L2** Level 2 activities should be within the ability range of the average to above-average student.

**L3** Level 3 activities are designed for the ability range of above-average students.

**LEP** LEP activities should be within the ability range of Limited English Proficiency students.

**COOP LEARN** Cooperative Learning activities are designed for small group work.

**P** These strategies represent student products that can be placed into a best-work portfolio.

## ADDITIONAL MATERIALS

**Software**
*Investigating Models of Light,* IBM.
*Investigating Wave Interference,* IBM.
*Light,* Queue.
*Light Waves,* EME.
*Waves,* J&S Software.
*Waves,* Sunburst.

**Audiovisual**
*Exploring Light and Color,* video, United Learning.
*Light and the Electromagnetic Spectrum,* video, Coronet/MTI.
*Radiation,* video, Hawkhill Science.
*The Story of Radiation,* video, Hawkhill Science.

**Laserdisc**
*The Living Textbook, Principles of Physical Science,* Optical Data Corp.
*Physics at Work,* Videodiscovery.

**Readings**
Oxlade, Chris, et al., *The Usborne Illustrated Dictionary of Physics.* Great Britain: Usborne Publishing.

*Performance Assessment in Middle School Science

*Science and Technology Videodisc Series

# Electromagnetic Waves

## THEME DEVELOPMENT

The themes that this chapter supports are energy, and scale and structure. Waves are rhythmic disturbances that carry energy. They can be described in terms of characteristics such as frequency or wavelength. Waves can also be described on a larger scale, in terms of the effects they have on matter.

## CHAPTER OVERVIEW

In this chapter, students will study the nature and characteristics of electromagnetic waves. Students will compare and contrast waves in various parts of the electromagnetic spectrum and explore everyday uses of electromagnetic energy. Finally, students will study the properties of visible light that have led scientists to classify light as an electromagnetic wave.

### Tying to Previous Knowledge

Have students recall types of energy and how each is used. Emphasize that electromagnetic waves carry energy. Have students list as many ways to use this energy as they can think of. Examples include lighting a home, cooking food in a microwave oven, operating a solar-powered calculator, taking X rays of bones, operating a radio or television.

## INTRODUCING THE CHAPTER

Have students look at the photograph on pages 80 and 81. Ask them to describe what they see. Tell students that the light they see and the warmth of the sun they would feel are just two of the kinds of waves they will study in this chapter.

# ELECTROMAGNETIC waves

### Did you ever wonder...

✓ How walkie talkies send signals through the air?

✓ Why people in warm climates wear white clothing?

✓ Why you see colors on a black oil slick in the street?

Before you begin to study about electromagnetic waves, think about these questions and answer them *in your Journal.* When you finish the chapter, compare your Journal write-up with what you have learned.

**W**aves carrying energy surround you every day. Some waves can be seen, the presence of others felt, but most can't be observed directly with your senses.

Have you ever listened to music on a portable radio, warmed your hands in front of a fire, or had your teeth checked for cavities at a dentist's office? You've heard about radio waves, microwaves, and X rays. But what are they? Are they very different, or related in some way?

▶ **This chapter will help you find answers to these questions. In the activity on the next page, explore one of the characteristics of electromagnetic waves.**

80

### Did you ever wonder...

• Walkie talkies send signals using electromagnetic waves that travel through space. (p. 86)

• White reflects light and, therefore, less heat is absorbed from the sun, (pp. 88–89)

• Light reflected from the two surfaces of a thin film produces a rainbow effect. (p. 94)

### STUDENT JOURNAL

Have students write their responses to the Did You Ever Wonder questions in their journals. After they have read the chapter, students should read their journal entries again to see what they have learned about electromagnetic waves.

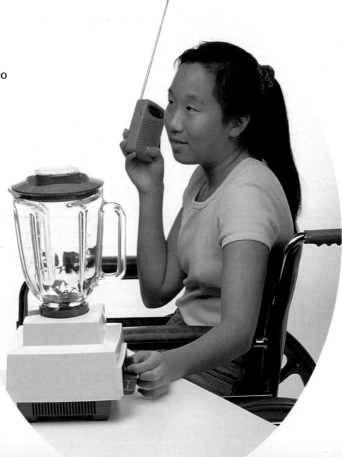

# Explore! ACTIVITY

## Do electrical appliances create disturbances?

### What To Do

1. Tune a small, battery-powered AM radio between two stations so that you hear only noise.

2. Carry the radio around your house. Listen closely to the noise coming from the radio as you turn on and off a lamp, the television or vacuum cleaner, or a fluorescent light. Use any electrical appliances that are handy.

3. In Chapter 1, you learned that these appliances depend on moving electrical charges or the effects of magnetic fields. *In your Journal*, explain how you think electricity or magnetism is related to what you heard on the radio.

81

## Uncovering Preconceptions

Students may confuse sound waves with radio waves. Explain that sound waves require a medium such as air to transfer energy. Radio waves can travel without a medium such as air.

# Explore!

## Do electrical appliances create disturbances?

**Time needed** 10 minutes

**Materials** portable radio and several household appliances

**Thinking Processes** observe and inferring

**Purpose** To relate electrical charges and magnetic fields, in preparation for learning about electromagnetic waves.

### Teaching the Activity

**Troubleshooting** Bring a portable radio to class and allow students who do not have access to one at home to perform the activity in class.

**Student Journal** Have students draw their explanations in their journals. L1

### Expected Outcome
Students will conclude that some electrical effect from the appliances interfered with radio reception.

### Answer to Question
Students should conclude that moving electric charges or magnetic fields are affecting the radio.

### ✔ Assessment

**Process** Arrange students in cooperative learning groups to compare their observations from this activity. Students can create cartoons showing the interference in radio reception. Use the Performance Task Assessment List for Cartoon/Comic Book in **PAMSS**, p. 61. L1 **COOP LEARN** P

## PREPARATION

### Concepts Developed

Electromagnetic radiation is energy emitted by vibrating electric charges. Electromagnetic waves are composed of an electric field and a magnetic field oscillating at right angles to each other. This section describes the characteristics of electromagnetic waves and explains how energy is carried by such waves.

### Planning the Lesson

Refer to the Chapter Organizer on pages 80A–B.

## 1 MOTIVATE

**Activity** Guide students to model various waves. First have the class make a wave like those that spectators make at ball games. Then have students join hands in a circle and move their arms so that the wave goes around the circle. Emphasize that in each instance there is a certain rhythm to the wave. Experiment with how many ways you can change the appearance of the wave to simulate changes in wavelength, frequency, amplitude, and speed. L1 LEP

## 2 TEACH

### Tying to Previous Knowledge

Ask students whether they have ever made waves in a swimming pool. Ask what they had to do to make a wave. *A person must move his or her hands or body to put energy into the water.*

---

### Section Objectives

■ Describe the nature of electromagnetic waves.
■ Compare and contrast the characteristics of waves in various parts of the electromagnetic spectrum.
■ Recognize the uses of energy carried by electromagnetic waves.

### Key Terms

electromagnetic wave
electromagnetic spectrum
radiation

---

# The Electromagnetic Spectrum

## What's an Electromagnetic Wave?

In Chapter 1, you learned that an electric charge exerts a force on other electric charges. The charge produces an electric field, a region around the charge in which the electric force acts. From your observations and what you learned in Chapters 1 and 2, you can see that there may be a connection between electric and magnetic fields.

When you made an electromagnet, you used an electric current to produce a magnetic field. You also learned that magnetic fields exert a force on moving electric charges.

**Figure 3-1** shows how an oscillating electric charge makes a combination of electric and magnetic fields called an **electromagnetic wave**.

**Figure 3-1**

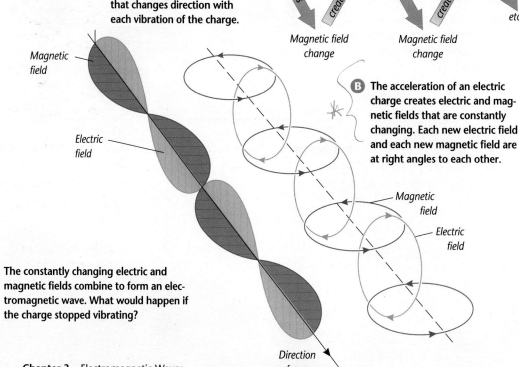

Ⓐ A vibrating electric charge produces an electric field. The electric field, in turn, produces a magnetic field that changes direction with each vibration of the charge.

Ⓑ The acceleration of an electric charge creates electric and magnetic fields that are constantly changing. Each new electric field and each new magnetic field are at right angles to each other.

Ⓒ The constantly changing electric and magnetic fields combine to form an electromagnetic wave. What would happen if the charge stopped vibrating?

**82** Chapter 3 Electromagnetic Waves

---

## Program Resources

**Study Guide,** p. 15
**Concept Mapping,** p. 11, Waves L1
**Take Home Activities,** p. 8, Visible Light Effects L1
**Making Connections: Technology & Society,** p. 9, Food Irradiation L2

## Meeting Individual Needs

**Limited English Proficiency** Invite students to make models. Give pairs of students a piece of string about two feet long. Instruct them to form the string into the shape of transverse waves. Count the number of waves and measure the average wavelength. Now change the waves so they have a greater wavelength. Change them again so they have a shorter wavelength. LEP

---

# Characteristics of Electromagnetic Waves

In the opening Explore activity with the portable radio, you detected electromagnetic waves coming from a variety of appliances as you changed the electrical and magnetic fields in the appliances. More elaborate experiments show that electromagnetic waves have properties of transverse waves and do not need a medium through which to travel. **Figure 3-2** below contrasts transverse and longitudinal waves.

**Figure 3-2**

**A** Moving the ribbon end creates a transverse wave, the type of wave in which the motion of the wave disturbance is at right angles to the direction the wave is traveling. Electromagnetic waves are transverse waves resembling this one, but with one difference—electromagnetic waves require no medium through which to travel.

Direction of wave

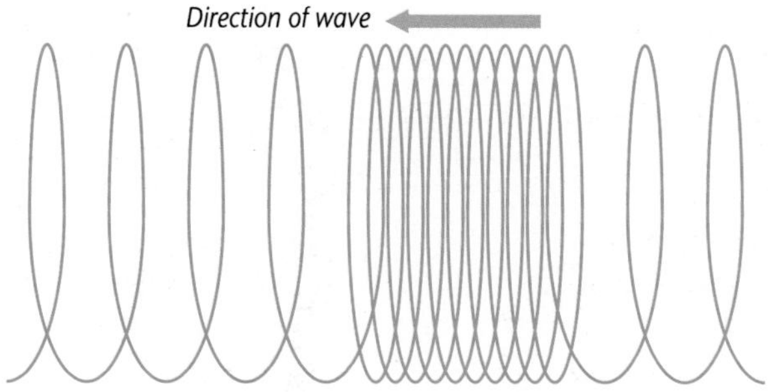

**B** This spiral spring illustrates a longitudinal wave. The area of compressed coils, or wave disturbance, travels in the same direction as the wave. Sound waves are longitudinal waves and require a medium through which to travel.

3-1 The Electromagnetic Spectrum **83**

**Visual Learning**

**Figure 3-1** Have students identify the cause and effect shown in Figure 3-1. *Cause: acceleration of an electric charge, Effect: formation of electromagnetic wave.* Then pose the question in the third caption. **What would happen if the charge stopped vibrating?** *The interacting electric and magnetic fields, and hence, the electromagnetic wave, would disappear.*

**Figure 3-2** Have students compare and contrast transverse and longitudinal waves. *Student responses should include the motions of wave disturbance and the necessity of a medium for a longitudinal wave.*

**Demonstration** Allow students to observe how a wave moves outward from its source.

You will need a wide pan, water, a table tennis ball and a small rock.

Place a table tennis ball in a wide pan of water about halfway between the center of the pan and the edge. When the water is still, drop a rock into the pan. The wave moves, but the ball remains in the same place. The energy generated by the falling rock moves in waves. The ball rises and falls as the waves pass. L1

**Activity** To reinforce comprehension of the major features of a transverse wave, let students make models that demonstrate how amplitude, wavelength, and frequency can be varied by making waves on a long (3m) rope, one end of which is tied to a fixed object such as a doorknob. Students move the free end to produce waves. The waves made with the rope can be described by their characteristics. When the rope is snapped up and down, high points and low points are formed. The highest points of a wave are the crests, and the lowest points are the troughs. L1

Like all waves, electromagnetic waves can be described by their frequency, their wavelength, and speed as **Figure 3-3** shows.

**Figure 3-3**

Ⓐ Every time the source of an electromagnetic wave vibrates, it creates one wave that moves away from the source at the speed of light, 300 million meters per second.

Ⓑ The distance from a point on one wave to the same point on the next wave is called the wavelength.

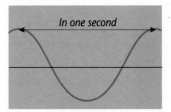
Low-frequency
In one second

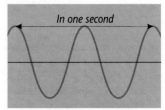
High-frequency
In one second

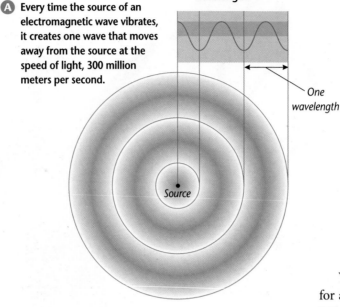
Source
One wavelength

Ⓒ The more times per second an electric charge vibrates, the higher the frequency of the resulting electromagnetic wave. Because an electromagnetic wave moves out at a constant speed, its wavelength is inversely proportional to its frequency. If the frequency of a wave increases, does its wavelength get longer or shorter?

We can figure out the relationship between these three by using the units in which each is measured. Speed is distance divided by time—meters/second. Wavelength is the length, in meters, of one wave. We could express this as meters/wave. Finally, frequency is in hertz, or the number of waves per second. What mathematical relationship can we uncover by examining these units?

$$\frac{meters}{second} = \frac{meters}{wave} \times \frac{waves}{second}$$

$$speed = wavelength \times frequency$$

You can then solve this equation for any of the terms you wish to find. What is the frequency of an electromagnetic wave which has a wavelength of 100 m?

$$speed = wavelength \times frequency$$

Dividing both sides by wavelength, we get

$$frequency = speed/wavelength$$

The speed of light is a constant.

$$= \frac{300\ 000\ 000\ m/s}{100\ m/wave}$$

$$= 3\ 000\ 000\ \frac{waves}{second}$$

$$= 3\ 000\ 000\ Hz$$

Electromagnetic waves come in a wide range of wavelengths and frequencies. Each wavelength is useful in a different way. We've mentioned electricity, light, and radio. At the beginning of the chapter, we also talked about X rays and microwaves. Do the Find Out activity below to see how the frequencies and wavelengths of these waves compare.

### DID YOU KNOW?

The frequency of stations on your radio dial are marked in kilohertz (kHz) and megahertz (MHz). A station at 800 on the AM radio dial has a frequency of 800 kHz, or 800 000 Hz. On the FM dial, a station at 103 MHz has a frequency of 103 million hertz, 103 000 000 Hz.

## Find Out! ACTIVITY

### How do frequencies of electromagnetic waves compare?

**What To Do**

Use the equation you've just learned about to find the frequency of the electromagnetic waves listed to the right.

**Conclude and Apply**

1. Which wave has the lowest frequecy? The highest?

2. What is the relationship between wavelength and frequency?

| Wavelength vs. Frequency | | |
|---|---|---|
| Wave source | Wavelength | Frequency _Hz_ |
| AM radio | 500 m | 600,000 (.6×10⁶) |
| VHF TV | 5.0 m | 60,000,000 (.6×10⁸) |
| FM radio | 3.33 m | 9,009,009 |
| UHF TV | 1.0 m | 30,000,000 |
| Radar | 0.03 m | 10,000,000,000 |
| Visible Light | 0.000 000 5 m | 600,000,000,000,000 |
| X rays | 0.000 000 009 m | 33,333,333,333,333,333 _quad_ |

In the Find Out activity, you discovered that there is an inverse relationship between the frequency and wavelength of electromagnetic waves. In other words, as long as the speed of the wave is constant, the longer the wavelength, the lower its frequency and the shorter the wavelength, the higher its frequency.

3-1   The Electromagnetic Spectrum   **85**

---

### Find Out!

### How do frequencies of electromagnetic waves compare?

**Time needed**   15 minutes

**Thinking Process**   making and using tables, interpreting data, classifying, sequencing, comparing and contrasting

**Purpose**   To calculate the frequencies of various kinds of waves.

**Teaching the Activity**

**Demonstration**   Review the wavelength equation and make sure students understand it. Calculate the frequency for the AM radio along with students or use a hypothetical wave source and wavelength as an example.

**Student Journal**   Have students do the calculations in their journals. Allow students to exchange journals and check one another's calculations. L1 **COOP LEARN**

**Expected Outcome**

Students will conclude that the waves with the shortest wavelength have the highest frequency.

**Conclude and Apply**

1. AM radio, X rays

2. The shorter the wavelength the higher the frequency; that is, the two are inversely proportional.

### ✔ Assessment

**Performance**   Have students work in cooperative groups to do research that allows them to expand the table on page 85 to include microwaves and gamma rays. Use the Performance Task Assessment List for Data Table in **PAMSS**, p. 37. L1 **COOP LEARN**

### ENRICHMENT

**Demonstration**   Demonstrate for the class how a cellular telephone operates or invite a guest to do so. Discuss the equipment, the frequency of the transmission, and what causes interference. If possible, include information on the evolution of this technology. L2

### Program Resources

**Transparency Master,**   p. 13, and **Color Transparency** Number 5, Electromagnetic Spectrum L2

**Critical Thinking/Problem Solving,** p. 11, Microwave Television L2

**Critical Thinking/Problem Solving,** p. 5, Flex Your Brain

**How It Works,**   p. 7, Remote Control Units L3

**Flex Your Brain**   Have students use the Flex Your Brain activity to explore RADIATION. L1

**Math**

Students have learned that as wavelength increases, frequency decreases if the speed of the wave is constant. Ask them to identify the mathematical relationship between wavelength and frequency. *They are inversely proportional.*

L3

**Discussion** Remind students that electromagnetic waves all travel at the same constant speed in a given medium. Ask what characteristics can vary. *Frequencies and wavelengths can vary.* The shorter the wavelength of a wave, the higher its frequency. Electromagnetic waves are classified according to their wavelengths on the electromagnetic spectrum.

# Use of Electromagnetic Waves

In the Find Out activity you calculated frequencies for different types of waves. The entire range of electromagnetic waves, from extremely low to extremely high frequencies, is called the **electromagnetic spectrum**. Parts of the spectrum have been given names. A diagram of the electromagnetic spectrum is shown in **Figure 3-4** below.

**A** A cellular phone uses radio waves to enable people to talk to each other.

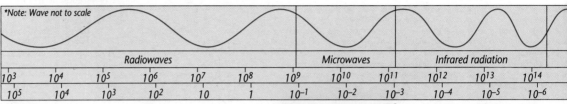

*Note: Wave not to scale

| Radiowaves | Microwaves | Infrared radiation |

| $10^3$ | $10^4$ | $10^5$ | $10^6$ | $10^7$ | $10^8$ | $10^9$ | $10^{10}$ | $10^{11}$ | $10^{12}$ | $10^{13}$ | $10^{14}$ |
| $10^5$ | $10^4$ | $10^3$ | $10^2$ | $10$ | $1$ | $10^{-1}$ | $10^{-2}$ | $10^{-3}$ | $10^{-4}$ | $10^{-5}$ | $10^{-6}$ |

**Figure 3-4**

**B** A microwave oven cooks food using microwaves.

# Life Science CONNECTION

## Sunscreens

As summer approaches, the lure of summer sports brings you outdoors. If you are health conscious, however, you apply a good sunscreen to protect yourself from the sun's radiation. The greatest danger lies in the solar radiation you cannot see—ultraviolet (UV) rays.

UV rays have wavelengths about half as long as light. A wave of 0.00000028 meters wavelength (or $280 \times 10^{-9}$ m) would be UV radiation.

In recent years, scientists have vigorously studied the effect of UV radiation. Sunscreens have been developed to block ultraviolet B (UVB). UVB is the name given to shorter-wavelength ultraviolet waves. UVB causes sunburn and can cause cancer in people with a history of sunburn. Now, scientists warn that a longer wavelength of UV—UVA—penetrates the skin even more deeply than UVB. UVA causes wrinkling and aging of the skin and increases the chances that UVB will cause skin cancer.

### ■ Protecting Yourself

Whether or not your skin is harmed by UV depends on your type of skin. Darker skin has more melanin, the pigment that protects the skin against UV. Fair skin has less melanin. Fair skin burns quickly and

**86** Chapter 3 Electromagnetic Waves

**Purpose**
This excursion expands on the information in Section 3-1 that discusses types of radiation and their applications to everyday life. The sun's radiant energy can have harmful effects.

**Content Background**
Sunburn is not as prevalent in the winter months as it is in summer because, during winter, the rays of the sun reach Earth at an oblique angle and must, therefore, pass through a greater depth of atmosphere. The exception to this is in areas of high elevation, where the atmosphere is less dense and the air is clearer than at sea level. Sunburning under these conditions is greatly accelerated.

Filtering of ultraviolet rays also occurs during the early morning and evening hours at any time of the year, making this the safest time to be outdoors.

Unlike the mechanical waves that you learned about previously, electromagnetic waves need no medium through which to travel. The energy is transferred from one point to another without matter carrying it. The transfer of energy by electromagnetic waves is called **radiation**.

The amount of energy transferred by radiation is affected by many things. The Investigate on the next pages examines some of those factors.

**C** A lamp lights up a room by radiating electromagnetic waves in the visible part of the spectrum.

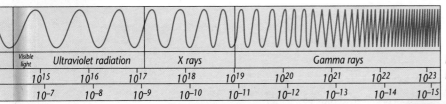

| Visible light | Ultraviolet radiation | | X rays | | Gamma rays | | | | Electromagnetic spectrum |

| $10^{15}$ | $10^{16}$ | $10^{17}$ | $10^{18}$ | $10^{19}$ | $10^{20}$ | $10^{21}$ | $10^{22}$ | $10^{23}$ | Frequency (f) in hertz |
| $10^{-7}$ | $10^{-8}$ | $10^{-9}$ | $10^{-10}$ | $10^{-11}$ | $10^{-12}$ | $10^{-13}$ | $10^{-14}$ | $10^{-15}$ | Wavelength (λ) in meters |

**D** In an infrared photograph, portions of an object that radiate at slightly different frequencies show up as different colors.

painfully, then peels. Light brown skin burns little and tans easily. Dark brown skin doesn't burn unless exposed to the sun for a long period.

To choose the right sunscreen, you have to understand how the sunscreen works and how your skin reacts to it. Think about the shortest exposure needed to cause your skin to become slightly red 24 hours later. This time varies according to skin type, geographic location, and time of the year. For example, suppose you burn after 10 minutes in the sun. If you use a sunscreen with Sun Protection Factor (SPF) 15, you could stay in the sun for 150 minutes before burning.

### You Try It!

In order to absorb UVA rays, a sunscreen must contain a chemical called Parsol 1789. Another chemical, Benzophenone-3, absorbs some UVA. PABA, an active ingredient in sunscreens, absorbs no UVA. The graph to the right compares these three chemicals. Study the sunscreens available in your area. List those containing Parsol 1789, PABA, and Benzophenone-3. Also list the SPF of the sunscreens. Which sunscreen would you buy for maximum protection?

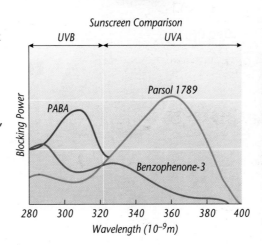

Sunscreen Comparison

UVB ← → UVA

Blocking Power

PABA

Parsol 1789

Benzophenone-3

280  300  320  340  360  380  400

Wavelength ($10^{-9}$m)

---

### Visual Learning

**Figure 3-4** Review the illustration of the electromagnetic spectrum shown in Figure 3-4. Visible radiation is the only part of the electromagnetic spectrum you can see. Point out that it covers a very small range compared to other types of radiation. Hot objects, such as the sun, radiate a great deal of electromagnetic energy. Much of this energy is in the visible range of the electromagnetic spectrum.

**Theme Connection** As students read about the electromagnetic spectrum, they should be reminded of the theme of energy. Point out that all electromagnetic waves carry energy.

**Demonstration** Allow students to observe the cooking pattern in a microwave oven. Cut several identical pieces of margarine and arrange them randomly on a large plate. Cook in five-second intervals until some pieces begin to melt. Guide students to infer that microwaves are not evenly distributed in the oven, which is why some pieces melted before others. Therefore, food must be rotated as it cooks to cook evenly. L2

**Inquiry Question** Why shouldn't you use metal containers in microwave ovens? *Metal containers would reflect the microwaves. Reflected microwaves can cause damage to the oven.*

---

Ultraviolet radiation also has its biological benefits. It enables the skin to produce vitamin D, an essential nutrient. Ultraviolet radiation is also useful in promoting healing of wounds and can kill bacteria.

### Teaching Strategy

Have students analyze why having a suntan is associated with health, wealth, and enjoyment of life. What can be done to encourage more people to protect themselves with sunscreens? L2

### Answers to
You Try It!

The one that protects against both UVA and UVB and has an SPF of 15 or higher is best for most people.

### Going Further ▌▌▌▌▶

Have the class work in small groups to gather information on how the sun's radiation causes the skin to get darker. They should answer the following questions: What is the pigment melanin? How does melanin interact with ultraviolet radiation to cause the skin to get tan? How does melanin protect the skin from burning? Use the Performance Task Assessment List for Group Work in **PAMSS**, p. 97. L2 **COOP LEARN**

## 3-1 Infrared Radiation

**Time needed** 40 minutes

**Purpose** To measure the rate at which water in different-colored containers absorbs infrared radiation.

**Process Skills** observing, forming a hypothesis, designing experiment to test your hypothesis, separating and controlling variables, interpreting data, making and using graphs

**Materials** See student activity.

**Preparation** Set up several work stations and have the class work in groups. If materials are limited, demonstrate the activity while students record data. **COOP LEARN**

### Teaching Strategies

**Discussion** Review the steps in the activity and ask students to form hypotheses concerning the solution to the problem. Record their hypotheses on the board and review them at the end of the lesson. **L1**

**Process Reinforcement** Have students brainstorm a list of data that they will need in order to make a meaningful graph. Students should note that they need temperature readings taken often enough to show all changes over time.

**Possible Hypotheses** Students may incorrectly hypothesize that the black can absorbs more infrared radiation and, therefore, will cool more slowly than the shiny can.

**Possible Procedures** Stress the importance of observing each can under the same conditions. Students should measure and record the temperature of each can at precise, identical intervals (such as 0 minutes, 5 minutes, 10 minutes) after exposure to the light. The procedure should be repeated as the cans cool.

**Troubleshooting** This will work best if you start with water at room temperature.

---

# Infrared Radiation

*You probably know that dark materials get hotter faster than shiny or white materials when exposed to sunlight. How much of a difference is there, though? Do different materials also cool differently?*

### Problem

Which colors of material absorb and release infrared (heat) radiation best?

### Materials

3 aluminum cans of equal size: one black, one white, one shiny

water

3 thermometers

clock or stopwatch

heat lamp

graph paper

### Safety Precautions

Be careful when using the heat lamp to avoid burns. Keep water away from the lamp and cord.

## What To Do

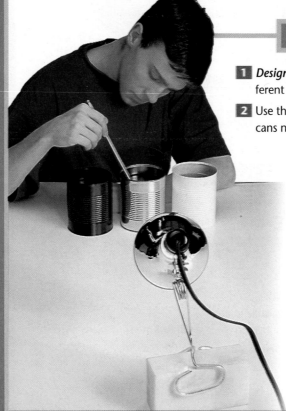

**1** *Design an experiment* to measure how well the three different colors of cans absorb and release infrared radiation.

**2** Use the materials provided. Keep in mind that each of the cans needs to be observed under the same conditions.

**3** Be sure to plan your data collection so that you can make a meaningful *graph*.

**4** You may need to make a quick trial to see how often you need to collect data during the actual experiment.

---

## Program Resources

**Activity Masters,** pp. 15–16, Investigate 3-1

**Laboratory Manual,** pp. 13–16, Light Intensity **L3**

**Multicultural Connections,** p. 9, Spanish Television in the United States **L1**

**Multicultural Connections,** p. 10, Korea and Microwave Ovens **L1**

**Science Discovery Activities,** 3-1, Catching Rays

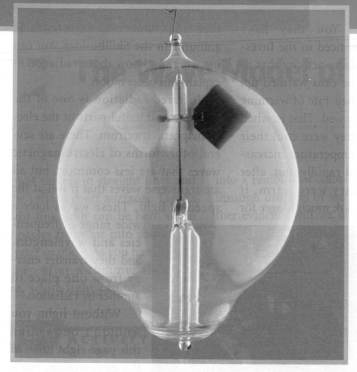

A radiometer converts radiant energy into mechanical energy as light waves from the sun heat the vanes and make them spin.

**5** Show your experiment design to your teacher. If you are advised to revise your plan, be sure to check with your teacher again before you begin. Look at all the safety precautions before you begin. Carry out your plan.

## Analyzing

1. Which can became warmer faster?

2. Which can became the warmest?

3. Which can cooled most quickly?

4. Did the temperature of any can increase or decrease the same amount during each data collection interval?

## Concluding and Applying

5. If you wanted the roof of your home to absorb the sun's radiation to help heat your house, would you buy black or white shingles?

6. What color shingles would you buy if you lived in a climate that was always sunny and warm?

7. **Going Further** Builders often use insulation covered with shiny aluminum foil. *Infer* how this would help to keep a house warm or cool.

**Student Journal** Have students write the answers to the Analyzing/Concluding and Applying questions in their journals. L1

**Expected Outcome**

Students will see that water in the black can becomes warm most quickly and cools most quickly. They will infer that dark colors absorb and radiate infrared radiation at a faster rate than light colors.

**Answers to Analyzing/ Concluding and Applying**

1. the black one

2. the black one

3. The black can should cool faster than the others.

4. See student data.

5. black

6. either white or silver

7. It will reflect energy away from the walls. If it is cold out, the heat will stay in. If it is warm out, the heat will stay out.

## ✔ Assessment

**Content** Have students place their answers to the Analyzing/Concluding and Applying questions, together with a copy of the graph that their group made, in their portfolios. Then have students write summaries of their graphs. Use the Performance Task Assessment List for Written Summary of a Graph in **PAMSS**, p. 41. L1 P

## Meeting Individual Needs

**Learning Disabled** Have students roll or fold a piece of black paper and a piece of white paper into tubes. Have them place each tube ten inches from a light source, such as a lamp. Insert a thermometer into each tube and leave it for ten minutes. Record the temperature on each thermometer and compare the difference between the two. Be sure they note that the thermometer in the black paper shows a higher temperature reading. L1 LEP

## Critical Thinking

**1.** The vibrations simultaneously produce an alternating magnetic field and an alternating electric field.

**2.** View the light source through the diffraction grating. Then match the pattern you see to patterns you have seen.

**3.** If the opening were wider, the wave would not be as diffracted. If there were two small openings, a pattern like Reviewing Main Ideas, item 3 would form.

**4.** The right-hand side is thicker.

## Problem Solving

**1.** Silver side up to reflect infrared back to you.

**2.** Adding another layer of insulation will keep you warmer.

**3.** Students' answers will vary. Lighter colors reflect more sunlight and darker colors absorb more sunlight.

## Connecting Ideas

**1.** Electricity requires an object or conductor to move from place to place. Electromagnetic waves require no medium. Electricity is observed in only one form, while electromagnetic waves include many forms.

**2.** Yes, because they are electromagnetic waves. Waves of any frequency or wavelength still produce interference patterns.

**3.** You should consider skin type, location, time of day, and time of year when determining which SPF to use. Generally, though, the lighter your skin color, the higher SPF value you need to prevent sunburn.

**4.** Many new technologies make use of the same part of the spectrum (radio waves). Signals can't overlap if clear communiction is to be maintained.

**5.** X rays are useful for locating broken bones or cavities in teeth. Overexposure to X rays may cause cancer or other cell deformities.

## Critical Thinking

In your Journal, *answer each of the following questions.*

**1.** How does a vibrating charge create an electromagnetic wave?

**2.** How would you use a diffraction grating to identify the source of a light?

**3.** Describe the appearance of a wave after passing through a narrow slit and after passing through a much wider slit. What pattern would result if a wave passed through two narrow, side by side slits?

**4.** The color blue is seen in the left portion of a thin film and the color red in the right portion of the same film. Which portion of the film is thicker?

## Problem Solving

*Read the following problem and discuss your answers in a brief paragraph.*

**You are going camping with a friend and expect it to get quite cold during the night. You are taking with you a foam sleeping pad that is silver on one side to put under your sleeping bag. You are also taking a "space blanket"—a very thin, shiny silver plastic blanket.**

**1.** Which side of the sleeping pad should face up when you put it on the ground? Why?

**2.** Why will wrapping yourself in the plastic blanket before climbing into your sleeping bag keep you warmer than the sleeping bag alone?

**3.** Should you take light or dark colored clothing for your trip, or does it matter? Explain.

## CONNECTING IDEAS

Discuss each of the following in a brief paragraph.

**1. Theme—Energy** Discuss two ways in which electromagnetic waves differ from the electricity discussed in Chapters 1 and 2.

**2. Theme—Systems and Interactions** If you were able to see radio waves, do you think they would produce interference patterns? Explain your answer.

**3. Life Science Connection** How would you decide which SPF value of sunscreen to select?

**4. Science and Society** Explain why the spectrum is becoming crowded.

**5. Health Connection** Describe one positive and one negative health effect of X rays.

## ✔ Assessment

**Portfolio** Review the portfolio options that are provided throughout the chapter. Encourage students to select one product that demonstrates their best work for the chapter. Have students explain what they learned and why they chose this example for placement into their portfolios.

Additional portfolio options can be found in the following **Teacher Classroom Resources:**

**Making Connections: Integrating Sciences, p. 9**

# ELECTRICITY AND MAGNETISM

In Unit 1, you worked with electricity and magnetism. You discovered that electrical energy is used in many appliances around the home. You found out that an electric current produces a magnetic field and a changing magnetic field produces an electric current. You also learned how electromagnetic waves are created. You explored the different ways that electromagnetic waves carry information and energy for our use and enjoyment.

Try the exercises and activity that follow—they will challenge you to use and apply some of the ideas you learned in this unit.

## CONNECTING IDEAS

**1.** Do you think that pushing the button of an electric doorbell completes a circuit or opens one? If you were designing a doorbell button, would you use an electrical conductor, an insulator, or both? Explain your answer. Describe the purpose of the coil of copper wire found inside an electric doorbell.

**2. Analyzing Data:** Suppose your electric bill rose by twenty dollars the month after your family bought an air conditioner. If the electric company charges 10 cents for each kilowatt-hour of energy, how many extra kilowatt-hours are used by the air conditioner in one month?

## Exploring Further ACTIVITY

### Design a circuit with a bulb, an electromagnet, a switch, and a D-cell.

Connect the circuit elements so that changing the position of the switch turns on the electromagnet and turns off the bulb. Then, draw a diagram of your circuit design.

## Electricity and Magnetism

### THEME DEVELOPMENT

Unit 1 explored the themes of energy, and scale and structure. Students learned that one common way of transferring energy is through electricity. In this unit, students focused on electromagnetic waves that bring energy to Earth from the sun and electrical currents that convey energy from power plants. Students also learned about two phenomena that illustrate scale and structure—static cling and lightning. Although their scale and structure make these two phenomena seem unrelated, they share a common origin.

### Connecting Ideas
#### Answers

**1.** A closed circuit activates a doorbell. The wiring for the doorbell requires both an insulator and a conductor to be safe and effective. The coil of wire is an electromagnet, which pulls the striker against the bell.

**2.** $20 = (E \text{ kwh}) \times (\$0.10/\text{kwh})$, or $E = \$20/(\$0.10/\text{kwh}) = 200$ kwh. This question illustrates a calculation involving a rate. Guide students to solve this problem using dimensional analysis.

## Exploring Further

**Design a circuit with a bulb, an electromagnet of a switch, and a D-cell**

**Purpose** To assemble a working electric circuit that has more than one pathway for current.

**Suggested Materials** D-cells, bulb, socket, insulated wire, three-way switch

### Answers
Circuit diagrams should show a path that branches at the switch, so that the bulb and electromagnet are on separate circuits.

### ✔ Assessment

**Process** Challenge students to diagram a circuit that would allow them to turn on the bulb and electromagnet separately or together. Use the Performance Task Assessment List for Scientific Drawing in **PAMSS**, p. 55. L1

# Atoms and Molecules

## UNIT OVERVIEW

Chapter 4    Structure of the Atom

Chapter 5    The Periodic Table

Chapter 6    Combining Atoms

Chapter 7    Molecules in Motion

## UNIT FOCUS

In Unit 1, students learned about electrical and magnetic properties of matter. In Unit 2, students will learn about the basic structure of matter and will discover how the internal structure of matter determines its physical properties. They will learn how the structure of matter affects its behavior and how substances interact with one another. Students will also become familiar with the kinetic molecular theory of matter and be able to explain changes in state and the characteristics of solids, liquids and gases in terms of this theory.

## THEME DEVELOPMENT

A key theme in Unit 2 is stability and change. For example, in Chapter 5, students will explore how the Periodic Table shows the organization of elements based on the arrangements of their subatomic particles, and how these arrangements are responsible for both stability and change on the atomic and molecular levels. Energy is also a key theme in this unit. Students will learn how energy relates to the structure of the atom, to changes in state of matter, and to the characteristic behavior of matter in the three states.

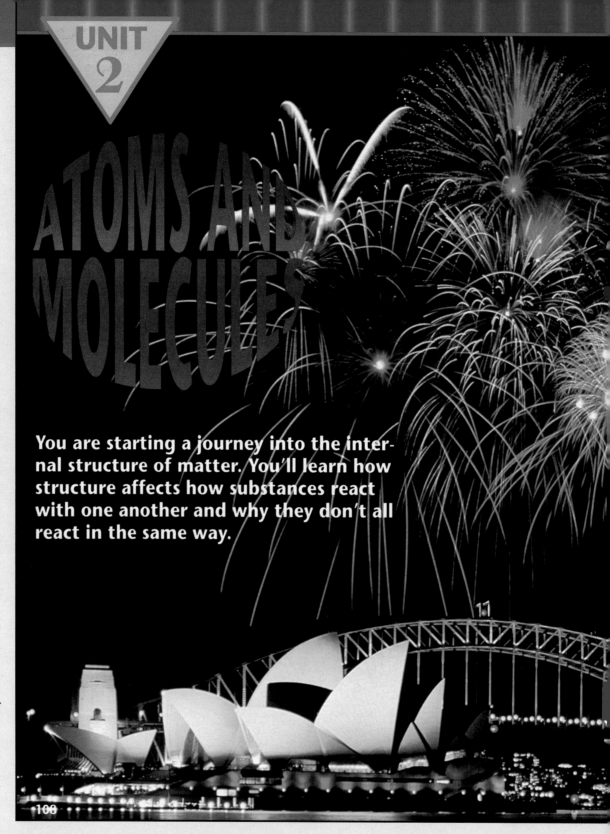

**You are starting a journey into the internal structure of matter. You'll learn how structure affects how substances react with one another and why they don't all react in the same way.**

### VIDEODISC

Use the **Integrated Science Videodisc** to reinforce and enhance concepts in this unit.

**108**    Unit 2   Atoms and Molecules

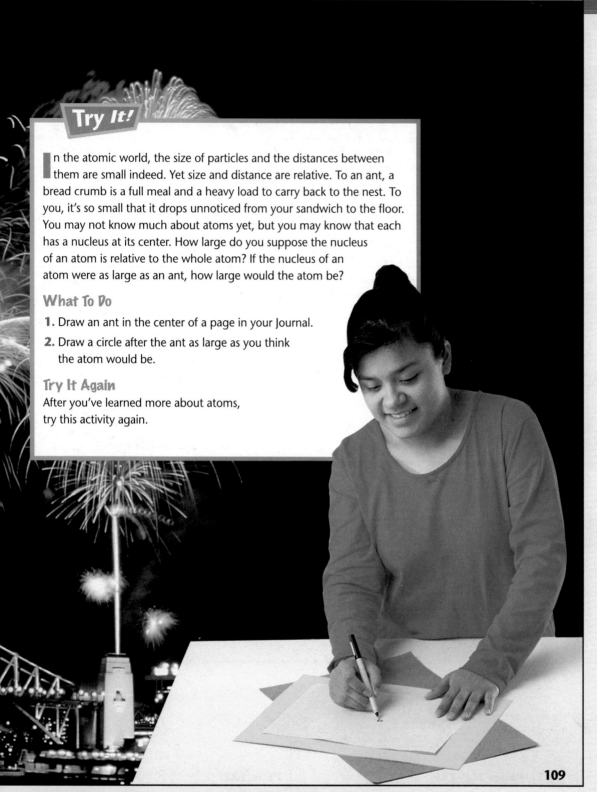

### Try It!

In the atomic world, the size of particles and the distances between them are small indeed. Yet size and distance are relative. To an ant, a bread crumb is a full meal and a heavy load to carry back to the nest. To you, it's so small that it drops unnoticed from your sandwich to the floor. You may not know much about atoms yet, but you may know that each has a nucleus at its center. How large do you suppose the nucleus of an atom is relative to the whole atom? If the nucleus of an atom were as large as an ant, how large would the atom be?

#### What To Do

1. Draw an ant in the center of a page in your Journal.

2. Draw a circle after the ant as large as you think the atom would be.

#### Try It Again

After you've learned more about atoms, try this activity again.

---

### Connections to Other Units

The concepts developed in this unit are related to Unit 1, where types of electrical and magnetic energy were explored. The effects of these types of energy are transferred through atoms and molecules, which make up matter. Students will build on what they learned about electricity to find out how atoms are structured and how molecules move.

### GETTING STARTED

**Discussion** Some questions you may want to ask your students are

1. **What is an atom?** *Some students may know that an atom is the smallest particle into which matter can be divided without extraordinary means.*

2. **What are the parts of an atom?** *Some students may know that atoms consist of protons and neutrons in the nucleus and orbiting electrons. Most will probably be unable to describe their relationship. The answers to these questions will help you establish any misconceptions students may have.*

3. **What is the smallest particle of matter?** *Most students will probably be unaware that when hit with rapidly accelerating neutrons, atoms have been found to consist of even smaller particles called quarks.*

---

### Try It!

**Purpose** To help students use spatial relationships to model the proportions of an atom.

#### Background Information

Students will call on information from Unit 1 concerning electrons and protons to develop a visual image of an atom. They will use familiar images, such as the ant and bread crumb, to infer the size of an atom relative to its nucleus. Be prepared for misconceptions in students' grasp of this relationship.

#### Answers

Student drawings should show an atom larger than the "nuclear" ant, although the size relationship between the two may be inaccurate.

#### ✔ Assessment

**Process** Students will draw the sketches in their journal. After completion of Sections 4-1 and 4-2, students should draw a second sketch based on their increased knowledge about atomic structure. Comparisons of the two sketches can be used to generate a class discussion about their findings. L1 P

# Chapter Organizer

| SECTION | OBJECTIVES | ACTIVITIES |
|---|---|---|
| **Chapter Opener** | | **Explore!** How can you determine the shape of an object you cannot see? p. 111 |
| **4-1 Early Discoveries** (4 days) | 1. **Relate** the contributions of Crookes, Thomson, Becquerel, and Rutherford to the study of the structure of the atom. <br> 2. **Describe** radioactivity. <br> 3. **List** the characteristics of alpha and beta particles and gamma rays. | **Skillbuilder:** Making and Using Tables, p. 117 <br> **Investigate 4-1:** Parts of an Atom, pp. 118–119 |
| **4-2 A Model Atom** (5 days) | 1. **Trace** the development of the model of the atom. <br> 2. **Distinguish** among electrons, protons, and neutrons. | **Find Out!** How can you make a mental picture of an atom? p. 122 <br> **Explore!** Does a magnet hold everything with the same strength? p. 129 <br> **Investigate 4-2:** Models of Atomic Structure, pp. 132–133 |

## EXPAND your view

**A Closer Look** Radon Testing, pp. 114–115
**Physics Connection** Quirk, Quork, Quark! pp. 128–129
**Science and Society** Can You Give Me a Float to School? p. 135

**Literature Connection** Wisdom in Many Forms, pp. 136–137
**Health Connection** Nuclear Medicine, p. 137
**Leisure Connection** Your Nose Knows, p. 138

## ACTIVITY MATERIALS

| EXPLORE! | INVESTIGATE! | FIND OUT! |
|---|---|---|
| **Page 111\*** <br> paper clip, pencil, brick, small bag of sand, piece of cardboard, marbles <br> **Page 129\*** <br> horseshoe magnet, bowl of ball bearings or tacks | **Pages 118–119** <br> regular-size aluminum pie pan, 4 glass marbles, 12-mm steel ball, 4 steel marbles, grooved ruler <br> **Pages 132–133** <br> magnetic board about 20 cm × 27 cm, one 0.5-cm piece and 24 2-cm pieces of rubber magnetic strips, circle of white paper 4 cm wide, marker | **Page 122\*** <br> nuts, bolts, and/or washers; modeling clay, toothpicks |

\*For adequate development of the concepts presented, we recommend that students do the activities with an asterisk.

# Chapter 4 Structure of the Atom

## TEACHER CLASSROOM RESOURCES

| Student Masters | Teaching Aids |
|---|---|
| **Study Guide**, p. 17<br>**Multicultural Connections**, p. 11<br>**Making Connections: Across the Curriculum**, p. 11<br>**Making Connections: Technology & Society**, p. 11<br>**Activity Masters, Investigate 4-1**, pp. 19–20<br>**Making Connections: Integrating Sciences**, p. 11<br>**Science Discovery Activities**, 4-1 | **Color Transparency and Master 7**, Types of Radiation<br>**\*STVS:** *Images of Atoms*, Chemistry (Disc 2, Side 1)<br>**\*STVS:** *PETT Scanner*, Human Biology (Disc 7, Side 1)<br>**\*STVS:** *Radon Danger*, Chemistry (Disc 2, Side 2) |
| **Study Guide**, p. 18<br>**Critical Thinking/Problem Solving**, p. 12<br>**Multicultural Connections**, p. 12<br>**Take Home Activities**, p. 10<br>**Activity Masters, Investigate 4-2**, pp. 21–22<br>**Concept Mapping**, p. 12<br>**Flex Your Brain**, p. 5<br>**How It Works**, p. 8<br>**Science Discovery Activities**, 4-2, 4-3 | **Laboratory Manual**, pp. 17–18, Atomic Spectra<br>**Color Transparency and Master 8**, Atomic Models<br>**\*STVS:** *Carbon-14 Dating of the Shroud of Turin*, Chemistry (Disc 2, Side 2) |

| ASSESSMENT RESOURCES | |
|---|---|
| **Review and Assessment**, pp. 23–28<br>**Performance Assessment**, Ch. 4<br>**PAMSS\***<br>**MindJogger Videoquiz**<br>**Alternate Assessment in the Science Classroom**<br>**Computer Test Bank** | **Spanish Resources**<br>**Cooperative Learning Resource Guide**<br>**Lab and Safety Skills**<br>**Integrated Science Videodisc** |

## KEY TO TEACHING STRATEGIES

The following designations will help you decide which activities are appropriate for your students.

- **L1** Level 1 activities should be within the ability range of all students.
- **L2** Level 2 activities should be within the ability range of the average to above-average student.
- **L3** Level 3 activities are designed for the ability range of above-average students.
- **LEP** LEP activities should be within the ability range of Limited English Proficiency students.
- **COOP LEARN** Cooperative Learning activities are designed for small group work.
- **P** These strategies represent student products that can be placed into a best-work portfolio.

## ADDITIONAL MATERIALS

**Software**
*Atoms*, J&S Software.
*Families of Atoms*, J&S Software.
*Investigating Atomic Models*, IBM.
*Radioactivity*, J&S Software.

**Audiovisual**
*Atoms*, video, Educational Activities.
*The Atom*, video, Hawkhill Science.
*A Brief History of Chemistry*, Hawkhill Science.
*How We Found Out About Atoms*, Hawkhill Science.
*Chemical Bonding and Atomic Structure*, video, Coronet/MTI.
*The Story of Radiation*, video, Hawkhill Science.

**Laserdisc**
*Chemistry at Work*, Videodiscovery.
*Windows on Science, Physical Science*, Optical Data Corp.

**Readings**
Gray, Harry B. *Chemical Bonds: An Introduction to Atomic and Molecular Structure*. Benjamin-Cummings.
Hazen, Robert and James Trefil. *Science Matters: Achieving Scientific Literacy*. Doubleday.

\*Performance Assessment in Middle School Science

\*Science and Technology Videodisc Series

## Structure of the Atom

### THEME DEVELOPMENT

The predominant theme in this chapter is energy. Radiation is a form of energy that can be harmful or useful. Scientists studied the behavior of electrons before and after energy was added to a vacuum tube. It was found that radioactive elements release high-energy particles, giving them a clue to understanding the structure of atoms. The theme of scale and structure is also evident in this chapter in the arrangement of particles within an atom. A spherical cloud of electrons surrounds a small, compact nucleus containing larger particles, protons and neutrons.

### CHAPTER OVERVIEW

In this chapter, students will learn about the early studies that contributed to the understanding of the atom. The development of atomic models by Crookes, Thomson, Becquerel, and Rutherford is then presented. Students consider the value of a model and how models can be developed based on the behavior of matter rather than on direct observation.

#### Tying to Previous Knowledge

Have students work in groups of three or four to brainstorm various models used today, and why they are of value. Have each group share one or two models with the class. **COOP LEARN**

### INTRODUCING THE CHAPTER

Have students refer to the photograph of an early globe on pages 110 and 111. Discuss how these early models were constructed. Relate this to making a model of an atom—something you cannot see with your eyes alone.

# structure OF THE atom

### Did you ever wonder...

✓ **Why bones can be seen on X rays?**

✓ **Where radiation comes from?**

✓ **What an atom looks like?**

Before you begin to study about the structure of the atom, think about these questions and answer them *in your Journal*. When you finish the chapter, compare your Journal write-up with what you have learned.

When you look at a globe, you know you're not looking at Earth itself. The globe is a model, a small and very useful representation of a much larger and more complicated object— Earth. A globe is an actual physical model that you can see and touch. You can also make mental pictures of things you want to understand—mental models. In this chapter, you'll follow the story of how scientists have developed the model of the atom.

▶ *In the activity on the next page, explore how you can determine the shape of an object without seeing it.*

**110**

### Did you ever wonder...

• X rays can travel through soft tissues but not through harder tissues, such as bone. (p. 114)

• Radiation comes from an object giving off heat, light, or beams of small particles. (p. 115)

• Atoms have a nucleus that contain protons and neutrons. Around this nucleus, electrons move in a spherical cloud. (p. 127)

### STUDENT JOURNAL

Have students write their responses to the Did You Ever Wonder questions in their journals. After they have read the chapter, students should read their journal entries to see what they have learned about X rays and radiation, and how these are related to the structure of an atom.

**ACTIVITY**

## How can you determine the shape of an object you cannot see?

**What To Do**

1. Place a paper clip, a pencil, a brick, or a small bag of sand on the floor. Hold a large piece of cardboard about six inches above the object.

2. Without looking under the cardboard, take turns rolling a marble under the cardboard.

3. Compare the direction the marble rolled toward the object with the direction the marble rolled after it hit the object.

4. Roll the marble into the object from several different directions. Record and diagram your observations *in your Journal*. Can you determine which object is under the cardboard, based on your observations?

111

### ASSESSMENT PLANNER

**PORTFOLIO**
Refer to page 141 for suggested items that students might select for their portfolios.

**PERFORMANCE ASSESSMENT**
Process, pp. 111, 119, 129, 133
Skillbuilder, p. 117
Explore! Activities, pp. 111, 129
Find Out! Activity, p. 122
Investigate, pp. 118–119, 132–133

**CONTENT ASSESSMENT**
Oral, p. 122
Check Your Understanding, pp. 121, 134
Reviewing Main Ideas, p. 139
Chapter Review, pp. 140–141

**GROUP ASSESSMENT**
Opportunities for group assessment occur with Cooperative Learning Strategies.

**Explore!**

**How can you determine the shape of an object you cannot see?**

**Time needed** 10-15 minutes

**Materials** paper clip, pencil, brick, small bag of sand, cardboard, marbles

**Thinking Processes** observing and inferring, modeling, comparing and contrasting

**Purpose** To infer certain physical characteristics of an object from indirect evidence.

**Teaching the Activity**

This activity is best performed on the floor with students working in pairs.
**COOP LEARN**

**Troubleshooting** Advise students not to roll the marbles too hard to avoid having them fly off in all directions. Place unused objects out of sight so that students cannot guess what is under the cardboard by what is missing from the materials.

**Student Journal** Suggest that students include in their journals a written description of the different trials in addition to the diagrams of the observed motions of the marble. Students should also include the reasoning behind their selection of the hidden object.
**L1**

**Expected Outcome**

Students should be able to identify the objects under the cardboard based on the marble's behavior.

✔ **Assessment**

**Process** Have students observe the behavior of a rolling marble as it strikes and rebounds from several objects of different size, shape, and rigidity. In their journals, have them compare and contrast the behavior of the marbles for each trial. Use the Performance Task Assessment List for Making Observations and Inferences in **PAMSS**, p. 17. **L1**

## PREPARATION

### Concepts Developed

In this section, students will learn that present-day models of the atom are based on extensive research carried out by a number of scientists over the last 150 years. They will also learn that radioactivity is the release of high-energy particles or rays by certain elements.

### Planning the Lesson

Refer to the Chapter Organizer on pages 110A-B.

## 1 MOTIVATE

**Demonstration** This activity introduces students to the concept of divisibility of matter. Hold up a sheet of paper and ask students how many times it could be divided into smaller pieces. Use scissors or simply tear the sheet in half. Then, cut one of the halves in half, and so on. Do this until it is no longer possible to subdivide the paper efficiently. You may also have a student perform this activity for the class. Then discuss whether the cutting tool used limits the amount of subdivisions one can produce and whether there is a point at which the paper would no longer be paper. L1

## 2 TEACH

### Tying to Previous Knowledge

A review of the material on electricity presented in Chapter 1 and magnetism in Chapter 2 will help students better understand Crookes's experiments. Ask students what type of charges attract each other (*unlike*) and repel each other (*like*) and when they may have experienced these.

---

4-1
# Early Discoveries

## Discovering Atoms

### Section Objectives

- Relate the contributions of Crookes, Thomson, Becquerel, and Rutherford to the study of the structure of the atom.
- Describe radioactivity.
- List the characteristics of alpha and beta particles and gamma rays.

### Key Terms

*electron*
*radioactivity*
*beta particle*
*alpha particle*
*gamma ray*

More than 2400 years ago, Greek philosophers discussed the idea of atoms. The Greeks imagined what might happen if a material was cut repeatedly. Eventually, the piece of material would be so small it could not be cut again and still have the properties of the material. The Greeks called this basic part of matter an atom, meaning indivisible.

#### ■ The Atomic Theory

According to the atomic theory, atoms are the building blocks of matter. Acceptance of this theory of matter was slow, and understandably so. How can you prove the existence of something you can't see? You know from the Explore activity how difficult it is to determine the shape of something invisible. It was in the mid-1800s before most scientists accepted the existence of atoms. The atomic theory offered a simple and useful explanation for the behavior of gases. It was also useful in explaining chemical compounds and the products of chemical reactions. In all, the atomic theory accounted for observations about matter better than any earlier theory had. Yet, scientists wondered if the atoms involved in chemistry could be further divided. The answer came from an unlikely experiment.

#### ■ Discovery of the Electron

William Crookes was a British physicist. In the late 1800s, he was interested in the vacuum tube. A vacuum tube is a sealed glass tube with the air removed from it. **Figures 4-1** and **4-2** demonstrate some of his vacuum tube experiments.

**Figure 4-1**

The vacuum tube William Crookes used in his experiments had a positive terminal at one end and a negative terminal at the other end. When the terminals were connected to a battery, a greenish glow formed at the negative end of the tube and then gradually moved toward the positive end of the tube.

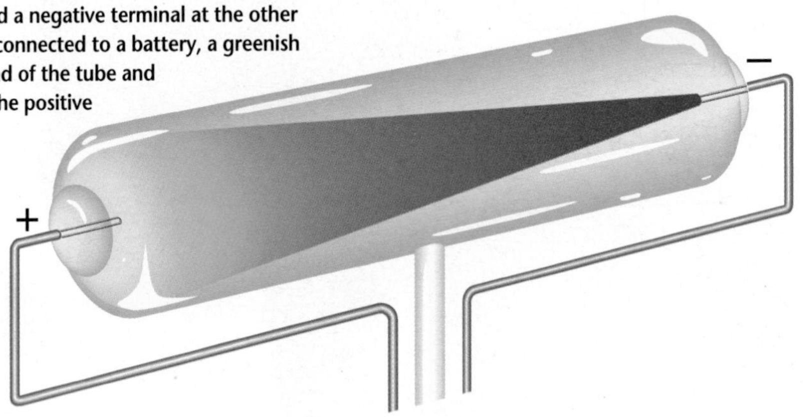

---

### Program Resources

**Study Guide,** p. 17
**Making Connections: Across the Curriculum,** p. 11, Low-level radiation L2
**Making Connections: Technology & Society,** p. 11, Boron Neutron Capture Therapy L3
**Science Discovery Activities,** 4-1, Magnetic Models

### Meeting Individual Needs

**Learning Disabled** Allow students to handle a sample of lead or some other metal. Ask them what they believe the smallest part of this sample could be and whether this part would have the same properties as the larger sample. Accept any answers that students can justify.

**Figure 4-2**

**In another experiment, an object placed in the path of the green glow cast a shadow. Crookes knew that shadows are cast by waves or particles that travel in straight lines. Knowing that, what could Crookes conclude about the green glow?**

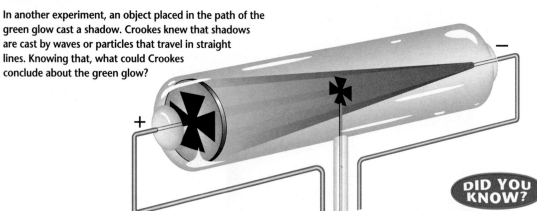

Nearly 20 years after Crookes' work, the British physicist J. J. Thomson repeated the experiment with Crookes' vacuum tube, which was now called a cathode-ray tube. Thomson observed that the waves, or beam of particles, formed inside the tube were bent when they passed through an electric field. Similar observations were made with magnetic fields, as shown in **Figure 4-3**.

In addition to showing that the beam was made up of charged particles, Thomson showed that the particles had much less mass than any atoms have. Thomson also found that the kind of material used for the tube's metal plates did not seem to affect how many charged particles were produced or how they behaved. Thomson had shown that particles even smaller than atoms existed. The particle was given the name **electron**. In 1906, Thomson received the Nobel Prize in physics for his discovery of the electron.

## Radiation

The electrons Crookes and Thomson observed are a form of radiation. The term radiation is commonly used to describe any form of energy—heat, light, or even beams of small particles—given off by an object. What caused the negative terminal in the vacuum tube to radiate these particles? Does radiation only occur when there is a voltage present? Is there any type of radiation that occurs naturally?

**DID YOU KNOW?**

The tube Crookes used was the ancestor of the television tube and the computer screen. Each of these modern devices relies on a vacuum tube with positive and negative metal plates. The inside of each tube is coated with materials that glow when they are struck by electrons, making the beam easy to see.

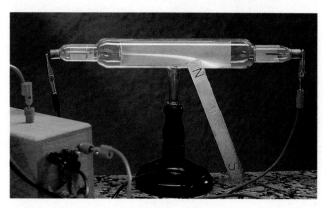

**Figure 4-3**

**In this experiment, a cathode-ray tube was placed in a magnetic field. The magnetic field caused the beam of particles inside the tube to bend. What do you think would happen to the rays if the tube were removed from the magnetic field?**



**Theme Connection** The theme of systems and interactions is developed in this section during the Investigate activity (pages 118–119) where students explore how objects interact with matter in a system. Much of what we know about the atom comes from work done by Rutherford to see how alpha, beta, and gamma radiation interact with matter.

### Visual Learning

**Figure 4-1** Have students infer from their knowledge of electricity what kind of particles might be present at the negative terminal. *negative particles.*
**Figure 4-2** To help students visualize what is happening in the vacuum tube, ask them what kind of energy produces shadows. *Light; electromagnetic.* **Knowing that, what could Crookes conclude about the green glow?** *Crookes could infer that the green is produced by some type of electromagnetic energy moving through the tube.*
**Figure 4-3** Help students to recall that electricity and magnetism are closely related. Ask why the stream of negatively charged particles bends. *The particles are attracted to the positively charged plate (and repelled by the negatively charged plate).* **What do you think would happen to the rays if the tube were removed from the magnetic field?** *The beam of particles would travel in a straight line if removed from the magnetic field.*

**Inquiry Question** What might Crookes have concluded if he had used a negatively charged plate in his vacuum tube and the green glow bent toward this plate? *The glow was caused by positively charged particles.*

### ENRICHMENT

**Research** Have students research the lives and contributions of Marie and Pierre Curie and Enrico Fermi, scientists who conducted extensive research on radiation. Students should prepare a report for presentation to the class. You may wish to have students work in groups to develop posters for classroom display. The posters could show the scientists and their major contributions. L1 P

4-1 Early Discoveries 113

# Natural Radiation

Perhaps you've had a broken arm X-rayed. Maybe you've seen an X ray photograph of a person's lungs or

**Figure 4-4**

X rays pass through soft tissues such as skin and muscle but are stopped by hard tissue, thereby revealing the bones underneath.

hand. X rays can even show cracks or breaks in steel bridges and building supports. The material to be tested is placed between the X-ray source and a sheet of film. Wherever the X rays pass through the material, the film clouds as though it has been exposed to light.

There are other forms of radiation that can affect film. Nearly a hundred years ago, a French physicist, Henri Becquerel, accidentally left a small sample of a uranium compound on top of a photographic plate. The plate was in a drawer, wrapped tightly in

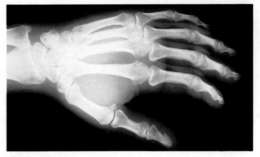

# Radon Testing

In the past few years, many people began to worry that their homes might be hazardous to their health. Reports in the newspapers warned people that their homes might contain dangerous levels of radon.

## What is Radon?

Radon is a radioactive gas that is produced from uranium and thorium. Radon produces charged particles that are attracted to dust. When inhaled, these particles can produce a higher risk of cancer than normal. Some homes built over rocks containing uranium and thorium have been found to have high levels of radon gas.

## Sources of Radon

The problem of radon gas in homes was discovered by accident. A construction worker helping to build a nuclear power plant in Pennsylvania kept setting off the radiation alarms at the plant. After it was found that he was not being exposed to radiation at work, investigators checked out his home. They found that his house was built on radioactive rocks that were filling the air in his home with radon gas.

There are other sources of radon gas. Some modern lightning rods contain radon gas that can leak into the attics of homes.

light-colored paper. Yet, when Becquerel went to use the plate, he found it fogged. It seemed as if the compound were giving off radiation that could go through paper. Becquerel began to study the radiation further. The radiation penetrated matter just as X rays did, and it was given off in all directions by the compound. The radiation could even be deflected by a magnetic field. Becquerel inferred that the radiation had to be—at least partly—made up of tiny, charged particles. Eventually, he concluded that the negatively charged part of the radiation was due to negatively charged particles. Becquerel further concluded that these particles were identical to those in Thomson's experiment. They were electrons. Where were the electrons coming from? The only possible source was the uranium compound, or rather the atoms of the uranium compound. Here was more evidence that the atom must have smaller parts. Furthermore, one of those parts must be a light, negatively charged particle—an electron.

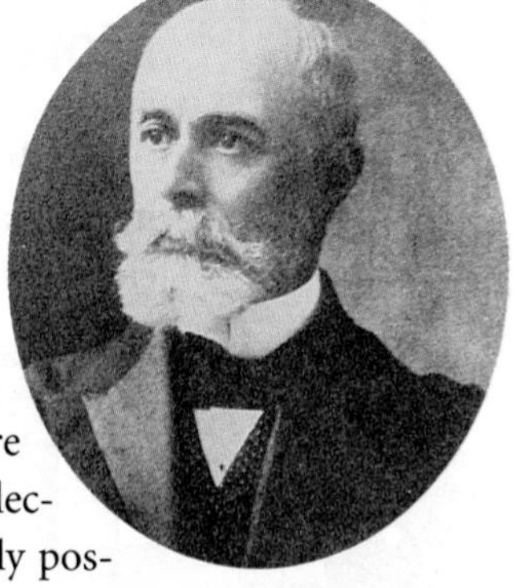

**Figure 4-5**

**Henri Becquerel discovered that atoms of uranium gave off negatively charged particles, which provided evidence that atoms are made up of smaller particles.**

### Testing for Radon

Kits are now available to test for high radon levels. Most kits contain activated charcoal, which attracts radon particles. The kit is then sent to a laboratory for an interpretation of the results.

### What To Do

People who find that their homes contain high amounts of radon gas are advised to make modifications in their homes. In some cases, added ventilation solves the problem. In other cases, walls, ceilings, or floors must be sealed against the gas.

### You Try It!

Get a radon testing kit either from your state or local health department. Check your home or school for radon gas. Usually, buildings that are well insulated collect gases more than those that are built off the ground or are not so tightly built. Compare the results of a test on a new building with those of a test on an old building.

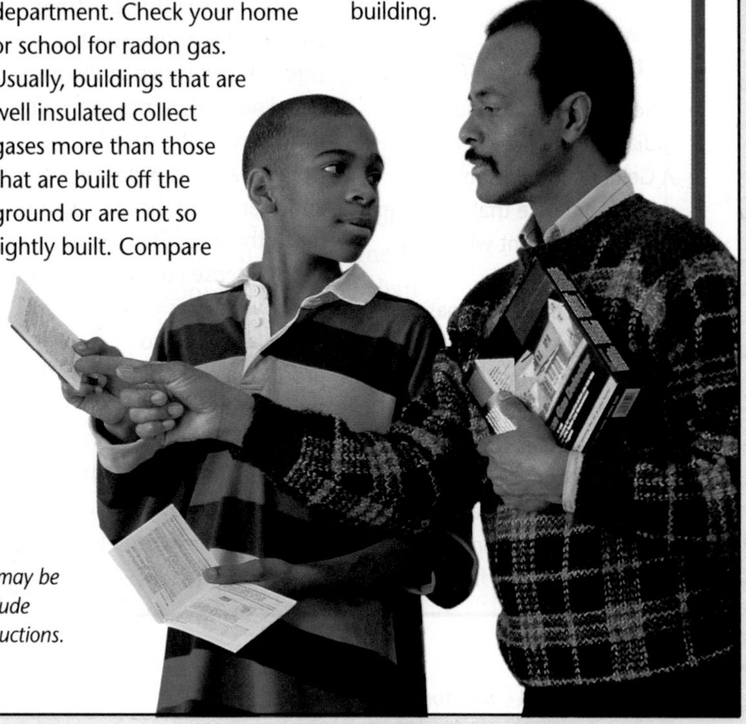

*Radon-testing kits may be purchased and include easy-to-follow instructions.*

**Answer to You Try It!**

Results will vary, but students should use scientific methodology in conducting their tests.

**Going Further**

Have students write your local health department requesting additional information on the symptoms of radon exposure. The address and phone number can be found in your local phone book or municipal directory. Students should know what changes to look for in their health that might suggest exposure to radon.

### Visual Learning

**Figure 4-4** Ask students what the photograph shows. *an image of the bones in a human hand* Ask how this image is like a shadow. *As X rays pass through the hand, some of the rays are blocked by the bones in much the same way that light rays are blocked by solid objects, producing shadows.*

**Discussion** Use Becquerel's discovery to reveal the role that accidental discovery may occasionally play in science, illustrating the fact that the scientific method is not a fixed set of rules that are followed regardless of external factors in all instances. Discuss the role of imagination, creativity, and chance, along with logic in conducting scientific investigations. L3

**Activity** Have students survey local tanning salons for information regarding the types of rays emitted from their tanning beds. Then have them contact their local Cancer Society for information on the types of rays that are harmful. Have them compare the effect of sun versus tanning bed and, presented in a written report, make recommendations for safety. L2 P

Act
pro
is al

Y
cou
are
fens
or
haz
tals
cou
tair
mal

of v
atic
hav
mo
ma
sur
the
gro
stu
cou
tur
nu
ute
wh
tio
der
of
tha
cou
hav
dia
det
dia
fin

## 4-1 Parts of an Atom

### Planning the Activity

**Time Needed** 20-30 minutes

**Purpose** To use a model to investigate the interaction of alpha particles with the parts of an atom.

**Process Skills** observing and inferring, recognizing cause and effect, hypothesizing, interpreting data, making and using models, forming operational definitions, comparing and contrasting

**Materials** See reduced student text.

### Teaching the Activity

Have students work in pairs. One student can roll the steel ball while the other records its effects on the glass marbles. Students can reverse roles for the second part of the activity. **COOP LEARN**

**Discussion** Ask students to share experiences in which they learned about an object or person by observing the behavior of other objects or people that interact with it. Point out that many scientific ideas have been formulated by observing how objects interact with each other.

**Process Reinforcement** Ask students to tell what each part of their model represents. *Rolling steel ball—beta particle, rolling marble—alpha particle, stationary balls and marbles—atomic nuclei*

---

# Parts of an Atom

*Think back to the Explore activity you did at the beginning of this chapter. Suppose you were absolutely certain the brick was under the cardboard, but the marble seemed to roll as if nothing were under the cardboard. What would you think?*

### Problem
What's inside an atom?

### Materials
| | |
|---|---|
| regular-size aluminum pie pan | 12-mm steel ball |
| | 4 steel marbles |
| 4 glass marbles | grooved ruler |

### What To Do

**1** Gently press the 4 glass marbles into the pie pan so that they make small indentations near the center of the pan (see photo **A**).

**2** Roll the 12-mm steel ball down the grooved ruler, (see photo **B**). Try to hit the marbles.

**3** *Observe* and record what happens to the steel ball. Does it ever change its path? Does the steel ball ever bounce back?

---

## Meeting Individual Needs

**Behaviorally Disordered** For the Investigate activity on pages 118–119, you may wish to have students work with a partner. Give clear instructions as to the role of each student in the activity. For example, one student should set up the marbles in the pan and the other student can roll it down the slope. Then have students switch roles. Both students, however, should record their observations. **COOP LEARN**

---

## Program Resources

**Activity Masters,** pp. 19–20, Investigate 4-1

**A**          **B**          **C**

**4** Place the ruler at different slopes (see photo **C**). Record any effect this has on your observations.

**5** Now put steel marbles into the indentations in the pie pan.

**6** Repeat Steps 2, 3, and 4 rolling a glass marble down the grooved ruler.

## Analyzing

1. *Compare* and *contrast* the results in Step 6 with the previous observations.

2. Why were the results different?

3. What effect did the slope of the ruler have on the way the rolling ball or marble behaved? What *hypothesis* can there be for your observation?

## Concluding and Applying

4. Which has a greater effect on the way the rolling ball acts after a collision, the mass of the rolling ball or the mass of the ball in the indentation?

5. **Going Further** How would your observations change if the steel marbles and the rolling steel ball were all positively charged?

### Building Blocks of Matter

People have long tried to discover and understand the basic building blocks of matter. Different cultures developed different theories. The ancient Chinese and the Jains of ancient India developed theories of dualism, wherein two major forces or elements balanced one another. One Chinese philosophy, Naturalism, viewed the universe as governed by a balance between two opposing forces—the yin and yang.

In India during the sixth century B.C.E., the Jains believed that living matter "swam" around in particles of inert (non-living) matter. These two essential elements (Life and Non-Life) comprised the universe. Have students research these early theories. L2

---

**Student Journal** Have students record their data, observations, and answers in their journals. L2

**Expected Outcome**

Students should find that the deflection of the rolling glass marble when it strikes the steel marbles is considerably greater than that of the steel ball when it strikes the glass marbles. They should also note that the greater the slope, the less the deflection.

**Answers to** Analyzing/ Concluding and Applying

**1.** The massive steel ball is relatively unaffected by collision with less massive glass marbles. The less massive glass marble is more likely to change velocity when it collides with the more massive steel marbles.

**2.** The amount of deflection is related to the masses of the moving ball and the stationary marbles.

**3.** The greater the slope of the ruler, the greater the velocity of the rolling ball. Rolling balls with greater velocity are less likely to be affected by collisions.

**4.** In most cases the mass of the ball in the indentation has a greater effect on the velocity of the rolling ball.

**5.** If the steel marbles and steel ball were positively charged, they would repel each other, and the rolling ball would move away from any stationary marble it approached.

### ✔ Assessment

**Process** Have student pairs extend the activity by investigating different arrangements of balls and marbles. For example, they could roll a glass marble at other glass marbles and a steel ball at steel marbles, and they could add more marbles to the pie pan. Students should describe their setups and results in their student journals. Select the appropriate Performance Task Assessment List from **PAMSS**. **COOP LEARN** L1

# Alpha Particle Experiments

In this Investigate, you learned that the way objects interact is affected by their mass, their velocity, and whether or not they are charged. Rutherford used a similar experiment to study the way alpha particles interacted with matter.

Rutherford and his colleagues wanted to learn more about alpha particles. They designed an experiment to study the ability of alpha particles to pass through different metals. The setup is shown in **Figure 4-8**.

Rutherford, talking about his gold foil experiment some years later, was quoted: "It was about as believable as if you had fired a 15-inch shell at a piece of tissue paper, and it came back and hit you."

Rutherford's team set out to learn more about alpha particles. Instead, they made one of history's most important observations about atoms. Look at **Figure 4-9**.

Rutherford's team concluded from their gold foil experiments that somewhere in the gold atom was a very massive charged object that would repel the positively charged alpha particles. After they made these observations, other scientists became very interested in just what an atom looked like and how the parts of an atom were arranged. The problem was that they had no tools to directly observe the atom. Instead, they had to rely on mental pictures of the atom.

**Figure 4-8**

In his experiment, Rutherford fired a beam of positively charged alpha particles at a very thin sheet of gold foil. He expected the particles to pass straight through the foil. The alpha particles appeared as tiny flashes of light on the fluorescent screen. However, the boundary of the circle formed by the flashes was fuzzy, which meant that some of the particles had been bent. A few alpha particles even bounced back from the foil. Observing this, Rutherford concluded that an atom is mostly empty space, with a dense, positively charged center.

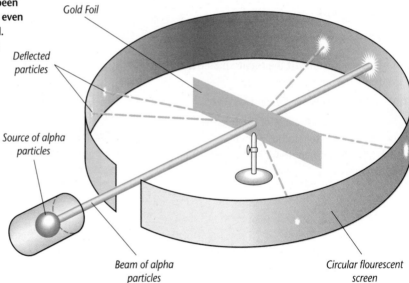

Gold Foil

Deflected particles

Source of alpha particles

Beam of alpha particles

Circular flourescent screen

**R**eview the statements below about the big ideas presented in this chapter, and try to answer the questions. Then, re-read your answers to the Did You Ever Wonder questions at the beginning of the chapter. *In your Journal*, write a paragraph about how your understanding of the big ideas in the chapter has changed.

❶ Using cathode-ray tubes, Thomson demonstrated the existence of a negatively charged particle he called the electron. *How did he arrive at this conclusion?*

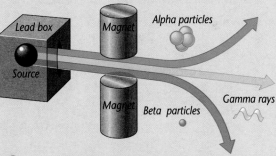

Lead box
Magnet
Source
Magnet
Alpha particles
Beta particles
Gamma rays

❷ Rutherford observed the existence of alpha particles, beta particles, and gamma rays. *How do these particles and rays compare?*

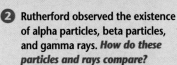
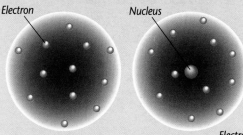

Electron
Nucleus

Orbit
Nucleus
Electron

Electron Cloud

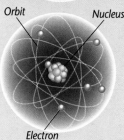
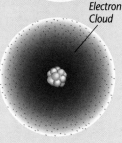

❸ Our model of the structure of the atom has been changed as new experiments provided more information. *What model do we generally refer to now?*

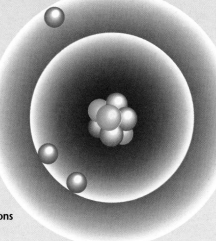

❹ The atom consists of a nucleus containing protons and neutrons surrounded by electrons in energy levels within their electron cloud. *Draw a model of a helium atom.*

Have students look at the illustrations on this page. Direct them to read the statements to review the main ideas in this chapter.

### Teaching Strategies

Divide the class into four groups. Assign each group one of the illustrations. Have students write a brief paragraph interpreting their particular illustration. Then have each group share its paragraph with the class by reading it aloud, or you can photocopy it and pass out a copy to each student. **COOP LEARN**

You may also have pairs of students write essays that describe what each Find Out, Explore, and Investigate activity contributed to their understanding of the structure of an atom. Display these essays in the classroom or conduct a contest in which the best essay receives a prize. **P**

### Answers to Questions

**1.** Thomson placed a cathode-ray tube in a magnetic field. The magnetic field caused the beam of particles to bend, indicating that the beam was made up of charged negative particles. He showed that these particles had much less mass than any atoms have and that they were present in many kinds of materials.

**2.** Refer to Skillbuilder answer table on page 117.

**3.** We generally refer to the electron cloud model.

**4.** The model should show two protons and two neutrons in the nucleus, and a pair of electrons orbiting the nucleus in the shell closest to the nucleus.

## Project

Have students construct posters displaying the various experiments conducted by Crookes, Rutherford, Becquerel, and Thomson, along with the atomic model proposed by each scientist. Display these around the classroom. Use the Performance Task Assessment List for Poster in **PAMSS**, p. 73 **L1** **P**

## Science at Home

Have each student locate three newspaper or magazine articles pertaining to work done by scientists regarding the atom and its electrons, protons, neutrons, and even smaller subatomic particles. Direct students to write a brief summary of each article to the best of their understanding. **L2** **P**

chapter 4
**CHAPTER REVIEW**

## Using Key Science Terms

**1.** radioactivity; the others are all types of particles or rays given off by matter.

**2.** gamma ray; the others are all negative

**3.** electron; the others are positively charged

**4.** proton; the others are given off by radioactive matter

**5.** radioactivity; the others are parts of an atom

## Understanding Ideas

**1.** The atom has 4 electrons, because the number of electrons is equal to the number of protons.

**2.** Eight electrons is the maximum number that can be found in an atom's second energy level.

**3.** John Dalton formulated the billiard ball model; J.J. Thomson formulated the blueberry muffin model.

**4.** Gold atoms consist mostly of empty space with dense, positively charged centers.

**5.** A model is an idea, system, or structure that represents something being explained or described.

**6.** More energy is needed to remove an electron in the first energy level because it is closer to the nucleus and held more tightly than an electron in the third energy level.

## Developing Skills

**1.** Rutherford would have concluded that most of the atom consisted of dense matter, probably positively charged.

**2.** Both particles will curve in the same direction, but the path of the omega particle will curve more because of its greater charge.

**3.** See reduced student page for completed concept map.

---

## Using Key Science Terms

| | |
|---|---|
| alpha particle | neutron |
| beta particle | nucleus |
| electron | proton |
| gamma ray | radioactivity |

*For each set of terms below, choose the one term that does not belong and explain why it does not belong.*

**1.** radioactivity, alpha particle, beta particle, gamma ray

**2.** electron, beta particle, gamma ray, negative charge

**3.** alpha particle, proton, neutron, electron

**4.** radioactivity, proton, alpha particle, gamma ray

**5.** neutron, radioactivity, proton, electron

## Understanding Ideas

*Answer the following questions in your Journal using complete sentences.*

**1.** If an atom has 4 protons and 5 neutrons, how many electrons does it have? Explain.

**2.** What is the maximum number of electrons that can be found in an atom's second energy level?

**3.** Who formulated:
   **a.** the billiard ball model of the atom?
   **b.** the blueberry muffin model of the atom?

**4.** What did the gold foil experiment reveal about gold atoms?

**5.** What is a model?

**6.** Which requires more energy to remove from the nucleus, an electron in the first energy level or an electron in the third energy level? Explain.

## Developing Skills

*Use your understanding of the concepts developed in this chapter to answer each of the following questions.*

**1. Observing and Inferring** In the gold foil experiment, most of the alpha particles went through the foil. Suppose that, instead, only a few particles had gone through the foil. How would Rutherford's conclusion have been different?

**2. Predicting** Imagine an omega particle that has the same mass as an alpha particle and a positive charge of three. If an alpha particle and an omega particle pass through a magnetic field, how will their paths differ?

**3. Concept Mapping** Create a spider concept map that depicts the atom through a description of its component particles.

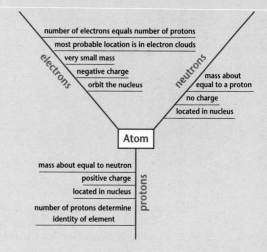

electrons
- number of electrons equals number of protons
- most probable location is in electron clouds
- very small mass
- negative charge
- orbit the nucleus

neutrons
- mass about equal to a proton
- no charge
- located in nucleus

Atom

protons
- mass about equal to neutron
- positive charge
- located in nucleus
- number of protons determine identity of element

---

### Program Resources

**Review and Assessment,** pp. 23–28 [L1]
**Performance Assessment,** Ch. 4 [L2]
**PAMSS**
**Alternate Assessment in The Science Classroom**
**Computer Test Bank**

## Critical Thinking

In your Journal, *answer each of the following questions.*

**1.** Three particles are fired into a box that is positively charged on one side and negatively charged on the other. The result is shown in the picture. Which particle is the proton? Which particle is the electron? Which particle is the neutron? Explain.

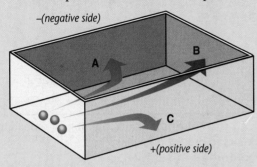

–(negative side)

A    B

C

+(positive side)

**2.** If you wanted to repeat an experiment to test a hypothesis you didn't believe, what is most important for you to find out and do?

## Problem Solving

*Read the following problem and discuss your answers in a brief paragraph.*

Carbon-14 (14 particles in the nucleus) atoms are unstable. Carbon-14 is a radioactive form of carbon. Normal carbon atoms are carbon-12 (12 particles in the nucleus). It takes 5700 years for half the atoms in a sample of carbon-14 to release their extra energy and particles and become stable. In another 5700 years, half of the remaining atoms in the sample would become stable, and so on every 5700 years.

All living things have carbon atoms in them. Living organisms absorb some carbon-14 from the atmosphere. When the organisms die, no new atoms are taken in. The carbon-14 atoms present begin to break down into stable atoms.

How could these facts be used to determine the age of a mummy found in a newly discovered ancient Egyptian tomb?

## Critical Thinking

**1.** Particle A is the positively charged proton, which is attracted to the negative side. Particle C is the negatively charged electron, which is attracted to the positive side. Particle B is the uncharged neutron, which is not affected by the charged sides.

**2.** You must find out how the experiment was done and repeat the steps exactly.

## Problem Solving

The age of a newly discovered mummy could be found by measuring the amount of radioactive carbon-14 present in it. Using the known half-life of carbon-14 left in the mummy, the number of years since carbon-14 first began breaking down can be calculated. That is, the age of the mummy can be determined.

## Connecting Ideas

**1.** A beta particle, which has a negative charge, would be attracted to the positive region of the electric field.

**2.** Size and distance relationships are not accurate, because not enough space is available.

**3.** Accept all reasonable responses.

**4.** Responses may include testing for radon, checking for adequate ventilation, and sealing off portions of the house to prevent radon gas from entering.

## CONNECTING IDEAS

Discuss each of the following in a brief paragraph.

**1. Theme—Systems and Interactions** What would happen to beta particles in an electric field? Explain.

**2. Theme—Scale and Structure** Figure 4-12D on page 124 shows a model of an atom. Is the size of the nucleus accurate in relation to the size of the electron cloud? Explain.

**3. Literature Connection** "This can't be true because science has never proven it." Describe how you might respond to such a statement.

**4. Technology Connection** What steps can be taken to reduce the level of radon in a home?

## ✔ Assessment

**Portfolio** Review the portfolio options that are provided throughout the chapter. Encourage students to select one product that demonstrates their best work for the chapter. Have students explain what they learned and why they chose this example for placement into their portfolios.

Additional portfolio options can be found in the following **Teacher Classroom Resources:**

**Concept Mapping,** p. 12

**Making Connections: Integrating Sciences,** p. 11

**Multicultural Connections,** pp. 11–12

**Making Connections: Across the Curriculum,** p. 11

**Critical Thinking/Problem Solving,** p. 12

**Take Home Activities,** p. 10

**Laboratory Manual,** pp. 17–18

**Performance Assessment** [P]

# Chapter Organizer

| SECTION | OBJECTIVES | ACTIVITIES |
|---|---|---|
| **Chapter Opener** | | **Explore!** Can you organize your classmates? p. 143 |
| **5-1 Structure of the Periodic Table** (4 days) | 1. **Describe** the arrangement of the elements in the periodic table. <br> 2. **Find** the number of protons and electrons in an atom using the periodic table. <br> 3. **Explain** atomic number. <br> 4. **Identify** mass number and calculate atomic mass. | **Investigate 5-1:** Two-Dimensional Classification, pp. 146–147 <br> **Investigate 5-2:** Isotopes and Atomic Mass, pp. 152–153 |
| **5-2 Families of Elements** (2 days) | 1. **Identify** a family of elements. <br> 2. **Recognize** the alkali family. <br> 3. **Describe** the alkaline earth family. | **Find Out!** How are elements alike and different? p. 155 |
| **5-3 Periods of Elements** (3 days) | 1. **Describe** a period on the periodic table. <br> 2. **Identify** where metals, nonmetals, and metalloids are located on the periodic table. <br> 3. Use the periodic table to **classify** an element. | **Find Out!** How can you use a table of repeating events to predict or explain? p. 161 <br> **Skillbuilder:** Classifying, p. 166 |

## EXPAND your view

**A Closer Look** Medical Uses of Radiation, pp. 150–151
**Life Science Connection** The Chernobyl Disaster, pp. 162–163

**Science and Society** Synthetic Elements, pp. 168–169
**History Connection** Experimental Disproof, p. 170

## ACTIVITY MATERIALS

| EXPLORE! | INVESTIGATE! | FIND OUT! |
|---|---|---|
| **Page 143** <br> No special materials are needed. | **Pages 146–147** <br> 20 squares of colored paper with numbers from 1 through 20, envelope <br> **Pages 152–153*** <br> 4 red and 3 green candy-coated peanuts, 2 red and 3 green candy-coated chocolates | **Page 155*** <br> 2 index cards, objects or pictures of objects made of elements, tape <br> **Page 161*** <br> No special materials are needed. |

*For adequate development of the concepts presented, we recommend that students do the activities with an asterisk.

# Chapter 5 The Periodic Table

## TEACHER CLASSROOM RESOURCES

| Student Masters | Teaching Aids |
|---|---|
| **Study Guide**, p. 19<br>**Making Connections: Integrating Sciences**, p. 13<br>**Making Connections: Technology & Society**, p. 13<br>**Activity Masters, Investigate 5-1**, pp. 23–24<br>**Activity Masters, Investigate 5-2**, pp. 25–26<br>**Science Discovery Activities**, 5-1, 5-2 | **Laboratory Manual**, pp. 19-20, Relationships Among Elements<br>**\*STVS:** *Photo Acoustic Cell*, Physics (Disc 1, Side 1) |
| **Study Guide**, p. 20<br>**Critical Thinking/Problem Solving**, p. 13<br>**Take Home Activities**, p. 11<br>**Making Connections: Across the Curriculum**, p. 13<br>**Multicultural Connections**, p. 13 | **\*STVS:** *Sea Urchins and Power Plants*, Chemistry (Disc 2, Side 1)<br>**\*STVS:** *Composite Materials*, Chemistry (Disc 2, Side 1) |
| **Study Guide**, p. 21<br>**Concept Mapping**, p. 13<br>**Flex Your Brain**, p. 5<br>**Multicultural Connections**, p. 14<br>**How It Works**, p. 10<br>**Science Discovery Activities**, 5-3 | **Laboratory Manual**, pp. 21-24, Chemical Activity<br>**Color Transparency and Masters 9 and 10**, The Periodic Table<br>**\*STVS:** *Hydrogen Sponge*, Chemistry (Disc 2, Side 1) |
| **ASSESSMENT RESOURCES** | **Spanish Resources**<br>**Cooperative Learning Resource Guide**<br>**Lab and Safety Skills**<br>**Integrated Science Videodisc** |
| **Review and Assessment**, pp. 29–34<br>**Performance Assessment**, Ch. 5<br>**PAMSS\***<br>**MindJogger Videoquiz**<br>**Alternate Assessment in the Science Classroom**<br>**Computer Test Bank** | |

## KEY TO TEACHING STRATEGIES

The following designations will help you decide which activities are appropriate for your students.

**L1** Level 1 activities should be within the ability range of all students.

**L2** Level 2 activities should be within the ability range of the average to above-average student.

**L3** Level 3 activities are designed for the ability range of above-average students.

**LEP** LEP activities should be within the ability range of Limited English Proficiency students.

**COOP LEARN** Cooperative Learning activities are designed for small group work.

**P** These strategies represent student products that can be placed into a best-work portfolio.

## ADDITIONAL MATERIALS

**Software**
*Chemicals of Life I*, EduQuest.
*Chemistry, The Periodic Table*, MECC.
*Periodic Table*, EME.
*Periodic Table*, J&S Software.

**Audiovisual**
*Periodic Table*, video, EME.
*The Periodic Table and Periodicity*, video Coronet/MTI.

**Laserdisc**
*Chemistry at Work*, Videodiscovery.
*Periodic Table Videodisc: Reactions of the Elements*, JCE Software.

**Readings**
Gray, Harry B. *Chemical Bonds: An Intro-* *duction to Atomic and Molecular Structure*. Benjamin Cummings.
Hazen, Robert and James Trefil. *Science Matters: Achieving Scientific Literacy*. Doubleday.

# The Periodic Table

## THEME DEVELOPMENT

Scale and structure are exemplified by the organization of the elements in the periodic table. The arrangement of elements in the table makes patterns of size and structure obvious.

A secondary theme presented in this chapter is stability and change. The elements discussed in this chapter possess a certain amount of stability in their neutral state. However, the number of electrons an element has in its outer energy level determines the reactivity of that element.

## CHAPTER OVERVIEW

In this chapter, students will see how elements are arranged on the periodic table. The atomic mass of an atom is defined and related to the arrangement of elements in the periodic table. Next, students will examine the alkali metals and the alkaline earth metals as examples of families found in the periodic table. Finally, students learn to classify elements as metals, nonmetals, or metalloids, based on their positions in the periodic table.

### Tying to Previous Knowledge

Have students recall what they learned about the structure of an atom in Chapter 4: the nucleus contains protons and neutrons, and electrons equal in number to the number of protons in the nucleus orbiting the nucleus. Divide the class into small groups and have groups brainstorm ways in which atoms might be classified. Suggestions might include arranging atoms according to the number of protons and neutrons in the nucleus or by the number of electrons in the outer energy level. Have groups present their ideas for discussion. **COOP LEARN**

# THE periOdic TABLE

### Did you ever wonder...

✓ How the pioneers made soap?

✓ Why racing bicycles are so light?

✓ What is used to mark the white lines on baseball diamonds and football fields?

Before you begin to study about the periodic table, think about these questions and answer them *in your Journal*. When you finish the chapter, compare your Journal write-up with what you have learned.

**T**he movement of a metronome, a playground swing, and the seasons—all have something in common. What do you think it is? What kind of patterns exist in the examples above? In the swing, it is the height and direction of the seat. In the seasons, the pattern could be the number of daylight hours or the growth of trees and plants. To make sense of the world, your brain always looks for such patterns—patterns in the properties of things.

In this chapter, you will discover some similarities and patterns among elements. You'll also see how the elements can be placed in a pattern based on their characteristics.

▶ *In the activity on the next page, explore different ways of organizing your classmates.*

142

### Did you ever wonder...

• They collected water that had run through ashes, and cooked it with grease. (p. 159)

• They are made of a magnesium aluminum alloy that is lightweight yet strong. (p. 160)

• Calcium hydroxide (p. 160)

### STUDENT JOURNAL

Have students write their responses to the Did You Ever Wonder questions in their journals. After they have read the chapter, students should read their journal entries to see what they have learned about families of elements and their properties.

## Explore! ACTIVITY

### Can you organize your classmates?

**What To Do**

1. Work in groups to identify the different characteristics of your classmates. In addition to physical appearance, don't forget things like birth month or date, or telephone number. Be creative. Record these characteristics *in your Journal.*

2. Use your list to arrange your classmates in some pattern.

3. Compare your group's arrangement to that of others.

---

## INTRODUCING THE CHAPTER

As students look at the pictures on pages 142–143, ask how they would describe the patterns that are represented. *They are repeating patterns. The pendulum swings back and forth, and the seasons repeat in a cycle.*

### Explore!

**Can you organize your class-mates?**

**Time needed** 15–20 minutes

**Materials** No special materials or preparation are required for this activity.

**Thinking Processes** comparing and contrasting, classifying

**Purpose** To develop and use a classification scheme.

**Teaching the Activity**

**Demonstration** Show students a variety of nuts and bolts and ask how they might be classified.

**Student Journal** Have students record their organization scheme in their journals. L1

**Expected Outcome**

Students should find that their classmates can be organized in different ways depending on the factors used to categorize them.

### ✔ Assessment

**Process** Have students select some group of related objects and devise a scheme to organize them in some way. Objects may be leaves, rocks, metallic items, and the like. Use the Performance Task Assessment List for Carrying Out a Strategy and Collecting Data in **PAMSS**, p. 25. L1

---

## ASSESSMENT PLANNER

**PORTFOLIO**
Refer to page 173 for suggested items that students might select for their portfolio.

**PERFORMANCE ASSESSMENT**
Process, pp. 143, 153, 155, 161
Skillbuilder, p. 162
Explore! Activity, p. 143
Find Out! Activities, pp. 155, 161
Investigate, pp. 146–147, 152–153

**CONTENT ASSESSMENT**
Check Your Understanding, pp. 154, 160, 167
Reviewing Main Ideas, p. 171
Chapter Review, pp. 172–173

**GROUP ASSESSMENT**
Opportunities for group assessment occur with Cooperative Learning Strategies.

# PREPARATION

## Concepts Developed

In this section, students will trace the development of the periodic table. They will see that as more and more elements were discovered, the need to classify them in an orderly fashion became necessary. Students will then use an element's atomic number shown on the periodic table to find the number of protons and electrons in an atom of that element. Students will also find that because of isotopes, the atomic mass of an element is not simply the mass number, or total protons and neutrons, but an average of the mass of all isotopes of the element.

## Planning the Lesson

Refer to the Chapter Organizer on pages 142A–B.

# 1 MOTIVATE

**Demonstration** Begin a discussion about the need to classify elements.

You will need a battery-powered conductivity tester and samples of elements.

Touch the instrument's probes to each element sample. Have students classify each element as a conductor or nonconductor. L1

# Structure of the Periodic Table

## Section Objectives

- Describe the arrangement of the elements in the periodic table.
- Find the number of protons and electrons in an atom using the periodic table.
- Explain atomic number.
- Identify mass number and calculate atomic mass.

## Key Terms

*periodic table*
*atomic number*
*mass number*
*isotopes*
*atomic mass*

## Decisions, Decisions

You've been asked to design a new product for a very successful company. You find out that the material must be lightweight, strong, flexible, and resistant to heat and weather. How do you decide what to use? One way would be to obtain a list of all the thousands of available substances and start checking out their properties. Wow! What a job! Perhaps if you started with the elements in these substances, you could at least narrow the list down to a hundred or so.

You may remember from learning about elements that metals have many of the desired properties, but that still leaves a lot of work. Wouldn't it be nice if someone arranged those elements so that you could quickly find the one you want? Properties such as

**Figure 5-1**

In making new products, different materials are selected based on the usefulness of their properties.

144

## Meeting Individual Needs

**Visually Impaired, Learning Disabled** To develop classification skills, give students some nuts and bolts of different sizes and shapes or coins and ask them to organize them in some way. Encourage them to feel the different shapes and textures to help them in their organization. Have students work in small groups to create a chart showing the different ways the objects are organized. **COOP LEARN**

flexibility, resistance to heat, strength, and ability to combine with other elements need to be considered. These elements need to be arranged based on such properties and repeating patterns in these properties. In such an arrangement, you'd be able to predict which elements would have the properties you want to make your revolutionary new product.

### ■ The Birth of the Periodic Table

In the late 1800s, as more and more elements were discovered, the need arose to arrange them into a pattern that would simplify their study. Dmitri Mendeleev, a Russian chemist, searched for a meaningful way to organize the elements. He decided to put them in order of increasing masses.

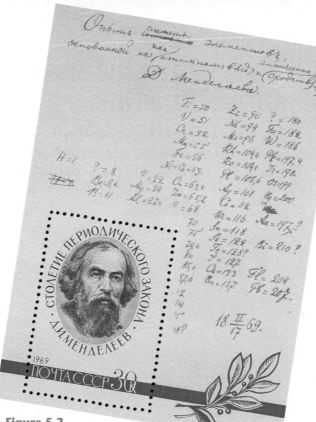

**Figure 5-2**

The Russian chemist Dmitri Mendeleev arranged the elements in order of increasing mass, forming one of the first periodic tables.

When Mendeleev put the elements in order by mass, he found that other properties, such as density, malleability, and the ability to react with other elements, seemed to repeat over and over. This repeating pattern is called periodic, and he called his table the **periodic table** of the elements.

In the following Investigate, try to develop a good strategy for arranging and identifying characteristics of elements by arranging something more common instead.

5-1   Structure of the Periodic Table   **145**

## 5-1 Two-Dimensional Classification

### Planning the Activity

**Time Needed**  30–35 minutes

**Purpose**  To identify a missing object based on its position in an organized arrangement.

**Process Skills**  organizing information, classifying, predicting, modeling, sequencing, observing and inferring

**Materials**  20 squares of paper (see student list), envelopes

**Preparation**  You can cut out the squares or have students cut them out the previous day. Place each set of squares in an envelope. For the missing square remove one of the following squares: 7, 8, 9, 12, 16, 17, 20. You may wish to remove the same number from all to make checking the answers easy, or you may wish to remove different ones so students do not copy.

### Teaching the Activity

**Process Reinforcement**  Have students discuss possible ways to order the cards. Responses may include by color; by increasing/decreasing numerical order; or prime numbers in one row, composites in another, and 1 in the last row. Encourage students to determine which method is easiest to arrange and use.

**Possible Procedures**  After ordering the cards by number, students may attempt any of several rearrangements, based on color, number, or combinations of the two.

---

# INVESTIGATE!

# Two-Dimensional Classification

*You classify things and people every day. Edible, tall, red, hard, smart, magnetic—these are all properties used to put things in groups. Let's find out how a scientist can use this tool.*

### Problem

How can you arrange properties to predict and explain?

### Materials

20 squares of paper to include:
  11 yellow squares with the numbers 1, 2, 6-10, 15-18;
  7 blue squares with the numbers 3, 4, 11-13, 19, 20; and
  2 green squares with the numbers 5, 14

## What To Do

**1** Imagine you have never seen these squares organized in any meaningful way. These squares have some things in common, but they are different in other ways. You have two jobs. One is to **organize** the squares in a way that organizes their properties, and the other is to **identify** the one square that is missing.

**2** Put the squares in order. Try to do this in one long row (see **photo**). Record your pattern *in your Journal.*

## Program Resources

**Activity Masters,**  pp. 23–24, Investigate 5-1

**Laboratory Manual,**  pp. 19–20, Relationships Among Elements  **L2**

**3** How would you arrange your squares in several rows, without changing the order in which you already have them? Try to arrange them so that every square in a row has something in common and/or every square in a column has something in common. Where would you break your original arrangement and begin a new row? Do this now.

**4** Continue until you have used all the squares. Remember, you can't change the order you have them in already. Record your final pattern.

## Analyzing

1. What pattern did you use to organize your squares the first time?

2. When you completed your arrangement of rows and columns, what properties did the squares in a row have in common? In a column?

## Concluding and Applying

3. *Predict* the properties (number and color) of the missing square.

4. *Observe* and *infer* which property of the numbers shows a repeating pattern.

5. **Going Further** If you were able to arrange the elements as you did the numbers, predict what properties you might use to group them.

**Expected Outcomes**
Results may vary. Accept all reasonable organizations. The students may have initially placed their squares in numerical order and then divided into rows based on patterns of color. Each row may have a series of yellow squares, followed by blue and then green.

The missing square can be determined by looking at the numerical order and at the color of the squares preceding and following the missing square.

The particular squares represent the first 20 elements of the periodic table, with appropriate atomic numbers and colors representing whether the elements are metals, nonmetals, or metalloids.

**Answers to** Analyzing/
Concluding and Applying
Note: answers may vary depending on individual arrangements of squares.

**1.** Each number increases by one

**2.** rows: identical patterns of color—yellow, blue and green. columns: same color

**3.** It fills in the missing number and reflects the colors of the squares preceding and following

**4.** color

**5.** Answers include ability to react, malleability, hardness, luster, color

## ✔ Assessment

**Process** Have students work in pairs, and provide each pair with numbered pieces of paper of different shapes—squares, circles, and triangles. Have students organize the pieces into some logical two-dimensional classification scheme and include a written description of how the arrangement is used. Select the Performance Task Assessment List for writing in science in **PAMSS,** p. 87. L1
**COOP LEARN**

# Arrangement of the Periodic Table

Mendeleev arranged the elements by increasing mass. When he did this, some of the elements' properties didn't match with what was expected in the pattern of periods. The periodic table we now use today takes care of that problem.

Remember that atoms are composed of protons, neutrons, and electrons. In the periodic table each element has one more proton in its nucleus than the one before it. The number of protons in an atom of an element is called the **atomic number** of the element. Since atoms are electrically neutral, there must be the same number of electrons (negative charges) in the atom as there are protons (positive changes). The atomic number tells you both the number of protons and the number of electrons. The modern periodic table shown on pages 164-165 is arranged in order of increasing atomic number.

Look at the information given in one box of the periodic table, shown in **Figure 5-3**.

**Figure 5-4**

Since each of these eggs has about the same mass, the "mass" of a carton of eggs could be defined as twelve egg mass units (12e).

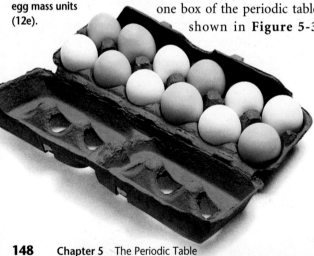

This box represents the element boron. The box contains the atomic number (5), the chemical symbol (B), the name, and the atomic mass (10.811) of the element. What do we mean by atomic mass?

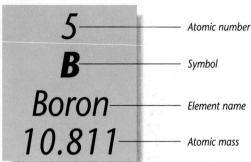

Atomic number
Symbol
Element name
Atomic mass

**Figure 5-3**

This is how the element boron is listed in the periodic table, showing its atomic number, its symbol, the name of the element, and its atomic mass.

### ■ Atomic Mass

Imagine you are asked the mass of a carton of eggs that contains six white eggs and six brown eggs, as shown in **Figure 5-4**. You decide that each egg has about the same mass and the carton is very light by comparison, so you decide to measure the mass of the eggs in terms of the number of eggs. That is, you define the mass of an egg as one egg mass unit (e). You tell the person that the mass of the carton of eggs is twelve! Twelve egg mass units—12 e!

Since atoms are so small, the easiest way to describe their mass is by describing the total number of protons and neutrons in the nucleus—the

**Figure 5-5**

An atom of carbon-12 has 6 protons and 6 neutrons, so the mass of the atom is 12 atomic mass units.

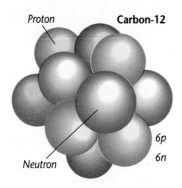

Proton  Carbon-12

Neutron

6p
6n

**mass number**. Protons and neutrons are like the brown and white eggs. They have different properties, but just about the same mass. If there are 6 protons and 6 neutrons in the nucleus, you say that the mass of the atom is 12 atomic mass units (u). Why aren't the electrons included? Even if we counted all the electrons in the biggest atom, their total mass would be only a fraction of the mass of a proton.

If an atom has a mass number of 23 and contains 12 neutrons, how many protons does it have? In other words, what is its atomic number, and what element is it? Remember that the mass number, 23, is the total number of protons and neutrons in the nucleus. If 12 of them are neutrons, how many are protons? 23-12=11 protons. That is the atomic number. Find that number on the periodic table on pages 164-165. The element is Na—sodium.

Try this. An atom has 9 protons and 10 neutrons. Look at the periodic table and figure out what element it is. Use the number of protons—the atomic number. What element has an atomic number of 9? Fluorine!

What is the mass number of this flourine atom? That's right—19.

What if you looked for the mass number on the table? Oops! There is no element with a mass number of 19. Fluorine is listed at 18.998. And 18.998 is called the atomic mass, not the mass number. Are atomic mass and mass number the same? If so, how come the atomic mass is not a whole number when you are counting protons and neutrons? Are there pieces of protons and neutrons?

**Figure 5-6**

The combined number of individual chocolates and peanuts in this pile of candy would determine the candy's "mass number."

### ■ Isotopes

Imagine that you have 100 pieces of candy, 60 are candy-coated chocolates, each having a mass of 1 candy mass unit, and 40 of them are candy-coated peanuts, each with a mass of 2 candy mass units (c). First, what is the total mass of the 100 pieces of candy?

$$60 \times 1\,c = 60\,c$$
$$\underline{40 \times 2\,c = 80\,c}$$
$$100 \text{ pieces } = 140\,c$$

The average mass of one piece is:
140 c / 100 pieces = 1.4 c/piece

**Activity** In this activity, students will use a model of isotopes to explore finding the atomic mass of an element.

Materials needed for this activity are dried lima beans and a pan or beam balance.

Give each group of students 50 dried beans. Direct them to find the total mass of the 50 beans to the nearest tenth of a gram and the average mass of the beans by dividing the total mass by the total number of beans. Then have them sort the beans into three groups according to size and find the mass of one bean from each group. Have students compare the masses of the smaller and larger beans with the average bean mass. Then discuss how the beans in this activity are like the isotopes of an element. L1

Atoms of the same element always have the same number of protons—their atomic number. This identifies them as the element they are. But all atoms of the same element don't necessarily have the same number of neutrons. For example, boron is a dark, gray solid. All boron atoms have 5 protons. Four-fifths of them have 6 neutrons. What is their mass number? The other one-fifth of all boron atoms found in nature have 5 neutrons. What is their mass number? Atoms of the same element with different numbers of neutrons are called **isotopes** of that element. The two isotopes of

boron discussed above are referred to as boron-11 and boron-10 and are illustrated in **Figure 5-7**. The numbers indicate the mass number of that isotope.

What is the average mass of 100 boron atoms? It would be closer to 11 than to 10, because there are more boron atoms with a mass of 11 than there are with a mass of 10.

$$4/5 \times 100 \text{ atoms} = 80 \text{ atoms}$$
$$1/5 \times 100 \text{ atoms} = 20 \text{ atoms}$$
$$80 \text{ atoms} \times 11 \text{ u/atom} = 880 \text{ u}$$
$$20 \text{ atoms} \times 10 \text{ u/atom} = \underline{200 \text{ u}}$$
$$100 \text{ atoms} = 1080 \text{ u}$$

$$1080 \text{ u/100 atoms} = 10.8 \text{ u/atom}$$

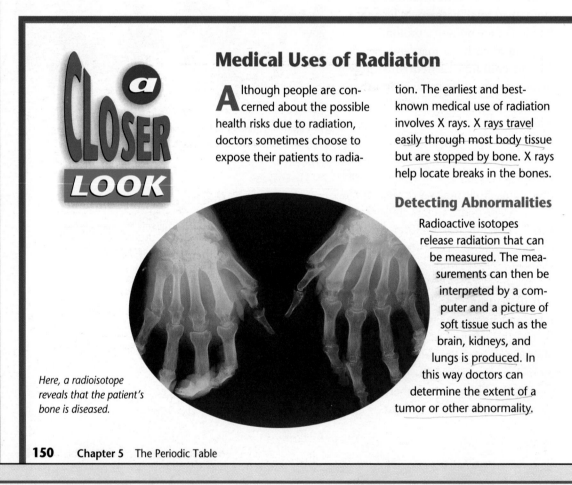

## Medical Uses of Radiation

Although people are concerned about the possible health risks due to radiation, doctors sometimes choose to expose their patients to radiation. The earliest and best-known medical use of radiation involves X rays. X rays travel easily through most body tissue but are stopped by bone. X rays help locate breaks in the bones.

### Detecting Abnormalities

Radioactive isotopes release radiation that can be measured. The measurements can then be interpreted by a computer and a picture of soft tissue such as the brain, kidneys, and lungs is produced. In this way doctors can determine the extent of a tumor or other abnormality.

*Here, a radioisotope reveals that the patient's bone is diseased.*

### Purpose

A Closer Look reinforces Section 5-1 which introduces isotopes by describing some medical uses of radiation.

### Content Background

All materials can absorb X rays to some degree. The amount absorbed depends on the atomic numbers of the elements in the material. Bone contains a large amount of calcium. Bone absorbs X rays better than the soft tissue that surrounds it because

calcium has a higher atomic number than the elements making up the soft tissue. Lead shields are used to protect people who work with X rays. Lead has a high atomic number indicating that it can absorb both X rays and gamma rays better than materials with lower numbers.

Sodium-24 is a radioactive isotope that can be used to detect diseases of the circulatory system, and iron-59 can be used to study blood circulation because the iron

Note boron's atomic mass shown on the periodic table. The **atomic mass** is the average mass of the isotopes of an element found in nature which explains why they are not whole numbers. Let's investigate more about the way isotopes and atomic mass are related.

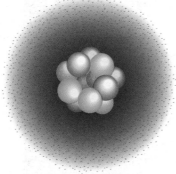
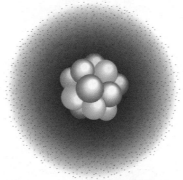

**Figure 5-7**

The most common isotope of boron has six neutrons, but some boron atoms have five neutrons, making them a different isotope.

## Detecting Viruses, Hormones, and Drugs

Radioactive isotopes can also be used to determine—very precisely—how much of a virus, hormone, or drug is in a patient's body. The technique, radioimmunoassay (RIA), was pioneered in the 1950s by Rosalyn Yalow and Soloman Berson. Yalow was awarded a Nobel Prize for her work. In an RIA test, the patient is given a precise amount of a radioactive compound. Compounds used in the test are chosen for their ability to take the place of the virus, hormone, or drug normally present in the body's fluids. Then a precise measurement of the radioactivity given off by the patient's blood or

*In this photograph, a radioisotope shows that the patient's bone is healthy.*

urine is made. By comparing the measurements, physicians can determine the amount of the substance under study present in a patient's body. For example, it was widely believed that diabetes was a condition that resulted from a total lack of insulin in the patient's blood. RIA showed that diabetes can occur even if insulin is present.

RIA has been used successfully to treat diabetes, reduce the risk of transmitting hepatitis in transfused blood, and in identifying infectious diseases such as tuberculosis.

### What Do You Think?

Survey the members of your family to learn if any of them have had any radiation treatment. How does that make you feel about the dangers of radiation?

will be incorporated into the hemoglobin in red blood cells. Radioactive cobalt-60 is used to treat cancer cells which it kills without harming healthy tissue cells.

### Teaching Strategy

Ask students about the diagnostic procedures they underwent the last time they visited the dentist for a checkup. Most will have experienced the use of a lead apron to protect them from X rays. Ask them why only the main part of their bodies was shielded with the lead apron. Dentists are primarily concerned with the protection of the patient's major organs, especially their reproductive glands. X rays can damage the genetic make-up of sex cells. L2

### Answers to

**What Do You Think?**

Students may have family members who have benefitted from ultrasound or magnetic resonance treatments; thus, they may feel the benefits outweigh the dangers of radiation.

### Going Further ⫸

Try to obtain discarded X rays from a hospital or physician's office. Have students work in small groups to examine these X rays. Have students try to differentiate between soft tissues and bone and look for any gross abnormalities such as a broken bone. X rays can be taped to the classroom windows for better viewing. Ask students to record their observations using words and sketches. **COOP LEARN**

## Planning the Activity

**Time Needed** 20–30 minutes

**Purpose** Develop and use a model to explore the relationship between isotopes and atomic mass

**Process Skills** interpreting data, making and using tables, sampling and estimating, comparing and contrasting, forming operational definitions, making models

**Materials** red and green candy-coated peanuts, red and green candy-coated chocolates

**Preparation** Use any of several popular brands of candy available in most food stores. Organize the candy into small paper cups or plastic bags before the activity.

Have students work in pairs, dividing the duties of arranging the candies and record keeping. Each pair should work together to calculate averages.
**COOP LEARN**

## Teaching the Activity

**Troubleshooting** Before students begin the activity, complete an example as a class, using different candy ratios than are used in the activity. Discourage students from eating the candy.

**Process Reinforcement** To reinforce critical thinking, ask **why red and green candies can't be mixed.** *Because each color represents a particular element.*

**Student Journal** Have students copy the data table and record all observations and calculations in their journals. ⏢L1⏢

## Expected Outcome

Students should find that the average mass of the red candies is 1.7 units and the average mass of the green candies is 3.5 units.

# Isotopes and Atomic Mass

*In this Investigate, you'll use a model of isotopes to help you understand the concept of atomic mass.*

## Problem

How do isotopes affect average atomic mass?

## Materials

4 red and 3 green candy-coated peanuts
2 red and 3 green candy-coated chocolates

## What To Do

**1** Copy the data table *into your Journal.*

**2** Make a pile of four red candy-coated peanuts and two red candy-coated chocolates (see photo **A**). The two different kinds of candy represent two isotopes of the same element.

**3** Assume that a red peanut has a mass of 2 candy units, and a red chocolate has a mass of 1 candy unit. *Calculate* the average mass of the red candy as follows:

    **a.** Multiply the number of red peanuts by the mass in candy units.

*Sample Data*

### Data and Observations

| | Peanut (candy × candy unit) | Chocolate (candy × candy unit) | Average (total mass) / (total candies) |
|---|---|---|---|
| Red | 4 × 2 = 8 | 2 × 1 = 2 | $\frac{8+2}{4+2}$ = 1.7 |
| Green | 3 × 4 = 12 | 3 × 3 = 9 | $\frac{12+9}{3+3}$ = 3.5 |

## Program Resources

**Activity Masters,** pp. 25–26, Investigate 5-2

**Science Discovery Activities,** 5-2, What's in the Bag?

## ENRICHMENT

Have students construct a table like the one shown on the next page. Provide them with the headings for the rows and columns, and have them fill in the grid. ⏢L2⏢

A                  B

**b.** Multiply the number of red chocolates by the mass in candy units.

**c.** Add the masses and divide by the total number of candies.

**4** Repeat Steps 2 and 3, but use three green peanuts and three green chocolates. Assume a green peanut has a mass of 4 units, and a green chocolate has a mass of 3 units.

**5** Record your calculations *in your Journal* (see photo *B*).

## Analyzing

**1.** There were six red and six green candies. Why were their calculated average masses not the same?

**2.** If a sample of element X contains 100 atoms of X-12 and 10 atoms of X-14, *calculate* the average mass of X.

## Concluding and Applying

**3.** An element needed for most nuclear reactors is uranium. Its two major isotopes are U-235 and U-238. Look up the mass of uranium on the periodic table. *Infer* which isotope is the most common. Explain.

**4.** *Compare* and *contrast* mass number and atomic mass.

**5.** ~~Going Further~~ Hydrogen has three isotopes. The most common one, protium, has no neutrons. Deuterium, the second isotope, has one neutron. Tritium has two neutrons. Using this information, *calculate* the mass number of these isotopes.

| Term | Meaning | Characteristics | Examples |
|---|---|---|---|
| Atomic Number | # of Protons | Same for all atoms of the same element | Carbon (C) Atomic # = 6 |
| Mass Number | # of Protons plus # of Neutrons | Changes for different isotopes of an element | C-12 (6p + 6n) C-13 (6p + 7n) C-14 (6p + 8n) |
| Atomic Mass | Avg. mass of atoms of the element | Usually not a whole # because many isotopes are present | Atomic mass of C = 12.011 |

## Check for Understanding

Ask volunteers to share the calculations they used to complete the table in the Apply question.

## Reteach

Materials needed are different-sized nuts or bolts and a pan balance. Have students find the total mass of nuts or bolts and then calculate the average mass of one nut or bolt. Students should be able to tell you that the different-sized nuts or bolts represent the different isotopes of an element. Help them to understand that the average mass represents the element's atomic mass. **L1**

## Extension

Have students use the periodic table to find the atomic number and atomic mass of the elements in the following pairs: tellurium (Te) and iodine (I); cobalt (Co) and nickel (Ni); argon (Ar) and potassium (K). Ask them to determine the order in which the elements in each pair would have been placed in Mendeleev's periodic table. *iodine, tellurium; nickel, cobalt; potassium, argon* Then have them compare this with the way they are arranged in the modern periodic table. **L3**

# 4 CLOSE

## Discussion

Discuss with students how a card catalog and the library are arranged like the periodic table. *Books are categorized with other books with which they are similar. Science books are grouped together as are works of fiction, nonfiction, magazines, encyclopedias, etc. The card catalog is organized to help you find the book you are looking for.* **L1**

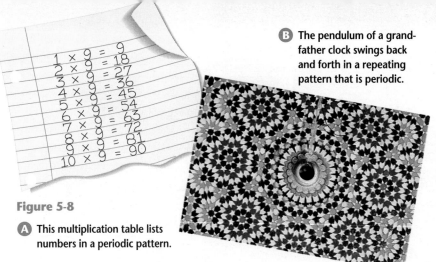

**Figure 5-8**

**A** This multiplication table lists numbers in a periodic pattern.

**B** The pendulum of a grandfather clock swings back and forth in a repeating pattern that is periodic.

**C** These tiles are arranged in a repeating pattern much like the elements are arranged in the periodic table.

You just used a candy mass unit as a model for atomic mass. The calculations you used to find the average candy mass are similar to the calculations you used to find the atomic mass of an element. Some elements may have only identical atoms, while several elements have as many as 6 or 7 isotopes. The atomic mass is found by calculating the average mass of a sample of atoms. Carbon has 6 isotopes, with mass numbers ranging from 10 to 15. However, almost 99 percent of carbon atoms have 6 protons and 6 neutrons—mass number 12. This is referred to as carbon-12.

The days of the week, the pendulum of a clock, and multiplication tables, shown in **Figure 5-8**, all occur in repeating patterns that are periodic. Elements can also be organized into a table that shows repeating patterns of properties. In the next section, you'll take a closer look at the organization of the periodic table and how it is used.

### check your UNDERSTANDING

1. How does the arrangement of the modern periodic table differ from Mendeleev's table?
2. Use the periodic table to find the name, atomic number, and atomic mass of the following elements: O, N, Ca, Ba, and Br.
3. Name three pieces of information that you can learn from an atomic number.

4. **Apply** Complete the following table.

| Symbol | Atomic No. | Mass No. |
|--------|-----------|----------|
| N | 7 | 14 |
| F | 9 | 19 |
| K | 19 | 39 |
| Co | 27 | 59 |

### check your UNDERSTANDING

1. It is arranged by atomic number rather than mass.

2. oxygen, 8, 15.999; nitrogen, 7, 14.0067; calcium, 20, 40.078; barium, 56, 137.33; bromine, 35, 79.904

3. name of element, number of protons, number of electrons

4. 1st row: 14; 2nd row: 9, 3rd row: 19; 4th row: 27

# Families of Elements

## Organizing the Elements

We began this chapter by using properties to organize elements in a way that would allow us to quickly locate them and to predict other properties. These might be density, strength, or any other chemical or physical characteristic of the element. What else do the elements have in common? You'll examine the periodic table in the next activity to find out.

### Find Out! ACTIVITY

## How are elements alike and different?

**What To Do**

1. Select two elements from the list provided by your teacher.

2. For each of your chosen elements, prepare an index card. In the upper left-hand corner of the card, place a box like the one on the periodic table. This should show the atomic number, symbol, name, and atomic mass of the element.

3. Do some research on the element and write a few sentences about its properties and uses.

4. Attach either an object or a picture to the card that shows its properties. For example, for iron, you could attach a nail. For helium, you might have a picture of a floating balloon.

5. Make a large periodic table using your cards and those of your classmates.

**Conclude and Apply**

1. *In your Journal,* record what you notice about the properties of elements on the left side of your table.

2. What about the right side?

Library

---

### Find Out!

## How are elements alike and different?

**Time Needed** 30 minutes

**Materials** teacher list of elements, index cards, objects made of elements, pictures of elements or objects made of or utilizing elements, tape

**Thinking Processes** observing, comparing and contrasting, interpreting data, using reference materials, forming operational definitions

**Purpose** To compare and contrast the properties of elements.

**Preparation** Have students find objects and/or pictures of objects made of elements or that utilize elements (such as an oxygen tank).

## Teaching Strategy

Make sure that, in piecing together their Periodic Table, students leave gaps for any elements that have not been chosen.

---

# PREPARATION

## Concepts Developed

In this section, students will explore families of elements including halogens, alkali metals, and alkaline earth metals. The members of a family of elements share common characteristics and properties. Students will see how dot diagrams represent the relationship between members of a periodic family. Students will use these diagrams to predict how certain members of a family combine with members of another family.

## Planning the Lesson

Refer to the Chapter Organizer on pages 142A–B.

---

**Student Journal** Have students record their research notes about their selected elements in their journals. **L1**

## Expected Outcome

Once the cards are arranged to simulate the periodic table, students should observe that elements have properties that are related to their positions in the table.

## Conclude and Apply

1. These elements have metallic properties.

2. Most of the elements are nonmetallic gases.

## ✔ Assessment

**Process** Have interested students select and research remaining elements and prepare index cards to complete the Periodic Table. Use the Performance Task Assessment List for Carrying Out a Strategy and Collecting Data in **PAMSS**, p. 25. **L1**

# 1 MOTIVATE

**Discussion** Have students give some of the ways books are classified. (by author, subject, title, Dewey Decimal system) Lead students to see that elements are classified in the periodic table. It contains a "library" of useful information for the scientist. L1

# 2 TEACH

## Tying to Previous Knowledge

In Chapter 4, students learned that electrons are arranged in energy levels around the nucleus of an atom. In this section, students will learn that all elements of a family have the same number of electrons present in their outer energy level. Ask students to describe the number of electrons allowed in each of the energy levels.

**Student Text Question**
**What other elements would you expect to behave in the same way?** *krypton, xenon, and radon*

**Activity** This activity will allow students to focus on grouping items based on their properties.

Materials needed are assorted pencils and pens, and a large table surface.

Ask students to arrange similar pens and pencils in columns and in order of mass. Discuss with students the reasons for their arrangements. Make sure they have examined the properties of objects as they are arranged in columns. Then ask students to describe how their columns are like the columns of the periodic table. *They are based on similar properties.*

## Columns of the Periodic Table

On the periodic table, elements in the same column are called a **family of elements**. Do you recognize the three elements in Family 11 on the periodic table? Copper, silver, and gold, shown in **Figure 5-9,** are called the coinage metals. Although they are different colors, they have similar physical and chemical properties. They are all malleable, shiny, and resistant to change.

Noble gases—such as helium and neon—are called noble because, like royalty refusing to associate with common people, these elements rarely combine with other elements. What other elements would you expect to behave in the same way? On the other hand, members of Family 17, the halogens, are very reactive and often combine with other elements.

Why do elements in the same family have similar properties? Electrons in an atom are arranged in energy levels around the nucleus, as shown in **Figure 5-10**. The number of electrons in the outer energy level of an atom determines if and how an element will combine with other elements. These outer electrons are so important that a special system is used to represent them.

**Figure 5-9**

**A** The Navajo turquoise and silver jewelry are among the treasures found at a Shiprock, New Mexico trading post. Bogata's Gold museum displays fine art and jewelry made by Indian goldsmiths.

**B** The tetradrachm, a coin of ancient Greece, had an owl on the back and was made of silver. Others, like these Canadian coins, were made of gold. The coin to the left is from the Ching Dynasty and is made of copper.

**156** Chapter 5 The Periodic Table

## Program Resources

**Study Guide,** p. 20
**Critical Thinking/Problem Solving,** p. 13, Radon Detectors L2

## ENRICHMENT

**Research** To reinforce their skills in using reference sources, assign each student a noble gas or halogen to research. Have them report orally to the class who discovered each and practical applications of these gases in everyday life. Use the Performance Task Assessment List for Oral Presentations in **PAMSS**, p. 71. L2

Figure 5-10

These diagrams of lithium, boron, sodium, and chlorine show the different arrangements of electrons in the energy levels around the nucleus of the atom.

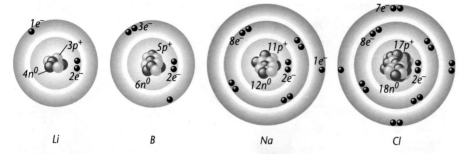

Li      B      Na      Cl

## ■ Dot Diagrams

A dot diagram is simply the symbol for an element surrounded by as many dots as there are electrons in the outer energy level. How can you tell how many electrons there will be? If you skip the elements in Families 3 through 12 on your periodic table, the other columns have a very simple pattern. There will be one electron in the outer level of column 1, two in column 2, three in column 13, and so on until you reach column 18, which has eight electrons in the outer level, except for helium which has two electrons in its one energy level. The pattern of outer electrons is simply one through eight. How many electrons are in the last energy level of the halogens? They are in Family 17, so it's seven. **Figure 5-11** shows examples of dot diagrams.

How would you write dot diagrams for the element sulfur? First, write the symbol for the element—S. Then look at its position on the periodic table. What column is it in? Family 16. How many electrons does it have in its outer energy level? Using the pattern mentioned above, we see that it has six. **Figures 5-11** shows how dot diagrams are drawn.

Figure 5-11

Ⓐ These are dot diagrams of potassium and aluminum. Potassium is represented by the symbol K and has one electron in its outer energy level. Aluminum is represented by the symbol Al. How many electrons are in the outer energy level of an atom of aluminum?

K ·

Ⓑ Sulfur is in Family 16 of the periodic table, so it has six electrons in its outer energy level. These are shown as six dots around the symbol for sulfur, S. There are five dots around the symbol for phosphorus, P. What family of the periodic table is phosphorus in?

## Meeting Individual Needs

**Learning Disabled, Visually Impaired**
Have students model dot diagrams for elements by using an object like a dish or watch glass to represent the nucleus. Have them place pennies around this object corresponding to the electrons in the outer energy level.

**Theme Connection** The number of electrons in the outer energy level of an atom determines the interaction of an element with other elements. All elements of a family, except for helium, have the same number of electrons in this outer level and, therefore, interact the same way with other elements. This strongly supports the theme of interactions and systems.

**Activity** Have students spend some time drawing electron dot diagrams. Some students will catch on to this skill more quickly than others so have groups of students work together.

Point out the rule for drawing electron dots around the symbol of an atom. Then demonstrate by drawing the diagrams shown in Figure 5-11. **COOP LEARN**

Content Background
Until recently, groups or families in the periodic table were labeled with a Roman numeral and the capital letter A or B. Now, based on a decision made by IUPAC (International Union of Pure and Applied Chemistry), groups are labeled 1 through 18. Also, the names lanthanide and actinide have been changed to lanthanoid and actinoid.

### Visual Learning

**Figure 5-10** To reinforce student's ability to interpret scientific illustrations, have them compare the number of electrons in the first energy level of the four atoms shown. Students may infer that two is the maximum number of electrons this level can accommodate. Repeat with the second energy level, leading students to infer that eight is the maximum for that level. **L1**

**Figure 5-11 How many electrons are in the outer energy level of an atom of aluminum?** *3* **What family of the periodic table is phosphorus in?** *15*

If the sodium gives its electron to chlorine, how many electrons will chlorine have in its outer level? *8* How many will sodium have after it loses that electron? *8*

**Demonstration** This activity demonstrates the flame test by which different alkali metals can be identified.

Materials needed are ionic solution of cesium, rubidium, potassium, and sodium; nichrome wire; Bunsen burner; and goggles.

When an alkali metal is heated, some of the electrons in its atoms gain energy and move to a higher energy level. When these electrons fall back to their original positions, they lose their energy in the form of light. The characteristic color of the light identifies the alkali metal. Dip the nichrome wire into each solution, one at a time, and insert it into the flame of a Bunsen burner. The cesium solution will produce a red/violet flame, the rubidium a red flame, the potassium a blue/violet flame, and the sodium a bright yellow flame.

Notice that, with the exception of helium, all of the noble gases have eight electrons in their outer energy level. Once eight is reached, the next element adds an energy level and begins again with one electron. It

xenon        neon        argon        krypton

**Figure 5-12**

The elements xenon, neon, argon, and krypton are noble gases. As these dot diagrams show, each of these elements already has eight electrons in its outer energy level. As a result, these gases do not combine easily with other elements.

### ■ Combining Atoms

By observation, we find that when other elements combine, they tend to do so in a way that will give them eight electrons in their outer energy level. Let's look at one example. **Figure 5-14** shows dot diagrams of an atom of sodium and an atom of chlorine. If the sodium gives its electron to chlorine, how many electrons will chlorine have in its outer level? How many will sodium have after it loses that electron?

There is an exception to this rule of having eight electrons in the outer level. Hydrogen and helium are so

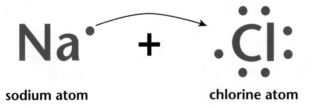

sodium atom                chlorine atom

would seem that the presence of eight electrons makes the energy level full, or complete. You know that noble gases do not combine easily with other elements. They seem very stable—that is, they resist change.

**Figure 5-13**

Xenon and other noble gases are often used in electric lamps. Many lighthouses use xenon arc lamps, which produce an intense blue-white light.

small that they only have electrons in the first energy level. In this first energy level, there is only room for two electrons. Therefore, the noble gas helium is complete with two electrons in its outer energy level. When elements such as lithium (Li) and beryllium (Be) lose their outer electrons, their outer levels become like helium, and they are stable.

**Figure 5-14**

This diagram shows one atom of sodium combining with one atom of chlorine to form sodium chloride. The sodium atom gives up one electron to the chlorine atom. The chlorine atom then has eight electrons in its outer energy level, making it complete, while the sodium atom is left with eight electrons in its outer energy level. Do you think sodium chloride is a stable compound?

**158**    **Chapter 5**    The Periodic Table

# Some Important Families

## ■ Alkali Metals

Since each Family 1 element has one outer electron to lose, they will all behave like sodium and combine with chlorine. What other elements, in addition to sodium, would you expect to react with chlorine?

The column 1 elements belong to a Family known as the **alkali metals.** They differ from typical metals because they are so soft they can be cut with a knife. They have a metallic luster, conduct heat and electricity, and are malleable.

In nature, alkali metal atoms immediately react with air, water, or other substances in the environment as shown in **Figure 5-15B**. Pure alkali metals must therefore be stored in kerosene or some other liquid that doesn't react with them.

**DID YOU KNOW?**

Compounds of sodium are used in the manufacture of detergents and soaps. Pioneers made soap by collecting water that ran through ashes and cooking it with grease. The water contained mainly potassium hydroxide. Alkali means to roast ashes in a pan.

**Figure 5-15**

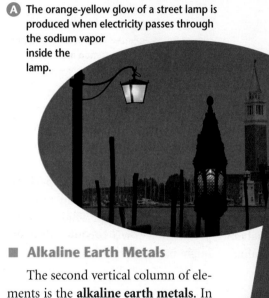

**A** The orange-yellow glow of a street lamp is produced when electricity passes through the sodium vapor inside the lamp.

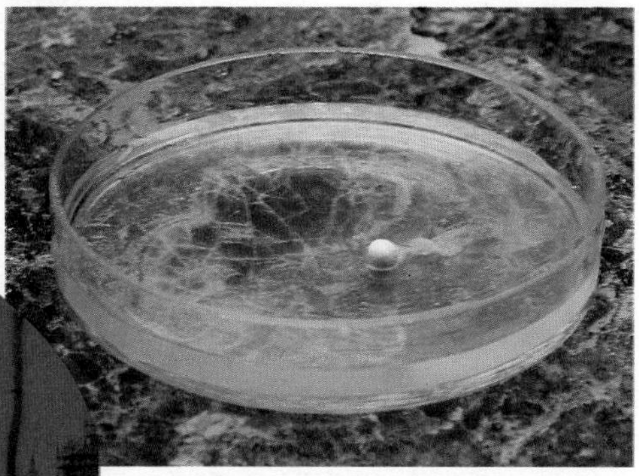

**B** The atoms of the alkali metals, such as the sodium shown here, react immediately with water or other substances in the environment.

## ■ Alkaline Earth Metals

The second vertical column of elements is the **alkaline earth metals.** In what ways do their properties seem different from those of the alkali metals? **Figure 5-16** shows a reaction between magnesium nitrate and a solution of baking soda. What do you expect will happen if strontium nitrate were added to a baking soda solution? What other nitrates should behave in the same way?

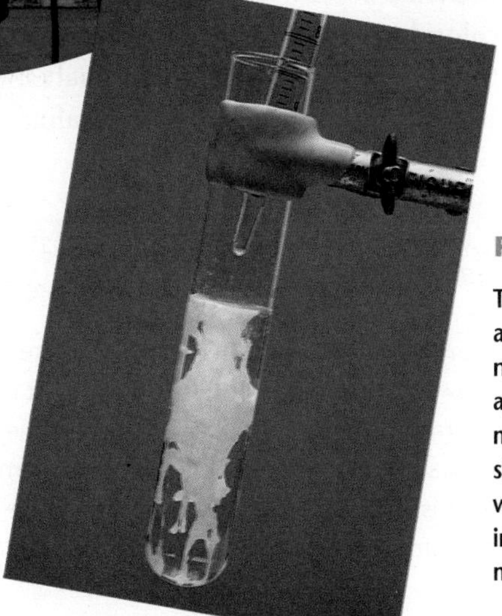

**Figure 5-16**

The alkaline earth metals, which include magnesium, are not quite as reactive as the alkali metals. This photograph shows what happens when a solution of baking soda is added to magnesium nitrate.



***Across the Curriculum***

**Daily Life**

Alkali metals have many uses in industry. Sodium is used in streetlights. Students may have noticed a yellowish glow in sodium vapor lamps. Compounds of sodium are used in the manufacture of detergents, paper, petroleum products, glass, and soaps. Potassium is used in the manufacture of fertilizer.

Potassium chloride can be used in place of table salt for people who need to reduce the amount of sodium in their diet. Sodium and potassium are also very important to the proper functioning of our nervous systems. These elements are lost in perspiration, which is why people use special sports drinks containing these elements during and after heavy workouts.

**Student Text Questions**

**What other elements, in addition to sodium, would you expect to react with chlorine?** *H, Li, L, Rb, Cs, Fr* **In what ways do their properties seem different from those of the alkali metals?** *They are harder and less reactive.* **What do you expect will happen if strontium nitrate were added to a baking soda solution?** *A white solid will form.* **What other nitrates should behave in the same way?** *Nitrates of any other Family 2 element.*

**ENRICHMENT**

**Research** The hardness of water actually refers to the calcium and magnesium content of the water. Assign students to find out how a water softner operates. *Sodium and potassium ions replace the calcium and magnesium ions. Sodium and potassium are more soluble and consequently do not precipitate out like calcium and magnesium salts.* Have students research why certain areas of the country have harder water than others. P

5-2 Families of Elements 159

# 3 ASSESS

## Check for Understanding

The intent of the Apply question under Check Your Understanding is for students to apply what they know about the characteristics of elements to make a prediction.

## Reteach

Show students a Bohr diagram of each of the elements found in the families studied. Ask them to look for similarities in these diagrams. The diagrams in Figure 5-10 are Bohr diagrams. L1

## Extension

Have students work in groups to make a chart exhibiting the alkali and alkaline earth metals. Encourage them to be as artistic and creative as possible. They could draw pictures of materials or objects that utilize these elements as well as provide structural information regarding each element's atom. COOP LEARN L3

# 4 CLOSE

## Activity

Provide students with some properties of lithium, sodium, and potassium, the first three members of the alkali metal family. Then ask students to find rubidium on the periodic table and tell what properties they think it would have as well as the number of electrons an atom of rubidium would have in its outer energy level. L1

**Figure 5-17**

**A** The bright colors you see in a fireworks display are produced mainly by alkaline earth metals. Magnesium is used in some fireworks to produce a brilliant white light. Strontium is used to produce a crimson light, and barium is used to produce green light. Would other alkaline earth metals produce different colors?

**B** Magnesium is often mixed with aluminum in alloys. These alloys are used in products such as tennis rackets and bicycle frames because they are strong but lightweight. Why do you think alkali metals such as sodium are not used in these products?

**Connect to...**

## Life Science

Some coral polyps secrete calcium carbonate skeletons. These are called hard corals. Make a diagram of three different types of hard corals.

Calcium compounds, found in dairy products, are an essential building block for strong bones and teeth. Calcium hydroxide is a white powder used to make baseball diamond and football field lines. It is also used to neutralize acidity in soil. Calcium chloride is used in winter to keep ice from forming on roads and walks. Uses of magnesium, another alkaline earth metal, are discussed in **Figure 5-17**.

Because members of a chemical family have the same number of outer electrons, they also have similar abilities to form compounds with other elements. Rather than having to test each individual element, you can simply look at the periodic table and identify the family to which an element belongs. Then you can predict how it will behave and how it might be used.

## check your UNDERSTANDING

1. List four of the elements in Family 16 of the periodic table. Draw dot diagrams for them.
2. Compare and contrast the properties of alkali metals and alkaline earth metals.
3. **Apply** An element is shiny, but easily cut with a knife. When dropped in water, it reacts immediately, giving off a flash of light. It is placed in a container with another element that is a gas. Nothing happens. What families would you guess these two elements are in? Explain your answer using the periodic table on pages 164-165.

160    **Chapter 5**   The Periodic Table

## check your UNDERSTANDING

1. oxygen (O), sulfur (S), selenium (Se), tellurium (Te), or polonium (Po); each dot diagram should have the same dot arrangement as this diagram for oxygen:

:Ö:

2. Alkaline earth metals are harder and less reactive than alkali metals.
3. Family 1 and Family 18 because their properties correspond to those described for these families.

# Periods of Elements

## What's the Period in the Periodic Table?

You know that the elements in a column of the periodic table are related as members of the same family. What about the rows of the periodic table? What information can you infer about the elements in a particular row? Do they share similar properties as well? Do this next activity to see how you can use a familiar table to infer information.

**Section Objectives**
■ Describe a period on the periodic table.
■ Identify where metals, non-metals, and metalloids are located on the periodic table.
■ Use the periodic table to classify an element.

**Key Terms**
*period*

### Find Out! ACTIVITY

## How can you use a table of repeating events to predict or explain?

### What To Do

1. The figure shows a familiar table of repeating properties. What is it? Of course, it's a calendar, but one with a difference. This calendar has some missing information.

2. Determine what is missing by examining the information surrounding the spot where the missing information goes. This periodic table is made up of families of days, Sunday through Saturday, and by horizontal periods called weeks.

### Conclude and Apply

1. Two of the days in Families 3 and 4 are marked with an @ and a #. What dates should go in these positions? Explain your reasons *in your Journal*.

2. Family 5 doesn't have a name. What is the correct name for this family?

3. What dates are included in the third period of the table?

4. Assuming that the previous month had 30 days, what day would the 28th of that month have been? What period of this table would it appear in?

| SUN | MON | TUE | WED | | FRI | SAT |
|---|---|---|---|---|---|---|
| | | | | 1 | 2 | 3 |
| 4 | 5 | 6 | 7 | 8 | 9 | 10 |
| 11 | 12 | @ | # | 15 | 16 | 17 |
| 18 | 19 | 20 | 21 | 22 | 23 | 24 |
| 25 | 26 | 27 | 28 | 29 | 30 | 31 |

### Find Out!

**How can you use a table of repeating events to predict or explain?**

**Time needed** 5–10 minutes

**Thinking Processes** organizing information, making and using tables, thinking critically, observing and inferring, sequencing, modeling

**Purpose** To interpret a table of repeating events and use the pattern to make deductions and predictions about missing information.

### Teaching the Activity

**Student Journal** Have students enter their responses and reasoning in their journals. [L1]

### Expected Outcomes

Students should recognize patterns in the arrangement of the calendar and use these to find the missing information.

## PREPARATION

### Concepts Developed

In this section, students will examine the relationships within the rows, or periods, of the periodic table. They will locate metals, nonmetals, and metalloids. And they will use the periodic table to compare the reactivities of different elements.

### Planning the Lesson

Refer to the Chapter Organizer on pages 142A–B.

## 1 MOTIVATE

**Activity** Give students an opportunity to practice classifying. Materials needed are metals and nonmetals such as a metal spoon, aluminum foil, piece of charcoal, etc.

Number the samples for easy reference. Allow students to examine these samples and write the observable properties of each such as color, luster, hardness, etc. Then ask students to group the samples into metals and nonmetals according to their properties. [L1]

### Conclude and Apply

**1.** 13 and 14; they are consecutive days that fit between 12 and 15

**2.** Thursday

**3.** 11–17

**4.** Monday; period 1

### ✓ Assessment

**Process** To reinforce formulating models and making tables, tell students they are on a space trip to a planet that has 400 days in a year. Have students construct a calendar to use on the planet. Use the Performance Task Assessment List for Carrying Out a Strategy and Collecting Data in **PAMSS**, p. 25. [L1]

**Tying to Previous Knowledge**

In the last section, students learned about the alkali and alkaline earth metals. This can be related directly to the metals covered in this section. Use their understanding of these highly reactive metals to introduce other, less reactive ones.

**Theme Connection** The reactivity of an element depends on the electrons in its outer energy level, thus supporting the energy theme. The electrons around the nucleus of an atom are held there by a force of attraction between opposite charges. It requires energy to pull an electron away from its orbit around the nucleus.

The calendar is just one example of a table of periodic events. One repeat of a pattern is called a **period**. On the periodic table of elements, shown on pages 164-165, each row begins as the pattern of physical and chemical properties of elements begins to repeat itself. When arranged in this manner, the 100+ known elements form 7 horizontal rows, or periods, because of the periodic repetition of properties as you move from left to right. Breaking the sequence of elements into periods created 18 columns called families. This is similar to the calendar in the Find Out activity.

On the periodic table, locate the stair-step line toward the right side that divides the table. The elements to the left of this line are metals, except hydrogen. Notice that the box containing hydrogen is slightly above the rest of the table. Although hydrogen has one electron in its outer energy level, you might also say that it has one less than it needs to become nonreactive like helium. In that case, it would be placed at the top of the halogen family. As you know, hydrogen is a gas and has properties of a nonmetal. It is placed in Family 1 because the formulas for its compounds are similar to those formed by Family 1 elements.

You've learned that most metals are solid at room temperature, shiny,

## The Chernobyl Disaster

History's worst accident at a nuclear power plant occurred on April 26, 1986, in Chernobyl in the Soviet Union.

This reactor used graphite to regulate the nuclear reaction, and water to carry the thermal energy to the turbine, which then produced electrical energy. On that day, the water flow past the core (where the nuclear reaction occurs) was stopped. Part of the reactor got so hot that the graphite caught fire and caused an explosion that ripped apart the reactor and released large amounts of radioactive material into the

*The explosion at the Chernobyl nuclear reactor caused considerable damage and released large amounts of harmful radioactive material into the atmosphere.*

**162**

**Purpose**

The Life Science Connection describes the possible long-range effects of the Chernobyl disaster, particularly the effect of strontium-90. Because of the concept presented in Section 5-2 that members of a family of elements have similar properties, scientists have used their knowledge of calcium to predict the behavior of strontium, an element in the same family.

**Content Background**

It is estimated that the Chernobyl accident may result in the eventual death of up to 4000 people.

The same accident that occurred at Chernobyl would not happen in a nuclear power plant in the United States because U.S. power plants are moderated with water rather than graphite. The moderator is a material used to regulate the flow of neutrons in a nuclear reactor.

and good conductors of heat and electricity. In your index card periodic table, locate examples of metals you are familiar with, such as iron, zinc, copper, and silver. Elements in Families 3 through 12 are called transition elements. They include many of the metals found in everyday objects.

The elements to the right of the stair-step line are the nonmetals. Many of them are gases. The solids, such as carbon and sulfur, are easily crushed and do not shine.

The properties of elements change gradually as they move from left to right. On either side of the stair-step line is a special group of elements called metalloids, elements that have

some properties of both metals and nonmetals. They are dull in color, not malleable or ductile, but they do conduct a current. Because metalloids, such as silicon and germanium, do not conduct as well as a metal, they are called semiconductors. These elements are used to make transistors, integrated circuits, and other critical parts of electronic devices, such as computers and video games.

**Figure 5-18**

A Like most of the transition elements, titanium is hard and has a high melting point.

B Vanadium, another of the transition elements, is often used to form alloys such as vanadium steel.

**Activity** Allow students to compare and contrast the conductivity of heat by metals and materials that are not metals.

Materials needed are aluminum foil, metal spoon, iron nail, wooden strip, plastic spoon, plastic cup, and hot water.

Roll the foil into a small cylinder about the size of a pencil. Stand the foil, spoons, nail, and wooden strip upright in a plastic cup. Add hot water to the cup, leaving the tops of the objects above the water level. Wait one minute. Then have students carefully touch the exposed ends of each object. Students should find that the metal objects conduct the heat well, while the objects that are not metal do not.
L1

atmosphere. At least 31 people died from radiation sickness or burns. Many more may die in the coming years as a result of this accident.

### Strontium-90

People who lived in the Soviet Union were not the only ones affected by the Chernobyl disaster. Some radioactive material was carried by wind into northern and central Europe. Health experts in Europe were particularly concerned about strontium-90, an isotope of the element strontium that has a half-life of 28 years.

If you look at the periodic table, you will notice that strontium is just beneath calcium. Elements that belong to the

same group in the periodic table have many similar characteristics. Strontium, therefore, can take the place of calcium in many chemical reactions.

### Effects on the Human Body

Our bones are made up almost entirely of calcium compounds. If strontium-90 enters the human body, it replaces some of that calcium and exposes the bones to radiation. Constant exposure to this type of radiation can seriously damage bone marrow, causing diseases such as leukemia.

Strontium-90 enters our bodies the same way that calcium enters our bodies. When grass grows, it absorbs calcium from

the soil. Cows eat the grass and produce milk. When we drink milk or eat milk products, such as butter and cheese, our bodies absorb the calcium.

That's why, in the aftermath of the Chernobyl explosion, European health officials carefully monitored the level of strontium-90 in milk. Some milk had to be thrown away because it contained too much of the radioactive material.

### What Do You Think?

Many people were evacuated from the vicinity of the Chernobyl nuclear power plant when it caught fire in 1986. From what you've learned about strontium-90, do you think they have been allowed to return?

Extra Credit

**Teaching Strategy**
Besides reading the excursion, discuss the 1979 Three Mile Island incident of near meltdown due to the workers mistakenly turning off most of the automatic safeguards in the plant. Then hold a class debate regarding the use of nuclear energy and the hazards as well as the benefits it provides. L3

**Answers to**
**What Do You Think?**
A probable answer is no. The concentration of strontium-90 in the soil is most likely greater in the vicinity of Chernobyl than elsewhere. Because this isotope has a half-life of 28 years, it will remain a danger to health for many years to come.

**Going Further ▶**
Have students work in pairs or small groups to research the uptake of certain radioactive isotopes by living organisms. Suggest that they research the studies being done with strontium-90 or the studies of the people of Hiroshima and Nagasaki. Have students present their findings in the form of written or oral reports. Select the appropriate Performance Task Assessment list in **PAMSS**. L3 COOP LEARN

**Activity** To help students interpret the periodic table, draw electron dot diagrams of lithium (Family 1) and fluorine (Family 17) on the chalkboard. Have student volunteers show the electron transfer that occurs and tell how many electrons each atom has after the transfer takes place. Then ask students to name other elements that would combine in this way. *Accept all pairings of Family 1 and Family 17 elements.* You might wish to repeat this activity with a Family 2 atom and a Family 17 atom. L1

**Figure 5-19**

In the periodic table, all of the known elements are arranged in rows and columns according to their properties. Elements arranged in the same column make up a family of elements. One of the elements in Family 11 is gold, which has the symbol Au. What is the atomic number of gold?

**Metallic Properties**

| Alkali Metals 1 | Alkaline Earth Metals 2 | | Transition Elements | | | | | | |
|---|---|---|---|---|---|---|---|---|---|
| | | | | | | | | | |
| 1 **H** Hydrogen 1.007 94 | | | | | | | | | |
| 3 **Li** Lithium 6.941 | 4 **Be** Beryllium 9.012 182 | | | | | | | | |
| 11 **Na** Sodium 22.989 77 | 12 **Mg** Magnesium 24.305 | 3 | 4 | 5 | 6 | 7 | 8 | 9 | |
| 19 **K** Potassium 39.0983 | 20 **Ca** Calcium 40.078 | 21 **Sc** Scandium 44.955 91 | 22 **Ti** Titanium 47.88 | 23 **V** Vanadium 50.9415 | 24 **Cr** Chromium 51.9961 | 25 **Mn** Manganese 54.9380 | 26 **Fe** Iron 55.847 | 27 **Co** Cobalt 58.9332 | |
| 37 **Rb** Rubidium 85.4678 | 38 **Sr** Strontium 87.62 | 39 **Y** Yttrium 88.9059 | 40 **Zr** Zirconium 91.224 | 41 **Nb** Niobium 92.9064 | 42 **Mo** Molybdenum 95.94 | 43 **Tc** Technetium 97.9072* | 44 **Ru** Ruthenium 101.07 | 45 **Rh** Rhodium 102.9055 | |
| 55 **Cs** Cesium 132.9054 | 56 **Ba** Barium 137.33 | 71 **Lu** Lutetium 174.967 | 72 **Hf** Hafnium 178.49 | 73 **Ta** Tantalum 180.9479 | 74 **W** Tungsten 183.85 | 75 **Re** Rhenium 186.207 | 76 **Os** Osmium 190.2 | 77 **Ir** Iridium 192.22 | |
| 87 **Fr** Francium 223.0197* | 88 **Ra** Radium 226.0254 | 103 **Lr** Lawrencium 260.1054* | 104 **Unq** Unnilquadium 261* | 105 **Unp** Unnilpentium 262* | 106 **Unh** Unnilhexium 263* | 107 **Uns** Unnilseptium 262* | 108 **Uno** Unniloctium 265* | 109 **Une** Unnilennium 266* | |

— Metallic properties —

| Lanthanoid Series | 57 **La** Lanthanum 138.9055 | 58 **Ce** Cerium 140.12 | 59 **Pr** Praseodymium 140.9077 | 60 **Nd** Neodymium 144.24 | 61 **Pm** Promethium 144.9128* | 62 **Sm** Samarium 150.36 |
|---|---|---|---|---|---|---|
| Actinoid Series | 89 **Ac** Actinium 227.0278* | 90 **Th** Thorium 232.0381 | 91 **Pa** Protactinium 231.0359* | 92 **U** Uranium 238.0289 | 93 **Np** Neptunium 237.0482 | 94 **Pu** Plutonium 244.0642* |

*Mass of isotope with longest half-life that is the most stable isotope of the element

---

## Program Resources

**Study Guide,** p. 21

**Multicultural Activities,** p. 14, Gold and the Yanomami Indians L1

**How It Works,** p. 10, Aluminum Production L1

**Transparency Masters,** pp. 21 and 23, and **Color Transparencies,** Numbers 9 and 10, The Periodic Table L2

**Concept Mapping,** p. 13, Elements of the Periodic Table L1

**Laboratory Manual,** pp. 21–24, Chemical Activity L1

**Science Discovery Activities,** 5-3, Dot Marks the e⁻

**Teacher F.Y.I.**

The nonmetal oxygen is the most abundant element by mass in the human body (approximately 65 percent). Calcium is the most abundant metal by mass at only 1.4 percent.

Noble Gases
18

| | | | | | Halogens 17 | 2 He Helium 4.002 602 |
|---|---|---|---|---|---|---|

| 13 | 14 | 15 | 16 | 17 | 18 |
|---|---|---|---|---|---|

| 5 B Boron 10.811 | 6 C Carbon 12.011 | 7 N Nitrogen 14.0067 | 8 O Oxygen 15.9994 | 9 F Fluorine 18.998 403 | 10 Ne Neon 20.1797 |

Transition Elements

| 10 | 11 | 12 |
|---|---|---|

| 13 Al Aluminum 26.981 54 | 14 Si Silicon 28.0855 | 15 P Phosphorus 30.973 76 | 16 S Sulfur 32.07 | 17 Cl Chlorine 35.453 | 18 Ar Argon 39.948 |

| 28 Ni Nickel 58.69 | 29 Cu Copper 63.546 | 30 Zn Zinc 65.39 | 31 Ga Gallium 69.723 | 32 Ge Germanium 72.61 | 33 As Arsenic 74.9216 | 34 Se Selenium 78.96 | 35 Br Bromine 79.904 | 36 Kr Krypton 83.80 |

| 46 Pd Palladium 106.42 | 47 Ag Silver 107.8682 | 48 Cd Cadmium 112.41 | 49 In Indium 114.82 | 50 Sn Tin 118.710 | 51 Sb Antimony 121.757 | 52 Te Tellurium 127.60 | 53 I Iodine 126.9045 | 54 Xe Xenon 131.29 |

| 78 Pt Platinum 195.08 | 79 Au Gold 196.9665 | 80 Hg Mercury 200.59 | 81 Tl Thallium 204.383 | 82 Pb Lead 207.2 | 83 Bi Bismuth 208.9804 | 84 Po Polonium 208.9824* | 85 At Astatine 209.987 12* | 86 Rn Radon 222.017* |

Nonmetallic properties

Metals    Metalloids    Nonmetals

Lettering:    ■ Solids    □ Synthetics (solid)    Liquids    Gases

| 63 Eu Europium 151.96 | 64 Gd Gadolinium 157.25 | 65 Tb Terbium 158.9253 | 66 Dy Dysprosium 162.50 | 67 Ho Holmium 164.9303 | 68 Er Erbium 167.26 | 69 Tm Thulium 168.9342 | 70 Yb Ytterbium 173.04 |

| 95 Am Americium 243.0614* | 96 Cm Curium 247.0703* | 97 Bk Berkelium 247.0703* | 98 Cf Californium 251.0796* | 99 Es Einsteinium 252.0828* | 100 Fm Fermium 257.0951* | 101 Md Mendelevium 258.0986* | 102 No Nobelium 259.1009* |

5-3    Periods of Elements    **165**

---

| **Meeting Individual Needs** |
|---|

**Visually Impaired**   To assist the visually impaired and to start students thinking about observation through senses other than sight, provide students with as many samples of metals and nonmetals as possible. Allow them to handle these and feel the textural differences. Provide them with copper wire as well as a thin sheet of aluminum to illustrate the properties of ductility and malleability.

## ■ Reactivity of Elements

You learned that the metals in Family 1, or alkali metals are so reactive that they are never found uncombined in nature. Of the alkali metals, those nearest the bottom are the most active. The most active metals are in the lower left corner of the periodic table. Their outer electrons are so far away from the nucleus that the attraction between the electrons and the protons is much weaker. Therefore, these elements easily lose electrons.

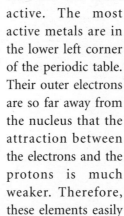
The opposite is true of the nonmetals. If you don't count the noble gases, Family 18, the most active nonmetals are found in the upper right corner. Recall that nonmetals gain electrons from other elements, rather than losing them. Since the nucleus is positive and will attract electrons, the closer the outer energy level is to the nucleus, the easier it is for the atom to attract electrons. In the case of fluorine, the outer energy level is closer to the nucleus than any of the larger atoms in Family 17. Therefore, fluorine is the most active nonmetal.

You've taken a short trip through the periodic table. If you had the task of designing the new product mentioned at the beginning of the chapter, you can see how it would be simplified by using the table.

**Figure 5-20**

Like the other nonmetals in Family 17 of the periodic table, chlorine is very active, which is why a chlorine spill can be quite dangerous.

**166** **Chapter 5** The Periodic Table

You may have noticed that there's one section we haven't discussed. What are those two rows doing down at the bottom of the table? The atomic numbers would indicate they should be placed between Families 2 and 3 in periods 6 and 7. Why aren't they there? Simple—the table wouldn't fit on the page! The table is made more compact and useful by placing them at the bottom.

As you continue your education, you'll find that organizing information according to systematic patterns can help you study, learn, and recall important facts more easily. Lists and tables are one way to do this. You're sure to discover other methods of organization that will also work well for you. Even now, you can probably recall the names of families of elements that appear in columns one, two, and eighteen of the periodic table. Working with an organized system can make studying fun. **Figure 5-21** illustrates

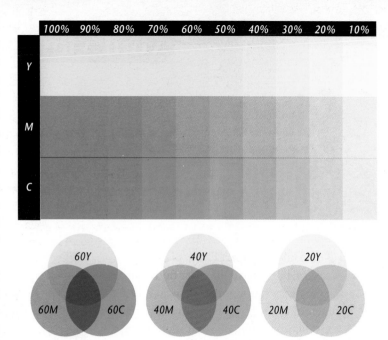

**Figure 5-21**

Pigments are coloring materials used to make paints. The three primary pigments are yellow; magenta, which is a reddish color; and cyan, which is a bluish color. The figure shows that each pigment family—cyan, magenta, and yellow—is made up of several shades of the pigment. By mixing different percentages of these three pigments, different colors can be produced. Note the color patterns created.

another such system. You may want to experiment with a system something like this in some of your other classes.

## check your UNDERSTANDING

1. What happens to atomic numbers as you follow a period across the periodic table? Why is it called a period?
2. Locate the positions on the periodic table for metals, nonmetals, and metalloids. Sequence these three categories from the one containing the largest number of elements to the smallest.
3. Give the period and family in which each of the following elements are found: nitrogen, sodium, iodine, and mercury. Tell whether the element is a metal, nonmetal, or transition element.
4. **Apply** Which element is more reactive?
   a. potassium or magnesium
   b. phosphorus or chlorine

**Check for Understanding**

As you discuss the Apply question, ask students to state in their own words a generalization for determining which of two elements is more active by referring to the periodic table.

**Reteach**

**Activity** Have students make a list of all the metals with which they are now familiar. Next to the name of the metal, have them list objects they see or use that are made from that metal. Lead a discussion about how the uses of metals are derived from their properties. L1

**Extension**

Have students put together their own chart showing the metals and nonmetals by using index cards with information regarding the specific element on each. Ask each student to design a different card for a different element. Display this metal/nonmetal chart in class. L3

## 4 CLOSE

**Activity**

Provide each small group of students with a small sample of a metal and of a nonmetal. Allow students a few minutes to determine which is the metal and nonmetal. Then have them write their conclusion. COOP LEARN

---

### ENRICHMENT

**Research** To reinforce using reference materials, ask students to find out about the cyclotron and other instruments currently being used to investigate the atom. Students should determine the purpose of each instrument, what the instrument does that a person could not do, and how the instrument is operated. P

### check your UNDERSTANDING

1. It increases by one each time. It is one repetition of a repeating pattern.
2. metals, nonmetals, metalloids
3. nitrogen: Period 2, Family 15, nonmetal; sodium: 3, 1, metal; iodine: 5, 17, nonmetal; mercury: 6, 12, metal.
4. Potassium; chlorine

## Science and Society

**Purpose**

Section 5-3 mentions two rows of elements placed below the periodic table of elements rather than within the table. These are the lanthanoid and actinoid series. Science and Society discusses elements in these series and details the problems with disposing of one of the elements, plutonium.

**Content Background**

There are several methods used to dispose of nuclear waste. Low-level radiation wastes are often released into the air, water, or ground where they disperse and become diluted in the environment. Radioactive wastes with short half-lives are stored in tanks and allowed to decay and then are released. High-level radioactive waste can be held in storage under water in large pools or buried, as discussed in the excursion. One idea that is currently being researched is the mixing of nuclear waste in glass or ceramic capsules, sealing these in tanks, and burying them. Another problem with nuclear waste involves their transport. A nuclear waste carrier involved in an accident might release deadly radioactive wastes into the environment. Any disposal or transport system must be protected from wars, terrorist acts, and natural disasters during the long period of decay.

## Science and Society
# Synthetic Elements

You could take apart Earth, piece by piece, but you would never find even the slightest trace of an element called promethium. That's because promethium is a synthetic element, one that is produced only in laboratories. Like all other synthetic elements, promethium is radioactive. It has been used as a miniature electric power source for pacemakers and artificial hearts like the one shown.

### The Lanthanoid Series

Promethium belongs to a part of the periodic table known as the lanthanoid series, a group of elements with atomic numbers from 57 through 71. These elements share similar chemical properties. The same is true of elements belonging to the actinoid series, which includes atomic numbers from 89 through 103. Most synthetic elements are found in the actinoid series, and most are known as transuranium elements. Transuranium literally means "beyond uranium." A transuranium element has an atomic number greater than uranium's atomic number, 92.

Some of the first physicists to create transuranium elements began bombarding uranium with slow neutrons. The element was named neptunium because uranium was named after the planet Uranus, and Neptune is the next planet in the solar system. Another transuranium element, discovered later that year, was named plutonium after the planet Pluto.

### The Plutonium Problem

Plutonium is perhaps the best known of all the synthetic elements. It has been used in nuclear warheads. Small amounts of plutonium provided electric power for the Voyager I spacecraft that went to the moon.

Nearly 40 metric tons of plutonium are produced each year. Most of it is in the form of nuclear waste. Finding ways to dispose of plutonium is one of society's most challenging problems. Plutonium is one of the most toxic substances on Earth—a lump the size of an orange could poison an entire city and it remains radioactive for more than 24 000 years.

*Made 110 (for 1/1000 of second)*
*Oct, '94 Germany*
*bombarded lead nuclei w/ nickel nuclei*
*82 + 28 = 110 protons*

## Methods of Disposal

How, then, do you dispose of plutonium? One suggestion would be to load it up on rockets and launch it into space. But what if the rocket explodes or crashes shortly after lift-off? Another idea is to bury containers filled with nuclear waste beneath the polar ice caps. But what if the radioactive heat melts the polar ice caps and causes worldwide flooding?

Many experts believe that the safest way to dispose of plutonium would be to bury it deep underground. The United States government is considering a place to bury highly radioactive nuclear waste beneath the Yucca Mountain in Nevada shown in the photo.

Before the plutonium is buried, it has to be sealed in specially constructed stainless steel canisters. These canisters have been dropped from a height of 600 meters, crashed into a concrete wall at 128 kilometers per hour, and submerged in burning fuel. Despite all of this punishment, none of the containers ever sprang a leak. Even so, no one can be certain what would have happened if the containers had been filled with plutonium when they were tested.

The canisters may be placed in tunnels dug more than 300 meters beneath the Yucca Mountain. Most of the mountain is composed of volcanic rock, which will carry heat away from the canisters as they cool down.

After 60 years, the canisters would be inspected. If there are no leaks, the tunnels would be permanently sealed. In all, the dump site would contain more than 187 kilometers of tunnels, enough to hold nearly 70 000 metric tons of radioactive waste.

### Worries

Some people who live in Nevada are worried about the dump site. What would happen if there were ever a volcanic eruption? Or an earthquake? What if the canisters ever came in contact with underground water? Can these canisters resist corrosion over a period of 24 000 years? Only time will tell.

### What Do You Think?

Energy creates pollution. When you burn fossil fuels—such as natural gas, coal, and oil—you release toxic chemicals into the air. Nuclear power, by comparison, is a very clean source of energy. But nuclear waste, such as plutonium, is a potential threat to the environment. Some people feel that no more nuclear power plants should be constructed until scientists develop a foolproof way to store nuclear wastes. How do you feel about the use of nuclear power?

### Going Further ▮▮▮▮▶

## Using Key Science Terms

1. Change *total* to *average*.
2. Change *alkaline earth* to *alkali*.
3. Change *family* to *period*.
4. Change *period* to *family of elements*.
5. Change *neutrons* to *protons*.
6. Change *alkali metals* to *alkaline earth metals*.

## Understanding Ideas

1. Answers may include any three of the following:
   a. lithium, sodium, potassium, rubidium, cesium, francium.
   b. helium, neon, argon, krypton, xenon, radon.
   c. beryllium, magnesium, calcium, strontium, barium, radium.
2. 19
3. Atomic numbers of elements in period 4 range from 19 to 36.
4. Possible answers include boron, silicon, germanium, arsenic, antimony, tellurium, polonium, astatine.
5. It has 7 neutrons; nitrogen.
6. Halogens have 7 outer electrons.
7. All are metals.
8. Each has the same number of electrons in its outer energy level.
9. 1st level—2 electrons; 2nd level—8 electrons; 3rd level—5 electrons

---

## Using Key Science Terms

| | |
|---|---|
| alkali metals | isotopes |
| alkaline earth metals | mass number |
| atomic mass | period |
| atomic number | periodic table |
| family of elements | |

*The sentences below include terms that have been used incorrectly. Change the incorrect terms so that the sentence reads correctly. Underline your change.*

1. The atomic mass of an element represents the total mass of all its isotopes.
2. Family 1 on the periodic table is called the alkaline earth metals.
3. A horizontal row in the periodic table is called a family of elements.
4. The halogens are a very reactive period in the periodic table.
5. The atomic number of an element is the number of neutrons in its nucleus.
6. Magnesium and calcium are alkali metals.

## Understanding Ideas

*Answer the following questions in your Journal using complete sentences. Use the periodic table on pages 164-165 as needed.*

1. Name three elements in each of the following families of elements.
   a. alkali metals
   b. noble gases
   c. alkaline earth metals
2. An element has an atomic number of 11. What is the atomic number of the next heaviest element with similar properties?

3. What are the atomic numbers of the elements in period four?
4. Name three metalloids.
5. An element has an atomic number of 7 and a mass number of 14. How many neutrons are in the nucleus? What is the element?
6. How many electrons do the halogens have in their outer energy level?
7. What do all of the transition elements have in common?
8. Why do elements in the same family have similar properties?
9. How many electrons are in each of the energy levels of a phosphorus atom?

## Developing Skills

*Use your understanding of the concepts developed in this chapter to answer each of the following questions.*

1. **Concept Mapping** Using the word list, complete the following concept map: *metals, metalloids, nonmetals*

**metals, metalloids, nonmetals**
Elements

metals   metalloids   nonmetals

2. **Making and Using Graphs** Suppose a sample of 200 atoms of an element contains the isotopes listed in the following table. List the isotopes and make a pie graph representing this data.

---

**Program Resources**

**Review and Assessment,** pp. 29–34 [L1]
**Performance Assessment,** Ch.5 [L2]
**PAMSS**
**Alternate Assessment in the Science Classroom**
**Computer Test Bank**

| Isotope Sampling | |
|---|---|
| Mass Number of Isotopes | Number of Atoms |
| 34 | 72 |
| 35 | 46 |
| 36 | 82 |

**3. Recognizing Cause and Effect** A helium atom has only two electrons. Why does helium behave as a noble gas?

## **C**ritical Thinking

In your Journal, *answer each of the following questions.*

1. A silver sample contains 52 atoms, each having 60 neutrons, and 48 atoms, each having 62 neutrons. What is the sample's average atomic mass?

2. According to the periodic table, what is the most active metal? The most active nonmetal? What would you expect if these two elements were brought together?

3. What are the family numbers of the elements diagrammed below?

## **P**roblem Solving

*Read the following problem and discuss your answers in a brief paragraph.*

**You are a public official in a town that has been isolated by a natural disaster. A major factory in your town uses cadmium in a process that is vital to the town's survival. All sources of cadmium have been cut off.**

1. Suggest two elements that might replace cadmium in the factory's process. Explain your suggestions.

2. The town workers must handle this element in the manufacturing process. Explain which of your two choices from Question 1 you would recommend.

## CONNECTING IDEAS

Discuss each of the following in a brief paragraph.

1. **Theme—Stability and Change** When an atom of element X emits an alpha particle, one product is Pb-214. What are the atomic number and mass number of element X? What element is it?

2. **Theme—Scale and Structure** Atoms in a family of elements increase in size as you move downward in the periodic table. Explain why this is so.

3. **Life Science Connection** What radioactive element could easily replace the calcium in human bones?

4. **Science and Society** List four benefits and four risks associated with synthetic elements. Do you think the benefits outweigh the risks? Explain.

## ✔ Assessment

**Portfolio** Review the portfolio options that are provided throughout the chapter. Encourage students to select one product that demonstrates their best work for the chapter. Have students explain what they learned and why they chose this example for placement into their portfolios.

Additional portfolio options can be found in the following **Teacher Classroom Resources:**
**Concept Mapping,** p. 13

### Developing Skills

1. See reduced student page

2.

*Pie chart showing: mass number 34 (72 atoms), mass number 35 (46 atoms), mass number 36 (82 atoms)*

3. Helium has only one energy level, which can hold a maximum of 2 electrons. Therefore, the outer energy level of helium is full, making the element chemically inactive.

### Critical Thinking

1. 107.96

2. Francium; fluorine. The would combine violently.

3. Family 14; Family 16

### Problem Solving

1. Zinc and mercury; they are in the same family as cadmium.

2. Zinc; mercury is a liquid, difficult to handle, and poisonous.

### Connecting Ideas

1. Po-218, atomic number 84

2. Going down a family in the periodic table, the number of protons in the nucleus of an element increases. Adding an equal number of electrons, forming new energy levels, makes the atoms larger.

3. strontium-90

4. Synthetic elements have found uses in medicine, in space exploration, on nuclear warheads, and in other technologies. However, synthetic elemnets are radioactive, toxic substances that produce nuclear waste and a problem of disposal. The importance of benefits versus risks is a matter of opinion.

# Chapter Organizer

| SECTION | OBJECTIVES | ACTIVITIES |
|---|---|---|
| **Chapter Opener** | | **Explore!** How can a fire be extinguished? p. 175 |
| **6-1 Kinds of Chemical Bonds** (3 days) | 1. **Describe** ionic and covalent bonds.<br>2. **Identify** particles produced by ionic and covalent bonding.<br>3. **Distinguish** between a nonpolar covalent and a polar covalent bond. | **Explore!** Can you see an ionic reaction? p. 179<br>**Investigate 6-1:** Models of Combining Atoms, pp. 182–183<br>**Skillbuilder:** Comparing and Contrasting, p. 184 |
| **6-2 Chemical Shorthand** (2 days) | 1. **Explain** how to determine oxidation numbers.<br>2. **Give** formulas for compounds from their names.<br>3. **Name** compounds from their formulas. | **Explore!** What's it made of? p. 185<br>**Skillbuilder:** Making and Using Tables, p. 191 |
| **6-3 Balancing Chemical Equations** (3 days) | 1. **Explain** what is meant by a balanced chemical equation.<br>2. **Demonstrate** how to write a balanced chemical equation. | **Explore!** Must the sum of the reactant and product coefficients be equal? p. 192 |
| **6-4 Chemical Reactions** (3 days) | 1. **Describe** four types of chemical reactions, using their general formulas.<br>2. **Classify** various chemical reactions by type. | **Find Out!** How does a chemical reaction enable a space shuttle to be launched? p. 196<br>**Investigate 6-2:** Double Displacement Reactions, pp. 198–199 |

## EXPAND your view

**A Closer Look** Silver Streaks and Speeding Electrons, pp. 178–179
**Life Science Connection** Pond Scum Be Gone, pp. 190–191

**Science and Society** Chemical Detectives, pp. 201–202
**History Connection** Healthful Structures, p. 203
**Economics Connection** Using It Up, p. 204

## ACTIVITY MATERIALS

### EXPLORE!

**Page 175**
20 grams of baking soda, small test tube, 50 mL vinegar, 500-mL flask, one hole stopper containing piece of tubing, sink
**Page 179***
camera and flashbulb
**Page 185***
bag of lawn fertilizer, dog or cat food, can of paint, box of laundry detergent or bleach
**Page 192***
marked cards

### INVESTIGATE!

**Pages 182–183***
modified egg cartons, marbles
**Pages 198–199***
5 test tubes and rack, small beaker; saturated solutions of calcium sulfate, $CaSO_4$; magnesium sulfate, $MgSO_4$; soap solution 1%, sodium carbonate $Na_2CO_3$, graduated cylinder-25mL, funnel, filter paper, dropper, stirring rod, 3 stoppers, distilled water

### FIND OUT!

**Page 196***
No special materials are required.

*For adequate development of the concepts presented, we recommend that students do the activities with an asterisk.

# Chapter 6 Combining Atoms

## TEACHER CLASSROOM RESOURCES

| Student Masters | Teaching Aids |
|---|---|
| **Study Guide**, p. 22<br>**Multicultural Connections**, p. 15<br>**Take Home Activities**, p. 12<br>**Making Connections: Integrating Sciences**, p. 15<br>**Science Discovery Activities**, 6-1 | **Laboratory Manual**, pp. 25–28, Chemical Bonds<br>**\*STVS:** *Fire Safety Tests*, Chemistry (Disc 2, Side 1)<br>**\*STVS:** *Sand Blasting with Dry Ice*, Chemistry (Disc 2, Side 1) |
| **Study Guide**, p. 23<br>**Multicultural Connections**, p. 16<br>**Making Connections: Technology & Society**, p. 15<br>**Flex Your Brain**, p. 5<br>**Science Discovery Activities**, 6-2 | **\*STVS:** *Treating Acid Lakes*, Chemistry (Disc 2, Side 2) |
| **Study Guide**, p. 24<br>**Critical Thinking/Problem Solving**, p. 14<br>**Making Connections: Across the Curriculum**, p. 15 | **\*STVS:** *Advanced Composites*, Chemistry (Disc 2, Side 1) |
| **Study Guide**, p. 25<br>**Concept Mapping**, p. 14<br>**How It Works**, p. 11<br>**Science Discovery Activities**, 6-3 | **Laboratory Manual**, pp. 29–32, Chemical Reactions<br>**Laboratory Manual**, pp. 33–36, Reaction Rates and Temperature<br>**Color Transparency and Master 11**, Chemical Equations<br>**Color Transparency and Master 12**, Types of Chemical Reactions |

### ASSESSMENT RESOURCES

**Review and Assessment**, pp. 35–40
**Performance Assessment**, Ch. 6
**PAMSS\***
**MindJogger Videoquiz**
**Alternate Assessment in the Science Classroom**
**Computer Test Bank**

**Spanish Resources**
**Cooperative Learning Resource Guide**
**Lab and Safety Skills**
**Integrated Science Videodisc**

## KEY TO TEACHING STRATEGIES

The following designations will help you decide which activities are appropriate for your students.

- **L1** Level 1 activities should be within the ability range of all students.
- **L2** Level 2 activities should be within the ability range of the average to above-average student.
- **L3** Level 3 activities are designed for the ability range of above-average students.
- **LEP** LEP activities should be within the ability range of Limited English Proficiency students.
- **COOP LEARN** Cooperative Learning activities are designed for small group work.
- **P** These strategies represent student products that can be placed into a best-work portfolio.

## ADDITIONAL MATERIALS

**Software**
*Chemical Hotline*, Focus.
*Chemicals of Life I*, Eduquest.
*Chemistry: Balancing Equations*, MECC.
*Chemistry Help Series: Physical vs. Chemical Changes*, Focus.
*Reactions*, J& S Software.
*The Structure of Matter*, Educational Activities.

**Audiovisual**
*Catalytic Reactions*, video, EBEC.
*Chemical Bonding and Atomic Structure*, video, Coronet/MTI.
*Elements, Compounds and Mixtures*, video, Coronet/MTI.
*Reaction Rates and Equilibrium*, video, Coronet/MTI.

**Laserdisc**
*Chemical Energy*, Churchill.
*Science Discovery Middle School*, Videodiscovery.
*Windows on Science: Physical Science*, Optical Data Corp.

**Readings**
Carona, P. B. *Chemistry and Cooking*. Prentice-Hall.
Hazen, Robert and James Trefil. *Science Matters: Achieving Science Literacy*. Doubleday.

**\*Performance Assessment in Middle School Science**

**\*Science and Technology Videodisc Series**

# Combining Atoms

## THEME DEVELOPMENT

The predominant theme of this chapter is systems and inter-actions. Each chemical reaction could be considered a system in which there is an interaction of elements or compounds.

Stability and change is anoth-er theme of this chapter. Change occurs when elements or com-pounds react to produce a new substance that is different from the original substances.

## CHAPTER OVERVIEW

In this chapter, students will differentiate two types of chemi-cal bonds—ionic and covalent—that can form between two or more atoms. Students will write chemical formulas for various compounds by using oxidation numbers. Then, they will discov-er how to write and balance chemical equations by utilizing coefficients. Finally, students will classify chemical reactions according to type.

### Tying to Previous Knowledge

Arrange students in small groups to identify a list of com-mon chemical reactions that oc-cur in daily life. They might sug-gest such things as burning fuels, digesting food, and baking bread. Have the class discuss whether or not the reaction giv-en is indeed a chemical reaction.

**L1** **COOP LEARN**

## INTRODUCING THE CHAPTER

Challenge students to com-pare and contrast two types of reactions. Ask students if they have ever seen newspaper turn yellow or a piece of paper burn. Then have them describe the difference between the reactions. *They occur at different rates. One releases a greater amount of ener-gy than does the other.*

# combining Atoms

**D**id you ever dream of being a fire fighter? Today's fire fighters do more than just pour water on fires. If a tanker truck full of chemicals has an accident, the fire department may spray a special foam over the truck. If there is a gas leak, fire fighters decide what precautions to use until the leak is stopped. Perhaps they should be renamed "chemical reaction technicians."

Fire is a very rapid chemical reaction that releases heat and produces new compounds. Putting out a fire may also involve chemical reactions. In this chapter, you'll learn more about the language scientists use to describe such reactions.

▶ **In the activity on the next page, explore an example of how atoms combine.**

### Did you ever wonder...

✓ Why water puts out fire?
✓ Why water is called H₂O?
✓ How a detergent gets your clothes clean?

Before you begin to study about combining atoms, think about these questions and answer them *in your Journal.* When you finish the chapter, compare your Journal write-up with what you have learned.

174

### Did you ever wonder...

• Water lowers the temperature of the burn-ing material and reduces the oxygen supply to the fire. (p. 176)

• Water is made up of molecules, each of which is composed of two hydrogen atoms and one oxygen atom. (p. 190)

• Water and grease will not combine. The de-tergent will combine with both the water and the grease, so the grease can be washed away. (p. 184)

### STUDENT JOURNAL

Have students write their responses to the Did You Ever Wonder questions in their journals. After they have read the chapter, students should read their journal entries again to see what they have learned about how atoms combine.

## How can a fire be extinguished?

**M**odern fire extinguishers do not contain these specific chemicals, but you can use this activity to see how a fire can be put out by a chemical reaction.

### What To Do

1. Put 20 grams of baking soda into a small test tube.

2. Pour 50 mL of vinegar into a 500-mL flask.

3. Carefully lower the test tube into the flask, making sure the baking soda does not contact the vinegar.

4. Put a one-hole stopper containing a piece of tubing into the mouth of the flask.

5. While pointing the tubing into the sink, tilt the flask so that the vinegar wets the baking soda. Record your observations *in your Journal.* **CAUTION:** *If the contents react too fast, the stopper can blow out.*

175

### Uncovering Preconceptions

Guide students to differentiate physical and chemical changes. Explain to students that a chemical change occurs only if electrons are gained, lost, or shared to combine the two materials in a chemical bond.

## Explore!

### How can a fire be extinguished?

**Time needed** 15 minutes

**Materials** vinegar, test tube, baking soda, flask, one-hole stopper fitted with a piece of tubing

**Thinking Processes** observing and inferring, measuring in SI, modeling, comparing and contrasting, recognizing cause and effect

**Purpose** To observe the chemical reaction released by a fire extinguisher.

### Teaching the Activity

**Discussion** Ask students to predict what will happen when the baking soda contacts the vinegar. L1

**Student Journal** Have students draw their observations in their journals. L1

### Expected Outcome

Students should observe bubbling carbon dioxide gas as a result of the chemical reaction taking place.

### ✔ Assessment

**Process** Challenge students to compare the reaction that they created to the reaction that occurs in a fire extinguisher. Then, working in cooperative learning groups, have students research the environmental issue of whether lightning-caused forest fires should be put out or should be allowed to burn themselves out. Use the Performance Task Assessment List for Investigating an Issue Controversy in **PAMSS**, p. 65. L1 **COOP LEARN**

## ASSESSMENT PLANNER

### PORTFOLIO
Refer to page 207 for suggested items that students might select for their portfolios.

### PERFORMANCE ASSESSMENT
Process, pp. 175, 185, 192, 196
Skillbuilder, pp. 184, 191
Explore! Activities, pp. 175, 179, 185, 192
Find Out! Activity, p. 196
Investigate, pp. 182–183, 198–199

### CONTENT ASSESSMENT
Check Your Understanding, pp. 184, 191, 195, 200
Reviewing Main Ideas, p. 205
Chapter Review, pp. 206–207

### GROUP ASSESSMENT
Opportunities for group assessment occur with Cooperative Learning Strategies.

# PREPARATION

## Concepts Developed

After studying this section, students should be able to differentiate the different ways elements combine to form compounds. In order to fill their outermost energy levels, some atoms will lose or gain electrons as they form ionic bonds between one another. Other atoms become electrically stable by sharing electrons as they form a covalent bond. The concept of polar and nonpolar molecules is also discussed in this section. Students will learn to identify a molecule that has a slightly uneven charge at either end as a polar molecule.

## Planning the Lesson

Refer to the Chapter Organizer on pages 174A–B.

# 1 MOTIVATE

**Demonstration** CAUTION: *Handle lead compound with care and dispose of heavy metal waste properly.* Allow students to observe a very simple chemical reaction. You will need lead nitrate solution, $Pb(NO_3)_2$, (33 g/L); sodium iodide solution, NaI, (17 g/L); 2 flasks; and filter paper. Hold up two flasks, one containing lead nitrate solution and the other sodium iodide solution. Have students note the clarity and the state (liquid) of the two solutions. Next, while all watch carefully, mix the two solutions. Instantly you will get a heavy yellow precipitate of $PbI_2$ as the double replacement reaction occurs, giving evidence of the chemical change. Filtering will show the solid nature of the $PbI_2$ precipitate. L1

---

## 6-1 Kinds of Chemical Bonds

### Section Objectives
- Describe ionic and covalent bonds.
- Identify particles produced by ionic and covalent bonding.
- Distinguish between a nonpolar covalent and a polar covalent bond.

### Key Terms
ion
ionic bond
molecule
covalent bond
polar molecule
nonpolar molecule

## Atomic Glue

Three different products were formed when you mixed ordinary vinegar, also called acetic acid, with baking soda, also called sodium hydrogen carbonate, in the Explore activity. These products were water, carbon dioxide, and sodium acetate, a salt. Each of these products can put out a fire. The salt cuts off the oxygen supply and suffocates the fire. Water lowers the temperature of the burning materials below their ignition point and reduces the oxygen supply to the fire. Carbon dioxide is more dense than air, so it forms a blanket over the flames and cuts off the supply of oxygen. Some fire extinguishers work just like the one you made.

### ■ Why Atoms Combine

How and why do the atoms in these chemicals join together in the first place? Is there some atomic glue that keeps them together? And why do some elements form compounds much more easily than others do?

**Figure 6-1**

Ⓐ When sodium gives up an electron to chlorine, its outermost energy level has eight electrons and is complete.

Ⓑ When chlorine takes on an electron from sodium, its outermost energy level has eight electrons, and it then is complete.

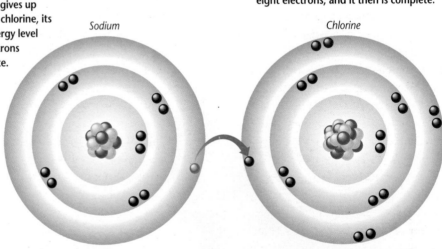
Sodium    Chlorine

Ⓒ This makes the resulting charged sodium and chlorine atoms very stable. What is the common name for sodium chloride?

---

## Program Resources

**Study Guide,** p. 22
**Multicultural Connections,** p. 15, The Chemistry of Colors L1
**Take Home Activities,** p. 12, Bonding L1

Recall from Chapter 5 that having a complete outer energy level makes an atom very stable. **Figure 6-1** shows how this stability is achieved when sodium chloride, common table salt, is formed during a reaction between atoms of sodium and chlorine. When sodium gives its outer level electron to chlorine, both will have filled outer electrons levels. **Figure 6-2** shows what happens when a small amount of the metal sodium is placed in a flask of chlorine gas.

Recall from Chapter 4 that atoms are neutral—that is, they have equal numbers of positive and negative charges. Sodium has 11 protons (11+) and 11 electrons (11-). When it loses one of those electrons, what happens to the overall charge? It now has only 10 electrons (10-) and thus has an overall charge of 1+. (11+) + (10-) = 1+. This charged atom is called an **ion**. In this case the ion is positively charged because it has one fewer electron than proton. It is written Na$^+$.

In the meantime, what has happened to the chlorine atom with its 7 outer level electrons? When chlorine gains one electron from sodium, it has 8 electrons in its outermost energy level. Sodium and chlorine now both have full outer energy levels. But chlorine has 17 protons with a charge of 17+ and 18 electrons with a charge of 18-. If you add the charges, you can see that (17+) + (18-) = 1-. Chlorine is a negative ion because it contains one more electron than proton. Scientists call it a chloride ion and write it as Cl$^-$.

**Figure 6-2**

Sodium is a metal, and chlorine is a gas. When a small amount of sodium is placed in a flask of chlorine, the metal bursts into a bright yellow flame and a white powder, which is sodium chloride, is formed.

### ■ Formulas for Ions

Notice that when we write the shorthand for the ions Na$^+$ and Cl$^-$, the sign is slightly above the symbol. This is called a superscript, *super-* meaning above. You'll see superscripts, such as those in Al$^{3+}$ and O$^{2-}$ throughout the chapter. They describe the charge on the ion. When the superscript is + or -, it is understood to mean 1+ or 1-.

The charges of the two ions are opposite. Therefore, they attract each other to make up the compound NaCl. NaCl is the white smoke you see as the reaction in **Figure 6-2** takes place. Because the positive charge of the sodium ion is equal, but opposite in sign, to the negative charge of the chloride ion, the compound NaCl, sodium chloride, is neutral.

## Meeting Individual Needs

**Visually Impaired** To help the visually impaired differentiate the inner and outer energy levels of an atom, provide large cutout nuclei of various atoms, such as sodium and chlorine. Have students place one penny outside the sodium nucleus and seven pennies around the outside of the chlorine nucleus. To model the ionic bonding of sodium and chlorine, have them move the one penny from the sodium over to join the other seven. L1 LEP

## Visual Learning

**Figure 6-1** Have students compare and contrast what happens to atoms of sodium and chlorine as these atoms react to form sodium chloride. *Both types of atoms acquire a charge. Sodium loses one electron, acquiring a positive charge, and chlorine gains one electron, acquiring a negative charge.* **What is the common name for sodium chloride?** *table salt*

**Figure 6-2** Have students use Figure 6-2 to recognize cause and effect. Ask them to identify the substance shown in Figure 6-2. *sodium chloride* Then have them tell what caused this substance to form. *a reaction between sodium and chlorine* LEP

# 2 TEACH

**Tying to Previous Knowledge**

In the previous chapter, reactivity was discussed and related to the placement of elements in the periodic table. Certain elements will more readily combine with other elements, based on the number of electrons in their outer energy level. Ask students how they can find the number of electrons in the outer energy level of an element using the periodic table. To visualize how atoms combine, ask students to think of how the pieces of a jigsaw puzzle interlock to form a complete picture. In a similar way, atoms bond together in a definite ratio and in a definite order to form compounds.

**Theme Connection** An atom has the most stability when its outer energy level is complete. When ionic bonds are formed, atoms gain or lose electrons to achieve complete outer energy levels. When covalent bonds are formed, atoms become more stable by sharing electrons. Students will observe this in the Investigate on pages 182–183.

## Visual Learning

**Figure 6-3** Ask students to use a hand lens and table salt to compare the shape of the table salt crystals to that of the large crystal in the photo. Students should notice that both are cubic.

# Ionic Bonding

There are many compounds that form in a way similar to the way sodium chloride is formed. When atoms gain or lose electrons, they become ions. Because some of these ions are positively charged and some are negatively charged, they attract one another. This attraction of positive ions for negative ions is called an **ionic bond**.

**Figure 6-3**

This salt crystal is an example of an ionic compound.

## ■ Ionic Compounds

Compounds that are made up of ions are ionic compounds. Although there are exceptions, most ionic compounds have certain properties. Ionic compounds will conduct an electric current when the compounds are melted or dissolved in water. Most of them are solid crystals with high melting points. Is NaCl, as is shown in **Figure 6-3**, an ionic compound? Yes, it is, because it is made up of ions, and the bonds that hold it together are ionic bonds—not atomic glue!

## Silver Streaks and Speeding Electrons

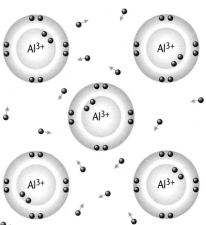

The properties of aluminum are determined by the action of its electrons. The atoms in every element contain a specific number of electrons around the nucleus of the atom. An atom of aluminum has 13 electrons. The electrons nearest the nucleus are relatively stable and closely bound to the nucleus. Those in the outer energy levels, however, are farther from the nucleus and they are more loosely held. They easily move away from their own atom to bond with other atoms.

*In metallic bonding, the electrons in the outer energy levels of an atom of aluminum move away from the nucleus easily and freely bond with other atoms that make up the piece of aluminum.*

### Roving Electrons

The electrons in the outer energy levels of aluminum and many other metals actually move freely among all the millions of atoms that make up a

### Purpose

A Closer Look explains how the arrangement of electrons in atoms of aluminum give aluminum its properties. This is an example of a concept presented in Section 6-1. Elements bond by gaining, losing, or sharing electrons.

### Content Background

Because metals tend to lose electrons, they react with elements in the atmosphere and water. A chemical reaction of this na- ture is often referred to as corrosion. Corrosion involves a chemical reaction that changes the metal element into a metallic compound and causes the gradual wearing away of the metal. The rusting of iron and the tarnishing of silver are examples of corrosion. Gold is more valuable than silver because it is scarce and does not corrode.

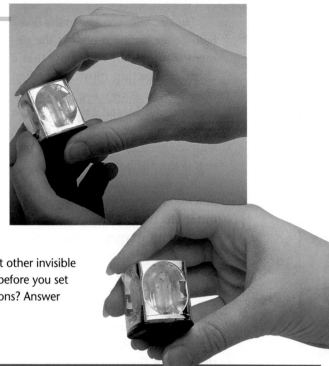

## Explore! ACTIVITY

### Can you see an ionic reaction?

Examine a camera flashbulb.

#### What To Do

1. List the properties of the substance(s) inside the bulb.

2. Without looking directly at the bulb, set it off. After it has cooled, examine it again.

3. How have the properties changed? What other invisible substance do you think was in the bulb before you set it off? Have you seen other similar reactions? Answer these questions *in your Journal.*

---

piece of aluminum. In fact, they form a kind of sea of electrons that makes aluminum lustrous,

*The chemical reaction that takes place here can remove tarnish from silver.*

as well as a good conductor of heat and electricity.

The ability of these roving electrons to combine with other elements, however, allows metals such as silver to become easily tarnished. Silver atoms bond readily with sulfur in the air to create silver sulfide. Silver polishes remove the silver sulfide, but every time you polish silver, you take a little of the silver away.

#### You Try It!

Can you take the tarnish off silver

without losing the silver? Line a glass bowl with aluminum foil. Place a tarnished silver spoon or fork into the bowl. Dissolve several tablespoons of baking soda in enough boiling water to cover the silver. Pour the water over the silver. With a wooden or plastic spoon, press the ends of the aluminum foil loosely over the silver. It only has to touch the silver in a few places.

After fifteen minutes, pour out the water and rinse off the silver. How do the silver and aluminum foil look? Write down "in the presence of baking soda" and the word equation for the reaction that you think might have occurred here. What is the black substance on the aluminum?

---

### Answers to
#### You Try It!

In the presence of baking soda,
$$3Ag_2S + 2Al \rightarrow 6Ag + Al_2S_3.$$
Aluminum sulfide is the black substance.

#### Going Further ▮▮▮▮▶

Have interested students research corrosive forces and their effect on the Statue of Liberty. Students should find that the salty environment, acid rain, and other factors caused the iron and copper involved in the structure to corrode and weaken. Major renovations have since been performed on the statue. Have students share their findings with the class. Have students work in small groups. Provide them with samples of metals that corrode, such as iron, zinc, and aluminum. Have students refer to the periodic table, then draw dot diagrams for these metals to verify that the metals might easily lose the electrons in their outer levels. Use the Performance Task Assessment List for Scientific Drawing in **PAMSS**, p. 55. L2 P
COOP LEARN

---

## 6-1 Models of Combining Atoms

**Time needed** 25–30 minutes

**Purpose** To model the bonding of atoms.

**Process Skills** organizing information, classifying, concept mapping, representing and applying data, making models, predicting

**Materials** modified egg cartons, marbles

**Preparation** Modify the egg cartons by blocking the second cup in each row with tape. Buttons, candy, or beans could be substituted for marbles.

### Teaching the Activity

Give students different numbers of marbles, representing the electrons for all elements from lithium to neon. For example, if a student's model will be representing lithium, he or she will need three marbles. This students would then fill the first two cups of the egg carton and one of the next eight. Guide students so that they discover simple matchups such as LiF and progress to compounds such as $BeF_2$, $Li_2O$, BeO, and $Be_3N_2$. **LEP** **L2**

# Models of Combining Atoms

*You know that atoms combine in order to fill their outer energy levels. Let's use models to see how this can happen.*

**Problem**

How can a model show the way atoms gain, lose, or share electrons?

**Materials**

modified egg carton
marbles

### What To Do

**1** Obtain a modified egg carton and marbles from your teacher. The carton represents the first and second energy levels of an atom, and the marbles represent electrons.

**2** Put one marble in each of the depressions of the carton that represent the first energy level.

**3** Place the remaining marbles in depressions representing the second energy level. What is the element? In which column of the periodic table would your element appear?

---

### Meeting Individual Needs

**Learning Disabled** To help students to model the sharing of electrons in covalent bonds, use polystyrene balls and toothpicks. A large polystyrene ball can represent the nucleus and smaller polystyrene balls the electrons. **L1** **COOP LEARN**

**4** Compare your model with those of your classmates. Find one or more other cartons that, when combined with yours, will make it possible for one of the cartons to have eight marbles in its second energy level and the other to have only the two in the first energy level. You may not, however, have more than two different elements represented.

**For example:**

If you have five marbles in your second energy level, you may not take one marble from a carton that has one in its second level and two from another carton that has two in the second level. You would have to find three separate cartons with one marble to fill the three spaces in your carton.

**5** Make a list of combinations that you made with your classmates' models.

**6** Observe your classmates' models again. Are there any combinations that could make it possible for both cartons to have eight marbles in the second energy level? What are they?

## Analyzing

**1.** Would you *infer* that your model is a metal or a nonmetal? How did you know?

**2.** Which of the combinations that you made in Steps 4 and 6 were ionic bonds and which were covalent? How do you know?

## Concluding and Applying

**3.** *Predict* what combinations of boron and fluorine will give you complete energy levels.

**4.** **Going Further** How would you have to change your model to show how sodium (Na) combines?

**Process Reinforcement** Allow students to make and use models of two or more elements, as time permits.

**Possible Hypotheses** Students may hypothesize that they can use their models in two ways to show the two types of chemical bonds that they have studied.

**Student Journal** Have students sketch their models in their journals. L1

### Expected Outcome

Students should be able to combine their model with one or more students' models in numerous ways.

### Answers to Analyzing/ Concluding and Applying

**1.** This depends on the number of marbles in the second energy level. If there are fewer than four, it is a metal. If there are four or more, it is a nonmetal.

**2.** The combinations in Step 4 were ionic because marbles were transferred. Those in Step 6 were covalent because marbles were shared.

**3.** one B and three F—$BF_3$

**4.** Add another energy level.

### ✔ Assessment

**Content** Have students review their lists of combinations. Students can then make a concept map that shows the combinations on their lists and the reactions that form these combinations. Use the Performance Task Assessment List for Concept Map in **PAMSS**, p. 89. L1 P

## Program Resources

**Activity Masters,** pp. 27–28, Investigate 6–1

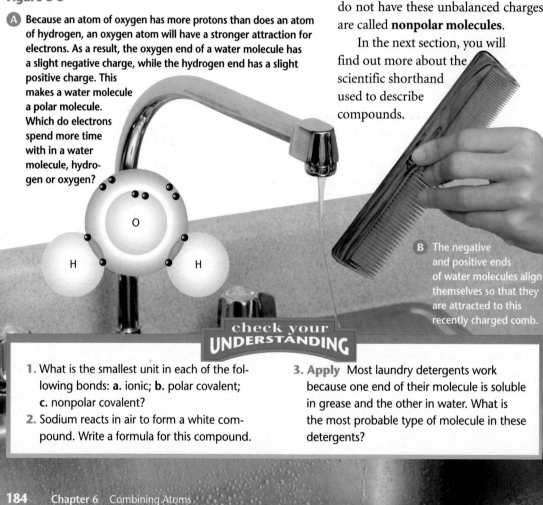

## Visual Learning

**Figure 6-6** Challenge students to identify a cause and effect shown in Figure 6-6. *Cause: A charged comb is held near a thin stream of water. Effect: The water is bending toward the comb.* Have a volunteer explain the effect in terms of polar molecules. **Which do electrons spend more time with in a water molecule, hydrogen or oxygen?** *oxygen*

### SKILLBUILDER

Each of these bonds results from an attractive force. In ionic bonding, electrons are gained or lost, and ions attract each other; electrons are shared in covalent bonding as molecules are formed. Polar covalent molecules are slightly positive at one end and slightly negative at the other; nonpolar covalent molecules do not have these differences at their ends. **L1**

# 3 Assess

## Check for Understanding

Have students answer the questions in Check Your Understanding.

## Reteach

Utilize electron dot diagrams to help students understand the concept of ionic and covalent bonds. Use dots around the atom of one element and X's around the other atom to clarify the sharing of electrons in covalent bonds and their transfer in ionic bonding. **L1** **LEP**

## Extension

Have students who have mastered the concepts in this section construct a chart showing diagrams (dot or Bohr) of various common molecules. **L2** **LEP**

# Polar and Nonpolar Molecules

In the Investigate, you could see how atoms can lose, gain, or share electrons to become stable.

Do atoms always share electrons equally? You know that an atom such as oxygen has more protons than an atom such as hydrogen. For this reason, an oxygen atom will have a greater attraction for electrons than will hydrogen. As is shown in **Figure 6-6**, electrons are not shared equally when hydrogen and oxygen form water. This makes the oxygen end a little more negative and the hydrogen end a little more positive than if the electrons were shared equally. We call this type of bond a *polar bond*. Polar means having two opposite ends or poles. A polar bond may result in a **polar molecule**, which has a slightly positive end and a slightly negative end. Molecules that do not have these unbalanced charges are called **nonpolar molecules**.

In the next section, you will find out more about the scientific shorthand used to describe compounds.

### SKILLBUILDER

**Comparing and Contrasting**

Compare and contrast ionic, polar covalent, and nonpolar covalent bonds. If you need help, refer to the **Skill Handbook** on page 683.

**Figure 6-6**

**A** Because an atom of oxygen has more protons than does an atom of hydrogen, an oxygen atom will have a stronger attraction for electrons. As a result, the oxygen end of a water molecule has a slight negative charge, while the hydrogen end has a slight positive charge. This makes a water molecule a polar molecule. Which do electrons spend more time with in a water molecule, hydrogen or oxygen?

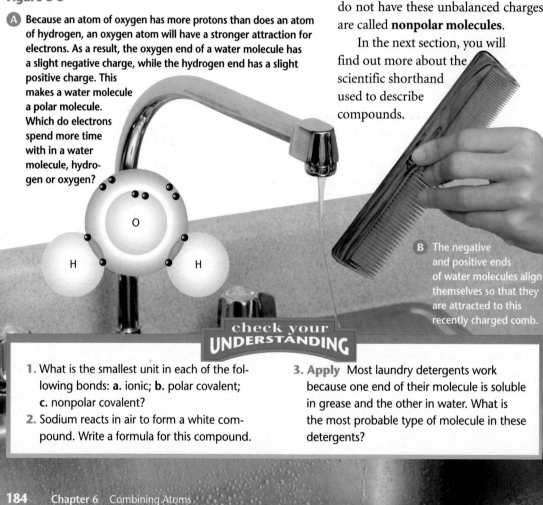

**B** The negative and positive ends of water molecules align themselves so that they are attracted to this recently charged comb.

### check your UNDERSTANDING

1. What is the smallest unit in each of the following bonds: **a.** ionic; **b.** polar covalent; **c.** nonpolar covalent?
2. Sodium reacts in air to form a white compound. Write a formula for this compound.
3. **Apply** Most laundry detergents work because one end of their molecule is soluble in grease and the other in water. What is the most probable type of molecule in these detergents?

# 4 Close

## Demonstration

Blow up a balloon and rub it with a cloth to give it a charge. Stick the balloon to the wall. Ask students how this is like ionic bonding. They should understand that by rubbing the balloon, you gave it a charge opposite to that of the wall. **L1**

### check your UNDERSTANDING

1. a) ion; b) molecule; c) molecule
2. $Na_2O$
3. polar molecules

## The World of Alphabet Soup

If you take a close look at many of the containers around your home and school, you'll find enough combina- tions of letters and numbers to fill a can of alphabet soup. Let's explore several possibilities.

**Section Objectives**

- Explain how to determine oxidation numbers.
- Give formulas for compounds from their names.
- Name compounds from their formulas.

**Key Terms**

*oxidation number*
*binary compound*
*polyatomic ion*

### Explore! ACTIVITY

## What's it made of?

### What To Do

1. Study the chemical content on a bag of lawn fertilizer, dog or cat food, a can of paint, and a box of laundry detergent or bleach.

2. *In your Journal*, list the ingredients by name and include any symbols or numbers used to describe the ingredient.

3. Do these products have any elements in common?

Was it easy for you to know what made up each ingredient that was list- ed on each label? How could the lists of chemicals you saw on the packages have been written in a shorter form so that everyone would still understand them? You have learned that all mat- ter is made up of elements and that each element can be represented by a symbol. Let's see how we can combine symbols to describe how elements form compounds.

6-2 Chemical Shorthand **185**

---

## PREPARATION

### Concepts Developed

In this section, students will explore the writing of chemical formulas for binary compounds and compounds with polyatom- ic ions. The formula of a chemi- cal compound indicates how much of each atom is present in one unit of the compound. Stu- dents will apply a procedure for naming a compound, given its formula.

### Planning the Lesson

Refer to the Chapter Organiz- er on pages 174A–B.

## 1 MOTIVATE

**Discussion** Ask students to list the formulas for as many compounds as they know. Write the name and formula for each compound on the chalkboard. Have students describe what each formula represents. L1

### Expected Outcome

Students should find that some chemical compounds are common to numerous household products.

### Answer to Question

**3.** Most will have carbon, oxy- gen, and hydrogen in com- mon.

### ✔ Assessment

**Process** Have students iden- tify additional products that contain elements they ob- served in this activity. Students could then make a data table showing elements common to household products. Use the Performance Task Assessment List for Data Table in **PAMSS**, p. 37. L1 P

---

### Explore!

## What's it made of?

**Time needed** 10–15 minutes

**Materials** ingredient list for fertilizer, dog or cat food, paint, bleach

**Thinking Processes** thinking critically, ob- serving and inferring, comparing and contrast- ing, classifying

**Purpose** To investigate the lists of chemical ingredients in common household products.

**Preparation** Any variety of household prod- ucts that contain chemicals may be used. Try to use products that have a few formulas and/or names of compounds in common.

### Teaching the Activity

Show students what to look for on the prod- uct labels by listing the ingredients for a repre- sentative item.

**Student Journal** Have students record their answers in their journals. L1

**Figure 6-7** Have students study Figure 6-7. Then pose the following inquiry questions. Many alchemists tried to find a way to change lead into a precious metal. What precious metal was this? *gold* Why do you think modern chemists wear goggles while they are working? *to protect their eyes from health-hazardous by-products of chemical reactions*

**Figure 6-8** Have students examine Figure 6-8. Then ask what element is represented by the modern symbol Fe. *iron*

# 2 TEACH

## Tying to Previous Knowledge

The key to writing correct subscripts in chemical formulas is correct identification of the oxidation numbers of elements. In the previous section, students learned that atoms may gain, lose, or share electrons during bonding. The number of such electrons is an element's oxidation number. Ask students to describe how they know how many electrons will be gained, lost, or shared in bonding.

**Theme Connection** A theme that this section supports is scale and structure. In a clear, concise way understood by all scientists, chemical formulas describe the number and type of atoms found in the structure of one molecule of a compound. Students will learn to write a formula showing this structure by following the rules on page 188.

**Figure 6-7**

**A** Alchemists practiced a form of "chemistry" in the Middle Ages. In fact, alchemists were the ancestors of modern chemists.

**B** Like the alchemist, the modern chemist investigates the structure of matter. But chemistry has come a long way since the days of the ancient alchemist.

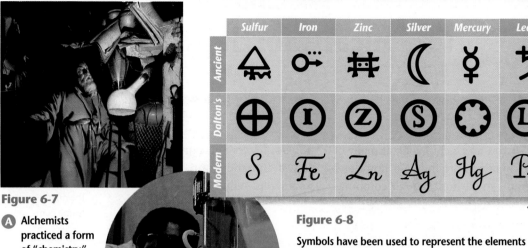

**Figure 6-8**

Symbols have been used to represent the elements since the times of the alchemists. John Dalton, who helped develop the atomic theory, came up with his own symbols. Modern chemists use symbols that can be understood by scientists around the world.

## ■ Chemical Shorthand

The two people in **Figure 6-7** seem to have little in common. Yet, in a sense, the medieval alchemist is the ancestor of the modern chemist. Both are shown at work investigating matter. Notice how each would write symbols for the elements silver and sulfur. If the alchemist knew the composition of tarnish, how might he write its formula? The modern chemist does know its composition. She would write it $Ag_2S$. Being able to use this kind of shorthand can enable you to write a great deal of information in just a short time.

When you write $Ag_2S$, chemists around the world know exactly what you mean. Chemical formulas allow scientists to communicate and share research. Where do formulas come from, and what do they mean?

## ■ Chemical Formulas

Recall the fire extinguisher you made at the beginning of this chapter. A scientist would write the reaction like this:

*vinegar     baking soda*
acetic acid + sodium hydrogen carbonate →
*a salt*
sodium acetate + water + carbon dioxide

*Put on board*

$HC_2H_3O_2 + NaHCO_3 →$
$NaC_2H_3O_2 + H_2O + CO_2$

The words you've used before to name compounds have been replaced by a kind of chemical shorthand called a formula. The formula of a compound tells a chemist how much of each element is present. For example, in the formula, $H_2O$, the subscript 2 shows 2 atoms of the element hydrogen. Because there is no subscript on the O, 1 atom is present. How are these numbers determined?

# Oxidation Number

Recall that you can tell how many electrons an element has in its outermost energy level from its family number on the periodic table. Most atoms will tend to lose, gain, or share these electrons to become stable.

The number of electrons that an atom gains, loses, or shares when bonding with another atom is called its **oxidation number**. For example, when sodium forms an ion, it loses an electron and has a charge of 1+, so the oxidation number of sodium is 1+. When chlorine forms an ion, it gains an electron and has a charge of 1-, so its oxidation number is 1-.

The red numbers printed on the periodic table shown in **Figure 6-10** are the oxidation numbers for many elements that form binary compounds. The prefix *bi*–means two. Thus, a **binary compound** is one that is composed of two elements. The oxidation numbers of the transition elements may change from compound to compound.

Some elements have more than one oxidation number, as shown in **Figure 6-9**. When an element can have more than one oxidation number, a Roman numeral is used in the name of the compound to indicate the oxidation number.

| | |
|---|---|
| copper(I) | $Cu^+$ |
| copper(II) | $Cu^{2+}$ |
| iron(II) | $Fe^{2+}$ |
| iron(III) | $Fe^{3+}$ |
| chromium(II) | $Cr^{2+}$ |
| chromium(III) | $Cr^{3+}$ |
| lead(II) | $Pb^{2+}$ |
| lead(IV) | $Pb^{4+}$ |

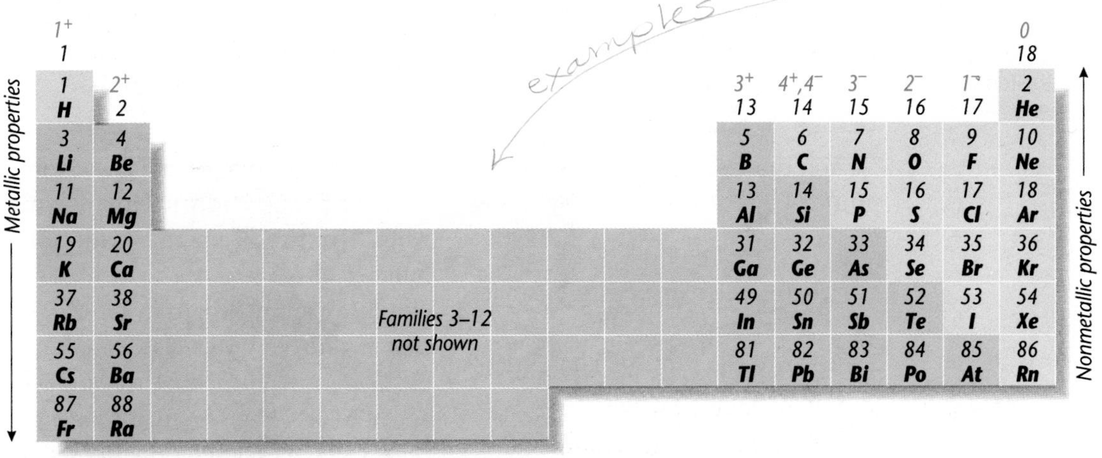

*examples*

**Figure 6-10**

| | | | | | | | | |
|---|---|---|---|---|---|---|---|---|
| $1^+$ 1 | | | | | | | | 0 18 |
| 1 **H** | $2^+$ 2 | | $3^+$ 13 | $4^+,4^-$ 14 | $3^-$ 15 | $2^-$ 16 | $1^-$ 17 | 2 **He** |
| 3 **Li** | 4 **Be** | | 5 **B** | 6 **C** | 7 **N** | 8 **O** | 9 **F** | 10 **Ne** |
| 11 **Na** | 12 **Mg** | | 13 **Al** | 14 **Si** | 15 **P** | 16 **S** | 17 **Cl** | 18 **Ar** |
| 19 **K** | 20 **Ca** | Families 3–12 not shown | 31 **Ga** | 32 **Ge** | 33 **As** | 34 **Se** | 35 **Br** | 36 **Kr** |
| 37 **Rb** | 38 **Sr** | | 49 **In** | 50 **Sn** | 51 **Sb** | 52 **Te** | 53 **I** | 54 **Xe** |
| 55 **Cs** | 56 **Ba** | | 81 **Tl** | 82 **Pb** | 83 **Bi** | 84 **Po** | 85 **At** | 86 **Rn** |
| 87 **Fr** | 88 **Ra** | | | | | | | |

← Metallic properties    Nonmetallic properties →

In the periodic table, all the elements are arranged in rows and columns according to their properties. The elements with metallic properties are listed on the left side of the table, and the elements with nonmetallic properties are listed on the right side. Based on the table, is magnesium classified as a metal or a nonmetal?

# Formulas and Names for Binary Compounds

Once you know how to find the oxidation numbers of elements when they are in binary compounds, you can write the formulas for these compounds by using the rules that are shown below in **Table 6-1**.

**Table 6-1**

| How to Write Formulas for Binary Compounds | |
|---|---|
| 1. Write the symbol of the element with the positive oxidation number. Hydrogen and all metals have positive oxidation numbers. | Ca |
| 2. Then write the symbol of the element with the negative oxidation number. | F |
| 3. Look up the oxidation numbers on the periodic table and write them above the symbols. | $Ca^{2+}F^-$ |
| 4. In the completed formula, there must be an equal number of positive and negative charges. The charge is calculated by multiplying the number of atoms of the element by its oxidation number. When $Ca^{2+}$ and $F^-$ combine, we see that one Ca atom will combine with two F atoms. We know this because one atom of Ca times a charge of 2+ equals 2+. Two atoms of F times a charge of 1– equals 2–. The sum of 2+ and 2– is zero, and the compound is neutral. | *Criss-Cross* $Ca^{2+} + 2 F^-$ |
| 5. The last step is to put subscripts in so that the sum of the charges in the formula is zero. | $CaF_2$ |

You can also name a binary compound from its formula by using these rules.

1. Write the name of the first element.
2. Write the root of the name of the second element.
3. Add the suffix *-ide* to the root.

To name the compounds of elements having two oxidation numbers, you must first figure out the oxidation numbers of each of the elements. For example, suppose you wanted to name CrO. Because Cr can have more than one oxidation number, you would first look up the oxidation number of the negative element. The oxidation number of oxygen is 2-. Next, figure out the oxidation number of the positive element. That number added to 2- will give a total charge of zero. (2+) + (2-) = 0. Finally, write the name of the compound, using a Roman numeral for the positive oxidation number. In this case the positive oxidation number is 2 and the compound is chromium(II) oxide.

*transition elements*

# Compounds with Polyatomic Ions

Have you ever used baking soda in cooking, as a medicine, or to brush your teeth? You'll remember that baking soda was one of the ingredients in our homemade fire extinguisher. Some compounds, including baking soda, contain polyatomic ions. The prefix *poly-* means many, so polyatomic means having many atoms. A **polyatomic ion** is a group of positively or negatively charged covalently bonded atoms. In the case of baking soda, $Na^+$ is the positive ion, and $HCO_3^-$ is the negative, polyatomic ion.

*acts as a single ion*

## ■ Naming

**Table 6-2** lists several polyatomic ions. To name a compound that contains one or more of these ions, use the name of the polyatomic ion. Other than that, use the same rules used for a binary compound. For example $K_2SO_4$ is potassium sulfate. What are the names of $Sr(OH)_2$ and $NH_4Cl$?

## ■ Writing Formulas

To write formulas for compounds containing polyatomic ions, follow the rules for writing formulas for binary compounds, with one addition. Use parentheses around the group representing the polyatomic ion when more than one of that ion is needed, such as $Mg(OH)_2$. Without the parentheses, it appears as though there are two hydrogen atoms, rather than two hydroxide ions.

*Example Problem:*
Writing a Formula with Polyatomic Ions

*Problem Statement:*
What is the formula for calcium nitrate?

*Problem-Solving Steps:*
1. Write symbols and oxidation numbers for calcium and the nitrate ion.
$$2+ \quad 1-$$
$$Ca \quad NO_3$$

2. Write in subscripts so that the sum of the oxidation numbers is zero. Enclose the $NO_3$ in parentheses.
$$2+ \quad 1-$$
$$Ca \quad (NO_3)_2$$

*Solution:*
Final Formula: $Ca(NO_3)_2$

**Table 6-2**

| Common Polyatomic Ions | | |
|---|---|---|
| Charge | Name | Formula |
| 1+ | Ammonium | $NH_4^+$ |
| 1– | Acetate | $CH_3CO_2^-$ |
| 1– | Chlorate | $ClO_3^-$ |
| 1– | Hydroxide | $OH^-$ |
| 1– | Nitrate | $NO_3^-$ |
| 2– | Carbonate | $CO_3^{2-}$ |
| 2– | Sulfate | $SO_4^{2-}$ |
| 3– | Phosphate | $PO_4^{3-}$ |

This table lists eight polyatomic ions, showing each ion's formula and charge.

## Program Resources

**Critical Thinking/Problem Solving,** p. 5, Flex Your Brain

## Meeting Individual Needs

**Learning Disabled** To help students relate chemical compounds to their uses in everyday life, display a box of baking soda on which is listed its many uses as a deodorizer, cleaning agent, and antacid. Explain that baking soda's chemical formula is what makes it good for all these uses. It is made up of the polyatomic ion $HCO_3^-$ and sodium. Guide students in using oxidation numbers to write the formula for baking soda, $NaHCO_3$. L1

**Activity** Challenge students to identify elements and compounds, to communicate, and to write formulas for binary compounds. Divide the class into two teams. Have a student on one team name an element. Have a student from the other team name an element that, when placed with the first, produces a compound. Finally, ask a volunteer to write the formula for the compound on the chalkboard, using the oxidation numbers provided on the periodic table. Allow team members to consult before writing the formula. L2 **COOP LEARN**

**Student Text Question**
What are the names of $Sr(OH)_2$ and $NH_4Cl$? *strontium hydroxide; ammonium chloride*

**Flex Your Brain** Use the Flex Your Brain activity to have students explore COMPOUNDS. L1

**Using the Table** Ask students to find the oxidation number of sulfur in a sulfate ion, $SO_4^{2-}$, listed in Table 6-2. By looking at the formula for the polyatomic ion, they should realize that the sum of the oxidation numbers of 4 oxygen atoms and 1 sulfur atom must be 2-. Oxygen has an oxidation number of 2-.

$$\underline{\quad\quad} + 4(2-) = 2-$$
$$\underline{\quad 6 \quad} + 8- = 2-$$

The oxidation number of sulfur is 6+. L2

**Activity** Challenge students who have mastered the concepts in this section to write the chemical formulas for these compounds found in common household products.

• A compound containing ammonium ions and selenate ions is used as a mothproofing agent. The selenate ion is $SeO_4^{-2}$. *$(NH_4)_2 SeO_4$*

• A compound containing oxygen and titanium is used as a white pigment in the production of paint, plastic, and paper. Titanium has an oxidation number of 4+ in this compound. *$TiO_2$* L3

lithium sulfide, magnesium fluoride, iron(II) oxide, copper(I) chloride L1

# Life Science CONNECTION

## Purpose

This Life Science Connection describes the effect of phosphates on ponds. Phosphate is one type of polyatomic ion mentioned in Section 6-2. This excursion describes a chemical reaction with phosphate ions that cleans up scummy ponds. It is one of the four types of chemical reactions explained in Section 6-4.

## Content Background

Phosphorus is utilized by plants and animals to form high-energy compounds. Additions of these compounds can cause a surprising burst in plant growth. The bloom of algae in a pond is actually not a problem until the algae begin to die and decay in large amounts. The decaying process is what uses up the available oxygen in the water. This oxygen is life-sustaining to many aquatic organisms such as fish, tadpoles, and aquatic insects that in turn are food for herons, frogs, raccoons, and a host of other animals. Thus, phosphates can result in the ultimate death of a pond. For this reason, many soap industries are reducing the amount of phosphates in their detergents, and many areas have made the use of phosphate-containing detergents illegal.

## Teaching Strategy

Have students observe algae growth. Obtain some water from a nearby pond or stream. Place the water in two large

# Names of Compounds

## How Do We Know?

### Common and Systematic Names

A systematic name gives a lot of useful information. When you're thirsty, you wouldn't ask for a glass of ice cold dihydrogen monoxide! You would go by the common name and ask for a glass of water. However, if you need to plan a scientific experiment involving water, you'll be glad that the systematic name for water tells you its exact composition.

Why do we need standards and rules for naming compounds? Early in the history of chemistry, the discoverer of a new compound would name it. Often the discoverer would choose a name that described some chemical or physical property of the new compound. For example, a common name for potassium carbonate, $K_2CO_3$, is potash because the compound could be produced by boiling wood ash in iron pots. Laughing gas was named for the effect it has on humans when it is inhaled. Sodium hydrogen carbonate, written $NaHCO_3$, is commonly called baking soda. It's one of the compounds that helps baked goods rise. Sulfuric acid was once called oil of vitriol. Lye and plaster of paris are other common names of compounds. While these names may be very descriptive, they tell us nothing about the chemical composition of the compound.

# Life Science CONNECTION

*This photograph of algae was taken using a microscope.*

## Pond Scum Be Gone!

If your pond is green and scummy, just throw in a few bales of rotting straw. Scientists in England have discovered that rotting straw produces a chemical that initiates a reaction that destroys pond scum.

### What Is Pond Scum?

Algae—microscopic protists—flourish in water that is high in phosphates. Phosphates are compounds that contain the phosphate ion. Phosphates run into water from many sources. They are found in detergents. They come from fertilizers that are spread on crops in the country and on lawns and golf courses in the city. Phosphates are present in the manure that farm animals deposit on the ground and in sewage that has been treated by city treatment plants. The phosphorus from the phosphate ion acts as fertilizer for the algae and encourages it to grow with incredible speed. Soon the entire surface of the water is covered with green pond scum.

The result of this speedy growth is that the algae use up all the oxygen that is in the water and that is necessary for other life. Fish of all sizes must have oxygen to survive. In ponds and lakes where algae are rampant, the other life-forms die out.

containers. To one container add a few mL of detergent water. Add nothing to the other container. Place both containers under a strong light source. Within a few weeks, algae should appear to grow in both. However, the growth will be more robust in the treated container. L2

### Going Further ▐▐▐▐▐▶

Have students work in groups of two or three to compile a list of products found at home that contain phosphates. Students can examine the contents label to determine the existence and amount of phosphates in each product. They can also visit garden supply, hardware, or grocery stores to check the labels of other detergent and fertilizer containers. Another source is consumer reports that discuss detergents and fertilizers. Have students use their findings to conduct their own Consumer Decision Making Study. Use the Performance Task Assessment List in **PAMSS**, p. 43. L2

**COOP LEARN**

## The Need for a System

As the number of known compounds grew, it became necessary to establish a system for naming, part of which you have learned. For example, there are 217 different known compounds that have the simple formula $C_6H_6$. Each of them has a unique name based on a system accepted by chemists worldwide. Because hundreds of thousands of new compounds are made each year, it's clear that a systematic naming system is necessary.

### SKILLBUILDER

**Making and Using Tables**

Name the following compounds: $Li_2S$, $MgF_2$, $FeO$, $CuCl$. Strategy Hint: For names of elements with more than one oxidation number, remember to include the Roman numeral. If you need help, refer to the **Skill Handbook** on page 680.

### check your UNDERSTANDING

1. Name the following compounds: $NaI$, $FeI_3$, $NH_4Br$.
2. Write formulas for compounds composed of (a) lithium and sulfur, (b) calcium and the acetate ion, and (c) barium and oxygen.
3. Assign an oxidation number to each element in the following: $Al_2O_3$; $ZnCl_2$; $FeBr_2$.
4. **Apply** The label on a package of plant food lists potassium nitrate as one ingredient. What is the formula for potassium nitrate?

### Getting Rid of Scum

Scientists decided to follow up on a lead from a farmer who accidentally dropped rotten bales of straw into his lake and was amazed to see the algae disappear. They found that rotting straw produces a chemical that stops algae growth. They don't yet know the exact identity of the chemical, and are still studying it. They have, however, found that fish and plants do not seem to be affected by it. Different kinds of straw work differently. Barley straw works best. Wheat straw works, but more slowly.

Researchers recommend throwing straw into the pond twice a year, once in the fall, and again in the spring before algae start growing.

*Phosphorus in water causes algae to grow extremely fast, until the entire surface of the water is covered with green pond scum.*

### What Do You Think?

Find a lake or pond in your area. Look for algae growing on the water. Then look around you. Are there farms or manicured lawns nearby? What could be leading to phosphorus runoff that encourages the growth of algae?

*What do they see around wetlands?*

---

### check your UNDERSTANDING

1. sodium iodide, iron(III) iodide, ammonium bromide
2. $Li_2S$, $Ca(C_2H_3O_2)_2$, $BaO$
3. $Al^{3+}O^{2-}$, $Zn^{2+}Cl^{1-}$, $Fe^{2+}Br^{1-}$
4. $KNO_3$

---

## 3 ASSESS

### Check for Understanding

Have students answer the questions in Check Your Understanding. In discussing question 4, the Apply question, help them understand the function of chemical compounds by pointing out that nitrogen is an essential plant nutrient. Although nitrogen is present in the air, plants are unable to use it in this form. It must be changed to a nitrogen compound and absorbed from the soil.

### Reteach

Write the formulas below on the chalkboard. Have students state what is wrong with the formulas as written. Then have students rewrite them correctly.

**Al3Cl** *Formulas should use subscripts, not coefficients; $AlCl_3$ is correct.*

**NaO** *Oxidation numbers do not sum to zero: $Na_2O$ is correct.*

**$(Ca)_1(Br)_2$** *The numeral 1 is not used in formulas. Parentheses are used only with polyatomic ions; $CaBr_2$ is correct.* L1 LEP

### Extension

Have students apply what they have learned in this section to write an operational definition of the word *chemical*. L2

## 4 CLOSE

Have students work cooperatively to review the concepts presented in this section. Divide the class into two groups. Give one group flash cards showing positive ions and the names of the ions. Give the other group a similar set of flash cards, showing negative ions. Then have groups get back together and draw one card from each set. Have them determine the formula and name of the resulting compound. Repeat until all cards have been used. **COOP LEARN**

# PREPARATION

## Concepts Developed

In this section, students will use numbers in writing balanced chemical equations. A chemical equation is a way of showing, by numbers and symbols, what is taking place during a chemical reaction. A chemical equation is balanced when the same number of each type of atom appears on both sides of the equation.

## Planning the Lesson

Refer to the Chapter Organizer on pages 174A–B.

---

## Explore!

**Must the sum of the reactant and product coefficients be equal?**

**Time needed** 10–15 minutes

**Materials** marked cards

**Thinking Processes** observing and inferring, representing and applying data, making a model

**Purpose** To make models showing that coefficients of reactants and products need not be equal.

**Preparation** Prepare twice as many *guard* and *forward* as *center* cards.

## Teaching the Activity

Lead students to represent this reaction with symbols. $2G + 2F + C = G_2F_2C$.

**Student Journal** In their journals, have students make and use symbols to show

---

**6-3**

## Section Objectives
- Explain what is meant by a balanced chemical equation.
- Demonstrate how to write a balanced chemical equation.

**Key Terms**

*balanced chemical equation*

# 6-3 Balancing Chemical Equations

## Checking for Balance

If you were to write an equation for making applesauce, you might say that 10 apples + 1 pound of sugar = 3 cups of applesauce. The apples and sugar represent reactants. When heated together, they make applesauce, the product. Another example is shown in **Figure 6-11**, where several ingredients, representing reactants, produce one cake, representing the product. The numbers in front of each item are called coefficients. They describe how many units of that substance are involved in the recipe. Let's learn more about this type of equation in the following activity.

### Explore! ACTIVITY

**Must the sum of the reactant and product coefficients be equal?**

**What To Do**

1. Obtain a marked card from your teacher.

2. With others in your class, assemble all the cards to represent a basketball team. When you write this as an equation, you have something like this: 2 guards + 2 forwards + 1 center = 1 team.

3. Why aren't the sums of the coefficients on each side of the equation equal?

4. What other examples like this can you think of?

*Milk*

*Eggs*

*Cake mix*

**Figure 6-11**

Combining several different ingredients — milk, eggs, and cake mix — results in one new product, a cake.

---

graphically the "basketball team" that they assembled with the marked cards. **L3**

### Expected Outcome

Students should see that the coefficients of the reactants include 1 and 2, and the coefficient of the product is 1.

### Answers to Questions

**3.** Coefficients represent only numbers of units (players, teams). Each unit contains a specific number of components. In this case, there is one component to a player, but five to a team.

**4.** Answers will vary but may include sports teams and other food products such as pizza.

### ✔ Assessment

**Process** Have students make a model of one of the examples that they gave in answering Question 4. Use the Performance Task Assessment List for Model in **PAMSS**, p. 51. **L1**

Let's see how the coefficients for the reactants and products in a chemical reaction compare to the Explore activity. Have you ever seen silver polish in the supermarket? It's used to remove tarnish from silver. Tarnish can make silver appear almost black. Where does tarnish come from? It forms when sulfur-containing compounds in air or food react with silver to form silver sulfide, the black tarnish.

## Matter is Conserved

Let's write the chemical equation for tarnishing:

$Ag + H_2S \rightarrow Ag_2S + H_2$.

Look at the equation closely. Remember that matter is never created or destroyed in an ordinary chemical reaction. Notice that one silver atom appears in the reactants, $Ag + H_2S$. However, two silver atoms appear in the product, $Ag_2S + H_2$. As you know, one silver atom can't just become two. The equation must be balanced so that it shows a true picture of what takes place in the reaction. A **balanced chemical equation** has the same number of atoms of each element on both sides of the equation. In the Explore activity, even though there were 2 guards, 2 forwards, and 1 center on one side and 1 team on the other, no players had been lost. The player "equation" was balanced. To find out if the equation for tarnishing is balanced, make a chart like that shown in **Table 6-3**.

**Table 6-3**

Atoms in an Unbalanced Equation

| Kind of Atom | Number of Atoms $Ag + H_2S = Ag_2S + H_2$ | |
|---|---|---|
| Ag | 1 | 2 |
| H | 2 | 2 |
| S | 1 | 1 |

This table shows an unbalanced equation, in which the number of atoms of each element on one side of the equation is not equal to the number of atoms of that element on the other side of the equation.

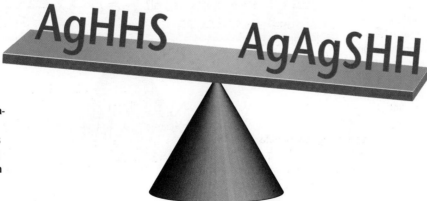

**Figure 6-12**

This diagram shows the unbalanced equation from Table 6-3. There are two atoms of silver on the right side, but only one on the left.



## Program Resources

**Study Guide,** p. 24

**Critical Thinking/Problem Solving,** p. 14, Metal Corrosion L2

**Making Connections: Across the Curriculum,** p. 15, Writing Chemical Equations L1

## Meeting Individual Needs

**Learning Disabled** Invite students to make models that illustrate the concept of a balanced chemical equation and conservation of mass, provide students with two sets of colored-paper shapes: square, circle, triangle, and rectangle. On one side of their "equation," have them tape together the square and circle and tape together the triangle and rectangle. Use the same shapes on the other side of the arrow, but in different configurations. LEP

# 1 Motivate

**Activity** Invite students to communicate what takes place in a chemical reaction. Remind students that a flashbulb contains magnesium and oxygen. Ask a volunteer to write in words the chemical reaction that takes place when a flashbulb is set off. *Student's choice of words should convey that magnesium reacts with oxygen to produce magnesium oxide and energy in the form of light.* Use this description to lead into a discussion of a more accurate method of depicting a chemical reaction—the chemical equation.

# 2 Teach

### Tying to Previous Knowledge

Students will apply the skill of writing formulas for chemical compounds, developed in Section 6-2, to writing balanced chemical equations. Give students an addition example presented in horizontal form and ask them to write the entire example including its solution. Inform them that if they do this correctly, they can balance equations.

**Theme Connection** A balanced chemical equation accurately represents what actually happens when molecules interact during a chemical reaction, thus supporting the theme of systems and interactions.

## Visual Learning

**Figure 6-11** Have students draw on their prior experience as they study Figure 6-11. Challenge them to infer what a baker must do to initiate a chemical reaction using the ingredients shown. *Add heat*

6-3 Balancing Chemical Equations 193

# Using Coefficients

The number of hydrogen and sulfur atoms are balanced, as is shown in **Figure 6-13**. However, there are two silver atoms on the right side of the equation and only one on the left side. We cannot change the subscripts of a correct formula in order to balance an equation. Instead, we place whole-number coefficients to the left of the formulas of the reactants and products so that there are equal numbers of silver atoms on both sides of the equation. If the coefficient is one, no coefficient is written. How do we choose which coefficients to use to balance this or any other equation?

**Table 6-4**

| Atoms in a Balanced Equation | | |
|---|---|---|
| Kind of Atom | Number of Atoms $2Ag + H_2S = Ag_2S + H_2$ | |
| Ag | 2 | 2 |
| H | 2 | 2 |
| S | 1 | 1 |

**Figure 6-13**

This diagram shows the balanced equation from Table 6-4. There are two atoms of silver, two atoms of hydrogen, and one atom of sulfur on each side.

## ■ Choosing Coefficients

The decision for choosing coefficients is often a trial-and-error process. With practice, however, the process becomes simple to perform.

In the chemical equation for tarnishing, you found that both the sulfur atoms and the hydrogen atoms were already balanced. So look at the formulas containing silver atoms: Ag and $Ag_2S$. There are two atoms of silver on the right side and only one silver atom on the left side. If you put a coefficient of 2 before Ag, the equation is balanced, as shown in **Table 6-4** and **Figure 6-13**.

This table depicts a balanced equation, the coefficients showing that the kinds of atoms and the number of each kind are equal on both sides of the equation.

## Writing Balanced Equations

**Figure 6-14** shows that when a silver nitrate solution is mixed with a sodium chloride solution, a white, insoluble solid, silver chloride, is formed. This silver chloride solid falls to the bottom of the container. The sodium nitrate formed remains in solution. Here are some guidelines to follow if you are to write a balanced equation for this reaction.

1. Describe the reaction in words. Silver nitrate plus sodium chloride produces silver chloride plus sodium nitrate.

2. Write a chemical equation for the reaction using formulas and symbols for each term. Review Section 6-2 on how to write formulas for compounds. The formulas for elements are generally just their symbols.

$$AgNO_3 + NaCl \rightarrow AgCl + NaNO_3$$

3. Check the equation for balance. Set up a chart similar to **Table 6-5** to help you. Notice that there are already equal numbers of atoms of each element on both sides of the

equation. This equation is balanced.

4. Determine coefficients. This equation is balanced, so no coefficients need to be changed.

In the next section, you will take a closer look at a number of familiar and unfamiliar types of chemical equations and how they are classified.

**Figure 6-14**

Silver and chloride ions combine to form a solid. The sodium and nitrate ions remain in the solution.

**Table 6-5**

| Atoms in a Balanced Equation | | |
|---|---|---|
| Kind of Atom | Number of Atoms | |
| | $AgNO_3$ + NaCl → AgCl + $NaNO_3$ | |
| Ag | 1 | 1 |
| N | 1 | 1 |
| O | 3 | 3 |
| Na | 1 | 1 |
| Cl | 1 | 1 |

This table depicts the balanced equation describing the reaction that takes place when silver nitrate is mixed with sodium chloride.

### check your UNDERSTANDING

1. Write balanced chemical equations for the following reactions: (a) copper plus sulfur produces copper(I) sulfide, (b) sodium plus water produces sodium hydroxide plus hydrogen gas.

2. Rust, iron(III) oxide, can be formed when iron is exposed to oxygen in the air. Write a balanced equation for this reaction.

3. **Apply** When charcoal burns, it appears that the ashes have less mass and take up less space than the charcoal did. How can this be explained in terms of a balanced equation?

# PREPARATION

## Concepts Developed

In this section the students will study four general types of chemical reactions: synthesis, decomposition, single displacement, and double displacement.

## Planning the Lesson

Refer to the Chapter Organizer on pages 174A–B.

# 1 MOTIVATE

**Demonstration** Invite students to observe a decomposition reaction.

Materials needed are sugar (sucrose), a test tube, a test tube holder, and a Bunsen burner.

Place some sucrose in a test tube and heat it until it burns. Carbon will remain. Water vapor and carbon dioxide gas will be released. Compare this reaction to what happens when sugar is metabolized in cells. In cells, glucose combines with oxygen to produce carbon dioxide, water, and energy. L1

### Find Out!

**How does a chemical reaction enable a space shuttle to be launched?**

**Time needed** 5–10 minutes

**Materials** No special materials or preparation are required for this activity.

**Thinking Processes** predicting, forming operational definitions, interpreting data

**Purpose** To write an equation to describe a synthesis reaction.

### Teaching the Activity

Point out that energy must be released by the reaction in order to propel the shuttle.

# Chemical Reactions

## Classifying Chemical Reactions

Scientists have developed a system of classification for chemical reactions. It is based on the way that atoms rearrange themselves in the reaction. Most reactions can be placed in one of four groups: synthesis, decomposition, single displacement, or double displacement reactions.

You've worked with three of these in word equations. Now you'll be able to write balanced chemical equations for these reactions.

In the following Find Out activity, you'll discover how chemical reactions enable a space shuttle to be launched.

### Section Objectives
- Describe four types of chemical reactions, using their general formulas.
- Classify various chemical reactions by type.

### Find Out! ACTIVITY

#### How does a chemical reaction enable a space shuttle to be launched?

#### What To Do
Read the following information.
A space shuttle is powered by a chemical reaction between pure liquid hydrogen and pure liquid oxygen. Liquid hydrogen actually serves as the fuel. The fuel tank contains 1 464 000 liters of $H_2$. The oxidizer tank contains 544 734 liters of $O_2$. The reaction between $H_2$ and $O_2$ is a synthesis reaction that produces large amounts of energy. In a synthesis reaction two or more reactants produce a single product.

#### Conclude and Apply

1. What do you predict the product of $H_2$ and $O_2$ will be?

2. Write a balanced equation for the reaction.

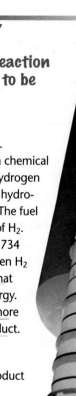

544,734
× 2
1089468

$2H_2 + O_2 \rightarrow 2H_2O$

**Student Journal** Have students write their responses in their journals. L1

### Expected Outcome

Students should write a balanced equation for the reaction in which liquid hydrogen and liquid oxygen produce energy and water.

### Conclude and Apply
1. water
2. $2H_2 + O_2 \rightarrow 2H_2O$

### ✔ Assessment

**Process** Working in pairs, have students check each other's equations. Students could then make their own cartoon that relates a chemical reaction to a space shuttle launch. Use the Performance Task Assessment List for Cartoon/Comic Book in **PAMSS**, p. 61. **COOP LEARN** L1 P

## Synthesis Reactions

The easiest reaction to recognize is a synthesis reaction, where two or more substances combine, forming another substance. Typically, synthesis reactions give off energy in the form of heat and light. The general formula for a synthesis reaction is: A + B → AB.

**Figure 6-15**

**A** The corrosion on this wheel is a product of a synthesis reaction.

**B** This equation describes the synthesis reaction in which aluminum and oxygen combine to form aluminum oxide.

$$4Al + 3O_2 \rightarrow 2Al_2O_3$$

## Decomposition Reactions

In a decomposition reaction, one substance breaks down into simpler substances. The general formula for this type of reaction is: AB → A + B. Most decomposition reactions require the addition of energy.

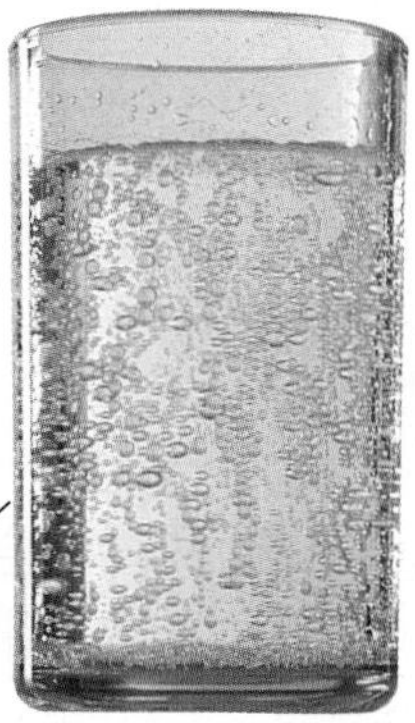

**Figure 6-16**

**A** This equation describes the decomposition reaction in which carbonic acid breaks down to form water and carbon dioxide, causing bubbles in the soda.

$$H_2CO_3 \rightarrow H_2O + CO_2$$

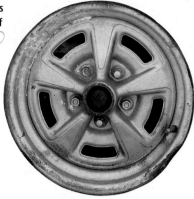

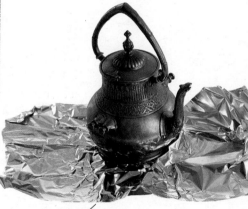

**B** The bubbles in this soda are a product of a decomposition reaction.

## Single Displacement Reactions

A single displacement reaction occurs when one element replaces another in a compound, such as A + BC → AC + B or D + BC → BD + C.

In the first case the positive ion is replaced, and in the second case the negative ion is replaced.

The following Investigate shows yet another type of reaction.

**Figure 6-17**

**A** The tarnish that has formed on this silver is an example of a single displacement reaction.

$$2Al + 3Ag_2S \rightarrow Al_2S_3 + 6Ag$$

**B** This equation describes the single displacement reaction in which aluminum and silver sulfide react to form aluminum sulfide and silver.



# 2 TEACH

### Tying to Previous Knowledge

In the previous section, students used numbers to write balanced chemical equations. In this section, students will learn that these equations can provide information on the type of reaction that occurs.

You may also want to discuss what students have learned in health class or life science class about chemical reactions associated with digestion.

**Theme Connection** In the four types of reactions presented, energy is either used or released. For example, the energy stored in molecules of hydrogen and oxygen are released when they combine to form water.

### *Across the Curriculum*

**Language Arts**

Have students look up the definition of the word *decompose* in a dictionary. Have them write a poem or paragraph relating decomposition reactions to a possible solution of the problem of solid waste disposal caused by the closing of landfills. Encourage students to include reference to nature's own decomposers, bacteria and fungi, and their role in decomposition. L1

### Visual Learning

**Figures 6-15, 6-16, and 6-17** Help students practice communication skills. Make photocopies of the pictures and equations shown in Figures 6-15, 6-16, and 6-17. Divide the class into cooperative learning groups. Shuffle the pictures and equations, then distribute one picture and one equation to each group. Have groups trade equations as necessary to obtain the correct equation for their picture. L1 COOP LEARN LEP

### Program Resources

**Study Guide,** p. 25

**Laboratory Manual,** pp. 29–32, Chemical Reactions L2; pp. 33–36, Reaction Rates and Temperature COOP LEARN

**Concept Map,** p. 14, Types of Chemical Reactions L1

**How It Works,** p. 11, Photography L2

**Science Discovery Activities,** 6–3, Bubble, Bubble, Bubble

### Meeting Individual Needs

**Learning Disabled** Challenge students to use different-shaped blocks or paper to model the single displacement process. Combine three blocks in such a way as to have a shape, a plus sign, and then two other shapes combined to represent the reactants. On the other side of the arrow, switch the shapes that are paired with the single shape to represent the products. LEP L1

**Time needed** 25–30 minutes

**Purpose** To cause a double displacement reaction and write an equation to describe it.

**Process Skills** observing and inferring, recognizing cause and effect, measuring in SI, forming operational definitions, comparing and contrasting, interpreting data, classifying, designing an experiment, separating and controlling variables

**Materials** See student activity.

**Preparation** Dissolve approximately a gram of calcium sulfate in 100 mL of water to obtain the desired solution. Do the same for the magnesium sulfate and the sodium carbonate solutions. To make a 1-percent soap solution, add 10 drops of liquid soap to 100 mL of water. Make sure enough solution has been made for the whole class. Double or triple mixtures as needed.

### Teaching the Activity

**Demonstration** You may want to do this entire activity as a demonstration and allow students to record their observations. L2

**Process Reinforcement** To help students recognize cause and effect and to assist them with Concluding and Applying Question 4, have students identify a cause and effect that they observed in this activity. *Cause: Hard water ions were filtered from the calcium/magnesium carbonate + sodium sulfate solution. Effect: More soap suds were produced with the same solution.*

**Possible Hypotheses** Students may correctly hypothesize that more suds form in soft water than in hard water.

**Student Journal** Have students write their responses in their journals. L1

---

# INVESTIGATE!

# Double Displacement Reactions

*One other type of reaction is called double displacement. Let's investigate one way you can tell when this type of reaction occurs.*

### Problem
How does a water softener work?

### Materials
| | |
|---|---|
| 5 test tubes and rack | sodium carbonate, |
| small beaker | $Na_2CO_3$ |
| saturated solutions | 25-mL graduated |
| of calcium sulfate, | cylinder |
| $CaSO_4$, and | filter paper |
| magnesium | funnel |
| sulfate, $MgSO_4$ | stoppers |
| distilled water | dropper |
| soap solution—1% | stirring rod |

### Safety Precautions

## What To Do

**1** The $CaSO_4$ and $MgSO_4$ solutions represent hard water. Place 10 mL of distilled water and 10 mL of each of the hard water solutions in separate test tubes.

**2** Place 2 mL (about 40 drops) of soap solution in each tube. Stopper each tube and shake. Observe the amount of suds formed.

**A**          **B**          **C**

**3** Place 15 mL of one of the hard water samples in a small beaker. Add 5 mL of sodium carbonate solution. Stir thoroughly. Record your observations.

**4** Filter the solution, collecting the clear liquid in a test tube. Add 2 mL of soap solution and shake. Compare the suds formed with the suds formed before the reaction in Step 3.

**5** Repeat Steps 3 and 4 with the other hard water solution.

## Analyzing

**1.** What evidence of a chemical reaction did you *observe* in Step 3?

**2.** *Compare* the suds formed in the hard water solutions before the reaction with sodium carbonate with the suds formed after the reaction.

**3.** How would you account for the fact that more suds formed after the reaction in Step 4?

## Concluding and Applying

**4.** Write a word equation for the reaction in Step 3. Based on your knowledge of single displacement reactions, what would you *infer* the products to be in this double displacement reaction? Write a balanced equation for what you see.

**5.** Going Further In terms of cleanliness and cost, what are the advantages of having a water softener?

---

### Expected Outcome

Students should see that the sodium carbonate softened the water enough to produce suds from the soap solution.

**Answers to** Analyzing/Concluding and Applying

**1.** A precipitate forms.

**2.** More suds were produced after the reaction.

**3.** The hard water ions were removed.

**4.** calcium sulfate/magnesium sulfate + sodium carbonate → calcium/magnesium carbonate + sodium sulfate; calcium carbonate and sodium sulfate or magnesium carbonate and sodium sulfate; $CaSO_4 + Na_2CO_3 \rightarrow CaCO_3 + Na_2SO_4$ or $MgSO_4 + Na_2CO_3 \rightarrow MgCO_3 + Na_2SO_4$

**5.** Less soap is needed to do wash, and clothes do not have soap scum and discoloration on them.

### ✔ Assessment

**Performance** Have students design an experiment to further investigate how a water softener works. Use the Performance Task Assessment List for Designing an Experiment in **PAMSS,** p. 23. L1 P

---

**Figure 6-18** Before students examine Figure 6-18, invite volunteers to describe a symptom for which they might have taken an antacid tablet. Ask volunteers whether the medication was effective and, if so, why. Challenge students to relate the alleviation of a physical discomfort to a chemical reaction. **L2**

# 3 ASSESS

## Check for Understanding

Have students answer the questions in Check Your Understanding. In discussing question 3, the Apply question, ask students to identify the type of chemical reaction discussed. *synthesis*

## Reteach

Provide students with a series of chemical reactions representative of the four types discussed. An introductory chemistry text is a good source. Have students write the balanced chemical equation for each reaction and classify it by type. **L1**

## Extension

Have students who have mastered the concepts in this section research the controversy that surrounds the use of sodium nitrite and sodium nitrate in foods. Specifically, have them find out if these compounds can produce damaging chemical reactions in the body. **COOP LEARN** **L3**

## DID YOU KNOW?

Of prime importance to fire fighters is this reaction:
$$C + O_2 \rightarrow CO_2 + heat.$$
Most combustible materials are made of carbon-based compounds. When something burns, this reaction is the key reaction.

## Double Displacement Reactions

In a double displacement reaction, the positive ion of one compound replaces the positive ion of the other compound, forming two new compounds. The general formula for this type of reaction is:
$$AB + CD \rightarrow AD + CB.$$
The two reactions in the Investigate are both double displacement.

calcium sulfate + sodium carbonate = calcium carbonate + sodium sulfate
$$CaSO_4 + Na_2CO_3 \rightarrow CaCO_3 + Na_2SO_4$$

The reaction with magnesium is identical except that Mg is used instead of Ca.

Life could not exist without chemical reactions. You get up in the morning, wash your face, and brush your teeth. Toothpaste and soap are both made with chemicals. Eating involves more chemical reactions occurring within your body.

Chemistry is all around you. Understanding how chemical reactions occur can help you understand your world.

**Figure 6-18**

**A** Most acid-based reactions are double displacement reactions. Drinking some antacids results in a reaction that involves the antacid (base) and stomach acid.

**B** This equation describes the double displacement reaction in which the magnesium hydroxide in the antacid combines with hydrochloric acid in the stomach to form magnesium chloride and water.

$$Mg(OH)_2 + 2HCl \rightarrow MgCl_2 + 2H_2O$$

*Tell why antacid did not work for me!*

## check your UNDERSTANDING

**1.** Which type of reaction is each general formula?
 **a.** $XY \rightarrow X + Y$
 **b.** $XY + Z \rightarrow XZ + Y$
 **c.** $X + Z \rightarrow XZ$
 **d.** $WZ + XY \rightarrow WY + XZ$

**2.** Classify the following reactions by type:

**a.** $2KClO_3 \rightarrow 2KCl + 3O_2$
**b.** $CaBr_2 + Na_2CO_3 \rightarrow CaCO_3 + 2NaBr$

**3. Apply** The copper bottoms of some cooking pans turn black after being used. The copper reacts with oxygen forming black copper(II) oxide. Write a balanced chemical equation for this reaction.

# 4 CLOSE

Have students write the names of the four types of chemical reactions they learned about in this section. Then have them write one or two characteristics of each reaction. **L1** **LEP**

## check your UNDERSTANDING

**1.** (a) decomposition; (b) single displacement; (c) synthesis; (d) double displacement

**2.** a) decomposition
b) double displacement

**3.** $2Cu + O_2 \rightarrow 2CuO$ (copper (II) oxide is CuO)

## ENRICHMENT

**Activity** Have students explore the possibility of preventing a chemical reaction. Provide them with two iron nails. Have them paint one nail with clear nail polish, and then place both in a beaker of water. Students should see that the rusting reaction was greatly retarded by the fact that the polish separates the nail from the water. Have students research how ship hulls are protected from rusting. **L2** **LEP**

# Science and Society

## Chemical Detectives

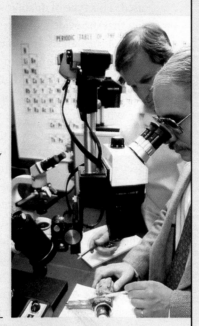

In recent times science, particularly chemistry, has provided law enforcement agencies with a powerful tool. This tool, known as forensic chemistry, not only helps police to understand more about the crime itself, but often leads to identification of the criminal.

Who does the blood found at the scene of the crime belong to? Was the fire an accident or was it deliberately set? Is the piece of art or the letter from Abraham Lincoln real or a forgery? The forensic chemist can answer those questions.

### Collecting and Using Evidence

Law enforcement agencies are becoming more and more systematic and careful about collecting and preserving evidence at the scene of a crime. Police now often call in evidence technicians to collect the evidence rather than do it themselves.

Forensic chemists work with the tiniest bits of hair, skin, and fibers from clothing or rugs, blood, or other materials that the untrained eye might overlook. Evidence is sent to one of several hundred crime labs around the United States and Canada. These labs are fully equipped with the latest computerized testing equipment, such as the electron microscope shown in the photo, and

staffed with highly trained personnel who examine evidence from crime scenes.

Other laboratories work solely on evidence in cases concerning violations of federal or state laws. These may involve identifying pollutants, testing imported materials or products sold to the public, or verifying that a particular substance is an illegal drug.

### Types of Evidence

In crime labs, body fluids and internal organs are commonly analyzed for poisons, drugs, and alcohol. Even knowing what the victim ate at his or her last meal can provide information as to where he or she might have been before the crime. Blood, saliva, and hair can be classified as to type. While once it was only possible to identify a couple of different blood types, it is now possible to compare 30 or more characteristics of a tissue sample.

Evidence can be divided into several categories. For example, the paint from a car can be identified as to the car manufacturer who

# Science and Society

**Purpose** This Science and Society excursion describes the work of forensic chemists. These people use many concepts of elements, chemical compounds, and reactions to help determine the cause of a crime or accident and identify the criminal.

**Content Background** The most recent forensic process used to solve certain criminal cases is DNA fingerprinting. In this process, blood, saliva, or other body fluids found at the scene of a crime can be analyzed for the DNA the cells contain. No two people have exactly the same DNA structure. If a suspect's DNA structure matches tissue found at the scene, this fact can be used as admissible evidence in a court of law.

EXPAND
your view

EXPAND
your view

**Teaching Strategies** Read aloud or provide students with the description of a crime from your local newspaper or a Sherlock Holmes mystery. Ask students to suggest how forensic chemistry might be used to help solve this crime. If the crime has been solved, present the solution and discuss it in light of students' suggestions.

**Answer to**
**What Do You Think?**

Answers will vary but should include a straight, nonjudgmental statement.

uses it and possibly the years in which it was used. This type of qualitative testing identifies that the evidence comes from a certain class of substances. It cannot, however, show that the sample came from a specific car. The sample could come from any car from that manufacturer produced during those years.

What if the car has been repainted on several occasions? If the sequence of paint colors in the sample matches that of the suspect car, there is a much greater probability that they are from the same car.

The composition of the water in the lungs of a drowning victim could, if not identify where the victim drowned, at least rule out bodies of water that did not possess the same composition.

Forensic chemists can restore charred documents and analyze debris from a fire scene. This residue may be an indication of arson.

### In the Future

While the present techniques are excellent, new forensic chemistry equipment is constantly being developed. It's possible to identify a substance if it is present in

A career in forensic chemistry, the study of evidence connected with criminal activity, requires a degree in chemistry. Forensic chemists need to be good problem solvers to be able to explain complex procedures in simple terms.

amounts of only a few parts per million. That's like finding one specific person in a city with a population of a million people.

When forensic chemists testify in court, they are considered expert witnesses. They can testify to what their tests have shown and under what circumstances one could expect to observe the same findings.

### What Do You Think?

Imagine that you are a forensic chemist. You have tested some fibers found at the scene of a murder and fibers from the jacket of the person arrested. The fibers match. What would you say when you testified in court?

By analyzing this skeleton, forensic chemists determined that it is the remains of an eight-year-old girl who was murdered.

Using the data gathered, artists reconstructed a likeness of the person with precision.

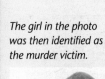
The girl in the photo was then identified as the murder victim.

Such a test could determine whether Abraham Lincoln had a disease called Marfan's syndrome, which used to be called gigantism.

### Going Further ▐▐▐▶
Have students research blood types. Specifically, ask them to find out what causes different blood types and what portion of the population has each major blood type. Encourage students to contact a local chapter of the American Red Cross for information about out what types of blood can be used in transfusions for people with various blood types and how blood banks operate and screen potential donors.

Have students present their findings in a

newspaper article. Use the Performance Task Assessment List for Newspaper Article in **PAMSS**, p. 69. **COOP LEARN** **P** **L1**

# Healthful Structures

HISTORY
CONNNECTION

When you eat healthful foods or take a daily vitamin supplement, each vitamin taken into your body has a necessary job to do. How can scientists identify a vitamin and know what each vitamin does to keep us healthy? Dorothy Crowfoot Hodgkin, an English chemist, worked to answer such questions.

### Finding the Structure

If scientists know what elements are present in a substance and how the atoms are arranged, they can predict how that substance will

react with other materials in the body. Vitamin $B_{12}$, for example, has a very complicated structure. Dr. Hodgkin used X rays to determine what atoms vitamin $B_{12}$ contains and how they are arranged.

### Pernicious Anemia

The body uses this vitamin to build red blood cells and to prevent the disease pernicious anemia. When people have this disease, they have severe problems with digesting food and may have numbness or paralysis in their hands or legs. After Dr. Hodgkin discovered the structure of vitamin $B_{12}$, its reactions could be predicted and it was used in prevention of and treatment for pernicious anemia. Before the use of vitamin $B_{12}$, people who suffered from this disease frequently died.

### Other Work

Dr. Hodgkin did not limit her X-ray studies to vitamin $B_{12}$. She also used this technique to determine the structure of many other complicated molecules that could be used to treat disease.

One of the molecular structures Dr. Hodgkin discovered was that of penicillin, a common antibiotic. She also discovered the structure of insulin, the hormone that regulates blood sugar level. Not only did all these discoveries help scientists learn how chemical changes take place in the body, they also helped chemists make (synthesize) these medications in the laboratory. These synthetic medications are usually more plentiful and cost less than medications produced from living organisms.

For her accomplishment in determining the structure of vitamin $B_{12}$, Dr. Hodgkin was awarded the Nobel Prize for Chemistry in 1964.

## Purpose

Section 6-1 describes different kinds of chemical bonds. Section 6-4 describes different types of chemical reactions. This History Connection relates the structure formed by the bonds between the atoms in vitamin $B_{12}$ and the chemical reactions that this vitamin undergoes with other materials in the body.

## Content Background

Vitamin $B_{12}$ occurs in dairy products, eggs, and meats but is not found in other foods. As a result, people who limit their intake of these foods may need a vitamin $B_{12}$ supplement. Some people, however, eat virtually none of these foods but have adequate vitamin $B_{12}$ in their bodies. This is because only a very small amount (3 mcg) of the vitamin is needed by the body, and colonies of bacteria in the digestive tract produce the vitamin from other materials ingested.

## Teaching Strategies
Guide students to relate vitamins to disease prevention and treatment. Invite a nutritionist to speak to your students on vitamin deficiencies and their symptoms and treatments and other diseases that can be treated with vitamin therapy. Allow time for students to ask questions after the presentation. L2

### Going Further ▐▐▐▐▐➡
Have interested students investigate how a person can have adequate supply of the vitamin in his or her body yet suffer from a deficiency. In order for vitamin $B_{12}$ to be effective, it must be absorbed by the digestive tract. Hydrocholoric acid and a substance called "intrensic factor" are produced by the stomach and are necessary for proper absorption. People who are deficient in these substances or who have had intestinal or stomach surgery may need massive supplements.

A number of medications and drugs such as alcohol can also interfere with absorption. L2

## economics connection

### Purpose
This Economics Connection expands Section 6-4 by considering how our increased knowledge of producing chemical reactions could exhaust supplies of certain minerals.

### Content Background
Minerals, such as quartz, are used in various chemical reactions to produce materials such as glass, sandpaper, telephones, radios, and watches. To preserve mineral resources, conservation measures must be taken. There are several ways of doing this. One way involves the use of alternative materials. For example, large amounts of steel are used in the car industry. Engineers are working to replace metal engines with a type of plastic engine. Another way of conserving resources is recycling. The metal in discarded cars can be recycled and used to make new cars.

### Teaching Strategies
Show students some objects that have been made from recycled materials, such as certain cans and paper. Then ask students to suggest ways they can personally work to conserve mineral resources.

### Debate
Have students evaluate an economic theory about mineral resources. Many economists believe that prices of a mineral rise when it becomes scarce. This encourages the use of lower grades of the mineral substitutes. Have students debate the use of lower-grade minerals. Do they cost more to process because more energy is required to do so? Is the finished product the same?

## economics connection

# Using It Up

As our knowledge of chemistry and chemical reactions has improved, we have found many ways of using these reactions to produce the products we all use. As the technology of such production improves and spreads throughout the world's countries, there is increased competition for raw materials. In many countries, these raw materials are found as minerals in Earth. But the supply of these minerals is limited.

The graph shows three different possible outcomes for how soon the raw materials from which metals are produced might be used up in the United States. Line A shows what will happen if, in the future, we continue to use raw materials at the present rate. What would produce the lines shown in B and C?

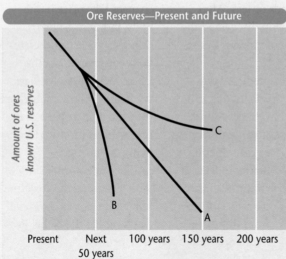

Ore Reserves—Present and Future

*Amount of ores known U.S. reserves*

Present | Next 50 years | 100 years | 150 years | 200 years

### You Try It!
Your teacher will divide the class into small groups and will assign each group a certain course of action. Discuss this action with your group and answer the following questions.
1. Which of the lines on the graph would indicate the results of the action you take?
2. What are the advantages and disadvantages of this action in terms of the country's economy? In terms of the environment?
3. How would this action affect your own personal lifestyle?

After discussing your action, share your results with the class. Since most of these actions would probably require government action, what groups might oppose the passage of each of the laws? Working with your team, think of several other actions that will move our use of metal-containing resources toward line C on the graph.

### Going Further
Organize the class into small groups of two or three students. Ask each group to record the items they typically use in a 24-hour period that are made from minerals. Have them identify what these minerals are and determine which are becoming scarce. They can discuss alternative materials to be used in place of the scarce minerals, alternative items, or life-style changes that would help conserve those minerals. Have students present the conclusions that they reached

in their discussions in a skit. Use the Performance Assessment List for Skit in **PAMSS,** p. 75.

L2 **COOP LEARN**

**R**eview the statements below about the big ideas presented in this chapter, and try to answer the questions. Then, re-read your answers to the Did You Ever Wonder questions at the beginning of the chapter. *In your Journal,* write a paragraph about how your understanding of the big ideas in the chapter has changed.

**1** Ions and covalent molecules are found in all living things. *Which of the symbols shown represent ions, and which represent molecules?*

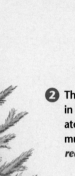

$Na^+$
$K^+$
$Fe^{2+}$
$O_2$
$H_2O$
$CO_2$

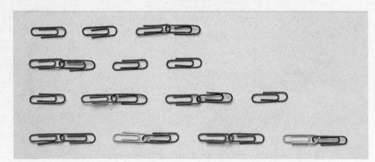

AgAgHHS   AgAgHHS

**2** The total number of atoms of each element in the reactants equals the total number of atoms in the products. All chemical reactions must be balanced. *Why must a chemical reaction be balanced?*

**3** Four major types of reactions are synthesis (a), decomposition (b), single displacement (c), and double displacement (d). All can be expressed as balanced chemical equations. *Which type of reaction is the opposite of synthesis?*

Have students look at the four figures on this page. Direct them to read the statements to review the main ideas in this chapter.

### Teaching Strategies

Prepare a list of 20 to 25 chemical equations, including the four types of chemical reactions discussed in this chapter. Divide the class into two or three teams. Have one member of each team approach the chalkboard. Call out a chemical reaction such as "Silver plus hydrogen sulfide." The first student to write the balanced equation on the board scores a point. Meanwhile, the rest of the class should be trying to write the equation at their desks. For a bonus point, have the team member identify the equation as a synthesis, decomposition, single displacement, or double displacement reaction. Start the contest with easier equations and make them progressively more difficult. At the end of the contest, the team that scored the most points should receive some kind of recognition. The entire list of equations can be given for homework as a reinforcement.
**COOP LEARN**

### Answers to Questions

**1.** Ions are $Na^+$, $K^+$, and $Fe^{2+}$. Molecules are represented by $O_2$, $H_2O$, and $CO_2$.

**2.** Matter is neither created nor destroyed in a chemical reaction.

**3.** decomposition

## Project

Provide each student with a chemical equation to balance. Provide examples of all four types of reactions. Have students make small posters showing their equations and listing the numbers of atoms on both sides, as shown on page 194, to show the balance. Display these posters in the classroom, grouped by reaction type. Use the Performance Task Assessment List for Poster in **PAMSS**, p. 73. **L1** **P**

## Science at Home

Have students copy warning labels from cans and other product containers such as paint, turpentine, and medicine. Have them bring their findings to class and discuss the importance of understanding that certain chemical reactions can be hazardous. **L1**

    MINDJOGGER
VIDEOQUIZ

**Chapter 6** Have students work in groups as they play the videoquiz game to review key chapter concepts.

## Using Key Science Terms

**1.** A polar molecule, such as $H_2O$, is slightly positive on one end and slightly negative on the other end. A nonpolar molecule, such as $O_2$, is not.

**2.** There is an equal number of each type of atom on both sides of the equation.

**3.** A sodium atom gives up an electron to a chlorine atom, forming ions, not molecules.

**4.** a. ionic b. covalent

**5.** Water is a binary compound because it contains only two different types of atoms.

**6.** Answers may include copper, iron, chromium, or lead.

**7.** Answers, such as ammonium sulfate or ammonium nitrate, should include compounds formed from the ammonium ion and a negative ion.

## Understanding Ideas

**1.** A subscript is a small number written to the lower right of a chemical symbol to tell how many atoms of that element are in a molecule. A coefficient is a number written to the left of a chemical formula that tells how many atoms or molecules are represented. For example, in $3N_2$, 3 is a coefficient, and 2 is a subscript.

**2.** $Fe(ClO_3)_3$

**3.** No; both are negatively charged ions.

**4.** $3^+$

**5.** 2, 1, 2; the 1 would not be written.

**6.** synthesis

**7.** Decomposition is the only type of reaction that could result in two elements.

**8.** six

## Developing Skills

**1.** a. single displacement
b. double displacement
c. synthesis
d. decomposition

---

## Using Key Science Terms

balanced chemical equation

binary compound

covalent bond

ion

ionic bond

molecule

nonpolar molecule

oxidation number

polar molecule

polyatomic ion

*Use what you know about the above terms to answer the following questions.*

**1.** How does a polar molecule differ from a nonpolar molecule? Give an example of each.

**2.** How do you know whether a chemical equation is balanced?

**3.** Can sodium and chlorine combine to form a molecule of sodium chloride? Explain.

**4.** What type of bond exists:
a. in calcium chloride?
b. in chlorine gas?

**5.** Your friend says that water is not a binary compound because a water molecule contains three atoms. Is she right? Explain.

**6.** Name three elements that have more than one oxidation number.

**7.** Name a compound formed by combining two polyatomic ions.

## Understanding Ideas

*Answer the following questions in your Journal using complete sentences.*

**1.** In a chemical equation, explain the difference between a subscript and a coefficient.

---

**2.** What is the formula for iron(III) chlorate?

**3.** Could a nitrate ion and a sulfate ion combine to form a compound? Explain.

**4.** What is the oxidation number of Fe in $Fe_2S_3$?

**5.** $Mg + O_2 \rightarrow MgO$.
What coefficients would balance this equation?

**6.** $H_2 + S \rightarrow H_2S$ is an example of which type of reaction?

**7.** A chemical reaction yields two elements as products. What type of reaction has probably occurred? Explain.

**8.** When a benzene molecule, $C_6H_6$, burns, how many carbon dioxide molecules are formed?

## Developing Skills

*Use your understanding of the concepts developed in the chapter to answer each of the following questions.*

**1. Classifying** Classify the following reactions by reaction type.
a. $Zn + CuSO_4 \rightarrow Cu + ZnSO_4$
b. $NaOH + HCl \rightarrow NaCl + H_2O$
c. $CaO + H_2O \rightarrow Ca(OH)_2$
d. $2H_2O_2 \rightarrow 2H_2O + O_2$

**2. Making Models** Draw a picture of a methane ($CH_4$) molecule, showing how electrons are shared by the atoms.

**3. Predicting** Suppose that equal masses of copper(I) chloride and copper(III) chloride are decomposed into their component elements, copper and chlorine. Predict which compound will yield more copper. Explain your answer.

---

**2.**

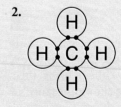

**3.** Copper (I) chloride contains a greater number of copper atoms compared to the number of chlorine atoms and will thus yield more copper.

---

### Program Resources

**Review and Assessment,** pp. 35–40 L1
**Performance Assessment,** Ch. 6 L2
**PAMSS**
**Alternate Assessment in the Science Classroom**
**Computer Test Bank**

**4. Sequencing** Sequence the following compounds in order of increasing oxidation number of the metal in the compound. $Fe_2(SO_4)_3$, $Cu(CH_3CO_2)_2$, $SnCl_4$, $Hg_2O$

## Critical Thinking

In your Journal, *answer each of the following questions.*

1. The diagram shows the reactants in a chemical reaction. Write a balanced equation for this reaction.

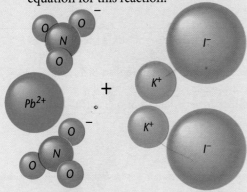

2. Element X has oxidation numbers of 3+ and 5+. Element Z has oxidation numbers of 2- and 3-. Write formulas for the four different compounds of X and Z.

3. Balance the following equation:
$Fe_3O_4 + H_2 \rightarrow Fe + H_2O$

## Problem Solving

*Read the following problem and discuss your answers in a brief paragraph.*

**You are living on the shore of a body of water and you get 250 days of sunshine a year. The problems of storing and transporting hydrogen have been solved.**

Suggest how you would use the electricity from solar cells to produce a clean, nonpolluting fuel. What use(s) could you make of any other products of this reaction?

---

### CONNECTING IDEAS

Answer each of the following.

1. **Theme—Stability and Change** In nature, tin is found in ore as tin(IV) oxide. When the tin(IV) oxide is heated with carbon, the products are tin and carbon dioxide. Write a balanced equation for this reaction. What type of reaction is this?

2. **Theme—Systems and Interactions** The unbalanced reaction involved in photosynthesis is $CO_2 + H_2O \rightarrow C_6H_{12}O_6$ (sugar) + $O_2$. This takes place in the presence of light energy and chlorophyll. What set of coefficients will balance this equation?

3. **Science and Society** What's the difference between forensic and other laboratories?

4. **Earth Science Connection** Why do phosphates cause ponds to be overrun with plant growth?

5. **A Closer Look** How does the behavior of silver's outer electrons contribute to the properties of silver?

---

4. $Hg_2O$, $Cu(CH_3CO_2)_2$, $Fe_2(SO_4)_3$, $SnCl_4$

**Critical Thinking**

1. $Pb(NO_3)_2 + 2KI \rightarrow PbI_2 + 2KNO_3$
2. $X_2Z_3$, $XZ$, $X_2Z_5$, $X_3Z_5$
3. $Fe_3O_4 + 4H_2 \rightarrow 3Fe + 4H_2O$

**Problem Solving**

Decompose water using solar cells for power to produce hydrogen fuel. Oxygen is the other product that could have various uses.

**Connecting Ideas**

1. $SnO_2 + C \rightarrow Sn + CO_2$; single displacement
2. 6, 6, 1, 6
3. The work done in forensic laboratories all relates to matters of law.
4. Phosphates serve as fertilizer for algae, causing them to grow rapidly and cover the surface of a pond.
5. The loosely held electrons in the outer energy level of silver allow it to readily combine with other elements.

---

## ✔ Assessment

**Portfolio** Review the portfolio options that are provided throughout the chapter. Encourage students to select one product that demonstrates their best work for the chapter. Have students explain what they learned and why they chose this example for placement into their portfolios.

Additional portfolio options can be found in the following **Teacher Classroom Resources: Concept Mapping,** p. 14

**Making Connections: Integrating Sciences,** p. 15
**Multicultural Connections,** pp. 15-16
**Making Connections: Across the Curriculum,** p. 15
**Critical Thinking/Problem Solving,** p. 14
**Take Home Activities,** p. 12
**Laboratory Manual,** pp. 25-28; 29-32; 33-36
**Performance Assessment** P

# Chapter Organizer

| SECTION | OBJECTIVES | ACTIVITIES |
|---|---|---|
| **Chapter Opener** | | **Explore!** Do hot things move? p. 209 |
| **7-1 Solids and Liquids** (5 days) | **1. Describe** the molecular structure of solids. **2. Explain** how solids and liquids expand when heated. **3. Discuss** melting in terms of kinetic theory. **4. Explain** evaporation, condensation, and sublimation. | **Investigate 7-1:** High Temperature Straws, pp. 212–213 **Find Out!** How do the molecular forces within liquids compare? p. 216 **Explore!** Do cooling liquids shrink or swell? p. 218 **Explore!** Do you need sunlight to make a liquid change state? p. 219 |
| **7-2 Kinetic Theory of Gases** (3 days) | **1. Describe** pressure in terms of kinetic theory. **2. Explain** the meaning of temperature in gases. **3. Discuss** what absolute zero means. | **Find Out!** How do collisions produce pressure? p. 222 **Investigate 7-2:** Ballooning Size, pp. 224–225 **Skillbuilder:** Making and Using Graphs p. 229 |

## EXPAND your view

**Life Science Connection** Sounds Fishy to Me, pp. 214–215
**A Closer Look** Crystal Clear, pp. 228–229
**Science and Society** Keeping Your Cool, p. 231
**Literature Connection** Ancient Wisdom, p. 232
**Technology Connection** Sweet Evaporation, p. 233

## ACTIVITY MATERIALS

| EXPLORE! | INVESTIGATE! | FIND OUT! |
|---|---|---|
| **Page 209** 3 75-mL beakers, ice water, tap water, hot water, thermometer, 3 pieces brightly colored hard candy **Page 218*** tray or square cake pan, water, freezer, permanent marker, paraffin, pan for melting paraffin, hot plate; small, clear container **Page 219** dropper, rubbing alcohol | **Pages 212–213** 2 plastic drinking straws, cardboard sheet, 2 drinking cups, tape, very hot water, cooking syringe, pencil, thermal mitt **Pages 224–225** 2 medium-sized round balloons, 1 m string, felt-tipped marking pen, meter stick, container of ice water, tongs, heat-proof glove, beaker of boiling water, thermometer | **Page 216*** 25 mL water, 3 clear glasses, 3 large plates or pie pans; 2 or 3 liquids such as syrup, molasses, motor oil, salad oil, or liquid soap **Page 222*** 2 large cardboard boxes, tennis balls |

*For adequate development of the concepts presented, we recommend that students do the activities with an asterisk.

# Chapter 7 Molecules in Motion

## TEACHER CLASSROOM RESOURCES

| Student Masters | Teaching Aids |
|---|---|
| **Study Guide**, p. 36<br>**Multicultural Connections**, p. 17<br>**How It Works**, p. 12<br>**Activity Masters**, Investigate 7-1, pp. 31–32<br>**Flex Your Brain**, p. 5<br>**Making Connections: Integrating Sciences**, p. 17<br>**Take Home Activities**, p. 13<br>**Making Connections: Across the Curriculum**, p. 17<br>**Critical Thinking/Problem Solving**, p. 15<br>**Concept Mapping**, p. 15<br>**Science Discovery Activities**, 7-1, 7-2 | **Color Transparency and Master 13**, States of Matter<br>**Laboratory Manual**, pp. 37–40, Density of a Liquid<br>**Laboratory Manual**, pp. 41–44, Viscosity<br>**\*STVS:** *Cloud Chemistry*, Chemistry (Disc 2, Side 1)<br>**\*STVS:** *Geothermal Wells*, Chemistry (Disc 2, Side 2) |
| **Study Guide**, p. 37<br>**Activity Masters**, Investigate 7-2, pp. 33–34<br>**Making Connections: Technology & Society**, p. 17<br>**Multicultural Connections**, p. 18<br>**Science Discovery Activities**, 7-3 | **Color Transparency and Master 14**, Boyle's Law<br>**\*STVS:** *Greenhouse Effect*, Earth and Space (Disc 3, Side 2) |
| **ASSESSMENT RESOURCES**<br>**Review and Assessment**, pp. 41–46<br>**Performance Assessment**, Ch. 7<br>**PAMSS\***<br>**MindJogger Videoquiz**<br>**Alternate Assessment in the Science Classroom**<br>**Computer Test Bank** | **Spanish Resources**<br>**Cooperative Learning Resource Guide**<br>**Lab and Safety Skills**<br>**Integrated Science Videodisc** |

## KEY TO TEACHING STRATEGIES

The following designations will help you decide which activities are appropriate for your students.

**L1** Level 1 activities should be within the ability range of all students.

**L2** Level 2 activities should be within the ability range of the average to above-average student.

**L3** Level 3 activities are designed for the ability range of above-average students.

**LEP** LEP activities should be within the ability range of Limited English Proficiency students.

**COOP LEARN** Cooperative Learning activities are designed for small group work.

**P** These strategies represent student products that can be placed into a best-work portfolio.

## ADDITIONAL MATERIALS

**Software**
*Boyle's Law, Absolute Zero Unit,* EME.
*Earth's Water,* Queue.
*Exploring Gas Laws,* MECC.
*Gas Relationships,* J&S Software.
*Kinetics,* J&S Software.
*Science 3: Matter: Gas, Liquid & Solids,* Ellen Nelson Learning Library.

**Audiovisual**
*Heat, Temperature and The Properties of Matter,* video, Coronet/MTI.
*Mr. Wizard's World, Change of State,* video, Mr. Wizard Institute.
*Mechanical Energy,* video, Churchill Media.

*Particles in Motion: States of Matter,* filmstrip, National Geographic.

**Laserdisc**
*Chemistry at Work,* Videodiscovery.
*Density in Gases/Density in Liquids,* AIMS.
*Density in Solids/Phase Changes,* AIMS.
*Heat Molecules in Motion,* AIMS.

**Readings**
Hazen, Robert and Trefil, James. *Science Matters: Achieving Scientific Literacy.* Doubleday.

\*Performance Assessment in Middle School Science

\*Science and Technology Videodisc Series

# THEME DEVELOPMENT

Students learn how kinetic energy changes can affect the stability of solid, liquid, and gaseous states of matter. In the Investigate on pages 212–213 students observe how an increase in the temperature in a solid increases the kinetic energy of its particles. They observe how this change in motion affects the stability of the solid. The chapter also describes how the interactions of particles in a system can account for the behavior of gases, liquids, and solids over a range of different temperatures.

# CHAPTER OVERVIEW

All matter can change phases. When energy is given to it or taken away, matter can change from solid to liquid to gas and back again. This phenomenon is seen in the world in freezing, melting, evaporation, condensation, and sublimation. The behavior of gas particles—and the relationships they demonstrate between temperature, pressure, and volume—also illustrate matter's sensitivity to energy.

## Tying to Previous Knowledge

Write these headings on the board: *Gases, Liquids, Solids.* As a group, have students list anything that they associate with each heading. Under *Liquids,* for example, they might include runny, wet, cold, no shape, seeks lowest level, heavy, and so on. After the lists are complete, check if any word(s) appear on more than one list. If so, have the class discuss whether this is appropriate or significant.

# MOLECULES in MOTION

## Did you ever wonder...

✓ **Why you feel cooler if you splash yourself with water?**

✓ **Why water pours faster than catsup or syrup?**

✓ **Why the tar squeezes out of street cracks in warm weather?**

Before you begin to study about how moving molecules affect you, think about these questions and answer them *in your Journal.* When you finish the chapter, compare your Journal write-up with what you have learned.

I t's a warm, clear, sunny day, and you and your friends are on the way home from the beach. You had arrived early enough in the day to get a choice spot on the beach and put on a sunscreen. Then you waded knee deep into the water to test the temperature. Perfect!

After lying in the sun for 20 minutes, you were so warm that you began to sweat. You decided it would be a good time for a swim. You dove into the surf, but started shivering when you got out of the water. Why?

Now, walking home, you are starting to get hot again. You and your friends decide to buy ice cream cones. But you must finish the cones fast before they melt all over your hands.

▶ ***What causes all these changes? You'll find out in this chapter with the help of the kinetic-molecular theory. You can begin your discoveries with this Explore activity.***

**208**

## Did you ever wonder...

• Thermal energy transfers from your skin to water molecules, allowing some to escape. The loss of energy cools the skin. (p. 218)

• The attractive forces between molecules of catsup or syrup are stronger than those that hold water molecules together. (p. 217)

• Heating during warm weather causes tar and pavement to expand. This thermal expansion forces tar up through cracks. (p. 214)

## STUDENT JOURNAL

Have students write their responses to the Did You Ever Wonder questions in their journals. After they have read the chapter, students should read their journal entries again to see how their perceptions of molecular motion changed.

# Explore! ACTIVITY

## Do hot things move?

### What To Do

1. Place 75 mL of ice water into one beaker, 75 mL of tap water into a second beaker, and 75 mL of hot water into a third.

2. Measure and record the temperature in each beaker.

3. Drop a piece of brightly colored hard candy into each beaker. Observe the beakers. Is there a pattern to what you observed?

4. *In your Journal*, record your observations. What can you infer to explain your observations?

209

## INTRODUCING THE CHAPTER

Have students look at the photograph and describe what they see. Ask students how the water differs from the sand beneath it or from the air in the raft.

## Explore!

### Do hot things move?

**Time needed** 20 minutes

**Materials** 3 75-ml beakers, ice water, tap water, hot water, thermometer, 3 pieces of brightly colored hard candy

**Thinking Processes** thinking critically, observing and inferring, recognizing cause and effect, measuring in SI, designing an experiment

**Purpose** To observe how heat affects motion in matter.

### Teaching the Activity

**Student Journal** Invite students to write about their observations in their journals. Possible topics might include how their observations differed from their expectations and the patterns formed by the dissolving candies. L1

### Expected Outcome

Students should have observed the candy color spreading most rapidly in the hot water, and inferred that heat aided that process.

### Answer to Question

4. The motion of water molecules was transferred to the dissolving candy, which was dispersed to varying extents, depending on how hot the water was.

### ✔ Assessment

**Performance** Have students develop an experiment to find out if all solids dissolve and disperse faster in hot water than in cold water. Students could test ice, boullion cubes, or bath salts. Use the Performance Task Assessment List for Designing an Experiment in **PAMSS**, p. 23. L1 P

---

## ASSESSMENT PLANNER

### PORTFOLIO ASSESSMENT
Refer to page 236 for suggested items that students might select for their portfolios.

### PERFORMANCE ASSESSMENT
Process, pp. 213, 219, 222, 225
Skillbuilder, p. 229
Explore! Activities, pp. 209, 218, 219
Find Out! Activities, pp. 216, 222
Investigate, pp. 212–213, 224–225

### CONTENT ASSESSMENT
Check Your Understanding, pp. 221, 230
Reviewing Main Ideas, p. 234
Chapter Review, pp. 235–236

### GROUP ASSESSMENT
Opportunities for group assessment occur with Cooperative Learning Strategies.

# PREPARATION

## Concepts Developed

The kinetic-molecular theory is introduced to explain much of the behavior of solids and liquids. The particles in matter are constantly moving. In this section, students investigate the effect of temperature on this motion. In a solid, there is enough force between molecules for the matter to keep its shape. However, as temperature increases, the motion of the molecules increases, resulting in a liquid and eventually in a gas. The processes that occur as matter changes from one state to another—melting, freezing, boiling, evaporation, condensation, and sublimation—are also explained using the kinetic-molecular theory.

## Planning the Lesson

Refer to the Chapter Organizer on pages 208A–B.

# 1 MOTIVATE

**Demonstration** Students will observe the effect of an increase in kinetic energy on the temperature of a liquid.

Put equal amounts of water at the same temperature in two identical blender jars. Ask students how they think the temperature of each sample will compare after one has been blended for several minutes. Blend one sample at a rapid speed for several minutes. Place a thermometer into each sample. The blended water should have a higher temperature. Ask students why they think this temperature difference occurred. **L1**

---

**7-1** **Solids and Liquids**

**Section Objectives**

■ Describe the molecular structure of solids.
■ Explain how solids and liquids expand when heated.
■ Discuss melting in terms of kinetic theory.
■ Explain evaporation, condensation, and sublimation.

**Key Terms**

kinetic-molecular theory
thermal expansion
viscosity
evaporation
boiling
sublimation
condensation

## The Kinetic-Molecular Theory

In the 1800s, a scientist named James P. Joule discovered that the increase in thermal energy produced by a given amount of mechanical work was always the same. The experiment shown in **Figure 7-1** below demonstrates that work can be changed into thermal energy.

Joule used the idea that all matter is made up of vibrating atoms and molecules to explain what happened.

In his experiment, the movement of the paddle wheel eventually caused the water molecules to vibrate faster.

The explanation of thermal energy as the random movement of atoms or molecules is part of what is called the **kinetic-molecular theory**.

In this section, you'll see how the kinetic-molecular theory explains the properties and behavior of matter with which you're familiar.

**Figure 7-1**

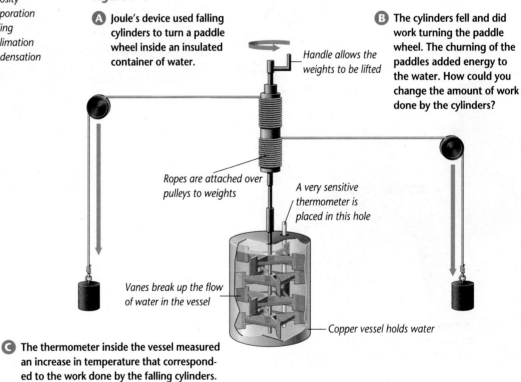

**A** Joule's device used falling cylinders to turn a paddle wheel inside an insulated container of water.

Handle allows the weights to be lifted

Ropes are attached over pulleys to weights

A very sensitive thermometer is placed in this hole

Vanes break up the flow of water in the vessel

Copper vessel holds water

**B** The cylinders fell and did work turning the paddle wheel. The churning of the paddles added energy to the water. How could you change the amount of work done by the cylinders?

**C** The thermometer inside the vessel measured an increase in temperature that corresponded to the work done by the falling cylinders.

---

**Program Resources**

---

## What Makes a Solid Solid?

During your day at the beach, you might buy a soft drink to cool off. The paper cup, ice, and coins you get as change are examples of solids. A solid has a definite shape and fills a definite amount of space. Because solids are rigid, there must be forces of attraction that hold their particles in a definite shape. Although solids appear rigid and unmoving, the kinetic-molecular theory says that the ions, atoms, or molecules in solid matter are in constant motion. **Figure 7-2** below shows how this apparent contradiction is resolved.

What effect does this internal motion have on a solid when its temperature rises? You can investigate this question on the next pages using common drinking straws.

**Figure 7-2**

Ⓐ This diagram shows a model of a solid. In this model, the particles of the solid are represented by small balls, and forces between the particles are represented by springs.

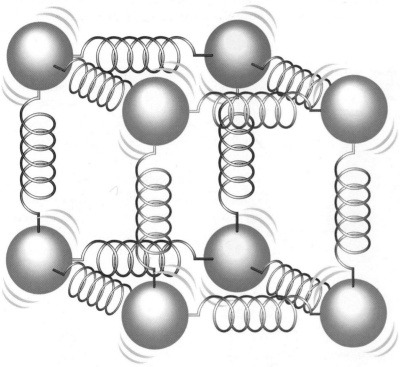

Ⓑ Springs hold the balls in position. If you push or pull on any ball, the springs resist the motion. When you release the ball, it vibrates around its rest position. This shows how particles in a solid can move while the solid retains its shape and volume.

Ⓒ An increase in temperature is represented by greater vibration of the particles in the framework. The particles vibrate faster and move further from their rest positions.

---

---

## INVESTIGATE!

### 7-1 High Temperature Straws

#### Planning the Activity

**Time needed** 20 minutes

**Purpose** To demonstrate the thermal expansion of a solid.

**Process Skills** thinking critically, observing and inferring, comparing and contrasting, recognizing cause and effect, drawing in science, predicting, forming a hypothesis, modeling, forming operational definitions

**Materials** See reduced student text.

**Preparation** Before using the hot water, have students test their system to see if water runs smoothly through it without spilling or coming into contact with the second straw.

#### Teaching the Activity

**Process Reinforcement** Before students begin the activity, ask them to try to predict the results. Ask, if one straw undergoes thermal expansion and the other does not, what configuration might you expect?

**Safety** Cooking syringes should be handled with care to prevent accidental punctures.

**Possible Hypotheses** Students may hypothesize that the expanding hot straw may deform the static cool straw, or that the tape holding the two together may become loose or break.

**Student Journal** Have students record their observations and answer the questions in their journals. L1

# High Temperature Straws

*An increase in temperature of a solid indicates an increase in the kinetic energy of the particles in the solid. What are some effects of this increased motion?*

### Problem
What happens to a solid as its temperature rises?

### Materials
2 plastic drinking straws
cardboard sheet
2 drinking cups
tape

very hot water
cooking syringe
pencil
thermal mitt

### Safety Precautions

Be careful with the hot water to avoid being burned. Use the syringe carefully to avoid injury.

## What To Do

1. Tape two of the straws tightly together as shown below. Make sure the ends are even. Then, tape these straws to the cardboard.

2. Mark the positions of the bottoms of the straws.

3. Use the cooking syringe and the thermal mitt to inject the hot water into one of the straws (see Photo **A**). Use a cup to catch the water as it runs out the other end. Make sure that the hot water only comes in contact with one straw.

## Program Resources

**Activity Masters,** pp. 31–32, Investigate 7-1

**Science Discovery Activities,** 7-1, Where does the Energy Go?

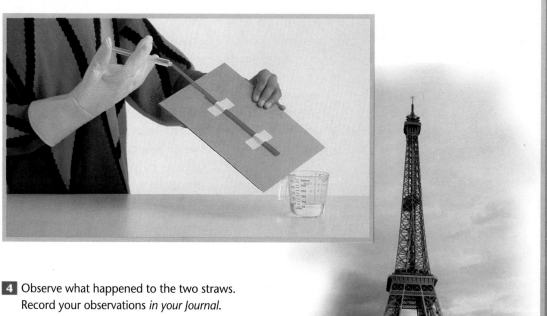

**4** Observe what happened to the two straws. Record your observations *in your Journal*.

*Heat causes the particles in solids to vibrate faster, which explains why the Eiffel Tower in Paris grows 7.5 centimeters (about 3 inches) every summer.*

## Analyzing

1. Describe the motion of the two-straw combination when one straw was heated.

2. Make a drawing that shows the two straws after the hot water was injected. Indicate which straw was heated and which straw was not.

## Concluding and Applying

3. Did the heated straw get larger or smaller? Use the kinetic-molecular theory to *hypothesize* why this happened.

4. *Predict* two ways to make the straws return to their normal shape.

5. **Going Further** You have a metal storm door that opens and closes very easily in the winter, but sticks in the summer. Explain why this happens.

**Expected Outcome**

The straws will bend. The hot straw will occupy the outer layer of the curve because it has lengthened while its cooler counterpart has not.

**Answers to** Analyzing/ Concluding and Applying

**1.** The straws bent into a curve, with the hot straw on the outside of the curve.

**2.** Drawings should show the straws taped together and curved in such a way that the outer straw (hot) is on the outside of the curve and is slightly longer than the inner (cold) straw.

**3.** It got larger. Heating made its particles move faster and farther from one another.

**4.** Pour cold water through the heated straw or hot water through the unheated straw.

**5.** In the winter, because the temperature is lower, the particles do not have as much kinetic energy and are closer together. In the summer when the temperature is higher, the particles have more energy and take up more space.

✔ **Assessment**

**Process** To challenge students to formulate a hypothesis, present the following puzzler: I took a jar of olives out of the refrigerator. The aluminum lid was screwed on so tightly, I couldn't get the jar open. After running the mouth of the jar under warm running water, the lid came off easily. Why? *The lid expanded as it got hotter.* What does this tell us about the jar, in relation to the lid? *The glass jar expands less with added heat energy than the metal lid.* Use the Performance Task Assessment List for Formulating a Hypothesis in **PAMSS**, p. 21. **L1**

**Early Glassmaking**

When most crystalline solids are heated, they melt quickly over a narrow temperature range. Glass is different. When heated, glass can be softened without melting it into a puddle of liquid. This glowing 'dough' can be blown into various shapes and sizes. The ancient Egyptians were probably the first to exploit the remarkable qualities of glass about 5,000 years ago. They found that it made better containers than clay because it was transparent and not porous to water. They also found that adding different impurities resulted in different colors of glass.

Of course, you normally would have no reason to consider how drinking straws change when heated. When the temperature increases, a solid tends to expand. The expansion of the straw you observed was small, but it is important to the design of structures such

as highways, railroads, and bridges as **Figure 7-3** shows.

The expansion that occurs as a solid is heated is called **thermal expansion**. As the temperature of a solid increases, its atoms or molecules vibrate with greater speed and amplitude. The atoms move a little farther from their home position. In terms of the ball-and-spring model, the balls vibrate faster and with greater amplitude. The average length of the springs increases.

**Figure 7-3**

This railroad track wasn't designed to handle record-breaking summer temperatures. The expanding rails pushed one another out of line.

# Life Science CONNECTION

## Sounds Fishy to Me

Imagine fish living in the frigid Arctic waters near the North Pole. How do they survive without being frozen solid?

*The Alaskan blackfish can survive in freezing waters because it has a natural antifreeze that lowers the freezing point of its body fluids.*

Unlike humans, fish aren't able to increase or maintain a constant body temperature by breaking down foods. The reason many fish survive in freezing waters is because they have what scientists call a natural antifreeze.

Antifreeze in a car's radiator does not warm up the car. Instead, it keeps cars running in frigid weather by lowering the freezing temperature of water.

Water freezes at 0°C. If water turned to ice inside a car, it would expand and crack the radiator. If a fish's blood froze inside its body, the sharp ice crystals would break cell membranes and do all sorts of dam-

# Life Science CONNECTION

**Purpose**

The Life Science Connection emphasizes the concept presented in Section 7-1 that a liquid freezes into a solid because lowered temperatures cause the molecules to slow down to a point where they clump together. Antifreeze lowers the freezing point of a liquid.

**Content Background**

Adding solute to a pure liquid or to a solution lowers the freezing point of the solution. The identity of the solute is not as important as the number of particles that are added to the solution. Because ionic compounds dissociate as they dissolve, they add more particles to a solution than covalent compounds do. For example, for every formula unit of sodium chloride that dissolves, two particles, $Na^+$ and $Cl^-$, enter the solution.

# The Nature of Liquids

Early in your science studies, you probably learned that a liquid has a definite volume and tends to be hard to compress. A liquid also expands as its temperature rises. Kinetic theory explains this expansion in the same way that it explains the expansion of solids. The thermal expansion of some liquids like mercury and alcohol is regular over a wide temperature range. This regularity allows the liquids to be used in thermometers.

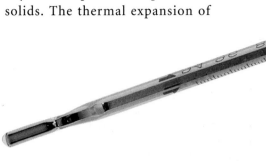

**Figure 7-4**

Either mercury or alcohol is used in thermometers like this one because each expands nearly the same amount for the change from -20 °C to -21°C as for the change from 40°C to 41°C.

age. A fish's natural antifreeze works by lowering the freezing point of its blood and other body fluids.

Some fish, like the Alaskan blackfish pictured, live near the bottom of freshwater lakes that are almost completely frozen.

The super-cooled lake bottom waters remain unfrozen—even at temperatures below 0°C—because flowing water currents prevent ice crystals from forming. Most fish avoid the higher waters where ice is forming to keep ice crystals from forming in their bodies. But fish with natural antifreeze can swim almost anywhere.

An active ingredient in car antifreeze is a substance called ethylene glycol. Scientists have discovered that an active ingredient in fish's natural antifreeze is a substance called glyco-protein. It's also been found that fish that live closer to the frozen surface, where ice crystals form, have more glyco-protein than fish that stay near the bottom, where ice crystals don't form.

*The antifreeze in this car's radiator keeps the car running during the cold winter.*

*Antifreeze contains ethylene glycol, which lowers the freezing temperature of the water in the radiator.*

## What Do You Think?

The Alaskan blackfish is one type of fish that lives in frigid waters. Read about other fish that live in frigid waters and share that information with your classmates.

Figure 7-5

Unlike a solid, the molecules in a drop of water are constantly touching and sliding over and around one another.

Attractive forces must exist between a liquid's molecules, or else the liquid would not stay together at all. As in solids, the molecules resist being squeezed together. In a liquid, however, the attractive forces between the molecules are too weak to maintain a particular shape.

Is this force between molecules the same for all liquids? Do the activity below and see for yourself.

## Find Out!

### How do the molecular forces within liquids compare?

**Time needed** 15 minutes

**Materials** 3 clear glasses, 3 large plates or pie pans, 25-mL water, 2 or 3 other liquids such as salad oil, motor oil, molasses, syrup, or liquid soap

**Thinking Processes** sequencing, observing and inferring, comparing and contrasting, recognizing cause and effect, predicting, designing an experiment, hypothesizing

**Purpose** To compare the attractive forces between molecules of various liquids.

**Preparation** Substitute liquids of varying viscosities including non-toxic paint, alcohol, corn syrup, or honey.

### Teaching the Activity

**Student Journal** Have students predict in their journals how they expect their experimental liquids to rank in terms of viscosity. Then have students compare their predictions to their final data and note any unexpected results.
L1

### Expected Outcome

Students should observe that thicker liquids pour more slowly than the others, and infer that the force of attraction between the molecules of those liquids is stronger.

### Answer to Questions

3. It spreads out.

### Conclude and Apply

1. Lists will vary depending on materials used. Example: water, salad oil, liquid soap, syrup, motor oil, molasses.

2. The liquids that are harder to pour must have stronger attractions between their molecules.

## Find Out! ACTIVITY

### How do the molecular forces within liquids compare?

You can't directly observe the forces between a liquid's molecules, but you can make inferences from properties of the liquid.

#### What To Do

1. Obtain from your teacher three clear glasses, three large plates, and liquid samples.

2. Put about 25 mL of water in one glass. Try to coat the inside of the glass with water.

3. Slowly turn the glass upside down and pour the water into one of the pie plates. Observe how long it takes all the water to pour out. What happens as the water reaches the pie plate?

4. Repeat Steps 2-3 for two or three other liquids.

#### Conclude and Apply

1. Make a list of liquids you tested, sequencing from fastest to slowest pouring.

2. Use your results to form a hypothesis about the attractive forces between the molecules in the liquids you tested.

**216** Chapter 7 Molecules in Motion

## ✔ Assessment

**Performance** Have student groups plan and carry out an experiment to test if a liquid's viscosity is affected by its temperature. Students might test molasses or shampoo. Use the Performance Task Assessment List for Designing an Experiment in **PAMSS**, p. 23. L1 COOP LEARN

## ENRICHMENT

**Research** Have students hypothesize how liquids behave in the weightless environment of outer space. For example, what shape does a liquid take if gravity is not affecting it? Does it hold together or fragment like a gas spreading out in a room? Have students share their findings with the class. (Activities in space show that liquids take on spherical shapes and do hold together if undisturbed.) L2

As you discovered in the Find Out activity, one liquid may change shape less readily than another. A liquid's resistance to changing shape is called its **viscosity**. As **Figure 7-6** shows, a liquid with high viscosity, such as syrup, pours more slowly than a liquid with low viscosity, such as water. Viscosity depends on the attractive forces between a liquid's molecules. The stronger the force, the more viscous the liquid. The temperature of the liquid affects the strength of this force. This is because when a liquid is cold, its molecules have less kinetic energy and are closer together. The force holding the molecules together depends on distance.

### ■ Freezing and Melting

If you heat almost any solid, it will melt into a liquid. You have to add energy to a solid to melt it. If you drop an ice cube into water, the ener-

**Figure 7-7**

**A** This chocolate was just heated. Some of the bonds holding the solid in a regular shape have been broken. The corners of the block are rounding and smoothing as the molecules in the chocolate start to move around one another.

**Figure 7-6**

Different liquids have different viscosities. Water has a low viscosity, so it runs down the board quickly. Paint and motor oil have higher viscosities, so they run down the board more slowly. Honey has a much higher viscosity, so it runs down the board very slowly. Which of these four liquids has the strongest attractive force between its molecules?

gy that melts the ice comes from the water. The water temperature drops as a result.

After you've examined **Figure 7-7**, turn the page and do the Explore activity to discover a unique property of one liquid.

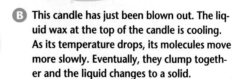

**B** This candle has just been blown out. The liquid wax at the top of the candle is cooling. As its temperature drops, its molecules move more slowly. Eventually, they clump together and the liquid changes to a solid.

7-1 Solids and Liquids **217**

## Explore!

**Do cooling liquids shrink or swell?**

**Time needed** 20 minutes and overnight

**Materials** water, square cake pan, paraffin, small clear container, marker, freezer, heat source

**Thinking Processes** observing and inferring, comparing and contrasting, recognizing cause and effect, designing an experiment, modeling

**Purpose** To compare the volume of a liquid to its volume as a solid.

**Preparation** Wax from candles or melted crayons can substitute for pure paraffin.

### Teaching the Activity

**Troubleshooting** Be sure to let the water chill overnight so that it freezes completely.

**Student Journal** Have students write their observations in their journals. Suggest that they discuss how the change in volume they anticipated might have differed from the final results. Ask them to note instances of change in volume of freezing water they are familiar with from the real world. L1

### Expected Outcome

The water will increase in volume as it freezes.

### Answers to Questions
**3.** The wax shrank.

### ✔ Assessment

**Performance** Have students work in groups to plan and carry out an experiment in which they test the change in volume for other liquids as they solidify. Students might test liquid soap, milk, juice, vinegar, or gelatin. Use the Performance Task Assessment List for Designing an Experiment in **PAMSS,** p. 23.
COOP LEARN L1

## Explore! ACTIVITY

**Do cooling liquids shrink or swell?**

### What To Do

1. Pour water into a tray or square cake pan until the tray is two-thirds full. Mark the level of the water on one side of the tray, then place the tray in the freezer.

2. Observe the tray after the water has completely frozen. Record your observations *in your Journal.*

3. Repeat the experiment using warmed paraffin and a small, clear container instead of water and a tray. Let the wax cool to room temperature. How did the wax change when it cooled?

4. *In your Journal,* compare your observations of solidifying water and wax.

### DID YOU KNOW?

There is more thermal energy locked up in a one-ton, -10°C iceberg than in a cup of boiling water. Each molecule of water has more kinetic energy than each molecule of ice. But, because the iceberg has trillions more molecules, the iceberg's total energy is greater than that of the boiling water.

Knowing how a drop in temperature affects the interaction of molecules, you might have accurately predicted the behavior of the wax. Generally, the solid phase of a substance occupies a smaller volume than the liquid phase does. Molecules do, on the whole, move more slowly and stay closer together as a substance freezes or solidifies. Water turns out to be the chief exception to this. As water cools its volume decreases, but only until the temperature reaches 4°C. Below that temperature, water does something unusual—it expands. It expands even more when it freezes. Can you explain why icebergs float?

Because water expands when it freezes, ice floats. Rivers and streams freeze from the top down. Many forms of life survive under the ice instead of being trapped on the surface. Scientists hypothesize that planets too cold to ever have had liquid water aren't likely to develop life. Liquids on such planets would all freeze from the bottom up. The floor of a non-water ocean would be a harsh place for developing life.

### ■ Evaporation

You've seen what happens when solids gain and lose energy. What happens to liquids as energy is added? If your T-shirt gets wet at the beach, it eventually dries out in the sun. Where does the water go? Why do you and the shirt feel cool? Try this Explore activity to experience and observe a similar change.

**218** Chapter 7 Molecules in Motion

## ENRICHMENT

**Activity** Materials needed are paraffin, heat source, and trays.

During the Explore activity, students learned that water is unusual because it is less dense in the solid phase than in the liquid phase. Have them place a piece of solid paraffin in liquid paraffin to compare its density in the solid and liquid phases. Repeat this test with other materials. If students use materials from their Performance Assessment experiments for this activity, have them look for a pattern. Ask students to predict which solids will float in their liquid forms and which will sink. *Liquids that shrank when solidified became more dense and therefore will sink. Liquids that expanded will float.* L2 P

## Do you need sunlight to make a liquid change state?

### What To Do

1. Using a dropper, place five drops of rubbing alcohol on the back of one hand.

2. Wait two minutes. *In your Journal,* describe what you saw and felt.

3. Has energy entered or left your hand? How do you know?

**Figure 7-8**

Ⓐ You feel cool when you come out of the water because your body is losing thermal energy to the water on your skin. You pass more thermal energy to the water on your skin than you usually do to surrounding air molecules.

### ■ Evaporation and Condensation

As energy moves from your skin to the alcohol, the alcohol molecules move faster. The fastest ones soon gain enough energy to break free into the open air as an invisible gas. The process of a liquid changing to a gas is called **evaporation**. Similarly, as **Figure 7-8** shows, water evaporates from your skin when you come out of the water at the beach and you also feel cool.

Ⓑ Evaporating sweat cools your body. During evaporation, the highest energy molecules escape from the surface first. This lowers the average energy of the molecules remaining in the liquid.

Explore!

**Do you need sunlight to make a liquid change state?**

**Time needed** 5 minutes

**Materials** dropper, rubbing alcohol

**Thinking Processes** observing and inferring, forming a hypothesis

**Purpose** To examine energy changes during evaporation.

**Preparation** Any liquid that evaporates quickly can be used.

**Teaching the Activity**

**Student Journal** Have students answer the questions in their journals. L1

**Expected Outcome**

Students should observe the evaporation of the alcohol, connecting it with the cold feeling it produces on their skin, and infer that the loss of energy on their skin is related to the increase in energy in the alcohol.

**Answers to Questions**

**3.** Energy has left your hand. The energy was used by the alcohol as it evaporated.

✔ **Assessment**

**Process** Help students to formulate a hypothesis by considering the following. If you washed one glass in hot water and another glass in cold water and then left them both to dry on the counter, would one dry first? Why? *The glass washed in hot water would dry first. The warm material in that glass would contribute more energy to evaporate the water on its surface than would the cool material in the other glass.* Use the Performance Task Assessment List for Formulating a Hypothesis in **PAMSS**, p. 21. L1

**220    Chapter 7    Molecules in Motion**

## Uncovering Preconceptions

Many people call the cloud that emerges from a teakettle or hangs over a bathtub "steam." Actually, steam is an invisible gas. Steam exists near the spout of a teakettle, where it is invisible. The cloud that appears just beyond the spout is tiny water droplets that form as the true steam begins to condense.

## Content Background

Scientists call the amount of energy it takes to change a substance completely from liquid to gas its *heat of vaporization*. For water, the heat of vaporization is 2260 kJ of energy to change one kg of water at 100°C to gas. The *heat of fusion* is the energy needed to take a substance from a solid to a liquid state. For water at 100°C it is 334 kJ per kilogram.

## ■ Boiling

Water evaporates faster from your warm skin than it does from a container at room temperature. If you warm the water on a stove, it evaporates even faster. If you heat the water further, bubbles form throughout it and rise to the surface. The water is **boiling** because the pressure of escaping water vapor equals air pressure.

#### Figure 7-9

**A** The water in the heated pot evaporates faster than the water in the unheated pot. More molecules in the heated pot have enough energy to escape from the water's surface.

**B** In the unheated pot, fewer water molecules have enough energy to overcome the forces holding them to one another and escape from the water's surface.

**C** In this pot, the water is boiling and many molecules are escaping the water's surface as invisible water vapor. The water vapor molecules are moving much faster and are much farther apart than water molecules.

## ■ Sublimation

Solids can undergo a process similar to evaporation. If you leave a tray of ice cubes in the freezer for several months, you find that the once-full tray now has only small cubes of ice in it. The temperature was below freezing, so the cubes couldn't have melted, and then evaporated in the normal way. Instead, the water changed directly from solid to gas. In this process, called **sublimation**, a solid changes into a gas without first becoming a liquid.

#### Figure 7-10

Solid carbon dioxide is usually called dry ice because it doesn't become a liquid before it becomes a gas. In other words, it sublimates. Dry ice is much colder than regular ice, so a fog of condensed water vapor forms as air surrounding it cools. This result is often used for special effects onstage.

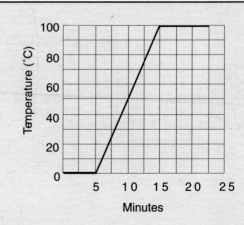

## Condensation

If you've had a cold glass of water on a hot day, you've probably noticed that water collects on the outside of the glass. Experiments have proved that since the water didn't move through the glass, it must have come from the surrounding air. Molecules of water vapor in the air must have changed into liquid. The process of a gas becoming a liquid is called **condensation**. **Figure 7-11** gives two examples of condensation.

**Figure 7-11**

Ⓐ The water drops on this window pane form as water vapor molecules transfer energy to the cold glass and condense.

Ⓑ The space shuttle's main fuel tank is so cold that even during a blazing hot day, water condenses and then freezes on it.

The kinetic-molecular theory can explain the properties of solids and liquids in terms of moving molecules and the forces between them. In solids, strong bonds between particles restrict their movement to vibrations about fixed points.

Heating a solid causes its particles to vibrate increasingly faster. Solids melt when the vibrations exert larger forces than those holding the particles together. Bonds between molecules of a liquid are strong enough to give it a definite volume but are too weak to give it a particular shape. If you boil a liquid, its particles gain enough kinetic energy to break away from the surface and become a gas.

### check your UNDERSTANDING

1. Compare and contrast the way the particles in a solid and liquid are arranged.
2. Suppose you have filled a gasoline can to the brim on a cool morning. You come back to it in the hot afternoon to find that some gasoline leaked from the can. The can isn't damaged. How can you explain it?
3. Explain melting and evaporation in terms of the kinetic-molecular theory.
4. **Apply** Experiments have shown that it takes more than five times as much energy to change 1 g of water at 100°C to water vapor at 100°C, as it does to heat that gram of water from 0°C to 100°C. In terms of energy transfer, why do you get a more severe burn from steam than you do from boiling water?

### check your UNDERSTANDING

**1.** Solid: particles arranged in a fairly rigid structure. While there is vibration, the particles cannot move far. Liquid: they have more energy, can move past one another. In both, there is particle motion.

**2.** The rise in temperature caused the gasoline to expand and it spilled out.

**3.** During melting, thermal energy gives molecules of a solid kinetic energy. They overcome the bonds that hold them in a fixed position and move apart with fluid-like properties.

**4.** Steam condenses. The greater kinetic energy in the steam transfers to the water that forms on your skin.

# 3 ASSESS

## Check for Understanding

Have students answer questions 1–4 in Check Your Understanding. As you discuss the answer to the Apply question, point out that people often think that water keeps getting hotter as it boils. In fact, while a substance is undergoing a phase change all energy added to it is used to make this change. Once water is boiling, it remains at 100°C.

## Reteach

Help students form a mental model of states of matter. Ask students to visualize a group of marbles on a Chinese-checkers board. As a gas, the marbles move much too quickly to settle into any of the little holes. There is complete freedom of movement. As a solid, all the marbles rest in holes, leaving no freedom of movement. A liquid state can be roughly explained as a state that is intermediate between a solid state and a gaseous state. There is some order and some freedom of movement. L1

## Extension

Bimetallic strips use differential thermal expansion rates to make thermostats function. Obtain a bimetallic strip and let students consult a sourcebook for a full explanation of thermostatic switches. L3

# 4 CLOSE

## Activity

Have students work in small groups to develop lists of states of matter in the human body. Solids—bones, teeth, and hair. Liquids—blood, sweat, and tears. Gases—oxygen and carbon dioxide. L1 **COOP LEARN**

# PREPARATION

## Concepts Developed

This section continues the kinetic-molecular theory, focusing on gases and their behavior. The pressure exerted by a gas is attributed to the force of many particles colliding with the walls of the vessel that holds the gas. Particles account for the inverse relationship between pressure and volume (Boyle's law) and the direct relationship between pressure and temperature and temperature and volume (Charles's law).

## Planning the Lesson

Refer to the Chapter Organizer on pages 208A–B.

### Find Out!

**How do collisions produce pressure?**

**Time needed**  15 minutes

**Materials**  2 large cardboard boxes, tennis balls

**Thinking Processes**  thinking critically, observing and inferring, comparing and contrasting, formulating models

**Purpose**  To model the effects of moving gas particles.

**Preparation**  Any kind of soft balls that will not cause injuries or damage if they veer off course can be used.

## Teaching the Activity

**Student Journal**  Have students answer the questions in their journals. They might describe the activity and relate it to the action of gas molecules, describing a situation (such as with a balloon) where such effects might be observed. L1

## Expected Outcome

Students should observe that the motion of the box increases as the number of balls and the force with which they are thrown increase.

---

# Kinetic Theory of Gases

## Section Objectives

- Describe pressure in terms of kinetic-molecular theory.
- Explain the meaning of temperature in gases.
- Discuss what absolute zero means.

## Key Terms

*absolute zero*

## Pressure

Consider how air behaves when you blow up a party balloon. You take a deep breath, put the balloon to your lips, and try to force air into the balloon. The balloon pushes the air back, and you feel it pushing against your cheeks. Finally, the rubber begins to stretch. The more air you can keep inside the balloon after each breath, the more readily the balloon expands. Try this activity to see how something like air, made up of tiny moving particles with relatively large spaces between them, exerts pressure.

### Find Out! ACTIVITY

## How do collisions produce pressure?

You can feel air move when the wind blows, but what keeps a balloon inflated?

### What To Do

1. Tape the bottoms of two identical cardboard boxes together and place them on a smooth floor so both open tops are exposed.

2. Have two groups stand about two meters away from each opening of the box and toss tennis balls into the box facing them. Find out what has to happen for the boxes to move toward a group and what has to happen for the boxes to remain centered between the groups.

### Conclude and Apply

1. How does the motion of the boxes change when the number of balls hitting the boxes increases?

2. Compare the effect of the fast balls and the slow balls on the boxes' motion.

3. If the tennis balls are air molecules, what might the boxes represent?

---

## Conclude and Apply

1. It moves farther.

2. The fast-moving balls made the box move farther.

3. Moving boxes might represent the sails of a boat or the vanes of a windmill. If the forces on boxes are balanced, they might represent a wall or balloon skin.

## ✔ Assessment

**Process**  To build students' understanding of cause and effect, position a pinwheel in front of a two-speed electric fan. Turn on the fan at a low setting and have students describe what is happening. Then turn up the speed and ask students to explain why the pinwheel is moving faster. *More faster-moving air molecules strike the pinwheel with greater force.* Use the Performance Task Assessment List for Making Observations and Inferences in **PAMSS**, p. 17. L1

You've seen that the force exerted on the boxes depended on the speed and number of balls thrown. In the same way, the force that molecules in the air exert is related to their kinetic energy, which depends on their mass and velocity. Although the motion of the box may have been uneven, moving only when a ball hit it, imagine billions of balls hitting both sides of the boxes at the same time. Your body is constantly experiencing those billions of collisions. Unlike the boxes, because the collisions are the same on all sides you don't feel any movement or impact. **Figure 7-12** below shows how this applies to a balloon. After you've studied the photos, do the activity on the next pages to see how temperature affects balloons.

**Connect to...**

# Earth Science

When the elastic limit of a balloon is exceeded, it bursts. Research what happens when the elastic limit of rocks on a fault is exceeded.

**Figure 7-12**

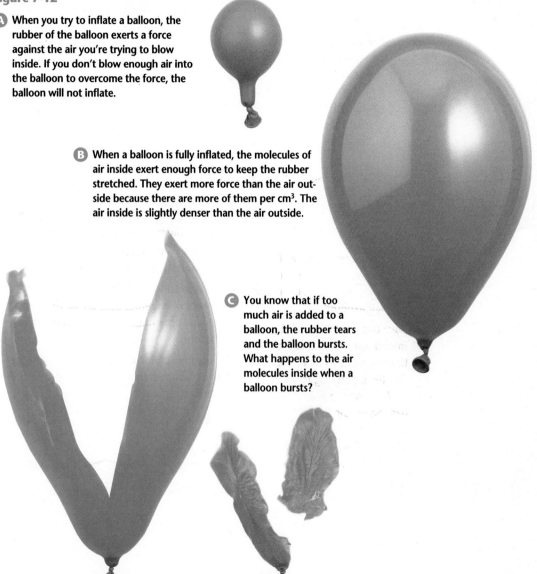

**A** When you try to inflate a balloon, the rubber of the balloon exerts a force against the air you're trying to blow inside. If you don't blow enough air into the balloon to overcome the force, the balloon will not inflate.

**B** When a balloon is fully inflated, the molecules of air inside exert enough force to keep the rubber stretched. They exert more force than the air outside because there are more of them per cm³. The air inside is slightly denser than the air outside.

**C** You know that if too much air is added to a balloon, the rubber tears and the balloon bursts. What happens to the air molecules inside when a balloon bursts?

7-2 Kinetic Theory of Gases **223**

---

## 1 MOTIVATE

**Demonstration** This activity provides an analogy for the behavior of a gas.

Materials needed are a microwave oven and a bag of microwave popcorn.

Have students identify that when popcorn kernels are cold, their kinetic energy is low. Pop the corn. Discuss that as the kernels' energy increased, they "vibrated until they finally shot out." The force of the impact on the bag's walls forces the volume of the bag to *increase*, in accordance with Charles's law. **L1 LEP**

## 2 TEACH

**Tying to Previous Knowledge**

The kinetic theory of particles used to explain the behavior of solids and liquids in the previous section is related to gas laws in this section. Ask students to state Boyle's law and Charles's law.

**Uncovering Preconceptions**

**Activity** Students may have difficulty appreciating that intangible, invisible air has mass and substance just as liquids and solids do. Instead, students may perceive the air around them to be empty space. Have students weigh an uninflated balloon on a sensitive balance scale. Then have them blow up the balloon, tie it off, and weigh it again. They should note that the added mass shown on the scale is that of the air trapped within the balloon. **L1**

---

**Meeting Individual Needs**

**Learning Disabled** Have students demonstrate what is meant by several of the difficult concepts covered in this section by having them role-play such terms as *kinetic, inversely, proportional, solidify,* and *attraction.* **LEP**

**Program Resources**

**Study Guide,** p. 37

**Transparency Master,** p. 31, and **Color Transparency,** Number 14, Boyle's Law **L2**

**Making Connections: Technology & Society,** p. 17, Aerodynamic Design **L2**

**Visual Learning**

**Figure 7-12 What happens to the air molecules inside when a balloon bursts?** *The collapsing balloon forced the molecules out. The molecules from inside the balloon spread out among the air molecules in the room.*

## 7-2 Ballooning Size

### Planning the Activity

**Time needed** 35–45 minutes

**Purpose** To observe the effects of changing temperature on gases.

**Process Skills** observing and inferring, comparing and contrasting, recognizing cause and effect, collecting and organizing data, making and using tables, making and using graphs, measuring in SI, interpreting data, designing an experiment, separating and controlling variables, observing, modeling, sampling and estimating, forming operational definitions

**Materials** See reduced student text.

**Preparation** Students should set water to boil at the beginning of the experiment so that it is ready to use when they need it.

### Teaching the Activity

**Process Reinforcement** Have students construct a two-column table itemizing all the ways that temperature affects molecules in solids and liquids. One column should detail the effects of raising the temperature, and the other should list the contrasting ways in which solids and liquids behave when their temperatures are lowered.

**Possible Hypotheses** Students may hypothesize that the air in the balloon expands in the heat and shrinks in the cold.

**Possible Procedures** Students may choose to immerse the balloons in the cold-water bath and hold balloons in steam above the boiling water in order to gather data.

**Troubleshooting** Use permanent (nonwater-based) markers for this exercise, so that students' circumference-markings are not washed off or blurred during the experiment.

**Student Journal** Have students record the volumes in a data table and make their graph in their journals. L1

# Ballooning Size

*The effect of temperature on gases is part of what makes steam engines work. Do gases react to temperature the same way solids do?*

## Problem

How does changing temperature affect the gas contained in a balloon?

## Materials

| | |
|---|---|
| 2 medium, round balloons | container of ice water |
| 1 m of string | tongs |
| felt-tipped marking pen | heat-proof glove |
| meter stick | beaker of boiling water |
| | thermometer |

## Safety Precautions

Use care when holding the balloons near hot water.

## What To Do

**1** Inflate two balloons to about the same size and tie them closed.

**2** Use the string and meter stick to measure the circumference of each balloon. For later reference, place an ink dot where the string went around each balloon.

**3** *Calculate* the volume of each balloon using this formula: $(circumference)^3/59 = $ Volume. Record the volumes.

Sample Data

### Data and Observations

| State | Circumference | Volume | Temperature |
|---|---|---|---|
| Room | 36cm | 780cm$^3$ | 24°C |
| Cold | 33cm | 609cm$^3$ | 1°C |
| Hot | 42cm | 1256cm$^3$ | 98°C |

## Program Resources

**Activity Masters,** pp. 33-34, Investigate 7-2

**Take Home Activities,** p. 13, Playing with Air Pressure L1 LEP

**Science Discovery Activities,** 7-3, What Happens if You Press on a Gas

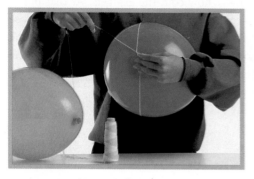

**A**

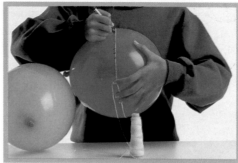

**B**

**4** Building on what you've just done, *design an experiment* to answer the problem. Plan data collection so you can produce a graph. Show your design to your teacher. If you are advised to revise your plan, be sure to check with your teacher again before you begin. Look at all safety precautions before you begin. Carry out your plan.

*The air molecules inside a hot-air balloon are moving very fast and are very far apart. This makes the air inside less dense than the surrounding air, which causes the balloon to be buoyed up.*

## Analyzing

**1.** Using the temperatures and volumes from your experiment, *make a line graph*. What is the relationship between temperature and volume of a gas?

**2.** If you extended the line of your graph to zero volume, to what temperature would it correspond?

## Concluding and Applying

**3.** Using the kinetic theory, explain how the movement of air molecules inside the balloons caused the effects you observed.

**4.** Going Further  Aerosol cans often bear the warning, "Do not incinerate, contents under pressure." How can you apply what you have seen in this activity to explain this caution?

**Expected Outcome**

Students should find in their measurements that the heated balloon gains circumference, while the cooled balloon loses circumference. They should infer that the volume of a given amount of a gas is affected by its temperature.

**Answers to** Analyzing/ Concluding and Applying

**1.** Students' graphs of temperature vs. volume should show a straight line. Temperature and volume of a gas are directly proportional. As one increases, so does the other.

**2.** Students' answers will vary depending on their graphs.

**3.** As they warmed, the gas molecules inside the balloon gained kinetic energy. Greater speed resulted in more forceful collisions with the balloon walls. The balloon walls were pushed out. Cooling produced the reverse effect.

**4.** Pressure builds inside aerosol cans as they're heated; eventually, they explode. The hot metal fragments and burning contents expelled are very dangerous.

**✔ Assessment**

**Process** Working in small groups, have students repeat the experiment using helium balloons, observing the effects of heating and cooling on helium. Have them compare their data with the data they collected in the original experiment and share their findings. Results should be qualitatively identical. Use the Performance Task Assessment List for Making Observations and Inferences in **PAMSS**, p. 17. L1  **COOP LEARN**
P

### ■ Volume Changes with Temperature

As you discovered in the Investigate activity, air takes up more space when heated and less when cooled. Charles' law describes this relationship. At constant pressure, volume and temperature are directly proportional. That is, as one increases the other increases. **Figure 7-13** below shows why this is so.

The volume of a gas can never be zero because matter takes up space.

**Figure 7-13**

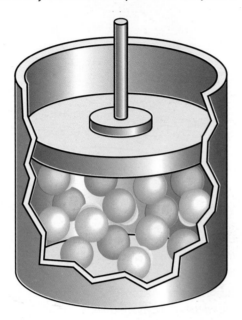

Ⓐ The pressure on these two cylinders is the same. In the unheated cylinder, the gas molecules aren't moving very fast so they don't exert much pressure on the cylinder.

Ⓑ At constant pressure, the volume of a gas increases as its temperature increases. In the heated cylinder, the gas molecules move faster. Their collisions push the piston up until the pressure they exert on the cylinder is the same as it was in Figure 7-13A.

The volume eventually reaches a level below which it can't go, no matter how cold the gas gets. At that point, the molecules in the gas are so close together that no matter how weak the forces of attraction between them, the gas condenses or even solidifies.

### ■ Pressure Changes with Volume

A physical principle called Boyle's Law describes the relationship between the pressure and volume of a gas. For a fixed amount of gas at a constant temperature, pressure and volume are inversely proportional. That is, as volume goes down, pressure goes up. **Figure 7-14** on the right demonstrates this.

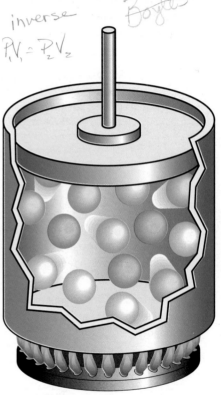

---

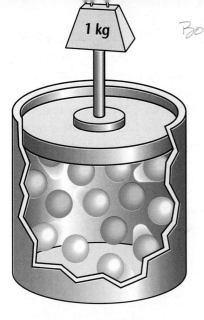

Boyle's $P_1V_1 = P_2V_2$

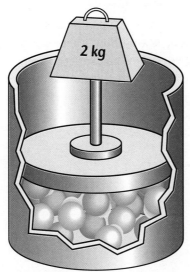

## ■ Pressure Changes with Temperature

**Figure 7-15** shows a sample of gas in a container with a fixed volume. If you heat the gas, its pressure increases. If you cool the gas, its pressure decreases. For a fixed amount of gas at a constant volume, the pressure is directly related to its temperature. The area of the container's surface did not change, but the energy of the gas molecules did.

This explains why you should never throw a container of pressurized gas, such as an aerosol can, into a fire. As the temperature of the gas inside the can rises, the pressure also rises until the container can no longer withstand the pressure and explodes.

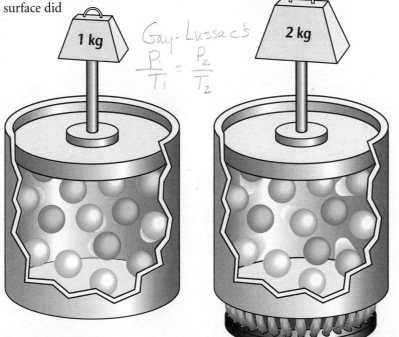

Gay-Lussac's
$$\frac{P_1}{T_1} = \frac{P_2}{T_2}$$

### Figure 7-15

The volume of these two gases is the same. In the unheated cylinder, the gas molecules exert enough pressure to lift up a 1 kilogram block. In the heated cylinder, the gas molecules exert greater pressure, so they are able to lift a 2 kilogram block. If the flame were turned up higher, would the gas molecules exert more pressure or less pressure?

**Activity** Scientists are constantly trying to produce temperatures closer and closer to absolute zero in the laboratory. Interested students might do research to find the latest achievements in this quest, detailing the results and the methods used to obtain them. L2

## Absolute Zero

As far as we know, there is no upper limit to how hot matter can get, but there is a limit to coldness. The temperature of a gas measures the average kinetic energy of the molecules. Suppose that a substance could be cooled to -273.15°C. At that temperature, known as **absolute zero**, the kinetic energy of molecules would have decreased to zero. And if the

Kelvin (absolute) scale                                                    Water freezes —        Water liquid

0          50          100          150          200          250  273.15K  300                350

Celsius (Centigrade) scale

-237.15          -200          -150          -100          -50          0°C          50

Thin slices of silicon crystal, like the one shown here, are used to make computer chips.

## Crystal Clear

**W**hat do salt, diamonds, and snowflakes all have in common? They are all crystals. The ancient Greeks thought

A snowflake is a common example of a crystal.

crystals were made from water that was frozen under intense cold. This belief lasted into medieval times. *Crystal* comes from the Greek word *krystallos*, which means frozen water. Even today, we call very clear water crystal clear.

Crystals are everywhere—even in your pencil. A pencil's lead is really clay mixed with graphite—a crystal form of carbon. Draw a line on a piece of paper with your pencil. Then look at that line under a magnifying glass. What do you see?

Today, we call solids whose atoms are arranged in a pattern repeated over and over again crystals. But, in ancient times,

### Purpose

A Closer Look reinforces Section 7-1's discussion of solids by identifying the origin of the word, *crystal,* and by looking at crystal structures.

### Content Background

Nearly all solids form crystals, from microscopic in size to several meters long. Crystals are made of atoms arranged in repeating patterns. As crystals grow, they simply add these repeating structures, and the final shape of a crystal (sides and an-

gles) reflects the internal atomic pattern. Crystals grow three ways: from melts (mineral crystals from magma or metal crystals from molten metals), from solutions (evaporated salt and sugar solutions), or from vapor deposits (snowflakes). Electrical charges bond atoms together in a crystal. Varied electrical charges and atom sizes make crystals vary in character. For example, carbon crystals can be extremely hard (diamond) or extremely soft (graphite).

## Try *It!*

**E**ven though molecules are on the move all around us, it's impossible to see the motion of individual molecules without the help of special equipment. You can, however, observe the motion of groups of them.

### What To Do

1. Make a loop in one end of a paper clip. Use the other end of the clip as a handle.

2. Dip the loop into liquid soap. Lift the loop and gently blow on the film inside the loop. A bubble will float into the air.

3. *In your Journal,* record the motion of your bubble throughout the room. In what direction were molecules moving around the bubble? How do you know? Repeat the activity several times in various places around the room.

### Try It Again

After you've learned more about the motions of molecules, try this activity again and see if the movements are easier to explain.

---

## Connections to Other Units

Chapter 8, *Weather,* relates to the information in Unit 4 on moving continents. The movement of air via convection currents and plate movement is caused by convection currents inside Earth. In addition, information on organic chemistry found in Chapter 10 provides background for changes in matter that students will learn about in Unit 5 on fission and fusion and the solar system.

## GETTING STARTED

**Discussion** Some questions you may want to ask your students are

**1. Why is weather constantly changing?** *Some students will be able to name some of the factors in weather change such as the constant movement of air and moisture in the atmosphere. Some students may mention the development and movement of air masses.*

**2. What causes tides?** *Some students will be able to relate tides to the sun-moon-Earth system and gravity.*

**3. What is an antibody?** *A few students may know that an antibody is a protein in the blood that destroys foreign substances.* The answers to these questions will help you establish any misconceptions students may have.

---

## Try *It!*

**Purpose** To infer the movement of individual molecules by making observations of molecules trapped in a container, a soap bubble.

### Background Information

This activity is designed to show students that molecules in the air are constantly moving. Encourage students to release their bubbles at different heights and at different locations around the classroom. For example, students might compare different distances from a heat vent or an open window.

**Materials** paper clip, liquid soap solution, shallow dish

**Preparation** Use liquid soap for washing dishes and dilute it with water until a paper-clip loop can pick up a thin film of soap solution.

### ✔ Assessment

**Process** Have students develop a hypothesis to explain why the bubbles moved. They can present their hypotheses in the form of drawings of written explanations. Use the appropriate Performance Task List in **PAMSS.** L1

# Chapter Organizer

| SECTION | OBJECTIVES | ACTIVITIES |
|---|---|---|
| **Chapter Opener** | | **Explore!** What kind of data can you find on a weather map? p. 241 |
| **8-1 What Is Weather?** (4 days) | 1. **Explain** the role of water vapor in the atmosphere and how it affects weather.<br>2. **Relate** relative humidity to weather.<br>3. **Explain** how clouds form. | **Explore!** What things make up the weather? p. 242<br>**Skillbuilder:** Determining Cause and Effect, p. 244<br>**Find Out!** What happens to air that is cooled to the point where it cannot hold any more water? p. 245<br>**Investigate 8-1:** Relative Humidity, pp. 246–247<br>**Explore!** How can you make a cloud? p. 249 |
| **8-2 Changes in Weather** (3 days) | 1. **Describe** the weather associated with different types of fronts.<br>2. **Explain** why high pressure systems usually bring clear weather and low pressure systems bring cloudy weather. | **Find Out!** What happens when two air masses meet? p. 252<br>**Skillbuilder:** Making and Using Tables, p. 254<br>**Explore!** How do pressure systems move? p. 254<br>**Investigate 8-2:** Reading a Weather Map, p. 258–259 |
| **8-3 Severe Weather** (2 days) | 1. **Describe** what causes thunderstorms.<br>2. **Relate** how tornadoes evolve from thunderstorms.<br>3. **Compare and contrast** tornadoes and hurricanes. | **Find Out!** How does air in a tornado move? p. 261 |

## EXPAND your view

**A Closer Look** Forecasting the Weather, pp. 258–259
**Physics Connection** A New Storm Detection Tool, pp. 262–263
**Science and Society** Is Cloud Seeding a Good Idea, p. 265

**How It Works** Barometers p. 266
**Literature Connection** Surviving an Everglades Hurricane, p. 267
**Teens in Science** Weather Watch, p. 268

## ACTIVITY MATERIALS

| EXPLORE! | INVESTIGATE! | FIND OUT! |
|---|---|---|
| **Page 241**<br>newspaper weather maps for three consecutive days<br>**Page 242***<br>no special materials are needed<br>**Page 249***<br>ice cube, hot water, soft drink bottle<br>**Page 254***<br>thermos bottle, freezer | **Pages 246–247***<br>2 identical Celsius thermometers, piece of gauze (2 cm$^2$), string, tape, cardboard, beaker of water<br>**Pages 258–259***<br>Appendix K | **Page 245***<br>shiny metal container such as cup or can, water, thermometer, ice<br>**Page 252***<br>aquarium with glass lid, cold bag of sand or marbles, pan, very hot water<br>**Page 261***<br>two 2-liter soft drink bottles, water, liquid dishwash soap, duct tape |

*For adequate development of the concepts presented, we recommend that students do the activities with an asterisk.

# Chapter 8 Weather

## TEACHER CLASSROOM RESOURCES

| Student Masters | Teaching Aids |
|---|---|
| **Study Guide,** p. 28<br>**Activity Masters,** Investigate 8-1, pp. 35–36<br>**Concept Mapping,** p. 16<br>**Flex Your Brain,** p. 5<br>**Take Home Activities,** p. 15<br>**How It Works,** p. 13 | **Laboratory Manual,** pp. 45–46, Clouds<br>**Color Transparency and Master 15,** Cloud Types<br>***STVS:** Reducing Hail Damage,* Earth and Space (Disk 3, Side 1)<br>***STVS:** World's Worst Weather,* Earth & Space (Disk 3, Side 1) |
| **Study Guide,** p. 29<br>**Critical Thinking/Problem Solving,** p. 16<br>**Multicultural Connections,** p. 19<br>**Making Connections: Across the Curriculum,** p. 19<br>**Making Connections: Technology & Society,** p. 19<br>**Activity Masters,** Investigate 8-2, pp. 37–38<br>**Science Discovery Activities,** 8-1, 8-2 | **Laboratory Manual,** pp. 47–48, Weather Forecasting<br>**Color Transparency and Master 16,** Types of Fronts<br>***STVS:** Global Weather Forecasting,* Earth and Space (Disc 3, Side 2) |
| **Study Guide,** p. 30<br>**Multicultural Connections,** p. 20<br>**Making Connections: Integrating Sciences,** p. 19<br>**Flex Your Brain,** p. 5<br>**Science Discovery Activities,** 8-3 | **Laboratory Manual,** pp. 49–52, Hurricanes<br>***STVS:** Hurricane Hunters,* Earth and Space (Disc 3, Side 1) |
| **ASSESSMENT RESOURCES** | **Spanish Resources**<br>**Cooperative Learning Resource Guide**<br>**Lab and Safety Skills**<br>**Integrated Science Videodisc** |
| **Review and Assessment,** pp. 47–52<br>**Performance Assessment,** Ch. 8<br>**PAMSS***<br>**MindJogger Videoquiz**<br>**Alternate Assessment in the Science Classroom**<br>**Computer Test Bank** | |

## KEY TO TEACHING STRATEGIES

The following designations will help you decide which activities are appropriate for your students.

- **L1** Level 1 activities should be within the ability range of all students.
- **L2** Level 2 activities should be within the ability range of the average to above-average student.
- **L3** Level 3 activities are designed for the ability range of above-average students.
- **LEP** LEP activities should be within the ability range of Limited English Proficiency students.
- **COOP LEARN** Cooperative Learning activities are designed for small group work.
- **P** These strategies represent student products that can be placed in a best-work portfolio.

## ADDITIONAL MATERIALS

**Software**
*Accuweather Forecaster,* Metacomet.
*Five Star Forecast,* MECC.
*Forecaster!: School Edition,* Mindscape.
*Weather,* Educational Activities.
*Weather,* J&S Software.
*Weather Academy,* Focus Media.
*Weather & Climate,* Queue.
*Weather Basics,* Yaker.
*Weather Fronts,* DEE.
*Weather Science,* Orange Cherry New
   Media Schoolhouse.

**Audiovisual**
*The Atmosphere in Motion,* video, United
   Learning.

*Climate, Weather & People,* video,
   Hawkhill Science.
*The Job of a Meterologist,* video, United
   Learning.
*Severe Weather,* video, United Learning.
*Precipitation, Storms, Why Weather
   Changes, Winds,* video, Coronet/MTI.

**Laserdisc**
*Science Discovery Middle School,*
   Videodiscovery.
*Understanding Weather & Climate,* SVE.
*What Makes Clouds?/What Makes Wind
   Blow?,* EBEC.

**Readings**
Ramsey, Dan. *Weather Forecasting: A
   Young Meterologist's Guide.* TAB.

***Performance Assessment in Middle School Science**

***Science and Technology Videodisc Series**

# Weather

## THEME DEVELOPMENT

One theme that this chapter supports is systems and interactions. Students learn that changing weather systems are related to the amount of water vapor in the air and the pressure of the air. Students also learn that the air masses are in a constant state of change, thus supporting the theme of stability and change.

## CHAPTER OVERVIEW

In this chapter, students will study the relationship between the global water cycle and weather. They will learn how air can contain water vapor, and how water vapor condenses to form clouds and precipitation. Then they will explore how moving air masses and high and low pressure systems cause changes in weather. Students also will learn to interpret a weather map. They will see how thunderstorms, tornadoes, and hurricanes form.

### Tying to Previous Knowledge

Ask the students to write a paragraph about how the weather has affected activities in which they have been involved. Have them share the paragraph with the class. Find out how many students wrote something negative about the weather and how many wrote positive responses. L1

## INTRODUCING THE CHAPTER

To help students relate clouds to weather, have them look at the photograph of clouds on page 240. Tell them that clouds are an indicator of weather. Have them describe clouds during fair weather. *high and thin or white and puffy* Ask them to describe storm clouds. *thick and dark.* L1

## Did you ever wonder...

✓ **What fog is?**

✓ **What causes clouds?**

✓ **Why weather changes?**

Before you begin to study about the weather, think about these questions and answer them *in your Journal.* When you finish this chapter, compare your Journal write-up with what you have learned.

**Y**ou look out the window at the beautiful, sunny day, daydreaming about your after-school plans. By three o'clock, the wind has blown huge storm clouds overhead, and the rain is coming down in sheets. Your plans for going to the park or playing basketball with your friends have to be cancelled.

Your first thought in the morning might be, "What's the weather going to be like today?" You'd want to know whether you needed to take an umbrella to school or whether you might need sweatpants for track practice afterward. Sometimes you might think you know what the weather will be like, but it changes!

▶ *In the following activity explore how weather maps help us in predicting the weather.*

## Did you ever wonder...

• Fog is a cloud that has formed at Earth's surface. (p. 249)

• Clouds form as air is cooled to the point at which the water vapor in the air condenses and forms tiny droplets around dust particles. When millions of these cloud droplets cluster together, a cloud is formed. (p. 248)

• Weather changes because air masses move. The movement and collision of air masses cause weather conditions to change. (p. 251)

## STUDENT JOURNAL

Have students write their responses to the Did You Ever Wonder questions in their journals. After they have read the chapter, students should read their journal entries to see what they have learned about weather.

## Explore! ACTIVITY

### What kind of data can you find on a weather map?

**W**eather maps can tell us many things, such as whether it will rain or be sunny or both. During this activity you'll discover how weather maps use symbols to show the weather for the day.

**What To Do**

1. Look at the weather map in a newspaper on three consecutive days.

2. *In your Journal*, write down the changes you observed in symbols and other graphics between the map from the first day and the map from the third day.

3. How did the symbols on the maps relate to the weather for the day?

4. How accurate of a prediction can you make for tomorrow based on today's weather map? Make a prediction and record it *in your Journal*. Check the next day to see if you were correct.

241

---

## Explore!

**What kind of data can you find on a weather map?**

**Time needed**  25 to 30 minutes

**Materials**  newspaper weather maps for 3 consecutive days

**Thinking Processes**  predicting, comparing and contrasting, interpreting data, interpreting scientific illustrations

**Purpose**  To see how the weather changes by comparing and contrasting weather maps from consecutive days.

**Preparation**  Have students cut weather maps from a local paper for three consecutive days.

### Teaching the Activity

**Student Journal**  Encourage students to draw the symbols and graphics in their journals. Students could also paste the newspaper weather maps into their journals. **L1** **LEP**

### Expected Outcome

Students will observe that weather systems move from day to day.

### Answers to Questions

**3.** Symbols should relate directly to the weather.

**4.** Answers will vary.

### ✔ Assessment

**Performance**  Have students work in groups to collect local weather data through observation or by calling the National Weather Service. Students could then present their data in newspaper format. Place student work on a bulletin board labeled "Reporting the Weather." Select the appropriate Performance Task Assessment List in **PAMSS**. **COOP LEARN** **L1**

---

### ASSESSMENT PLANNER

**PORTFOLIO**
Refer to page 271 for suggested items that students might select for their portfolios.

**PERFORMANCE ASSESSMENT**
Process, pp. 247, 249, 252, 254, 257
Skillbuilder, pp. 244, 254
Explore! Activities, pp. 241, 242, 249, 254
Find Out! Activities, pp. 245, 252, 261
Investigate, pp. 246–247, 258–259

**CONTENT ASSESSMENT**
Check Your Understanding, pp. 250, 259, 264
Reviewing Main Ideas, p. 269
Chapter Review, pp. 270–271

**GROUP ASSESSMENT**
Opportunities for group assessment occur with Cooperative Learning Strategies.
Performance, pp. 241, 242, 261

# PREPARATION

## Concepts Developed

In this section, students will learn the role of water vapor in the atmosphere and how it affects weather. They will learn how clouds form, and the differences between cirrus, cumulus and stratus clouds. This section is related to Chapter 7, Molecules in Motion, which explains evaporation and condensation.

## Planning the Lesson

Refer to the Chapter Organizer on pages 240A–B.

# 1 MOTIVATE

**Discussion** To reinforce the skill of recognizing cause and effect, discuss with students direct and indirect ways that the weather affects their lives. One indirect way is consumers having to pay more at the market for fruits and vegetables when an agricultural region experiences a very wet growing season, as with corn, or a very cold season, as with citrus fruits. [L1]

## Explore!

**What things make up the weather?**

**Time Needed** 10 to 15 minutes

**Materials** No special materials are needed.

**Thinking Processes** observing and inferring, defining operationally, classifying

**Purpose** To develop an operational definition of weather by observing the outdoor environment.

## Teaching the Activity

**Student Journal** Encourage students to draw pictures that show the weather. [L1] [LEP]

---

## 8-1 What Is Weather?

### Section Objectives
- Explain the role of water vapor in the atmosphere and how it affects weather.
- Relate relative humidity to weather.
- Explain how clouds form.

### Key Terms
*relative humidity*
*saturated*
*dew point*

## Water and Weather

Several factors determine what kind of weather you see outside the window each day. Some of these factors are plainly visible, such as cloud cover and the wind blowing the leaves on trees. Other factors can be felt, such as the temperature from the thermal energy of the sun or the amount of moisture in the air.

Weather is also greatly affected by one of Earth's most abundant substances: water. How do you think water affects weather?

You talk about weather all the time because it affects you every day. Can you explain what weather is? Try this next activity and find out.

### Explore! ACTIVITY

**What things make up the weather?**

**What To Do**

1. Look out the window and *in your Journal* write down everything you can about today's weather.

2. Observe the sky. Are there clouds? If so, what do they look like? Are they moving?

3. Observe objects near the ground. Is the ground wet? Are the leaves on the trees blowing?

4. Some of the things you should be describing are the presence and strength of the wind, the air temperature, the amount and type of

cloud cover, and whether it is raining, snowing, or clear.

5. What are some of the things you think of when you think of weather?

---

## Expected Outcomes

Students will observe the factors that make up daily weather.

## Answers to Questions

Answers will vary. Students should connect things such as sunshine, clouds, wind, temperature, and precipitation with weather.

## ✔ Assessment

**Performance** Have students classify activities that can be done in different types of weather. Students could then write a story showing how weather affects the main character's recreational plans. Use the Performance Task Assessment List for the Writer's Guide to Fiction in **PAMSS**, page 83. [L1] [P]

In the activity you probably mentioned clouds, rain, snow, wind and sunshine. Much of what you observed is related to how water moves. How much do you know about the water cycle? Water on Earth's surface does not stay in one place for long. Some water sinks into the ground. Other water runs off the surface into rivers and then into lakes and oceans. A great deal of water evaporates into the air.

The sun provides the energy to evaporate water from the oceans and other bodies of water. Then, as the water vapor cools in the upper atmosphere, it condenses and forms clouds. The water eventually falls back to Earth as precipitation such as rain or snow. This water cycle forms the basis of Earth's weather.

Water vapor is a large component of the water cycle. The amount of water vapor in the air is called humidity. You've probably heard this term used before. People sometimes comment about how humid it is on hot summer days.

**Figure 8-1**

A hayloft hygrometer is a homemade instrument used to help forecast the weather. When the moisture content of the air increases, the rope absorbs moisture and lengthens, and the stick gradually moves and points in a different direction.

■ **Humidity**

Think of air as a sponge. A sponge has holes that allow it to hold water. The holes can be completely or partially full of water. Air doesn't exactly have holes, but there are spaces between the molecules that make up air. Water vapor molecules are distributed within those spaces.

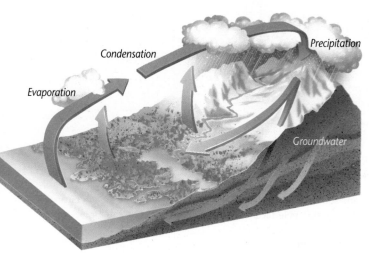

Condensation

Precipitation

Evaporation

Groundwater

**Figure 8-2**

The water cycle supplies living things with fresh water. Examine this diagram of the water cycle carefully. Is the water cycle a continuous chain of events? Explain.

**Tying to Previous Knowledge**

Have students discuss ways in which weather has altered their plans in the past.

**Theme Connection** The themes that this section supports are systems and interactions, and stability and change. This section focuses on changes and interactions in a large system, the atmosphere. Students will learn about the role of water vapor in weather system development, from humidity to clouds to precipitation. The water cycle is shown as an interactive system that continuously recycles water from the liquid and solid states to the gaseous state and back again.

**Discussion** Have students name the three states of matter and apply the names to water. They should know that water vapor is a gas, water is a liquid, and ice is a solid. Make sure students realize that the cloud above a pan of boiling water is not water vapor, but condensed water droplets. L2

**Demonstration** Place a large, flat pan in the center of the classroom. Tell students to sit very still. Turn off any air vents or close windows. Pour some after-shave lotion in the pan. Have students raise a hand when they smell the lotion. They will notice the odor spreads out in a circle. Ask students to relate this with the term **evaporation.** Ask students how the odor spreads through the room. *Vapor molecules are in constant motion in all directions, and move about, filling whatever space they are in.* L2

---

**ENRICHMENT**

**Demonstration** Make a model to show students that water is the substance that evaporates from Earth's surface to form clouds. Anything in the water is left behind. In front of students, mix some salt, potting soil, and water in a beaker. Ask students if it looks drinkable. Put the mixture on a ring stand and boil it. Pack some crushed ice into a clean flask. Put a ring stand clamp on the neck of the flask, secure it to the stand, and tilt the flask 45°. Place the flask above and near the boiling mixture. Water will condense and drip from the flask. Catch it in a paper cup. Ask students if they think it is drinkable. What happened in terms of evaporation, condensation, and precipitation? *Water evaporated from the mixture as it was heated and then boiled. The water vapor condensed on the surface of the cold flask, which is similar to condensation of water vapor in the air to form clouds. The dripping of the condensed water is similar to precipitation.* L3

**Visual Learning**

**Figure 8-2 Is the water cycle a continuous chain of events? Explain.** *Yes, water is constantly moving from place to place or changing from one state to another.*

### ■ Relative Humidity

No doubt you've also heard a weather forecaster mention relative humidity. **Relative humidity** is a measure of the amount of water vapor in the air at a particular temperature compared with the total amount of water vapor possible at that temperature.

For example if the relative humidity is 50 percent, the air contains only half of the water vapor possible at its current temperature. Weather forecasters have developed a simple instrument for measuring relative humidity.

The maximum amount of water vapor possible depends on the temperature of the air. Recall from Chapter 7 that the molecules in matter move more rapidly as matter is heated. In warm air water vapor molecules are moving rapidly. It is more difficult for water vapor molecules to join and condense in warm air than in cold air, where molecules are moving more slowly. Because water vapor condenses more easily out of cold air, the maximum amount of water vapor possible in cold air is less than the maximum amount of water vapor possible in warm air. This can be seen in **Figure 8-3**.

For example, a cubic meter of air can contain a maximum of 22 grams of water vapor at 25°C. On the other hand, the same air cooled to 15°C can contain only about 13 grams of water vapor. In the next Investigate, you will see more clearly how water vapor in the air is related to changes we see in temperature.

**Figure 8-3**

Ⓐ Even though the air and the water in this container have the same temperature, the speed of the water molecules is great enough to allow some of them to escape into the air and become water vapor.

Ⓑ The air in this container is saturated—it cannot contain any additional water vapor. If one water molecule moves from the air into the water, what will another water molecule do?

Ⓒ The water and the air are warmer. Would you expect there to be a greater or smaller number of water molecules in the air? Explain.

**244** Chapter 8 Weather

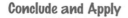
## What happens to air that is cooled to the point where it cannot hold any more water?

### What To Do

1. Partially fill a shiny metal container, such as a cup or can, with water at room temperature.

2. While slowly stirring the water with a thermometer, carefully add small amounts of ice. Watch the outside of the container.

3. *In your Journal* note the temperature at which a thin film of moisture first begins to form.

4. Repeat the procedure two more times, making sure that you start with water at room temperature and with the outside of the container dry. Calculate the average of the three temperatures.

### Conclude and Apply

1. Where did the water on the container come from?

2. What do you think happened to the air surrounding the container as you added ice to the water?

3. Why did the water on the outside of the container appear?

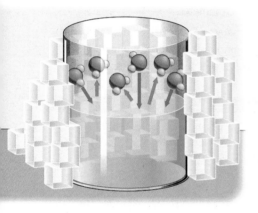

**D** If the air and the water in the container are allowed to cool, the water molecules and the air molecules will move more slowly.

When the relative humidity of air reaches 100 percent, the air contains all the moisture it possibly can at that temperature. When this happens, the air is **saturated**. As you saw in the Find Out activity, when the temperature of the air around the container was cooled to the point of saturation, water vapor in the air condensed on the container's outside surface. Dew forms on grass in the same way. When air near the ground is cooled to a point where the air is saturated with water, water vapor condenses and forms droplets on the grass. The temperature at which air is saturated and condensation takes place is called the **dew point**.

8-1 What Is Weather? **245**

**Discussion** Have a volunteer relate saturation and dew point. Be sure all students understand these concepts, because they are the basis for cloud formation and precipitation. L2

the temperature will fall so rapidly that an accurate determination of the temperature at which the water condenses cannot be made.

To avoid thermometer breakage, advise students not to let the thermometer rest on or strike the side or bottom of the container. As a precaution, you may wish to give students a craft stick to stir the water so that the thermometer can remain still.

**Student Journal** Have students record the temperatures from all three trials in a data table in their journals. L1

### Expected Outcomes

Students will observe that water in the air condenses when it reaches the dew point.

### Conclude and Apply

1. The water on the outside of the container came from the air next to the container.

2. Air surrounding the container became cooler.

3. Cool air can contain less water than warm air. The excess water condensed on the cool surface.

### ✔ Assessment

**Content** To help students recognize cause and effect, ask them what caused a film to form on the container. Have students list events, such as fog or clouds forming, that have a similar cause and effect. Students could then make an events chain showing the sequence of events that results in the condensation of water vapor. Events should include loss of kinetic energy, slowing of molecular movement, and the accumulation of molecules in droplets. Use the Performance Task Assessment List for Events chain in **PAMSS**, p. 91. L1 P

## What happens to air that is cooled to the point where it can not hold any more water?

**Time needed** 20 minutes

**Materials** shiny metal container, water, thermometer, ice

**Thinking Processes** observing and inferring, measuring in SI, recognizing cause and effect, collecting and organizing data, sampling and estimating, interpreting data, separating and

controlling variables

**Purpose** To conduct an experiment to measure average dew point

**Preparation** Break ice cubes into small pieces. Keep them in a freezer until you are ready to use them.

### Teaching the Activity

**Troubleshooting** Stress that the ice must be added slowly to the water. If it is added too fast,

**Planning the Activity**

**Time needed** 45 minutes

**Purpose** To interpret data on relative humidity.

**Process Skills** interpreting data, observing and inferring, measuring in SI, collecting and organizing data, comparing and contrasting, making and using tables, predicting

**Materials** 2 identical Celsius thermometers, piece of gauze (2 cm²), string, tape, cardboard, beaker of water

**Preparation** Check the calibration of the thermometers ahead of time. Test the thermometers in ice water (0°C) and boiling water (100°C) to be sure that they are marked correctly. Thermometers that are not calibrated correctly may be used if you match pairs that are calibrated the same way. You may wish to construct the psychrometer setups before class. The table referred to in the Going Further question is Table 8-1 on p. 246.

**Teaching the Activity**

**Process Reinforcement** Before doing the experiment, students should predict which areas will have the highest or lowest relative humidity. Have students compare their predictions with their findings.

**Possible Procedures** For best results, have students test an area that you know has a much different humidity and/or temperature from your classroom. Examples are the gym and the kitchen.

Make available a hygrometer to use as a standard for the measurements. Many barometers also contain hygrometers, which give a direct reading of relative humidity.

**Troubleshooting** Be sure there is a strong, steady flow of moving air. The psychrometers will not work if the temperature is less than 0°C.

**Student Journal** Have students make a data table in their journals and record their measurements for each trial. [L1]

# Relative Humidity

*In the following activity, you will make a psychrometer to measure the relative humidity in three different areas around your school.*

### Problem

How do you determine relative humidity?

### Materials

2 identical alcohol Celsius thermometers
piece of gauze, 2 cm²
string
tape
cardboard
beaker of water

## What To Do

**1** Attach the gauze to the bulb of one thermometer. Leave the other thermometer uncovered.

**2** Thoroughly wet the gauze on the thermometer by dipping it into the beaker of water (see photo **A**). This is called a wet bulb thermometer.

**3** Tape both thermometers side by side on the cardboard with the bulbs hanging over the edge of one end (see photo **B**). You have created a psychrometer.

| Relative Humidity | | | | | | | | | | |
|---|---|---|---|---|---|---|---|---|---|---|
| Dry Bulb Temp. | Dry Bulb Temperature Minus Wet Bulb Temperature, °C | | | | | | | | | |
| | 1 | 2 | 3 | 4 | 5 | 6 | 7 | 8 | 9 | 10 |
| 10°C | 88 | 77 | 66 | 55 | 44 | 34 | 24 | 15 | 6 | |
| 12°C | 89 | 78 | 68 | 58 | 48 | 39 | 29 | 21 | 12 | |
| 14°C | 90 | 79 | 70 | 60 | 51 | 42 | 34 | 26 | 18 | 10 |
| 16°C | 90 | 81 | 71 | 63 | 54 | 46 | 38 | 30 | 23 | 15 |
| 18°C | 91 | 82 | 73 | 65 | 57 | 49 | 41 | 34 | 27 | 20 |
| 20°C | 91 | 83 | 74 | 67 | 59 | 53 | 46 | 39 | 32 | 26 |
| 22°C | 92 | 83 | 76 | 68 | 61 | 54 | 47 | 40 | 34 | 28 |
| 24°C | 92 | 84 | 77 | 69 | 62 | 56 | 49 | 43 | 37 | 31 |
| 26°C | 92 | 85 | 78 | 71 | 64 | 58 | 51 | 46 | 40 | 34 |
| 28°C | 93 | 85 | 78 | 72 | 65 | 59 | 53 | 48 | 42 | 37 |
| 30°C | 93 | 86 | 79 | 73 | 67 | 61 | 55 | 50 | 44 | 39 |

## Meeting Individual Needs

**Learning Disabled** Reinforce the wet bulb's evaporative cooling effect. Have students place a wet paper towel on the back of one hand and a dry one on the other. After a few minutes, ask students which hand feels cooler. *The hand with the wet paper towel*

## Program Resources

**Activity Masters,** pp. 35–36, Investigate 8-1

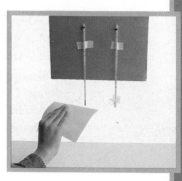

A      B      C

**4** Create air motion across both thermometer bulbs by quickly fanning them with a sheet of paper (see photo **C**).

**5** Wait until the alcohol in the thermometers stops moving and record the temperatures.

**6** Subtract the wet bulb temperature from the dry bulb temperature.

**7** *Use* the table on the opposite page to determine relative humidity . Find the temperature difference you computed in Step 6 by reading across the top of the table. Keep one finger on this number. Find the dry bulb temperature in the first column of the table. Look across this row until you find the column you marked with your finger. *In your Journal*, record the number where the row and column intersect. This is the percent relative humidity.

**8** Repeat Steps 4-7 at different locations inside and outside your school. Be sure to soak the wet bulb thermometer again at each new test site. Wait at least five minutes between trials in order to let the thermometers adjust to the new location.

## Analyzing

**1.** How did the wet bulb temperature *compare* with the dry bulb temperature at each site?

**2.** Which area in your school had the highest relative humidity? Which area had the lowest?

## Concluding and Applying

**3.** *Predict* the relative humidity if the wet bulb and dry bulb thermometers recorded the same temperature?

**4.** ~~Going Further~~ *Use the table* to determine whether two spots having the same relative humidity must also have the same temperature. Is there the same amount of water vapor in the air at both spots? Explain.

**Expected Outcomes**

Students will be able to take measurements with a psychrometer and interpret data from a relative humidity table.

**Answers to** Analyzing/ Concluding and Applying

**1.** It was lower.

**2.** Answers will vary; the gym and kitchen might be high, a classroom or office lower.

**3.** 100%

**4.** No. The table shows that the same relative humidity can be obtained at different temperatures. The same relative humidity means only that the percentage of the air's capacity to contain water vapor is the same at both spots, not that the amount of water vapor in the air is the same.

✔ **Assessment**

**Process** Have students compare and contrast relative humidities at different temperatures. At 10°C, a cubic meter of air can contain 11g of water. At 25°C, it can contain 22g of water. At 33°C, it can contain 33g of water. Have students calculate the relative humidity at each of these temperatures if a cubic meter of air contains 5.5g of water. Give them the following equation: (water vapor present ÷ maximum water vapor) × 100 = percent relative humidity. *50%, 25%, 17%.* Use the Performance Task Assessment List for Using Math in Science in **PAMSS,** page 29. L1

## Multicultural Perspectives

**Weather and Society**

Explain that weather has always played a major role in shaping human life, especially in agricultural economies, where changes in weather can be very important. By the third century B.C.E., the Chinese had learned to measure humidity using charcoal, which absorbs water vapor from the air. By weighing pieces of charcoal and recording the differences over time, the Chinese could measure changes in relative humidity. Have students visit the library to find out how other cultures sought to explain, predict, or control the weather. L1

### Content Background

Point out that although there are only four basic types of clouds—nimbus, stratus, cumulus and cirrus—many clouds are combinations of these types. For example, puffy rain clouds are cumulonimbus clouds.

### Visual Learning

**Figure 8-4 Describe the shapes of the cirrus clouds in the sky.** *They appear wispy or feathery.*
**Figure 8-6 What kind of clouds are in the sky above you today?** *Answers will vary.*
**Figure 8-7 How does fog form?** *Fog forms through condensation of water vapor in the air.*

**Flex Your Brain** Use the Flex Your Brain activity to have students explore CLOUDS. L1

## Clouds and Precipitation

When you think of a cloud, what kind of cloud do you imagine? Some people think of fluffy, white clouds, while others think of dark storm clouds. There are many different types of clouds. They vary in shape and in the altitude at which they form.

A similar process happens in the atmosphere. Clouds form as humid air is cooled to its dew point. The water vapor in the air condenses. The condensing water vapor forms tiny drops of water around dust particles in the atmosphere. These tiny drops of water in the atmosphere are called cloud droplets.

Cloud droplets are so small that the slightest air movement keeps them from falling to the ground. When millions of these drops cluster together, a cloud forms.

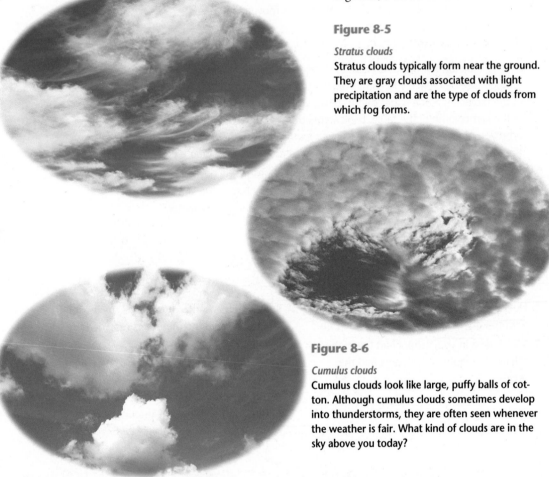

**Figure 8-4**

*Cirrus clouds*

**Clouds have different shapes and sizes. Cirrus clouds are usually found at very high altitudes. Cirrus clouds contain ice crystals. Describe the shapes of the cirrus clouds in the sky.**

**Figure 8-5**

*Stratus clouds*

**Stratus clouds typically form near the ground. They are gray clouds associated with light precipitation and are the type of clouds from which fog forms.**

**Figure 8-6**

*Cumulus clouds*

**Cumulus clouds look like large, puffy balls of cotton. Although cumulus clouds sometimes develop into thunderstorms, they are often seen whenever the weather is fair. What kind of clouds are in the sky above you today?**



### Meeting Individual Needs

**Visually Impaired** To help a visually impaired student interpret observations of clouds, have the student work with a sighted partner. Give the students rolls of cotton with which to make clouds. Tell the visually impaired student to fashion a cloud from the cotton after hearing a description of the cloud. Have the sighted student close his or her eyes and try to identify the clouds by touch. LEP COOP LEARN

### ENRICHMENT

**Activity** Have paired partners observe clouds and record the weather for three consecutive days. Tell students to draw or write a list of the clouds they observe and the weather the clouds bring with them. Have the students write a general rule which describes how the cloud types relate to the weather observed. L3 COOP LEARN

248 Chapter 8 Weather

# Explore! ACTIVITY

## How can you make a cloud?

**W**ould you like to walk through a cloud? Then walk outside on a foggy day. Fog is simply a stratus cloud that has formed at Earth's surface. How do fog and other clouds form?

### What To Do

1. Make a cloud using hot water, a bottle, and an ice cube.

2. Put about 25 mL of hot water in the bottom of a tall, slender bottle such as a soft drink bottle.

3. Then place an ice cube so that it rests on top of the bottle.

4. *In your Journal* explain what happens.

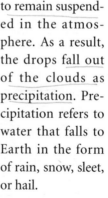

In the last Explore activity, you made a cloud. Do you think you could also make rain? Actually, you did make rain. Did you notice that where the fog came in contact with the inside of the bottle, water droplets joined together and slid down the sides of the bottle? These large droplets were rain.

Water droplets in a cloud swirl around and bump into one another. When they collide, they merge into bigger droplets. When these water droplets reach a diameter of 0.2 mm, they are too heavy to remain suspended in the atmosphere. As a result, the drops fall out of the clouds as precipitation. Precipitation refers to water that falls to Earth in the form of rain, snow, sleet, or hail.

### DID YOU KNOW?

Arica, Chile, is the driest place on Earth. During one 14-year period, no rain fell at all. During a 59-year period, the average annual rainfall was 0.76 mm.

**Figure 8-7**

Fog is a cloud that forms very close to Earth's surface. How does fog form?.

---

## How can you make a cloud?

**Time needed** 15 to 20 minutes

**Materials** Soft drink bottle, hot water, ice cube

**Thinking Processes** recognizing cause and effect, observing and inferring, formulating models, measuring in SI, interpreting scientific illustrations

**Purpose** To make a model of a cloud by cooling warm, moist air.

**Preparation** Use large ice cubes for this activity.

### Teaching the Activity

**Discussion** Have the students review dew point determination. Focus on condensation from the cooling of moist air. L1

**Student Journal** Students should draw the apparatus in their journals and record all of their observations. L1

### Expected Outcomes

Students will observe how a cloud forms during the cooling process of moist air.

### Answers to Question

A cloud forms in the top of the bottle and gradually descends lower.

### ✔ Assessment

**Process** If there are clouds, have students go outside and draw and label the clouds they observe. Then have students find pictures of different types of clouds. Students could include their drawings on a bulletin board labeled "Clouds." Use the Performance Task Assessment List for Bulletin Board in **PAMSS**, page 59. L1 P

---

## Program Resources

**Study Guide,** p. 28

**Laboratory Manual,** pp. 45–46, Clouds L1

**Concept Mapping,** p. 16, Rain L1

**Transparency Master,** p. 33, and **Color Transparency,** Number 15, Cloud Types L1

**Take Home Activities,** p. 15, Rain Gauge L1

**How It Works,** p. 13, Measuring Wind Speed L2

**Critical Thinking/Problem Solving,** p. 5 Flex Your Brain

## Check Your Understanding

To help students answer the Apply question, have them explain how temperature affects humidity. *If the amount of water in the air stays the same, increasing the temperature decreases the humidity.* L1

## Reteach

Have students practice sequencing skills by making flash cards, each with a step in the process from water on Earth to precipitation. Tell them to arrange the cards so the steps are in ascending order on the desk. Have them shuffle and repeat until they succeed two times in a row. L1 LEP

## Extension

For students who have mastered the concepts in this section, have them build a hair hygrometer to measure humidity. Have them tie a 15 to 20 gram mass to one end of a long strand of hair and tie the other end to a ring stand. Tell them to measure the distance from the base of the stand to the mass. Direct them to place a beaker with hot water directly below the apparatus for 5 minutes. Have them measure the distance again. The distance will be less, because hair stretches in high humidity. L3

# 4 CLOSE

Have students sequence the steps of one complete turn of the water cycle starting with ocean water and ending with precipitation. *Ocean water evaporates and rises. It cools and condenses to form cloud droplets. Droplets join together and may become too heavy to float in the cloud. Water or ice falls from the cloud as precipitation. The precipitation either sinks into the ground, evaporates, or runs off to the ocean.* L1 P

**Figure 8-8**

When water vapor in the air collects on a nucleus to form water droplets, the type of precipitation that is received on the ground depends on the temperature of the air.

| | A | B | C | D |
|---|---|---|---|---|
| Condensation by cooling | Nucleus | Nucleus | Nucleus | Nucleus |
| Freezing | | | | |
| Water vapor condensing on ice crystals | | | Cloud Droplet | |
| Accumulating cloud droplets | | | Ice Crystal | |
| Softening and merging of snowflakes | Cloud Droplet | Cloud Droplet | | Ice Crystal |
| Melting | | | | |
| Low-level freezing | | | Snowflake | |
| Ground temperature | Warm | Rain Drop — Cold | Cold | Warm |
| | Rain | Sleet | Wet snow | Hail |

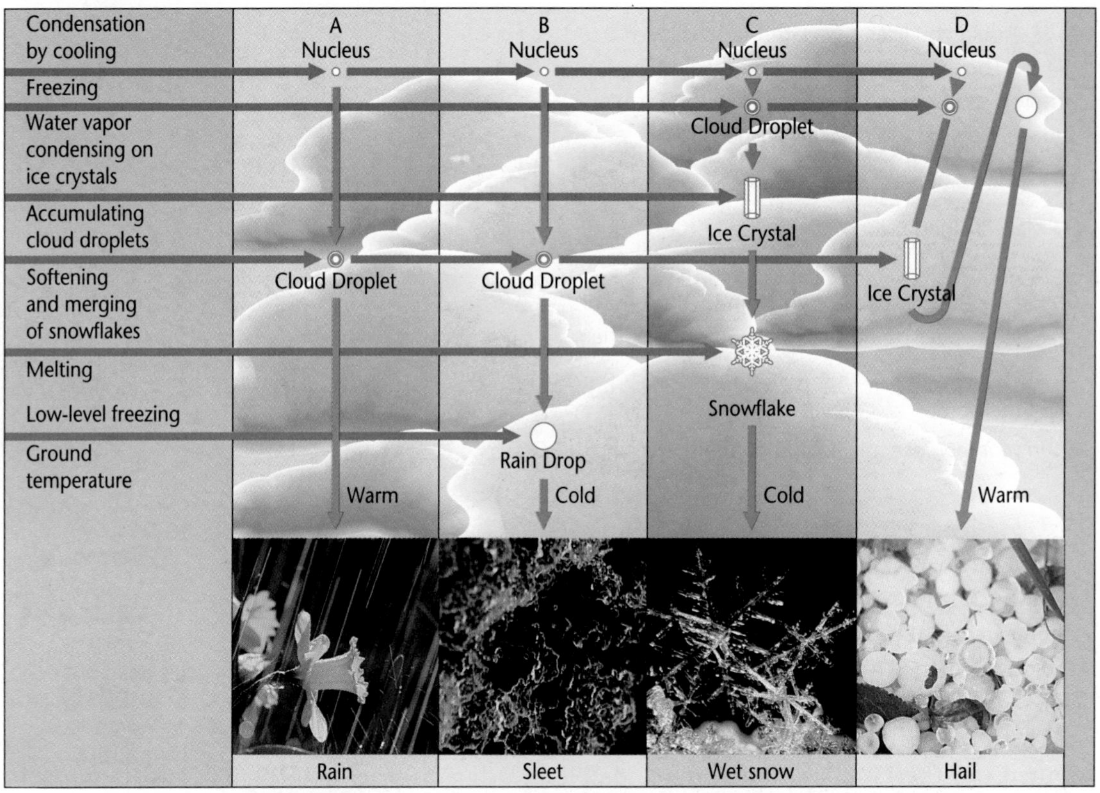

**A** When water vapor collects and forms raindrops that fall to the ground, the temperature of the air near the ground is warm.

**B** Sleet is made up of many small ice pellets that form when the temperature of the air near the ground is cold.

**C** The temperature of the air when water vapor forms snowflakes that fall to the ground is very cold.

**D** Hailstones are pellets of ice made up of many layers. A water droplet in the air forms a hailstone by going through the cycle several times.

## check your UNDERSTANDING

1. How does air temperature affect the type of precipitation that falls?

2. What is the relative humidity when dew forms? Explain.

3. Explain why cold air can hold less moisture than warm air.

4. Use the terms evaporation and condensation to explain how clouds form.

5. **Apply** Two rooms of the same size have the same humidity. It is colder in room A than room B. Which room has the higher relative humidity?

**250** Chapter 8 Weather

## check your UNDERSTANDING

1. Air temperature determines whether precipitation is snow, sleet, rain, or hail.

2. 100%; dew forms when air cools to the point where it is saturated with water vapor and it starts to condense.

3. The molecules in cold air have less kinetic energy so water vapor molecules condense more easily.

4. Water evaporated from Earth's surface rises, cools, and condenses around dust particles in the atmosphere to form cloud droplets. When millions of these drops cluster together, a cloud forms.

5. Room A

# Changes in Weather

## Air Masses

Have you ever noticed that the weather you're having today may be gone tomorrow? That's because the air is moving. The changes in weather are caused by the development and movement of large air masses.

An **air mass** is a large body of air whose properties are determined by the part of Earth's surface over which it develops. For example, an air mass that develops over land is dry compared with one that develops over water. An air mass that develops near the equator is warmer than one that develops at a higher latitude. What characteristics might you expect of an air mass that forms over northern Canada compared to one that forms over Mexico?

Air masses move and swirl over the surface of Earth. Because they move in different directions and at different speeds, they often bump into each other. Rain, thunderstorms, snow, tornadoes—all of these weather-related events can result when air masses meet. When an air mass moves and collides with another air mass, a boundary forms between the two air masses. This boundary is called a **front**. The next activity will show you what happens at the boundary.

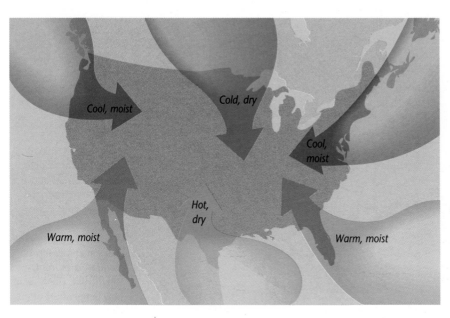

Cool, moist

Cold, dry

Cool, moist

Hot, dry

Warm, moist

Warm, moist

**Section Objectives**

- Describe the weather associated with different types of fronts.
- Explain why high pressure systems usually bring clear weather and low pressure systems bring cloudy weather.

**Key Terms**

air mass
front

**Figure 8-9**

During the year, different air masses will dominate the weather. In the United States during winter, the cold, dry air masses meet with a warm, moist air mass to bring snow to the northern sections.

# PREPARATION

## Concepts Developed

In section 2, students will learn to describe weather associated with frontal systems, and correlate clear and cloudy weather to pressure systems. This section will introduce technologies used in weather forecasting and teach students to read a weather map.

### Planning the Lesson

Refer to the Chapter Organizer on pages 240A–B.

# 1 MOTIVATE

**Discussion** Review air's capacity to hold moisture. Ask students how they think water vapor in the atmosphere affects the type of weather associated with an air mass. *Moist air masses are more likely to produce precipitation than are dry air masses.* L1

# 2 TEACH

### Tying to Previous Knowledge

Ask students if they have ever heard a weather forecaster say that the barometer is falling. What sort of weather is expected when the barometer "falls?" *precipitation*

**Student Text Question** **What characteristics might you expect of an air mass that forms over northern Canada compared to one that forms over Mexico?** *Both air masses would be dry. The one over Canada would be cold and the one over Mexico would be hot.*

## Multicultural Perspectives

### El Niño

Students can learn to better recognize cause and effect by researching how El Niño causes climatic change. Every few years a massive warm ocean current known as El Niño (the child) moves east through the Pacific Ocean. Peruvians named the phenomenon for the Christ Child because it usually occurs around Christmastime. The huge current has a higher temperature on average than normal Pacific Ocean water. Most meteorologists believe El Niño is one of the most important climate events beyond the annual cycle of seasons.

Have students research the effects of El Niño in 1990-1992. Each group should report on a section of the world El Niño affected. L2
**P COOP LEARN**

## What happens when two air masses meet?

**Time needed** 15 to 20 minutes

**Materials** aquarium with a glass lid, cold bag of sand or marbles, pan, hot water

**Thinking Processes** observing and inferring, formulating models, predicting

**Purpose** To model a front.

**Preparation** Chill plastic food storage bags filled with sand or marbles. Very hot tap water works, but boiling water is more dramatic.

### Teaching the Activity

**Troubleshooting** Be sure students have the hot and cold sources near each other. You may want to do this activity as a demonstration to avoid having students handle very hot water.

**Student Journal** Have students predict what will happen when a warm air mass meets a cool air mass. L1

### Expected Outcomes

Students will observe that condensation forms where air masses of different temperatures meet.

### Conclude and Apply

A cloud forms because the warm, saturated air over the pan of hot water meets the cold air over the bag. As the warm air cools, it reaches its dew point and forms condensation.

### ✔ Assessment

**Process** Give students the following scenario. An air mass from northern Canada moves south, while an air mass from the Pacific Ocean moves north. They meet over Denver, Colorado. Have students predict the weather for Denver for that day (*rainy*) and include an Events Chain in the explanation. Use the Performance Task Assessment List for Events Chains in **PAMSS**, page 91. L1

---

## Find Out! ACTIVITY

## What happens when two air masses meet?

### What To Do

1. For this activity, you will need an aquarium with a glass lid, a cold bag of sand or marbles, and a pan of very hot water.

2. Place the pan of water inside the aquarium next to the cold bag.

3. Cover the aquarium with the glass lid. Observe and record what happens *in your Journal*.

### Conclude and Apply

1. What happened above the pan of hot water? Why do you think this occured?

*yes* ★

You created a model of a front in the Find Out activity. Although you couldn't see it, the front formed where the cool air and warm air meet.

Much of what we think of as weather occurs along these fronts. The following diagrams show how weather is affected by the fronts that are formed.

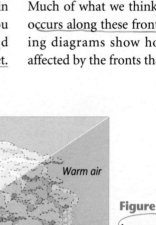

*Warm air*

*Cold air*

**Figure 8-10**

A warm front forms when a warm air mass meets, and rises above, a cold air mass. As the warm air rises, its temperature falls. Rain and other forms of precipitation sometimes form along a warm front. Why? (Hint: Think about how temperature affects water vapor.)

---

## Meeting Individual Needs

**Limited English Proficiency** Have groups of students interpret their observations by making a diorama of different kinds of weather. Give them cotton, and gray, yellow, and black paint. Also give them construction paper, blue for cold air masses and pink for warm air masses. They will also need glue, string and stiff wire, (for lightning bolts). Snowflakes made of paper cutouts can be suspended with thread. **COOP LEARN**

## Program Resources

**Study Guide,** p. 29

**Making Connections: Across the Curriculum,** p. 19, Adiabatic Lapse Rate L2

**Making Connections: Technology & Society,** p. 19, The Global Warming Debate L2

Figure 8-11

When a cold air mass overtakes and moves underneath a warm air mass, warm air is forced quickly upward, and a cold front forms. The most violent storms often occur along cold fronts.

Warm air

Cold air

**Theme Connection** The themes that this section supports are Interactions and Systems and Stability and Change. Section 2 describes how weather results from the interaction of air masses. Because air masses are systems in a continual state of change, stability is short lived.

### Content Background

The stability of an air mass is one factor that determines the weather of an area. Warm, moist air masses are said to be unstable. The warm air at the surface, because it is less dense, will tend to be forced aloft, producing clouds, precipitation, and storms. Cold, dry air masses are more stable because cold air is more dense than warm air and will tend to remain at the surface.

### Figure 8-12

A stationary front occurs when a cold air mass meets a warm air mass, and neither mass moves. Precipitation sometimes forms along the front between these masses. If a stationary front is located near where you live, and it is raining, will it rain for a short time, or a long time? Why?

Warm air

Cold air

---

| Visual Learning |
| --- |

**Figure 8-10 Rain and other forms of precipitation sometimes form along a warm front. Why?** *As the warm air rises and the temperature falls, and water vapor condenses and falls.*

**Figure 8-12 If a stationary front is located near where you live, and it is raining, will it rain for a short time, or a long time? Why?** *It will rain for a long time because the air masses will not be moving.*

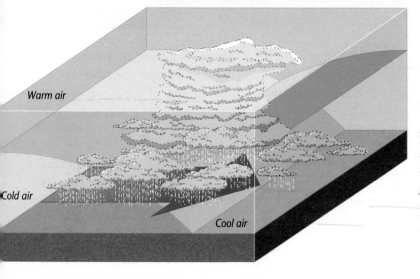

Warm air

Cold air

Cool air

### Figure 8-13

An occluded front forms when two cold air masses meet, and force a warm air mass between them to rise completely off the ground. Weather that forms along an occluded front is often difficult to predict because three air masses are involved.

8-2 Changes in Weather **253**

---

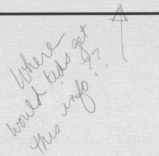
# Pressure Systems

## SKILLBUILDER

**Making and Using Tables**
Make a table that shows the four types of fronts and the weather associated with each. If you need help, refer to the **Skill Handbook** on page 680.

Differences in pressure have a great effect on the weather. High pressure usually means clear weather, and low pressure might bring cloudy, rainy weather.

As you learned in chapter 7, air molecules have mass, and as they collide, they exert pressure on one another. When air molecules are less densely packed, high pressure occurs. Air molecules are less densely packed in low pressure. Let's explore how such an air mass moves.

## Explore! ACTIVITY

### How do pressure systems move?

**What To Do**

1. Place an empty, capped thermos bottle in the freezer for several hours.

2. Remove the thermos from the freezer and take off the cap.

3. Hold the thermos upside down above your head. What are you feeling?

4. *In your Journal*, describe what is taking place.

Dense air sinks. You felt this for yourself in the Explore activity. The cold air in the thermos was more dense than the air in the room, so it flowed out and down onto your head.

This also happens in high pressure systems. As cool, dense air sinks toward Earth's surface, it starts to become warmer. As the air becomes warmer, it can hold more water vapor.

Although the amount of water vapor in the air remains the same, the relative humidity of warmer air decreases. Droplets of water in clouds evaporate. That is why high pressure usually means fair weather. Moisture in the air is evaporated, so few clouds form.

The reverse is true with low pressure systems. Because its density is low, warm air of a low pressure sys-

## ✔ Assessment

**Process** Have students observe the effects of falling cold air on the surrounding air. Have them repeat the activity holding the chilled thermos bottle over a table. Using a feather or a strip of tissue paper as a draft detector, students should locate air currents near the side of the flask. They should infer that sinking cold air pushes warm air upward. Use the Performance Task Assessment List for Making Observations and Inferences in **PAMSS**, page 55. **L1**

## ENRICHMENT

**Research** To reinforce their understanding of cause and effect, ask students if any of them suffer from sinus headaches. The ones who do may experience discomfort in extremes of barometric pressure. Sudden changes in pressure, especially, may cause painful headaches. Have students research the cause of sinus headaches, and report on the reasons air pressure may affect this condition. **L2**

tem is forced upward by surrounding, denser air. As it gains altitude, the air cools. As the air cools, its relative humidity increases. The air eventually reaches its dew point. Condensation takes place, and clouds form. You can see how low pressure often leads to rain, snow, sleet or hail in the forecast.

**Figure 8-14**

**A** **Air pressure is not constant on Earth. It is different in one place than it is in another. In a high pressure system, what prevents warm, moist air from rising?** cold air sinking

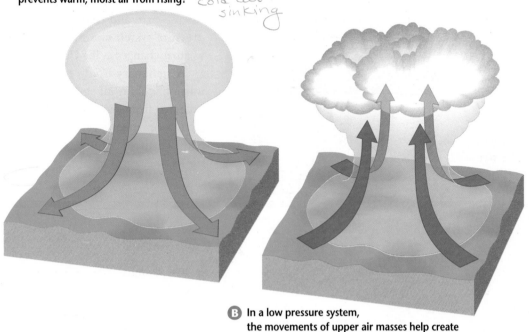

**B** **In a low pressure system, the movements of upper air masses help create low air pressure near the ground.**

Because high and low pressure systems are constantly moving and shifting, the National Weather Service uses information gathered at many different locations. Each location communicates its data, and the Weather Service combines them to make weather maps used to forecast the weather. The information is shown in symbols on the map is called a station model. A key to the symbols is shown in Appendix I. Symbols are used because if words were written on such maps, they would be too cluttered to read.

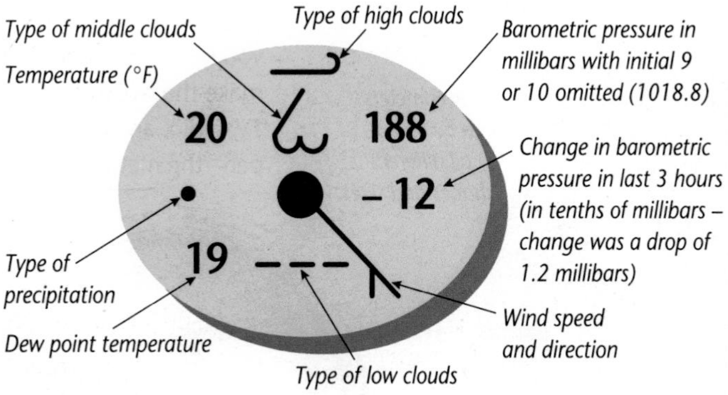

Type of middle clouds
Type of high clouds
Temperature (°F)
Barometric pressure in millibars with initial 9 or 10 omitted (1018.8)
20
188
Change in barometric pressure in last 3 hours (in tenths of millibars – change was a drop of 1.2 millibars)
– 12
19
Type of precipitation
Dew point temperature
Wind speed and direction
Type of low clouds


**Figure 8-15**

**Symbols like these are used to describe and forecast the weather.**



**Discussion** Ask students to name kinds of technologies that are used to help predict the weather. Possible areas of discussion are radar, weather satellites, ground weather stations, airplanes, weather balloons, and rockets. It might be helpful to videotape a weather report the day before the lesson or, if you can, the day of the lesson, and then play it for the class. L1

## Visual Learning

**Figure 8-14** Have students study the illustrations and explain the relationship between altitude change, temperature, relative humidity, and precipitation in a low pressure system. *As warm air rises, it cools. This increases the relative humidity, causing condensation and precipitation.* **In a high pressure system, what prevents warm, moist air from rising?** *Cold air is sinking.* L2

Study Appendix I

Do Weather Map activity

## Program Resources

**Laboratory Manual,** pp. 47–48, Weather Forecasting L1

**Critical Thinking/Problem Solving,** p. 16, Weather Forecasting Folklore L2

**Multicultural Connections,** p. 19, They Call the Wind . . . What? L1

**Transparency Master,** p. 35, and **Color Transparency** Number 16, Types of Fronts L2

**Science Discovery Activities,** 8-1, Can Water "Float" on Water? and 8-2, Mapping Weather

## ■ Moving Fronts

When you witness a change in the weather from one day to the next, it is due to the movement of air masses.

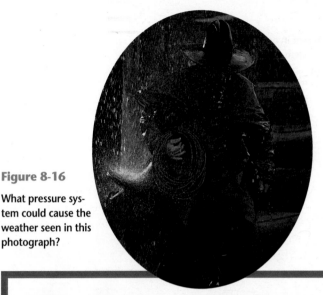

**Figure 8-16**

What pressure system could cause the weather seen in this photograph?

The movement and collision of air masses cause weather conditions to change. The boundary formed between moving air masses is a front.

A warm front develops when a warm air mass meets a cold air mass. A cold front forms when a cold air mass invades a warm air mass. Low pressure usually forms along fronts where warm and cold air meet. Low pressure systems cause most of the weather changes in the United States.

A stationary front results when a warm or cold front stops moving. An occluded front results when two cold air masses meet and trap warm air between them. Along each of these fronts, the warm air is being cooled.

## Forecasting the Weather

You can tell what current weather conditions are by simply making observations. However, the weather is continually changing, so you can't always rely on your own observations to predict what the weather will be like later. Instead you rely on the people who make the weather forecasts on TV, radio, and in the newspaper—the meteorologists.

*Thermometers can be found in all different shapes and sizes.*

You've learned that thermometers measure temperature and that psychrometers measure relative humidity. In the How it Works section you'll learn how barometers measure atmospheric pressure. In addition to these instruments, meteorologists use satellites, radar, and computers to help them forecast the weather.

### Uses of Satellites

Some satellites gather information on global weather patterns by recording information

*Barometers are sensitive instruments that are used to measure atmospheric pressure.*

**256** Chapter 8 Weather

the data and patterns indicated on the map to forecast the weather for the fourth day. Then give students the map for the fourth day so they can check their forecast. **COOP LEARN** **L2**

When the air becomes saturated, precipitation falls.

You'll learn more about the severe weather associated with low pressure systems in the next section.

Figure 8-17

Sunny days are caused by what kind of pressure system?

### check your UNDERSTANDING

1. Compare and contrast warm fronts and cold fronts.
2. Suppose a weather report states that a high pressure system will cover your area tomorrow. Why can you expect the skies to become clear?
3. What weather might you expect if cool, dry air from Canada meets warm, moist air from Gulf.
4. **Apply** Air that stays over the Gulf of Mexico for a period of time forms an air mass. Describe the humidity and temperature of that air mass in general terms.

on the temperature and moisture of the air at different heights. Stationary satellites remain at the same spot above the equator and record air currents and cloud formation. Information from these satellites is entered into computers and the data are shared with weather stations around the world. Radar, or radio wave pictures, is used by meteorologists to detect raindrops and ice particles up to 400 kilometers away, revealing what type of weather is approaching.

Once these data are gathered, meteorologists can make predictions, or forecasts, about the weather. To make short-range forecasts, meteorologists use a combination of computer

analysis of data and human interpretation. Long-range forecasts are made by computers that compare current weather information with information from previous years.

**You Try It!**

Make your own observations of the weather in your city. Observe such things as temperature, barometric pressure, clouds, rainfall, and wind direc-

*Weather satellites help make weather forecasts more accurate.*

Percent Cloud Cover

tion and speed. Record your observations at the same time each day, over a period of several days or a week. Based on your data, forecast the weather for the next three days. Check your results against actual weather forecasts.

8-2 Changes in Weather **257**

### check your UNDERSTANDING

1. Both are caused by the meeting of two air masses. A cold front forms when a cold, dense air mass overtakes and pushes under a warm one. Weather is violent. A warm front forms when a warm air mass overtakes and rides up over a cold, dense one. Rain or snow is produced. Warm fronts move slowly, while cold fronts move rapidly.

2. A high pressure system is composed of cool, dense air that sinks and warms. As it warms, the air can hold more moisture so water in clouds evaporates. The weather becomes clear under these conditions.

3. You would expect clouds and precipitation along the frontal system where the air masses meet.

4. Air takes on the characteristics of the area over which it develops. The air would be warm and humid because it is developing over a warm, wet environment.

### Planning the Activity

**Time needed** 45 minutes

**Purpose** To interpret weather map symbols and measurements.

**Process Skills** observing and inferring, interpreting data, interpreting scientific illustrations, predicitng, modeling

**Materials** Appendix K, hand lens

**Preparation** Some students will need to review the locations of the states and major cities prior to performing this activity. Have the students refer to the map of the United States. Students may wish to use hand lenses to read the small details on the map.

### Teaching the Activity

**Process Reinforcement** Have students record the weather data from the maps in a data table in their journals. L1

**Troubleshooting** If an opaque projector is available, project the weather map on a screen.

Review the weather map symbols found in Appendix K with the class. Be sure students understand the meanings of the flags used to denote wind speed and the shorthand notation for air pressure (only the last three digits of the millibar reading are written; the initial 9 or 10 is dropped). L3

**Student Journal** Have students answer all questions in their journals.

### Expected Outcome

Students will be able to analyze and interpret weather station models.

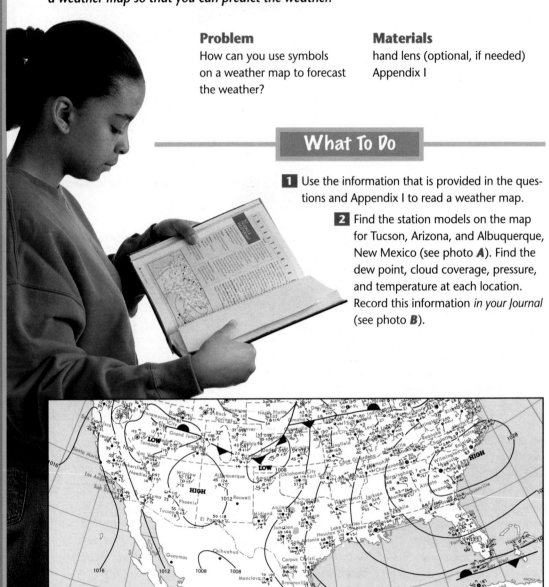

## INVESTIGATE!

# Reading a Weather Map

*In this activity, you'll read and interpret the symbols on a weather map so that you can predict the weather.*

**Problem**

How can you use symbols on a weather map to forecast the weather?

**Materials**

hand lens (optional, if needed)
Appendix I

### What To Do

**1** Use the information that is provided in the questions and Appendix I to read a weather map.

**2** Find the station models on the map for Tucson, Arizona, and Albuquerque, New Mexico (see photo **A**). Find the dew point, cloud coverage, pressure, and temperature at each location. Record this information *in your Journal* (see photo **B**).

### Meeting Individual Needs

**Gifted** Students can better learn to interpret weather maps by working in pairs to make a board game using weather map symbols. Mark one space START and another space FINISH. Have students label some of the spaces on the board with a weather phenomenon and a short description or fact about it. For example, a space could be labeled "Hurricane—Blow back 2 spaces". Then have students make cards on which weather map symbols appear on one side. The other side should have a verbal explanation of the symbol. Students should take turns drawing cards. Correct responses will allow students to move ahead the number of spaces indicated by the roll of a die. The first student to reach the space marked FINISH wins. **COOP LEARN** P L3

**A**                    **B**                    **C**

**3** Determine the type of front located near Key West, Florida.

**4** The triangles or half circles on the weather front symbol are on the side of the line that indicates the direction the front is moving. Determine the direction that the cold front located over Colorado and Kansas is moving.

## Analyzing

1. *In your Journal*, record the dew point, cloud coverage, pressure and temperature at each location.

2. What type of front is located near Key West, Florida?

3. What direction is the cold front moving that is located over Colorado and Kansas?

## Concluding and Applying

4. The prevailing westerlies are the winds responsible for the movement of weather across the United States and Canada. Based on this fact, would you *predict* that Charleston, South Carolina, will continue to have clear skies over the next several days? Explain your answer.

5. The line on the station model that indicates wind speed shows from which direction the wind is blowing, and the wind is named according to the direction from which the wind blows. What is the name of the wind at Jackson, Mississippi?

6. ~~Going Further~~ Locate the pressure system over Winslow, Arizona. *Infer* the effect this system would have on the weather of Wichita, Kansas, if it moved there.

**Answers to** Analyzing/ Concluding and Applying

**1.** Tucson: dew point 18, no cloud cover, barometric pressure 1011.6 mb., 55° F; Albuquerque: dew point 7, one tenth or less cloud cover, barometric pressure 1012.4 mb., 45°F

**2.** stationary front

**3.** southeast

**4.** No, a cold front and low pressure area over Oklahoma are moving toward Charleston.

**5.** southeast

**6.** The skies would clear and there would be fair weather.

✔ *Assessment*

**Process** Using the data from the map, have students work in groups and write out a complete description of the weather for a location. Students could then present and video tape mock television weather reports. Select the appropriate Performance Task Assessment List from **PAMSS.** L1 COOP LEARN

## Program Resources

**Activity Masters,** pp. 37–38, Investigate 8-2

## ENRICHMENT

**Activity** Explain that to approximate Fahrenheit temperature from Celsius temperature, double the Celsius temperature and add 32. Give students this example. Approximate 20° C to its Fahrenheit equivalent. $20° \times 2 = 40°$, $40° + 32° = 72°$. The actual conversion equation is $(9/5 \times °C) + 32 = F$ so the actual Fahrenheit temperature is 68°. $(9/5 \times 20) + 32 = F$, $36 + 32 = 68°F$. Have students work the math out on the board. L2

## PREPARATION

### Concepts Developed

In section 3, students will learn what causes a thunderstorm and relate how tornadoes evolve from thunderstorms. Students will compare and contrast tornadoes and hurricanes.

### Planning the Lesson

Refer to the Chapter Organizer on pages 240A–B.

## 1 MOTIVATE

**Discussion** Discuss the effects of severe thunderstorms, hurricanes, and tornadoes. Have students list the kinds of destruction that might result from severe storms. *Students may mention damage from flooding, lightning, or high winds that blow down houses or power lines.* L1

## 2 TEACH

### Tying to Previous Knowledge

Ask students to sequence the events leading up to an afternoon thunderstorm. Guide them to list the development stages on the chalkboard. *Very warm, humid air is rapidly pushed up by cooler air. Strong convection currents form. The rising warm air cools to its dew point and cumulonimbus clouds form. Water droplets stick together, and rain and hail start to fall.* L1

**Discussion** Ask students what safety rules should be followed when lightning is seen or conditions that produce lightning are present. *Avoid high spots in open land. Avoid metal objects and bodies of water.*

---

8-3 **Severe Weather**

### Section Objectives

- Describe what causes thunderstorms.
- Relate how tornadoes evolve from thunderstorms.
- Compare and contrast tornadoes and hurricanes.

### Key Terms

*tornado*
*hurricane*

## Thunderstorms

Thunderstorms are formed by the rapid upward movement of warm, moist air. They can occur within warm, moist air masses but often occur at cold fronts. As the warm, moist air is forced upward, it cools, and its water vapor condenses, forming cumulus clouds that can reach heights of 10 kilometers. A thunderstorm can cause a great deal of damage.

Water droplets that form in the clouds begin falling the long distance toward Earth's surface. As the droplets fall through the clouds, they collide with other droplets and become larger. These falling droplets create a downward motion of air that spreads out at Earth's surface and causes some of the strong winds associated with thunderstorms.

  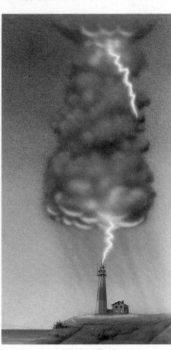

**Figure 8-18**

**A** Lightning is a sudden, violent discharge of electricity.

**B** Lightning occurs because an attraction exists between positive and negative electrical charges.

**C** Lightning strikes taller objects such as trees and buildings.

**260    Chapter 8    Weather**

---

## Program Resources

**Study Guide,** p. 30 L1
**Laboratory Manual,** pp. 49–52, Hurricanes
**Critical Thinking/Problem Solving,** p. 5, Flex Your Brain
**Multicultural Connections,** p. 20, Bangladesh and Killer Cyclones L1

**Making Connections, Integrating Sciences,** p. 19, Air Force L2
**Science Discovery Activities,** 8-3, Tracking a Hurricane

---

### ■ Lightning

Lightning is also associated with thunderstorms. Lightning, which is nothing more than electricity, occurs when current flows between regions of opposite electrical charge. Bolts of lightning can leap from cloud to cloud, from a cloud to Earth's surface, or from Earth's surface to a cloud.

**Figure 8-19**

Lightning strikes Earth about 100 times each second.

If you've seen lightning, you've probably heard thunder, too. Thunder results from the rapid heating of the air around a lightning bolt. The air close by expands rapidly, forming a sound wave. It's hard to believe, but lightning can reach temperatures of about 28 000°C.

Heavy rains from thunderstorms sometimes cause flooding and mudslides. Lightning can strike trees and other objects, setting them on fire, and can electrocute people and animals. Strong winds can also cause damage.

If a thunderstorm has winds traveling faster than 80 kilometers per hour and often hail more than 2 centimeters in diameter, weather forecasters classify it as a severe thunderstorm. Hail this size can dent cars and the siding on houses. It can also flatten and destroy a crop in a matter of minutes.

## Find Out! ACTIVITY

### How does air in a tornado move?

**What To Do**

1. Obtain two 2-liter plastic bottles.
2. Fill one about three-quarters full of water and add one drop of dishwashing soap.
3. Tape the mouth of the empty bottle to the mouth of the bottle with water in it. Make sure the tape secures the bottles together so that they won't leak.
4. Now, flip the bottles so that the one with the water is on top.

5. Move the top bottle in a circular motion.

**Conclude and Apply**

1. *In your Journal,* record what you see forming in the bottle?
2. How is this model of a tornado similar to a real tornado?

## Find Out!

### How does air in a tornado move?

**Time needed** 15 to 20 minutes

**Materials** 2 2-liter soft drink bottles, liquid dishsoap, water, duct tape (Scientific supply houses sell a device that can be used in place of the tape.)

**Thinking Processes** formulating models, observing and inferring, recognizing cause and effect

**Purpose** To model a tornado.

**Preparation** Several days before this activity, have students bring 2-L, clear, plastic soft drink bottles (labels and glue removed) to class. Be sure the bottles are rinsed thoroughly. Tell students to soak the bottles in warm water to remove any label glue. Be sure the outsides of the bottles are dry before beginning. Paper-punch cutouts dropped in the bottles beforehand will simulate airborne debris.

**Flex Your Brain** Use the Flex Your Brain activity to have students explore WEATHER SYSTEMS. [L1]

### Teaching the Activity

Do not discourage students from creating their tornadoes over and over again. Each time, they will notice something different related to tornado formation.

**Troubleshooting** Be sure students wrap the tape tightly around the necks of the bottles, especially on the first wrap. Be sure students hold the apparatus at the tape joint to keep it from falling apart.

**Student Journal** Have students explain in their journals how their model compares to a real tornado. [L1]

### Expected Outcome

By observing their model, students will be able to describe the shape and motion of a tornado.

### Conclude and Apply

1. A spiral-shaped, soapy funnel which looks like a tornado forms in the bottle.
2. Both this model and a real tornado rotate, and are turbulent and spiral-shaped.

### ✔ Assessment

**Content** Have student groups use reference materials to explore tornadoes. Have students research where tornadoes occur, how they form, and how their high winds and low pressure can cause destruction. Students can include their information on a bulletin board titled "Twisters." Use the Performance Task Assessment List for Bulletin Boards in **PAMSS**, page 59. [L1]
**COOP LEARN**

## Tornadoes

A **tornado** is a violent, funnel-shaped storm whose whirling winds move in a narrow path over land. Tornadoes form from severe thunderstorms. As with regular thunderstorms, tornado-producing thunderstorms involve the rapid upward movement of warm, moist air.

Scientists aren't exactly sure what causes this upward-moving air to rotate. They think the upward-moving air is twisted when it comes in contact with the cooler winds moving in a different direction at the top of the cloud. As the speed of the rotating air mass increases, even more warm air is drawn into the low pressure at the center. A funnel-shaped cloud then extends from the bottom of the storm cloud, sometimes touching the ground. The funnel cloud picks up dirt and debris from the ground, which give the funnel its dark gray or black color.

Although tornadoes average only 200 meters in diameter and usually last less than 10 minutes, they are one of the most destructive types of storms.

## Physics CONNECTION

### A New Storm Detection Tool

When people are warned in time that tornadoes and severe thunderstorms are approaching, not as many people die. There are also fewer injuries and less property damage. That's reason enough for scientists to study tornados and hurricanes and try to develop better tools for predicting their paths. One such tool is a new kind of radar.

*Doppler weather radar measures precipitation and wind speed and direction and allows meteorologists to predict and track storms.*

**Figure 8-20**

Although tornadoes tend to occur more often during spring than during any other season of the year, they can occur anytime.

### *Across the Curriculum*
**Math**

Have students use numbers to calculate when a hurricane will hit land. Tell them they are in an east coast city of the United States. A hurricane, 400 km directly to the southeast, is moving northwest at 25 km per hour. It is now 3:00 P.M. on Tuesday. If the storm moves in a straight line, what time will it hit land? *400 km ÷ 25 km/hr = 16 hr so landfall will be at 7 A.M., Wednesday.* L2

## Doppler Weather Radar

Doppler radar uses the Doppler effect, named after Dr. Christian Johann Doppler. (Dr. Doppler discovered why a moving train whistle seems to change its pitch as it passes you.) If a source of sound is moving, the sound waves are bunched up ahead of it and stretched out behind it. As the source passes you, you hear the bunched-up sound waves as higher pitch and the stretched-out sound waves as lower pitch.

Doppler radar uses the Doppler effect to measure the relative velocity, that is, the relative speed and direction of itself and the radar target. Airplanes equipped with Doppler radar can study thunderstorms, tor-nados, and even hurricanes, and determine their speeds and directions. A storm may contain several different wind speeds and wind directions; the Doppler-radar screen shows them in different colors. It can also tell the difference between the small drops of rain that a normal cloud produces and the big drops that a thunderhead produces. It can even distinguish rain clouds from dust clouds and clouds of mosquitoes or birds.

When installed at airports, Doppler radar can detect wind shear regions and warn planes not to take off or land. Wind shear regions are places where the wind speed or direction changes greatly in a small area. Wind shear near Earth's surface is usually caused by strong downdrafts of air. When the downdraft strikes the surface, it blows out strongly in all directions across the surface, thus making a wind shear region. Wind shear near or on an airport runway can cause serious accidents, but with Doppler radar, wind shear can be detected and accidents prevented.

## What Do You Think?

You know that the Doppler effect causes an outside listener to hear first high, then low pitches from the moving siren. What do you think the siren would sound like to a listener who was moving along with the siren?

## Teaching Strategy

Discuss with students the types of information a meteorologist might want to know before issuing a hurricane or tornado warning. *Students may mention wind speed and direction, location of the tornado, or land fall of the hurricane.* Discuss why an early warning system is important for people living in areas prone to hurricanes or tornadoes. L2

## Answer to
### What Do You Think?

The sound of the siren would not change.

## Going Further ⅢⅢ➧

To help students observe how this technology works, explain that Doppler radar detects the difference in reflected radio waves that have bounced off ice particles in clouds. If the frequency is higher than it should be, the cloud is moving toward the radar station. If the frequency is lower than it should be, the cloud is moving away. Have a student volunteer attach a 1.5 m strong cord firmly to a tuning fork. Use a heavy-duty tape such as duct tape. Have the student strike the tuning fork, then set it in circular motion above his or her head. Ask students to describe what happens. *As the tuning fork moves toward other students, its pitch raises. As it moves away from the students, the pitch lowers.* L1

# 3 ASSESS

## Check for Understanding

As preparation for the Apply item, have students compare hurricanes and tornadoes. *Winds spin around a low pressure area; both are associated with warm, moist air.* L1

## Reteach

Have pairs of students contrast tornadoes and hurricanes, using the following terms: Relative size, Origin, Type of pressure system, Damage, Cause. Have them set up a chart using these terms as heads for each column. Under each head, write the characteristics of tornadoes and hurricanes. L1 P

## Extension

Have students use reference books to find the areas of Earth where hurricanes form and the general directions in which they move. L3 P

# 4 CLOSE

Show the film *Countdown to Survival* by Screenscope, Inc. It emphasizes precautions to take during a tornado. If the movie is not available, ask students to prepare a list of classroom steps to be taken in case a severe hurricane, tornado, or other weather extreme occurs while they are in school. L1

# Hurricanes

The largest storm that occurs on Earth is the hurricane. A **hurricane** is a very large, swirling, low pressure system that forms over tropical oceans. For a storm to be called a hurricane, it must have winds that blow at least 120 kilometers per hour. Hurricanes may be many kilometers in diameter. Because they form over large bodies of water and have a steady supply of energy, they may go on for many days, until they reach land.

Hurricanes form over warm, tropical oceans where two opposing winds meet and begin to swirl. A low pressure area forms in the middle of the swirl and begins rotating. Warm, moist air is forced up into the middle of the low pressure area. You already know what happens when warm, moist air rises. It cools, and moisture starts to condense.

Just as in a tornado, the dropping air pressure inside the low pressure area pulls air toward the center, causing even greater winds and lower air pressure. Hurricanes weaken when they strike land because they no longer receive energy from the warm water.

**Figure 8-21**

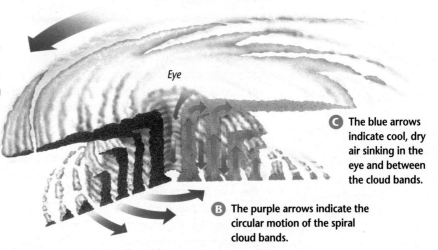

**A** In this hurricane cross-section, the red arrows indicate rising warm, moist air forming cumulus clouds in bands around the eye.

*Eye*

**C** The blue arrows indicate cool, dry air sinking in the eye and between the cloud bands.

**B** The purple arrows indicate the circular motion of the spiral cloud bands.

## check your UNDERSTANDING

1. Describe how thunderstorms occur and why they cause the damage they do.
2. Explain how tornadoes evolve from thunderstorms.
3. How does a tornado differ from a hurricane? What are the similarities between the storms?
4. **Apply** Tornadoes sometimes form when hurricanes come onto land. Discuss how the tornadoes might form.

## check your UNDERSTANDING

1. Thunderstorms result from the rapid, upward movement of warm, moist air. As this air cools, the moisture in it begins to condense into water droplets and form cumulonimbus clouds. The moisture forms drops, which fall as rain. Thunderstorms cause damage because they bring destructive high winds, heavy rains, hail, and lightning.

2. In severe thunderstorms, warm air is forced upward at great speeds. If this air collides with wind moving in a different direction at the top of the thunderstorm, a swirling motion begins.

3. Both are low pressure areas and both can cause damage. A tornado is smaller. A tornado forms over land, a hurricane forms over warm ocean water.

4. Strong winds from a hurricane may continue to swirl over land if there is warm, moist air. As the air is drawn into the low pressure area, a tornado forms.

# Science *and* Society

## Is Cloud Seeding a Good Idea?

**A**s you know, weather is extremely changeable and often difficult to predict. Human activities can cause weather changes. Cloud seeding is an example of how people intentionally try to change the weather.

### The Seeding Process

The process of seeding clouds was pioneered in 1946. Dry ice, or frozen carbon dioxide, was first used to cause the moisture in supercooled clouds (temperatures below -5°C) to adhere to the dry ice crystals. The crystals get heavier and soon begin to fall as snow or rain. Silver iodide is now the most common chemical used for cloud seeding. Silver iodide's crystalline structure is like that of dry ice and causes silver iodide to act like dry ice. Ice crystals form, grow, absorb the moisture in the clouds, and eventually drop out of the clouds as rain.

Cloud-seeding aircraft, as shown here feed smoke

trails of silver iodide into the updrafts of clouds. In other cases, rockets filled with silver iodide are shot from the ground into clouds, where water droplets are collecting, to prevent the formation of large hailstones.

While the results seem positive, there are problems. Some cloud-seeding projects have led to court battles. Some communities accuse the seeders of "cloud rustling" because they take the water out of clouds that normally drop moisture on their towns.

### What Do You Think?

You love to ski, but the ski resort nearest your home hasn't had enough snow this year to open. Should they seed the clouds?

### Going Further ⫸

To highlight the effects of cloud seeding, review air mass movements as shown in Figure 8-9 with students and ask where they think the rain-producing air masses for the midsection of the United States come from. *The West or the Gulf of Mexico* Have students hypothesize what would happen if cloud seeding was used in arid western regions. Then have each group draft a letter to Congress in support or nonsupport of cloud seeding in these regions. Ask groups to share their letters. **COOP LEARN** [L1]

# EXPAND *your view*

# Science *and* Society

**Purpose**
The role of water vapor and clouds in our weather is presented in Section 8-1. Science and Society discusses cloud seeding, a method used to encourage clouds to release precipitation.

**Content Background**
Explain that cloud seeding is performed in an effort to increase Earth's surface water supply. It has been a controversial environmental issue for almost five decades. Proponents of cloud seeding claim that the process actually raises the amount of precipitation by up to 20 percent. Opponents challenge that claim.

Some of the questions being asked are: (1) Who is entitled to the water in clouds? (2) Does the silver iodine pose a threat to the environment? People downwind from a cloud seeding operation feel that they are being robbed of water they would have, under normal circumstances, received. No one has determined the effects of silver iodine on the environment.

**Teaching Strategies** To allow students to communicate their ideas about cloud seeding, divide your class into groups to debate the question raised in the What Do You Think? activity. Have one group represent skiers and another represent residents of the resort area. Also discuss what other groups of people might have an interest in this situation. **COOP LEARN** [L1]

**Answer to**
**What Do You Think?**
Answers will vary, but students should be able to justify their responses.

# HOW IT WORKS

## Purpose

Section 8-2 discusses the effect of atmospheric pressure on weather. How It Works describes how an aneroid barometer measures atmospheric pressure.

## Content Background

The SI unit of air pressure is the millibar. Weather reports give the barometric pressure in inches of mercury. This measurement is based on the original Toricellian barometer invented over three centuries ago. A 30.3 inch tube, closed at one end and open at the other, is filled with mercury and inverted in a bowl of mercury. The column of mercury in the tube falls, leaving a vacuum at the closed top of the tube. When air pressure increases, it pushes down on the mercury in the bowl, forcing the mercury in the tube to rise. The opposite happens when pressure decreases. Normal atmospheric pressure at sea level is 29.92 inches of mercury. The SI equivalent is 1013.2 millibars. A pressure of 1013.6 millibars is shown as 136 on an isobaric (air pressure) map.

## Discussion

Have students refer to the face of the barometer in the photo on this page to discuss what weather conditions are associated with high, low, rising, and falling barometer readings.

## Answers to

*You Try It!*

Graphs will vary. Increasing pressure indicates that weather will be clear. Decreasing pressure indicates that there will be clouds and probably precipitation.

# HOW IT WORKS     Barometers

Atmospheric pressure influences weather patterns all around the world. These pressure systems help us predict what our weather will be. Barometers are instruments used to determine atmospheric pressure. How do barometers work?

One common type of barometer, pictured on the right here, is an aneroid barometer. It works on the principle that a sealed metal chamber contracts and expands with changes in the atmospheric pressure. For example, if high pressure moves in, pressure outside the chamber is greater than pressure inside the chamber, and the chamber contracts. If low pressure moves in, pressure outside the chamber is less than pressure inside the chamber, and the chamber expands.

A small chain extends between the chamber to a pointer on a dial that is read on the face of the barometer.

### You Try It!

Take barometric pressure readings regularly each morning and evening for a week. Be sure it is about the same time each day. Draw a graph to show the pressure readings. Based on what you know about high- and low-pressure systems, what can you predict using only the pressure data?

*Chain   Needle   Spindle   Dial*

*Lever*

*Lever*

*Vacuum chamber*

## Going Further

Reinforce data interpretation skills by having students make an isobaric data map. First explain that equal value atmospheric pressure readings from all over the world can be connected with lines called isobars. The lines close to form outlines indicating points of equal pressure, just as contour lines close on a topographic map showing equal elevation. Have students label a 10-by-10 grid 0 at the origin, A through J on the vertical axis, and 1 through 10 on the horizontal axis. Then have them plot these data, connecting the points for each location having the same pressure. Have them label the isobars.

Pressure = 135; Locations = C3, C4, D5, E6, F5, F4, E3, D2

Pressure = 134; Locations = D1, C1, B2, B3, B4, B5, C6, D7, E7, F7, G6, G3, F2, E1

Pressure = 133; Locations = 05, A6, B7, E8, F8, H7, H5, H3, G1, F0, C0, A1, 02

Pressure = 134; Locations = 07, A8, B9, C10, G10, H9, I8, J7, J4, I2, H0

Then discuss how the map shows a mass of high pressure. **L3** **P**

# Literature Connection

# Surviving an Everglades Hurricane

# Literature Connection

**N**owadays many of us spend most of our time indoors. If we hear warnings of an approaching weather disaster such as a blizzard, tornado or hurricane, we rush around protecting our property. Then we move into the safest part of our homes and wait out the storm. But what if you were spending the summer camping out in the Florida Everglades and suddenly you learned that a hurricane was approaching? To make it even more interesting, what if you were camping out on your own?

Well, at least you wouldn't have to rush around closing garage doors or putting tape on your windowpanes. You'd have only yourself to worry about. What would you do?

For a hurricane in the Everglades, of course, one must plan for high water as well as high wind. One must find a place of refuge thirteen feet above sea level in order to be safe from the tidal wave associated with hurricanes there. That requirement makes your task even trickier.

If you're having trouble coming up with a hurricane safety plan for the Everglades, read *The Talking Earth* by Jean Craighead George (Harper & Row, 1983). In this novel Billie Wind, a thirteen-year-old Seminole, finds herself in the Everglades during both a fire and a hurricane. Somehow she keeps herself and her animal companions (an otter, a panther cub, a turtle, and others) alive.

## What Do You Think?

Before you read The Talking Earth, list some things you would do to survive a hurricane in the Everglades. Write down supplies you would hope to have along that would help you survive. Then, after you have read The Talking Earth, go back to your list and evaluate it. What survival tips do you need to add to your list?

## Purpose

The Literature Connection reinforces Section 8-3 on severe weather through the novel *The Talking Earth* by Jean Craighead George.

## Content Background

Hurricanes are watched carefully by people who live on the Gulf and East coasts of the United States. These hurricanes originate off the coast of Africa and move westward over the Atlantic. They start as storms called tropical depressions and intensify by drawing energy from the warm ocean water. They continue to intensify as they move across the ocean. Even in an age of technology and early warnings, property damage can be very high as a result of a hurricane passing over inhabited land. Hurricane Andrew in August, 1992 first struck the Bahamas and then hit southern Florida, where 13 people were killed and 250,000 people were left homeless.

Satellites provide us with the best data on the movement of hurricanes, but they cannot provide us with the physical data we need to know. The National Oceanic and Atmospheric Administration uses the eyewitness accounts of people in spotter aircraft for physical measurements.

## Discussion

Hold a class discussion of the types of dangerous weather your area receives. Ask the students what they could do to survive a hurricane or dangerous storm. L1

## Going Further ⫸

Have students write to the National Hurricane Center, 1320 S. Dixie Highway, Room 631, Coral Gables, FL, 33146-2967 or call 305-667-3108 to obtain information on all aspects of hurricanes, including tracking charts. Have paired partners brainstorm a list of common sense precautions to take before the onset of a hurricane. Have students compare their lists with the information found in the literature and revise them if necessary. L2 COOP LEARN P

## Answer to

**What Do You Think?**

Accept all reasonable answers. After reading this feature, students will probably have an increased awareness of the dangers associated with a hurricane.

## Teens in SCIENCE

### Purpose

Teens in Science describes how one teen uses the concepts of weather presented in Sections 8-1 and 8-2 to predict weather from his high school's weather station and how he disseminates this information to the public.

### Content Background

Some students may wish to build a weather station. If possible, build a shed with a white roof and with a vent and walls that allow air to flow through. However, the walls should limit light and block precipitation. It is best to use overlapping boards, set on angles, not touching. To equip the weather station, students will need a thermometer, barometer, psychrometer, relative humidity chart, wind vane, anemometer, and rain gauge. In addition, students will need ice and a can of water to measure dew point each time they make observations. For a two-week period, have them compare their data to the data from a local television or radio station in order to calibrate their equipment. At that point students should be ready to collect their own weather information.

### Teaching Strategy

Invite a meteorologist to your class to describe his or her work and how he or she got interested in doing this work. `L2`

## Teens in SCIENCE

### Weather Watch

Christopher Maiorino's science teacher invited him to see the Lakeland High School's weather station three and a half years ago. "I thought, 'Why not?'" said Chris. "I never left. I'd like to do this as a career."

Chris and his teacher, Tim Maloy, arrive at the weather station every day at 6:30 A.M. Together they call weather stations from Salt Lake City to Connecticut, which are equipped with satellite weather maps as shown in the photo, for the daily weather data. The station has a fully equipped weather laboratory with a computer and modem, barometer, weather radio, and other equipment for measuring temperature, air pressure, wind, and humidity. More members of the Weather Club come in later to discuss the predictions. Then Chris broadcasts the weather forecast in the morning and in the afternoon over the local radio station.

Maloy, Chris's teacher, took over the Lakeland High School Weather Club in 1976, and since that time has installed a lot of new equipment, including a satellite dish. "Weather prediction gets exciting," he says, "when there's a potential for a good storm."

0601 09JA92 29E-4HF 01072 13491 CC2

### Going Further ⅢⅢ➡

Have students start a weather club at school. Interested students should generate a list of equipment on hand and needed equipment for their studies. Assign the responsibility for obtaining or building each piece of equipment to pairs of students. Some weather instruments such as rain gauges and anemometers can be built from easily obtainable materials. A psychrometer can be constructed as directed in this chapter. Students may wish to construct a weather station outside the school to house their equipment. See Content Background for instructions. Have them gather information from the local weather bureau on suggested designs. Tell students to research and report on the costs involved and form a group to try to find donors or funding for the building project. Also have students contact a local radio or television station to arrange to broadcast weather information. `L3` **COOP LEARN**

R eview the statements below about the big ideas presented in this chapter, and try to answer the questions. Then, re-read your answers to the Did You Ever Wonder questions at the beginning of the chapter. In your Journal, write a paragraph about how your understanding of the big ideas in the chapter has changed.

**1** Water evaporates into the atmosphere and condenses to form clouds. *How does air temperature effect how much water vapor is contained in the air?*

**2** Different processes control what form of precipitation falls. *Using figure 8-8, compare the processes that form hail to the processes that form snow.*

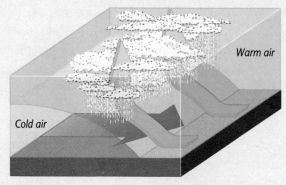

Warm air

Cold air

**3** Weather at a front depends on the types of air masses that meet. *Compare weather along a cold front to the weather that occurs along a stationary front.*

**4** Hurricanes and tornadoes both form from low pressure systems. *How do hurricanes differ from tornadoes?*

Have students look at the photographs and diagrams on this page. Direct them to read the statements to review the main ideas.

### Teaching Strategies

Divide the class into four equal groups. Assign each group one of the photographs or diagrams. Have students answer the question and interpret what their photograph or diagram shows by writing a brief paragraph of explanation.

**1.** This diagram shows the water cycle.

**2.** This figure shows the formation of hailstones.

**3.** This figure shows how air masses collide.

**4.** This figure shows a tornado. It is a very small but intense storm. Low pressure systems bring cloudy conditions, precipitation, and sometimes, severe storms.

### Answers to Questions

**1.** The higher the temperature, the more water vapor possible in the air.

**2.** Hailstones move up and down through the cloud, adding a layer of ice on each trip.

**3.** Cold fronts bring thunderstorms or snow showers. Stationary fronts bring light winds and precipitation that lasts for days.

**4.** Hurricanes are much larger and form over oceans. Tornadoes are smaller and form over land.

---

## Project

Have students collect and organize weather data by placing an outdoor thermometer and a narrow diameter, graduated beaker (to be used as a rain gauge) at an appropriate location outside of your school. Have students record temperature and rainfall data for one week. Have them compare their data to those reported in newspaper, radio, or TV weather reports. **L1**

## Science at Home

Have students collect and interpret weather data by keeping track of the temperature at 3 specific times of the day for a week. Have them create a table with a special data column to note precipitation. Have them also prepare a graph to show the high temperatures in red and the low temperatures in blue. Have them use the graph to find the day with the greatest temperature range and the day with the least temperature range. **L2**

 **MINDJOGGER VIDEOQUIZ**

**Chapter 8** Have students work in groups as they play the videoquiz game to review key chapter concepts.

## Using Key Science Terms

1. Fronts are formed where air masses meet.

2. The temperature at which air is saturated and condensation takes place is the dew point.

3. When the relative humidity reaches 100%, the dew point has been reached.

4. Both are swirling masses of air, but hurricanes are formed over tropical oceans and are much larger than tornadoes.

## Understanding Ideas

1. 33%

2. Dew forms when air is cooled until its relative humidity is 100%.

3. Weather around the world would remain relatively constant. Changes might occur along the edges of the air masses.

4. You would need weather maps of the areas west of you to find the location of fronts, cloud cover and air temperature information to the west, and instruments such as the Beaufort wind scale, a thermometer, and a barometer.

5. Wind speeds are usually higher in a tornado. Tornadoes occur over land, hurricanes develop over water. Tornadoes last a short time while hurricanes can last up to several days. Both are strong circular winds around low pressure centers.

6. They no longer get warm humid air from the ocean water.

## Developing Skills

1. See reduced student page for completed concept map.

2. Predictions should be based on features such as fronts and areas of precipitation continuing in a west to east pattern.

3. By increasing the temperature or by using a dehumidifier to remove moisture from the air.

## Using Key Science Terms

| | |
|---|---|
| air mass | relative humidity |
| dew point | saturated |
| front | tornado |
| hurricane | |

*For each set of terms below, explain the relationship that exists.*

1. air mass, front
2. dew point, saturated
3. relative humidity, dew point
4. hurricane, tornado

## Understanding Ideas

*Answer the following questions* in your Journal *using complete sentences.*

1. If one cubic meter of air at 25°C can contain 15 g of water vapor, but it only contains 5 g, what is its relative humidity?

2. When does dew form?

3. If air masses stayed in their source areas, how would this affect weather conditions?

4. If you were given the task of predicting the weather for your area over the next few days, what information and instruments would you need to determine the upcoming weather conditions?

5. How does a tornado differ from a hurricane? How are they alike?

6. Why do hurricanes weaken as they move over land?

## Critical Thinking

1. The original air mass contained moisture. As it moved up over the Rocky Mountains, it would cool and lose its moisture.

2. The air near the glasses was cooled to its dew point and condensed, causing the glasses to fog up.

## Developing Skills

*Use your understanding of the concepts developed in this chapter to answer each of the following questions.*

1. **Concept Mapping** Complete the concept map of clouds.

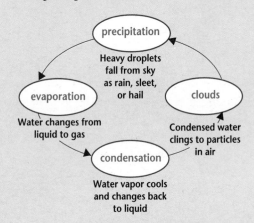

2. **Predicting** Using the information you collected from weather maps for three consecutive days in the Explore activity on page 241, predict what the weather map might look like on the fourth day. What trends of weather features did you notice and continue for your prediction?

3. **Interpreting Data** Reviewing the data you collected in the Investigate activity on relative humidity on page 246, how could the relative humidity in your classroom be lowered?

## Program Resources

**Review and Assessment,** pp. 47–50
**Performance Assessment,** Ch. 8 L2
**PAMSS**
**Alternate Assessment in The Science Classroom**
**Computer Test Bank**

## Critical Thinking

In your Journal, *answer each of the following questions.*

1. Why would an air mass formed off the coast of Oregon have different qualities after it moved across the western United States and crossed the Rockies?
2. Fred walks out of an air-conditioned building. His eyeglasses immediately fog up. Why?
3. You go into the basement of your school building. In the ceiling, you see two identical copper pipes. You know one carries cold water, the other hot water. The left pipe is moist on the outside. Without touching the pipes, how can you tell which pipe has the hot water?
4. The relative humidity of the air outside has remained 50 percent all day, despite an increase in temperature. Explain why this can happen.

5. Describe the weather conditions shown on the station model in the diagram. The initial 10 is omitted from the barometer reading.

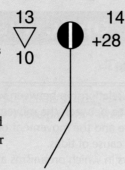

## Problem Solving

*Read the following problem and discuss your answers in a brief paragraph.*

**Jason and Kim were helping their father by fixing spaghetti for supper. They filled a pot two-thirds full of water and put it on the stove to heat. Then they went to watch television. When Jason went to check the pot a while later, it was only half full of water. On the wall above the stove were droplets of water. What had happened? What happened to the relative humidity of the room as the water boiled?**

3. The pipe that is moist on the outside carries the cold water.
4. Evaporation of water into the air is keeping pace with the temperature increase, so the relative humidity remains the same.
5. Sky is overcast with openings. Barometric pressure is 1014 mb and has increased 28 mb in the last 3 hours. Temperature is 13° C and there are showers. Winds are from the south at 13-17 knots. Dew point temperature is 10° C.

### Problem Solving

The heat caused some of the water to evaporate. Some of the water vapor in the air condensed on the cooler wall. The relative humidity of the room increased.

### Connecting Ideas

1. Convection in the atmosphere is a process by which heated air is forced aloft, cools, and sinks. The interaction of warm and cool air masses causes weather systems to develop.
2. Water evaporates, condenses to form clouds, and falls back to Earth as precipitation.
3. Cooler air is denser, so a cool air mass is associated with high pressure. Warmer air is less dense and is associated with low pressure.
4. Such factors as temperature, relative humidity, atmospheric pressure, air currents, and cloud formation.
5. In cloud seeding, a substance such as frozen carbon dioxide or silver iodide is added to supercooled clouds, causing the moisture in the air to adhere to the substance's crystals.

---

## CONNECTING IDEAS

Discuss each of the following in a brief paragraph.
1. **Theme—Systems and Interactions** Explain how convection is related to the formation of weather systems.
2. **Theme—Systems and Interactions** How is the water cycle related to the weather?
3. **Theme—Systems and Interactions** How are temperature and pressure related in air masses?
4. **A Closer Look** What are some of the weather factors that forecasters must collect data on in order to predict the weather?
5. **Science and Society** Explain how the process of cloud seeding works.

---

## ✔ Assessment

**Portfolio** Review the portfolio options that are provided throughout the chapter. Encourage students to select one product that demonstrates their best work for the chapter. Have students explain what they learned and why they chose this example for placement into their portfolios.

Additional portfolio options can be found in the following **Teacher Classroom Resources:**

**Making Connections: Integrating Sciences,** p. 19
**Multicultural Connections,** pp. 19–20
**Making Connections: Across the Curriculum,** p. 19
**Concept Mapping,** p. 16
**Critical Thinking/Problem Solving,** p. 16
**Take Home Activities,** p. 15
**Laboratory Manual,** pp. 45–46; 47–48; 49–52
**Performance Assessment** P

# PREPARATION

## Concepts Developed

Students will differentiate between the movement of water particles in a wave and the movement of wave energy.

## Planning the Lesson

Refer to the Chapter Organizer on pages 272A–B.

# 1 MOTIVATE

**Demonstration** Help students learn to interpret their observations. Obtain a large spring and a ribbon. Tie the ribbon to the middle of the spring. Have two students shake the spring to create a wave while another student holds the ribbon. Ask students what they observe. *The ribbon does not move with the wave, but energy moves through the ribbon nonetheless.* What does this suggest about the movement of a wave? *Energy moves through the water but the water itself does not move forward with the wave.* L1

# 2 TEACH

## Tying to Previous Knowledge

Arrange students in small groups to create diagrams showing how heat from the sun creates convection currents that cause wind. Have each group share its diagram with the class. Explain to students that they will now learn how wind affects waves. **COOP LEARN** L2 LEP

**Theme Connection** This section focuses on the theme of energy. Students will learn that wind provides the energy that produces most waves in an ocean. In the Investigate on page 276, students will see how wind affects the height of waves.

## Section Objectives

- Explain the relationship between wind and waves.
- Differentiate between the movement of water particles in a wave and the movement of wave energy.
- Explain the cause of tides.
- Discuss ways in which organisms are adapted to life in intertidal zones.

## Key Terms

*intertidal zone*

## Waves

It's a great day for the beach. You've protected yourself from the sun and spread out your blanket. With your radio to your left and a can of soda to your right, you sit and watch the waves roll in.

Water waves are movements in which the water alternately rises and falls. Water waves have a lot in common with light waves and sound waves. You may remember that all waves have a crest and a trough and that waves can be measured in terms of height and length. These wave characteristics are shown in **Figure 9-3**. But what causes water waves to form, and why are some waves very tall, while others are barely ripples?

### Find Out! ACTIVITY

#### How do waves move?

**What To Do**

1. Fill a clear plastic storage container or a glass baking dish with water.

2. Place a cork in the middle of the container. Use tape to mark the approximate location of the cork on each side of the container.

3. At one end of the container, gently lower and raise a small wooden block in and out of the water to create waves. Record *in your Journal* your observations of the effect on the cork.

**Conclude and Apply**

How and where does the cork move? Explain.

## Program Resources

**Study Guide,** p. 31
**Multicultural Connections,** p. 21, Riding the Ocean Waves L1

# How Waves Move

When you watch a wave, it looks like the water is moving forward with the wave. The water is moving, but not in the way you may think.

Water waves actually consist of two motions. One is the forward progress of the energy of the wave. The other is the circular motion of the water particles this energy displaces as it passes by. These two motions are shown in **Figure 9-2**. The activity you did with the cork demonstrates that as the crest of a wave passes, water particles are lifted and moved briefly forward before they sink back down to their original position. The cork, along with the water, was only temporarily moved as the energy of the wave passed by.

## ■ How Waves Break

Have you ever heard the sound of waves tumbling on the beach? You cannot hear waves as they move over the ocean. Only when they break do they make sound. What do you think causes a wave to break? **Figure 9-1** illustrates the cause.

**Figure 9-1**

You may have noticed that, unless the wind is very strong, waves out at sea roll instead of break. In shallower waters, the water at the bottom of the wave rubs against the ocean floor, and the friction slows the wave down. The wave gets taller and narrower, until it is so tall, it breaks.

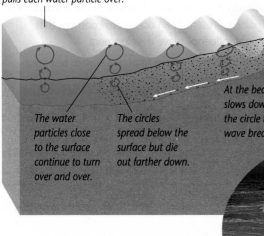

Wind blowing over the water surface pulls each water particle over.

(Beach)

The water particles close to the surface continue to turn over and over.

The circles spread below the surface but die out farther down.

At the beach, the movement slows down. The top part of the circle falls down, and the wave breaks.

The immense power of pounding waves changes the face of rocky coastlines.

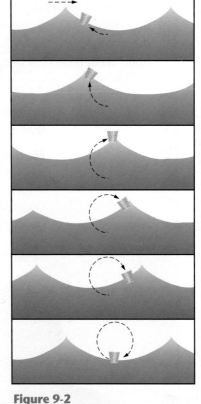

**Figure 9-2**

This wave's energy briefly draws the cork up to its top, or crest. Then the cork drifts back down to the bottom, or trough. How far has the cork traveled?

**275**

## Visual Learning

**Figure 9-2  How far has the cork traveled?** *The cork's total displacement is zero.*

### Student Text Question

**What do you think causes a wave to break?** *The friction of water against the ocean floor.*

## Find Out!

### How do waves move?

**Time needed**  20 minutes

**Materials**  clear plastic storage containers, corks, tape, small wooden blocks, water

**Thinking Processes**  observing and inferring, recognizing cause and effect, modeling

**Purpose**  To infer that as the crest of a wave passes, water moves up and down.

**Preparation**  The wooden blocks must be smaller than the storage containers.

### Teaching the Activity

**Troubleshooting**  Caution students to move the wooden block gently.

**Student Journal**  Suggest that students draw a diagram in their journals of how the wave and cork move. L1

### Expected Outcome

Students will observe that the cork does not move forward with the waves.

### Conclude and Apply

The cork moves up and then down as each wave passes.

### ✔ Assessment

**Oral**  Ask students to describe their observations of the cork's movement and infer how water particles in waves move. Have students prepare oral reports on how waves move. Use the Performance Task Assessment List for Oral Presentations in the **PAMSS**, page 71. L1

### Meeting Individual Needs

**Physically Challenged**  A physically challenged student can make a model that shows how waves move by working with a partner to complete the Find Out activity on page 274. Make sure that the partner allows the physically challenged student to do as much of the activity as he or she is able. The partner may need to assist with marking the location of the cork or moving the block in and out of the water. The physically challenged student should observe the effect of the waves on the cork. Have partners interpret the data together, completing the Conclude and Apply question as a team. **COOP LEARN**

I

9-

Pl

Ti

Pu
wi

Pr
inf
eff
ing
ex
tro

M
far
or
we
pla
ric

Pr
so

Te

Pr
he
an
ab
m
sh
th

Sa
de
fro
we
th
wi

Pe
de
w

Po
de
at
w
ho
ar
fo

St
de
th

# How Waves Form

In the ocean, waves are usually caused by the wind. The same stiff breeze that uproots your beach umbrella causes waves to form. As wind blows across a body of water, friction causes the water to move along with it. With enough wind speed, the water will pile up on itself and form a wave.

Once a wave forms, it will continue to travel over long distances, even after the wind stops blowing. The waves you see at the beach may have originated many thousands of kilometers away.

As you learned in the Investigate, the height of wind-generated waves depends on the speed of the wind as well as the length of time the wind blows.

A third factor that affects wave height is the distance over which the wind blows. The greater the distance, the higher the wave. This is why waves on the oceans can reach greater heights than waves on smaller bodies of water.

Another way waves can form is by underwater earthquakes. These waves, called tsunamis, can reach enormous heights. Some have been over 30 meters high! The energy to create such large waves comes from the movement of the ocean floor, rather than wind.

**Figure 9-3**

To find wave length (L), it is necessary to locate comparable points on two waves next to each other and measure the distance between them. In this diagram, what points are being used? What points are used to measure wave height (H)?

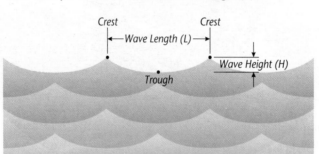

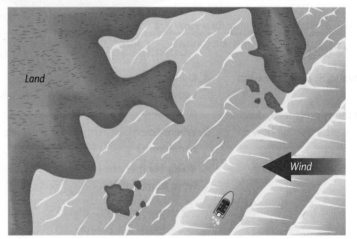

**Figure 9-4**

Even though the wind speed is the same, wave size varies greatly in this diagram. Why do you think the waves on the shore side of the peninsula are smaller than the waves on the sea side?

# Tides

If you have ever spent an entire day at the seashore, then you have probably seen the tides. Tides are long, slow waves that result in an alternate rise and fall of the surface level of the ocean. Tides can change the sea level by as much as 15 meters (50 feet). As you can imagine, such a drop in sea level can leave crabs, starfish, and other sea organisms stranded in puddles called tidal pools.

Tides are mainly an ocean phenomenon; people who live inland rarely observe tides on lakes and ponds. Even the largest lakes don't contain the volume of water necessary to be affected by the same forces that cause water levels along coastal areas to rise and fall. What are the forces that cause tides?

## ■ The Gravitational Pull of the Moon

Tides are caused by the gravitational attraction among the sun, the moon, and Earth. The gravitational force of the moon pulls on all parts of Earth including the oceans. **Figure 9-6** on page 282 shows how the moon's gravity affects the oceans.

**Figure 9-5**

**Ⓐ** *Mont-Saint-Michel at High Tide*
At high tide, the Mont-Saint-Michel, a large rock peninsula off the northwest coast of France, looks like an island. Why do you suppose the tides at the Mont-Saint-Michel once played a part in its strategic defense?

**Ⓑ** *Mont-Saint-Michel at Low Tide*
As soon as high tide is reached, the water begins to go out again. At low tide, the island is connected to the mainland and tourists drive up the rock to sightsee. Why do you suppose they have to keep an eye on the tide schedule?

9-1 Waves and Tides **279**

**Uncovering Preconceptions**
Ask students to estimate the wavelengths of tides. Most students will not realize that the average wavelength is 10,000 km.

**Content Background**
Tell students that the tides have been used to provide power for centuries. In the 1700s, for example, tidal mills along the coast of Europe trapped incoming tidal water in a reservoir. At high tide the sluices were closed. As the tide fell, the water escaped by propelling a water wheel. The same principle was used in a power station built in La Rance, France, about 30 years ago. Today, it generates about 240,000 kw at peak output, enough to power the city.

**Student Text Question**
What are the forces that cause tides? *The gravitational forces among the earth, moon, and sun.*

### Visual Learning

**Figure 9-5** Help students learn to identify the effects of tidal shifts by directing their attention to the photographs which show the difference between high and low tide at Mont-Saint-Michel. Ask how these clear shifts in tides might affect the area. *Students might suggest that they had an impact on fishing, shipping, and water travel. They might also infer that the dramatic shift in tides attracts tourists, as is the case in the Bay of Fundy, for instance.* L2
**Why do you suppose the tides at the Mont-Saint-Michel once played a part in its strategic defense?** *At high tide, the only access would be by boat.* **Why do you suppose they have to keep an eye on the tide schedule?** *At high tide the island becomes cut off from the mainland, preventing tourists from getting back.*

**280** **Chapter 9** Ocean Water and Life

**Theme Connection** Students will learn how the ebb and flow of the tides create an ecosystem known as the intertidal zone, where a variety of organisms interact. The interdependency between these organisms and the tides reinforces the theme of interaction and systems.

## Visual Learning

**Figure 9-7 What is the effect on the tides when the sun, Earth, and moon are lined up?** *High tides are higher, and low tides are lower.*

## Content Background

Explain that the wave crest closest to the moon is called direct tide; the crest on the opposite side of Earth is called opposite tide. Although the high and low waters in the Atlantic Ocean are generally about the same height, in other bodies of water the heights of the tides vary greatly. This is especially true in the Bay of Fundy, for example.

**Activity** If your school is located near an ocean, have students determine the times of low and high tides. Then have students record the position of the moon each day and relate it to the high and low tides. It may be possible to obtain tidal information from coastal weather stations, newspapers, or Navy or Coast Guard installations if you do not live near a seacoast. L1 P

## Teacher F.Y.I.

Point out that at most shores throughout the world, two high and low tides occur every lunar day. The average length of a lunar day is 24 hours, 50 minutes, and 28 seconds.

**Figure 9-6**

As with all forces, there is a pair of forces affecting ocean tides. One of the forces, gravity, pulls the moon and Earth closer together. The other force acts to keep them apart. The second force is a result of Earth's movement around the common center of mass between the Earth and moon. This interaction of forces causes both tidal bulges. While gravity causes oceans to bulge towards the moon, the second force creates the tidal bulge on the opposite side of Earth.

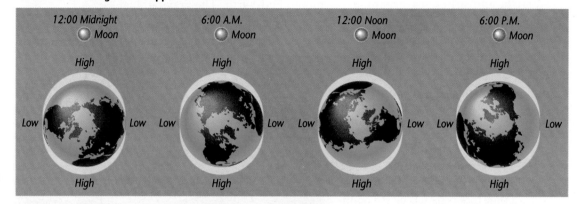

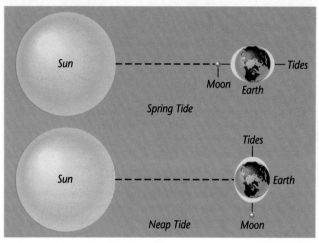

**Figure 9-7**

*Spring and Neap Tides*

This figure demonstrates the sun's effect on the moon's gravitational pull on Earth. What is the effect on the tides when the sun, Earth, and moon are lined up?

**280** **Chapter 9** Ocean Water and Life

Looking at **Figure 9-6** might lead you to think that a high tide should occur at a location when the moon is directly overhead. But high tides occur from four to six hours later than that. The delay is due to the interference of continents, inertia of the water, friction, and the distance the water must travel to form a tidal bulge. Thus, by the time high tide occurs, the moon is no longer overhead.

The sun strengthens or weakens the moon's effects. When the moon, Earth, and the sun are aligned, high tides are higher and low tides are lower than normal. These are called spring tides. When the moon, Earth, and the sun form a right angle, high tides are lower and low tides are higher than normal. These are called neap tides. Spring tides and neap tides are shown in **Figure 9-7**.

**Activity** Have students find out how one of the following hydrologic instruments works: drift bottle, neutrally buoyant float, or swallow float. Then invite students to work in small groups to build a working model of one of these instruments. When all the models are complete, have students hold an invention fair to demonstrate their instruments. You may wish to invite students from other classes, administration, family members, and community members to see the inventions. **COOP LEARN** L3 P

## Life in The Intertidal Zone

You may think that few organisms could live in an area that is pounded by waves and raked over by rocks and sand day after day.

However, a wide variety of plants and animals thrive in the **intertidal zone**, the area of a coastline between high and low tide. For the organisms that live in the intertidal zone, it's a dangerous way of life. They are threatened daily with the possibility of being dried up, eaten by birds and other animals, or washed out to sea. But the intertidal organisms have adapted to these conditions in some surprising ways.

**Figure 9-8**

*Life in Different Tidal Zones*

The intertidal zone is one of Earth's ecosystems. In this rocky intertidal zone, you can see the shoreline along which oysters, mussels, and barnacles grip the rocks so tightly that even storm waves can't pry them loose. What three things do you suppose these animals' hard shells protect them from? Since they don't move, how do you suppose they get food?

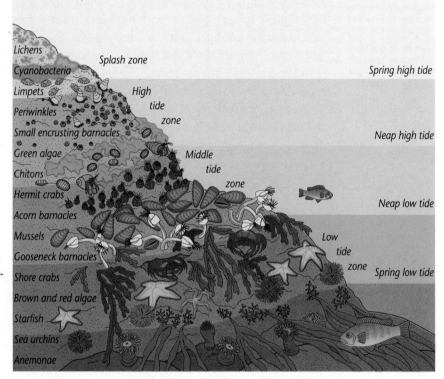

Lichens
Cyanobacteria
Limpets
Periwinkles
Small encrusting barnacles
Green algae
Chitons
Hermit crabs
Acorn barnacles
Mussels
Gooseneck barnacles
Shore crabs
Brown and red algae
Starfish
Sea urchins
Anemonae

Splash zone
High tide zone
Middle tide zone
Low tide zone

Spring high tide
Neap high tide
Neap low tide
Spring low tide

### check your UNDERSTANDING

1. How does wind affect water waves?
2. What effect does the moon have on Earth's oceans?
3. Describe the living conditions in the intertidal zone and name two characteristics that enable animals to survive there.
4. **Apply** When a wave passes, why do harbor markers bob up and down in the water?

### check your UNDERSTANDING

1. Waves are usually caused by the wind.
2. The gravitational force of the moon pulls the oceans to form two tidal bulges.
3. The intertidal zone is exposed at low tide and under water at high tide. Some animals burrow or have shells to keep their bodies moist at low tide. Other animals attach themselves to objects to keep from being washed away at high tide.
4. The water particles travel in a circular pattern, ending where they started and carrying floating objects in the same way.

**Visual Learning**

**Figure** 9-8 Have students identify the animals that are found in the intertidal zone. **What three things do you suppose these animals' hard shells protect them from?** *Predators, heat from the sun, and sand and rocks washing up on shore.* **Since they don't move, how do you suppose they get food?** *Food is washed in by the tides.*

# 3 ASSESS

## Check for Understanding

Before students answer the Check Your Understanding questions, have students work in small groups to contrast the effects of the sun and moon on Earth's tides. COOP LEARN L2

## Reteach

Using an overhead projector, show students a picture of a wave. Ask students to brainstorm factors that affect the origin of the wave and explain how the wave displaces water and energy. L1

## Extension

Have students who have mastered the concepts in this section research tsunamis and explore why they cause so much destruction. Direct students to find out why tsunamis are mistakenly called "tidal waves." L3 P

# 4 CLOSE

## Activity

Have students work in small groups to create children's storybooks showing the relationship of winds, the moon, the sun, and Earth to the formation of waves and the movement of tides. L1 COOP LEARN P

# PREPARATION

## Concepts Developed

In this section, students will explore the origin and composition of ocean water. They will also learn how seawater sustains the organisms it contains.

## Planning the Lesson

Refer to the Chapter Organizer on pages 272A–B.

# 1 MOTIVATE

**Discussion** To help students recognize cause and effect, ask them to describe what Earth would be like without its oceans. At first, they may say that the world would be dry. After more thought, they may describe Earth as having no life as we know it. Finally, students should realize that even the weather patterns would be different without oceans. L1

# 2 TEACH

## Tying to Previous Knowledge

To help students relate what they will learn in this section to what they already know, have them work in small groups to make a diagram of the water cycle. Have them use these terms in their diagram: *condenses, falls as precipitation, collects in basins,* and *evaporates.* The following is a possible solution: **COOP LEARN** L2

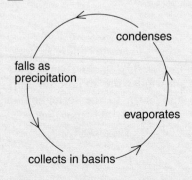

condenses

falls as precipitation

evaporates

collects in basins

# The Origin and Composition of Oceans

## Section Objectives

- Describe the origin of ocean water.
- Discuss the origin of ocean salts, and explain why the salinity of the ocean does not change.
- Describe the benefits that organisms get from seawater.

## Key Terms

*salinity*

## The Origin of Ocean Water

Ocean water covers nearly three-quarters of Earth's surface. Where do you think all this water came from? Scientists can only hypothesize about the origin of ocean water. They think that in Earth's younger years, it was much more volcanically active than it is today, and that the water in our oceans came from volcanoes.

Not only do volcanoes spew lava and ash, but they also give off water vapor, as you can see in **Figure 9-9.** About 4 billion years ago, water vapor from volcanoes began to accumulate in Earth's atmosphere. The vapor eventually cooled enough to condense. Precipitation began to fall, and oceans formed over millions of years as this water filled low areas. Now, almost three-fourths of Earth's surface is covered by water. But why is ocean water so salty?

**Figure 9-9**

*Origin of Ocean Water and Ocean Salt*

**A** As Earth's surface cooled about 4 billion years ago, it formed a thin crust. Water vapor and other gases from volcanic eruptions formed the early atmosphere. Cooling of Earth caused moisture to condense in the atmosphere, and storm clouds soaked the planet. It took tens of millions of years for these rains to gradually cease.

**B** As the clouds thinned and the sun again shone on Earth, volcanic eruptions and Earth's shifting crust molded the ocean basins.

## Program Resources

**Study Guide,** p. 32
**Laboratory Manual,** pp. 53–54, Salt Concentration in Ocean Water L2
**Concept Mapping,** p. 17, Salinity of Ocean Water L1
**Critical Thinking/Problem Solving,** p. 17, Freshwater Resources L2
**Science Discovery Activities,** 9-2, What Factors Affect Ocean Salinity?

## ENRICHMENT

**Activity** Help students relate what they have learned about oceans to how oceans are depicted in literature. Suggest that students read a novel, poem, short story, or nonfiction work about the ocean. Students can then write reviews of the work, relating its contents to what they have learned about oceans. L3 P

# The Origin of Ocean Salts

If you've ever accidentally swallowed a mouthful of ocean water, you could tell immediately that it was different from the water you drink at home. Ocean water contains many dissolved materials, including sodium, chlorine, silicon, and calcium. Where do these materials come from? Look at **Figure 9-10** to find out.

## Salinity

**Salinity** is a measure of the amount of solids—primarily salts—dissolved in ocean water. On average, every 1000 grams of ocean water contains about 35 grams of dissolved salts. Do the following experiment to compare the characteristics of different saltwater solutions.

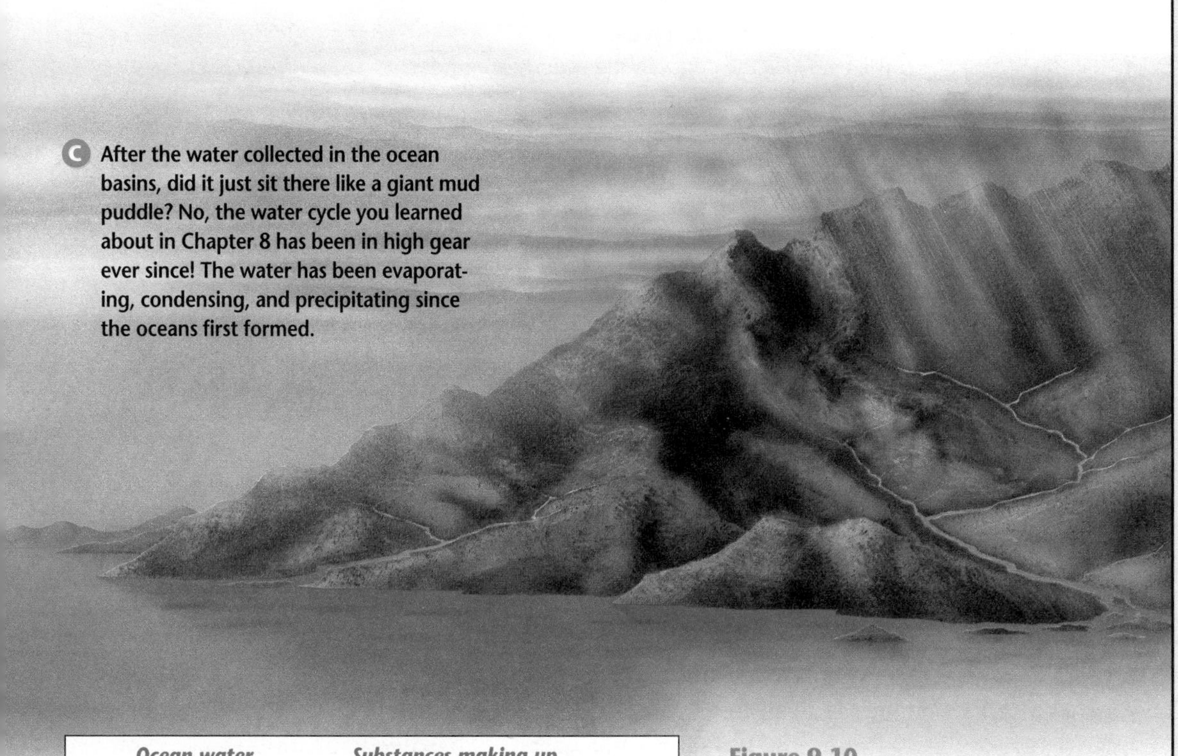

**C** After the water collected in the ocean basins, did it just sit there like a giant mud puddle? No, the water cycle you learned about in Chapter 8 has been in high gear ever since! The water has been evaporating, condensing, and precipitating since the oceans first formed.

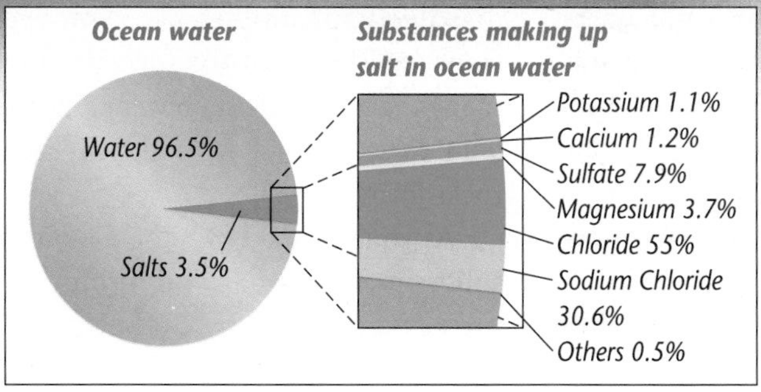

Ocean water
Substances making up salt in ocean water
Water 96.5%
Salts 3.5%
Potassium 1.1%
Calcium 1.2%
Sulfate 7.9%
Magnesium 3.7%
Chloride 55%
Sodium Chloride 30.6%
Others 0.5%


**Figure 9-10**

The constant runoff of water gradually dissolved many elements and minerals, depositing them in the oceans. Other elements came from the atmosphere and volcanic eruptions. As they collected, the oceans became saltier until they reached their current salinity. The most abundant sea salts are chlorine and sodium. They combine to form halite which you might know better as common table salt.



**Theme Connection** Throughout the history of Earth, changes in its crust and atmosphere have led to the formation of its oceans and the concentration of salts in them. Today, that concentration remains relatively stable since the amount of both water and minerals in the oceans is more or less constant. Thus this section supports the theme of stability and change.

### Content Background

Explain to students that seawater whips into more whitecaps than fresh water because the salt content produces more air bubbles and sustains them longer.

### Visual Learning

**Figure 9-9** To help students recognize cause and effect, have them read the figure captions and describe the effects volcanic eruptions had on the newly formed Earth. *Eruptions released gases, which formed an atmosphere and condensed to form the oceans. Eruptions also released lava, which helped to mold the ocean basins.*

### ENRICHMENT

**Research/Activity** Have students formulate models that show how a salinometer works, by looking at encyclopedias, reference texts, and related science articles. Arrange students in groups to build working models of this instrument. Ask each group to summarize its work and demonstrate its model to the class. **COOP LEARN** P L3

### Program Resources

**Take Home Activities,** p. 17, Drinking Water from Salt Water L1

**How It Works,** p. 15, Desalination by Flash Distillation L3

**Making Connections: Technology & Society,** p. 21, Salt Marshes L3

**Inquiry Questions** Where does the calcium in seashells come from? *The calcium is leached from rocks and minerals by streams and rivers, whose water eventually flows into the ocean. Animals remove the calcium from the water to make their shells.* **What happens to the wastes of organisms that live in the ocean?** *The wastes dissolve in seawater and some are then used as nutrients by other organisms.*

## Find Out! ACTIVITY

### How does salt affect the density of water?

**What To Do**

1. Carefully stick a thumbtack into the eraser end of a pencil.
2. Fill a tall, narrow jar 1 cm from the top with water.
3. Place the pencil in the water, eraser end first. Mark the water level on the floating pencil with a grease pencil.
4. Add 1 tablespoon of salt to the water, and stir until the salt is completely dissolved. Predict *in your Journal* where the water level on the pencil will be. Place the pencil in the water and mark the new water level. How did your prediction compare with your observations? How can you explain the difference in water levels?
5. Add another tablespoon of salt and find out what the level will be.

**Conclude and Apply**

Is seawater more or less dense than fresh water?

As this experiment showed, the saltier the water, the higher the pencil floated. This is because the presence of salt in water causes the water to become denser, and objects float more easily in dense water.

Generally, the salinity of ocean water does not change. Although substances are added constantly by rivers, volcanoes, and the atmosphere, they are being removed at the same rate by plants and animals, or they are forming solids on the ocean bottom.

Some marine animals use calcium to form bones, while others use silicon and calcium to form shells. Because there are so many sea plants and animals, calcium, silicon and other minerals are constantly removed from seawater.

Another way minerals and other dissolved substances are removed from seawater is in the formation of manganese nodules. Look at **Figure 9-11** to see how these golf ball-sized rocks form.

As you've found out, the dissolved solids in seawater are important for the survival of many ocean organisms. For land animals and plants,

water. Have students explain why there are differences. Students could then form small groups to research and present oral reports that explain issues such as how life jackets help you float, why lean muscular people have a harder time floating than people with more body fat, why it's easier to float when your lungs are full of air, and so on. Students could also include information about water safety in their reports. Use the Performance Task Assessment List for Oral Presentations in the **PAMSS**, page 71. L1 P COOP LEARN

### ENRICHMENT

**Discussion** Help students recognize cause and effect by having them discuss the following question. How can the rate of evaporation affect density differences in large bodies of water? *High rates of evaporation increase the concentration of salts in water and, hence, increase the water's density.* L2 however, seawater salinity can be harmful. In order to drink the water in Earth's oceans, the salts and other solids must first be removed. In the next Investigate, you will explore one method of removing salt from salt water.

**Recognizing Cause and Effect**

Discuss what would happen to the composition of seawater if all organisms having bones or shells suddenly died. If you need help, refer to the **Skill Handbook** on page 684.

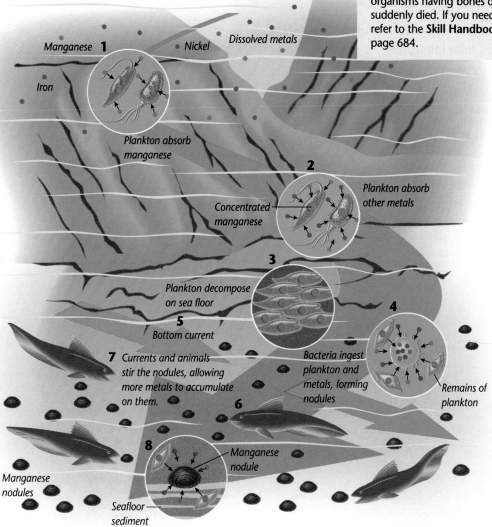

Manganese **1**
Nickel
Dissolved metals
Iron
Plankton absorb manganese

**2**
Concentrated manganese
Plankton absorb other metals

**3**
Plankton decompose on sea floor

**5**
Bottom current

**4**
Bacteria ingest plankton and metals, forming nodules
Remains of plankton

**7**
Currents and animals stir the nodules, allowing more metals to accumulate on them.

**6**

**8**
Manganese nodule
Manganese nodules
Seafloor sediment

**Figure 9-11**

*Manganese Nodules*
What's at the heart of manganese nodules? Maybe a shark's tooth—or some plankton! How do they get there? Solids in sea water—mainly oxides of iron and manganese—precipitate out of their solution and fall to the ocean floor. But how the metals concentrate is still a mystery. One theory is shown above. These minerals then collect around a small object until they've formed a rounded rock the size of a golf or tennis ball.

9-2   The Origin and Composition of Oceans   **285**

---

The calcium content of the seawater would increase. [L1]

**Activity** Encourage students to suggest ways to allocate resources wisely by informing them that there are many valuable mineral resources on the ocean floor. Arrange students in small groups to learn more about these deposits and to share their findings with the class. In addition to presenting reports, students might also want to bring in pictures, slides, articles, and samples of products that use ores mined from the seas. After completing the activity, divide the class in half and have teams debate how these valuable resources should be allocated. Who now has the rights to these deposits? Is this system equitable? Students might also want to look into the United Nations Law of the Sea conference that began in 1958. [L1]
**COOP LEARN** [P]

**Inquiry Question** Why is ocean water low in silicon and calcium? *Many marine organisms use these elements in their life processes, thus removing them from the ocean.* [L2]

### Visual Learning

**Figure 9-11** Have students sequence one way the earth recycles its minerals by making an events chain that shows the movement of manganese from land to the ocean floor. The events chain should also show how these manganese deposits might, over a period of billions of years, end up on land again. Use the Performance Task Assessment List for Events Chains in the **PAMSS**, page 91. [P] [L1]

---

### ENRICHMENT

**Research** Have students use research materials to explore early beliefs about the ocean. Point out that by the 1400s, most people knew that the world was round, but they didn't agree on how big the world was or how wide the oceans were. People thought Earth included only the continents of Europe, Africa, and Asia, and one great "Ocean Sea," which we today call the Atlantic Ocean. Ask students to explain why they think sailors often refused to sail in unknown waters. Have students find pictures of early maps. Ask students to suggest how religion, politics, and trade influenced beliefs about Earth.

9-2   The Origin and Composition of Oceans   **285**

INVESTIGATE!

9-2 Fresh Water From Salt Water

## Planning the Activity

**Time needed** 60–90 minutes

**Purpose** To model one way to remove salt from salt water.

**Process Skills** observing and inferring, recognizing cause and effect, formulating models, measuring in SI

**Materials** See reduced student text.

**Preparation** Check that the plastic tubing has been cut and bent and fits the holes in the rubber stopper.

## Teaching the Activity

**Process Reinforcement** Encourage students to use their observations to infer what would remain in the flask and the beaker if they boiled all of the water out of the flask.

**Safety** Make sure students wear goggles, and tell them to be careful when using the hot plate. Glassware should be allowed to cool before it is moved.

**Troubleshooting** Stress that students be careful when inserting plastic tubing into the stopper and the rubber tubing into the plastic tubing.

**Student Journal** Have students predict in their journals whether the water in the beaker will be more or less salty than the water in the flask. Have students compare their predictions with their observations. [L1]

# Fresh Water From Salt Water

*In this activity, you'll learn one way of removing salt from salt water.*

## Problem

How can you make drinking water from ocean water?

## Materials

| | | |
|---|---|---|
| pan balance | table salt | water |
| 2 500-mL beakers | 1000-mL flask | 1-hole rubber |
| rubber tubing | hot plate | stopper |
| cardboard | ice | shallow pan |
| polyethylene | glycerine | towel |
| plastic tubing | scissors | washers |
| conductivity tester | | |

## Safety Precautions

Be careful when using the hot plate. It should be cool before moving glassware.

## What To Do

**1** Be sure the glassware is clean before beginning this experiment. *Measure* and dissolve 18 g of table salt into a beaker containing 500 mL of water. Test the solution with a conductivity tester. Record the results *in your Journal*. Pour the soulution into the flask.

**2** Rub a small amount of glycerine on both ends of the plastic tubing. Hold the tubing with a towel, and gently slide it into the stopper and rubber tubing as shown in the photo.

## Program Resources

**Activity Masters,** pp. 41–42, Investigate 9-2

**Science Discovery Activities,** 9-3, "Water, Water Everywhere . . ."

**A**

**B**

**C**

**3** Insert the tube-stopper assembly into the flask. Make sure the plastic tubing is above the surface of the solution.

**4** Cut a small hole in the cardboard. Insert the free end of the rubber tubing through the hole. Be sure to keep the tubing away from the hot plate.

**5** Place the flask on a hot plate, but do not turn on the hot plate yet. Set the beaker in a shallow pan filled with ice.

**6** Place the cardboard over a clean beaker. Add several washers to the cardboard to hold it in place.

**7** Turn on the hot plate. Bring the solution to a boil. Observe the flask and the beaker. Continue boiling until the solution is almost boiled away. Turn off the hot plate, remove the flask, and let them cool.

**8** Test the water in the beaker with the conductivity tester. Plain water does not conduct electricity as well as salt water. What kind of water can you *infer* is in the beaker?

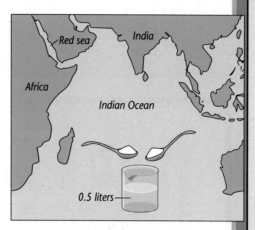

*The Red Sea's salinity is equal to two teaspoons of salt dissolved in 1 pint of water.*

## Analyzing

**1.** What happened to the water in the flask as you boiled the solution?

**2.** What happened inside the beaker? Explain.

**3.** What remains in the flask?

## Concluding and Applying

**4.** Explain how evaporation can be used to obtain fresh water from salty water.

**5.** ~~Going Further~~ *Infer* how this process could be used to extract minerals from seawater.

Students will observe how salt can be removed from salt water through distillation. Using conductivity, students should infer that the water in the beaker is plain water.

**Answers to** Analyzing/ Concluding and Applying

**1.** The volume of water decreased.

**2.** Water began to fill the beaker as the water vapor condensed.

**3.** concentrated salt water

**4.** Fresh water is evaporated from salt water, leaving behind salt.

**5.** Evaporation and condensation can be used to remove fresh water from sea water leaving the minerals behind.

## ✔ Assessment

**Process** Have students create scientific drawings showing the causes and effects of evaporation and condensation. Student drawings could show energy and state changes. Use the Performance Task Assessment List for Scientific Drawing in the **PAMSS,** page 55. L1 P LEP

### Meeting Individual Needs

**Visually Impaired** Assist visually impaired students in completing the Investigate activity on by pairing them with fully sighted students. Have the visually impaired partner help set up the apparatus. The fully sighted student can observe the results in the flask and beaker, test the conductivity of the water in the beaker, and note what remains on the sides of the flask. Have partners interpret the data as a team. **COOP LEARN**

## Ocean Water Supports Life

You've already seen how marine organisms need the calcium and silicon dissolved in ocean water to survive. Oxygen and carbon dioxide, also necessary for life, are dissolved in ocean water too. Animals use oxygen to breathe. Protists, such as the green algae shown in **Figure 9-12B**, need carbon dioxide to photosynthesize.

In the next section, you will learn about how changes in the salinity and temperature of ocean water affect the way it moves.

**Figure 9-12**

**A** A coral reef

## A Long Drink of Water

**Y**ou just discovered in the Investigate a method for removing salt from seawater to produce fresh water. Desalination plants use a similar method for producing fresh water. These plants are an important source of fresh water for people living in desert areas, near an ocean.

Although there are many different ways desalination can occur, the most efficient is a process called flash distillation. **Figure 9-13** is a diagram of a flash distillation plant. Follow the diagram as you read how it works. It all begins by heating sea water to around 80° Celsius (A). The hot water then enters a series of chambers (B) which have very little air pressure in them. The low air pressure causes some of the water to evaporate into water vapor. Just

*A distillation plant*

**288** Chapter 9 Ocean Water and Life

 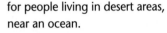

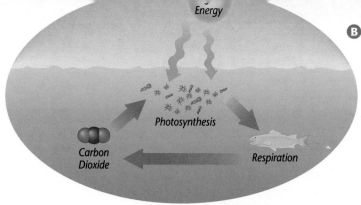

**B** Through photosynthesis, phytoplankton take in dissolved carbon dioxide and release oxygen, using energy from sunlight. Other organisms then use this oxygen and release carbon dioxide in the process of respiration.

## 3 ASSESS

### Check for Understanding

To help students answer the Apply question, remind them that green algae produce oxygen.

### Reteach

Arrange students in small groups. Have each group develop an operational definition of seawater by writing a "recipe" for making seawater, using the elements detailed in this lesson. Suggest they use cooking terms such as *add*, *combine*, and *blend*.
**L1** **COOP LEARN**

### Extension

Have students who have already mastered the concepts in this section use reference materials to research and report on chemical oceanography. **L3**

## 4 CLOSE

### Discussion

Show students a seashell and ask students to explain where the calcium in the shell came from. *Calcium was dissolved from rocks and minerals and then carried by rivers into the ocean. The animal then removed it to make its shell.* **L1**

## check your UNDERSTANDING

1. What role do scientists think volcanoes played in the formation of the oceans?
2. What makes ocean water salty, and where do these substances come from? Why doesn't the salinity of the ocean change?
3. Discuss how organisms benefit from ocean water and its dissolved substances.
4. **Apply** What might happen to sea animals if all the green algae in the ocean died? Explain.

as in the Investigate you just did, this water vapor doesn't contain the salts and other dissolved elements found in seawater. The vapor then condenses on cold coils (C) at the top of the chamber. The condensed fresh water drips into a collector (D) and is ready for drinking. As the sea water moves from chamber to chamber, it becomes a more concentrated brine.

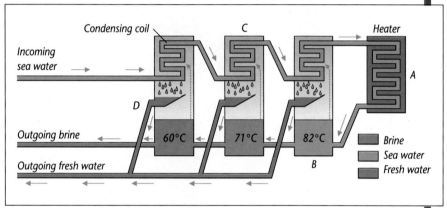

**Figure 9-13**

### What Do You Think?

Imagine you live in a desert region along the ocean. You are on the committee to investigate options for how to meet your community's increasing need for fresh water. You suggest a desalination plant would be a worthwhile investment. Before you present your plan to the city council, brainstorm some ways to improve the benefits of the desalination plant. How could you heat the water economically? What could you do with the brine that's produced? How would you protect the plant from pollution such as oil spills? Assemble your ideas in a report to city council.

9-2 The Origin and Composition of Oceans **289**

## check your UNDERSTANDING

1. Water vapor released into the atmosphere by volcanoes cooled, condensed, and precipitated. Over millions of years, this process filled the ocean basins with water.

2. Sodium is dissolved in river water and chlorine comes from volcanoes. The elements combine to form sodium chloride, a salt. It is this compound and a few others that make ocean water salty. The salinity remains constant because the salts are removed from the water at the same rate they are added.

3. Some animals use the calcium and silicon in ocean water to make shells. Ocean plants need carbon dioxide in ocean water for photosynthesis. The water itself provides nutrients, washes away wastes, and provides the moisture marine animals need to live.

4. Green algae produce oxygen. If the algae died, the oxygen level of the water would decrease and sea animals would suffocate.

# PREPARATION

## Concepts Developed

Students have read how sea-water supports the organisms that it contains. Here, they will complete the unit by learning about currents and upwellings and find out how currents affect organisms.

## Planning the Lesson

Refer to the Chapter Organizer on pages 272A–B.

# 1 MOTIVATE

**Demonstration** Students can infer how currents flow by observing the following demonstration. Materials needed are a glass, a spoon, 250 mL of milk, and chocolate syrup. Pour the milk into the glass. Add the chocolate syrup and stir. Point out the dark swirl of chocolate as you stir. Tell students that the swirl is similar to ocean currents. Ask students if currents flow the same way that waves do. *no* How are currents different? *The water particles appear to flow in one direction in a current, not in circles like waves.* L1

# 2 TEACH

## Tying to Previous Knowledge

To help students recognize cause and effect ask them to study the map on page 303, which shows the earth's surface currents. Ask students why sailors would want to know the location of currents such as the Gulf Stream. *Sailing with the current would speed their journey; sailing against it would impede them. Students might also realize that currents affect climate and fishing.* L1

---

## Section Objectives

- Contrast surface currents and density currents.
- Discuss ways that ocean currents affect organisms.
- Describe the movement of water in an upwelling.

## Key Terms

*surface current*
*plankton*
*nekton*
*density current*
*upwelling*

---

## 9-3 Ocean Currents

## What Are Currents?

When you stir chocolate syrup into a glass of milk, you make currents. These currents are shown by the dark swirls of chocolate made by stirring with your spoon.

Oceans have currents too. You know that water particles in ocean waves do not travel forward. Rather, they move in a circle as the energy of the wave temporarily displaces them. In currents, however, water particles flow in one direction like giant rivers in the ocean.

**Figure 9-14**

*Current Movement Around the World*
**Many factors influence the directions and temperatures of the ocean currents that travel about Earth. In the figure, examine the currents north and south of the equator. Which move clockwise? Counterclockwise?**

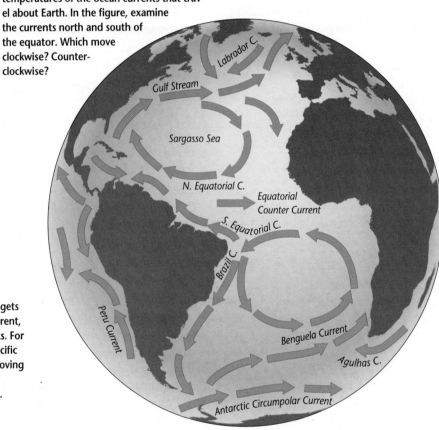

**A** When a continent gets in the way of a current, the current deflects. For example, in the Pacific Ocean, currents moving west are deflected northward by Asia.

**290** Chapter 9 Ocean Water and Life

---

## Program Resources

**Study Guide,** p. 33
**Making Connections: Integrating Sciences,** p. 21, Biology Mammals of the Deep L1
**Making Connections: Across the Curriculum,** p. 21, Amelia Earhart's Last Grand Adventure L2
**Critical Thinking/Problem Solving,** p. 5, Flex Your Brain

**Laboratory Manual,** pp. 55-56, Ocean Life L1
**Multicultural Connections,** p. 22, El Niño L1
**Transparency Master,** p. 39, and **Color Transparency,** Number 18, Ocean Currents L2

---

# Surface Currents

In the late 1760s, the American colonists noticed that it took their mail ships two weeks longer to travel from England to America than it took whaling ships to make the same trip. It was learned that the whalers knew of a place in the ocean where the water moved in a northeasterly direction. When they wanted to travel southwest from Europe to America, the whalers sailed outside this area.

The current was mapped so mail ship captains could avoid it on their way back to America. Because it seemed to flow out of the Gulf of Mexico, the current was named the Gulf Stream.

The Gulf Stream is one of several surface currents in Earth's oceans. A **surface current** is movement of water that affects only the upper few hundred meters of seawater. Most surface currents are caused by wind.

## ■ Surface Currents and Climates

If you live near a seacoast, how do you think the warm or cold currents off your coastline affect your climate? Do you know that currents can have an effect on you even if you don't live along the coast?

Iceland is located near the Arctic Circle, so you would expect it to have a very frigid climate. But the Gulf Stream flows past Iceland, carrying with it warm water from the Equator. The current's warm water heats the surrounding air, causing the entire country to have a surprisingly mild climate.

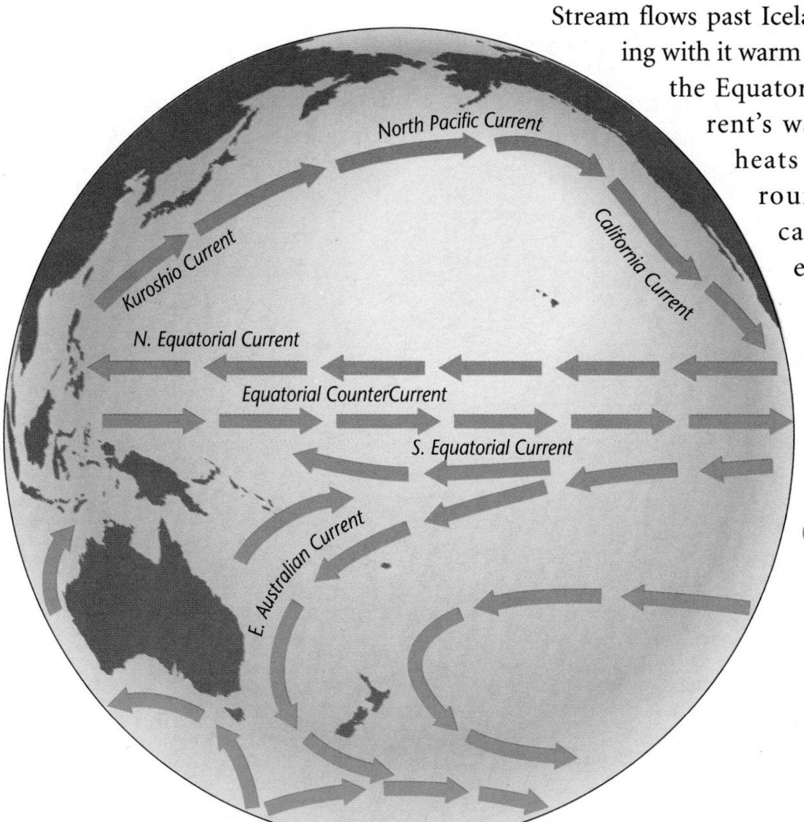

**B** Many surface currents on the western coasts of continents are cold because they generally originate in the cooler latitudes, far from the equator. What does this tell you about the probable temperature of currents on the eastern coasts?

*North Pacific Current*
*Kuroshio Current*
*California Current*
*N. Equatorial Current*
*Equatorial CounterCurrent*
*S. Equatorial Current*
*E. Australian Current*

9-3 Ocean Currents **291**

### Riding the Wind

Help students recognize the effect of wind on sailors by explaining that ancient explorers had many beliefs about the wind.

Chinese sailors thought a red moon meant a good, strong wind. Whistling mocked the devil and he answered the insult with wild winds, so whistling was believed to be good when winds were mild but deadly in a storm. If the gulls flew inland, there was sure to be a storm. Beliefs aside, the explorers knew a great deal about how the wind works. Have student groups research sailing and explain how the wind affected ships. Students should explain how sailors used the wind to stay on course and what happened when there was no wind.

**COOP LEARN** L1

**Activity** Have students research and classify the many medicines made from marine organisms. To share the results of their findings, have students create a chart showing various marine organisms, the medicines that can be made from them, and the diseases that are treated by the medicines. **L1** **P**

**Inquiry Question** Why is a fish considered plankton at one stage of its life and nekton at another stage? *When it is still inside an egg or is a young hatchling, it drifts with the surface currents and can be considered plankton. When it matures, a fish can move from one depth and place to another and is considered nekton.*

**Interpreting Scientific Illustrations**

The latitudes of San Diego, California, and Charleston, South Carolina, are exactly the same. However, the average yearly water temperature in the ocean off Charleston is much higher than the water temperature off San Diego. Use Figure 9-14 to help explain why. If you need help, refer to the **Skill Handbook** on page 691.

## ■ Surface Currents and Marine Organisms

Surface currents also greatly affect marine life. Most photosynthetic plants and protists live in the upper 140 meters of the ocean because this is about how far sunlight will penetrate ocean water. Most animals live where there are algae because of the food and oxygen the algae provide. Therefore, most marine organisms live where there are surface currents.

One way of classifying marine organisms is by how they move. Drifting organisms are called **plankton**. Most plankton are microscopic and depend largely on dissolved substances in the seawater for their survival. The currents carry nutrients to these organisms and carry the wastes away.

**Nekton** include all swimming forms of fish and other animals, from tiny herring to huge whales. Nekton are able to easily move from one depth to another. Their ability to move reduces the effects surface currents have on them. However, some animals use surface currents for migrating and searching for food.

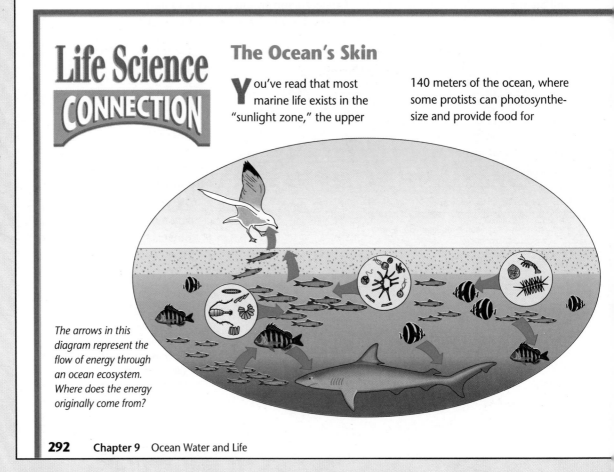

## Life Science CONNECTION

### The Ocean's Skin

You've read that most marine life exists in the "sunlight zone," the upper 140 meters of the ocean, where some protists can photosynthesize and provide food for

*The arrows in this diagram represent the flow of energy through an ocean ecosystem. Where does the energy originally come from?*

### Purpose

This Life Science Connection adds to Section 9-3 by describing some organisms that inhabit the ocean's surface.

### Content Background

Point out that one liter of seawater may contain as many as ten million diatoms, a type of one-celled algae that represent the primary food of the ocean. In recognition of their capacity to nourish, these diatoms are sometimes called "the grass of the sea." All land-dwelling creatures are in their debt as well, for the diatoms that teem in the upper few meters of the ocean make, through photosynthesis, much of the oxygen we breathe.

Diatoms can be divided into two basic types. The first are found most often near the ocean's surface. The second type inhabit freshwater streams and swamps.

### Teaching Strategy

Students can hone their skills at recognizing cause and effect by working in teams to discuss

**Figure 9-15**

Is there a pasture in the sea? Some people say there is—the huge masses of plankton on the ocean's surface. Plankton means "wandering"—why is this an appropriate name? Nekton means "swimming." Why is this name appropriate for the fishes swimming below the plankton?

**Across the Curriculum**

**Mathematics**

To provide students with practice converting SI units, use this exercise and Appendix A and Appendix B on pages 657–658.

Each adult blue whale can consume more than 1800 kg of krill a day. The whales can grow up to 30 meters in length and can weigh more than 136 000 kg. How many grams of krill can a blue whale consume in one day? How many centimeters long can a blue whale become? *A blue whale can consume 1.8 million grams of krill a day and can grow up to 3000 centimeters long.* L2

marine animals. A narrower, paper-thin habitat exists on the surface of the ocean that separates the water from the atmosphere. This microlayer or, "skin," is a rich ecological niche where thousands of insects, fish, crustacean larvae, protists, and monerans—most invisible to the naked eye—cluster near the water's surface.

### A Marine Nursery

Because of its special ability to nurture life, the surface serves as a nursery for many fish species. Billions of fish eggs float to the surface where they attach themselves with fat globules to the film until they hatch. Shellfish larvae seek the surface to feed on the microscopic plankton. Bacteria adhere to the underside of the surface film. Other organisms use air bubbles to float on the film.

### The Oceanic Buffet

This surface area is like a large dining room for multitudes of species. Tiny life-forms inhabiting the water's surface, invisible to the naked eye, are the base of an extensive food web. Small fish feed on these plankton, only to constitute a meal for larger and larger fish that swim upward to feed at the top. Seabirds feast by skimming food from the water's surface.

### You Try It!

You can see for yourself that water that appears clear and empty can be full of life. Take a trip to an ocean, pond, lake, or stream and collect some water in a glass jar. If possible, get some samples from different water sources.

Look at your samples through magnifying glasses and microscopes, slowly increasing the magnification as you view the samples.

Take a drop of water from one of your samples with an eyedropper. Make a slide and look through a high-powered microscope. How many more organisms can you find?

Draw pictures of what you see. Try to identify the organisms from a field guide.

**Visual Learning**

**Figure 9-15** **Plankton means "wandering"—why is this an appropriate name?** *Because plankton are organisms that drift.* **Nekton means "swimming." Why is this name appropriate for the fishes swimming below the plankton?** *Because nekton include fish and other animals that can swim.*

what influence people might have on the proliferation of the creatures that live in the ocean's "skin." Have each team share one example with the class. **COOP LEARN** L2

### Answers to
**You Try It!**

What students will see depends on whether they get their water samples from an ocean, pond, lake, or stream. Ocean water, for example, will be full of round *Centrales,* while pond, lake, and stream water will have many *Pennales.*

### Going Further ⫸

Help students recognize cause and effect as they work in small groups to research how the organisms that lived in the ocean created the world's petroleum supply. How did these organisms store their food supplies? Where did they go after they died? What forces caused the oil to coalesce into pools? Have students create poster-sized events chains to illustrate how petroleum formed. Use the Performance Task Assessment List for Events Chains in the **PAMSS,** page 91. L3 **COOP LEARN** P

## Content Background

Explain that oceans can be divided into three layers based on temperature. Heat in the surface layer is evenly distributed because of the mixing of waves and the turbulence of currents. The depth of this layer averages 200 to 300 meters below the surface. Below the surface layer is the thermocline, where the temperature is about 5°C. In the lowest layer, temperature decreases to about 1°C.

**Student Text Question**
**Can you think of something else besides temperature that might affect the density of seawater?** *Salinity*

## Explore!

### Can temperature affect water density?

**Time needed** 15 minutes

**Materials** large glass jars, warm water, food coloring, ice cubes

**Thinking Processes** observing and inferring, comparing and contrasting, recognizing cause and effect

**Purpose** To observe how temperature affects the density of water.

**Preparation** Use red, blue, or green food coloring for the most dramatic results.

### Teaching the Activity

**Demonstration** Show students how to squeeze one drop of food coloring at a time from the container. Remind them to follow the directions carefully, using one drop for the first part of the activity and two drops for the second half.

**Student Journal** Have students relate their observations to what happens when ocean water cools. L1

# Density Currents

Water below a few hundred meters is too deep to be affected by winds, and yet it also has currents. These currents are called density currents. A **density current** is movement of water that occurs when dense seawater moves toward an area of less dense seawater. What do you think would cause differences in the density of seawater?

## Explore! ACTIVITY

### Can temperature affect water density?

#### What To Do

1. Fill a large glass jar with warm water. Gently add a drop of food coloring in the center.

2. Now carefully float an ice cube on top of the food coloring. Observe for one minute. What happens to the food coloring?

3. Add two drops of food coloring directly on the ice cube to help you see what is happening. Record your observations *in your Journal.*

In the Explore activity, you saw that temperature affects the movement of water. The molecules in cold water are less active and are closer together than molecules in warm water, making the cold water more dense. Dense water sinks, forming a vertical current.

In the ocean, cold air near the North and South poles cools the water, causing it to become more dense than water in nonpolar areas. Can you think of something else besides temperature that might affect the density of seawater?

## Expected Outcome

Students will observe that the food coloring disperses rather uniformly in the warm water but tends to be carried downward when an ice cube is added. This happens because the ice cube cools part of the water, which becomes more dense and sinks.

## Answer to Question

2. The food coloring sinks.

## ✔ Assessment

**Process** Have student groups use research materials to explore the ocean's heat transfer system. Students could them make displays using photographs, drawings, and text to explain how the ocean transfers heat between its equatorial and polar regions. Displays should explain the roles of the sun, wind, and currents. Use the appropriate Performance Task Assessment List from the **PAMSS.** COOP LEARN L1 P

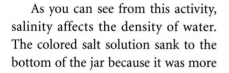

## Explore! ACTIVITY

### How are density and salinity related?

1. Fill a large jar three-quarters full with water at room temperature.

2. Mix several teaspoons of table salt into a small glass of water of the same temperature as the water in the jar.

3. Add a few drops of food coloring to the salt water and pour the solution very slowly and gently into the jar of water. Describe what happens *in your Journal*.

As you can see from this activity, salinity affects the density of water. The colored salt solution sank to the bottom of the jar because it was more dense than the fresh water around it. What do you think causes salinity differences in the ocean?

**Figure 9-16**

*Warm and Cold Currents*

**A** This diagram demonstrates the effect of temperature on sea water. Compare this to air in a freezer. At what latitudes is the surface water the coldest? Why might it then move away from its original location, producing density current?

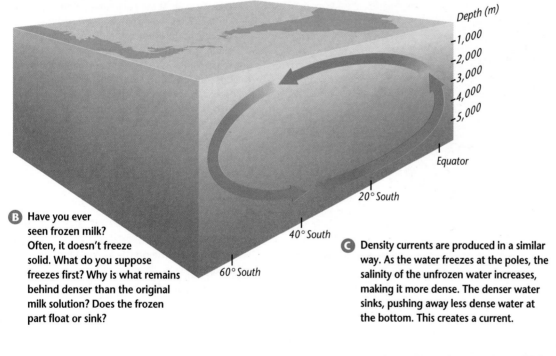

**B** Have you ever seen frozen milk? Often, it doesn't freeze solid. What do you suppose freezes first? Why is what remains behind denser than the original milk solution? Does the frozen part float or sink?

**C** Density currents are produced in a similar way. As the water freezes at the poles, the salinity of the unfrozen water increases, making it more dense. The denser water sinks, pushing away less dense water at the bottom. This creates a current.

### Visual Learning

**Figure 9-16 At what latitudes is the surface water the coldest?** *At 60–80 degrees North or South.* **Why might it then move away from its original location, producing density currents?** *Cold surface waters are more dense and sink.* **What do you suppose freezes first?** *The water.* **Why is what remains behind denser than the original milk solution?** *Because it contains milk solids.* **Does the frozen part float or sink?** *It floats.*

### Expected Outcome

Students will observe that the colored salt water sinks to the bottom and spreads out toward the sides of the container.

### ✔ Assessment

**Process** Reinforce students' ability to recognize cause and effect by having them explain how heat from the sun can result in an increase in salinity of ocean water and thus cause density currents. Have students work in groups to design experiments that explain this process. Use the Performance Task Assessment List for Designing an Experiment from the **PAMSS**, page 23. [L1] [P] **COOP LEARN**

## Explore!

### How are density and salinity related?

**Time needed** 15 minutes

**Materials** large jars, water at room temperature, table salt, food coloring, small glass

**Thinking Processes** observing and inferring, comparing and contrasting, recognizing cause and effect, making models

**Purpose** To observe how the salinity of water affects its density.

**Preparation** Have a strong cleaner on hand to remove any food coloring stains.

### Teaching the Activity

**Troubleshooting** Remind students that food coloring can stain hands and clothing. Caution them to be careful when they use it, and to wipe up any spills quickly.

**Student Journal** Have students predict in their journals what will happen when the salt water is added to the fresh water. [L1]

# 3 ASSESS

## Check for Understanding

To help students answer the Apply question, have them create a chart comparing the two types of currents.

## Reteach

Ask students why adding hot water to a bucket of cold water would result in a layer of warmer water over a layer of cooler water. *Because the hot water is less dense than the cold water, it remains on the top of the colder, denser water.* L1

## Extension

Have students who have mastered the concepts in this section research how the Coriolis effect affects surface currents in the Northern Hemisphere. L3

# 4 CLOSE

## Discussion

Ask students how density currents affect the circulation of water in the deeper parts of the ocean. *Cold water at the poles sinks and moves along the ocean bottom toward the equator.* L1

# Upwellings

In some regions of the world, the density current cycle is interrupted. This happens where strong, wind-driven surface currents carry warm surface water away from an area. In such an area, cold water from deep below rises to replace water at the surface. This upward movement of cold water is called an **upwelling**.

Whether your family makes its living from the ocean, or you occasionally visit the coast, or you have never even seen the ocean, the composition and movement of the ocean has a tremendous effect on your daily life. What would life on Earth be like without oceans?

**Figure 9-17**

If you roil up the water in a fish bowl, any food laying on the bottom will float back up. How does this phenomenon apply to the effect of warm wind in the diagram? How does it differ?

*Upwelling in Peru*
Northward along the Peruvian coast flows the Peru Current. At the same time, a transport of surface water away from the coast occurs because of the southeast trade winds blowing along the northern and central parts of the coast. Nutrients from the ocean floor are stirred up, enriching the diet of plankton in the surface water. The herringlike Peruvian anchoveta's diet is 99 percent plankton. How does this tie to the success of the Peruvian fishing industry with the southeast trade winds?

## check your UNDERSTANDING

1. What is the difference between surface currents and density currents?
2. How do ocean currents affect organisms?
3. What causes an upwelling? Why might commercial fisheries be on the lookout for upwellings?
4. **Apply** How are density currents similar to convection currents?

## check your UNDERSTANDING

1. Surface currents are caused by wind. Density currents, which occur much deeper in the oceans, are caused by changes in salinity and temperature of ocean water.
2. Ocean currents transport organisms, carry away wastes, and carry food and nutrients to organisms.
3. An upwelling is caused by a strong surface current that carries warm water away from an area, replacing it with nutrient-rich water from below. Upwellings are fertile fishing grounds.
4. In both, the warmer, less dense substances are forced up, while the cooler, more dense substances sink.

# Science and Society

# Aquaculture

# Science and Society

One of the most difficult problems facing the world of tomorrow is how to feed our growing population when food-producing areas on land remain the same size or get smaller. Where will we turn for new food sources?

A good place to find them is under water. Aquaculture is the controlled raising, or farming, of shellfish, fish, and plants that live in water. Aquaculture is done in both fresh water and seawater, and is done in both natural bodies of water and enclosures built on land. By controlling the environment—providing proper nutrients, providing protection from predators, and controlling breeding—farm-raised plants and animals often grow faster and larger than those in the wild.

In Japan's Inland Sea, oysters, clams, and mussels, are cultivated on ropes hanging into the water from rafts. The Hanging Gardens of the Inland Sea are really very large undersea fields for growing bivalves. Hundreds of oysters are hung into the sea from floating rafts that give the animals a place on which to grow and mature. The oysters get their food in the form of algae and are ready to harvest in a few months to a couple of years, depending on the animal.

Besides shellfish, many types of fish are also raised as aquaculture crops. Fish farms in the United States raise mostly salmon, catfish and trout. Many other countries—including China, India, Chile, and Norway—also have fish farms.

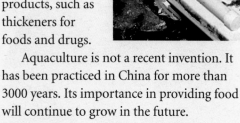

Plants are also often cultivated through aquaculture. Seaweeds are raised most often. They are used as food or as other products, such as thickeners for foods and drugs.

Aquaculture is not a recent invention. It has been practiced in China for more than 3000 years. Its importance in providing food will continue to grow in the future.

### What Do You Think?

Shellfish, fish, and plants raised through aquaculture are often raised in a controlled environment. That means their eating and breeding habits may be controlled. What effects do you think this may have on these plants and animals?

### Going Further ⑩⑩⑩➧

Seaweed is present in a wide variety of food products as an emulsifier and stabilizer. Have students work in teams to list as many products as they can that use seaweed. Tell students that seaweed is often called *agar, alginic, acid,* and *nori* on food labels. Recognize the team that found the most. If possible, have students bring in unopened containers of these products for volunteers to taste. Use the Performance Task Assessment List for Group Work in the **PAMSS,** page 97. **COOP LEARN** **L1**

### Purpose

Science and Society reinforces Section 9-3 by explaining how some species of ocean organisms can be raised commercially for human consumption. Although not a new method of farming, aquaculture may prove to be an important source of food in the future.

### Content Background

Point out that in Japan, shrimp are raised from egg to market size in less than a year. To achieve this remarkable success, the shrimp must be nurtured in a carefully controlled environment. After the female shrimp spawns—between a third and half a million eggs—the eggs are removed from the tanks so the shrimp do not eat them. When temperature and salinity are right, the eggs hatch in 13 to 14 hours. The larvae are first fed tiny diatoms, then oyster and clam eggs and brine shrimp. Technicians add oxygen to the tanks, which makes the shrimp grow quickly. The animals are then packed live in chilled, dry, cedar sawdust and shipped to markets and restaurants.

### Teaching Strategy

Students can work with a partner to list all the fish and shellfish they enjoy eating or would like to try. Then have them research where these fish and shellfish are harvested. **COOP LEARN** **L2**

### Answers to
### What Do You Think?

Students should suggest that marine organisms can grow better under controlled environments, safe from predators, fluctuations in food supply, weather, and currents.

EXPAND
your view

Literature
Connection

## Purpose

This Literature Connection enhances section 9-2 by describing how Samuel Taylor Coleridge's ancient mariner and marine biologist Rachel Carson feel about the composition of the ocean.

## Content Background

Coleridge was twenty-five years old when his neighbor told him about a strange dream concerning "A skeleton ship, with figures on it." This, together with some suggestions from his friend William Wordsworth, aroused in Coleridge a desire to write a sea ballad.

In 1952, Rachel Carson was awarded the National Book Award for nonfiction for *The Sea Around Us*. Her prose is distinguished not only by scientific accuracy, but also by its graceful style. Critics hailed *The Sea Around Us* as "one of the most beautiful books of our time." Carson is credited for arousing worldwide concern about the environment.

**Teaching Strategy** Student pairs can read the two stanzas from Coleridge's poem aloud and then list words that describe their feelings about the mariner's plight. **COOP LEARN** L2

## Discussion

After students read the chapter "A Changing Year" from Carson's book, have teams discuss how *The Sea Around Us* might affect people's perception of the ocean. **COOP LEARN** L2

## Answers to

## What Do You Think?

To capture Coleridge's style, students can use four line stanzas with an *abab* rhyme scheme. Remind them to select adjectives and adverbs other than Carson's to avoid plagiarism. **P**

---

Literature
Connection

# Two Views of the Ocean

**W**riters have written about water and the seas for thousands of years. The images they have presented have brought clear pictures, even to those who have never seen the ocean. Read the following excerpt from "The Rime of the Ancient Mariner" by Samuel Taylor Coleridge.

> Day after day, day after day,
> We stuck, nor breath nor motion;
> As idle as a painted ship
> Upon a painted ocean.
> Water, water, everywhere,
> And all the boards did shrink;
> Water, water, everywhere,
> Nor any drop to drink.

Rachel Carson (1907-1964) presented another view of the ocean. As a marine biologist who spent most of her life working for the United States Fish and Wildlife Service, the author was especially interested in the sea.

In her writing, Carson emphasized how all living things are interrelated. You can see an example of this by reading the chapter "A Changing Year" from Carson's book The Sea Around Us. The book tells about the history, geography, biology, and chemistry of the sea. "A Changing Year" describes life in the sea as the seasons change. It tells us that nothing is ever wasted in the sea. Instead, it is used and then passed on from one creature to another. The minerals in the sea water are vital to the life of even the smallest of marine protists. Everything in the ocean in necessary for the survival of something else in the ocean.

### What Do You Think?

Using information from Carson's book, write a poem in the style of Samuel Taylor Coleridge.

---

**Going Further** ⫸

Students might also enjoy comparing and contrasting the ways different writers depict the ocean. Have them read part or all of famous works that contain images of the ocean. Some possibilities include the following:
*Moby Dick,* by Herman Melville
"The Open Boat," by Stephen Crane
*The Tempest,* by William Shakespeare
*The Sea Wolf,* by Jack London

Students can then write essays comparing the impression of the ocean in the work they chose with that of the stanzas from Coleridge's *The Rime of the Ancient Mariner.* Use the Performance Task Assessment List for the Writer's Guide to Nonfiction in the **PAMSS**, page 85. **P**
L2

## HISTORY CONNNECTION

# Did Columbus Sail West?

If you were an explorer in the days before steamships, would you take advantage of the strong currents in the ocean? Columbus did. Look at the world map shown below. America is west of Europe. But Columbus did not sail due west from Europe. His ships could only sail with the wind, and the winds off the coast of Spain did not blow in the direction of America. Therefore, he had to take a southerly route to the Canary Islands before he turned west toward what he thought was Asia.

Had Columbus sailed 20 degrees farther south in latitude, he would have met both the equatorial current moving east and areas where winds seldom blow, making the crossing impossible. The southward-moving Canaries current took him to the area of the westward-moving North Equatorial trade winds and current. The expedition sighted land—possibly what we now call San Salvador—on the 36th day of the journey. Columbus wrote in his journal, "my people were very much excited because they thought that in these seas no winds ever blew to carry them back to Spain." Indeed, returning the way they came would have been impossible because the current flowed westward, and he took advantage of a north-blowing wind to sail northeast and then due east to the Azores and Portugal.

### You Try It!

Using a map of worldwide currents, plan a trip—short or long—that you could undertake in a vehicle that must drift or sail.

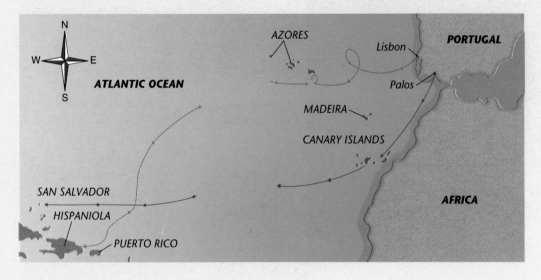

### Going Further ⟩⟩⟩⟩⟩

Few topics have generated as much controversy as Columbus's initial landing in the New World. Exactly where did he land? To practice analyzing conflicting information, students should review the different theories on the subject and then make up their own minds based on the currents, wind, and evidence of artifacts. Direct students to cite specific details in their analysis. For a thorough overview of the subject, students can consult the November, 1986 issue of *National Geographic* (vol. 170, No. 5). Students could then give oral presentations explaining their views. Select the appropriate Performance Task Assessment List from the **PAMSS**. L2 P

## HISTORY CONNNECTION

### Purpose
This History Connection reinforces section 9-3 by describing how the currents determined Columbus's route to the New World. Due to the wind, Columbus was forced to sail in a southerly direction to the Canary Islands.

### Content Background
In 1485, Columbus submitted his plan to the King of Portugal, John II, but was rejected. Soon after, Columbus tried Spain. As in Portugal, his request for funding was turned down. But Columbus persevered, and in 1492, Queen Isabella and King Ferdinand agreed to subsidize the expedition.

### Teaching Strategy
Have small groups of students make lists of items they would stock the ship with if they were planning Columbus' journey. COOP LEARN L2

### Debate
Columbus is often credited with discovering America. Actually he was possibly the first European to come to America. North and South America were already populated with thousands of Native Americans. Columbus and many Europeans that followed him put many Native Americans into slavery and took their land. Many Native Americans don't see Columbus' "discovery" as a great feat. Ask students why not? Can you relate to this point of view? COOP LEARN L3

### Answers to
**You Try It!**

Answers will depend on the location students select for their trip across the ocean. Make sure that students accurately follow the currents, regardless of their destination.

## EXPAND your view

### Teens in SCIENCE

**Purpose** Teens in Science reinforces Section 9-3 by describing the work of an aquarium volunteer with some organisms that live in the ocean, such as plankton and algae.

**Content Background** Established in 1853, the London Zoological Gardens was the first scientific and popular aquarium. Other large aquariums of the same era were built in Plymouth, England; Paris and Nice, France; and Berlin, Germany.

The best-known contemporary American aquariums are the Steinhart Aquarium in San Francisco, the Shedd Aquarium in Chicago, and the New York Aquarium in Brooklyn. Originally the latter was located in Battery Park in Manhattan, had nearly 200 tanks containing 3.8 million liters of water, and exhibited 11,000 fish at a time. In 1957, the aquarium moved to new, larger quarters in Coney Island.

The Miami Seaquarium and Marineland of the Pacific (Los Angeles) represent a new phase in the development of aquariums. Located by the ocean, they feature huge outdoor tanks and have portholes so visitors can see large fish such as sharks and dolphins from above and below the surface of the water.

**Teaching Strategy** Have pairs of students briefly discuss their own career plans, what type of volunteer positions might be available in their field, and whether they would be interested in taking them. COOP LEARN L2

**Debate**
Have teams debate whether hands-on experience or formal study would be more valuable to Desiree in learning about marine life. COOP LEARN L2

## EXPAND your view

### Teens in SCIENCE

# Desiree Siculiano

At the age of 12, Desiree Siculiano started as a volunteer guide in the New York City Aquarium. She worked at the touching tank, a large tank holding various aquatic animals, such as horseshoe crabs, that visitors are encouraged to touch. She was the youngest volunteer at the Aquarium when she started. How did she have the self-confidence to volunteer at such a young age? "My science teacher said it would be a good program for me for the summer. If he thought I could do it, so did I." Desiree convinced her brother to volunteer with her, and they worked as a team for four years.

Desiree is in the College Now program at John Dewey High School in Brooklyn. She takes college-level courses after the regular school day and plans to study marine biology in college. To help her reach this goal, she works in the culture room at the aquarium where she studies brown algae, which are used to feed small aquatic animals, and fry—baby fish—at the aquarium. Microscopic animals also eat algae. "This type of organism (algae) is at the very bottom of the food chain," says Desiree, whose task is purifying the water in which the algae grow.

**Going Further**
Students might enjoy working together to set up a class aquarium. Here are some questions for students to consider when planning the aquarium:

- How big a tank do they want to set up?
- How might they use aquatic plants to supply oxygen for the fish?
- Will they need a separate aerating device?
- What fish do they want to exhibit?
- Which fish need cool water? Warmer water?

Students might want to speak to the staff at local aquarium supply stores or write to these aquariums:

John G. Shedd Aquarium
1200 South Lake Shore Drive
Chicago, IL 60605

Sea World
1720 South Shores Road, Mission Bay
San Diego, CA 92109 L2 COOP LEARN

**R**eview the statements below about the big ideas presented in this chapter, and try to answer the questions. Then, reread your answers to the Did You Ever Wonder questions at the beginning of the chapter. *In your Journal*, write a paragraph about how your understanding of the big ideas in the chapter has changed.

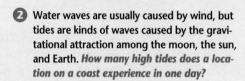

**1** In a water wave, water particles are temporarily displaced while the energy of the wave passes. The water itself does not move forward with the wave. *What is the shape water particles move in as a wave passes?*

**2** Water waves are usually caused by wind, but tides are kinds of waves caused by the gravitational attraction among the moon, the sun, and Earth. *How many high tides does a location on a coast experience in one day?*

**3** Scientists think that oceans were formed when water vapor from volcanoes condensed and fell to Earth as precipitation. Ocean water contains dissolved solids such as salt and dissolved gases such as oxygen and carbon dioxide. *Where did many of the dissolved solids found in the ocean come from?*

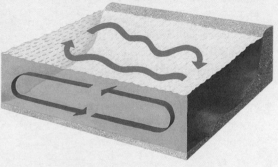

**4** Ocean currents are like rivers of water in the sea. Marine protists and animals depend on currents to bring them food, carry away waste, and provide them with transportation. *What are two types of ocean currents?*

Direct the class to study the illustrations on this page. Ask volunteers to read the captions and answer the questions to review the main ideas of this chapter.

**Teaching Strategy**

Divide the class into four equal groups. Assign to each group one of the four illustrations on this page. Then give each group a large sheet of poster board, pencils, and colored markers. Direct each group to redraw the illustration from a different vantage point. They may wish to draw the tides from the viewpoint of a fish under the ocean, an organism in the intertidal zone, or a person traveling in an oceanliner, for example. Then have students write a new caption reflecting the shift in point of view. Urge each group member to participate fully. Those who are uncomfortable drawing, for example, might wish to color the illustration and help draft the new caption. Have each group share its work with the class. **L2** **COOP LEARN** **P**

**Answers to Questions**

**1.** Water particles move in a circle.

**2.** Most coastal locations will experience two high tides each day.

**3.** Most of the dissolved solids found in the oceans came from minerals dissolved by water and transported to the oceans by runoff.

**4.** There are density currents and surface currents.

## Project

Have students work in pairs to find and read a novel, play, short story, poem, or movie in which the ocean plays an important role. Direct students then to write a one-page summary describing what they learned about the ocean. Then have a member of each group in turn read its summary to the class and explain its assessment. Students may also want to display the literature. Use the Performance Task Assessment List for Group Work in the **PAMSS**, page 97. **COOP LEARN**

**P**

## Science at Home

Have students create a collage at home that explains the interaction of ocean water and life. They should include representations of the interaction of the sun, the moon, and Earth to create tides and an explanation of the formation of waves and tides. Encourage students to use found objects such as sand and shells as well as pictures from newspapers and magazine. Invite students to display their collages in the classroom. Use the Performance Task Assessment List for Displays in the **PAMSS**, page 63. **L2**

## Using Key Science Terms

**1.** A density current is the movement of water when dense water moves toward less dense water. A surface current is the movement of the upper few hundred meters of seawater, mostly caused by the wind.

**2.** Nekton are swimming forms of fish and other animals. Nekton can move from one depth to another. Plankton are drifters that depend on currents to bring nutrients to them, carry wastes away, and move them from place to place.

**3.** Salinity is the amount of solids dissolved in ocean water. Manganese nodules form when minerals precipitate out and collect around a small object. This is one process that helps keep the salinity of the ocean water the same.

**4.** Upwellings bring an abundance of food from the deeper, colder water that takes the place of water that has blown away. Fish and other marine animals thrive in these areas because of the high nutrient concentration.

## Understanding Ideas

**1.** There would be higher high tides and lower low tides.

**2.** The water from the Mediterranean Sea would have a higher salinity and would therefore be more dense than the ocean water that was diluted by rainfall and had low evaporation.

**3.** The Gulf Stream moderates the climate making warmer winters than might otherwise be expected.

**4.** Materials used will vary but the answer should include the evaporation/condensation method of desalination.

**5.** The higher the salinity of water, the more dense it is. As the water becomes more dense, its buoyancy increases.

## Developing Skills

**1.** See reduced student page.

---

## Using Key Science Terms

| | |
|---|---|
| density current | intertidal zone |
| nekton | plankton |
| salinity | surface current |
| upwelling | |

*Use the terms from the list to answer the following questions.*

**1.** How does a density current differ from a surface current?

**2.** How do the movements of nekton and plankton differ?

**3.** What is salinity and how do manganese nodules affect the salinity of ocean water?

**4.** Why is fishing so successful in areas of upwellings?

## Understanding Ideas

*Answer the following questions* in your Journal *using complete sentences.*

**1.** If the pull of gravity between Earth and the moon increased, how would it affect tides on Earth?

**2.** The Mediterranean Sea has high evaporation and low precipitation. How would its water density compare to ocean water from an area where there is a lot of rainfall and temperatures are lower?

**3.** How does the Gulf Stream affect the climate in England and Ireland?

**4.** If your drinking water ran out as you were sailing around the world, how could you get more?

**5.** What is the relationship between the density of water and its salinity? How does this relationship affect buoyancy?

---

## Developing Skills

*Use your understanding of the concepts developed in this chapter to answer each of the following questions.*

**1. Concept Mapping** Complete the concept map of Ocean Water.

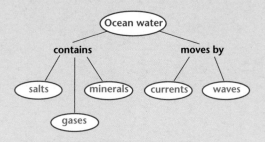

**2. Predicting** Repeat the density experiment on page 284 using an egg. Predict if more or less salt will be required to make the egg float in the water than it did to make the pencil float. Compare your results with your prediction.

**3. Predicting and Sequencing** Repeat the Explore activity on density and salinity on page 295 using three jars of water with different salinities and one jar with plain tap water. Make each jar of salt water a different color and leave the plain water clear. Using what you have learned about salinity and density, sequence the water samples from highest/lowest density to least density. Using a clear straw, test your prediction and see if you can layer the colored water in the straw.

---

**2.** The egg will require a denser solution to float.

**3.** When layering the water in the straw, start with the least dense first (the clear water will be on top) and continue to the most dense (on the bottom).

**4.** The food coloring dropped into the hot water will spread throughout the water more rapidly than the food coloring dropped into the ice water. This shows the faster molecular movement in the hot water than in the cold water.

---

**Program Resources**

**Review and Assessment,** pp. 53-58 L1
**Performance Assessment,** Ch. 9 L2
**PAMSS**
**Alternate Assessment in the Science Classroom**
**Computer Test Bank**

## Critical Thinking

In your Journal, *answer each of the following questions.*

1. In which direction would you expect a surface current off the southern coast of Africa to flow?
2. Thermo refers to temperature and haline to salinity. Why do you think density currents are sometimes called thermohaline currents?
3. Look at the map below. How are fishing grounds related to the location of surface currents, as shown in **Figure 9-14**

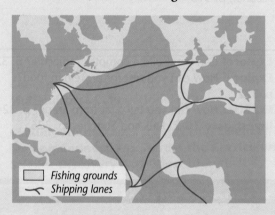

☐ Fishing grounds
〜 Shipping lanes

4. How are the shipping lanes shown on the map related to the location of surface currents?
5. Why do you think 80 percent of the kinds of seaweed found off the east coast of North America are also found off the west coast of Great Britain?

## P roblem Solving

*Read the following problem and discuss your answers in a brief paragraph.*

**Suppose your local park district is running a contest to design a water amusement park for the city. After reading this chapter, you decide to enter the contest. Using what you know about the movement of water in currents and waves, describe in words and pictures three different water rides you would design.**

1. Identify the source of energy for each ride.
2. Discuss how objects or people move in the ride.
3. Make diagrams of your rides.

## CONNECTING IDEAS

Discuss each of the following in a brief paragraph.
1. **Theme - Energy**  What do ocean waves and sound waves have in common? How are they different?

2. **Theme - Systems and Interactions**  If the moon is full, what kind of tide would you expect? Why?
3. **A Closer Look**  Why is the fresh water trapped in icebergs largely free from organic matter?

4. **History Connection**  What kind of movement of ocean water did Columbus use to sail to America? How did he use this movement?

### Critical Thinking

1. The surface current moves counterclockwise because the prevailing winds blow counterclockwise at this location.

2. Temperature and salinity both affect density, and as a result, density currents.

3. Commercial fishing grounds run along coastlines where surface currents are deflected by the continents. Fishing grounds are also found at upwellings.

4. Shipping lanes follow major surface currents such as the Gulf Stream.

5. Both places are in the path of the Gulf Stream, which affects the climates of the places. As a result, the conditions are favorable for the same types of plants. Answers may also include that the Gulf Stream may have carried/transported the seaweed from one coast to another.

### Problem Solving
Answers will vary.

### Connecting Ideas

1. Both have troughs and crests and can be measured. Their sources of energy are different.

2. You would expect normal high and low tides. Spring tide occurs at a new moon.

3. Because the temperature is too cold for most living things.

4. Columbus used surface currents. He gained speed by sailing with the currents instead of against them.

### ✔ Assessment

**Portfolio**  Review the portfolio options that are provided throughout the chapter. Encourage students to select one product that demonstrates their best work for the chapter. Have students explain what they learned and why they chose this example for placement into their portfolios.

Additional portfolio options can be found in the following **Teacher Classroom Resources:**

**Concept Mapping,** p. 17

**Making Connections: Integrating Sciences,** p. 21
**Multicultural Connections,** pp. 21-22
**Making Connections: Across the Curriculum,** p. 21
**Critical Thinking/Problem Solving,** p. 17
**Take Home Activities,** p. 17
**Laboratory Manual,** pp. 53-54; 55-56
**Performance Assessment** P

CHAPTER 10

# Organic Chemistry

## THEME DEVELOPMENT

Scale and structure is a major theme developed in this chapter. Structure on a molecular scale determines the properties of the many organic molecules introduced in this chapter. The theme of energy is supported by the fact that it takes more thermal energy to cause a change of state in hydrocarbons with long carbon chains than short carbon chains.

## CHAPTER OVERVIEW

The term "organic" is used to describe nearly all carbon-containing substances. The atomic structure of carbon allows it to combine with many different elements. Compounds formed when carbon combines with hydrogen are called *hydrocarbons*. When one or more of the hydrogen atoms is replaced with another element, a *substituted hydrocarbon* is formed. *Polymers* are huge organic molecules made up of many smaller molecules. Examples of polymers include proteins, carbohydrates, and lipids.

## Tying to Previous Knowledge

Draw this on the chalkboard:

$$
\begin{array}{ccc}
& H & H \\
& | & | \\
H - & C - & C \\
& | & | \\
& H & H \\
\end{array}
$$

Now, add two hydrogens and an -OH on the "empty" carbon to create ethanol, a common alcohol. Next, replace the two hydrogens you just added with one double-bonded oxygen. Inform students that you have now made acetic acid, vinegar. Discuss the impact that "small" changes can have on the properties of a compound. **L1**

# Organic chemistry

Did you ever wonder...

✓ **What gas is carried in that pipeline under your street?**

✓ **What causes the pain when you are stung by a bee or wasp?**

✓ **What the difference is between a saturated and an unsaturated fat?**

Before you begin to study about organic chemistry, think about these questions and answer them *in your Journal*. When you finish the chapter, compare your Journal write-up with what you have learned.

*E*very day you wake up, get dressed, eat something, and head out the door. Maybe you listened to music on the radio. Do you ride a bus to school? Your nylon backpack holds your books, notebook paper, pens and pencils.

Is carbon a part of your life? Most things you come in contact with today involve carbon in some way. The clothes you wear, the food you eat, the fuel in the bus, the cassette tape you use to listen to music, even the basketball you play with are made of carbon compounds. Why is carbon found in so many different compounds? How can carbon be used to make fuels and foods? In this chapter you will learn about some carbon compounds and what they mean to you.

▶ **In the activity on the next page, explore one way that foods can be tested for carbon.**

**304**

## Did you ever wonder...

• Methane, $CH_4$, is the gas that is piped into houses and used in furnaces and stoves. (page 308)

• Formic acid, $CH_3COOH$, causes the "sting" in a bee sting or wasp sting. (page 315)

• Unsaturated fats have double or triple bonds between carbon atoms; saturated fats have only single bonds. (page 325)

## STUDENT JOURNAL

Have students write their responses to the Did You Ever Wonder questions in their journals. After they have read the chapter, students should read their journal entries to see what they have learned about the chemistry of organic substances. **L1**

## Explore! ACTIVITY

### How can you test for carbon?

**C**arbon is a part of many things including clothes, fuels, sporting equipment, and foods. Test some different foods for the presence of carbon.

### What To Do

1. Take a small piece of marshmallow, tomato, bread, apple, and sugar.

2. Carefully heat each one separately in an open crucible, over a flame. The food will appear to change a couple of times. Keep heating until you do not see any more changes.

3. *In your Journal*, record what each substance looked like after it was heated.

**305**

## INTRODUCING THE CHAPTER

Have students identify the objects in the photograph on page 304. Ask what they have in common. Lead them to see that these objects all involve carbon in some way.

## Explore!

### How can you test for carbon?

**Time needed** 40 minutes

**Materials** marshmallow, tomato, bread, apple, sugar, crucible, Bunsen burner, tongs

**Thinking Processes** observing and inferring, recognizing cause and effect, comparing and contrasting

**Purpose** To compare properties of organic substances.

### Teaching the Activity

**Discussion** Compare the differences in appearance of each of the substances before and after heating. Point out that carbon must have been part of the original substances if it is left over after oxidation.

**Student Journal** Suggest that students note all the changes each substance undergoes. L1

### Expected Outcome

A black substance, carbon, should be left after oxidizing the substances.

### Answer to Question

3. Each substance looks blackened and fragile.

### ✔ Assessment

**Process** Have students draw one of the substances in this activity as it is heated. Their drawings should show the substance before, during, and after heating. Use the Performance Task Assessment List for Scientific Drawing in **PAMSS**, p. 55. L1

---

## ASSESSMENT PLANNER

### PORTFOLIO ASSESSMENT
Refer to page 335 for suggested items that students might select for their portfolios.

### PERFORMANCE ASSESSMENT
Process, pp. 305, 310, 314, 321
Skillbuilder, p. 313
Explore! Activities, pp. 305, 312, 314, 321, 322, 324
Find Out! Activities, pp. 307, 310
Investigate, pp. 318–319, 326–327

### CONTENT ASSESSMENT
Check Your Understanding, pp. 313, 320, 328
Reviewing Main Ideas, p. 333
Chapter Review, pp. 334–335

### GROUP ASSESSMENT
Opportunities for group assessment occur with Cooperative Learning Strategies.

# PREPARATION

## Concepts Developed

This section introduces organic compounds, compounds that contain carbon. Students will observe that carbon's ability to form covalent bonds with itself and other elements in long chains makes it a unique element. It allows the creation of millions of different organic compounds. Students will compare saturated and unsaturated hydrocarbons, and be able to name them. Students will recognize isomers, molecules with the same chemical formula that have different molecular structures.

## Planning the Lesson

In planning your lesson on simple organic compounds, refer to the Chapter Organizer on pages 318 A–B

# 1 MOTIVATE

**Demonstration** This activity will show that all *organic* items are not necessarily *natural* and vice versa.

Materials you will need are cotton cloth, synthetic cloth, plastic bag, insect spray, a piece of glass, and a piece of stone.

Display the items in front of the class. Ask which items are *natural* and which are organic. Point out that the first four are organic, while answers may vary on which are natural. L1

---

10-1 **Simple Organic Compounds**

### Section Objectives

- Describe structures of organic compounds and explain why carbon forms so many compounds.
- Distinguish between saturated and unsaturated hydrocarbons.
- Identify isomers of organic compounds.

### Key Terms

*organic compound*
*hydrocarbon*
*isomers*

## Organic Compounds

Would you eat a piece of charcoal? If you have ever eaten a marshmallow, you might be surprised to learn that both marshmallows and charcoal are composed mainly of the element carbon. A substance that contains carbon is called an **organic compound**. For years, scientists thought that living things were needed to make organic compounds. In 1828, a German scientist accidentally formed the organic compound urea from inorganic materials. This made other scientists realize that living organisms weren't always necessary to form organic compounds.

Today, the term organic is used to describe nearly all carbon-containing substances, whether or not they are found in living organisms. Most of the millions of different organic compounds that exist can be synthesized from carbon-containing raw materials such as wood, oil, natural gas, and coal.

You have already seen how you can turn simple substances, such as bread and apple, into carbon. How can you make other forms of carbon, such as charcoal?

**Figure 10-1**

Ⓐ An interesting reaction occurs when concentrated sulfuric acid is poured into a beaker containing sugar, or sucrose.

Ⓑ How would you describe the reaction that is occurring?

Ⓒ Carbon is produced when sulfuric acid pulls the water out of sucrose. What happened to the water in this reaction?

**306** Chapter 10 Organic Chemistry

---

### Visual Learning

**Figure 10-1 How would you describe the reaction that is occurring?** *The white sugar is disappearing, a black substance is forming and filling the beaker, and a vapor is being given off.* **What happened to the water in the reaction?** *It evaporated.*

### Meeting Individual Needs

**Learning Disabled** Students might benefit from a list of the prefixes used to name hydrocarbons and what they mean. Have students make flash cards with the number on one side and the prefix on the other. Have pairs of students take turns showing a prefix and identifying the number. LEP COOP LEARN

### Program Resources

**Study Guide,** p. 34.
**Multicultural Connections,** p. 23, Prescription: Charcoal L1
**Science Discovery Activities,** 10-1, Modeling Hydrocarbons.

## How do you make charcoal from wood?

**A**lthough wood and charcoal appear different, they both contain carbon.

### What To Do

1. Fill a clean, empty 1/4-pint varnish or paint can with sawdust from either a white pine or an oak.

2. Punch a small round hole (about 1/4" in diameter) through the center of the lid with a nail. Press the lid firmly in place and place the can on a hot plate.

3. Begin heating until white smoke comes out of the hole. Carefully light the smoke with a match until a yellow flame appears.

4. Continue heating until the flame disappears from the hole.

5. Turn off the hot plate and allow the can to cool overnight. Open the can the following day.

### Conclude and Apply

1. What do you observe?

2. *In your Journal,* record what happened to the sawdust.

Carbon forms many different compounds because it has an atomic structure that allows it to combine with a tremendous number of different elements. A carbon atom has four electrons in its outer energy level. This electron arrangement means that the carbon atom can form four covalent bonds, as shown in **Figure 10-2**, with other carbon atoms or with atoms of other elements such as hydrogen and nitrogen.

In chapter 6 you learned that a covalent bond forms when two atoms share a pair of electrons. Carbon can form single, double, or triple covalent bonds with other atoms. Single covalent bonds contain one pair of shared electrons. Double bonds contain two shared electron pairs. Triple bonds contain three shared electron pairs.

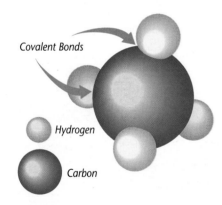

*Covalent Bonds*

*Hydrogen*

*Carbon*

**Figure 10-2**

This model of a carbon atom is bonded covalently with four hydrogen atoms. Is there a limit to the number of covalent bonds this carbon atom can form? Why or why not?

10-1 Simple Organic Compounds **307**

## 2 TEACH

**Tying to Previous Knowledge**

Review chemical bonding from Chapter 6. Emphasize covalent bonding, which is key to organic compounds.

### Visual Learning

**Figure 10-2 Is there a limit to the number of covalent bonds this carbon atom can form? Why or why not?** *Yes, because carbon has four outer electrons, which allow it to form four covalent bonds.*

### Find Out!

**How do you make charcoal from wood?**

**Time needed** 30 minutes and overnight

**Materials** 1/4-pint varnish or paint can with lid, sawdust (white pine or oak), nail, hammer, hot plate, match

**Thinking Processes** observing and inferring, modeling

**Purpose** To synthesize an organic compound from a raw material that contains carbon.

**Teaching the Activity**

**Safety** Perform this activity in an extremely well-ventilated area. Leave charcoal in the can after cooling.

**Student Journal** Have students record their observations and answer the questions in their journals. **L1**

**Expected Outcomes**

Sawdust contains carbon, the element that is charcoal.

**Conclude and Apply**

1. The can contains powdered charcoal.

2. It broke down into carbon and gases.

### ✓ Assessment

**Content** Ask students what was added to the sawdust to change it to charcoal. *heat energy* **L1**

# Hydrocarbons

Carbon atoms form an enormous number of compounds with hydrogen alone. A **hydrocarbon** is a compound that contains only carbon and hydrogen. Hydrocarbons form the basis for the structure and chemistry of a number of other organic compounds.

The shorter hydrocarbons are lighter molecules. In general, these compounds have low boiling points, and so they evaporate and burn more easily. This makes them useful as fuel gases. Longer hydrocarbons are heavy molecules that form solids or liquids at room temperature. They can be used as oils, waxes, or in asphalt.

Does the furnace, stove, or water heater in your home burn natural gas? This fuel, methane, is brought to homes through the pipeline underneath the street. Why do you suppose it's called natural gas?

Methane is the first and simplest member of the hydrocarbon family. Each line between atoms in a structural formula represents a single covalent bond. In methane, the carbon atom has four single covalent bonds to hydrogen atoms.

Other hydrocarbon molecules in this family are made by joining additional carbon and hydrogen atoms to methane. Every time another carbon atom is added, a new molecule is formed with its own set of properties.

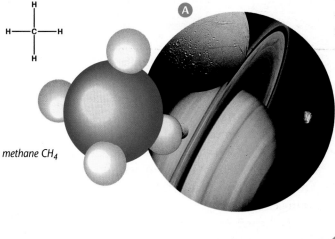

methane CH$_4$

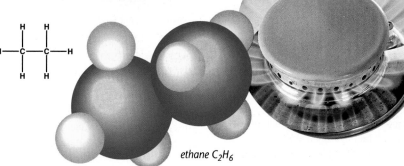

**Figure 10-3**

Methane has been discovered on distant planets such as Saturn (A). On Earth, natural gas (B) is a fuel that is mostly methane, CH$_4$.

**Figure 10-4**

Ethane is formed by adding a -CH$_2$ group to methane. Compare the structural formulas of methane and ethane. In what ways are they similar?

ethane C$_2$H$_6$

### Program Resources

**Transparency Master,** p. 41 and **Color Transparency,** Number 19, Hydrocarbon Structure L1

**How It Works,** p. 16, Petroleum Refinery L3

**Making Connections: Technology & Society,** p. 23, Technology: Bucky balls L3

### Meeting Individual Needs

**Physically Challenged** To help students identify structural models, have a set of pre-made drawings of the molecules discussed in this section at their disposal. Structure is key to understanding organic chemistry. Having quick and convenient access to diagrams may be extremely helpful to the students.

## ■ Saturated Hydrocarbons

Methane, ethane, propane, and their cousins make up a family of molecules known as saturated hydrocarbons. A hydrocarbon that is saturated contains only single covalent bonds. What would be the chemical and structural formulas for the next members of the methane family? **Table 10-1** shows formulas for some saturated hydrocarbons.

Have you ever opened your refrigerator and wondered why some foods seem to spoil quickly? How can you find out how this process works?

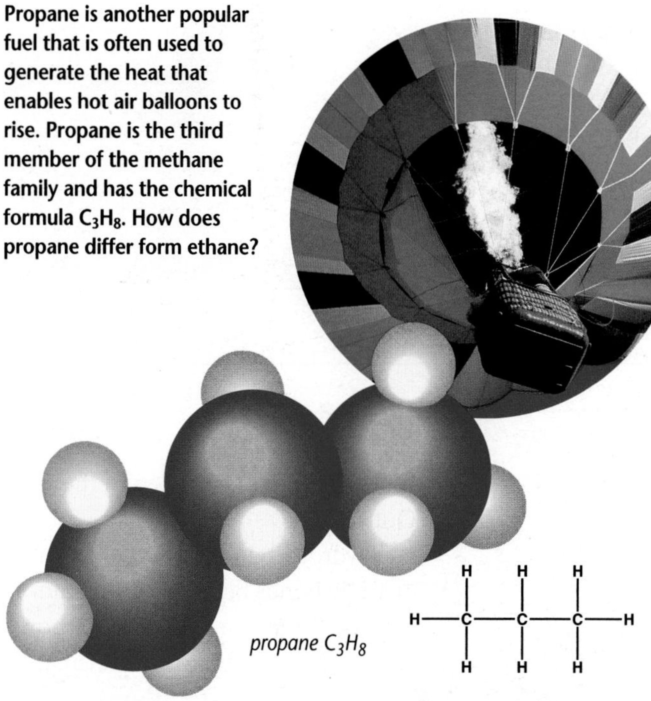

**Figure 10-5**

Propane is another popular fuel that is often used to generate the heat that enables hot air balloons to rise. Propane is the third member of the methane family and has the chemical formula $C_3H_8$. How does propane differ form ethane?

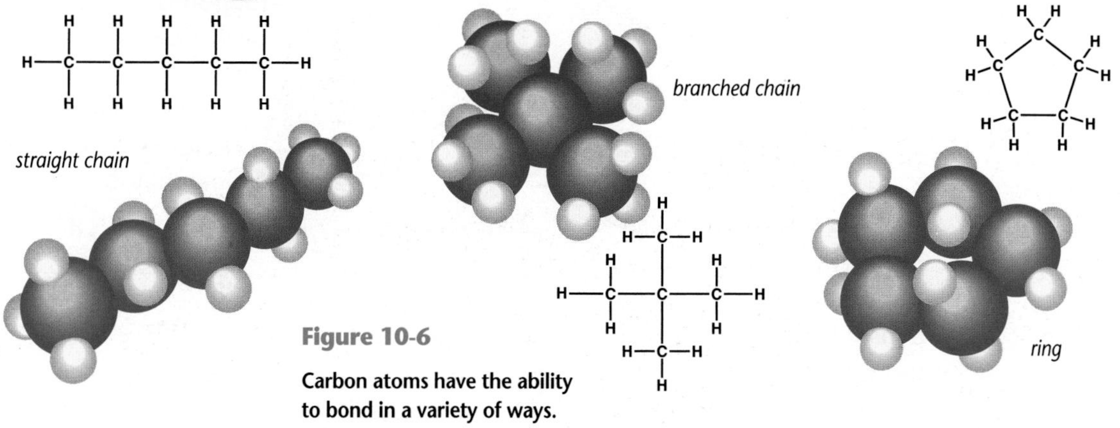

**Table 10-1**

| Hydrocarbon Series | |
|---|---|
| NAME | FORMULA |
| Methane | $CH_4$ |
| Ethane | $C_2H_6$ |
| Propane | $C_3H_8$ |
| Butane | $C_4H_{10}$ |
| Octane | $C_8H_{18}$ |

A saturated hydrocarbon can be described as one in which all carbon atoms are bonded to the maximum number of hydrogen atoms. Think about the structural formulas of these hydrocarbons. Are all of their carbon atoms bonded to the maximum number of hydrogen atoms?

propane $C_3H_8$

straight chain

branched chain

ring

**Figure 10-6**

Carbon atoms have the ability to bond in a variety of ways.

### Across the Curriculum

**Math**

Have students use the information in Figure 10-6 to devise a formula for determining how many hydrogen atoms exist in a saturated hydrocarbon molecule. Encourage them to experiment with different formulas until they come up with one that works. *Algebraically the formula can be written: H = 2C + 2, where H is the number of hydrogen atoms and C is the number of carbon atoms The number of hydrogen atoms is twice the number of carbon atoms plus two.* **L3**

**Inquiry Question** Propane's boiling point is about -40°C. A space probe on Planet X found that the planet had a large supply of liquid propane. Do you think that life as we know it on Earth is likely to exist on Planet X? Why or why not? *Since propane boils at about -40°C, the temperature on Planet X must be colder than that. Life as we know it cannot exist at such a low temperature.*

### Visual Learning

**Figure 10-5** Have students compare and contrast the structures of the hydrocarbons shown here. **How does propane differ from ethane?** *Propane has one more carbon atom and two more hydrogen atoms than ethane.* **Are all of their carbon atoms bonded to the maximum number of hydrogen atoms?** *Yes*

### ENRICHMENT

**Activity** Have students make a model of methane using toothpicks and polystyrene balls. The atoms in methane (or in any unsaturated hydrocarbon) are arranged in a pyramid shape with the carbon atom in the center and the four hydrogen atoms radiating from it, equidistant from one another. Then have students measure the angle between any two toothpicks. *If the bonds are equally spaced, each angle should measure 109.5°.* **L3**

### Meeting Individual Needs

**Visually Impaired** To help students formulate models, provide them with modeling materials that clearly differentiate among carbon atoms, hydrogen atoms, and other atoms. The carbon atoms should be considerably larger than the hydrogen atoms, for example, to minimize confusion. Etched markings on the sides of atoms might also be helpful.

## What causes fruits and vegetables to ripen?

Fruits and vegetables change as they ripen although the cause of the change is not readily apparent.

### What To Do

1. Place a rotten apple in a clear plastic box along with a fresh unripe apple.
2. Seal the lid of the box with aluminum foil and a rubber band.
3. Set another unripe apple on top of the box.
4. Observe the changes in each apple over the course of a week.
5. Repeat this experiment with two green tomatoes instead of apples.

### Conclude and Apply

1. Which apple ripens faster?
2. Does the same thing occur when you use tomatoes instead of apples?

### Find Out!

**What causes fruits and vegetables to ripen?**

**Time needed** 10 minutes to set up, then 20 minutes one week later

**Materials** 1 rotten apple, 2 unripe apples, 1 rotten tomato, 2 green tomatoes, clear plastic box, aluminum foil, rubber band

**Thinking Processes** observing and inferring, recognizing cause and effect, comparing and contrasting, separating and controlling variables, interpreting data

**Purpose** To observe a property of ethylene gas.

**Preparation** The rotten apple should have at least one open "spot" that is soft and decomposing. A container that seals tightly works best.

### Teaching the Activity

**Discussion** Encourage students to account for what happens to the unripe apple. Give clues like these: The ripe apple must be influencing the unripe apple somehow. Are the two touching? How can one influence the other without touching? **LEP**

**Student Journal** Students may wish to include drawings with their observations. **L1**

### Expected Outcomes

The unripe apple in the box will ripen faster than the apple outside the box.

### Conclude and Apply

**1.** The apple in the box; the rotten apple has an effect on the unripe apple next to it.
**2.** Yes; the fruit or vegetable in the box always ripens faster than the one outside of it.

### ✓ Assessment

**Process** Ask students to develop guidelines for storing produce at home based on this activity. Use the Performance Task Assessment List for Analyzing the Data in **PAMSS**, p. 27. **L1**

### ■ Unsaturated Hydrocarbons

In some of the hydrocarbons, some of the carbon atoms form double or triple covalent bonds with other carbon atoms. These new molecules have different properties from the molecules that have a single carbon-carbon bond.

The hydrocarbon ethene, $C_2H_4$, has a double bond between the carbon atoms. This gas, commonly called ethylene, helps ripen fruits and vegetables at warehouses before they are sold. Foods that spoil in your refrigerator produce this gas, which causes other foods to spoil. You saw this happen in the Find Out activity.

Hydrocarbons that contain double or triple bonds between carbon atoms are called unsaturated hydrocarbons. Remember that saturated hydrocarbons contain only single bonds. Fats and oils can also be classified as saturated or unsaturated.

**Figure 10-7**

This is the structural formula for ethene, showing the double bond.

*ethene $C_2H_4$*

### ENRICHMENT

**Activity** Have students make charts like these to determine how many carbons and hydrogens exist in hydrocarbons with:

no double bonds

| C | 1 | 2 | 3 | 4 | 5 | 6 |
|---|---|---|---|---|---|---|
| H | 4 | 6 | 8 | 10 | 12 | 14 |

one double bond

| C | – | 2 | 3 | 4 | 5 | 6 |
|---|---|---|---|---|---|---|
| H | – | 4 | 6 | 8 | 10 | 12 |

**L3**

# Isomers

Imagine that you could move the desks around in your classroom. You might place them all in two long rows or in six short rows. How many combinations can you think of?

Just as you could move your desks into different arrangements, the atoms in a hydrocarbon can form several different molecular structures, all having identical chemical formulas. Each carbon atom will still have four covalent bonds, but the overall shape of the molecule may vary. **Isomers** are compounds that have identical chemical formulas but different molecular structures, or shapes. Can you make isomers from any other hydrocarbons?

## ■ Properties of Isomers

The properties of isomers of a substance may not be identical, even though the chemical formulas are the same. The shape of the molecule seems to determine some of the properties. **Figure 10-8** shows the structures of butane and isobutane.

Isomers, such as those you will make for pentane and hexane, are still members of the methane family. They are all formed by adding more carbon and hydrogen atoms to methane. A double or triple covalent bond in a compound, instead of a single bond, makes an entirely new hydrocarbon, each with its own unique properties.

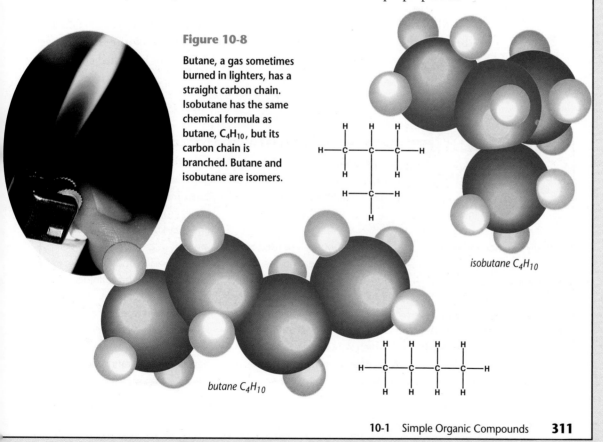

**Figure 10-8**

Butane, a gas sometimes burned in lighters, has a straight carbon chain. Isobutane has the same chemical formula as butane, $C_4H_{10}$, but its carbon chain is branched. Butane and isobutane are isomers.

isobutane $C_4H_{10}$

butane $C_4H_{10}$

**Program Resources**

**Critical Thinking/Problem Solving,** p. 5, Flex Your Brain

## Meeting Individual Needs

**Behaviorally Disordered**  To reinforce observing, have students make clay models to explore isomers. Identical isomers can seem different when twisted at unfamiliar angles. Have students make clay models to differentiate among different isomers.

### Across the Curriculum
#### History

In 1865, the German organic chemist August Kekule was wrestling with the problem of the structure of benzene, $C_6H_6$. Until Kekule, it was presumed that organic molecules could exist only in either straight or branched *chains*. The three possible structures that had been suggested so far proved incorrect. One night in Ghent he dozed by the fire:

"Again the atoms were gamboling before my eyes. This time the smaller groups kept modestly in the background. My mental eye, rendered more acute by repeated visions of the kind, could now distinguish larger structures of manifold conformation: long rows, sometimes more closely fitted together, all twining and twisting in snake-like motion. But look! What was that? One of the snakes had seized hold of its own tail, and the form whirled mockingly before my eyes. As if by a flash of lightning I awoke; and this time also I spent the rest of the night in working out the consequences of my hypothesis."

After his dream, Kekule proposed a new structure for benzene. Have students use the description of Kekule's dream and their own insight to draw what they think it might be. [L3]

# SKILLBUILDER

The number of carbon atoms should be plotted on the x-axis, and the number of hydrogen atoms should be plotted on the y-axis. The data points would be: carbon 1, hydrogen 4; carbon 2, hydrogen 6; carbon 3, hydrogen 8; carbon 4, hydrogen 10; carbon 8; hydrogen 18. The formula for the saturated hydrocarbon that contains eleven carbon atoms is $C_{11}H_{24}$.

# Explore!

**Do pentane and hexane have isomers?**

**Time needed**   20 minutes

**Materials**   gumdrops, raisins, toothpicks

**Thinking Processes** representing and applying data, making models, forming operational definitions, making and using tables, classifying, comparing and contrasting, interpreting scientific illustrations

**Purpose** To model the structure of isomers.

**Preparation** Any ball-shaped candies or fruits in which toothpicks can be solidly anchored can be used in this activity. Since carbon atoms have a greater atomic weight than hydrogen atoms, use the larger candy or fruit to represent carbon atoms. Save the hexane models for use in the Explore activity on page 314.

## Teaching the Activity

**Discussion** Encourage students to experiment with different forms of each molecule. Point out that appearances can be deceiving. When making pentane isomers, for example, there is no chemical difference between a four-carbon chain with a branch coming off the second or off the third carbon. They are both

# Explore! ACTIVITY

## Do pentane and hexane have isomers?

### What To Do

1. Using gum drops for carbon atoms, raisins for hydrogen atoms, and toothpicks for covalent bonds, try to make a model of pentane, $C_5H_{12}$. Remember that each carbon atom must have four bonds, while each hydrogen atom can have only one bond.

2. How many different models of pentane can you build?

3. Try to make a model of hexane, $C_6H_{14}$. Follow the same rules as for pentane.

4. How many different models can you build now?

Most hydrocarbons form isomers. Because the larger molecules have more carbon atoms they form more isomers. Octane, $C_8H_{18}$, the hydrocarbon used in gasoline, has 18 possible isomers. These isomers can have straight chains or branched chains.

## How Do We Know?

### How are octane numbers assigned?

When fuel burns in an engine, small amounts of it will occasionally explode rather than burning evenly. These tiny explosions can be heard and are referred to as knocking. You might also notice that the car does not run as smoothly when knocking occurs. Fuels are rated on their ability to burn evenly, rather than explode. The rating is called the octane number.

### Rating Fuels

Two compounds are used as standards in creating the scale for octane numbers. Isooctane, which resists knocking very well, is assigned an octane number of 100. Heptane, which knocks very badly, has an octane number of 0. The amount of knocking in a fuel is compared with a known mixture of these two compounds. For example, a sample of gasoline that knocks the same amount as a mixture of 90 percent isooctane and 10 percent heptane would have an octane number of 90. If a fuel knocks less than pure isooctane, it can have an octane number greater than 100. Gasoline pumps have an octane rating on them.

the same; they are not isomers. Similarly, a single "branch" coming off one of the ends is not really a branch; it is an end. L2 LEP

**Student Journal** In their journals, have students sketch each isomer model they build. L1

## Expected Outcomes

Each molecule can be structured in several different ways. Each model of $C_5H_{12}$ is an isomer of pentane.

## Answers to Questions

**2.** Three different pentane isomers can be built.

**4.** Five different isomers of hexane can be built.

## ✔ Assessment

**Content** Ask students to practice using a table by having them look at the table on page 309. Ask, Which hydrocarbon is likely to have more isomers, octane or ethane? *octane, because it has more carbon atoms* L1

You may have heard of octane rating applied to gasoline. Octane rating does not measure the amount of octane in the fuel, but rather the tendency of fuel to knock. Knocking occurs when a fuel does not burn evenly.

Hydrocarbons directly affect you. The major source of energy in the world comes from chemicals made from organic compounds found in petroleum or natural gas. Over 90 percent of the energy used in homes, schools, industry, and transportation comes from methane and the other hydrocarbons. Products ranging from fertilizer to skateboards are manufactured from hydrocarbons. Can hydrocarbons be used to make more complicated molecules? In the next section, you will learn how three special types of organic compounds are synthesized from hydrocarbons.

## SKILLBUILDER

**Making and Using Graphs**

Make a graph of the information in Table 10-1. For each compound, plot the number of carbon atoms on one axis and the number of hydrogen atoms on the other axis. Use this graph to predict the formula for the saturated hydrocarbon that has 11 carbon atoms. If you need help, refer to the **Skill Handbook** on page 681.

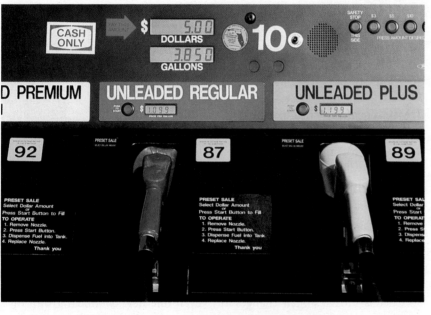

**Figure 10-9**

Each of the different kinds of gasoline is given an octane rating. You can see the octane ratings, 92, 87, and 89, in this photo.

## check your UNDERSTANDING

1. Why can carbon form so many different organic compounds?
2. How is an unsaturated hydrocarbon different from a saturated hydrocarbon?
3. How many isomers can you make from heptane, $C_7H_{16}$?

4. **Apply** Cyclopropane is a saturated hydrocarbon containing three carbon atoms. In this compound, each carbon atom is bonded to two other carbon atoms. Draw its structural formula. Are cyclopropane and propane isomers? Explain.

# 3 ASSESS

**Check for Understanding**

In discussing question 4, the Apply question, you may want to point out that unlike propane, which has a chain structure, cyclopropane is a ring compound. Cyclopropane is used as an anesthetic. Because it is highly flammable, extreme caution must be taken when it is used during surgery.

**Reteach**

Have students construct models of five saturated hydrocarbons. Use a ball-and-stick model system with four-holed balls for carbon atoms and one-holed balls for hydrogen atoms. Using models with a limited number of holes, it will be impossible for students to make incorrect configurations, as long as they have the right number of carbon atoms. L1

**Extension**

Have students who have mastered the concepts in this section draw all eighteen isomers of octane. L3

# 4 CLOSE

**Activity**

Tell students to suppose they are given a formula for an unknown hydrocarbon. From the formula above, have them list the characteristics they would be able to infer for this compound. *Sample answer: molecular weight, number of single and double bonds, number of isomers* L3

## check your UNDERSTANDING

1. Because its atomic structure allows it to combine with a great many different elements, carbon can form four stable covalent bonds with other carbon atoms or with atoms of other elements.
2. Unsaturated hydrocarbons contain double or triple bonds, whereas saturated hydrocarbons contain only single bonds. Unsaturated hydrocarbons have fewer hydrogen atoms per carbon atom than do saturated hydrocarbons.
3. 9
4. They are not isomers because they do not have the same chemical formula. Cyclopropane has two fewer hydrogen atoms than propane because of the extra carbon-carbon bond.

**Concepts Developed**

This section explores substituted hydrocarbons, hydrocarbons with one or more of their hydrogen atoms replaced by atoms, or groups of atoms, of different elements.

**Planning the Lesson**

Refer to the Chapter Organizer on pages 304A–B.

# 1 MOTIVATE

**Discussion** Write these structures on the chalkboard.

Methane       Formic acid

Have students point out differences in these molecules. Methane is used for heating and cooking, and formic acid causes the painful stings from bees and wasps. [L1]

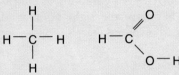

**Can you make new models from your hexane structures?**

**Time needed** 15 minutes

**Materials** raisins, gumdrops, minimarshmallows, toothpicks, hexane models from Explore, page 312

**Thinking Processes** representing and applying data, making models, comparing and contrasting, interpreting scientific illustrations

**Purpose** To model the relationship between a hydrocarbon and a substituted hydrocarbon.

**Preparation** Use any ball-shaped candies or fruits in which toothpicks can be solidly anchored.

---

10-2   **Section Objectives**

■ Classify substituted hydrocarbons as belonging to the alcohol, carboxylic acid, or amine family.

■ Describe the structure of an alcohol, a carboxylic acid, and an amine.

■ Draw the structural formula for the simplest alcohol, carboxylic acid, and amine.

**Key Terms**

*alcohol*
*carboxylic acid*
*amines*

# Other Organic Compounds

## Substituted Hydrocarbons

Usually a cheeseburger is a hamburger covered with American cheese and served on a bun. However, you can make a cheeseburger with Swiss cheese and serve it on slices of rye bread. If you ate this cheeseburger, you would notice that the substitutions affected the taste.

**Explore! ACTIVITY**

### Can you make new models from your hexane structures?

**What To Do**

1. Make a gumdrop/raisin/toothpick model for hexane.

2. Remove a hydrogen raisin and replace it with a mini marshmallow.

3. Then exchange the marshmallow with a raisin already on your model.

4. Replace another raisin with a gummy candy.

5. Make as many different models as you can.

Chemists make similar changes to organic compounds. These changes produce compounds called substituted hydrocarbons. A substituted hydrocarbon has had one or more of its hydrogen atoms replaced by atoms or groups of atoms of other elements.

In the Explore activity, you substituted marshmallows and gummy candy for the raisin/hydrogen in the gumdrop/hexane model. Substituting even one new chemical group on a hydrocarbon forms an entirely new class of compounds with chemical properties different from those of the original compound. Sometimes two or more chemical groups can replace hydrogen atoms. You can imagine how complicated these new molecules can become. This is why millions of organic compounds exist in our world.

---

**Teaching the Activity**

**Discussion** Talk about whether the substitution of a minimarshmallow for a raisin would significantly change the properties of the compound. Have students predict the change. [L2]

**Expected Outcomes**

Substituting any "atom" for one of the molecule's hydrogen atoms changes the shape and properties of the compound.

**✔ Assessment**

**Process** Have students work in small groups to develop a list of at least three methods that could be used to classify substituted hydrocarbons. Answers may include by number of atoms substituted or by types of materials used as substitutes. Use the Performance Task Assessment List for Making and Using a Classification System in **PAMSS**, p. 49. **COOP LEARN** [L1]

## ■ Alcohols

Ethanol, shown in **Figure 10-10A**, is an example of an alcohol. **Alcohol** is the name of a family of compounds formed when a hydroxyl (-OH) group replaces one or more hydrogen atoms in a hydrocarbon. Ethanol is produced naturally by sugar fermenting in corn, grains, and fruits. You will learn more about mixing ethanol with gasoline to fuel cars.

**Table 10-2** lists some common alcohols and their uses.

**Table 10-2**

| | METHANOL | ETHANOL | ISOPROPYL ALCOHOL |
|---|---|---|---|
| Uses | H<br>H–C–OH<br>H | H H<br>H–C–C–OH<br>H H | H OH H<br>H–C–C–C–H<br>H H H |
| Fuel | √ | √ | |
| Cleaner | √ | √ | √ |
| Disinfectant | | √ | √ |
| Manufacturing chemicals | √ | | √ |

*Some Common Alcohols*

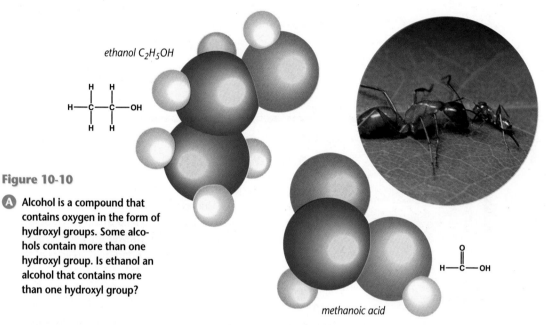

*ethanol C$_2$H$_5$OH*

**Figure 10-10**

Ⓐ Alcohol is a compound that contains oxygen in the form of hydroxyl groups. Some alcohols contain more than one hydroxyl group. Is ethanol an alcohol that contains more than one hydroxyl group?

*methanoic acid*

## ■ Carboxylic Acid

If you have ever tasted salad dressing made with too much vinegar, you probably made a face because of the sour taste. Acetic acid in vinegar causes that sour taste.

A **carboxylic acid** is formed when a -CH$_3$ group is displaced by a carboxyl (-COOH) group. The simplest carboxylic acid is methanoic acid or

Ⓑ Methanoic acid is an example of a carboxylic acid. The carbon has a double bond to the oxygen atom, a single bond to the hydroxyl (-OH) group, and a single bond to what remains of the original hydrocarbon molecule. Some ants have a gland that makes formic acid, which is connected to a powerful stinger at the end of their abdomen.

formic acid, as seen in **Figure 10-10B**. This acid is made by ants and other insects and causes the pain when you are stung by a bee or wasp.

# 2 TEACH

## Tying to Previous Knowledge

This section continues the system for categorizing organic compounds begun in Section 10-1. Review how organic molecules are named and distinguished from one another.

**Activity** Have students do a research project on polymers. They might delve into the history of polymers, learning that the initial push to make synthetic materials came in World War II when the Allies desperately needed a synthetic replacement for natural rubber. Or they might look into the substituted hydrocarbons that are used for modern plastics. A list is shown below:

polyester
polyvinyl alcohol
polystyrene
polyethylene
polypropylene L2

---

### Visual Learning

**Figure 10-10** Have students locate the hydroxyl group in each alcohol molecule. **Is ethanol an alcohol that contains more than one hydroxyl group?** *no*

---

### Program Resources

**Study Guide,** p. 35
**Critical Thinking/Problem Solving,** p. 18, Denatured Alcohol

### ENRICHMENT

**Research** Have students research how the chlorofluorocarbons such as Freon have been involved in the destruction of Earth's ozone layer. Chlorofluorocarbons are substituted hydrocarbons. Ask students to find out how serious the problem really is, and what can and is being done to rectify the situation. (A treaty has been signed to phase out all use of chlorofluorocarbons throughout the world by the year 2000.) L2

In another group of substituted hydrocarbons, nitrogen forms covalent bonds with the carbon and hydrogen in the molecule. When the amine group, $-NH_2$, replaces the hydrogen in a hydrocarbon, organic compounds called **amines** are formed.

Methylamine, $CH_3NH_2$, shown in **Figure 10-11**, is the simplest amine. Have you ever been given novocaine at a dentist's office? Do you take vitamins that include niacin? Does your soft drink contain caffeine? These are all hydrocarbons substituted with nitrogen.

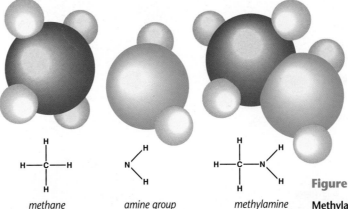

*methane*     *amine group*     *methylamine*

**Figure 10-11**

Methylamine, $CH_3NH_2$, is formed when an amine group ($-NH_2$) replaces a hydrogen in methane.

## Sidebar (left column)

**Theme Connection** Stability and change are demonstrated in the investigate activity on page 318 which shows students how one organic molecule can be changed into another in a natural process.

**Inquiry Question** Tell students that hydrocarbon Z is identical to Compound Z, except that one hydrogen in Hydrocarbon Z has been replaced by an -OH group in Compound Z. Both compounds are liquids at room temperature. If heated, which one do students think would boil first? Why? *Hydrocarbon Z would boil first. Alcohols seem to have higher boiling points than their corresponding hydrocarbons. Ethane, for example, is a gas at room temperature, while ethanol is a liquid. By the same reasoning, one would expect Hydrocarbon Z to have a lower boiling point than Compound Z, so it would boil first.*

**Student Text Question** Can one of these types of hydrocarbons be converted into another? *Yes*

### Visual Learning

**Figure 10-12 Why are proteins important to you?** *Proteins are found in every living cell.*

## A Closer Look

# Organic Motor Fuels

Did you know that about 90 percent of the total United States energy needs are met by fossil fuels, such as oil and natural gas?

Oil, of course, is used for a variety of purposes, from plastics production to the food manufacturing industry. One of the most important uses of oil is as a fuel to power the engines of automobiles and other forms of transportation.

## Fossil Fuels

As you know, fossil fuels are considered to be nonrenewable energy sources. In other words, once they have been used up, they're gone forever. Right now, we are using up fossil fuels much faster than can be replaced by Earth. What fuels will power the engines of the transportation vehicles of the future?

Since the energy crisis of the 1970s, scientists have been working on the development of new sources of energy, especially ones that can be used to power engines.

## Gasohol

Did you ever see a sign like the one pictured here? Gasohol is a combination of the alcohol ethanol and gasoline. The gasohol used currently contains about 90 percent gasoline and

**Purpose**
A Closer Look expands upon the discussion of hydrocarbons in Section 10-1 and alcohols in Section 10-2 by looking at the future of gasohol.

**Content Background**
There is an attraction to using renewable fuel in cars and trucks even if it is only 10% renewable. Gasohol already makes up about 7% of the U.S. motor fuel market. Because of ozone pollution in major cities like Los Angeles, New York and Chicago, federal agencies want to require more people to use gasohol. Gasohol-powered cars are harder to start in cold weather and gasohol causes some car parts to wear out faster. Oil companies would have to build new facilities to process gasohol, which would make it more expensive. Gasohol is a short-term solution to the long-term problems. A better solution might be the use of the electric car.

## ■ Amino Acids

As well as being in novocaine, niacin, and caffeine, amines occur in many other biological compounds. A special type of amine-substituted hydrocarbon forms when both the $-NH_2$ group and the $-COOH$ group replace hydrogens on the same molecule. This type of compound is called an amino acid, which is a building block for the formation of proteins. You may have eaten an amino acid lately if you like gelatin desserts.

Many organic compounds are composed of different combinations of carbon, hydrogen, oxygen, and nitrogen atoms. You have already learned about alcohols, carboxylic acids, and amines. Can one of these types of hydrocarbons be converted into another?

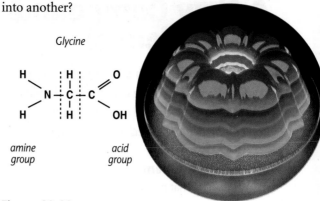

Glycine

amine group     acid group

**Figure 10-12**

Gelatin desserts contain glycine, an amino acid. Amino acids are a key ingredient of proteins. Why are proteins important to you?

10 percent ethanol. As you recall, ethanol is the substituted hydrocarbon found in all alcoholic beverages.

Gasohol has many advantages over gasoline. Ethanol is produced commercially by the fermentation of potatoes, sugar cane, and grains, such as corn and wheat. Because it is produced from plant materials, ethanol is considered to be a renewable energy source.

Another advantage of using gasohol is that most car engines do not have to be modified to burn the gasohol manufactured today. In fact, car engines can be made to burn pure ethanol, and engineers are working hard to design engines that can use ethanol efficiently.

### What Do You Think?

Clearly, we need to develop new sources of fuel for our transportation vehicles. Gasohol shows some promise as an alternative fuel, but there are some disadvantages to gasohol as well. Commercial production of ethanol results in numerous environmental problems. Among these are disruption of the ecosystem, fertilizer runoff, and erosion. Do you think gasohol is an answer to our fossil fuel problems? Explain your answers.

10-2   Other Organic Compounds   **317**

### Check for Understanding

To answer question 4, the Apply question, in Check Your Understanding, students will need to find out the meaning of the prefix *iso-*.

### Reteach

Use "R" notation to help students identify alcohols, carboxylic acids, and amines. Thus, the formula for an alcohol is ROH, for a carboxylic acid RCOOH, and for an amine RNH₂. The "R" in each case stands for any hydrocarbon group. When students seek to identify a compound, they should first name R, then go on to name the substitution group. [L1]

### Extension

Have each student diagram a mystery chemical on a piece of paper and then play the Mystery Chemical Game. Each diagram should be displayed to the class. The person who correctly names the chemical first wins a point. [L3]

# 4 CLOSE

### Activity

Encourage students to identify the hydrocarbons and substituted hydrocarbons on the labels of foods, household cleansers, paints, solvents, and so on that they bring from home. On the chalkboard make a list of all substituted hydrocarbons that students find. [L1]

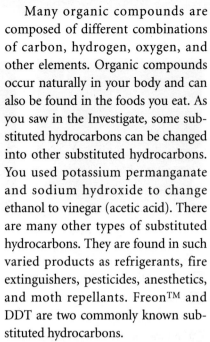

**Figure 10-13**

Substituted hydrocarbons have had one or more of the hydrogen atoms replaced by atoms or groups of atoms of other elements. Some examples of substituted hydrocarbons are shown here.

Many organic compounds are composed of different combinations of carbon, hydrogen, oxygen, and other elements. Organic compounds occur naturally in your body and can also be found in the foods you eat. As you saw in the Investigate, some substituted hydrocarbons can be changed into other substituted hydrocarbons. You used potassium permanganate and sodium hydroxide to change ethanol to vinegar (acetic acid). There are many other types of substituted hydrocarbons. They are found in such varied products as refrigerants, fire extinguishers, pesticides, anesthetics, and moth repellants. Freon™ and DDT are two commonly known substituted hydrocarbons.

In the following section of this chapter, you will find out more about the complicated hydrocarbons that make up your body and why you need to eat foods to rebuild yourself.

### check your UNDERSTANDING

1. What major chemical group is characteristic of an alcohol? A carboxylic acid? An amine?
2. Can a substituted hydrocarbon have more than one chemical group replacing its hydrogen atoms at one time? Give an example.
3. Methylamine is a compound in which one hydrogen in ammonia has been replaced with a -CH₃ group, another hydrogen has been replaced with a -CH₂CH₃ group, and a third hydrogen remains. Draw its structural formula.
4. **Apply** Rubbing alcohol is isopropyl alcohol. How does its structure differ from propyl alcohol?

### check your UNDERSTANDING

1. -OH, -COOH, -NH₂
2. Yes; Amino acids have both -COOH and -NH₂ groups.
3. CH₃NHCH₂CH₃

4. In isopropyl alcohol, the -OH group is on the middle carbon of the three-carbon chain. It is on the end carbon in propyl alcohol. They are isomers and therefore differ in their structural formulas.

# Biological Compounds

## Polymers

Milk, muscle, blood, cassette tapes, and athletic shoes are made of organic compounds which are made of very large molecules. In the Explore activity, you will see one way that large molecules can be formed from many different molecules. **Polymers** are huge molecules made up of many smaller organic molecules that are linked together to form new bonds. The smaller molecules, called monomers, are usually similar in size and structure.

Polymers are also found in the biological compounds that make up living things. There are three major groups of biological compounds: proteins, carbohydrates, and lipids.

### Section Objectives

■ Describe polymers and examine their importance as biological compounds.

■ Compare and contrast proteins, carbohydrates, and lipids.

### Key Terms

*polymers*
*proteins*
*carbohydrates*
*lipids*

## PREPARATION

### Concepts Developed

Organic molecules that are important as biological compounds are surveyed in this section. Many of them are polymers, huge molecules of repeated organic compounds held together by chemical bonds. The structures of proteins, carbohydrates, and lipids are compared.

### Planning the Lesson

Refer to the Chapter Organizer on pages 304A–B.

## 1 MOTIVATE

**Activity** Allow students to practice their classifying skills by giving small groups of students one or two food packages each. Ask students to look at the nutritional information on each package and write each item in one of three lists: Elements, Vitamins, or Other. Then compile master lists based on the findings of each group. Point out that the carbohydrates, protein, and fats found on the "Other" list are biological compounds L1

COOP LEARN

### Explore! ACTIVITY

### Can you build a complex molecule?

#### What To Do

1. Loop together different colored strips of paper into a chain, or string colored paper clips together.

2. How many different combinations can be made?

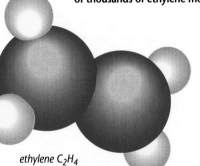

#### Figure 10-14

The polyethylene polymer is synthesized by linking together ethylene molecules, $C_2H_4$. The resulting polyethylene molecule could have a continuous chain of thousands of ethylene molecules linked as one.

*ethylene $C_2H_4$*

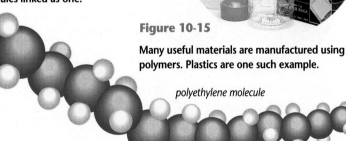

#### Figure 10-15

Many useful materials are manufactured using polymers. Plastics are one such example.

*polyethylene molecule*

### Expected Outcome

Only the number of subunits available and time should limit the length and complexity of the chains.

### ✔ Assessment

**Process** Ask students how they would evaluate the complexity of the chains. Is the longest chain also the most complex? Why or why not? Use the Performance Task Assessment list for Model in **PAMSS**, p. 51. L2

### Explore!

#### Can you build a complex molecule?

**Time needed** 30 minutes

**Materials** strips of colored paper, glue, colored paper clips

**Thinking Processes** representing and applying data, making models

**Purpose** To make a model of a complex arrangement created from repeating subunits.

**Preparation** Cut colored paper strips ahead of time.

#### Teaching the Activity

**Discussion** Encourage students to think about the different patterns they can create with individual units. Emphasize that the chains should be composed of repeating units, not random strings. LEP L1

**Student Journal** Have students sketch in their journals the repeating units they used. L1

# 2 TEACH

### Tying to Previous Knowledge

This section follows directly from the previous two in this chapter. Molecules described in the previous sections are combined to form important biological polymers.

Milk and fish contain protein, a particular kind of hydrocarbon polymer that is a necessary part of all living cells. **Proteins** are polymers formed by linking together various amino acids.

Proteins are in your muscles, hair, bones, fingernails–in every living cell. Eight of the twenty-two or more amino acids used by the body are absolutely essential for your body to function properly, but your body cannot make them. You need to eat protein-rich foods every day for your body to get adequate protein so it can grow and renew itself. How can you tell whether a certain food contains proteins or not?

---

## Visual Learning

**Figure 10-17** Have students identify the amine (-NH₂) and acid (-COOH) groups of both amino acids shown in Figure 10-17.

---

**Student Journal** Have students consult food labels, then keep a diary in their journals of their protein, fat, and carbohydrate intake over a period of time. Then have students write how their diets can be improved (if improvement is needed). L1

---

## Explore!

### How can you test for protein in food?

**Time needed** 30 minutes

**Materials** sodium hydrogen sulfate, potassium nitrate, 4 large test tubes, milk, dropper, burner, test tube holder, egg white, meat sample, chocolate

**Thinking Processes** recognizing cause and effect, comparing and contrasting, observing and inferring, making and using tables, classifying, measuring in SI, interpreting data

**Purpose** To use a chemical test

**Preparation** Dilute nitric acid could be substituted for the two reagents used.

### Teaching the Activity

**Troubleshooting** Students should use small pieces of the solids. **CAUTION:** *Have students be aware of eye safety and using a test tube holder to heat the test tube.*

---

## Explore! ACTIVITY

### How can you test for protein in food?

#### What To Do

1. Add 5 g of sodium hydrogen sulfate and 5 g of potassium nitrate to a large test tube.

2. Add one drop of milk to the test tube and heat the contents gently over a burner.

3. Describe what happens inside the test tube. Yellow indicates the presence of protein in your milk sample. Record your results *in your Journal*.

4. Repeat this test with samples of egg white, meat, and chocolate.

5. Do all of these foods contain protein? Record your answer *in your Journal.*

**Figure 10-16**

Eggs, meat, tofu, and milk are examples of foods that are rich in proteins.

**Figure 10-17**

Amino acids combine to make a protein segment. Even though there are only about 200 different amino acids, millions of different proteins can be made from them. Proteins account for 15% of your total weight.

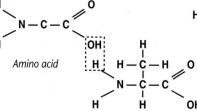

*Amino acid*

*Amino acid*

*Protein segment*

**322**  Chapter 10  Organic Chemistry

---

**Student Journal** Have students answer the questions in their journals. L1

### Expected Outcomes

A yellow color appears when milk, egg white, and meat are added to the test tube, but not when chocolate is added.

### Answers to Questions

3. The material in the test tube turns yellow.

5. No. All but chocolate contain protein.

---

### ✔ Assessment

**Performance** Have students construct a data table to record the results of this activity. Use the Performance Task Assessment List for Data Table in **PAMSS,** p. 37. L1

---

# Carbohydrates

What do you think of when you hear the word carbohydrate? Do you think of pasta or bread? Maybe you think of your diet and good nutrition. Sugars and starches are known as **carbohydrates**; this class of food provides energy for your body.

Glucose ($C_6H_{12}O_6$) and sucrose ($C_{12}H_{22}O_{11}$) are common sugars. Glucose is found in many sweet foods such as grapes and honey. In your body, glucose is broken down into simpler substances that enter the mitochondria to provide energy to all of your cells. Another sugar found in foods is sucrose, the white table sugar produced from sugarcane. Sucrose breaks down into glucose and other simple sugars during digestion.

Starches are larger molecule carbohydrates that occur naturally in plants like wheat, rice, and corn.

Carbohydrates are organic compounds in which there are twice as many hydrogen atoms as oxygen atoms. Count the hydrogen and oxygen atoms in the formulas for yourself to prove that this is true. The simple sugars are straight-chain polymers, but the larger molecule sugars and starches can be branched and are more complex.

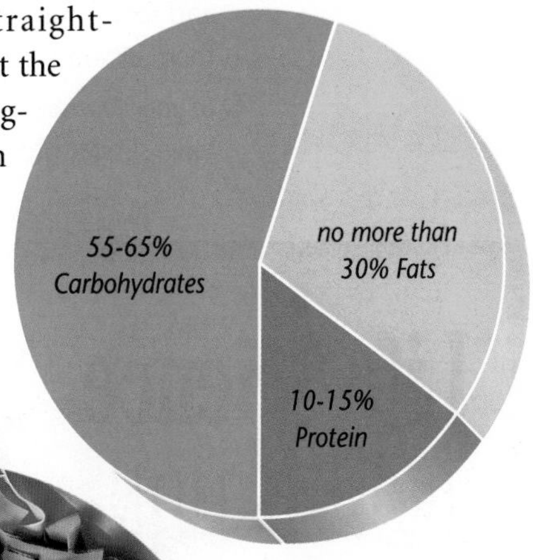

**Figure 10-18**

Starch is the major component of pasta.

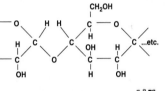

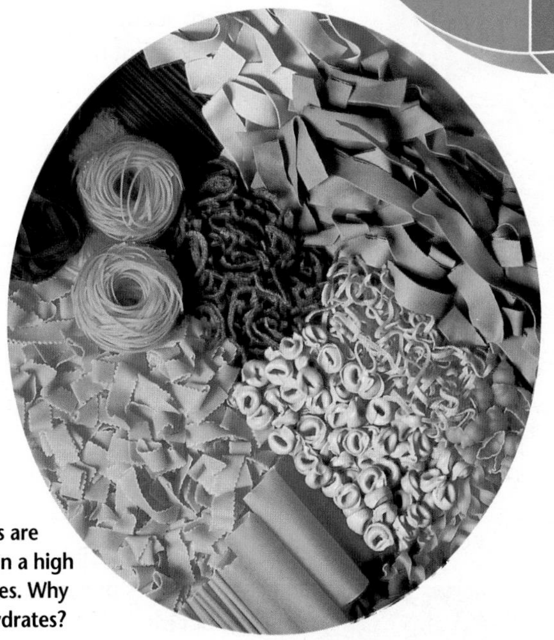

**Figure 10-20**

Pasta, rice, corn, and potatoes are examples of foods that contain a high concentration of carbohydrates. Why does your body need carbohydrates?

**55-65% Carbohydrates**

**no more than 30% Fats**

**10-15% Protein**

**Figure 10-19**

This graph shows the recommended percentage of calories that come from carbohydrates, protein, and fats. Why is a balanced diet important?

**Theme Connection** Biological compounds provide energy, stability, and change to our bodies. Energy is provided by carbohydrates and lipids. Proteins, parts of all body cells, are necessary for the growth and renewal of our bodies. Without adequate and balanced levels of each of these compounds, our bodies would change in unfavorable ways.

**Inquiry Question** On the morning of a marathon race, a runner finds out that the race will be held at 10 A.M. instead of 4 P.M. How should she change her eating strategy? *She has less time to digest starches and break them down to sugar. Therefore, she should eat more "sugary" foods, whose glucose she can have immediate access to.*

## Across the Curriculum

### Math

Nutritionists claim that a healthful diet should not include more than 30 percent of its calories from fat. You can calculate the percentage of calories from fat by using the "9 Rule." Each gram of fat contains approximately 9 calories, so multiply the number of grams of fat per serving (see nutrition information on food container) by 9. Divide this by the number of calories per serving and change the decimal to a percent. L1

### Visual Learning

**Figure 10-19** **Why is a balanced diet important?** *A balanced diet provides your body with everything it needs to function properly.*

**Figure 10-20** **Why does your body need carbohydrates?** *Carbohydrates provide energy for your body.*

## Multicultural Perspectives

### Refining Sugar

Norbert Rillieux was born on a plantation in New Orleans in 1806. He studied engineering and revolutionized the sugar refining business. At that time, sugar was crude and lumpy. Rillieux's evaporating pans changed that, producing the sweet, white, uniform granulated sugar that is used throughout the world today. L1

## Lipids

What do butter, margarine, the oil part of salad dressings, and some vitamins have in common? They are all included in the third major type of biological compound called a lipid. **Lipids** are organic compounds that

# Explore! ACTIVITY

## How can you tell a fat from an oil?

### What To Do

1. Obtain small samples of butter, soybean oil, margarine, olive oil, and solid shortening. Observe them at room temperature.

2. *In your Journal*, list which ones have similar properties.

---

# Life Science CONNECTION

## Poisonous Proteins

The next time you visit the zoo to learn about the exotic animals, you just might want to bring along a chemistry book! Why?

### Biological Compounds

In this chapter, you learned that living organisms are made of the biological compounds—proteins, carbohydrates, and lipids. As you know, these compounds are important for the metabolic processes of cells. Cell structures are made primarily of proteins, and lipids and carbohydrates are important for the functioning of cells. Lipids and carbohydrates provide energy for cells.

### Biotoxins

It's clear that if the cells of organisms did not manufacture proteins from amino acids, organisms couldn't stay alive. But would you believe that there are many animals and plants that produce proteins that can mean immediate death for other organisms? Such proteins are organic poisons that are known as biotoxins, and they are produced and used by animals, plants, fungi, and bacteria for defense against predators and for obtaining food.

The reptile house at the zoo is a great place to learn about animals that produce biotoxins. Many species of snakes, includ-

---

# Life Science CONNECTION

### Purpose

Life Science Connection expands the discussion of proteins in Section 10-3 to include biotoxins.

### Content Background

Most snakes are nonpoisonous. The ones that do have venom use it to stun their prey and to defend themselves. Rattlesnakes provide warning by rattling their tails, but other poisonous species provide no warnings. When a poisonous snake coils up and strikes, it embeds its two hypodermic-needle-like fangs in its victim, and venom flows from poison glands through the teeth into the wounds. The amount and concentration of venom varies, as does an individual's sensitivity to it. In North America, most snakebites are not fatal. But *all* bites should be treated immediately, for even nonpoisonous snakebites can become infected.

feel greasy and will not dissolve in water. Fats, oils, waxes, and related compounds make up this group of biological compounds.

Although lipids contain the same elements—carbon, hydrogen, and oxygen—that carbohydrates do, they are put together in different proportions. Lipids are a more concentrated source of energy for the body than carbohydrates. They provide twice as much energy per gram as carbohydrates.

Have you ever heard that eating too much saturated fat can be unhealthy? Fats and oils are classified as saturated or unsaturated according to the types of bonds in their carbon chains. Let's test for the presence of fats and starches in various foods.

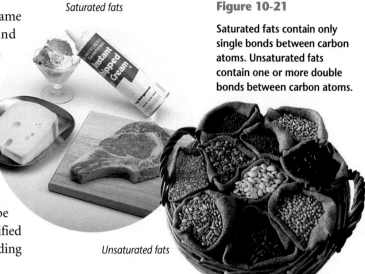

*Saturated fats*

*Unsaturated fats*

### Figure 10-21

Saturated fats contain only single bonds between carbon atoms. Unsaturated fats contain one or more double bonds between carbon atoms.

---

ing North American snakes, produce a substance called venom. Some types, similar to the snake shown in the photo at the left, are more poisonous to humans than others.

### Snake Venom

Scientists know more about the chemical makeup of snake venom than any other animal biotoxin. Proteins in snake venom are of a special group called enzymes. Enzymes are large and complex protein molecules that work by breaking down other organic molecules. The most common protein in snake venom is an enzyme called cholinesterase, which disrupts the functioning of the nervous system.

The most poisonous land snake in the world is the tiger snake from Australia, shown in the photo at the right. Tiger snake venom is extremely poisonous. It only takes about one-half a milligram of tiger snake venom to kill an adult human.

### What Do You Think?

Besides snakes, many other species of animals, including insects, frogs, toads, and fish produce biotoxins that are poisonous to humans. More is known about snake venom for two reasons. First, scientists are able to obtain more venom from snakes than

biotoxins from other animals. More importantly, the enzymes in snake venom are important for the development of drugs to treat illness. How do you suppose studying the proteins found in snake venom can help scientists develop new types of drugs?

---

## 10-2 Fats and Starches

### Planning the Activity

**Time needed** 30 minutes

**Purpose** To predict the content of food samples and analyze data to test the predictions.

**Process Skills** making and using tables, observing and inferring, comparing and contrasting, predicting, classifying, interpreting data

**Materials** liquid cooking oil, iodine solution in dropper bottle, raw potato slice, cooked bacon, large brown paper bag, bread, cheese, cooked egg white samples, potato chip, scissors, marker

### Teaching the Activity

**Discussion** Encourage students to use their knowledge about a food to make their predictions. For example, they may have heard that potatoes are starchy or that eggs contain a lot of fat. But do egg whites contain much fat? And what happens to a potato when it becomes a potato chip? Warn them to think carefully before they predict. L2

**Process Reinforcement** Be sure that students copy the data table correctly. Foods to be tested should be listed down the left side of the table, with space to record predictions and tests under columns arranged along the top of the table. Use the Performance Task Assessment List for Data Table in **PAMSS**, p. 37.

**Possible Hypothesis** Students may hypothesize that the cheese, bacon, and potato chip contain fat and that the potato, bread, and potato chip contain starch.

**Possible Procedure** Be sure that students make their predictions for each food sample before actually testing the sample.

---

# INVESTIGATE!

# Fats and Starches

*Simple tests can be performed to discover if lipids and carbohydrates are present in foods.*

### Problem

Which foods contain starch and fats?

### Materials

| | |
|---|---|
| liquid cooking oil | bread |
| iodine solution | cheese |
| in dropper bottle | cooked egg |
| raw potato slice | white samples |
| cooked bacon | potato chip |
| large brown | scissors |
| paper bag | marker |

### Safety Precautions

Wear safety goggles and an apron when working with liquids.

Be careful when working with poisonous substances.

Be careful when using scissors.

## What To Do

**1** Copy the data table *into your Journal.*

**2** Open a brown bag and cut it in half. Mark one part Fat and the other part Starch. Mark off each part into six sections. Label each section with the food name. All foods are to be named on both papers, and checked for both fat and starch. **CAUTION:** *Put on an apron and goggles to protect clothing and eyes.*

### Data and Observations

| | FAT | | STARCH | |
|---|---|---|---|---|
| | Predict | Result | Predict | Result |
| Test food | yes/no | yes/no | yes/no | yes/no |
| Bread | no | no | yes | yes |
| Cheese | yes | yes | no | no |
| Egg white | no | no | no | no |
| Raw potato | no | no | yes | yes |
| Bacon | yes | yes | no | no |
| Potato Chip | yes | yes | yes | yes |

**326** Chapter 10 Organic Chemistry

---

## Program Resources

**Activity Masters,** pp. 45–46, Investigate 10-2

**Transparency Master,** p. 43, and **Color Transparency,** Number 20, Biological Polymers L2

**Take Home Activities,** p. 18, Making Plastics L1

**Making Connections: Integrating Sciences,** p. 23, Drug-Producing Tree L2

**Making Connections: Across the Curriculum,** p. 23, How Risky Are Pesticides? L2

**Science Discovery Activities,** 10-2, Food for Thought, and 10-3, How is Soap Made?

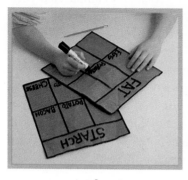

**A**  **B**  **C**

**3** Place a drop of oil in a corner of the paper marked Fat. Hold the paper up to a light and observe the spot. Foods with fat leave a grease spot like this on brown paper.

**4** *Predict* which test foods contain fat.

**5** Rub each food on its labeled section (see photo **B**). Let the spots dry.

**6** Hold the paper up to a light source. Record your observations.

**7** *Predict* which foods contain starch. Foods that contain starch turn dark blue when iodine solution is dropped on them. **CAUTION:** *Iodine is poisonous and will stain clothing and skin.*

**8** Place foods on the labeled sections of the Starch paper. Place a drop of iodine solution on each food on the paper (see photo **C**). Observe and record any color changes.

## Analyzing

**1.** What evidence did you have that fat was present in the food?

**2.** What evidence did you have that starch was present in the food?

## Concluding and Applying

**3.** Which of the foods would you *infer* contained fat?

**4.** **Going Further** What might you do to test whether the fat present was saturated or unsaturated?

**Student Journal** Have students enter the data table and answer the questions in their journals. **L1**

### Expected Outcomes

Cheese, bacon, potato chips, and perhaps bread should leave grease spots on the bag. Bread, potato, and the potato chip should turn dark blue in the presence of the iodine solution.

### Answers to Analyzing/ Concluding and Applying

**1.** Foods with fat made grease spots on the bag.

**2.** Foods with starch turned dark blue in the presence of the iodine solution.

**3.** cheese, bacon, potato chip, possibly bread

**4.** Observe whether it is liquid or solid at room temperature.

### ✔ Assessment

**Content** Ask students which of the foods that were tested contained neither fat nor starch. *egg white* What does that food contain? *protein* (Refer students back to the Explore activity on page 322 if they have trouble remembering that egg whites are rich in protein.)

---

### ENRICHMENT

**Activity** Iodine reacts with lipids and starches and forms double bonds in their carbon chains. Materials needed are iodine solution in dropper bottle; samples of lipids. Put drops of iodine on various lipid samples. The more iodine that is needed to cause a reaction, the more double bonds a lipid will have. Animal fat would need little iodine. Sunflower oil would require a great deal of iodine. **L2**

# 3 ASSESS

## Check for Understanding

When assigning the Check Your Understanding questions you may need to describe and review photosynthesis with students as they work on question 4, the Apply question. As a hint, ask what plants need to survive? *light, air, water*

## Reteach

Have students evaluate the role of different foods in a healthful diet. List two or three healthful menus on the chalkboard. Obtain these from a health text or from pamphlets published by a reputable health organization. Have students identify each item as a contributor of protein, lipid, or carbohydrate. L1

## Extension

**Demonstration** Allow students to recognize how the structure of protein can be changed without adding heat or chemicals.

Materials needed are egg white, whisk, and bowl. Have students whisk egg whites until they change from clear in color to white. Explain that the whisking "denatures" the protein by disrupting its polymer structure. L3

# 4 CLOSE

## Activity

Ask a representative from your school's food service department to explain to the class how the menu items are selected for the school lunch program and how the menus meet the nutritional needs of a teenager. L1

---

Rubber is a polymer that we sometimes chew. Bubble gum is stretchy because it contains a little synthetic rubber, other synthetic polymers, flavoring, and vegetable oil for softening.

## ■ Cholestrol

Besides saturated fats, animal foods contain another lipid called cholesterol. Do you know that even if you never eat foods containing cholesterol, your body will still make its own supply? Cholesterol is needed by your body to build cell membranes and is also found in bile, a fluid made by the liver and needed for digestion. Too much cholesterol is not good and can result in a build-up of cholesterol in arteries.

We have discussed three important classes of biological hydrocarbon compounds: proteins, carbohydrates, and lipids. Many of these compounds are very long and complicated polymers. Carbohydrates and lipids are in foods that provide energy for the body. Proteins are present in every living substance and are needed in food for growth and to renew the body. Each of these compounds exists because of carbon's ability to form covalent bonds with other atoms such as oxygen or nitrogen.

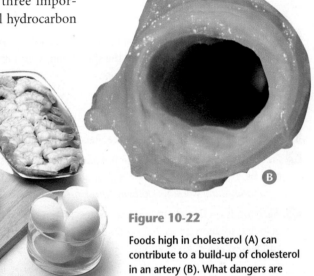

**Figure 10-22**

Foods high in cholesterol (A) can contribute to a build-up of cholesterol in an artery (B). What dangers are posed when cholesterol builds-up and clings to walls of the arteries?

## check your UNDERSTANDING

1. How are polymers formed?
2. Name some examples of biological compounds. Where are they found?
3. What do proteins, carbohydrates, and lipids in the foods you eat provide for your body?

4. **Apply** Unlike animals, plants cannot digest the foods necessary to form biological compounds. Explain how plants make the biological compounds they need.

---

## check your UNDERSTANDING

1. Smaller organic molecules called monomers are chemically bonded together.

2. Possible answers: Proteins make up muscles. Glucose is found in grapes and honey. Vegetables contain carbohydrates in the form of starch.

3. Proteins provide growth and renewal. Carbohydrates and lipids provide energy.

4. Plants can make carbohydrates through photosynthesis. Using energy from the sun, they convert water and carbon dioxide into organic compounds containing carbon, hydrogen, and oxygen.

## Technology Connection

# The Discovery of DNA Structure

Almost everyone has heard of DNA today, but in the 1950s, DNA structure was a mystery. In fact, one of the major scientific events of the 20th century was the discovery of the structure of DNA. Much of the research that led to this discovery was based on the work of an English scientist, Rosalind Elsie Franklin.

### X-ray Crystallography

From 1947 to 1950, Franklin studied the basics of a technique called X-ray crystallography. In X-ray crystallography, X rays are sent through a substance to find out how atoms are arranged. She used this technique to research changes in the arrangement of carbon atoms when coal is heated. Her work was invaluable to the coking and atomic technology industries.

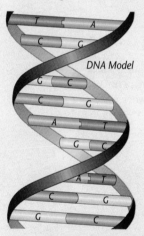
DNA Model

In 1951, Franklin applied X-ray crystallography techniques to the study of DNA. She is credited with discovering the density of DNA and its double-strand structure. She died of cancer at the age of 37.

### DNA Structure

Using Franklin's invaluable discoveries, other scientists continued the study of DNA. They started their work knowing that DNA is a large molecule composed of sugar and phosphate groups linked in long chains plus nitrogen-containing compounds called bases. They did not know, however, how all these components fit together.

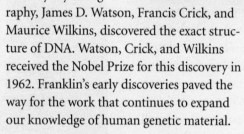

With further use of X-ray crystallography, James D. Watson, Francis Crick, and Maurice Wilkins, discovered the exact structure of DNA. Watson, Crick, and Wilkins received the Nobel Prize for this discovery in 1962. Franklin's early discoveries paved the way for the work that continues to expand our knowledge of human genetic material.

### What Do You Think?

Do you always work straight through a problem from beginning to end? Did you ever wake up in the middle of the night knowing just how to solve a problem? Can you draw any conclusions from these experiences about how the mind works?

### Going Further ▸

Genetic diseases are encoded right into DNA, meaning that people are born with them. Have each student select a genetic disease and write a brief report on its symptoms, who can be or is usually affected, and what treatment is available. Examples are Down syndrome, cystic fibrosis, sickle-cell anemia, hemophilia, Tay-Sachs disease, and muscular dystrophy. Genetic engineering is a controversial subject. Have students research genetic engineering in recent magazine articles. Then form teams to debate this question: **Should we allow genetic engineers to change the DNA in organisms to create new medicines, eliminate disease, correct genetic disorders, and improve our food, when there is the risk of abuse such as creating killer bacteria or mutant humans?** COOP LEARN L3

## Science and Society

**Purpose** Science and Society connects the biological compounds discussed in Section 10-3 with the part they play in recycling and composting.

### Content Background

When thoroughly mixed over several years, compost creates a black, porous, easy-to-work garden soil that holds water for growing plants. It may be acidic, so gardeners add lime to neutralize some of the acid. Compost is a mild fertilizer that releases nutrients to growing plants at a rate they can use efficiently. Some gardeners add a stronger commercial fertilizer. The main advantage of composting lies in recycling plant waste.

### Teaching Strategies

Discuss any experiences students may have had with gardening. What was done to prepare the soil for planting? Why? Was a commercial fertilizer or compost used? If compost was used, how and where was it made? **L2**

## Science and Society

# Pile It On!

Do you have a compost pile in your backyard? Compost is one of the best fertilizers available to gardeners and is free for the making. In fact, compost has been produced for eons without any help from people. Before farmers and homeowners began moving things around, leaves and weeds fell on the ground, rotted there, and provided a constant source of food for growing plants. Without knowing it, landowners created an ideal environment for encouraging growth. When we rake leaves, plant grass, and pull weeds and throw them away, we break that natural cycle.

### Composting

Composting is the process of breaking down waste material and changing it into useful products. The main ingredients in compost are carbon and nitrogen. All plant materials contain both of these elements.

Some are higher in carbon, such as twigs, sawdust, dried leaves, and hay. Others are higher in nitrogen, such as green grass clippings, kitchen vegetable waste, and animal by-products. The ratio of carbon to nitrogen determines how quickly the waste will be turned into useful fertilizer. Most materials have more carbon than nitrogen, so adding nitrogen makes the process go faster. A pile of sawdust, which is mostly carbon, can take years to break down, but if you mix the sawdust with green grass and animal manure, it will turn into rich compost in a matter of several months.

### Anaerobic and Aerobic Composting

The process of composting is done in two ways. Anaerobic composting (without air) is done in closed bins. By keeping the air out, you are able to prevent the loss of valuable nitrogen. Nitrogen is necessary for all plant growth and is the main ingredient in most fertilizers. With this kind of composting, methane gas is produced and can then be used as a fuel for heating or lighting. Many small farms use this free source of fuel gained from anaerobic composting.

Most composting, however, is done aerobically (with air). The materials are piled in bins or simply in piles and turned occasionally to let the air circulate through and speed up the decomposition process. Heat is produced from the chemical reaction that makes the compost.

### Benefits

In either method of composting, the result is nitrogen-rich soil that will feed your plants and encourage them to grow. Addition of many different kinds of materials to your compost heap will also add beneficial minerals, such as calcium, phosphates, and potash.

Composting is also one of the easiest and most beneficial ways everyone can protect the environment. Many communities now have laws that prohibit yard waste from being put in landfills. It takes up space and is wasteful! Instead of throwing all these valuable resources away, you can easily return them to nature to help the trees, grass, flowers, and vegetables grow healthier and faster.

### *You Try It!*

Build a compost pile in the corner of your yard and watch a bunch of trash turn into rich soil. Layer kitchen scraps (vegetable only) with grass clippings, leaves, and whatever other waste you find in the yard. Keep the pile damp but not wet and turn it every few days to keep the materials well mixed. Notice that the middle of the pile gets hot as the compost is being formed. In a few weeks, you will have a free supply of the best fertilizer available.

### Demonstration

Explain to students that making compost is like running a "humus factory." Humus is the decayed plant and animal matter that makes soil dark and porous. If possible, arrange for students to observe an area which the soil is disturbed, such as a construction site, road cut, or trench. Or, with the school's permission, dig a hole in the school yard. (Be sure to refill it.) Have students describe the soil profile they see. This should include a dark layer at the top with lighter layers below. Explain that the dark layer is topsoil that contains humus. L1

### Going Further ⅢⅢ▶

Have students determine whether composting at your school is done, or is feasible. Point out that composting, like all recycling, needs both a source and a market. *Source:* Have a group of students interview cafeteria personnel to determine the quantity of vegetable waste generated per week. Have another group interview maintenance personnel to determine the quantity of grass clippings that might be available. *Market:* Also have students ask maintenance personnel if there is a use for composted material around the school property. Hold a class discussion of whether there is a market at your school for compost and how well the demand matches the possible supply. If your school looks like a candidate for composting, have a group of students draft a proposal and present it to your building principal. L2 **COOP LEARN**

### Teens in SCIENCE

**Purpose**
Teens in Science continues the concern for the environment that runs through this chapter by describing some recycling efforts of teens.

**Content Background**
Recycling is an ideal fund-raiser for organizations since everyone benefits from it. However, a key problem organizations don't always recognize is that there may not be a market for the metal, glass, paper, plastic, cardboard, and other recyclable materials that they collect. For example, if a recycling facility is privately owned, it won't accept or pay for scrap paper unless it can resell the waste for a profit. If a recycling facility is government-operated, it will accept waste because tax money is paying for the operation. However, it may not pay for it.

**Teaching Strategies** Have students find out whether or not your school recycles. Have students find out which materials are recycled, where they go, and whether the school receives money for them. [L1]

**Discussion**
Brainstorm with students the possible groups in your school that might profit from gathering recyclable materials. [L1]

### Teens in SCIENCE

## Cleaning up Earth

Teenagers may be more environmentally sensitive than their parents were at the same age. They know that the world they are inheriting needs cleaning up, and they want it to be in good shape when they hand it over to their own children. Individuals and groups such as bands, scouts, and science clubs routinely gather up recyclable material such as newspapers and aluminum cans and raise money by taking them to recycling centers. Many others are going even farther to clean up the environment.

### Testing River Water

Teenagers from Quincy High School in Illinois monitor the Mississippi River for pollutants. They use tests that show levels of dissolved oxygen. If there is a low level of oxygen, life in the river suffers. The students are working directly with The Illinois Rivers Project to make sure that the river is clean and that those who use the water do so responsibly.

### Roland Ng

Eighteen-year-old Roland Ng of Tracy, California, headed up a recycling project that collected throw-aways—cans, bottles, and paper all over town. Roland coaches a team of seven year olds at the Boys and Girls Club in Tracy, and uses the money earned from recycling to buy basketballs and other sports equipment for the children.

### *You Try It!*

Locate the recycling centers in your area. Do they take aluminum, glass, plastic, and paper? Start recycling materials from your own home.

**CAREER connection**

**Environmental scientists** have many options. They monitor bodies of water, air, and industry for possible pollutants. They research ways to control or eliminate pollutants. They work for government agencies, industry, or have their own consulting or research businesses.

CLEAN GLASS ONLY

### Going Further ▶

Everyone knows about the trash their families generate. But how many students have visited a landfill to see just how huge the problem of garbage disposal is? Plan a field trip to your local landfill. Before you do so, have a group of student volunteers research and report on the anatomy of a landfill—how plastic-sheet liners are used and how trash is layer-caked with clay and dirt—so that students will better understand what they see. [L2] **COOP LEARN**

One person's trash is another person's treasure! Have student volunteers research "garbology" (garbage archeology) in which archeologists learn about a city's or culture's past by carefully excavating ancient dumping grounds. Ask them to describe a specific excavation and what was found. Then ask students to write a brief summary of what archeologists could discover in the future by an excavation of our present landfills. [L3]

Review the statements below about the big ideas presented in this chapter, and try to answer the questions. Then, reread your answers to the Did You Ever Wonder questions at the beginning of the chapter. *In your Journal*, write a paragraph about how your understanding of the big ideas in the chapter has changed.

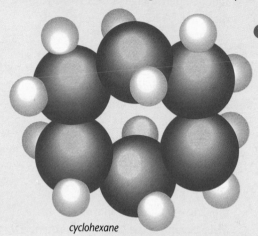

cyclohexane

**1** Carbon's unique ability to form four covalent bonds with other atoms enables it to make a huge number of compounds. *How does the structure of a compound determine its properties?*

**2** Hydrocarbons can be composed of hydrogen and carbon alone, or other chemical groups may be substituted for hydrogen on the molecule to form new compounds, as with vitamin C. *Compare and contrast the three types of substituted hydrocarbons.*

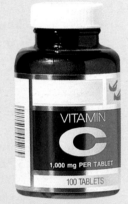

**3** Biological compounds are complex hydrocarbons that make up living things. Your body needs the proteins, carbohydrates, and lipids that are found in food to provide energy and to repair or replace cells. *What are two examples of foods that provide protein? carbohydrates? lipids?*

Direct students' attention to the diagrams. Use the diagrams to review the main ideas presented in the chapter.

## Teaching Strategies

Have students use pencil and paper or models to explore the structure of hydrocarbons by posing these situations.

**a.** Suppose carbon could form only three bonds instead of four.

**b.** Suppose carbon could form only two bonds instead of four.

**c.** Suppose carbon could form only one bond instead of four.

Discuss why carbon's ability to form four bonds allows it to form a variety of complex molecules such as lipids, proteins, vitamins, and carbohydrates. **COOP LEARN** **L2**

## Answers to Questions

**1.** Shorter hydrocarbons are lighter molecules and in general have low boiling points and they evaporate and burn easier. Longer hydrocarbons are heavy molecules and exist as solids or liquids at room temperature.

**2.** *alcohol:* hydroxyl group (-OH) replaces 1 or more hydrogen atoms, produced naturally by sugar fermentation in fruit and grain

*carboxylic acid:* carboxyl (-COOH) replaces a $CH_3$ group, oxygen double bonds to carbon, sour taste, used for fuels, as a disinfectant and cleaner

*amine:* amine group ($-NH_2$) replaces a hydrogen, found in caffeine, novocaine, and in some vitamins

**3.** Answers will vary but can include the following:

foods providing protein - milk, fish, meat, poultry

foods providing carbohydrates - pasta, bread, vegetables, sugar

foods providing lipids - butter, margarine, oils, solid shortening

## Project

Make glue from milk: Add 6 tablespoons of vinegar to 2 cups of skim milk. Let the mixture sit overnight (or longer) until curds form. When curds form, pour off the liquid (whey) and leave the solid curds. Milk souring is a result of lactic acid produced by bacteria. Here, the vinegar soured the milk. Add 1/4 cup of water and 1 level teaspoon of baking soda to the curds. The baking soda neutralizes the remaining vinegar and leaves glue. **L1**

## Science at Home

When poured into water, the chlorine in bleach combines with the hydrogen. This frees up the oxygen in the water to oxidize or combine with any stains in a fabric to produce a colorless compound. Do a "magic" trick using bleach. Pour a very small amount of bleach into a glass. In an identical glass, mix enough red food coloring with water to get a deep red color. Now pour the red liquid into the other cup. After a few minutes, the colored liquid turns colorless! **L1**

## Using Key Science Terms

1. amines do not belong because they contain nitrogen, while alcohol and carboxylic acid contain oxygen

2. hydrocarbon does not belong because it contains only hydrogen and carbon, and no other substituted groups

3. polymers do not belong because they are made up of many smaller molecules such as alcohols and amines

4. isomers do not belong because they are not a type of biological compound

## Understanding Ideas

1. alcohol, amine, carboxylic acid

2. 32

3. Hexane is a longer and heavier hydrocarbon than butane so it has a higher boiling point.

4. amino acid monomers

5. lipids—30% or less
proteins—10–15%
carbohydrates—55–65%

## Developing Skills

1. From the graph, the boiling point of pentane is about 34°C. (The actual value is 36°C.)

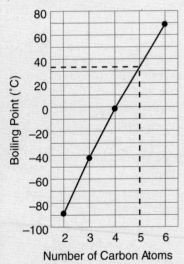

2. a) alcohol b) carboxylic acid c) amine d) alcohol e) carboxylic acid

3. Peanut and kidney bean contain protein; apple does not contain protein.

---

### U sing Key Science Terms

| | |
|---|---|
| alcohol | isomers |
| amines | lipids |
| carbohydrates | organic compound |
| carboxylic acid | polymers |
| hydrocarbon | proteins |

*For each set of terms below, choose the one term that does not belong and explain why it does not belong.*

1. alcohol, amines, carboxylic acid
2. hydrocarbon, alcohol, amines
3. polymers, alcohol, amines
4. proteins, lipids, isomers

### U nderstanding Ideas

*Answer the following questions in your Journal using complete sentences.*

1. Name three types of substituted hydrocarbons.

2. If a carbohydrate has 16 oxygen atoms, how many hydrogen atoms does it have?

3. Do you expect hexane or butane to have a higher boiling point? Explain.

---

4. Monomers of which type make up a protein polymer?

5. A healthy diet includes lipids, proteins, and carbohydrates. What is the recommended percentage of calories in your diet from each of these three groups?

### D eveloping Skills

*Use your understanding of the concepts developed in this chapter to answer each of the following questions.*

1. **Making and Using Graphs** - The boiling points of ethane, propane, butane, and hexane are as follows:

   ethane -89°C   butane -1°C
   propane -42°C   hexane 69°C

   Make a graph of the data. Plot the number of carbon atoms on the x-axis and the boiling point on the y-axis. Use your graph to estimate the boiling point of pentane.

2. **Classifying** - For each of the following tell whether the compound given is an alcohol, amine, or carboxylic acid:
   a. $C_3H_7OH$
   b. $CH_3CH_2COOH$
   c. $CH_3CH_2NH_2$
   d. $CH_3OH$
   e. $C_8H_{17}COOH$

3. **Comparing and Contrasting** - Repeat the test for protein in the Explore activity on page 322 using different foods. Use a piece of apple, a peanut, and a kidney bean. Compare the results of this activity with those made in the original activity.

---

### Program Resources

**Review and Assessment,** pp. 59–64 [L1]
**Performance Assessment,** Ch. 10 [L2]
**PAMSS**
**Alternate Assessment in The Science Classroom**
**Computer Test Bank**

## Critical Thinking

In your Journal, *answer each of the following questions.*

1. Compare and contrast saturated and unsaturated fats.
2. Why do butane and isobutane have different properties?
3. How does an amino acid differ from a carboxylic acid?
4. Describe the substitution process in which butane changes to butyl alcohol.

## Problem Solving

*Read the following problem and discuss your answers in a brief paragraph.*

**Maria bought some green, unripe bananas at the store. She needs to make a banana cake tomorrow but the bananas are too green to mash. She wants to eat some bananas during the week.**

1. What can she do to help the bananas for the cake ripen faster between now and tomorrow?
2. What can she do to keep the bananas she wants to eat from ripening too quickly?

## CONNECTING IDEAS

Discuss each of the following in a brief paragraph.

1. **Theme—Scale and Structure** Octane number is used as a measure of a gasoline's ability to burn evenly. The higher the octane number for a gasoline, the less likely it is to cause an engine to knock or ping when driving. Look at the diagram. It shows three types of gasolines, and their octane numbers. What do you think is the relationship between even burning and molecular structure?

a. Heptane 0

$$H - \overset{\overset{\displaystyle H}{|}}{\underset{\underset{\displaystyle H}{|}}{C}} - \overset{\overset{\displaystyle H}{|}}{\underset{\underset{\displaystyle H}{|}}{C}} - \overset{\overset{\displaystyle H}{|}}{\underset{\underset{\displaystyle H}{|}}{C}} - \overset{\overset{\displaystyle H}{|}}{\underset{\underset{\displaystyle H}{|}}{C}} - \overset{\overset{\displaystyle H}{|}}{\underset{\underset{\displaystyle H}{|}}{C}} - \overset{\overset{\displaystyle H}{|}}{\underset{\underset{\displaystyle H}{|}}{C}} - \overset{\overset{\displaystyle H}{|}}{\underset{\underset{\displaystyle H}{|}}{C}} - H$$

b. 2-methylheptane 23

c. Isooctane 100

2. **Theme—Energy** One gram of a lipid yields about 9 calories in energy, while one gram of a carbohydrate only yields 4 calories. If lipids produce more energy than carbohydrates, why shouldn't they make up the larger part of a healthful diet?

3. **Life Science CONNECTION** What are biotoxins, and of what organic molecules are many of them composed?

4. **Science and Society** Describe some of the benefits of composting.

## Critical Thinking

1. Saturated fats are found mostly in foods that come from animal sources. They contain only single bonds between carbon atoms and are usually solid at room temperature. Oils from plants are mostly unsaturated. They contain at least one double or triple bond and are liquid at room temperature.

2. They are isomers with the same formulas, but different structures.

3. An amino acid has a $-NH_2$ group as well as an acid group in its structure.

4. Replace a hydrogen (H) with a hydroxyl group (-OH).

## Problem Solving

1. Put them in a sealed container with any other ripening fruit that will emit ethene.

2. Keep them in an open place where air can circulate, away from other ripening fruit.

## Connecting Ideas

1. Hydrocarbons in straight chains tend to explode more than branched hydrocarbons, causing knocks and pings. 2,2,4-trimethylpentane, with 3 branches in its structure, burns more evenly and has a higher octane number than n-heptane, with no branches.

2. Eating too much fat (lipid) is associated with heart disease, high blood pressure, and certain kinds of cancer. Lipids can cause a person to be overweight, which initiates all of the problems above and puts a strain on many systems in the body.

3. Biotoxins are substances made by plants or animals that can kill other organisms. Many are composed of protein.

4. Some benefits of composting are rich soil for plants, less garbage in landfills, and the return of natural resources to the environment.

## ✔ Assessment

**Portfolio** Review the portfolio options that are provided throughout the chapter. Encourage students to select one product that demonstrates their best work for the chapter. Have students explain what they learned and why they chose this example for placement into their portfolios.

Additional portfolio options can be found in the following **Teacher Classroom Resources:**

**Concept Mapping,** p. 18

Making Connections: Integrating Sciences, p. 23

**Multicultural Connections,** pp. 23–211

**Making Connections: Across the curriculum,** p. 23

**Critical Thinking/Problem Solving,** p. 18

**Take Home Activities,** p. 18

**Laboratory Manual,** pp. 57–60; 61–64; 65–66

**Performance Assessment** P

CHAPTER 11

# Fueling the Body

## THEME DEVELOPMENT

The theme of this chapter is energy—the use of food as fuel to provide energy for the body. The second section focuses on systems and interactions, as the enzymes of the digestive system interact with foods, breaking them down into a form that can be used by the body.

## CHAPTER OVERVIEW

Six nutrients are essential to health: proteins, carbohydrates, fats, vitamins, minerals, and water. The process of digesting these nutrients from foods begins in the mouth and continues as food travels through the esophagus, stomach, and intestines. Other organs, such as the liver, gall bladder, and pancreas, assist in the process of digestion by secreting or storing enzymes.

### Tying to Previous Knowledge

Ask students what a car needs to run. Elicit the idea that a variety of fuels might make the car run, but it will run best if it is given the kind of fuel that is right for its engine. Now ask if the same is true of humans. Point out that this chapter is about the fuel that works best to power the human engine, and how that engine uses its fuel.

## INTRODUCING THE CHAPTER

Have students look at the photograph on page 336. How many of the foods pictured can they identify? Make a list on the chalkboard and ask for a show of hands for who likes each vegetable listed. Ask students to add foods that are not pictured. *meats, grains, dairy products, for example.* Point out that we need various types of food, and this chapter will show why.

# FUELING the BODY

**W**elcome to Blanca Hidalgo's garden. Those red-ripe tomatoes soon will find their way into a spicy salsa. The carrots and zucchini will become part of a fresh vegetable salad. And those onions and peppers will add zip to tonight's tacos.

Animals benefit from Blanca's garden too. Pesky crows swoop down to sample the ripening corn. A rabbit nibbles at the lettuce and aphids suck juices from the tomato stems.

All living things—from the largest animal to the tiniest cell—require nourishment. In this chapter you will learn about the fuel your body needs and how your body processes that fuel to keep you healthy!

▶ *In the Explore activity you will learn about different diets that people eat.*

### Did you ever wonder...

✓ **How long someone could live without food?**

✓ **Why your stomach makes noises when you're hungry?**

✓ **How large the area of your small intestine is?**

Before you begin to study about fueling the body, think about these questions and answer them *in your Journal.* When you finish the chapter, compare your Journal write-up with what you have learned.

### Did you ever wonder...

Students will explore these questions as they progress through the chapter.

• A person could live without food for weeks, perhaps months, but only a few days without water. (p. 341)

• An empty stomach acts as an amplifier for the sounds that are always present in the digestive tract. (p. 361)

• The surface area of the small intestine is over 264 square meters. (p. 360)

### STUDENT JOURNAL

Have students write their responses to the Did You Ever Wonder questions in their journals. After they have read the chapter, students should read their journal entries to see what they have learned about the role of nutrients in human digestion.

## Explore! ACTIVITY

### How is your diet different from that of your classmates?

**N**ot everyone eats the same kinds of food. You have favorite foods, foods you tolerate, and foods you do not care for at all.

**What To Do**

1. Make a list of the foods you eat most often at home. Be honest about your snacking habits, too.

2. Compare your list with your classmates'.

3. What foods are common to everyone's lists?

4. What foods are different?

5. What foods are on your classmates' lists that you would be willing to try?

### ASSESSMENT PLANNER

**PORTFOLIO**
Refer to 369 for suggested items that students might select for their portfolios.

**PERFORMANCE ASSESSMENT**
Process, pp. 337, 338, 355, 359, 361
Skillbuilder, p. 344
Explore! Activities, pp. 337, 340, 341, 343, 353
Find Out! Activities, pp. 338, 345, 356, 358, 361
Investigate, pp. 348–349, 354–355

**CONTENT ASSESSMENT**
Check Your Understanding, pp. 350, 362
Reviewing Main Ideas, p. 367
Chapter Review, pp. 368–369

**GROUP ASSESSMENT**
Opportunities for group assessment occur with Cooperative Learning Strategies.

### Uncovering Preconceptions

People tend to have many misconceptions about food. Have students write one thing they think they know about nutrition and digestion on a piece of paper and seal it in an envelope with their name on the outside. Collect the envelopes. At the end of the chapter, return the envelopes and have students discuss whether their ideas were true or false.

## Explore!

### How is your diet different from that of your classmates?

**Time needed** 20 minutes

**Thinking Processes** interpreting data, comparing and contrasting

**Purpose** To interpret data about diets.

### Teaching the Activity

**Troubleshooting** Many students have poor diets because their families cannot afford nutritious foods. Handle this issue sensitively in this and all activities in this chapter.

**Student Journal** Have students make their list in their journals. L1

### Expected Outcome

People have varied eating patterns.

### Answers to Questions

Answers will vary. Be sure that students respect each other's food choices and do not ridicule others for eating foods that they do not like.

### ✓ Assessment

**Process** Have students make a graph that allows them to show how many "votes" different foods received. They may do this in small groups or as a class. Use the Performance Task Assessment List for Graph from Data in **PAMSS**, p. 39. **COOP LEARN** L1

## Concepts Developed

In Chapter 10, students learned about the chemistry of organic compounds, including proteins and carbohydrates—two nutrients needed by the human body. This section discusses all six nutrients and the importance of each. Students will evaluate their own diet and plan a healthy one.

## Planning the Lesson

Refer to the Chapter Organizer on pages 336A–B.

---

### Find Out!

**Does your diet include a healthful variety of foods?**

**Time needed**  15 minutes

**Thinking Processes** making and using tables, observing and inferring, interpreting data

**Purpose** To interpret data about diet.

**Preparation** Remind students periodically during the week to keep up their charts.

### Teaching the Activity

**Discussion** Lead students in a discussion of the importance of accurate data collection. Emphasize that data will be private.

**Student Journal** Have students make their charts in their journals. L1

### Expected Outcome

Students should identify their diets' strengths and weaknesses.

---

# Nutrients: The Spice of Life

## Section Objectives

■ Identify types of nutrients and describe the importance of each.

■ Evaluate your own diet and plan a healthy one.

## Key Terms

*nutrients*
*minerals*
*vitamins*

## Nutrients and Your Diet

You've probably heard the expression "you are what you eat." No, it doesn't mean that you'll turn into a pizza if that's your favorite food. What would happen to your body if you didn't eat certain foods? Do you know what happens to a body when it doesn't get the food it needs?

Your body requires the right kind of nourishment—a healthful variety of foods. Exactly what does food do for you?

### Find Out! ACTIVITY

### Does your diet include a healthful variety of foods?

**Y**ou may think that you are eating a well-balanced diet that includes a variety of foods. How can you be sure?

### What To Do

1. Make a chart. Across the top of the chart write the days of the week. Along the left side of the chart write Breakfast, Lunch, Dinner, and Snacks.

2. Fill out the chart for an entire week, listing every food you eat at every meal and the foods you eat between meals.

3. Analyze your chart.

4. Do you know which foods came from animal sources? Which foods came from plants?

5. Which food choices came from grain sources, such as bread or pasta?

6. Which foods do you think had a great deal of fat?

### Conclude and Apply

1. Based on your analysis, explain why you think you are or are not eating a healthful variety of foods.

2. Based on your analysis, what foods should you add to your diet to make it more healthful?

---

### Conclude and Apply

**1.** Diets rich in fruits, vegetables, and grains may be identified as being healthful. Those containing excessively fatty, sweet, or salty foods should be identified as being unhealthful.

**2.** Students may wish to add more fruits and vegetables, whole grains, and low-fat or non-fat dairy products.

### ✔ Assessment

**Process** Ask students who succeed in collecting data for the whole week to explain how they remembered to collect data and what motivated them to keep their records. Use the Performance Task Assessment List for Carrying Out a Strategy and Collecting Data in **PAMSS**, p. 25. L1 P

## Nutrition Information Labels

In the Find Out activity, you discovered whether or not you are eating a healthful variety of foods. Some foods are more healthful than others. How can you tell?

Take a look at a box of breakfast cereal. Besides the colorful images and the free offers, you'll also notice a label on the side panel listing nutritional information, like the one in **Figure 11-1.** You may think you're just eating toasted corn with raisins, but you're actually taking in nutrients. **Nutrients** are substances in food that provide energy and materials for the development, growth, and repair of cells. Nutrients are the fuel your body needs to function efficiently.

## Proper Nutrients Or . . .

Suppose your body doesn't get the proper mix of nutrients. Take a look at the two skeletons in **Figure 11-2.** The skeleton on the left is normal. The skeleton on the right, however,

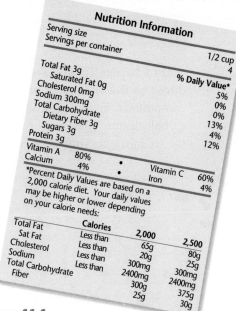

**Figure 11-1**

Nutrition labels display many valuable pieces of information.

shows evidence of a disease called rickets. Rickets is caused by the lack of an important nutrient, vitamin D. How did the lack of vitamin D affect the development of this person?

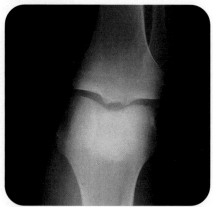

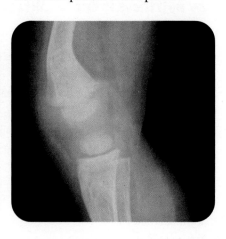

**Figure 11-2**

**Ⓐ** A balanced diet is essential for building a normal, healthy skeleton such as the one shown above.

**Ⓑ** This skeleton shows evidence of the disease rickets, which is caused by a lack of vitamin D.

11-1 Nutrients: The Spice of Life **339**

## Explore!

**How nutritious is one breakfast cereal?**

**Time needed** 10 minutes

**Thinking Processes** interpreting data, measuring in SI, using tables

**Purpose** To interpret data about nutrients in a cereal.

### Teaching the Activity

**Troubleshooting** Be sure students distinguish between the nutrients listed for cereal alone and cereal with milk.

**Student Journal** Have students record their answers in their journals. L1

### Expected Outcome

Students will accurately read the table of nutrients.

### Answers to Questions

The nutrients present will vary. The minerals will be absorbed quickly because they are inorganic compounds.

### ✔ Assessment

**Performance** Have students examine nutrition labels on cereal boxes at home or in a store. Have them compare and contrast the nutritional value of kind of cereal by listing maximum and minimum amounts of nutrients in the cereals they examine. Use the Performance Task Assessment List for Analyzing the Data in **PAMSS**, p. 27. L1

# Six Important Nutrients

In Chapter 10, you were introduced to the chemistry of organic compounds, including proteins and carbohydrates. These are just two of the six nutrients your body needs to function properly. The other nutrients are fats, vitamins, minerals, and water. Fats and vitamins are also organic compounds because they contain carbon atoms. Water and minerals are inorganic compounds. They contain no carbon atoms.

Look at the size and complexity of the diagrams of water, carbohydrate, and protein in **Figure 11-3**. What do you notice?

Carbohydrates, fats, and proteins in foods are usually in a form that must be broken down into simpler molecules before they can be absorbed and used by your body. In contrast, smaller molecules, such as water, vitamins, and minerals, are absorbed quickly.

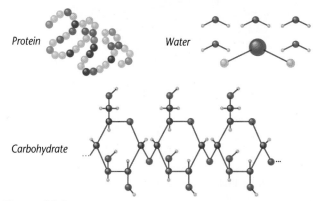

**Figure 11-3**

Organic molecules, such as protein and carbohydrate, are large and more complex than inorganic molecules, such as water.

## Explore! ACTIVITY

### How nutritious is one breakfast cereal?

**What To Do**

1. Look again at the list of nutrients on the cereal box label in Figure 11-1.

2. Which of the six nutrients does the cereal contain?

3. How much of each nutrient is present in the cereal? Nutrients are measured in grams and milligrams.

4. To get a better idea of just how much of each nutrient is present, measure out a gram of salt or sugar for comparison.

5. What vitamins are present? In what amounts?

6. What minerals are present?

7. Which of the nutrients will be absorbed most quickly by your body? Why?

**340** Chapter 11 Fueling the Body

## ■ Water

Water is a critical nutrient for life. Your body might function for weeks on limited amounts of food. But without water, your body would remain alive only for a few days.

Why is water so important? All of the cells of your body are mostly water. All chemical reactions and other cellular functions take place in the cell's cytoplasm, a substance that is primarily water.

### Explore! ACTIVITY

## How much of you is water?

Believe it or not, by weight, your body is nearly two-thirds water. Generally, when a person diets, the first pounds lost are actually pounds of water.

### What To Do

1. To figure out how much of you is water, multiply your weight by 66 percent.

2. What figure do you get? Record your answer *in your Journal.*

**Figure 11-4**

Why do you drink liquid when you feel thirsty? Your body is trying to maintain a balanced internal condition. Exercise, perspiration, and urination deplete your body's supply of water. Messages are sent to your brain and you feel thirsty. After you replenish your water supply, more messages are sent to your brain and you no longer feel thirsty.

**Figure 11-5**

Your body cells all contain water. The amount of water in the cells depends on the type of tissue they make up.

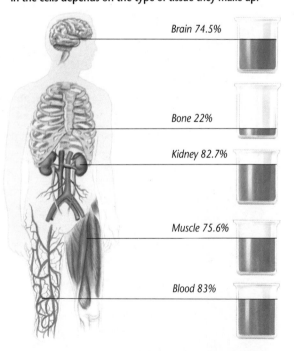

Brain 74.5%

Bone 22%

Kidney 82.7%

Muscle 75.6%

Blood 83%

## Across the Curriculum

### Health

Some foods were invented to cure diseases (though they probably did not do so). Have students research the origins of Graham crackers, Kellogg's wheat flakes, or Post Toasties. These products were invented by Rev. Graham, Dr. Kellogg, and Mr. Post in hopes of curing such ailments as alcoholism, malaria, tuberculosis, and even appendicitis. More information on food and health can be found in *Jane Brody's Nutrition Book* (NY: Norton, 1986).

### Content Background

During strenuous exercise, an athlete loses fluid. Sudden loss of as little as 2 percent of your body weight through perspiration can impair your body's circulation and temperature regulation. Weigh yourself before and after exercise. For every pound lost, drink two cups of water to maintain adequate hydration.

### Visual Learning

**Figure 11-6** Ask students to name some foods that are sources of minerals. Be sure students understand the importance of minerals to the proper development and maintenance of the body.

**Figure 11-7 How do the starches found in carbohydrates help fulfill your long-term energy needs?** *Because starches break down slowly, they provide energy over a period of time.*

**DID YOU KNOW?**

Blood supplies nutrients, including sodium, protein, and iron. In some cultures, blood is used as food, a regular part of the diet. The Slavic people make a soup from duck's blood. The British make blood sausage. And the Masai people of Africa milk blood from the cattle they herd to supplement their diet during the dry season.

## Minerals

Like water, minerals are also important nutrients for your body. Salt is a mineral, and minerals come from Earth. **Minerals** are inorganic compounds that regulate many of the chemical reactions that take place in your body. But why is your body composed of molecules from Earth?

Scientists think that all life on Earth began in the sea. The sea is rich in minerals, so it makes sense that organisms that began life in this "mineral soup" are mineral-rich themselves. In fact, the water in your body contains dissolved minerals that make it chemically similar to the water in the ocean.

Of all the elements listed in the periodic table, your body requires about 14 to regulate its chemical reactions. These include calcium, phosphorous, sodium, potassium, magnesium, and iron. They are required by your body in small amounts. A deficiency in any one mineral, however small, can result in disease such as osteoporosis or goiter.

**Figure 11-6** shows some of the most important minerals your body needs, how they function in your body, and which foods contain them. Look back at the chart of foods you've been eating during the past week. Is your body being provided with the minerals it needs?

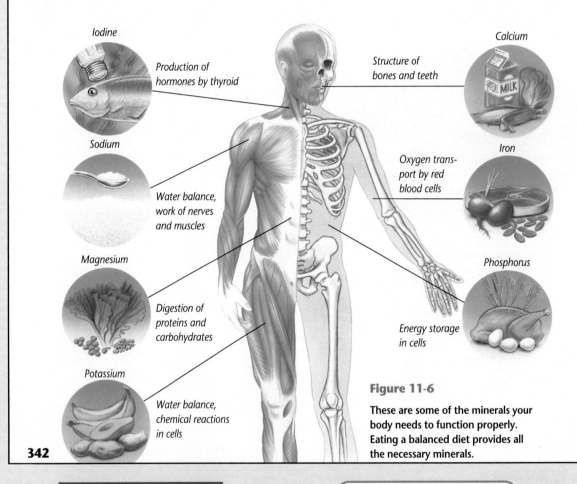

Iodine
Production of hormones by thyroid
Sodium
Water balance, work of nerves and muscles
Magnesium
Digestion of proteins and carbohydrates
Potassium
Water balance, chemical reactions in cells
Calcium
Structure of bones and teeth
MILK
Iron
Oxygen transport by red blood cells
Phosphorus
Energy storage in cells


**Figure 11-6**

**These are some of the minerals your body needs to function properly. Eating a balanced diet provides all the necessary minerals.**

342

### ENRICHMENT

**Discussion** If there are athletes among your students, have them tell the class about the need for water or other fluids during sports training and performance. Do they drink water or a special sports drink? What is in commercially available sports drinks that may make them more beneficial than water? Coaches can help with information for this discussion. Ideas to consider include: fluid needs for different sports and the effects of heat and humidity.

### Program Resources

**Making Connections: Integrating Sciences,** p. 25, Advertising and Anorexia L2

**Making Connections: Across the Curriculum,** p. 25, Using the Food Guide Pyramid L2

**Science Discovery Activities,** 11-1, Weighing Curds and Accounting for Whey

### Carbohydrates

The next time you come home from school feeling tired, do what the nutrition pros do for an energy boost. Eat a potato, a dish of three-bean salad, or a plate of spaghetti. All of these foods contain carbohydrates. Carbohydrates are organic compounds and are the main source of energy for most organisms.

Carbohydrates come in three forms: sugars, starches, and cellulose. Sugar is a simple carbohydrate. Sugar comes in many forms, including glucose, dextrose, fructose, corn syrup, and molasses. Energy that you use for all your body's activities is released from simple carbohydrates when they are broken down in your cells.

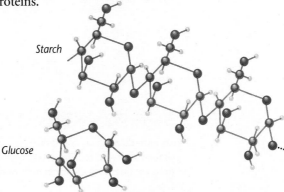

#### Explore! ACTIVITY

### Which foods contain carbohydrates?

**What To Do**

1. Look at the nutrition labels on the packages of ten foods that you eat often, such as frozen pizza, pasta, orange juice, bread, and so on.

2. Which foods contain carbohydrates?

3. How many total grams of carbohydrates does a serving contain?

Starches, found in foods such as pasta, potatoes, and cassava root are complex carbohydrates. So is cellulose, the tough fiber that makes up the cell walls in plants. Complex carbohydrates are made up of large molecules that have to be broken down into smaller forms, simple carbohydrates,

before they can be used by your body. Complex carbohydrates, especially grains, are important foods in diets all over the world because they are more plentiful and less expensive than fats and proteins.

**Figure 11-7**

Carbohydrates are the main source of energy for you and other animals. Sugars that are found in carbohydrates can be used almost immediately by your body and help to fulfill your short-term energy needs. How do the starches found in carbohydrates help fulfill your long-term energy needs?

*Starch*

*Glucose*

**344** Chapter 11 Fueling the Body

**Activity** Challenge students to find the "hidden" fat. Using food labels or nutrition books, have students look for a food with over 75 percent of its calories from fat (butter); a food labeled "no cholesterol" with at least 50 percent of its calories from fat (salad oil, mayonnaise); a food that they thought had little or no fat, but in fact has at least 20 percent of its calories from fat (coconut); a food they thought was very fatty but has 20 percent or less of its calories from fat (buttermilk). L1

**Uncovering Preconceptions**
There is a tendency to think that it is all right to eat some fats but not others. For example, some people think if you cut out red meat with its high fat content, you can eat all the potato chips you want, no matter what they're fried in. Pose this question to students: **Is it OK to eat fatty foods as long as they have a label saying that they have "no cholesterol"?** In fact, all fat intake should be limited. Butter is fat; so are cooking oil and margarine. Saturated fats increase the body's cholesterol level.

**SKILLBUILDER**

**Student Journal** Have students record their nutritional tables in their journals.

**Visual Learning**

**Figure 11-8** Ask students to predict some other foods that get more than 75 percent, more than 40-50 percent, and less than 20 percent of their calories from fat.

## ■ Fats

Fats are large organic molecules—some larger than carbohydrates. Like carbohydrates, fats are broken down to release energy to fuel your body. In fact, fats release more energy per molecule than carbohydrates do. Usually, however, you get your energy from carbohydrates because they make up the largest part of your diet. Only in an emergency, when your supply of carbohydrates is low, does your body turn to its fat reserves for energy.

**SKILLBUILDER**

**Making and Using Tables**

As you learn about the six nutrients needed by your body, organize this information into a table that lists each nutrient, its sources, and its nutritional value. If you need help, refer to the **Skill Handbook** on page 680.

The next time you're in your kitchen, open the refrigerator and see just how "fat" it is. Chances are you'll see some butter, margarine, or cheese in there. All of these foods contain fats.

Solid vegetable shortening, corn oil, and olive oil are fats too. In addition, fats are present in meat, nuts, ice cream and cookies.

## ■ How Much Fat?

Just how much fat do you need? Most nutritionists thought that 30 percent of your calories should come from fats. Today, some think that figure should be 20 percent or lower. Your body does need some fat. Excess fat contributes to becoming overweight, and saturated fats—found in meat, dairy products, and some tropical oils—increase the risk of heart and artery disease. The result may be a narrowing of the arteries, preventing an adequate blood supply from reaching the heart muscle. Unsaturated fats, found in vegetable oils, are much more healthy.

**Figure 11-8**

| More than 75% Calories from fat | 40-50% Calories from fat | Less than 20% Calories from fat |
|---|---|---|
| 1 medium avacado - 31 g | 1/2 cup ice cream - 7g | 1 medium white fish - 1g |

An avocado contains unsaturated fat, while ice cream and white fish contain saturated fat. The percentage and type of fat in a food needs to be considered in determining how good it is for your body.

## Program Resources

**Laboratory Manual,** pp. 67–70, Thermal Energy from Foods L2
**Multicultural Connections,** p. 26, Rice—Food for Billions L1
**Making Connections: Technology & Society,** p. 25, The Cholesterol Controversy L2

## Find Out! ACTIVITY

### What percentage of the calories you consume comes from fat?

You can use a simple mathematical formula to calculate your fat intake from certain foods. You can find the information that you need to know on nutrition labels, such as the total number of Calories per serving and the total grams of fat per serving.

#### What To Do

1. Suppose that you're eating one serving of breakfast cereal. One serving has 65 Calories and 1 gram of fat.
2. To find out what percentage of your breakfast Calories comes from fat, multiply the grams of fat by 9. There are 9 Calories in each gram of fat. Then divide the result by the total Calories:

   $1 \times 9 = 9$

   $9 \div 65 = 0.1384$, or 14 percent
3. Is your breakfast a healthful one? What makes you think so?

#### Conclude and Apply

1. Suppose you ate cheesecake that has 300 Calories and 25 grams of fat. What percentage of the Calories comes from fat?
2. Is this a healthful food choice? Explain your answer?

### ■ Protein

How do you feel about insects? If you're like most people, the fewer insects you see, the better. In some cultures, however, insects play an important role in diet. You'd probably be surprised to learn that in parts of Africa, for example, termites are considered quite a delicacy. African termites are much larger than those found in the United States, and they are enjoyed both fresh and fried.

Why termites? Well, termites are an important source of protein. Termites are just about 50 percent protein. Protein is an organic compound containing nitrogen that is used throughout the body for growth and to replace and repair cells. Proteins are the building blocks of body tissue.

You learned in Chapter 10 that proteins are composed of long chains of molecules called amino acids. Your body requires twenty different kinds of amino acids. Sixteen of these amino acids, called nonessential amino acids, can be made in the cells in your body. The other eight, called essential amino acids, have to be supplied by the food you eat.

**Connect to...**

## Chemistry

When a leech feeds on an organism, it may take in and store enough blood to keep itself alive for four months. Research and explain to your class the function of an anticoagulant. Explain why an anticoagulent benefits the leech.

11-1  Nutrients: The Spice of Life  **345**

---

**Content Background**

Fats can be divided into two groups—saturated fats and unsaturated fats. Saturated fats are generally found in meats and other animal products. Eating too much saturated fat can raise the level of cholesterol in the body. Unsaturated fats are generally found in plant products, such as corn oil or peanut oil. Unsaturated fats do not raise the body's cholesterol level. Some unsaturated fats actually lower cholesterol levels.

**Connect to...**

## Chemistry

The function of an anticoagulant is to keep blood from clotting. This works while the leech feeds and keeps stored blood from clotting while it is being digested.

**Student Journal** Have students perform their calculations in their journals. [L1]

**Expected Outcomes**

Many foods get many of their calories from fat.

**Conclude and Apply**

1. 75 percent of the cheesecake's calories come from fat.
2. This is not a healthful food choice because it contains more than twice the daily recommended percentage of fat.

### ✔ Assessment

**Content** Have students list a sample menu for one day. Have them use the nutritional information on packaged foods to list the calories and grams of fat provided by foods on their menus. Then have them determine the total percentage of fat provided by their menu. Select the appropriate Performance Task Assessment List in **PAMSS**. [L1]

---

## Find Out!

### What percentage of the calories you consume comes from fat?

**Time needed**  10 minutes

**Materials**  calculator

**Thinking Process**  calculating, interpreting data, classifying

**Purpose**  To calculate the percentage of calories from fat in a given food.

### Teaching the Activity

**Troubleshooting**  Help students with the mathematics: Multiply grams of fat by 9 to get calories from fat. Divide calories from fat by total calories to determine the percentage.

**Discussion**  Ask students whether the cereal is within the recommended guidelines for percent of calories from fat. *It is, because 14 percent is below the recommended 20 (or 30) percent.*

The Recommended Dietary Allowances (RDAs) were established by the National Research Council of the National Academy of Sciences, an independent research organization based in Washington, DC. The Food and Drug Administration (FDA) adapted these requirements and called them USRDA. USRDAs are available for four age levels.

Four steps were used to determine the USRDAs: (1) Estimate the average requirements for a given age group; (2) Increase the average to an amount that will meet the needs of almost everyone in that group. (3) Increase the requirement to allow for inefficient use of the nutrient by the body; (4) Use judgment to interpret and extrapolate requirements where information is limited. You can find the USRDA for four age groups in Dunne, Lavon J. *Nutrition Almanac*, 3rd ed., NY: McGraw-Hill, 1990.

## ■ Complete and Incomplete Protein

The protein in meat, eggs, and dairy products contains the eight essential amino acids your body cannot produce. That's why the protein in these foods is called complete protein. The protein in plants is incomplete—that is, it contains some, but not all, of the eight essential amino acids. **Figure 11-9b** shows examples of vegetables that do not have all of the essential amino acids. By combining different types of plant proteins, however, you can get all eight essential amino acids in your diet. Beans, rice, and grains are all excellent sources of protein.

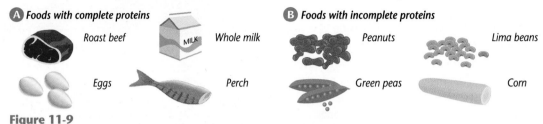

**A** Foods with complete proteins — Roast beef, Whole milk, Eggs, Perch

**B** Foods with incomplete proteins — Peanuts, Lima beans, Green peas, Corn

**Figure 11-9**

Complete proteins (A) such as roast beef, perch, eggs, and whole milk provide some of the eight essential amino acids that your body needs. Peanuts, green peas, lima beans and corn each have some, but not all, of the essential amino acids and are therefore incomplete proteins (B).

# Eating Like a Bird

The expression "eats like a bird" describes someone who eats very little. Birds, however, eat a lot of food because flying requires a lot of energy.

Hummingbirds beat their wings up to 90 times a second when they are hovering at a flower. This activity burns energy so quickly that hummingbirds need to eat 70 percent of their body weight each day.

*Some large organisms eat large things, while others eat small things. What do you think this blue whale eats?*

## Amount and Type of Food

How much food an animal needs to eat depends on both the kind of animal and the kind of food. Animals that eat berries eat more than animals that eat nuts and seeds. Berries contain a lot of water but do not supply energy. Nuts and seeds are mostly dry and are packed full of nutrients.

Whether an animal eats plants or other animals also affects how much food is consumed. In general, animals that feed on plants eat larger quantities of food to get the nutrients they need than meat-eating

### Purpose

A Closer Look reinforces Section 11-1 on nutrients and diet by describing how much food different animals need to fuel their bodies.

### Content Background

The energy value of food is measured in calories. Every pound of body weight is equal to 3,500 calories.

Different foods provide different amounts of energy and so have different caloric values. Fat supplies more calories per gram than carbohydrates or proteins. Water and cellulose (fiber) have no calories. This is why foods highest in fat are highest in calories, and foods high in water and cellulose (such as fresh vegetables) are lowest in calories.

### Teaching Strategies

Have students try to determine the approximate amount of time they spend eating every day. L2

## Vitamins

If you're not getting the right vitamins, you might actually be suffering from malnutrition! **Vitamins** are organic nutrients necessary to your continued good health. Most vitamins are required in extremely small amounts. However, a deficiency in any one vitamin can sometimes cause serious health problems. Each vitamin is needed and contributes to the functioning of your body.

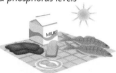

*Vitamin D* controls calcium & phosphorus levels
*Vitamin A* healthy skin & eyes, growth
*Vitamin E* reproduction, cell growth, wound healing
*Vitamin B* growth, healthy skin & mucous membrane


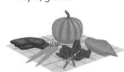

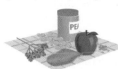

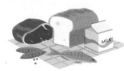

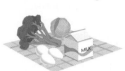

*Vitamin K* blood clotting
*Vitamin C* healing, maintains body cell connections


**Figure 11-10**

**Vitamins are classified as fat-soluble A, D, E and K, and water-soluble B and C. Fat-soluble vitamins are stored in fat tissues. Water-soluble vitamins are not stored by the human body.**

animals do. Plants are harder to digest than meat. Plant cells contain cellulose, a rigid substance that gives support to stems and leaves.

### Time Spent Eating

A 6000-kilogram African bull elephant, for example, eats about 170 kilograms of plants a day. Consequently, elephants spend a lot of time grazing—17 to 19 hours a day. Cows, deer, horses, and other grazing animals also spend almost all of the time they are awake eating.

Meat eaters, on the other hand, spend much less time eating. An adult male lion weighing between 150 and 250 kilograms eats about 32.5 kilograms of food each day.

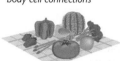

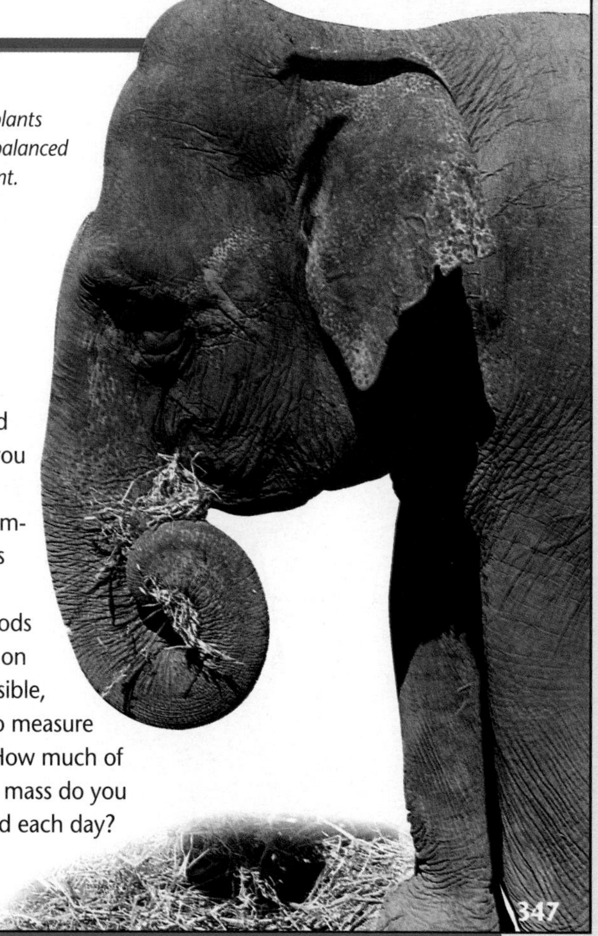

*About 170 kg of plants provides a tasty, balanced diet for an elephant.*

### You Try It!

Keep a record of all the food you eat in one day. Estimate the number of kilograms you consume. Prepackaged foods list the amount on the label. If possible, use a balance to measure food servings. How much of your total body mass do you consume in food each day?

347

**Activity** Students can read the selection in small groups and then make a list of the foods they feed to their pets or have seen animals in the classroom or a zoo eat. L2 COOP LEARN

**Answers to You Try It!**

Answers will vary according to body mass and eating habits.

**Going Further**

Every year, thousands of people go on diets and lose thousands of pounds—and then gain them back within a short time. Divide the class into small groups and have each team evaluate one kind of diet fad or crash diet. For information, students can contact:

American Dietetic Association
430 North Michigan Avenue
Chicago, IL 60611
(312) 280-5000 COOP LEARN L1

**Activity** Allow students to practice using the tables of nutritional values by having them bring in a variety of boxes and cans (or their labels) and notice the nutrition charts on each. They can also use the material from the Explore activity on page 343. Many will point out the percentage of the recommended RDAs that the product supplies. L1

### Content Background

Vitamins are usually classified as water-soluble or fat-soluble. The water-soluble vitamins (B complex, C, and compounds called "bioflavonoids") are usually measured in milligrams (mg). Fat-soluble vitamins (A, D, E, and K) are measured in International Units (IU) or United States Pharmacopeia Units (USP).

Vitamins taken in excess of the amount needed by the body are either excreted in the urine or stored in the body. Fat-soluble vitamins are stored in body fat; some however, such as vitamin A, can be toxic in large amounts.

### Visual Learning

**Figure 11-9** Have students compare and contrast a diet high in complete proteins and lacking in incomplete proteins with one high in incomplete proteins and lacking in complete proteins.

**Figure 11-10** Have students work in pairs to discuss the foods they eat that they believe contain each of the vitamins A, B, C, D, E, and K. Would it be more important for you to eat foods containing fat-soluable or water-soluable vitamins every day? Why? *water-soluable vitamins; because they are not stored in the body*

# INVESTIGATE!

## 11-1 Vitamin C

### Planning the Activity

**Time needed** one class period

**Purpose** To experiment with substances to infer their nutritional value.

**Process Skills** making and using tables, observing and inferring, comparing and contrasting, recognizing cause and effect, measuring in SI, separating and controlling variables, interpreting data, hypothesizing

**Materials** See reduced student text.

**Preparation** Label the dropper bottles clearly. Indophenol is available from chemical supply houses. To prepare the indophenol solution dissolve 1 gram of indophenol in 1000 mL of water. To prepare vitamin solution, dissolve a 250 mg vitamin C tablet in 200 mL water.

### Teaching the Activity

**Troubleshooting** Label the dropper bottles clearly. Go over all instructions in the text to be sure that students understand what they are to do.

**Discussion** Before starting, ask students if they think that fresh foods are more nutritious than preserved foods. This activity will enable them to find out if they are for one food, the orange, and for one nutrient, vitamin C.

**Safety** Remind students to be very careful not to get indophenol on skin or clothing.

**Process Reinforcement** Be sure that students set up their data tables so they can record results for all four liquids.

**Possible Hypotheses** Students may hypothesize that age and processing destroy some nutrients and that, therefore, the fresh juice will have more vitamin C than the bottled or frozen juices.

**Possible Procedures** Have students work in cooperative groups. Students may take turns adding drops of the different juices and the water to the indophenol. Students may also

# Vitamin C

*At the store, you have seen bottled orange juice and frozen orange juice concentrate. At some time you may have squeezed your own orange juice. Orange juice contains vitamin C.*

### Problem

How can you determine whether each type of orange juice contains the same amount of vitamin C?

### Materials

| | |
|---|---|
| 10 test tubes | 4 dropper bottles |
| test-tube rack | containing: |
| masking tape | (A) refrigerated |
| safety goggles | tap water, |
| apron | (B) frozen orange |
| 25mL graduated | concentrate mixed |
| cylinder | according to |
| indophenol solution | directions, |
| | (C) bottled orange |
| | juice, and |
| | (D) fresh squeezed |
| | orange juice |

### Safety Precautions

Wear safety goggles.

Dispose of materials properly.

Wear protective clothing to prevent stains.

Handle indophenol solution carefully.

## What To Do

**1** Copy the data table *into your Journal*. Put on safety goggles and an apron.

Sample Data

### Data and Observations

DROPS OF JUICE TO CHANGE INDICATION

| Trail | Frozen (B) | Bottled (C) | Fresh (D) |
|---|---|---|---|
| 1 | 14 | 10 | 8 |
| 2 | 16 | 12 | 7 |
| 3 | 15 | 11 | 6 |
| Ave. | 15 | 11 | 7 |

share responsibility for checking one another's count of drops of juice and recording the data.
**COOP LEARN**

**Student Journal** Have students write their hypotheses and answer the questions in their journals. L2

### Program Resources

**Activity Masters,** pp. 47-48, Investigate 11-1

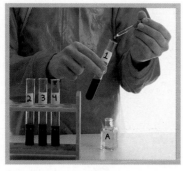

**A**       **B**       **C**

**2** Label four test tubes 1 through 4.

**3** Measure 15 mL indophenol solution into each of the four test tubes.
**CAUTION:** *Indophenol is poisonous, and can stain skin and clothing.* Notify your teacher if any is spilled. Indophenol is an indicator that changes from blue to colorless when enough vitamin C is present.

**4** Add 20 drops of water from dropper bottle A to test tube 1 as in photo **B**. Swirl the mixture carefully. The solution will stay blue. This will be your color control.

**5** Add orange juice B, one drop at a time, to test tube 2 as in photo **C**. Keep an accurate count. Compare with your control after each drop. Add one drop at a time until the indicator changes from blue to colorless. Record the number of drops of juice B it took to make the indicator colorless.

**6** Repeat Step 5 for juice C, then for juice D.

**7** Test each juice, B, C, and D, two more times.

**8** Average the data for the three trials.

## Analyzing

1. ***Compare and contrast*** the amount of vitamin C in the orange juices tested. Which orange juice contained the most vitamin C? Which contained the least? How do you know?

2. Why did you test each juice three different times and average the results?

## Concluding and Applying

3. What can you ***infer*** about the amount of vitamin C in the different forms of orange juice?

4. **Going Further** *Hypothesize* what would happen to the vitamin C content of orange juice that was not refrigerated for several days. How would you test your hypothesis?

---

The fresh juice should require the fewest drops to change the indicator.

**Answers to** Analyzing/ Concluding and Applying

**1.** From most to least—fresh, bottled, and frozen, because fewer drops of each (in this sequence) were required to indicate the presence of vitamin C.

**2.** Retesting and averaging corrects for errors in measurement.

**3.** The amount of vitamin C varies because vitamin C deteriorates as it ages.

**4.** Unrefrigerated juice would lose vitamin C faster than juice that is kept cold. To test the hypothesis, repeat the investigation once or twice a day for several days. Use two samples of the same kind of orange juice. Put one sample in the refrigerator; keep the other sample at room temperature.

## ✔ Assessment

**Performance** Have students determine the cost per ounce of the three types of juice. They should figure out the cost of each ounce of reconstituted frozen juice. Then they should figure out how many oranges are needed to make 4 ounces of fresh juice and divide to get the cost per ounce. Then have them determine, based on the drops of each type of juice required to change the indicator, what the relative vitamin C content is per ounce of each type of juice. For example, the fresh juice may contain twice as much vitamin C per ounce as does the frozen. Students can then determine which type of juice is the most economical source of vitamin C. Use the Performance Task Assessment List for Consumer Decision Making Study in **PAMSS**, p. 43. [L1] [P]

---

## ENRICHMENT

**Research** Some people with eating disorders binge and purge, ultimately starving themselves, sometimes to death. Divide the class in half and have one group research anorexia nervosa; the other, bulimina. Then have students share their findings with the class. Be sensitive to the fact that a student in your class, or in the school, may have an eating disorder.

Students can contact:
American Institute of Nutrition
9650 Rockville Pike
Bethesda, MD 20814
(301) 530-7050   **COOP LEARN** [L2]

## Check for Understanding

Assign questions 1 and 2 in Check Your Understanding. Question 3, Apply, is well suited to cooperative learning group work. Have students review their answers to question 2 before planning their meals. Meals could be illustrated with drawings or magazine pictures. [L1]

## Reteach

**Activity** To reinforce their understanding of nutritional values, have students plan a meal. To limit the options, offer two choices for each group of nutrients. One choice should be clearly better than the alternative. Discuss the reason for each choice. For protein and fat: hamburger patty (60 percent of calories from fat) or chicken breast (23 percent of calories from fat) For carbohydrates: baked potato (33 grams) or two dinner rolls (16 grams). [L1]

## Extension

Challenge teams to use "nutritional counter" books and plan meals for an entire day. Meals should have no more than 2,200 calories, and no more than 25 percent of the calories from fat. [L2] **COOP LEARN**

# 4 CLOSE

## Activity

Have students return to the food diaries they kept for a week at the beginning of the section and write an analysis of the nutritional value of the food they ate. Have them include two changes they could make to make their diet more nutritionally sound. Have volunteers share their results. [L1]

---

In the Investigate, you tested the vitamin C content in various forms of orange juice. There are similar tests that can be done to test for the presence of other vitamins, minerals, and nutrients in foods. Tests such as these help provide accurate nutritional information that can then be listed on food labels.

### ■ Nutrient Content Change

The nutrient content of many foods can change greatly from the time they are harvested until they are consumed. Tests show that certain methods of storage and preparation can cause a significant decrease in the amount of useful nutrients in a food. Oxygen from the air and excessive cooking are two culprits that break certain nutrients down into less useful substances or remove them from the foods.

As you can see in **Figure 11-11**, all of the nutrients that we have discussed in this section are essential to your good health. The more scientists study the relationship between diet and health, the more convinced they are that what we eat has a direct effect on how we feel and how our bodies respond to daily stresses. In this sense, you really are what you eat! In the next section, you'll learn how the human digestive system breaks down the foods that you have eaten so your body can use the nutrients to maintain itself.

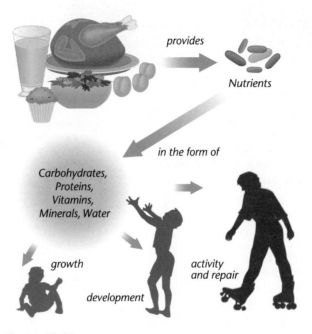

**Figure 11-11**

Eating a balanced diet provides necessary nutrients that result in growth and development. Nutrients also supply a healthy body with raw materials to effectively repair wounds, such as scrapes, cuts, or broken bones.

---

### check your UNDERSTANDING

1. It has been said that we "cannot live by bread alone." Explain why this statement is true from a nutritional point of view.

2. Describe the six different types of nutrients and explain how your body uses each type.

3. **Apply** Using what you've learned about nutrients, plan a healthful meal for you and your classmates. Explain which nutrients are present in your meal and why you think it is healthful.

---

### check your UNDERSTANDING

1. In order to be healthy, people need a variety of nutrients, not only carbohydrates.

2. Protein, carbohydrates, fats, vitamins, minerals, and water. The body uses these nutrients in many ways. Students should be able to name at least one for each nutrient.

3. Meals should include plenty of carbohydrates, some protein, and less than 20 percent fat.

# Digestion: A Disassembly Line

## The Disassembly Line

Remember all the nutritious foods growing in Blanca Hidalgo's garden? All those fruits and vegetables were packed with all the nutrients your body needs to grow strong and healthy. But how does your body "get to" those nutrients so it can use them for energy, tissue growth and repair, and other important body functions? The answer is a remarkable process called digestion.

You've heard of assembly lines in factories where products are put together quickly and efficiently? Your digestive system, shown in **Figure 11-12**, works in reverse. Digestion is a disassembly line where foods you eat are taken apart. **Digestion** is the process that breaks down carbohydrates, fats, and proteins into smaller and simpler molecules that can be absorbed and used by the cells in your body. Later, your cells use these molecules as building blocks for growth and repair and as fuel from which energy is released. Any molecules that are not absorbed by your cells eventually pass out of your body as solid wastes.

Chemical digestion works on individual molecules, breaking down large molecules into smaller molecules using chemicals produced by your body. Chemical digestion is one process of metabolism, which includes all of the chemical changes that take place in your body—including the breakdown of fuel molecules for energy.

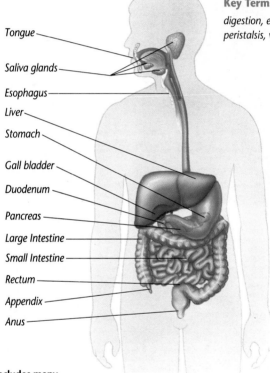

Tongue
Saliva glands
Esophagus
Liver
Stomach
Gall bladder
Duodenum
Pancreas
Large Intestine
Small Intestine
Rectum
Appendix
Anus

**Figure 11-12**

The human digestive system includes many organs that work to break down the food you eat.

### Section Objectives

- Describe the purpose of the mechanical breakdown of food in your digestive system.
- Explain the role of enzymes in chemical digestion.
- Describe what happens to food as it passes through each organ of the digestive system.

### Key Terms

*digestion, enzyme, peristalsis, villi*

---

---

## PREPARATION

### Concepts Developed

In the last section, the nutritive components of food were discussed. This section examines the digestive processes, which make those nutrients available to the body.

### Planning the Lesson

Refer to the Chapter Organizer on pages 336A–B.

## 1 MOTIVATE

**Discussion** Help students begin to form an operational definition of digestion by displaying a common food, such as a carrot. Ask students what nutrients it contains. After students have answered, break the carrot into four pieces. Ask students if they think you have just "broken down" the carrot so that each piece represents one of the four nutrients listed. Students should let you know quickly that this is not how food is "broken down." Point out that this section explains how foods are chemically broken down to let the body get the various nutrients and to release energy available from the bonds in these nutrients. L1 LEP

## 2 TEACH

**Tying to Previous Knowledge**

From their study of Section 11-1, students are aware of the role of nutrients in food. Ask what happens to food after it is swallowed. Write the reasonable responses on the chalkboard to get an idea of how much students know about digestion. L1

**Theme Connection** The themes supported by this section are energy and scale and structure. Food contains nutrients, but their structure must be changed in order to be used by the body as building materials or sources of energy. Students will see how the organs of the digestive system take part in this process.

# The Mouth

You've just returned home from gymnastics practice, and you're ready for a snack. You pop two slices of pepperoni pizza in the microwave, and in a few minutes you're biting into a delicious treat. Let's follow that pizza as it moves through your digestive system, beginning in your mouth.

Digestion begins as teeth start to work on food. Teeth are adapted to the kinds of food an animal eats. Look at the illustration of human teeth in **Figure 11-15**. You'll use your incisors to take that first bite of pizza. Then you'll use your molars at the back of your mouth to grind the pizza into smaller bits. This is mechanical digestion. But that's not all that's going on in your mouth.

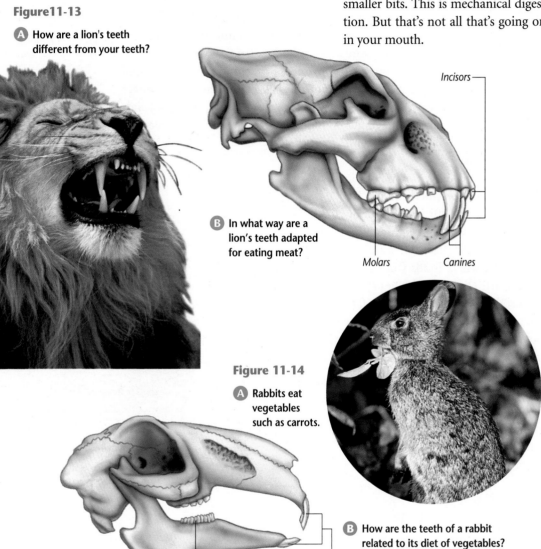

**Figure 11-13**

Ⓐ How are a lion's teeth different from your teeth?

Ⓑ In what way are a lion's teeth adapted for eating meat?

*Incisors*

*Molars*   *Canines*

**Figure 11-14**

Ⓐ Rabbits eat vegetables such as carrots.

Ⓑ How are the teeth of a rabbit related to its diet of vegetables?

*Molars*   *Incisors*

## ENRICHMENT

**Activity** Have students look in an encyclopedia or chemistry book to find out what starch and sugar molecules look like. Have them make models of starch molecules and use them to show how starch molecules can break down into sugar molecules. If stick-and-ball molecular model kits are available, allow students to use these. L3

**Activity** Humans are *omnivorous*—they eat both meat and vegetable foods. Have students use a mirror to look at their teeth. How are human teeth shaped for a variety of actions? If possible, get a model of human teeth from a dentist and use it to help students answer this question. Have students compare the sharp incisors with the flat molars. Ask which shape is better for cutting and which is better for grinding. L2

## Explore! ACTIVITY

### Where does digestion begin?

**Y**ou just learned that mechanical digestion starts in your mouth as you chew your food. Is that all that happens in your mouth?

#### What To Do

1. Chew a saltine cracker or large hard pretzel, but don't swallow it. It won't be too easy, but hold it in your mouth for about five minutes.
2. After five minutes, how does the cracker taste?
3. Why has the taste of the cracker changed?

The cracker you chewed was made from wheat flour or some other grain and contains complex carbohydrates. Remember, carbohydrates are broken down into smaller sugar molecules before they can be used as fuel for your body. What's going on in your mouth? Let's investigate.

#### Figure 11-15

When food is mechanically digested by your teeth, it is broken down into smaller pieces. In what way are your teeth like knives and forks?

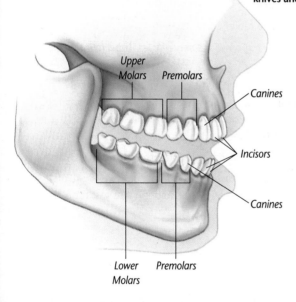

Upper Molars
Premolars
Canines
Incisors
Canines
Lower Molars
Premolars

#### Figure 11-16

Organisms eat a great variety of foods. Analyze how teeth are suited for eating various foods.

11-2 Digestion: A Disassembly Line **353**

---

---

## Explore!

**Where does digestion begin?**

**Time needed** 10 minutes

**Materials** saltine crackers or hard pretzels

**Thinking Processes** observing and inferring, forming a hypothesis

**Purpose** To observe that carbohydrates are broken down into sugar by the action of saliva.

**Preparation** Alternative Materials: Any plain cracker or white bread can be used.

### Teaching the Activity

Because students will not be able to talk during this activity, you might assign a quiet, independent activity, like reading, for these five minutes.

**Troubleshooting** Students may swallow the cracker before the five minutes are up. Chewing more than one cracker at a time may help keep them from swallowing, because one is too easy to swallow.

**Student Journal** Have students note their observations and answer the questions in their journals. [L2]

### Expected Outcome

The taste of the cracker becomes sweet as the saliva begins the process of digestion.

### Answers to Questions

**2.** sweet

**3.** saliva in the mouth has started the digestion process, changing the chemical makeup of the cracker.

### ✔ Assessment

**Content** After students complete this activity, have them work in pairs or small groups to create a cartoon panel that explains to younger children why chewing food well is important. Use the Performance Task Assessment List for Cartoon/Comic Book in **PAMSS,** p. 61. [L1] **COOP LEARN**

### Planning the Activity

**Time needed** 45 minutes

**Purpose** To recognize that saliva causes starch to change to sugar

**Process Skills** making and using tables, observing and inferring, measuring in SI, recognizing cause and effect, interpreting data, separating and controlling variables

**Materials** See Student activity. Do not use table sugar. For best results, use glucose (available in drug stores) or dextrose (honey).

### Teaching the Activity

**Troubleshooting** Direct students to follow the instructions in the textbook carefully. Before beginning the activity, review each step with students and answer any questions they may have. During the activity, circulate around the room, providing assistance as needed.

**Process Reinforcement** Be sure that students copy the data table correctly. Test tubes should be carefully numbered, and each number should be keyed on the data table to a description of the contents of the test tube. Careful labeling and recording will help students develop the ability to control constants and variables during experiments. L2

**Possible Hypothesis** Students may hypothesize that adding saliva to a starch causes chemical digestion to begin.

**Possible Procedure** Since the procedure has many detailed steps, encourage students to work in cooperative groups, checking one another's work and making sure instructions are followed. **COOP LEARN** L1

**Student Journal** Have students enter the data table and answer the questions in their journals. L1

---

# INVESTIGATE!

# Chemical Digestion

*While eating you usually chew your food. This mechanical digestion breaks the food into smaller particles. In the Explore activity you kept a chewed cracker in your mouth for a few minutes. During that time the taste of the cracker changed.*

## Problem

How can you determine if chemical digestion begins in the mouth?

## Materials

| | |
|---|---|
| 4 test tubes | sugar |
| test-tube rack | teaspoon |
| 100-mL graduated cylinder | medicine dropper |
| | iodine solution |
| 10-mL graduated cylinder | Benedict's solution |
| 250-mL beaker | hot plate |
| tap water | safety goggles |
| non-instant oatmeal | test-tube clamp |
| | apron |

## Safety Precautions

Be careful when handling hot objects and using electrical equipment.

Wear safety goggles.

Handle chemicals carefully.

Wear protective clothing to prevent stains.

## What To Do

1. Make a data table *in your Journal.*

2. **CAUTION:** *Put on your safety glasses. Label four test tubes 1 through 4.*

3. Fill a beaker with 100 mL of water. Soak a handful of oatmeal in the water. Allow to stand for 10 minutes, stirring once or twice. Pour off the milky-white liquid. Use this as your starch solution.

4. *Measure* 10 mL starch solution into test tubes 1, 3, and 4.

5. Completely dissolve 1 teaspoon of sugar in 25 mL of water. *Measure* 10 mL sugar solution into test tube 2.

---

## Program Resources

**Activity Masters,** pp. 49–50, Investigate 11-2

**Concept Mapping,** p. 19, Digestion L1

**Science Discovery Activities,** 11-3, Higher When Drier

---

**A**

**B**

**C**

**6** Wash the starch solution out of the beaker, fill it half full with hot tap water, and place it on a hot plate.

**7** Add 4 drops of iodine solution to test tube 1. Iodine will turn blue-black in the presence of starch. Observe the test tube and record your observations by indicating a positive (starch present) or a negative (no starch present) result.

**8** Add 4 drops of Benedict's solution to test tube 2 and heat it in the hot water in the beaker. Benedict's solution is an indicator. If sugar is present, it turns muddy green to yellow to rust to red. Record your observations in the data table.

**9** Add several drops of saliva to test tubes 3 and 4, and swirl carefully. Wait 5 minutes.

**1 0** Add 4 drops of iodine solution to test tube 3. Record your observations.

**1 1** Add 4 drops of Benedict's solution to test tube 4. Wait for the water bath to boil. Using a test-tube clamp, place test tube 4 in the water bath and leave it there for 5 minutes. Record your observations.

## Analyzing

**1.** How did you test for the presence of starch?

**2.** How did you test for sugar?

## Concluding and Applying

**3.** What can you *conclude* from your data table? What process begins as you chew food?

**4.** Going Further *Infer* why chewing your food is an important part of the digestive process.

### Expected Outcome

Results may vary, depending on the concentration of the starch solution and the amount of saliva added. The liquid in test tube 1 will turn blue-black; test tube 2, muddy green, yellow, or rust-colored; test tube 3, probably blue-black, indicating that starch is still present; test tube 4 will probably indicate that sugar is present.

### Answers to Analyzing/Concluding and Applying

**1.** by adding iodine

**2.** by adding Benedict's solution

**3.** Saliva begins to break down carbohydrates. Chewing food begins the process of mechanical digestion.

**4.** Chewing food breaks it into small bits, thus increasing the surface area exposed to saliva and accelerating the process of digestion.

### ✔ Assessment

**Process** Allow students to develop their skills in controlling constants and variables by asking them to explain why different groups of students may have gotten different results when they tested the liquids in test tubes 3 and 4. Use the Performance Task Assessment List for Analyzing the Data in **PAMSS**, p. 27. **L1**

### Multicultural Perspectives

**Supplying Fresh Foods**

Fresh fruits and vegetables are better sources of vitamin C and other vitamins than are canned fruits. We have many more sources of fresh food than people had a few generations ago. Before 1949, fresh food could not be shipped long distances without spoiling. In that year, an African American, Frederick McKinley Jones, received a patent for a cooling device that enabled trucks to be refrigerated. Ask students to name some foods they enjoy that would not be available to them without refrigerated shipping. **L2**

**Figure 11-17**

**How are the actions of enzymes like putting together and taking apart a jigsaw puzzle?**

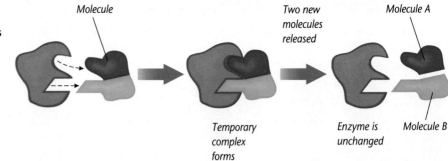

Molecule

Temporary complex forms

Two new molecules released

Molecule A

Enzyme is unchanged

Molecule B

**DID YOU KNOW?**

One enzyme molecule can break down millions of starch molecules.

The Investigate showed that digestion begins in your mouth. Saliva contains an enzyme that begins the process. An **enzyme** is a protein molecule that controls the rate of hundreds of different processes in your body. Enzymes are a vital part of chemical digestion. They work on nutrient molecules like a key in a lock. Each enzyme fits just one type of molecule, breaking the nutrient into smaller molecules, as in **Figure 11-17**.

You have over 700 different enzymes in your body, each with a unique function. When an enzyme in your saliva mixes with the starchy wheat crust of the pizza you're eating, chemical digestion begins and starch is broken down to sugar.

Is gravity responsible for getting food from your mouth to your stomach? Let's find out.

**Find Out! ACTIVITY**

## Does gravity move food to your stomach?

**Y**ou are usually sitting or standing when you eat or drink something. Is it possible to eat when you are lying down with your head lower than your stomach?

### What To Do

1. Get a glass of water with a flexible straw.

2. Lie down on an exercise slant board with your head at the lower end.

3. Lift up your head and take a small mouthful of water through the straw. Don't swallow it yet!

4. Rest your head back on the slant board and carefully swallow the water in your mouth.

**Conclude and Apply**
What role does gravity play in digestion?

**✔ Assessment**

**Process** Have students list animals who do not normally eat in an upright position and could not rely on gravity to move food through their digestive systems. (Most four-legged mammals, for example fall into this category.) Use the Performance Task Assessment List for Making Observations and Inferences in **PAMSS**, p. 17. L1

**Meeting Individual Needs**

**Learning Disabled** Help students to visualize the analogy of enzyme action to keys in a lock by displaying an actual lock and key. The body and shackle of the lock are parts of a molecule and the key is the enzyme. Start with the lock closed and show how the key enables the two parts to separate. The key is then removed and can be used again.

## From Mouth to Stomach

Even though your head was tilted downward, you were still able to swallow the water. **Figure 11-18** illustrates the process of **peristalsis**. During peristalsis, the smooth muscles of the esophagus contract in waves, carrying

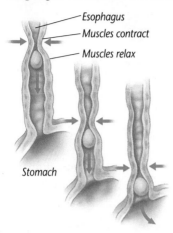

- Esophagus
- Muscles contract
- Muscles relax

Stomach

**Figure 11-18**

Food is moved through the esophagus to the stomach by waves of contractions of the esophagus muscles. Are these contractions voluntary?

food to your stomach. This same muscle action moves food through your entire digestive system.

The muscle action of your esophagus slowly fills your stomach where mechanical and chemical digestion continues. Your stomach muscles churn and mix the partially digested pizza. Meanwhile, the cells in your stomach wall produce hydrochloric acid and enzymes that attack the pizza chemically.

**Figure 11-19**

The inner lining of an empty stomach has many wrinkles and folds. Do you think a full stomach is the same? Why or why not?

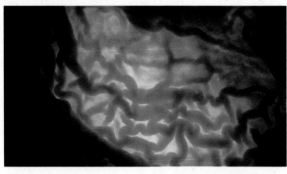

### How Do We Know?

**The Stomach Observed**

Much of what we know about the actions of the stomach is based on an accident. In 1822, a young French Canadian fur trapper named Alexis St. Martin was shot in his left side. An army surgeon named William Beaumont successfully removed the bullet and saved Alexis's life. However, Dr. Beaumont could not close the wound completely, and Alexis was left

with a hole in his side leading straight into his stomach.

*Observing and Analyzing*

Dr. Beaumont was a scientist as well as a physician. For a number of years, he observed the activity in Alexis's stomach under various conditions. For instance, he tied different kinds of foods on strings and lowered them into Alexis's stomach to observe the effect of stomach fluids on the different foods.

Dr. Beaumont also removed samples of these fluids and had them analyzed. He identified hydrochloric acid in the fluid. More importantly, he discovered that although meats are chemically digested in the stomach, other types of food are not.

Dr. Beaumont published his observations in a book that is still referred to today. Alexis, by the way, lived to be 83.

11-2 Digestion: A Disassembly Line **357**

## How do enzymes work?

**Time needed** 45 minutes (5 for preparation, 30-minute wait, 10 to observe and answer questions)

**Materials** two small plastic plates for each student or group, water, two small cubes of beef for each student or group, commercial brand of meat tenderizer

**Thinking Processes** observing, comparing and contrasting, recognizing cause and effect, foming operational definitions, modeling

**Purpose** To observe the effect of an enzyme

**Preparation** Any raw meat can be used. Cut the meat into very small cubes. Distribute two plates and two cubes of meat to each student or group.

### Teaching the Activity

**Troubleshooting** The meat should only be slightly moist. Having more than one container of tenderizer will speed the preparation of samples. Some students may not want to handle the meat; have toothpicks or other implements available for them to use. Dispose of the meat properly.

**Student Journal** Have students answer the question and note their observations in their journals. L1

### Expected Outcome

The two pieces will be different because the enzyme in the tenderizer is breaking down the muscle fibers.

---

## How do enzymes work?

**Y**ou have already learned that enzymes convert starch to sugar. How can you tell if an enzyme is working?

### What To Do

1. Obtain two beef samples. Moisten each with water. Sprinkle one sample generously with tenderizer. The other sample will not be treated. It is your control.

2. After one half hour, examine the two samples. Feel the texture of each one.

### Conclude and Apply

1. Do you detect any differences in the samples?

2. As a result of your observations, what is the function of enzymes?

Meat tenderizer contains an enzyme that breaks down protein. Your stomach also contains enzymes to break down protein. Your stomach produces a coating of slimy mucus that protects it from digesting itself.

---

# Physics CONNECTION

## Do You Always Have a Temperature?

**Y**ou might think that the only time you have a temperature is when you are sick. Even when you are healthy, your body has a temperature of about 37°C. Where does that warmth come from?

The process of celllular respiration releases energy. Only a small amount of this energy is captured in a form that is used by your body for daily activities. Most of the energy released from stored nutrients is thermal energy. Some of this energy maintains a constant body temperature.

For birds and mammals, a constant body temperature makes it possible to live and be active in a wide range of habitats, no matter what the temperature of the environment is. Birds and mammals can live in the Arctic, where winter temperatures are below freezing. Amphibians and reptiles, which depend on heat from the environment to regulate their body temperature, cannot live in such a cold habitat.

### Amount of Energy Loss

Not all of the energy released by metabolism of food is used by an animal, however. Much is lost to the environment through the skin. Just how much energy is lost depends on an animal's size.

---

# Physics CONNECTION

## Purpose

This Physics Connection adds to Section 11-2 by describing how the body uses energy to maintain the body's temperature. It also expresses the amount of energy lost through an animal's skin in a surface area-to-volume ratio.

## Content Background

In spite of all the external temperature changes they experience in an average day, most people maintain a fairly consistent internal body temperature of 37°C, the temperature at which body processes work best. This regulation is accomplished with the help of a biological thermostat in the base of the brain, the hypothalamus. This organ monitors the temperature of the blood flowing through it and triggers changes in the diameter of blood vessels. If metabolism is producing a lot of heat, for example, the blood vessels in the skin will expand or dilate. Therefore, the volume of

# Traveling Through the Intestines

Your pizza will spend about four hours in your stomach being mechanically and chemically changed into a thin, watery liquid. Then, little by little, the muscles in your stomach push this liquid into your small intestine.

## ■ Small Intestine

Most chemical digestion takes place in your small intestine. Your liver, gallbladder, and pancreas supply different digestive juices needed for chemical digestion to your small intestine, shown in **Figure 11-20**.

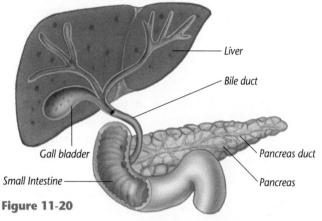

**Figure 11-20**

Bile is an important digestive juice that breaks up large fat particles found in foods. Bile is produced in the liver and stored in the gall bladder. When needed, bile moves through a duct into the small intestine. What is a duct?

---

Small animals lose energy faster than larger ones do, because small animals have a large surface area-to-volume ratio. (Surface area is how much surface is exposed to the environment.) The larger the ratio, the more surface there is through which heat can be lost from the inside. Small animals that have a higher rate of metabolism than larger animals do lose heat more rapidly. The graph shows the relationship between body size and metabolism for several different species.

## Rate of Metabolism

A higher rate of metabolism in turn requires more food consumption. So small animals also eat more, relative to body size.

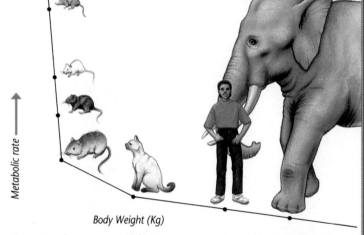

*Metabolic rate →*

*Body Weight (Kg)*

For example, a mouse with a mass of 3 grams eats 30 times more food per gram of body mass than a 5000-kilogram elephant.

## You Try It!

Freeze 1 L of water into a single block. Freeze another 1 L of water as small cubes. Place the large block in one pan and the small cubes in another pan. Allow all the ice to melt. Keep track of how long it takes. Which melts faster, the large block or the small cubes? Explain your answer in terms of surface area-to-volume ratio.

11-2 Digestion: A Disassembly Line **359**

---

blood moving through them increases and carries the heat to the surface, where it dissipates. If, on the other hand, the internal temperature falls, the blood vessels on the skin will shrink or contract, reducing the blood flow to the surface of the body, thus conserving heat.

## Teaching Strategies

Based on this selection, have students debate whether or not it is important to wear a hat in cold weather. L2 **COOP LEARN**

Discuss why indoor shopping malls and other large, crowded areas are generally not heated but are almost always air conditioned. *The body heat of the crowds has a warming effect.* L1

## Answer to
**You Try It!**

The small cubes of ice will melt faster than the large block because they have a greater surface area-to-volume ratio.

## Going Further ▸

Ask students to record their temperature by mouth at set times during an average day. They may wish to use three-hour intervals from 6 A.M. until 9 P.M., for example. Compile the results by having everyone add his or her readings to a class chart. At what times during the day did most temperatures fluctuate? What is the average daily body temperature? L2

Figure 11-21

The many villi of your small intestine increase the surface area dramatically. The surface area of your small intestine is over 264 square meters. Why is this important for digestion?

Your small intestine is less than two centimeters in diameter but is over six meters long! It is lined with many ridges and folds, and the folds are covered with tiny finger-like projections called **villi** as seen in **Figure 11-21**.

Notice the many blood vessels in the villi. By the time your snack reaches your small intestine, its molecules have been broken down into a size small enough to pass through the walls of your villi and into your bloodstream. As the muscles of your small intestine move the liquid nutrient mixture along, the villi are completely bathed in the liquid, and nutrient molecules move from your digestive system into your circulatory system. From here, nutrients will be carried to cells throughout your body.

## ■ The End of the Line—Your Large Intestine

The last stage of digestion is about to take place. The thin, watery liquid that's been moving through your small intestine is now pushed into your large intestine. This digestive organ is almost two meters long and six to seven centimeters in diameter. Muscle contractions here are much slower than they were in your small intestine. The large intestine absorbs large amounts of water. The liquid that isn't absorbed is concentrated into a somewhat solid mass of undigested material.

The solidified wastes also contain large numbers of bacteria that are beneficial. They consume some of the last microscopic bits of food and produce vitamins—vitamin K and some of the B vitamins. Finally, the solidified wastes are eliminated from your body as feces.

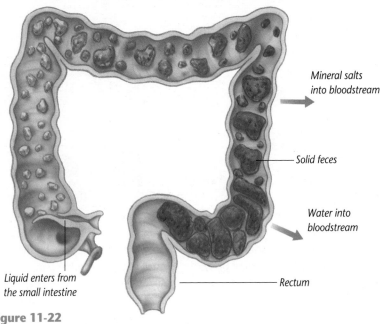

Mineral salts into bloodstream

Solid feces

Water into bloodstream

Rectum

Liquid enters from the small intestine

**Figure 11-22**

The words "small" and "large" are used to describe the two intestines of the human body. Do these words refer to the diameter or the length of the intestine they are used to describe?

**360** Chapter 11 Fueling the Body

# The Nutritional Payoff

The pizza you snacked on provided your body with starch, protein, fat, vitamins, water and minerals. Once these nutrients have been distributed throughout your body by your circulatory system, how are they used?

Some of the nutrients you've taken in act as fuel for a variety of metabolic processes, including cell growth, development and repair. They provide your body with the energy it needs to function and maintain itself.

## Find Out! ACTIVITY

### How much energy do you need?

You can calculate the rate at which your body uses energy. First you need to know that a Calorie is a unit of measurement of the energy available in food. Males use about 1.0 Calories per kilogram of body mass per hour. Females use less—about 0.9.

### What To Do

1. Convert your mass in pounds to kilograms by multiplying your weight by 0.453.

2. Then multiply your mass in kilograms by 1.0 if you're a male and 0.9 if you're a female.

3. The result is the energy in Calories you use per hour. Record this in your Journal.

### Conclude and Apply

1. How many Calories of food energy do you use per day?

2. Compare the Calories needed per day by a 100 pound woman and a 150 pound man.

3. What factors would affect the calories you need on a given day?

These daily energy requirements are averages. If you're more active, you'll use more energy. If you take in more Calories of energy than you use in any given time period, the extra will be stored as fat. If you don't take in as many Calories as you require, your body will take them from your fat reserve, and you'll start to lose weight.

## Find Out!

### How much energy do you need?

**Time needed** 10 minutes

**Materials** calculators, bathroom scale

**Thinking Process** interpreting data, calculating, interpreting scientific illustrations, comparing and contrasting

**Purpose** To calculate daily caloric requirements.

**Preparation** Provide a scale so that students can weigh themselves if they need to.

### Teaching the Activity

**Discussion** Ask students to estimate how many calories they use each day.

Point out that the constants given (0.9 calories per kilogram for females and 1.0 for males) are only an average—the actual caloric usage depends on individual factors such as metabolism and age.

**Troubleshooting** Have students write their information anonymously to protect their privacy. If students know their weight in pounds only, be sure they convert their weight to kilograms using the correct factor for multiplication.

**Student Journal** Have students write their estimates and do their calculations in their journals. L2

### Expected Outcome

Students will see that daily calorie requirement varies with the individual's weight.

### Conclude and Apply

Results will vary. Accept all answers that derive from correct data and calculations.

### ✔ Assessment

**Process** Have students use Figure 11-24 to estimate how many calories they use in a day. Multiply the number of hours for each activity by the number of calories. Finally, add the calories. Use the Performance Task Assessment List for Using Math in Science in **PAMSS**, p. 29. L1 P

## ENRICHMENT

**Discussion** The text uses pepperoni pizza as an example of a food being digested. Have students list other kinds of pizza. Ask students if any of these pizzas would be digested differently. For example, pepperoni and sausage pizza tend to be greasier than meatless pizza. As a result, meatless pizza might be digested more easily. Extra-cheese pizza might take longer to be digested because of the extra protein and fat. L2

# Calories and Calorie Use

Tomato
1 medium
**25**

Whole Milk
1 cup
**150**

Cheese Pizza
1 slice
**290**

Egg
1 large
**80**

Apple
1 medium
**80**

Green Pepper
1 medium
**20**

Wheat Bread
1 slice
**65**

Potato
1 medium
**145**

Ice Cream
1 cup
**270**

Orange
1 medium
**60**

**Figure 11-23**

The foods you eat contain different numbers of Calories. How many apples would you need to eat to equal the Calories in one cup of ice cream?

## Visual Learning

**Figure 11-23** How many apples would you need to eat to equal the calories in one cup of ice cream? *almost 3½*

**Figure 11-24** Has there ever been a moment in your life when you did not use energy in the form of Calories? *No; Even when you are asleep, your body is using Calories.* **Using the table to the right and the calories listed in Figure 11-23, how long would it take you to use the calories in one slice of cheese pizza if you were running? Sitting?** *male 29 minutes, 192 minutes female 41 minutes, 216 minutes*

# 3 ASSESS

## Check for Understanding

Have students answer the Check Your Understanding questions.

## Reteach

**Activity** Push a small ball through an inner tube to demonstrate peristalsis. Have students discuss what this process represents. L1

## Extension

**Research** Assign short research papers. Allow students to choose among topics such as digestive system disorders, enough food for everyone, keeping food safe to eat, and what's the appendix for? L3

# 4 CLOSE

## Activity

Have students turn to the food diary they have been keeping in their journals. Ask them to write for five minutes on the subject "How I made (or did not make) some changes toward a healthier diet." Ask for a few volunteers to share what they have written. L1 P

**Figure 11-24**

Has there ever been a moment in your life when you did not use energy in the form of Calories? Using the table to the right and the Calories listed in Figure 11-23, how long would it take you to use the calories in one slice of cheese pizza if you were running? Sitting?

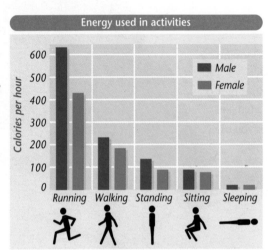

Energy used in activities

A sample listing of some foods and their calories are given in **Figure 11-23**. **Figure 11-24** shows the Calories used up during some different physical activities.

Your digestive system is an incredible machine. It will process thousands of pounds of food for you during your lifetime. It will break down the nutrients you need and send them off across the villi into your blood stream for transport throughout your body. What it can't use, it will efficiently eliminate. Supply it with useful nutrients, and your digestive system will help you remain healthy and strong.

### check your UNDERSTANDING

1. What is the difference between mechanical and chemical digestion?
2. How do enzymes work?
3. **Apply** Suppose you ate a cheeseburger with lettuce and tomato for lunch. Identify the various types of nutrients it contains and explain what is happening to them on the way from your mouth to your cells.

### check your UNDERSTANDING

1. Both break down food nutrients. Mechanical digestion tears, grinds, and mashes food. Chemical digestion breaks down nutrients so they can be absorbed.

2. There is an enzyme for each type of nutrient molecule; the enzyme molecule breaks the nutrient molecule into smaller molecules. The enzyme molecule is unchanged.

3. A cheeseburger contains proteins, fats, vitamins, and minerals. The bun contains carbohydrates. From the mouth to the intestine these nutrients are mechanically and/or chemically digested into subunits small enough to be absorbed across the intestinal wall into the bloodstream. The blood transports them throughout the body.

# Health CONNECTION

# Eating a Balanced Diet

A healthy body needs proteins, fats, carbohydrates, vitamins, and minerals. How much of each of these nutrients does your body need each day?

## Specific Nutrients

Nutrition experts recommend that people pay more attention to the specific nutrients they eat. For example, no more than 30 percent of the calories in your daily food intake should be from fat. The average American diet has 48 percent of the calories from fat. Scientists have long known that too much fat in the diet can increase the risk of heart disease. A high level of dietary fat is also associated with breast and colon cancer.

Americans need to cut down on meat consumption as well. Current research now links too much protein from meat to heart disease and cancer. Just about 30 grams of protein are needed each day, but most people eat around 100 grams.

## Healthful Diet

A healthful diet should be high in complex carbohydrates, fiber, vitamins, and minerals. To eat a healthful diet, there are certain guidelines you should follow. Think of your diet as a pyramid. At the bottom, which is the

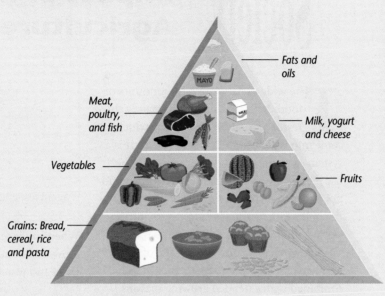

Fats and oils

Meat, poultry, and fish

Milk, yogurt and cheese

Vegetables

Fruits

Grains: Bread, cereal, rice and pasta

widest part, are grains. Grains include bread, cereal, rice, and pasta.

Your diet should also contain large amounts of fresh fruits and vegetables, the next layer in the pyramid. A much smaller portion of your diet should be dairy products and meat because these foods are high in fat. Even lean meat and chicken can contribute too much fat to your diet. The protein they provide can be obtained as easily by eating grains and beans instead. Grains and beans contain little fat.

### You Try It!

Draw a diagram that shows the proportions of the different nutrients in your diet. How does your diet compare to what is recommended for a healthful diet?

## Going Further ⅢⅢⅢ▶

Have students use a data table like the one shown here to record how many grams of protein are contained in foods they eat on a regular basis.

| food | serving size | grams of protein |
|------|--------------|------------------|
| milk | 8 oz. | 8 |
| egg | 1 | 6 |
| chicken | 1 breast | 52 |

# Health CONNECTION

## Purpose

By explaining which nutrients people need in order to have a balanced diet, this excursion focuses on Section 11-1.

## Content Background

Carbohydrates make up the most abundant and least expensive kinds of food. They represent the body's main source of energy. In addition, carbohydrates are metabolized more efficiently than fats and proteins and put less stress on the body when oxidized. When fat is metabolized, in contrast, it leaves large amounts of toxic metabolites in the blood, burdening the kidneys. Complex carbohydrates—unrefined grains, vegetables, tubers, and fruits—are the most nutritious.

Sometimes, canned and frozen foods purchased in a supermarket have a higher nutritive value than corresponding "fresh" foods, for the latter may not have become available until many days after harvesting, while the former are preserved at the peak of nutritional value.

## Teaching Strategies

Pairs of students can work together to complete the You Try It activity and discuss what changes they plan to make in their diet after having completed this chapter. **COOP LEARN** | **L2**

## Activity

Have students work with partners to design a week of nutritionally balanced meals for their families. You may wish to collate all the menus and create a class book to distribute. **COOP LEARN** **L2**

## Answers to

You Try It!

As a result of this activity, students may recognize that their diets need improvement.

# Science and Society

## Purpose

The first half of this Science and Society excursion adds to Section 11-1 by describing modern agriculture, the source of most of our foods, and explaining its environmental drawbacks. The conclusion of this excursion explains numerous techniques available to make modern agriculture "sustainable." These methods include the use of animal and green manure in place of chemical fertilizers, and diversity and rotation of crops.

## Content Background

In 1942, Dr. Paul Muller discovered the insecticidal properties of DDT, for which he received the Nobel Prize. World War II research on poison gas led to the discovery of yet more powerful insecticides. Crop losses were cut sharply, and it seemed that almost any farm pest, disease, or weed problem could be eliminated.

Problems appeared in the early 1950s. Standard doses of DDT, parathion, and similar pesticides proved suddenly ineffective on cotton crops and had to be doubled or trebled against newly resistant insects. The pesticides also destroyed natural predators and helpful parasites. It was found that birds retained considerable amounts of DDT in their bodies. The unease over the use of pesticides in farming flared in 1962 when American biologist Rachel Carson published *Silent Spring*, which sparked a reappraisal of the use of these chemicals.

## Teaching Strategy

Have students work with partners to debate the advantages and disadvantages of chemical fertilizers and pesticides. Then have each pair share its conclusion with the class. **L2** **COOP LEARN**

# Science and Society

# Environmental Impact of Modern Agriculture

The wide variety and large amounts of food that are available are mainly the result of modern agriculture which came into wide use after World War II. It is a system of farming that relies heavily on the use of machinery and chemical fertilizers and pesticides to increase crop yields.

In the last 30 years, modern agriculture has become associated with a number of serious problems. For example, use of large heavy machines to manage vast fields, combined with extended growing seasons, depletes soil fertility. Eventually, the soil breaks down and can no longer be farmed.

**CAREER connection**

An agronomist is an agricultural scientist. Agronomists study biology. They work for corporations, government agencies, and colleges and universities.

When soil is severely damaged, nothing grows in it, and often it is carried away by wind and water.

## Fertilizers and Pesticides

The use of chemical fertilizers and pesticides is associated with environmental contamination and threats to human and animal health. In California's San Joaquin Valley, for example, about one million people have been exposed to the pesticide DBCP in their drinking water. This chemical, created to eliminate pests on the roots of farm crops, is known to cause cancer and sterility. Its use has been banned. Water from 1500 wells in the region cannot be used for drinking, bathing, or cooking because of contamination with other pesticides known to cause kidney and liver damage, cancer, sterility, and genetic damage. About half the states in the country have some contamination of water supplies from farm chemicals.

## Going Further ▐▐▐▐▐➔

Students can work in small groups to make a large map of the United States' ten major farming areas. Then have students describe the variations in soil, slope of land, and climate to determine which sustainable farming methods would be best suited to each individual area. Students can include these methods on their map through the use of symbols and a symbol key. **COOP LEARN** **L3**

## ENRICHMENT

**Activity** Many home gardeners know that some plants help repel insects from other plants. Marigolds and garlic, for example, when interplanted with tomatoes, repel garden pests from the tomatoes. Invite students to find out more about interplanting from gardening centers, books, and pamphlets and work in small groups to design a small home garden using these principles. **L2** **COOP LEARN**

## Sustainable Farms

Many techniques are available to make agriculture sustainable. A sustainable farm is one that produces good quality food at a profit while keeping the soil fertile and healthy. To save energy, reduce pollution, and cut costs, farm chemicals and fuels are replaced whenever possible by resources found on the farm.

For example, some farmers use solar or wind power to generate electricity. Chemical pesticides are replaced by biological pest controls, such as insect predators and microorganisms that infect insect pests. Animal and green manure are used instead of chemical fertilizers.

## Crop Rotation and Diversity

Another important method in sustainable agriculture is crop rotation. Over the course of several growing seasons, a planned series of different crops is grown in a given field.

Diversity is another key characteristic of sustainable farms. Unlike standard farms, which grow huge fields of only one or a few kinds of crops, sustainable farms have livestock, trees, and a mixture of species and varieties of crops.

In case of a natural disaster or a sudden drop in prices for a single crop, farmers with more diverse crops are less likely to lose their entire yield for a season.

In 1980, there were between 20 000 and 30 000 farmers using sustainable agriculture methods, according to the U.S. Department of Agriculture. Farm experts estimate that today there may be two to three times that number. However, that is still just a tiny percent of the country's two million farmers.

## Converting to Sustainable Methods

Converting from standard farming to sustainable methods is not easy or quick. The more damaged the soil is and the more dependent on chemicals the farm is, the longer it takes the soil to be returned to a productive condition without the use of applied fertilizers.

Government policies have also worked to discourage farmers from using sustainable methods. For example, the federal government purchases a handful of crops and sets prices for them. So farmers who want to be certain of a profit are, in a way, trapped by a system of federal price supports. Because so many farmers are heavily in debt, they are unable to switch to sustainable methods. To do so would mean risking economic loss.

### You Try It!

Should the federal government help farmers convert to sustainable methods? Explain your answer. How might the government help with this change?

**Going Further** ▸
Suggest that students work with partners to find out which crops are grown in their area and why. What soil, climate, transportation, and market conditions make these crops suitable? Were there different crops grown in the past? If so, why did farmers decide to plant something else at this time? Encourage students to get samples of local farm products, if possible, and bring them to class to display. **COOP LEARN** **L2**

## ENRICHMENT

**Activity** After the post-World War II agriculture boom, overproduction of food became a serious problem. The Agriculture Department authorized payments to farmers if they reduced production of certain crops. Have students find out more about the crop subsidy program in their social studies books, encyclopedias, and magazine articles and then debate the advantages and disadvantages of this program. **L3**

**Content Background**
Scientists have now identified more than a thousand viruses, bacteria, fungi, and protozoa that can be used to control insect infestation in crops. Many of these organisms are specific to a particular insect but are harmless to people and animals. Another solution is to plant crop varieties that are resistant to insect attack. However, such varieties are not universally available and development takes a long time. Still another method is to sterilize insects by irradiating them and then release them into a population of wild insects. This technique has shown success in controlling fruit flies. Scientists have also developed chemical attractants that lure insects into small amounts of pesticides or sterilant.

**Teaching Strategies** Have pairs of students make a list of the sustainable farming methods described in this excursion and rank them from easiest to most difficult to adapt to conventional farming practices. Have groups exchange papers and discuss their rankings. **COOP LEARN** **L2**

**Discussion**
Students can discuss in small groups why they would or would not consider farming as a career. **L1**

**Answers to**
**You Try It!**
Answers will vary. Students might suggest that the government help farmers by teaching them more about sustainable farming and giving them grants to try these methods.

### ■ White Blood Cells

In contrast to red blood cells, there are only about five to ten thousand white blood cells in a cubic millimeter of blood. This means that for every 500 red cells in your blood, you will find only one white cell! That is quite a difference, isn't it? Is their function different from red blood cells?

**White blood cells**, like the one you see in **Figure 12-5**, fight bacteria, viruses, and other foreign substances that constantly try to invade your body. Your body responds to infections by increasing its number of white blood cells. In the next section, you will learn more about how white blood cells destroy bacteria, virus, or foreign substances that invade your body.

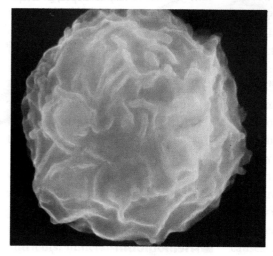

**Figure 12-5**

White blood cells are important in helping your body fight bacteria, viruses, and other foreign substances.

# Physics CONNECTION

## Oxygen and Carbon Dioxide Transport

The average red blood cell contains about 265 million hemoglobin molecules. Because each hemoglobin molecule can carry four oxygen atoms, each red blood cell can carry an enormous amount of oxygen. What makes hemoglobin such a good carrier of oxygen?

As you know, hemoglobin contains iron, which has a strong attraction for oxygen. Within hemoglobin, oxygen attaches to iron very loosely. Under certain conditions, these loosely attached oxygen molecules can be released from the iron.

### Partial Pressure

Whether oxygen is held or released by hemoglobin depends on a property called

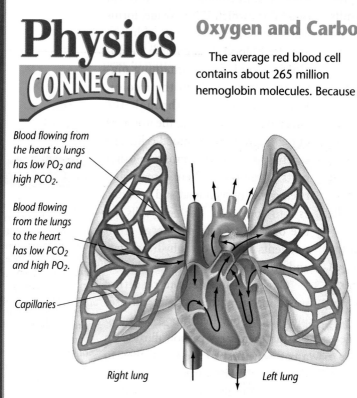

*Blood flowing from the heart to lungs has low $PO_2$ and high $PCO_2$.*

*Blood flowing from the lungs to the heart has low $PCO_2$ and high $PO_2$.*

*Capillaries*

*Right lung*        *Left lung*

# Physics CONNECTION

### Purpose

Section 12-1 explains that red blood cells transport oxygen and carbon dioxide throughout the body. This Physics Connection describes how a property of gases called partial pressure makes this transport possible.

### Content Background

When oxygen is in short supply, the kidneys, which monitor blood as it flows through them, step up their production of a hormone called *erythropoietin*. This hormone flows to the bone marrow, causing the production of red blood cells to increase. If people remain at an altitude of 4,267 meters or higher for a month or more, the production of red blood cells in their body will increase by 30 to 40 percent. This increased volume of blood cells helps oxygen flow to the body's organs.

Carbon monoxide's extraordinary ability to combine with hemoglobin has an im-

# our fluid ENVIRONMENT

In this unit, you investigated how movements of air and water molecules are affected by differences in temperature and density, and by Earth's rotation.

You studied the chemistry of carbon compounds and the chemistry that occurs in your digestive system to break down some of these compounds. Finally, you saw how blood circulates these compounds to all other parts of your body.

Try the exercises and activity that follow—they will challenge you to use and apply some of the ideas you learned in this unit.

## CONNECTING IDEAS

**1.** What is being measured when you obtain a reading of air pressure, water pressure, or blood pressure? How are these readings similar? In what way is a measurement of blood pressure different than the measurements of air or water pressure?

**2.** Organisms living in the oceans depend on sea water for certain things in order to survive. In a similar way, your cells depend on your blood for some of these same things. Make a list of those things that both sea water and blood provide.

## Exploring Further ACTIVITY

### How are people affected by changes in the weather?

Many people are affected by changes in the weather. Sometimes this is just the inconvenience of dealing with storms, but sometimes changes in weather affect their well being.

### What To Do

**1.** Design a research project to study the effects of dark, dreary, rainy days on the moods that people project as related to the moods of these same people on bright, sunny days.

**2.** Conduct your research project and record your observations *in your Journal.*

**3.** Are your moods affected by changes in the weather?

## Our Fluid Environment

### THEME DEVELOPMENT

In Unit 3, students explored the themes of systems and interactions, and energy. Fluid movement was shown to be the result of molecules interacting with each other and with energy to form the basis for a larger system.

### Connections to Other Units

The information students learned in Unit 1 about electricity as a naturally occurring energy force applies to what they learned here about weather, fueling the body, and blood transport. Kinetic energy, described in Unit 2, applies to an understanding of air movements and ocean currents. Unit 3 expands upon the structure of the atom and the characteristics of chemicals, taught in the previous unit, through an exploration of organic chemistry in Chapter 10 and nutrients and the process of digestion in Chapter 11.

### Connecting Ideas
### Answers

**1.** All pressure readings show the force per unit area exerted by a gas or liquid on a surface. Unlike air or water pressure, blood pressure is measured during two phases of the heart's cycle.

**2.** Both sea water and blood provide fluid, nutrients, trace metals, salts, and oxygen.

## Exploring Further

### How are people affected by changes in the weather?

**Purpose** To determine whether there is a cause and effect relationship between weather and people's moods.

### Background Information

Many people are affected by the weather. Some people are affected by sea-sons. Seasonal Affective Disorder, SAD, is related to the short period of daylight during winter months.

**Troubleshooting** Remind students to construct their questions carefully, avoiding any wording that could influence the subjects' answers.

### Answers to Questions

**3.** Answers will vary, depending on the personality of the individual.

### ✔ Assessment

Encourage students to represent their data graphically. Students might make a graph to compare number of people affected and number of people not affected. Students may subdivide the affected people into categories, such as those affected physiologically and those affected psychologically. Use the Performance Task Assessment List for Graph from Data in **PAMSS**, p. 39. [L1] [P]

# Changes in Life and Earth Over Time

## UNIT OVERVIEW

## UNIT FOCUS

In Unit 3, students learned about the movement of materials on Earth and in the human body. In this unit, they will study the movements of continents and the forces that cause these movements. Students will explore the dramatic changes that have occurred on Earth and in its living things over time. By studying reproduction and heredity, students will investigate the processes that make many of the changes in living things possible.

## THEME DEVELOPMENT

Unit 4 addresses the themes of energy and scale and structure. Forces within Earth, fueled by nuclear reactions within the mantle and core, move through the crust. This energy is responsible for the processes that create mountains, continental drift, volcanic eruptions, and earthquakes. Understanding how long Earth has been evolving to its present state is based on an understanding of scale and structure as it relates to time.

## Connections to Other Units

The concepts developed in this unit are related to Unit 5. There, students will build on what they learned in this unit about moving continents and geologic time to explore events and processes that formed Earth, the solar system, stars, and galaxies.

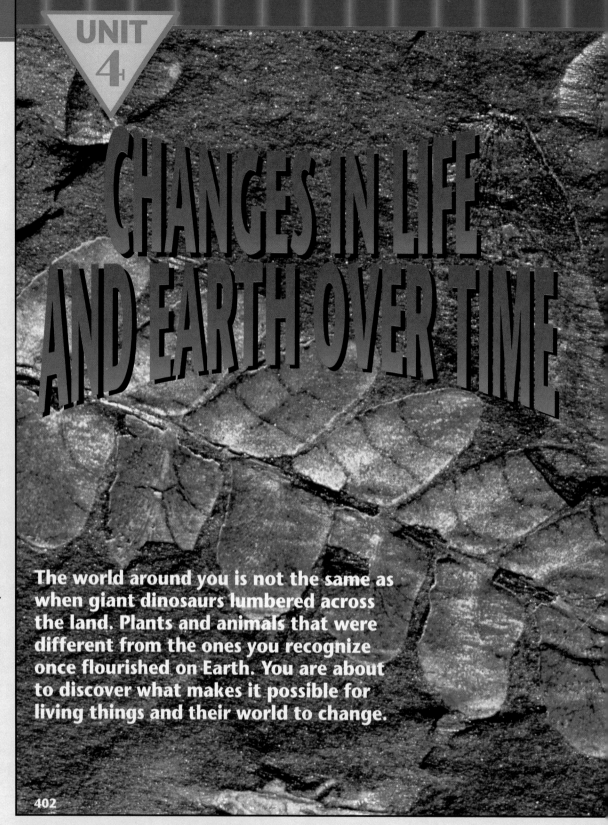

**UNIT**
**4**

**CHANGES IN LIFE AND EARTH OVER TIME**

The world around you is not the same as when giant dinosaurs lumbered across the land. Plants and animals that were different from the ones you recognize once flourished on Earth. You are about to discover what makes it possible for living things and their world to change.

402

⊙ VIDEODISC

Use the **Integrated Science Videodisc** to reinforce and enhance concepts in this unit.

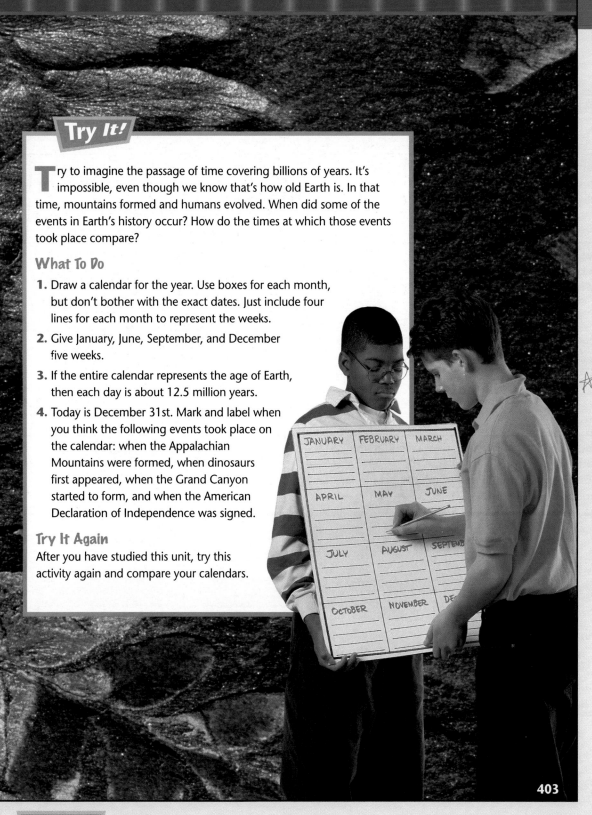

## Try It!

Try to imagine the passage of time covering billions of years. It's impossible, even though we know that's how old Earth is. In that time, mountains formed and humans evolved. When did some of the events in Earth's history occur? How do the times at which those events took place compare?

### What To Do

1. Draw a calendar for the year. Use boxes for each month, but don't bother with the exact dates. Just include four lines for each month to represent the weeks.

2. Give January, June, September, and December five weeks.

3. If the entire calendar represents the age of Earth, then each day is about 12.5 million years.

4. Today is December 31st. Mark and label when you think the following events took place on the calendar: when the Appalachian Mountains were formed, when dinosaurs first appeared, when the Grand Canyon started to form, and when the American Declaration of Independence was signed.

### Try It Again

After you have studied this unit, try this activity again and compare your calendars.

## GETTING STARTED

**Discussion**  You may want to pose the following questions.

**1. How does sexual reproduction differ from asexual reproduction?** *Students may have some ideas but be unable to describe sexual reproduction as involving the joining of two cells, each containing half the genes of the new organism, and the recombination of genetic material involved.*

**2. What is a gene?** *Many students will know that genes have something to do with heredity. The definition of a gene as a segment of DNA that carries the information for one protein will probably be new to them.*

**3. What evidence do you have that continents are still moving today?** *Plate movement is monitored by laser measuring devices and by satellites. Movement along some plate boundaries can be seen by the naked eye.*

The ways in which students answer these questions will help you establish any misconceptions that students may have.

## Try It!

**Purpose**  To describe Earth's age and sequence some events that have occurred on Earth. **L1**

**Troubleshooting**  Students may have difficulty placing events. Remind students that they will have a chance to try this activity again, after they have acquired more information.

**Answers**

Suggested responses are: Appalachian Mountains formed about 225 million years ago, (18 days, second week of Dec.); dinosaurs appeared about 180 million years ago (14.5 days, third week in Dec.), Grand Canyon formed 600 million years ago (48 days, third week in Nov.); and Declaration of Independence was signed 0 million years ago (last day of Dec.).

**✔ Assessment**

**Oral**  Have students place their completed calendars in their portfolios. Students can then write a story from Earth's point of view, describing changes that Earth has experienced over time. Ask volunteers to read their stories aloud. Use the Performance Task Assessment List for Writer's Guide to Fiction in **PAMSS**, p. 83. **L1** **P**

# Chapter Organizer

| SECTION | OBJECTIVES | ACTIVITIES |
|---|---|---|
| **Chapter Opener** | | **Explore!** What's an egg? p. 405 |
| **13-1 Sex Cells—A Different Story** (2 days) | 1. **Compare and contrast** eggs and sperm. 2. **Contrast** chromosome number in body cells and sex cells. | **Find Out!** Does a relationship exist between chromosome number and the complexity of an organism? p. 407 **Explore!** How do the number of chromosomes in body cells and sex cells compare? p. 410 |
| **13-2 Meiosis Makes Sex Cells** (3 days) | 1. **Describe** the process of meiosis. 2. **Determine** the results of meiosis and why it is needed. 3. **Determine** where and when meiosis occurs. | **Explore!** How are sex cells formed? p. 411 **Investigate 13-1:** Mitosis and Meiosis, pp. 414–415 **Skillbuilder:** Interpreting Scientific Illustrations, p. 417 |
| **13-3 Plant Reproduction** (3 days) | 1. **Diagram** the structure of a typical flower. 2. **Describe** how flowering plants reproduce. | **Investigate 13-2:** Parts of a Flower, pp. 420–421 |
| **13-4 Animal Reproduction** (3 days) | 1. **Compare and contrast** external and internal fertilization in animals. 2. **Demonstrate** an understanding of how humans reproduce. | **Explore!** What is the pathway of sperm through the male reproductive system? p. 424 |

## EXPAND *your view*

**A Closer Look** Which Came First—The Chicken or the Egg? pp. 408–409

**Chemistry Connection** Chemicals and Birth Defects, pp. 426–427

**Science and Society** Curing Infertility, pp. 429–430

**Technology Connection** Saving Endangered Species, p. 431

**How It Works** Adaptations for Pollination, p. 432

## ACTIVITY MATERIALS

| EXPLORE! | INVESTIGATE! | FIND OUT! |
|---|---|---|
| **Page 405** chicken egg, dish **Page 410\*** No special materials are required. **Page 411\*** package of colored candies, 5 paper cups | **Pages 414–415\*** Figure 13-5, yarn strands, four different colors; tape or glue; scissors; large sheets of paper **Pages 420–421** gladiolus, fresh or preserved; scalpel, hand lens, microscope, microscope slide, water, eyedropper, coverslip, forceps | **Page 407\*** No special materials are required. |

\*For adequate development of the concepts presented, we recommend that students do the activities with an asterisk.

# Chapter 13 Reproduction

## TEACHER CLASSROOM RESOURCES

| Student Masters | Teaching Aids |
|---|---|
| **Study Guide,** p. 41<br>**Science Discovery Activities,** 13-1 | |
| **Study Guide,** p. 42<br>**Flex Your Brain,** p. 5<br>**Science Discovery Activities,** 13-2 | **Laboratory Manual,** pp. 79–82, Chromosomes<br>**Color Transparency and Master 25,** Meiosis<br>***STVS:** *Genetic Engineering in Barley,* Plants and Simple Organisms (Disc 4, Side 1) |
| **Study Guide,** p. 43<br>**Take Home Activities,** p. 23<br>**Making Connections: Integrating Sciences,** p. 29<br>**Making Connections: Across the Curriculum,** p. 29<br>**Concept Mapping,** p. 21<br>**Science Discovery Activities,** 13-3 | **Laboratory Manual,** pp. 83–86, Overproduction<br>***STVS:** *Super Trees,* Plants and Simple Organisms (Disc 4, Side 2)<br>***STVS:** *Plant Clones,* Plants and Simple Organisms (Disc 4, Side 2) |
| **Study Guide,** p. 44<br>**Critical Thinking/Problem Solving,** p. 21<br>**Multicultural Connections,** p. 29, 30<br>**Making Connections: Technology & Society,** p. 29 | **Laboratory Manual,** pp. 87–88, Fetal Development<br>**Color Transparency and Master 26,** Fertilization and Early Development |

| ASSESSMENT RESOURCES | **Spanish Resources**<br>**Integrated Science Videodisc**<br>**Cooperative Learning Resource Guide**<br>**Lab and Safety Skills** |
|---|---|
| **Review and Assessment,** pp. 77–82<br>**Performance Assessment,** Ch. 13<br>**PAMSS***<br>**MindJogger Videoquiz**<br>**Computer Test Bank** | |

## KEY TO TEACHING STRATEGIES

The following designations will help you decide which activities are appropriate for your students.

**L1** Level 1 activities should be within the ability range of all students.

**L2** Level 2 activities should be within the ability range of the average to above-average student.

**L3** Level 3 activities are designed for the ability range of above-average students.

**LEP** LEP activities should be within the ability range of Limited English Proficiency students.

**COOP LEARN** Cooperative Learning activities are designed for small group work.

**P** These strategies represent student products that can be placed into a best-work portfolio.

## ADDITIONAL MATERIALS

**Software**
*Cell Functions, Growth and Mitosis,* IBM.
*Describing Patterns in Reproduction, Growth and Development,* Queue.
*Human Life Processes III,* IBM.
*The Human Systems, Series 3,* Focus Media.
*Meiosis,* EME.
*Reproduction in Plants,* J & S Software.
*The Reproduction System: A Baby is Born,* Marshware.

**Audiovisual**
*Asexual Reproduction,* video, Educational Activities.
*Human Body: Reproductive System,* video, Coronel/MTI.

*Pollination,* video, National Geographic.
*Sexual Reproduction,* video, Educational Activities.

**Laserdisc**
*Cell Biology I,* Videodiscovery.
*Life Cycles,* Videodiscovery.
*Meiosis and Mitosis,* EBEC.
*Pollination Biology,* Videodiscovery.
*Reproduction in Organisms,* AIMS.

**Readings**
Aronson, Billy. *They Came from DNA.* W.H. Freeman.

Parker, Steve. *The Body Atlas.* Dorling Kindersley.

*Performance Assessment in Middle School Science

*Science and Technology Videodisc Series

## Reproduction

### THEME DEVELOPMENT

This chapter explores the theme of stability and change. The process of meiosis is necessary for sexual reproduction and ensures that there is variation among organisms. Variation within an organism helps the stability of the species.

Scale and structure is another theme supported in this chapter. In the Investigate on pages 420–421, students explore the size and structure of a flower.

### CHAPTER OVERVIEW

Students begin the chapter by comparing and contrasting characteristics of egg and sperm cells and comparing the chromosome number in body cells to that of sex cells. Next, students will see where, when, and why meiosis occurs.

Students will come to understand how fertilization occurs in plants by studying the anatomy of a flower. They will learn about external and internal fertilization in animals, focusing on the human reproductive system.

### Tying to Previous Knowledge

Review the process of mitosis on pages 411–412, in which a cell nucleus divides into two new nuclei, each of which contains the same number of chromosomes as the parent cell. Tell students that an understanding of mitosis will be applied when they learn about meiosis.

### INTRODUCING THE CHAPTER

Have students observe the close-up photograph on page 404 and discuss what parts of the flower stand out most sharply. Have students explain what the bee is doing. How might the bee's actions be beneficial to the flower and the bee?

---

# Reproduction

A blur of buzzing yellow and black zips by Linda like a miniature B-52 bomber. Its destination? The zinnias beckoning with their bright red and yellow blooms from the Orozcos' flower garden. Why do bees visit zinnias? They drink the nectar and collect the pollen that zinnias produce. Bees use nectar and pollen for food. While collecting pollen, bees also transfer pollen from one flower to another, helping flowers make seeds and reproduce. Both plants and animals, including human beings, need to reproduce if their species are to survive. Plants and animals don't reproduce in exactly the same way, of course. But for both, the process almost always begins with the union of a female egg and a male sperm. How does this union take place? How are the egg and the sperm produced? How do insects help plants reproduce? In this chapter, you'll discover the answers as you learn about the life process called reproduction.

▶ *In the activity on the next page, explore some of the characteristics of a chicken egg.*

### Did you ever wonder...

✓ **Why you resemble other members of your family?**

✓ **Why insects, such as bees, are attracted to flowers?**

✓ **How a single flower makes seeds?**

Before you begin to study about how organisms reproduce, think about these questions and answer them *in your Journal*. When you finish the chapter, compare your Journal write-up with what you have learned.

404

---

### Did you ever wonder...

• You resemble family members because both you and your siblings have received chromosomes from your parents. (p. 406)

• Insects drink nectar and eat pollen. (p. 422)

• Pollen lands on the stigma; a pollen tube grows down the style to the ovary. Sperm travel down pollen tube and join the eggs to create a fertilized egg, which becomes a seed. (p. 422)

### STUDENT JOURNAL

Have students write their responses to the Did You Ever Wonder questions in their journals. After they have read the chapter, students should read their journal entries again to see what they have learned about reproduction.

## Explore! ACTIVITY

### What's an egg?

**A**n egg may be just breakfast to you, but it is much more to a chicken.

### What To Do

1. Your teacher will provide you with a chicken egg. Look at the physical traits of the egg, such as its size, color, and presence of a shell.

2. What do your observations indicate about the habitat of chickens?

3. Now examine the internal structure of the egg. Break open the chicken egg and pour the contents into a dish. What does the membrane just inside the shell look like?

4. Carefully examine the yolk and egg white. Based on what you can see, might this egg have grown into a chicken?

5. Make a drawing of the parts of the egg.

6. *In your Journal,* describe the appearance and possible functions of the parts of the chicken egg.

405

# PREPARATION

## Concepts Developed

This section builds on students' knowledge of mitosis and extends what they learned about cells and cell reproduction. Students will compare and contrast egg and sperm cells and compare chromosome number in body cells versus sex cells. By organizing data, they will learn that there is no correspondence between the type of organism and its number of chromosomes.

## Planning the Lesson

Refer to the Chapter Organizer on pages 404A–B.

# 1 MOTIVATE

**Activity** Allow students to make a model showing the division of sex cells and its effect on chromosome number.

Materials needed are one pound each of red and blue clay.

Have students break off a small chunk of each color clay and roll it into a ball. If each ball represents a cell of the same species, how can you show meiosis? *Break each ball into equal pieces.* What can be said about the number of chromosomes in each piece? *Each piece contains half the number of chromosomes that were in the undivided "cell."* Ask students to combine one red and one blue daughter cell. How many chromosomes does this new cell have? *Same number of chromosomes as the parent cells.* What might the new color indicate about the red and blue cell? *It has inherited traits from both the red and blue parent cells.* L1

---

### Section Objectives

- Compare and contrast eggs and sperm.
- Contrast chromosome number in body cells and sex cells.

### Key Terms

*body cell, sex cells, sperm, eggs*

## Cell Types

Your body contains trillions and trillions of cells, the basic unit of structure in all living things. Just as whole organisms grow and die, individual cells grow and die. In the short time it takes you to read this paragraph, millions of the cells within your body will die.

### ■ Body Cells

How can your body continue to work properly even as millions of its cells are dying? Your body is constantly producing new cells. Even as cells are dying, new cells are being produced at a faster rate. Most of the cells that make up your body,

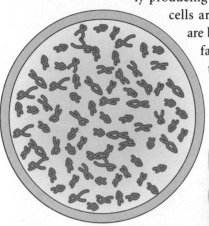

your **body cells**, reproduce exact copies of themselves by mitosis. You may recall that in mitosis, one parent cell forms two identical new cells. The instructions that "tell" a cell how to develop, whether to be a blood cell or skin cell or some other kind of cell, are contained in the cell's chromosomes. All human body cells contain 46 chromosomes. Mitosis produces two new body cells, each with 46 chromosomes, just like the parent cell.

All species of organisms have a certain number of chromosomes in their body cells. This number is the same for all members of the species. For example, a body cell of a dog, whether it is a poodle or a collie, contains 78 chromosomes.

**Figure 13-1**

The 78 chromosomes in a puppy's body cells are what tells it to grow up to be a 0.5 kilogram chihuahua or a 66 kilogram wolfhound. How is this cell like a human body cell? How is it different?

---

## Program Resources

**Study Guide,** p. 41
**Laboratory Manual,** pp. 79–82, Chromosomes L1
**Science Discovery Activities,** 13-1, Eggstra Protection?

## Find Out! ACTIVITY

### Does a relationship exist between chromosome number and the complexity of an organism?

**A**re you more complex than a fruit fly? What about a goldfish? Does complexity of an organism depend on the number of chromosomes in its body cells?

### What To Do

1. List the following organisms according to chromosome number, beginning with the smallest number of chromosomes: grasshopper—24, giant sequoia—22, fruit fly—8, tomato—24, guinea pig—64, goldfish—94, spider plant—24, dog—78, human—46.

2. Next to each organism, indicate the kingdom to which it belongs.

### Conclude and Apply

1. Which organisms listed have the same chromosome number?

2. Are the organisms in Question 1 in the same kingdom?

3. *In your Journal*, state what you can conclude about a relationship between chromosome number and complexity of an organism.

Fruitfly
8 chromosomes

Sequoia
22 chromosomes

Grasshopper
24 chromosomes

### ■ Sex Cells

Body cells are not the only kind of cell in your body, and mitosis is not the only kind of cell reproduction. In order for many organisms to produce offspring, they must produce **sex cells**. If you are a male, your body produces sex cells called **sperm**. If you are a female, your body produces sex cells called **eggs**. Offspring may be produced only when egg and sperm have united. Sex cells play an important role in reproduction. In the next section, you will learn how sex cells are produced.

**407**

**Tying to Previous Knowledge**

Have students diagram the process of mitosis to help them understand it more clearly. First have students recall what they know about cell reproduction and mitosis. Challenge them to explain how and why mitosis occurs.

### Visual Learning

**Figure 13-1** Check students' understanding of the information presented by asking them how many chromosomes there are in a Cairn terrier's body cell. In a cocker spaniel's body cell? *A body cell of any dog contains 78 chromosomes.* **How is this cell like a human body cell?** *It reproduces by mitosis.* **How is it different?** *It has a different number of chromosomes (A human's body cell has 46.)* **L1**

### Expected Outcome

Students should conclude that the number of chromosomes in an organism is not related to its complexity.

### Conclude and Apply

**1.** grasshopper, tomato, spider plant

**2.** The grasshopper is in a different kingdom from the other two.

**3.** The number of chromosomes in an organism is not related to its apparent complexity.

### ✔ Assessment

**Process** Have students make a data table that gives the information that they recorded in What To Do. Use the Performance Task Assessment List for Data Table in **PAMSS**, p. 37. **L1**

## Find Out!

### Does a relationship exist between chromosome number and the complexity of an organism?

**Time needed** about 15 minutes

**Thinking Processes** making and using tables, classifying, sequencing, recognizing cause and effect

**Purpose** To infer that there is no connection between the type of organism and the number of chromosomes it possesses.

**Preparation** Before students begin, make sure they have their textbooks so they can check whether they have put each organism in the right kingdom.

### Teaching the Activity

**Troubleshooting** Before students start, have volunteers describe any unfamiliar organisms.

**Student Journal** Have students write their answers to the Conclude and Apply questions in their journals. **L2**

Students may erroneously believe that mitosis is a continually recurring process in all the cells of an organism. Explain that once certain cells are formed, mitosis does not occur in them again. In humans, spinal cord injuries are often irreversible because nerve cells do not undergo mitosis and cannot form new cells. In plants, mitosis is an ongoing in growth regions, but not throughout the entire plant.

## Visual Learning

**Figures 13-2 and 13-3** Have students compare and contrast the cells shown in Figures 13-2 and 13-3. Explore with students how the shape of the sperm, as shown in Figure 13-2, might relate to its function. Guide students to see that the tail gives the sperm mobility. Contrast this to shape of the egg as shown in Figure 13-3. Make sure that students understand that even though the egg is much larger than the sperm, both contain the same number of chromosomes. **Why can't it produce a baby alone?** *The egg is produced by the human female. Because humans reproduce sexually, it must join with a sex cell from a male human to produce a baby. This process restores the chromosome number (i.e., 2n).*

# Sperm and Eggs – Alike and Different

**Figures 13-2** and **13-3** show a human sperm and a human egg. As you can see, sex cells are quite different from each other. Look closely at the

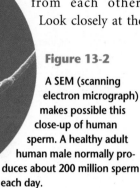

**Figure 13-2**

A SEM (scanning electron micrograph) makes possible this close-up of human sperm. A healthy adult human male normally produces about 200 million sperm each day.

physical traits of these cells. Sperm have tails and can swim, like tadpoles; eggs cannot. Sperm are very tiny and can be seen only under a microscope; eggs are one of the few human cells that can be seen with the naked eye. (Nerve cells are another.) A human egg is about the size of the point of a needle. Eggs contain a food supply in the form of a yolk. Tiny sperm do not.

### ■ Numbers Don't Lie

Another way that sperm and eggs differ is in the number produced. A bull can produce as many as five bil-

## Which Came First— The Chicken or the Egg?

The first group of vertebrates able to lay its eggs on dry land appeared around 310 million years ago. Those eggs were encased in leathery shells, similar to the shells found on eggs laid by modern reptiles. The first land vertebrates were successful in the new environment because the shell protected the egg from predators and prevented it from drying out.

### Parts of the Egg

In the Explore activity on page 405, you looked at the shelled egg of a chicken. In animals that lay shelled eggs, the

Bird eggs come in all colors and sizes, but they all have protective shells.

**408** Chapter 13 Reproduction

**Purpose**

A Closer Look explains the role of a shelled egg in internal fertilization. This excursion also discusses the importance of water in fertilization and embryo development.

**Content Background**

The structure and development of eggs of different species vary with the conditions under which the egg is produced and matures. The water flea, for example, lays both small "summer eggs" and larger "winter eggs." Under normal conditions, the summer eggs hatch, but in times of extreme cold or drought, when the pools in which the animals live dry up, the winter eggs are fertilized and deposited. These eggs can remain dormant for years until conditions are favorable for their hatching.

lion sperm at one time. But a cow usually produces only one egg at a time. This is the case with most mammals, including humans. Human males produce lots of sperm, while females produce relatively few eggs. Although the traits of sperm and eggs are quite different, the main job of these sex cells is the same; to join together to produce a new organism.

### ■ Chromosome Number

You have learned that a human body cell contains 46 chromosomes. You have also learned that body cells are produced through mitosis. Remember, through the process of mitosis, each new human body cell

**Figure 13-3**

Again using SEM, this human egg has been made large enough to see in detail. Why can't it produce a baby alone?

contains 46 chromosomes, just like the parent body cell. This ensures that the new cells look and function exactly like the parent cell. Sex cells are formed by a different process. Do you think that a human sex cell contains 46 chromosomes like a body cell? You will discover the answer to this question in the following activity.

shell is deposited around the fertilized egg cell just before it leaves the animal's reproductive tract. Packaged along with the fertilized egg is a large food supply called the yolk. Albumen, a protein in the white of the egg, provides water and additional nutrients.

Shelled eggs have several <sup>4</sup> protective membranes. The first membrane to form encloses the yolk. Another membrane surrounds the embryo and is liquid-filled. This liquid-filled space acts as a shock absorber, cushioning the developing embryo.

A third membrane lines the eggshell and allows the embryo to exchange oxygen and carbon dioxide with the air outside. The remaining membrane

*Like birds, reptiles lay shelled eggs.*

forms a sac into which the embryo excretes wastes.

Shelled eggs provide a developing embryo with everything it needs to survive. Why do you think they were such an important adaptation for the evolution of land vertebrates?

### What Do You Think?

In most animals that lay unshelled eggs in water, fertilization is external. What kind of fertilization occurs in animals that lay shelled eggs? What is the advantage of this kind of fertilization?

13-1    Sex Cells—A Different Story    **409**

**Across the Curriculum**

**Language Arts**

Have students look up the words *sperm* and *ovum* and find out how their Latin roots are appropriate to their meaning. Then have students look up the words *exogamy* and *endogamy* and discuss the different ideas about marriage expressed by these words. Challenge students to contrast the meaning of *exogamy* as a biological and social term. **L2**

**Theme Connection**  Energy is a central theme in this section. It drives biological systems and is involved in the reproduction, growth, and development of organisms. The unique functioning of the human reproductive system is dependent on energy for cell division and the subsequent growth and differentiation of cells.

---

**Teaching Strategy**

Working in small groups, have students carefully break open a hen's egg to identify its contents. In their journals, have students make a labeled sketch of their findings. **COOP LEARN** **L2**

**Answers to**

**What Do You Think?**

internal; Not as many eggs and sperm need to be released to assure fertilization.

**Going Further ⅢⅢⅢ▸**

Salmonella, a bacterium that causes food poisoning, can be transmitted through contaminated eggs. Have students list guidelines for storing and cooking eggs. How should eggs be stored? How long should they cook? For information, students can contact:

Human Nutrition Information Service
Food and Consumer Services
6505 Belcrest Road
Hyattsville, MD 20782

Invite students to create a display that shows what they found out about salmonella and how to avoid contact with it. Use the Performance Task Assessment List for Display in **PAMSS**, p. 63. **COOP LEARN** **L1**

Have students explain what they learned from section 13-1 about the formation of body cells through mitosis. Then have them review the numbers of chromosomes in body cells and in sex cells. Ask volunteers to diagram egg and sperm cells, showing the number of chromosomes in each.

**Flex Your Brain** Use the Flex Your Brain activity to have students explore MEIOSIS. L2

**Teacher F.Y.I.**

With 23 pairs of chromosomes in the human body, there are more than 8 million different combinations of chromosomes possible for every human cell formed by meiosis.

---

### Visual Learning

**Figure 13-4** Give students an opportunity to communicate. Divide the class into cooperative learning groups to answer the questions in Figure 13-4. Use the Performance Task Assessment List for Group Work in **PAMSS**, p. 97.

**A.** 4 chromosomes; 8 chromatids

**B.** across the center of the cell

**C.** Chromosomes are pulled to opposite ends of the cell. The chromosomes that are pulled to one end are unlike.

**D.** Each cell has one chromosome from each pair. Each chromosome is composed of sister chromatids.

**E.** Chromosomes are not paired.

**F.** Sister chromatids separate as they do in mitosis.

**G.** Four new cells are formed. Each has half the number of chromosomes found in the original cell.

---

# Meiosis – A Closer View

Now that you have a general idea of what occurs during meiosis, let's look at the process in detail. **Figure 13-4** shows the steps that make up this process. Meiosis begins in a cell in the reproductive organs of an organism. The number of chromosomes in the cell varies among different species of organisms. For this example, the cell in **Figure 13-4** has two pairs of chromosomes for a total of four chromosomes.

**Figure 13-4**
All reproductive cells reproduce the same way, through the process of meiosis. Meiosis involves two divisions of the chromosomes in the original cell.

**A** Each chromosome doubles itself, forming a sister chromatid. How many chromosomes are in the diagram? How many chromatids?

**B** The doubled chromosomes come together in matching pairs. Where do they line up?

**C** The chromosomes now separate. Where are they pulled? Are the chromosomes that have been pulled to one end like one another, or are they different?

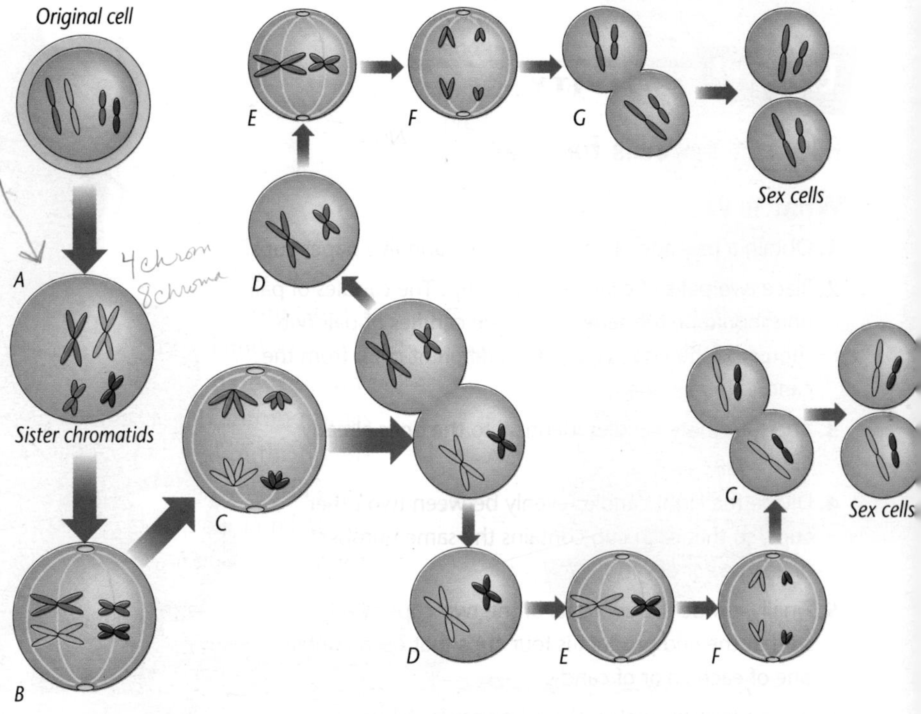

**D** The first division in meiosis has occurred as the cell divides, forming two new cells. What are the contents of these cells?

**E** The chromosomes again line up along the center of each new cell. How does this differ from step B?

**F** Now the sister chromatids separate and move to opposite ends of the cell. How is this stage of meiosis very similar to mitosis?

**G** The cells divide. How many new cells are formed? Compared to the original cell, how many chromosomes do the four new cells have?

**412** Chapter 13 Reproduction

---

### Program Resources

**Study Guide,** p. 42
**Critical Thinking/Problem Solving,** p. 5, Flex Your Brain
**Transparency Master,** p. 53, and **Color Transparency,** Number 25, Meiosis L2

### Meeting Individual Needs

**Learning Disabled** Show students a model of chromosome thickening. Remove a telephone cord from a phone. Have students stretch out the cord. Discuss how it is long and thin when stretched out. Allow the cord to return to its usual position. Make sure students understand that the cord shortens and thickens when it goes back into position. This is comparable to what happens to chromosomes during the first stages of meiosis. **LEP**

Once you understand meiosis, study **Figure 13-5**, which shows a comparison of mitosis and meiosis. In the following Investigate, you will take a closer look at these two processes.

**Figure 13-6**

As in other sexually reproducing animals, meiosis produces egg and sperm in these two cats.

**Figure 13-5**

The end products of mitosis and meiosis are very different even though the two process start out similarly.

**Ⓐ** The chromosomes double in both mitosis and meiosis.

**Ⓑ** The chromosomes line up in pairs in meiosis, but not in mitosis.

**Ⓒ** In meiosis, the chromosomes separate but chromatids remain joined. In mitosis, chromatids separate.

**Ⓓ** Chromatids are still joined in meiosis, but not in mitosis.

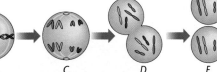

*Mitosis*

*Original cell*   A   B   C   D   E

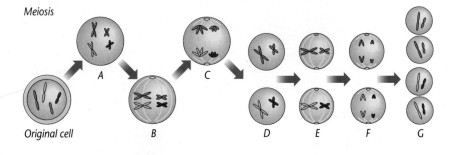

*Meiosis*

*Original cell*   A   B   C   D   E   F   G

**Ⓔ** Mitosis is complete, but another division is about to take place in meiosis. The chromosomes line up along the center of the cell.

**Ⓕ** The chromatids separate.

**Ⓖ** Compare the end products of meiosis with the end products of mitosis. How do they differ?

13-2   Meiosis Makes Sex Cells   **413**

INVESTIGATE!

## 13-1 Mitosis and Meiosis

### Planning the Activity

**Time needed**   45–60 minutes

**Purpose**   By making a model, to infer that cells formed by meiosis have half the chromosomes of the original cell, while cells formed by mitosis contain the same number of chromosomes as the original cell.

**Process Skills**   making models, observing and inferring, comparing and contrasting, making and using tables, forming operational definitions, predicting, interpreting scientific illustrations, sequencing

**Materials**   Figure 13-5, four different colors of yarn, tape, scissors, large sheets of paper

**Preparation**   Use contrasting colors of yarn for a clearer demonstration. Be sure that yarn strands are of the same thickness.

### Teaching the Activity

**Possible Procedures**   Have students use small pieces of tape to place the yarn on the dashed outlines in figures B and C. **LEP** **L1**

**Process Reinforcement**   Have students discuss in their groups how their models helped them complete the data table. **COOP LEARN**

**Student Journal**   Have students write the answers to the Analyzing/Concluding and Applying questions in their journals. **L1**

# Mitosis and Meiosis

*You can make models of the steps of mitosis and meiosis. Your model will allow you to compare the end results of mitosis and meiosis.*

### Problem
How is meiosis different from mitosis?

### Materials
yarn strands, four different colors
tape or glue
scissors
large sheets of paper

### Safety Precautions

### What To Do

**1** Copy the data table *into your Journal.*

**2** In your group, develop a plan for *modeling* the steps of mitosis and meiosis using the materials provided. Refer to the data table for the number of chromosomes to include in your model. You may also want to sketch diagrams of your plan to use as patterns. If you need additional help, the steps of mitosis and meiosis are shown in Figure 13-5 on page 413.

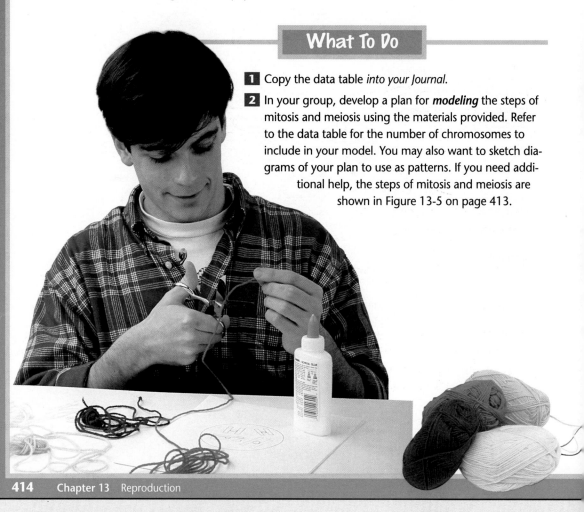

414   Chapter 13   Reproduction

## Program Resources

**Activity Masters,**   pp. 55–56, Investigate 13-1

**Science Discovery Activities,**   13-2, Comparing Chromosomes

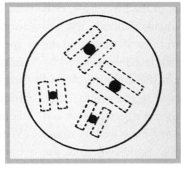

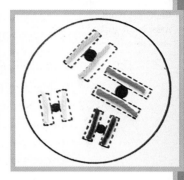

A          B          C

**3** Before you make your model, have your teacher check your plan.

**4** Make your model following the plan you have developed.

**5** When you are finished with your model, complete your data table.

### Data and Observations

| COMPARING MITOSIS AND MEIOSIS | MITOSIS | MEIOSIS |
|---|---|---|
| Type of cell undergoing reproduction | Body Cell | Sex Cell |
| Number of chromosomes before cell begins to reproduce | 4 | 4 |
| Chromosome pairs in the original cell | 2 | 2 |
| Final number of chromosomes in each new cell at the end of reproduction | 4 | 2 |
| Chromosome pairs in each new cell at conclusion of reproduction | 2 | None |

## Analyzing

1. **Compare** the location and arrangement of chromosomes in the cell during Step B of mitosis and meiosis.

2. **Compare** the location and arrangement of chromosomes in the cell during Step C of mitosis and meiosis.

## Concluding and Applying

3. How do the end results of mitosis and meiosis differ?

4. **Going Further** Predict what would occur if sex cells were produced by mitosis rather than by meiosis.

**Expected Outcome**

Students will observe that cells formed by meiosis have half the chromosomes of the original cell, while cells formed by mitosis contain the same number of chromosomes as body cells from the same organism.

**Answers to** Analyzing/Concluding and Applying

**1.** In mitosis, chromosomes are not paired, but do line up along the cell center. In meiosis, chromosomes first pair up and then become arranged along the cell center.

**2.** The locations are the same, but in meiosis, in each pair of sister chromatids, the original and copy are still attached to each other.

**3.** Mitosis produces two cells identical to the original one; meiosis produces four cells with half the chromosomes of the original cell.

**4.** The resulting organism would have twice the normal number of chromosomes.

✔ **Assessment**

**Performance** Have students place their answers to the Analyzing/Concluding and Applying questions, together with a sketch of the model that their group made, in their portfolios. Then have students use what they learned in this activity to make a bulletin board comparing and contrasting mitosis and meiosis. Use the Performance Task Assessment List for Bulletin Board in **PAMSS**, p. 59. L1 P

**Meeting Individual Needs**

**Physically Challenged/Visually Impaired** Visually impaired students can make three-dimensional models of mitosis and meiosis on poster board. Direct them to show each stage of each process on a separate poster. L1 LEP

COOP LEARN

### DID YOU KNOW?

Meiosis comes from the Greek word meaning reduction.

# Where and When Meiosis Occurs

As you saw in the Investigate, cells produced by meiosis contain half the number of chromosomes found in the original cell, while cells produced by mitosis contain the same number of chromosomes as in the original cell. Because sperm and eggs are produced by meiosis, they have half as many chromosomes as body cells from the same organism.

**Figure 13-7**

Although these family members are each unique, they display many similar characteristics.

### How Do We Know?

**How do scientists count chromosomes?**

Various cell staining techniques help scientists examine and even count chromosomes within a cell. Counts can be made from a body cell and a sex cell of an organism and then compared. Scientists are also able to stop meiosis or mitosis at a particular stage to observe exactly what is occurring at that time in each process.

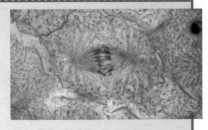

Meiosis can occur only in the sex organ of a living thing. In humans, sperm are produced in a male sex organ called a **testis**. A male usually has two testes. Eggs are produced in a female sex organ called an **ovary**. Females usually have two ovaries. Where does meiosis occur in your body?

### ■ Sexual Maturity

From the time you were an embryo, mitosis has been occurring in most of your body cells. This is not true of meiosis. For males, meiosis begins when the organism reaches sexual maturity. For females, meiosis begins before birth. Chromosomes duplicate themselves, but cells remain in this stage until the female is sexually mature. Then the process of meiosis continues. Cells divide to form eggs, usually one at a time.

The time of your own sexual maturity is marked by the production of sex cells by your sex organs. If you are a male, your testes will be producing sperm for the rest of your life.

However, the number of sperm your body produces will decrease as you age. If you are a female, your ovaries will produce eggs until between the ages of 45 and 55.

The time of sexual maturity differs in all living things. For humans, sexual maturity usually occurs between the ages of 10 and 14. A mouse can reach sexual maturity at the age of 2 months. Sexual maturity in a corn plant occurs when the plant is between 3 and 4 months old, while most dandelion plants reach sexual maturity when 4 to 5 weeks old.

### ■ Why Meiosis Is Needed

Did you ever wonder why you resemble some members of your family more than others? You probably share physical traits with each of your parents because you inherited genetic material from each of them. Half of the 46 chromosomes in each of your body cells resemble half of the chromosomes in your mother's body cells. The other half of the chromosomes in your body cells resemble half of the chromosomes in your father's body cells.

In order to understand why this happens, think again about meiosis. Meiosis produces sex cells that contain half the number of chromosomes found in a body cell. Human eggs contain 23 chromosomes. Human sperm also contain 23 chromosomes. During fertilization, an egg and a sperm join. The cell that results contains 46 chromosomes. You should now understand why sex cells must divide by meiosis. If human sex cells formed by mitosis, each would contain 46 chromosomes. The cell produced by fertilization would contain 92 chromosomes!

In this section, you have compared two methods of cell division. You have learned why it is important that sex cells divide by meiosis rather than mitosis. In the next section, you will discover how sex cells meet during fertilization.

## SKILLBUILDER

**Interpreting Scientific Illustrations**

Make a diagram to illustrate meiosis in humans. At the top of your diagram draw a circle around the number 46. This represents an original cell with its full number of chromosomes. Continue the diagram by drawing additional circles to represent each change the original cell undergoes. Be sure you write the number of chromosomes or chromatids each new cell contains. If you need help, refer to the **Skill Handbook** on page 691.

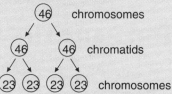
## 3 ASSESS

**Check for Understanding**

Make sure that students can explain what happens in the cell cycle. Before having students answer the Check Your Understanding questions, give them an outline drawing of the cell cycle. Have them draw in the chromosomes and write what occurs at each stage.

**Reteach**

Have students make a chart comparing mitosis and meiosis in humans. L1

| Feature | Mitosis | Meiosis |
|---|---|---|
| Cell Type | body cell | sex cell |
| Number of Cells Produced | two | four |
| Number of Chromosomes in end Product | same as parent | half of parent |

**Extension**

Have students who have mastered the concepts in this section explain why the time of sexual maturity differs between kinds of living things. *It depends on their life span.* L3

## 4 CLOSE

**Activity**

Use an overhead transparency to show the stages of meiosis *out of sequence.* Have students identify each stage and sequence the stages. L1

### check your UNDERSTANDING

1. How many times in meiosis do chromosomes double themselves? How many times do matching pairs of chromosomes line up along the cell center in groups of four? How many times do sister chromatids separate?

2. Why must an egg and sperm have half the number of chromosomes as the fertilized egg?

3. Where does the process of meiosis occur in your body?

4. **Apply** Cells from the muscle of a cat's thigh contain 38 chromosomes each. Based on this information, how many chromosomes does a cat sperm contain? Explain how you arrived at your answer.

13-2  Meiosis Makes Sex Cells  **417**

### check your UNDERSTANDING

1. They copy themselves once, line up in groups of four once, and separate once.

2. The egg and sperm of an organism contain half the normal number of chromosomes so that the fertilized egg can contain the total number of chromosomes of the particular species.

3. Meiosis occurs only in an individual's sex organs, the male's testes or female's ovaries.

4. A cat sperm cell contains 19 chromosomes. Since this sex cell is formed by meiosis, it contains half the number of chromosomes found in a cat's body cell.

## Plant Reproduction

# PREPARATION

## Concepts Developed

The previous lesson explored how sex cells are formed by meiosis and how that process differs from mitosis. Here, students will study the anatomy of a flower to learn where flowering plants produce sex cells and how fertilization occurs in plants. Finally, students will study how pollination occurs.

## Planning the Lesson

Refer to the Chapter Organizer on pages 404A–B.

# 1 MOTIVATE

Allow tactile learners and other students to manipulate and identify parts of a plant. You will need peanuts in their shells. The nut is the seed and the shell is the dried ovary. Have students open the shells and remove the seeds. Ask students to identify the paper-thin covering. *the seed coat* Tell students to pull apart the two halves of the peanut, working carefully. Have them locate and identify the small bump on one half. *the embryo plant* Finally, have students find the parts they think will become the leaves, stem, and roots. L1 LEP

# 2 TEACH

## Tying to Previous Knowledge

Have students communicate the overall process of meiosis. Then have volunteers describe when and why meiosis occurs. Ask students if they know how plants reproduce. Have a volunteer describe the process or draw it on the chalkboard. L2

## Section Objectives

- Diagram the structure of a typical flower.
- Describe how flowering plants reproduce.

## Key Terms

*stamen*
*pistil*

## The Need for Fertilization

On its own, a single egg or sperm cannot form a new offspring. An egg and sperm must come together. But the joining of an egg and a sperm is no easy task. In most plants and animals, a sizeable distance lies between the male and female sex organs. Most organisms have structures that aid the fertilization process. In this section, you'll learn about fertilization in plants. In the next section, you'll read about fertilization in animals.

**Figure 13-8**
Flowers seem like pretty decorations, but they have important work to do.

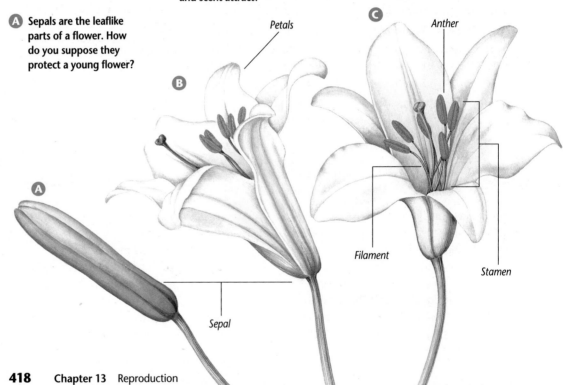

**B** Petals are the colored parts that protect the flower's sex organs. What do their color and scent attract?

**C** The stamen is the male reproductive organ. The saclike anther at the top is held up by a long filament. Anthers produce pollen. What reproductive cell is in this pollen?

**A** Sepals are the leaflike parts of a flower. How do you suppose they protect a young flower?

Petals

Anther

Filament

Stamen

Sepal

**418** Chapter 13 Reproduction

## Program Resources

**Study Guide,** p. 43
**Take Home Activities,** p. 23, Reproduction in Plants L1
**Making Connections: Integrating Sciences,** p. 29, A Natural Attraction L2
**Making Connections: Across the Curriculum,** p. 29, Linnaeus's Plant Classification System L3

# Plant Reproduction

Nearly all the plants you are familiar with are seed plants. Like animals, seed plants have both body cells and sex cells. A plant's body cells grow and divide by mitosis. The body cells develop into roots, stems, and leaves. A plant's sex cells are produced by meiosis in the reproductive organs of the plant. If a seed plant's male and female sex cells join, a new seed develops.

## ■ Flowering Plants

Have you ever stopped to admire a flower in bloom? **Figure 13-8** shows the anatomy of a flower. In this figure,

you will notice the male reproductive organ, the **stamen**. You'll also notice the female reproductive organ, the **pistil**. Study and read about these and other flower parts in the figure.

All of the structures shown in **Figure 13-8** are found in flowers. Some flowers contain both male and female structures, while others have only male or female parts. Whether an egg and sperm come from the same plant or different plants, pollen must be transferred from the male part to the female part for a new organism to develop. This process is called pollination.

**Connect to...**

## Earth Science

Rhododendrons and azaleas prefer cool, moist soil that contains humus, and is acidic, with a pH between 4.5 and 6.5. Prepare a table that shows how soil, climate, and moisture conditions in your area compare with the requirements for Rhododendrons and azaleas.

**Theme Connection** The theme of stability and change is apparent in plant reproduction. Meiosis allows recombination of genetic material to produce new, genetically different offspring. Thus, although the individual organisms are different, this gives greater stability to the species so it can respond to changes in its environment.

### Visual Learning

**Figure 13-8** Divide the class into small groups. Challenge each group to be the first to answer all the caption questions in Figure 13-8 correctly. **How do you suppose they protect a young flower?** *by covering or sheltering the flower* **What do their color and scent attract?** *Insects, birds, and moths* **What reproductive cell is in this pollen?** *sperm* **How do you suppose the stigma's sticky surface helps ensure pollination?** *The sticky surface helps the stigma trap pollen formed by the male part of the flower.* **What reproductive cells are produced there?** *eggs* **What reproductive cells will be deposited there?** *sperm* `COOP LEARN` `L2`

**D** The pistil is the female reproductive organ. Its top end is called the stigma. How do you suppose the stigma's sticky surface helps ensure pollination?

**E** The pistil, like the stamen, has a long, stalk-like structure. It's called the style. The pistil's base is rounded. It is the flower's ovary. What reproductive cells are produced there? What reproductive cells will be deposited there?

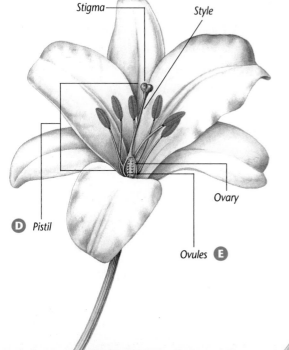

Stigma — Style

**D** Pistil

Ovary

Ovules **E**

Pollen

13-3 Plant Reproduction **419**

### Across the Curriculum

**Fine Arts**

Bring in some prints of paintings of flowers, such as those by Georgia O'Keeffe or Vincent van Gogh. Display real flowers, such as dandelions, clover, and daisies and have students make drawings of a real flower, using both the real flower and the prints as guides. Display these for others to share. `L1`

## Multicultural Perspectives

### Native American Cures

Many Native American nations had a medicine man or shaman who treated people with curative plants. The Dakota used the powdered root of skunk cabbage to relieve asthma. To cure upset stomachs, the Cheyenne drank water in which wild mint had been boiled. The Cree chewed tiny spruce cones to soothe an inflamed throat. Indigenous rainforest peoples also use plants as remedies. Have interested students research and report on scientists' attempts to gather and preserve indigenous people's medical knowledge about rainforest plants. An ecology or biology department at a local college or university might be one good source of information. `COOP LEARN` `L3` `P`

## 13-2 Parts of a Flower

### Planning the Activity

**Time needed** 60–90 minutes (1–2 class periods)

**Purpose** To infer how pollination occurs by locating and observing a flower's male and female reproductive organs.

**Process Skills** observing and inferring, hypothesizing, making and using tables, comparing and contrasting, interpreting scientific illustrations

**Materials** tulip, scalpels, hand lenses, microscopes and slides, water, eyedroppers, coverslips, forceps

**Preparation** Other flowers, such as lilies or gladiolas, may be used, depending on availability. Some flowers will have petals fused together. Others will have fused anthers.

### Teaching the Activity

You may be able to obtain free or inexpensive flowers from a florist or a grocery store.

**Troubleshooting** If you cannot find tulips, you may use other flowers.

**Process Reinforcement** Invite students to compare and contrast their observations of the flower, first with the naked eye and then with the hand lens. L1

**Student Journal** Have students complete the data table and record their answers to the Analyzing/Concluding and Applying questions in their journals. L1

---

# INVESTIGATE!

# Parts of a Flower

*Many plants are both male and female. In this activity, you will identify the male and female reproductive organs of a flower and hypothesize how pollination occurs.*

### Problem
How does pollination occur?

### Materials
tulip, fresh or preserved

| | |
|---|---|
| scalpel | water |
| hand lens | eyedropper |
| microscope | coverslip |
| microscope slide | forceps |

### Safety Precautions

Use caution with microscope and slides.

## What To Do

1 Copy the data table *into your Journal*.

2 Remove the flower's sepals. Record their number and color in your table.

3 Remove the flower's petals, and record their number and color.

4 Remove the stamens. Look at one with a hand lens. *Observe* its top part, or anther,

*dissecting scope*

### Data and Observations

| FLOWER PART | NUMBER | COLOR |
|---|---|---|
| Sepals | Student | answers will |
| Petals | depend | on specimen. |
| Stamens | | |
| Anthers | | |
| Pollen grains | | |
| Pistil | | |
| Inside ovary | | |

---

## Program Resources

**Activity Masters,** pp. 57–58, Investigate 13-2

**Concept Mapping,** p. 21, Reproductive Organs of Flowers L1

**Laboratory Manual,** pp. 83–86, Overproduction COOP LEARN

**Science Discovery Activities,** 13-3, Pollinate It!

**A**

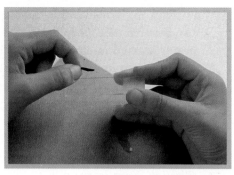

**B**

and also its filament. Record the number and color of stamens.

**5** Hold the anther over a drop of water on a microscope slide, and tap it gently. Add a coverslip. Observe the pollen grains under a ~~microscope~~ and make a drawing of them. ✮

**6** The structure that remains is the pistil, the female reproductive structure. Record the pistil's color.

**7** The stigma is located at the top of the style. Touch the stigma. Describe how it feels. *—Use lens paper*

**8** The round base of the pistil is the ovary. Cut the ovary in half crosswise. **CAUTION:** *Always be careful with sharp instruments such as a scalpel.*

**9** Examine the inside of the ovary with a hand lens. Make a drawing of what you see. Note the number of compartments.

*Hummingbird beaks are well suited for obtaining nectar from flowers.*

## Analyzing

**1.** *Compare and contrast* the numbers and sizes of the male and female reproductive organs.

**2.** How many compartments did you see in the cross-section of the ovary?

**3.** What did you observe inside the ovary?

## Concluding and Applying

**4.** What is the function of the petals?

**5.** How is the stigma adapted for attracting pollen?

**6.** ~~Going Further~~  You probably have seen bees travel among flowers in a garden. *Hypothesize* how the movement of a bee might aid in pollination.

**Answers to** Analyzing/ Concluding and Applying

**1.** Stamens are in groups of three. There is usually one pistil.

**2.** three

**3.** There are eggs inside the ovary.

**4.** The petals protect the stamen and pistil and attract insects.

**5.** Its stickiness traps pollen.

**6.** As they move about the flowers, bees pick up pollen, which they transfer to the stigmas of other flowers.

## ✔ Assessment

**Performance** Have students expand the drawings that they made in Step 9 by making a scientific drawing of the flower they observed. Use the Performance Task Assessment List for Scientific Drawing in **PAMSS**, p. 55. L1 P

---

## ENRICHMENT

**Discussion**  List these flowers on the board. Challenge students to explain how the seeds are dispersed in each instance: dandelion, touch-me-not, wood sorrel, cherry, apple. *Dandelion seeds are borne by the wind. Touch-me-not and wood sorrel are scattered by pods that pop open. Cherry and apple seeds are found inside fruit, which is eaten by birds and other animals. These seeds pass through the animal's body and reach the soil.* L3

# 3 ASSESS

## Check for Understanding

To help students answer the Apply question have them identify all the ways pollen can be transported.

## Reteach

Using an overhead projector, show students a picture of a flowering plant that has both male and female sexual organs. Working as a class, have students identify each organ and explain its function. L1 **COOP LEARN**

## Extension

Have students who have mastered the concepts in this section predict how a corn plant is pollinated. *The pollen grains are carried by wind.* Invite interested students to research the various colors of corn and their significance in different cultures. Students might, for example, research the significance of blue corn to the Hopi. L3

# 4 CLOSE

**Demonstration** Invite students to observe a composite flower and infer the reason for the term *composite*. A composite looks like one flower, but is actually made up of many flowers. Composites include daisies, sunflowers, and carnations. L2

# Getting Sperm and Egg Together

Eggs are located inside the ovary of a flower. Sperm are found in pollen grains located in stamens. Usually, sperm from one flower fertilize the eggs of a different flower of the same species. How do sperm and egg get together?

**Figure 13-9** shows the events that take place during pollination and fertilization. Keep in mind that pollination is the transfer of pollen from the male anther to the female stigma. Fertilization is the actual union of egg and sperm and takes place inside the pistil.

After fertilization, the ovary grows and develops into a fruit. The fertilized egg becomes an embryo within a future seed. This embryo will eventually develop into a new plant.

**Figure 13-9**

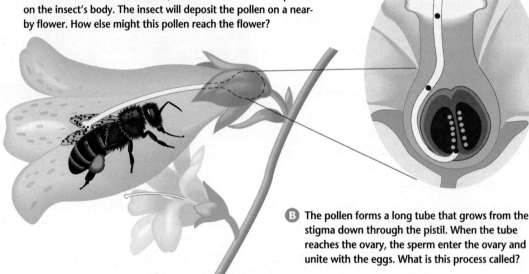

Ⓐ The insect can't resist this flower's colorful petals and sweet scent. As the insect moves about, the flower's anther rubs pollen on the insect's body. The insect will deposit the pollen on a nearby flower. How else might this pollen reach the flower?

Ⓑ The pollen forms a long tube that grows from the stigma down through the pistil. When the tube reaches the ovary, the sperm enter the ovary and unite with the eggs. What is this process called?

**check your UNDERSTANDING**

1. Diagram a typical flowering plant. Label all the parts of the flower, including the reproductive organs.
2. What are the roles of stamens and pistils in plant reproduction?
3. Describe the process of reproduction in a flowering plant.
4. **Apply** Could pollination occur in an ecosystem that didn't contain any insect populations? Explain your answer.

**check your UNDERSTANDING**

1. Diagrams should reflect Figure 13-8, pages 418–419.
2. Stamens are the male reproductive organs and produce sperm in pollen grains. The pistil is the female reproductive organ, where eggs are produced.
3. The sticky stigma traps pollen released from the anthers. The pollen forms a long tube and grows to reach the ovary, where the sperm in the pollen fertilize eggs in the ovary.
4. Yes, but not for all plant species. Pollen can be carried by the wind, water, or by animals, such as hummingbirds or bats.

# Animal Reproduction

## Animal Reproduction

Unlike many plants, a frog does not have both male and female reproductive structures. A frog is either a male or a female. This is not the case, however, for all animals. Each earthworm, sponge, and flatworm contains both male and female parts in the same animal. But animals in most species are either male or female.

### ■ External Fertilization

Because a frog is either male or female, certain actions are necessary for fertilization to occur. The joining of a sperm and an egg occurs outside the bodies of the two frogs. This type of fertilization is called external fertilization. Follow the steps of fertilization in **Figure 13-10**.

**Section Objectives**

■ Compare and contrast external and internal fertilization in animals.

■ Demonstrate an understanding of how humans reproduce.

**Key Terms**

*menstrual cycle, menstruation*

**Figure 13-10**

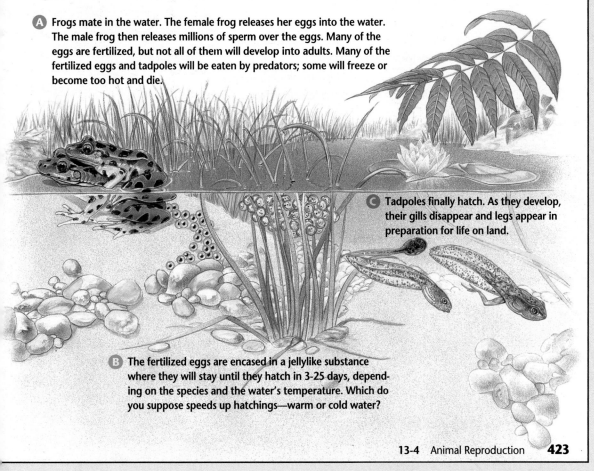

**A** Frogs mate in the water. The female frog releases her eggs into the water. The male frog then releases millions of sperm over the eggs. Many of the eggs are fertilized, but not all of them will develop into adults. Many of the fertilized eggs and tadpoles will be eaten by predators; some will freeze or become too hot and die.

**C** Tadpoles finally hatch. As they develop, their gills disappear and legs appear in preparation for life on land.

**B** The fertilized eggs are encased in a jellylike substance where they will stay until they hatch in 3-25 days, depending on the species and the water's temperature. Which do you suppose speeds up hatchings—warm or cold water?

13-4 Animal Reproduction **423**

# PREPARATION

**Concepts Developed**

In 13-3, students explored how fertilization occurs in plants, how and where flowering plants produce sex cells, and how the living and nonliving parts of a flower's environment help pollination occur. In this section, students will extend this knowledge to compare and contrast external and internal fertilization in animals, focusing on human reproduction.

**Planning the Lesson**

Refer to the Chapter Organizer on pages 404A–B.

# 1 MOTIVATE

**Discussion** Challenge students to determine probability. Flip a coin 20 times, each time recording on the board whether it landed on heads or tails. Lead students to observe and infer that there is an equal chance that the penny will land on heads or tails. Then ask if there is sometimes a run of heads before tossing a tail. *yes* If heads represents a girl being born and tails a boy, what are the chances of having a girl? *1 out of 2* a boy? *1 out of 2* According to what you learned, what are the chances of a family having a girl after they have had six boys? *1 out of 2*

**Visual Learning**

**Figure 13-10** After students examine Figure 13-10, challenge them to identify one drawback of external fertilization. *Fertilized eggs are vulnerable to predators and weather.* **Which do you suppose speeds up hatchings—warm or cold water?** *warm water*

# 2 TEACH

## Tying to Previous Knowledge

First, draw or post a diagram of a flower. Have different students identify each of the flower's organs involved in pollination. Then have students compare and contrast the number and sizes of the male and female reproductive organs. A thorough understanding of plant reproduction will help students make the transition to animal reproduction.

**Figure 13-11** After students have studied Figure 13-11, challenge them to describe the parts of the male reproductive system and their functions. Remind students to use scientific terminology to identify body parts.

## Teacher F.Y.I.

If an egg were enlarged to the size of a dime, the relative size of a sperm would be a dot.

## Explore!

### What is the pathway of sperm through the male reproductive system?

**Time needed** 15 minutes

**Materials** Figure 13-11 on page 424; pencil eraser; colored pencils, pens, or markers

**Thinking Processes** observing and inferring, sequencing, interpreting scientific illustrations

**Purpose** To make a diagram showing how sperm travels through the male reproductive system.

**Preparation** Caution students to trace Figure 13-11 neatly and carefully. **LEP**

## Teaching the Activity

**Troubleshooting** Before students color or shade their diagram, suggest they sketch

the sperm's path in pencil, so they can erase if they make an error in their diagrams. **L1**

**Student Journal** Have students make their diagrams in their journals. Then have students trade journals and check each other's response to question 3. **COOP LEARN** **L1**

### Expected Outcome

Students should conclude that sperm are created in the testes.

---

## Human Reproduction

### ■ Male Reproductive System

Like frogs, humans are either male or female. In humans, however, as in many other animals, fertilization occurs inside the body of the female. This is called internal fertilization because internal means inside. The male reproductive system consists of organs and tissues that produce sperm and move them out of the body. **Figure 13-11** shows the parts of the male reproductive system. Study **Figure 13-11** and then do the Explore activity.

## Explore! ACTIVITY

### What is the pathway of sperm through the male reproductive system?

### What To Do

1. Trace the figure of the male reproductive system in Figure 13-11.

2. Use arrows to show the pathway that sperm follow through the system.

3. *In your Journal*, list in order the structures sperm pass through to reach the female reproductive system.

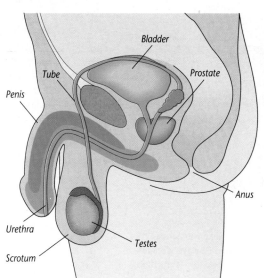

### Figure 13-11

The testes are a pair of reproductive organs, each covered and protected by the scrotum. The testes produce sperm, which are carried out of the body via the tube and urethra. The prostate produces fluids that enable the sperm to swim and keep them from drying out.

### ■ Female Reproductive System

The main job of the male reproductive system is to produce sex cells. The female reproductive system has two jobs—to produce sex cells and to provide a home to a developing

---

### Answer to Question

**3.** Sperm leave the testes through a duct, move into the urethra, and then leave the body.

### ✔ Assessment

**Performance** Working in cooperative learning groups, have students make a poster showing the male reproductive system and the pathway that sperm pass through. Use the Performance Task Assessment List for Poster in **PAMSS**, p. 74. **L1** **COOP LEARN**

embryo. **Figure 13-12** shows the parts of the female reproductive system that carry out these jobs. As you study **Figure 13-12**, think about the process of fertilization. Then, read the next section about where fertilization occurs.

### ■ Where Does Fertilization Occur?

You already know that fertilization in humans takes place internally. During mating, the male releases sperm directly into the female's vagina. Internal fertilization increases the chance that egg and sperm will meet. Millions of sperm are deposited into the female's reproductive system. A fertilized egg results only if a sperm joins with an egg and fertilizes it. It only takes one sperm to fertilize an egg. About every 28 days, the female reproductive system goes through a cycle that prepares an egg for fertilization.

**Figure 13-12**

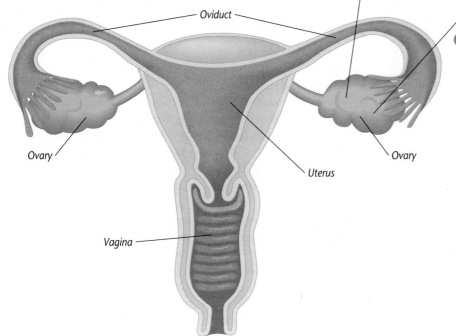

**A** The female reproductive system includes the thick-walled uterus, two ovaries, two oviducts, and the vagina. Eggs develop within the ovaries, and are then released into the oviducts. From there, they travel to the uterus. Why do you suppose the uterus has thick, muscular walls?

Oviduct

Ovary

Uterus

Vagina

Ovary

**B** Eggs develop in the ovaries and are usually released one at a time. One egg is released about every 28 days. The large, bulging structure is an egg that is about to rupture from the ovary.

**Multicultural Perspectives**

**Blessing or Curse?**
The menstrual period has been surrounded by myth from the beginning of time. The very word *taboo* may come from the Polynesian word for menstruation. Not all the myths are negative, however. A girl's first period is greeted with celebration in some cultures, for it means that she can now have children. Canada's Naskapi, for example, create elaborate caribou veils for women during their first menses. Apache girls kneel on a sacred deerskin during a four-day celebration of their first menstrual period.

## Visual Learning

**Figure 13-13** Figure 13-13 charts the changes that occur in the uterus during an average 28-day menstrual cycle. After students have examined Figure 13-13 and studied the text, have volunteers explain what is happening to the uterine lining during each part of the cycle. Ask students what purpose the thickening lining of the uterus serves. *If ovulation occurs and the egg implants successfully, the uterine lining will provide initial nourishment for the embryo.*

**Inquiry Question** How are ovulation and menstruation related? *Menstruation is the shedding of the uterine lining after ovulation if the egg has not been fertilized.*

# Menstrual Cycle

When a human female is born, there are nearly half a million undeveloped eggs in her ovaries. Only about 500 of these eggs will ever develop. Beginning between the ages of 10 and 14, the ovaries begin to release an egg about once every 28 days. The egg is either fertilized, or it

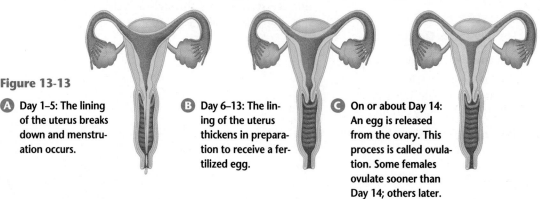

**Figure 13-13**

Ⓐ **Day 1–5:** The lining of the uterus breaks down and menstruation occurs.

Ⓑ **Day 6–13:** The lining of the uterus thickens in preparation to receive a fertilized egg.

Ⓒ **On or about Day 14:** An egg is released from the ovary. This process is called ovulation. Some females ovulate sooner than Day 14; others later.

# Chemistry CONNECTION

## Chemicals and Birth Defects

Although scientists do not know what causes the majority of birth defects in humans, they do know that certain chemicals and other substances pose risks to a developing fetus. How does a fetus come into contact with these substances?

### Female Reproductive Health

Until recently, most attention to preventing birth defects focused on women while they were pregnant. Scientists had long assumed that most children born with birth defects had suffered some kind of damage while they were developing inside their mothers.

### Male Reproductive Health

New research shows, however, that men's reproductive health also affects their children. For example, men exposed to lead may produce defective sperm. Defective sperm usually cannot fertilize an egg. If, however, fertilization does occur, the result may be a deformed fetus.

Men who smoke cigarettes or drink alcohol heavily may also have fertility problems or may have children with birth

# Chemistry CONNECTION

### Purpose

This chemistry connection extends Section 13-4 by describing factors that could cause damage to developing embryos.

### Content Background

About one in ten birth defects is the result of an external factor such as infection, radiation, or chemicals. The most widely known infection to affect the fetus is German measles, which can result in children with damaged sight or hearing or mental retardation. The effects of radiation were shown by the increased numbers of birth defects in the children of Japanese women exposed to the atomic bomb. The belief that the placenta affords the fetus protection from chemicals was tragically disproven in the early 1960s when children were born with missing limbs after their mothers took the antinausea drug thalidomide.

is shed from the body in a monthly cycle called the menstrual cycle. The **menstrual cycle** is a cycle in which the ovary releases an egg and the uterus prepares to receive it, then discards it if the egg is not fertilized. The monthly discharge of egg, uterine lining, and blood through the vagina is called **menstruation**. This event and the other changes that take place during the menstrual cycle are shown in **Figure 13-13**.

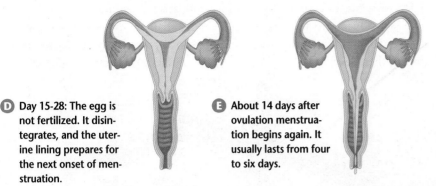

**D** Day 15-28: The egg is not fertilized. It disintegrates, and the uterine lining prepares for the next onset of menstruation.

**E** About 14 days after ovulation menstruation begins again. It usually lasts from four to six days.

defects that result from these habits. It has long been known, for example, that women who smoke during pregnancy risk having low birth weight babies. Research now indicates that low birth weight in babies can also result from fathers who smoke. Heavy drinking by men one month before fertilization can also cause low birth weight in babies.

Exactly how chemicals affect men's reproductive health is still mostly unknown. A toxin (poison) may directly damage sperm-producing cells in the testes, so not enough sperm are produced, and sterility results. Other times defective sperm are produced, which also may cause sterility. Or, the defective sperm might fertilize an egg and result in a damaged fetus. Men also might pass toxins in their semen to women. These toxins can then damage the egg.

### What Do You Think?

Some employers have fetal protection policies. These policies keep women of child-bearing age from working at jobs where they might be exposed to toxic chemicals. What is the problem with focusing only on women when it comes to toxins in the workplace?

*Healthy parents increase the likelihood of healthy babies.*

# Fertilization

If sperm are deposited in the vagina, they move up into the oviducts. If sperm are present as an egg leaves the ovary, fertilization can take place. When these sex cells unite, the fertilized egg moves into the uterus and attaches itself to the lining, where an embryo then develops.

You've learned that reproduction using sex cells and fertilization of an egg is called sexual reproduction. Seed plants and most animals—including humans—reproduce sexually. In the next chapter, you will learn how offspring produced by sexual reproduction inherit traits from both parents.

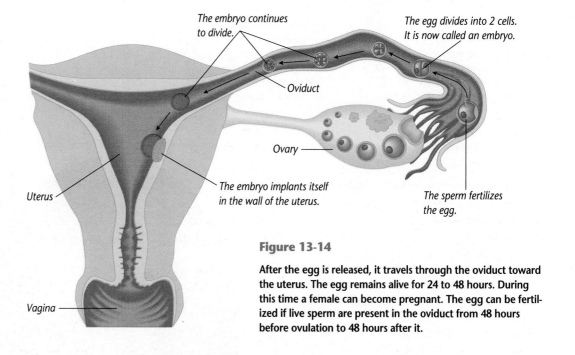

The embryo continues to divide.

The egg divides into 2 cells. It is now called an embryo.

Oviduct

Ovary

The embryo implants itself in the wall of the uterus.

Uterus

Vagina

The sperm fertilizes the egg.

**Figure 13-14**

**After the egg is released, it travels through the oviduct toward the uterus. The egg remains alive for 24 to 48 hours. During this time a female can become pregnant. The egg can be fertilized if live sperm are present in the oviduct from 48 hours before ovulation to 48 hours after it.**

## check your UNDERSTANDING

1. What is the difference between internal and external fertilization?
2. Why can animals that reproduce through internal fertilization afford to produce so few eggs at a time?
3. **Apply** For each time period given below, indicate whether fertilization can occur and briefly explain why it can or can't occur. Assume sperm are present.
   a. 24 hours after ovulation;
   b. 48 hours after menstruation has ended;
   c. during menstruation.

## check your UNDERSTANDING

**1.** In internal fertilization, sperm are deposited directly into the female reproductive system. In external fertilization, sperm are deposited onto eggs that are outside the female.

**2.** The eggs are protected and the chances of fertilization are better.

**3. a.** Yes; the egg is viable. **b.** Usually no (no egg to fertilize), varies with the individual. **c.** not likely, but possible

# Science and Society

## Curing Infertility

For a variety of reasons, one in twelve couples in the United States is experiencing infertility. They are unable to conceive a child. The number of people going to a doctor because of fertility problems recently exceeded one million.

### Causes of Infertility

As the number of people dealing with infertility increases, new techniques are being developed for treatment. For example, one cause of infertility is that sperm are too weak to swim or don't have the right enzymes to break through the egg's outer membrane. To overcome this problem, doctors can now use a needle viewed under a powerful microscope to inject sperm directly into the egg.

Sometimes a woman fails to ovulate. When a woman does not release an egg through ovulation, she can be given hormones. Then she will produce many eggs, increasing her chances of getting pregnant.

Sometimes infertility occurs because the fertilized egg does not implant itself in the uterus. One-third of all pregnancies may end because implantation does not occur. To correct this problem, doctors pierce a tiny hole in the egg's protective outer layer. For some reason, eggs that are pierced attach better than those that aren't.

### In Vitro Fertilization

The use of technology to assist in reproduction has increased dramatically since the first test tube baby was born over a decade ago. At that time, in vitro fertilization (IVF—fertilization in a glass dish) was revolutionary. Since then, more than 10 000 babies in the United States have been produced through IVF.

IVF is used when a woman is unable to conceive naturally. It can also be used when a man or woman is infertile but the woman is

## Science and Society

### Purpose
Science and Society extends Section 13-4 by explaining several new treatments for infertility, the inability of a couple to conceive a child. It also presents some of the ethical questions prompted by the new developments in reproductive technology.

### Content Background
The two major causes of female infertility are a failure to ovulate or an obstruction in a Fallopian tube. A male's fertility most often depends on three conditions: an adequate number of sperm, normally-shaped sperm, and mobile sperm. Of these, the most common problem is poor sperm production, which is usually caused by a swollen or varicose vein surrounding one of the testes. Oddly enough, wearing tight, heavy clothing can also impair fertility. The temperature in the testicles may also rise above the optimum level for sperm production (34°C to 35°C) if a man takes frequent hot baths or works in an overheated environment.

## Content Background

The technique known as *in vitro* fertilization had its first success in Bristol, England, in 1978. The mother-to-be received daily hormone injections to accelerate the production of eggs, since normally only one egg is produced at a time. The eggs were then surgically removed and put into a glass dish. Six hours later, the father's sperm were added to the dish. The fertilized egg incubated for two days before it was implanted in the mother's uterus. Louise Brown was the result, the first child born through this method.

## Teaching Strategy

Have students discuss the advantages and disadvantages of the reproductive technology they read about. They should include how this technology might change the world for better or for worse. Students could also examine how people's ways of life shape their attitudes toward population. They could, for example, compare the population needs of hunting and gathering societies and industrialized nations. **L3**

still able to carry a developing child. Different combinations of egg and sperm are possible using IVF. The couple themselves may contribute eggs and sperm. Or the woman may give eggs that will be fertilized by sperm from a male donor. If the woman is infertile, her partner's sperm may be used to fertilize eggs donated by another woman.

### Whose Embryo Is It?

As reproductive technology has become more complex and more widely used, it has raised many ethical questions. For example, more than one egg is fertilized during the

IVF procedure because not all fertilized eggs will survive. So several eggs are used to ensure that there will be at least one embryo that can be placed into the mother's uterus. The remaining embryos are frozen.

But questions have come up concerning what to do with these extra embryos. In one court case, a divorced couple fought about whether the woman can have custody of the embryos that were created while the couple was still married.

### The High Cost of Having Children

Other questions relate to the cost of the treatment. IVF can cost from $6000 to $50,000 to produce one child. This means that only wealthy people or those with good health insurance have access to the procedure. Only nine states have laws that require insurance companies to pay for infertility treatments.

Still other concerns about the development of reproductive technology have to do with larger questions of world population growth. The world's population is currently 5.4 billion and is expected to double around the year 2030. There is growing concern that Earth cannot support such a large human population. Thus the use of scientific resources and millions of dollars to help certain people have children is seen by some as unwise.

### What Do You Think?

In 1980, the federal government cut funding for research on IVF. Do you think that the government should support research in reproductive technology? To what extent is society responsible for helping couples who are infertile?

**Nurse-midwives** study biology, chemistry, and medicine. They work at hospitals, clinics, and at birthing centers assisting women in childbirth.

**CAREER** connection

### Going Further ⫸

Have students hold a mock trial to decide the disposition of the extra embryos in the case of the divorcing couple. Appoint the divorced couple, a judge, court officers, teams of lawyers, a jury, and reporters. After students try the case, they can research to find the actual outcome of the dispute. Use the Performance Task Assessment List for Investigating an Issue Controversy in **PAMSS**, p. 65. **L2** **COOP LEARN**

# Chapter 15 Moving Continents

| Student Masters | Teaching Aids |
|---|---|
| **Study Guide,** p. 49<br>**Take Home Activities,** p. 25<br>**Making Connections: Integrating Sciences,** p. 33<br>**Science Discovery Activities,** p. 15-1 | **\*STVS:** *Map Science,* Earth and Space (Disc 3, Side 2)<br>**\*STVS:** *Moving Continents,* Earth and Space (Disc 3, Side 2) |
| **Study Guide,** p. 50<br>**Making Connections: Technology & Society,** p. 33<br>**Flex Your Brain,** p. 5<br>**Science Discovery Activities,** p. 15-2 | **Color Transparency and Master 29,** Earth's Layers<br>**Laboratory Manual,** pp. 93–94, Earth's Magnetism<br>**\*STVS:** *Underwater Seismograph,* Earth and Space (Disc 3, Side 2) |
| **Study Guide,** p. 51<br>**Concept Mapping,** p. 23<br>**Critical Thinking/Problem Solving,** p. 23<br>**Multicultural Connections,** p. 33 | **Color Transparency and Master 30,** Converging/Diverging Plates<br>**\*STVS:** *Deep Hole Research,* Earth and Space (Disc 3, Side 2) |
| **Study Guide,** p. 52<br>**Multicultural Connectionss,** p. 34<br>**How It Works,** p. 20<br>**Making Connections: Across the Curriculum,** p. 33<br>**Science Discovery Activities,** p. 15-3 | **\*STVS:** *Miniature Volcanoes,* Earth and Space (Disc 3, Side 2) |
| **ASSESSMENT RESOURCES** | **Spanish Resources**<br>**Cooperative Learning Resource Guide**<br>**Lab and Safety Skills**<br>**Integrated Science Videodisc** |
| **Review and Assessment,** pp. 89–94<br>**Performance Assessment,** Ch. 15<br>**PAMSS\***<br>**Computer Test Bank**<br>**MindJogger Videoquiz** | |

## KEY TO TEACHING STRATEGIES

The following designations will help you decide which activities are appropriate for your students.

- [L1] Level 1 activities should be within the ability range of all students.
- [L2] Level 2 activities should be within the ability range of the average to above-average student.
- [L3] Level 3 activities are designed for the ability range of above-average students.
- [LEP] LEP activities should be within the ability range of Limited English Proficiency students.
- [COOP LEARN] Cooperative Learning activities are designed for small group work.
- [P] These strategies represent student products that can be placed into a best-work portfolio.

## ADDITIONAL MATERIALS

**Software**
*Earth: The Inside Story,* Educational Activities, Inc.
*The Earth Moves,* Aquarius.
*Forces in the Earth,* Queue.

**Audiovisual**
*Earthquakes and Moving Continents,* video, Educational Activities.
*Formation of Continents and Mountains,* video, United Learning.
*Planet Earth—The Living Machine,* video, The Annenberg/CPB Project.
*Plate Tectonics—The Puzzle of the Continents,* video, Nystrom.
*The Story of the Changing Earth,* video, Hawkhill Science.

**Laserdisc**
*The Living Textbook, Geology and Meteorology,* Optical Data Corp.
*Physics at Work,* Videodiscovery.
*STV: Restless Earth,* National Geographic.

**Readings**
Aylesworth, Thomas G. *Moving Continents: Our Changing Earth.* Enslow.

\*Performance Assessment in Middle School Science

\*Science and Technology Videodisc Series

## Moving Continents

### THEME DEVELOPMENT

The themes that this chapter supports are interactions and systems and energy. Students investigate how Earth's tectonic plates interact. The energy involved in moving such massive slabs of crust and upper mantle can cause volcanoes and earthquakes.

### CHAPTER OVERVIEW

In this chapter, students will study and assess Alfred Wegener's hypothesis of continental drift. In an Investigate, students will reconstruct the supercontinent Pangaea, using continental outlines and other data similar to those used by Wegener.

Students will also examine the hypothesis of sea-floor spreading. They will compare and contrast the three types of tectonic plate boundaries. Students will observe convection currents, which scientists believe to be the driving mechanism of plate tectonics.

Finally, students will relate plate tectonics and the occurrence of earthquakes and volcanoes.

### Tying to Previous Knowledge

In Chapter 2, students learned about magnetism. Remind students that a magnet is surrounded by a magnetic field. Ask what happens to iron or other magnetic materials when placed in a magnetic field. *They become magnetized.* The discovery of magnetic patterns on the ocean floor was one piece of evidence that led scientists to propose the theory of plate tectonics. Have students recall from Chapter 9 how convection currents form. *Convection currents occur within Earth.*

# Moving Continents

**Did you ever wonder...**

- ✓ **What the bottoms of the oceans look like?**
- ✓ **Why California has so many earthquakes?**
- ✓ **How a dormant volcano could suddenly erupt after 600 years?**

Before you begin to study about moving continents, think about these questions and answer them *in your Journal.* When you finish the chapter, compare your Journal write-up with what you have learned.

You can hardly imagine how beautiful Earth must look from space. Then you see the satellite photo of Earth on the jigsaw puzzle you were given. The picture is spectacular! You can't wait to begin working on the puzzle.

For days, you fit pieces together, and ever so slowly the puzzle begins to take shape. You easily finish North America and Europe. They are now intact on the puzzle. You turn your attention to completing the African continent, and you make an interesting discovery. You notice that although the pieces you've placed all fit together well, the continent doesn't look like the picture on the puzzle box. You recheck your work and discover that some of the pieces you placed on the western coast of Africa actually belong on the eastern coast of South America. How could you have made this mistake? Is it possible that your puzzle pieces fit in two different places?

▶ *In the next activity, you'll explore the information you use to help you put together a puzzle.*

468

---

### Did you ever wonder...

- The bottoms of oceans have mountains and valleys just like those on the continents. (p. 477)
- Earthquakes are common in California because of plate movement along faults. (pp. 492–493)
- Plate movements are largely responsible for volcanic activity. Plate movements are relatively slow so, it could take hundreds of years for enough pressure to build up to cause an eruption. (p. 495)

### STUDENT JOURNAL

Have students write their responses to the Did You Ever Wonder questions in their journals. After they have read the chapter, students should read their journal entries to see how their perceptions of moving continents have changed.

## Explore! ACTIVITY

### What clues are used to piece together puzzles?

**What To Do**

1. Cut a picture out of an old magazine and paste it on lightweight cardboard.

2. Then cut the picture into pieces of different sizes and shapes. Try to piece it back together again. *In your Journal*, record the clues you used to help you put the picture together.

**469**

## INTRODUCING THE CHAPTER

Ask students to make observations of a world map. Lead them to make the observation of the puzzle-like fit of South America and Africa.

### Uncovering Preconceptions

Students may think that earthquakes and volcanic eruptions are random events. Although their prediction is not always possible, there is a general pattern to their occurrence.

## Explore!

**What clues are used to piece together puzzles?**

**Time needed** 20 minutes

**Materials** lightweight cardboard, old magazines with colorful pictures, glue, scissors

**Thinking Processes** comparing and contrasting, observing and inferring, formulating models

**Purpose** To infer how scientists formed the hypothesis of continental drift.

**Preparation** Have enough magazines so that each group of five students has one.

### Teaching the Activity

**Student Journal** Suggest that students sketch in their journals the shapes of puzzle pieces that fit together. **L1**

### Expected Outcome

Students should list clues such as the matching of color, lines, and shapes on puzzle pieces, as well as the fitting together of the edges of the pieces.

### ✔ Assessment

**Content** Invite students to select several puzzles for a bulletin board on how scientists use clues. Students can add to the bulletin board as they study this chapter. Use the Performance Task Assessment List for Bulletin Board in **PAMSS** page 59. **L1**

---

### ASSESSMENT PLANNER

**PORTFOLIO**
Refer to page 501 for suggested items that students might select for their portfolios.

**PERFORMANCE ASSESSMENT**
Process, pp. 479, 481, 491
Skillbuilder, p. 495
Explore! Activities, pp. 469, 479, 491
Investigate, pp. 472–473, 480–481

**CONTENT ASSESSMENT**
Check Your Understanding, pp. 475, 483, 490, 495
Reviewing Main Ideas, p. 499
Chapter Review, pp. 500–501

**GROUP ASSESSMENT**
Opportunities for group assessment occur with Cooperative Learning Strategies.

# PREPARATION

## Concepts Developed

Discuss with students the role of amassed evidence in acceptance of a scientific hypothesis. In the early 1900s, Alfred Wegener, a German meteorologist, proposed that all Earth's continents were once part of a single landmass. His hypothesis of continental drift was rejected by most of his peers because Wegener was unable to explain the mechanism responsible for the movement of Earth's plates.

## Planning the Lesson

Refer to the Chapter Organizer on pages 468A–B.

# 1 MOTIVATE

**Activity** This activity will help students identify and discuss the evidence that led to belief in Wegener's hypotheses.

You will need small jigsaw puzzles with about 50 pieces. Without any indications of what the completed puzzles look like, hand out puzzles and ask groups of students to put them together. After 10 minutes, discuss the clues students used to fit the pieces together. L1

# 2 TEACH

## Tying to Previous Knowledge

Challenge students to make inferences from assembled information. Ask them if they like to read murder mysteries or watch detective shows on television. Discuss how the detective looks for connections between clues. As students read about Wegener's hypothesis, have them compare his use of clues to that of a detective.

---

# The Moving Continents

**Section Objectives**

- Explain the hypothesis of continental drift.
- Identify and discuss four pieces of evidence used to support the hypothesis of continental drift.

**Key Terms**

*continental drift*

## Continental Drift

Have you ever told your friends a true story that they did not believe? Maybe you gave them all kinds of specific details to support your story—and they still wouldn't believe you.

The same sort of thing happened to the people who first said that the continents move. No one would believe them.

Alfred Wegener observed the similarity in the shapes of continental coastlines. Wegener thought that the fit of the continents wasn't a coincidence. He hypothesized that all the continents were once joined as one large supercontinent called Pangaea, which means "all Earth." Wegener believed that Pangaea broke apart about 200 million years ago, and that the continents had since moved. In 1912, Wegener proposed his hypothesis known as **continental drift**.

Because of lack of proof, however, Wegener's hypothesis was not taken seriously by other scientists. One reason Wegener's ideas were scoffed at was because he was not a geologist. He had been trained as a meteorologist. After his hypothesis was rejected by other scientists, Wegener decided

**Figure 15-1**

**A** Fossils and fossil remains of the plants and animals shown here have been found on more than one continent. Mesosaurus fossils, for example, have been discovered in South America and in Africa.

**B** One explanation for the fact that some animal fossils have been found on more than one continent is that they swam from one continent to another. This hypothesis, however, is believed to be incorrect. Look at the animals pictured in the diagram. Why is it hard to believe they could swim across oceans?

*Kannemeyerid*

*Kannemeyerid*

*Glossopteris*

*Mesosaurus*

*Glossopteris*

**470** Chapter 15 Moving Continents

---

### Program Resources

**Study Guide,** p. 49
**Take Home Activities,** p. 25, Travelling Continents L1 LEP
**Making Connection: Integrating Sciences,** p. 33, What's the Difference? L2

---

to gather more data to support his idea.

### ■ Fossil Evidence

To develop his supercontinent idea, Wegener also started with the puzzle-like fit of the continents, but then he gathered additional information to help in the reconstruction of Pangaea. One type of data he gathered was fossil information. Wegener discovered something unusual about two types of fossils, a reptile called Mesosaurus, and a fern called Glossopteris. What was so unusual is that Mesosaurus fossils are found in South America and Africa, and Glossopteris fossils are found in Africa, South America, India, Australia, and Antarctica. What could explain how these organisms got from one continent to another? And, how could Glossopteris live in climates as different as tropical Africa and polar Antarctica? **Figure 15-1** shows some of the fossil evidence Wegener had.

### ■ Glacier Evidence

Wegener believed these answers could be explained by his hypothesis of continental drift. But he needed more evidence. Wegener gathered evidence of deposits of glacial sediment and grooved bedrock in the southern parts of South America, Africa, India, and Australia. Although these areas are now located in middle and low latitudes, and their climates are quite different from one another, Wegener thought these areas must have been connected and covered by glaciers.

In the next Investigate, you will explore the fit of the continents using the evidence Wegener had.

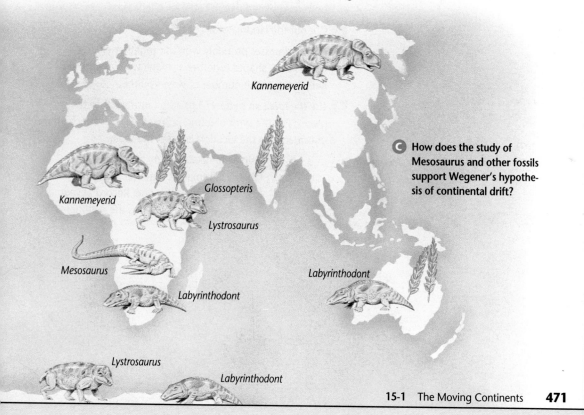

Kannemeyerid

Kannemeyerid

Glossopteris

Lystrosaurus

Mesosaurus

Labyrinthodont

Lystrosaurus

Labyrinthodont

Labyrinthodont

**C** How does the study of Mesosaurus and other fossils support Wegener's hypothesis of continental drift?

15-1   The Moving Continents   **471**

**Theme Connection** The theme that this section supports is systems and interactions. Students trace how Wegener integrated all his evidence—continental outlines, fossils, climate data, and rock structures—to support his hypothesis of continental drift. Wegener saw Earth as a system of landmasses that move and interact.

### Visual Learning

**Figure 15-1** Have students compare and contrast the fossils found on different continents. **Why is it hard to believe they could swim across oceans?** *Except for Mesosaurus, the thick, short legs and large bodies of the animals would make it difficult for them to swim great distances.* **How does the study of Mesosaurus and other fossils support Wegener's hypothesis of continental drift?** *The presence of similar fossils on separate continents is expected if the continents were once joined.* L1

### Teacher F.Y.I.

*Mesosaurus* was a freshwater reptile that lived in cool regions and probably hibernated in lake bottoms during winter.

**Student Text Questions**
**What could explain how these organisms got from one continent to another?** *Accept all reasonable answers. Scientists have puzzled over many different explanations, beyond continental drift. One explanation theorized they drifted between continents on logs carried by swift ocean currents.* **And, how could *Glossopteris* live in climates as different as tropical Africa and polar Antarctica?** *Accept all reasonable answers at this time. Apart from continental drift pushing plates into different climates, some scientists hold that the global climate was more uniform at one time, therefore, a plant such as Glossopteris could survive in many places.*

**Time needed** 45 minutes

**Purpose** To make a model of the super-continent Pangaea

**Process Skills** observing and inferring, interpreting data, interpreting scientific illustrations, sequencing, formulating models, making and using tables, comparing and contrasting, forming operational definitions

**Materials** world map (Appendix H), five sheets of unlined paper, large sheet of paper, scissors, glue

## Teaching the Activity

**Process Reinforcement** Before students begin Step 4, challenge them to infer the potential significance of the data provided in the table. **L2**

**Troubleshooting** Group physically challenged students with students who are able to cut out the landmasses. **COOP LEARN**

**Student Journal** Have students compare their reconstruction of Pangaea with that of other students and record their observations their journals. **L1**

---

# INVESTIGATE!

# Reconstruct Pangaea

*You know that a scientist must have evidence to support a hypothesis. In this activity, you will examine evidence that Pangaea existed.*

### Problem
What evidence is helpful in reconstructing Pangaea?

### Materials
| | |
|---|---|
| world map (Appendix H) | large sheet of paper |
| 5 sheets unlined paper | scissors |
| | glue |

## What To Do

**1** Trace the continents and Greenland from the world map onto the unlined paper. Label each landmass.

**2** Cut out the landmasses.

**3** The landmasses probably won't fit together exactly, but try to fit the shapes together as many ways as you can. Keep track of the number of ways you try.

**4** *Use the table* on page 473 to add information to the pieces. Put the symbol found in parentheses for each type of evidence in the location listed in the table.

**5** Using the new data, try again to fit the labeled landmasses together. *Compare* your first attempt with this one. Record *in your Journal* the number of ways the continents fit together.

---

## Meeting Individual Needs

**Physically Challenged** In the Investigate activity on pages 472–473, if physically challenged students are unable to manipulate the landmasses, be sure that these students are actively involved in interpreting data and making decisions on how to line up the continents.

## Program Resources

**Activity Masters,** pp. 63–64, Investigate 15-1

**Science Discovery Activities,** 15-1, Drifting Away

A               B               C

**6** When you have the best fit, glue the assembled pieces to the large piece of paper. This is your reconstruction of Pangaea.

| TYPE OF EVIDENCE | SYMBOL | LOCATION |
|---|---|---|
| **Evidence of Pangaea** | | |
| Type A mountains | (AAAA): | eastern North America, western Europe, southern tip of Greenland |
| Type C mountains | (CCCC): | southern end of South America, southern end of Africa |
| Evidence of glaciers | (XXXX): | western Australia, southern tip of India, southern Africa, southeastern South America, Antarctica |
| Type G fossils | (GGGG): | western Australia, southern tip of India, southern Africa, southeastern South America, Antarctia |
| Type M fossils | (MMMM): | southern tip of Africa, southern tip of South America |

## Analyzing

1. Using only the shapes of the landmasses as evidence, how many ways did they fit together?

2. Using the shapes plus the evidence from the data table, how many ways did the landmasses fit?

## Concluding and Applying

3. How did the additional evidence help you *construct a model* of Pangaea?

4. How does this reconstruction of Pangaea help explain the evidence of glaciers in Africa where no glaciers currently exist?

5. ~~Going Further~~ From what evidence can you *infer* that India may once have been separated from Asia?

**Figure 15-2** Have students use figure 15-2 to describe how the world's oceans have changed over time. **What continents can be found in the southern portion of Pangaea?** *South America, India, Africa, and Australia* **In which direction is India moving in this diagram?** *north and east* **Will this arrangement ever change in the future? Explain.** *Yes, it will change as the continents continue to drift.*

**Inquiry Question** Why do you think there isn't an exact fit of the continental outlines? *Students should be able to infer that continental edges change due to Earth processes such as weathering and erosion.*

**Discussion** As students read through the section and the rest of the chapter, make sure that they can differentiate between a hypothesis and a theory. Have students hypothesize why Wegener's idea—which is often incorrectly referred to as the theory of continental drift—was a hypothesis, *not* a theory. A theory is an idea that is tested many times and produces the same results. A hypothesis is an educated guess based on a number of observations.

**Student Text Questions** Is it possible that those parts could have been covered by glaciers? *yes*

## ■ Reconstructing Pangaea

Think back to the Explore activity at the beginning of this chapter. How did you fit the pieces of the magazine picture together? One clue you probably used was their shapes. What other clues did you use? Wegener also used the shapes of the continents to build his model of Pangaea. But just as you also used the picture on the pieces of each puzzle as clues, Wegener used the fossil and glacier evidence as "pictures" to put together Pangaea.

Look at the **Figure 15-2** below. Notice where the southern parts of South America, Africa, India, and Australia are located when the continents were joined. Is it possible that those parts could have been covered by glaciers?

**Figure 15-2**

Ⓐ About 250 million years ago, the arrangement of the continents formed the supercontinent Pangaea. Modern day Europe, Asia, and North America can be found in the northern portion of Pangaea. What continents can be found in the southern portion of Pangaea?

Ⓑ About 125 million years ago, Pangaea began to separate into smaller pieces. Think of the way our continents are arranged today. In which direction is India moving in this diagram?

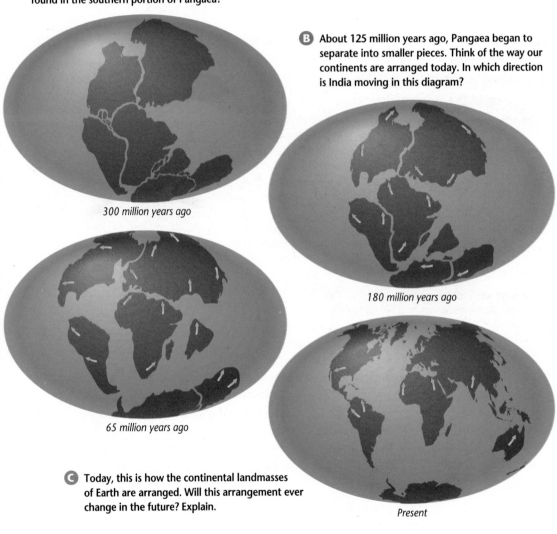

*300 million years ago*

*180 million years ago*

*65 million years ago*

Ⓒ Today, this is how the continental landmasses of Earth are arranged. Will this arrangement ever change in the future? Explain.

*Present*

---

## Meeting Individual Needs

**Visually Impaired** Allow visually impaired students to use and manipulate models as you discuss continental drift. Obtain foam about 1/2" thick from a crafts store. Make large models of the present-day continents and cut them out. Invite more able students to help you. Use different-colored Velcro circles to represent the different lines of evidence used to support continental drift. For example, mountain chains can be represented by a thin chain of red dots, glacial deposits by blue dots, and so on. Have more able students attach the circles in the correct geographic positions.

## Clues From Rocks

If the continents were once all part of the same supercontinent, shouldn't the rock structures of continents that were once joined be similar along the place they split apart? **Figure 15-3** and **15-4** show some of the rock clues that supported Wegener's hypothesis. You would expect to find similar types, ages, and structures of rocks along the coastal areas of two continents that were once joined.

Unfortunately, Wegener was never able to explain how or why the continents move. However, additional evidence found in the 1950s and 1960s revived the hypothesis. Today, the hypothesis of continental drift has been largely accepted. In the following section, you will read about the evidence that has helped support it.

### Figure 15-4

A lot can be discovered about the geologic history of an area by studying its rock layers. What can you infer about continental movement by comparing the layers of these two rock columns from Brazil and Africa?

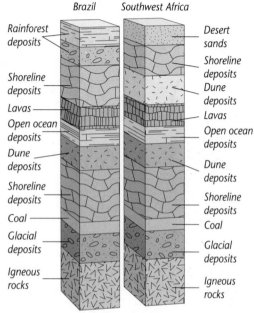

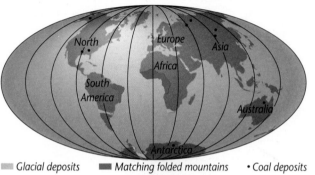

Glacial deposits ■ Matching folded mountains • Coal deposits

### Figure 15-3

Similar rocks and rock formations can be found scattered throughout the world as shown in the map above.

### check your UNDERSTANDING

1. How did Wegener use four types of evidence to help support his hypothesis of continental drift?

2. Fossils indicate that tropical plants once lived on what is now Antarctica. What two explanations can you give for this?

3. **Apply**  Continental slopes are the steep edges of the continents that plunge deep to the ocean floor. If continental slopes, not shorelines, mark the true edges of continents, how would it change your reconstruction of Pangaea?

### check your UNDERSTANDING

1. Wegener used the fit of the continents and the fact that similar fossils, rock structures, and climate clues exist on different continents.

2. Antarctica was once at the equator and has moved to its present position, or Earth was once warm enough for the polar regions to have tropical climates.

3. Including the continental slopes on the outlines will result in a better fit of the landmasses that made up Pangaea.

**PREPARATION**

### Concepts Developed

After studying this section, students should be able to explain how sonar studies of the seafloor, magnetic studies of rocks on the ocean bottom, and age information from ocean floor core samples support Wegener's hypothesis of continental drift.

### Planning the Lesson

Refer to the Chapter Organizer on pages 468A–B.

# 1 MOTIVATE

**Demonstration** Cut a peach and its pit in half lengthwise and have students observe the layers of the peach. Have them compare Earth's layers to those of the peach. L1 LEP

# 2 TEACH

### Tying to Previous Knowledge

In Chapter 2, students learned about magnetic materials. Ask students to name some magnetic materials. When the elements iron and nickel are mentioned, point out that these metals are found in Earth's core. Ask what happens to magnetic materials in a magnetic field. *The domains line up with the field lines.*

# 15-2 Sea-Floor Spreading

<blockquote>
</blockquote>

## The Layered Earth

If Wegener had possessed more information about what lay beneath the continents, he might have been better able to explain how continents can move. **Figure 15-5** shows a model of Earth's inner structure. The layered structure of Earth can be compared to the structure of a peach. Earth is made of many layers just as a peach seed is surrounded by the pit, the juicy flesh, and the skin.

The extremely dense inner core is made of mostly iron and nickel. While the surrounding outer core is made of the same material, it's liquid. The next layer, the mantle, has some unusual properties. While it is solid, it can flow like a liquid because of the tremendous heat and pressure. The outermost layer, the one we live on, is the crust. The crust is the thinnest of all of Earth's layers.

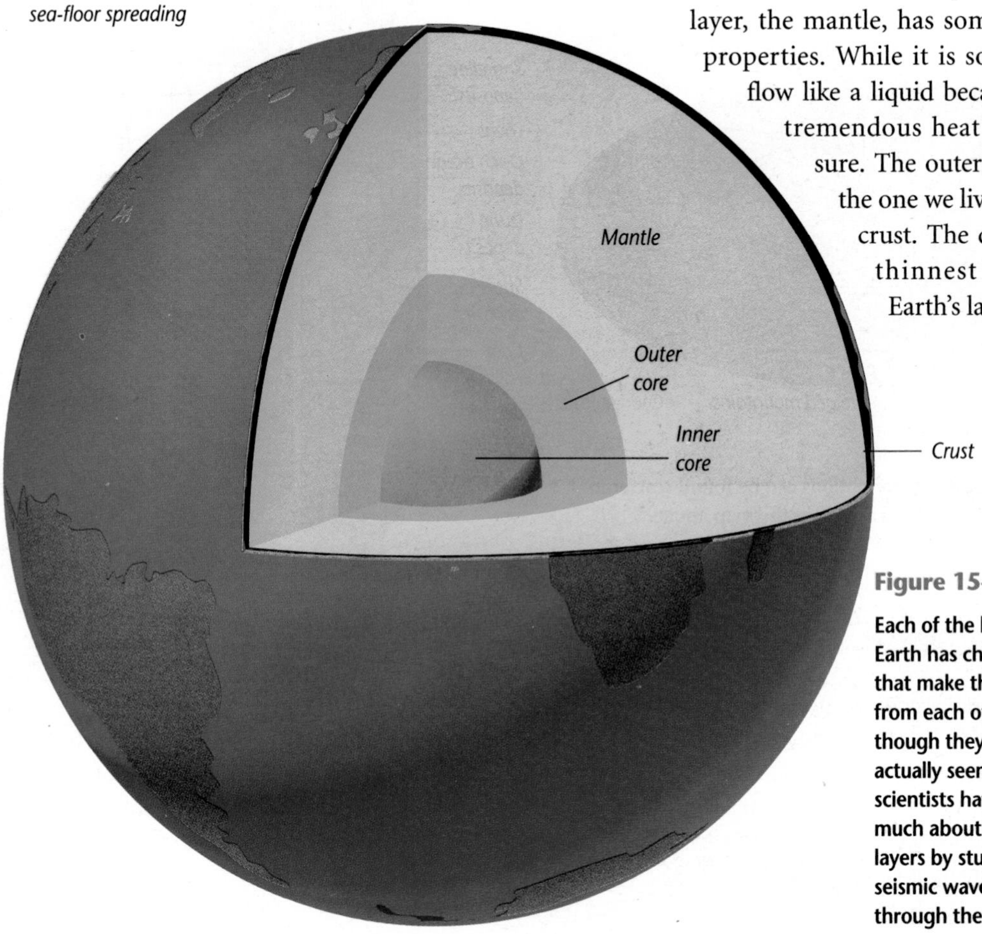

*Mantle*

*Outer core*

*Inner core*

— *Crust*

**Figure 15-5**

Each of the layers of Earth has characteristics that make them different from each other. Even though they have never actually seen inside Earth, scientists have learned much about its different layers by studying how seismic waves travel through them.

# Clues on the Ocean Floor

During Wegener's lifetime, little was known about the ocean floor. However, by the late 1950s, research vessels had crisscrossed Earth's oceans, taking thousands of echo soundings. Echo sounding was made possible by sound wave technology. Scientists would send a sound wave to the seafloor, and the sound would echo back up to the ship. Scientists could time the returning sound and determine how far from the surface the seafloor was. The resulting maps showed mountains and valleys just like those on the continents. The most amazing discovery was mountain chains thousands of kilometers long as shown in **Figure 15-6**. These mountain chains are called mid-ocean ridges. Along the crests of these ridges are narrow regions called rift valleys.

The seafloor maps also showed the location of deep trenches. The deepest trench, the Marianas Trench in the Western Pacific Ocean, is over 11 kilometers deep in some parts.

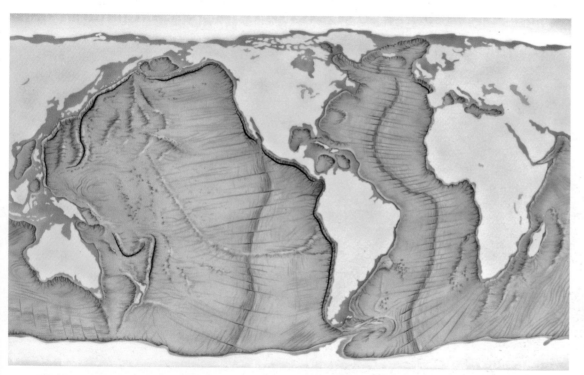

**Figure 15-6**

Many people think the ocean floor is smooth and flat. But if you drained the water from the oceans, it would look like the diagram above. Look at the features of the ocean floor. How are the features of the ocean floor similar to, and different from, the features of continents?

## Visual Learning

**Figure 15-6** Have students compare and contrast the seafloor map shown in Figure 15-6, with how they imagined a seafloor to be. Then pose the question in the caption. **How are the features of the ocean floor similar to, and different from, the features of continents?** *Like continents, the ocean floor has valleys and mountains. Unlike the continents, the ocean features are found under water.*

**Inquiry Question** How does echo sounding determine the depth of the ocean? *Sound waves are sent to the bottom of the ocean, where they are reflected. The time it takes for the waves to return is measured. This distance is divided by two to find the travel time to the floor. Then, the distance is computed using a mathematical equation.*

## Across the Curriculum

### Math

Have students contrast the depth of the Marianas Trench (*about 11,000 m*) with the highest peak on Earth's surface—Mount Everest (*about 9000 m*). Ask students to calculate the total difference in elevation from the bottom of the trench to the top of Mount Everest (*about 20,000 m*). **L2**

## Multicultural Perspectives

**Native-American Heritage**

Have students find out about Native-American legends that describe the origins of Earth's oceans and ocean basins. Students may wish to present their findings in the form of an oral presentation, poster, or illustrated booklet. **P**

## ENRICHMENT

**Research** Have students find out about the work done by the Scottish scientist James Hutton. Hutton was one of the first to propose that Earth was much older than the then accepted age of a few thousand years. Based on his principle of uniformitarianism, which states that Earth processes occurring today are similar to those that took place in the past, Hutton concluded that Earth is millions of years old. **L2**

**478** Chapter 15 Moving Continents

Giant tube worms live by deep undersea vents that occur along mid-ocean ridges. Make a report that explains how the tube worms obtain nutrients, since there is no light where they live.

**Discussion** Use the analogy of a supermarket conveyor belt to help students define seafloor spreading operationally. Have students recall how the belt at the end of the counter "ascends" from below the counter, travels laterally, then "descends" beneath the counter near the cashier. Ask students to correlate the positions and events involved in the belt's movements with what happens on the ocean floor.

**Student Text Question**
**Why were the rocks near the ridges younger?** *They hardened from magma more recently.*

Teacher F.Y.I.

Spreading rates in the Atlantic Ocean range from 2 to 3 cm/yr. Spreading rates in the Pacific range from 6 to 12 cm/yr.

**Connect to . . .**

# Life Science

Hot water from the undersea vents contains hydrogen sulfide. Some bacteria are able to use the energy in hydrogen sulfide to make organic matter. This process is chemosynthesis. Giant tube worms have symbiotic bacteria in their feeding tubes. The giant tube worms supply the bacteria with hydrogen sulfide and the bacteria provide organic matter for the giant tube worms.

**Flex Your Brain** Use the Flex Your Brain activity to have students explore the OCEAN FLOOR. L2

**How Do We Know?**

Earth's magnetic field has reversed more than a dozen times. When the field was oriented as it exists today, it is said to be normal. When the magnetic poles are opposite their current positions, the field is said to be reversed.

# Age Evidence

In the 1960s, scientists on board the research ship Glomar Challenger began gathering information about rocks in the ocean crust. The scientists used a hollow drill bit and drill pipe to drill into the seafloor and pull out samples, in the same way you could stick a straw into gelatin and pull out a sample. None of the ocean floor rock samples was older than 200 million years. This was surprising because some rocks have been found on the continents that are more than three billion years old! Rocks at the mid-ocean ridges were very young, but rocks became increasingly older farther away from the ridges. This was true in both directions from the mid-ocean ridges. Why were the rocks near the ridges younger than those further away?

In the 1960's, a hypothesis known as **sea-floor spreading** emerged. This hypothesis states that molten material from Earth's mantle is forced upward to the surface at mid-ocean ridges and cools to form new seafloor. New magma slowly pushes this material away from the ridges. **Figure 15-7** shows how sea-floor spreading works.

**Figure 15-7**

**A** Sea-floor spreading occurs when two plates underneath the ocean floor pull apart and form a rift valley.

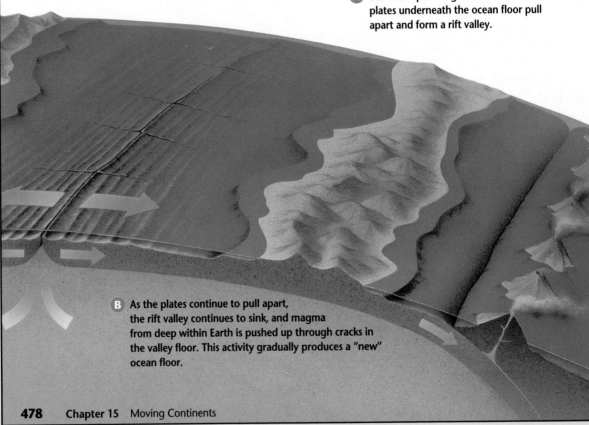

**B** As the plates continue to pull apart, the rift valley continues to sink, and magma from deep within Earth is pushed up through cracks in the valley floor. This activity gradually produces a "new" ocean floor.

**Program Resources**

**Critical Thinking/Problem Solving,**
p. 5 , Flex Your Brain
**Science Discovery Activities,**
15-2, Pudding Plates

# Magnetic Clues

Like any hypothesis, sea-floor spreading had to be able to explain new information as it became available. The next information available, in this case, was magnetic informa-tion locked within the ocean floor rocks. But how can magnetic infor-mation become locked? The next Explore activity will help you under-stand the magnetic nature of rocks.

## Explore! ACTIVITY

### How does a magnet affect iron filings?

**What To Do**

1. Divide a stiff piece of cardboard into two sections. Carefully place a small amount of iron filings on one of the sections. Place a large bar magnet flat on a table.

2. Place the cardboard and filings on top of the magnet. Record *in your Journal* how the filings align themselves. Lightly spray the filings with clear lacquer in a well-ventilated area, covering the opposite side of the cardboard to keep it dry.

3. Change the position of the magnet by 90°. Spread a small amount of iron filings on the other section. Move this section on top of the magnet. *In your Journal,* describe what happens to the lacquered filings in the first section? To the filings you added?

Earth has a magnetic field much like that of a bar magnet. While lava is still liquid, the iron particles in it are free to move and align themselves with Earth's magnetic field. When the lava hardens into rock, the iron is no longer free to move. The hardened rock contains a record of how Earth's magnetic field was aligned at the time the lava cooled. In the Investigate, you will discover how magnetic evidence can support sea-floor spreading.

### ····· How Do We Know? ·····

**Earth's Magnetic Record**

The iron particles in igneous rock align with Earth's magnet-ic field as the rock forms. This means that the iron exhibits its own magnetic field. By using a magnetometer—an instrument that detects and measures the presence of weak magnetic fields—scientists can tell in which direction Earth's north and south magnetic poles were located when a rock formed.

15-2 Sea-floor Spreading **479**

---

---

## Explore!

### How does a magnet affect iron filings?

**Time needed** 20 minutes

**Materials** iron filings, thin stiff cardboard, bar magnets, clear lacquer

**Thinking Processes** Ob-serving and inferring, recog-nizing cause and effect

**Purpose** To observe how iron filings align and become fixed in a permanent record.

### Teaching the Activity

Stress that the can of lac-quer should not be held too close to the filings. The pres-sure will scatter the filings.

**Safety** Caution students to use the spray can only in a well-ventilated place. Be sure that students do not point the spray can at each other. Have students wear goggles when they spray the lacquer.

**Student Journal** In their journals, have students sketch the filings in Procedures 2 and 3 and compare the two sketches. L1

### Expected Outcomes

Students should observe that the iron filings take the shape of force lines that ap-pear to wrap around the bar magnet.

### Answers to Questions

**3.** The lacquered filings re-main fixed in their original ori-entation. The added filings align themselves relative to the bar magnet at a 90° angle to the fixed filings.

### ✔ Assessment

**Process** Have students iden-tify a cause and an effect that they recognized in this activi-ty. *Cause: The field of a bar magnet exerts a force on iron filings. Effect: Iron filings align themselves with a magnet's field.* Then have students make a poster that relates their ob-servations to igneous rocks. Use the Performance Task As-sessment List for Poster in **PAMSS** page 73. **COOP LEARN** L1

**Time needed** 45 minutes

**Purpose** To model magnetic data present along a mid-ocean ridge

**Process Skills** observing and inferring, measuring in SI, formulating models, interpreting scientific illustrations, comparing and contrasting, interpreting data

**Materials** metric ruler, paper, tape, 2 small magnetic compasses, 2 bar magnets, pen or marker

**Preparation** Obtain enough compasses and magnets so that each pair of students has two of each item.

**Process Reinforcement** Challenge students to infer what the reversed bar magnets represent. *Earth's shifting magnetic poles*

**Possible Hypotheses** Students may correctly hypothesize that the compass needle will reverse direction as the magnets are turned 180°.

**Troublshooting** Demonstrate how to record the magnetic data by showing students how to draw the first pair of lines.

**Student Journal** Have students record their answers in their journals. L1

---

# INVESTIGATE!

# Magnetic Data

*Magnetic data can be used to support the hypothesis of sea-floor spreading. What other information do the magnetic data provide?*

### Problem
How do rocks show locations of Earth's magnetic poles?

### Materials
| | |
|---|---|
| metric ruler | paper |
| tape | 2 small magnetic |
| 2 bar magnets | compasses |
| pen or marker | |

## What To Do

**1** Tape several sheets of paper together, end to end, to produce a strip 40 to 60 cm long.

**2** Fold the strip of paper in the middle as shown in the figure and place it between two desks or piles of books. The paper represents oceanic crust that forms as lava comes out of the mid-ocean ridge.

**3** Place the two small magnets and the compasses on the paper as shown in the figure.

**4** Draw lines on the paper along each side of the space to represent the edges of the mid-ocean ridge. Beside each line, draw an arrow that shows the direction of north as shown on the compass needle.

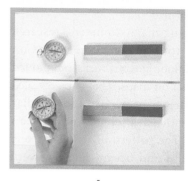

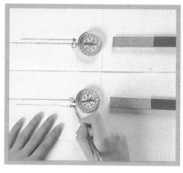

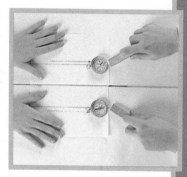

A         B         C

**5** Spread the seafloor by pulling paper up from the space and away from the center. Pull the paper out about 3 cm on each side.

**6** Reverse the magnets by turning them 180°.

**7** Move the compasses so that they are again aligned. Draw new arrows on the paper to represent the direction that the compass needles are now pointing.

**8** Repeat Steps 5-7 several times, but vary the amount of paper you pull out each time. Be sure to move the same amount of paper on each side of the space.

**9** Number the stripes you made when you drew the lines. Use 1 to represent the oldest stripe, 2 the next, and so on.

## Analyzing

**1.** Where are the oldest stripes on your paper?

**2.** *Compare* your paper to the patterns in Figure 15-8 on page 482. What are the similarities?

**3.** What do the arrows on the paper represent?

## Concluding and Applying

**4.** Why were you instructed to pull the same amount of paper out from both sides of the middle space?

**5.** **Going Further** A rock that is 50 million years old is found 3000 km west of a mid-ocean ridge. What can you *infer* about a rock found 4000 km west of the ridge? 3000 km east?

---

### Program Resources

**Activity Masters,** pp. 65–66, Investigate 15-2

**Laboratory Manual,** pp. 93–94, Earth's Magnetism **L2**

---

## Expected Outcome

Students should produce a model of normal and reversed magnetic data as they would appear on both sides of a mid-ocean ridge.

### Answers to Analyzing/ Concluding and Applying

**1.** farthest from the space between the two desks or piles of books

**2.** Students' models will not show the variety of line widths shown in the figure. However, their drawings will have stripes that reflect alternating polarity that are parallel to the space between the two desks.

**3.** the direction to the north magnetic pole at the time the lines were drawn

**4.** In reality, about the same amount of seafloor forms on either side of a rift.

**5.** older; the same age

## ✔ Assessment

**Process** Have students make a scientific drawing that shows how magnetic data can be used to support the hypothesis of sea-floor spreading. Use the Performance Task Assessment List for Scientific Drawing in **PAMSS**, page 55. **L1** **P**

## Visual Learning

**Figure 15-8** Invite students to infer the relative age of three rocks from the rocks' position relative to a mid-ocean ridge.

Just as you found a pattern to the stripes in the Investigate, scientists examining seafloor rocks found an interesting pattern in the magnetic records of the rocks. This pattern is shown in **Figure 15-8**. The rocks show that Earth's magnetic field has reversed itself many times. Each time the magnetic field switched, rocks recorded the new field. The magnetic properties of rocks aligned with the magnetic orientation at the time that they formed.

Using magnetometers, research ships took magnetic readings on ocean floor igneous rocks and plotted the data on maps. The maps revealed that stripes of magnetically similar rock run parallel to a mid-ocean ridge. The pattern of stripes on one side of a mid-ocean ridge was very similar to the pattern on the other side. Radiometric dating revealed that the age of the rocks on either side of a rift is also very similar. What do these findings suggest about what happens at a mid-ocean ridge?

**Figure 15-8**

Rocks formed on both sides of mid-ocean ridges recorded the change in magnetic polarity each time the Earth's magnetic field reversed itself.

Normal Polarity

Reversed Polarity

## Purpose

This activity allows students to calculate an average spreading rate for a portion of the Mid-Atlantic Ridge, where two of Earth's plates are forced apart.

## Teaching Strategy

It may be useful for you to make a transparency of the graph on this page and perform Procedure step 1 using the overhead projector so that students who are unsure about the procedure can see how they should proceed with the rest of the activity. **L2**

| Peak | 1 | 2 | 3 | 4 | 5 | 6 |
|---|---|---|---|---|---|---|
| Distance west normal polarity | 45 | 65 | 80 | 105 | 120 | 135 |
| Distance east normal polarity | 35 | 55 | 80 | 95 | 115 | 150 |
| Average distance | 40 | 60 | 80 | 100 | 117 | 142 |
| Distance west reversed polarity | 25 | 50 | 70 | 90 | 115 | 130 |
| Distance east reversed polarity | 25 | 45 | 65 | 80 | 100 | 125 |
| Average distance | 25 | 47 | 67 | 85 | 108 | 127 |
| Age from scale (millions of years) | 3.5 | 4.7 | 7.0 | 8.0 | 9.0 | 11.0 |
| Rate of movement (cm/year) | 1.1 | 1.3 | 1.1 | 1.2 | 1.3 | 1.3 |

## Figure Caption Question

**What happens to the magma that erupts through cracks of rift valleys?** *It forms new rock on the sea floor.*

## Sea-Floor Spreading

You have learned that changes in Earth's magnetic field help support the idea of sea-floor spreading. In this activity, you'll use data from the magnetic field profile of the Mid-Atlantic Ridge to measure how fast the seafloor is spreading. You will work with six major peaks east and west of the Mid-Atlantic Ridge, for both normal and reversed polarity.

### You Try It!

Materials
paper
pencil
metric ruler
Procedure

1. Place the ruler through the first major peak west of the Mid-Atlantic Ridge. This peak shows reverse polarity and extends downward on the profile. Determine and record *in your Journal* the distance in kilo-

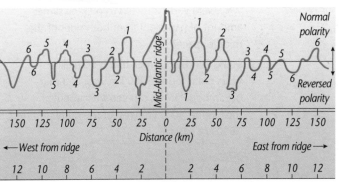

Normal polarity

Reversed polarity

Mid-Atlantic ridge

150 125 100 75 50 25 0 25 50 75 100 125 150
Distance (km)

←West from ridge          East from ridge→

12 10 8 6 4 2    2 4 6 8 10 12

*Age (millions of years)*

**482** Chapter 15 Moving Continents

## Answers to You Try It!

**6.** The average rate should be between 1.2 and 1.3 cm/yr. Accept any rate that is within a reasonable range from these two values.

**7.** Using a rate of 1.2 cm/yr, it would take about 25 million years.

## Going Further ⅢⅢ⯈

Challenge students to interpret scientific illustrations and make and use graphs. Make photocopies of Figure 15-6 on page 477. Then have students use reference books to label the major ridges on their photocopies. Next, have them plot on graph paper the spreading rates of each. Use the Performance Task Assessment List for Graph from Data in **PAMSS,** page 39. **L3** **P**

The discovery of similar magnetic records and ages of rock on both sides of a mid-ocean ridge helped support the hypothesis of sea-floor spreading. For one thing, the magnetic reversal showed that new rock was being formed at the mid-ocean ridges. For another, if the floor were not spreading, the ages and magnetic records of rocks on either side of a mid-ocean would probably not be the same.

While Wegener believed that the continents were moving, others believed that the seafloor was moving. Was it possible that both were correct? Like putting pieces of a puzzle together, scientists fit the two hypotheses together to show us the big picture of Earth in continual motion.

### check your UNDERSTANDING

1. How are the ideas of continental drift and sea-floor spreading related?
2. Discuss two pieces of data used to support the idea of sea-floor spreading.

3. **Apply** Imagine a seafloor that is spreading. How could it be possible for the seafloor to spread, while the ocean remains the same width?

meters to the Mid-Atlantic Ridge using the distance scale.

2. Repeat Step 1 for each of the six major peaks east and west of the main ridge, for both normal and reversed polarity.

3. Find the average distance from peak to ridge for each pair of peaks on either side of the ridge. Record these values.

4. Place the ruler through each of the normal polarity peaks and find the age of the rocks.

5. Using the normal polarity readings, calculate the rate of

movement in centimeters per year. You will need to convert kilometers to centimeters. Use this formula:

distance = rate x time.

6. Find the average rate of sea-floor spreading in both directions in one year, based on the rate of movement in one direction you determined in Step 5.

7. How many years would it take rock to move from the ridge to a trench 300 km away?

*Underwater mountain chains like the Mid-Atlantic Ridge can be found on the floor of all of our oceans. Rift valleys extend the length of these mountain chains. What happens to the magma that erupts through the cracks of rift valleys?*

### check your UNDERSTANDING

1. Continental drift suggests that the continents move; sea-floor spreading suggests that the seafloor moves.

2. Age data show young rock near the mid-ocean ridges and older rock farther from the ridges. The age and magnetic records for rocks on both sides of the ridges are similar.

3. New plate materials are formed as plate boundaries diverge. Old plate materials are forced down into Earth's mantle as other plates are pushed together.

## 3 ASSESS

**Check for Understanding**

1. Use Figure 15-8 to quiz students about sea-floor spreading. **Where is the rift?** *in the center of the illustration* **What do the arrows represent?** *the direction of sea-floor spreading* **Where is the oldest rock relative to the ridge?** *farthest from the rift* **What does the large vertical arrow just below the rift represent?** *the upward movement of magma*

2. Have students work in small groups to discuss the Apply question under Check Your Understanding. Then have groups report their answers to the class. **COOP LEARN**

**Reteach**

Obtain and show the film *Famous Boundary of Creation: Mid-Atlantic Ridge* from the National Oceanographic and Atmospheric Administration. **L1**

**Extension**

Have students examine a globe and note the positions of oceans and continents. Then have them hypothesize where sea-floor spreading might be occurring today. **L3**

## 4 CLOSE

Use the answer to Question 1 in Check Your Understanding to summarize what was learned in the first two sections of the chapter. It is critical that students understand the relationship between these two concepts in order to understand the theory of plate tectonics presented in Section 15-3. **L1**

# PREPARATION

## Concepts Developed

Earth's crust and solid upper mantle are divided into large plates that move because of convection currents. Points where plates interact are called plate boundaries.

## Planning the Lesson

Refer to the Chapter Organizer on pages 468A-B.

# 1 MOTIVATE

**Demonstration** Allow students to observe energy transfer in a convection current.

Materials needed are a large glass beaker, a hot plate, rice, and water.

Put about 1/4 cup of rice into the beaker, which should be three-fourths full of water. Bring the water to a boil and have students observe how the rice moves through the water. L1

# 2 TEACH

## Tying to Previous Knowledge

Have students recall from Chapter 9 how density currents form. Then explain that convection currents form for similar reasons and move in the same manner.

---

### Visual Learning

**Figure 15-9** To help students in interpreting scientific illustrations, ask the following questions. Which layers make up the lithosphere? *continental crust, oceanic crust, upper mantle* Which layers make up the asthenosphere? *upper mantle*

---

---

15-3 # Colliding Plates

### Section Objectives

- Explain how plate tectonics accounts for the movement of continents.
- Compare and contrast divergent, convergent, and transform plate boundaries.
- Explain how convection currents inside Earth might be the cause of plate tectonics.

### Key Terms

plate tectonics
lithosphere
divergent boundary
convergent
    boundary
transform fault
    boundary
asthenosphere

## Tectonic Plates

Do you enjoy reading mystery stories? Usually, the characters piece together clues or evidence. Think of the hypotheses of continental drift and sea-floor spreading as clues to a mystery. How can the two hypotheses be explained?

In the late 1960s, geologists developed a new theory to explain the apparent movement of the continents. The theory of **plate tectonics** suggests that Earth's crust and upper mantle are broken into sections called plates

that move. But what are the plates made of, and why do they move?

You already know that Earth's crust is a layer of solid rock. The uppermost portion of the mantle is also solid. Together, these two areas are the **lithosphere**.

How are these solid plates able to move around? As you can see in **Figure 15-9**, below the lithosphere is a portion of the mantle that is less solid. The material here behaves almost like putty; it's a solid that can flow. This putty-like layer is called the **asthenosphere**. The plates can be thought of as rafts that slide around on the asthenosphere. Because they cover the entire planet, there are always places where the plates are in contact with each other. The place where two plates meet is called a plate boundary. The directions of plate movement determine what occurs at a plate boundary. Let's look at the basic types of plate boundaries.

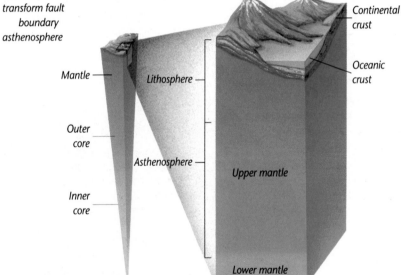

**Figure 15-9**

This diagram shows the different layers of the crust and the mantle of Earth. The rigid lithosphere moves around on top of the asthenosphere, which is capable of flowing gradually.

**484** Chapter 15 Moving Continents

---

### Meeting Individual Needs

**Learning Disabled** Obtain a tectonics globe and have learning-disabled students manipulate the pieces as they study this section. These globes are available from scientific supply houses. L1 LEP

### Program Resources

**Study Guide,** p. 51
**Transparency Master,** p. 63, and **Color Transparency** Number 30, Converging/Diverging Plates, L2

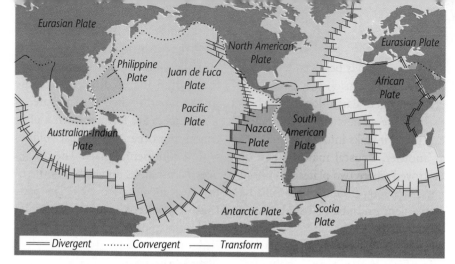

**Figure 15-10**

This map displays the lithospheric plates on which all of the oceans and continents of Earth move. Are all of the lithospheric plates of Earth the same size? On which plate do you live?

Divergent ——————
Convergent ········
Transform ——

**Visual Learning**

**Figure 15-10** What type of plate boundary separates the Indo-Australian Plate from the Antarctic Plate? *a divergent boundary* **In which direction is the South American Plate moving relative to the African Plate?** *to the west* **What is the movement of the North American Plate relative to the Eurasian Plate?** *The North American Plate is moving west relative to the Eurasian Plate.*

### ■ Divergent Boundaries

The boundary between two plates that are moving away from each other and spreading apart is called a **divergent boundary**. Magma is forced upward to Earth's surface in the rift valley that forms between the two plates, creating new crust. Mid-ocean ridges are divergent boundaries. In the Atlantic Ocean, the North American Plate is moving away from the Eurasian and African plates. This divergent boundary is the Mid-Atlantic Ridge discussed earlier. This boundary is shown in **Figure 15-11.**

**Uncovering Preconceptions**
Some students may think that the rates of plate movements are the same. Plates move at various rates from as little as 1.3 cm/yr at the southern tip of the African Plate to as much as 18.3 cm/yr along the divergent boundary of the Nazca Plate.

**Figure 15-11**

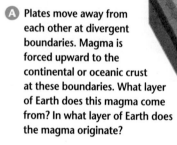

**A** Plates move away from each other at divergent boundaries. Magma is forced upward to the continental or oceanic crust at these boundaries. What layer of Earth does this magma come from? In what layer of Earth does the magma originate?

**B** The diagram above displays a more detailed look at a divergent boundary. Divergent boundaries are also called constructive boundaries. In what sense are divergent boundaries "constructive?"

**Visual Learning**

**Figure 15-11** After studying Figure 15-11, have students compare and contrast convergent and divergent boundaries. **What layer of Earth does this magma come from?** *upper mantle or asthenosphere* **In what layer of Earth does the magma originate?** *upper mantle or asthenosphere* **In what sense are divergent boundaries "constructive?"** *Divergent boundaries "construct" new plate material as the two plates spread apart.*

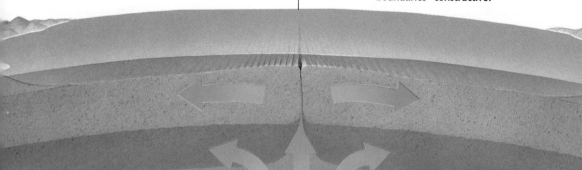

### Meeting Individual Needs

**Gifted** Have gifted students obtain and read the classic article by J. F. Dewey, "Plate Tectonics" (*Scientific American,* May 1972). Have students then form small groups and discuss the article, helping one another, if necessary, with any difficult concepts or terms. **COOP LEARN** L3

### ENRICHMENT

Challenge students to use numbers. Tell students that in the past 130 million years, as much as 7000 km of the Pacific Ocean floor may have been thrust under the North American Plate. This implies that an area approximately equal to the present-day ocean has been subducted. Have students compute the average rate, in cm/yr, of subduction. *(7000 km × 100,000 cm/km) ÷ 130,000,000 yr = 5.4 cm/yr* L3

486

■ **Convergent Boundaries**

If new crust is being added at the divergent boundaries, why isn't Earth getting bigger? Earth doesn't get bigger because as new crust is added in one place, it sinks into Earth's interior at another. Crustal material can be destroyed where two plates meet head on. This type of boundary is called a **convergent boundary**. It is shown in **Figure 15-12**.

What do you think happens when two plates containing continental crust collide? The two plates crumple, forming mountain ranges. The Himalaya Mountains formed when the Indian Plate collided with the southern part of the Eurasian Plate.

Trenches are formed when a plate containing ocean floor crust collides with a continental plate. The denser ocean crust sinks under the continental crust, forming a trench. The plate that is pushed underneath melts under the tremendous heat and pressure. Trenches can also form when two plate of ocean floor crust collide.

**Figure 15-12**

At convergent boundaries, much of what happens when two plates collide depends on the type of crust at the leading edge of each plate. Continental crust is thicker and less dense than oceanic crust. How does this explain what's happening in these diagrams?

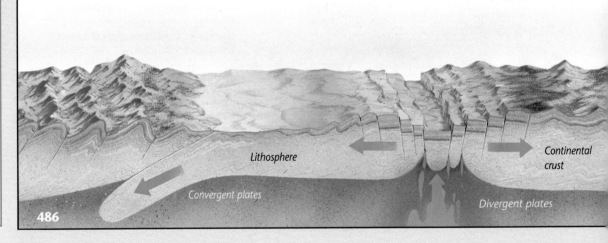

Lithosphere

Convergent plates

Continental crust

Divergent plates

486

---

## ■ Transform Fault Boundaries

A third type of plate boundary is shown in **Figure 15-13**. Called a **transform fault boundary**, it is formed when two plates slide past one another in opposite directions or in the same direction at different rates. Look back at **Figure 15-10**. Find where the North American and Pacific plates meet in California. This is the San Andreas Fault. The San Andreas is a transform fault boundary. Along this boundary, the Pacific Plate moves northwest compared with the North American Plate. The part of California that is on the Pacific Plate is actually moving northward in relation to the North American Plate at an average of two centimeters per year.

The formation of many landforms occurs as plates move around the surface of Earth, pulling apart from each other, colliding, and sliding past each other. **Figure 15-14** shows how boundaries can create landforms. From the majestic Himalayan Mountains, to the Great Rift Valley in Africa, plate movement shapes the land we live on. But what causes the plates to move? Next we will explore the driving force behind plate movements.

### Figure 15-13

A fault is a line along which rocks or rock formations move. Faults can be so small that you have to look closely to see them, or they can be large enough to be seen from an airplane. How is the movement of material at a transform fault boundary different from the movement of material at convergent and divergent boundaries?

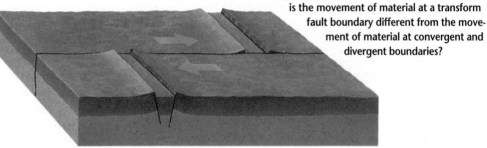

### Figure 15-14

Convergent, divergent, and transform boundaries exist in various places along Earth's crust. Look at this diagram to find what kinds of landforms are typically created at such boundaries.

*Trench*

*Divergent oceanic plates*

**487**

## Causes of Plate Tectonics

How does the theory of plate tectonics explain the cause of plate movements? The driving force behind that movement is heat. A material that is hot is less dense than the same material that is cold. This is because the same mass takes up more volume when the material is heated. Remember that less dense material is forced up by more dense material. Think about how a room is heated. A radiator heats air in the room. The heated air is forced upward by cool, denser surrounding air. As it loses heat, the air becomes cooler and more dense.

The cooler air sinks to the floor, where it forces more warm air upward and the cycle is repeated. This cycle is called a convection current.

**Figure 15-15** describes how this process occurs within Earth's asthenosphere. Remember that this layer can flow gradually like a thick liquid, even though it's more like a solid. Heat from the core warms the asthenosphere, causing convection currents to form. As these currents flow underneath the lithosphere, they pull on the plates, causing them to slowly move.

### Moving Fluids and Moving Plates

Convection currents deep inside Earth provide energy that moves plates in Earth's lithosphere.

In the familiar environment of your home, convection is one of the main ways in which thermal energy is transferred in fluids. You've seen water move in a current as it boiled, and you've experienced that air is warmer near the ceiling and cooler near the floor. These are examples of the movement of fluids due to their different densities. Let's build a model of convection in action.

**You Try It!**

**Materials**
clear glass baking dish
immersion heater
plastic sandwich bag with
  wire tie
ice cubes
tape
2 eyedroppers
red and blue food coloring
water

**Procedure**
1. Fill the baking dish with cool water to about 2 cm from the top.
2. Put six ice cubes in the sandwich bag and close the bag with a wire tie.

**Purpose**
This activity, which reinforces and extends the material presented in Section 15-3, provides a model for the convection currents thought to be the driving mechanisms of plate tectonics.

**Content Background**
Plates are essentially produced at a mid-ocean ridge. As they move laterally across the planet, they cool and may eventually become consumed at trenches. As a plate descends into the asthenosphere, it partially melts and becomes a source of magma. As the magma cools and becomes more dense it sinks and forces other, less dense magma up toward Earth's surface.

**Teaching Strategy**
Have students work in small groups of three to do this activity. Before students plug in their heaters, check to see that each group has properly assembled the apparatus. Assign one student in each group to be responsible for handling the heater. **L2** **COOP LEARN**

**Figure 15-15**

Convection cells within the mantle cause the various plates in Earth's lithosphere to move around. As the plates bump into each other, boundaries form.

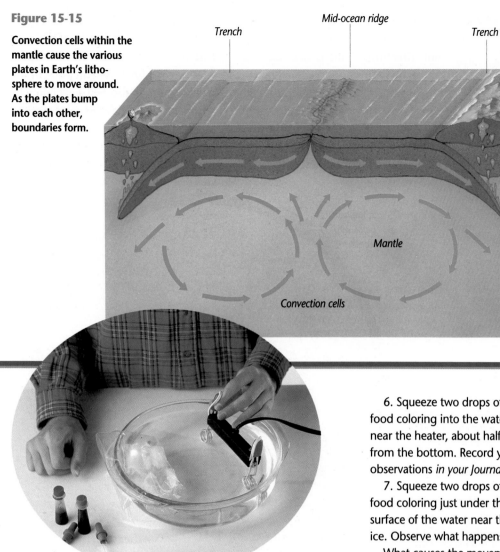

Trench    Mid-ocean ridge    Trench

Mantle

Convection cells

## Visual Learning

**Figure 15-15** Ask students to observe and infer what happens to subducting plate material at converging boundaries. *Because it is more dense, it sinks under the less dense material of the crust. As it continues to sink in the mantle, it melts, becoming part of the mantle and its convection cells.*

### Across the Curriculum

**Geography**

Have groups of students find out that part of the Mid-Atlantic Ridge is exposed at Earth's surface in Iceland. Using geothermal energy is a common way to heat homes and other buildings in Iceland. You may wish to have students research this alternative to burning fossil fuels and its connection to the divergent boundary. **L1  COOP LEARN**

**Inquiry Questions** Why is the Mid-Atlantic Ridge classified as a divergent boundary? *The ridge represents an area where two plates are moving apart and forming new crust.* **What kinds of features result from the collision of two plates?** *Trenches form either when oceanic and continental plates collide or when two oceanic plates converge. Mountain ranges form when two continental plates collide.*

3. Put the bag in the water at one end of the pan. Tape the top of the bag to the outside of the pan to hold the bag in place.

4. Place the immersion heater in the water at the other end of the pan and plug it in. Wait about a minute for the water to heat. **CAUTION:** *Not all heaters can be used as immersion heaters. Use only approved* immersion heaters. The heater is very hot. Do not touch it. Do not put any part of the heater in the water except the coil. Unplug the heater before you remove it from the water.

5. While you're waiting for the water to heat, fill one eyedropper with red food coloring and the other with blue food coloring.

6. Squeeze two drops of red food coloring into the water near the heater, about halfway from the bottom. Record your observations *in your Journal.*

7. Squeeze two drops of blue food coloring just under the surface of the water near the ice. Observe what happens.

What causes the movement of the red-colored water? What causes the movement of the blue-colored water? Ongoing convection currents are produced as liquids are heated, are pushed up by cooler, denser liquids, then cool and once again sink. Use your knowledge of Earth's mantle and lithosphere to explain how convection currents could produce plate movement.

15-3  Colliding Plates    **489**

---

**Student Journal**

Have students make a sketch of their setups in their journals. Colored pencils should be used to record how the water moved.

**Answers to**

*You Try It!*

The difference in water temperature causes the colored water to flow in a cyclic manner. Magma in Earth's mantle is pushed up in a similar way because it is less dense than surrounding materials.

**Going Further** ▥▥▥▥▶

Have students give additional examples of convection currents and describe how fluids move through each. Examples might include atmospheric circulation, deep ocean currents (density currents), conventional ovens, or forced-air heating systems. Then have students share their example by making a model or a poster or by writing a research report. Use the appropriate Performance Task List in the **PAMSS.** **L2**

# 3 ASSESS

## Check for Understanding

Assign questions 1, 2, and the Apply question under Check Your Understanding. Discuss the answer to the Apply question. To help students answer this question, have them compare normal conditions beneath ridges and trenches with the conditions given in the question.

## Reteach

Challenge student volunteers to demonstrate for the class what happens at divergent and convergent margins. Obtain some flexible foam padding about 8 cm thick. Cut the foam in half to form two "plates." Volunteers should demonstrate the folding that occurs when two plates with continental crust collide. They can also demonstrate subduction. L2

## Extension

Have students discuss what climate and culture would have been like if the continents had remained together as Pangaea. L2

# 4 CLOSE

Discuss with students the major difference between Wegener's continental drift and the theory of plate tectonics. Students should realize that Wegener did not have sea-floor spreading data to support his idea. They should also be aware that plate tectonics has proved that the continents move with the ocean floor and in fact with part of the mantle. L1

If convection explains why plates move, how can plates move in different directions? This is because there are many convection cells within the mantle, pushing the plates in different directions. However, geologists aren't sure how many and how big these cells are. **Figure 15-16** shows one possible arrangement of these cells.

The theory of plate tectonics explains the puzzle-like fit of the continents as well as how the seafloors change over time. As you'll see in the next section, it also helps explain why some parts of Earth's surface can change at any moment, as Earth erupts to form a volcano or shakes with the power of an earthquake.

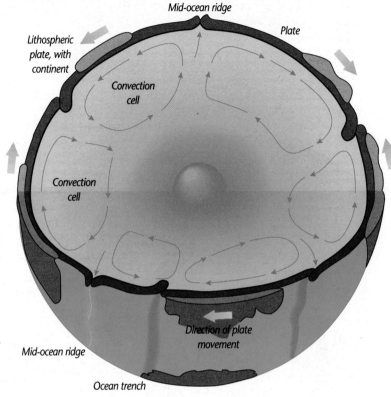

**Figure 15-16**

The material in convection cells rises and sinks, completing cycles. These convection cycles occur in different locations around Earth. Because this process is not thoroughly understood, scientists debate the exact size and number of convection cells. Is such debate, or disagreement, healthy for the scientific community? Why or why not?

## check your UNDERSTANDING

1. Describe continental drift and relate it to plate tectonics.
2. Compare and contrast the types of movements that occur at divergent, convergent, and transform fault plate boundaries.
3. **Apply** Suppose that a change takes place inside the asthenosphere. The areas beneath the mid-ocean ridges become cold; the areas beneath the trenches become hot. Draw a before-and-after diagram showing the direction of plate movement and the convection within the asthenosphere.

## check your UNDERSTANDING

1. According to continental drift, all continents were once joined and have moved and still move. Plate tectonics explains how plates move and why the seafloor spreads. The mechanism of this is convection currents.
2. Plates come together and collide at a convergent boundary. Plates pull apart at a divergent boundary. Plates move laterally at a transform fault boundary.
3. The diagrams should show currents in opposite directions. The second diagrams should show new mid-ocean ridges at old trench locations, and new subduction zones at old mid-ocean ridge locations.

# Dynamic Earth

## Changes in Earth's Surface

When Earth's plates meet, mountains form, volcanoes erupt, and earthquakes rumble through the ground. Let's look at the connections between earthquakes, volcanoes, and plate boundaries.

### Section Objectives

■ Relate the occurrence of earthquakes and volcanoes to plate tectonics.

■ Compare and contrast the three types of regions where volcanoes occur.

### Key Terms

*hot spots*

### Explore! ACTIVITY

#### How are plate boundaries related to earthquakes and volcanoes?

**What To Do**

1. Review Figure 15-10, which shows the locations of known plate boundaries.

2. Now look at the diagram to the right, which shows the locations of active volcanoes and areas of high earthquake activity. *In your Journal* record any similarities you find between the two diagrams. How do the locations of earthquake epicenters and active volcanoes relate to the location of plate boundaries?

**Conclude and Apply**

How might you explain the relationship between earthquakes, volcanoes, and plate boundaries?

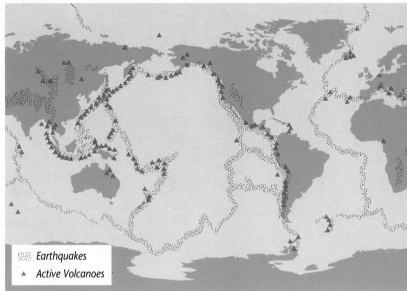

&#9617; *Earthquakes*

▲ *Active Volcanoes*

### Find Out!

#### How are plate boundaries related to earthquakes and volcanoes?

**Time needed**  10–15 minutes

**Materials**  No special materials are required.

**Thinking Processes**  interpreting scientific illustrations, recognizing cause and effect, predicting

**Purpose**  To relate the occurrence of earthquakes and volcanoes to plate boundaries

**Teaching the Activity**

Have students work in pairs to do this activity. **COOP LEARN**

**Student Journal**  Have students record the answers to their questions in their journals. L1

#### Expected Outcome

Students should note a correlation between plate boundaries and earthquakes and volcanoes.

---

## PREPARATION

**Concepts Developed**

Two of Earth's most dramatic processes—volcanic eruptions and earthquakes—occur because of plate tectonics. Earthquakes are the results of movements along plate boundaries. Volcanoes are common at mid-ocean ridges, certain types of convergent boundaries, and above hot spots in the mantle.

**Planning the Lesson**

In planning your lesson on earthquakes and volcanoes, refer to the Chapter Organizer on pages 468A–B.

## 1 MOTIVATE

**Discussion**  Allow students to define Earth's movements operationally. Ask students to remain perfectly still. Then ask them whether they are moving. Some students may recognize that Earth is rotating, revolving, and changing via plate tectonics. L1

### Conclude and Apply

Most earthquakes and volcanoes occur near plate boundaries. The movement of plates puts stress on rocks, causing earthquakes. Subducted material melts and forms volcanoes.

### ✔ Assessment

**Process**  Have students use the figure to determine the likelihood of earthquake and volcanic activity in the area where they live. Students could then make a slide show or photo display that shows recent earthquake and volcanic activity in the United States. Use the Performance Task Assessment List for Slide Show or Photo Display in **PAMSS** page 77. L1

# 2 TEACH

## Tying to Previous Knowledge

Have students recall hearing about any recent earthquakes and/or volcanic eruptions around the world. Help them find the locations of these events on a world map. Then use the map to show students that these Earth phenomena are related to plate boundaries, which were studied in Section 15-3.

**Theme Connection** The themes of energy and stability and change can be seen in this lesson. Tremendous amounts of energy are released during both earthquakes and volcanic eruptions. Both of these events are related to the changes that occur as tectonic plates move over Earth's surface.

---

## Visual Learning

**Figure 15-17** Use Figure 15-17 to help students realize why seismic information from fewer than three stations does not allow scientists to pinpoint the location of an earthquake. Point out that if only two stations are used, there are two points of overlap and you cannot tell which point is the epicenter. Then have students verify this by measuring with a metric ruler the data shown in Figure 15-17. Students will find that the radius of each circle is equal to the distance to the epicenter from each seismograph station. L1

**Figure 15-18** Have students compare the types of movement seen at different faults. **In how many different directions does the lithosphere move at each of these faults?** *two* **What might happen if the lithosphere of Earth did not contain faults?** *The lithosphere would buckle.*

---

## Where Do Earthquakes Occur?

As you saw in the Find Out activity, earthquakes are common at plate boundaries. Think about what you know about earthquakes. Rocks under pressure can break or snap suddenly along faults. Movement along the faults releases energy that shakes the ground.

How do we know where earthquakes occur? You know that the energy released by a quake is in the form of waves. Primary earthquake waves travel faster than secondary waves. The time that elapses between primary and secondary waves is used to determine an earthquake's distance from a given location. To help you understand how this is done, think of two runners. In a 50 meter race, Miguel always beats Greg by two seconds. In a 100 meter race, Miguel always wins by four seconds. You can figure out how far the race is by knowing how many seconds Miguel wins by. For example, if Miguel wins by two seconds, you know the race was 50 meters long. How long would a race be that Miguel wins by 3 seconds? The winning margin is like the lag time of earthquake waves. Because we know the speed of each wave, we can calculate how far away the waves started by measuring the lag time. The farther away the earthquake is from you, the longer the lag time between the two kinds of waves. **Figure 15-17** shows how seismologists pinpoint the location of an earthquake.

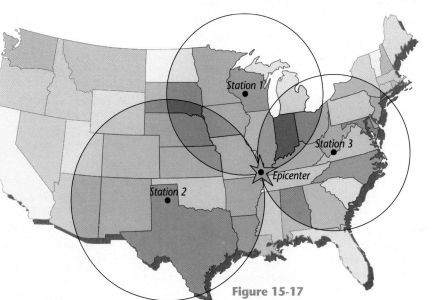

**Figure 15-17**

The exact location of an earthquake is found by measuring the earthquake's distance by using lag times from three separate locations on the surface of Earth. A circle representing the distance is drawn from each location, and the point where all three circles intersect, or meet, identifies the epicenter of the earthquake. Somewhere beneath the epicenter is the origin of the earthquake.

**492** Chapter 15 Moving Continents

---

## Program Resources

**Study Guide,** p. 52

**Multicultural Connections,** p. 34, Tsunami—Seismic Sea Wave L1

**How It Works,** p. 20, The Seismograph L1

**Making Connections: Across the Curriculum,** p. 33, Are Volcanic Areas Populated? L1

**Figure 15-18**

Although earthquakes can occur deep within Earth, they occur most often near faults in the lithosphere. The diagram displays how movement can occur at various faults. In how many different directions does the lithosphere move at each of these faults? What might happen if the lithosphere of Earth did not contain faults?

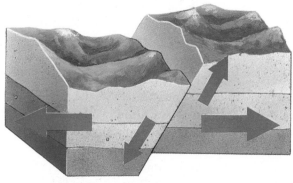

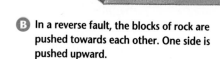

**B** In a reverse fault, the blocks of rock are pushed towards each other. One side is pushed upward.

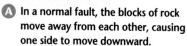

**A** In a normal fault, the blocks of rock move away from each other, causing one side to move downward.

**D** In a strike-slip fault, the blocks of rock move horizontally past each other.

**C** Earthquakes can also occur at plate boundaries like this one. Here, one plate is sliding underneath another. This can cause earthquakes deep within Earth.

While it may seem peaceful, Earth's crust is subjected to all sorts of bending, pushing and pulling caused by plate movement. Earthquakes are felt when movement occurs at a break in the crust called a fault. Just as there are different kinds of plate boundaries, there are different kinds of faults. **Figure 15-18** shows the main types of faults. Even the bending caused by rising magma at subduction zones can result in earthquakes.

---

## Across the Curriculum

### Daily Life

Although most earthquakes occur near plate boundaries, two of the most severe earthquakes in the United States occurred far removed from tectonic boundaries. Thus, everyone should be aware of what to do and what not to do during an earthquake.

Have students find out how their homes and your school can be "earthquake-proofed" and what people should do to protect themselves in the event of an earthquake. **L1**

**Activity** Use this simulation to demonstrate for tactile learners what happens during an earthquake.

Materials needed are two wooden blocks that are each sanded smooth on one side and rough—with saw marks—on another.

Allow students to slide the smooth surfaces against each other gently, noting that there is little friction produced. Then have students try to slide the rough surfaces against each other. Students should "feel" the surfaces catch or snag. Relate this activity to what causes some earthquakes. This action is similar to what happens along the San Andreas fault. **L1** **LEP**

**Uncovering Preconceptions**
Some people, perhaps including some of your students, have been misinformed that, during an earthquake, huge cracks form that "swallow" people, cars, buildings, and so forth. Cracks may develop in the crust during an earthquake but few are large enough to pose real threats to people and structures.

---

## Meeting Individual Needs

**Behaviorally Disordered** Invite students to make a model of an earthquake. Have students place a piece of long plastic tubing into the neck of a thick rubber balloon and secure the tube so that no air can escape the balloon. Have them then place the balloon at the bottom of an empty aquarium, with the tubing extending out of the tank. Have students add alternating layers of moist sand and dry sand, each about 1 cm deep. This task will help students focus on one part of the activity. Have one student in each group slowly inflate the balloon until the sand cracks, simulating an earthquake. Remind students that the expanding balloon does not represent what actually occurs during an earthquake. Earth's interior does not expand. The balloon is used to produce the movement needed to model the earthquake. **COOP LEARN**

# Where Do Volcanoes Occur?

Volcanoes, like those shown in **Figure 15-19**, form in three kinds of places related to plate tectonics: divergent plate boundaries, convergent plate boundaries, and locations called hot spots.

### ■ Divergent Boundaries

Where the plates pull apart, magma is forced upward to Earth's surface and erupts as lava. Lava that flows from underwater rifts cools quickly in the cold ocean water. As eruptions continue over time, layers of cooled lava accumulate. Iceland was formed when the layers of lava accumulated to form an island.

### ■ Convergent Boundaries

Earth's most well-known volcanoes are found at convergent plate boundaries.

When one of the converging plates is forced underneath the other, it's called a subduction zone. Melting of the subducted plate creates magma, which is forced upward to the surface. When the magma reaches the surface, it erupts as lava, forming volcanoes.

Today, plates continue to collide and subduct. Find Japan and the Philippines on your map of plate boundaries. Which plates are colliding?

### ■ Hot Spots

The Hawaiian Islands are actually the tips of volcanoes that have risen from the ocean floor. However, unlike Iceland, these islands did not form at a plate boundary. The Hawaiian Islands are in the middle of the Pacific Plate. How then are these islands related to plate tectonics?

**Figure 15-19**

Ⓐ This is a new island forming off the coast of Iceland

Ⓑ In what ways can the eruption of Mount Saint Helens, or other volcanoes, be dangerous?

**494**    Chapter 15   Moving Continents

Some areas of Earth's mantle are hotter than others. In these areas, magma is forced up by surrounding denser material. The magma is forced up through cracks in the solid lithosphere and spills out as lava. These areas are known as **hot spots. Figure 15-20** shows how hot spots can form an island chain. The Hawaiian Islands were formed as the Pacific plate moved over a hot spot in the middle of the Pacific Ocean.

Plate tectonics is a story of energy transfer. The thermal energy from inside Earth is transferred to Earth's surface. Some is released as heat creating lava. Some is changed into energy of motion, causing the plates to move. Throughout geologic time, plate movements form and reform oceans, continents, and mountains.

## SKILLBUILDER

**Forming a Hypothesis**

Mount Unzen in Japan and Mount Pinatubo in the Philippines both erupted in the spring of 1991. Use Figure 15-10 and the diagram in the Explore activity on page 491 to hypothesize how these volcanoes may have formed. If you need help, refer to the **Skill Handbook** on page 687.

## SKILLBUILDER

The volcanoes formed when two oceanic plates collided. [L1]

**Visual Learning**

**Figure 15-20** Help students use the figure to recognize cause and effect. Ask what will happen over the hot spot as the lithospheric plate continues to move. *New islands will form.*

# 3 ASSESS

**Check for Understanding**

Discuss students' answers to the Apply question. If they have trouble with this question, indicate on a map of Hawaii the direction of plate movement and the stationary position of the hot spot.

**Reteach**

Obtain and show the video *Earthquakes and Moving Continents* from Educational Activities. [L1]

**Extension**

Have students use what they have learned in this chapter along with Figure 15-10 to draw maps predicting where and what kinds of landmasses and landforms may be located on Earth's surface in the future. [L2]

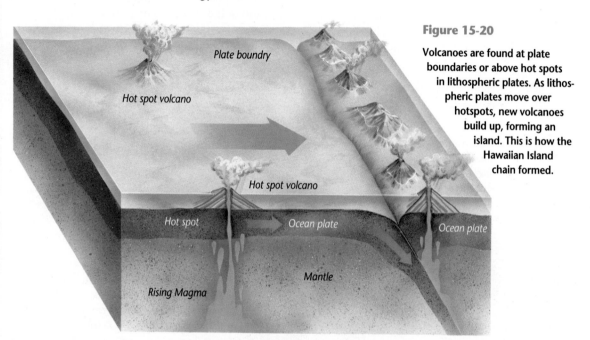

**Figure 15-20**

Volcanoes are found at plate boundaries or above hot spots in lithospheric plates. As lithospheric plates move over hotspots, new volcanoes build up, forming an island. This is how the Hawaiian Island chain formed.

## check your UNDERSTANDING

1. Both Japan and California are prone to earthquakes. Explain this fact using plate tectonics.
2. Where does lava come from that flows out of a rift? A convergent boundary?
3. **Apply**  Today, a new Hawaiian volcano, Loihi Seamount, is forming. Look at a map of the Hawaiian islands. If Kauai is the oldest island of the chain, predict where Loihi Seamount is forming.

## check your UNDERSTANDING

**1.** Japan is on a convergent plate boundary. California is on a transform fault boundary. Plate movement along these boundaries can produce earthquakes.
**2.** Magma from Earth's mantle surfaces as lava in both cases.
**3.** It is probably forming southeast of Hawaii.

# 4 CLOSE

Have students pretend that they are real-estate developers. If they could live 200 million years, how would they use a map of Earth plates today to invest in what will eventually be valuable beach-front property in the distant future? Students can use information on the direction and speed of plate movement to see where new beaches will appear. [L1]

## Science and Society

### Purpose

In this feature, students learn more about one of Earth's most dramatic events—volcanic eruptions. The feature extends what was learned in Section 15-4. Although volcanic eruptions can last several minutes, hours, or days, the events that lead up to the explosion can take hundreds or thousands of years to occur.

### Content Background

The bulge that formed on the north flank of Mount Saint Helens prior to the 1980 eruption was monitored and showed a very slow but steady growth rate of a few meters per day from March until the May eruption. Because the growth rate was slow, geologists were unable to determine when the volcano would erupt. In many cases, if such a bulge changes size abruptly, an eruption usually follows quickly. In the case of Mount Saint Helens, however, seismic activity actually *decreased* two days prior to the May 18th explosion. The tremors associated with the May 1980 eruption of Mount Saint Helens registered 5.1 on the Richter scale, which is a scale of earthquake magnitude based on the motions recorded by a seismograph. Volcanic ejecta spewed by the 1980 Mount Saint Helens eruption is estimated to have had a volume of approximately 4 km$^3$.

### Teaching Strategies

Challenge students to infer how physical and chemical changes within a volcano and the nearby crust can be precursors of volcanic eruptions. Earthquakes often precede volcanic eruptions because of the underground movement of magma and gases. These movements can be indications of an upcoming eruption.

## Science and Society

# Volcanoes and Saving Lives

**B**arry Voigt adjusts a sensitive scientific instrument. He's in the midst of a landscape so alien that it could be on another planet. The rocks have edges as sharp as razors. He has to wear a mask for protection against poisonous fumes. It is truly hostile territory.

Voigt is on Merapi, a dangerous, active volcano in Indonesia. Here, 5890 meters above sea level, he risks his life carrying out research that may someday save thousands of lives.

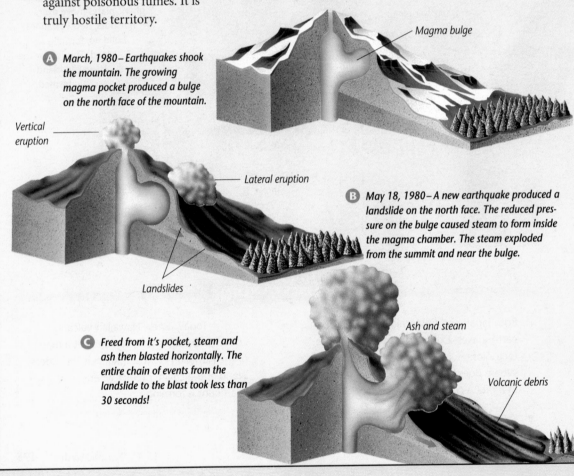

**A** March, 1980 – Earthquakes shook the mountain. The growing magma pocket produced a bulge on the north face of the mountain.

Magma bulge

Vertical eruption

Lateral eruption

Landslides

**B** May 18, 1980 – A new earthquake produced a landslide on the north face. The reduced pressure on the bulge caused steam to form inside the magma chamber. The steam exploded from the summit and near the bulge.

**C** Freed from it's pocket, steam and ash then blasted horizontally. The entire chain of events from the landslide to the blast took less than 30 seconds!

Ash and steam

Volcanic debris

An increase in the sulfur dioxide emission of a volcano, which can be monitored by chemical sensors, can be indicative of magma very near the surface. Bulging, is another indication of a potential volcanic eruption. **L2**

### Going Further ⫸

Have students work in small groups to prepare and act out an evacuation plan should a hypothetical volcanic eruption be predicted for your area. Explain that they have about seven days to evacuate the area. Students can present their plans in a booklet or pamphlet. Use the Performance Task Assessment List for Booklet or Pamphlet in **PAMSS,** page 57. Evaluate students on their ability to work cooperatively within the group as well as on the thoroughness of the proposed plan. **L2** **COOP LEARN**

## Predicting Explosions

Voigt wants to reliably predict volcanic explosions weeks before they happen. That way, people in the path of a volcano's destruction would have plenty of time to get out of the way.

As recently as 1985, nearly 22 000 people died in the town of Armero in Colombia when a nearby volcano erupted. Authorities were hesitant to order an evacuation because they were not sure when the volcano would erupt. Reliable prediction could have prevented this and many similar tragedies.

## An Unusual Eruption

Voigt began studying volcanoes in 1980, when earthquakes started to shake Mount Saint Helens in Washington. A specialist in rockslides and avalanches, Voigt predicted that rockslides caused by the earthquakes could make Mount Saint Helens erupt sideways. And that's what happened. The diagram on these two pages shows the sequence of the eruption.

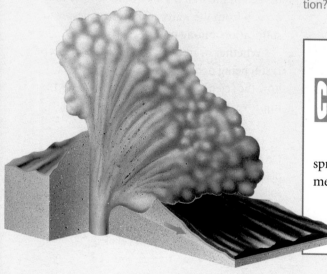

## Tools of the Trade

Voigt has developed new techniques for analyzing information from the special instruments he uses and for predicting when the rock in a volcano will give way and allow an eruption to take place.

To collect the data that he needs, Voigt uses an array of instruments such as laser measuring devices, seismographs, and instrments that measure tilt and movement of Earth.

### *What Do You Think?*

At times, government officials have forced the evacuation of an area when a volcanic eruption was predicted. The eruption may never have happened or may have been much less severe than predicted. The evacuation may have produced many hardships that some people would consider unnecessary.

At other times, government officials have waited too long, as was the case in Armero.

Imagine you're in the government of a country with many active volcanoes. What factors would you use to decide when to order evacuation? Explain your choices.

**CAREER connection**

**Volcanologists** are geologists who specialize in volcanoes. They examine lava flows, rock formations, geysers, and hot springs, collecting samples and measurements as they work. Volcanologists attempt to determine the kind of eruptions that might occur in the future.

### Content Background

The changing chemistry of a volcano, as well as seismic data, can indicate a future eruption. Changes in the levels of chlorine and sulfur, in most cases, indicate an eruption.

A laser is a light source that produces a very narrow beam of light of only one color or wavelength.

A tiltmeter is a device that measures slight changes in the tilt of Earth's surface relative to a liquid-level surface or to the rest position of a pendulum.

### Teaching Strategies
Challenge students to investigate technologies used for predicting volcanic eruptions. Have interested students find out about early-warning systems (RSAM and SSAM) used by the United States Geological Survey (USGS) to predict eruptions. Students can present their findings to the class and should be prepared to answer any questions that arise. **L3**

### Discussion

Guide students to infer that lasers are found in some welding torches, automated checkout counters at the supermarket or department store, compact disk players, optical fibers used in communications, and are used by physicians to perform delicate surgery and by surveyors building bridges, roads, and tunnels. Most students think of the laser as a high-tech device used only in theoretical research such as that described in this feature.

### Answers to
### What Do You Think?

Factors that should be considered include the estimated severity of the future eruption, the volcanic history of the area, any scientific evidence that an eruption may occur, and so on. Make sure students are able to justify their responses with scientific facts.

EXPAND
*your view*

## HISTORY CONNNECTION

### Purpose

This excursion allows students to think critically about some hypotheses that suggest why sea level has changed over geologic time. It expands what was learned in Sections 15-3 and 15-4 about changes in Earth during its long history, including changes in sea level.

### Teaching Strategies

Make sure students realize that the water molecules present on Earth today are the same water molecules that were present when the water molecules first formed. Over the past 4.6 billion years, water has merely changed state as it cycles through the water cycle. Demonstrate this concept with the activity below. **L2**

### Activity

Allow students to observe that Earth's water doesn't "disappear" during sea level falls but rather changes state.

Materials needed are a container with a definite amount of water (2 cups); 1/4 c measuring cup. Show students the container of water. Ask them what it represents. *Earth's oceans* Carefully remove 1/4 c and freeze it. Ask students what the frozen water represents. *a continental glacier* Ask students to describe the change in water level. *It dropped.* Allow the ice to melt. Return it to the container. Have students observe that water level rises. Have a volunteer summarize the relationship between glaciations and changes in sea level. Elicit from students that this relationship is a hypothesis, not a demonstrated fact.

## HISTORY CONNNECTION

# Changing Sea Levels

One branch of science may shed light on another. You've seen how fossil records contributed to the theory of plate tectonics. Knowledge from different fields may help explain changing sea levels.

Ocean levels have sometimes changed by as much as 150 feet. It has long been assumed that this change came from the melting and refreezing of polar ice caps. However, evidence from geologic and fossil records suggests than changes in the ice cap aren't large enough to account for it.

### Deeper Oceans

One hypothesis proposes that the sea's rise and fall may have been caused by changes in the ocean floor plates. Like the continents, the ocean bottoms are rocky plates adrift on a convecting mantle. If the plates pulled apart, deep rifts and depressions would open in the seafloor. Ocean water would fill the depressions, creating a drop in levels around the world. Molten rock from the mantle would then slowly refill the rift, pushing sea levels back up.

Look at the map below of the Pacific Ocean basin. It is not too hard to imagine how changes in the topography of this vast area of the ocean floor might have a major effect on sea levels.

### Fossil Evidence

Fossil records suggest that this idea may have some merit. They indicate that during the time of sea level changes, huge numbers of sea creatures became extinct. Magma filling in a rift would combine with dissolved oxygen in the water. This would remove the oxygen from the water and cause widespread suffocation among marine life.

Whether or not this hypothesis is correct is still being debated. This shows, however, how the sciences can work together to try to improve our understanding of our world.

### What Do You Think?

On a human time scale, changes in sea level take place slowly. However, what if a very dramatic shift in ocean levels took place? What do you think the effects would be of an extremely sharp rise or drop in sea level on coastal cities? What might the effects be on Earth's ecology?

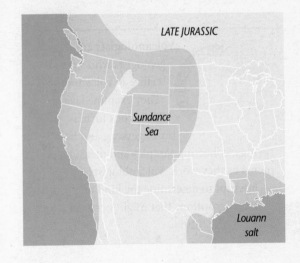

LATE JURASSIC

Sundance Sea

Louann salt

### Going Further ▸▸▸▸▸

Most materials, like Earth's crust, expand when heated. Have students come up with examples in their every day lives of expansion. Responses might include joints in bridges, hot air balloons, spaces between adjacent railroad tracks and slabs of concrete in roads and sidewalks, thermometers, thermostats, and so on. Elicit from students that magma expands when heated. As it expands and is pushed upward, magma pushes Earth's plates apart, causing sea-floor spreading. Working in cooperative groups, have students make a bulletin board on expansion. Each group can take responsibility for presenting one of the examples that students identified. Use the Performance Task Assessment List for Bulletin Board in **PAMSS** page 59. **L1** **COOP LEARN**

Review the statements below about the big ideas presented in this chapter, and try to answer the questions. Then, reread your answers to the Did You Ever Wonder questions at the beginning of the chapter. *In your Journal,* write a paragraph about how your understanding of the big ideas in the chapter has changed.

**1** The first evidence for continental drift was the obvious fit of some continents. *How does the fit of the continents suggest they have moved?*

**2** A plate is a piece of lithosphere that usually contains both seafloor and part of a continent. *What causes the plates to move around?*

Ocean crust

Continental crust

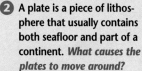

Lava

Magma

**3** Horizontal movement of mantle material causes sea-floor spreading. Magma is forced upward, pouring out of rift valleys and creating new sea-floor. *How could an ocean floor spread, yet the size of the ocean remain the same?*

**4** In subduction, one plate is forced beneath another. At a depth of 700 km, the subducted plate is mostly melted. *What can happen to the subducted plate after it has melted?*

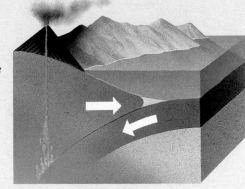

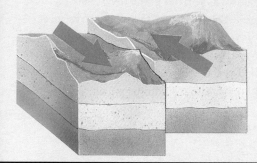

**5** Most earthquakes and volcanoes occur near plate boundaries. *How can volcanoes occur in places other than plate boundaries?*

Have groups of students use the figures on this page to teach a short lesson on each topic.

## Teaching Strategies

Divide students into five groups. Assign each group one of the topics given. Each group should prepare a 10 minute lesson to be taught to the class. Each member of the group should contribute to the lesson by orally presenting some material or by preparing supplementary materials (transparencies, models, work sheets). Encourage groups to use handouts, models, and demonstrations to present the group's topic. **COOP LEARN**

## Answers to Questions

**1.** If one continent broke apart into several continents, you would expect their shapes to fit together, as they do in places.

**2.** Convection within the mantle causes movement in the plates floating on top of them.

**3.** Because the ocean floor could be subducting at convergent boundaries at the same rate that it is spreading.

**4.** The low density magma can be pushed toward the surface, where it erupts in volcanoes or hardens at mid-ocean ridges.

**5.** They can occur at hot spots and anywhere where magma can reach the surface.

**◎◎ MINDJOGGER VIDEOQUIZ**

**Chapter 15** Have students work in groups as they play the videoquiz game to review key chapter concepts.

## Project

Challenge students to plot data on a map. Have students find out about 10 to 15 of the most recent volcanic eruptions and earthquakes that have occurred around the world. Obtain a world map and have students plot earthquake locations with green sticky dots and volcanoes with red sticky dots. Have them add to the map using information from the chapter. Students should notice a pattern evolving as more data are added. Completed maps should look similar to the map on page 491. **L1** **LEP**

## Science at Home

Have students model the movement of Earth's plates, using a large baking pan of water, an immersion heater, and two floating objects such as pieces of wood or plastic foam. Fill the pan and place the heater in the center. Place the pan on a heatproof surface and float the two objects about an inch apart near the center of the pan. Allow the water to come to rest, then turn on the heater and observe how the "plates" move. This activity should be done under adult supervision. **L2**

## Using Key Science Terms

1. convergent boundary
2. sea-floor spreading
3. lithosphere
4. convergent boundary
5. plates

## Understanding Ideas

**1.** convergent, divergent, and transform fault

A convergent boundary is where two plates meet head on. A divergent boundary is where two plates moving away from each other. A transform fault boundary is formed when two plates slide past one another in opposite directions or in the same direction at different rates.

**2.** Pangaea was the original supercontinent composed of the present-day continents. Pangaea formed and broke up due to plate movement.

**3.** The relative shapes of continents and their fits are probably the most obvious clues to continental drift.

**4.** Continental plates, being less dense, tend to override the more dense oceanic plates, which are subducted into the mantle.

## Developing Skills

**1.** See reduced student page for completed concept map.

**2.** Some background information would make putting together an unknown puzzle easier. Knowing what the picture is and the colors involved would probably be the most helpful knowledge. Background information is useful to scientists as they try to put pieces of knowledge together to make a whole "picture."

**3.** Results will vary. Suggest that resource books be used to determine the average speed and directions of movement of the continents.

---

## U sing Key Science Terms

| | |
|---|---|
| asthenosphere | hot spots |
| continental drift | lithosphere |
| convergent | plate tectonics |
| boundary | sea-floor spreading |
| divergent | transform fault |
| boundary | boundary |

*An analogy is a relationship between two pairs of words generally written in the following manner: a:b::c:d. The symbol : is read "is to," and the symbol :: is read "as." For example, cat:animal::rose:plant is read "cat is to animal as rose is to plant." In the analogies that follow, a word is missing. Complete each analogy by providing the missing word from the list above.*

**1.** hot spots:Hawaii:: _____ :Mount Pinatubo

**2.** Fossil evidence:continental drift:: Magnetic evidence:_____

**3.** _____:solid:: asthenosphere:putty-like

**4.** divergent boundary:rift:: _____:trench

**5.** gasoline:automobiles:: convection:_____

## U nderstanding Ideas

*Answer the following questions in your Journal using complete sentences.*

**1.** List the three types of plate boundaries and what makes them different.

**2.** Explain the history of Pangaea.

**3.** Of the evidence gathered by Wegener and others, which was most obvious and led to the hypothesis of continental drift?

---

**4.** What generally appears to occur when oceanic and continental plates collide?

## D eveloping Skills

*Use your understanding of the concepts developed in this chapter to answer each of the following questions.*

**1. Concept Mapping** Complete the concept map of moving continents.

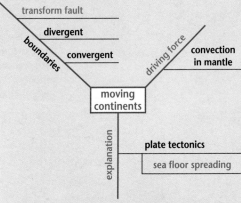

**2. Observing and Inferring** Repeat the Explore activity on page 469 using another student's puzzle pieces. Without asking any questions, put the puzzle together. Would this task be easier if you had some background knowledge? What information would be helpful?

**3. Predicting** Cut out another set of landmasses as you did in the Investigate on page 472-473. Place them on a large sheet of paper in their current relative positions. Predict their positions in 10 million years. Show your predicted positions of the landmasses on the paper.

---

## Program Resources

**Review and Assessment,** pp. 89–94 L1
**Performance Assessment,** Ch. 15 L2
**PAMSS**
**Alternate Assessment in the Science Classroom**
**Computer Test Bank**

## Critical Thinking

In your Journal, *answer each of the following questions.*

1. Projections of where the continents will be in 100 million years are based on what evidence?
2. If a sudden and tremendous increase in the temperature of rocks within the asthenosphere occurred, how would plate movement be affected?
3. The diagram shows convection currents in the upper mantle. Explain why the features labeled A and B occur at those positions.

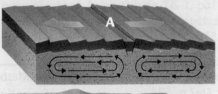

4. How did fossil data help support Wegener's hypothesis of continental drift?

How did magnet rock data help support the hypothesis of sea-floor spreading?

## Problem Solving

*Read the following problem and discuss your answers in a brief paragraph.*

**Mapmakers Shelly and Luis are updating a topographic map of the Banquo Valley. Shelly and Luis measure the distance from Smitty on the western side of the valley to Hazy on the eastern side. Oddly, they find the distance has changed since 1920.**

| | Measurement Data | |
|---|---|---|
| Year | Distance from Smitty to Hazy | Angle from Smitty to Hazy |
| 1920 | 1.0 km | 60° |
| 1992 | 1.4 km | 45° |

Draw two figures representing the data. One should represent the locations of Smitty and Hazy in 1920, and the other should represent the locations of these places in 1992.

1. What explanation can you give for the changes in locations?
2. In which direction is Smitty moving relative to Hazy?

## Critical Thinking

1. current directions and rates of plate movement
2. Plates would probably move faster as the rate of convection within the asthenosphere increases.
3. A ridge occurs at A because two plates are moving apart, causing a rift where magma rises to the surface and piles up, forming new crust. A trench occurs at B because one plate is being forced below another plate.
4. Wegener compared fossils found on separate continents and saw similarities in some. The magnetic orientation of rocks on the sea floor is not constant, which indicates that some parts of the sea floor are older than others.

## Problem Solving

1. The places appear to be on opposite sides of a north-south or north-west-southeast trending transform fault boundary.
2. south or southwest

## Connecting Ideas

1. The "drifting" of continents is caused by the movements of plates. The flow of lava at divergent boundaries in the ocean, as well as subduction at convergent plate boundaries, account for sea-floor spreading.
2. Water temperatures near and over the rift would be warmer than elsewhere. Warm water would be forced upward by cooler, denser water.
3. Sea-floor spreading and plate tectonics may have contributed to variances in sea level over the years as shorelines and plate boundaries changed.

## CONNECTING IDEAS

Discuss each of the following in a brief paragraph.

1. **Theme—Systems and Interactions** How does plate tectonics help explain continental drift and sea-floor spreading?

2. **Theme—Energy** How would the thermal energy reaching the seafloor surface at a mid-ocean ridge affect water temperature? Describe a possible density current set up over a rift valley.

3. **HISTORY Connection** How can seafloor spreading help account for the periodic rise and fall of ocean water levels?

## Assessment

**Portfolio** Review the portfolio options that are provided throughout the chapter. Encourage students to select one product that demonstrates their best work for the chapter. Have students explain what they learned and why they chose this example for placement into their portfolios.

Additional portfolio options can be found in the following **Teacher Classroom Resources:**

**Multicultural Connections,** pp. 33-34

**Making Connections: Integrating Sciences,** p. 33
**Making Connections: Across the Curriculum,** p. 33
**Concept Mapping,** p. 23
**Critical Thinking/Problem Solving,** p. 23
**Take Home Activities,** p. 25
**Laboratory Manual,** pp. 93-94
**Performance Assessment** P

## Geologic Time

### THEME DEVELOPMENT

The themes that are supported by this chapter are systems and interactions, and stability and change. Layers of rock form a system. Interactions between layers leave clues to the ages of different rock layers. By studying these systems, scientists find evidence of changes in Earth over time.

### CHAPTER OVERVIEW

Earth's history is recorded in layers of rock and fossils. The appearances and disappearances of organisms in the fossil record are some of the evidence that has been used to construct the geologic time scale. Earth is about 4.6 billion years old. We know little about Precambrian time, which covers the time from Earth's formation until 545 million years ago. The appearance of organisms with hard parts marks the beginning of the Paleozoic. During the Mesozoic Era, dinosaurs, mammals, and flowering plants appeared. Mammals and flowering plants have dominated the last geologic era, the Cenozoic.

### Tying to Previous Knowledge

Over time, Earth's climates have changed. Living things that could not survive such changes became extinct. Have students who have moved from other climates, or those who might vacation in other climates, discuss differences in climate. Relate this discussion to changes in an organism's environment as plates moved into latitudes with different climates. Then have students hypothesize how changes in climate may have affected organisms that lived long ago.

# CHAPTER 16

# GEOLOGIC TIME

### Did you ever wonder...

✓ How old Earth is?

✓ How fossils are formed?

✓ How we know what dinosaurs looked like?

Before you begin to study geologic time, think about these questions and answer them *in your Journal.* When you finish the chapter, compare your Journal write-up with what you have learned.

*Imagine you've built a machine that can take you back in time. You strap yourself in, set the controls, and away you go. Each minute by your watch takes you another million years back in time. Finally, after traveling for just over an hour, your time machine grinds to a halt. You've reached your time journey's end.*

*Outside your machine is lush green vegetation. Suddenly, you see a large, fierce-looking animal with long, sharp teeth eyeing you. A Tyrannosaurus! You've traveled back to the age of dinosaurs!*

▶ **In this chapter, you'll see how scientists travel back in geologic time.**

502

### Did you ever wonder...

• Earth is approximately 4.6 billion years old. (p. 520)

• Fossils form through replacement of minerals or a mold and cast process. (p. 506)

• Based on the size and structure of fossilized bones, scientists can reconstruct what the organisms looked like. (p. 505)

### STUDENT JOURNAL

Have students write their responses to the Did You Ever Wonder questions in their journals. After they have read the chapter, students should read their journal entries to see what they have learned about geologic time.

# Explore! ACTIVITY

## How can you discover and organize events that happened in the past?

**W**ithout knowing an exact date how can you figure out when one event occurred in relation to another?

### What To Do

1. Examine a stack of last week's newspapers with the dates cut off. The papers may be in the order in which they were read—oldest papers on the bottom, more recent toward the top. Some papers may be out of order.

2. Make a time line of all the front page stories during the past week.

3. *In your Journal* record the difficulties you had and the clues you used to organize your time line.

4. Without the dates on the papers, how do you know the correct order in which the events occurred? What clues did you use to tell if one of your papers was out of order? Record your answers *in your Journal.*

**503**

# PREPARATION

## Concepts Developed

Fossils are the remains or traces of once-living organisms preserved in Earth's crust. Fossil formation is affected by the rate of burial of the organic remains as well as the amount of "hard parts" possessed by the organism. Earth's fossil record is used to study events and organisms of the geologic past.

## Planning the Lesson

Refer to the Chapter Organizer on pages 502A–B.

# 1 MOTIVATE

**Activity** Obtain some fossils for students to compare and contrast. After students have examined the fossils, discuss any similarities and differences. L1

## Find Out!

**What clues do organisms leave that they've been here?**

**Time needed** 25 minutes to prepare and observe the "fossils" and 24 hours for the plaster to set

**Materials** plaster of paris; small, clean, empty cardboard milk cartons; water; fresh leaves, bones, shells, or other organism "parts"; petroleum jelly; scissors; spoon

**Thinking Processes** observing and inferring, recognizing cause and effect, formulating models

**Purpose** To model a fossil

## Teaching the Activity

**Troubleshooting** Make sure students thoroughly cover the objects with petroleum jelly.

**Student Journal** Have students list other "fossil" impres-

---

16-1 **Fossils**

## Traces from the Past

In the opening Explore activity, you used newspapers to model how scientists learn about events in Earth's past. You've probably read about dinosaurs and other previous inhabitants of Earth. You've also probably seen them depicted, not always accurately, in science fiction movies. But how do we know dinosaurs existed? What "newspaper stories" do scientists use as evidence of past life on Earth? The following Find Out activity will help you begin to answer these questions.

### Section Objectives

- Explain the conditions necessary for fossils to form.
- Describe two processes of fossil formation.

### Key Terms

*fossil*

### Find Out! ACTIVITY

## What clues do organisms leave that they've been here?

Earth scientists use many different types of clues to figure out what happened in Earth's past. One type of clue is fossils. But how do fossils form?

### What To Do

1. Cut the top off a small milk carton and add enough plaster of paris to fill it halfway.

2. Mix in enough water to make the plaster smooth.

3. Coat a leaf, shell, bone, or other plant or animal part with petroleum jelly.

4. Press the coated object into the plaster of paris.

5. Allow the plaster to dry at least 24 hours before removing the object.

6. Examine and describe the plaster now. Record your observations *in your Journal.*

### Conclude and Apply

1. How do the object and the plaster impression differ? How are they similar?

2. What kind of details can you see in the plaster impression?

3. What parts of the original object aren't preserved in the impression?

**504**   Chapter 16   Geologic Time

---

sions they have made, such as hand prints in clay or foot prints in mud. L1

### Expected Outcome

The impressions left by the organism part will depend on the pressure applied.

### Conclude and Apply

1. The object has a raised surface, whereas the plaster impression is like a depression. Both are the same size and shape.

2. details of surface texture

3. the other side of the object and the object's color and original material

### ✔ Assessment

**Process** Have students work in pairs or small groups to develop a list of questions they would have about the original organism if they found a fossil like the one they have made. Use the Performance Task Assessment List for Asking Questions in **PAMSS,** p. 19. L1

# How Fossils Form

In the Find Out activity, you made plaster imprints of parts of organisms that were once alive. Such imprints in nature are one kind of fossil. A **fossil** is the remains or trace of an organism that was once alive. A fossil can show us what an organism looked like when it was alive. It also can tell us when, where, and how an organism once lived. In fact, fossils have helped geologists determine approximately when life on Earth began and what types of plants, animals, and other organisms lived in the past.

How are fossils formed? Study **Figure 16-1** to find out.

## Connect to...
### Life Science

Fossils are evidence of life of the past. Look on pages 520-521, choose one of the geologic periods and find out what kind of fossils are commonly found in rocks from that period.

**Figure 16-1**

*Formation of a Dinosaur Fossil*

When an animal dies, scavengers and bacteria eat away the soft tissues of the animal. What parts of its body will be left to fossilize?

The sediment collecting on the dinosaur's remains protect its bones and teeth. Slowly over time, the remains become encased in sediments, and minerals replace them.

Layer on layer of sediment begin to compress deeper layers and rock forms. If shifts in the earth move and lift the rock, how might the dinosaur fossil be affected?

After tens of millions of years, the dinosaur fossil is near the earth's surface again. Erosion may expose the fossil by wearing away the rock in which it is buried. What factors on Earth's surface cause this erosion?

---

# 2 TEACH

**Tying to Previous Knowledge**

Lead students in a discussion of news stories about endangered species or recent visits to a zoo, where they may have seen animals that are listed as endangered. If necessary, define the term *endangered* and differentiate among threatened, endangered, and extinct species. Endangered species are in serious danger of becoming extinct. Threatened species are also in danger of extinction, but they are not as close to extinction as are species classed as endangered.

## Visual Learning

**Figure 16-1** Have students use sequencing skills and illustrations and captions to describe and list in order events that form a dinosaur fossil. **What parts of its body will be left to fossilize?** *bones, teeth, and other hard parts* **If shifts in the earth move and lift the rock, how might the dinosaur fossil be affected?** *The fossil could be moved to the same level as a layer of rock that was put down before or after the dinosaur actually lived.* **What factors on Earth's surface cause this erosion?** *The action of wind, water, glaciers, and gravity can cause erosion.*

## Connect to...
# Life Science

You can extend this activity by having students work together to construct an illustrated, mural-sized geologic time scale for a classroom or hallway bulletin board. Use the Performance Task Assessment List for Bulletin Board in **PAMSS**, p. 59. **L1 COOP LEARN**

---

## Program Resources

**Study Guide,** p. 53
**Laboratory Manual,** pp. 95–96, Volcanic Preservation **L2** pp. 97–98, Carbon Impressions **L2**
**Critical Thinking/Problem Solving,** p. 24, Fossil Clues to the Origin of Life **L2**
**Multicultural Connections,** p. 35, Preserved in Amber **L1**

## ENRICHMENT

**Activity** Have students experiment to determine which types of sediments would best preserve fossils by pressing shells or clean chicken bones into various thick mixtures, such as sand and water; clay and water; and gravel, clay, and water. The ability of a mixture to "preserve" should be judged on the clarity of the imprint made. Clay will hold the best imprint. Gravel will be the least able to hold an imprint. **L1**

## 16-1 Determining Relative Ages of Rock Layers

### Planning the Activity

**Time needed** 20 minutes

**Purpose** To infer a sequence of events from a diagram of the geologic history of an area

**Process Skills** sequencing, observing and inferring, interpreting scientific illustrations, predicting

**Materials** pen or pencil, paper

### Teaching the Activity

Ask students to review what they have learned about determining the relative ages of different rocks. Have them recall the law of superposition and the importance of unconformities.

**Process Reinforcement** As students look at the diagram, help them use the key to identify the materials that make up each layer.

**Possible Procedures** After students write down the sequence of events that they think led to the geologic formation portrayed in the illustration, have them meet in small groups of three or four to compare their accounts. Have them discuss any differences in their accounts and try to develop a scenario that everyone in the group agrees on.

**Student Journal** Have students compare their inferred sequence of events with that of other students and describe what they think they did wrong or why they think their sequence is correct. L1

### Expected Outcome

The lower layers are older except when disturbed by a fault or intrusion.

# Determining Relative Ages of Rock Layers

*You've learned that clues in rock layers can be used to determine the relative ages of the rocks in those layers. In this activity, you will observe and infer the ages of rock layers.*

**Problem**

How do you determine the relative ages of rock layers?

**Materials**

pen or pencil    paper

## What To Do

**1** Study the figure at the bottom of this page. The key will help you interpret the scientific illustration of the different types of rock layers.

■ Granite    ▦ Limestone    ▧ Sandstone    ■ Shale

**A**

**B**

**2** *Infer* the relative ages of the rock layers, unconformities, and the fault in the figure.

**3** *In your Journal,* write down the sequence of events that resulted in the cross-section you see here.

*Volcanic eruptions can rearrange layers of rock, and the lava flow creates new landforms*

## Analyzing

**1.** Where can you observe an unconformity? What is your evidence?

**2.** Determine which layer is incomplete because of the unconformity. Explain your answer.

**3.** Is it possible that there were originally more layers of rock between the top and bottom of the figure than are now shown? Explain your answer.

## Concluding and Applying

**4.** What can you *infer* caused the unconformity?

**5.** Assume that the layers have not been overturned. Based on the figure alone, do you know whether the shale was deposited before or after the fault occurred? Explain.

**6.** ~~Going Further~~ *Predict* what may happen to the top limestone layer above the fault. Explain your prediction.

### Answers to Analyzing/ Concluding and Applying

**1.** between the uppermost sandstone and the lowermost limestone; The wavy nature of the top of the lower limestone suggests that erosion has taken place.

**2.** The lower limestone is "missing" some of its history because erosion removed some of the top of the rock layer. After erosion, the sandstone was deposited. The erosional surface is an unconformity.

**3.** Yes. Unconformities are surfaces of nondeposition or erosion. One or more layers may have been eroded to form the unconformity.

**4.** uplift and erosion.

**5.** Because the shale is beneath layers of rock that have been disturbed by the fault, the shale had to have been deposited before faulting occurred.

**6.** Because this layer is closest to the surface of Earth, it may become exposed to agents of weathering and may be eroded.

### ✔ Assessment

**Performance** Have students create a three-dimensional model of the cross-section portrayed in this activity, using clay, flour and salt dough, corrugated cardboard, styrofoam, or other materials. Use the Performance Task Assessment List for Model in **PAMSS,** p. 51. **L1**

## Program Resources

**Activity Masters,** pp. 67–68, Investigate 16-1

## ENRICHMENT

**Research** Have students write to your state geological survey and request publications on the fossils and rock types found in your area. Then have students work in small groups to prepare short presentations on the geologic history of your area. **COOP LEARN** **P**

# 3 ASSESS

## Check for Understanding

To evaluate students' comprehension of relative dating and unconformities, have them answer the questions in Check Your Understanding. Collect students' diagrams from the Apply question for display in the classroom.

## Reteach

**Activity** Students will make models of unconformities.

Materials needed for this activity are sand, gravel, silt, and small plastic storage containers.

Have students work in groups of three or four. Have each group make two models—one that represents a "complete" hypothetical geologic section and one in which unconformities are present. After the sections are complete, have groups exchange models and describe the unconformities present and the possible causes for them. **COOP LEARN** **L1**

## Extension

Refer students to the diagram of rock layers on page 512. Have students determine when the granite intrusion was formed. Discuss its age relative to the rock layers into which it intruded. Students should be able to conclude that the intrusion is younger than the shales, limestones, sandstone, and unconformity that it cross-cuts. It is impossible from the information given in the figure to determine the age of the fault relative to the intrusion. **L3**

# 4 CLOSE

## Demonstration

Show students photographs of road cuts and have them determine the relative ages of the rocks exposed. **L1**

## Rock Layers and Geologic Time

The Investigate gave you a chance to apply what you've learned about rock layers. It showed you how much you've already learned about rock layers and geologic time. The more people learn, however, the harder it becomes to keep information organised. Eventually, there are so many things we know and want to remember that we have to put all the pieces of information in some sort of order.

As scientists learned more and more about rock layers and geologic time, they too needed some way to organize the information they had gathered. In the next section, you'll learn about a system geologists use to organize the information they've learned about rock layers and geologic time. You'll also look at some of the discoveries they've made concerning these different spans of time.

**Figure 16-7**

**Rocks in Bryce Canyon National Park, show distinct layers that can be used to interpret the geologic history of the area.**

### check your UNDERSTANDING

1. Describe how fossils can be used to determine the ages of rock layers.
2. Describe how the law of superposition is used to determine the relative ages of rock layers.
3. Give two examples of situations that can cause an unconformity.
4. **Apply** A geologist finds a series of rocks. The sandstone contains a fossil that is 400 million years old. The shale contains some fossils that are between 540 and 500 million years old. The limestone contains fossils that are between 500 and 400 million years old. Which rock bed is oldest? Which rock bed is most likely below the others? Explain. Draw an illustration to help you.

### check your UNDERSTANDING

1. By knowing relative ages of the fossils, you can determine relative ages of rock layers that contain them; the rock layers must be approximately the same age as the fossils.
2. According to the law of superposition, older rocks are near the bottom of undistrubed rock layers. The rocks get progressively younger toward the top of the sequence.
3. Periods of erosion and/or nondeposition, as well as earthquakes and volcanoes, can cause unconformities.
4. The shale is oldest because it contains the oldest fossils. The shale is most likely below the limestone and sandstone.

# Early Earth History

## Time Brings Change

At one time, you may have thought that mountains existed forever. But based on what you learned in Chapter 15 and in Section 16-2 of this chapter, you now know that the geological features of Earth change constantly.

Not only the geologic features, but Earth's climates also change continually. At various times in the past, Earth has been both warmer and colder than it is now.

How did changes in Earth's geology and climate affect the plants and animals on Earth? What happened to the dinosaurs pictured in **Figure 16-8**.

We have a geologic record of Earth's past preserved in Earth's rocks. Geologists organized this record by developing a geologic time scale that is similar to a calendar. The following Explore activity will show you how you could organize events in your life by constructing a personal time scale.

### Section Objectives

- Give examples of the different life-forms of Precambrian Time and the Paleozoic Era.
- Describe the major geologic changes of Precambrian time and the Paleozoic Era.
- Explain the subdivisions of the Paleozoic Era.

### Key Terms

*era*
*Precambrian Time*
*Paleozoic Era*
*period*

**Figure 16-8**

Time brings change in the living things on Earth. For instance, you can see the differences in living things during two eras of Earth's history. This change in life forms and in the fossils found in rocks is one of the important pieces of evidence scientists use to help divide geologic time.

Boundary between two time spans

Life in the Age of Dinosaurs

Life in the Age of Mammals

## PREPARATION

### Concepts Developed

The fossil record has allowed scientists to divide geologic time into segments. The geologic time scale is a record of many of the changes and events in Earth's 4.6-billion-year life.

### Planning the Lesson

Refer to the Chapter Organizer on pages 502A–B.

## 1 MOTIVATE

**Activity** Tell students that plants and animals have existed on Earth's surface for only about 10 percent of Earth's existence. Have students prepare a diagram (a pie chart or drawing) that portrays this fact. L1

## 2 TEACH

### Tying to Previous Knowledge

Have students recall from Chapter 15 the tectonic events that occurred to shape and change Earth's surface over geologic time. Ask a volunteer to list suggested events on the chalkboard.

### Visual Learning

**Figure 16-8** Help students practice interpreting scientific illustrations by asking them to describe how time periods and boundaries between time periods are represented in the figure. *Time periods are represented as different landmasses separated by a boundary represented as a body of water.* Emphasize that these animals did not exist at the same time.

### ENRICHMENT

**Activity** Have students interview a grandparent or other senior citizen. Students should ask the person to list the major changes in the world the person has experienced in his or her lifetime. Changes might include inventions, transportation, communications, the environment, advances in medicine, and changes in political and philosophical issues. Students could then develop a time scale of some of these events in this person's "era." Then have students attempt to divide the "era" into "periods" based on certain events or characteristics. LEP L1 P

**INVESTIGATE!**

# Geologic Time Scale

*In this activity, you'll see the types of events scientists use to help construct a time line. You'll only use a very few events, but over time scientists have used thousands!*

### Planning the Activity

**Time needed** 35–40 minutes

**Purpose** To construct a geologic time scale

**Process Skills** measuring in SI, formulating models, comparing and contrasting, sequencing, interpreting data, forming operational definitions

**Materials** meterstick, adding machine paper, scissors, pencil

**Preparation** A roll of butcher paper may be substituted for adding machine tape. Cut rolls into narrower widths of between 15 and 30 cm before distributing, or have students measure and cut the strips themselves.

### Teaching the Activity

**Process Reinforcement** Be sure that students measure carefully to plot the events to scale. Use the Performance Task Assessment List for Scientific Drawing in **PAMSS**, p. 55.

**Troubleshooting** Point out that the apparent clustering of events in recent times is a function of available evidence in the fossil and geologic records and not a change in the rate of geologic or life processes.

**Possible Procedure** You may wish to allow students to work in pairs or small groups to plot events on a single tape or strip of paper. **COOP LEARN**

**Student Journal** Have students record their answers in their journals. **L1**

## Problem

How can you arrange the geologic time scale on a proportional time line?

## Materials

adding machine paper     meterstick     pencil
scissors

### What To Do

**1** Using a scale of 1 mm = 1 000 000 years, measure and cut a piece of adding machine paper equal to the approximate age of Earth (4.6 billion years).

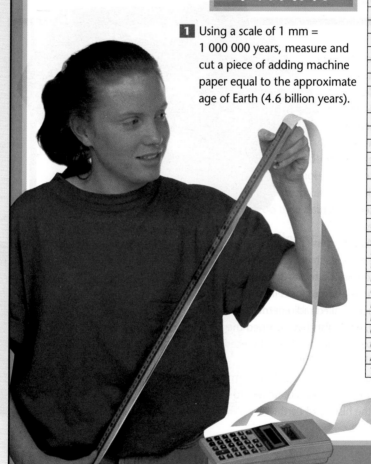

| Earth History Events | Approximate years before present |
|---|---|
| Oldest known rocks | 3900 million |
| Oldest microfossils | 3600 million |
| Early sponges | 600 million |
| Beginning of the Cambrian period (Paleozoic Era) —animals evolve hard parts | 545 million |
| First vertebrates | 510 million |
| Beginning of the Ordovician | 505 million |
| Beginning of the Silurian Period | 438 million |
| First land plants | 435 million |
| Beginning of Devonian Period | 408 million |
| First amphibians | 367 million |
| Beginning of the Mississippian Period | 360 million |
| Appalachian Mountains rise | 330 million |
| Beginning of Pennsylvanian Period | 320 million |
| First reptiles | 315 million |
| Beginning of Permian Period | 286 million |
| Extinction of trilobites —largest mass Extinction in Earth's history | 246 million |
| Beginning of Triassic Period (Mesozoic Era) | 245 million |
| First dinosaurs and mammals | 225 million |
| Beginning of Jurassic Period | 208 million |
| First birds | 150 million |
| Beginning of Cretaceous Period | 144 million |
| Rocky Mountains begin to rise | 80 million |
| Extinction of the dinosaurs | 66 million |
| Beginning of Paleocene Epoch (Cenozoic Era) | 66 million |
| First horses | 50 million |
| First elephants | 40 million |
| Early human ancestors | 5 million |
| Beginning of the most recent ice age | 1 million |
| First modern humans | 500 000 |
| Continental ice retreats from North America | 10 000 |
| Eratosthenes calculates Earth's circumference | 2100 |
| Pompeii destroyed | 1900 |
| Columbus lands in America | 500 |
| U.S. Civil War | 135 |
| Astronauts land on the moon | 25 |
| Today | 0 |

**A**                **B**               **C**

**2** Mark one end of the paper "Today" and the other end "4.6 billion years ago."

**3** Use the chart on previous page to *measure* and mark the places on the paper that represent the time when each era began.

**4** Choose ten other events from the table and mark their position on the time line. You may choose to mark the event with a label. However, you may choose to draw a small picture of the event and attach it to the time line.

*Crinoids, which are related to starfish, were common during the Paleozoic Era.*

## Analyzing

1. Identify the events that were most difficult to plot.

2. *Compare* the length of time humans have existed on Earth with the total geologic time.

3. Approximately what percent of geologic time occurred during the Precambrian? Use this formula.

$$\frac{\text{Precambrian}}{\text{total geologic time}} \times 100\%$$

## Concluding and Applying

4. *Compare* your time line with the geologic time scale in **Figure 16-9** on pages 520-521. Which time scale is easier to read information from? Which time line gives the better sense of the actual age of the world and of the relative time spans of the individual eras, periods, and epochs?

5. Going Further Think of different events you might want to display graphically on your time line. What kinds of illustrations would best present your data effectively?

# Precambrian Time

You've had a chance to get a feel for the vast length of time in Earth's history. Let's begin to explore it at the beginning. The geologic time scale begins with Earth's beginning—about 4.6 billion years ago. The first major division of geologic time was more than 4 billion years long. In fact, this first division, **Precambrian Time,** makes up about 90 percent of Earth's history to date.

However, information about life and events in the Precambrian can be difficult to get. In the past, Precambrian rocks may have been buried deep within Earth where they were

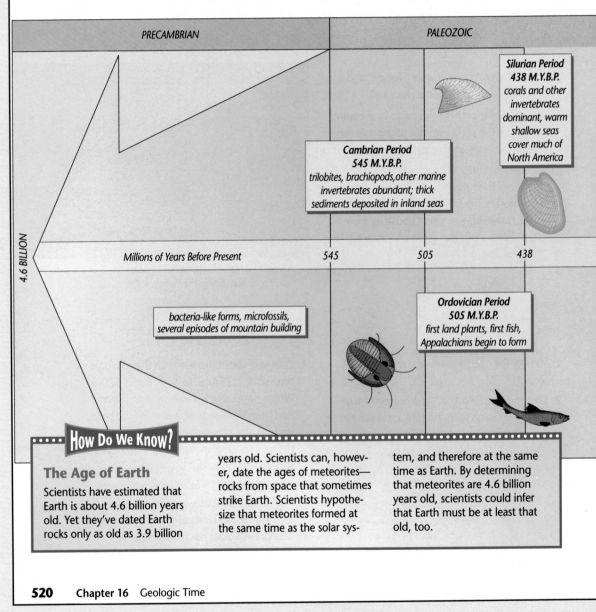

PRECAMBRIAN · PALEOZOIC

4.6 BILLION

Millions of Years Before Present          545          505          438

**Cambrian Period**
**545 M.Y.B.P.**
trilobites, brachiopods, other marine invertebrates abundant; thick sediments deposited in inland seas

**Silurian Period**
**438 M.Y.B.P.**
corals and other invertebrates dominant, warm shallow seas cover much of North America

bacteria-like forms, microfossils, several episodes of mountain building

**Ordovician Period**
**505 M.Y.B.P.**
first land plants, first fish, Appalachians begin to form

## How Do We Know?

**The Age of Earth**
Scientists have estimated that Earth is about 4.6 billion years old. Yet they've dated Earth rocks only as old as 3.9 billion years old. Scientists can, however, date the ages of meteorites—rocks from space that sometimes strike Earth. Scientists hypothesize that meteorites formed at the same time as the solar system, and therefore at the same time as Earth. By determining that meteorites are 4.6 billion years old, scientists could infer that Earth must be at least that old, too.

changed by heat and pressure so that information is lost, even if the rocks are eventually exposed by erosion. Precambrian rocks that were not buried have been exposed to water, wind, and ice longer than younger rocks, and so have been eroded significantly.

The Precambrian rocks we do find have fossils that show that through much of Precambrian Time the dominant form of life on Earth was cyanobacteria. These bacteria altered Earth's ancient atmosphere, which had little oxygen, by adding large amounts of oxygen through photosynthesis. Oxygen made it possible for the soft-bodied animals that evolved near the end of the Precambrian Time to live on Earth.

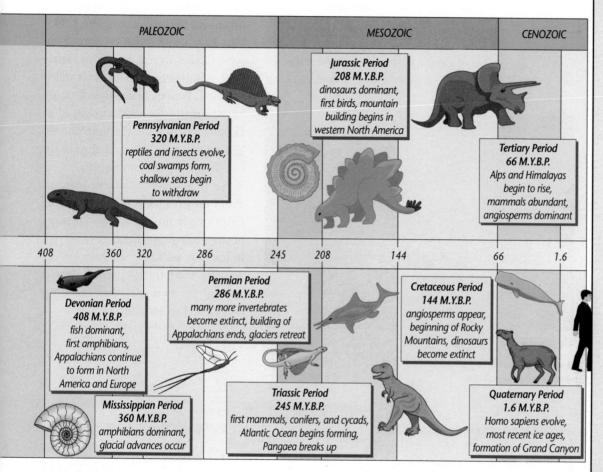

Figure 16-9

This geologic time scale has been adjusted to show all of Earth's history in a small space. Note how each of the eras is divided into periods. The Paleozoic Era has 7 periods:—what are they? The Mesozoic Era has 3 periods, and the Cenozoic Era has 2 periods. Using eras, periods, and smaller time divisions geologists are able to organize the geologic time scale.

## Visual Learning

**Figure 16-9** Help students develop their ability to interpret and analyze information from a scientific illustration by distributing three-by-five cards or pieces of paper. Ask each student to use the figure to make six "flashcards," each with a fact about the appearance or dominance of a life form or the occurrence of a geologic event on the front of the card. The back of the card will have the period and era when the event occurred, along with the number of years before the present. For example, the front of a flashcard that said "fish dominant," would have "Devonian period of the Paleozoic, 408–365 M.Y.B.P." on the back. A card that said "angiosperms appear" on the front would say "Cretaceous Period of the Mesozoic, 144–66 M.Y.B.P." on the back. Have students form small groups of three or four to take turns showing each other their flashcards and learning to match events and their dates. L1 P

**The Paleozoic Era has 7 periods:—What are they?** *Cambrian, Ordovician, Silurian, Devonian, Mississippian, Pennsylvanian, and Permian*

## Across the Curriculum

**Language Arts Connection**

Have students work in pairs to select the name of a period or era and research the meaning or background of the name. In addition to reference books, students may consult local experts at museums or universities for clues as to why the periods and eras have the names they have. Have students present their findings to the class. COOP LEARN L2

## ENRICHMENT

**Discussion** Although little is known about the Precambrian, one of Earth's most significant resources was formed during this time. Precambrian banded iron formations (BIFs) provide much of the iron used in the world today. The BIFs are alternating bands of iron compounds. The green bands contain compounds with little oxygen and the red bands contain compounds with more oxygen. Ask students what these alternating bands indicate about Earth's early atmosphere. *The amount of oxygen available to combine with iron varied from time to time.* L2

**Check for Understanding**

Assign questions 1-2 and the Apply question under Check Your Understanding.

**Reteach**

Have students work in pairs to make tables listing the life-forms present and geologic events that took place during the Precambrian and Paleozoic eras.

COOP LEARN  L1  P

**Extension**

Have students use reference books to identify as many organisms as possible in Figure 16-10. Students should also find out how each organism lived, fed, and whether or not it became extinct.  L3

# 4 CLOSE

Inform students that trilobites once dominated Earth's early seas but they became extinct near the end of the Permian Period. Have students hypothesize why these organisms may have become extinct. One hypothesis suggests that *as the shallow seas began to disappear, trilobites, were not able to adjust to the changing conditions and eventually became extinct.*  L1

## DID YOU KNOW?

Throughout geologic time, the average temperature of Earth has been from 1° to 3°C warmer than current average temperatures.

## The Paleozoic Era

When organisms have hard parts, fossil formation is easier. The appearance of fossils formed by organisms with hard parts marks the beginning of the second major geologic time scale division, the **Paleozoic Era.** The Paleozoic Era began about 545 million years ago. Examine **Figure 16-9**, or look at your time line. How long did the Paleozoic Era last?

Warm shallow seas covered much of Earth's surface during the early part of the Paleozoic Era. Therefore, most life-forms were marine. Examples of Paleozoic life forms include trilobites (distant relatives of the horseshoe crab), brachiopods (animals similar in shape to clams), and crinoids (relatives of starfish, which you can see in the photograph on page 519). The first fish evolved during the Paleozoic Era.

To better classify events and organisms of the Paleozoic Era, geologists have divided this era into seven subdivisions, as you can see in **Figure 16-9.** A subdivision of an era is called a **period.** Periods in geologic time are based on life-forms that existed at approximately the same time and on geologic events, such as mountain building and plate movements.

In this section, you've learned about the organisms that lived during Earth's early history and about some of the geologic events that occurred. In the next section, you'll journey forward in time to the present. You'll look at the two eras that make up middle and recent Earth history.

**Figure 16-10**

A variety of marine organisms existed during the Paleozoic Era.

## check your UNDERSTANDING

1. What life-forms existed during the Paleozoic Era that did not exist during Precambrian Time?
2. What changes in Earth's geology during early Earth history can still be recognized now?
3. **Apply** When were trilobites abundant? What does the presence of trilobite fossils in a rock layer tell you about the age of the rock layer? What do they tell you about the geologic history of the area?

## check your UNDERSTANDING

1. marine invertebrates, fish and land plants, amphibians, reptiles, and insects
2. the Appalachian Mountains
3. 545–505 M.Y.B.P., although trilobites continued to be common throughout most of the Paleozoic. It means the area was covered by seas during the time trilobites existed.

# Chapter 17 Evolution of Life

## TEACHER CLASSROOM RESOURCES

| Student Masters | Teaching Aids |
|---|---|
| **Study Guide,** p. 57<br>**Flex Your Brain,** p. 5<br>**Science Discovery Activities,** 17-1 | *STVS: *Sea Turtle Mystery,* Animals (Disc 5, Side 2) |
| **Study Guide,** p. 58<br>**Making Connections: Across the Curriculum,** p. 37<br>**Activity Masters: Investigate 18-1,** pp. 71–72<br>**Making Connections: Technology & Society,** p. 37<br>**Science Discovery Activities,** 17-2 | **Color Transparency and Master 34,** How Species Are Formed<br>*STVS: *Kit Fox,* Animals (Disc 5, Side 2) |
| **Study Guide,** p. 59<br>**Concept Mapping,** p. 25<br>**Take Home Activities,** p. 27<br>**Multicultural Connections,** p. 37<br>**Multicultural Connections,** p. 38<br>**Critical Thinking/Problem Solving,** p. 25<br>**Making Connections: Integrating Sciences,** p. 37<br>**Activity Masters, Investigate 18-2,** pp. 73–74<br>**Science Discovery Activities,** 17-3 | **Color Transparency and Master 33,** Homologous Structures<br>**Laboratory Manual,** pp. 103-104, DNA and Evolution<br>*STVS: *Brain Development,* Human Biology (Disc 7, Side 1) |

| ASSESSMENT RESOURCES | |
|---|---|
| **Review and Assessment,** pp. 101–106<br>**Performance Assessment,** Ch. 17<br>**PAMSS***<br>**MindJogger Videoquiz**<br>**Alternate Assessment in the Science Classroom**<br>**Computer Test Bank** | **Spanish Resources**<br>**Integrated Science Videodisc**<br>**Cooperative Learning Resource Guide**<br>**Lab and Safety Skills** |

## KEY TO TEACHING STRATEGIES

The following designations will help you decide which activities are appropriate for your students.

**L1** Level 1 activities should be within the ability range of all students.

**L2** Level 2 activities should be within the ability range of the average to above-average student.

**L3** Level 3 activities are designed for the ability range of above-average students.

**LEP** LEP activities should be within the ability range of Limited English Proficiency students.

**COOP LEARN** Cooperative Learning activities are designed for small group work.

**P** These strategies represent student products that can be placed into a best-work portfolio.

## ADDITIONAL MATERIALS

**Software**
*Evolutionary Trail,* Queue.
*Natural Selection,* EME.
*Survival of the Fittest,* EME.
*Tracking Changes in Organisms Through Time: Evolution,* Queue.

**Audiovisual**
*Adaptations of Animals,* video, Coronet/MTI.
*Evolutionary Biology,* video, Coronet/MTI.
*Evolution by Natural Selection,* video, Hawkhill Science.
*The Story of Evolution,* video, Hawkhill Science.
*Theories of Evolution,* video, Educational Activities.

**Laserdisc**
*Evolution: Inquiries into Biology and Earth Science,* Videodiscovery.
*The Living Textbook: Mechanisms of Stability and Change,* Optical Data Corp.
*Science Discovery Middle School,* Videodiscovery.

**Readings**
Erikson, John. *Dying Planet: The Extinction of a Species.* McGraw-Hill.
Lasky, Kathryn. *Traces of Life: The Origins of Humankind.* Morrow Junior Books.
Skelton, Renee. *Charles Darwin and the Theory of Natural Selection.* Barron's Educational Series.

*Performance Assessment in Middle School Science

*Science and Technology Videodisc Series

# Evolution of Life

## THEME DEVELOPMENT

Systems and interactions and stability and change are the themes developed in this chapter. The interaction of living species with the environmental systems in their surroundings leads to the selection of certain variations, or adaptations, in the species. In this process, certain traits remain stable within a species while others change.

## CHAPTER OVERVIEW

Variations improve the chances that some individuals will survive in their environments. Individuals who survive are more likely to produce offspring that have the same variations in traits that helped them survive. This process is called natural selection. Over time, this process allows species to change and evolve into new species. Evidence for the evolution of species can be found in the fossil record, in the structure of cells of ancient and modern organisms, in the chemical makeup of related species, in homologous body parts of different organisms, and in the similar development of vertebrate embryos.

### Tying to Previous Knowledge

Relate the topic of this chapter to the study of genetics in Chapter 14. Genetics provides the mechanism for evolution to work in a population. If traits were not inherited, there could be no evolution as we understand it.

## INTRODUCING THE CHAPTER

Direct students' attention to the chapter opening photographs and lead the class in a discussion of how animals are adapted to their environment.

# CHAPTER 17

# EVOLUTION OF LIFE

### Did you ever wonder...

- ✓ How a new species of animal evolves from a single ancestor?
- ✓ What you can learn from fossils about how and where an organism lived?
- ✓ How similar you might be to other animals or organisms?

Before you begin to study how living things evolve, think about these questions and answer them *in your journal.* When you finish the chapter, compare your journal write-up with what you have learned.

**A** sidewinder loops sideways over the desert sand. A camel munches noisily on a tall desert plant. A lizard perched atop a rock keeps watch like an armored guard. The sidewinder, lizard, camel, and even the desert plant are adapted to the hot, dry, desert climate. Many kinds of snakes exist besides the sidewinder—garter snakes, rattlesnakes, king snakes, and water snakes. These snakes display a variety of shapes, sizes, and colors, and they don't all live in the desert. What accounts for these differences in snakes? What accounts for the huge variety of plants and animals? In this chapter, you will examine a process that offers an explanation—evolution.

*In the activity on the next page, explore the variation in the lengths of pine needles.*

534

### Did you ever wonder...

- A variation occurs in a member of the species and this new trait is passed on to offspring. Eventually, two different species develop, each with its own traits. (p. 544)
- Fossils are remains of life from earlier times. Different fossils can be found in different parts of the world and in different rock layers. (p. 548)
- Humans have DNA structure and physical structures that are similar (homologous) to those of other primates. (p. 556)

### STUDENT JOURNAL

Have students write their responses to the Did You Ever Wonder questions in their journals. After they have read the chapter, students should read their journal entries to see what they have learned about the process and evidence of evolution.

# Technology Connection

# When Were Rock Pictures Painted?

When scientists find a prehistoric site, they want to learn as much as they can about the people who lived there. They study the pots, spears, and other objects that are scattered around such places. They also study the paintings, called pictographs, on cave walls and other rocks.

## Carbon-14 Dating

Carbon-14 dating helps scientists calculate just how long ago a basket was woven or a piece of horn was carved. However, until recently, they could not use carbon-14 dating to learn the age of pictographs. Carbon-14 dating was impossible because of the similarity between the carbon in the paint and the carbon in the limestone rock the paintings are on. Because of this problem, scientists had to use the carbon-14 dates of objects near the paintings and the style of the art to estimate the age of pictographs.

## Rock Dating Updated

A few years ago, some scientists used a limestone chip from an ancient pictograph to invent a way to separate the two kinds of carbon. First, the scientists scraped paint from the rock and put it in a container. Next, they filled the container with a gas that changed the carbon from the paint into carbon dioxide but left the carbon from the rock alone. Finally, they measured the carbon-14 that originated from the carbon dioxide in the paint.

Using the earlier method, the scientists would have estimated the age of the pictograph to be from 2000 to 6000 years old.

Using their new method, the scientists calculated that the paint was 3865 years old, plus or minus 100 years.

### What Do You Think?

What could scientists thousands of years from now learn about our society from studying murals painted on the sides of buildings?

*Radiocarbon dating uses isotopes of carbon to date rocks or fossils. Which isotope of carbon is used in carbon-14 dating?*

## Going Further ⫸

Divide the class into small groups and have them discuss the following questions: **Why do scientists study the past? How does the knowledge acquired about past civilizations affect our world today? What are the practical applications of studying past civilizations?** COOP LEARN

L2

EXPAND
*your view*

# Technology Connection

### Purpose
This excursion gives students a more in-depth understanding of the techniques scientists use to determine the age of fossils and other prehistoric data. It is an extension of section 17-3.

### Content Background
Carbon-14 is a heavy radioactive isotope of carbon used to determine the date of archaeological and geological material. The rate of radioactive decay is sufficiently slow for some elements so that the ages of ancient events can be determined by measuring the amounts of radioactive elements and the decay products present in a given sample. Because the rate of radioactive decay is independent of the physical environment of the sample, materials in all types of environments can be dated.

Prior to the discovery and use of radioactivity, estimates of absolute prehistoric time were impossible. Early geologists could only estimate time based on calculating the relative ages of rocks and events.

### Teaching Strategies
Obtain a photograph of a pictograph from an excavation in France, Egypt, or some other ancient area. Have students interpret the meaning of the pictures and discuss the information that can be inferred about the culture that produced them. L2

### Answers to
**What Do You Think?**

Possible answers: what people looked like; how they dressed; foods and beverages they consumed; their values; their language.

Direct students to look at the illustrations and think about how each main idea that is depicted contributes to the available evidence supporting the theory of evolution.

## Teaching Strategies

Have students create a plant, animal, or other life form from the past or future. Students should give the species a history and describe its fossil record. Finally, students should describe the changes that may have occurred within the species and make a time line showing major physical changes and ecological events that coincided with changes in the species. **COOP LEARN**

## Answers to Questions

**1.** Variations include coat color, eye color, length of fur, length of claws, size of teeth. For domestic cats, coat color, eye color, and length of fur generally are not adaptations, but are artificially selected. Fur length could be adaptive for feral cats living in cold climates. Claw length and tooth size could be adaptive.

**2.** Organisms with variations that are favorable in a given environment survive and reproduce. These variations are inherited by their offspring. Changes in the environment can affect which organisms, with their particular variations, survive. Over time, there may be a shift in the number of organisms with certain variations. This shift is the basis of evolution.

**3.** fossil record, similarities among embryos, homologous structures, similarities in cell structure and chemistry among organisms

### MINDJOGGER VIDEOQUIZ

**Chapter 17** Have students work in groups as they play the videoquiz game to review key chapter concepts.

Review the statements below about the big ideas presented in this chapter, and try to answer the questions. Then, re-read your answers to the Did You Ever Wonder questions at the beginning of the chapter. *In your Journal*, write a paragraph about how your understanding of the big ideas in the chapter has changed.

**①** Variations are differences in inherited traits among members of the same species. Variations that allow an organism to be better suited to its environment are adaptations. *What are some variations in the organisms shown in the photograph? Are these variations adaptations?*

**②** Charles Darwin is credited with developing the theory of natural selection. This theory states that natural selection is a process in which living things that are better adapted to their environment are more likely to survive and reproduce. *How does natural selection lead to evolution?*

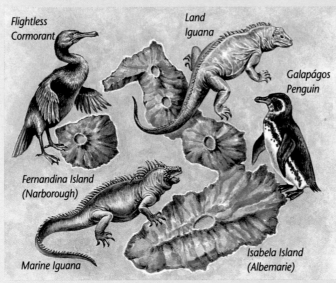

Flightless Cormorant

Land Iguana

Galápagos Penguin

Fernandina Island (Narborough)

Marine Iguana

Isabela Island (Albemarie)

**③** Scientists get evidence for evolution from fossils, the chemical structure of organisms, and the physical structure of cells and body parts. Evolution is an ongoing process. *What are some examples of scientific evidence of evolution?*

## Project

Have students collect pictures of flowers. They can cut photographs from old magazines or seed catalogs. As students progress through the chapter, they should identify characteristics of the flower that are adaptations that attract insect pollinators or that make wind pollination possible. You may wish to have students make a scrapbook of flower adaptations, or to have them arrange their pictures on a bulletin board. [L1]

## Science at Home

Have students observe an animal, such as a cat, dog, or bird. Students should look for ways that the animal's body structure and behavior help it survive. If students observe a pet, have them think about what might happen if the pet had to survive on its own outside. Students may observe defensive or threatening behaviors used for protection against enemies, food-getting behaviors, and structural traits such as coloration or beak shape. [L1]

## Using Key Science Terms

| | |
|---|---|
| evolution | natural selection |
| homologous structure | primate |
| mutation | variation |

*Explain the differences in the terms given below. Then, explain how the terms are related.*

1. mutation, variation
2. natural selection, evolution
3. variation, homologous structure

## Understanding Ideas

*Answer the following questions in your Journal using complete sentences.*

1. What does "survival of the fittest" mean?
2. Why is variation important?
3. How are humans adapted to their environment?
4. How are mutations important in the process of evolution?
5. How do wolves function as selecting agents?

## Developing Skills

*Use your understanding of the concepts developed in this chapter to answer each of the following questions.*

1. **Observing and Inferring** To further examine how a trait can improve or decrease survival potential of a species as in the Find Out activity on page 537, use a large (22 x 28 cm) piece of green paper, green thread, 3 other colors of thread, tweezers (forceps), and a watch with a second hand. Cut 2-cm pieces of each color of thread and scatter them on the paper. Taking turns, use the tweezers and count how many pieces of thread can be picked up in 10 seconds. Which color of thread was picked up most often? Which color was picked up least often? Which is the most beneficial trait for the thread animals?

2. **Concept Mapping** Complete the concept map of evolution. Use the following terms: size, natural selection, adaptations, drought-resistant plant, type of feet, type of beak, variations, color, faster deer.

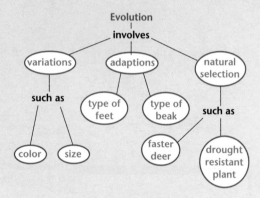

3. **Observing and Inferring** Find variations within a species as you did in the Explore activity on page 535. Collect 25 leaves from different trees of the same species. Measure the leaves and record the measurements. Note the shortest and longest measurements in addition to the most common length of the leaves. What other traits might vary within the species?

4. **Recognizing Cause and Effect** Recalling the findings from the Investigate on page 546, list other examples of animals that rely on color for survival.

most often, with the green color of thread being picked up least often. A green color closest to the green color of the paper would be the most beneficial trait.

2. See reduced student page.

3. Answers will vary but might include width, margin (smooth or serrated), pattern of veins, and depth of color.

4. Answers will vary but might include the snowshoe rabbit, anoles, walking stick, and praying mantis.

## Using Key Science Terms

1. A mutation is a permanent change in a gene or chromosome. A variation is an appearance of an inherited trait or behavior that makes one organism different from the others of the same species. Variations are often caused by mutations.

2. The process by which living things that are better adapted to their environment are more likely to survive and reproduce is known as natural selection. Evolution is the change in hereditary features of a population of organisms over time. Evolution may be the result of natural selection.

3. See the answer question 1 for an explanation of variation. Body parts of different organisms that are similar in origin and structure are called homologous structures. Homologous structures may exhibit variations.

## Understanding Ideas

1. The organism best adapted to its environment will survive to reproduce. The offspring will have inherited traits that make survival in that environment possible.

2. A variation may provide a survival advantage.

3. Humans have the ability to stand upright, opposable thumbs, speech, and binocular vision.

4. Mutations lead to variations. Natural selection acts on variations among individuals, whereby individuals with variations favorable to an environment survive to reproduce. Over time, this process of natural selection may result in evolution.

5. As predators, wolves feed on poorly adapted animals, thereby reducing their numbers.

## Developing Skills

1. The thread that contrasts most with the green paper would probably be picked up the

## Critical Thinking

**1.** Adaptations could be more nasal hairs to filter out pollutants, or lung tissue that resists chemicals in the air.

**2.** The variation in ear sizes and coat color evolved when ancestral foxes were faced with different environmental conditions. Mutations caused the variations and within each environment the individuals that had the variations best adapted for survival were able to reproduce.

**3.** A and C

**4.** Darwin's observations caused him to think about the way each species is adapted to survive.

## Problem Solving

Compare the skeleton to skeletons of similar fossils and living species; date the skeleton to determine its age.

## Connecting Ideas

**1.** These two continents were once connected. The identical fossils probably formed while the continents were connected, or shortly after they separated.

**2.** Farmers can breed cows for producing milk or meat. The characteristics selected by the breeder might not be advantageous for survival, as is the case in natural selection.

**3.** Studies of homologous structures, similar cell structures, natural selection (life science), fossil formation, plate tectonics (earth science), chemistry of DNA, radioactive dating techniques (physical science) all contribute

**4.** The amount of carbon-14 in an object indicates the object's age. Scientists can tell if organisms lived at the same time.

**5.** Some students may say that changes in genes of humans could be used to eliminate genetic diseases. Others may say that society will not permit scientists to alter human genes.

## Critical Thinking

In your Journal, *answer each of the following questions.*

**1.** Use what you've learned about evolution through natural selection to hypothesize how humans might evolve over time if our atmosphere keeps becoming more polluted.

**2.** Study the sketches of the Arctic fox (A), red fox (B), and desert fox (C). How might the variations you observe have evolved?

**3.** Animal A and animal B share 89 percent of the DNA code. Animal A and animal C share 91 percent of the DNA code. Which animals are more closely related?

**4.** Why were Darwin's observations of the Galapagos finches important to his theory of natural selection?

## Problem Solving

*Read the following problem and discuss your answers in a brief paragraph.*

Rumors of a primitive human-like animal have circulated in a remote wilderness area for over 100 years. An individual brings the remains of what appears to be a human-like animal and claims that this is the mysterious beast. The remains consist of some long hairs and a partial skeleton. As a scientist, what could you do to prove that the beast was real or a hoax?

## CONNECTING IDEAS

Discuss each of the following in a brief paragraph.

**1. Theme—Systems and Interactions** Fossils of two almost identical animals that lived millions of years ago were found in both Africa and South America. How do you explain this from what you have learned about evolution and plate tectonics?

**2. Theme—Scale and**

**Structure** Farmers often breed domestic animals and plants to have certain characteristics. Give an example of this type of breeding and tell how it is different from natural selection.

**3. Theme—Systems and Interactions** How do the disciplines of life science, Earth science, and physical science all contribute evidence of evolution?

**4. Technology Connection** Describe the method of carbon-14 dating. How can carbon-14 dating help scientists learn about life in the past?

**5. Science and Society** Scientists have discovered ways to modify the genes of some living organisms. Do you think human evolution will be affected by these techniques?

## ✔ Assessment

**Portfolio** Review the portfolio options that are provided throughout the chapter. Encourage students to select one product that demonstrates their best work for the chapter. Have students explain what they learned and why they chose this example for placement into their portfolio.

Additional portfolio options can be found in the following **Teacher Classroom Resources:**

**Concept Mapping,** p. 15

**Multicultural Connections,** pp. 17-18

**Making Connections: Integrating Sciences,** p. 17

**Making Connections: Across the Curriculum,** p. 17

**Critical Thinking/Problem Solving,** p. 15

**Take Home Activities,** p. 13

**Laboratory Manual,** p. 39-44

**Performance Assessment** P

# CHANGES IN LIFE AND EARTH OVER TIME

In this unit, you learned that the face of Earth and the living things on it are very different today than they were in the distant past. In geologic time, measured in millions of years, continents have moved, mountains have appeared and disappeared, and many life forms have flourished and then become extinct. Also, you explored in depth the processes that produce the genetic diversity on which natural selection works.

Try the exercises and activity that follow—they will challenge you to use and apply some of the ideas you learned in this unit.

## CONNECTING IDEAS

1. Coal deposits are located in some very cold regions of the world near the Arctic Circle. Relate the appearance of coal in these areas to the climate that must have existed when the coal beds started forming and why the coal appears in these areas today.

2. Suppose that conditions in an area change so much that certain easily chewed and digested plants died off over a short period of time. The only plants remaining as a supply of food had extremely tough cell walls that could be easily chewed. What characteristics would better prepare one organism to survive this sudden change in the environment better than another?

## Exploring Further

### ACTIVITY

### What would you say to Darwin if he were alive today?

#### What To Do

1. *In your Journal,* write a letter to Charles Darwin. Provide him with evidence that he was not aware of that would support his ideas on evolution and natural selection.

2. Using what you know about heredity, evolution, and natural selection, how would you answer someone who claims that evolution could not occur because we have never found an organism that is half of one species and half of another?

## Exploring Further

### What would you say to Darwin if he were alive today?

**Purpose** To identify information that supports the theory of natural selection.

#### Background Information

Although Darwin and Mendel lived at the same time, Darwin never learned of Mendel's work in the field of genetics. Information on genetics would have helped Darwin explain why offspring of well adapted parents were usually also well adapted.

#### Answers to Questions

**2.** Students might explain to the critic that the evolution of a species is a complex process involving "side branches" and some "dead ends." Thus, one cannot expect to find fossil evidence of a creature that is exactly half of one species and half of another.

## Changes in Life and Earth Over Time

### THEME DEVELOPMENT

In this unit, students learned that chemical reactions that occur beneath Earth's surface produce energy. When released, this energy can create mountain ranges, volcanoes, and other changes in land masses. By studying the scale and structure of genes and DNA, students better understand the changes that occur in organisms over time.

### Connections to Other Units

The concepts of reproduction and heredity related to the information in Unit 3 on the relationship of chemicals to life. Unit 4 developed these concepts further by relating them to changes that occur within Earth.

### Connecting Ideas
#### Answers

**1.** Coal beds are the remains of ancient tropical forests. Since the Arctic is no longer a tropical region, land masses that were originally in a tropical climate moved to the Arctic.

**2.** The types of traits that may be useful adaptations in this situation include strong teeth, a muscular stomach for grinding, a longer intestinal tract, and intestinal bacteria able to digest tough-shelled foods.

### ✔ Assessment

Have students take the role of Darwin, and use the information they just provided to defend the theory of natural selection. The defense can take the form of a letter or a speech. Use the appropriate Performance Task Assessment List from **PAMSS.** L1

# Observing the World Around You

## UNIT OVERVIEW

## UNIT FOCUS

In Unit 5, students will see how changes in elements occur because of fission and fusion reactions. They will see how fusion reactions produce the energy we receive from the sun each day. Students will also study how the solar system and the universe itself have changed over time. They will learn that the structure of our solar system is related to the energy produced by fusion and the movement of molecules.

## THEME DEVELOPMENT

The main themes developed in Unit 5 are energy, and scale and structure. Nuclear fusion releases energy in stars and the sun. Seeing the universe from the smallest atom to the solar system and galaxies gives students a perspective on their scale and structure.

## Connections to Other Units

Chapter 18, *Fission and Fusion*, relates to information in Unit 2 on the structure of the atom. Information on the development of the universe extends students' study of changes in Earth over time in Unit 4.

### VIDEODISC

Use the **Integrated Science Videodisc** to reinforce and enhance concepts in this unit.

# observing THE WORLD around you

As you study planets, stars, and galaxies, you'll see how changes in elements occur because of fission and fusion reactions. You will see how fusion reactions produce the energy you receive from the sun each day. You will also study how the solar system and the universe itself have changed over time. You will learn that the structure of our solar system is related to the energy produced by fusion and the movement of molecules you learned about earlier.

564

a

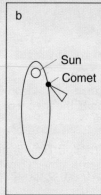

b

Sun
Comet

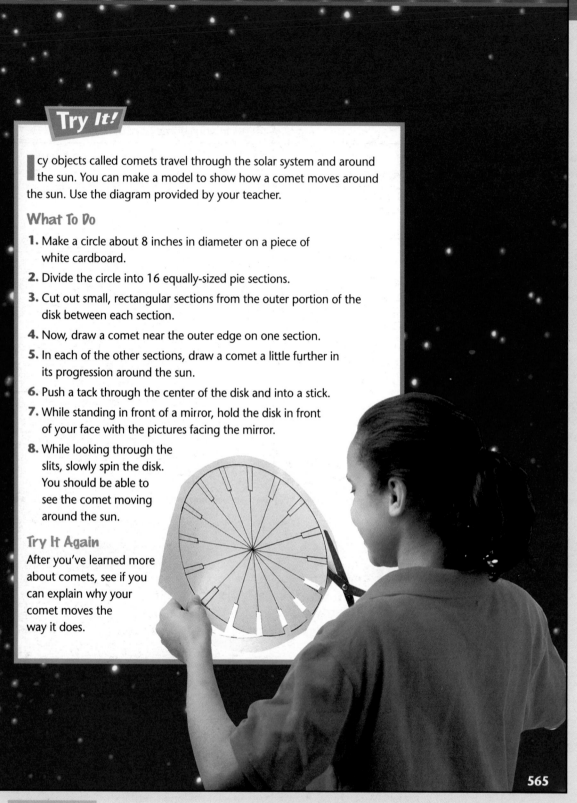

## Try It!

Icy objects called comets travel through the solar system and around the sun. You can make a model to show how a comet moves around the sun. Use the diagram provided by your teacher.

### What To Do

1. Make a circle about 8 inches in diameter on a piece of white cardboard.

2. Divide the circle into 16 equally-sized pie sections.

3. Cut out small, rectangular sections from the outer portion of the disk between each section.

4. Now, draw a comet near the outer edge on one section.

5. In each of the other sections, draw a comet a little further in its progression around the sun.

6. Push a tack through the center of the disk and into a stick.

7. While standing in front of a mirror, hold the disk in front of your face with the pictures facing the mirror.

8. While looking through the slits, slowly spin the disk. You should be able to see the comet moving around the sun.

### Try It Again

After you've learned more about comets, see if you can explain why your comet moves the way it does.

565

## GETTING STARTED

**Discussion** Some questions you may want to ask your students are

**1. How do fission reactions differ from fusion reactions?** *Students may easily mix up these two similar sounding reactions. Fission is splitting of nuclei. Fusion is joining nuclei together.*

**2. How do large, gaseous planets like Jupiter differ from smaller planets like Earth?** *Students may name some ways these planets differ: in size, composition, and position in relation to sun in solar system.*

The answers to these questions will help you establish any misconceptions that students may have.

## Try It!

**Purpose**   To model the movement of a comet.

### Background Information

Students will be using a phenakistoscope to simulate the movement of a comet around the sun. A phenakistoscope is a pinwheel-like device that creates the illusion of a motion picture. Each section of the device will show the sun and an elliptical orbit around it. These elements of the drawings are always the same. What varies from one drawing to the next is the position of the comet and the length of its tail. In the 16 drawings, the comet should travel through one complete orbit. A partially completed phenakistoscope and a sample orbit are shown to the left.

**Materials**   white cardboard, scissors, tack, stick, large mirror

### ✔ Assessment

**Oral**   Ask students to suggest other patterns in nature that could be demonstrated with a phenakistoscope. Help students focus their suggestions on phenomena related to astronomy, such as phases of the moon, the path of the moon or sun across the sky, or the changes that can be seen during an eclipse. [L1]

# Chapter Organizer

| SECTION | OBJECTIVES | ACTIVITIES |
|---|---|---|
| **Chapter Opener** | | **Explore!** Is there a use for radioactive elements in your home? p. 567 |
| **18-1 Radioactivity, Natural and Artificial** (3 days) | 1. **Describe** an artificial transmutation.<br>2. **Compare** artificial and natural transmutations. | **Explore!** How do protons stick together in an atom's nucleus? p. 568<br>**Investigate 18-1:** Measuring Half-Life, pp. 572–573 |
| **18-2 Fission** (3 days) | 1. **Describe** nuclear fission.<br>2. **Outline** a nuclear fission reaction.<br>3. **Model** a chain reaction. | **Skillbulider:** Comparing and contrasting, p. 580<br>**Find Out!** What is a chain reaction? p. 582 |
| **18-3 Fusion** (3 days) | 1. **Explain** nuclear fusion.<br>2. **Distinguish** between nuclear fusion and nuclear fission.<br>3. **Outline** a nuclear fusion reaction. | **Investigate 18-2:** Nuclear Fusion, pp. 586–587 |

## EXPAND your view

**Life Science Connection** Has Your Food Been Irradiated? pp. 574–575
**A Closer Look** Nuclear Reactors, pp. 582–583

**How It Works** Healing Radiation, p. 589
**Science and Society** No Nuclear Dumping, pp. 590–591
**Technology Connection** Fusion Reactors, p. 592

## ACTIVITY MATERIALS

| EXPLORE! | INVESTIGATE! | FIND OUT! |
|---|---|---|
| **Page 567**<br>smoke detector<br>**Page 568***<br>10 BB pellets, cookie tray, salad oil | **Pages 572–573***<br>100 pennies, container with cover, graph paper, colored pencils<br>**Pages 586–587***<br>6 balls of green clay, 6 balls of white clay | **Page 582***<br>no special materials required |

*For adequate development of the concepts presented, we recommend that students do the activities with an asterisk.

# Chapter 18 Fission and Fusion

## TEACHER CLASSROOM RESOURCES

| Student Masters | Teaching Aids |
|---|---|
| **Study Guide,** p. 60<br>**Concept Mapping,** p. 26<br>**Multicultural Connections,** p. 39<br>**Activity Masters,** Investigate 18-1, pp. 75–76<br>**Science Discovery Activities,** 18-1, 18-2 | **Laboratory Manual,** pp. 105–108, The Effect of Radiation on Seeds<br>**Laboratory Manual,** pp. 109–112, Radioactive Decay—A Simulation<br>**\*STVS:** *Dating by Thermoluminescence,* Chemistry (Disc 2, Side 2) |
| **Study Guide,** p. 61<br>**Take Home Activities,** p. 29<br>**Flex Your Brain,** p. 5<br>**Multicultural Connections,** p. 40<br>**Making Connections: Integrating Sciences,** p. 39<br>**Making Connections: Technology & Society,** p. 39<br>**Science Discovery Activities,** 18-3 | **Color Transparency and Master 35,** Controlled Fission<br>**Color Transparency and Master 36,** Nuclear Reactor<br>**\*STVS:** *Neutron Activation Analysis of Paintings,* Chemistry (Disc 2, Side 2) |
| **Study Guide,** p. 62<br>**Critical Thinking/Problem Solving,** p. 26<br>**Making Connections: Across the Curriculum,** p. 39<br>**Activity Masters,** Investigate 18-2, pp. 77–78 | **\*STVS:** *Micro Machine Shop,* Physics (Disc 1, Side 2) |

## ASSESSMENT RESOURCES

**Review and Assessment,** pp. 107–112
**Performance Assessment,** Ch. 18
**PAMSS\***
**MindJogger Videoquiz**
**Alternate Assessment in the Science Classroom**
**Computer Test Bank**

**Spanish Resources**
**Cooperative Learning Resource Guide**
**Lab and Safety Skills**
**Integrated Science Videodisc**

## KEY TO TEACHING STRATEGIES

The following designations will help you decide which activities are appropriate for your students.

**L1** Level 1 activities should be within the ability range of all students.

**L2** Level 2 activities should be within the ability range of the average to above-average student.

**L3** Level 3 activities are designed for the ability range of above-average students.

**LEP** LEP activities should be within the ability range of Limited English Proficiency students.

**COOP LEARN** Cooperative Learning activities are designed for small group work.

**P** These strategies represent student products that can be placed into a best-work portfolio.

## ADDITIONAL MATERIALS

**Software**
*Radioactivity,* J&S Software.

**Audiovisual**
*Atoms,* Educational Activities, Inc.
*Cold Fusion,* video, NOVA (PBS).
*Energy from the Atom—Nuclear Power,* video, United Learning.
*Fusion: The Energy Promise,* video, NOVA (PBS).
*Matter Into Energy* (Revised) *video,* Coronet/MTI.
*Nuclear Power, video,* Hawkhill Science.
*Radiation,* video, Hawkhill Science.
*Radiation & Environment,* video, EME.

*"Time Out" For Science: Benefits and Uses of Nuclear Technology,* video, United Learning.

**Laserdisc**
*Energy at Work,* Churchill Media.
*Physics at Work,* Videodiscovery.

*\*Performance Assessment in Middle School Science

*\*Science and Technology Videodisc Series

# Fission and Fusion

## THEME DEVELOPMENT

The themes supported by this chapter are energy and stability and change. Students learn how certain unstable atoms change, or transmute, into other atoms, which may or may not be stable. Students further learn that such transmutations are accompanied by the release of energy, which under certain conditions can be harnessed for use by people.

## CHAPTER OVERVIEW

In this chapter, students will define the two kinds of nuclear reaction, fission and fusion. Students will investigate natural and artificial transmutation, and infer that transmutation is governed by the stability or instability of atomic nuclei. They will apply the concepts of transmutation and chain reaction to develop an understanding of how nuclear fission can produce energy. Students will compare and contrast fission and fusion and consider the effects of both on human life and the environment.

## Tying to Previous Knowledge

Ask students to recall what they learned about the atom in Chapter 4. Ask them to identify and describe the three kinds of subatomic particles—proton, neutron, and electron. Then lead students to discuss why scientists would want to split the atom, one considered the smallest unit of matter. Help students relate this question to their daily lives by asking them what they have heard or read in the news about limited and diminishing energy resources.

# FISSION AND FUSION

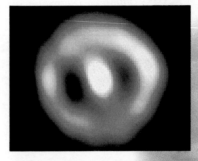

**Y**ou're outdoors. The sun is providing you with the light and warmth that makes life possible, thanks to nuclear reactions. On your way to school, you pass by a woman out jogging. She could have died a year ago from thyroid cancer, but she's alive today thanks to medical breakthroughs made possible by nuclear science.

Just what are nuclear reactions? How and why will they play an important role in your life and in the decisions you will be asked to make? In this chapter you'll learn about this important source of energy.

▶ **In the Explore activity on the next page, find out where you may have some radioactive material in your home.**

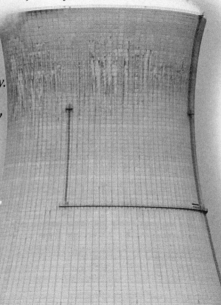

### Did you ever wonder...

✓ How all the positive particles stay in an atom's nucleus even though they repel each other?

✓ What happens to naturally occuring radioactive elements?

✓ What happens in a nuclear reaction?

Before you begin your study of fission and fusion, think about these questions and answer them in your Journal. When you have finished the chapter, compare your Journal write-up with what you have learned.

### Did you ever wonder...

• A strong nuclear force holds neutrons to protons, protons to protons, and neutrons to neutrons. (p. 569)

• The nucleus spontaneously expels a particle to become more stable. (p. 569)

• In a nuclear reaction, large nuclei are split (fission) or small nuclei are joined (fusion). In either case, new elements are formed. (pp. 580, 585)

### STUDENT JOURNAL

Have students write their responses to the Did You Ever Wonder questions in their journals. After they have read the chapter, students should read their journal entries again to see what they have learned about fission and fusion.

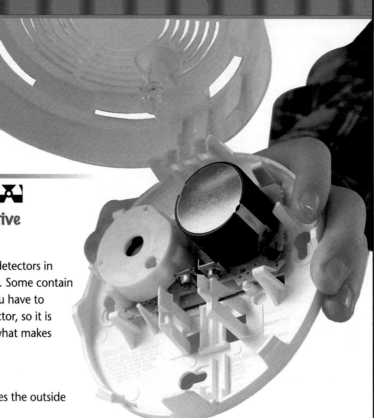

## Explore! ACTIVITY

### Is there a use for radioactive elements in your home?

You have probably seen smoke detectors in your home and other buildings. Some contain radioactive material. Periodically, you have to replace the battery in a smoke detector, so it is possible to take one apart and see what makes it work.

### What To Do

1. Watch while your teacher removes the outside cover of a smoke detector.

2. Look for a small metal cover or cage. **CAUTION:** *Don't take this metal cage apart!*

3. Most home smoke detectors contain information about the radioactive material as shown in the photo. The symbol indicates an area where radioactive materials are located. Look for this symbol inside the smoke detector.

4. Describe it *in your Journal*. What does it say?

**567**

### INTRODUCING THE CHAPTER
Have students identify the subjects of the photographs. *a nuclear reactor and a super nova.* Then ask what they have in common. *Both involve nuclear reactions.*

## Explore!

### Is there a use for radioactive elements in your home?

**Time needed** 10 minutes

**Materials** non-electronic smoke detector

**Thinking Process** observing

**Purpose** To observe that radioactive elements are used in the home.

### Teaching the Activity

**Troubleshooting** Some smoke detectors are electronic and do not contain radioactive materials.

**Safety** Warn students not to tamper with the inside of the smoke detector. An adult should help students.

**Student Journal** Have students draw in their journals the symbol they see. L1

### Expected Outcomes
Students will observe that a smoke detector contains radioactive material.

### Answers to Questions
Detectors that contain the radioactive element amerecium have the symbol for radiation.

### ✔ Assessment

**Process** Ask students how important it is to consider radioactive elements and how well shielded those elements are when purchasing smoke detectors. Use the Performance Task Assessment List for Consumer Decision Making Study in **PAMSS**, p. 43. L1

## ASSESSMENT PLANNER

### PORTFOLIO
Refer to page 595 for suggested items that students might select for their portfolios.

### PERFORMANCE ASSESSMENT
Process, pp. 567, 573, 587
Skillbuilder, p. 580
Explore! Activities, pp. 567, 568
Find Out! Activity, p. 582
Investigate, pp. 572–573, 586–587

### CONTENT ASSESSMENT
Check Your Understanding, pp. 578, 584, 588
Reviewing Main Ideas, p. 593
Chapter Review, pp. 594–595

### GROUP ASSESSMENT
Opportunities for group assessment occur with Cooperative Learning Strategies.

### Concepts Developed

This section describes how nuclear decay causes one element to change into another element. Students will distinguish the natural transmutation of unstable elements from the artificial transmutation of stable elements and the manufacture of radioactive isotopes.

### Planning the Lesson

Refer to the Chapter Organizer on pages 566A-B.

## 1 MOTIVATE

**Activity** Have students model using a Geiger counter. Hide several small jars of coins representing uranium ore around the room. Tell four students where they are. These students will act as Geiger counters. Divide the class into four teams. Have each team search for the jars using their "Geiger counter." The "Geiger counters" should signal if students are close or far by making fast or slow clicking noises. L1

## Explore!

### How do protons stick together in an atom's nucleus?

**Time needed** 10 minutes

**Materials** 10 BB pellets, cookie tray, salad oil

**Thinking Processes** Observing and inferring, comparing and contrasting, recognizing cause and effect, modeling, forming operational definitions

**Purpose** To observe and interpret a model of the force that holds particles together.

### Teaching the Activity

**Student Journal** Students may wish to include drawings. L1 LEP

# Radioactivity, Natural and Artificial

### Section Objectives
- Describe an artificial transmutation.
- Compare artificial and natural transmutations.

### Key Terms
*transmutation*
*artificial*
  *transmutation*

## Getting to the Source of Nuclear Energy

When you talk about nuclear energy, radioactivity, and nuclear reactions, you are talking about changes that are taking place in the nucleus of an atom. You are going to take a closer look at the forces inside the nucleus of an atom. You will see that changes may occur in the nucleus naturally, but that humans can also cause changes.

## Explore! ACTIVITY

### How do protons stick together in an atom's nucleus?

**What To Do**

1. Group ten BB pellets in a pile on a tray.

2. Roll one BB pellet along the tray toward the pile. What happens to the BBs in the pile when they are struck?

3. Now lightly coat the ten BB pellets with salad oil.

4. Regroup the BB pellets and roll a pellet towards the pile. Observe the behavior of the BBs when they are struck.

5. Did the pile of BBs in steps 2 and 4 break apart in the same way?

6. Why did they behave differently?

In the Explore activity, you observed a model for the behavior of nuclear particles. The uncoated BBs rolled apart. The BBs coated with oil behave in a similar manner to protons in the nuclei of atoms. A force, modeled by the oil, seems to be holding them together.

### Expected Outcomes

Students will observe that uncoated pellets roll apart and the coated pellets clump together.

### Answers to Questions

2. They scatter.

5. no

6. Something (the oil) held the pellets in step 4 together.

### ✔ Assessment

**Performance** Have students place ten uncoated BB pellets at one end of a tray and ten coated pellets at the other end. Students should shake the tray and observe what happens. Ask which group of pellets is more like a nucleus. *The coated pellets.* Use the Performance Task Assessment List for Making Observations and Inferences in **PAMSS**, p. 17. L1

An atomic nucleus contains positively charged protons. Just like any objects with similar electric charge, the protons repel one another. Yet the protons in a nucleus are very close to each other. Some force must be holding the protons together.

There are neutrons in the nucleus as well. Neutrons aren't charged so they don't repel protons. Neutrons don't attract protons either. Neutrons do, however, help to hold the nucleus together. Protons and neutrons share a force that holds the nucleus together. It's an extremely strong force that holds neutrons to protons, protons to neutrons, and neutrons to neutrons. Although this force is very strong it works only over extremely short distances. It's called the strong nuclear force. As shown in **Figure 18-2**, the protons and neutrons must be nearly touching or the strong force has no effect. As a result, this strong force can't hold every nucleus together.

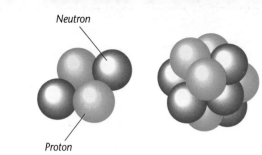

**Figure 18-1**

The atomic nucleus of hydrogen is the simplest and consists of one positively charged proton. The nucleus of helium contains two protons and two neutrons. The force that holds protons and neutrons together is called the strong nuclear force. A more massive element needs more neutrons so that the strong force can hold the nucleus together. If there are not enough neutrons, the nucleus will become unstable and decay. The heaviest elements are always unstable. Uranium has 92 protons. Is uranium stable or unstable?

The nucleus of a lighter element stays together if it has roughly equal numbers of protons and neutrons. For example, the most common isotopes of He, C, N, and O have exactly as many neutrons as protons. In a more massive element, more neutrons are needed so that the strong force can balance the repulsion between the protons. If there are too few or too many neutrons, the nucleus is unstable. The nucleus will expel a particle to become more stable. When this happens, we say that the element is radioactive and it decays. Some elements of light and medium mass are radioactive. Unlike the lighter elements, elements with more than 83 protons are always unstable, whatever the number of neutrons.

**Figure 18-2**

Because both of these protons have a positive charge, the electric force causes them to repel each other. However, when they are very close together, the strong nuclear force overcomes the force of repulsion. As a result, the protons and neutrons are held together in the nucleus. What would happen to the protons if the neutrons were removed from the nucleus?

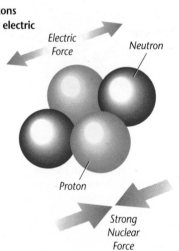

Electric Force

Neutron

Proton

Strong Nuclear Force

18-1  Radioactivity, Natural and Artificial  **569**

---

## 2 TEACH

**Tying to Previous Knowledge**

Remind students of their study of atomic structure. They learned that chemical reactions depend mostly on electron configurations. In this section students will see that nuclear reactions involve particles in the nucleus, protons and neutrons.

**Theme Connection** One theme this section supports is stability and change. For elements to remain stable, a certain ratio of protons to neutrons must exist. As students study this page, they will see what happens if such a ratio does not exist. The element will lose one or more protons and/or neutrons. This causes a change in the element to a more stable element.

### Visual Learning

**Figures 18-1 and 18-2**
**Is uranium stable or unstable?** *unstable* Allow students to make a model of the forces illustrated in Figure 18-2. Have students divide into cooperative groups, and provide each group with two magnets. Have students touch the magnets together, like pole to like, so that the magnets repel when released. Ask students to identify which of the forces in Figure 18-2 behaves like the magnets. *The electric force of the protons.* Now have students force the magnets together, the force of their hands overcoming the magnets' force of repulsion. Ask students to relate the force exerted by their hands on the magnets to one of the forces in Figure 18-2. *The strong nuclear force.* **What would happen to the protons if the neutrons were removed from the nucleus?** *The protons would probably fly apart.* L1

# Decay Transmutes Elements

In the first Explore activity, you looked inside a smoke detector. The most common radioactive element used in smoke detectors is americium-241, element number 95.

### ■ Transmutation—Ejecting Protons

Americium decays by expelling an alpha particle. An alpha particle is helium nucleus without its electrons. It contains two protons and two neutrons. An element is defined by its atomic number, the number of protons in its nucleus. Americium has 95. If an americium atom loses two pro-

tons, it's not americium anymore. As shown in **Figure 18-3**, it becomes an atom with 93 protons—an atom of the element neptunium. When a nucleus emits an alpha particle, it loses two protons, so it becomes a lighter element two numbers lower on the periodic table. Because the alpha particle has a mass number of 4, the nucleus must also lose two neutrons, and the new element has a mass number that is 4 smaller than the original. When an atom changes from one element to another by emitting particles, or decaying, it's called **transmutation**.

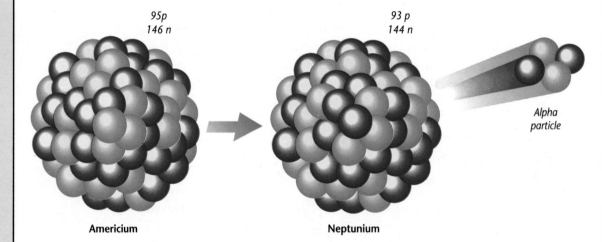

95p
146 n

93 p
144 n

Alpha particle

Americium

Neptunium

**Figure 18-3**

Americium has 95 protons, so it is an unstable element. When an atom of americium decays, it ejects an alpha particle. An alpha particle is a helium nucleus, which consists of two protons and two neutrons. After emitting an alpha particle, an atom of americium is left with 93 protons. It has changed into an atom of the element neptunium. Will the atom of neptunium itself decay?

**570** Chapter 18 Fission and Fusion

**Figure 18-4**

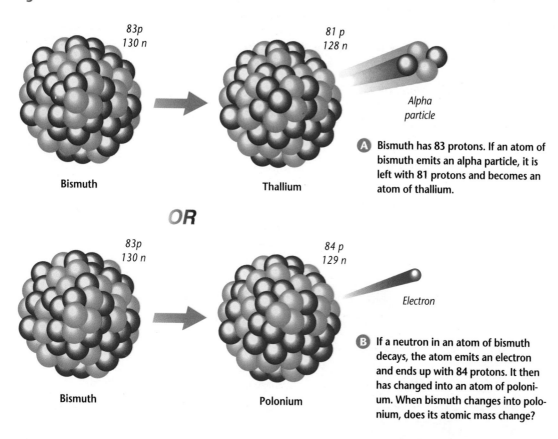

83p
130 n

Bismuth

81 p
128 n

Thallium

*Alpha particle*

**Ⓐ** Bismuth has 83 protons. If an atom of bismuth emits an alpha particle, it is left with 81 protons and becomes an atom of thallium.

**OR**

83p
130 n

Bismuth

84 p
129 n

Polonium

*Electron*

**Ⓑ** If a neutron in an atom of bismuth decays, the atom emits an electron and ends up with 84 protons. It then has changed into an atom of polonium. When bismuth changes into polonium, does its atomic mass change?

### ■ Transmutation—Ejecting Electrons

Transmutation also occurs when a nucleus emits an electron. But there are no electrons in a nucleus. How can a nucleus emit a particle it doesn't have? If there are too many neutrons in a nucleus, a neutron can become unstable. This neutron decays into an electron and a proton. The nucleus now has one more proton. The atom turns into an atom of an element one number higher on the periodic table. Because the mass of the electron is so small, the atomic mass of the element doesn't change much. For example, an

isotope of bismuth (83) can either emit an alpha particle to become thallium (81), or decay a neutron and emit an electron to become polonium (84). These alternatives are illustrated in **Figure 18-4.**

The spontaneous radioactive decay that occurs in certain isotopes of all elements is an example of natural transmutation. The time it takes for a given mass of an element to transmute can be determined. A time interval known as half-life measures this length or period of time. In the next Investigate you will make a model of half life.

---

## Visual Learning

**Figure 18-4** Have students describe and explain the transmutation of bismuth-213 to thalium-209 and polonium-213. They may wish to draw a diagram in addition to consulting the periodic table. **When bismuth changes to polonium, does its atomic mass change?** *no* ⌷L2⌷

**Activity** Give students an opportunity to predict the stability of an atom.

Material needed is a periodic table of the elements.

Have students locate (1) aluminum, (2) carbon, (3) gold, (4) krypton, (5) nickel, (6) plutonium, (7) radon, and (8) zirconium on the periodic table. Ask students to arrange the elements in order of their number of protons. Then ask which elements are probably stable or unstable. *The order should be 2, 1, 5, 4, 8, 3, 7, 6. The unstable elements are radon and plutonium. Ask students to generalize from this list. Elements with high atomic numbers are more likely to be unstable than elements with low atomic numbers.* ⌷L1⌷

## Planning the Activity

**Time needed** 30 minutes

**Purpose** To make and analyze a model that demonstrates the regularity of half-life decay.

**Process Skills** making and using tables, observing and inferring, making models, making and using graphs, predicting, sampling and estimating, comparing and contrasting

**Materials** 100 pennies, a container with a cover, graph paper, colored pencils

## Teaching the Activity

**Troubleshooting** Guide students to determine which variable goes on which axis of their graph, and the proper range for each.

**Discussion** Help students to recognize probability by asking if it is possible to predict whether any one penny will "decay" in a given throw. *No; it is only possible to predict that approximately half of the pennies will "decay."*

**Process Reinforcement** Have students reinforce their observations by repeating the experiment with a different number of pennies. Discuss how or whether the results of the second trial differ from the first. Guide students to recognize that the decay proceeds in a regular fashion for a sample of any size.

**Possible Hypotheses** Students may hypothesize that, while it is not possible to know which nuclei will decay during one half-life, it is possible to predict that approximately half of them will.

**Possible Procedures** Help students to sequence their observations by having them make a series of diagrams to show what they have observed on one of the trials. Students should make one diagram for each of the throws.

**Student Journal** Have students make their data tables and draw their graphs in their journals. L1

---

# Measuring Half Life

*All radioactive materials decay at a steady rate. The rate differs from element to element and from isotope to isotope. Radioactive decay is measured in terms of half-life.*

### Problem
How can coin tossing simulate radioactive decay?

### Materials
100 pennies            container with cover
graph paper            colored pencils

## What To Do

1. *In your Journal,* prepare a data table to record the shake number and the number of heads.

2. Place the 100 coins in the container and cover it. Shake for serveral seconds.

3. Gently pour the coins in a single layer on a desk top. Separate the coins into piles with heads up and tails up.

4. Count the coins with heads up and record the number in the data table.

5. Put only the coins with heads up back into the container. Shake the container.

**572** Chapter 18 Fission and Fusion

---

## Program Resources

**Activity Masters,** pp. 75–76, Investigate 18-1

**Science Discovery Activities,** 18-2, Here Today, Gone Tomorrow?

**A**  **B**  **C**

**6** Repeat steps 3, 4, and 5 until no more coins remain.

**7** *Predict* the number of coins that will be heads up after each shake. *Make a graph* of the shake number on the horizontal axis versus the number of heads on the vertical axis.

**8** On the same axis, with a different colored pencil, plot your actual results.

**9** Work with other groups in your class to *calculate* the class number of heads remaining for each shake number. Plot a graph of these numbers in the same way as you plotted your own results.

**10** Plot the predicted class results on the same graph.

## Analyzing

**1.** Each penny represents one atom. Are the atoms represented stable or unstable?

**2.** How many shakes represent one half-life?

**3.** Are there still unstable atoms after one half-life? After two or more half-lives?

## Concluding and Applying

**4.** *Compare* the number of heads actually remaining to the predicted numbers on your graphs for both your results and for the class results. For which set of data were the actual results closer to the predicted results? Why do you think this was so?

**5.** **Going Further** *Infer* whether a radioactive sample is safe once it is one half-life old. Justify your answer.

**Data table (Sample data)**

| Shake Number | Number of Heads |
|:---:|:---:|
| 1 | 60 |
| 2 | 28 |
| 3 | 13 |
| 4 | 5 |
| 5 | 3 |
| 6 | 2 |
| 7 | 1 |
| 8 | 1 |
| 9 | 0 |

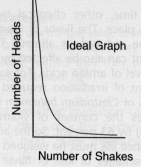

Ideal Graph

Number of Heads

Number of Shakes

---

**Expected Outcome**

Students will observe that approximately one half of the nuclei will decay with each shake. They will infer that nuclear decay is a regular process. Student graphs should resemble the graph shown below.

**Answers to** Analyzing/ Concluding and Applying

**1.** The atoms are unstable.

**2.** one shake

**3.** yes; yes

**4.** The average for the class set of data should be closer to the predicted ideal than the individual sets. Because it cannot be predicted which coins will be heads, only that about half of them will, the greater the number of coins, the closer the result will be to the prediction.

**5.** A radioactive element would not be safe after one half-life because half of the radioactive atoms would remain.

## ✔ Assessment

**Process** Challenge students to relate their observations to the process of nuclear decay by having students work in pairs to make a poster showing nuclear decay. Ask each pair to choose one of the elements americium, bismuth, or neptunium, pictured in Figures 18-3 and 18-4. Have students write the name of their element and number of protons it has at the top of the poster. Underneath the name, have students draw at least ten nuclei of their element, showing how many will decay in the first half-life, then include one panel to illustrate each subsequent half-life until the transmutation is complete. At the bottom of the poster, have students write the name of the element after the transmutation, the number of protons it has, and the type of decay (alpha or beta) which produced it. Use the Performance Task Assessment List for Poster, in **PAMSS**, page 73. **COOP LEARN** L1

**Tying to Previous Knowledge**

To encourage students to analyze what they know about nuclear power, pose the following question. "If this community were facing a power shortage, would you want to have a nuclear power plant supply electricity?" Those who say no should suggest ways that the community can provide energy or reduce consumption. Those who say yes should suggest how nuclear waste should be disposed of.

**Theme Connection** By triggering changes in atomic nuclei, scientists have been able to produce both controlled and uncontrolled supplies of energy. One way this is done is through nuclear fission, in which unstable atoms are transformed into other, stable atoms. Thus this section deals with the themes of energy, and stability and change.

**Flex Your Brain** Use the Flex Your Brain activity to have students explore FISSION REACTIONS. L2

## SKILLBUILDER

Both devices accelerate charged particles. In a linear accelerator, particles are propelled in a straight line by impulses from a succession of electric fields. A cyclotron accelerates particles around in a circle with an alternating electric field in a constant magnetic field.

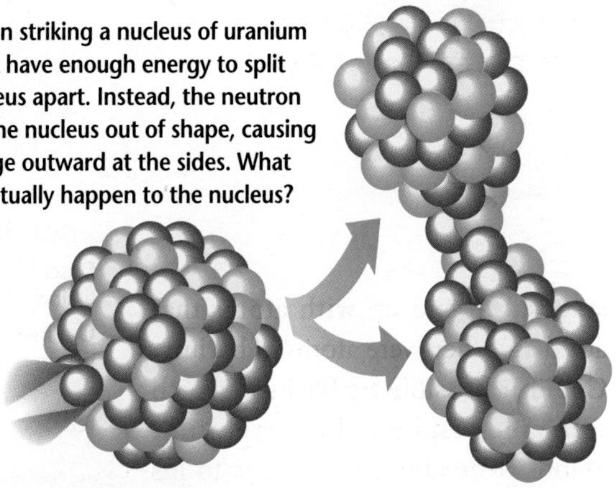

---

**Figure 18-11**

A neutron striking a nucleus of uranium does not have enough energy to split the nucleus apart. Instead, the neutron knocks the nucleus out of shape, causing it to bulge outward at the sides. What will eventually happen to the nucleus?

## SKILLBUILDER

**Comparing and Contrasting**

Atomic particles can be accelerated by means of a linear accelerator or a cyclotron. Compare and contrast a linear accelerator and a cyclotron. If you need help, refer to the **Skill Handbook** on page 659.

A neutron hitting a uranium nucleus might not have the energy to split the nucleus in two, but it may have enough energy to knock it out of shape for an instant, as shown in **Figure 18-11**. Imagine squeezing a balloon, as in **Figure 18-12**. Your fingers don't cut the balloon in half, but they do press the middle in and make the ends bulge out.

If the impact of a neutron has a similar effect on a larger nucleus, such as uranium's, the nucleus might never go back to its original shape.

### ■ Breaking Apart the Nucleus

Remember that the electric forces between the protons in the nucleus make the protons repel each other while the strong force is holding the protons together. But the strong nuclear force works only over a very short distance. Where the sides of the nucleus are squeezed together, there might not be enough force to hold the

two bulges together anymore. The repelling force among the protons is stronger than the attraction of the strong force and the two bulges tear away from each other to form two smaller nuclei. Thinking of the way cells divide, Meitner named this process nuclear **fission**. A uranium-235 nucleus could therefore split into a barium-141 nucleus and a krypton-92 nucleus. That would leave three neutrons to go flying free—two from the uranium-235 nucleus and the original one fired into the U-235 nucleus. This reaction is shown in **Figure 18-14**.

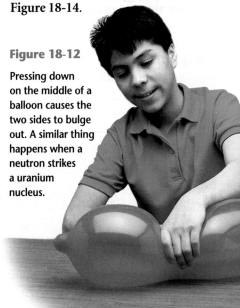

**Figure 18-12**

Pressing down on the middle of a balloon causes the two sides to bulge out. A similar thing happens when a neutron strikes a uranium nucleus.

There's no reason why uranium must split into barium and krypton rather than other elements. All that matters is that all the protons and neutrons are accounted for in the split. In fact, Hahn and Strassman found traces of lanthanum as well as barium in the products of their reaction.

---

## ENRICHMENT

**Discussion** Discuss with the class the importance of publishing the results of study and experiments, so that scientists may share information. Invite students to share what they might have heard or read in the news about recent scientific discoveries around the world. Point out that the development of atomic power was an international effort. Antoine Becquerel and Marie Curie were French. Ernest Rutherford lived in New Zealand. Niels Bohr of Denmark

came up with a theory of atomic structure. James Chadwick of Great Britain discovered the neutron. Max Planck, Otto Hahn, and Fritz Strassmann were from Germany. Lise Meitner and Otto Frisch lived in Austria. The first nuclear chain reaction was performed at the University of Chicago. The United States was the first place to generate electricity from atomic energy—in Arco, Idaho. L1

# The Power of Fission

However the nucleus splits, two important things happen. First, a great deal of energy is released. When you add up the mass of a barium-141 nucleus, a krypton-92 nucleus, and three neutrons, you find there is not as much mass as was in the uranium-235 nucleus before it split. What happened to the missing mass? It turned into energy. How much energy? One uranium molecule splitting into barium and krypton puts out more energy than the chemical energy released in the explosion of 6 600 000 molecules of TNT.

The second important thing that happens is that neutrons are produced by the reaction. And each of these neutrons is available to bombard another uranium nucleus. What if the three neutrons emitted when the uranium nucleus split each hit another uranium nucleus and caused it to split? The result could be what's known as a chain reaction.

**Figure 18-13**

These stamps were printed to honor Otto Hahn and Lise Meitner for their contributions to our knowledge of nuclear fission.

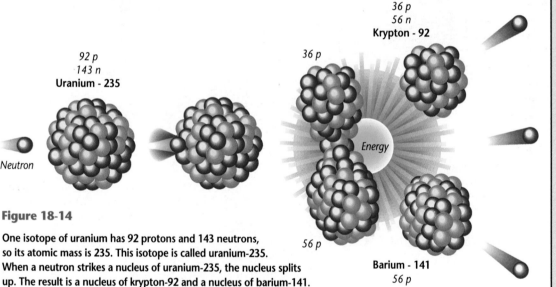

92 p
143 n
**Uranium - 235**

Neutron

36 p
56 n
**Krypton - 92**

36 p

Energy

56 p

**Barium - 141**
56 p
85 n

**Figure 18-14**

One isotope of uranium has 92 protons and 143 neutrons, so its atomic mass is 235. This isotope is called uranium-235. When a neutron strikes a nucleus of uranium-235, the nucleus splits up. The result is a nucleus of krypton-92 and a nucleus of barium-141. This process releases three neutrons and a huge amount of energy.

## Program Resources

**Critical Thinking/Problem Solving,** p. 5, Flex Your Brain

**Multicultural Connections,** p. 40, Mexico and Nuclear Power L1

**Transparency Master,** p. 75, and **Color Transparency,** Number 36, Nuclear Reactor L2

**Making Connections: Integrating Sciences,** p. 39, Nuclear Reactor Design L2

## Discussion
**Discussion** Have students analyze the following prediction made by Einstein in 1939: "For the first time in history men will use energy that does not come from the sun." Remind students that most of the energy used in 1939 came from the burning of fossil fuels. Students should be aware that these fuels are formed from once-living things. All living things depend on plants for energy (food), and plants depend on the sun for energy.

## Visual Learning

**Figure 18-11 and 18-12** Guide students to sequence the reaction shown in Figure 18-11. Have students work in cooperative learning groups. Ask each group to identify the force that holds together the bulges after the collision illustrated in Figure 18-11. *Strong nuclear force.* **What will eventually happen to the nucleus?** *It will divide into two.* Point out that only after the collision do the bulges simulated by the balloon in Figure 18-12 separate from each other to form two smaller nuclei. Challenge students to identify the force that eventually will overcome the strong nuclear force, and discuss why the strong force is no longer sufficient to hold the bulges together. Have each group draw a diagram of what will happen to the nucleus in Figure 18-11 after the protons' force of repulsion overcomes the strong force. COOP LEARN L1

**Figure 18-14** Review with students the meaning of the term "isotope" by asking what the difference is between a nucleus of uranium-235 and one of uranium-238.

## What is a chain reaction?

**Time needed** 10 minutes

**Thinking Processes** making models, sequencing, forming operational definitions, recognizing cause and effect

**Purpose** To make a model of a fission chain reaction.

### Teaching the Activity

**Troubleshooting** For this activity, arrange to use the gymnasium or other open space where there are no obstacles to students' movements. You might want to do a practice demonstration with one group first.

**Safety** Remind students not to shove one another or run.

**Student Journal** Have students describe in their journals how their chain reaction proceeded. `L1` `LEP` `COOP LEARN`

### Expected Outcome

Students will observe how one action causes another.

### Conclude and Apply

**1.** Students probably can keep track of people for only three or four collisions.

**2.** After the third collision, things probably proceed faster than students can easily follow.

### ✔ Assessment

**Process** Have students draw a series of diagrams to sequence what they observed in their chain reaction. Use the Performance Task Assessment List for Scientific Drawing in **PAMSS**, p. 55. `L1`

---

**Find Out!** ACTIVITY

## What is a chain reaction?

### What To Do

**1.** Select one classmate to be the first free neutron.

**2.** The rest of the class should divide into groups of three. Each group represents a radioactive nucleus.

**3.** In each group, two students will be neutrons. The third person represents both a proton and energy.

**4.** To start, the first free neutron will collide with any nucleus.

**5.** That nucleus then splits and the two neutrons rush off to collide with two other nuclei. The proton should indicate the energy accompanied with this split by raising both arms above his/her head. Each time a neutron hits a nucleus, the student representing that neutron stays with the third student in the nucleus, the proton. They'll represent the two nuclei and the energy from the collision.

**6.** Continue colliding and splitting until each nucleus has undergone fission. Be sure that you move in straight lines.

### Conclude and Apply

**1.** How long were you able to keep track of who was going where?

**2.** How quickly did the process build?

---

## Nuclear Reactors

**Y**ou probably already know that a nuclear reactor is a device that produces electrical energy from a controlled nuclear chain reaction. A diagram of a reactor is shown in the figure.

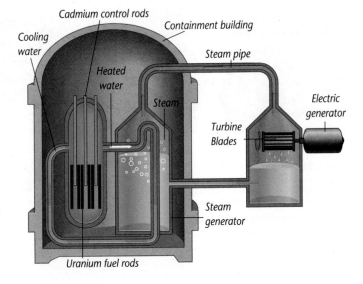

*The fission taking place in a nuclear reactor makes the reactor extremely hot. That thermal energy is used to heat water, causing it to boil. Steam from the boiling water turns the turbine. The turbine then turns the generator, which produces electricity.*

Cadmium control rods
Containment building
Cooling water
Steam pipe
Heated water
Steam
Electric generator
Turbine Blades
Steam generator
Uranium fuel rods

---

### Purpose

A Closer Look extends the discussion of nuclear fission in Section 18-2 by explaining how the chain reaction resulting from fission is used to produce electricity in nuclear reactors.

### Content Background

Not long ago, nuclear reactors seemed to be the answer to the world's energy problems. Fission plants do not pollute the atmosphere. But scientists soon found many disadvantages in the process. The most important one concerns safety. The use of either uranium or plutonium involves radioactivity. Workers in nuclear fission plants risk exposure to high radiation levels. Also, the reaction used must be carefully contained and controlled. If the cooling process fails, the fuel materials can melt and produce a radioactive dust harmful to plant and animal life for miles around.

When each reaction causes more reactions, energy released can grow at a fantastic rate. When the neutron released by one reaction creates the next reaction, and that reaction creates the reaction after that, you have a **chain reaction. Figure 18-15** shows the special way that nuclei are pictured. As shown in **Figure 18-16**, a chain reaction can occur at a steady rate if each reaction creates just one more reaction. In the case of uranium fission, each reaction can create three more. The reactions multiply very rapidly.

You saw how quickly the energy increased in your classroom. Imagine, then, what it would be like on the atomic scale. If only two neutrons from one reaction caused another

**Figure 18-15**

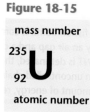

mass number

$^{235}_{92}U$

atomic number

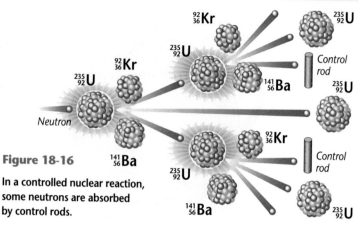

**Figure 18-16**

In a controlled nuclear reaction, some neutrons are absorbed by control rods.

## Reactor Design

Modern nuclear reactors vary in design, but they all work on the same principle. In the core of the reactor is fuel, usually pellets of uranium oxide. The fuel pellets are surrounded by water, which slows down the neutrons produced by the fission reaction. Only slow neutrons can cause U-235 to undergo fission. As soon as one nucleus undergoes fission, a chain reaction can start. Cadmium rods absorb enough neutrons to keep the reaction from going out of control. But how do we use the energy that the reactions release?

## Generating Electrical Energy

Most nuclear reactors make electricity. Look at the diagram again. The fission taking place in the reactor makes the reactor intensely hot. The thermal energy heats the water surrounding the fuel rods. Because the water is pressurized, it doesn't boil. The superheated water passes through a heat exchanger where it heats other water, causing it to boil. The reactor water, now much cooler, is then pumped back to the reactor. Steam from the boiling water in the heat exchanger turns the turbine that turns the

generator that makes the electricity. Trace the flow. See if you can tell where nuclear energy becomes thermal energy, where thermal energy becomes mechanical energy, and where mechanical energy becomes electrical energy.

## What Do You Think?

Trace the path of the water that is used inside the reactor. Is this the same water that goes to the cooling towers? Is it the same water that turns the turbines? Why do you think the water from the reactor core is contained in the core and not pumped through the turbines?

# 3 ASSESS

## Check for Understanding

Have students answer the Check Your Understanding questions. As students answer question 4, the Apply question, remind them that fission and fusion are opposite processes, but the nuclear reactions in each case produce energy. Have students locate hydrogen and thorium on the periodic table to see how different they are.

## Reteach

**Activity** Have students draw a "close-up" of a nuclear reaction on the sun using different-colored crayons or pencils. Drawings should be similar to Figure 18-16. L1 LEP

## Extension

Have students who have mastered this section do research into possible careers in the field of atomic energy. L2

# 4 CLOSE

Have the class compose a poem that compares and contrasts fission and fusion. Write it on the board and revise it as students come up with new ideas. L1

As you saw in the second Investigate, the particles resulting from a fusion reaction have less mass than the original particles. The clay-ball model does not show what happens to that mass, but you already know. The difference in mass becomes the energy for the sun's light and heat. In fact, the energy released is more than enough to cause two other nuclei to fuse. This may sound similar to what happened during fission reactions —the makings of another chain reaction. That's exactly what a star is—a gigantic thermonuclear fusion chain reaction.

While fission releases energy by splitting larger nuclei into smaller ones, fusion does just the opposite. It fuses smaller nuclei into larger ones. Fusion of hydrogen into helium releases vast amounts of energy. It's the source of energy in stars. Researchers are working on peaceful uses of nuclear fusion. Many believe that fusion can be a clean, safe source of energy for the future. In the meantime, researchers also continue to study the thermonuclear fusion reactions that occur in the stars. In the last chapter of this book, you will learn more about the sun, the stars, and the other systems in outer space.

**Figure 18-19**

Nuclear fusion on the sun is a result of the extreme temperature and pressure conditions.

## check your UNDERSTANDING

1. Compare and contrast nuclear fusion with nuclear fission.
2. What happens to extra mass when hydrogen is fused into helium?
3. What is the sequence of events that must occur for fusion to take place?
4. **Apply** Would thorium (element number 90) be better suited for a fission or fusion reaction?

## check your UNDERSTANDING

1. Nuclear fusion combines two nuclei. Fission splits a large nucleus. Both produce large amounts of energy.
2. The mass is converted into energy.
3. Two nuclei must be forced close together. If they get close enough, the strong force overcomes the electric force and holds the nuclei together. One nucleus results.
4. fission, because thorium has a very large nucleus.

## HOW IT WORKS

# Healing Radiation

Radiation and natural radioactive decay are useful for treating a variety of cancers. Cancers are a group of disorders involving cells that divide much more rapidly than normal cells. These abnormal cells form masses called tumors. Researchers have shown that cancer cells are more sensitive to radiation than are normal cells. This means that radiation can be used to kill cancer cells within a tumor and leave surrounding normal cells unharmed.

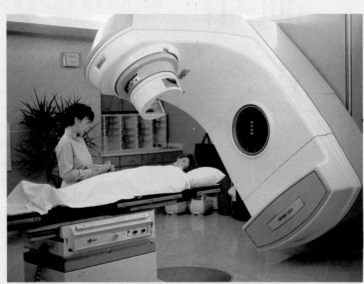

*Special equiment that delivers controlled doses of radiation is used to treat certain forms of cancer.*

### Radioactive Beams

For instance, gamma radiation from cobalt-60 and cesium-137 are often directed at cancerous tumors. The beams of radiation are finely focused so that they are directed at only cancer cells and avoid healthy cells. This treatment requires expensive equipment, and the patient must go to the hospital every few days for another dose of radiation.

### Radioactivity in a Tube

Another treatment uses the radioactive isotope sealed in a gold tube. The tube is implanted in the patient's tumor. The radiation kills the surrounding cancer cells, destroying the tumor from the inside out. This treatment is not dependent on expensive equipment and allows the patient some independence during treatment. Because the radioactive material is sealed in a capsule, materials with relatively long half-life may be used.

### What Do You Think?

Manganese is a trace element needed by the body. Manganese-56 emits a beta particle and has a half-life of 2.6 hours. After 10.4 hours, what fraction of manganese would be in the patient's body? What other element would be in the patient's body as a result of treatment with manganese? Do you think manganese would be a good choice for radiation therapy?

---

### Purpose

How It Works reinforces Section 18-1 by describing an important use scientists have found for naturally radioactive materials—the treatment of cancer.

### Content Background

Treatments with radioactive iodine have reduced the need for surgery in patients with hyperthyroidism. Radioactive iodine has a half-life of 8.08 days, so it remains in the body for only a short time. It can be given orally or intravenously. Over 20,000 patients a year are treated with iodine-131, resulting in a drop in surgeries from 3,000 to 50 a year.

### Teaching Strategy
Divide the class into several groups. Ask each group to present an argument supporting or rejecting the use of radioactive isotopes as a treatment for cancer. Students should consider the time, pain, and expense involved in treatments. L2

### Answers to
#### What Do You Think?

After 10.4 hours, one-sixteenth of the initial dose of manganese would be left in the body. Radioactive manganese would decay into iron. Suggest to students that manganese might not be a good choice for radiation therapy because the iron resulting from its decay could build up to toxic levels in the body.

---

### ENRICHMENT

**Discussion** Have students work in small groups to develop questions they would like answered about the use of radiation and radioactive materials in medicine. Then invite a member of your hospital's nuclear medicine department to visit your class, describe his or her medical training, and answer student questions. Use the Performance Task Assessment List for Asking Questions in **PAMSS**, p. 19. **COOP LEARN** L1

### Going Further ▸

Have students research the effectiveness of various cancer treatments. Suggest that students interview an oncologist in your area or contact the local chapter of the American Cancer Society. Have students present their findings to the class along with any personal experiences with people who have had cancer. Use the Performance Task Assessment List for Oral Presentation in **PAMSS**, p. 71. L2

# Science and Society

### Purpose
Science and Society extends Section 18-2 and the use of fission by discussing the problem of nuclear waste disposal.

### Content Background
As of January 1992, there were at least 31,000 hazardous waste sites in the United States. This number means that there is a one-in-six chance that you live close to a hazardous waste dump. While most of these are not sites for radioactive waste, some might be. Three low-level radioactive waste dumps were closed in 1978. West Valley, N.Y., Maxey Flats, KY, and Sheffield, IL were closed because of clear evidence that radioactive materials had leaked from the dump. For years, only three commercial dumpsites in Nevada, Washington, and South Carolina accepted radioactive wastes. These states still have the option to close. Because these states may stop accepting radioactive wastes, new sites must be established. States contributing to nuclear waste will be subject to heavy federal fines if they cannot come up with a solution to the waste problem.

It has been proposed that safe storage can be achieved. Nuclear wastes could be dried and stored in glass canisters. The canisters would be enclosed in copper or cast iron. They would then be buried at least several hundred meters deep and covered with bentonite, which limits the escape of radioactive material. Experts estimate that radioactivity could be contained for about 1000 years. At that point, the radioactivity of the materials would have decayed to a manageable point.

# Science and Society

# No Nuclear Dumping

One of today's most hotly debated issues is the location of nuclear dump sites. As evidenced by a number of unpleasant incidents, nuclear waste is coming back to haunt us.

A startling example of the effects of nuclear waste occurred near Oak Ridge National Laboratory in Tennessee. In the 1940s, Oak Ridge was a research center for atomic weapons. The research produced several highly radioactive materials.

*Protesters gather at the site of a new nuclear reactor.*

The government and researchers in charge of the facility decided to sink the radioactive wastes under water. A 50-acre pond was created, and solid waste and drums of the liquid waste were placed at the bottom of the pond.

### Radioactivity Spreads

In the 1960s, scientists working near Oak Ridge noticed turtles had traveled as far as five miles from the pond. More amazing was the realization that these animals had high concentrations of radioactive cesium in their tissues and organs.

Despite the intentions of the original researchers, the radioactivity had spread. Small plants and organisms beneath the water and at the facility's edge had absorbed some of the products of radiation. The plants were eaten by the small animals, such as turtles, that lived at the storage pond. The plants that carried radioactivity had entered the food chain.

The problem was one not only of the spread of radioactivity, but also of its concentration. As an animal, such as a small fish, repeatedly eats contaminated food, the radioactive elements concentrate in its tissues and organs. If a larger fish or bird feeds on the small fish, the radioactive elements are concentrated further. Animals feeding on plants and other animals from the storage pond had cesium concentration levels a thousand times higher than the cesium concentration levels of the storage pond. The increase in concentration as a result of the natural feeding process is called amplification.

### Going Further ▻
Nuclear waste disposal is a NIMBY problem. NIMBY is a way of saying that the responsibility belongs to someone else. People agree that we should have waste disposal sites, but *"Not In My Back Yard!"* Have students give examples of other situations where the NIMBY problem appears. Students may mention the location of sewage-treatment plants or high-security prisons. Have students work in small groups to create a phrase and acronym that suggests we take responsibility for our own actions. Have each group make a poster displaying its phrase and acronym. Use the Performance Assessment Task List for Poster in **PAMSS**, p. 73. **L1** **COOP LEARN**

## Nuclear Reactors Produce Waste

Oak Ridge is a single example of the problems that accompany high-level nuclear waste. High-level waste is a by-product of the operation of nuclear reactors. Each reactor produces solid wastes, usually from the fuel rods of the reactors. Liquid waste is an acid-based substance produced during the treatment of the rods. For years, there were fewer than a dozen of these reactors. They were used for research and all were under the control of the government. But, as the nation's demand for electricity increased, the number of nuclear reactors also increased. Today's reactors are scattered across the country and are owned and operated by a number of widespread commercial interests.

Government scientists have suggested that high-level waste be buried two or three thousand feet beneath Earth's surface, in a geologically stable rock formation. They think this will be safe, but they cannot be sure.

In addition to the high-level waste, reactors also produce low-level waste. Hospitals, too, produce low-level waste. The half-life

*Nuclear waste is transported to storage facilities*

of some of these materials is a few days, while other waste products have half-lives of 500 years.

Occasionally, metal drums filled with low-level radiation are dumped in shallow trenches. These sites are often affected by rainwater, and the containers may corrode, allowing the radioactive substances to leak into the ground and reach the groundwater supply. Drums stored in shuttered warehouses have leaked or corroded and contaminated the surrounding ground and water.

The federal government has authority over the disposal of high-level nuclear waste, while the states have control of low-level radiation sites. If waste is transported across state lines, the federal government can be asked to intercede.

## Not in My Back Yard

Leaders across the country are meeting intense opposition to nuclear disposal sites. At every proposed site, the community protests. Voters promise to turn the political leaders out of office for approving the site. Yet every voter is, in some sense, responsible for creating nuclear waste. The nuclear reactors exist to supply an increased demand for electrical energy. Nuclear medicine has flourished, employing technology to cure illness or prolong life. Each of us benefits in some way from nuclear technology.

### What Do You Think?

In 1982, the federal government ordered that construction of a solid nuclear waste depository site should be completed by 1998. What would you do if a proposed site were three miles from your home?

**Content Background**
Closures of nuclear power plants add to the problem. Worldwide, somewhere between 100 to 200 plants will shut down between now and 2010. A plant closure involves three options. The plant can be taken apart and decontaminated immediately. Its radioactive materials can be temporarily stored for fifty to one hundred years so that nuclear decay can continue. Or the plant and its materials can be isolated in a permanent storage area. None of these are easy. Workers must be extremely careful. All possible radiation has to be tracked at all times. Cleaning materials have to be regulated because they become radioactive. Whatever approach is taken, the pile of radioactive wastes increases with each plant closure. And as we learn more and more about the problems of leakage, the cost of disposal becomes greater. The safe closure of a plant is estimated to cost anywhere between $50 million and $3 billion.

**Teaching Strategy** Review the nature of radioactivity and how it can seriously affect plant and animal life. Then have students discuss the value of scientific advances involving nuclear power and materials in light of the potential problems involving nuclear wastes. Remember that there are no clear answers. [L2]

**Answer to**
**What Do You Think?**
Many students will probably say they would try to get the site changed. This might include writing letters to government officials or newspapers. Other students may say that they would want to find out about proposed design and safety features before forming an opinion.

## Multicultural Perspectives

### Keep Out!

Because of the long half-lives of some isotopes in radioactive wastes, scientists are concerned that future generations may not understand warning signs posted near waste storage sites. Some sites may remain dangerously radioactive for as long as 10 000 years. Scientists fear that languages will continue to evolve, and Twentieth Century words may be misunderstood thousands of years from now. Some people have suggested developing folklore and myths about waste sites, hoping that an oral tradition, much like Native-American legends, will survive. Other people have suggested that fierce masks or other icons could serve as warnings. Have students design warning devices and share them with the class. [L1]

## Technology Connection

## Technology Connection

# Fusion Reactors

Nuclear fusion requires temperatures of more than 100 million degrees Celsius. No material can contain anything at such a temperature. However, scientists have been able to use a magnetic field to contain charged particles.

### Magnetic Containment

When energy is added to hydrogen atoms, their electrons may be stripped away, forming a fluidlike material called a plasma that is comprised of electrons and ions. A design that might accomplish this is shown in the illustration.

A sudden increase in the magnetic field will compress the plasma, raising its temperature. This causes hydrogen nuclei to be fused into helium. The energy released by the reaction would be used to heat some other material, possibly liquified lithium, at 186°C. The lithium, in turn, would boil water, producing steam to turn electric generators. Unfortunately, more energy is used by the equipment than is produced by the reaction.

### Laser Fusion

A technique that doesn't require a sustained reaction uses pellets of frozen hydrogen-2 and hydrogen-3 dropped into a chamber. Here they are blasted by several high-powered laser beams. The concentrated laser light compresses the hydrogen and heats the pellets to fusion point.

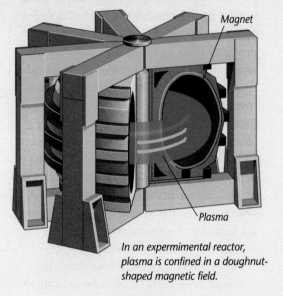

Magnet

Plasma

*In an experimental reactor, plasma is confined in a doughnut-shaped magnetic field.*

### Tritium

In late 1991, British researchers reported results of an experiment using tritium, an isotope of hydrogen that has two neutrons and one proton in its nucleus. They were able to produce a sustained fusion reaction for two seconds—a long time in nuclear circles. The reaction generated 2 million watts.

### What Do You Think?

Very expensive research is needed for a fusion reactor to become a reality. If a corporation funds a researcher who finds a solution, that corporation could make a huge profit from the discovery. If a government-funded researcher finds the solution, the government would share the development with all citizens. Do you think research should be funded by corporations or by the government? Why do you think as you do?

**R**eview the statements below about the big ideas presented in this chapter, and try to answer the questions. Then, re-read your answers to the Did You Ever Wonder questions at the beginning of the chapter. *In your Journal*, write a paragraph about how your understanding of the big ideas in the chapter has changed.

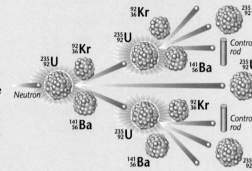

**1** One element can change into another by emitting particles and changing its number of protons. This is called transmutation. You can force nuclei to transmute by bombarding them with alpha particles. *What is this process called?*

**2** A collision with a neutron can cause a heavy nucleus to split into two lighter nuclei. This process is called nuclear fission. *Why is fission a useful process?*

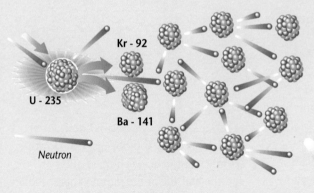

**3** If the neutrons freed by one split can cause fission in other nuclei, a chain reaction can result. *What would happen if the chain reaction were uncontrolled?*

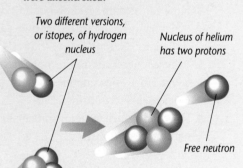

Two different versions, or isotpes, of hydrogen nucleus

Nucleus of helium has two protons

Free neutron

**4** It's possible to fuse smaller nuclei into larger ones. Fusion of hydrogen into helium releases vast amounts of energy. *When does fusion take place in nature?*

Have students look at the four illustrations. Direct them to read the captions to review the main ideas of the chapter. Students will then write science fiction stories related to the main ideas.

**Teaching Strategies**

Divide students into four groups. Assign each group one of the illustrations. Have each group formulate an answer to the question and explain the importance of the idea. Suggest they think about what each has meant or could mean to humanity. Then ask each group to imagine a future use for the idea. Have group members cooperate in writing a science fiction story in which the idea plays a major role. They should be sure their scientific facts are accurate. After the stories are written, have them typed. With student help, photocopy the stories and bind them into a book for each student.

Some students might want to provide additional illustrations for their story.

**Answers to Questions**

**1.** Artificial transmutation

**2.** In controlled circumstances, nuclear fission can be used to produce energy.

**3.** An uncontrolled chain reaction can release enough energy to cause a violent explosion.

**4.** Natural fusion reactions require an extremely high density of particles such as can be found in the core of the sun and the other stars.

---

## Project

Have students work in groups to research the Chernobyl and Three Mile Island nuclear reactor accidents. The former occurred in the Ukraine in 1986, the latter in Middletown, Pennsylvania, in 1979. Use the Performance Task Assessment List for Investigating an Issue Controversy in **PAMSS**, p. 65. L2 **COOP LEARN**

## Science at Home

Have students ask relatives and neighbors whether they know anyone who has had radioiotopic diagnosis or treatment. What was the purpose of the diagnosis or treatment? What kinds of isotopes were used? Students should report their findings to the class. Use the Performance Task Assessment List for Oral Presentations in **PAMSS**, p. 71. L1

## Using Key Science Terms

1. transmutation
2. fission
3. chain reaction
4. fusion
5. artificial transmutation

## Understanding Ideas

1. The electrical forces tear the nucleus apart after it has been deformed by a collision with a neutron.

2. The energy and particles released by a nuclear reaction cause other nuclei to fission.

3. by adding some material that will absorb some the free neutrons

4. It becomes energy.

5. The protons in the nucleus of heavier elements strongly repel the protons in the alpha particles.

6. A neutron can decay into a proton and an electron, and the electron is emitted.

## Developing Skills

1. See reduced student page for completed concept map.

2. There is no relationship between mass-number and half-life. Bismuth and polonium have the same mass number and widely different half-lives. You could not predict the half-life from the graph.

3. One year is 365/91 = 4 half-lives, so the fraction of the original element remaining would be $1/2 \times 1/2 \times 1/2 \times 1/2 = 1/16$. $1/16 \times 10 \text{ g} = 0.63 \text{ g}$.

## Critical Thinking

1. Both are self-sustaining reactions for a finite amount of time. The energy released by one reaction allows the next reaction to take place.

2. samarium-149

3. $^{222}_{86}$Rn decays to produce $^{218}_{84}$Po + alpha particle ($^{4}_{2}$He)

## Using Key Science Terms

artificial transmutation   fusion
chain reaction                     transmutation
fission

*Which science term describes each of the following processes?*

1. Astatine-215 decays into bismuth-211.
2. Uranium-235 splits into lanthanum and rubidium.
3. Neutrons freed by the splitting of a plutonium nucleus cause other plutonium nuclei to split.
4. Two helium-3 nuclei combine to create helium-4 plus two free protons.
5. Molybdenum is bombarded with alpha particles to create technetium.

## Understanding Ideas

*Answer the following questions in your Journal using complete sentences.*

1. What do electrical forces have to do with nuclear fission?
2. What causes a chain reaction?
3. How can a chain reaction be slowed?
4. What happens to the mass lost in a fission or fusion reaction?
5. Why is it necessary to fire alpha particles at extremely high energies to cause heavier elements to transmute?
6. How can a nucleus decay into an element with more protons?

## Developing Skills

*Use your understanding of the concepts developed in this chapter to answer each of the following questions.*

1. **Concept Mapping** Create a spider concept map that describes nuclear reactions by summarizing the types, characteristics, and uses of the reactions described in the chapter. Use transmutation, artificial transmutation, fission, and fusion as the four main legs.

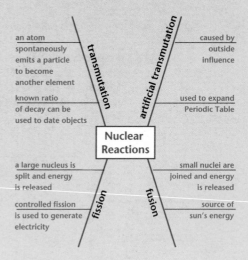

2. **Making and Using Graphs** Look closely at the table at the top of page 595. Do you see any relation between mass number and the half-life of the radioisotopes? Plot the mass numbers versus half-lives. Is it possible to predict the half-life of a radioisotope given its mass number?

**Program Resources**

**Review and Assessment,** pp. 107–112 [L1]
**Performance Assessment,** Ch. 18. [L2]
**PAMSS**
**Alternate Assessment in the Science Classroom**
**Computer Test Bank**

| Mass | | |
|---|---|---|
| Radioisotope | Number | Half–Life |
| Radium | 222 | 4 days |
| Thorlum | 234 | 25 days |
| Iodine | 131 | 8 days |
| Bismuth | 210 | 5 days |
| Polonium | 320 | 138 days |

**3. Interpreting Data** If you have a 10-gram sample of a radioactive element with a half-life of 91 days, how much of this element will remain after one year of radioactive decay?

## Critical Thinking

In your Journal, *answer each of the following questions.*
1. How is a fire similar to a nuclear chain reaction?
2. Promethium-149 can transmute by the decay of a neutron and the ejection of an electron. What is the resulting element?

**3.** Write a nuclear reaction to show how radon-222 decays to give off an alpha particle and another element. What is the other element?

## Problem Solving

*Read the following problem and discuss your answers in a brief paragraph.*

Kristine found an old alarm clock and put it next to her bed. During the night, Kristine was surprised by a greenish-white glow coming from the clock. Kristine did some research and found that the numerals and the hands of the clock were coated with a paint containing zinc sulfide and radium, a radioactive element with a half-life of 1600 years. The zinc sulfide emits little flashes of light when excited by radiation. These tiny flashes of light make the hands and numerals of the clock glow.

Will the glow of the hands change over time? Could uranium-238 have been used instead of radium? Explain your answer.

### CONNECTING IDEAS

Discuss each of the following in a brief paragraph.

1. **Theme—Stability and Change** How can uranium-238 be used in the life and earth sciences? Why is it such an important tool?
2. **Theme—Energy** Compare and contrast the benefits and disadvantages of using nuclear reactions.
3. **A Closer Look** Design an events chain for the generation of electricity in a nuclear reactor. Begin with the bombarding neutrons and end with electric transmission lines.
4. **Life Science Connection** How can irradiation help combat the problem of starvation in third-world countries?
5. **Science and Society** Explain what effects biomagnification might have on society.

## Problem Solving

The glow of the hands will become dimmer as the radium decays, this change will occur very slowly over many hundreds of years. Uranium-235 has a half-life of 4.5 billion years, so its rate of decay is too slow to provide enough radiation to cause the paint to glow.

## Connecting Ideas

1. Uranium-235 is used for absolute dating, a method of determining the age of geological objects. It is used to find the age of very old rocks, which provide information about the geological history of Earth and the solar system. Uranium-235 is also used to date fossils, which helps scientists to understand how species have evolved.

2. The benefits of using nuclear reactions are that tremendous amounts of energy can be produced, and that it provides an alternative to fossil fuels. Among the disadvantages are the danger of a reactor going out of control and the problem of storage and disposal of toxic wastes.

3. Neutron bombards a nucleus; nucleus splits; energy is released; water is heated; turbine water boils; steam turns turbine; turbine turns generator; electric current is produced; current leaves on transmission lines.

4. Irradiation of foods kill bacteria living in and on the surfaces of foods, keeping food fresh longer. This would allow food to be shipped to third-world countries without spoiling.

5. Biomagnification can have a major effect on society because humans consume large amounts of animals and plants that may have been exposed to radiation. A high radiation concentration can destroy human cells and lead to cancer, premature aging, and genetic mutations.

## ✔ Assessment

**Portfolio** Review the portfolio options that are provided throughout the chapter. Encourage students to select one product that demonstrates their best work for the chapter. Have students explain what they learned and why they chose this example for placement in their portfolios.

Additional portfolio options can be found in the following **Teacher Classroom Resources:**

**Multicultural Connections,** pp. 39–40

**Making Connections: Integrating Sciences,** p. 39
**Making Connections: Across the Curriculum,** p. 39
**Concept Mapping,** p. 26
**Critical Thinking/Problem Solving** p. 26
**Take Home Activities,** p. 29
**Laboratory Manual,** pp. 105–108; 109–112
**Performance Assessment** [P]

# Chapter Organizer

| SECTION | OBJECTIVES | ACTIVITIES |
|---|---|---|
| **Chapter Opener** | | **Explore!** How do the different bodies that travel around the sun compare with one another? p. 597 |
| **19-1 The Solar System** (2 days) | 1. **Explain** one hypothesis of how the solar system formed. 2. **Compare and contrast** Earth with Mercury, Venus, and Mars. 3. **Relate** studies of Venus and Mars to concerns about global warming and atmospheric ozone on Earth. | **Investigate 19-1:** Orbits, pp. 600–601 **Explore!** How do the atmospheres of Venus, Earth, and Mars compare? p. 605 **Skillbuilder:** Interpreting Data, p. 607 |
| **19-2 The Outer Planets** (3 days) | 1. **Compare** the gaseous giant planets with the terrestrial planets. 2. **Recognize** that Pluto differs from the other planets and is therefore not classified with either group. | **Explore!** Solar System Facts and Figures, p. 609 **Skillbuilder:** Recognizing Cause and Effect, p. 609 **Investigate 19-2:** Distances in the Solar System, pp. 610–611 |
| **19-3 Other Objects in the Solar System** (3 days) | 1. **Explain** where a comet comes from and describe how a comet develops as it approaches the sun. 2. **Differentiate** between comets, asteroids, and meteors. | |

## EXPAND your view

**A Closer Look** Rehearsal for Mars, pp. 606–607
**Physics Connection** Out Beyond Pluto, pp. 614–615
**Science and Society** Will Humans or Robots Explore Mars? pp. 620–621

**Literature Connection** Life in a Solar System Colony, p. 621
**Teens in Science** The Space Station Project, p. 622

## ACTIVITY MATERIALS

| EXPLORE! | INVESTIGATE! | FIND OUT! |
|---|---|---|
| **Page 597** No special materials are required. **Page 605*** No special materials are required. **Page 609** No special materials are required. | **Pages 600–601** thumbtacks or pins, string, cardboard (21.5 cm × 28 cm), metric ruler, pencil, paper **Pages 610–611*** adding machine tape, meterstick, scissors, pencil | |

*For adequate development of the concepts presented, we recommend that students do the activities with an asterisk.

# Chapter 19 The Solar System

## TEACHER CLASSROOM RESOURCES

| Student Masters | Teaching Aids |
|---|---|
| **Study Guide**, p. 63<br>**Multicultural Connections**, p. 41<br>**Take Home Activities**, p. 30<br>**Concept Mapping**, p. 28<br>**Activity Masters, Investigate 19-1**, pp. 79–80<br>**Flex Your Brain**, p. 5<br>**Science Discovery Activities**, 19-1 | **Laboratory Manual**, pp. 113–116, Venus—The Greenhouse Effect<br>**Color Transparency and Master 37**, Relative Sizes of the Planets<br>**\*STVS:** *Meteorites in the Antarctic*, Earth and Space (Disc 3, Side 1)<br>**\*STVS:** *Indian Medicine Wheels*, Earth and Space (Disc 3, Side 1) |
| **Study Guide**, p. 64<br>**Critical Thinking/Problem Solving**, p. 27<br>**How It Works**, p. 21<br>**Making Connections: Integrating Sciences**, p. 41<br>**Making Connections: Across the Curriculum**, p. 41<br>**Making Connections: Technology & Society**, p. 41<br>**Activity Masters, Investigate 19-2**, pp. 81–82<br>**Science Discovery Activities**, 19-2 | **Laboratory Manual**, pp. 117-118, Jupiter and Its Moons<br>**Color Transparency and Master 38**, Relative Distances Between the Planets<br>**\*STVS:** *Video Astronomy*, Physics (Disc 1, Side 1) |
| **Study Guide**, p. 65<br>**Multicultural Connections**, p. 42<br>**Science Discovery Activities**, 19-3 | **\*STVS:** *Flying Observatory*, Earth and Space (Disc 3, Side 1)<br>**\*STVS:** *Mars Ball*, Earth and Space (Disc 3, Side 1)<br>*Vehicle for the Disabled*, Earth and Space (Disc 3, Side 1) |

| ASSESSMENT RESOURCES | |
|---|---|
| **Review and Assessment**, pp. 113–118<br>**Performance Assessment**, Ch. 19<br>**PAMSS\***<br>**MindJogger Videoquiz**<br>**Alternate Assessment in the Science Classroom**<br>**Computer Test Bank** | **Spanish Resources**<br>**Cooperative Learning Resource Guide**<br>**Lab and Safety Skills**<br>**Integrated Science Videodisc** |

## KEY TO TEACHING STRATEGIES

The following designations will help you decide which activities are appropriate for your students.

**L1** Level 1 activities should be within the ability range of all students.

**L2** Level 2 activities should be within the ability range of the average to above-average student.

**L3** Level 3 activities are designed for the ability range of above-average students.

**LEP** LEP activities should be within the ability range of Limited English Proficiency students.

**COOP LEARN** Cooperative Learning activities are designed for small group work.

**P** These strategies represent student products that can be placed into a best-work portfolio.

## ADDITIONAL MATERIALS

**Software**
*Astronomy*, Orange Cherry New Media Schoolhouse.
*Planetarium on Computer: The Solar System*, Focus Media.
*Sky Lab*, MECC.
*The Solar System*, Queue.
*The View from Earth*, CD-ROM, Warner New Media.

**Audiovisual**
*Close-up on the Planets*, video, Disney Educational Productions.
*Comets, Meteors, and Asteroids*, video, Coronet/MTI.
*Discovering Our Planet Earth*, video, United Learning

*Introducing Astronomy*, video, SVE.

**Laserdisc**
*AstroVision*, Houghton Mifflin.
*The Living Textbook: Astronomy and the Sun*, Optical Data Corp.
*Exploring Our Solar System*, AIMS.
*STV: Solar System*, National Geographic.

**Readings**
Branley, Franklyn M. *Mysteries of the Planets*. Dutton.
Fisher, David E. *The Origin and Evolution of Our Own Particular Universe*. Atheneum.
Kelch, Joseph W. *Small Worlds: Exploring the 60 Moons of Our Solar System*. Julian Messner.

\*Performance Assessment in Middle School Science

\*Science and Technology Videodisc Series

## The Solar System

### THEME DEVELOPMENT

One theme that this chapter supports is stability and change. Although the planets formed relatively stable bodies when they condensed from the dust and gas of the early solar system, they underwent change depending on their size and distance from the sun. The theme of scale and structure is illustrated by the differences in size and composition of the gaseous giants when compared with the terrestrial planets.

### CHAPTER OVERVIEW

First, students learn how the solar system formed from a cloud of gas and dust. Characteristics of the terrestrial planets—Mercury, Venus, Earth, and Mars—are covered.

Then, the remaining planets of the solar system are explored, namely, Jupiter, Saturn, Uranus, Neptune, and Pluto. Finally, the movement of comets, asteroids, and meteoroids through the solar system is discussed.

#### Tying to Previous Knowledge

Arrange students into small groups and have them write what they know about the solar system. Have them concentrate on the planets, but also include comets, meteors, and asteroids. Allow students to draw on knowledge from science fiction books and movies. **COOP LEARN**
**P**

### INTRODUCING THE CHAPTER

Have students look at the photo on page 597. Ask them what planet is the easiest to identify. Most will say Saturn because of the rings. Tell students that in this chapter they will learn about all of the planets.

### Did you ever wonder...

✓ **Where the solar system came from?**
✓ **What it's like on other planets?**
✓ **If there's life on other planets?**

Before you begin to study the solar system, think about these questions and answer them *in your Journal*. When you finish the chapter, compare your Journal write-up with what you have learned.

# THE solar SYSTEM

**C**ould it really happen to you? Probably not, but who doesn't like to dream about it? You suit up one day, board a spacecraft, and head out—way out. In a flash, you've left the atmosphere and entered the hushed, dark world of outer space.

After a while, you look back. There's the sun, shining steady and bright. Nine planets move around it. Some are huge, though not nearly as large as the sun. Others are tiny and pretty unimpressive. There's Earth, a small deep-blue globe with white, wispy clouds. Don't we Earthlings have a unique home in space? Yes, we do.

▶ *Once you read this chapter, you'll understand how special Earth is. Start your exploration with the activity on the next page.*

*Uranus*

*Neptune*

*Jupiter*

### Did you ever wonder...

• Many scientists hypothesize that the solar system began as a slowly rotating cloud of dust and gas. (p. 599)

• All planets are much hotter or colder than Earth. Some are solid, others are gaseous. (pp. 603–616)

• Living things have not yet been discovered on any planet except Earth. (p. 608)

### STUDENT JOURNAL

Have students write their responses to the Did You Ever Wonder questions in their journals. After they have read the chapter, students should read their journal entries to see what they have learned about the origin of the solar system, the properties of the planets, and whether life exists on any planet except Earth.

# Explore! ACTIVITY

## How do the different bodies that travel around the sun compare with one another?

**W**here can you start to make comparisons among objects that orbit the sun? You can start with careful observation and recording of observed differences.

### What To Do

1. Using observable characteristics and the information in appendix J on page 671, compare Earth with the other planets shown in the photographs on these two pages.

2. How does Earth compare in color? In shape? In size? Write your answers *in your Journal*.

*Earth*

*Saturn*

*Venus*

*Images of the planets on these pages are not to scale.*

**597**

## ASSESSMENT PLANNER

**PORTFOLIO**
Refer to page 625 for suggested items that students might select for their portfolios.

**PERFORMANCE ASSESSMENT**
Process, pp. 597, 605
Content, pp. 601, 609
Skillbuilder, pp. 607, 609
Explore! Activities, pp. 597, 605, 609
Investigate, pp. 600–601, 610–611

**CONTENT ASSESSMENT**
Oral, p. 611
Check Your Understanding, pp. 608, 616, 619
Reviewing Main Ideas, p. 623
Chapter Review, pp. 624–625

**GROUP ASSESSMENT**
Opportunities for group assessment occur with Cooperative Learning Strategies.

---

## Explore!

**How do the different bodies that travel around the sun compare with one another?**

**Time needed** 15–20 minutes

**Materials** No special materials or preparation are required for this activity.

**Thinking Processes** observing and inferring, classifying, comparing and contrasting, interpreting scientific illustrations

**Purpose** To compare and contrast major bodies of the solar system.

### Teaching the Activity

**Student Journal** In their journals, have students make colored drawings (approximately to scale) of the planets shown. L1

### Expected Outcome

Students should be able to identify similarities and differences among the planets in the photograph.

### Answers to Questions

**3.** Earth is blue-green and cloudy. Other planets are different colors, though all shown on these pages have clouds. Earth is about the same size as Venus but smaller than Jupiter, Saturn, Uranus, and Neptune.

### ✔ Assessment

**Process** Have students use previous knowledge of research to compare and contrast the planets by size and make a generalization concerning size and distance from the sun. *With the exception of Pluto, the smaller planets (Mercury, Earth, Venus, and Mars) are nearest the sun whereas the largest planets (Jupiter, Saturn, Uranus, and Neptune are farthest from the sun.)* Use the Performance Task Assessment List for Making Observations and Inferences in **PAMSS**, p. 17. L1

## Planning the Activity

**Time needed** 35 minutes

**Purpose** To compare and contrast ellipses of various eccentricities that represent the shape of planetary orbits.

**Process Skills** observing and inferring, measuring in SI, hypothesizing, separating and controlling variables, interpreting data, formulating models, making and using tables, formulating operational definitions, comparing and contrasting, recognizing cause and effect,

**Materials** See student activity.

**Preparation** Although thumbtacks are easier for students to control, hat pins are excellent for this activity, since they allow students to observe all parts of the taut string. Time can be saved by having a number of pieces of string already tied in loops of various sizes.

## Teaching the Activity

**Process Reinforcement** Have students do research to determine the eccentricities of the various planetary orbits. Students should then compare these orbits to the ones they have drawn.

**Student Journal** Have students trace the ellipses they have made in their journals. **L3**

**Troubleshooting** As an example, provide students with values for *d* (2 cm) and *L* (6 cm) for an ellipse and ask them to solve for *e*. 2 ÷ 6 = 0.3 Some students may become frustrated attempting to construct an ellipse with Earth's orbital eccentricity of 0.017, thinking it impossible. If so, discuss with them the answers to questions 1 and 2, and then apply their answers to this task.

---

**INVESTIGATE!**

# Orbits

*You've learned that the planets travel around the sun along fixed paths called orbits. In this activity, you'll construct a model of a planetary orbit.*

## Problem

What's the shape of a planetary orbit?

## Materials

thumbtacks or pins    metric ruler
string    pencil
cardboard    paper
 (21.5 cm x 28 cm)

## Safety Precautions

Exercise care with thumbtacks or pins.

## What To Do

1 Copy the data table *into your Journal.*

2 Place a blank sheet of paper on top of the cardboard and stick two thumbtacks or pins in the paper about 3 cm apart.

3 Tie a string into a circle with a circumference of about 15-20 cm. Loop the string around the tacks. As someone holds the tacks in place, place the pencil inside the loop and pull it taut.

Sample Data

### Data and Observations

| Constructed Ellipse | d (cm) | L (cm) | e |
|---|---|---|---|
| 1 | 3 | 15.6 | 0.19 |
| 2 (widen tacks) | 5 | 13.5 | 0.37 |
| 3 (shorten string) | 5 | 8.7 | 0.57 |
| Earth's orbit | .48 | .28 | 0.017 |

---

**Multicultural Perspectives**

### Keeping an Eye on Venus

Many civilizations, including the Babylonian, Egyptian, and Mayan, developed techniques for viewing and recording the movements of celestial bodies. The Maya were one of pre-Columbian America's most advanced civilizations. At a site called Chichén Itzá on the Yucatan Peninsula in Mexico, the Maya built their greatest observatory. Through windows in the 41-foot-high tower, they could observe the movements of the planet Venus. The Maya built a temple to Venus in their southern-most city of Copán in Honduras. Many cultures considered the movements of planets religious omens and guides to planting crops. Have students research other ancient astronomical sites. **L2**

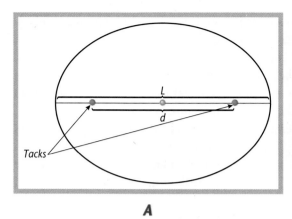

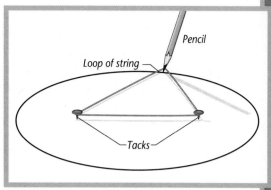

**A**                                                    **B**

**4** Keeping the string taut, move the pencil around the tacks until you
have completed an elongated, closed curve, also known as an ellipse.

**5** Repeat Steps 2 through 4 twice. First vary the distance between the
tacks; then vary the circumference of the loop of string. Determine
the effect of each change on the size and shape of the ellipse.

**6** Planetary orbits are usually described in terms of eccentricity (e).
You drew the ellipse around the two thumbtacks. The two points
around which an ellipse is drawn are called the foci. The eccentricity
of any ellipse is determined by dividing the distance between the
foci (f) by the length of the major axis (L). See the diagram above.

**7** Refer to Appendix J on page 671 to find the eccentricities of
the planetary orbits.

**8** Construct an ellipse with the same eccentricity as Earth's orbit.

## Analyzing

**1.** What effect does a change in length of the
string or distance between the tacks have on
the ellipse?

**2.** Describe the shape of Earth's orbit. Where is
the sun located within the orbit?

## Concluding and Applying

**3.** What must be done to the string or placement of tacks to decrease the eccentricity
of an ellipse?

**4.** ~~Going Further~~ *Hypothesize* what effect
a change that made Earth's orbit more
elliptical might have.

## Expected Outcomes

Students' data will vary depending on the lengths of string
and distances between tacks
that the students choose. However, students should find that
lengthening the string or shortening the distance between the
tacks will decrease the eccentricity of an ellipse.

**Answers to** Analyzing/
Concluding and Applying

**1.** Increasing the length of the
string or decreasing the distance
between the tacks makes the ellipse more circular. Decreasing
the string's length or increasing
the distance between foci makes
the shape more elliptical.

**2.** It appears to be an ellipse
that is very nearly circular, with
the sun near one of the foci.

**3.** Lengthen the string or move
the tacks closer to each other.

**4.** There would be no noticeable
effect of such a change. Seasons
are due to Earth's tilt, not its orbital position.

## ✔ Assessment

**Content**   Have students make
posters that compare Earth's orbit with that of two other planets in terms of their size and eccentricity. Use the Performance
Task Assessment List for Poster
in the **PAMSS,** p. 73. L1 P

## Program Resources

**Activity Masters,** pp. 79–80, Investigate
19-1

**Concept Mapping,** p. 27, Planets of the
Solar System L1

**Science Discovery Activities,** 19-1, Turning Up the Heat

## Motions of the Planets

In the Investigate you constructed a model of the path of planets around the sun. Planets move in a counterclockwise direction around the sun.

For much of history, people thought that Earth was at the center of the universe. They were certain the sun, moon, and planets were embedded in the surface of a large sphere that revolved around Earth. Ptolemy, an Egyptian astronomer, developed a different slant on this idea, as shown in **Figure 19-3**.

A Polish scientist, Copernicus, was the first to hypothesize that the planets, including Earth, orbit the sun. He published this revolutionary idea in 1543. As shown in **Figure 19-4**, Copernicus' model of the solar system had the planets traveling around the sun in circular orbits. Later observers discovered that certain planetary motions could not easily be explained by circular orbits. In the early 1600s, Johannes Kepler, a German mathematician, determined that planetary orbits were ellipses, and that the sun is offset from the exact center of an orbit. The orbit you constructed in the Investigate was in the shape of an ellipse.

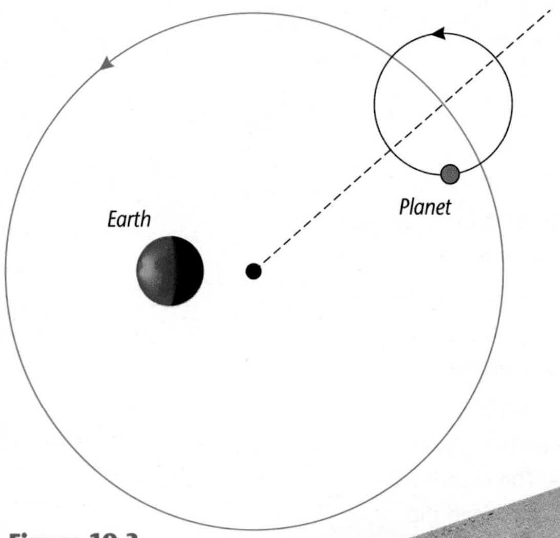

*Earth*      *Planet*

**Figure 19-3**

Ptolemy hypothesized that Earth was near the center of the universe and the planets moved around Earth in a complex orbit.

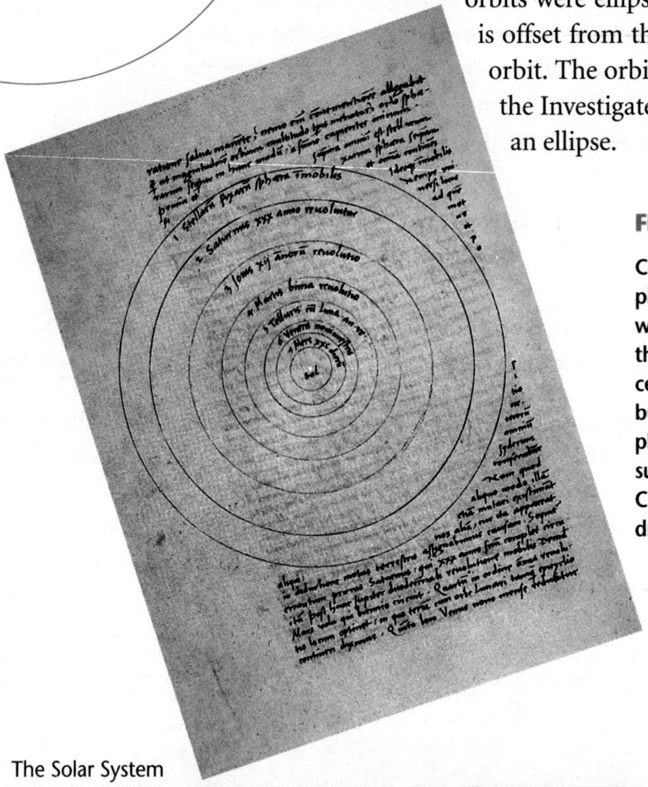

**Figure 19-4**

Copernicus changed people's view of the universe when he pointed out that Earth was not the center of the universe, but one of a number of planets that orbited the sun. This is a copy of Copernicus' orginal drawing of his theory.

# Terrestrial Planets

Except for the fact that planets all orbit the sun, do they have much else in common? Let's compare Earth with its nearest planetary neighbors. Earth and its three nearest planetary neighbors have one thing in common: their surfaces are made up of solid rock. With the proper equipment, you could travel across their surfaces, collecting rock samples. Because of the size and composition of these planets, they are classified as Earth-like, or **terrestrial planets**.

### ■ Mercury

Mercury, Venus, Earth, and Mars make up the group of planets known as the terrestrial planets. Although Mercury is quite a bit smaller than the other members of this group, it is included because it has much more in common with Venus, Earth, and Mars than it does with the other planets of the solar system.

If you look back at **Figure 19-1** on page 598, you'll see that Mercury is the planet closest to the sun. It's the second smallest planet in diameter. Our first close look at Mercury came in 1974, when *Mariner 10* passed close to the planet and sent pictures back to Earth. As shown in **Figure 19-5**, the surface of Mercury looks much like the surface of Earth's moon.

**Figure 19-5**

Ⓐ Even from a great distance the craters on Mercury's surface are apparent.

Ⓑ Mercury's craters are similar to those of the moon. Because Mercury has a stronger gravitational pull than the moon, large walls do not form around the craters on Mercury. As a result, craters tend to be shallower on Mercury.

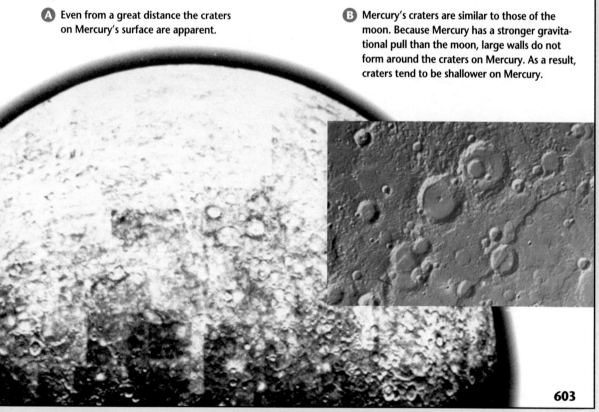

603

Most of the recent evidence about the nature of Venus has been gathered by the *Pioneer Venus* satellite and the *Magellan* spacecraft, which made a radar survey of the planet. Since radar penetrates the thick clouds of the planet, it is able to reveal what lies on its surface. For example, there is no water on the surface of Venus.

**Discussion** Discuss what special equipment would be necessary for humans to successfully explore the surface of Venus. Since the atmospheric pressure compares to the pressure on Earth found at an ocean depth of one kilometer, would deep-sea diving vehicles be needed? How would we deal with the tremendously high temperatures and dangerous atmospheric gases? **L2**

Because of its small mass, Mercury exerts a weak gravitational force compared to other planets. Thus, as you might expect, it has almost no atmosphere. And as you might also expect from its nearness to the sun, Mercury can get very hot. Daytime temperatures reach as high as 450°C. Mecury's thin atmosphere, however, allows thermal energy to radiate away from the planet; nighttime temperatures fall as low as -170°C.

**Figure 19-6**

Ⓐ Radar-imaging makes it possible for us to "see" through the clouds in Venus's atomosphere. The radar image below shows the surface of Venus.

Ⓑ Radar images have shown us that Venus has landforms similar to those of Earth. This volcano is a good example.

**■ Venus**

Venus, which orbits the sun at an average distance of 108 million kilometers, is the second planet from the sun (See **Figure 19-1** on page 598). This planet is sometimes called Earth's twin because it is similar in diameter and mass to Earth. Venus has a thick blanket of dense clouds high up in the planet's atmosphere. These clouds contain sulfuric acid, which gives them a yellowish color.

Beneath this cloud layer lies an atmosphere made up mostly of carbon dioxide gas. This gas is much denser than the mixture of nitrogen and oxygen gases that makes up most of Earth's atmosphere. In fact, atmospheric pressure on the surface of Venus is 91 times greater than that exerted by Earth's atmosphere. You'd have to dive down nearly one kilometer in the ocean to experience pressure this great on Earth.

**604** Chapter 19 The Solar System

## ENRICHMENT

**Activity** To encourage students to observe the night sky and record their observations, locate a nearby observatory or amateur astronomy club. Arrange for an evening field trip for the class. Ask someone from the observatory to recommend a time that is likely to produce relevant observations such as an early evening viewing of one or more planets, or a good view of the moon. Ask if meteor showers are expected during the time students will be studying this chapter. Have students write a report or poem or draw a picture of their observations. Use the appropriate Performance Task Assessment List in **PAMSS**. **L1** **P**

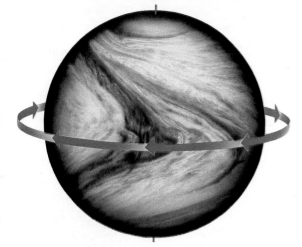

**Figure 19-7**

Venus rotates, or spins on its axis, from east to west. All of the other planets in our solar system rotate from west to east.

The temperature on Venus's surface is 470°C! This temperature is high enough to melt lead! Compare this temperature with the highest temperature ever recorded on Earth, 58°C.

"Why is Venus so hot?" you ask. "Doesn't its cloud cover and dense atmosphere block out most of the sunlight?" You're right, but don't forget the high percentage of carbon dioxide gas in the atmosphere. Carbon dioxide, as you know, is one of the gases that contributes to the greenhouse effect. It acts something like the glass in a greenhouse. Like the glass, carbon dioxide traps the heat from solar radiation and holds it near the planet's surface. Hence, the temperature of the atmosphere rises higher and higher. You know this process is called the greenhouse effect, and it contributes to Venus' very high surface temperature.

## Explore! ACTIVITY

### How do the atmospheres of Venus, Earth, and Mars compare?

Venus, Earth, and Mars all have atmospheres that are quite different from one another. As you do this activity you'll find out how they differ.

#### What To Do

1. Study the data in this table.

2. Which planets have fairly similar atmospheres? Do all three planets have anything in common? Would you expect life as we know it to be present on Venus or Mars?

3. Answer the questions and explain your answers *in your Journal.*

| Atmospheres of Terrestrial Planets | | | | | |
|---|---|---|---|---|---|
| **Venus** | | **Earth** | | **Mars** | |
| Gas | % of total | Gas | % of total | Gas | % of total |
| $CO_2$ | 96.5 | $CO_2$ | 0.03 | $CO_2$ | 95.0 |
| $N_2$ | 3.5 | $N_2$ | 78.1 | $N_2$ | 2.7 |
| $O_2$ | 0.002 | $O_2$ | 20.9 | $O_2$ | 0.15 |
| $H_2O$ | 0.01 | $H_2O$ | 0.05–4.0 | $H_2O$ | 0.03 |

19-1 The Solar System **605**

---

To provide practice using numbers, have students calculate how many years it would take to travel from Earth's orbit to Mars's orbit, if they were traveling at 88 km/hr, the speed of a car on a highway. The average distance between the orbits is about 78 million km. *The trip would take about 100 years.* **L1**

### Uncovering Preconceptions

In the 1870s, the Italian astronomer Giovanni Schiaparelli reported seeing *canali*, or channels, on Mars. A Bostonian, Percival Lowell, mistranslated the word as *canals*, which implied that they were constructed. Lowell built an observatory in Arizona, at least partially to find out if there indeed was life on Mars. Ask students if they have ever read a science fiction book or seen a movie that included life on Mars or visits to Earth by Martians.

**Inquiry Questions** **Why isn't Earth's surface marked by a large number of craters like the surface of Mars?** *Water on Earth's surface, along with other agents of erosion, is constantly eroding the surface. Moving wind, water, and ice may have "erased" the ancient craters.* **If oxygen ever did exist in the Martian atmosphere, where might it be now?** *The oxygen might have combined with iron in the rocks of Mars's surface to form the red iron oxide surface visible from Earth.*

## Mars

Mars is the fourth planet from the sun, orbiting the sun at an average distance of 228 million kilometers (see **Figure 19-1** on page 598). This means that Earth, which orbits the sun at an average distance of 150 million kilometers, is situated between Venus and Mars.

Much of the information we have about Mars came from the *Viking* probes. In 1976, *Viking 1* and *2* landed on Mars and changed our ideas about this planet completely.

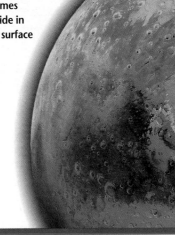

**Figure 19-8**

The distinct red color of Mars is visible from Earth even without a telescope. This color comes from iron oxide in rocks on the surface of Mars.

### Rehearsal for Mars

The first crewed landing on Mars will follow years of planning and practice. Astronauts will have to practice their roles and even their research acitvities many times before the launch. To do this, they will need to know exactly where they will be landing and what the area looks like.

*This photograph of the surface of Mars was taken by a spacecraft that did not carry any astronauts.*

### Purpose

A Closer Look prompts students to evaluate the terrain of Mars in terms of a landing site for a future human mission to the planet.

### Content Background

One of the objectives of the *Mars Observer* mission, launched in September of 1992, was to map the surface of Mars. Its cameras were designed to reveal objects as small as 1.4 meters across, which would have helped astronauts choose a safe landing spot for future human missions to Mars. Unfortunately, something went wrong and all contact was lost with the spacecraft.

### Teaching Strategy

Ask students to compare preparations for the first human landings on the moon with those that would have to be undertaken for similar landings on Mars. **L2**

### ■ Craggy, Barren Surface

The *Viking* probes sent back pictures of a reddish-colored, barren, rocky, windswept surface with many craters.

The *Viking* probes also revealed long channels on the surface of Mars. These channels look as if they were carved by flowing water at some time in Mars's past. Some of the information retrieved by the *Viking* missions is summarized in **Figure 19-9** on page 608.

### ■ Polar Ice Caps

Have you ever used dry ice? People place chunks of dry ice in water to make the foglike clouds that you see at concerts or plays. Dry ice is really frozen carbon dioxide. It's much colder than frozen water, and it's called dry ice because it doesn't melt to form

## SKILLBUILDER

**Interpreting Data**

Use the information in Appendix J on page 671 to explain how Mars is like Earth. If you need help, refer to the **Skill Handbook** on page 689.

### Exploring Mars by Robot

Robots with cameras and sensors will be sent to explore possible landing sites. These robots will be controlled by people on Earth and will send back pictures of the Martian surface along with information about its atmosphere.

### Remote Sample Retrieval

A mission specialist and assistant will operate remote controls that will enable the robot surface probe to move around on the Martian surface. A second mission specialist will operate the Remote Sample Retrieval (RSR) System and collect samples for study. A successful mission is one in which the lander explores all parts of

*Robots will be useful in preparing for human exploration of Mars.*

the Martian surface within range, without colliding with boulders or falling into craters. A successful mission also involves retrieving rock samples from the planet's surface and returning them to Earth for study.

After the mission is complete, scientists and astronauts will study the photos and rock samples. This information will be used to help prepare a crewed mission to Mars.

### What Do You Think?

Discuss the difficulties of exploring another planet. Talk about the steps needed to make sure everything is successful.

## SKILLBUILDER

Both Mars and Earth have similar periods of rotation and average orbital speeds. They both have at least one moon and neither planet has rings.

### Visual Learning

**Figure 9-8** To help with comparing and contrasting skills, have students compare the appearance of the Martian surface with that of Earth and its moon. *Like the moon, but unlike Earth, the surface of Mars is pockmarked with craters. Unlike either body, Mars appears red in color.* Ask students to account for any differences. *The thin atmosphere of Mars, and the lack of atmosphere of the moon, allow objects from space to reach the surface unimpeded, causing craters to form on impact. In addition, the absence of flowing water on Mars and the moon reduces the erosion of craters so they persist for millions of years. The red color of Mars is due to the presence of rocks rich in iron-oxide.*

---

### Answers to
#### What Do You Think?

The discussion should include preparations such as staff training and data gathering about the planet. It should also include the need for adequate food and oxygen supplies for the journey and adequate equipment for surviving the planet's adverse conditions.

### Going Further ⫸

Have students do research to find out how robots are used in the auto industry, the nuclear industry, and in space exploration. Have students suggest how industrial robots or others with which the students are familiar might be used to explore the surface of Mars. **L2** **P**

# 3 ASSESS

## Check for Understanding

Before beginning the table in the Apply question, discuss with students what the important characteristics of the planets should be.

## Reteach

Show the filmstrip, *Exploration of the Universe, Inner Planets,* available from the National Geographic Society, Washington, DC. L1

## Extension

Divide students into four groups. Assign one of the terrestrial planets to each group and have them devise an advertising campaign to encourage travel to their planet. Suggest the creation of posters, slogans, and songs to promote their planet. Call on students from each group to share their advertisements with the class. L2 **COOP LEARN**

# 4 CLOSE

## Activity

Have students summarize information about planets. Materials needed are a baseball, tennis ball, golf ball, and grape. Have students place the objects in size order and indicate which planet each object represents. Then have students arrange the models according to their distances from the sun. *Mercury (grape), Venus (tennis ball), Earth (baseball) Mars (golf ball).* L1

---

a liquid. It just changes back to carbon dioxide gas. The northern polar ice cap on Mars is made up of frozen water and carbon dioxide. During the Martian summer, the carbon dioxide vaporizes, and the size of the polar cap decreases considerably. However, the southern polar cap of Mars changes little throughout the Martian year.

The surface of Mars is quite cold, mostly because the planet is so far from the sun. Actual temperatures range from a high of about -20°C to a low of -140°C.

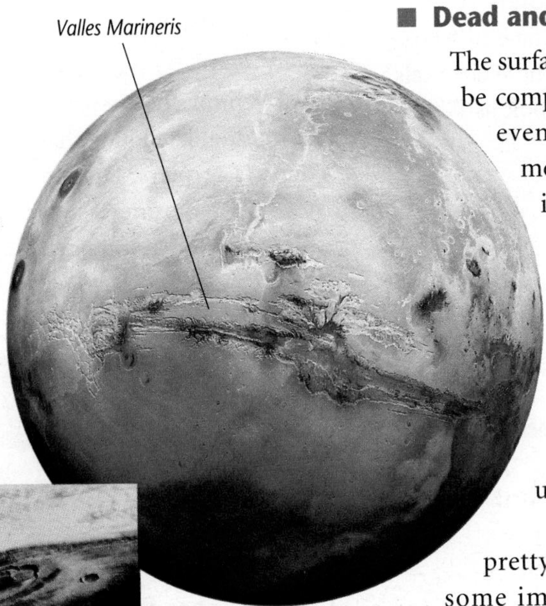

Valles Marineris

**Figure 19-9**

**A** Valles Marineris is Mars' largest canyon. If placed on Earth, Valles Marineris would stretch from New York City to Los Angeles. How might this large canyon have been formed?

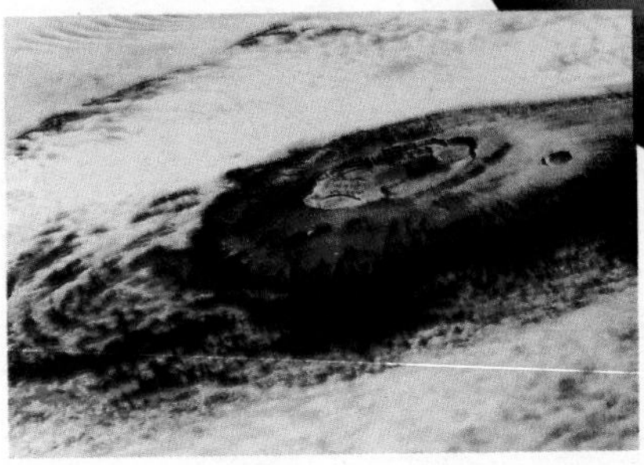

**B** Located on Mars, Olympus Mons is the largest known volcano in the solar system. It is about three times taller than the tallest mountain on Earth. If this volcano were on Earth its base would stretch from Washington D.C. to Boston.

### ■ Dead and Dusty

The surface of Mars is thought to be completely lifeless and lacks even the simplest organic molecules. Lack of ozone in Mars's atmosphere could be one reason for no life. Ozone absorbs harmful ultraviolet rays from the sun. Without this protection, organic molecules cannot survive ultraviolet radiation.

By now, Earth looks pretty good. It certainly has some impressive distinctions. Earth is the only planet where the range of surface temperatures allows water to exist in all three of its physical states. The presence of liquid water is essential for life as we know it. Also, Earth has a great enough mass to hold an atmosphere, which you know is also essential to life.

---

**check your UNDERSTANDING**

1. Explain the current hypothesis of how the solar system formed.
2. In what ways are Venus, Earth, and Mars similar? In what ways are they different?
3. Why are temperatures higher on Venus than on Mercury, which is much closer to the sun?
4. **Apply** Make a table showing the important characteristics of the Earth-like planets.

---

**check your UNDERSTANDING**

1. A slowly rotating cloud of dust and gases contracted. Its core became hot enough to cause hydrogen to fuse into helium, creating the sun. Other particles formed the planets.

2. All are terrestrial planets. Differences: Earth's atmosphere is less dense than that of Venus and denser than that of Mars. Venus and Mars do not show evidence of life.

3. Mercury's thin atmosphere allows heat to radiate back into space; the carbon dioxide in Venus's dense atmosphere holds heat close to the planet's surface.

4. Students should include planet's distance from the sun, atmospheric composition, temperature, and surface conditions.

# 19-2 The Outer Planets

## The Gaseous Giants

Besides the four planets closest to the sun, there are five other planets in the solar system. These other planets are in orbits beyond that of Mars. How do these planets compare with the terrestrial planets?

**Section Objectives**

■ Compare the gaseous giant planets with the terrestrial planets.

■ Recognize that Pluto differs from the other planets and is therefore not classified with either group.

**Key Terms**

*gaseous giant planets*

### Explore! ACTIVITY

#### Solar System Facts and Figures

**O**ne way to learn about planets is to analyze information collected by other scientists. Here's your chance to learn about planets.

#### What To Do

1. Use Appendix J on page 671 to compare each planet's size with Earth's. What is the largest planet in the solar system?

2. Distances within the solar system are often measured in astronomical units, AU for short. Earth's average distance from the sun is 1 AU. How many AUs is Neptune from the sun?

3. Compare the periods of revolution and the periods of rotation for the planets. On which planet is a period of rotation longer than a period of revolution?

4. Record your answers *in your Journal.*

You've visited four planets so far. Now you'll leave the terrestrial planets and travel to the gaseous giants.

The **gaseous giant planets** are huge, low-density planets composed mainly of gases. Much of what we know about these planets was learned from the *Voyager* space probes. Launched in 1977, *Voyager 1* and *Voy-* *ager 2* provided a wealth of new information about Jupiter, Saturn, Uranus, and Neptune. Begin your travel out to the far planets by making a model in the Investigate on the following pages.

**Recognizing Cause and Effect**

Look at the figures for period of revolution and average distance to the sun for the planets in Appendix J on page 671. How are these two aspects of a planet related? If you need help, refer to the **Skill Handbook** on page 684.

---

### 19-2

## PREPARATION

### Concepts Developed

The other planets in the solar system, the gaseous giants (Jupiter, Saturn, Uranus, and Neptune) and Pluto, are presented in this section.

### Planning the Lesson

Refer to the Chapter Organizer on pages 596A–B.

## 1 MOTIVATE

**Discussion** Write this sentence on the chalkboard: My Very Exceptional Mother Just Served Us Nutritious Pizza. Tell the students that this sentence will help them remember the planets in their order from the sun.

## 2 TEACH

### Tying to Previous Knowledge

Students have studied or experienced storms on Earth. Have students compare storms on Earth with storms on Jupiter.

### SKILLBUILDER

As the average distance to the sun increases, so does the period of revolution. L1

the sun, and that Venus's day is longer than a year.

**Answers to Questions**
1. Jupiter
2. 30.061
3. Venus

### ✔ Assessment

**Content** Have students analyze the data to determine the length of the seasons on Mars. Use the Performance Task Assessment List for Analyzing the Data in **PAMSS**, p. 27. L1

### Explore!

#### Solar System Facts and Figures

**Time needed**   5–10 minutes

**Thinking Processes**   interpreting data, making and using tables, comparing and contrasting, forming operational definitions

**Purpose**   To interpret data about the solar system

#### Teaching the Activity

**Troubleshooting**   Some students may fail to realize that the period of revolution is measured in days for the first four planets and in years for the last five.

**Student Journal**   Have students record their answers in their journals. L1

#### Expected Outcome

Students should determine that Jupiter is the largest planet, that Neptune is 30.061 AUs from

# INVESTIGATE!

## 19-2 Distances in the Solar System

### Planning the Activity

**Time needed**  40 minutes

**Purpose**  To formulate a scale model of the distances between the sun and planets.

**Process Skills**  collecting and organizing data, making and using tables, measuring in SI, interpreting data, formulating models, using numbers, comparing and contrasting, sequencing

**Materials**  adding machine tape, meterstick, scissors, pencil, construction paper

**Preparation**  Divide students into pairs.  COOP LEARN

### Teaching the Activity

**Process Reinforcement**  Have students outline a plan for constructing a scale model of planetary sizes.

**Suggested Procedures**  In developing a model, the first step is deciding on a scale. Because the astronomical unit (AU) is a scale that has already been derived, many students will base their models on that scale, with I AU equal to 1 cm. Students may elect to equate 1 AU to more than 1 cm. However, a scale of 1 AU equal to more than 10 cm will result in a model that is about 3 m long.

**Student Journal**  Have students record their observations, drawings, and answers in their journals.  L1

### Expected Outcome

As long as they have done the calculations properly, each pair of students should get the same results.

---

# Distances in the Solar System

*The distances between planets and between the planets and the sun vary considerably throughout the solar system. In this activity, you'll make a scale model of the solar system and use it to discover how these distances are related.*

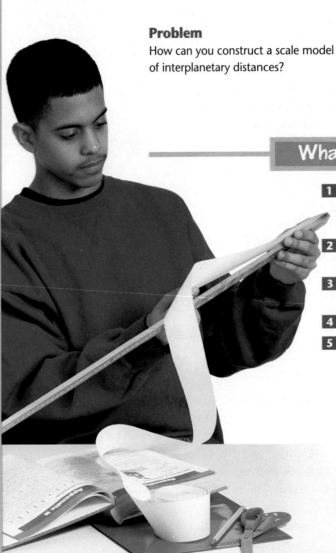

### Problem

How can you construct a scale model of interplanetary distances?

### Materials

adding machine tape  pencil
meterstick  construction
paper
scissors

## What To Do

**1** Use the information in Appendix J on page 671, to make a table that lists the distances of the planets from the sun.

**2** Design a plan to *make a model* of the distances in the solar system.

**3** Write your plan *in your Journal* after your teacher approves it.

**4** Use your plan to construct your model.

**5** *In your Journal*, record your observations, a drawing of your completed model, and the answers to the following questions.

## Program Resources

**Activity Masters,**  pp. 81–82, Investigate 19-2

**Transparency Master,** p. 79, and **Color Transparency,**  Number 38, Relative Distances Between the Planets  L1

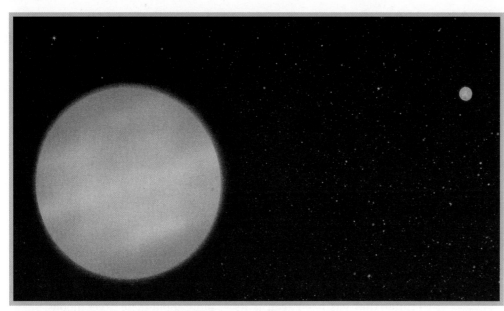

The planet Neptune at left above, as photographed by *Voyager 2*.
To the right you can see Neptune's moon Triton.

## Analyzing

1. Explain how scale distance is determined.

2. On your model, *observe* the four planets closest to the sun, then the five farthest away. *Compare* the closeness of the planets in each group to each other.

3. Would you *predict* that the surface temperature of Neptune would be greater or less than the surface temperature of Mars? Why?

4. Summarize distance in the solar system. *Compare* distances within each group to the group's distance from the sun.

## Concluding and Applying

5. In addition to scale distances, what other information would you need to construct an exact scale model of the solar system?

6. What might be some problems with constructing scale models of the planets using the same scale you used to construct your scale model of distances?

7. ~~Going Further~~ Proxima Centauri, the closest star to the solar system, is about 40 trillion (40 x 10$^{12}$) km from the sun. Using a scale of 10 cm = 1 AU, *calculate* the length of tape you would you need to include this star on your scale model.

**1.** The Earth-sun distance is set as 1, and a scale is selected to give you an overall size you can work with.

**2.** The four terrestrial planets closest to the sun are much closer to one another than the five farthest giant planets are to one another.

**3.** Less; Neptune is much farther from the sun.

**4.** The planets in the group that is farther away are farther apart from one another.

**5.** the diameter of each planet and the sun

**6.** The models of the planets would be too small.

**7.** 27 km (If 10 cm = 1 AU, 1 lightyear would equal 6.3 km.)

**Student Journal** Have students record their data in their journals.

## ✔ Assessment

**Oral** Have students write and present to the class stories, poems, or songs about what they have learned about the distances between, the sizes of, or the features of the planets. Select the appropriate Performance Task Assessment List from **PAMSS.** L1 P

# Jupiter

Jupiter is one and a half times larger than all the other planets put together and contains more than twice their total mass. The planet is surrounded by very strong magnetic and gravitational fields.

Jupiter is composed mainly of gaseous and liquid hydrogen and helium, with smaller amounts of ammonia, methane, and water vapor. Because of its strong gravity, the atmosphere of hydrogen and helium gases may become a liquid ocean as you travel deeper into the planet. Below this ocean is a solid rocky core about the size of Earth. The only part of Jupiter that has been seen is its outer covering of clouds. The *Voyager* probes provided vivid pictures of bands of red, white, tan, and brown clouds. Within these clouds are continuous storms of swirling gas. The most spectacular storm is the Great Red Spot, which was first seen through a telescope in 1664. See page 596 for a picture of Jupiter.

Sixteen moons revolve around Jupiter. Four of them are quite large. Io is the closest large moon to the surface of the planet. Ganymede, another moon, is the largest satellite in the solar system. It's larger than the planet Mercury. Examine **Figure 19-10** learn more about these larger moons.

**Figure 19-10**

## Moons of Jupiter

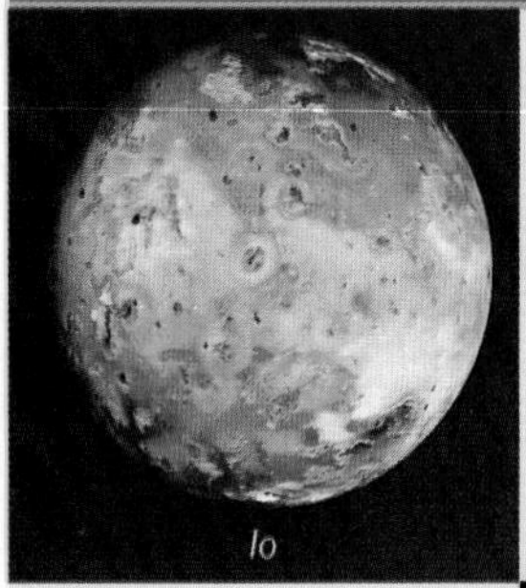

**Io**

**Europa**
Rocky interior is covered by a 100 km thick ice crust, which has a network of cracks, indicating tectonic activity.

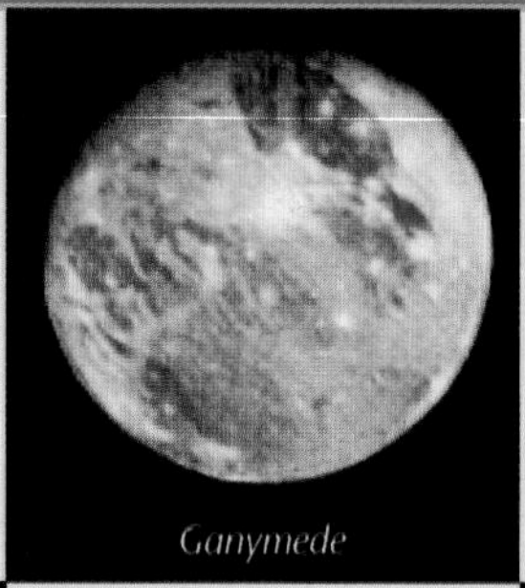

**Ganymede**

**Callisto**
Has a heavily cratered ice-rock crust several hundred km thick. Crust surrounds a water or ice mantle around a rocky core.

**Io**
The most volcanically active object in the solar system. Sulfur lava gives it its distinctive red and orange color.

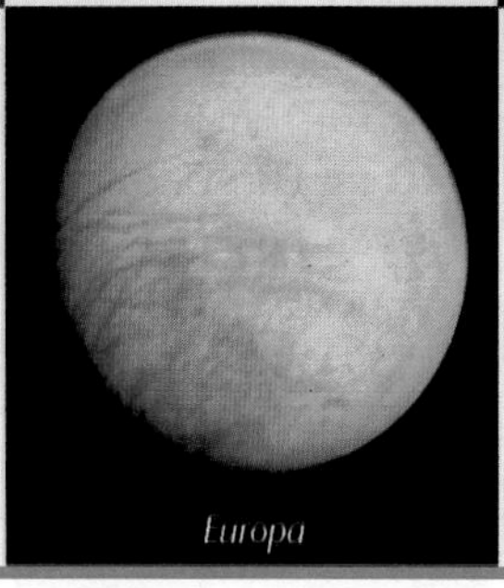

**Europa**

**Ganymede**
Has an ice crust about 100 km thick, covered with grooves. Crust surrounds a 900 km thick slushy mantle of water and ice. Has a rocky core.

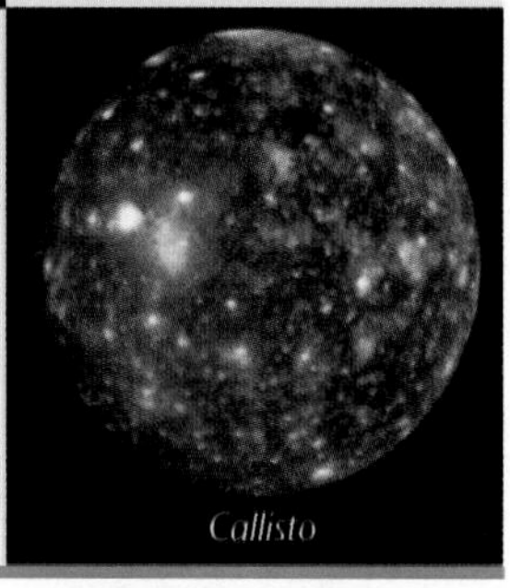

**Callisto**

## Saturn

Saturn is the second largest planet in the solar system, but it has the lowest density. If Saturn were placed in water, it would float. Saturn's structure is similar to that of Jupiter. Its atmosphere contains the same gases. Below the atmosphere is an ocean of liquid helium and hydrogen that surrounds a small rocky core. Look at **Figure 19-11** to see what Saturn looks like.

Saturn is circled by several broad rings, each of which is made up of hundreds of smaller, narrower rings. Each ring is composed of millions of particles ranging in size from specks of dust to chunks of rock several meters in diameter. Saturn also has at least 18 moons orbiting it. The largest of these, Titan, is larger than the planet Mercury. Titan is surrounded by a dense atmosphere of nitrogen, argon, and methane, and it may have organic molecules on its surface.

Figure 19-11

**A** Saturn is the second largest planet in the solar system. In addition to its rings, it has at least 18 moons.

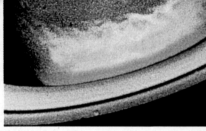

**B** Amateur astronomers and the Hubble Space Telescope photographed this rapidly-growing "white spot" on Saturn in the early 1990s. What do you think this white spot might be?

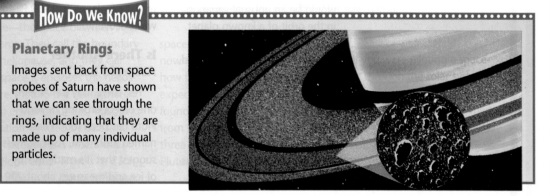

### How Do We Know?

**Planetary Rings**

Images sent back from space probes of Saturn have shown that we can see through the rings, indicating that they are made up of many individual particles.

19-2   The Outer Planets   **613**

**Demonstration** Although Saturn's ring system had been observed from Earth many years ago, the ring structures of the other gaseous giants have been detected only recently. Ask students why they think this is so. *Students may state that the rings are not solid and also very thin.* To illustrate how thin even the rings of Saturn are, hold up a phonograph record. Inform students that if a record was used as a scale model of the rings, and the width of the record represented the thickness of the rings, the diameter of the record would have to be over 12 km.

### Across the Curriculum

**Math**

*Voyager 2* traveled 7 billion km in 12 years. Have students determine the average speed of the satellite in kilometers per hour.

$$\frac{7\,000\,000\,000 \text{ km}}{12 \text{ yr}} \times \frac{1 \text{ yr}}{365 \text{ days}} \times \frac{1 \text{ day}}{24 \text{ hr}} =$$

66 591 km/hr

### Connect to...
## Physics

Find out how gravitational acceleration of an object is related to the mass of the object. Would you expect the asteroids to have a large gravitational acceleration or a small one? Why?

## Asteroids

An **asteroid** is a large chunk of rock traveling through space. As shown in **Figure 19-17** most asteroids are located in an area between the orbits of Mars and Jupiter known as the asteroid belt. The asteroids in this belt may be material that might have combined into another planet were it not for the strong influence of Jupiter's gravity. Some of the larger asteroids have been thrown out of the belt and are now scattered throughout the solar system. It's likely that many asteroids have been captured by planetary gravity to become moons of the planets.

Most asteroids in the asteroid belt are about 1 kilometer or less in diameter. The largest asteroid, Ceres, is 940 kilometers in diameter.

Not all asteroids are found in the asteroid belt. Large asteroids pass close to Earth from time to time. In 1972, an asteroid estimated to be about 10 meters in diameter and weighing more than 1000 tons passed within 60 kilometers of Earth's surface.

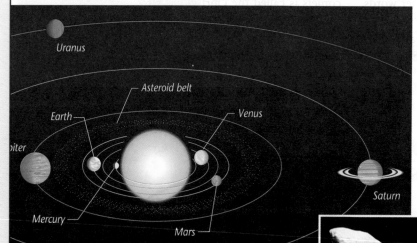

**Figure 19-17**

**A** Most asteroids orbit the sun in a belt between Jupiter and Mars. Do you think "runaway" asteroids could be responsible for some of the surface features that appear on many of our planets? Explain.

**B** Gaspra is one of the larger asteroids in the asteroid belt.

*Gaspra*

### How Do We Know?

**How large are asteroids?**

Most of the asteroids in the Solar System are too small and too distant to be observed and measured with conventional Earth-based telescopes. Astronomers can use the amount of thermal radiation given off by asteroids to determine their size, much in the same way as they use the same kind of radiation to measure the surface temperatures of planets.

## Meteoroids, Meteors, and Meteorites

While the space between planets is mostly empty, space does contain millions of solid particles. Most of these particles come from comet nuclei that have broken up or collisions that have caused asteroids to break up. These small pieces of rock moving through space are then called meteoroids. Meteoroids range in size from grains of sand to huge fragments of rock.

Sometimes, a meteoroid enters Earth's gravitational field and is pulled toward Earth's surface. When a meteoroid enters the atmosphere, it becomes a **meteor**. Friction causes the meteor to glow as it streaks across the sky.

Most meteoroids burn up completely in Earth's atmosphere. However, occasionally a meteoroid survives and strikes Earth's surface. A meteoroid that strikes Earth's surface is called a **meteorite**. A few large meteorites have produced enormous craters on Earth's surface, such as the one shown in **Figure 19-18**.

Comets, meteoroids, and asteroids are probably all composed of material that formed early in the history of the solar system. Thus, a study of meteorites is also a study of the materials in comets and asteroids. Scientists study the structure and composition of these space objects in order to learn what the solar system was like long ago. Such knowledge could help us understand the formation and development of Earth and its relationship to other objects in the solar system.

**Figure 19-18**

This crater was created when a meteorite struck the ground in Arizona. Impacts of this size are relatively rare. They happen only once in hundreds of thousands or millions of years.

### check your UNDERSTANDING

1. How does a comet distant from the sun differ from one that is close to the sun?
2. Compare and contrast comets, meteoroids, and asteroids.
3. **Apply** Why is it unlikely that a comet would ever orbit a planet?

Many people incorrectly refer to meteors as "shooting stars." Explain that meteors are relatively small, rocklike bodies. When they enter our atmosphere, friction with air causes them to give off light, making them visible from Earth.

**Inquiry Question** What causes a meteor shower? *A meteor shower occurs when Earth passes within the orbit of a comet that has broken apart.*

## 3 ASSESS

### Check for Understanding

Have students answer the Check Your Understanding questions. In answering the Apply question, students should be aware that gravitational acceleration decreases with distance. Only objects much more massive than the planets could exert the force necessary to attract an object such as a comet now hundreds of millions of kilometers away.

### Reteach

**Activity** Have students use a small fan and strips of paper fastened to a rubber ball to demonstrate why a comet's tail always points away from the sun. The "wind" generated by the fan is analogous to the solar wind. [L1]

### Extension

Have students research and report on Sir Edmund Halley's study of the comet that is named for him. [L2]

## 4 CLOSE

### Activity

Review the objects of the solar system with the class. Describe size, composition, and other characteristics of an object and have the class guess the category and/or name of the body you are describing. [L1]

### check your UNDERSTANDING

1. Far from the sun, a comet has no coma or tail; a coma forms as a comet approaches the sun, and near the sun, solar winds force gases of the coma into a tail.
2. All are bodies in the solar system; comets are made of frozen gas, ice, and dust; asteroids and meteoroids are rocky. Most comets form in a region beyond the orbit of Pluto and orbit the sun in long, eccentric orbits. Most asteroids are located in the asteroid belt between the orbits of Mars and Jupiter.
3. Only the sun has enough gravitational pull to attract objects so far out in the solar system.

## Science and Society

## Science and Society

# Will Humans or Robots Explore Mars?

### Purpose
Science and Society links the material presented on Mars in Section 19-1 with the issue of whether it makes scientific and economic sense to send a human crew to explore Mars or to send robots to do the same job.

### Content Background
The surface of Mars is not hospitable to human life. Temperatures are too low, there is insufficient oxygen to support human life, the atmosphere is too thin to protect people from lethal solar radiation, there are no sources of food, there are few if any sources of water, and the terrain is rugged and dangerous. In addition, the round trip for a crewed mission to Mars would take many months, which would severly challenge astronauts physically and psychologically.

Other problems and dangers would also be encountered. For example, a crewed mission to Mars would require two liftoffs, one from Earth and one from Mars. Each of these presents special problems that could threaten the lives of the crew. Furthermore, unexpected solar activity or dust storms on Mars could also endanger the lives of the crew.

### Teaching Strategy
Set up two debating teams of four to six students each from members of the class. The issue of the debate should be: Should we send human crews or robots to explore the surface of Mars? The members of each team should thoroughly familiarize themselves with physical conditions on Mars and with factors related to the survival and health of astronauts who must spend many months in space, including the effects of prolonged weightlessness and isolation in relatively

Space scientists today are beginning to talk about sending astronauts to Mars. But talk of resuming crewed exploration has started a hot debate among those who believe humans should explore space and those who think space probes can do the job as well as humans.

### Space Probes

Those in favor of using space probes say the cost of exploration would be much less than crewed exploration. They also point out that astronauts will not have to risk their lives if space probes are used.

**CAREER connection** Engineers design and help build spacecraft for exploring other planets. They work with computer scientists who develop software that guides the spacecraft and helps it conduct experiments.

### Living In Space—Health Problems

Astronauts who survive a trip to another planet might suffer the health problems that have been suffered by astronauts in Earth orbit. For example, bones and muscles become weaker within a few days. Just imagine how weak they would be after a three-year trip to Mars!

Other health problems also result from prolonged weightlessness. The kidneys can eliminate too much fluid from the body. This could cause dehydration in an astronaut.

You may also wonder how a machine could explore as well on another planet as a human could. Scientists who prefer robots have an answer for that question as well.

confined quarters. Allow about 30 minutes for the debate followed by a full class discussion and a vote to determine which team was the most convincing. **L2** **COOP LEARN**

### Answer to
### What Do You Think?

Students should be able to support their reasons with accurate science facts or well-thought-out opinions.

### Going Further ⑄⑄⑄⬥
Have students do library research to determine the positions taken by various scientists, legislators, and others regarding a crewed versus an uncrewed mission to Mars. **L3**

## Being in Space on Earth

In the future, scientists on Earth will be able to wear goggles and data gloves that will allow them to see what the probe sees and to feel what the probe feels. Earth-bound scientists would be able to experience the probe's visit almost as though they were there themselves. Space scientists are already experimenting with these techniques, which they call virtual reality because the experience seems real.

Also, the space probe will mimic the motions of the person wearing the special data gloves. In this way, the glove wearer could carefully control the probe millions of kilometers away.

## Crewed Missions

Many people firmly believe humans, not robots, should be the space travelers. Dr. Carl Sagan, an astronomy professor, admits that robots could do the work of humans on Mars, but he feels that we should conduct crewed exploration if there is enough money to do so. One reason he favors this is because it would "provide an exciting, adventure-rich, and hopeful future for young people."

### *What Do You Think?*

If robots can explore other planets more cheaply and as effectively as humans can, what reasons can you give for crewed exploration?

# Life in a Solar System Colony

Choose one of the books below to read.
*The Martian Chronicles* by Ray Bradbury
*The Rolling Stones* by Robert A. Heinlein
*Farmer in the Sky* by Robert A. Heinlein

In each of these science-fiction books, humans have colonized places in our solar system. In *The Martian Chronicles* the colony is on Mars. *The Rolling Stones* live in colonies on the moon, Mars, and the Asteroid Belt. In *Farmer in the Sky* the colonists live on Ganymede, Jupiter's third satellite.

Use the book you read as a model, and write your own science-fiction story about an adventure on the same planet or satellite. Use your imagination to tell the story, but include accurate scientific information about the planet or satellite itself.

### *What Do You Think?*

How long ago did the author write the book you read? (Find the copyright year on the back of the title page.) Were some facts in the book inaccurate according to what we know now? If the author were writing the book now, how might it be different? Write a short essay about your book telling why you did or did not like it. Also tell how accurate you thought the science was.

### Going Further ▌▌▌▌▶

Have students share the stories they wrote in small groups and select one story per group to dramatize. Have each group rewrite their selection as a short play and present it to the class with some appropriate, but simple, scenery and costumes. **COOP LEARN** **L2**

### Purpose

The Literature Connection reinforces the material in this chapter by having students imagine how it would be to live on another object in the solar system.

### Content Background

Many writers and filmmakers have created works of science fiction involving travel to other planets and visits from extraterrestrial life-forms. They include H.G. Wells *War of the Worlds*, Arthur Clarke's *2001: A Space Odyssey*, C. S. Lewis's space trilogy, and the works of Ursula K. LeGuin.

### Teaching Strategies Before students start writing, have them identify the purpose of their stories and make a brief outline. Encourage them to illustrate their stories.

### Answers to

#### What Do You Think?

*The Martian Chronicles* was published in 1950, *The Rolling Stones* in 1952, and *Farmer in the Sky* in 1950.

Responses will vary. Some of the "facts" in the book were inaccurate. For example, in *The Martian Chronicles*, Ray Bradbury depicts a Martian surface much like those of Earth inhabited by a Martian civilization.

Authors may have written their stories today with the current understanding of the planets or objects involved; thus the stories might have been more accurate. Accept all student responses. **L2** **P**

## Teens in SCIENCE

### Purpose

Teens in Science reinforces this entire chapter by showing one way that students like themselves can become involved in space science. It also discusses how present studies prepare students for the field of engineering.

### Content Background

Currently in the works is a space station planned to be a permanently crewed base in orbit around Earth. It will enable scientists to conduct laboratory research, study the effects on humans of prolonged space travel, and focus telescopes on Earth and the rest of the universe free from the limitations imposed by Earth's atmosphere. In addition to the United States, Belgium, Canada, Denmark, France, Germany, Italy, Japan, the Netherlands, Norway, Spain, and the United Kingdom are providing major program elements at an estimated cost of nearly $8 billion.

A voltmeter is an instrument used to measure the difference in electric potential between two points in a circuit. An ohmmeter measures the resistance to a flow of current. A diode is a device that has a low resistance in one direction and a high resistance in the other direction and can be used to convert alternating current (AC) to direct current (DC).

### Teaching Strategy

Have students discuss whether the classes they are now taking could help to prepare them for the SHARP program. Although they are not studying calculus now, will the math they learn now be needed in advanced math courses? How? What other skills must Candace have had in order to succeed in the program? Which classes build these skills? L2

## Teens in SCIENCE

# The Space Station Project

Candace Kendrick was still in high school when she began working on NASA's space station project at Johnson Space Center. Although she was just 17 years old, she had already put in years of hard work in math and science, her favorite subjects.

### Apprentice Engineer

Candace was one of 17 students chosen to participate in the space center's eight-week summer program called SHARP (Summer High School Apprenticeship Program). The NASA program selects young people to work with engineers and scientists on projects at space research facilities in the United States.

In her NASA job, Candace studied ways of calibrating electrical instruments on the Space Station Freedom. "The calibration devices at NASA are great," she says. "But they're too big and generate too much heat to put on the already crowded space station."

Her project was to find ways to overcome heat and size problems. She also had to find ways to prevent electromagnetic interference among instruments aboard the station.

### Calibration Problems

From day to day, she calibrated electrical instruments, such as voltmeters and ohmmeters. She spent her lunch hour studying at the library. She also learned from NASA electrical engineers and electricians.

The effort paid off for Candace, who wrote a research paper recommending use of a diode to calibrate space station equipment. Her report was well received by NASA personnel, and she hopes to participate in future NASA programs for college students.

Candace's friends describe her as serious and meticulous, and Candace agrees. "I really hate surface learning. That's one thing about physics and math. If you don't understand one thing, it's hard to go on to the next thing."

Her advice to those who want to follow in her footsteps? "Concentrate on math. If you really want to go into engineering, math is really important. It's probably important for anything you go into, but it's really important for engineering. And take the honors classes because they'll help you a lot, even if it's scary."

### What Do You Think?

What specialized courses should you take to pursue the career of your dreams? In what ways can you use the courses you are taking now to help you in the future?

### Answers to
#### What Do You Think?

Answers will vary, but should include a need for specialized math, science, language arts, social studies, and history courses of some kind. The courses the students are now taking provide the foundation for the specialized courses they will take in the future.

### Going Further ▸

Have students write to NASA to acquire information about SHARP or explore apprenticeship programs in other areas that they find interesting. Ask them to report on the name of the program, its location, cost, application requirements, and whether they are qualified for the program. If not, ask students what they might do to prepare themselves to enter the program or obtain exposure to their chosen areas in other ways. L1

Review the statements below about the big ideas presented in this chapter, and try to answer the questions. Then, re-read your answers to the Did You Ever Wonder questions at the beginning of the chapter. *In your Journal*, write a paragraph about how your understanding of the big ideas in the chapter has changed.

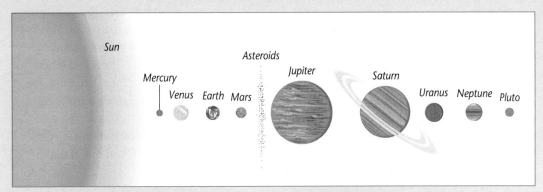

Sun

Asteroids

Mercury    Jupiter    Saturn

Venus  Earth  Mars    Uranus  Neptune  Pluto

**1** The major components of the solar system are the sun and the nine planets that revolve around the sun. *What is the shape of the orbital path of planets?*

**2** The planets are classified into two groups—Earth-like, or terrestrial, planets, and gaseous giant planets. *Why might gaseous giant planets have more moons than terrestrial planets?*

**3** The solar system formed more than 4.6 billion years ago from a huge rotating cloud of gas and dust that condensed to form the sun and planets. *How does the formation of the solar system explain observed orbits of planets?*

**4** Comets and asteroids are other important components of the solar system. *How might the position of the asteroid belt explain how it originated?*

## Project

Divide students into teams to research and report on the history of exploration of one of the planets. Encourage teams to write to NASA to acquire material about past, present, and planned future missions to their planet. Use the Performance Task Assessment List for Group Work in **PAMSS**, p. 97. **COOP LEARN** **L1**

## Science at Home

Have each student produce a model of one of the planets. These models can be constructed of any material but should be three-dimensional. Encourage students to illustrate as many of the surface or observable features of their planet as possible, such as cratering, ring systems, atmospheric features, satellites, etc. **L1**

---

Students will use the text and illustrations on this page to play a game that tests their knowledge of the chapter contents.

### Teaching Strategies

Have students work in pairs to play twenty questions. Each student writes something about three members of the solar system on an index card or piece of paper. The components should be only one, two, or three words long. They can be the name of a planet or other body in the solar system or a structure found on one of those bodies, such as a crater, rings, or the Great Red Spot. When both students are ready, have one try to guess what the other has written on his or her first card in twenty questions or fewer. The questions must be phrased so that the answer is either yes or no or a guess at the contents of the card. For example, a question might be "Is it between Mars and Venus?" The student continues to ask questions until he or she guesses correctly or has asked twenty questions. Then students reverse roles. Repeat until all three cards are guessed. Students get one point for every question or guess that they make. The student with the *lowest* total points from the three questions wins.

### Answers to Questions

**1.** The shape is an ellipse.

**2.** Because they are larger, have greater mass, and thus greater gravitational attraction.

**3.** Because the solar system formed from a swirling gas cloud, the current orbits of the planets are around the sun (which was once the center of the gas cloud).

**4.** The position of the asteroid belt may be related to its origin because Jupiter and the Sun may have exerted enough gravitational pull such that the fragments in the asteroid belt never came together to form a planet.

## Using Key Science Terms

**1.** Meteors are rocks that enter Earth's atmosphere. Meteorites are meteors that strike Earth's surface.

**2.** Both asteroids and comets are chunks of matter traveling through space. Asteroids are rock and are found between the orbits of Mars and Jupiter. Comets are large chunks of ice, dust, frozen gases, and rock fragments whose orbits cut across those of the planets.

**3.** Mercury, Venus, Earth, Mars. The surfaces of these four terrestrial planets are made of rock.

**4.** Jupiter, Saturn, Uranus, Neptune. The gaseous planets are large, low-density planets composed mainly of gases.

**5.** A planet is a body of matter that travels in an orbit around a star. A solar system consists of a star, planets, and smaller objects traveling around the star.

## Understanding Ideas

**1.** The high density of the atmospheres would crush any space probe before it could reach the planet's surface.

**2.** The greenhouse effect on Venus is much greater than that on Earth because the clouds are so dense and the amount of carbon dioxide is great.

**3.** An asteroid belt is a region where many asteroids are found. In the solar system, this is a bond between the orbits of Mars and Jupiter.

**4.** Neptune and Uranus are similar in size and composition and have ring systems. Uranus has 15 moons and is tilted on its axis to be almost parallel to the plane of its orbit. Neptune is less tilted on its axis and has eight moons.

**5.** Until 1999, Pluto is closer to the sun. Because Pluto's orbit is so elliptical, it will cross Neptune's orbit again in 1999 and Neptune will then be closer to the sun.

## Using Key Science Terms

| | |
|---|---|
| asteroid | meteorite |
| comet | planet |
| gaseous giant planets | solar system |
| meteor | terrestrial planets |

**1.** Distinguish between a meteor and a meteorite.

**2.** What are some similarities and differences between asteroids and comets?

**3.** What are the four terrestrial planets and what do they have in common?

**4.** What are the four gaseous planets and what do they have in common?

**5.** How is a planet related to a solar system?

## Understanding Ideas

*Answer the following questions* in your Journal *using complete sentences.*

**1.** Why are surface probes or landings on Jupiter or Saturn unlikely events?

**2.** Why is the surface temperature on Venus so much higher than on Earth?

**3.** What is an asteroid belt?

**4.** Compare and contrast the characteristics of Neptune and Uranus.

**5.** Which planet is presently closer to the sun, Neptune or Pluto? Will this change? Why or why not?

## Developing Skills

*Use your understanding of the concepts developed in this chapter to answer each of the following questions.*

**1. Concept Mapping** Develop an illustration that will help you organize information about the solar system including: relative position of planets and other objects, relative distances from the sun, relative sizes, and periods of rotation and revolution.

**2. Comparing and Contrasting** Refer to Appendix J again as you did in the Explore activity on page 609. What happens to the average orbital speed of the planets as they get farther away from the sun? Are these differences related to the sizes of the planets? Explain.

**3. Making Models** After making a model of distances in the solar system to scale in the Investigate on page 610, develop a scale to make a model of the planets (the scale will have to be different) and add the number of known satellites around each planet. Cut out the planets and satellites and attach them to the adding machine tape model of the distances between planets. Do any of the distances between planets or planet sizes surprise you? Is this an accurate scale model of the solar system? Explain.

## Developing Skills

**1.** Students should include an orbital diagram with planets and orbits labelled correctly.

**2.** The average orbital speed decreases as the planets get farther away from the sun. No; if they were related to the size of the planets, Pluto would move as fast as Mercury or faster.

**3.** Answers to the first part will vary. No, this is not an accurate scale model since the planets are constructed to a different scale than are the distances between objects in the solar system.

> ## Program Resources
>
> **Review and Assessment,** pp. 113–118 [L1]
> **Performance Assessment,** Ch. 19 [L2]
> **PAMSS**
> **Alternate Assessment in the Science Classroom**
> **Computer Test Bank**

## Critical Thinking

In your Journal, *answer each of the following questions.*

1. Why are scientists concerned about the possible destruction of the ozone layer of Earth's atmosphere?

2. We are able to see Mercury and Venus only in the early morning or early evening sky. Study the diagram below. Then explain why we cannot see these two planets at midnight.

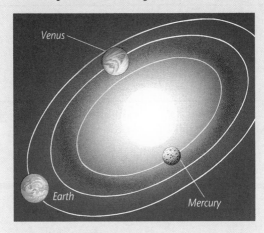

Venus

Earth

Mercury

3. Why is the sun's gravitational acceleration so much stronger than that of any of the planets?

4. What might happen if an object the size of Io passed close to Earth?

## Problem Solving

*Read the following problem and discuss your answers in a brief paragraph.*

**A new planet has been discovered and you have been asked to calculate information on its speed and orbit.**

1. What factors do you need to know in order to calculate the average speed of the planet along its orbit?

2. If you know the average orbital speed of the planet and its period of revolution, how could you calculate the length of its orbit?

## CONNECTING IDEAS

Discuss each of the following in a brief paragraph.

1. **Theme—Systems and Interactions** Assuming the rotating cloud theory correctly describes the formation of the solar system, how might it relate to the Oort cloud?

2. **Theme—Scale and Structure** How is it possible for a day to be longer than a year?

3. **A Closer Look** Why might astronauts need to rehearse what they might do while on a planet?

4. **Science and Society** Do you think it will ever be possible to change the environment on Mars so that it can support a colony? Why or why not?

## Assessment

**Portfolio** Review the portfolio options that are provided throughout the chapter. Encourage students to select one product that demonstrates their best work for the chapter. Have students explain what they learned and why they chose this example for placement into their portfolios. Additional portfolio options can be found in the following **Teacher Classroom Resources: Concept Mapping,** p. 27

**Making Connections: Integrating Sciences,** p. 41
**Multicultural Connections,** pp. 41-42
**Making Connections: Across the Curriculum,** p. 41
**Critical Thinking/Problem Solving,** p. 27
**Take Home Activities,** p. 30
**Laboratory Manual,** pp. 113-116; 117-118
**Performance Assessment** P

## Critical Thinking

1. This layer absorbs some of the ultraviolet rays, which are harmful to all living things.

2. At midnight, we are on the side of Earth facing away from the sun. Since the orbits of Venus and Mercury lie close to the sun, we can only see these planets for a relatively short period of time after sunset or before sunrise.

3. The sun is much more massive than any planet.

4. The gravitational attraction between the two bodies could change the object's orbit, perhaps even causing a collision.

## Problem Solving

1. length of the orbit and time required to make one revolution

2. Multiply the average speed by the period of revolution, because *rate × time = distance.*

## Connecting Ideas

1. Leftover cloud material was probably pushed outward to form the Oort cloud.

2. A planet may take longer to rotate once on its axis (a day) than to complete one revolution around the sun (a year). On Venus, a day is longer than a year.

3. Rehearsing will allow them to plan time, work more efficiently, and plan how to respond in the event of an emergency.

4. Accept all answers with support. An example follows. We have already shown that we can change the environment on Earth, so the environment on Mars could possibly be changed. To change the atmosphere so that it has enough oxygen to maintain life, it may be best to start with a massive plant-growing program.

# Chapter Organizer

| SECTION | OBJECTIVES | ACTIVITIES |
|---|---|---|
| **Chapter Opener** | | **Explore!** What stars can you identify? p. 627 |
| **20-1 Stars** (3 days) | 1. **Compare and contrast** a star's actual brightness with how bright it appears from Earth.<br>2. **Explain** the process by which a star produces energy.<br>3. **Relate** the temperature of a star to its color. | **Find Out!** What factors affect the observable brightness of stars? p. 628<br>**Investigate 20-1:** Analyzing Spectra, pp. 634–635 |
| **20-2 Sun** (3 days) | 1. **Describe** phenomena on the sun's surface and recognize that sunspots, prominences, and solar flares are related.<br>2. **Describe** how phenomena on the sun's surface affect Earth. | **Skillbuilder:** Making and Using Graphs, p. 639<br>**Investigate 20-2:** Tracking Sunspots, pp. 640–641 |
| **20-3 Galaxies** (3 days) | 1. **Describe** a galaxy and list three main types of galaxies.<br>2. **Identify** several characteristics of the Milky Way galaxy. | **Explore!** Why is determining the shape of the Milky Way so difficult? p. 647 |

## EXPAND your view

**A Closer Look** Stellar Evolution, pp. 630–631
**Physics Connection** The Doppler Shift, pp. 644–645
**Science and Society** A Look at Light Pollution, pp. 648–649

**Technology Connection** Questions about Quasars, p. 650
**Teens in Science** Space Camp, p. 651

## ACTIVITY MATERIALS

| EXPLORE! | INVESTIGATE! | FIND OUT! |
|---|---|---|
| **Page 627**<br>star charts, flashlight<br>**Page 647***<br>20 paper cups | **Pages 634–635**<br>ruler or straightedge, pencil, paper<br>**Pages 640–641***<br>several books, cardboard, clipboard, drawing paper, small tripod, scissors, small refracting telescope | **Page 628***<br>small flashlight, 2 large flashlights, new batteries |

*For adequate development of the concepts presented, we recommend that students do the activities with an asterisk.

# Chapter 20  Stars and Galaxies

## TEACHER CLASSROOM RESOURCES

| Student Masters | Teaching Aids |
|---|---|
| **Study Guide,** p. 66<br>**Critical Thinking/Problem Solving,** p. 28<br>**Take Home Activities,** p. 31<br>**Making Connections: Across the Curriculum,** p. 43<br>**Making Connections: Technology & Society,** p. 43<br>**Concept Mapping,** p. 29<br>**Flex Your Brain,** p. 5<br>**Making Connections: Integrating Sciences,** p. 43<br>**Science Discovery Activities,** 20-1 | **Color Transparency and Master 39,** Birth of a Main Sequence Star<br>**Laboratory Manual,** pp. 119–120, Star Colors<br>**Laboratory Manual,** pp. 121–122, Star Trails<br>**Laboratory Manual,** pp. 123–124, Star Positions<br>**\*STVS:** *Modeling Black Holes,* Earth and Space (Disc 3, Side 1) |
| **Study Guide,** p. 67<br>**Multicultural Connections,** p. 43<br>**Science Discovery Activities,** 20-2 | **Color Transparency and Master 40,** Layers of the Sun<br>**\*STVS:** *Monitoring the Sun,* Earth and Space (Disc 3, Side 1) |
| **Study Guide,** p. 68<br>**Multicultural Connections,** p. 44<br>**How It Works,** p. 22<br>**Science Discovery Activities,** 20-3 | **\*STVS:** *Shape of Galaxies,* Earth and Space (Disc 3, Side 1) |

| ASSESSMENT RESOURCES | |
|---|---|
| **Review and Assessment,** pp. 119–124<br>**Performance Assessment,** Ch. 20<br>**PAMSS\***<br>**MindJogger Videoquiz**<br>**Alternate Assessment in the Science Classroom**<br>**Computer Test Bank** | **Spanish Resources**<br>**Cooperative Learning Resource Guide**<br>**Lab and Safety Skills**<br>**Integrated Science Videodisc** |

## KEY TO TEACHING STRATEGIES

The following designations will help you decide which activities are appropriate for your students.

- **L1** Level 1 activities should be within the ability range of all students.
- **L2** Level 2 activities should be within the ability range of the average to above-average student.
- **L3** Level 3 activities are designed for the ability range of above-average students.
- **LEP** LEP activities should be within the ability range of Limited English Proficiency students.
- **COOP LEARN** Cooperative Learning activities are designed for small group work.
- **P** These strategies represent student products that can be placed into a best-work portfolio.

## ADDITIONAL MATERIALS

**Software**
*Stars,* Aquarius.
*Stars and Galaxies,* Queue

**Audiovisual**
*Discovering Our Universe,* video, United Learning.
*The Expanding Universe,* video, Hawkhill Science.
*Introducing Astronomy,* video, SVE.
*Space,* video, Coronet/MTI.
*The Story of the Expanding Universe,* video, Hawkhill Science.
*William Shatner's "The Universe,"* video, Kid Time Video.

**Laserdisc**
*The Night Sky/The Universe: Beyond the Solar System,* EBEC.
*Windows in Science: Earth Science,* Vol. II, Optical Data Corp.

**Readings**
Lancaster-Brown, Peter. *Skywatch.* Sterling Publishing Co.
Moore, Patrick. *The Universe for the Beginner.* Cambridge.

\*Performance Assessment in Middle School Science

\*Science and Technology Videodisc Series

# Stars and Galaxies

## THEME DEVELOPMENT

The universe and all the structures in it are interrelated, if on a vast scale. Stars, such as our sun, vary in size, heat and light produced, age, and distance from Earth. Galaxies, huge families of stars whirl far out in space at distances so great that a new unit of measurement, the light year, had to be invented to describe such distances. Thus, the theme of this chapter is scale and structure.

## CHAPTER OVERVIEW

First, students learn how the brightness, temperature, and color of stars relate to their composition, size and distance from Earth. Star groupings are also named. Students get a close-up view of the nearest star to Earth—the sun. A technique is given to measure sunspots on the solar surface.

Then, students learn how to describe their position in the universe as living within the Milky Way galaxy of the Local Group. Other types of galaxies are described as well as the difficulty of observing the shape of the Milky Way from inside of it.

### Tying to Previous Knowledge

Using a model of the solar system from the previous chapter, ask students to imagine what lies outside of the model. If students respond that there are other stars, inquire whether they are grouped or randomly scattered. Ask them if they can see the true picture from Earth. Remind them that for centuries people assumed that Earth was the center of the universe. From Earth, it is also easy to imagine that the solar system is the center of the universe because from Earth it appears as if all objects in the sky revolve around our planet.

# STARS AND GALAXIES

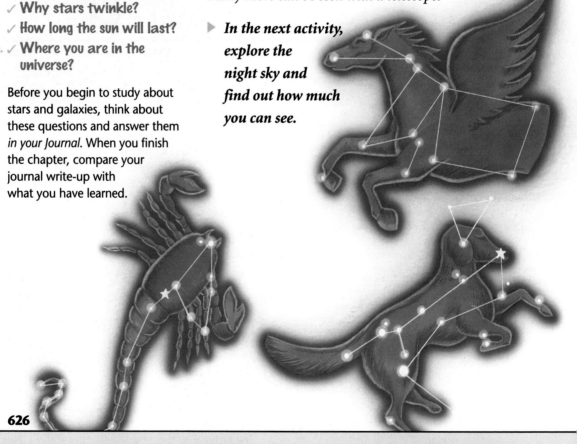

## Did you ever wonder...

✓ Why stars twinkle?

✓ How long the sun will last?

✓ Where you are in the universe?

Before you begin to study about stars and galaxies, think about these questions and answer them *in your Journal.* When you finish the chapter, compare your journal write-up with what you have learned.

**W**hen you look up at the sky at night, what do you see? Perhaps the blinking red lights on a jumbo jet, or the thin trail of a meteor as it streaks across the sky. How many stars can you see?

On a dark, clear night, away from street lamps, headlights, and house lights, you might see over 3000 stars. Many more can be seen with a telescope.

▶ *In the next activity, explore the night sky and find out how much you can see.*

626

## Did you ever wonder...

• Stars twinkle because their light is bent and scattered by dust in Earth's atmosphere. (p. 629)

• The sun will last as long as there is sufficient fuel for fusion. (pp. 630–631)

• Earth is the third planet from the sun in a solar system in the Milky Way Galaxy. The Milky Way is one of a cluster of galaxies called the Local Group. (p. 643)

## STUDENT JOURNAL

Have students write their responses to the Did You Ever Wonder questions in their journals. After they have read the chapter, students should read their journal entries to see what they have learned about stars, the sun, and galaxies.

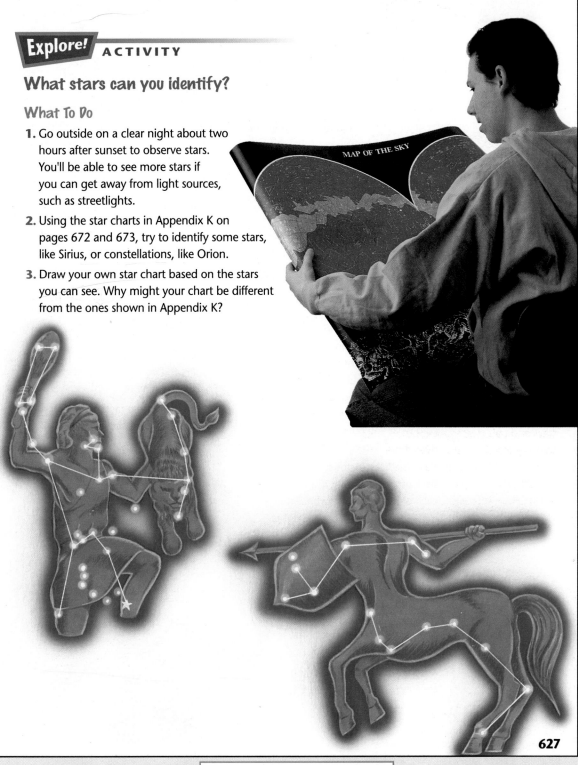

## Explore! ACTIVITY

### What stars can you identify?

#### What To Do

1. Go outside on a clear night about two hours after sunset to observe stars. You'll be able to see more stars if you can get away from light sources, such as streetlights.

2. Using the star charts in Appendix K on pages 672 and 673, try to identify some stars, like Sirius, or constellations, like Orion.

3. Draw your own star chart based on the stars you can see. Why might your chart be different from the ones shown in Appendix K?

MAP OF THE SKY

**627**

## INTRODUCING THE CHAPTER

Have students look at the stars in the constellations on page 626. Ask them whether the stars in a constellation are the same distance from Earth. Discuss the apparent brightness, size, and distribution of the stars in the constellations and how these might be affected by distance and perspective.

## Explore!

### What stars can you identify?

**Time needed** 25–30 minutes

**Materials** star charts, flashlight

**Thinking Processes** observing and inferring, interpreting scientific illustrations

**Purpose** To observe stars and constellations using a star chart.

### Teaching the Activity

**Troubleshooting** Assist students in determining where north is so they can align their charts.

**Student Journal** Suggest that students draw their star charts in their journals. P L2

### Expected Outcome

Several prominent stars and constellations should be observable if the sky is clear.

### Answer to Question

View depends on factors such as latitude, time of year and day, lights, and obstruction by objects.

### ✔ Assessment

**Process** Ask students to identify characteristics of the stars that suggest differences in size, distance from Earth, or energy output. *Brightness and color might suggest such differences.* Use the Performance Task Assessment List for Making Observations and Inferences in **PAMSS**, p. 17. L1

# PREPARATION

## Concepts Developed

In this section students will differentiate between actual and apparent brightness. They will explain how stars produce energy and how the color of a star is related to its temperature.

## Planning the Lesson

Refer to the Chapter Organizer on pages 626A–B.

# 1 MOTIVATE

**Demonstration** The following model shows how stars that are different distances from Earth are seen as constellations.

Materials needed are foam balls and sticks.

Construct a model of the Big Dipper in three dimensions so that the stars are not all on the same plane. It should look like the constellation when viewed from head on, but not at all when viewed from the top or the side. Inform the students that stars vary widely in their distance from Earth. L1

## Explore!

### What factors affect the observable brightness of stars?

**Time needed** 15 minutes

**Materials** 2 utility flashlights, 1 penlight, new batteries

**Thinking Processes** observing and inferring, comparing and contrasting, classifying, sequencing, recognizing cause and effect, making models

**Purpose** To relate distance and actual brightness to the apparent brightness of an object.

**Preparation** The penlight and flashlights must be **significantly** different in actual brightness.

---

## 20-1 Stars

### Section Objectives

■ Compare and contrast a star's actual brightness with how bright it appears from Earth.

■ Explain the process by which a star produces energy.

■ Relate the temperature of a star to its color.

### Key Terms

*star*
*nebula*
*supernova*
*light-year*

## The Brightness of Stars

If you've ever lain down in a field away from city lights and gazed at the night sky, you may have felt what it's like to be covered with a blanket of stars. Above you lie thousands of twinkling points of light. Some stars are bright, like holiday lights, while others are so faint they seem to disappear if you look directly at them. Have you ever wondered why some stars look brighter than others? Explore this question in the next activity.

### Find Out! ACTIVITY

#### What factors affect the observable brightness of stars?

**What To Do**

1. Have a classmate stand at the back of the classroom holding one small and one large flashlight (for example, a penlight and a utility flashlight). Turn off the overhead lights and have your classmate turn on the flashlights. Record what you notice about the brightness of the two lights *in your Journal*.

2. Have two classmates stand at the back of the classroom holding identical flashlights with new batteries. Have them turn on the flashlights. Turn off the overhead lights. Compare the brightness of the two flashlights. Next, have one of these classmates approach you with a lighted flashlight. What do you notice about the comparative brightness of the two lights now?

3. Ask the student closest to you to exchange his or her flashlight for the penlight. Again, compare the brightness of the two lights.

**Conclude and Apply**

1. What are two factors that affect the brightness of light?

2. How might these factors relate to the brightness of stars?

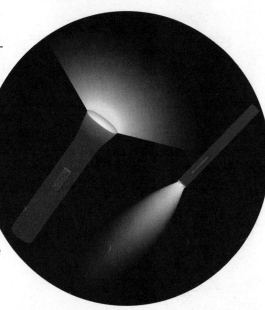

---

## Teaching the Activity

**Student Journal** Have students record their observations and answers in their journals. L1

## Expected Outcome

Distance and actual brightness affect the apparent brightness of the flashlights and also stars.

## Conclude and Apply

1. actual brightness (size) and distance

2. Stars that appear brightest may actually be brightest (largest) or closest to Earth.

### ✔ Assessment

**Process** Have students invent a magnitude scale, from 1 to 5, for identical and different flashlights positioned at given distances from an observer. Use the Performance Task Assessment List for Making and Using a Classification System in **PAMSS**, p. 49. L1

In the Find Out activity, you discovered how size and distance can affect how bright an object appears. The same is true of stars. One star can appear brighter than another simply because it is larger than the other star.

One star can also appear brighter than another because it is closer to Earth, just as in Step 2, when one of two identical flashlights looked brighter because it was moved closer to you. However, the closest stars aren't necessarily the brightest stars, as you observed in Step 3.

In order to understand the brightness of stars, you need to know what a star is. A **star** is a hot, glowing sphere of gas that produces energy by fusion, a process you learned about in Chapter 18. Some stars produce more energy and are therefore hotter than other stars of the same size. The hotter the star, the greater the energy, and therefore the greater the amount of light the star produces; just as the light from a flashlight with new batteries is brighter than the light from a flashlight with weak batteries.

## ■ Actual vs. Apparent Brightness

Because of the variables of star size, distance, and temperature, astronomers talk about the brightness of stars in two ways: actual brightness and apparent brightness.

The apparent brightness of a star is the amount of light received on Earth from the star. A star's apparent brightness is affected by its size and temperature as well as its distance from Earth. For example, a small, cool star can appear quite bright in the sky if it's close to Earth while a large, hot star can appear dim if it's far away. Apparent brightness can even be temporarily affected by conditions in Earth's atmosphere such as dust and moisture.

Look at **Figure 20-1**, for example. The apparent brightness of Sirius is greater than the apparent brightness of Rigel. In fact, Rigel is a much bigger and hotter star, but it's farther away from Earth. If the two stars were the same distance from Earth, Rigel would be much brighter.

**Figure 20-1**

**A** Sirius appears as one of the brightest stars in the sky.

**B** Although it's actually much bigger and brighter than Sirius, Rigel is almost 100 times farther away than Sirius, and so it does not appear as bright.

### Connect to...

## Physics

The stars closest to Earth are much farther away than the sun is. Nearby stars appear to change position throughout the year or exhibit parallax. Draw a diagram that helps define parallax.

# 2 TEACH

**Tying to Previous Knowledge**

In this section, students will learn about the brightness, temperature, and composition of stars. This relates to the study of electromagnetic waves in Chapter 3, particularly in the use of a spectrograph. The source of a star's energy is the fusion of hydrogen atoms in its core. Ask students to explain nuclear fusion, which was presented in Chapter 18.

**Theme Connection** One theme that this section supports is scale and structure. The distances in space are so great that a special unit of measure, the light-year, had to be defined.

### Connect to

## Physics

Parallax is the apparent shift in positions in the sky of a star relative to stars much further away. This effect can be seen when watching your finger and a distant object while moving your head from side to side.

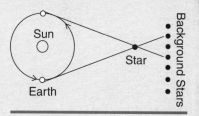

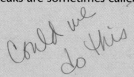

Content Background

As the force of gravity draws hydrogen particles inward in a nebula, the center of the nebula becomes more and more dense with these particles and temperatures rise higher and higher. When the temperature reaches 10 000 000°C, the hydrogen particles begin to fuse. This fusion produces particles of helium and enormous amounts of energy, some of which is given off as heat and light.

## The Origin of Stars

A star forms from a large cloud of gas and dust called a **nebula.** Look at the nebula in **Figure 20-2**. How would you describe its shape?

Even though gas and dust particles are very small, they exert a gravitational force on each other just as all matter does. As the gravitational force

**Figure 20-2**

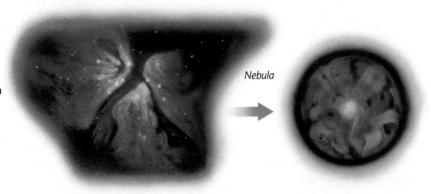

Ⓐ The particles of gas and dust in a nebula exert a gravitational force on each other causing the nebula to contract.

Nebula

## Stellar Evolution

**Y**ou learned that stars begin as nebulas and eventually evolve. A massive star uses up its hydrogen supply rapidly, causing the star's core to contract. The temperature and pressure in the core rise, while the outer temperature slowly

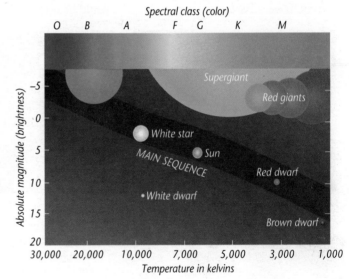

The Hertzsprung-Russell diagram shows the relationships among a star's color, temperature, and brightness. Stars in the main sequence run from hot, bright stars in the upper left corner of the diagram to cool, faint stars in the lower right corner. What type of star listed in the diagram is the coolest, faintest type of star?

*Spectral class (color)*

O  B  A  F  G  K  M

Supergiant

Red giants

White star

MAIN SEQUENCE

Sun

Red dwarf

White dwarf

Brown dwarf

*Absolute magnitude (brightness)*

−5  0  5  10  15  20

*Temperature in kelvins*

30,000  20,000  10,000  7,000  5,000  3,000  1,000

**630**   **Chapter 20**   Stars and Galaxies

### Purpose

A Closer Look will help students distinguish the fates of stars of different masses.

### Content Background

The life cycle of a star depends on its starting mass. All medium sized stars end up as white dwarfs, but a very massive star has a different fate. Its end comes in a spectacular explosion called a supernova. The most spectacular supernova on record occurred in 1054 A.D. It could be seen even in daylight for 23 days and at night for 600 days. What is now left of that great explosion is a fuzzy patch of light called the Crab Nebula.

### Teaching Strategy

To generate student interest in the topics, invite students to relate anything they may already know about stellar evolution and black holes from reading or watching television or movies. **L2**

pulls the particles closer and closer together, the temperature inside the nebula increases. Once the temperature reaches 10 000 000°C fusion begins to take place. The energy released from fusion radiates outward through the condensing ball of gas.

The release of energy into space signals the birth of the star.

After a new star is formed, it does not stay the same forever. Like organisms, stars have a type of life cycle. You'll learn more about the life of stars in the "A Closer Look" article below.

**Inquiry Question** What would you expect to happen to the sun when most or all of the hydrogen in it has fused to form helium? *The helium core begins to shrink. As it does so, temperatures soar, reaching perhaps 200 000 000°C. At these temperatures, the helium particles fuse to form carbon. The sun no longer produces either heat or light.*

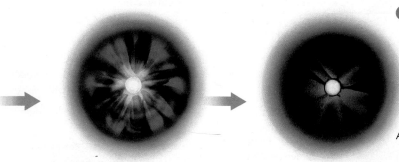

**B** As the particles move closer together, the temperature inside the nebula rises. When the temperature reaches 10 000 000°C, fusion begins, and a star is born.

*Average star*

---

falls. The star expands and becomes a red giant. In very large stars, the core heats up to a much higher temperature, elements heavier than helium can form by fusion, and the star expands into a supergiant.

As the core of a star about the size of our sun uses up its supply of helium and contracts, the outer layers escape into space. The remaining core is white-hot and is called a white dwarf. White dwarfs were first observed in 1915. But it was 1939 before researchers, such as Subrahmanyan Chandrasekhar, an astrophysicist from India, offered an explanation of their evolution.

Chandrasekhar also hypothesized that stars much more

massive than the sun have cores so dense that fusion continues even when the supplies of hydrogen and helium have been used up. Elements as heavy as iron are produced. Once there is no more material left in the core to be transformed, the star explodes into a **supernova**. What remains depends on the mass of the star. It may end up as a neutron star—a small, dense core of neutrons with an average radius of 15 kilometers.

The most massive stars, however, may collapse into black holes after the explosion. A black hole is so dense, not even light can escape its gravitational field. If a light shines at a black hole, the light simply disappears.

## Classifying Stars

When you look up into the sky at night, you see stars that are in all different stages of their life cycles. Just as you can classify living things, you can classify stars. In the early 1900s, two scientists developed a system for classifying stars based on their surface temperatures and their absolute brightness. The Hertzsprung-Russell diagram shows that most stars fall along a line called the main sequence.

## What Do You Think?

If black holes can't be seen using light telescopes, how do you think scientists could try to find them?

20-1 Stars **631**

---

**Figure Caption Question**
**What type of star listed in the diagram is the coolest, faintest type of star?** *A brown dwarf* How, specifically, would you classify the sun? *It is a main sequence star. Its spectral class is G. Its temperature is about 7,000°K. Its absolute magnitude is about +5.* Then ask students how they would describe a red supergiant. *A red supergiant is a relatively cool, bright, and very large star whose spectral class is M.*

**Answers to**
**What Do You Think?**
A black hole can only be detected by inference. Some astronomers suggest that as the gases of a nearby star are drawn into a black hole, radiation in the form of X-rays with unusual properties may be given off. This radiation can be detected and may provide a clue to the presence of a black hole.

**Going Further** ⅢⅢⅢ➤
Have students research and write reports on the supernova that occurred in the Large Magellanic Cloud and was visible during 1987. Have them include some of the data astronomers were able to gather from this event. Use the Performance Task Assessment List for Writing in Science in **PAMSS**, p. 87. [L2]

## Content Background

The color of a star is related to its surface temperature. M-type stars such as Betelgeux and Antares are red or orange-red and have surface temperatures between 3000–3400°C. K-type stars such as Arcturus and Aldebaran are orange and have surface temperatures between 4000–4900°C. G-type stars such as the sun and Capella are yellow and have surface temperatures between 5300–5800°C. F-type stars such as Canopus and Polaris are yellowish and have surface temperatures of about 7500°C. A-type stars such as Altair and Vega are white and have surface temperatures of about 11 000°C. Finally, B-type stars such as Rigel and Spica are white to bluish and have surface temperatures of about 25 000°C or higher.

**Flex Your Brain** Use the Flex Your Brain activity to have students explore STARS. L1

# Determining a Star's Temperature

The stars you see from your backyard or bedroom window probably look white. But if you examined those stars with a powerful telescope, you would see that they appear from bluish white to yellow, orange, and red.

**Figure 20-3**

As steel is heated and its temperature increases, it changes color. Here, the steel has turned red. If the steel continues to be heated, what color will it turn?

Star color reveals the temperature of the star. Scientists have determined that very hot stars are bluish white. A relatively cool star looks orange or red. Stars the temperature of our sun have a yellow color.

The same is true of any object that gives off its own thermal energy. The difference in temperature shows up as a gradual change in color in the spectrum of light coming from the glowing object—whether that object is a nail or a star. **Figure 20-4** shows the progression of color in stars of progressively higher temperatures.

Red dwarf

Yellow giant

White dwarf

Orange giant

Blue giant

**Figure 20-4**

The temperature of a star determines the color of its light. The hottest stars have a bluish-white light, while cooler stars glow with a red light. Stars with a medium temperature, like the sun, have a yellow light. Which type of star is hotter, a red giant or a white dwarf?

**632     Chapter 20   Stars and Galaxies**

---

## Program Resources

**Study Guide,**  p. 66
**Critical Thinking/Problem Solving,** p. 28, Astrology L2
**Critical Thinking/Problem Solving,** p. 5, Flex Your Brain
**Take Home Activities,**  p. 31, Starry Nights L1
**Making Connections: Across the Curriculum,**  p. 43, Astronomical Distances L2

**Science Discovery Activities,**  20-1, The View from Space
**Making Connections: Integrating Sciences,**  p. 43, Black Holes L2
**Laboratory Manual,**  pp. 119–120, Star Colors L2

# Hydrogen Fusion: Energy of the Stars

All of the heat and light produced by stars requires an amazing amount of energy. But where does all of this energy come from?

Stars have large amounts of hydrogen gas. The extremely high temperature and pressure found in the core of a star causes four hydrogen atoms to fuse, forming helium. However, the mass of four hydrogens is slightly greater than the mass of one helium atom. What happens to the missing mass? It is converted to a tremendous amount of energy.

Fusion continues in a star's core until all of the hydrogen is used up. Then helium fuses to form carbon. This also releases an incredible amount of energy. Together, hydrogen fusion and helium fusion can power a star for billions of years, depending on how big the star is.

### DID YOU KNOW?

Like all stars, someday the sun will run out of hydrogen fuel. However, don't get too worried. Although roughly half of its hydrogen has fused into helium, the sun will keep shining for another 5 billion years!

### Visual Learning

**Figure 20-5 Why do you think we don't use fusion power on Earth?** *To use the energy of fusion in a controlled way is very difficult since extremely high temperatures of reaction are involved.*

### Across the Curriculum

**Math**

The mass of a hydrogen nucleus is 1.008 atomic mass units (amu). A helium nucleus' mass is 4.004 amu. Have the students calculate the mass that is lost when four hydrogen nuclei fuse to form one helium nucleus. *0.028 amu* Ask them what happens to this mass. *It is converted into energy.* **L1**

### Content Background

Each type of star has its own spectral signature. For example, the spectra of bluish stars have prominant helium lines, which indicates that such stars are very rich in helium. The spectra of white stars have prominant hydrogen lines. Yellow stars, such as the sun have spectra that show many lines of metalic elements. So it is logical to conclude that the sun is at a stage in its life cycle when it is producing metals.

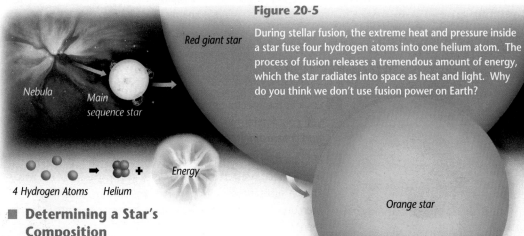

Red giant star
Nebula
Main sequence star
4 Hydrogen Atoms   Helium   Energy
Orange star

**Figure 20-5**

During stellar fusion, the extreme heat and pressure inside a star fuse four hydrogen atoms into one helium atom. The process of fusion releases a tremendous amount of energy, which the star radiates into space as heat and light. Why do you think we don't use fusion power on Earth?

## ■ Determining a Star's Composition

Starlight, like any other light, separates into bands of color called a spectrum when it passes through a prism. However, a star's spectrum has dark bands along the spectrum. This is caused by the absorption of certain wavelengths of light by gas in the star's atmosphere. Each element leaves a certain "fingerprint" of dark bands on a spectrum. By studying the bands in a star's spectrum, astronomers can tell what elements are in the star's atmosphere. Discover how this is done in the next Investigate.

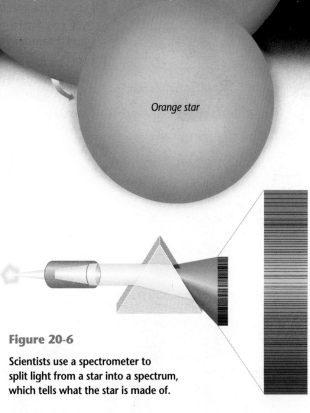

**Figure 20-6**

Scientists use a spectrometer to split light from a star into a spectrum, which tells what the star is made of.

INVESTIGATE!

## Analyzing Spectra

*In this activity, you will observe spectra and determine the compositions of the sun and unknown objects by comparing the dark lines in their spectra with those in the spectra of known substances. The spectra have been greatly simplified for this activity so that line patterns can be easily identified.*

### Planning the Activity

**Time Needed** 20–25 minutes

**Purpose** To analyze spectra and determine the elements present in a star.

**Process Skills** observing and inferring, collecting and organizing data, interpreting scientific illustrations, comparing and contrasting, interpreting data

**Materials** ruler or straightedge, pencil, paper

**Preparation** Students can perform this activity individually or in small groups of two or three. **COOP LEARN**

### Teaching the Activity

**Process Reinforcement** Ask students to discuss the significance of a dark line in the spectrum of a star; that is, what process produces a dark line? A dark line is produced when light in a particular part of the visible spectrum is absorbed by the atoms of an element in a star. Thus, dark lines indicate the presence of certain elements.

**Safety** Remind students that they should never look at the sun with the unaided eye or through any instrument. The sun should be observed by projecting its image or light on a surface such as a sheet of paper.

### Problem

What do dark lines in the spectrum of light emitted from an object tell us?

### Materials

ruler or straightedge
pencil
paper

### What To Do

**1** Look at the spectra on page 635. *In your Journal*, describe how you could determine the composition of the sun by *comparing and contrasting* the spectra.

**2** Using a ruler or straightedge, try to match the vertical lines in the spectrum of the sun with lines in the spectra of the five known substances: hydrogen, helium, calcium, sodium, and mercury. A matching line indicates the presence of that element in the sun.

**3** Record your findings *in your Journal*.

**4** Repeat Steps 2 and 3 for the spectra of the unknown objects.

## Program Resources

**Activity Masters,** pp. 83–84, Investigate 20-1

**Making Connections Technology & Society,** p. 43, Telescopes **L2**

**Transparency Master,** p. 81, and **Color Transparency** Number 39, Birth of a Main Sequence Star **L1**

**Concept Mapping,** p. 29, Formation of Stars **L1**

**Laboratory Manual,** pp. 121–122, Star Trails **L1**

**Laboratory Manual,** pp. 123–124, Star Positions **L3**

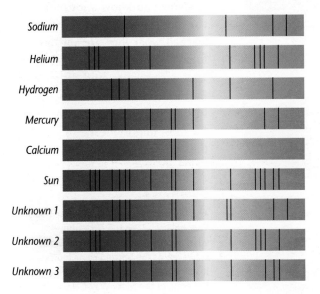

Sodium
Helium
Hydrogen
Mercury
Calcium
Sun
Unknown 1
Unknown 2
Unknown 3

## Analyzing

**1.** What elements are contained in the sun?

**2.** What elements can you *infer* are contained in the unknown objects?

## Concluding and Applying

**3.** How is a substance's spectrum like a fingerprint?

**4.** Going Further How could scientists find out if stars within a newly discovered galaxy are composed of the same elements as stars within the Milky Way galaxy?

To answer the Apply question, remind students that a light-year is a measure of the distance that light travels in one year.

**Reteach**

Obtain a series of slides or pictures of many different types of nebulas with dark globules contained in them (the Eagle, Lagoon, and Trifid Nebulas are good examples). Explain that these dark globules are thought to be places where stars are presently forming. Show slides or pictures of the Crab Nebula and other supernova remnants. Ask students what these objects look like. Students should recognize evidence of massive explosions. L1 LEP

**Extension**

Provide students who have mastered the concepts in this section with star charts and ask them to try to identify particularly bright stars. Ask them if they can distinguish color in some of the stars and, if so, have them attempt to locate and name at least one blue, red, white, and yellow star. This activity must be done at night. Have students write their findings and share them with the class the next day. L2 LEP

**4 CLOSE**

**Discussion**

Based upon what they have learned about stars in this section, ask students to write down as many facts and processes as they can about our sun. Facts and processes can include the sun's temperature, what it was formed from, how it produces energy, what elements it contains, and why it appears brighter than any other object in the sky. L1

## Light-Years

Distances to even the closest stars, aside from the sun, are too large to measure in kilometers. For this reason, astronomers use an extremely large unit called a light-year to measure distances in space. A **light-year** is the distance light travels in one year.

Light travels faster than anything else in the universe, including sound. You may know this from watching lightning storms. Often, you see the flash of light before you hear the rumble of thunder. In space, light travels at 300 000 kilometers per second, or about 9.5 trillion kilometers in one year. One light-year, then, is about 9.5 trillion kilometers.

Now you know a lot more about the stars you see at night. You've learned what they are and how they form. You've discovered that their size, temperature, and distance from Earth affect how bright they appear. In the next section, you will explore the most important star in your life—the sun.

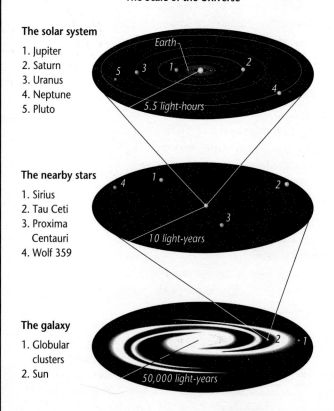

**The Scale of the Universe**

**The solar system**
1. Jupiter
2. Saturn
3. Uranus
4. Neptune
5. Pluto

*Earth*

*5.5 light-hours*

**The nearby stars**
1. Sirius
2. Tau Ceti
3. Proxima Centauri
4. Wolf 359

*10 light-years*

**The galaxy**
1. Globular clusters
2. Sun

*50,000 light-years*

**Figure 20-7**

This diagram shows how large the Milky Way galaxy is. The top circle shows what is within 5.5 light hours of Earth. However, as the bottom circle indicates, it's 50 000 light years from the center to the edge of the Milky Way Galaxy. To compare these distances, calculate how many light hours there are in a light year.

### check your UNDERSTANDING

1. How can two stars that have the same actual brightness look different to an observer on Earth?
2. Describe the process in which the sun produces energy.
3. What is true of the color of visible stars as you go from cooler to hotter?
4. **Apply** Suppose you observe an object explode that is 10 light-years away. When would the explosion have actually occurred?

**636** Chapter 20 Stars and Galaxies

### check your UNDERSTANDING

1. One star might be closer to Earth than the other star.

2. The sun produces energy by fusion. Hydrogen atoms in the core of the sun are forced together, fuse, and form helium atoms. This fusion gives off energy.

3. The color ranges from red to orange to yellow to bluish-white, with red being the coolest and bluish-white being the hottest.

4. ten years ago

# 20-2 Sun

## The Sun and You

The sun supplies Earth and the entire solar system with energy. Energy from the sun warms air and water masses, causing global wind patterns, changes in weather, and ocean currents. We can harness the energy from the sun for use in heating and lighting our homes, schools, and businesses. What are some other positive ways in which the sun affects your life?

Although the sun is extremely beneficial to us, solar radiation can be harmful. If you've ever gotten a blistering sunburn, you've felt the harmful effects of the sun's radiation on your body. Prolonged exposure to ultraviolet rays from the sun can cause skin cancer. About 27 000 Americans develop skin cancer each year, and about 6000 die from it. Think of some ways that the sun has had a negative effect on you.

### ■ An Average Star

As you observed on the H-R diagram on page 630, most stars are known as main sequence stars. Our sun is just such a star. It is considered to be of average age and temperature. The actual brightness of our star is also about average for a star of its fairly average size, though it is a bit on the small side.

As you can see in **Figure 20-9** on page 638, the sun has many layers surrounding a dense core like a gigantic, gaseous onion. The core is the site of hydrogen fusion. Just outside of the core is a radiation zone in which energy bounces back and forth before it escapes to the convection zone. This is a cooler layer of gas that is constantly rising to the surface and sinking back to the radiation zone, transferring energy to the photosphere. The photosphere is the incredibly bright source of much of the light we see on Earth. The chromosphere is an active layer, which is home to magnificent solar displays that we'll discuss later. The outer layer is the corona, which is a gradual boundary between the sun and space.

**Figure 20-8**

Using sunscreen when you are out in the sun can help prevent ultraviolet rays from damaging your skin.

---

### Program Resources

**Study Guide,** p. 67

**Multicultural Activities,** p. 43, Jai Singh and His Observatories [L1]

**Transparency Master,** p. 83, and **Color Transparency** Number 40, Layers of the Sun. [L1]

---

## Section Objectives

■ Describe phenomena on the sun's surface and recognize that sunspots, prominences, and solar flares are related.

■ Describe how phenomena on the sun's surface affect Earth.

### Key Terms

*sunspot*

---

## 20-2

# PREPARATION

### Concepts Developed

Stars in general were introduced in the previous section. In this section, the composition and interior structure of one star, our sun, is presented along with a more detailed exploration of surface phenomena. Sunspots are areas of intense magnetic activity whose variability follows an 11-year cycle. Active prominences may last from a few days to many months, and can extend more than one-half million km into space. Solar flares occur when a magnetic loop becomes unstable and explodes, emitting X-rays, gamma rays, and high-energy particles. In addition to producing auroras, flares can affect power transmission, radar, and electrical equipment on Earth.

### Planning the Lesson

Refer to the Chapter Organizer on pages 626A–B.

# 1 MOTIVATE

**Activity** Pair students into partners and have them compare and contrast the sun with Earth. Students should consider any factors they studied in Chapter 19 (The Solar System) and the previous section. [L1]

**COOP LEARN**

**Tying to Previous Knowledge**

Help students recall from Chapter 8 that the sun affects our weather. Remind them that interactions of air, water, and the sun cause Earth's weather. Have students explain what role the sun plays in the formation of clouds. Connect the information provided in this chapter with what they have learned about the sun's position in the solar system in Chapter 19, and the more general study of stars in the previous section of this chapter.

**Theme Connection** The theme that this section supports is stability and change. The sun provides a constant presence and stability in our lives, warming the surface of Earth on a daily basis. And yet it is undergoing change on a massive scale. Seen with special telescopes, sunspots, flares, and prominences prove that the surface of the sun has a variety of features that constantly change.

**Activity** This activity allows students to compare the relative sizes of Earth, a star, and the sun. Materials needed are string (190-cm and 55-cm) chalk, and a meterstick.

Do this activity outside on pavement. Tie a piece of chalk to one end of the 190-cm string. Have one student hold the other end of the string to the pavement while another student pulls the string tight and draws a circle around the first student. Use the same technique with the 55-cm string to draw a second circle within the first. In the middle of the circle, have another student draw a circle by hand with a 1 cm diameter. The large circle represents a star like Sirius; the circle within it shows our sun; and the tiny circle in the middle is Earth, all drawn to scale. Inform students that it would take a piece of string about 178 m long to draw one of the largest stars, such as Betelgeuse, to this scale. L1

**Figure 20-9**

Ⓐ When you look at a picture of the sun, what you're seeing is actually the lowest layer of the sun's atmosphere. This layer is the photosphere, which is about 300 kilometers, or about 187 miles, thick.

Ⓑ The light from the corona is very faint, and it is clearly visible only when the moon moves between the sun and Earth and blocks out the photosphere. What is this event called?

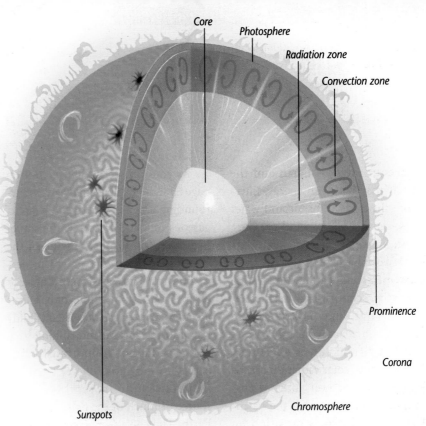

### ■ Sunspots

Often, the sun is pictured as a perfectly smooth sphere. It's not. There are many features that can be studied, including dark areas of the sun's surface that are cooler than surrounding areas. Such a cool, dark area on the sun's surface is called a **sunspot**. You can see examples of sunspots in **Figure 20-10**.

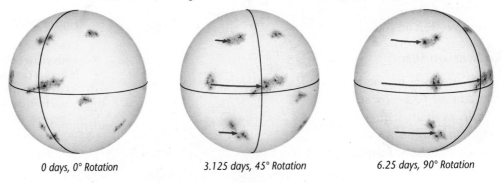

0 days, 0° Rotation    3.125 days, 45° Rotation    6.25 days, 90° Rotation

**Figure 20-10**

Because the sun is made up of gases, it does not rotate as a solid body, as Earth does. The sun rotates faster at its equator than at its poles. As a result, sunspots at the equator take about 25 days to go around the sun, while sunspots near the poles take up to 35 days.

**638    Chapter 20    Stars and Galaxies**

Galileo was the first to identify sunspots, and scientists have been fascinated by them ever since. One thing we've learned by studying sunspots is that the sun rotates. We can observe the movement of individual sunspots as they are carried by the sun's rotation.

Sunspots are not permanent features on the sun. They may appear and disappear over a period of several days or several months. Look at **Figure 20-11** and **Table 20-1**. The table shows the cycle of sunspot occurrences over a 25-year period.

Sometimes there are many large sunspots—a period called a sunspot maximum—while at other times there are only a few small sunspots or none at all—a sunspot minimum. Sunspot maximums occur about every 11 years. The next is expected in 2001. This 11-year cycle of sunspot occurrences is often called the cycle of solar activity.

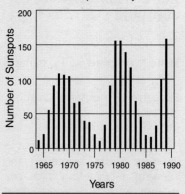
**Table 20-1**

| Recent Sunspot Activity | | | | | |
|---|---|---|---|---|---|
| Date | Number of Sunspots | Date | Number of Sunspots | Date | Number of Sunspots |
| 1964 | 11 | 1973 | 38 | 1982 | 116 |
| 1965 | 18 | 1974 | 35 | 1983 | 67 |
| 1966 | 53 | 1975 | 16 | 1984 | 46 |
| 1967 | 91 | 1976 | 13 | 1985 | 18 |
| 1968 | 106 | 1977 | 28 | 1986 | 14 |
| 1969 | 105 | 1978 | 93 | 1987 | 29 |
| 1970 | 104 | 1979 | 155 | 1988 | 100 |
| 1971 | 67 | 1980 | 155 | 1989 | 159 |
| 1972 | 69 | 1981 | 140 | | |

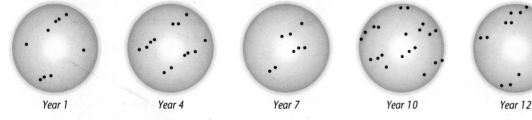

Year 1    Year 4    Year 7    Year 10    Year 12

**Figure 20-11**

As you can see from the pictures above, the number of sunspots changes from year to year. A year when there are a lot of large sunspots is called a sunspot maximum. Sunspot maximums occur about every 11 years. Based on the illustrations above, will there be many sunspots or few sunspots in year 21?

## 20-2 Tracking Sunspots

### Planning the Activity

**Time needed** 60 minutes over 5 days

**Purpose** To observe sunspots, estimate their size, and from their apparent motion estimate the sun's period of rotation.

**Process Skills** observing and inferring, interpreting data, collecting and organizing data, measuring in SI, using numbers, estimating, making and using tables, predicting

**Materials** several books, cardboard, clipboard, drawing paper, small tripod, scissors, small refracting telescope

**Preparation** If a telescope isn't available, substitute binoculars set on a window ledge with one of the eye-pieces covered. Divide students into groups of three or four. **COOP LEARN**

### Teaching the Activity

**Process Reinforcement** Make sure students realize that the sunspots are not moving independently across the sun's face. Rather, they are being carried along with the sun's gases as the sun rotates. Therefore, by calculating the time required for a sunspot to traverse the face of the sun and multiplying by two, the rotation of the sun at the sunspot's latitude can be inferred.

**Safety** Make sure that students understand the harmful effects of looking directly at the sun through the telescope, binoculars, or with the unaided eye. Serious damage to the eye, even blindness, can result.

**Troubleshooting** To ensure correct alignment, in the event the apparatus must be taken down or moved for any reason, mark the exact position of the telescope, books, and clipboard. Only in this way will students be able to accurately record the changing position of the sunspots. If no sunspots are visible, keep the setup in place until some are sighted.

# Tracking Sunspots

*In the activity, you will measure the movement of sunspots and use your findings to determine the sun's period of rotation.*

### Problem
How can you trace the movement of sunspots?

### Materials
| | |
|---|---|
| several books | cardboard |
| clipboard | drawing paper |
| small tripod | scissors |
| small refracting telescope | |

### Safety Precautions
Do not look through the telescope at the sun. Severe eye damage may result. Never look directly at the sun under any circumstances!

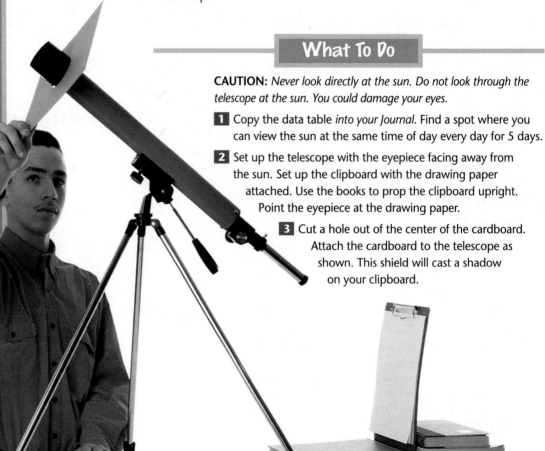

## What To Do

**CAUTION:** *Never look directly at the sun. Do not look through the telescope at the sun. You could damage your eyes.*

**1** Copy the data table *into your Journal.* Find a spot where you can view the sun at the same time of day every day for 5 days.

**2** Set up the telescope with the eyepiece facing away from the sun. Set up the clipboard with the drawing paper attached. Use the books to prop the clipboard upright. Point the eyepiece at the drawing paper.

**3** Cut a hole out of the center of the cardboard. Attach the cardboard to the telescope as shown. This shield will cast a shadow on your clipboard.

### Program Resources

**Activity Masters,** pp. 85–86, Investigate 20-2

**Science Discovery Activities,** 20-2, More Power to You!

**A**  **B**  **C**

**4** Move the clipboard back and forth until you have the largest possible image of the sun on the paper. Adjust the telescope to form a clear image. Trace the outline of the sun on the paper.

**5** Trace any sunspots that appear as dark areas on the sun's image. At the same time each day for a week, check the sun's image and trace the position of the sunspots.

**6** The sun's diameter is approximately 1 400 000 kilometers. Using this SI measure, *calculate* the scale of your image. Estimate the size of the largest sunspots you observed.

**7** *Calculate* and record how many kilometers any observed sunspots appear to move each day.

**8** At the rate determined in Step 7, *predict* how many days it will take for the same sunspots to return to the same position in which you first saw them.

*Plane mirror*
*Rays from the Sun*
*Plane mirror*
*Concave mirror*

Solar telescopes use a series of mirrors to reflect light from the sun down into an underground observation room where the light can be studied.

## Analyzing

1. Which part of the sun showed up in your image?

2. What was the average number of sunspots you observed each day?

## Concluding and Applying

3. How can the movement of sunspots be *predicted*?

4. How can sunspots be used to prove that the sun is rotating?

5. **Going Further** How can sunspots be used to *infer* that the sun's surface is not solid like Earth's?

---

**Student Journal** Have students record their data, drawings, and answers in their journals. L1

**Expected Outcome**

If weather or low sunspot activity prevents the students from completing the data table, they should at least observe that sunspots are transitory features of the sun's surface, apparently moving across the sun and disappearing within a relatively short period of time. However, if weather permits students should be able to estimate the sun's period of rotation by observing the apparent movement of specific sunspots.

**Answers to** Analyzing/ Concluding and Applying

**1.** its outer surface

**2.** Answers will vary, but should be approximately the same.

**3.** The movement of sunspots can be predicted by observing previous movements of sunspots.

**4.** Assuming that sunspots are stationary features, the only explanation for their apparent movement is that the sun rotates.

**5.** When viewed over a number of days, equatorial sunspots require less time to return to their original position than those near the sun's poles. This couldn't occur if the surface were solid.

**✔ Assessment**

**Process** Have students analyze their data to estimate the sun's period of rotation at or near its equator. *The sun's period of rotation at its equator is 25.38 days.* Use the Performance Task Assessment List for Analyzing Data in **PAMSS**, p. 27. L1

---

## ENRICHMENT

**Activity** Have students develop hypotheses concerning the period of rotation of the sun at various latitudes. Students should address questions such as: Does the period of rotation vary with latitude? If so, in what way? If so, what might account for the variations? Students should consult the data they collected in the Investigate! activity to see whether it supports or does not support the various hypotheses. *Because it is a gaseous object, the sun's period of ro-* *tation varies with latitude. It rotates more rapidly at its equator than at higher latitudes, which student data should reveal if the behavior of sunspots at various latitudes was observed.* L2

# 3 ASSESS

## Check for Understanding

To answer the Apply question, students should compare the information provided in this section to that which they learned in the previous section.

## Reteach

Refer students to Figures 20-10, 20-11 and 20-13. Have students use these illustrations and photographs to draw a cross section of the sun's interior as well as phenomena on its surface. **L1**

**LEP**

## Extension

Have students who have mastered the concepts of this section make a model of the sun emphasizing its surface features, such as solar flares, prominences, and sunspots. Models can be made from clay, papier-mache, or other materials. **L3**

# 4 CLOSE

## Discussion

You may find that some students in your class (or their parents) are ham radio operators. Have them discuss how solar activity affects their radios. **L2**

■ **Prominences and Flares**

Sunspots are related to other phenomena on the sun—prominences and solar flares. A prominence is a huge arching column of gas.

Gases near a sunspot sometimes brighten suddenly, shooting outward at high speed. These violent eruptions are called solar flares. **Figure 20-12A** is a photograph of a solar flare.

Solar flares can also interact with Earth's magnetic field, producing a beautiful, eerie light show. This spectacular display of lights is called the *aurora borealis*, or northern lights, in the Northern Hemisphere, and the *aurora australis* in the Southern Hemisphere. Next, you will observe some more spectacular light displays that can be seen only through the lens of a powerful telescope.

**Figure 20-12**

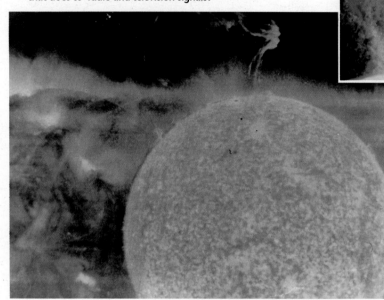

Ⓐ Solar flares are typically a few thousand kilometers across. Most flares increase to their maximum brightness in a few seconds or minutes, and then fade out over several minutes or hours. A flare releases huge amounts of X rays and particles that stream towards Earth. What do you think that does to radio and television signals?

Ⓑ Some prominences are so powerful that they eject matter from the sun out into space at speeds up to 1000 kilometers per second. Other prominences form huge loops over sunspot areas that can reach heights of hundreds of thousands of kilometers. Would there be more prominences during a sunspot maximum or a sunspot minimum?

**check your UNDERSTANDING**

1. In what ways are sunspots, prominences, and solar flares related?

2. What effect do solar phenomena have on Earth?

3. **Apply** How does our sun differ from most other stars? In what ways is our sun average? How would life be affected on Earth if the sun was larger or smaller?

**check your UNDERSTANDING**

1. They are all solar disturbances in the surface gases of the sun.

2. Solar flares can disrupt telephone and radio communication. They also produce the aurora borealis and aurora australis.

3. It is the star closest to Earth. It is an average star in size, temperature, and age. Life on Earth requires, among other things, just the right amount of heat and other radiation from the sun. If the sun were larger, it might engulf and burn up Earth. If the sun were smaller, it might not produce enough light and heat to make life possible on Earth.

# Galaxies

## Earth's Galaxy—and Others

One reason to study astronomy is to learn about your place in the universe. Through centuries of studying space, we know there's a lot more to the universe than the sun and planets in our solar system.

Suppose you need to give directions to your house to a distant cousin who lives in another country. You could probably do it. But suppose your cousin lives in a galaxy millions of light-years away. Look at **Figure 20-13**. What other information would you need to give your cousin?

You are living on a planet in a giant galaxy called the Milky Way. A **galaxy** is a large group of stars, gas, and dust held together by gravity. Our galaxy contains about 200 billion stars. The sun is just one of those stars, and Earth revolves around it.

Just as stars are grouped together within galaxies, galaxies are grouped into clusters. Even so, the galaxies in a cluster are separated by huge distances—often millions of light-years. The cluster the Milky Way belongs to is called the Local Group. It contains about 25 galaxies of various shapes and sizes. However, there are three major types of galaxies: elliptical, spiral, and irregular.

### Section Objectives

- Describe a galaxy and list three main types of galaxies.
- Identify several characteristics of the Milky Way galaxy.

### Key Terms

*galaxy*

**Figure 20-13**

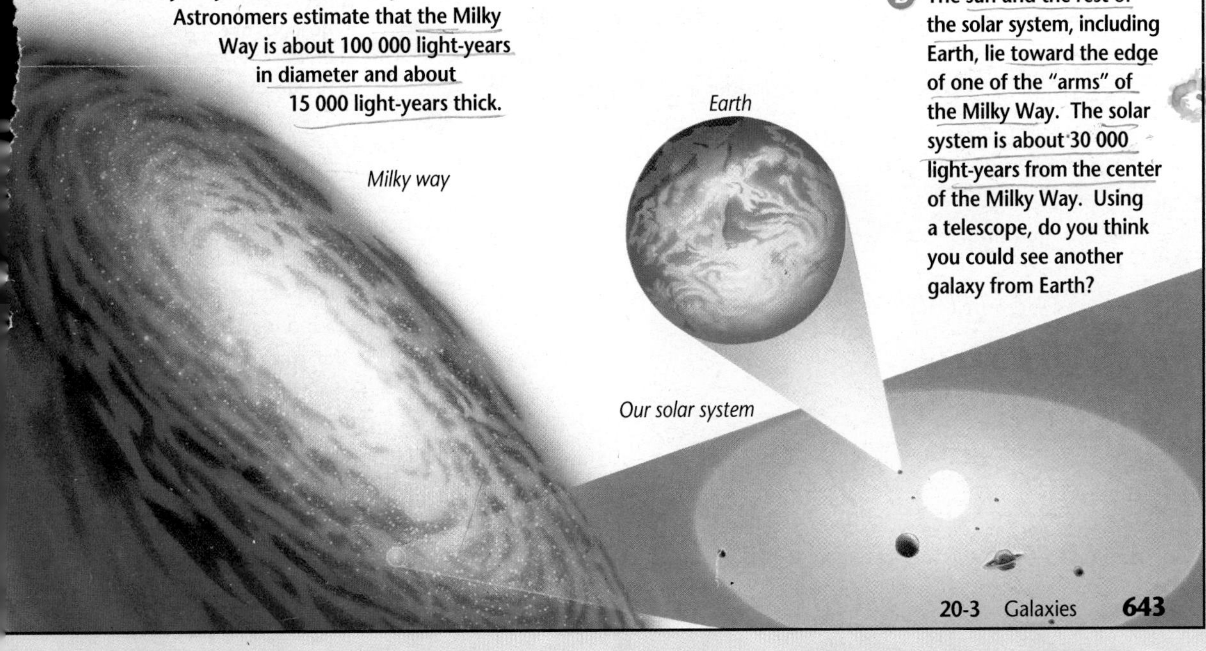

**A** The Milky Way galaxy contains about 200 billion stars, one of which is the sun. The Milky Way also contains many nebulas. Astronomers estimate that the Milky Way is about 100 000 light-years in diameter and about 15 000 light-years thick.

*Milky way*

*Earth*

*Our solar system*

**B** The sun and the rest of the solar system, including Earth, lie toward the edge of one of the "arms" of the Milky Way. The solar system is about 30 000 light-years from the center of the Milky Way. Using a telescope, do you think you could see another galaxy from Earth?

20-3 Galaxies **643**

## Program Resources

**Study Guide,** p. 68
**Multicultural Activities,** p. 44, Ancient Astronomers [L1]
**How It Works,** p. 22, Radio Telescope [L2]
**Science Discovery Activities,** 20-3, Starry, Starry Night

### ENRICHMENT

**Research** Have students research the work of Margaret Geller and John Huchra, of the Harvard-Smithsonian Center for Astrophysics, on mapping the universe. The work of these two astronomers has led to the realization that great voids and large concentrations of galaxies alternate throughout the universe. They discovered that many galaxies lie in an enormous sheet now called the "Great Wall." [L1]

# PREPARATION

## Concepts Developed

In this section, students will describe the characteristics of a galaxy and compare and contrast types of galaxies. Students will also identify our location in the Milky Way galaxy.

## Planning the Lesson

Refer to the Chapter Organizer on pages 626A–B.

# 1 MOTIVATE

**Demonstration** Obtain a set of astronomy slides showing several galaxies. Demonstrate the different types of galaxies by showing slides of each type. Include a slide of the galaxy M31 in the Andromeda constellation. This is the closest large galaxy to the Milky Way. [L1]

# 2 TEACH

## Tying to Previous Knowledge

Review with students the systems of objects in space they have already studied. Galaxies and the Local Group are still larger groupings of gravitationally-bound objects moving together through space.

### Visual Learning

**Figure 20-13 Using a telescope, do you think you could see another galaxy from Earth?** *yes*

**Student · Text Question** What other information would you need to give your cousin? *the direction and distance to the Milky Way Galaxy and its location in the Local Group.*

## Elliptical Galaxies

**Figure 20-14**

**A** Elliptical galaxies, like the one shown here, contain mostly older, dimmer stars.

The most common type of galaxy is the elliptical galaxy. These galaxies are like large, three-dimensional ellipses. Many are football-shaped. Some elliptical galaxies are quite small, but others are so large that the entire Local Group of galaxies would fit inside them. **Figure 20-14A** shows an elliptical galaxy.

## Spiral Galaxies

Spiral galaxies have arms that curve outward from a central hub, making them look something like a pinwheel. The spiral arms are made up of stars and dust. In between the arms are fewer stars. **Figure 20-14B** shows a typical spiral galaxy.

The fuzzy patch you can see on a clear night in the constellation of Andromeda is actually a spiral galaxy. It's so far away that you can't see its

**B** Spiral galaxies, like the one shown here, contain a complete mixture of young and old stars.

# Physics CONNECTION

The red shift in the light from stars means that they are moving away from Earth, so eventually, some of these stars might no longer be visible from Earth.

## The Doppler Shift

Have you ever heard the horn of a train or car as it approached you and then passed? If you have, you know the sound becomes louder and louder as it approaches and then becomes fainter as it leaves. But the volume is not all that changes. The sound also changes, from lower to higher, then back to lower pitches as the train moves away. The change in pitch is called the Doppler shift. Scientists have been able to associate the Doppler shift with sound waves and with light waves.

### Shifty Light

Astronomers understand that the change in wavelength on a light spectrum is similar to the change in pitch of the train's horn. The wavelength of light from an object becomes shorter as the object approaches, just as the sound waves did.

If a star were approaching, the dark lines of its spectrum would move toward the blue-violet part of the spectrum. But if the star were traveling away, the lines would move toward the red part of the spectrum.

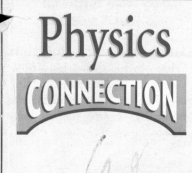

individual stars. Instead, it appears as a hazy spot in the night sky. The Andromeda galaxy is a member of the Local Group and is about 2 million light-years away from the Milky Way.

As you saw in **Figure 20-14B**, arms in a typical spiral galaxy start close to the center of the galaxy. Barred spiral galaxies have two spiral arms extending from a large bar that passes through the center of the galaxy. **Figure 20-15A** shows a barred spiral galaxy.

### ■ Irregular Galaxies

The third type of galaxy includes all those galaxies that don't fit into the other two categories. Irregular galaxies come in many different shapes and are smaller and less common than ellipticals or spirals. The Large Magellanic Cloud, shown in **Figure 20-15B**, is an irregular galaxy that orbits the Milky Way galaxy at a mere distance of about 170 000 light-years.

**Figure 20-15**

Ⓐ The bar in a barred spiral galaxy contains gas and dust clouds and bright stars.

Ⓑ Irregular galaxies, like the one shown here, contain from 100 million to a few billion stars.

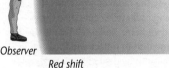

Observer
Red shift

Moving
light source

Observer
Blue shift

### The Expanding Universe

In 1924, Edward Hubble noticed that there is a red shift in the light from galaxies beyond the Local Group. What did this tell him about the universe? Because all galaxies beyond the Local Group show a red shift in their spectra, they must be moving away from Earth. Hubble then concluded that, for so many galaxies to be traveling away from Earth, the universe must be expanding.

### You Try It!

You can get an idea of how distances between stars change by inflating a balloon slightly and then closing it with a clothespin. Use a felt-tipped pen to put dots in a number of places on the balloon. Next, inflate the balloon some more and watch how distances between dots change.

The dots move away from each other, just as galaxies in the universe are doing. Such

*This diagram illustrates the Doppler shift of a moving object. An observer would note a red shift in the spectrum as an object moves away and a blue shift as it moves closer.*

observations led scientists to the "big bang" theory, which states that our universe began with an incredibly large explosion. Matter was blown apart by the explosion and even today the universe continues to expand.

20-3 Galaxies **645**

**646    Chapter 20    Stars and Galaxies**

# 3 ASSESS

### Check for Understanding

To answer the Apply question, make sure students can sequence the hierarchy of systems from planets, to solar system, galaxy, and cluster.

### Reteach

Have students draw and label pictures of the four galaxies illustrated in this section. Be sure that each drawing contains the unique characteristics of each galaxy. L1

### Extension

Ask students who have mastered the concepts in this section to further research the Doppler effect which shows whether distant objects are moving toward or away from us. L3

# 4 CLOSE

### Discussion

Discuss the most recent NASA research-based space mission. Bring in periodical articles. Talk about any satellite launches made and whether telescopes or other instrumentation was aboard. L1

# The Milky Way Galaxy

Our galaxy—the Milky Way—is about 100 000 light-years wide and contains more than 200 billion stars. These stars all orbit a central hub. You're familiar with one of these stars—the sun. The sun is located about 30 000 light-years from the center of the Milky Way galaxy. It orbits that center once every 240 million years.

The Milky Way is usually classified as a normal spiral galaxy. However, recent evidence suggests that it might be a barred spiral. It is difficult to know for sure because we have never seen our galaxy from the outside. We have an "insider's" view of the arrangement of the stars within the Milky Way. The next activity shows you why it is difficult to determine the shape of our galaxy while viewing it from inside.

**Figure 20-16**

In addition to light and heat, stars also give off energy in other forms, such as radio waves. Astronomers study the radio energy from stars by using radio telescopes, like those shown here. Radio telescopes use a large dish to reflect and focus radio waves. Why do you think radio telescopes have to be much larger than optical telescopes?

### How Do We Know?

**The Position of the Solar System in the Galaxy**

When plotting stars in the Milky Way, astronomers noted that there is a large concentration of stars about 30 000 light-years away. They hypothesize this concentration of stars is the center of the galaxy.

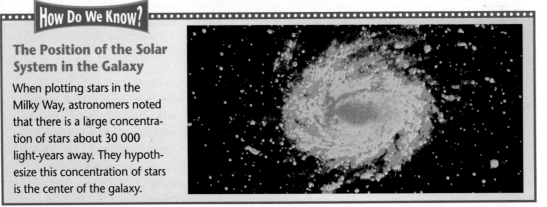

### Meeting Individual Needs

**Visually Impaired** Create solid clay models of the overall shape of the different types of galaxies. Allow students to feel the models in order to comprehend their general structure.

## Why is determining the shape of the Milky Way so difficult?

**What To Do**

1. Place about 20 cups upside down on a table. Arrange them in the shape of a spiral galaxy. Look at the arrangement from above.

2. Next, kneel down so that you are at eye level with the cups. Look at the arrangement from this angle. From which view did the cups seem to be arranged in a pattern? Imagine that these cups are stars in the Milky Way galaxy. Which view represents what we see when we look at our galaxy from Earth?

As the activity showed, you can't see the normal spiral (or perhaps barred spiral) shape of the Milky Way because you are located within one of its spiral arms. What you can see of this galaxy is a faint band of light stretching across the sky.

Will we ever be able to travel into the center of the Milky Way and beyond? Probably not. It would take many generations of people to make a trip that long. What we can expect is to improve on the methods we now use to view it from Earth and from space. Astronomers are already doing this by using unique telescopes that examine the waves of radio and heat energy that come from the center of the Milky Way galaxy. And the more information that is gathered, the better you can understand your place in the universe.

### check your UNDERSTANDING

1. List and describe the shapes of the three major types of galaxies. What do they all have in common?
2. Name and describe the shape of the galaxy that you live in. How do the stars in this galaxy move?
3. Why is the Large Magellanic Cloud classified as an irregular galaxy?
4. **Apply** Specify Earth's location as much as possible by identifying, in order of size from smallest to largest, the systems of planets and stars to which it belongs.

**Why is determining the shape of the Milky Way so difficult?**

**Time needed** 10 to 15 minutes

**Materials** about 20 paper cups

**Thinking Processes** observing and inferring, making models

**Purpose** To investigate the appearance of a spiral arrangement of objects from two different viewpoints.

**Teaching the Activity**

Arrange students in groups of three or four. COOP LEARN

**Student Journal** Have students record their observations and answers in their journals. L1

**Expected Outcome**

The cups will appear different when viewed from different locations.

**Answers to Questions**

2. The cups appeared to be in a spiral pattern when seen from above. When viewed from eye-level, the cups represented how the Milky Way galaxy looks from Earth.

### ✔ Assessment

**Oral** Have students repeat the activity using the solar system as a model. Students should give oral reports of what an extraterrestrial might see and conclude. Use the Performance Task Assessment List for Oral Reports in **PAMSS**, p. 71. L1

### check your UNDERSTANDING

1. Elliptical, spiral, irregular, they are all large groups of stars, gases, and dust held together by gravity.
2. The Milky Way Galaxy; spiral-shaped; the stars orbit around a central hub.
3. It is neither elliptical nor spiral in shape.
4. solar system, Milky Way Galaxy, the Local Group

# Science and Society

## Purpose

Science and Society reinforces Section 20-1 about stars and Section 20-3 about galaxies by explaining the difficulty of conducting astronomical observations near large cities.

## Content Background

Optical telescopes form an image of a light source such as a star or galaxy in a part of the telescope called the *objective*. The objective consists of a lens and/or mirror in which light rays are refracted through a lens and/or reflected from a mirror. The *focus* is the position where the light rays meet; the *focal length* is the distance behind the lens or from the mirror to the focus. An eyepiece can be used to magnify the image or a photographic plate can be inserted to use the telescope as a camera.

Light pollution is not the only problem confronted by astronomers using optical telescopes. Light passing through the lower layers of Earth's atmosphere is distorted by turbulence which causes the "twinkling" of stars. Smog, dust, weather conditions, air glow, and atmospheric haze can also obscure the view of the night sky.

Optical telescopes are ideally located on mountain tops where the humidity, wind velocity, and atmospheric turbulence are low. Other factors are considered when making observations of electromagnetic radiation other than that of visible light. Radio and microwave radiation pass through our atmosphere easily, while gamma ray, X ray, ultraviolet, and infrared radiation are largely filtered out. Balloon and space-based instruments are required to detect such radiation above Earth's atmosphere.

# Science and Society

# A Look at Light Pollution

Some people love to visit rural areas where many stars can be seen against a dark, moonless night sky. They may travel for miles to reach a mountaintop for clear viewing.

Other people love to watch city lights from a distance. In their eyes, the nighttime view of Los Angeles from nearby hills is beautiful—much like a galaxy on Earth.

## Blinding Lights

But the sky and city lights don't always mix. Urbanites must have lights for reading, safety, and thousands of other needs. And while the lights serve their purpose in the city, they also obscure the night sky.

That's a problem for astronomers and other star watchers who refer to the city's glow as light pollution. You can see a good example of light pollution while watching a nighttime football game in an outdoor stadium. The stars in the sky seem to disappear because of the glow of the lights.

It's obvious that cities can't do without light, and that astronomers can't view the night sky through light pollution. Does this mean that scientific research must stop? Can compromise solve the problem for astronomers and city dwellers?

## Environmentally Friendly Lighting

Some cities have taken measures to control light pollution. For example, one Arizona city near a mountaintop observatory has replaced its streetlights with lamps shining at wavelengths that can be filtered out by astronomers. The lamps are less expensive to operate, so the city is saving money while helping the pollution problem.

Light pollution might also be reduced by putting covers above some bright outdoor lights. This would allow the light to hit its target without illuminating the sky.

If such measures do not completely eliminate interference from light pollution, how can we solve the conflict between those who want to observe the stars and those who need

lights? Do you think the conflict could become as severe as disagreements over noise and air pollution?

### Light vs. Night

To get a better idea of arguments that could be made about light pollution, pretend that your classroom is a courtroom. Some of your classmates are attorneys for a group of astronomers who say new lighting near their observatory has stopped their astronomy projects.

The attorneys also represent a neighborhood association that is upset over the new floodlights and neon lights near their homes. They say the lights keep them awake at night and make their neighborhood look cheap.

Defense attorneys should represent the businesses that added the new lighting. They say the businesses would lose business without all the bright signs. They also claim that the new lights have reduced the number of burglaries in the area.

Select classmates to serve as a judge and jury to hear the arguments. Other classmates can be witnesses for the neighborhood association, while others can be owners of the well-lit businesses. Reporters from newspapers and TV should be present.

Both teams of attorneys should talk to their clients (the astronomers, neighborhood association, and business owners) before the trial begins. The attorneys and judge should know the local zoning laws that concern lighting.

After questioning their witnesses during the trial, the attorneys should make their closing arguments before the jury.

Remember that the news media should take notes for news coverage throughout the trial and when the jury announces its decision.

Remember also that some trials end when the plaintiffs and defendants finally reach an agreement outside of court.

### What Do You Think?

Did you agree with the outcome of the trial? What other viewpoints could you have added to the courtroom arguments? Were press reports of the trial accurate? Did they seem to support one side of the argument?

**Teaching Strategies** Have one student shine a bright flashlight at a wall so that the beam of light can be seen by the entire class. Cover the beam with colored transparent paper. Have a second student shine a small or weak flashlight so that it points close to the same spot on the wall as the other flashlight. Students should see that the colored light totally obscures the second light. Ask the students to separate the two beams gradually until they produce distinct spots. Repeat the activity by having the student with the bright light move away from the wall while the other student moves closer. L2

### Activity

Ask students to go outside and observe the sky on a clear night. Have them report to the class on how many stars they could see, particularly near the horizon. They can measure this by holding a meter stick or ruler at arms length while pointing in a predetermined direction-due north, for example-and finding the number of centimeters from the horizon to the first visible star. Compare the students' responses. Determine what factors may have produced the differences in their observations. How far do they live from city lights? Do they live on a hill or in a valley? L2

### Answers to
### What Do You Think?

While answers should vary, students should relate scientific principles, legal practices, and the role of the media in their responses.

### Going Further ⅢⅢ➡

Using a large political and/or topographical map of the world, pinpoint the location of the world's largest optical telescopes. An encyclopedia should have this information. Divide the class into teams, assigning one of the observatories to each team. Have the students research the factors that caused the observatory to be constructed there. Have them consider altitude, proximity to nearest large city, climatic conditions in the area, general accessibility. **COOP LEARN**

For additional information on the problem of light pollution in astronomy, see World Magazine, "Theft of the Night," by David Wallace (p. 78), Feb. 1991 or Sky Telescope of July 1990 for several good articles. For information concerning health and stress problems relating to light pollution see Woman's Day, Sept. 24, 1991, (p. 38), and USA Today Magazine, volume 120, issue 2555, Aug. 1991 (p. 4).

## EXPAND
### your view

# Technology
## Connection

### Purpose

The Technology Connection reinforces Section 20-1 by describing quasars, or star-like objects, as sources of energy whose behavior was partly determined by an analysis of their spectra.

### Content Background

The first star-like object that was identified as a source of strong radio emissions was actually found by scientists observing the moon. The moon, in its passage around the sky, blocked out the light from stars in its path. Scientists noticed that the moon cut in front of a strong radio emitter at the same time as it blacked out a "star". This "star" proved indeed to be, not a star, but a star-like object. This provided a key to locating other radio sources by using large optical telescopes to capture their light.

### Teaching Strategy The

term "quasi" may be too abstract for some students. Have students use a large, unabridged dictionary to define other "quasi" terms and relate these meanings to those of the genuine article. Examples of terms might be quasi-accidental, quasi farmer, quasi owner, or quasi tradition. **L2**

### Answers to
#### What Do You Think?

Accept any answers that students can adequately explain and justify.

# Technology
## Connection

# Questions About Quasars

In the 1960s, radio telescopes detected starlike energy sources that were too small to be pinpointed by the best radio instruments of the time. Astronomers then began using optical instruments and searched photographs of suspected areas for objects that could be the source of the energy. Then, by using the best available instruments on large telescopes, scientists were able to identify starlike objects as the source of the energy emissions. The objects, however, did not behave like stars; their brightness was greater than that of an average star and appeared to vary rapidly from time to time. The spectra lines of the objects showed a Doppler red shift, indicating that the objects were moving away at great velocity and were at great distances from Earth. These objects were called quasars, which stands for quasi–stellar radio source. Quasi means having a resemblance to, and stellar means star.

### Quasar Pioneer

Eleanor Margaret Burbidge, an English astronomer, has contributed greatly to current knowledge about quasars and to ideas about how elements are formed in stars through nuclear fusion. Margaret Burbidge left England and took a research assignment at the California Institute of Technology. Later she served as research astronomer at Yerkes Observatory at Williams Bay, Wisconsin, and was elected a Fellow of the Royal Society of London in 1964. She then served as the first woman director of the Royal Greenwich Observatory at London.

### Mighty Quasars

Quasars appear to be extremely luminous objects with relatively small sizes, great mass, and a great deal of energy. Quasars also appear to be traveling away from us at speeds up to nine-tenths of the speed of light, which is 300 000 km per sec. The light seen from quasars was given off many billions of years ago. Where they come from is still puzzling. Scientists have proposed a variety of causes for quasars including the collapse of stars 100 000 times more massive than the sun, collisions of stars in dense clusters, or the destruction of matter by antimatter.

### What Do You Think?

Do you think studying quasars is important? What could quasars tell us about the universe? Do you think the study is worth the time and money? Should money be spent in other ways?

### Going Further ▸

Through spectral studies, scientists have determined that all elements from helium through iron are produced by fusion reactions in stars. Heavier elements are not so produced. Have students research stellar fusion reactions and predict what reactions would produce any of the elements from helium through iron. **L3**

# Space Camp

Would you be interested in training the way a real astronaut does? Thousands of fourth to twelfth graders who attend Space Camp/Space Academy in Huntsville, Alabama, receive five days of this type of training. They learn about the development of the space program and even build and launch their own model rockets.

### 3, 2, 1....

Space campers get to try many different kinds of simulators—devices that provide test conditions much like real experiences. The Microgravity Training Chair gives its occupant the feeling of walking on the moon. This seat, suspended from the ceiling with springs and pulleys, alters the results of average movements. Taking steps as we normally do simply causes the tester to bounce in place. "Moon-walking" requires slow, giant steps.

### ...Ignition...

Further practice in moving without gravity comes with the Five Degrees of Freedom Simulator. In this activity, campers are strapped into a chair that floats on a cushion of air. This chair can swivel in any direction, so the slightest movement may bring surprising consequences, like a sudden tip upside down!

### Blast Off!

The primary activity at both Space Camp and Space Academy is the team mission, shown here. Campers get specific assignments during this two-hour simulation of an actual space shuttle flight. They may direct take-off or landing, fly the shuttle, launch satellites, make repairs, or monitor life-support systems. Trainers radio changes and

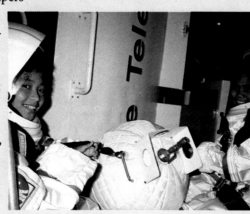

problems to campers from a computer as the campers follow a script of what to say and do in certain situations. Each crew member must think and follow directions carefully in order to complete a successful mission.

At the end of their five days, campers receive Space Camp diplomas and badges (a pair of wings) at a graduation ceremony. Many of them may return in future years for Space Academy I or II. One thing is sure—if any of them have dreams about becoming an astronaut, after Space Camp they have a much better idea of what it would be like!

### What Do You Think?

Imagine that you are on a mission to explore the surface of the moon. What is your greatest thrill in doing this?

## Going Further ⅢⅢⅢ➡

Students may wonder about the types of people who are chosen for space travel. Divide students into groups to produce a profile of the astronauts in five different space programs: the first astronauts of the U.S. *Mercury* and *Gemini* missions, the crew members of the *Apollo* flights to the moon, the *Skylab* missions, and the space shuttle astronauts. Have students determine the average age, ratio of men to women, and occupations and education. L2 **COOP LEARN**

**Purpose**
Teens in Science reinforce this entire chapter by describing some special training techniques for scientists and astronauts and how students may prepare for careers in fields related to astronomy by attending Space Camp.

**Content Background**
The U.S. Space Camp and the U.S. Space Academy provide educational programs that combine lectures, seminars, tours, and simulations related to space flight. Programs are offered in two locations—Huntsville, Alabama and Orlando, Florida. The Alabama program was begun in 1986, with the one in Florida starting two years later.

The Space Camp in Alabama is for students in grades 4–6, while the Space Camp in Florida is for grades 4–7. Space Academy Levels I and II are designed for students in grades 7–9 and 10–12, respectively. There are also courses for teachers in both locations that can be used for university credit or as an in-service program.

**Teaching Strategy** Ask students to write for more information about the U.S. Space Camp/Academy. The address is:

Alabama Space Science Exhibit Commission
The Space & Rocket Center
U.S. Space Camp
One Tranquility Base
Huntsville, AL 35807-7015 L2

**Discussion**
Discuss with students the kinds of careers—scientific and otherwise—that might be benefitted by the kind of training offered at the Space Camp. L2

chapter 20
REVIEWING MAIN IDEAS

Students should examine the main ideas on this page—both pictures and text—and write a creative story about one of them. Suggest a length of three to five pages for the story.

## Teaching the Activity

Students who choose the first main idea could write about travel to a star other than the sun. The story should include a description of the star visited, including the color, temperature, and size, and show how these factors would affect the journey. If they select the second main idea, students should write a story in which life on Earth is changed by having a different sun. For example, what would life be like if the sun were one of a binary pair, or if it were a different size, color, and temperature? Students who write about the third main idea should include a view of the night sky if our planet were either in a differently shaped galaxy or in another part of the Milky Way galaxy.

## Answers to Questions

**1.** Most stars arise from nebulas. The core of the star contracts until hydrogen begins to undergo fusion into helium. The star then begins to give off light and heat. Eventually fusion stops when the star's fuel is used up.

**2.** Temperatures would be much colder; there might not be enough light for the growth of plants; living things that feed on plants or on other living things that feed on plants might not be able to survive or evolve.

**3.** eliptical and irregular

MINDJOGGER
VIDEOQUIZ

**Chapter 20** Have students work in groups as they play the videoquiz game to review key chapter concepts.

---

**R**eview the statements below about the big ideas presented in this chapter, and try to answer the questions. Then, re-read your answers to the Did You Ever Wonder questions at the beginning of the chapter. *In your Journal*, write a paragraph about how your understanding of the big ideas in the chapter has changed.

**1** There are more stars in the universe than you could count in a lifetime. Some are brighter than others, depending on how big, how hot, and how far away from Earth they are. The temperature and composition of a star can be determined by its color and by examining the dark-line spectrum of the light it emits. *How do most stars change as they go through their life cycle?*

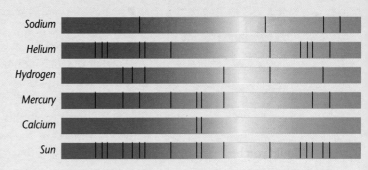

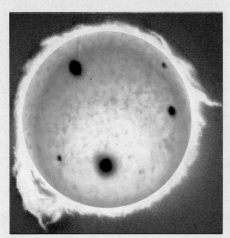

**2** All life on Earth depends on one star—the sun. It is an average star in terms of its size and temperature. The surface of the sun contains sunspots, prominences, and solar flares. *How would things be different on Earth if the sun was much farther away?*

**3** Our solar system belongs to the Milky Way galaxy. The Milky Way is a spiral-shaped galaxy in a cluster of galaxies called the Local Group. *What shapes are other galaxies?*

---

### Project

Have students use the star charts in Appendix K on pages 672–673. Assign a section on the chart to pairs of students. Students should attempt to view their sections two hours after sunset and identify the names and colors of stars within their sections, either through direct observation or by research. Have students keep a journal, noting each star and its color. **COOP LEARN** **L2**

### Science at Home

Direct students to make pinholes in 4-cm squares of black construction paper in the shape of major constellations. By placing the constellation squares at one end of a cardboard tube pointed toward a light source, students should be able to view constellations through the tube. Have students switch constellation squares and make a game of identifying the constellations. **L1**

## Using Key Science Terms

| | |
|---|---|
| galaxy | star |
| light-year | sunspot |
| nebula | supernova |

*For each set of terms below, explain the relationship that exists.*
1. nebula, star, supernova
2. star, sunspot
3. light-year, galaxy

## Understanding Ideas

*Answer the following questions in your Journal using complete sentences.*
1. How does our sun compare in size and brightness to other stars?
2. Why would light from an explosion far out in space be "old news"?
3. How are galaxies classified? What are the three kinds of galaxies?

## Developing Skills

*Use your understanding of the concepts developed in this chapter to answer each of the following questions.*
1. **Observing and Inferring** Observing the stars/constellations again as you did in the Explore activity on page 627, find a point of reference to stand near such as the edge of a building or a tree. Watch the star/constellation with respect to your point of reference for 30 minutes. What happens? Why?

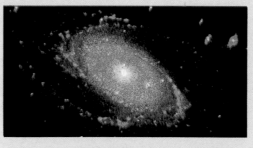

2. **Concept Mapping** Create an events chain concept map of the birth of a main sequence star.

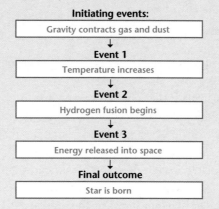

**Initiating events:**
Gravity contracts gas and dust
↓
**Event 1**
Temperature increases
↓
**Event 2**
Hydrogen fusion begins
↓
**Event 3**
Energy released into space
↓
**Final outcome**
Star is born

3. **Recognizing Cause and Effect** Using the two flashlights from the Find Out activity on page 628, find a way to make the flashlights look the same brightness.
4. **Observing, Interpreting Data** To discover how objects can be identified by the substance's spectrum, a spectroscope can be made and used. Cover the ends of a cardboard or paper tube with paper. Make a small slit in the paper on one end of the tube and a small hole in the paper on the other end. Cover the hole with diffraction grating and tape it to the tube.

### Using Key Science Term

1. A nebula is a cloud of gas and dust that may contract to form a star. After fusion has ended, the star may explode, forming a supernova.

2. Both terms describe the sun.

3. A light-year is a unit of measurement to describe the distances between galaxies, between a galaxy and Earth, and from one end of a galaxy to another.

### Understanding Ideas

1. No. It looks the biggest and brightest because it's the closest. Other stars are much bigger and brighter but are farther away.

2. The explosion might have happened years or hundreds of years ago. Because distances are so great in space, the light is just now reaching Earth.

3. By shape. spiral, elliptical, irregular.

### Developing Skills

1. Students should observe the change of position of the star/constellation as compared to their point of reference. Students should then infer that Earth's rotation causes this apparent motion.

2. See reduced student page.

3. By moving the small flashlight closer to the observer than the larger flashlight they will look the same brightness. Students will see that not only size and temperature affect a star's brightness, but also distance.

4. All light sources should have color bands separated by dark bands. Each light source should have its own characteristic spectrum by which it can be identified. Each substance has a unique spectrum by which it can be identified.

## Critical Thinking

**1.** It might be farther away.

**2.** The small star may be much closer to Earth than is the large star, or it may be hotter than the large star.

**3.** The amount of sunlight reaching Earth would decrease. This would probably make the planet too cold for life to exist.

**4.** The forces balance each other, so the star remains about the same size.

## Problem Solving

**1.** 30 years

**2.** In the 15 years it takes light from the star to reach Earth, the star could have burned out.

## Connecting Ideas

**1.** Since the sun is mostly hydrogen, only the fusion of light elements into heavier ones could be occurring. Fission could only occur if heavy elements were splitting to form lighter ones.

**2.** The sun warms water near the equator. This warm water forms density currents. The sun also warms air, causing wind. Surface currents are caused by wind.

**3.** By analyzing the sun's spectrum through a spectroscope, we see lines that correspond with those of hydrogen

**4.** Stars that are more than 30 times the mass of the sun can become black holes. When they use up their fuel, their mass collapses to form a black hole.

**5.** A red shift in light spectra means that an object is moving away from Earth. Since all galaxies show a red shift in their spectra, they must all be moving away from Earth, and universe is expanding.

Looking through the diffraction grating, aim the slit at a light source. (Light sources should include a halogen light bulb, fluorescent light bulb, Bunsen burner or candle, but NOT the sun.) Move the spectroscope side-to-side slightly. Sketch the light patterns using colored pencils or crayons. What similarities did you see? Can light patterns be used for identification? How?

### Critical Thinking

In your Journal, *answer each of the following questions.*

**1.** Explain why a hotter star might appear dimmer than a cooler star.

**2.** Explain why a small and a large star may appear to have the same brightness.

**3.** Describe the effects on life on Earth if the sun were to move one light-year away.

**4.** The diagram shows the forces that act within a star such as our sun. What do you think the overall effect of these forces is on the size of the star?

### Problem Solving

*Read the following problem and discuss your answers in a brief paragraph.*

**Suppose you had a rocket that could travel at the speed of light.**

**1.** How long would it take you to complete a round-trip journey to a star that is 15 light-years from Earth?

**2.** Explain why it might be possible to take off for the star without realizing that it no longer exists.

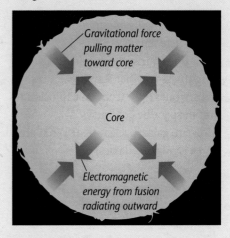

Gravitational force pulling matter toward core

Core

Electromagnetic energy from fusion radiating outward

## CONNECTING IDEAS

Discuss each of the following in a brief paragraph.

**1. Theme—Energy** Recall from chapter 18 the difference between fusion and fission. How do we know fusion and not fission occurs in the sun?

**2. Theme—Systems and Interactions** How does Earth's closest star affect its ocean currents?

**3. Theme—Energy** How do we know that the sun contains hydrogen?

**4. A Closer Look** What kind of stars may become black holes? Why?

**5. Physics Connection** How is a red shift in light spectra evidence for the expansion of the universe?

### Assessment

**Portfolio** Review the portfolio options that are provided throughout the chapter. Encourage students to select one product that demonstrates their best work for the chapter. Have students explain what they learned and why they chose this example for placement into their portfolios.

Additional portfolio options can be found in the following **Teacher Classroom Resources:**

**Multicultural Connections,** pp. 43–44

**Making Connections: Integrating Sciences,** p. 43

**Making Connections: Across the Curriculum,** p. 43

**Concept Mapping,** p. 29

**Critical Thinking/Problem Solving,** p. 28

**Take Home Activities,** p. 31

**Laboratory Manual,** pp. 119–120; 121–122; 123–124

**Performance Assessment** **P**

# observing THE WORLD around you

In this unit, you investigated how transmutations of elements occur by fission and fusion. You learned that during fission, atoms split apart and during fusion, they are forced together. You explored the idea that the solar system began as a huge rotating cloud of gas and dust, and that the universe is composed of small particles and huge galaxies of stars. You have investigated how humans are attempting to artificially cause and control nuclear processes to produce energy for human use.

Try the exercises and activity that follow—they will challenge you to use and apply some of the ideas you learned in this unit.

## CONNECTING IDEAS

1. Imagine you are planning a space mission to build a research base on another planet in our solar system. Pick the planet you would choose and describe the reasons for your choice and obstacles you would have to overcome to make your mission successful.

2. When four hydrogen nuclei undergo fusion to form a helium nucleus, mass is lost. Explain what happens to account for the loss of mass and how this demonstrates the conservation of mass and energy. How does this explain how stars produce so much energy?

## Exploring Further   ACTIVITY

### How do the diameters of the planets in the solar system compare?

**What To Do**

1. Obtain charts or tables to provide information on the diameters of the planets.

2. Determine how many times bigger in diameter each planet is than Pluto, the smallest.

3. Mix up some cookie dough and cut out cookies having diameters based on this scale. Decorate your planet cookies and bake them. **CAUTION:** *Be sure to have an adult help you with this activity.*

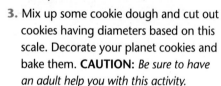

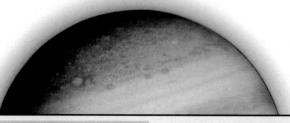

## Planets, Stars, and Galaxies

### THEME DEVELOPMENT

Scale and structure was used to describe the size and composition of atoms, planets, the solar system, stars, and galaxies. Students learned that some of the matter in fission and fusion changes into energy.

### Connections to Other Units

Learning about the structure of the atom and the Kinetic Theory of Matter in Unit 2 provided a foundation for the concepts of nuclear fission and fusion in Chapter 18. A comparative study of planets in Chapter 19 was enriched by information in Unit 3 on Earth's weather and oceans. Changes in Earth and its life forms, as presented in Unit 4, related to the evolution of stars as they change from one stage to another.

### Connecting Ideas
**Answers**

1. Students should consider distance from Earth and how long it would take to get there. Also, the structure of the planet, the atmospheric conditions of the planet, and characteristics such as gravitational force should be considered.

2. Most of the mass forms the helium nucleus, but a small amount is converted to energy. The fusion process created energy in the cores of stars.

## Exploring Further

**How do the diameters of the planets in the solar system compare?**

**Purpose**   To compare and contrast the sizes of the planets.

**Background Information**

Students can find information about the diameters of planets in Appendix J on page 671.

**Materials**   bowls, spoons, rolling pin, cardboard scissors, knife, baking sheets, ingredients for cookie dough or pre-mixed refrigerated cookie dough.

**Troubleshooting**   Use a recipe for cookies that are rolled out, not dropped from a spoon. Arrange in advance to use the home economics classroom. Premixed refrigerated cookie dough can be used. For planet templates, have students cut circles from cardboard.

**Answers to Questions**

2. Students should divide the diameter of each planet by the diameter of Pluto.

**✔ Assessment**

Have students "recycle" the cardboard circles that were used as cookie templates to make a visual display of the planets. Use the appropriate Performance Task Assessment List from **PAMSS**. [L1]

# APPENDICES

## Table of Contents

# International System of Units

The International System (SI) of Measurement is accepted as the standard for measurement throughout most of the world. Three base units in SI are the meter, kilogram, and second. Frequently used SI units are listed below.

| Table A-1: Frequently used SI Units | |
|---|---|
| Length | 1 millimeter (mm) = 1000 micrometers (µm) |
| | 1 centimeter (cm) = 10 millimeters (mm) |
| | 1 meter (m) = 100 centimeters (cm) |
| | 1 kilometer (km) = 1000 meters (m) |
| | 1 light-year = 9 460 000 000 000 kilometers (km) |
| Area | 1 square meter ($m^2$) = 10 000 square centimeters ($cm^2$) |
| | 1 square kilometer ($km^2$) = 1 000 000 square meters ($m^2$) |
| Volume | 1 milliliter (mL) = 1 cubic centimeter ($cm^3$) |
| | 1 liter (L) = 1000 milliliters (mL) |
| Mass | 1 gram (g) = 1000 milligrams (mg) |
| | 1 kilogram (kg) = 1000 grams (g) |
| | 1 metric ton = 1000 kilograms (kg) |
| Time | 1 s = 1 second |

Temperature measurements in SI are often made in degrees Celsius. Celsius temperature is a supplementary unit derived from the base unit kelvin. The Celsius scale (°C) has 100 equal graduations between the freezing temperature (0°C) and the boiling temperature of water (100°C). The following relationship exists between the Celsius and kelvin temperature scales:

$$K = °C + 273$$

Several other supplementary SI units are listed below.

| Table A-2: Supplementary SI Units | | | |
|---|---|---|---|
| Measurement | Unit | Symbol | Expressed in Base Units |
| Energy | Joule | J | $kg \cdot m^2/s^2$ or $N \cdot m$ |
| Force | Newton | N | $kg \cdot m/s^2$ |
| Power | Watt | W | $kg \cdot m^2/s^3$ or J/s |
| Pressure | Pascal | Pa | $kg/(m \cdot s^2)$ or $N/m^2$ |

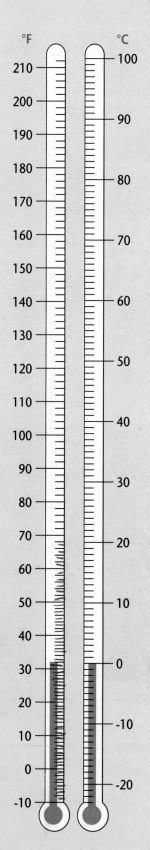

| Table B-1: SI/Metric to English Conversions | | | |
|---|---|---|---|
| | **When You Want to Convert:** | **Multiply By:** | **To Find:** |
| **Length** | inches | 2.54 | centimeters |
| | centimeters | 0.39 | inches |
| | feet | 0.30 | meters |
| | meters | 3.28 | feet |
| | yards | 0.91 | meters |
| | meters | 1.09 | yards |
| | miles | 1.61 | kilometers |
| | kilometers | 0.62 | miles |
| **Mass and Weight** | ounces | 28.35 | grams |
| | grams | 0.04 | ounces |
| | pounds | 0.45 | kilograms |
| | kilograms | 2.2 | pounds |
| | tons | 0.91 | tonnes (metric tons) |
| | tonnes (metric tons) | 1.10 | tons |
| | pounds | 4.45 | newtons |
| | newtons | 0.23 | pounds |
| **Volume** | cubic inches | 16.39 | cubic centimeters |
| | cubic centimeters | 0.06 | cubic inches |
| | cubic feet | 0.03 | cubic meters |
| | cubic meters | 35.3 | cubic feet |
| | liters | 1.06 | quarts |
| | liters | 0.26 | gallons |
| | gallons | 3.78 | liters |
| **Area** | square inches | 6.45 | square centimeters |
| | square centimeters | 0.16 | square inches |
| | square feet | 0.09 | square meters |
| | square meters | 10.76 | square feet |
| | square miles | 2.59 | square kilometers |
| | square kilometers | 0.39 | miles |
| | hectares | 2.47 | acres |
| | acres | 0.40 | hectares |
| **Temperature** | Fahrenheit | 5/9 (°F – 32) | Celsius |
| | Celsius | 9/5 °C + 32 | Fahrenheit |

$K = C + 273$

# APPENDIX C

# Safety in the Science Classroom

1. Always obtain your teacher's permission to begin an investigation.
2. Study the procedure. If you have questions, ask your teacher. Understand any safety symbols shown on the page.
3. Use the safety equipment provided for you. Goggles and a safety apron should be worn when any investigation calls for using chemicals.
4. Always slant test tubes away from yourself and others when heating them.
5. Never eat or drink in the lab, and never use lab glassware as food or drink containers. Never inhale chemicals. Do not taste any substances or draw any material into a tube with your mouth.
6. If you spill any chemical, wash it off immediately with water. Report the spill immediately to your teacher.
7. Know the location and proper use of the fire extinguisher, safety shower, fire blanket, first aid kit, and fire alarm.
8. Keep materials away from flames. Tie back hair and loose clothing.
9. If a fire should break out in the classroom, or if your clothing should catch fire, smother it with the fire blanket or a coat, or get under a safety shower. NEVER RUN.
10. Report any accident or injury, no matter how small, to your teacher.

Follow these procedures as you clean up your work area.
1. Turn off the water and gas. Disconnect electrical devices.
2. Return all materials to their proper places.
3. Dispose of chemicals and other materials as directed by your teacher. Place broken glass and solid substances in the proper containers. Never discard materials in the sink.
4. Clean your work area.
5. Wash your hands thoroughly after working in the laboratory.

| Table C-1: First Aid | |
| --- | --- |
| **Injury** | **Safe Response** |
| Burns | Apply cold water. Call your teacher immediately. |
| Cuts and bruises | Stop any bleeding by applying direct pressure. Cover cuts with a clean dressing. Apply cold compresses to bruises. Call your teacher immediately. |
| Fainting | Leave the person lying down. Loosen any tight clothing and keep crowds away. Call your teacher immediately. |
| Foreign matter in eye | Flush with plenty of water. Use eyewash bottle or fountain. Call your teacher immediately. |
| Poisoning | Note the suspected poisoning agent and call your teacher immediately. |
| Any spills on skin | Flush with large amounts of water or use safety shower. Call your teacher immediately. |

## Table D-1: Safety Symbols

**Disposal Alert**
This symbol appears when care must be taken to dispose of materials properly.

**Animal Safety**
This symbol appears whenever live animals are studied and the safety of the animals and the students must be ensured.

**Biological Hazard**
This symbol appears when there is danger involving bacteria, fungi, or protists.

**Radioactive Safety**
This symbol appears when radioactive materials are used.

**Open Flame Alert**
This symbol appears when use of an open flame could cause a fire or an explosion.

**Clothing Protection Safety**
This symbol appears when substances used could stain or burn clothing.

**Thermal Safety**
This symbol appears as a reminder to use caution when handling hot objects.

**Fire Safety**
This symbol appears when care should be taken around open flames.

**Sharp Object Safety**
This symbol appears when a danger of cuts or punctures caused by the use of sharp objects exists.

**Explosion Safety**
This symbol appears when the misuse of chemicals could cause an explosion.

**Fume Safety**
This symbol appears when chemicals or chemical reactions could cause dangerous fumes.

**Eye Safety**
This symbol appears when a danger to the eyes exists. Safety goggles should be worn when this symbol appears.

**Electrical Safety**
This symbol appears when care should be taken when using electrical equipment.

**Poison Safety**
This symbol appears when poisonous substances are used.

**Plant Safety**
This symbol appears when poisonous plants or plants with thorns are handled.

**Chemical Safety**
This symbol appears when chemicals used can cause burns or are poisonous if absorbed through the skin.

# Care and Use of a Microscope

**Coarse Adjustment** *Focuses the image under low power*

**Fine Adjustment** *Sharpens the image under high and low magnification*

**Arm** *Supports the body tube*

**Low-power objective** *Contains the lens with low-power magnification*

**Stage clips** *Hold the microscope slide in place*

**Base** *Provides support for the microscope*

**Eyepiece** *Contains a magnifying lens you look through*

**Body tube** *Connects the eyepiece to the revolving nosepiece*

**Revolving nosepiece** *Holds and turns the objectives into viewing position*

**High-power objective** *Contains the lens with the highest magnification*

**Stage** *Platform used to support the microscope slide*

**Diaphram** *Regulates the amount of light entering the body tube*

**Light source** *Allows light to reflect upward through the diaphram, the specimen, and the lenses*

## Care of a Microscope

1. Always carry the microscope holding the arm with one hand and supporting the base with the other hand.
2. Don't touch the lenses with your finger.
3. Never lower the coarse adjustment knob when looking through the eyepiece lens.
4. Always focus first with the low-power objective.
5. Don't use the coarse adjustment knob when the high-power objective is in place.
6. Store the microscope covered.

## Using a Microscope

1. Place the microscope on a flat surface that is clear of objects. The arm should be toward you.
2. Look through the eyepiece. Adjust the diaphragm so that light comes through the opening in the stage.
3. Place a slide on the stage so that the specimen is in the field of view. Hold it firmly in place by using the stage clips.
4. Always focus first with the coarse adjustment and the low-power objective lens. Once the object is in focus on low power, turn the nosepiece until the high-power objective is in place. Use ONLY the fine adjustment to focus with the high-power objective lens.

## Making a Wet Mount Slide

1. Carefully place the item you want to look at in the center of a clean glass slide. Make sure the sample is thin enough for light to pass through.
2. Use a dropper to place one or two drops of water on the sample.
3. Hold a clean coverslip by the edges and place it at one edge of the drop of water. Slowly lower the coverslip onto the drop of water until it lies flat.
4. If you have too much water or a lot of air bubbles, touch the edge of a paper towel to the edge of the coverslip to draw off extra water and force air out.

# Periodic Table

Alkali Metals
1

Metallic Properties →

| 1 |
|---|
| **H** |
| Hydrogen |
| 1.007 94 |

Alkaline Earth Metals
2

Transition Elements

| | | 3 | 4 | 5 | 6 | 7 | 8 | 9 |
|---|---|---|---|---|---|---|---|---|
| 3 **Li** Lithium 6.941 | 4 **Be** Beryllium 9.012 182 | | | | | | | |
| 11 **Na** Sodium 22.989 77 | 12 **Mg** Magnesium 24.305 | | | | | | | |
| 19 **K** Potassium 39.0983 | 20 **Ca** Calcium 40.078 | 21 **Sc** Scandium 44.955 91 | 22 **Ti** Titanium 47.88 | 23 **V** Vanadium 50.9415 | 24 **Cr** Chromium 51.9961 | 25 **Mn** Manganese 54.9380 | 26 **Fe** Iron 55.847 | 27 **Co** Cobalt 58.9332 |
| 37 **Rb** Rubidium 85.4678 | 38 **Sr** Strontium 87.62 | 39 **Y** Yttrium 88.9059 | 40 **Zr** Zirconium 91.224 | 41 **Nb** Niobium 92.9064 | 42 **Mo** Molybdenum 95.94 | 43 **Tc** Technetium 97.9072* | 44 **Ru** Ruthenium 101.07 | 45 **Rh** Rhodium 102.9055 |
| 55 **Cs** Cesium 132.9054 | 56 **Ba** Barium 137.33 | 71 **Lu** Lutetium 174.967 | 72 **Hf** Hafnium 178.49 | 73 **Ta** Tantalum 180.9479 | 74 **W** Tungsten 183.85 | 75 **Re** Rhenium 186.207 | 76 **Os** Osmium 190.2 | 77 **Ir** Iridium 192.22 |
| 87 **Fr** Francium 223.0197* | 88 **Ra** Radium 226.0254 | 103 **Lr** Lawrencium 260.1054* | 104 **Unq** Unnilquadium 261* | 105 **Unp** Unnilpentium 262* | 106 **Unh** Unnilhexium 263* | 107 **Uns** Unnilseptium 262* | 108 **Uno** Unniloctium 265* | 109 **Une** Unnilennium 266* |

← ——— Metallic properties ———

Lanthanoid Series

| 57 **La** Lanthanum 138.9055 | 58 **Ce** Cerium 140.12 | 59 **Pr** Praseodymium 140.9077 | 60 **Nd** Neodymium 144.24 | 61 **Pm** Promethium 144.9128* | 62 **Sm** Samarium 150.36 |
|---|---|---|---|---|---|
| 89 **Ac** Actinium 227.0278* | 90 **Th** Thorium 232.0381 | 91 **Pa** Protactinium 231.0359* | 92 **U** Uranium 238.0289 | 93 **Np** Neptunium 237.0482 | 94 **Pu** Plutonium 244.0642* |

Actinoid Series

*Mass of isotope with longest half-life that is the most stable isotope of the element

Noble Gases
18

| | | | | | Halogens | 2 |
| | | | | | | **He** |
| 13 | 14 | 15 | 16 | 17 | | Helium |
| | | | | | | 4.002 602 |

| 13 | 14 | 15 | 16 | 17 | 18 |
|---|---|---|---|---|---|
| 5 | 6 | 7 | 8 | 9 | 10 |
| **B** | **C** | **N** | **O** | **F** | **Ne** |
| Boron | Carbon | Nitrogen | Oxygen | Fluorine | Neon |
| 10.811 | 12.011 | 14.0067 | 15.9994 | 18.998 403 | 20.1797 |

Transition Elements

| 10 | 11 | 12 | 13 | 14 | 15 | 16 | 17 | 18 |
|---|---|---|---|---|---|---|---|---|
| | | | **Al** | **Si** | **P** | **S** | **Cl** | **Ar** |
| | | | Aluminum | Silicon | Phosphorus | Sulfur | Chlorine | Argon |
| | | | 26.981 54 | 28.0855 | 30.973 76 | 32.07 | 35.453 | 39.948 |
| 28 | 29 | 30 | 31 | 32 | 33 | 34 | 35 | 36 |
| **Ni** | **Cu** | **Zn** | **Ga** | **Ge** | **As** | **Se** | **Br** | **Kr** |
| Nickel | Copper | Zinc | Gallium | Germanium | Arsenic | Selenium | Bromine | Krypton |
| 58.69 | 63.546 | 65.39 | 69.723 | 72.61 | 74.9216 | 78.96 | 79.904 | 83.80 |
| 46 | 47 | 48 | 49 | 50 | 51 | 52 | 53 | 54 |
| **Pd** | **Ag** | **Cd** | **In** | **Sn** | **Sb** | **Te** | **I** | **Xe** |
| Palladium | Silver | Cadmium | Indium | Tin | Antimony | Tellurium | Iodine | Xenon |
| 106.42 | 107.8682 | 112.41 | 114.82 | 118.710 | 121.757 | 127.60 | 126.9045 | 131.29 |
| 78 | 79 | 80 | 81 | 82 | 83 | 84 | 85 | 86 |
| **Pt** | **Au** | **Hg** | **Tl** | **Pb** | **Bi** | **Po** | **At** | **Rn** |
| Platinum | Gold | Mercury | Thallium | Lead | Bismuth | Polonium | Astatine | Radon |
| 195.08 | 196.9665 | 200.59 | 204.383 | 207.2 | 208.9804 | 208.9824* | 209.987 12* | 222.017* |

Nonmetallic properties

Metals    Metalloids    Nonmetals

Lettering: Solids    Synthetics (solid)    Liquids    Gases

| 63 | 64 | 65 | 66 | 67 | 68 | 69 | 70 |
|---|---|---|---|---|---|---|---|
| **Eu** | **Gd** | **Tb** | **Dy** | **Ho** | **Er** | **Tm** | **Yb** |
| Europium | Gadolinium | Terbium | Dysprosium | Holmium | Erbium | Thulium | Ytterbium |
| 151.96 | 157.25 | 158.9253 | 162.50 | 164.9303 | 167.26 | 168.9342 | 173.04 |
| 95 | 96 | 97 | 98 | 99 | 100 | 101 | 102 |
| **Am** | **Cm** | **Bk** | **Cf** | **Es** | **Fm** | **Md** | **No** |
| Americium | Curium | Berkelium | Californium | Einsteinium | Fermium | Mendelevium | Nobelium |
| 243.0614* | 247.0703* | 247.0703* | 251.0796* | 252.0828* | 257.0951* | 258.0986* | 259.1009* |

# Diversity of Life: Classification of Living Organisms

Scientists use a five kingdom system for the classification of organisms. In this system, there is one kingdom of organisms, Kingdom Monera, which contains organisms that do not have a nucleus and lack specialized structures in the cytoplasm of their cells. The members of the other four kingdoms have cells each of which contains a nucleus and structures in the cytoplasm that are surrounded by membranes. These kingdoms are Kingdom Protista, Kingdom Fungi, the Plant Kingdom, and the Animal Kingdom.

## Kingdom Monera

**Phylum Cyanobacteria** one celled prokaryotes; make their own food, contain chlorophyll, some species form colonies, most are blue-green

**Bacteria** one-celled prokaryotes; most absorb food from their surroundings, some are photosynthetic; many are parasites; round, spiral, or rod shaped

## Kingdom Protista

**Phylum Euglenophyta** one-celled; can photosynthesize or take in food; most have one flagellum; euglenoids

**Phylum Chrysophyta** most are one-celled; make their own food through photosynthesis; golden-brown pigments mask chlorophyll; diatoms

**Phylum Pyrrophyta** one-celled; make their own food through photosynthesis; contain red pigments and have two flagella; dinoflagellates

**Phylum Chlorophyta** one-celled, many-celled, or colonies; contain chlorophyll and make their own food; live on land, in fresh water or salt water; green algae

**Phylum Rhodophyta** most are many-celled and photosynthetic; contain red pigments; most live in deep saltwater environments; red algae

**Phylum Phaeophyta** most are many-celled and photosynthetic; contain brown pigments; most live in saltwater environments; brown algae

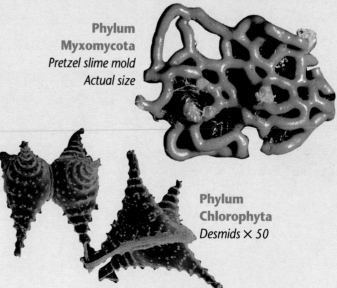

**Bacteria**
*Clostridium botulinum*
× 13 960

**Phylum Myxomycota**
*Pretzel slime mold
Actual size*

**Phylum Chlorophyta**
*Desmids × 50*

**Phylum Sarcodina** one-celled; take in food; move by means of pseudopods; free-living or parasitic; amoebas

**Phylum Mastigophora** one-celled; take in food; have two or more flagella; free-living or parasitic; flagellates

**Phylum Ciliophora** one-celled; take in food; have large numbers of cilia; ciliates

**Phylum Sporozoa** one-celled; take in food; no means of movement; parasites in animals; sporozoans

**Phyla Myxomycota and Acrasiomycota** one- or many-celled; absorb food; change form during life cycle; cellular and plasmodial slime molds

## Kingdom Fungi

**Phylum Zygomycota** many-celled; absorb food; spores are produced in sporangia; bread mold

**Phylum Ascomycota** one- and many-celled; absorb food; spores produced in asci; sac fungi; yeast

**Phylum Ascomycota**
*Yeast × 7800*

**Lichens**
*Old Man's Beard lichen*

**Phylum Basidiomycota** many-celled; absorb food; spores produced in basidia; mushrooms

**Phylum Deuteromycota** members with unknown reproductive structures; penicillin

**Lichens** organisms formed by symbiotic relationship between an ascomycote or a basidiomycote and a green alga or a cyanobacterium

## Plant Kingdom
### Spore Plants

**Division Bryophyta** nonvascular plants that reproduce by spores produced in capsules; many-celled; green; grow in moist land environments; mosses and liverworts

**Division Lycophyta** many-celled vascular plants; spores produced in cones; live on land; are photosynthetic; club mosses

**Division Sphenophyta** vascular plants with ribbed and jointed stems; scalelike leaves; spores produced in cones; horsetails

**Division Pterophyta** vascular plants with feathery leaves called fronds; spores produced in clusters of sporangia called sori; live on land or in water; ferns

**Division Bryophyta**
*Liverwort*

## Seed Plants

**Division Ginkgophyta** deciduous gymnosperms; only one living species called the maiden hair tree; fan-shaped leaves with branching veins; reproduces with seeds; ginkgos

**Division Cycadophyta** palmlike gymnosperms; large compound leaves; produce seeds in cones; cycads

**Division Coniferophyta** deciduous or evergreen gymnosperms; trees or shrubs; needlelike or scalelike leaves; seeds produced in cones; conifers

**Division Gnetophyta** shrubs or woody vines; seeds produced in cones; division contains only three genera; gnetum

**Division Anthophyta** dominant group of plants; ovules protected at fertilization by an ovary; sperm carried to ovules by pollen tube; produce flowers and seeds in fruits; flowering plants

## Animal Kingdom

**Phylum Porifera** aquatic organisms that lack true tissues and organs; they are asymmetrical and sessile; sponges

**Phylum Cnidaria** radially symmetrical organisms with a digestive cavity with one opening; most have tentacles armed with stinging cells; live in aquatic environments singly or in colonies; includes jellyfish, corals, hydra, and sea anemones

**Phylum Platyhelminthes** bilaterally symmetrical worms with flattened bodies; digestive system has one opening; parasitic and free-living species; flatworms

**Phylum Cnidaria**
*Jellyfish*

**Division Coniferophyta**
*Slash Pine cones*

**Division Anthophyta**
*Fairyslipper*

**Division Anthophyta**
*Blackberries*

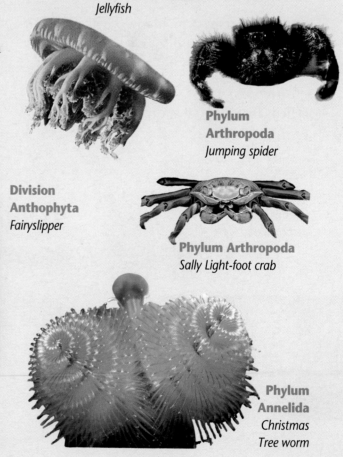

**Phylum Arthropoda**
*Jumping spider*

**Phylum Arthropoda**
*Sally Light-foot crab*

**Phylum Annelida**
*Christmas Tree worm*

**Phylum Nematoda** round bilaterally symmetrical body; digestive system with two openings; some free-living forms but mostly parasitic; roundworms

**Phylum Mollusca** soft-bodied animals, many with a hard shell; a mantle covers the soft body; aquatic and terrestrial species; includes clams, snails, squid, and octopuses

**Phylum Annelida** bilaterally symmetrical worms with round segmented bodies; terrestrial and aquatic species; includes earthworms, leeches, and marine polychaetes

**Phylum Arthropoda** very large phylum of organisms that have segmented bodies with pairs of jointed appendages and a hard exoskeleton; terrestrial and aquatic species; includes insects, crustaceans, spiders, and horseshoe crabs

**Phylum Echinodermata** saltwater organisms with spiny or leathery skin; water-vascular system with tube feet; radial symmetry; includes starfish, sand dollars, and sea urchins

**Phylum Chordata** organisms with internal skeletons, specialized body systems, and paired appendages; all at some time have a notochord, dorsal nerve cord, gill slits, and a tail; includes fish, amphibians, reptiles, birds, and mammals

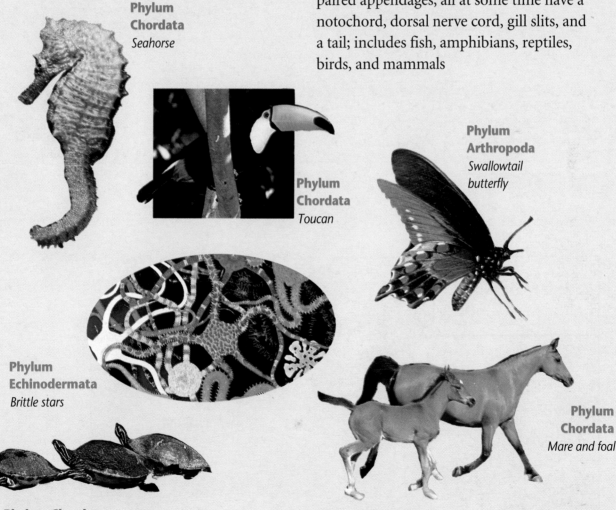

**Phylum Chordata**
*Seahorse*

**Phylum Chordata**
*Toucan*

**Phylum Arthropoda**
*Swallowtail butterfly*

**Phylum Echinodermata**
*Brittle stars*

**Phylum Chordata**
*Mare and foal*

**Phylum Chordata**
*Peninsula turtles*

# APPENDIX H

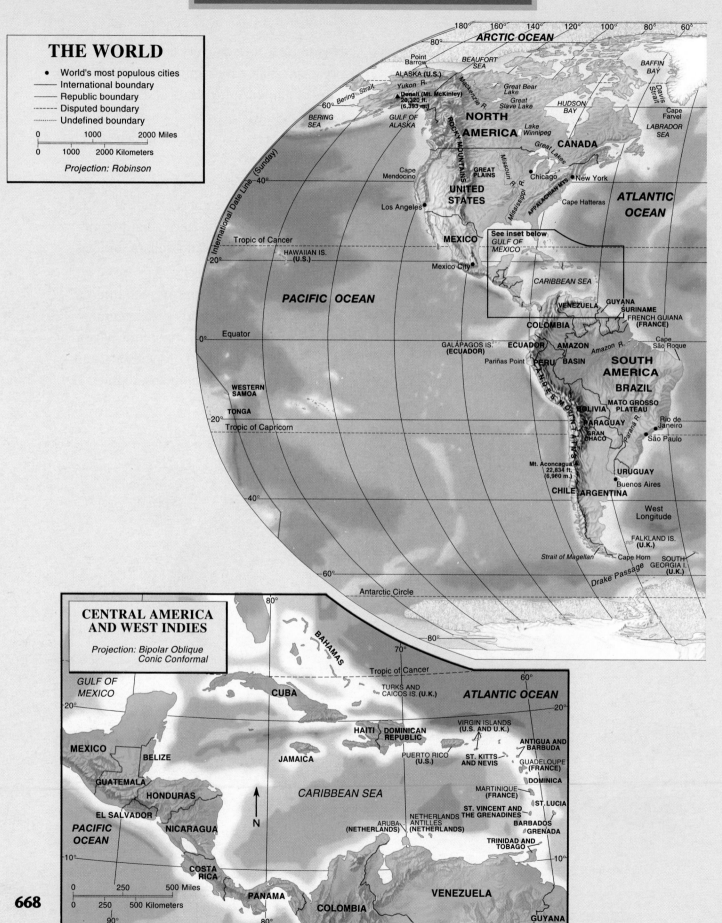

## THE WORLD

- • World's most populous cities
- —— International boundary
- —— Republic boundary
- ---- Disputed boundary
- ······ Undefined boundary

0  1000  2000 Miles
0  1000  2000 Kilometers

*Projection: Robinson*

ARCTIC OCEAN

Point Barrow
BEAUFORT SEA
BAFFIN BAY

ALASKA (U.S.)
Yukon R.
Mackenzie R.
Great Bear Lake
Great Slave Lake
HUDSON BAY
Davis Strait
Cape Farvel
LABRADOR SEA

Bering Strait
Denali (Mt. McKinley) 20,320 ft. (6,393 m.)
ROCKY MOUNTAINS
NORTH AMERICA
Lake Winnipeg
Great Lakes
CANADA

BERING SEA
GULF OF ALASKA
GREAT PLAINS
Missouri R.
Chicago
New York

Cape Mendocino
UNITED STATES
Mississippi R.
Appalachian Mts.
Cape Hatteras
ATLANTIC OCEAN

Los Angeles
MEXICO

International Date Line (Sunday)

Tropic of Cancer

See inset below
GULF OF MEXICO

HAWAIIAN IS. (U.S.)
Mexico City
CARIBBEAN SEA

VENEZUELA  GUYANA
SURINAME
FRENCH GUIANA (FRANCE)

PACIFIC OCEAN
COLOMBIA

Equator

GALÁPAGOS IS. (ECUADOR)
ECUADOR  AMAZON
Amazon R.
Cape São Roque

Pariñas Point
PERU  BASIN
AMAZON BASIN
SOUTH AMERICA

WESTERN SAMOA
BRAZIL

MATO GROSSO PLATEAU
Rio de Janeiro

TONGA
BOLIVIA
Tropic of Capricorn
PARAGUAY
GRAN CHACO
Paraná R.
São Paulo

Mt. Aconcagua 22,834 ft. (6,960 m.)
URUGUAY
Buenos Aires

CHILE  ARGENTINA
West Longitude

FALKLAND IS. (U.K.)

Strait of Magellan  Cape Horn
SOUTH GEORGIA I. (U.K.)
Drake Passage

Antarctic Circle

## CENTRAL AMERICA AND WEST INDIES

*Projection: Bipolar Oblique Conic Conformal*

GULF OF MEXICO

BAHAMAS

Tropic of Cancer

CUBA
TURKS AND CAICOS IS. (U.K.)
ATLANTIC OCEAN

MEXICO
BELIZE
HAITI  DOMINICAN REPUBLIC
VIRGIN ISLANDS (U.S. AND U.K.)
ANTIGUA AND BARBUDA

JAMAICA
PUERTO RICO (U.S.)
ST. KITTS AND NEVIS
GUADELOUPE (FRANCE)

GUATEMALA
DOMINICA

HONDURAS
CARIBBEAN SEA
MARTINIQUE (FRANCE)
ST. LUCIA

EL SALVADOR
N
ST. VINCENT AND THE GRENADINES
BARBADOS

PACIFIC OCEAN
NICARAGUA
NETHERLANDS ANTILLES (NETHERLANDS)
GRENADA

ARUBA (NETHERLANDS)
TRINIDAD AND TOBAGO

COSTA RICA
0  250  500 Miles
0  250  500 Kilometers
PANAMA
VENEZUELA

COLOMBIA
GUYANA

668

# APPENDIX H

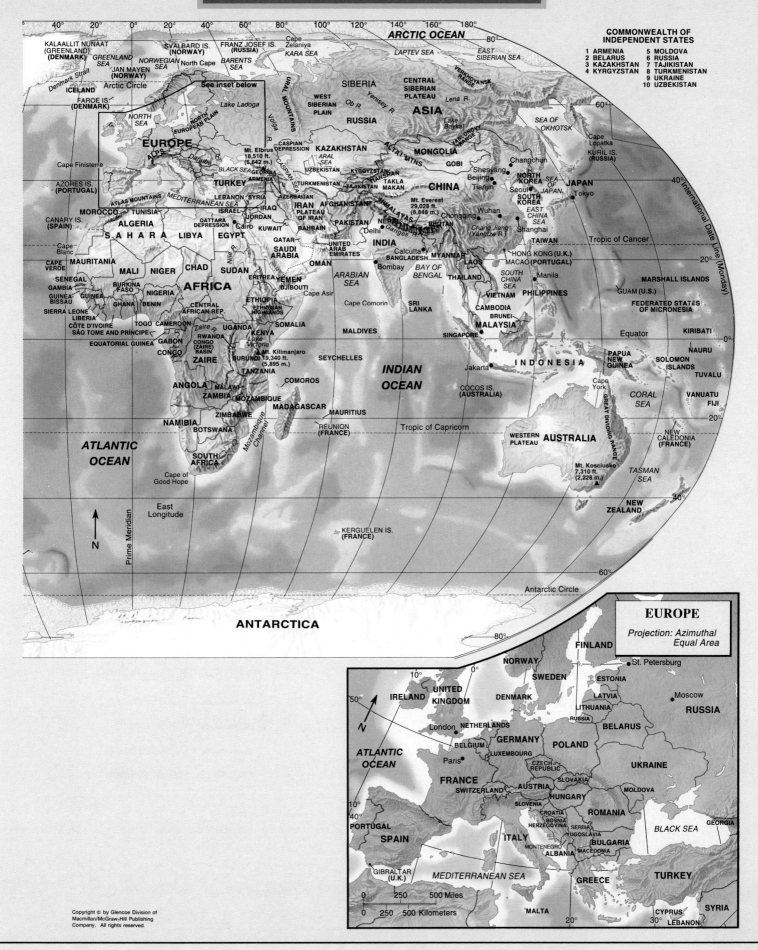

ARCTIC OCEAN

**COMMONWEALTH OF INDEPENDENT STATES**

1 ARMENIA    5 MOLDOVA
2 BELARUS    6 RUSSIA
3 KAZAKHSTAN    7 TAJIKISTAN
4 KYRGYZSTAN    8 TURKMENISTAN
                    9 UKRAINE
                  10 UZBEKISTAN

### EUROPE

*Projection: Azimuthal Equal Area*

# Weather Map Symbols

## Sample Plotted Report at Each Station

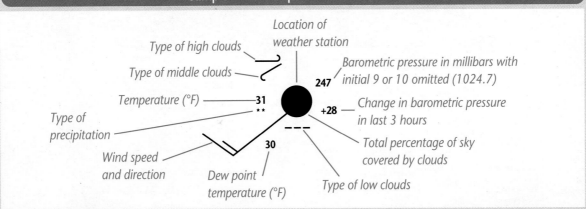

Type of high clouds

Location of weather station

Type of middle clouds

Barometric pressure in millibars with initial 9 or 10 omitted (1024.7)

**247**

Temperature (°F) — **31**

**+28** — Change in barometric pressure in last 3 hours

Type of precipitation

Total percentage of sky covered by clouds

Wind speed and direction

**30**

Dew point temperature (°F)

Type of low clouds

## Symbols Used in Plotting Report

### Precipitation

≡ Fog

\* Snow

• Rain

Thunder-storm

, Drizzle

∇ Showers

### Wind Speed and Direction

○ 0 calm

1–2 knots

3–7 knots

8–12 knots

13–17 knots

18–22 knots

23–27 knots

48–52 knots

1 knot = 1.852 km/h

### Sky Coverage

No cover

1/10 or less

2/10 or 3/10

4/10

1/2

6/10

7/10

Overcast with openings

Complete overcast

### Some Types of High Clouds

Scattered cirrus

Dense cirrus in patches

Veil of cirrus covering entire sky

Cirrus not covering entire sky

### Some Types of Middle Clouds

Thin altostratus layer

Thick altostratus layer

Thin altostratus in patches

Thin altostratus in bands

### Some Types of Low Clouds

Cumulus of fair weather

Stratocumulus

Fractocumulus of bad weather

Stratus of fair weather

### Fronts and Pressure Systems

**(H) or High**
**(L) or Low**
Center of high or low pressure system

▲▲▲▲ Cold front

●●●● Warm front

▲●▲● Occluded front

Stationary front

# APPENDIX J

## Solar System Information

### Table J-1: Solar System Information

| Planet | Mercury | Venus | Earth | Mars | Jupiter | Saturn | Uranus | Neptune | Pluto |
|---|---|---|---|---|---|---|---|---|---|
| Diameter (km) | 4878 | 12104 | 12756 | 6794 | 142796 | 120660 | 51118 | 49528 | 2290 |
| Diameter (E = 1.0)* | 0.38 | 0.95 | 1.00 | 0.53 | 11.19 | 9.46 | 4.01 | 3.88 | 0.18 |
| Mass (E = 1.0)* | 0.06 | 0.82 | 1.00 | 0.11 | 317.83 | 95.15 | 14.54 | 17.23 | 0.002 |
| Density (g/cm$^3$) | 5.42 | 5.24 | 5.50 | 3.94 | 1.31 | 0.70 | 1.30 | 1.66 | 2.03 |
| Period of rotation days hours minutes R = retrograde | 58 15 28 | 243 00 14$_R$ | 00 23 56 | 00 24 37 | 00 09 55 | 00 10 39 | 00 17 14$_R$ | 00 16 03 | 06 09 17 |
| Surface gravity (E = 1.0)* | 0.38 | 0.90 | 1.00 | 0.38 | 2.53 | 1.07 | 0.92 | 1.12 | 0.06 |
| Average distance to sun (AU) | 0.387 | 0.723 | 1.000 | 1.524 | 5.203 | 9.529 | 19.191 | 30.061 | 39.529 |
| Period of revolution | 87.97d | 224.70d | 365.26d | 686.98d | 11.86y | 29.46y | 84.04y | 164.79y | 248.53y |
| Eccentricity of orbit | 0.206 | 0.007 | 0.017 | 0.093 | 0.048 | 0.056 | 0.046 | 0.010 | 0.248 |
| Average orbital speed (km/s) | 47.89 | 35.03 | 29.79 | 24.13 | 13.06 | 9.64 | 6.81 | 5.43 | 4.74 |
| Number of known satellites | 0 | 0 | 1 | 2 | 16 | 18 | 15 | 8 | 1 |
| Known rings | 0 | 0 | 0 | 0 | 1 | thou-sands | 11 | 4 | 0 |

* Earth = 1.0

# Star Charts

Shown here are star charts for viewing stars in the Northern Hemisphere during the four different seasons. These charts are drawn from the night sky at about 35° north latitude, but they can be used for most locations in the Northern Hemisphere. The lines on the charts outline major constellations. The dense band of stars is the Milky Way. To use, hold the chart vertically, with the direction you are facing at the bottom of the map.

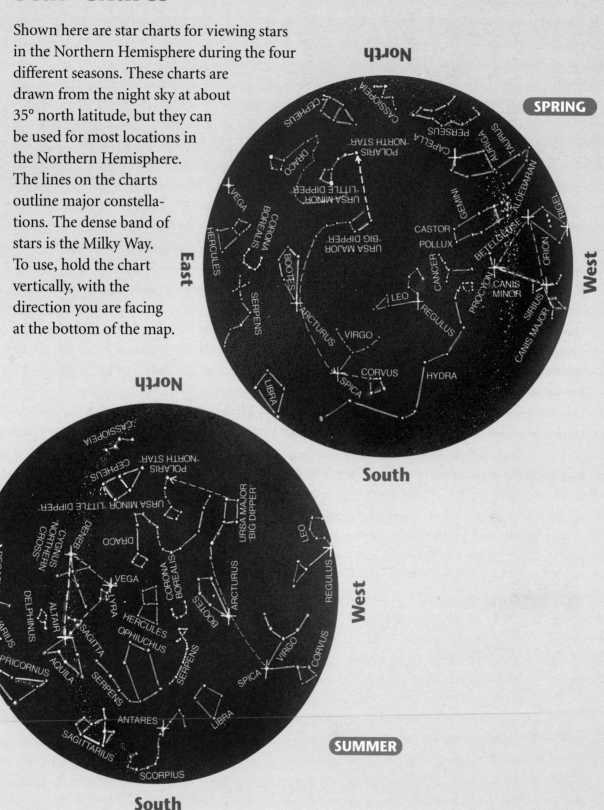

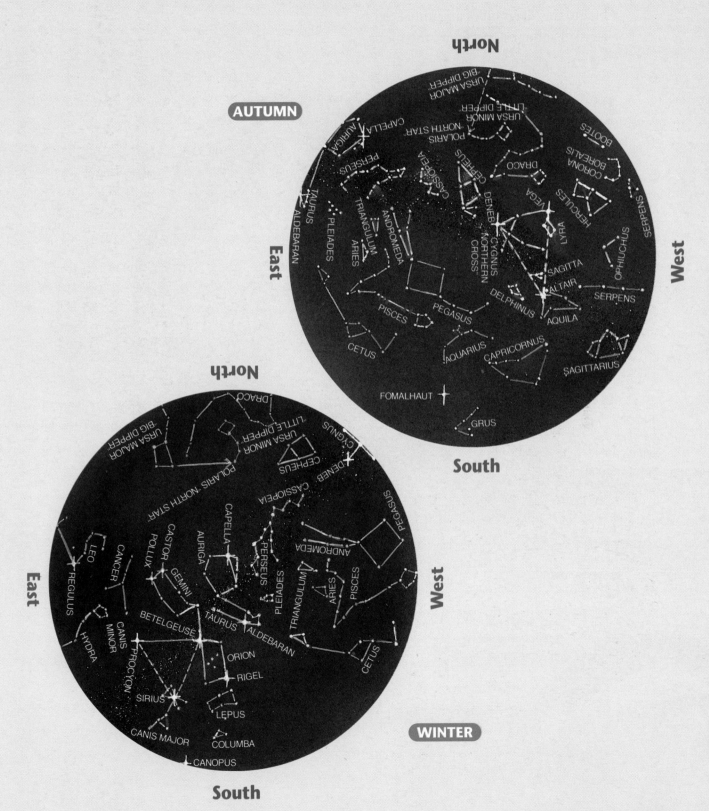

# Animal Cell

Refer to this diagram of an animal cell as you read about cell parts and their jobs.

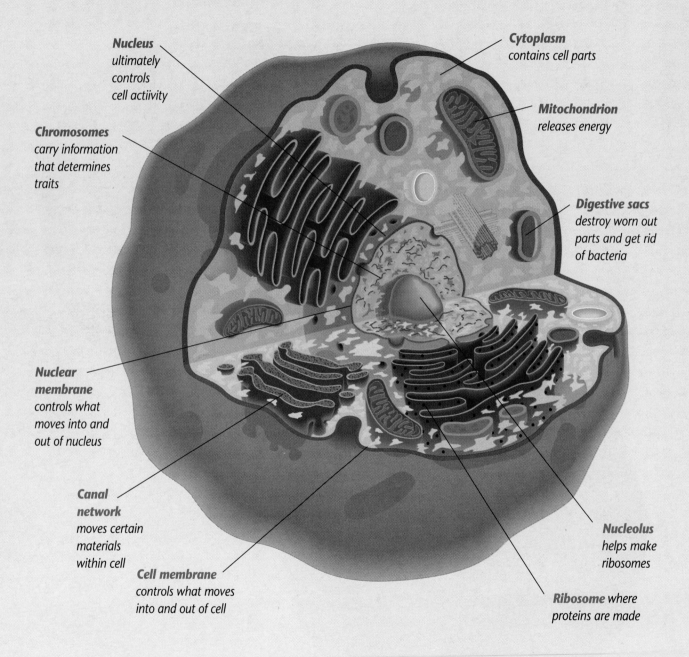

**Nucleus**
ultimately controls cell actiivity

**Chromosomes**
carry information that determines traits

**Nuclear membrane**
controls what moves into and out of nucleus

**Canal network**
moves certain materials within cell

**Cell membrane**
controls what moves into and out of cell

**Cytoplasm**
contains cell parts

**Mitochondrion**
releases energy

**Digestive sacs**
destroy worn out parts and get rid of bacteria

**Nucleolus**
helps make ribosomes

**Ribosome** where proteins are made

## Plant Cell

Refer to this diagram of a plant cell as you
read about cell parts and their jobs.

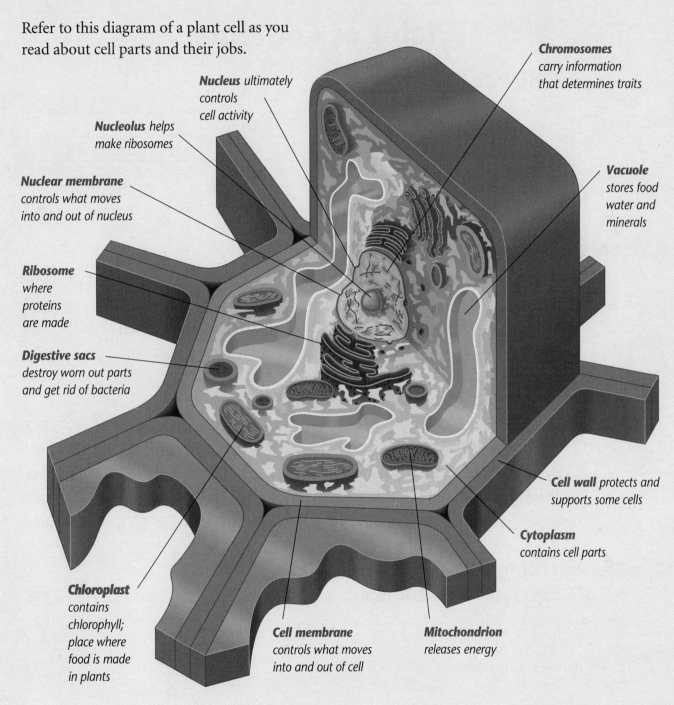

**Nucleus** ultimately controls cell activity

**Nucleolus** helps make ribosomes

**Nuclear membrane** controls what moves into and out of nucleus

**Ribosome** where proteins are made

**Digestive sacs** destroy worn out parts and get rid of bacteria

**Chloroplast** contains chlorophyll; place where food is made in plants

**Cell membrane** controls what moves into and out of cell

**Mitochondrion** releases energy

**Chromosomes** carry information that determines traits

**Vacuole** stores food water and minerals

**Cell wall** protects and supports some cells

**Cytoplasm** contains cell parts

# Table of Contents

## Organizing Information

## Thinking Critically

## Practicing Scientific Processes

## Representing and Applying Data

# Organizing Information

## ▶ Classifying

You may not realize it, but you make things orderly in the world around you. If you hang your shirts together in the closet, if your socks take up a particular corner of a dresser drawer, or if your favorite CDs are stacked together, you have used the skill of classifying.

Classifying is the process of sorting objects or events into groups based on common features. When classifying, first observe the objects or events to be classified. Then, select one feature that is shared by most members in the group but not by all. Place those members that share the feature into a subgroup. You can classify members into smaller and smaller subgroups based on characteristics.

How would you classify a collection of CDs? You might classify those you like to dance to in one subgroup and CDs you like to listen to in the next column, as in the diagram. The CDs you like to dance to could be subdivided into a rap subgroup and a rock subgroup. Note that for each feature selected, each CD only fits into one subgroup. Keep select-

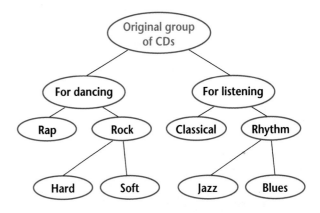

ing features until all the CDs are classified. The diagram above shows one possible classification.

Remember, when you classify, you are grouping objects or events for a purpose. Keep your purpose in mind as you select the features to form groups and subgroups.

## ▶ Sequencing

A sequence is an arrangement of things or events in a particular order. A sequence with which you are most familiar is the use of alphabetical order. Another example of sequence would be the steps in a recipe. Think about baking chocolate chip cookies. Steps in the recipe have to be followed in order for the cookies to turn out right.

When you are asked to sequence objects or events within a group, figure out what comes first, then think about what should come second. Continue to choose objects or events until all of the objects you started out with are in order. Then, go back over the sequence to make sure each thing or event in your sequence logically leads to the next.

## ▶ Concept Mapping

If you were taking an automobile trip, you would probably take along a road map. The road map shows your location, your destination, and other places along the way. By looking at the map and finding where you are, you can begin to understand where you are in relation to other locations on the map.

A concept map is similar to a road map. But, a concept map shows relationships among ideas (or concepts) rather than places. A concept map is a diagram that visually shows how concepts are related. Because the concept map shows relationships among ideas, it can make the meanings of ideas and terms clear, and help you understand better what you are studying.

**Network Tree**   Look at the concept map about Protists. This is called a network tree. Notice how some words are circled while others are written across connecting lines. The circled words are science concepts. The lines in the map show related concepts. The words written on the lines describe the relationships between concepts.

**Network Tree**

```
          Protists
             |
          include
      /      |      \
animal-like  plant-like  fungus-like
 protists    protists    protists
    |          |           |
known as    known as    known as
    |          |         /    \
protozoans   algae   water molds  slime molds
```

When you are asked to construct a network tree, write down the topic and list the major concepts related to that topic on a piece of paper. Then look at your list and begin to put them in order from general to specific. Branch the related concepts from the major concept and describe the relationships on the lines. Continue to write the more specific concepts. Write the relationships between the concepts on the lines until all concepts are mapped. Examine the concept map for relationships that cross branches, and add them to the concept map.

**Events Chain**   An events chain is another type of concept map. An events chain map, such as the one on the effects of gravity, is used to describe ideas in order. In science, an

**Events Chain**

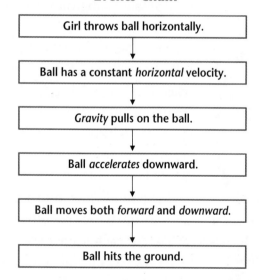

| Girl throws ball horizontally. |
| --- |
| Ball has a constant *horizontal* velocity. |
| *Gravity* pulls on the ball. |
| Ball *accelerates* downward. |
| Ball moves both *forward* and *downward*. |
| Ball hits the ground. |

events chain can be used to describe a sequence of events, the steps in a procedure, or the stages of a process.

When making an events chain, first find the one event that starts the chain. This event is called the initiating event. Then, find the

next event in the chain and continue until you reach an outcome. Suppose you are asked to describe what happens when someone throws a ball horizontally. An events chain map describing the steps might look like the one on page 678. Notice that connecting words are not necessary in an events chain.

**Cycle Map**   A cycle concept map is a special type of events chain map. In a cycle concept map, the series of events does not produce a

**Cycle Map**

Plants undergoing photosynthesis

use

carbon dioxide

which is released by

respiration in animals and plants

in the presence of

oxygen

which has been released by

final outcome. Instead, the last event in the chain relates back to the initiating event.

As in the events chain map, you first decide on an initiating event and then list each event in order. Since there is no outcome and the last event relates back to the initiating event, the cycle repeats itself. Look at the cycle map for photosynthesis shown above.

**Spider Map**   A fourth type of concept map is the spider map. This is a map that you can use for brainstorming. Once you have a central idea, you may find you have a jumble of ideas that relate to it, but are not necessarily clearly related to each other. By writing these

**Spider Map**

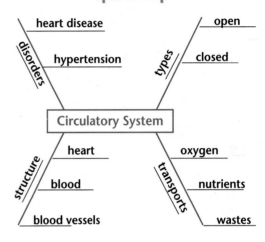

ideas outside the main concept, you may begin to separate and group unrelated terms so that they become more useful.

There is usually not one correct way to create a concept map. As you construct one type of map, you may discover other ways to construct the map that show the relationships between concepts in a better way. If you do discover what you think is a better way to create a concept map, go ahead and use the new way. Overall, concept maps are useful for breaking a big concept down into smaller parts, making learning easier.

## ▶ Making and Using Tables

Browse through your textbook, and you will notice tables in the text and in the activities. In a table, data or information is arranged in such a way that makes it easier for you to understand. Activity tables help organize the data you collect during an activity so that results can be interpreted more easily.

**Parts of a Table** Most tables have a title. At a glance, the title tells you what the table is about. A table is divided into columns and rows. The first column lists items to be compared. In the table shown to the right, different magnitudes of force are being compared. The row across the top lists the specific characteristics being compared. Within the grid of the table, the collected data is recorded. Look at the features of the table in the next column.

What is the title of this table? The title is "Earthquake Magnitude." What is being compared? The distance away from the epicenter that tremors are felt and the average number of earthquakes expected per year are being compared for different magnitudes on the Richter scale.

**Using Tables** What is the average number of earthquakes expected per year for an earthquake with a magnitude of 5.5 at the focus? Locate the column labeled "Average number expected per year" and the row "5.0 to 5.9." The data in the box where the column and row intersect is the answer. Did you answer "800"? What is the distance away from the epicenter for an earthquake with a

| Earthquake Magnitude | | |
|---|---|---|
| Magnitude at Focus | Distance from Epicenter that Tremors are Felt | Average Number Expected Per Year |
| 1.0 to 3.9 | 24 km | >100 000 |
| 4.0 to 4.9 | 48 km | 6200 |
| 5.0 to 5.9 | 112 km | 800 |
| 6.0 to 6.9 | 200 km | 120 |
| 7.0 to 7.9 | 400 km | 20 |
| 8.0 to 8.9 | 720 km | <1 |

magnitude of 8.1? If you answered "720 km," you understand how to use the parts of a table.

**Making Tables** To make a table, list the items to be compared down in columns and the characteristics to be compared across in rows. Make a table and record the data comparing the mass of recycled materials collected by a class. On Monday, students turned in 4 kg of paper, 2 kg of aluminum, and 0.5 kg of plastic. On Wednesday, they turned in 3.5 kg of paper, 1.5 kg of aluminum, and 0.5 kg of plastic. On Friday, the totals were 3 kg of paper, 1 kg of aluminum, and 1.5 kg of plastic. If your table looks like the one shown below, you are able to make tables to organize data.

| Recycled Materials | | | |
|---|---|---|---|
| Day of Week | Paper (kg) | Aluminum (kg) | Plastic (kg) |
| Mon. | 4 | 2 | 0.5 |
| Wed. | 3.5 | 1.5 | 0.5 |
| Fri. | 3 | 1 | 1.5 |

## Making and Using Graphs

After scientists organize data in tables, they may display the data in a graph. A graph is a diagram that shows how variables compare. A graph makes interpretation and analysis of data easier. There are three basic types of graphs used in science—the line graph, the bar graph, and the pie graph.

**Line Graphs** A line graph is used to show the relationship between two variables. The variables being compared go on two axes of the graph. The independent variable always goes on the horizontal axis, called the *x*-axis. The dependent variable always goes on the vertical axis, called the *y*-axis.

Suppose a school started a peer study program with a class of students to see how science grades were affected.

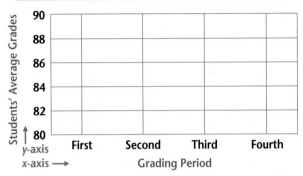

| Average Grades of Students in Study Program | |
|---|---|
| Grading Period | Average Science Grade |
| First | 81 |
| Second | 85 |
| Third | 86 |
| Fourth | 89 |

You could make a graph of the grades of students in the program over the four grading periods of the school year. The grading period is the independent variable and is placed on the *x*-axis of your graph. The average grade of the students in the program is the dependent variable and would go on the *y*-axis.

After drawing your axes, you would label each axis with a scale. The *x*-axis simply lists the four grading periods. To make a scale of grades on the *y*-axis, you must look at the data values. Since the lowest grade was 81 and the highest was 89, you know that you will have to start numbering at least at 81 and go through 89. You decide to start numbering at 80 and number by twos through 90.

Next, plot the data points. The first pair of data you want to plot is the first grading period and 81. Locate "First" on the *x*-axis and locate "81" on the *y*-axis. Where an imaginary vertical line from the *x*-axis and an imaginary horizontal line from the *y*-axis would meet, place the first data point. Place the other data points the same way. After all the points are plotted, connect them with straight lines.

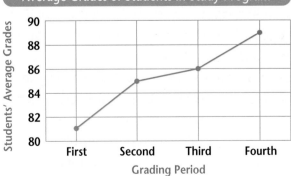

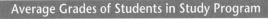

**Bar Graphs**   Bar graphs are similar to line graphs. They compare data that do not continuously change. In a bar graph, vertical bars show the relationships among data.

To make a bar graph, set up the *x*-axis and *y*-axis as you did for the line graph. The data is plotted by drawing vertical bars from the *x*-axis up to a point where the *y*-axis would meet the bar if it were extended.

Look at the bar graph comparing the masses lifted by an electromagnet with different numbers of dry cell batteries. The *x*-axis is the number of dry cell batteries, and the *y*-axis is the mass lifted.

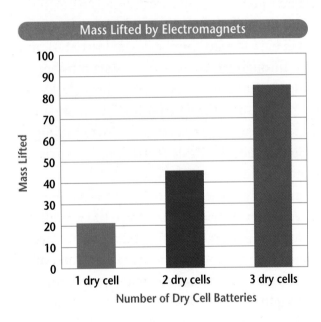

**Mass Lifted by Electromagnets**

**Pie Graphs**   A pie graph uses a circle divided into sections to display data. Each section represents part of the whole. All the sections together equal 100 percent.

Suppose you wanted to make a pie graph to show the number of seeds that germinated in a package. You would have to count the total number of seeds and the number of seeds that germinated out of the total.

You find that there are 143 seeds in the package. This represents 100 percent, the whole pie.

You plant the seeds, and 129 seeds germinate. The seeds that germinated will make up one section of the pie graph, and the seeds that did not germinate will make up the remaining section.

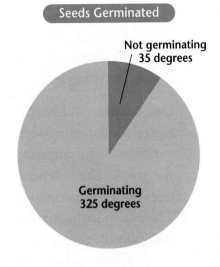

**Seeds Germinated**

Not germinating 35 degrees

Germinating 325 degrees

To find out how much of the pie each section should take, divide the number of seeds in each section by the total number of seeds. Then multiply your answer by 360, the number of degrees in a circle, and round to the nearest whole number. The section of the pie graph in degrees that represents the seeds germinated is figured below.

$$\frac{129}{143} \times 360 = 324.75 \text{ or } 325 \text{ degrees}$$

Plot this group on the pie graph using a compass and a protractor. Use the compass to draw a circle. Then, draw a straight line from the center to the edge of the circle. Place your protractor on this line and use it to mark a point on the edge of the circle at 325 degrees. Connect this point with a straight line to the center of the circle. This is the section for the group of seeds that germinated. The other section represents the group of 14 seeds that did not germinate. Label the sections of your graph and title the graph.

# Thinking Critically

## ▶ Observing and Inferring

Imagine that you have just finished a volleyball game. At home, you open the refrigerator and see a jug of orange juice on the back of the top shelf. The jug feels cold as you grasp it. Then you drink the juice, smell the oranges, and enjoy the tart taste in your mouth.

As you imagined yourself in the story, you used your senses to make observations. You used your sense of sight to find the jug in the refrigerator, your sense of touch when you felt the coldness of the jug, your sense of hearing to listen as the liquid filled the glass, and your senses of smell and taste to enjoy the odor and tartness of the juice. The basis of all scientific investigation is observation.

Scientists try to make careful and accurate observations. When possible, they use instruments such as microscopes and thermometers or a pan balance to make observations. Measurements with a balance

or thermometer provide numerical data that can be checked and repeated.

When you make observations in science, you'll find it helpful to examine the entire object or situation first. Then, look carefully for details. Write down everything you observe.

Scientists often make inferences based on their observations. An inference is an attempt to explain or interpret observations or to say what caused what you observed. For example, if you observed a CLOSED sign in a store window around noon, you might infer the owner is taking a lunch break. But, it's also possible that the owner has a doctor's appointment or has taken the day off to go fishing. The only way to be sure your inference is correct is to investigate further.

When making an inference, be certain to use accurate data and observations. Analyze all of the data that you've collected. Then, based on everything you know, explain or interpret what you've observed.

## ▶ Comparing and Contrasting

Observations can be analyzed by noting the similarities and differences between two or more objects or events that you observe. When you look at objects or events to see how they are similar, you are comparing them. Contrasting is looking for differences in similar objects or events.

Suppose you were asked to compare and contrast the planets Venus and Earth. You would start by looking at what is known about these planets. Arrange this information in a table, making two columns on a piece of paper and listing ways the planets are similar in one column and ways they are different in the other.

| Comparison of Venus and Earth | | |
|---|---|---|
| Properties | Earth | Venus |
| Diameter (km) | 12 756 | 12 104 |
| Average density (g/cm³) | 5.5 | 5.3 |
| Percentage of sunlight reflected | 39 | 76 |
| Daytime surface temperature (degrees) | 300 | 750 |
| Number of satellites | 1 | 0 |

Similarities you might point out are that both planets are similar in size, shape, and mass. Differences include Venus having a hotter surface temperature that reflects more sunlight than Earth refelects. Also, Venus lacks a moon.

## ▶ Recognizing Cause and Effect

Have you ever watched something happen and then made suggestions as to why it happened? If so, you have observed an effect and inferred a cause. The event is an effect, and the reason for the event is the cause.

Suppose that every time your teacher fed the fish in a classroom aquarium, she or he tapped the food container on the edge of the aquarium. Then, one day your teacher just happened to tap the edge of the aquarium with a pencil while making a point about an ecology lesson. You observed the fish swim to the surface of the aquarium to feed. What is the effect, and what would you infer to be the cause? The effect is the fish swimming to the surface of the aquarium. You might infer the cause to be the teacher tapping on the edge of the aquarium. In determining cause and effect, you have made a logical inference based on your observations.

Perhaps the fish swam to the surface because they reacted to the teacher's waving hand or for some other reason. When scientists are unsure of the cause of a certain event, they design controlled experiments to determine what causes the event. Although you have made a logical conclusion about the behavior of the fish, you would have to perform an experiment to be certain that it was the tapping that caused the effect you observed.

## ▶ Measuring in SI

The metric system is a system of measurement developed by a group of scientists in 1795. It helps scientists avoid problems by providing standard measurements that all scientists around the world can understand. A modern form of the metric system, called the International System, or SI, was adopted for worldwide use in 1960.

| Metric Prefixes | | | |
|---|---|---|---|
| Prefix | Symbol | Meaning | |
| kilo- | k | 1000 | thousand |
| hecto- | h | 100 | hundred |
| deka- | da | 10 | ten |
| deci- | d | 0.1 | tenth |
| centi- | c | 0.01 | hundreth |
| milli- | m | 0.001 | thousandth |

The metric system is convenient because unit sizes vary by multiples of 10. When changing from smaller units to larger units, divide by 10. When changing from larger units to smaller, you multiply by 10. For example, to convert millimeters to centimeters, divide the millimeters by 10. To convert 30 millimeters to centimeters, divide 30 by 10 (30 millimeters equals 3 centimeters).

Prefixes are used to name units. Look at the table for some common metric prefixes and their meanings. Do you see how the prefix *kilo-* attached to the unit *gram* is *kilogram*, or 1000 grams? The prefix *deci-* attached to the unit *meter* is *decimeter*, or one-tenth (0.1) of a meter.

**Length** You have probably measured lengths or distances many times. The meter is the SI unit used to measure length. A baseball bat is about one meter long. When measuring smaller lengths, the meter is divided into smaller units called centimeters and millimeters. A centimeter is one-hundredth (0.01) of a meter, which is about the size of the width of the fingernail on your ring finger. A millimeter is one-thousandth of a meter (0.001), about the thickness of a dime.

Most metric rulers have lines indicating centimeters and millimeters. The centimeter lines are the longer, numbered lines, and the shorter lines are millimeter lines. When using a metric ruler, line up the 0 centimeter mark with the end of the object being measured, and read the number of the unit where the object ends.

**Surface Area** Units of length are also used to measure surface area. The standard unit of area is the square meter (m²). A square that's one meter long on each side has a surface area of one square meter. Similarly, a square centimeter (cm²) is one centimeter long on each side. The surface area of an object is determined by multiplying the length times the width.

1 cm
1 cm

**Volume** The volume of a rectangular solid is also calculated using units of length. The cubic meter ($m^3$) is the standard SI unit of volume. A cubic meter is a cube one meter on each side. You can determine the volume of rectangular solids by multiplying length times width times height.

**Liquid Volume** During science activities, you will measure liquids using beakers and graduated cylinders marked in milliliters. A graduated cylinder is a cylindrical container marked with lines from bottom to top.

Liquid volume is measured using a unit called a liter. A liter has the volume of 1000 cubic centimeters. Since the prefix *milli-* means thousandth (0.001), a milliliter equals one cubic centimeter. One milliliter of liquid would completely fill a cube measuring one centimeter on each side.

**Mass** Scientists use balances to find the mass of objects in grams. You will use a beam balance similar to the one illustrated. Notice that on one side of the balance is a pan and on the other side is a set of beams. Each beam has an object of a known mass called a *rider* that slides on the beam.

Before you find the mass of an object, set the balance to zero by sliding all the riders back to the zero point. Check the pointer on the right to make sure it swings an equal distance above and below the zero point on the scale. If the swing is unequal, find and turn the adjusting screw until you have an equal swing.

Place an object on the pan. Slide the rider with the largest mass along its beam until the pointer drops below zero. Then move it back one notch. Repeat the process on each beam until the pointer swings an equal distance above and below the zero point. Add the masses on each beam to find the mass of the object.

You should never place a hot object or pour chemicals directly on the pan. Instead, find the mass of a clean beaker or a glass jar. Place the dry or liquid chemicals in the container. Then find the combined mass of the container and the chemicals. Calculate the mass of the chemicals by subtracting the mass of the empty container from the combined mass.

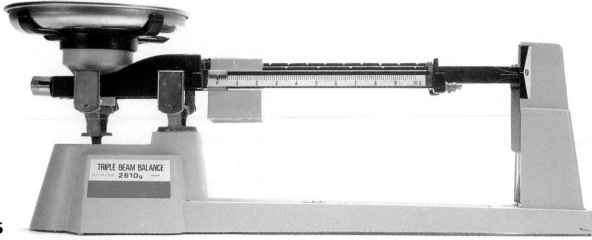

# Practicing Scientific Processes

You might say that the work of a scientist is to solve problems. But when you decide how to dress on a particular day, you are doing problem solving, too. You may observe what the weather looks like through a window. You may go outside and see if what you are wearing is warm or cool enough.

Scientists use an orderly approach to learn new information and to solve problems. The methods scientists may use include observing, forming a hypothesis, testing a hypothesis, separating and controlling variables, and interpreting data.

## ▶ Observing

You observe all the time. Any time you smell wood burning, touch a pet, see

lightning, taste food, or hear your favorite music, you are observing. Observation gives you information about events or things. Scientists try to observe as much as possible about the things and events they study so that they can know that what they say about their observations is reliable.

Some observations describe something using only words. These observations are called qualitative observations. If you were making qualitative observations of a dog, you might use words such as furry, brown, short-haired, or short-eared.

Other observations describe how much of something there is. These are quantitative observations and use numbers as well as words in the description. Tools or equipment are used to measure the characteristic being described. Quantitative observations of a dog might include a mass of 45 kg, a height of 76 cm, ear length of 14 cm, and an age of 283 days.

## ▶ Using Observations to Form a Hypothesis

Suppose you want to make a perfect score on a spelling test. Begin by thinking of several ways to accomplish this. Base these possibilities on past observations. If you put each of these possibilities into sentence form, using the words if and then, you can form a hypothesis. All of the following are hypotheses you might consider to explain how you could score 100 percent on your test:

If the test is easy, then I will get a perfect score.

If I am intelligent, then I will get a perfect score.

If I study hard, then I will get a perfect score.

Scientists make hypotheses that they can test to explain the observations they have made. Perhaps a scientist has observed that plants that receive fertilizer grow taller than plants that do not. A scientist may form a hypothesis that says: If plants are fertilized, then their growth will increase.

## ▶ Designing an Experiment to Test a Hypothesis

Once you state a hypothesis, you probably want to find out if it explains an event or an observation or not. This requires a test. A hypothesis must be something you can test. To test a hypothesis, you design and carry out an experiment. Experiments involve planning and materials. Let's figure out how to conduct an experiment to test the hypothesis

stated before about the effects of fertilizer on plants.

First, you need to write out a procedure. A procedure is the plan that you follow in your experiment. A procedure tells you what materials to use and how to use them. In this experiment, your plan may involve using ten bean plants that are each 15-cm tall (to begin with) in two groups, Groups A and B. You will water the five bean plants in Group A with 200 mL of plain water and no fertilizer twice a week for three weeks. You will treat the five bean plants in Group B with 200 mL of fertilizer solution twice a week for three weeks.

You will need to measure all the plants in both groups at the beginning of the experiment and again at the end of the three-week period. These measurements will be the data that you record in a table. A sample table has been done for you. Look at the data in the table for this experiment. From the data, you can draw a conclusion and make a statement about your results. If the conclusion you draw from the data supports your hypothesis, then you can say that your hypothesis is

| Growing Bean Plants | | |
|---|---|---|
| Plants | Treatment | Height 3 Weeks Later |
| Group A | no fertilizer added to soil | 17 cm |
| Group B | 3 g fertilizer added to soil | 31 cm |

reliable. Reliable means that you can trust your conclusion. If it did not support your hypothesis, then you would have to make new observations and state a new hypothesis, one that you could also test.

### ▶ Separating and Controlling Variables

In the experiment with the bean plants, you made everything the same except for treating one group (Group B) with fertilizer. In any experiment, it is important to keep everything the same, except for the item you are testing. In the experiment, you kept the type of plants, their beginning heights, the soil, the frequency with which you watered them, and the amount of water or fertilizer all the same, or constant. By doing so, you made sure that at the end of three weeks any change you saw was the result of whether or not the plants had been fertilized. The only thing that you changed, or varied, was the use of fertilizer. In an experiment, the one factor that you change (in this case, the fertilizer), is called the independent variable. The factor that changes (in this case, growth) as a result of the independent variable is called the dependent variable. Always make sure that there is only one independent variable. If you allow more than one, you will not know what causes the changes you observe in the dependent variable.

Many experiments also have a control, a treatment that you can compare with the results of your test groups. In this case, Group A was the control because it was not treated with fertilizer. Group B was the test group. At the end of three weeks, you were able to compare Group A with Group B and draw a conclusion.

## ▶ Interpreting Data

The word *interpret* means to explain the meaning of something. Information, or data, needs to mean something. Look at the problem originally being explored and find out what the data shows. Perhaps you are looking at a table from an experiment designed to test the hypothesis: If plants are fertilized, then their growth will increase. Look back to the table showing the results of the bean plant experiment.

Identify the control group and the test group so you can see whether or not the variable has had an effect. In this example, Group A was the control and Group B was the test group. Now you need to check differences between the control and test groups. These differences may be qualitative or quantitative. A qualitative difference would be if the leaf colors of plants in Groups A and B were different. A quantitative difference would be the difference in numbers of centimeters of height among the plants in each group. Group B was in fact taller than Group A after three weeks.

If there are differences, the variable being tested may have had an effect. If there is no difference between the control and the test groups, the variable being tested apparently

had no effect. From the data table in this experiment on page 688, it appears that fertilizer does have an effect on plant growth.

## ▶ What is Data?

In the experiment described on these pages, measurements have been taken so that at the end of the experiment, you had something concrete to interpret. You had numbers to work with. Not every experiment that you do will give you data in the form of numbers. Sometimes, data will be in the form of a description. At the end of a chemistry experiment, you might have noted that one solution turned yellow when treated with a particular chemical, and another remained clear, like water, when treated with the same chemical. Data therefore, is stated in different forms for different types of scientific experiments.

## ▶ Are All Experiments Alike?

Keep in mind as you perform experiments in science, that not every experiment makes use of all of the parts that have been described on these pages. For some, it may be difficult to design an experiment that will always have a control. Other experiments are complex enough that it may be hard to have only one dependent variable. Real scientists encounter many variations in the methods that they use when they perform experiments. The skills in this handbook are here for you to use and practice. In real situations, their uses will vary.

# Representing and Applying Data

## ▶ Interpreting Scientific Illustrations

As you read this textbook, you will see many drawings, diagrams, and photographs. Illustrations help you to understand what you read. Some illustrations are included to help you understand an idea that you can't see easily by yourself. For instance, we can't see atoms, but we can look at a diagram of an atom and that helps us to understand some things about atoms. Seeing something often helps you remember more easily. The text may describe the surface of Jupiter in detail, but seeing a photograph of Jupiter may help you to remember that it has cloud bands. Illustrations also provide examples that clarify difficult concepts or give additional information about the topic you are studying. Maps, for example, help you to locate places that may be described in the text.

**Captions and Labels** Most illustrations have captions. A caption is a comment that identifies or explains the illustration. Diagrams, such as the one of the feather, often have labels that identify parts of the item shown or the order of steps in a process.

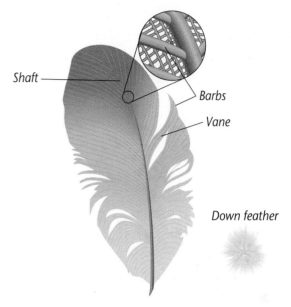

Shaft
Barbs
Vane
Down feather
Contour feather

**Learning with Illustrations** An illustration of an organism shows that organism from a particular view or orientation. In order to understand the illustration, you may need to identify the front (anterior) end, tail (posterior) end, the underside (ventral), and the back (dorsal) side of the organism shown.

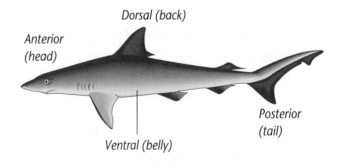

Dorsal (back)
Anterior (head)
Posterior (tail)
Ventral (belly)

You might also check for symmetry. Look at the illustration on the following page. A shark has bilateral symmetry. This means that drawing an imaginary line through the center of the animal from the anterior to posterior end forms two mirror images.

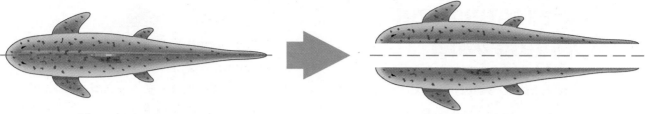

*Bilateral symmetry*                    *Two sides exactly alike*

Radial symmetry is the arrangement of similar parts around a central point. An object or organism such as a hydra can be divided anywhere through the center into similar parts.

Some organisms and objects cannot be divided into two similar parts. If an organism or object cannot be divided, it is asymmetrical. Regardless of how you try to divide a natural sponge, you cannot divide it into two parts that look alike.

Some illustrations enable you to see the inside of an organism or object. These illustrations are called sections.

Look at all illustrations carefully. Read captions and labels so that you understand exactly what the illustration is showing you.

### ▶ Making Models

Have you ever worked on a model car or plane or rocket? These models look, and sometimes work, just like the real thing, but they are usually much smaller than the real thing. In science, models are used to help simplify large processes or structures that may be difficult to understand. Your understanding of a structure or process is enhanced when you work with materials to make a model that shows the basic features of the structure or process.

In order to make a model, you first have to get a basic idea about the structure or process involved. You decide to make a model to show the differences in size of arteries, veins, and capillaries. First, read about these structures. All three are hollow tubes. Arteries are round and thick. Veins are flat and have thinner walls than arteries. Capillaries are very small.

Now, decide what you can use for your model. Common materials are often best and cheapest to work with when making models. Different

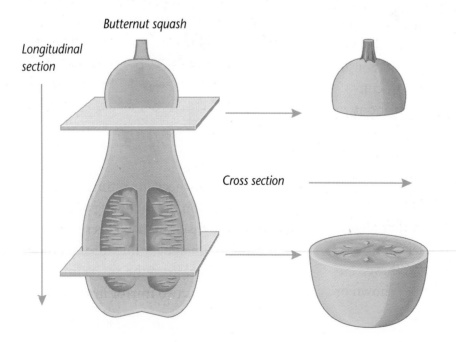

*Butternut squash*

*Longitudinal section*

*Cross section*

### ▶ Predicting

When you apply a hypothesis, or general explanation, to a specific situation, you predict something about that situation. First, you must identify which hypothesis fits the situation you are considering. People use prediction to make everyday decisions. Based on previous observations and experiences, you may form a hypothesis that if it is wintertime, then temperatures will be lower. From past experience in your area, temperatures are lowest in February. You may then use this hypothesis to predict specific temperatures and weather for the month of February in advance. Someone could use these predictions to plan to set aside more money for heating bills during that month.

### ▶ Sampling and Estimating

When working with large populations of organisms, scientists usually cannot observe or study every organism in the population. Instead, they use a sample or a portion of the population. Sampling is taking a small portion of organisms of a population for research. By making careful observations or manipulating variables with a portion of a group, information is discovered and conclusions are drawn that might then be applied to the whole population.

Scientific work also involves estimating. Estimating is making a judgment about the size of something or the number of something without actually measuring or counting every member of a population.

kinds and sizes of pasta might work for these models. Different sizes of rubber tubing might do just as well. Cut and glue the different noodles or tubing onto thick paper so the openings can be seen. Then label each. Now you have a simple, easy–to–understand model showing the differences in size of arteries, veins, and capillaries.

What other scientific ideas might a model help you to understand? A model of a molecule can be made from gumdrops (using different colors for the different elements present) and toothpicks (to show different chemical bonds). A working model of a volcano can be made from clay, a small amount of baking soda, vinegar, and a bottle cap. Other models can be devised on a computer.

Suppose you are trying to determine the effect of a specific nutrient on the growth of black-eyed Susans. It would be impossible to test the entire population of black-eyed Susans, so you would select part of the population for your experiment. Through careful experimentation and observation on a sample of the population, you could generalize the effect of the chemical on the entire population.

Here is a more familiar example. Have you ever tried to guess how many beans were in a sealed jar? If you did, you were estimating. What if you knew the jar of beans held one liter (1000 mL)? If you knew that 30 beans would fit in a 100-milliliter jar, how many beans would you estimate to be in the one-liter jar? If you said about 300 beans, your estimate would be close to the actual number of beans.

Scientists use a similar process to estimate populations of organisms from bacteria to buffalo. Scientists count the actual number of organisms in a small sample and then estimate the number of organisms in a larger area. For example, if a scientist wanted to count the number of microorganisms in a petri dish, a microscope could be used to count the number of organisms in a one square millimeter sample. To determine the total population of the culture, the number of organisms in the square millimeter sample is multiplied by the total number of millimeters in the culture.

# GLOSSARY

This glossary defines each key term that appears in bold type in the text. It also indicates the chapter number and page number where you will find the word used.

## A

**absolute zero:** coldness limit at which there can be no further cooling; at absolute zero, which is -273.15°C, the kinetic energy of molecules is decreased to zero; however, at absolute zero, matter still has a tiny amount of energy—representing the lowest possible energy that matter can have. (Chap. 7, p. 228)

**air mass:** large body of air whose temperature and amount of moisture result from the type of surface over which it developed; examples include cold and dry, hot and dry, or warm and moist air masses; day-to-day changes in the weather are caused by the movement and collision of air masses, which swirl over Earth's surface at different speeds and in various directions. (Chap. 8, p. 251)

**alcohol:** family of compounds that contain oxygen in the form of hydroxyl (—OH) groups; alcohols are formed when an —OH group replaces one or more hydrogen atoms in a hydrocarbon; examples are methanol, isopropyl alcohol, and ethanol; alcohols are used in fuel, disinfectants, and chemical manufacture. (Chap. 10, p. 315)

**alkali metals:** column 1 elements in the periodic table of elements; alkali metals are so reactive that they are never found uncombined in nature, can be cut with a knife, have a metallic lustre, conduct electricity and heat, are malleable, and in pure form must be stored in nonreactive liquids. (Chap. 5, p. 159)

**alkaline earth metals:** in the periodic table of elements, alkaline earth metals are column 2 elements such as magnesium, strontium, and barium and are not as reactive as alkali metals. (Chap. 5, p. 159)

**alpha particle:** positively charged particle—consisting of two protons and two neutrons—which is given off by a radioactive substance; alpha particles have more mass than beta particles and are unable to go through a thick sheet of paper. (Chap. 4, p. 117)

**amines:** organic compounds produced when an amine group (—NH$_2$) replaces one or more hydrogens in a hydrocarbon; amino acids, which are a type of amine-substituted hydrocarbon, form when both the —NH$_2$ and —COOH groups replace hydrogens on the same molecule. (Chap. 10, p. 316)

**antibodies:** specific substances produced by white blood cells in response to specific antigens; when the antibody on the surface of a B-cell, a type of white blood cell, meets its matching antigen, it bonds to it and produces antibodies to destroy it. (Chap. 12, p. 384)

**antigens:** proteins or chemicals or just about any large molecules— such molecules on the surface of bacteria and parasites—that are foreign to the body; when your body fights disease, it defends against antigens by producing a specific antibody to bind with a specific antigen, rendering it harmless. (Chap. 12, p. 384)

**artificial transmutation:** transmutation that does not happen spontaneously; scientists have forced nuclei to transmute by using particle accelerators, with the result that gaps in the periodic table have been filled in and more than a dozen new radioactive elements beyond uranium have been created. (Chap. 18, p. 575)

**asteroids:** traveling chunks of rock found mostly in the asteroid belt between the orbits of Mars and Jupiter; "runaway" asteroids may be captured by planetary gravity and become moons or may be responsible for some surface features of planets. (Chap. 19, p. 618)

**asthenosphere:** putty-like layer in Earth's crust on which plates slide around; capable of flow. (Chap 15, p. 484)

**atomic mass:** average mass of the isotope of an element found in nature; atomic mass of an element is calculated by determining the average mass of a sample of that element's atoms. (Chap. 5, p. 151)

**atomic number:** the number of protons in an atom of an element; atoms of the same element always have the same number of protons—for example, carbon always has an atomic number of 6 and strontium always has an atomic number of 38; elements appear in the periodic table of elements in order of increasing atomic number. (Chap. 5, p. 148)

## B

**balanced chemical equation:** equation with the same number of atoms of each element on both sides of the equation; whole-number coefficients can be written to balance a chemical equation. (Chap. 6, p. 193)

**beta particle:** high-speed electron given off by a radioactive substance; these negatively charged particles have less mass than alpha particles and can penetrate paper but are stopped by a 1.5-mm sheet of aluminum. (Chap. 4, p. 117)

**binary compound:** compound made up of atoms of two elements; calcium fluoride, CaF$_2$, is an example of a binary compound. (Chap. 6, p. 187)

**body cells:** most num
for example, bone
are body cells; a bo
copies of itself by m
somes in a body ce
for example, huma
tomatoes have 24,
tain twice the num
(Chap. 13, p. 406)

**boiling:** formation of bubbles rising to the surface of heated water that occurs when the pressure of water vapor escaping from the liquid's surface equals air pressure; boiling allows the water particles to gain enough kinetic energy to break away and become a gas. (Chap. 7, p. 220)

**carbohydrates:** organic compounds containing twice as many hydrogen atoms as oxygen atoms; carbohydrates provide energy for the body, and a balanced diet gets 50 percent of its calories from carbohydrate-rich foods such as pasta, rice, beans, and fruit. (Chap. 10, p. 323)

**carboxylic acids:** group of substituted hydrocarbons formed by displacement of a —CH₃ group by a carboxyl (—COOH) group; methanoic acid is the simplest carboxylic acid. (Chap. 10, p. 315)

**Cenozoic Era:** geologic division following the Mesozoic Era; the Alps formed and the Himalaya Mountains started to rise; life-forms included the first horses and elephants and the appearance of the first modern humans; because its geologic record is more complete, the periods of the Cenozoic are subdivided into epochs. (Chap. 16, p. 526)

**chain reaction:** reaction that can start if the neutrons freed by the split of one heavy nucleus into two lighter nuclei cause fission in other nuclei; in nuclear reactors, neutron-absorbing materials such as cadmium rods can be used so that fission chain reactions do not go out of control. (Chap. 18, p. 583)

**circuit:** any complete pathway through which electrical current flows; requires a source of potential difference, a conducting path, and resistance. (Chap. 1, p. 33)

**clotting:** process by which a broken blood vessel is sealed off by platelets, which release chemicals that react with substances in plasma and form sticky fibers that trap the blood cells—resulting in formation of a clot that seals the break and hardens into a scab. (Chap. 12, p. 381)

**comet:** large chunk of ice, dust, gases, and rock fragments that travels through space and is pulled into orbit by the sun's gravity. (Chap. 19, p. 617)

**condensation:** process in which a gas is changed into a liquid; for example, water droplets on a chilly window pane form as the result of water vapor molecules transferring energy to the cold surface of the glass and condensing. (Chap. 7, p. 221)

**conductor:** material that allows electrical charges to flow freely from place to place—examples include copper, gold, and silver; conductors are attracted to both positive and negative charges, and even very good conductors can offer some resistance to the flow of charges; power cables conduct electricity safely by wrapping conductors in such insulators as rubber. (Chap. 1, p. 28)

**continental drift:** hypothesis first proposed by Wegener that Earth's continents were once a single supercontinent called Pangaea, which broke into smaller landmasses about 200 million years ago and have since moved apart to form the present day arrangement of the continents. (Chap. 15, p. 470)

**convergent boundary:** boundary between two lithospheric plates colliding—for example, the head-on collision of plates with continental crust can form mountain ranges and plates with oceanic crust can form trenches; Earth's most famous volcanoes occur at convergent plate boundaries. (Chap. 15, p. 486)

**covalent bond:** type of bond formed between atoms when they share electrons; covalent bonds are strong and chemically stable—for example, when two atoms of Cl combine and share a pair of electrons, each atom, at some time, will have its outer energy level complete. (Chap. 6, p. 181)

**current:** rate at which electrical charges flow past a point in a circuit over a specific amount of time; the rate of current flowing through a bulb can be measured in amperes (A) by an instrument called an ammeter; current is equal to the potential difference divided by resistance, and can be found mathematically by V/R = I. (Chap. 1, p. 33)

**density current:** movement of ocean water produced when dense, more highly saline seawater sinks, pushing away less dense seawater at the ocean bottom; these vertical currents occur in water too deep to be affected by winds. (Chap. 9, p. 294)

**dew point:** temperature at which the water vapor in saturated air begins to condense; for example, clouds are formed when humid air cools to its dew point and condensed water clings to particles in the air. (Chap. 8, p. 245)

**diffraction:** bending of waves—such as light waves or water waves or sound waves—passing through openings, around obstacles, or by relatively sharp edges. (Chap. 3, p. 92)

**digestion:** mechanical and chemical breakdown of carbohydrates, fats, and proteins into smaller molecules that can be absorbed by the cells; the human digestive system includes the tongue, saliva glands, esophagus, liver, stomach, gall bladder, duodenum, pancreas, large and small intestines, rectum, and anus. (Chap. 11, p. 351)

**divergent boundary:** boundary between two lithospheric plates moving away from each other resulting in magma being forced upward to the continental or oceanic crust, where it erupts as lava and forms new crust; mid-ocean ridges are divergent boundaries; also called constructive boundaries. (Chap. 15, p. 485)

**DNA:** threadlike material making up the chromosomes within the cell nucleus; contains the master code that directs the cells in all their activities and passes on genetic information; the DNA of each species has a specific ladderlike sequence for the four types of paired bases—cytosine, guanine, thymine, and adenine. (Chap. 14, p. 457)

**dominant trait:** trait that seems to dominate, or cover up, a recessive trait; for example, when Mendel crossed pure tall with pure short pea plants, all plants in the first generation of offspring were tall, showing that the trait of tallness was dominant over shortness. (Chap. 14, p. 444)

**eggs:** female sex cells: a human egg can be seen with the unaided eye, contains a food supply, has 23 chromosomes, and develops in the ovaries in relatively small numbers; usually one human egg is released into the oviduct about every 28 days, and if fertilized by sperm, will implant into the uterine wall. (Chap. 13, p. 407)

**electric generator:** produces electricity for home and business use by inducing currents through rotating a coil within a magnetic field; in the United States, household alternating current changes direction 120 times/second. (Chap. 2, p. 72)

**electric motor:** motor that uses an electromagnet to change electric energy into mechanical energy, creating the ability of machines such as washers and vacuum cleaners to perform work. (Chap. 2, p. 70)

**electrical charge:** concentration of electricity; everything contains electrical charges, which can be either positive (+) or negative (-); electrical charges can be made to flow and do work in much the same way as water; can move easily through conductors but not through insulators. (Chap. 1, p. 23)

**electromagnet:** magnet produced by passing an electric current through a coil of wire wound around a core; for example, whenever you listen to a tape recording or ring an electric doorbell, you're using an electromagnet. (Chap. 2, p. 62)

**electromagnetic spectrum:** the entire range of electromagnetic waves as shown in both frequencies (103 to 1023 Hz) and wavelengths ($10^5$ to $10^{-15}$ m); for example, in the electromagnetic spectrum, gamma rays have the shortest wavelength and the highest frequency. (Chap. 3, p. 86)

**electromagnetic waves:** transverse waves that do not require a medium through which to travel and which are produced by an oscillating charge; an electromagnetic wave travels at a constant speed, so its wavelength is inversely proportional to its frequency; visible light, radio waves, and gamma waves are examples of electromagnetic waves. (Chap. 3, p. 82)

**electron:** negatively charged particle with a very small mass that orbits an atom's nucleus in an electron cloud; atoms contain an equal number of electrons and protons, resulting in an equal number of positive and negative charges. (Chap. 4, p. 113)

**engineers:** in the field of space exploration, engineers are individuals who work with scientists to help build and develop spacecraft to travel to other planets. (Chap. 19, p. 620)

**environmental scientists:** individuals working with environmental factors in a variety of ways—for example, monitoring air, water, and industry for pollutants. (Chap. 10, p. 332)

**enzyme:** protein molecule controlling the rate of different body processes; humans have over 700 enzymes—each with its own unique lock-and-key function—that are an essential part of chemical digestion and break nutrient molecules into smaller molecules; for example, an enzyme in saliva helps break down starch into sugar. (Chap. 11, p. 356)

**epochs:** subdivisions of the Tertiary and Quaternary Periods of the Cenozoic Era as the result of a more complete geologic record—the rocks are newer and have been exposed to fewer destructive geologic processes, so there is more information for geologists to organize. (Chap. 16, p. 526)

**era:** division of Earth's geologic time scale that is further divided into periods; the three major eras are the Paleozoic Era, the Mesozoic Era, and the Cenozoic Era; the fourth major division, Precambrian Time, covers such a huge time expanse that it is further divided into its own eras. (Chap. 16, p. 517)

**evaporation:** process of a liquid changing into a gas; molecules with the highest kinetic energy evaporate from the surface first, which lowers the average kinetic energy of the molecules still in the liquid. (Chap. 7, p. 219)

**evolution:** ongoing process of change in the inherited features of a population of organisms over time; evolutionary evidence can be drawn from such sources as fossil remains, the chemical structure of organisms, and the physical structure of cells. (Chap. 17, p. 544)

**family of elements:** organizational group in the periodic table of elements in which elements are listed in vertical columns based on their similar physical and chemical properties—for example, Family 17 (the halogens) is very reactive and often combines with other elements. (Chap. 5, p. 156)

**fission:** nuclear reaction in which a large nucleus is split and energy is released—for example, when a nucleus of uranium-235 is struck by a neutron, it splits into two lighter nuclei, and the process releases three neutrons and a huge amount of energy; nuclear reactors produce electrical energy from a controlled fission chain reaction. (Chap. 18, p. 580)

**fossil:** remains or traces of a once-living organism; can provide information about the organism's appearance, where and how it lived, and help divide geologic time; two methods of fossil formation are by replacement of minerals and mold-and-cast formation. (Chap. 16, p. 505)

**front:** boundary resulting from the collision between moving air masses, producing such weather events as rain, snow, or violent storms depending on the types of air masses that meet; fronts can be warm, cold, stationary, and occluded. (Chap. 8, p. 251)

**fusion:** joining of smaller nuclei into larger ones; fusion of hydrogen into helium releases vast amounts of energy and is the energy powering the stars, includ-

ing the sun; nuclear fusion is common in nature but not on Earth. (Chap. 18, p. 585)

**galaxy:** elliptical, spiral, or irregular shaped group of stars, dust, and gas held together by gravity and grouped into clusters; Earth belongs to the Milky Way galaxy, which contains about 200 000 stars, is about 100 000 light-years in diameter and about 15 000 light-years thick. (Chap. 20, p. 643)

**gamma rays:** electromagnetic waves given off by a radioactive substance; gamma rays are highly penetrating and can go through paper and a 1-mm sheet of aluminum but are stopped by a 1.5-cm sheet of lead. (Chap. 4, p. 117)

**gaseous giant planets:** huge, low density planets made mainly of gases; these planets were formed farther from the sun, where the effects of solar winds and thermal energy were less intense; Jupiter, Saturn, Uranus, and Neptune are gaseous giant planets. (Chap. 19, p. 609)

**gene:** specific location on a chromosome; chromosomes and genes usually occur in pairs, and in Mendelian inheritance there are two genes for each trait, one contributed by each parent; genes can be either dominant or recessive. (Chap. 14, p. 445)

**hemoglobin:** iron-containing pigment that gives red blood cells their color; oxygen attaches to the iron in hemoglobin as red blood cells move through the lungs and is carried throughout your body for diffusion into body cells. (Chap. 12, p. 375)

**heterozygote:** individual with one dominant and one recessive gene for a specific trait—for example, if one parent contributes the dominant *T* gene for tallness and the other parent contributes the recessive *t* gene for shortness, then the offspring will be tall (*tT* or *Tt*) but will have recessive genes for shortness. (Chap. 14, p. 446)

**homologous structure:** similarity in structure and origin of the body parts of different organisms; for example, a bat's wing, a human's arm, and a dolphin's flipper are homologous structures and suggest that the organisms evolved from a common ancestor. (Chap. 17, p. 552)

**hot spots:** areas of Earth's mantle that are hotter than others; as lithospheric plates move over hot spots, magma is forced up through cracks in the lithosphere, where it erupts as lava and volcanoes build up; the movement of the Pacific plate over a hot spot in the Pacific Ocean resulted in the formation of the Hawaiian Islands. (Chap. 15, p. 495)

**hurricane:** intense, highly destructive storm formed from a swirling, low pressure system over a warm, moist tropical ocean; hurricanes are very large, have high winds that can be accompanied by torrential rain, and weaken as they strike land. (Chap. 8, p. 264)

**hydrocarbon:** compound that can be composed only of hydrogen and carbon or can form new compounds when other chemical groups are substituted for one or more hydrogen atoms; complex hydrocarbons can form biological compounds that make up living things; saturated hydrocarbons contain only a single covalent bond; unsaturated hydrocarbons contain double or triple covalent bonds. (Chap. 10, p. 308)

**immunity:** occurs once your body produces a specific antibody to defend against a specific antigen, which protects you against the disease; memory cells—which are formed by B-cells—can provide lifelong immunity to certain diseases; immunity can be acquired actively or passively. (Chap. 12, p. 385)

**immunologists:** individuals who study immune system diseases and work on the development of vaccines; college and medical school are required to become an immunologist. (Chap. 12, p. 396)

**induced current:** electric current produced by using a magnet; results when a magnetic field is changed in a coil—the field can be changed by moving either the coil or the magnet; our homes and businesses have electricity because of induced current produced by electric generators. (Chap. 2, p. 72)

**induced magnetism:** magnetism that occurs only in the presence of a magnetic field—when the magnetized object is removed from the magnetic field, its poles soon disappear. (Chap. 2, p. 57)

**insulator:** material that does not allow electrical charges to flow freely from place to place; examples include paper, rubber, plastic, wood, and glass; insulators help to transmit electricity safely from one location to another. (Chap. 1, p. 27)

**intertidal zone:** coastal ecosystem that is under water at high tide and exposed at low tide; supports a wide variety of highly adapted organisms such as mussels, oysters, chitons, and limpets. (Chap. 9, p. 281)

**ion:** positively or negatively charged atom whose charge results from the gain or loss of one or more electrons; the more electrons an atom gains or loses, the higher its charge. (Chap. 6, p. 177)

**ionic bond:** type of bond formed by the attraction of positively charged ions for negatively charged ions; ionic bonds hold ionic compounds together—for example, the positively charged sodium ion, $Na^+$, and the negatively charged chloride ion, $Cl^-$, are attracted to each other and form the neutral compound NaCl, which is held together by ionic bonds. (Chap. 6, p. 178)

**isomers:** compounds with identical chemical formulas but different molecular shapes, which seem to determine some of an isomer's properties; for example, butane ($C_4H_{10}$) has a straight carbon chain and melts at -138°C, whereas isobutane ($C_4H_{10}$) has a branched carbon chain and melts at -160°C. (Chap. 10, p. 311)

**isotopes:** atoms of the same element with different numbers of neutrons—examples of common isotopes are carbon-14, which has 6 protons and 8 neutrons in its nucleus and carbon-12, which has 6 protons and 6 neutrons in its nucleus; radioactive isotopes can be used to precisely determine levels of drugs, hormones, or viruses in a patient's body. (Chap. 5, p. 150)

**kinetic-molecular theory:** states that all ions, atoms, or molecules composing all forms of matter are in constant motion; the higher the temperature, the faster the particles move; explains familiar behaviors of matter such as boiling, evaporation, melting, condensation, and expansion. (Chap. 7, p. 210)

**law of superposition:** states that the oldest rock layers are at the bottom and the youngest rock layers are at the top if the layers have not been disturbed by such processes as earthquakes, volcanoes, and mountain building; younger sedimentary rocks always form on top of older sedimentary rocks and can help date rock layers relative to one another. (Chap. 16, p. 509)

**light-year:** distance light travels in one year; a light-year is the unit astronomers use to measure distances in

# GLOSSARY

space; 1 light-year is about 9.5 trillion kilometers. (Chap. 20, p. 636)

**like charges:** similar electrical charges that repel each other; for example, when two glass rods are charged by being rubbed with silk and then brought toward each other, they will repel one another. (Chap. 1, p. 23)

**lipids:** greasy-feeling organic compounds that contain twice as much energy per gram as carbohydrates; lipids include waxes, oils, and fats; a balanced diet gets 30 percent of its calories from fats, which are present in such foods as meats, nuts, and ice cream, which provide energy for the body. (Chap. 10, p. 324)

**lithosphere:** Earth's rocky crust and solid, uppermost part of the mantle; all the oceans and continents of Earth move slowly over the asthenosphere on lithospheric plates. (Chap. 15, p. 484)

**loudspeaker:** changes variations in electric current into sound waves in radios and speakers. (Chap. 2, p. 67)

**magnetic field:** three-dimensional region where magnetic forces act; Earth's huge magnetic field, which resembles a large bar magnet, extends far out into space and protects us from showers of high-energy charged particles. (Chap. 2, p. 54)

**magnetic poles:** in a bar magnet, the two ends that point north-south—the places where the magnetic field is strongest; two north-seeking poles repel each other, but a north-seeking pole and a south-seeking pole attract each other; compass needles point north and south because Earth has magnetic poles—much like a bar magnet—which may be produced by material deep in Earth's core. (Chap. 2, p. 51)

**mass number:** the total number of protons and neutrons in the nucleus of an atom; for example, if the nucleus of an atom has 6 protons and 6 neutrons, the mass of the atom is 12 atomic mass units, or 12 u. (Chap. 5, p. 148-149)

**meiosis:** process of cell division of all reproductive cells; meiosis involves two divisions of the chromosomes in the original cell, producing four new cells, each with half the number of chromosomes found in a body cell of that organism. (Chap. 13, p. 411)

**menstrual cycle:** in human females, the monthly cycle that prepares the reproductive system for fertilization, during which the uterine lining thickens, an egg is released, and if unfertilized is discarded in a process called menstruation. (Chap. 13, p. 427)

**menstruation:** in human females, the monthly discharge of the disintegrated, unfertilized egg along with the uterine lining and blood through the vagina; menstruation usually lasts four to six days. (Chap. 13, p. 427)

**Mesozoic Era:** geologic division following the Paleozoic Era; life-forms included the first dinosaurs, birds, mammals, and flowering plants; during the Mesozoic, Pangaea separated and the Rocky Mountains began to rise; dinosaurs were extinct at end of the Mesozoic. (Chap. 16, p. 524)

**meteor:** space object formed of rock fragments; meteors are called meteoroids until they enter Earth's atmosphere; meteors glow as they streak across the night sky and most burn up completely due to friction. (Chap. 19, p. 619)

**meteorite:** meteoroids that survive passing through Earth's atmosphere and hit Earth's surface, sometimes producing craters. (Chap. 19, p. 619)

**minerals:** inorganic compounds essential for good health; minerals are needed by the body to regulate its chemical reactions and include, for example, calcium for strong bone and tooth structure, iron to make red blood cells and carry oxygen, and magnesium for digestion of carbohydrates and proteins. (Chap. 11, p. 342)

**molecules:** neutral particles formed when electrons are shared by atoms rather than being gained or lost. (Chap. 6, p. 181)

**mutation:** permanent change in a chromosome or gene; most mutations have little effect on organisms but some mutations can be harmful or helpful; variations in color, size, and shape are often caused by mutations. (Chap. 17, p. 545)

**natural selection:** process in which organisms with variations better adapted to their environments are more likely to survive and reproduce; Darwin formed the theory of natural selection to explain evolution. (Chap. 17, p. 540)

**nebula:** large cloud of dust and gas whose particles exert a gravitational force on each other, causing the cloud to contract and its internal temperature to rise until fusion begins, resulting in a star being born. (Chap. 20, p. 630)

**nekton:** free-swimming marine animals; nekton move through various depths, reducing the effects that surface currents can have on them; fish, whales, and sea turtles are examples of nektonic life-forms. (Chap. 9, p. 292)

**neutron:** uncharged particle in the nucleus of an atom; a neutron has a mass about equal to that of a proton; neutrons and protons are made up of even smaller particles called quarks. (Chap. 4, p. 127)

**nonpolar molecule:** molecule with balanced charges whose electrons are shared equally; nonpolar molecules are not water soluble; oil is an example. (Chap. 6, p. 184)

**nucleus:** positively charged, dense center of an atom made up of protons and neutrons around which a cloud of electrons moves. (Chap. 4, p. 123)

**nurse-midwives:** individuals trained to provide both physical and emotional assistance to a woman giving birth; nurse-midwives study biology, chemistry, and medicine. (Chap. 13, p. 430)

**nutrients:** substances in food that are needed by the body for growth, development, and repair; proteins, fats, carbohydrates, vitamins, minerals, and water are nutrients; a lack of nutrients can produce disease. (Chap. 11, p. 339)

**organic compound:** carbon-containing substance; millions of organic compounds can be synthesized from raw materials containing carbon because carbon's atomic structure allows it to combine with so many other elements; chemicals made from organic compounds in petroleum or natural gas provide the world's major energy source. (Chap. 10, p. 306)

**ovary:** in human females, ovaries are the two sex organs in which eggs are produced by meiosis, which in females begins before birth and continues at sexual maturity, when an egg is released from an ovary about every 28 days until the individual is 45 to 55 years old. (Chap. 13, p. 416)

**oxidation number:** number of electrons that an atom gains, loses, or shares when bonding with another atom; for example, when Cl forms an ion, it gains an electron, has a charge of 1-, and an oxidation number of 1-; some elements have more than one oxidation number, such as $Cr^{2+}$ and $Cr^{3+}$, or chromium(II) and chromium(III). (Chap. 6, p. 187)

**Paleozoic Era:** second major geologic time scale division; began about 545 million years ago and was characterized by warm, shallow seas covering much of Earth; life-forms included trilobites, the first fish, amphibians, land plants, and reptiles. (Chap. 16, p. 522)

**pedigree:** diagrammatic tool used to trace the existence of a specific trait among generations of a family; can show whether a trait has a pattern of appearance or is occurring randomly. (Chap. 14, p. 439)

**period:** geologic subdivision of an era based on the era's life-forms and geologic events; for example, the Mesozoic Era has three periods—Triassic, Jurassic, and Cretaceous—and the Cenozoic Era has two periods—Tertiary and Quaternary. (Chap. 16, p. 522; see also Chap. 5, p. 162)

**period:** one of the 7 horizontal rows in the periodic table of elements; each period starts as the pattern of chemical and physical properties of the elements begins to repeat itself; a period is made up of a series of elements with increasing atomic numbers. (Chap. 5, p. 162; see also Chap. 16, p. 522)

**periodic table:** organizes all the known elements into a table based on atomic mass and structure and helps you predict how elements will react with one another; the periodic table organizes elements into columns and rows and shows an element's atomic number, symbol, name, and atomic mass. (Chap. 5, p. 145)

**peristalsis:** smooth, muscular waves of contractions that move food through the esophagus, into the stomach, and through the entire digestive system. (Chap. 11, p. 357)

**pistil:** female reproductive organ of flowering plants composed of a sticky stigma, a stalk-like style, and a rounded base, which is its ovary; fertilization occurs when sperm-containing pollen grains deposited on the stigma forms a long tube that grows from the stigma through the pistil to the ovary, where the union of sperm and eggs takes place. (Chap. 13, p. 419)

**planet:** body of matter that moves around a star in a fixed, counterclockwise orbit; except for Pluto, which is small and formed of rock and ice, the planets of our solar system are classified as either Earth-like terrestrial planets or gaseous giant planets. (Chap. 19, p. 598)

**plankton:** microscopic life-forms that drift through the upper levels of the ocean and form the base of an extensive food web; plankton rely on currents to bring them nutrients and carry away wastes. (Chap. 9, p. 292)

**plasma:** liquid portion of your blood in which are suspended red and white blood cells and platelets; plasma is about 55 percent water and transports dissolved nutrients, minerals, and oxygen to all body cells and helps to carry away waste products to other organs for elimination; hormones are also transported by plasma. (Chap. 12, p. 373)

**plate tectonics:** geologic theory accounting for the movement of the continents, suggesting that the solid plates of the lithosphere are moved slowly by convection currents originating deep inside Earth. (Chap. 15, p. 484)

**platelets:** tiny, short-lived, non-nucleated, irregularly shaped cell fragments contained in blood; platelets help to prevent serious bleeding from broken blood vessels by the process of clotting. (Chap. 12, p. 381)

**polar molecule:** molecule with unbalanced charges as a result of electrons being shared unequally; for example, water is a polar molecule because its oxygen end has a slight negative charge and its hydrogen end has a slight positive charge. (Chap. 6, p. 184)

**polyatomic ion:** ammonium, nitrate, and phosphate are examples of polyatomic ions—all of which are made up of a group of positively or negatively charged covalently bonded atoms. (Chap. 6, p. 189)

**polymer:** large molecule composed of smaller organic molecules, called monomers, linked together, forming new bonds; some polymers are used in the manufacture of plastics; polymers are also found in biological compounds—mainly proteins, carbohydrates, and lipids. (Chap. 10, p. 321)

**potential difference:** change in total energy divided by the total electric charge; potential difference is measured in volts (V) or voltage; when potential difference stays the same, current decreases as resistance increases. (Chap. 1, p. 33)

**Precambrian Time:** first major division of geologic time that began more than 4 billion years ago and makes up about 90 percent of Earth's history to date; characterized by several episodes of mountain building and the altering of Earth's atmosphere by production of large amounts of oxygen by cyanobacteria, which were the dominant life-form during much of Precambrian Time. (Chap. 16, p. 520)

**primates:** mammalian group including apes, monkeys, and humans that shares many characteristics such as binocular vision, flexible shoulders, and opposable thumbs. (Chap. 17, p. 556)

**proteins:** organic compounds composed of long chains of amino acids; proteins are present in every living substance and are needed for growth and renewal of the body; a balanced diet gets 20 percent of its calories from such protein sources as milk, tofu, and fish. (Chap. 10, p. 322)

**proton:** positively charged particle in the nucleus of an atom; a proton's mass is about equal to that of a neutron; the number of protons in an element's nucleus determines the element's identity. (Chap. 4, p. 124)

**pure dominant:** trait resulting when the offspring receives the dominant form of a trait from each parent—for example, if both egg and sperm contain the dominant $T$ gene for tallness, then the tallness of the offspring will be a pure dominant trait, or $TT$. (Chap. 14, p. 446)

**pure recessive:** trait resulting when the egg and sperm of each parent contains the recessive form of a trait—for example, if both parents pass on the recessive $e$ gene for attached earlobes, then the attached earlobes of the offspring will be a pure recessive trait, or $ee$. (Chap. 14, p. 446)

**R**

**radiation:** transfer of energy by electromagnetic waves; for example, a lamp lights an area by radiating electromagnetic waves in the visible part of the spectrum. (Chap. 3, p. 87)

**radioactivity:** decay, or breaking apart, of unstable elements such as uranium and thorium, resulting in the release of high-energy particles; radiation from a radioactive source can be separated into alpha, beta, and gamma rays by using a magnetic field. (Chap. 4, p. 116)

**recessive trait:** trait that seems to disappear; for example, when Mendel crossed pure tall with pure short pea plants, the trait of shortness was recessive in the first generation of offspring but reappeared in about one-quarter of the second generation of offspring. (Chap. 14, p. 444)

**red blood cells:** tiny, most numerous type of blood cell in whole blood; your mature red blood cells lack a nucleus, are filled with iron-containing hemoglobin molecules, transport oxygen throughout the body, and return some carbon dioxide to the lungs for elimination; red blood cells are formed in the marrow of long bones. (Chap. 12, p. 375)

**relative humidity:** measure, expressed as a percentage, between the amount of water vapor in the air and the total amount of water vapor the air can hold at that specific temperature; an instrument called a psychrometer measures relative humidity. (Chap. 8, p. 244)

**resistance:** property of materials indicating how much energy is changed to thermal energy and light as an electrical charge passes through them; resistance depends on the material of the conductor in addition to the conductor's thickness and length. (Chap. 1, p. 34)

## S

**salinity:** in the ocean, the measure of dissolved materials, primarily salts, resulting from the accumulation of elements and minerals from the atmosphere, volcanic eruptions, and runoff of water from land; the most common sea salts are sodium and chlorine. (Chap. 9, p. 283)

**saturated:** 100 percent relative humidity of air; occurs when air cannot hold additional moisture at a specific temperature. (Chap. 8, p. 245)

**sea-floor spreading:** occurs when plates beneath the ocean floor pull apart and magma from Earth's mantle is forced upward at mid-ocean ridges where it cools and forms a new seafloor; similar ages and magnetic records of rocks on both sides of a rift support the idea of sea-floor spreading. (Chap. 15, p. 478)

**sex cells:** reproductive cells formed through meiosis, a process that begins in an organism's reproductive organs and results in the formation of eggs or sperm—each of which contains half the number of chromosomes as a body cell of the parent organism; the job of sex cells is to unite and to produce offspring. (Chap. 13, p. 407)

**sickle-cell anemia:** potentially fatal genetic disease in which the red blood cells are misshapen, are unable to carry as much oxygen as normal cells, and can become stuck in capillaries. (Chap. 14, p. 452)

**solar system:** system formed about 5 billion years ago from a rotating cloud of hydrogen and helium gases and dust particles that condensed to form its major components—the sun and its nine planets. (Chap. 19, p. 598)

**sperm:** male sex cells; human sperm are microscopic, have tails, can swim, contain 23 chromosomes, and are produced in large numbers by the testes; fertilization in humans and many other animals takes place internally, with the male releasing millions of sperm into the female's reproductive system, where it takes only one sperm to fertilize an egg. (Chap. 13, p. 407)

**stamen:** in flowering plants, the male reproductive organ whose saclike anther is held up by a long filament; anthers produce sperm-containing pollen grains, which are transferred to the female's sticky stigma by various means including wind, birds, and insects. (Chap. 13, p. 419)

**star:** glowing, hot sphere of gas, such as the sun, whose brightness depends on how big and hot it is and its distance from Earth; stars form from nebulas and produce energy by fusion; types of stars include blue supergiants, brown dwarfs, red giants, and white stars. (Chap. 20, p. 629)

**sublimation:** process in which a solid is changed into a gas without first becoming a liquid; for example, solid carbon dioxide (dry ice) sublimates, and because it is much colder than regular ice, a water vapor fog forms as the air surrounding it cools. (Chap. 7, p. 220)

**sunspots:** cool, dark areas on the surface of the sun that may appear and disappear over days or months; years in which there are many large sunspots are called sunspot maximums, which occur about every 11 years. (Chap. 20, p. 638)

**supernova:** explosion of a massive, dense-cored star that occurs when no more material remains in the core to be transformed, resulting in the formation of a small neutron star. (Chap. 20, p. 631)

**surface currents:** movement of ocean water produced primarily by winds; affect the upper few hundred meters of seawater, influence climate by their warming or cooling effects, and provide a home for most marine organisms; the Gulf Stream is a surface current. (Chap. 9, p. 291)

## T

**terrestrial planets:** the four small planets that were formed nearest the sun and whose surfaces are composed of dense, rocky material; Mercury, Venus, Earth, and Mars are terrestrial planets. (Chap. 19, p. 603)

**testis:** in human males, testes are the two sex organs that produce sperm by meiosis when the body reaches sexual maturity, usually at ages 10 to 14, with the amount of sperm decreasing gradually with age. (Chap. 13, p. 416)

**thermal expansion:** in a solid, the expansion that occurs as it is heated, resulting in its kinetic energy increasing and its particles moving farther apart; thermal expansion must be considered in designing such structures as railroad tracks, bridges, and highways. (Chap. 7, p. 214)

**tornado:** violent, funnel-shaped storm formed from a low pressure system; tornadoes are highly destructive, short-lasting, and move over land in a narrow path. (Chap. 8, p. 262)

**traits:** inherited characteristics of an organism; traits passed from one generation to another in a family may be nearly identical or similar and are controlled by genes carried on chromosomes; examples of traits are dimples, hitchhiker's thumb, and hair color. (Chap. 14, p. 438)

**transform fault boundary:** boundary formed when two plates slide past each other in the same direction at different speeds or slide past each other in opposite directions; the San Andreas Fault is a transform fault boundary. (Chap. 15, p. 487)

**transformer:** ensures that electricity produced by a power company has the correct voltage by raising (step-up transformer) or lowering (step-down transformer) the voltage to the needed level. (Chap. 2, p. 73)

**transmutation:** occurs when an atom of one element changes to an atom of another element by spontaneously emitting a particle, or by decaying—which changes its number of protons and its atomic number; the time it takes for a given mass of an element to transmute is known as its half-life. (Chap. 18, p. 570)

**unconformity:** occurs when layers of rock are missing, often because of such forces as plate tectonics, weathering and erosion, or lack of soil deposition, and results in an incomplete record of plants and animals that existed during that time. (Chap. 16, p. 510)

**unlike charges:** dissimilar electrical charges that attract one another; for example, rubbing a balloon with wool will enable the positively charged balloon to be stuck (attracted) to an uncharged wall. (Chap. 1, p. 23)

**upwelling:** interruption of the density current cycle resulting from the upward movement of cold water from deep in the ocean, replacing warmer surface water carried away by strong, wind-driven surface currents. (Chap. 9, p. 296)

**vaccine:** provides active immunity to a specific disease without having to get the disease first; vaccination introduces a dead or weakened form of the antigen to the body through inoculation or by mouth, and if the antigen later invades your body, it will be destroyed by antibodies already in your bloodstream. (Chap. 12, p. 386)

**variations:** differences in inherited traits or behaviors among members of the same species; advantageous variations help organisms survive in their environments and are called adaptations—examples are the webbed feet of ducks and the thick, white fur of polar bears. (Chap. 17, p. 536)

**villi:** tiny finger-like projections lining the folds of the small intestine; villi increase the surface area for absorption of nutrients into the bloodstream for delivery to individual cells. (Chap. 11, p. 360)

**viscosity:** resistance of a liquid to changing its shape; the stronger the attractive forces holding a liquid's molecules together, the higher its viscosity; different liquids have different viscosities—for example, water's low viscosity enables it to run down a grade quickly but honey has a high viscosity and runs down a grade slowly. (Chap. 7, p. 217)

**vitamins:** organic nutrients needed in small amounts by the body for good health; A, E, D, and K are fat-soluble vitamins and B and C are water-soluble vitamins; vitamins are found in such food sources as vegetables, meat, milk, fish, beans, and fruit; a deficiency in any one vitamin can sometimes result in a serious health problem. (Chap. 11, p. 347)

**volcanologists:** geologists who specialize in studying volcanoes in order to predict when and how a volcanic eruption will take place; volcanologists collect data using instruments such as laser measuring devices and seismographs. (Chap. 15, p. 497)

**white blood cells:** large, less numerous type of blood cell that fights bacteria, viruses, and other foreign substances—for example, when bacteria invade your body, blood carries white blood cells to the site, where they surround the bacteria and digest them. (Chap. 12, p. 376)

This glossary defines each key term that appears in bold type in the text. It also indicates the chapter number and page number where you will find the word used.

## A

**absolute zero/cero absoluto:** temperatura a la cual la energía cinética de las moléculas baja a cero; la temperatura más baja posible que puede tener la materia (Cap. 7, pág. 228)

**agronomist/agrónomo:** científico agrícola que estudia la biología (Cap. 11, pág. 364)

**air mass/masa de aire:** masa extensa de aire cuyas propiedades se determinan por la parte de la superficie terrestre sobre la cual se forma (Cap. 8, pág. 251)

**alcohol/alcohol:** nombre de una familia de compuestos que se forman cuando un grupo de hidroxilos reemplaza uno o más átomos de hidrógeno en un hidrocarburo (Cap. 10, pág. 315)

**alkali metals/metales alcalinos:** elementos en la columna 1 de la Tabla Periódica; son metales blandos que pueden cortarse fácilmente; poseen brillo metálico, son conductores del calor y de la electricidad y son maleables (Cap. 5, pág. 159)

**alkaline earth metals/metales alcalinotérreos:** metales en la segunda columna vertical de la Tabla Periódica; no son reactivos como los metales alcalinos (Cap. 5, pág. 159)

**alpha particle/partícula alfa:** partículas con carga positiva emitidas por sustancias radiactivas y con una masa mayor que las partículas beta (Cap. 4, pág. 117)

**amine/amina:** compuesto orgánico que se forma cuando el grupo de aminas, $-NH_2$, reemplaza el hidrógeno en un hidrocarburo (Cap. 10, pág 316)

**antibodies/anticuerpos:** sustancias que produce el cuerpo para responder a determinados antígenos (Cap. 12, pág. 384)

**antigens/antígenos:** proteínas y sustancias químicas que son agentes extraños para el cuerpo (Cap. 12, pág. 384)

**artificial transmutation/transmutación artificial:** reacción que se produce cuando una transmutación no ocurre espontáneamente, pero es causada por cualquier factor externo (Cap. 18, pág. 575)

**asteroid/asteroide:** trozo enorme de roca que viaja por el espacio (Cap. 19, pág. 618)

**asthenosphere/astenosfera:** capa menos sólida del manto terrestre en donde los materiales se comportan como masilla (Cap. 15, pág 484)

**atomic mass/masa atómica:** es la masa de un átomo medida en unidades de masa atómica (Cap. 5, pág. 151)

**atomic number/número atómico:** el número de protones en el átomo de un elemento (Cap. 5, pág. 148)

## B

**balanced chemical equation/ecuación química equilibrada:** ecuación que posee el mismo número de átomos de cada elemento a ambos lados de la ecuación (Cap. 6, pág. 193)

**beta particle/partícula beta:** electrón de alta velocidad emitido por una sustancia radiactiva (Cap. 4, pág. 117)

**binary compound/compuesto binario:** compuesto formado por dos elementos (Cap. 6, pág. 187)

**body cells/células corporales:** células que forman el cuerpo, las cuales producen copias exactas de sí mismas por medio de la mitosis (Cap. 13, pág. 406)

**boiling/ebullición:** cambio del estado líquido al estado gaseoso, como por ejemplo, cuando hierve el agua (Cap. 7, pág. 220)

## C

**carbohydrates/carbohidratos:** tipo de alimentos como azúcares y almidones que nos proporcionan energía (Cap. 10, pág. 323)

**carboxylic acid/ácido carboxílico:** ácido que se forma cuando un grupo $-CH_3$ es desplazado por un grupo carboxílico (-COOH) (Cap. 10, pág. 315)

**Cenozoic Era/Era Cenozoica:** era que comenzó después de terminar la Era Mesozoica (Cap. 16, pág. 526)

**chain reaction/reacción en cadena:** serie de reacciones que ocurren cuando el neutrón que libera una reacción desencadena la siguiente reacción y esa reacción desencadena la próxima reacción (Cap. 18, pág. 583)

**circuit/circuito:** trayectoria ininterrumpida por la cual fluye una corriente eléctrica (Cap. 1, pág. 33)

**clotting/coagulación:** proceso por el cual se cierra un vaso sanguíneo roto (Cap. 12, pág. 381)

**comet/cometa:** trozo enorme de hielo, polvo, gases congelados y fragmentos rocosos que se mueve por el espacio (Cap. 19, pág. 617)

**condensation/condensación:** proceso por el cual un gas se transforma en un líquido (Cap. 7, pág. 221)

**conductor/conductor:** material en el cual las cargas eléctricas pueden moverse libremente de un lugar a otro (Cap. 1, pág. 28)

**continental drift/deriva continental:** teoría de Alfred Wegener que dice que una vez todos los continentes estuvieron unidos en un solo supercontinente llamado Pangaea, el cual se separó hace cerca de 200 millones de años, provocando el movimiento de los continentes (Cap. 15, pág. 470)

**convergent boundary/límite convergente:** lugar donde chocan de frente dos placas (Cap. 15, pág. 486)

**covalent bond/enlace covalente:** enlace que se forma entre átomos que comparten electrones (Cap. 6, pág. 181)

**current/corriente:** la cantidad de carga eléctrica que se transmite a través de un punto de un circuito en un tiempo dado (Cap. 1, pág. 33)

**density current/corriente de densidad:** movimiento de agua que ocurre cuando el agua marina densa se mueve hacia un área de agua marina menos densa (Cap. 9, pág. 294)

**dew point/punto de rocío:** la temperatura a la cual el aire está saturado y se produce la condensación (Cap. 8, pág. 245)

**diffraction/difracción:** desviación de la luz alrededor de una barrera (Cap. 3, pág. 92)

**digestion/digestión:** proceso que descompone los carbohidratos, las grasas y las proteínas en moléculas más pequeñas y simples que pueden absorber y usar las células del cuerpo (Cap. 11, pág. 351)

**divergent boundary/límite divergente:** límite entre dos placas que se alejan y se separan una de la otra (Cap. 15, pág. 485)

**DNA/DNA:** siglas para el ácido ribonucleico; el DNA contiene el código maestro que imparte instrucciones a todas las células para sus funciones diarias (Cap. 14, pág. 457)

**dominant trait/rasgo dominante:** rasgo que parece dominar u ocultar por completo a otro rasgo (Cap. 14, pág. 444)

**eggs/óvulos:** células sexuales femeninas (Cap. 13, pág. 407)

**electric generator/generador eléctrico:** dispositivo que cambia la energía cinética de las rotaciones en energía eléctrica (Cap. 2, pág. 72)

**electric motor/motor eléctrico:** motor que usa un electroimán para cambiar la energía eléctrica en energía mecánica (Cap. 2, pág. 70)

**electrical charge/carga eléctrica:** concentración de electricidad (Cap. 1, pág. 23)

**electromagnet/electroimán:** imán fabricado con alambre conductor de corriente (Cap. 2, pág. 62)

**electromagnetic spectrum/espectro electromagnético:** la gama total de ondas electromagnéticas, desde las frecuencias extremadamente bajas hasta las frecuencias extremadamente altas (Cap. 3, pág. 86)

**electromagnetic wave/onda electromagnética:** combinación de un campo eléctrico y uno magnético que se forma de la oscilación de una corriente eléctrica (Cap. 3, pág. 82)

**electron/electrón:** partícula mucho más pequeña que el átomo (Cap. 4, pág. 113)

**enzyme/enzima:** molécula proteica que controla el ritmo de los diferentes procesos que se llevan a cabo en el cuerpo (Cap. 11, pág. 356)

**epoch/época:** subdivisión de los períodos de la Era Cenozoica (Cap. 16, pág. 526)

**era/era:** subdivisión principal de la escala del tiempo geológico (Cap. 16, pág. 517)

**evaporation/evaporación:** proceso por el cual un líquido cambia al estado gaseoso (Cap. 7, pág. 219)

**evolution/evolución:** cambio en los rasgos hereditarios de una población de organismos a través de cierto período de tiempo (Cap. 17, pág. 544)

**family of elements/familia de elementos:** elementos en la misma columna de la Tabla Periódica (Cap. 5, pág. 156)

**fission/fisión:** rompimiento del núcleo de un átomo acompañado de liberación de energía (Cap. 18, pág. 580)

**fossil/fósil:** restos de un organismo que una vez fue un ser vivo (Cap. 16, pág. 505)

**front/frente:** límite que se forma cuando una masa de aire en movimiento choca contra otra masa de aire (Cap. 8, pág. 251)

**fusion/fusión:** la unión de núcleos separados (Cap. 18, pág. 585)

**galaxy/galaxia:** gran agrupación de estrellas, gas, y polvo que se mantienen unidos debido a la gravedad (Cap. 20, pág. 643)

**gamma ray/rayo gama:** forma de radiación electromagnética (Cap. 4, pág. 117)

**gaseous giant planets/planetas gigantes gaseosos:** planetas inmensos de baja densidad compuestos principalmente de gases (Cap. 19, pág. 609)

**gene/gene:** ubicación específica en un cromosoma que controla un rasgo determinado (Cap. 14, pág. 445)

**hemoglobin/hemoglobina:** pigmento rojo que contiene hierro, el cual se encuentra en los glóbulos rojos (Cap. 12, pág. 375)

**heterozygote/heterocigoto:** organismo con un gene dominante y un gene recesivo para un rasgo (Cap. 14, pág. 446)

**homologous structure/estructura homóloga:** partes del cuerpo de organismos diferentes que tienen un origen y una estructura similares (Cap. 17, pág. 552)

**hot spots/puntos críticos:** zonas más calientes del manto terrestre, en las cuales el magma es forzado hacia la superficie por material más denso que se encuentra a su alrededor, a través de resquebrajaduras en la litosfera sólida (Cap. 15, pág. 495)

**hurricane/huracán:** sistema de baja presión, inmenso y turbulento, que se forma sobre los océanos tropicales (Cap. 8, pág. 264)

**hydrocarbon/hidrocarburo:** compuesto que contiene solamente carbono e hidrógeno (Cap. 10, pág. 308)

**immunity/inmunidad:** protección contra los efectos dañinos de sustancias causantes de enfermedades (Cap. 12, pág. 385)

**induced current/corriente inducida:** corriente eléctrica que se produce al usar un imán (Cap. 2, pág. 72)

**induced magnetism/magnetismo inducido:** magnetismo que ocurre solamente en presencia de un campo magnético (Cap. 2, pág. 57)

**insulator/aislador:** material en el cual las cargas eléctricas no se mueven libremente de un lugar a otro (Cap. 1, pág. 27)

**intertidal zone/zona entre mareas:** área del litoral entre la marea alta y la marea baja (Cap. 9, pág. 281)

**ion/ion:** partícula cargada formada por un átomo o por varios átomos que han ganado o perdido uno o más electrones (Cap. 6, pág. 177)

**ionic bond/enlace iónico:** la atracción entre iones positivos y negativos (Cap. 6, pág. 178)

**isomers/isómeros:** compuestos que poseen fórmulas químicas idénticas pero diferentes formas o estructuras moleculares (Cap. 10, pág. 311)

**isotopes/isótopos:** átomos del mismo elemento, pero con números diferentes de neutrones (Cap. 5, pág. 150)

**kinetic-molecular theory/teoría molecular cinética:** teoría que define, en parte, la energía térmica como un movimiento al azar de los átomos o las moléculas (Cap. 7, pág. 210)

**law of superposition/ley de superposición:** ley que asevera que, en las capas rocosas, las capas más antiguas se encuentran en la parte inferior y las capas más nuevas se encuentran en la parte superior, si las capas no han sido perturbadas (Cap. 16, pág. 509)

**light-year/año luz:** la distancia que viaja la luz en un año (Cap. 20, pág. 636)

**like charges/cargas iguales:** cargas que se repelen entre sí (Cap. 1, pág. 23)

**lipids/lípidos:** compuestos orgánicos que se sienten grasosos al tacto y que no se disuelven en agua (Cap. 10, pág. 324)

**lithosphere/litosfera:** parte de la superficie terrestre formada por la corteza y la parte superior del manto terrestres (Cap. 15, pág. 484)

**loudspeaker/altoparlante:** dispositivo en el cual las variaciones de la corriente eléctrica se transforman en energía sonora (Cap. 2, pág. 67)

**magnetic field/campo magnético:** región alrededor de un imán donde actúa la fuerza magnética (Cap. 2, pág. 54)

**magnetic poles/polos magnéticos:** los dos extremos de un imán que apuntan en dirección norte o sur (Cap. 2, pág. 51)

**mass number/número de masa:** el número total de protones y de neutrones en el núcleo de un átomo (Cap. 5, pág. 149)

**meiosis/meiosis:** proceso que forma las células sexuales (Cap. 13, pág. 411)

**menstrual cycle/ciclo menstrual:** ciclo en que el ovario libera un óvulo y el útero se prepara para recibirlo y luego lo desecha al no ser fecundado (Cap. 13, pág. 427)

**menstruation/menstruación:** descarga mensual del óvulo, del revestimiento uterino y de sangre a través de la vagina (Cap. 13, pág. 427)

**Mesozoic Era/Era Mesozoica:** llamada la "era de los dinosaurios", comenzó después de terminar la Era Paleozoica (Cap. 16, pág. 524)

**meteor/meteoro:** meteoroide que entra en la atmósfera terrestre (Cap. 19, pág. 619)

**meteorite/meteorito:** meteoroide que choca contra la superficie terrestre (Cap. 19, pág. 619)

**minerals/minerales:** compuestos inorgánicos que controlan muchas de las reacciones químicas que se llevan a cabo en el cuerpo (Cap. 11, pág. 342)

**molecule/molécula:** partícula neutra que se forma como resultado de átomos que comparten electrones (Cap. 6, pág. 181)

**mutation/mutación:** cambio permanente en un gene o en un cromosoma (Cap. 17, pág. 545)

**natural selection/selección natural:** proceso en el cual los organismos vivos mejor adaptados a su ambiente tienen mayores posibilidades de sobrevivir y producir progenie (Cap. 17, pág. 540)

**nebula/nebulosa:** nube inmensa de gas y polvo de la cual se forma una estrella (Cap. 20, pág. 630)

**nekton/necton:** organismos marinos que incluyen todas las formas de peces y otros animales que pueden nadar (Cap. 9, pág. 292)

**neutron/neutrón:** partícula sin carga, cuya masa es casi igual a la de un protón y que se encuentra en el núcleo de un átomo (Cap. 4, pág. 127)

**nonpolar molecule/molécula no polar:** molécula que no posee cargas desequilibradas como las de una molécula polar (Cap. 6, pág. 184)

**nucleus/núcleo:** centro denso de un átomo, el cual tiene carga positiva (Cap. 4, pág. 123)

**nutrients/nutrimientos:** sustancias en los alimentos que proporcionan energía y materiales para el desarrollo, crecimiento y reparación de las células (Cap. 11, pág. 339)

**organic compound/compuesto orgánico:** sustancia que contiene carbono (Cap. 10, pág. 306)

**ovary/ovario:** órgano sexual femenino donde se producen los óvulos (Cap. 13, pág. 416)

**oxidation number/número de oxidación:** número de electrones que un átomo gana o pierde o comparte con otro átomo (Cap. 6, pág. 187)

**Paleozoic Era/Era Paleozoica:** la segunda división principal del tiempo geológico que comenzó hace unos 545 millones de años (Cap. 16, pág. 522)

**pedigree/pedigrí:** diagrama que muestra la historia de un rasgo de una generación a la próxima (Cap. 14, pág. 439)

**period/período:** repetición de un patrón (Cap. 5, pág. 162); subdivisión de una era (Cap. 16, pág. 522)

**periodic table/tabla periódica:** diagrama organizado de los elementos que muestra un patrón repetitivo de sus propiedades (Cap. 5, pág. 145)

**peristalsis/peristalsis:** proceso durante el cual los músculos lisos del esófago se contraen en ondas llevando alimento al estómago (Cap. 11, pág. 357)

**pistil/pistilo:** órgano reproductor femenino de las plantas (Cap. 13, pág. 419)

**planet/planeta:** cuerpo celeste que viaja alrededor de una estrella en una trayectoria fija llamada órbita (Cap. 19, pág. 598)

**plankton/plancton:** organismos marinos que se mueven a la deriva (Cap. 9, pág. 292)

**plasma/plasma:** parte líquida de la sangre que consiste mayormente en agua (Cap. 12, pág. 373)

**plate tectonics/tectónica de placas:** teoría que sugiere que la corteza y el manto superior terrestres están separados en secciones llamadas placas, las cuales se encuentran en movimiento (Cap. 15, pág. 484)

**platelets/plaquetas:** fragmentos celulares que detienen el flujo de sangre que sale de un vaso sanguíneo roto (Cap. 12, pág. 381)

**polar molecule/molécula polar:** molécula que resulta de un enlace polar y que posee un polo ligeramente positivo y uno ligeramente negativo (Cap. 6, pág. 184)

**polyatomic ion/ion poliatómico:** grupo de átomos enlazados covalentemente ya sea que tengan una carga positiva o una negativa (Cap. 6, pág. 189)

**polymers/polímeros:** moléculas enormes formadas por muchas moléculas orgánicas más pequeñas que se unen para formar nuevos enlaces (Cap. 10, pág. 321)

**potential difference/diferencia de potencial:** cambio en la energía total dividido entre la carga total; llamada también voltaje (Cap. 1, pág. 33)

**Precambrian Time/Tiempo Precámbrico:** la primera división principal del tiempo geológico, la cual representa cerca del 90% de la historia de la Tierra hasta nuestros días (Cap. 16, pág. 520)

**primate/primate:** grupo de mamíferos que comprende a los monos, simios y seres humanos, quienes comparten características similares (Cap. 17, pág. 556)

**proteins/proteínas:** polímeros que se forman por la unión de varios aminoácidos (Cap. 10, pág. 322)

**proton/protón:** partícula con carga positiva en el núcleo de un átomo (Cap. 4, pág. 124)

**pure dominant/dominante puro:** rasgo que se produce al heredar la progenie dos genes dominantes (Cap. 14, pág. 446)

**pure recessive/recesivo puro:** rasgo que se produce al heredar la progenie dos genes recesivos (Cap. 14, pág. 446)

**radiation/radiación:** transferencia de energía por medio de ondas electromagnéticas (Cap. 3, pág. 87)

**radioactivity/radiactividad:** liberación de partículas de alta energía por elementos radiactivos (Cap. 4, pág. 116)

**recessive trait/rasgo recesivo:** rasgo que parece desaparecer en la progenie (Cap. 14, pág. 444)

**red blood cells/glóbulos rojos:** células sanguíneas cuya función principal es transportar oxígeno desde los pulmones hasta todas las demás células del cuerpo (Cap. 12, pág. 375)

**relative humidity/humedad relativa:** medida de la cantidad de vapor de agua en el aire en un momento determinado, comparada con la cantidad de vapor de agua que puede sostener el aire a esa temperatura (Cap. 8, pág. 244)

**resistance/resistencia:** propiedad de los materiales que indica la cantidad de energía que se transforma en energía térmica y en luz a medida que una carga eléctrica recorre los materiales (Cap. 1, pág. 34)

**salinity/salinidad:** medida de la cantidad de sólidos, especialmente sales, disueltos en el agua oceánica (Cap. 9, pág. 283)

**saturated/saturado:** aire que contiene toda la humedad que le es posible a una temperatura determinada (Cap. 8, pág. 245)

**sea-floor spreading/expansión del suelo oceánico:** hipótesis de Harry Hess que dice que la materia derretida del manto terrestre es forzada hacia la superficie en las dorsales oceánicas, donde se enfría para formar el nuevo suelo oceánico (Cap. 15, pág. 478)

**sex cells/células sexuales:** células que se producen por medio de la meiosis y cuya función es la de producir progenie (Cap. 13, pág. 407)

**sickle-cell anemia/anemia drepanocítica:** tipo de anemia en que los glóbulos rojos están deformados; muchos de estos glóbulos rojos tienen forma de hoz (Cap. 14, pág. 452)

**solar system/sistema solar:** sistema formado por el Sol, los planetas y muchos otros cuerpos más pequeños que viajan alrededor del Sol (Cap. 19, pág. 598)

**sperm/espermatozoide:** célula sexual masculina (Cap. 13, pág. 407)

**stamen/estambre:** órgano reproductor masculino de las plantas (Cap. 13, pág. 419)

**star/estrella:** esfera de gas brillante y caliente que produce energía por medio de la fusión (Cap. 20, pág. 629)

**sublimation/sublimación:** proceso por el cual un sólido se transforma directamente en un gas sin pasar por el estado de líquido (Cap. 7, pág. 220)

**sunspot/mancha solar:** área oscura en la superficie solar que es más fría que otras áreas a su alrededor (Cap. 20, pág. 638)

**supernova/supernova:** estrella masiva que explota después de agotar los materiales en su núcleo (Cap. 20, pág. 631)

**surface current/corriente de superficie:** movimiento de agua que afecta solamente unos cuantos metros de la parte superior del agua de mar (Cap. 9, pág. 291)

**terrestrial planets/planetas terrestres:** planetas cuyo tamaño y composición son parecidos a los de la Tierra (Cap. 19, pág. 603)

**testis/testículos:** órganos sexuales masculinos donde se producen los espermatozoides (Cap. 13, pág. 416)

**thermal expansion/expansión térmica:** expansión que ocurre a medida que se calienta un sólido (Cap. 7, pág. 214)

**tornado/tornado:** tormenta violenta en forma de embudo cuyos vientos arremolinados se mueven sobre la tierra en una trayectoria estrecha (Cap. 8, pág. 262)

**traits/rasgos:** características específicas de cada organismo vivo (Cap. 14, pág. 438)

**transform fault boundary/límite de falla transformante:** límite que se forma cuando dos placas se deslizan en direcciones opuestas o en la misma dirección, pero a velocidades diferentes (Cap. 15. pág. 487)

**transformer/transformador:** dispositivo que puede aumentar o disminuir el voltaje (Cap. 2, pág. 73)

**transmutation/transmutación:** cambio de un átomo de un elemento a otro al emitir partículas o al desintegrarse (Cap. 18, pág. 570)

**unconformity/discordancia:** brecha en la historia geológica de un área, en la cual faltan las capas rocosas que se formaron en ese lugar (Cap. 16, pág. 510)

**unlike charges/cargas desiguales:** cargas que se atraen entre sí (Cap. 1, pág. 23)

**upwelling/corrientes ascendentes:** movimiento ascendente de las aguas frías profundas que reemplazan las de la superficie (Cap. 9, pág. 296)

**vaccine/vacuna:** introducción en el cuerpo de un antígeno muerto o debilitado, ya sea por medio de inoculación o por vía oral, lo cual proporciona inmunidad activa contra una enfermedad específica (Cap. 12, pág. 386)

**variation/variación:** demostración de un rasgo o de un comportamiento heredado que hace que un organismo sea diferente a otros de la misma especie (Cap. 17, pág. 536)

**villi/microvellosidades:** pequeñísimas proyecciones en forma de dedos que cubren los pliegues del intestino delgado (Cap. 11, pág. 360)

**viscosity/viscosidad:** resistencia que presenta un líquido a cambiar de forma (Cap. 7, pág. 217)

**vitamins/vitaminas:** sustancias orgánicas que se necesitan para mantener la buena salud (Cap. 11, pág. 347)

**white blood cells/glóbulos blancos:** células sanguíneas que combaten las bacterias, los virus y otras materias extrañas que tratan de invadir el cuerpo constantemente (Cap. 12, pág. 376)

# INDEX

The Index for *Science Interactions* will help you locate major topics in the book quickly and easily. Each entry in the Index is followed by the numbers of the pages on which the entry is discussed. A page number given in **boldface type** indicates the page on which that entry is defined. A page number given in *italic type* indicates a page on which the entry is used in an illustration or photograph. The abbreviation *act.* indicates a page on which the entry is used in an activity.

# Credits

## Illustrations

**Bill Boyer/John Edwards** 482, 493, 499; **Cende Courtney-Hill/Morgan-Cain & Associates** 542, 544, 560, 562; **David De Gasperis/John Edwards** 296, 483, 489, 509; **John Edwards** 243, 269, 625, 632, 638, 643; **Chris Forsey/Morgan-Cain & Associates** (br) xx, 470-471, 478, 486, 495, 502-503, 505, 515, 524-525, 526-527, 528; **David Fischer/John Edwards** 485, 506, 511; **David Fischer/Morgan-Cain & Associates** 486, 487, 499, 501; **Tom Gagliano** (t) xiii, xvi, (t) xxii, (r) xxvi, 112, 113, 117, 120, 121, 123, 124, 125, 131, (bl, br) 139, 141, 149, 151, 211, 216, 219, 220, 226, 227, 230, 232, (c) 234, 569, 570, 571, 575, 580, 581, 583, 585, 593; **Henry Hill/John Edwards** 282-283, 599, 605, 617, 630, 633, 638; **Network Graphics** xxi, 205, 260, 341-342, 351, 352, 353, 357, 359, 360, 366, 367, 372, 374, 375, 376, 381, 382, 383, 393, 539, 552, 553; **Felipe Passalacqua** 423; **Stephanie Pershing/John Edwards** 548, 613; **Pond & Giles/Morgan-Cain & Associates** 418-419, 433, 540; **Precision Graphics** xv, xxv, (l) xxvi, 1, 23, 26, 28, 29, 31, 33, 34, 36-37, 41, (t) 45, 50, 52-53, 54, (tl, tr) 56, 58, (tl) 63, (lc) 64, (bl) 66, (rc) 67, (tr) 68, 70, 72, 73, 76, (tr, bl) 77, 82, (bl) 83, 84, 85, 86-87, 94, 98, 104, 116, 130, (tr) 139, 148, 154, 157, 161, 164, 165, 167, 171, 172, 173, 176, 178, 180, 181, 184, 186, 187, 188, 189, 192, 193, 194, 195, 204, 207, 210, 216, 228, 229, (bc) 234, (tr) 243, 244, 245, 246, 250, 251, 252, 253, 255, 265, 266, (tr, bl) 269, 272, 275, 278, 280, 281, (bl) 283, 285, 287, 289, 290, 291, 292, 293, 295, 299, (tl) 301, 303, 307, 308, 309, 311, 315, 316, 321, 323, 329, 333, 339, 340, 343, 344, 346, 350, 356, 362, 363, 369, 384, 400, 406, 420, 422, 424, 425, 426, 427, 428, 433, 439, 441, 442, 443, 445, 446, 447, 450, 453, 456, 459, 465, 467, 473, 474, 475, 476, 482, 485, 486, 487, 490, 491, 492, 498, 508, 509, 512, 518, 520-521, 525, 533, 550, 551, 554, 556, 577, 579, 582, 584, 586, 592, 595, 598, 601, 602, 605, 614, 616, 617, 618, 623, 626, 628, 630, 633, 635, 636, 639, 641, 645, 652, 654; **Max Ranft/John Walters & Associates** 298; **Chris Sahlin/John Edwards** 282, 301, 496, 626, 652; **Bill Singleton/John Edwards** 484, 510; **Charlie Thomas/ John Edwards** 529; **Sarah Woodward/Morgan-Cain & Associates** 477.

## Photographs

**Richard Hutchings** (t) x, (b) xi, (l) xv, (t) xvi, 2, 4, 6, 7, 8, 9, 12, 13, 14, 15, (c) 16, 23, 24, 25, (r) 49, 53, 57, 59, 60, 61, 65, 66, 67, 68, 69, 71, 91, 96, 97, (t) 99, (r) 109, (r) 111, (b) 115, 128, 129, (b) 131, 132, 133, 134, (b) 143, 144-145, 147, 152, 153, 155, (r) 175, (b) 179, 182, 185, 192, 195, 197, 198, 199, 200, (tr) 209, 212, (tl) 213, (cr) 215, 216, 217, 218, (t) 219, (t) 220, 222, 224, 225, 236, (r) 239, (r) 241, (t) 249, 274, 286, (t)287, 294, 295, (r) 305, 306, 312, 314, 318, 319, (l) 321, (r) 322, (t) 324, 326, 327, 337, 343, 356, 358, (r) 371, 373, 378, (r) 379, 383, 388, 390, 391, (r) 403, 411, 420, (t) 421, (r) 437, 440, 447, 448, (t) 449, 454, 455, (r) 460, 472, 473, 479, 480, 481, 489, 503, 512, (t) 513, (r)535, 554, (r)565, (t) 567, 568, 572, 573, 586, 587; **Jose L. Pelaez** (t) xi, (br) xiii, (t) xvii, xxiii, 20-21, 32, (br) 40, (bl) 45, 48, 138, (t)142, (t) 208, 246, 247, 250, 252, 258, 259, (r) 261, 320, 338, 340, 348, 349, (t) 353, 354, 355, 361, (r) 469, 600, 609, 610, 627, 634, 635, 640, 641, 647; **Peter Vadnai** (b) x, xxi, 19, (t) 21, (r) 22, 27, 29, 33, 35, 37, 38, 39, (l)40, (br) 45, (r) 50, (t) 51, 52, (t) 55, 58, (t) 62, (br) 77, (t) 81, 88, (t) 93, (b) 95, 118, 119, 122, (c) 131, (t) 179, (l) 230, 245, 254, 276, (t) 277, 284, (tr) 287, (tc) 304, 304-305, (r) 321, (tl) 321, (tl) 325, (l) 328, (l) 333, (t) 336, 345, (bl) 387, (t) 405, 410, 411, 414, 415, 424, 444, 457, 504, (t)

516, 518, (t)519, 523, 537, 546, (t) 547, (br) 549, (t) 555, (r) 556; **Cover,** (bk) Dennis Hallinan/FPG International, (tl) Nigel Dennis/Photo Researchers, Inc., (tr) Richard Small/Photo-op, (c) Hank Morgan/Photo Researches, Inc., (b) Mark Thayer Studio; **xii,** (l) Alfred Pasieka/Peter Arnold, Inc., (r) Lillian Gee/Picture It Corporation; **xiii,** Craig Aurness/Woodfin Camp & Associates, Inc.; **xiv,** (t) Bard Martin/The Image Bank, (b) Michael Groen/Picture It Corporation; **xxvi,** (l) Comstock; **xvii,** (b) Manfred Kage/Peter Arnold, Inc.; **xviii,** (l) David Phillips/Photo Researchers, Inc., (r) David Overcash/Bruce Coleman Inc.; **xix,** (t) Jon Feingersh/The Stock Market, (b) Tom Van Sant/The StockMarket; **xx,** (t) David Sumner/The Stock Market, (bl) John Cancalosi/OKAPIA/Photo Researchers, Inc.; **xxii,** (b) NASA/Photo Researchers, Inc.; **xxiv,** (tl) Kristian Hilsen/Tony Stone Worldwide, (tr) Patricia Lanz/F.J. Alsop III/Bruce Coleman Inc., (br) John Visser/Bruce Coleman Inc.; **xxv,** (l) Stanley Schoenberger/Grant Heilman Photography, Inc., (r) W. Eastep/The Stock Market; **xxvi,** (r) Rosemary Weller/Tony Stone Worldwide; **1,** (l) courtesy of U.S. Space Camp, (r) American Science and Engineering, Inc.; **3,** Jay Freis/Image Bank; **5,** (b) Dale Olson/ Thermo King. (t) courtesy of Thermo King; **6,** (r) The Bettmann Archive; **11,** (l) Gary Williams/Liaison International, (r) National Center for Atmospheric Research; **16,** (tr) Marvin E. Newman/The Image Bank, (bl) Mitchell Funk/The Image Bank; **17,** Tom Martin Photography/The Stock Market; **18-19,** Comstock; **20,** Hans Reinhard/Bruce Coleman Inc.; **22,** The Bettmann Archive; **30,** E.R. Degginger/Bruce Coleman Inc.; **42,** David Nunuk/First Light Toronto; **43,** Lewis H. Latimer/Stock Montage, Inc.; **44,** Courtesy of Sieu Ngo; **47,** Aaron Haupt; **48-49,** Courtesy of Ontario Science Center; **50,** (l) M. Claye Jacana/Photo Researchers, Inc.; **51,** (bl) The Bettmann Archive, (br) C. Padys/FPG International; **55,** (b) Pekka Parviainen/Photo Researchers, Inc.; **56,** Doug Martin; **62,** (b) David R. Frazier; **63,** (t) Comstock, (b) Kenji Kerins; **64,** (l) Manfred Kage/Peter Arnold, Inc., (r) Kodansha; **74,** (t) George Diebold/The Stock Market, (b) Roger Tully/Tony Stone Worldwide; **75,** Courtesy of the DuSable Museum of African American History; **77,** (t) Courtesy of General Electric Corporate Research and Development, (bl) Ken Ferguson; **78,** Ken Frick; **79,** Kodansha Ltd./Physical Phenomena; **80,** (t) Russell Ingram/The Stock Market; **80-81,** (b) Jan Cobb/ The Image Bank; **83,** Lillian Gee/ Picture It Corporation; **86,** (t) Robert Kristofik/The Image Bank, (c) Romilly Lockyer/The Image Bank, (b) Miguel Martin/The Image Bank; **87,** (t) G.K. & Vikki Hart/The Image Bank, (b) Alfred Pasieka/Peter Arnold Inc.; **89,** Leonard Lessin/Peter Arnold Inc.; **90,** NASA/Peter Arnold, Inc.; **92,** (l,r) Runk/Schoenberger/Grant Heilman Photography, Inc.; **93,** (b) Manfred Kage/Peter Arnold, Inc.; **94,** Peter Steiner/The Stock Market; **95,** (tl) Dr. Jeremy Burgess/Photo Researchers, Inc., (tc) Comstock, (tr) N. Smythe/Photo Researchers, Inc.; **98,** (b) Telegraph Colour Library/FPG International; **100,** John Lamb/Tony Stone Worldwide; **101,** (tl) Micheal Groen/Picture It Corporation, (bl) Micheal Groen/Picture It Corporation, (r) Stanley Schoenberger/Grant Heilman Photography, Inc.; **102,** (t) Patricia Ann Tesman/ The Image Bank, (b) Comstock; **103,** (l,r) American Science & Engineering, Inc.; **104,** David Parker/Science Photo Library/Photo Researchers, Inc.; **106,** Leonard Lessin/Peter Arnold, Inc.; **107,** Roy Morsch/The Stock Market; **108-109,** Paul Steel/The Stock Market; **110,**

(t) British Technical Films/Photo Researchers, Inc.; **110-111,** George DieBold/The Stock Market; **113,** Skip Comer; **114,** Steve Dunwell/ The Image Bank; **115,** (t) Science Photo Library/Photo Researchers, Inc.; **123,** Jock Pottle/Esto Photographics; **125,** (t) William E. Ferguson, (c) Doug Martin, (b) Ohio State University Archive; **126,** (t) stamps from collection of Professor C.M. Lang, photography by Gary Shulfer/University of Wisconsin-Stevens Point, (b) courtesy of IBM Corporate Research Division/Almaden Research Center; **131,** (t) Doug Martin; **135,** Gabe Palmer/The Stock Market; **136,** Lawrence Migdale; **137,** (l,r) CNFW/Science Photo Library/ Photo Reseachers, Inc.; **139,** Skip Comer; **142,** (l,r) Mug Shots/The Stock Market; **143,** (t,c) Mug Shots/The Stock Market; **145,** stamp from the collection of Professor C.M. Lang, photography by Gary Shulfer, University of Wisconsin-Steven's Point; **148,** First Image; **149,** Ken Ferguson; **150,** /Tony Stone Wordwide; **151,** Tony Stone Worldwide; **154,** (l) Craig Aurness/Woodfin Camp & Associates, Inc., (r) Chuck Savage/The Stock Market; **156,** (tl) Micheal Schneps/The Image Bank, (tr) Art Stein/Photo Researchers, Inc., (cl) Stuart Cohen/ Comstock, (cr)Paolo Koch/Photo Researchers, Inc., (bl) Runk/ Schoenberger/Grant Heilman, Inc., (br) Woodfin Camp & Associates, Inc.; **158,** Craig Tuttle Photography/The Stock Market; **159,** (tl) Masa Vemura/All Stock, (tr) Matt Meadows, (b) Chip Clark; **160,** (tl) Connie Hansen/The Stock Market, (r) Hank deLespinasse/ The Image Bank; **162,** Krostin/ Lehtikuva/Novosti/Woodfin Camp & Associates, Inc.; **163,** (t,b) Russ Lappa/Photo Researchers, Inc.; **166,** Comstock; **168,** Ed Tronic/Liaison International; **169,** (l) David R. Frazier Photolibrary, (r) EG& G/EM; **170,** /UPI Bettmann; **174,** (t) Bard Martin/The Image Bank; **174-175,** Morton Beebe/The Image Bank; **177,** Doug Martin; **178,** Doug Martin; **184,** Ralph Brunke; **186,** (t) W.W. Winter Ltd./The Derby Museum, (b) Jospeh Nettis/ Photo Researchers, Inc.; **190,** Ed Reschick/Peter Arnold, Inc.; **191,** Comstock; **196,** /Tony Stone Worldwide; **201,** Alvis Upitis/The Image Bank; **202,** (l) Hew Evans Picture Agency, (cl) sculpture by Richard Neve, photography by Jerry Young, (cr) Hew Evans Picture Agency, (r) Mathew Brady/The Bettmann Archive; **203,** The Bettmann Archive; **204,** FourByFive, Inc.; **205,** Aaron Haupt Photography; **206,** Doug Martin; **208-209,** (b) David Young-Wolff; **213,** (r) Stuart Cohen/Comstock; **214,** (t) AP/Wide World Photos, (b) R.H. Armstrong/Animals Animals; **215,** (cl) Clyde H. Smith/Tony Stone Worldwide, Ltd., (t) David McGlynn/ FPG International; **219,** (b) Robert Brenner/PhotoEdit; **220,** (b) Martha Swope Associates/Carol Rosegg; **221,** (l) Comstock, (r) Mark Reinstein/PhotoReporters; **223,** Michael Groen/Picture It Corporation; **225,** (b) Wes Thompson/The Stock Market; **228,** (l) Adam Hart-Davis/Photo Researchers, Inc., (r) Kristian Hilsen/Tony Stone Worldwide; **230,** (t) J. Irwin/All Stock, (r) Richard Fukuhara/ Westlight; **232,** (l) Rosemary Weller/Tony Stone Worldwide, (t) Tony Freeman/ PhotoEdit, (r) Emmet Bright/PhotoResearchers, Inc.; **233,** courtesy of the DuSable Museum of African American History; **234,** (t) Cabisco/ Visuals Unlimited, (r) Tardos Camesi/The Stock Market, (b) AP/Wide World Photos; **237,** (l) Alvis Upitis/The Image Bank, (r) Comstock; **238-239,** Klaus Mitteldorf/The Image Bank; **240,** (t) Greg L. Ryan/ Sally A. Beyer/All Stock; **240-241,** Fred Hirschmann; **242,** Julie Habel/ West Light/Woodfin Camp & Associates; **248,** (tl) Akhard Hamilton-

Smith/All Stock, (c) Vince Streano/The Stock Market, Inc., (bl) Lorentz Gullachsen/Tony Stone Worldwide; **249,** (b) Colin Raw/Tony Stone Worldwide, **250,** (l) Roy Morsch/The Stock Market, (cr) Mark McDermott/All Stock, (r) Nuridsany et Perennou/ Photo Researchers, Inc.; **256,** (t) Monte Funkhauser/The Stock Market, (bl) Barbara Van Cleve/Tony Stone Worldwide, (br) Bill Ivy/ Tony Stone Worldwide; **257,** (t) Tony Craddock/Tony Stone Worldwide, (bl) GSO Images/The Image Bank, (br) NASA; **261,** (tl) Keyphotos/The Stock Market; **262,** David R. Frazier; **263,** The Image Bank; **265,** Grant Heilman/Grant Heilman Photography, Inc.; **266,** Bill Ivy/Tony Stone Worldwide; **267,** Jim Anderson/ Woodfin Camp & Associates, Inc.; **268,** (t), (b) Daivd R. Frazier; **269,** The Image Bank; **272-273,** Don & Liysa King/ The Image Bank; **273,** (l) Don King/The Image Bank, (r) Stephen Wade/Allsport USA; **275,** George Schwartz/FPG International; **277,** (b) Dept. of Photo Service KYODO News; **279,** (l,r) Steve Vidler/Leo de Wys, Inc.; **288,** (t) Jeff Rotman, (b) Comstock; **296,** Comstock; **297,** Greg Vaughn/Tom Stack & Associates; **298,** Erich Hartmann/ Magnum Photos; **300,** (t) courtesy of LeAnn Gast/New York Aquarium, (b) Carl Purcell/Photo Reseachers, Inc.; **301,** Myrleen Ferguson/ PhotoEdit; **304,** (tl) Runk/Schoenberger/ Grant Heilman Photography, Inc., (tr) Breck P. Kent/Earth Scenes; **308,** (l) NASA, (r) Alan Marsh/First Light; **309,** Donovan Reese/Tony Stone Worldwide; **310,** Doug Martin; **311,** Alan Marsh/ First Light; **313,** W. Eastep/The Stock Market; **315,** J.H. Robinson/ Photo Researchers, Inc.; **317,** (t) Michael Waine/The Stock Market, (b) courtesy of Nebraska Ethanol Board; **322,** (l) Mike McCabe/Tony Stone Worldwide; **323,** Tony Stone Worldwide; **324,** (b) Tom McHugh/Photo Researchers, Inc.; **325,** (tr) Anthony Blake/Tony Stone Worldwide, (b) John Visser/Bruce Coleman Inc.; **328,** (r) B&B Photos/Custom Medical Stock Photo; **329,** Pictoral Parade; **330,** David Young-Wolff/PhotoEdit; **331,** (t) Ray Pfortner/Peter Arnold Inc., (b) GrantHeilman/Grant Heilman Photography, Inc.; **332,** courtesy of Stephen Wilkes, H.J. Heinz Company; **333,** (r) Tony Freeman/ PhotoEdit; **334,** Mike McCabe/Tony Stone Worldwide; **336,** (br) William Hubbel/Woodfin Camp & Associates, Inc., (b) Rucy Muller/ Envision; **339,** (l) Larry Mulvehill/Photo Researchers, Inc., (r) National Medical Slides/Custom Medical Stock Photo; **341,** (l) Joe McNally/The Image Bank, (r) Frank Siteman/ Monkmeyer Press; **344,** (l) Guy Powers/Envision, (c) Steven Mark Needham/Envision, (r) Nathan Benn/USA: Food & Drink; **346,** Comstock; **347,** Alon Reininger/Contact Press/The Stock Market; **352,** (l) Comstock, (r) Joe Van Os/The Image Bank; **353,** (b) Max Schneider/ The Image Bank; **357,** Lennart Nilsson/"Behold Man" Little, Brown & Company; **364,** Blair Seitz/Photo Researchers, Inc.; **365,** Randy Wells/ All Stock; **366,** Tony Freeman/PhotoEdit; **367,** Bruce Wilson/All Stock; **370,** (t) Manfred Kage/Peter Arnold, Inc.; **370-371,** Tony Freeman/PhotoEdit; **372,** Ken Eward/Science Source/Photo Researchers, Inc.; **373,** (l) Biophoto Associates/Photo Researchers, Inc., (r) Ocean Images/Giddings/ The Image Bank; **375,** Lennart Nilsson/"The Incredible Machine"/ National Geographic Society; **376,** Robert Becker, PhD/ Custom Medical Stock Photo; **377,** Biophoto Associates/Science Source/Photo Researchers, Inc.; **379,** (l) Comstock; **380,** (t) Stuart Westmorland/All Stock, (c) Jim Simmen/All Stock, (bl) Kevin Schafer/Martha Hill/ All Stock; **381,** Prof. P. Motta/Photo